NBA REGISTER

1990-91 EDITION

Editors/NBA Register

ALEX SACHARE
DAVE SLOAN

Contributing Editors/NBA Register

MIKE DOUCHANT
JOHN DUXBURY
TERRY LYONS
THERESA SANZARI

President-Chief Executive Officer

THOMAS G. OSENTON

Director, Specialized Publications

GARY LEVY

NBA Statistics by Elias Sports Bureau

Published by

The Sporting News

1212 North Lindbergh Boulevard
P.O. Box 56 — St. Louis, MO 63166

ISBN 0-89204-366-0 ISSN 0739-3067

Table of Contents

★ ★ ★

★ ★ ★

On the cover: San Antonio's David Robinson (50) and New York's Patrick Ewing were two of the NBA's premier centers in 1989-90, with Robinson unanimously winning the league's Rookie of the Year Award while Ewing was an All-NBA First Team selection.

Photo by Andrew Bernstein/NBA

Career Records of NBA Players

The following records are of players who appeared in at least one game during the 1989-90 NBA season. Also included are records of players with previous NBA experience who were invited to training camp this year or were on the injured list for the entire 1989-90 season.

†Indicates college freshman or junior varsity participant.

MARK RICHARD ACRES

Born November 15, 1962 at Inglewood, Calif. Height 6:11. Weight 225.
High School—Palos Verdes Estates, Calif., Palos Verdes.
College—Oral Roberts University, Tulsa, Okla.
Drafted by Dallas on second round, 1985 (40th pick).

Draft rights relinquished by Dallas, July 31, 1986; signed by Boston as a free agent, May 7, 1987.
Selected from Boston by Orlando in NBA expansion draft, June 15, 1989.
Played in Italy, 1985-86 and in Belgium, 1986-87.

—COLLEGIATE RECORD—

Year	G.	Min.	FGA	FGM	Pct.	FTA	FTM	Pct.	Reb.	Pts.	Avg.
81-82	22	702	186	109	.586	143	104	.727	178	322	14.6
82-83	28	976	368	203	.552	167	120	.719	269	526	18.8
83-84	31	...	482	266	.552	159	114	.717	324	646	20.8
84-85	29	959	380	221	.582	163	102	.626	280	544	18.8
Totals	110	...	1416	799	.564	632	440	.696	1051	2038	18.5

ITALIAN LEAGUE RECORD

Year	G.	Min.	FGA	FGM	Pct.	FTA	FTM	Pct.	Reb.	Pts.	Avg.
85-86—Pall. Varese	5	135	41	17	.415	20	17	.850	41	51	10.2

NBA REGULAR SEASON RECORD

									—Rebounds—									
Sea.—Team	G.	Min.	FGA	FGM	Pct.	FTA	FTM	Pct.	Off.	Def.	Tot.	Ast.	PF	Dq.	Stl.	Blk.	Pts.	Avg.
87-88—Boston	79	1151	203	108	.532	111	71	.640	105	165	270	42	198	2	29	27	287	3.6
88-89—Boston	62	632	114	55	.482	48	26	.542	59	87	146	19	94	0	19	6	137	2.2
89-90—Orlando	80	1691	285	138	.484	120	83	.692	154	277	431	67	248	4	36	25	362	4.5
Totals	221	3474	602	301	.500	279	180	.645	318	529	847	128	540	6	84	58	786	3.6

Three-Point Field Goals: 1988-89, 1-for-1 (1.000). 1989-90, 3-for-4 (.750). Totals, 4-for-5 (.800).

NBA PLAYOFF RECORD

									—Rebounds—									
Sea.—Team	G.	Min.	FGA	FGM	Pct.	FTA	FTM	Pct.	Off.	Def.	Tot.	Ast.	PF	Dq.	Stl.	Blk.	Pts.	Avg.
87-88—Boston	17	158	26	14	.538	18	9	.500	14	22	36	2	33	0	1	1	37	2.2
88-89—Boston	2	2	1	0	.000	0	0	.....	0	1	1	0	0	0	0	0	0	0.00
Totals	19	160	27	14	.519	18	9	.500	14	23	37	2	33	0	1	1	37	1.9

Three-Point Field Goals: 1987-88, 0-for-1. 1988-89, 0-for-1. Totals, 0-for-2.

MICHAEL ADAMS

Born January 19, 1963 at Hartford, Conn. Height 5:11. Weight 165.
High School—Hartford, Conn., Public.
College—Boston College, Chestnut Hill, Mass.
Drafted by Sacramento on third round, 1985 (66th pick).

Waived by Sacramento, December 17, 1985; signed by Washington as a free agent, May 13, 1986.
Waived by Washington, September 25, 1986; re-signed by Washington as a free agent, September 29, 1986.
Waived by Washington, October 28, 1986; re-signed by Washington as a free agent, November 21, 1986.
Traded by Washington with Jay Vincent to Denver for Mark Alarie and Darrell Walker, November 2, 1987.
Played in Continental Basketball Association with Bay State Bombardiers, 1985-86.

—COLLEGIATE RECORD—

Year	G.	Min.	FGA	FGM	Pct.	FTA	FTM	Pct.	Reb.	Pts.	Avg.
81-82	26	379	103	51	.495	61	36	.590	30	138	5.3
82-83	32	1075	405	195	.482	157	127	.809	86	517	16.2
83-84	30	1026	429	195	.455	172	130	.756	102	520	17.3
84-85	31	1044	413	193	.467	119	89	.748	102	475	15.3
Totals	119	3524	1350	634	.469	509	382	.750	320	1750	14.7

CBA REGULAR SEASON RECORD

			2-Point			3-Point									
Sea.—Team	G.	Min.	FGM	FGA	Pct.	FGM	FGA	Pct.	FTM	FTA	Pct.	Reb.	Ast.	Pts.	Avg.
85-86—Bay State	38	1526	241	487	.494	21	71	.296	125	164	.762	149	320	670	17.6

NBA REGULAR SEASON RECORD

									Rebounds									
Sea.—Team	G.	Min.	FGA	FGM	Pct.	FTA	FTM	Pct.	Off.	Def.	Tot.	Ast.	PF	Dq.	Stl.	Blk.	Pts.	Avg.
85-86—Sacramento	18	139	44	16	.364	12	8	.667	2	4	6	22	9	0	9	1	40	2.2
86-87—Washington	63	1303	393	160	.407	124	105	.847	38	85	123	244	88	0	85	6	453	7.2
87-88—Denver	82	2778	927	416	.449	199	166	.834	40	183	223	503	138	0	168	16	1137	13.9
88-89—Denver	77	2787	1082	468	.433	393	322	.819	71	212	283	490	149	0	166	11	1424	18.5
89-90—Denver	79	2690	989	398	.402	314	267	.850	49	176	225	495	133	0	121	3	1221	15.5
Totals	319	9697	3435	1458	.424	1042	868	.833	200	660	860	1754	517	0	549	37	4275	13.4

Three-Point Field Goals: 1985-86, 0-for-3. 1986-87, 28-for-102 (.275). 1987-88, 139-for-379 (.367). 1988-89, 166-for-466 (.356). 1989-90, 158-for-432 (.366). Totals, 491-for-1382 (.355).

NBA PLAYOFF RECORD

									Rebounds									
Sea.—Team	G.	Min.	FGA	FGM	Pct.	FTA	FTM	Pct.	Off.	Def.	Tot.	Ast.	PF	Dq.	Stl.	Blk.	Pts.	Avg.
86-87—Washington	3	82	25	8	.320	3	1	.333	0	7	7	10	6	0	7	0	19	6.3
87-88—Denver	11	406	130	47	.362	41	36	.878	9	27	36	64	19	0	18	2	147	13.4
88-89—Denver	2	75	36	15	.417	8	7	.875	5	12	17	9	6	0	3	0	47	23.5
89-90—Denver	3	105	34	13	.382	8	7	.875	0	6	6	18	10	0	4	0	39	13.0
Totals	19	668	225	83	.369	60	51	.850	14	52	66	101	41	0	32	2	252	13.3

Three-Point Field Goals: 1986-87, 2-for-9 (.222). 1987-88, 17-for-54 (.315). 1988-89, 10-for-22 (.455). 1989-90, 6-for-20 (.300). Totals, 35-for-105 (.333).

Holds NBA record for most three-point field goals in a season, 1989 . . . Named CBA Rookie of the Year, 1986 . . . CBA All-Star Second Team, 1986 . . . CBA All-Defensive Second Team, 1986.

MARK ANTHONY AGUIRRE

Born December 10, 1959 at Chicago, Ill. Height 6:06. Weight 235.

High Schools—Chicago, Ill., Austin (Sophomore) and Chicago, Ill., Westinghouse (Junior and Senior).

College—DePaul University, Chicago, Ill.

Drafted by Dallas on first round as an undergraduate, 1981 (1st pick).

Traded by Dallas to Detroit for Adrian Dantley and a 1991 1st round draft choice, February 15, 1989.

—COLLEGIATE RECORD—

Year	G.	Min.	FGA	FGM	Pct.	FTA	FTM	Pct.	Reb.	Pts.	Avg.
78-79	32	....	581	302	.520	213	163	.765	244	767	24.0
79-80	28	....	520	281	.540	244	187	.766	213	749	26.8
80-81	29	1069	481	280	.582	137	106	.774	249	666	23.0
Totals	89	....	1582	863	.546	594	456	.768	706	2182	24.5

NBA REGULAR SEASON RECORD

									Rebounds									
Sea.—Team	G.	Min.	FGA	FGM	Pct.	FTA	FTM	Pct.	Off.	Def.	Tot.	Ast.	PF	Dq.	Stl.	Blk.	Pts.	Avg.
81-82—Dallas	51	1468	820	381	.465	247	168	.680	89	160	249	164	152	0	37	22	955	18.7
82-83—Dallas	81	2784	1589	767	.483	589	429	.728	191	317	508	332	247	5	80	26	1979	24.4
83-84—Dallas	79	2900	1765	925	.524	621	465	.749	161	308	469	358	246	5	80	22	2330	29.5
84-85—Dallas	80	2699	1569	794	.506	580	440	.759	188	289	477	249	250	3	60	24	2055	25.7
85-86—Dallas	74	2501	1327	668	.503	451	318	.705	177	268	445	339	229	6	62	14	1670	22.6
86-87—Dallas	80	2663	1590	787	.495	557	429	.770	181	246	427	254	243	4	84	30	2056	25.7
87-88—Dallas	77	2610	1571	746	.475	504	388	.770	182	252	434	278	223	1	70	57	1932	25.1
88-89—Dal.-Det.	80	2597	1270	586	.461	393	288	.733	146	240	386	278	229	2	45	36	1511	18.9
89-90—Detroit	78	2005	898	438	.488	254	192	.756	117	188	305	145	201	2	34	19	1099	14.1
Totals	680	22227	12399	6092	.491	4196	3117	.743	1432	2268	3700	2397	2020	28	552	250	15587	22.9

Three-Point Field Goals: 1981-82, 25-for-71 (.352). 1982-83, 16-for-76 (.211). 1983-84, 15-for-56 (.268). 1984-85, 27-for-85 (.318). 1985-86, 16-for-56 (.285). 1986-87, 53-for-150 (.353). 1987-88, 52-for-172 (.302). 1988-89, 51-for-174 (.293). 1989-90, 31-for-93 (.333). Totals, 286-for-933 (.307).

NBA PLAYOFF RECORD

									Rebounds									
Sea.—Team	G.	Min.	FGA	FGM	Pct.	FTA	FTM	Pct.	Off.	Def.	Tot.	Ast.	PF	Dq.	Stl.	Blk.	Pts.	Avg.
83-84—Dallas	10	350	184	88	.478	57	44	.772	21	55	76	32	34	2	5	5	220	22.0
84-85—Dallas	4	164	89	44	.494	32	27	.844	16	14	30	16	16	1	3	0	116	29.0
85-86—Dallas	10	345	214	105	.491	55	35	.636	21	50	71	54	28	1	9	0	247	24.7
86-87—Dallas	4	130	62	31	.500	30	23	.767	11	13	24	8	15	1	8	0	85	21.3
87-88—Dallas	17	558	294	147	.500	86	60	.698	34	66	100	56	49	0	14	9	367	21.6
88-89—Detroit	17	462	182	89	.489	38	28	.737	26	49	75	28	38	0	8	3	214	12.6
89-90—Detroit	20	439	184	86	.467	52	39	.750	31	60	91	27	51	0	10	3	219	11.0
Totals	82	2448	1209	590	.488	350	256	.731	160	307	467	221	231	5	57	20	1468	17.9

Three-Point Field Goals: 1983-84, 0-for-5. 1984-85, 1-for-2 (.500), 1985-86, 2-for-6 (.333). 1986-87, 0-for-4. 1987-88, 13-for-34 (.382). 1988-89, 8-for-29 (.276). 1989-90, 8-for-24 (.333). Totals, 32-for-104 (.308).

NBA ALL-STAR GAME RECORD

								—Rebounds—								
Season—Team	Min.	FGA	FGM	Pct.	FTA	FTM	Pct.	Off.	Def.	Tot.	Ast.	PF	Dq.	Stl.	Blk.	Pts.
1984—Dallas	13	8	5	.625	4	3	.750	1	0	1	2	1	0	1	1	13
1987—Dallas	17	6	3	.500	3	2	.667	1	1	2	1	1	0	0	0	9
1988—Dallas	12	10	5	.500	3	3	1.000	0	1	1	1	3	0	1	0	14
Totals	42	24	13	.542	10	8	.800	2	2	4	4	5	0	2	1	36

Three-Point Field Goals: 1987, 1-for-2 (.500). 1988, 1-for-3 (.333). Totals, 2-for-5 (.400).

Member of NBA championship teams, 1989 and 1990 . . . Named THE SPORTING NEWS College Player of the Year, 1981. . . . THE SPORTING NEWS All-America First Team, 1980 and 1981. . . . Member of U.S. Olympic Team, 1980.

DANIEL RAY AINGE
(Danny)

Born March 17, 1959 at Eugene, Ore. Height 6:05. Weight 185.

High School—Eugene, Ore., North.

College—Brigham Young University, Provo, Utah.

Drafted by Boston on second round, 1981 (31st pick).

Traded by Boston with Brad Lohaus to Sacramento for Ed Pinckney and Joe Kleine, February 23, 1989.

Traded by Sacramento to Portland for Byron Irvin, a 1991 1st round draft choice and a 1992 2nd round draft choice, August 1, 1990.

—COLLEGIATE RECORD—

Year	G.	Min.	FGA	FGM	Pct.	FTA	FTM	Pct.	Reb.	Pts.	Avg.
77-78	30	....	473	243	.514	169	146	.864	173	632	21.1
78-79	27	922	376	206	.548	112	86	.768	102	498	18.4
79-80	29	984	430	229	.533	124	97	.782	114	555	19.1
80-81	32	1212	596	309	.518	199	164	.824	152	782	24.4
Totals	118	....	1875	987	.526	604	493	.816	541	2467	20.9

NBA REGULAR SEASON RECORD

									—Rebounds—									
Sea.—Team	G.	Min.	FGA	FGM	Pct.	FTA	FTM	Pct.	Off.	Def.	Tot.	Ast.	PF	Dq.	Stl.	Blk.	Pts.	Avg.
81-82—Boston	53	564	221	79	.357	65	56	.862	25	31	56	87	86	1	37	3	219	4.1
82-83—Boston	80	2048	720	357	.496	97	72	.742	83	131	214	251	259	2	109	6	791	9.9
83-84—Boston	71	1154	361	166	.460	56	46	.821	29	87	116	162	143	2	41	4	384	5.4
84-85—Boston	75	2564	792	419	.529	136	118	.868	76	192	268	399	228	4	122	6	971	12.9
85-86—Boston	80	2407	701	353	.504	136	123	.904	47	188	235	405	204	4	94	7	855	10.7
86-87—Boston	71	2499	844	410	.486	165	148	.897	49	193	242	400	189	3	101	14	1053	14.8
87-88—Boston	81	3018	982	482	.491	180	158	.878	59	190	249	503	203	1	115	17	1270	15.7
88-89—Bos.-Sac.	73	2377	1051	480	.457	240	205	.854	71	184	255	402	186	1	93	8	1281	17.5
89-90—Sacramento	75	2727	1154	506	.438	267	222	.831	69	257	326	453	238	2	113	18	1342	17.9
Totals	659	19358	6826	3252	.476	1342	1148	.855	508	1453	1961	3062	1736	20	825	83	8166	12.4

Three-Point Field Goals: 1981-82, 5-for-17 (.294). 1982-83, 5-for-29 (.172). 1983-84, 6-for-22 (.273). 1984-85, 15-for-56 (.268). 1985-86, 26-for-73 (.356). 1986-87, 85-for-192 (.443). 1987-88, 148-for-357 (.415). 1988-89, 116-for-305 (.380). 1989-90, 108-for-289 (.374). Totals, 514-for-1340 (.384).

NBA PLAYOFF RECORD

									—Rebounds—									
Sea.—Team	G.	Min.	FGA	FGM	Pct.	FTA	FTM	Pct.	Off.	Def.	Tot.	Ast.	PF	Dq.	Stl.	Blk.	Pts.	Avg.
81-82—Boston	10	129	45	19	.422	13	10	.769	6	7	13	11	21	0	2	1	50	5.0
82-83—Boston	7	201	72	28	.389	11	8	.727	2	12	14	25	24	0	5	1	66	9.4
83-84—Boston	19	253	90	41	.456	10	7	.700	4	12	16	38	36	0	9	2	91	4.8
84-85—Boston	21	687	208	97	.466	39	30	.769	20	38	58	121	76	1	32	1	231	11.0
85-86—Boston	18	652	193	107	.554	60	52	.867	22	54	76	93	57	0	41	1	280	15.6
86-87—Boston	20	762	238	116	.487	36	31	.861	13	39	52	92	62	0	24	4	295	14.8
87-88—Boston	17	670	184	71	.386	42	37	.881	15	38	53	109	64	2	9	1	198	11.6
Totals	112	3354	1030	479	.465	211	175	.829	82	200	282	489	340	3	122	11	1211	10.8

Three-Point Field Goals: 1981-82, 2-for-4 (.500). 1982-83, 2-for-5 (.400). 1983-84, 2-for-9 (.222). 1984-85, 7-for-16 (.438). 1985-86, 14-for-34 (.412). 1986-87, 32-for-73 (.438). 1987-88, 19-for-57 (.333). Totals, 78-for-198 (.394).

NBA ALL-STAR GAME RECORD

								—Rebounds—								
Season—Team	Min.	FGA	FGM	Pct.	FTA	FTM	Pct.	Off.	Def.	Tot.	Ast.	PF	Dq.	Stl.	Blk.	Pts.
1988—Boston	19	11	4	.364	2	1	.500	1	2	3	2	1	0	1	0	12

Three-Point Field Goals: 1988, 3-for-4 (.750).

RECORD AS BASEBALL PLAYER

Year	Club	League	Pos.	G.	AB.	R.	H.	2B.	3B.	HR.	RBI.	B.A.	PO.	A.	E.	F.A.
1978	Syracuse	Int.	SS-2B	119	389	33	89	10	1	4	30	.229	206	328	29	.948
1979	Syracuse	Int.	2B	27	101	10	25	4	2	0	8	.248	56	77	4	.971
1979	Toronto	Amer.	2B	87	308	26	73	7	1	2	19	.237	198	261	11	.977
1980	Syracuse	Int.	3-O-SS	80	295	37	72	9	1	2	17	.244	111	140	3	.988
1980	Toronto	Amer.	OF-3-2	38	111	11	27	6	1	0	4	.243	69	12	1	.988
1981	Toronto	Amer.	3-SS-O-2	86	246	20	46	6	2	0	14	.187	88	146	12	.951
Major League Totals				211	665	57	146	19	4	2	37	.220	355	419	24	.970

Member of NBA championship teams, 1984 and 1986. . . . Named to THE SPORTING NEWS All-America First Team, 1981. . . . Drafted by Toronto Blue Jays in 15th round of free-agent draft, June 7, 1977.

MARK STEVEN ALARIE

Born December 11, 1963 at Phoenix, Ariz. Height 6:08. Weight 217.
High School—Phoenix, Ariz., Brophy Prep.
College—Duke University, Durham, N.C.
Drafted by Denver on first round, 1986 (18th pick).

Traded by Denver with Darrell Walker to Washington for Michael Adams and Jay Vincent, November 2, 1987.

—COLLEGIATE RECORD—

Year	G.	Min.	FGA	FGM	Pct.	FTA	FTM	Pct.	Reb.	Pts.	Avg.
82-83	28	785	263	130	.494	128	104	.813	181	364	13.0
83-84	34	1129	400	230	.575	176	134	.761	245	594	17.5
84-85	31	935	352	206	.585	101	80	.792	158	492	15.9
85-86	40	1193	490	262	.535	197	162	.822	249	686	17.2
Totals	133	4042	1505	828	.550	602	480	.797	833	2136	16.1

Three-Point Field Goals: 1982-83, 0-for-2.

NBA REGULAR SEASON RECORD

Sea.—Team	G.	Min.	FGA	FGM	Pct.	FTA	FTM	Pct.	—Rebounds— Off.	Def.	Tot.	Ast.	PF	Dq.	Stl.	Blk.	Pts.	Avg.
86-87—Denver	64	1110	443	217	.490	101	67	.663	73	141	214	74	138	1	22	28	503	7.9
87-88—Washington	63	769	300	144	.480	49	35	.714	70	90	160	39	107	1	10	12	327	5.2
88-89—Washington	74	1141	431	206	.478	87	73	.839	103	152	255	63	160	1	25	22	498	6.7
89-90—Washington	82	1893	785	371	.473	133	108	.812	151	223	374	142	219	2	60	39	860	10.5
Totals	283	4913	1959	938	.479	370	283	.765	397	606	1003	318	624	5	117	101	2188	7.7

Three-Point Field Goals: 1986-87, 2-for-9 (.222). 1987-88, 4-for-18 (.222). 1988-89, 13-for-38 (.342). 1989-90, 10-for-49 (.204). Totals, 29-for-114 (.254).

NBA PLAYOFF RECORD

Sea.—Team	G.	Min.	FGA	FGM	Pct.	FTA	FTM	Pct.	—Rebounds— Off.	Def.	Tot.	Ast.	PF	Dq.	Stl.	Blk.	Pts.	Avg.
86-87—Denver	3	41	15	9	.600	2	2	1.000	0	5	5	1	9	0	2	2	20	6.7
87-88—Washington	1	4	2	1	.500	0	0	.000	0	1	1	0	0	0	0	0	3	3.0
Totals	4	45	17	10	.588	2	2	1.000	0	6	6	1	9	0	2	2	23	5.8

Three-Point Field Goals: 1987-88, 1-for-2 (.500).

STEPHEN TODD ALFORD
(Steve)

Born November 23, 1964 at Franklin, Ind. Height 6:02. Weight 185.
High School—New Castle, Ind., Chrysler.
College—Indiana University, Bloomington, Ind.
Drafted by Dallas on second round, 1987 (26th pick).

Waived by Dallas, December 13, 1988; signed by Golden State as a free agent, December 17, 1988.
Signed by Dallas as an unrestricted free agent, 1990.

—COLLEGIATE RECORD—

Year	G.	Min.	FGA	FGM	Pct.	FTA	FTM	Pct.	Reb.	Pts.	Avg.
83-84	31	....	289	171	.592	150	137	.913	82	479	15.5
84-85	32	....	431	232	.538	126	116	.921	101	580	18.1
85-86	28	....	457	254	.556	140	122	.871	75	630	22.5
86-87	34	....	508	241	.474	180	160	.889	87	749	22.0
Totals	125	....	1685	898	.533	596	535	.898	345	2438	19.5

Three-Point Field Goals: 1986-87, 107-202 (.530).

NBA REGULAR SEASON RECORD

Sea.—Team	G.	Min.	FGA	FGM	Pct.	FTA	FTM	Pct.	—Rebounds— Off.	Def.	Tot.	Ast.	PF	Dq.	Stl.	Blk.	Pts.	Avg.
87-88—Dallas	28	197	55	21	.382	17	16	.941	3	20	23	23	23	0	17	3	59	2.1
88-89—Dal.-Gol. St.	66	906	324	148	.457	61	50	.820	10	62	72	92	57	0	45	3	366	5.5
89-90—Dallas	41	302	138	63	.457	37	35	.946	2	23	25	39	22	0	15	3	168	4.1
Totals	135	1405	517	232	.449	115	101	.878	15	105	120	154	102	0	77	9	593	4.4

Three-Point Field Goals: 1987-88, 1-for-8 (.125). 1988-89, 20-for-55 (.364). 1989-90, 7-for-22 (.318). Totals, 28-for-85 (.329).

NBA PLAYOFF RECORD

Sea.—Team	G.	Min.	FGA	FGM	Pct.	FTA	FTM	Pct.	—Rebounds— Off.	Def.	Tot.	Ast.	PF	Dq.	Stl.	Blk.	Pts.	Avg.
87-88—Dallas	4	12	8	3	.375	0	0	....	1	1	2	2	0	0	0	0	6	1.5

Sea.—Team	G.	Min.	FGA	FGM	Pct.	FTA	FTM	Pct.	Off.	Def.	Tot.	Ast.	PF	Dq.	Stl.	Blk.	Pts.	Avg.
88-89—Golden State	6	52	22	9	.409	4	3	.750	2	2	4	5	7	0	2	0	25	4.2
89-90—Dallas	3	42	18	8	.444	5	5	1.000	1	2	3	8	4	0	1	0	23	7.7
Totals	13	106	48	20	.417	9	8	.889	4	5	9	15	11	0	3	0	54	4.2

Three-Point Field Goals: 1987-88, 0-for-2. 1988-89, 4-for-9 (.444). 1989-90, 2-for-6 (.333). Totals, 6-for-17 (.353).

Member of NCAA Division I championship team, 1987. . . . Led NCAA Division I in free-throw percentage, 1984. . . . Member of U.S. Olympic Team, 1984. . . . Named to THE SPORTING NEWS All-America Second Team, 1987.

JAMES RANDALL ALLEN
(Randy)

Born January 26, 1965 at Milton, Fla. Height 6:08. Weight 220.
High School—Milton, Fla.
College—Florida State University, Tallahassee, Fla.
Never drafted by an NBA franchise.

Signed by Sacramento as a free agent, October 5, 1988.

Waived by Sacramento, October 20, 1988; signed by Sacramento, March 3, 1989, to the first of consecutive 10-day contracts that expired, March 22, 1989.

Re-signed by Sacramento for remainder of season, March 23, 1989.

Played in Continental Basketball Association with Cedar Rapids Silver Bullets, 1988-89.

Played in Belgium, 1987-88.

—COLLEGIATE RECORD—

Year	G.	Min.	FGA	FGM	Pct.	FTA	FTM	Pct.	Reb.	Pts.	Avg.
83-84	30	879	211	109	.517	73	37	.507	148	255	8.5
84-85	28	901	352	187	.531	101	62	.614	190	436	15.6
85-86	27	849	330	152	.461	112	67	.598	163	371	13.7
86-87	30	954	312	144	.462	127	88	.693	235	376	12.5
Totals	115	3583	1205	592	.491	413	254	.615	736	1438	12.5

Three-Point Field Goals: 1986-87, 0-for-2.

CBA REGULAR SEASON RECORD

			—2-Point—			—3-Point—									
Sea.—Team	G.	Min.	FGM	FGA	Pct.	FGM	FGA	Pct.	FTM	FTA	Pct.	Reb.	Ast.	Pts.	Avg.
88-89—Cedar Rapids	46	1707	261	567	.460	0	1	.000	71	115	.617	508	56	593	12.9

NBA REGULAR SEASON RECORD

									—Rebounds—									
Sea.—Team	G.	Min.	FGA	FGM	Pct.	FTA	FTM	Pct.	Off.	Def.	Tot.	Ast.	PF	Dq.	Stl.	Blk.	Pts.	Avg.
88-89—Sacramento	7	43	19	8	.421	2	1	.500	3	4	7	0	7	0	1	1	17	2.4
89-90—Sacramento	63	746	239	106	.444	43	23	.535	49	89	138	23	102	0	16	19	235	3.7
Totals	70	789	258	114	.442	45	24	.533	52	93	145	23	109	0	17	20	252	3.6

Three-Point Field Goals: 1988-89, 0-for-1. 1989-90, 0-for-7. Totals, 0-for-8.

Named CBA Newcomer of the Year, 1989.

GREGORY WAYNE ANDERSON
(Greg)

Born June 22, 1964 at Houston, Tex. Height 6:10. Weight 230.
High School—Houston, Tex., Worthing.
College—University of Houston, Houston, Tex.
Drafted by San Antonio on first round, 1987 (23rd pick).

Traded by San Antonio with Alvin Robertson and future considerations to Milwaukee for Terry Cummings and future considerations, May 28, 1989.

—COLLEGIATE RECORD—

Year	G.	Min.	FGA	FGM	Pct.	FTA	FTM	Pct.	Reb.	Pts.	Avg.
83-84	35	414	101	49	.485	36	19	.528	123	117	3.3
84-85	30	931	344	197	.573	129	69	.535	244	463	15.4
85-86	28	1055	376	215	.572	181	106	.586	360	536	19.1
86-87	30	1057	409	215	.526	192	116	.604	318	546	18.2
Totals	123	3457	1230	676	.550	538	310	.576	1045	1662	13.5

NBA REGULAR SEASON RECORD

									—Rebounds—									
Sea.—Team	G.	Min.	FGA	FGM	Pct.	FTA	FTM	Pct.	Off.	Def.	Tot.	Ast.	PF	Dq.	Stl.	Blk.	Pts.	Avg.
87-88—San Antonio	82	1984	756	379	.501	328	198	.604	161	352	513	79	228	1	54	122	957	11.7
88-89—San Antonio	82	2401	914	460	.503	403	207	.514	255	421	676	61	221	2	102	103	1127	13.7
89-90—Milwaukee	60	1291	432	219	.507	170	91	.535	112	261	373	24	176	3	32	54	529	8.8
Totals	224	5676	2102	1058	.503	901	496	.550	528	1034	1562	164	625	6	188	279	2613	11.7

Three-Point Field Goals: 1987-88, 1-for-5 (.200). 1988-89, 0-for-3. Totals, 1-for-8 (.125).

GREG ANDERSON

NBA PLAYOFF RECORD

Sea.—Team	G.	Min.	FGA	FGM	Pct.	FTA	FTM	Pct.	—Rebounds— Off.	Def.	Tot.	Ast.	PF	Dq.	Stl.	Blk.	Pts.	Avg.
87-88—San Antonio	3	95	36	17	.472	9	4	.444	6	15	21	3	10	1	2	4	38	12.7
89-90—Milwaukee	4	101	19	13	.684	14	7	.500	6	18	24	0	19	2	1	4	33	8.3
Totals	7	196	55	30	.545	23	11	.478	12	33	45	3	29	3	3	8	71	10.1

Named to NBA All-Rookie Team, 1988.

NELISON ANDERSON (Nick)

Born January 20, 1968 at Chicago, Ill. Height 6:06. Weight 215.

High Schools—Chicago, Ill., Prosser (Fresh. and Soph.) and Chicago, Ill., Simeon (Jr. and Sr.).

College—University of Illinois, Champaign, Ill.

Drafted by Orlando on first round as an undergraduate, 1989 (11th pick).

—COLLEGIATE RECORD—

Year	G.	Min.	FGA	FGM	Pct.	FTA	FTM	Pct.	Reb.	Pts.	Avg.
86-87				Did Not Play—Proposition 48							
87-88	33	909	390	223	.572	120	77	.642	217	525	15.9
88-89	36	1125	487	262	.538	148	99	.669	285	647	18.0
Totals	69	2034	877	485	.553	268	176	.657	502	1172	17.0

Three-Point Field Goals: 1987-88, 2-for-6 (.333). 1988-89, 24-for-66 (.364). Totals, 26-for-72 (.342).

NBA REGULAR SEASON RECORD

Sea.—Team	G.	Min.	FGA	FGM	Pct.	FTA	FTM	Pct.	—Rebounds— Off.	Def.	Tot.	Ast.	PF	Dq.	Stl.	Blk.	Pts.	Avg.
89-90—Orlando	81	1785	753	372	.494	264	186	.705	107	209	316	124	140	0	69	34	931	11.5

Three-Point Field Goals: 1989-90, 1-for-17 (.059).

RICHARD ANDREW ANDERSON

Born November 19, 1960 at San Pedro, Calif. Height 6:10. Weight 240.

High School—Garden Grove, Calif., Rancho Alamitos.

College—University of California at Santa Barbara, Santa Barbara, Calif.

Drafted by San Diego on second round, 1982 (32nd pick).

Traded by San Diego to Denver for Billy McKinney, October 4, 1983.

Signed by Houston as a Veteran Free Agent, October 11, 1986; Denver agreed not to exercise its right of first refusal in exchange for a 1988 3rd round draft choice.

Waived by Houston, December 7, 1987; claimed off waivers by Portland, December 9, 1987.

Traded by Portland to Charlotte for Robert Reid, October 17, 1989.

Played in Italy, 1984-85 and 1985-86.

—COLLEGIATE RECORD—

Year	G.	Min.	FGA	FGM	Pct.	FTA	FTM	Pct.	Reb.	Pts.	Avg.
78-79	20	208	84	36	.429	16	7	.438	59	79	4.0
79-80	27	906	316	141	.446	77	58	.753	164	340	12.6
80-81	27	770	367	166	.452	98	72	.735	257	404	15.0
81-82	26	926	351	165	.470	121	87	.719	289	417	16.0
Totals	100	2810	1118	508	.454	312	224	.718	769	1240	12.4

ITALIAN LEAGUE RECORD

Year	G.	Min.	FGA	FGM	Pct.	FTA	FTM	Pct.	Reb.	Pts.	Avg.
84-85—Cantu	34	1162	431	222	.515	124	101	.815	309	620	18.2
85-86—Cantu	38	1280	278	156	.561	75	61	.813	320	547	14.4

NBA REGULAR SEASON RECORD

Sea.—Team	G.	Min.	FGA	FGM	Pct.	FTA	FTM	Pct.	—Rebounds— Off.	Def.	Tot.	Ast.	PF	Dq.	Stl.	Blk.	Pts.	Avg.
82-83—San Diego	78	1274	431	174	.404	69	48	.696	111	161	272	120	170	2	57	26	403	5.2
83-84—Denver	78	1380	638	272	.426	150	116	.773	136	270	406	193	183	0	46	28	663	8.5
86-87—Houston	51	312	139	59	.424	29	22	.759	24	55	79	33	37	0	7	3	144	2.8
87-88—Hou.-Port.	74	1350	439	171	.390	77	58	.753	91	212	303	112	137	1	51	16	448	6.1
88-89—Portland	72	1082	348	145	.417	38	32	.842	62	169	231	98	100	1	44	12	371	5.2
89-90—Charlotte	54	604	211	88	.417	23	18	.783	33	94	127	55	64	0	20	9	231	4.3
Totals	407	6002	2206	909	.412	386	294	.762	457	961	1418	611	691	4	225	94	2260	5.6

Three-Point Field Goals: 1982-83, 7-for-19 (.269). 1983-84, 3-for-19 (.158). 1986-87, 4-for-16 (.250). 1987-88, 48-for-150 (.320). 1988-89, 49-for-141 (.348). 1989-90, 37-for-100 (.370). Totals, 148-for-445 (.333).

NBA PLAYOFF RECORD

Sea.—Team	G.	Min.	FGA	FGM	Pct.	FTA	FTM	Pct.	—Rebounds— Off.	Def.	Tot.	Ast.	PF	Dq.	Stl.	Blk.	Pts.	Avg.
83-84—Denver	4	37	15	6	.400	6	4	.667	1	8	9	5	6	0	0	1	16	4.0
86-87—Houston	5	5	3	1	.333	2	2	1.000	1	0	1	0	1	0	0	0	5	1.0
87-88—Portland	3	63	24	11	.458	4	4	1.000	5	8	13	1	11	0	2	1	32	10.7
88-89—Portland	3	35	6	2	.333	0	0	....	0	3	3	4	2	0	0	1	5	1.7
Totals	15	140	48	20	.417	12	10	.833	7	19	26	10	20	0	2	3	58	3.9

Three-Point Field Goals: 1983-84, 0-for-1. 1986-87, 1-for-2 (.500). 1987-88, 6-for-14 (.429). 1988-89, 1-for-4 (.250). Totals, 8-for-21 (.381).

RONALD GENE ANDERSON
(Ron)

Born October 15, 1958 at Chicago, Ill. Height 6:07. Weight 215.
High School—Chicago, Ill., Bowen (Did not play basketball)
Colleges—Santa Barbara City College, Santa Barbara, Calif.,
and Fresno State University, Fresno, Calif.
Drafted by Cleveland on second round, 1984 (27th pick).

Traded by Cleveland to Indiana for a 1987 4th round draft choice, December 10, 1985.
Traded by Indiana to Philadelphia for the draft rights to Everette Stephens, October 4, 1988.

—COLLEGIATE RECORD—

Santa Barbara

Year	G.	Min.	FGA	FGM	Pct.	FTA	FTM	Pct.	Reb.	Pts.	Avg.
80-81	33	....	333	167	.502	75	56	.747	328	390	11.8
81-82	32	....	448	292	.652	84	66	.786	340	650	20.3
JC Totals	65	....	781	459	.588	159	122	.767	668	1040	16.0

Fresno State

Year	G.	Min.	FGA	FGM	Pct.	FTA	FTM	Pct.	Reb.	Pts.	Avg.
82-83	35	1303	426	234	.549	128	104	.813	204	572	16.3
83-84	33	1197	437	249	.570	104	82	.788	200	580	17.6
Totals	68	2500	863	483	.560	232	186	.802	404	1152	16.9

NBA REGULAR SEASON RECORD

Sea.—Team	G.	Min.	FGA	FGM	Pct.	FTA	FTM	Pct.	—Rebounds— Off.	Def.	Tot.	Ast.	PF	Dq.	Stl.	Blk.	Pts.	Avg.
84-85—Cleveland	36	520	195	84	.431	50	41	.820	39	49	88	34	40	0	9	7	210	5.8
85-86—Clev.-Ind.	77	1676	628	310	.494	127	85	.669	130	144	274	144	125	0	56	6	707	9.2
86-87—Indiana	63	721	294	139	.473	108	85	.787	73	78	151	54	65	0	31	3	363	5.8
87-88—Indiana	74	1097	436	217	.498	141	108	.766	89	127	216	78	98	0	41	6	542	7.3
88-89—Philadelphia	82	2618	1152	566	.491	229	196	.856	167	239	406	139	166	1	71	23	1330	16.2
89-90—Philadelphia	78	2089	841	379	.451	197	165	.838	81	214	295	143	143	0	72	13	926	11.9
Totals	410	8721	3546	1695	.478	852	680	.798	579	851	1430	592	637	1	280	58	4078	9.9

Three-Point Field Goals: 1984-85, 1-for-2 (.500). 1985-86, 2-for-9 (.222). 1986-87, 0-for-5. 1987-88, 0-for-2. 1988-89, 2-for-11 (.182). 1989-90, 3-for-21 (.143). Totals, 8-for-50 (.160).

NBA PLAYOFF RECORD

Sea.—Team	G.	Min.	FGA	FGM	Pct.	FTA	FTM	Pct.	—Rebounds— Off.	Def.	Tot.	Ast.	PF	Dq.	Stl.	Blk.	Pts.	Avg.
84-85—Cleveland	2	9	3	0	.000	0	0	.000	1	2	3	0	0	0	0	0	0	0.0
86-87—Indiana	4	24	4	2	.500	0	0	.000	2	1	3	0	2	0	0	0	4	1.0
88-89—Philadelphia	3	109	51	29	.569	5	4	.800	7	9	16	13	10	0	1	2	62	20.7
89-90—Philadelphia	10	256	93	40	.430	30	29	.967	6	31	37	14	22	0	4	0	112	11.2
Totals	19	398	151	71	.470	35	33	.943	16	43	59	27	34	0	5	2	178	9.4

Three-Point Field Goals: 1988-89, 0-for-1. 1989-90, 3-for-5 (.600). Totals, 3-for-6 (.500).

WILLIE LLOYD ANDERSON

Born January 8, 1967 at Greenville, S.C. Height 6:07. Weight 190.
High School—Atlanta, Ga., East Atlanta.
College—University of Georgia, Athens, Ga.
Drafted by San Antonio on first round, 1988 (10th pick).

—COLLEGIATE RECORD—

Year	G.	Min.	FGA	FGM	Pct.	FTA	FTM	Pct.	Reb.	Pts.	Avg.
84-85	13	80	39	19	.487	8	5	.625	19	43	3.3
85-86	29	493	197	99	.503	61	48	.787	98	246	8.5
86-87	30	1047	374	187	.500	97	77	.794	123	476	15.9
87-88	35	1161	482	241	.500	116	91	.784	177	583	16.7
Totals	107	2781	1092	546	.500	282	221	.784	417	1348	12.6

Three-Point Field Goals: 1986-87, 25-for-64 (.391). 1987-88, 10-for-44 (.227). Totals, 35-for-108 (.324).

NBA REGULAR SEASON RECORD

										—Rebounds—								
Sea.—Team	G.	Min.	FGA	FGM	Pct.	FTA	FTM	Pct.	Off.	Def.	Tot.	Ast.	PF	Dq.	Stl.	Blk.	Pts.	Avg.
88-89—San Antonio	81	2738	1285	640	.498	289	224	.775	152	265	417	372	295	8	150	62	1508	18.6
89-90—San Antonio	82	2788	1082	532	.492	290	217	.748	115	257	372	364	252	3	111	58	1288	15.7
Totals	163	5526	2367	1172	.495	579	441	.762	267	522	789	736	547	11	261	120	2796	17.2

Three-Point Field Goals: 1988-89, 4-for-21 (.190). 1989-90, 7-for-26 (.269). Totals, 11-for-47 (.234).

NBA PLAYOFF RECORD

										—Rebounds—								
Sea.—Team	G.	Min.	FGA	FGM	Pct.	FTA	FTM	Pct.	Off.	Def.	Tot.	Ast.	PF	Dq.	Stl.	Blk.	Pts.	Avg.
89-90—San Antonio	10	375	168	87	.518	36	29	.806	16	38	54	52	40	2	9	4	205	20.5

Three-Point Field Goals: 1989-90, 2-for-5 (.400).

Named to NBA All-Rookie First Team, 1989. . . . Member of U.S. Olympic team, 1988.

MICHAEL ANSLEY

Born February 8, 1967 at Birmingham, Ala. Height 6:07. Weight 225.
High School—Birmingham, Ala., Jackson-Olin.
College—University of Alabama, Tuscaloosa, Ala.
Drafted by Orlando on second round, 1989 (37th pick).

—COLLEGIATE RECORD—

Year	G.	Min.	FGA	FGM	Pct.	FTA	FTM	Pct.	Reb.	Pts.	Avg.
85-86	33	594	144	87	.604	39	21	.538	140	195	5.9
86-87	33	1009	243	145	.597	109	73	.670	259	363	11.0
87-88	31	1085	389	218	.560	171	125	.731	285	561	18.1
88-89	31	1053	446	255	.572	155	119	.768	284	630	20.3
Totals	128	3741	1222	705	.577	474	338	.713	968	1749	13.7

Three-Point Field Goals: 1987-88, 0-for-1. 1988-89, 1-for-4 (.250). Totals, 1-for-5 (.200).

NBA REGULAR SEASON RECORD

										—Rebounds—								
Sea.—Team	G.	Min.	FGA	FGM	Pct.	FTA	FTM	Pct.	Off.	Def.	Tot.	Ast.	PF	Dq.	Stl.	Blk.	Pts.	Avg.
89-90—Orlando	72	1221	465	231	.497	227	164	.722	187	175	362	40	152	0	24	17	626	8.7

BENJAMIN ROY ARMSTRONG JR.
(B.J.)

Born September 9, 1967 at Detroit, Mich. Height 6:02. Weight 175.
High School—Birmingham, Mich., Brother Rice.
College—University of Iowa, Iowa City, Ia.
Drafted by Chicago on first round, 1989 (18th pick).

—COLLEGIATE RECORD—

Year	G.	Min.	FGA	FGM	Pct.	FTA	FTM	Pct.	Reb.	Pts.	Avg.
85-86	29	232	66	32	.485	21	19	.905	16	83	2.9
86-87	35	995	295	153	.519	126	100	.794	89	434	12.4
87-88	34	1023	421	203	.482	146	124	.849	74	592	17.4
88-89	32	1015	403	195	.484	192	160	.833	79	596	18.6
Totals	130	3265	1185	583	.492	485	403	.831	258	1705	13.1

Three-Point Field Goals: 1986-87, 28-for-54 (.519). 1987-88, 62-for-137 (.453). 1988-89, 46-for-116 (.397). Totals, 136-for-307 (.443).

NBA REGULAR SEASON RECORD

										—Rebounds—								
Sea.—Team	G.	Min.	FGA	FGM	Pct.	FTA	FTM	Pct.	Off.	Def.	Tot.	Ast.	PF	Dq.	Stl.	Blk.	Pts.	Avg.
89-90—Chicago	81	1291	392	190	.485	78	69	.885	19	83	102	199	105	0	46	6	452	5.6

Three-Point Field Goals: 1989-90, 3-for-6 (.500).

NBA PLAYOFF RECORD

										—Rebounds—								
Sea.—Team	G.	Min.	FGA	FGM	Pct.	FTA	FTM	Pct.	Off.	Def.	Tot.	Ast.	PF	Dq.	Stl.	Blk.	Pts.	Avg.
89-90—Chicago	16	217	62	21	.339	24	22	.917	3	17	20	29	22	0	10	0	64	4.0

Three-Point Field Goals: 1989-90, 0-for-4.

JOHN EDWARD BAGLEY

Born April 23, 1960 at Bridgeport, Conn. Height 6:00. Weight 192.
High School—Bridgeport, Conn., Warren Harding.
College—Boston College, Chestnut Hill, Mass.
Drafted by Cleveland on first round as an undergraduate, 1982 (12th pick).

Traded by Cleveland with Keith Lee to New Jersey for Darryl Dawkins and James Bailey, October 8, 1987.
Traded by New Jersey to Boston for 1991 and 1993 2nd round draft choices, October 5, 1989.

—COLLEGIATE RECORD—

Year	G.	Min.	FGA	FGM	Pct.	FTA	FTM	Pct.	Reb.	Pts.	Avg.
79-80	29	....	270	130	.481	115	83	.722	91	343	11.8
80-81	30	965	418	209	.500	245	193	.788	115	611	20.4
81-82	32	1065	513	257	.501	202	161	.797	122	675	21.1
Totals	91	....	1201	596	.496	562	437	.778	328	1629	17.9

NBA REGULAR SEASON RECORD

									—Rebounds—									
Sea.—Team	G.	Min.	FGA	FGM	Pct.	FTA	FTM	Pct.	Off.	Def.	Tot.	Ast.	PF	Dq.	Stl.	Blk.	Pts.	Avg.
82-83—Cleveland	68	990	373	161	.432	84	64	.762	17	79	96	167	74	0	54	5	386	5.7
83-84—Cleveland	76	1712	607	257	.423	198	157	.793	49	107	156	333	113	1	78	4	673	8.9
84-85—Cleveland	81	2401	693	338	.488	167	125	.749	54	237	291	697	132	0	129	5	804	9.9
85-86—Cleveland	78	2472	865	366	.423	215	170	.791	76	199	275	735	165	1	122	10	911	11.7
86-87—Cleveland	72	2182	732	312	.426	136	113	.831	55	197	252	379	114	0	91	7	768	10.7
87-88—New Jersey	82	2774	896	393	.439	180	148	.822	61	196	257	479	162	0	110	10	981	12.0
88-89—New Jersey	68	1642	481	200	.416	123	89	.724	36	108	144	391	117	0	72	5	500	7.4
89-90—Boston	54	1095	218	100	.459	39	29	.744	26	63	89	296	77	0	40	4	230	4.3
Totals	579	15268	4865	2127	.437	1142	895	.784	374	1186	1560	3477	954	2	696	50	5253	9.1

Three-Point Field Goals: 1982-83, 0-for-14. 1983-84, 2-for-17 (.118). 1984-85, 3-for-26 (.115). 1985-86, 9-for-37 (.243). 1986-87, 31-for-103 (.301). 1987-88, 47-for-161 (.292). 1988-89, 11-for-54 (.204). 1989-90, 1-for-18 (.056). Totals, 104-for-430 (.242).

NBA PLAYOFF RECORD

									—Rebounds—									
Sea.—Team	G.	Min.	FGA	FGM	Pct.	FTA	FTM	Pct.	Off.	Def.	Tot.	Ast.	PF	Dq.	Stl.	Blk.	Pts.	Avg.
84-85—Cleveland	4	168	56	22	.393	10	7	.700	1	15	16	40	7	0	10	0	51	12.8
89-90—Boston	5	70	15	8	.533	4	3	.750	3	1	4	17	9	0	4	1	19	3.8
Totals	9	238	71	30	.423	14	10	.714	4	16	20	57	16	0	14	1	70	7.8

Three-Point Field Goals: 1984-85, 0-for-3. 1989-90, 0-for-1. Totals, 0-for-4.

THURL LEE BAILEY

Born April 7, 1961 at Washington, D. C. Height 6:11. Weight 232.

High School—Bladensburg, Md.

College—North Carolina State University, Raleigh, N. C.

Drafted by Utah on first round, 1983 (7th pick).

—COLLEGIATE RECORD—

Year	G.	Min.	FGA	FGM	Pct.	FTA	FTM	Pct.	Reb.	Pts.	Avg.
79-80	28	....	101	44	.436	55	37	.673	102	125	4.5
80-81	27	....	278	146	.525	53	39	.736	165	331	12.3
81-82	32	....	312	171	.548	118	96	.814	216	438	13.7
82-83	36	....	499	250	.501	127	91	.717	276	601	16.7
Totals	123	....	1190	611	.513	353	263	.745	759	1495	12.2

Three-Point Field Goals: 1982-83, 10-for-15 (.667).

NBA REGULAR SEASON RECORD

									—Rebounds—									
Sea.—Team	G.	Min.	FGA	FGM	Pct.	FTA	FTM	Pct.	Off.	Def.	Tot.	Ast.	PF	Dq.	Stl.	Blk.	Pts.	Avg.
83-84—Utah	81	2009	590	302	.512	117	88	.752	113	349	464	129	193	1	38	122	692	8.5
84-85—Utah	80	2481	1034	507	.490	234	197	.842	153	372	525	138	215	2	51	105	1212	15.2
85-86—Utah	82	2358	1077	483	.448	277	230	.830	148	345	493	153	160	0	42	114	1196	14.6
86-87—Utah	81	2155	1036	463	.447	236	190	.805	145	287	432	102	150	0	38	88	1116	13.8
87-88—Utah	82	2804	1286	633	.492	408	337	.826	134	397	531	158	186	1	49	125	1604	19.6
88-89—Utah	82	2777	1272	615	.483	440	363	.825	115	332	447	138	185	0	48	91	1595	19.5
89-90—Utah	82	2583	977	470	.481	285	222	.779	116	294	410	137	175	2	32	100	1162	14.2
Totals	570	17167	7272	3473	.478	1997	1627	.815	926	2376	3302	955	1264	6	298	745	8577	15.0

Three-Point Field Goals: 1984-85, 1-for-1 (1.000). 1985-86, 0-for-7. 1986-87, 0-for-2. 1987-88, 1-for-3 (.333). 1988-89, 2-for-5 (.400). 1989-90, 0-for-8. Totals, 4-for-26 (.154).

NBA PLAYOFF RECORD

									—Rebounds—									
Sea.—Team	G.	Min.	FGA	FGM	Pct.	FTA	FTM	Pct.	Off.	Def.	Tot.	Ast.	PF	Dq.	Stl.	Blk.	Pts.	Avg.
83-84—Utah	11	340	97	50	.515	21	17	.810	15	46	61	10	33	0	2	11	117	10.6
84-85—Utah	10	375	152	62	.408	55	45	.818	21	71	92	27	30	0	5	18	169	16.9
85-86—Utah	4	147	77	28	.364	11	8	.727	11	21	32	13	13	0	2	2	64	16.0
86-87—Utah	5	151	63	30	.476	18	18	1.000	14	16	30	9	12	1	3	6	78	15.6
87-88—Utah	11	449	203	99	.488	68	57	.838	21	42	63	18	32	0	6	23	255	23.2
88-89—Utah	3	122	34	12	.353	15	12	.800	10	15	25	3	11	0	1	4	36	12.0
89-90—Utah	5	190	88	43	.489	24	19	.792	8	24	32	7	19	1	5	6	105	21.0
Totals	49	1774	714	324	.454	212	176	.830	100	235	335	87	150	2	24	70	824	16.8

Three-Point Field Goals: 1983-84, 0-for-2. 1985-86, 0-for-1. 1987-88, 0-for-1. Totals, 0-for-4.

Named to NBA All-Rookie Team, 1984. . . . Member of NCAA Division I championship team, 1983.

KENNETH BANNISTER
(Ken)

Born April 1, 1960 at Baltimore, Md. Height 6:09. Weight 235.

High School—Baltimore, Md., Southwestern.

Colleges—Trinidad State Junior College, Trinidad, Colo.; Indiana State University, Terre Haute, Ind., and St. Augustine's College, Raleigh, N. C.

Drafted by New York on seventh round, 1984 (156th pick).

Waived by New York, October 21, 1988; signed by Los Angeles Clippers, April 5, 1989, to a 10-day contract that expired, April 14, 1989.

Re-signed by Los Angeles Clippers, April 14, 1989, for remainder of season.

Played in Continental Basketball Association with Quad City Thunder and Mississippi Jets, 1987-88, and with Wichita Falls Texans and Rockford Lightning, 1988-89.

Played in Israel, 1986-87 and 1987-88.

—COLLEGIATE RECORD—

Trinidad State J.C.

Year	G.	Min.	FGA	FGM	Pct.	FTA	FTM	Pct.	Reb.	Pts.	Avg.
79-80	Statistics Unavailable										
80-81	Statistics Unavailable										

Indiana State

Year	G.	Min.	FGA	FGM	Pct.	FTA	FTM	Pct.	Reb.	Pts.	Avg.
81-82	27	786	304	153	.503	117	69	.590	177	375	13.9

St. Augustine's

Year	G.	Min.	FGA	FGM	Pct.	FTA	FTM	Pct.	Reb.	Pts.	Avg.
82-83	Did Not Play—Transfer Student										
83-84	21	....	256	142	.555	117	64	.547	276	348	16.6
Totals	48	....	560	295	.527	234	133	.568	453	723	15.1

CBA REGULAR SEASON RECORD

			—2-Point—			—3-Point—									
Sea.—Team	G.	Min.	FGM	FGA	Pct.	FGM	FGA	Pct.	FTM	FTA	Pct.	Reb.	Ast.	Pts.	Avg.
87-88—Q.C.-Miss.	25	773	139	255	.545	0	1	.000	59	122	.483	175	42	337	13.4
88-89—Wich. F.-Rock	44	1115	238	465	.512	0	8	.000	122	244	.500	291	65	598	13.6
Totals	69	1888	377	720	.524	0	9	.000	181	366	.495	466	107	935	13.6

NBA REGULAR SEASON RECORD

									—Rebounds—									
Sea.—Team	G.	Min.	FGA	FGM	Pct.	FTA	FTM	Pct.	Off.	Def.	Tot.	Ast.	PF	Dq.	Stl.	Blk.	Pts.	Avg.
84-85—New York	75	1404	445	209	.470	192	91	.474	108	222	330	39	279	16	38	40	509	6.8
85-86—New York	70	1405	479	235	.491	249	131	.526	89	233	322	42	208	5	42	24	601	8.6
88-89—L.A. Clippers	9	130	36	22	.611	53	30	.566	6	27	33	3	17	0	7	2	74	8.2
89-90—L.A. Clippers	52	589	161	77	.478	110	52	.473	39	73	112	18	92	1	17	7	206	4.0
Totals	206	3528	1121	543	.484	604	304	.503	242	555	797	102	596	22	104	73	1390	6.7

Three-Point Field Goals: 1985-86, 0-for-1. 1988-89, 0-for-1. 1989-90, 0-for-1. Totals, 0-for 3.

CHARLES WADE BARKLEY

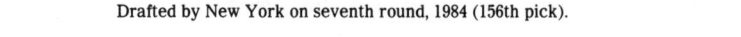

Born February 20, 1963 at Leeds, Ala. Height 6:06. Weight 253.

High School—Leeds, Ala.

College—Auburn University, Auburn, Ala.

Drafted by Philadelphia on first round as an undergraduate, 1984 (5th pick).

—COLLEGIATE RECORD—

Year	G.	Min.	FGA	FGM	Pct.	FTA	FTM	Pct.	Reb.	Pts.	Avg.
81-82	28	746	242	144	.595	107	68	.636	275	356	12.7
82-83	28	782	250	161	.644	130	82	.631	266	404	14.4
83-84	28	794	254	162	.638	145	99	.683	265	423	15.1
Totals	84	2322	746	467	.636	382	249	.652	806	1183	14.1

NBA REGULAR SEASON RECORD

									—Rebounds—									
Sea.—Team	G.	Min.	FGA	FGM	Pct.	FTA	FTM	Pct.	Off.	Def.	Tot.	Ast.	PF	Dq.	Stl.	Blk.	Pts.	Avg.
84-85—Philadelphia	82	2347	783	427	.545	400	293	.733	266	437	703	155	301	5	95	80	1148	14.0
85-86—Philadelphia	80	2952	1041	595	.572	578	396	.685	354	672	1026	312	333	8	173	125	1603	20.0
86-87—Philadelphia	68	2740	937	557	.594	564	429	.761	390	604	994	331	252	5	119	104	1564	23.0
87-88—Philadelphia	80	3170	1283	753	.587	951	714	.751	385	566	951	254	278	6	100	103	2264	28.3
88-89—Philadelphia	79	3088	1208	700	.579	799	602	.753	403	583	986	325	262	3	126	67	2037	25.8
89-90—Philadelphia	79	3085	1177	706	.600	744	557	.749	361	548	909	307	250	2	148	50	1989	25.2
Totals	468	17382	6429	3738	.581	4036	2991	.741	2159	3410	5569	1684	1676	29	761	529	10605	22.7

Three-Point Field Goals: 1984-85, 1-for-6 (.167). 1985-86, 17-for-75 (.227). 1986-87, 21-for-104 (.202). 1987-88, 44-for-157 (.280). 1988-89, 35-for-162 (.216). 1989-90, 20-for-92 (.217). Totals, 138-for-596 (.232).

NBA PLAYOFF RECORD

Sea.—Team	G.	Min.	FGA	FGM	Pct.	FTA	FTM	Pct.	—Rebounds— Off.	Def.	Tot.	Ast.	PF	Dq.	Stl.	Blk.	Pts.	Avg.
84-85—Philadelphia	13	408	139	75	.540	63	40	.635	52	92	144	26	49	0	23	15	194	14.9
85-86—Philadelphia	12	497	180	104	.578	131	91	.695	60	129	189	67	52	2	27	15	300	25.0
86-87—Philadelphia	5	210	75	43	.573	45	36	.800	27	36	63	12	21	0	4	8	123	24.6
88-89—Philadelphia	3	135	45	29	.644	31	22	.710	8	27	35	16	9	0	5	2	81	27.0
89-90—Philadelphia	10	419	162	88	.543	108	65	.602	66	89	155	43	36	0	8	7	247	24.7
Totals	43	1669	601	339	.564	378	254	.672	213	373	586	164	167	2	67	47	945	22.0

Three-Point Field Goals: 1984-85, 4-for-6 (.667). 1985-86, 1-for-15 (.067). 1986-87, 1-for-8 (.125). 1988-89, 1-for-5 (.200). 1989-90, 6-for-18 (.333). Totals, 13-for-52 (.250).

NBA ALL-STAR GAME RECORD

Season—Team	Min.	FGA	FGM	Pct.	FTA	FTM	Pct.	—Rebounds— Off.	Def.	Tot.	Ast.	PF	Dq.	Stl.	Blk.	Pts.
1987—Philadelphia	16	6	2	.333	6	3	.500	1	3	4	1	2	0	1	0	7
1988—Philadelphia	15	4	1	.250	2	2	1.000	1	2	3	0	2	0	1	1	4
1989—Philadelphia	20	11	6	.545	8	5	.625	3	2	5	0	0	0	2	1	17
1990—Philadelphia	22	12	7	.583	3	2	.667	2	2	4	0	1	0	1	1	17
Totals	73	33	16	.485	19	12	.632	7	9	16	1	5	0	5	3	45

Three-Point Field Goals: 1987, 0-for-2. 1988, 0-for-1. 1990, 1-for-1 (1.000). Totals, 1-for-4 (.250).

Named to All-NBA First Team, 1988, 1989, 1990. . . . All-NBA Second Team, 1986 and 1987. . . . NBA All-Rookie Team, 1985. . . . Led NBA in rebounding, 1987. . . . Recipient of Schick Pivotal Player Award, 1986, 1987, 1988.

DANA BRUCE BARROS

Born April 13, 1967 at Boston, Mass. Height 5:11. Weight 170.

High School—Westwood, Mass., Xaverian.

College—Boston College, Boston, Mass.

Drafted by Seattle on first round, 1989 (16th pick).

—COLLEGIATE RECORD—

Year	G.	Min.	FGA	FGM	Pct.	FTA	FTM	Pct.	Reb.	Pts.	Avg.
85-86	28	971	330	158	.479	86	68	.791	78	384	13.7
86-87	29	1145	424	194	.458	100	85	.850	85	543	18.7
87-88	33	1223	504	242	.480	153	130	.850	113	723	21.9
88-89	29	1096	484	230	.475	140	120	.857	103	692	23.9
Totals	119	4435	1742	824	.473	479	403	.841	379	2342	19.7

Three-Point Field Goals: 1986-87, 70-for-173 (.405). 1987-88, 109-for-240 (.454). 1988-89, 112-for-261 (.429). Totals, 291-for-674 (.432).

NBA REGULAR SEASON RECORD

Sea.—Team	G.	Min.	FGA	FGM	Pct.	FTA	FTM	Pct.	—Rebounds— Off.	Def.	Tot.	Ast.	PF	Dq.	Stl.	Blk.	Pts.	Avg.
89-90—Seattle	81	1630	738	299	.405	110	89	.809	35	97	132	205	97	0	53	1	782	9.7

Three-Point Field Goals: 1989-90, 95-for-238 (.399).

JOHN SIDNEY BATTLE

Born November 9, 1962 at Washington, D.C. Height 6:02. Weight 175.

High School—Washington, D.C., McKinley.

College—Rutgers University, New Brunswick, N.J.

Drafted by Atlanta on fourth round, 1985 (84th pick).

—COLLEGIATE RECORD—

Year	G.	Min.	FGA	FGM	Pct.	FTA	FTM	Pct.	Reb.	Pts.	Avg.
81-82	29	373	67	29	.433	28	12	.429	29	70	2.4
82-83	31	443	139	68	.489	51	37	.725	48	182	5.9
83-84	25	814	420	207	.493	153	111	.725	78	525	21.0
84-85	29	1017	470	231	.491	177	129	.729	115	608	21.0
Totals	114	2647	1096	535	.488	409	289	.707	270	1385	12.1

Three-Point Field Goals: 1982-83, 9-for-18 (.500). 1984-85, 17-for-58 (.293).

NBA REGULAR SEASON RECORD

Sea.—Team	G.	Min.	FGA	FGM	Pct.	FTA	FTM	Pct.	—Rebounds— Off.	Def.	Tot.	Ast.	PF	Dq.	Stl.	Blk.	Pts.	Avg.
85-86—Atlanta	64	639	222	101	.455	103	75	.728	12	50	62	74	80	0	23	3	277	4.3
86-87—Atlanta	64	804	315	144	.457	126	93	.738	16	44	60	124	76	0	29	5	381	6.0
87-88—Atlanta	67	1227	613	278	.454	188	141	.750	26	87	113	158	84	0	31	5	713	10.6
88-89—Atlanta	82	1672	628	287	.457	238	194	.815	30	110	140	197	125	0	42	9	779	9.5
89-90—Atlanta	60	1477	544	275	.506	135	102	.756	27	72	99	154	115	0	28	3	654	10.9
Totals	337	5819	2322	1085	.467	790	605	.766	111	363	474	707	480	0	153	25	2804	8.3

Three-Point Field Goals: 1985-86, 0-for-7. 1986-87, 0-for-10. 1987-88, 16-for-41 (.390). 1988-89, 11-for-34 (.324). 1989-90, 2-for-13 (.154). Totals, 29-for-105 (.276).

NBA PLAYOFF RECORD

									—Rebounds—									
Sea.—Team	G.	Min.	FGA	FGM	Pct.	FTA	FTM	Pct.	Off.	Def.	Tot.	Ast.	PF	Dq.	Stl.	Blk.	Pts.	Avg.
85-86—Atlanta	6	27	11	4	.364	4	3	.750	0	4	4	2	5	0	2	0	11	1.8
86-87—Atlanta	8	78	34	15	.441	23	21	.913	2	8	10	8	13	0	1	0	53	6.6
87-88—Atlanta	12	166	67	32	.478	25	17	.680	2	18	20	26	14	0	2	0	81	6.8
88-89—Atlanta	5	118	46	20	.435	12	9	.750	5	8	13	16	13	0	2	0	49	9.8
Totals	31	389	158	71	.449	64	50	.781	9	38	47	52	45	0	7	0	194	6.3

Three-Point Field Goals: 1985-86, 0-for-1. 1986-87, 2-for-5 (.400). 1987-88, 0-for-2. 1988-89, 0-for-6. Totals, 2-for-14 (.143).

KENNY BATTLE

Born October 10, 1964 at Aurora, Ill. Height 6:06. Weight 210.

High School—Aurora, Ill., West.

Colleges—Northern Illinois University, DeKalb, Ill., and University of Illinois, Champaign, Ill.

Drafted by Detroit on first round, 1989 (27th pick).

Draft rights traded by Detroit with Michael Williams to Phoenix for draft rights to Anthony Cook, June 27, 1989.

—COLLEGIATE RECORD—

Northern Illinois

Year	G.	Min.	FGA	FGM	Pct.	FTA	FTM	Pct.	Reb.	Pts.	Avg.
84-85	27	....	369	195	.528	234	154	.658	167	544	20.1
85-86	27	....	354	201	.568	193	126	.653	175	528	19.6
NIU Totals	54	....	723	396	.548	427	280	.656	342	1072	19.9

Illinois

Year	G.	Min.	FGA	FGM	Pct.	FTA	FTM	Pct.	Reb.	Pts.	Avg.
86-87	Did Not Play—Transfer Student										
87-88	33	1027	341	197	.578	179	122	.682	183	516	15.6
88-89	36	1105	361	218	.604	200	151	.755	174	596	16.6
Ill. Totals	69	2132	702	415	.591	379	273	.720	357	1112	16.1
Col. Totals	123	....	1425	811	.569	806	553	.686	699	2184	17.8

Three-Point Field Goals: 1987-88, 0-for-1. 1988-89, 9-for-17 (.529). Totals, 9-for-18 (.500).

NBA REGULAR SEASON RECORD

									—Rebounds—									
Sea.—Team	G.	Min.	FGA	FGM	Pct.	FTA	FTM	Pct.	Off.	Def.	Tot.	Ast.	PF	Dq.	Stl.	Blk.	Pts.	Avg.
89-90—Phoenix	59	729	170	93	.547	82	55	.671	44	80	124	38	94	2	35	11	242	4.1

Three-Point Field Goals: 1989-90, 1-for-4 (.250).

NBA PLAYOFF RECORD

									—Rebounds—									
Sea.—Team	G.	Min.	FGA	FGM	Pct.	FTA	FTM	Pct.	Off.	Def.	Tot.	Ast.	PF	Dq.	Stl.	Blk.	Pts.	Avg.
89-90—Phoenix	8	34	13	4	.308	1	1	1.000	1	4	5	0	5	0	0	0	9	1.1

WILLIAM BEDFORD

Born December 14, 1963 at Memphis, Tenn. Height 7:01. Weight 235.

High School—Memphis, Tenn., Melrose.

College—Memphis State University, Memphis, Tenn.

Drafted by Phoenix on first round as an undergraduate, 1986 (6th pick).

Traded by Phoenix to Detroit for a 1989 1st round draft choice, June 21, 1987.

—COLLEGIATE RECORD—

Year	G.	Min.	FGA	FGM	Pct.	FTA	FTM	Pct.	Reb.	Pts.	Avg.
83-84	26	684	187	108	.578	56	30	.536	137	246	9.5
84-85	35	1099	330	179	.542	101	68	.673	265	426	12.2
85-86	32	1038	389	227	.584	156	98	.628	273	552	17.3
Totals	93	2821	906	514	.567	313	196	.626	675	1224	13.2

NBA REGULAR SEASON RECORD

									—Rebounds—									
Sea.—Team	G.	Min.	FGA	FGM	Pct.	FTA	FTM	Pct.	Off.	Def.	Tot.	Ast.	PF	Dq.	Stl.	Blk.	Pts.	Avg.
86-87—Phoenix	50	979	358	142	.397	86	50	.581	79	167	246	57	125	1	18	37	334	6.7
87-88—Detroit	38	298	101	44	.436	23	13	.565	27	38	65	4	47	0	8	17	101	2.7
89-90—Detroit	42	246	125	54	.432	22	9	.409	15	43	58	4	39	0	3	17	118	2.8
Totals	130	1523	584	240	.411	131	72	.550	121	248	369	65	211	1	29	71	553	4.3

Three-Point Field Goals: 1986-87, 0-for-1. 1989-90, 1-for-6 (.167). Totals, 1-for-7 (.143).

NBA PLAYOFF RECORD

										—Rebounds—								
Sea.—Team	G.	Min.	FGA	FGM	Pct.	FTA	FTM	Pct.	Off.	Def.	Tot.	Ast.	PF	Dq.	Stl.	Blk.	Pts.	Avg.
89-90—Detroit	5	19	6	1	.167	2	2	1.000	0	2	2	0	4	0	0	1	4	0.8

Member of NBA championship team, 1990.

LENARD BENOIT BENJAMIN

(Known by middle name.)

Born November 22, 1964 at Monroe, La. Height 7:00. Weight 250.
High School—Monroe, La., Carroll.
College—Creighton University, Omaha, Neb.
Drafted by Los Angeles Clippers on first round as an undergraduate, 1985 (3rd pick).

—COLLEGIATE RECORD—

Year	G.	Min.	FGA	FGM	Pct.	FTA	FTM	Pct.	Reb.	Pts.	Avg.
82-83	27	871	292	162	.555	116	76	.655	259	400	14.8
83-84	30	1112	350	190	.543	144	107	.743	295	487	16.2
84-85	32	1193	443	258	.582	233	172	.738	451	688	21.5
Totals	89	3176	1085	610	.562	493	355	.720	1005	1575	17.7

NBA REGULAR SEASON RECORD

										—Rebounds—								
Sea.—Team	G.	Min.	FGA	FGM	Pct.	FTA	FTM	Pct.	Off.	Def.	Tot.	Ast.	PF	Dq.	Stl.	Blk.	Pts.	Avg.
85-86—L.A. Clippers	79	2088	661	324	.490	307	229	.746	161	439	600	79	286	5	64	206	878	11.1
86-87—L.A. Clippers	72	2230	713	320	.449	263	188	.715	134	452	586	135	251	7	60	187	828	11.5
87-88—L.A. Clippers	66	2171	693	340	.491	255	180	.706	112	418	530	172	203	2	50	225	860	13.0
88-89—L.A. Clippers	79	2585	907	491	.541	426	317	.744	164	532	696	157	221	4	57	221	1299	16.4
89-90—L.A. Clippers	71	2313	688	362	.526	321	235	.732	156	501	657	159	217	3	59	187	959	13.5
Totals	367	11387	3662	1837	.502	1572	1149	.731	727	2342	3069	702	1178	21	290	1026	4824	13.1

Three-Point Field Goals: 1985-86, 1-for-3 (.333). 1986-87, 0-for-2. 1987-88, 0-for-8. 1988-89, 0-for-2. 1989-90, 0-for-1. Totals, 1-for-16 (.063).

WINSTON GEORGE BENNETT III

Born February 9, 1965 at Louisville, Ky. Height 6:07. Weight 220.
High School—Louisville, Ky., Male.
College—University of Kentucky, Louisville, Ky.
Drafted by Cleveland on third round, 1988 (64th pick).

Played in Continental Basketball Association with Pensacola Tornados, 1988-89.
Played in Italy, 1988-89.

—COLLEGIATE RECORD—

Year	G.	Min.	FGA	FGM	Pct.	FTA	FTM	Pct.	Reb.	Pts.	Avg.
83-84	34	642	156	67	.429	126	88	.698	129	222	6.5
84-85	30	851	191	82	.429	77	52	.675	160	216	7.2
85-86	36	1129	338	171	.506	158	115	.728	252	457	12.7
86-87					Did Not Play—Knee Injury						
87-88	33	1091	380	195	.513	155	113	.729	258	504	15.3
Totals	133	3713	1065	515	.484	516	368	.713	799	1399	10.5

Three-Point Field Goals: 1987-88, 1-for-2 (.500).

ITALIAN LEAGUE RECORD

Year	G.	Min.	FGA	FGM	Pct.	FTA	FTM	Pct.	Reb.	Pts.	Avg.
88-89—Teo. Arese	7	253	131	55	.420	55	38	.691	54	148	21.1

CBA REGULAR SEASON RECORD

			—2-Point—			—3-Point—									
Sea.—Team	G.	Min.	FGM	FGA	Pct.	FGM	FGA	Pct.	FTM	FTA	Pct.	Reb.	Ast.	Pts.	Avg.
88-89—Pensacola	26	793	130	265	.491	0	0	.000	99	138	.717	288	28	359	13.8

NBA REGULAR SEASON RECORD

										—Rebounds—								
Sea.—Team	G.	Min.	FGA	FGM	Pct.	FTA	FTM	Pct.	Off.	Def.	Tot.	Ast.	PF	Dq.	Stl.	Blk.	Pts.	Avg.
89-90—Cleveland	55	990	286	137	.479	96	64	.667	84	104	188	54	133	1	23	10	338	6.1

NBA PLAYOFF RECORD

										—Rebounds—								
Sea.—Team	G.	Min.	FGA	FGM	Pct.	FTA	FTM	Pct.	Off.	Def.	Tot.	Ast.	PF	Dq.	Stl.	Blk.	Pts.	Avg.
89-90—Cleveland	5	135	47	23	.489	6	4	.667	14	7	21	5	11	0	3	1	50	10.0

WALTER BERRY

Born May 14, 1964 at New York, N.Y. Height 6:08. Weight 215.

High Schools—Bronx, N.Y., Morris; Bronx, N.Y., DeWitt Clinton and New York, N.Y., Benjamin Franklin.

Colleges—San Jacinto College (Central), Pasadena, Tex., and St. John's University, Jamaica, N.Y.

Drafted by Portland on first round as an undergraduate, 1986 (14th pick).

Traded by Portland to San Antonio for Kevin Duckworth, December 18, 1986.
Traded by San Antonio to New Jersey for Dallas Comegys, August 29, 1988.
Waived by New Jersey, January 30, 1989; signed by Houston as a free agent, February 2, 1989.

—COLLEGIATE RECORD—

St. John's

Year	G.	Min.	FGA	FGM	Pct.	FTA	FTM	Pct.	Reb.	Pts.	Avg.
82-83	Did Not Play—Ineligible										

San Jacinto

Year	G.	Min.	FGA	FGM	Pct.	FTA	FTM	Pct.	Reb.	Pts.	Avg.
83-84	35	....	625	419	.670	270	174	.644	489	1012	28.9

St. John's

Year	G.	Min.	FGA	FGM	Pct.	FTA	FTM	Pct.	Reb.	Pts.	Avg.
84-85	35	1200	414	231	.558	187	134	.717	304	596	17.0
85-86	36	1318	547	327	.598	248	174	.702	399	828	23.0
, St. John's Totals	71	2518	961	558	.581	435	308	.708	703	1424	20.1

NBA REGULAR SEASON RECORD

Sea.—Team	G.	Min.	FGA	FGM	Pct.	FTA	FTM	Pct.	—Rebounds— Off.	Def.	Tot.	Ast.	PF	Dq.	Stl.	Blk.	Pts.	Avg.
86-87—Port.-S.A.	63	1586	766	407	.531	288	187	.649	136	173	309	105	196	2	38	40	1001	15.9
87-88—San Antonio	73	1922	960	540	.563	320	192	.600	176	219	395	110	207	2	55	63	1272	17.4
88-89—N.J.-Hous.	69	1355	501	254	.507	143	100	.699	86	181	267	77	183	1	29	48	609	8.8
Totals	205	4863	2227	1201	.539	751	479	.638	398	573	971	292	586	5	122	151	2882	14.1

Three-Point Field Goals: 1986-87, 0-for-3. 1988-89, 1-for-2 (.500). Totals, 1-for-5 (.200).

NBA PLAYOFF RECORD

Sea.—Team	G.	Min.	FGA	FGM	Pct.	FTA	FTM	Pct.	—Rebounds— Off.	Def.	Tot.	Ast.	PF	Dq.	Stl.	Blk.	Pts.	Avg.
87-88—San Antonio	3	94	50	27	.540	15	12	.800	13	8	21	6	10	0	5	2	66	22.0
88-89—Houston	4	57	26	13	.500	8	7	.875	3	6	9	5	8	0	2	1	33	8.3
Totals	7	151	76	40	.526	23	19	.826	16	14	30	11	18	0	7	3	99	14.1

Three-Point Field Goals: 1987-88, 0-for-1. 1988-89, 0-for-1. Totals, 0-for-2.

Named THE SPORTING NEWS College Player of the Year, 1986. . . . THE SPORTING NEWS All-America First Team, 1986.

LARRY JOE BIRD

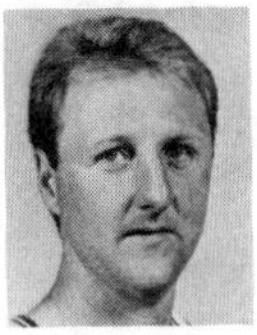

Born December 7, 1956 at West Baden, Ind. Height 6:09. Weight 220.

High School—French Lick, Ind., Springs Valley.

Colleges—Indiana University, Bloomington, Ind.; Northwood Institute, West Baden, Ind., and Indiana State University, Terre Haute, Ind.

Drafted by Boston on first round as junior eligible, 1978 (6th pick).

—COLLEGIATE RECORD—

Indiana

Year	G.	Min.	FGA	FGM	Pct.	FTA	FTM	Pct.	Reb.	Pts.	Avg.
74-75	Did Not Play										

Indiana State

Year	G.	Min.	FGA	FGM	Pct.	FTA	FTM	Pct.	Reb.	Pts.	Avg.
75-76	Did Not Play—Transfer Student										
76-77	28	1033	689	375	.544	200	168	.840	373	918	32.8
77-78	32	....	769	403	.524	193	153	.793	369	959	30.0
78-79	34	....	707	376	.532	266	221	.831	505	973	28.6
Totals	94	....	2165	1154	.533	659	542	.822	1247	2850	30.3

NBA REGULAR SEASON RECORD

Sea.—Team	G.	Min.	FGA	FGM	Pct.	FTA	FTM	Pct.	—Rebounds— Off.	Def.	Tot.	Ast.	PF	Dq.	Stl.	Blk.	Pts.	Avg.
79-80—Boston	82	2955	1463	693	.474	360	301	.836	216	636	852	370	279	4	143	53	1745	21.3
80-81—Boston	82	3239	1503	719	.478	328	283	.863	191	704	895	451	239	2	161	63	1741	21.2

LARRY BIRD

Sea.—Team	G.	Min.	FGA	FGM	Pct.	FTA	FTM	Pct.	Rebounds Off.	Def.	Tot.	Ast.	PF	Dq.	Stl.	Blk.	Pts.	Avg.
81-82—Boston	77	2923	1414	711	.503	380	328	.863	200	637	837	447	244	0	143	66	1761	22.9
82-83—Boston	79	2982	1481	747	.504	418	351	.840	193	677	870	458	197	0	148	71	1867	23.6
83-84—Boston	79	3028	1542	758	.492	421	374	.888	181	615	796	520	197	0	144	69	1908	24.2
84-85—Boston	80	3161	1760	918	.522	457	403	.882	164	678	842	531	208	0	129	98	2295	28.7
85-86—Boston	82	3113	1606	796	.496	492	441	.896	190	615	805	557	182	0	166	51	2115	25.8
86-87—Boston	74	3005	1497	786	.525	455	414	.910	124	558	682	566	185	3	135	70	2076	28.1
87-88—Boston	76	2965	1672	881	.527	453	415	.916	108	595	703	467	157	0	125	57	2275	29.9
88-89—Boston	6	189	104	49	.471	19	18	.947	1	36	37	29	18	0	6	5	116	19.3
89-90—Boston	75	2944	1517	718	.473	343	319	.930	90	622	712	562	173	2	106	61	1820	24.3
Totals	792	30504	15559	7776	.500	4126	3647	.884	1658	6373	8031	4958	2079	11	1406	664	19719	24.9

Three-Point Field Goals: 1979-80, 58-for-143 (.406). 1980-81, 20-for-74 (.270). 1981-82, 11-for-52 (.212). 1982-83, 22-for-77 (.286). 1983-84, 18-for-73 (.247). 1984-85, 56-for-131 (.427). 1985-86, 82-for-194 (.423). 1986-87, 90-for-225 (.400). 1987-88, 98-for-237 (.414). 1989-90, 65-for-195 (.333). Totals, 520-for-1401 (.371).

NBA PLAYOFF RECORD

Sea.—Team	G.	Min.	FGA	FGM	Pct.	FTA	FTM	Pct.	Rebounds Off.	Def.	Tot.	Ast.	PF	Dq.	Stl.	Blk.	Pts.	Avg.
79-80—Boston	9	372	177	83	.469	25	22	.880	22	79	101	42	30	0	14	8	192	21.3
80-81—Boston	17	750	313	147	.470	85	76	.894	49	189	238	103	53	0	39	17	373	21.9
81-82—Boston	12	490	206	88	.427	45	37	.822	33	117	150	67	43	0	23	17	214	17.8
82-83—Boston	6	240	116	49	.422	29	24	.828	20	55	75	41	15	0	13	3	123	20.5
83-84—Boston	23	961	437	229	.524	190	167	.879	62	190	252	136	71	0	54	27	632	27.5
84-85—Boston	20	815	425	196	.461	136	121	.890	53	129	182	115	54	0	34	19	520	26.0
85-86—Boston	18	770	331	171	.517	109	101	.927	34	134	168	148	55	0	37	11	466	25.9
86-87—Boston	23	1015	454	216	.476	193	176	.912	41	190	231	165	55	1	27	19	622	27.0
87-88—Boston	17	763	338	152	.450	113	101	.894	29	121	150	115	45	0	36	14	417	24.5
89-90—Boston	5	207	99	44	.444	32	29	.906	7	39	46	44	10	0	5	5	122	24.4
Totals	150	6383	2896	1375	.475	957	854	.892	350	1243	1593	976	431	1	282	140	3681	24.5

Three-Point Field Goals: 1979-80, 4-for-15 (.267). 1980-81, 3-for-8 (.375). 1981-82, 1-for-6 (.167). 1982-83, 1-for-4 (.250). 1983-84, 7-for-17 (.412). 1984-85, 7-for-25 (.280). 1985-86, 23-for-56 (.411). 1986-87, 14-for-41 (.341). 1987-88, 12-for-32 (.375). 1989-90, 5-for-19 (.263). Totals, 77-for-223 (.345).

NBA ALL-STAR GAME RECORD

Season—Team	Min.	FGA	FGM	Pct.	FTA	FTM	Pct.	Rebounds Off.	Def.	Tot.	Ast.	PF	Dq.	Stl.	Blk.	Pts.
1980—Boston	23	6	3	.500	0	0	.000	3	3	6	7	1	0	1	0	7
1981—Boston	18	5	1	.200	0	0	.000	1	3	4	3	1	0	1	0	2
1982—Boston	28	12	7	.583	8	5	.625	0	12	12	5	3	0	1	1	19
1983—Boston	29	14	7	.500	0	0	.000	3	10	13	7	4	0	2	0	14
1984—Boston	33	18	6	.333	4	4	1.000	1	6	7	3	1	0	2	0	16
1985—Boston	31	16	8	.500	6	5	.833	5	3	8	2	3	0	0	1	21
1986—Boston	35	18	8	.444	6	5	.833	2	6	8	5	5	0	7	0	23
1987—Boston	35	18	7	.389	4	4	1.000	2	4	6	5	5	0	2	0	18
1988—Boston	32	8	2	.250	2	2	1.000	0	7	7	1	4	0	4	1	6
1990—Boston	23	8	3	.375	2	2	1.000	2	6	8	3	1	0	3	0	8
Totals	287	123	52	.423	32	27	.844	19	60	79	41	28	0	23	3	134

Three-Point Field Goals: 1980, 1-for-2 (.500). 1983, 0-for-1. 1985, 0-for-1. 1986, 2-for-4 (.500). 1987, 0-for-3. 1988, 0-for-1. 1990, 0-for-1. Totals, 3-for-13 (.231).

NBA Most Valuable Player, 1984, 1985, 1986. . . . Named to All-NBA First Team, 1980, 1981, 1982, 1983, 1984, 1985, 1986, 1987, 1988. . . . All-NBA Second Team, 1990. . . . NBA All-Defensive Second Team, 1982, 1983, 1984. . . . NBA Rookie of the Year, 1980. . . . NBA All-Rookie Team, 1980. . . . Member of NBA championship teams, 1981, 1984, 1986. . . . NBA Playoff MVP, 1984 and 1986. . . . Holds NBA playoff record for most points in one year, 1984. . . . NBA's all-time three-point field goal leader. . . . Led NBA in free-throw percentage, 1984, 1986, 1987, 1990. . . . NBA All-Star Game MVP, 1982. . . . THE SPORTING NEWS College Player of the Year, 1979. . . . THE SPORTING NEWS All-America First Team, 1978 and 1979.

UWE KONSTANTINE BLAB

Born March 26, 1962 at Munich, West Germany. Height 7:01. Weight 255.
High School—Effingham, Ill.
College—Indiana University, Bloomington, Ind.
Drafted by Dallas on first round, 1985 (17th pick).

Signed by Dallas as an unrestricted free agent, 1990.
Traded by Golden State to San Antonio for Christian Welp, February 22, 1990.

—COLLEGIATE RECORD—

Year	G.	Min.	FGA	FGM	Pct.	FTA	FTM	Pct.	Reb.	Pts.	Avg.
81-82	24	....	124	69	.556	70	41	.586	89	179	7.5
82-83	30	....	220	114	.518	97	55	.567	148	283	9.4
83-84	31	....	284	150	.528	104	66	.635	190	366	11.8
84-85	33	....	375	212	.565	147	105	.714	207	529	16.0
Totals	118	....	1003	545	.543	418	267	.639	634	1357	11.5

NBA REGULAR SEASON RECORD

Sea.—Team	G.	Min.	FGA	FGM	Pct.	FTA	FTM	Pct.	—Rebounds— Off.	Def.	Tot.	Ast.	PF	Dq.	Stl.	Blk.	Pts.	Avg.
85-86—Dallas	48	409	94	44	.468	67	36	.537	25	66	91	17	65	0	3	12	124	2.6
86-87—Dallas	30	160	51	20	.392	28	13	.464	11	25	36	13	33	0	4	9	53	1.8
87-88—Dallas	73	658	132	58	.439	65	46	.708	52	82	134	35	108	1	8	29	162	2.2
88-89—Dallas	37	208	52	24	.462	25	20	.800	11	33	44	12	36	0	3	13	68	1.8
89-90—G.S.-S.A.	47	531	98	39	.398	37	20	.541	29	79	108	25	102	0	1	22	98	2.1
Totals	235	1966	427	185	.433	222	135	.608	128	285	413	102	344	1	19	85	505	2.1

NBA PLAYOFF RECORD

Sea.—Team	G.	Min.	FGA	FGM	Pct.	FTA	FTM	Pct.	—Rebounds— Off.	Def.	Tot.	Ast.	PF	Dq.	Stl.	Blk.	Pts.	Avg.
85-86—Dallas	1	6	3	2	.667	0	0	.000	0	1	1	0	1	0	0	0	4	4.0
86-87—Dallas	1	10	1	1	1.000	4	1	.250	1	2	3	0	4	0	1	1	3	3.0
87-88—Dallas	3	8	2	0	.000	2	2	1.000	1	0	1	1	1	0	0	0	2	0.7
89-90—San Antonio	2	5	1	0	.000	6	3	.500	0	2	2	0	0	0	0	0	3	1.5
Totals	7	29	7	3	.429	12	6	.500	2	5	7	1	6	0	1	1	12	1.7

Member of West German Olympic team, 1984.

ROLANDO ANTONIO BLACKMAN

Born February 26, 1959 at Panama City, Panama. Height 6:06. Weight 194.
High School—Brooklyn, N. Y., William Grady.
College—Kansas State University, Manhattan, Kan.
Drafted by Dallas on first round, 1981 (9th pick).

—COLLEGIATE RECORD—

Year	G.	Min.	FGA	FGM	Pct.	FTA	FTM	Pct.	Reb.	Pts.	Avg.
77-78	29	....	269	127	.472	93	61	.656	187	315	10.9
78-79	28	....	392	200	.510	113	83	.735	110	483	17.3
79-80	31	....	419	226	.539	145	100	.690	145	552	17.8
80-81	33	....	380	202	.532	115	90	.783	165	494	15.0
Totals	121	....	1460	755	.517	466	334	.717	607	1844	15.2

NBA REGULAR SEASON RECORD

Sea.—Team	G.	Min.	FGA	FGM	Pct.	FTA	FTM	Pct.	—Rebounds— Off.	Def.	Tot.	Ast.	PF	Dq.	Stl.	Blk.	Pts.	Avg.
81-82—Dallas	82	1979	855	439	.513	276	212	.768	97	157	254	105	122	0	46	30	1091	13.3
82-83—Dallas	75	2349	1042	513	.492	381	297	.780	108	185	293	185	116	0	37	29	1326	17.7
83-84—Dallas	81	3025	1320	721	.546	458	372	.812	124	249	373	288	127	0	56	37	1815	22.4
84-85—Dallas	81	2834	1230	625	.508	413	342	.828	107	193	300	289	96	0	61	16	1598	19.7
85-86—Dallas	82	2787	1318	677	.514	483	404	.836	88	203	291	271	138	0	79	25	1762	21.5
86-87—Dallas	80	2758	1264	626	.495	474	419	.884	96	182	278	266	142	0	64	21	1676	21.0
87-88—Dallas	71	2580	1050	497	.473	379	331	.873	82	164	246	262	112	0	64	18	1325	18.7
88-89—Dallas	78	2946	1249	594	.476	370	316	.854	70	203	273	288	137	0	65	20	1534	19.7
89-90—Dallas	80	2934	1256	626	.498	340	287	.844	88	192	280	289	128	0	77	21	1552	19.4
Totals	710	24192	10584	5318	.502	3574	2980	.834	860	1728	2588	2243	1118	0	549	217	13679	19.3

Three-Point Field Goals: 1981-82, 1-for-4 (.250). 1982-83, 3-for-15 (.200). 1983-84, 1-for-11 (.091). 1984-85, 6-for-20 (.300). 1985-86, 4-for-29 (.138). 1986-87, 5-for-15 (.333). 1987-88, 0-for-5. 1988-89, 30-for-85 (.353). 1989-90, 13-for-43 (.302). Totals, 63-for-227 (.278).

NBA PLAYOFF RECORD

Sea.—Team	G.	Min.	FGA	FGM	Pct.	FTA	FTM	Pct.	—Rebounds— Off.	Def.	Tot.	Ast.	PF	Dq.	Stl.	Blk.	Pts.	Avg.
83-84—Dallas	10	397	175	93	.531	63	53	.841	15	26	41	40	15	0	6	4	239	23.9
84-85—Dallas	4	169	92	47	.511	38	36	.947	11	15	26	19	8	0	2	2	131	32.8
85-86—Dallas	10	371	167	83	.497	53	42	.792	15	20	35	32	26	1	8	1	208	20.8
86-87—Dallas	4	153	73	36	.493	24	22	.917	4	10	14	17	7	0	2	0	94	23.5
87-88—Dallas	17	672	261	126	.483	62	55	.887	26	29	55	77	28	0	15	3	307	18.1
89-90—Dallas	3	127	54	24	.444	10	10	1.000	2	7	9	13	7	0	6	2	60	20.0
Totals	48	1889	822	409	.498	250	218	.872	73	107	180	198	91	1	39	12	1039	21.6

Three-Point Field Goals: 1984-85, 1-for-2 (.500). 1985-86, 0-for-1. 1986-87, 0-for-1. 1987-88, 0-for-3. 1989-90, 2-for-5 (.400). Totals, 3-for-12 (.250).

NBA ALL-STAR GAME RECORD

Season—Team	Min.	FGA	FGM	Pct.	FTA	FTM	Pct.	—Rebounds— Off.	Def.	Tot.	Ast.	PF	Dq.	Stl.	Blk.	Pts.
1985—Dallas	23	14	7	.500	2	1	.500	1	2	3	2	1	0	1	1	15
1986—Dallas	22	11	6	.545	0	0	.000	1	3	4	8	1	0	2	1	12
1987—Dallas	22	15	9	.600	13	11	.846	1	3	4	1	2	0	0	0	29
1990—Dallas	21	9	7	.778	1	1	1.000	1	1	2	2	1	0	2	0	15
Totals	88	49	29	.592	16	13	.813	4	9	13	13	5	0	5	2	71

Named to THE SPORTING NEWS All-America First Team, 1981. . . . Member of U.S. Olympic team, 1980.

DARON OSHAY BLAYLOCK
(Mookie)

Born March 20, 1967 at Garland, Tex. Height 6:00. Weight 180.
High School—Garland, Tex.
Colleges—Midland College, Midland, Tex., and University of Oklahoma, Norman, Okla.
Drafted by New Jersey on first round, 1989 (12th pick).

—COLLEGIATE RECORD—

Midland

Year	G.	Min.	FGA	FGM	Pct.	FTA	FTM	Pct.	Reb.	Pts.	Avg.
85-86	34	....	449	254	.566	84	62	.738	109	570	16.8
86-87	33	....	500	258	.516	83	60	.723	138	647	19.6
J.C. Totals	67	....	949	512	.540	167	122	.731	247	1217	18.2

Oklahoma

Year	G.	Min.	FGA	FGM	Pct.	FTA	FTM	Pct.	Reb.	Pts.	Avg.
87-88	39	1347	524	241	.460	114	78	.684	162	638	16.4
88-89	35	1359	598	272	.455	100	65	.650	164	700	20.0
Okla. Totals	74	2706	1122	513	.457	214	143	.668	326	1338	18.1

Three-Point Field Goals: 1986-87, 71. 1987-88, 78-for-201 (.388). 1988-89, 91-for-245 (.371). Oklahoma Totals, 169-for-446 (.379).

NBA REGULAR SEASON RECORD

									—Rebounds—									
Sea.—Team	G.	Min.	FGA	FGM	Pct.	FTA	FTM	Pct.	Off.	Def.	Tot.	Ast.	PF	Dq.	Stl.	Blk.	Pts.	Avg.
89-90—New Jersey	50	1267	571	212	.371	81	63	.778	42	98	140	210	110	0	82	14	505	10.1

Three-Point Field Goals: 1989-90, 18-for-80 (.225).

Named to THE SPORTING NEWS All-America Second Team, 1989.

TYRONE BOGUES
(Muggsy)

Born January 9, 1965 at Baltimore, Md. Height 5:03. Weight 140.
High School—Baltimore, Md., Dunbar.
College—Wake Forest University, Winston-Salem, N.C.
Drafted by Washington on first round, 1987 (12th pick).

Selected from Washington by Charlotte in NBA expansion draft, June 23, 1988.

—COLLEGIATE RECORD—

Year	G.	Min.	FGA	FGM	Pct.	FTA	FTM	Pct.	Reb.	Pts.	Avg.
83-84	32	312	46	14	.304	13	9	.692	21	37	1.2
84-85	29	1025	162	81	.500	44	30	.682	69	192	6.6
85-86	29	....	290	132	.455	89	65	.730	90	329	11.3
86-87	29	....	318	159	.500	93	75	.806	110	428	14.8
Totals	119	....	816	386	.473	239	179	.749	290	986	8.3

Three-Point Field Goals: 1986-87, 35-for-79 (.443).

NBA REGULAR SEASON RECORD

									—Rebounds—									
Sea.—Team	G.	Min.	FGA	FGM	Pct.	FTA	FTM	Pct.	Off.	Def.	Tot.	Ast.	PF	Dq.	Stl.	Blk.	Pts.	Avg.
87-88—Washington	79	1628	426	166	.390	74	58	.784	35	101	136	404	138	1	127	3	393	5.0
88-89—Charlotte	79	1755	418	178	.426	88	66	.750	53	112	165	620	141	1	111	7	423	5.4
89-90—Charlotte	81	2743	664	326	.491	134	106	.791	48	159	207	867	168	1	166	3	763	9.4
Totals	239	6126	1508	670	.444	296	230	.777	136	372	508	1891	447	3	404	13	1579	6.6

Three-Point Field Goals: 1987-88, 3-for-16 (.188), 1988-89, 1-for-13 (.077). 1989-90, 5-for-26 (.192). Totals, 9-for-55 (.164).

NBA PLAYOFF RECORD

									—Rebounds—									
Sea.—Team	G.	Min.	FGA	FGM	Pct.	FTA	FTM	Pct.	Off.	Def.	Tot.	Ast.	PF	Dq.	Stl.	Blk.	Pts.	Avg.
87-88—Washington	1	2	0	0	.000	0	0	.000	0	0	0	2	0	0	0	0	0	0.0

—DID YOU KNOW—

That former Lakers Coach Pat Riley posted 500 regular-season victories in just 684 games, faster than any coach in NBA history?

MANUTE BOL

Born October 16, 1962 at Gogrial, Sudan. Height 7:07. Weight 225.
High School—Attended Case Western Reserve English Language School, Cleveland, O.
College—University of Bridgeport, Bridgeport, Conn.
Drafted by San Diego on fifth round, 1983 (97th pick).
Declared ineligible for 1983 NBA draft.
Drafted by Washington on second round as an undergraduate, 1985 (31st pick).

Traded by Washington to Golden State for Dave Feitl and a 1989 2nd round draft choice, June 8, 1988.
Traded by Golden State to Philadelphia for a 1991 1st round draft choice, August 1, 1990.

—COLLEGIATE RECORD—

Year	G.	Min.	FGA	FGM	Pct.	FTA	FTM	Pct.	Reb.	Pts.	Avg.
84-85	31	....	496	303	.611	153	91	.595	419	697	22.5

NBA REGULAR SEASON RECORD

									—Rebounds—									
Sea.—Team	G.	Min.	FGA	FGM	Pct.	FTA	FTM	Pct.	Off.	Def.	Tot.	Ast.	PF	Dq.	Stl.	Blk.	Pts.	Avg.
85-86—Washington	80	2090	278	128	.460	86	42	.488	123	354	477	23	255	5	28	397	298	3.7
86-87—Washington	82	1552	231	103	.446	67	45	.672	84	278	362	11	189	1	20	302	251	3.1
87-88—Washington	77	1136	165	75	.455	49	26	.531	72	203	275	13	160	0	11	208	176	2.3
88-89—Golden State	80	1769	344	127	.369	66	40	.606	116	346	462	27	226	2	11	345	314	3.9
89-90—Golden State	75	1310	169	56	.331	49	25	.510	33	243	276	36	194	3	13	238	146	1.9
Totals	394	7857	1187	489	.412	317	178	.562	428	1424	1852	110	1024	11	83	1490	1185	3.0

Three-Point Field Goals: 1985-86, 0-for-1. 1986-87, 0-for-1. 1987-88, 0-for-1. 1988-89, 20-for-91 (.220). 1989-90, 9-for-48 (.188). Totals, 29-for-142 (.204).

NBA PLAYOFF RECORD

									—Rebounds—									
Sea.—Team	G.	Min.	FGA	FGM	Pct.	FTA	FTM	Pct.	Off.	Def.	Tot.	Ast.	PF	Dq.	Stl.	Blk.	Pts.	Avg.
85-86—Washington	5	152	17	10	.588	8	3	.375	16	22	38	1	15	0	3	29	23	4.6
86-87—Washington	3	43	10	4	.400	2	0	.000	5	4	9	0	6	0	0	5	8	2.7
87-88—Washington	5	44	7	4	.571	1	1	1.000	7	5	12	0	5	0	0	2	9	1.8
88-89—Golden State	8	148	36	7	.194	7	2	.286	5	26	31	1	21	0	2	29	18	2.3
Totals	21	387	70	25	.357	18	6	.333	33	57	90	2	47	0	5	65	58	2.8

Three-Point Field Goals: 1986-87, 0-for-1. 1988-89, 2-for-22 (.091). Totals, 2-for-23 (.087).

Named to NBA All-Defensive Second Team, 1986.... Led NBA in blocked shots, 1986 and 1989.

ANTHONY LEE BOWIE

Born November 9, 1963 at Tulsa, Okla. Height 6:06. Weight 190.
High School—Tulsa, Okla., East Central.
Colleges—Seminole Junior College, Seminole, Okla., and University of Oklahoma, Norman, Okla.
Drafted by Houston on third round, 1986 (66th pick).

Waived by Houston, November 4, 1986; re-signed by Houston as a free agent, June 11, 1987.
Waived by Houston, November 5, 1987; signed by New Jersey as a free agent, July 19, 1988.
Waived by New Jersey, November 1, 1988; signed by San Antonio, March 20, 1989, to the first of consecutive 10-day contracts that expired, April 8, 1989.
Re-signed by San Antonio, April 9, 1989, for remainder of season.
Traded by San Antonio to Houston for cash, August 15, 1989.
Played in Continental Basketball Association with Quad City Thunder, 1987-88 and 1988-89.

—COLLEGIATE RECORD—

Seminole

Year	G.	Min.	FGA	FGM	Pct.	FTA	FTM	Pct.	Reb.	Pts.	Avg.
82-83	40	....	....	....	.525	....	....	.770	....	712	17.8
83-84	38	....	....	....	.542	....	....	.793	....	707	18.6
J.C. Totals	78	....	....	....	.534	....	....	.782	....	1419	18.2

Oklahoma

Year	G.	Min.	FGA	FGM	Pct.	FTA	FTM	Pct.	Reb.	Pts.	Avg.
84-85	37	1282	392	202	.515	119	92	.773	215	496	13.4
85-86	35	1170	402	202	.502	78	63	.808	161	467	13.3
Totals	72	2452	794	404	.509	197	155	.787	376	963	13.4

CBA REGULAR SEASON RECORD

			—2-Point—			—3-Point—									
Sea.—Team	G.	Min.	FGM	FGA	Pct.	FGM	FGA	Pct.	FTM	FTA	Pct.	Reb.	Ast.	Pts.	Avg.
87-88—Quad City	37	1028	198	365	.542	7	23	.304	75	83	.903	163	105	492	13.3
88-89—Quad City	53	1959	442	878	.503	14	58	.241	171	213	.803	363	238	1097	20.7
Totals	90	2987	640	1243	.515	21	81	.259	246	296	.831	526	343	1589	17.7

NBA REGULAR SEASON RECORD

									—Rebounds—									
Sea.—Team	G.	Min.	FGA	FGM	Pct.	FTA	FTM	Pct.	Off.	Def.	Tot.	Ast.	PF	Dq.	Stl.	Blk.	Pts.	Avg.
88-89—San Antonio	18	438	144	72	.500	15	10	.667	25	31	56	29	43	1	18	4	155	8.6
89-90—Houston	66	918	293	119	.406	54	40	.741	36	82	118	96	80	0	42	5	284	4.3
Totals	84	1356	437	191	.437	69	50	.725	61	113	174	125	123	1	60	9	439	5.2

Three-Point Field Goals: 1988-89, 1-for-5 (.200). 1989-90, 6-for-21 (.286). Totals, 7-for-26 (.269).

NBA PLAYOFF RECORD

									—Rebounds—									
Sea.—Team	G.	Min.	FGA	FGM	Pct.	FTA	FTM	Pct.	Off.	Def.	Tot.	Ast.	PF	Dq.	Stl.	Blk.	Pts.	Avg.
89-90—Houston	2	4	1	0	.000	0	0	....	0	0	0	0	1	0	0	0	0	0.0

Named CBA Most Valuable Player, 1989. . . . CBA All-Star First Team, 1989.

SAMUEL PAUL BOWIE
(Sam)

Born March 17, 1961 at Lebanon, Pa. Height 7:01. Weight 240.
High School—Lebanon, Pa.
College—University of Kentucky, Lexington, Ky.
Drafted by Portland on first round, 1984 (2nd pick).

Traded by Portland with a 1989 1st round draft choice to New Jersey for Buck Williams, June 24, 1989.
Missed entire 1987-88 season due to injury.

—COLLEGIATE RECORD—

Year	G.	Min.	FGA	FGM	Pct.	FTA	FTM	Pct.	Reb.	Pts.	Avg.
79-80	34	886	311	165	.531	144	110	.764	276	440	12.9
80-81	28	895	356	185	.520	164	118	.720	254	488	17.4
81-82					Did Not Play—Injured						
82-83					Did Not Play—Injured						
83-84	34	980	258	133	.516	126	91	.722	313	357	10.5
Totals	96	2761	925	483	.522	434	319	.735	843	1285	13.4

NBA REGULAR SEASON RECORD

									—Rebounds—									
Sea.—Team	G.	Min.	FGA	FGM	Pct.	FTA	FTM	Pct.	Off.	Def.	Tot.	Ast.	PF	Dq.	Stl.	Blk.	Pts.	Avg.
84-85—Portland	76	2216	557	299	.537	225	160	.711	207	449	656	215	278	9	55	203	758	10.0
85-86—Portland	38	1132	345	167	.484	161	114	.708	93	234	327	99	142	4	21	96	448	11.8
86-87—Portland	5	163	66	30	.455	30	20	.667	14	19	33	9	19	0	1	10	80	16.0
88-89—Portland	20	412	153	69	.451	49	28	.571	36	70	106	36	43	0	7	33	171	8.6
89-90—New Jersey	68	2207	834	347	.416	379	294	.776	206	484	690	91	211	5	38	121	998	14.7
Totals	207	6130	1955	912	.466	844	616	.730	556	1256	1812	450	693	18	122	463	2455	11.9

Three-Point Field Goals: 1988-89, 5-for-7 (.714). 1989-90, 10-for-31 (.323). Totals, 15-for-38 (.395).

NBA PLAYOFF RECORD

									—Rebounds—									
Sea.—Team	G.	Min.	FGA	FGM	Pct.	FTA	FTM	Pct.	Off.	Def.	Tot.	Ast.	PF	Dq.	Stl.	Blk.	Pts.	Avg.
84-85—Portland	9	259	59	26	.441	25	14	.560	16	60	76	21	36	2	4	21	66	7.3
88-89—Portland	3	67	28	12	.429	8	6	.750	10	10	20	3	8	0	0	7	31	10.3
Totals	12	326	87	38	.437	33	20	.606	26	70	96	24	44	2	4	28	97	8.1

Three-Point Field Goals: 1988-89, 1-for-2 (.500).

Named to NBA All-Rookie Team, 1985. . . . Member of 1980 U.S. Olympic team. . . . THE SPORTING NEWS All-America Second Team, 1984.

ADRIAN FRANCIS BRANCH

Born November 17, 1963 at Washington, D.C. Height 6:07. Weight 190.
High School—Hyattsville, Md., DeMatha.
College—University of Maryland, College Park, Md.
Drafted by Chicago on second round, 1985 (46th pick).

Waived by Chicago, October 7, 1985; signed by Cleveland as a free agent, June 16, 1986.
Waived by Cleveland, August 22, 1986; signed by Los Angeles Lakers as a free agent, September 18, 1986.
Traded by Los Angeles Lakers to New Jersey for cash, November 5, 1987.
Waived by New Jersey, December 22, 1987; signed by Portland as a free agent, October 6, 1988.
Waived by Portland, October 13, 1989; signed by Minnesota as a free agent, October 20, 1989.
Waived by Minnesota, December 26, 1989.
Played in Continental Basketball Association with Baltimore Lightning, 1985-86, and Sioux Falls Skyforce, 1989-90.

—COLLEGIATE RECORD—

Year	G.	Min.	FGA	FGM	Pct.	FTA	FTM	Pct.	Reb.	Pts.	Avg.
81-82	29	976	346	164	.474	149	114	.765	125	442	15.2
82-83	29	1043	420	197	.469	165	118	.715	150	541	18.7
83-84	28	862	284	136	.479	121	91	.752	89	363	13.0
84-85	37	1298	529	270	.510	172	131	.762	182	671	18.1
Totals	123	4179	1579	767	.486	607	454	.748	546	2017	16.4

Three-Point Field Goals: 1982-83, 29-for-81 (.358).

CBA REGULAR SEASON RECORD

			—2-Point—			—3-Point—									
Sea.—Team	G.	Min.	FGM	FGA	Pct.	FGM	FGA	Pct.	FTM	FTA	Pct.	Reb.	Ast.	Pts.	Avg.
85-86—Baltimore	46	1630	430	842	.511	5	25	.200	295	388	.760	332	145	1170	25.4
89-90—Sioux Falls	15	490	150	325	.462	0	7	.000	57	88	.648	102	47	357	23.8
Totals	61	2120	580	1167	.497	5	32	.156	352	476	.739	434	192	1527	25.0

NBA REGULAR SEASON RECORD

									—Rebounds—									
Sea.—Team	G.	Min.	FGA	FGM	Pct.	FTA	FTM	Pct.	Off.	Def.	Tot.	Ast.	PF	Dq.	Stl.	Blk.	Pts.	Avg.
86-87—L.A. Lakers	32	219	96	48	.500	54	42	.778	23	30	53	16	39	0	16	3	138	4.3
87-88—New Jersey	20	308	134	56	.418	23	20	.870	20	28	48	16	41	1	16	11	133	6.7
88-89—Portland	67	811	436	202	.463	120	87	.725	63	69	132	60	99	0	45	3	498	7.4
89-90—Minnesota	11	91	61	25	.410	22	14	.636	8	12	20	4	14	0	6	0	65	5.9
Totals	130	1429	727	331	.455	219	163	.744	114	139	253	96	193	1	83	17	834	6.4

Three-Point Field Goals: 1986-87, 0-for-2. 1987-88, 1-for-5 (.200). 1988-89, 7-for-31 (.226). 1989-90, 1-for-1 (1.000). Totals, 9-for-39 (.231).

NBA PLAYOFF RECORD

									—Rebounds—									
Sea.—Team	G.	Min.	FGA	FGM	Pct.	FTA	FTM	Pct.	Off.	Def.	Tot.	Ast.	PF	Dq.	Stl.	Blk.	Pts.	Avg.
86-87—L.A. Lakers	11	42	21	4	.190	12	6	.500	3	7	10	5	10	0	2	0	14	1.3
88-89—Portland	1	5	3	0	.000	2	2	1.000	0	1	1	2	0	0	0	0	2	2.0
Totals	12	47	24	4	.167	14	8	.571	3	8	11	7	10	0	2	0	16	1.3

Three-Point Field Goals: 1986-87, 0-for-1. 1988-89, 0-for-1. Totals, 0-for-2.

Member of NBA championship team, 1987.

RANDALL W. BREUER
(Randy)

Born October 11, 1960 at Lake City, Minn. Height 7:03. Weight 258.

High School—Lake City, Minn.

College—University of Minnesota, Minneapolis, Minn.

Drafted by Milwaukee on first round, 1983 (18th pick).

Traded by Milwaukee with a conditional exchange of 2nd round draft choices in 1991 or 1992 to Minnesota for Brad Lohaus, January 4, 1990.

—COLLEGIATE RECORD—

Year	G.	Min.	FGA	FGM	Pct.	FTA	FTM	Pct.	Reb.	Pts.	Avg.
79-80	31	....	172	96	.558	74	48	.648	98	240	7.7
80-81	30	....	313	180	.575	141	97	.688	166	457	15.2
81-82	29	....	325	180	.554	168	127	.756	209	487	16.8
82-83	29	....	384	225	.586	186	143	.769	257	593	20.4
Totals	119	....	1194	681	.570	569	415	.729	730	1777	14.9

NBA REGULAR SEASON RECORD

									—Rebounds—									
Sea.—Team	G.	Min.	FGA	FGM	Pct.	FTA	FTM	Pct.	Off.	Def.	Tot.	Ast.	PF	Dq.	Stl.	Blk.	Pts.	Avg.
83-84—Milwaukee	57	472	177	68	.384	46	32	.696	48	61	109	17	98	1	11	38	168	2.9
84-85—Milwaukee	78	1083	317	162	.511	127	89	.701	92	164	256	40	179	4	21	82	413	5.3
85-86—Milwaukee	82	1792	570	272	.477	198	141	.712	159	299	458	114	214	2	50	116	685	8.4
86-87—Milwaukee	76	1467	497	241	.485	202	118	.584	129	221	350	47	229	9	56	61	600	7.9
87-88—Milwaukee	81	2258	788	390	.495	286	188	.657	191	360	551	103	198	3	46	107	968	12.0
88-89—Milwaukee	48	513	179	86	.480	51	28	.549	51	84	135	22	59	0	9	37	200	4.2
89-90—Milw.-Minn.	81	1879	696	298	.428	193	126	.653	154	263	417	97	196	2	42	108	722	8.9
Totals	503	9464	3224	1517	.471	1103	722	.655	824	1452	2276	440	1173	21	235	549	3756	7.5

Three-Point Field Goals: 1985-86, 0-for-1. 1989-90, 0-for-1. Totals, 0-for-2.

NBA PLAYOFF RECORD

									—Rebounds—									
Sea.—Team	G.	Min.	FGA	FGM	Pct.	FTA	FTM	Pct.	Off.	Def.	Tot.	Ast.	PF	Dq.	Stl.	Blk.	Pts.	Avg.
83-84—Milwaukee	12	66	26	11	.423	5	3	.600	6	11	17	4	18	0	0	6	25	2.1
84-85—Milwaukee	8	104	26	15	.577	21	14	.667	9	15	24	0	15	0	2	2	44	5.5

									—Rebounds—									
Sea.—Team	G.	Min.	FGA	FGM	Pct.	FTA	FTM	Pct.	Off.	Def.	Tot.	Ast.	PF	Dq.	Stl.	Blk.	Pts.	Avg.
85-86—Milwaukee	14	318	86	46	.535	38	26	.684	20	40	60	11	38	1	11	18	118	8.4
86-87—Milwaukee	12	156	33	16	.485	12	8	.667	9	22	31	4	32	1	7	9	40	3.3
87-88—Milwaukee	4	47	16	9	.563	6	1	.167	2	10	12	1	7	0	1	2	19	4.8
88-89—Milwaukee	9	162	32	17	.531	13	5	.385	9	31	40	5	17	0	2	6	39	4.3
Totals	59	853	219	114	.521	95	57	.600	55	129	184	25	127	2	23	43	285	4.8

FRANK BRICKOWSKI

Born August 14, 1959 at Bayville, N. Y. Height 6:10. Weight 240.

High School—Locust Valley, N. Y.

College—Penn State University, University Park, Pa.

Drafted by New York on third round, 1981 (57th pick).

Draft rights relinquished by New York, June 30, 1983; signed by Seattle as a free agent, September 23, 1984.

Signed by Los Angeles Lakers as a Veteran Free Agent, October 8, 1986; Seattle agreed not to exercise its right of first refusal in exchange for a 1988 3rd round draft choice and cash.

Traded by Los Angeles Lakers with Petur Gudmundsson, a 1987 1st round draft choice, a 1990 2nd round draft choice and cash to San Antonio for Mychal Thompson, February 13, 1987.

Traded by San Antonio to Milwaukee for Paul Pressey, August 1, 1990.

Played in Italy during 1981-82 season.

Played in France during 1982-83 season.

Played in Israel during 1983-84 season.

—COLLEGIATE RECORD—

Year	G.	Min.	FGA	FGM	Pct.	FTA	FTM	Pct.	Reb.	Pts.	Avg.
77-78	25	266	81	37	.457	25	21	.840	64	95	3.8
78-79	24	349	99	49	.495	48	38	.792	109	136	5.7
79-80	27	692	213	111	.521	105	82	.781	202	304	11.3
80-81	24	615	218	131	.601	63	49	.778	150	311	13.0
Totals	100	1922	611	328	.537	241	190	.788	525	846	8.5

NBA REGULAR SEASON RECORD

									—Rebounds—									
Sea.—Team	G.	Min.	FGA	FGM	Pct.	FTA	FTM	Pct.	Off.	Def.	Tot.	Ast.	PF	Dq.	Stl.	Blk.	Pts.	Avg.
84-85—Seattle	78	1115	305	150	.492	127	85	.669	76	184	260	100	171	1	34	15	385	4.9
85-86—Seattle	40	311	58	30	.517	27	18	.667	16	38	54	21	74	2	11	7	78	2.0
86-87—L.A.L.-S.A.	44	487	124	63	.508	70	50	.714	48	68	116	17	118	4	20	6	176	4.0
87-88—San Antonio	70	2227	805	425	.528	349	268	.768	167	316	483	266	275	11	74	36	1119	16.0
88-89—San Antonio	64	1822	654	337	.515	281	201	.715	148	258	406	131	252	10	102	35	875	13.7
89-90—San Antonio	78	1438	387	211	.545	141	95	.674	89	238	327	105	226	4	66	37	517	6.6
Totals	374	7400	2333	1216	.521	995	717	.721	544	1102	1646	640	1116	32	307	136	3150	8.4

Three-Point Field Goals: 1984-85, 0-for-4. 1986-87, 0-for-4. 1987-88, 1-for-5 (.200). 1988-89, 0-for-2. 1989-90, 0-for-2. Totals, 1-for-17 (.059).

NBA PLAYOFF RECORD

									—Rebounds—									
Sea.—Team	G.	Min.	FGA	FGM	Pct.	FTA	FTM	Pct.	Off.	Def.	Tot.	Ast.	PF	Dq.	Stl.	Blk.	Pts.	Avg.
87-88—San Antonio	3	113	44	22	.500	19	13	.684	7	15	22	14	12	0	6	2	58	19.3
89-90—San Antonio	10	161	54	31	.574	26	17	.654	16	28	44	11	31	0	8	1	79	7.9
Totals	13	274	98	53	.541	45	30	.667	23	43	66	25	43	0	14	3	137	10.5

Three-Point Field Goals: 1987-88, 1-for-1 (1.000).

SCOTT WILLIAM BROOKS

Born July 31, 1965 at French Camp, Calif. Height 5:11. Weight 165.

High School—Manteca, Calif., East Union.

Colleges—Texas Christian University, Fort Worth, Tex.; San Joaquin Delta College, Stockton, Calif., and University of California at Irvine, Irvine, Calif.

Never drafted by an NBA franchise.

Signed by Philadelphia as a free agent, September 23, 1988.

Traded by Philadelphia to Minnesota for a 1990 2nd round draft choice, June 25, 1990.

Played in Continental Basketball Association with Albany Patroons, 1987-88.

—COLLEGIATE RECORD—

Texas Christian

Year	G.	Min.	FGA	FGM	Pct.	FTA	FTM	Pct.	Reb.	Pts.	Avg.
83-84	27	....	87	46	.529	14	10	.714	32	102	3.8

San Joaquin Delta

Year	G.	Min.	FGA	FGM	Pct.	FTA	FTM	Pct.	Reb.	Pts.	Avg.
84-85	31	....	301	158	.525	102	90	.882	45	406	13.1

California-Irvine

Year	G.	Min.	FGA	FGM	Pct.	FTA	FTM	Pct.	Reb.	Pts.	Avg.
85-86	30	945	223	100	.448	88	78	.886	70	308	10.3
86-87	28	1027	431	206	.478	168	142	.845	50	665	23.8
UCI Totals	58	1972	654	306	.468	256	220	.859	120	973	16.8
Col. Totals	85	....	741	352	.475	270	230	.852	152	1075	12.6

Three-Point Field Goals: 1985-86, 30-for-80 (.375). 1986-87, 111-for-257 (.432). Totals, 141-for-337 (.418).

CBA REGULAR SEASON RECORD

			—2-Point—			—3-Point—									
Sea.—Team	G.	Min.	FGM	FGA	Pct.	FGM	FGA	Pct.	FTM	FTA	Pct.	Reb.	Ast.	Pts.	Avg.
87-88—Albany	52	1155	135	289	.467	25	76	.329	106	132	.803	94	116	451	8.6

NBA REGULAR SEASON RECORD

									—Rebounds—									
Sea.—Team	G.	Min.	FGA	FGM	Pct.	FTA	FTM	Pct.	Off.	Def.	Tot.	Ast.	PF	Dq.	Stl.	Blk.	Pts.	Avg.
88-89—Philadelphia	82	1372	371	156	.420	69	61	.884	19	75	94	306	116	0	69	3	428	5.2
89-90—Philadelphia	72	975	276	119	.431	57	50	.877	15	49	64	207	105	0	47	0	319	4.4
Totals	154	2347	647	275	.425	126	111	.881	34	124	158	513	221	0	116	3	747	4.9

Three-Point Field Goals: 1988-89, 55-for-153 (.359). 1989-90, 31-for-79 (.392). Totals, 86-for-232 (.371).

NBA PLAYOFF RECORD

									—Rebounds—									
Sea.—Team	G.	Min.	FGA	FGM	Pct.	FTA	FTM	Pct.	Off.	Def.	Tot.	Ast.	PF	Dq.	Stl.	Blk.	Pts.	Avg.
88-89—Philadelphia	3	21	6	1	.167	2	2	1.000	0	4	4	5	4	0	0	0	5	1.7
89-90—Philadelphia	9	99	19	6	.316	9	6	.667	2	6	8	16	13	0	3	0	21	2.3
Totals	12	120	25	7	.280	11	8	.727	2	10	12	21	17	0	3	0	26	2.2

Three-Point Field Goals: 1988-89, 1-for-2 (.500). 1989-90, 3-for-7 (.429). Totals, 4-for-9 (.444).

Named to CBA All-Rookie Team, 1988.

ANTHONY WILLIAM BROWN
(Tony)

Born July 29, 1960 at Chicago, Ill. Height 6:06. Weight 195.

High School—Chicago, Ill., Farragut.

College—University of Arkansas, Fayetteville, Ark.

Drafted by New Jersey on fourth round, 1982 (82nd pick).

Waived by New Jersey, October 25, 1982; signed by Detroit as a free agent, May 7, 1983.

Waived by Detroit, August 19, 1983; signed by Indiana as a free agent, September 28, 1984.

Waived by Indiana, October 22, 1985; signed by Chicago, February 22, 1986, to the first of consecutive 10-day contracts that expired, March 13, 1986.

Signed by New Jersey as a free agent, September 3, 1986.

Traded by New Jersey with Frank Johnson, Tim McCormick and Lorenzo Romar to Houston for Joe Barry Carroll and Lester Conner, November 2, 1988.

Waived by Houston, February 2, 1989; signed by Milwaukee as a free agent, February 7, 1989.

Missed entire 1987-88 season due to injury.

Played in Continental Basketball Association with Ohio Mixers, 1982-83, Kansas City Sizzlers, 1985-86, and Grand Rapids Hoops, 1989-90.

—COLLEGIATE RECORD—

Year	G.	Min.	FGA	FGM	Pct.	FTA	FTM	Pct.	Reb.	Pts.	Avg.
78-79	23	354	66	38	.576	14	11	.786	29	87	3.8
79-80	28	299	68	37	.544	23	13	.565	39	87	3.1
80-81	32	654	113	63	.558	46	29	.630	88	155	4.8
81-82	27	826	185	109	.589	68	52	.765	87	270	10.0
Totals	110	2133	432	247	.572	151	105	.695	243	599	5.4

CBA REGULAR SEASON RECORD

			—2-Point—			—3-Point—									
Sea.—Team	G.	Min.	FGM	FGA	Pct.	FGM	FGA	Pct.	FTM	FTA	Pct.	Reb.	Ast.	Pts.	Avg.
82-83—Ohio	44	1584	371	745	.497	0	5	.000	223	321	.694	304	115	965	21.9
85-86—Kansas City	23	767	181	370	.489	3	15	.200	130	178	.730	135	144	501	21.8
89-90—Grand Rapids	49	970	117	221	.529	0	1	.000	73	119	.613	380	30	307	6.3
Totals	116	3321	669	1336	.501	3	21	.143	426	618	.689	819	289	1773	15.3

NBA REGULAR SEASON RECORD

									—Rebounds—									
Sea.—Team	G.	Min.	FGA	FGM	Pct.	FTA	FTM	Pct.	Off.	Def.	Tot.	Ast.	PF	Dq.	Stl.	Blk.	Pts.	Avg.
84-85—Indiana	82	1586	465	214	.460	171	116	.678	146	142	288	159	212	3	59	12	544	6.6
85-86—Chicago	10	132	41	18	.439	13	9	.692	5	11	16	14	16	0	5	1	45	4.5
86-87—New Jersey	77	2339	810	358	.442	206	152	.738	84	135	219	259	273	12	89	14	873	11.3
88-89—Hou.-Milw.	43	365	118	50	.424	31	24	.774	22	22	44	26	42	0	15	4	128	3.0

Sea.—Team	G.	Min.	FGA	FGM	Pct.	FTA	FTM	Pct.	—Rebounds— Off.	Def.	Tot.	Ast.	PF	Dq.	Stl.	Blk.	Pts.	Avg.
89-90—Milwaukee	61	635	206	88	.427	56	38	.679	39	33	72	41	79	0	32	4	219	3.6
Totals	273	5057	1640	728	.444	477	339	.711	296	343	639	499	622	15	200	35	1809	6.6

Three-Point Field Goals: 1984-85, 0-for-6. 1985-86, 0-for-2. 1986-87, 5-for-20 (.250). 1988-89, 4-for-16 (.250). 1989-90, 5-for-20 (.250). Totals, 14-for-64 (.219).

NBA PLAYOFF RECORD

Sea.—Team	G.	Min.	FGA	FGM	Pct.	FTA	FTM	Pct.	—Rebounds— Off.	Def.	Tot.	Ast.	PF	Dq.	Stl.	Blk.	Pts.	Avg.
88-89—Milwaukee	6	69	11	4	.364	4	3	.750	2	5	7	6	9	1	2	0	11	1.8
89-90—Milwaukee	2	13	3	1	.333	0	0	....	0	0	0	0	3	0	2	0	3	1.5
Totals	8	82	14	5	.357	4	3	.750	2	5	7	6	12	1	4	0	14	1.8

Three-Point Field Goals: 1988-89, 0-for-1. 1989-90, 1-for-1 (1.000). Totals, 1-for-2 (.500).

Named to CBA All-Defensive Second Team, 1983.

CLARENCE BROWN
(Chucky)

Born February 29, 1968 at New York, N.Y. Height 6:07. Weight 230.
High School—Leland, N.C., North Brunswick.
College—North Carolina State University, Raleigh, N.C.
Drafted by Cleveland on second round, 1989 (43rd pick).

—COLLEGIATE RECORD—

Year	G.	Min.	FGA	FGM	Pct.	FTA	FTM	Pct.	Reb.	Pts.	Avg.
85-86	31	310	80	38	.475	34	21	.618	67	97	3.1
86-87	34	629	138	81	.587	80	61	.763	145	223	6.6
87-88	32	1024	395	226	.572	121	77	.636	193	530	16.6
88-89	31	1051	383	210	.548	125	81	.648	274	507	16.4
Totals	128	3014	996	555	.557	360	240	.667	679	1357	10.6

Three-Point Field Goals: 1986-87, 0-for-1. 1987-88, 1-for-6 (.167). 1988-89, 6-for-21 (.286). Totals, 7-for-28 (.250).

NBA REGULAR SEASON RECORD

Sea.—Team	G.	Min.	FGA	FGM	Pct.	FTA	FTM	Pct.	—Rebounds— Off.	Def.	Tot.	Ast.	PF	Dq.	Stl.	Blk.	Pts.	Avg.
89-90—Cleveland	75	1339	447	210	.470	164	125	.762	83	148	231	50	148	0	33	26	545	7.3

Three-Point Field Goals: 1989-90, 0-for-7.

MICHAEL BROWN
(Mike)

Born July 19, 1963 at Newark, N.J. Height 6:09. Weight 260.
High School—East Orange, N.J., Clifford Scott.
College—George Washington University, Washington, D.C.
Drafted by Chicago on third round, 1985 (69th pick).

Selected from Chicago by Charlotte in NBA expansion draft, June 23, 1988.
Traded by Charlotte to Utah for Kelly Tripucka, June 23, 1988.
Played in Italy during 1985-86 season.

—COLLEGIATE RECORD—

Year	G.	Min.	FGA	FGM	Pct.	FTA	FTM	Pct.	Reb.	Pts.	Avg.
81-82	27	926	350	174	.497	141	73	.518	230	421	15.6
82-83	29	1058	369	192	.520	171	112	.655	298	496	17.1
83-84	29	1049	355	190	.535	256	187	.730	351	567	19.6
84-85	26	937	321	154	.480	191	124	.649	287	432	16.6
Totals	111	3970	1395	710	.509	759	496	.653	1166	1916	17.3

ITALIAN LEAGUE RECORD

Year	G.	Min.	FGA	FGM	Pct.	FTA	FTM	Pct.	Reb.	Pts.	Avg.
85-86—Filanto Desio	30	1080	415	255	.614	185	142	.768	362	655	21.8

NBA REGULAR SEASON RECORD

Sea.—Team	G.	Min.	FGA	FGM	Pct.	FTA	FTM	Pct.	—Rebounds— Off.	Def.	Tot.	Ast.	PF	Dq.	Stl.	Blk.	Pts.	Avg.
86-87—Chicago	62	818	201	106	.527	72	46	.639	71	143	214	24	129	2	20	7	258	4.2
87-88—Chicago	46	591	174	78	.448	71	41	.577	66	93	159	28	85	0	11	4	197	4.3
88-89—Utah	66	1051	248	104	.419	130	92	.708	92	166	258	41	133	0	25	17	300	4.5
89-90—Utah	82	1397	344	177	.515	199	157	.789	111	262	373	47	187	0	32	28	512	6.2
Totals	256	3857	967	465	.481	472	336	.712	340	664	1004	140	534	2	88	56	1267	4.9

Three-Point Field Goals: 1987-88, 0-for-1. 1989-90, 1-for-2 (.500). Totals, 1-for-3 (.333).

NBA PLAYOFF RECORD

									—Rebounds—									
Sea.—Team	G.	Min.	FGA	FGM	Pct.	FTA	FTM	Pct.	Off.	Def.	Tot.	Ast.	PF	Dq.	Stl.	Blk.	Pts.	Avg.
86-87—Chicago	1	3	1	0	.000	0	0	.000	0	0	0	0	1	0	1	0	0	0.0
87-88—Chicago	1	4	0	0	.000	2	1	.500	0	0	0	1	0	0	1	0	1	1.0
88-89—Utah	2	11	2	0	.000	0	0	....	0	2	2	0	3	0	0	0	0	0.0
89-90—Utah	5	67	15	7	.467	5	4	.800	5	5	10	3	11	0	1	1	18	3.6
Totals	9	85	18	7	.389	7	5	.714	5	7	12	4	15	0	3	1	19	2.1

RAYMOND BROWN

Born July 5, 1965 at Atlanta, Ga. Height 6:08. Weight 220.
High School—Atlanta, Ga., Sylvan.
Colleges—Mississippi State University, Mississippi State, Miss., and University of Idaho, Moscow, Ida.
Never drafted by an NBA franchise.

Signed by Utah as a free agent, September 29, 1989.
Waived by Utah, October 30, 1989; re-signed by Utah, February 16, 1990, for remainder of season.
Played in Continental Basketball Association with Rapid City Thrillers, 1989-90.

—COLLEGIATE RECORD—

Mississippi State

Year	G.	Min.	FGA	FGM	Pct.	FTA	FTM	Pct.	Reb.	Pts.	Avg.
84-85	28	813	201	103	.512	48	33	.688	140	239	8.5
85-86	30	989	289	158	.547	67	39	.582	170	355	11.8
M.S. Totals	58	1802	490	261	.533	115	72	.626	310	594	10.2

Idaho

Year	G.	Min.	FGA	FGM	Pct.	FTA	FTM	Pct.	Reb.	Pts.	Avg.
86-87	Did Not Play—Transfer Student										
87-88	30	1039	394	195	.495	141	87	.617	184	482	16.1
88-89	31	1023	370	192	.519	144	96	.667	244	480	15.5
Ida. Totals	61	2062	764	387	.507	285	183	.642	428	962	15.8
Col. Totals	119	3864	1254	648	.517	400	255	.638	738	1556	13.1

Three-Point Field Goals: 1987-88, 5-for-9 (.556). 1988-89, 0-for-4. Totals, 5-for-13 (.385).

CBA REGULAR SEASON RECORD

			—2-Point—			—3-Point—									
Sea.—Team	G.	Min.	FGM	FGA	Pct.	FGM	FGA	Pct.	FTM	FTA	Pct.	Reb.	Ast.	Pts.	Avg.
89-90—Rapid City	39	1406	229	456	.502	0	0	.000	113	153	.739	363	87	571	14.6

NBA REGULAR SEASON RECORD

									—Rebounds—									
Sea.—Team	G.	Min.	FGA	FGM	Pct.	FTA	FTM	Pct.	Off.	Def.	Tot.	Ast.	PF	Dq.	Stl.	Blk.	Pts.	Avg.
89-90—Utah	16	56	28	8	.286	2	0	.000	10	5	15	4	11	0	0	0	16	1.0

NBA PLAYOFF RECORD

									—Rebounds—									
Sea.—Team	G.	Min.	FGA	FGM	Pct.	FTA	FTM	Pct.	Off.	Def.	Tot.	Ast.	PF	Dq.	Stl.	Blk.	Pts.	Avg.
89-90—Utah	3	6	0	0	....	0	0	....	0	0	0	0	2	0	0	0	0	0.0

Named to CBA All-Rookie Team, 1990.

STANLEY DWAYNE BRUNDY

Born November 13, 1967 at New Orleans, La. Height 6:06. Weight 210.
High School—Los Angeles, Calif., Crenshaw.
College—DePaul University, Chicago, Ill.
Drafted by New Jersey on second round, 1989 (32nd pick).

—COLLEGIATE RECORD—

Year	G.	Min.	FGA	FGM	Pct.	FTA	FTM	Pct.	Reb.	Pts.	Avg.
85-86	18	172	43	20	.465	17	5	.294	36	45	2.5
86-87	31	662	195	111	.569	51	26	.510	203	248	8.0
87-88	30	916	295	194	.658	100	52	.520	260	440	14.7
88-89	33	1052	441	286	.649	144	70	.486	336	642	19.5
Totals	112	2802	974	611	.627	312	153	.490	835	1375	12.3

NBA REGULAR SEASON RECORD

									—Rebounds—									
Sea.—Team	G.	Min.	FGA	FGM	Pct.	FTA	FTM	Pct.	Off.	Def.	Tot.	Ast.	PF	Dq.	Stl.	Blk.	Pts.	Avg.
89-90—New Jersey	16	128	30	15	.500	18	7	.389	15	11	26	3	24	0	6	5	37	2.3

MARK BRYANT

Born April 25, 1965 at Glen Ridge, N.J. Height 6:09. Weight 245.
High School—South Orange, N.J., Columbia.
College—Seton Hall University, South Orange, N.J.
Drafted by Portland on first round, 1988 (21st pick).

—COLLEGIATE RECORD—

Year	G.	Min.	FGA	FGM	Pct.	FTA	FTM	Pct.	Reb.	Pts.	Avg.
84-85	26	774	257	122	.475	114	74	.649	177	318	12.2
85-86	30	901	323	169	.523	121	82	.678	226	420	14.0
86-87	28	891	345	171	.496	180	127	.706	198	470	16.8
87-88	34	1105	473	267	.564	218	163	.748	311	698	20.5
Totals	118	3671	1398	729	.521	633	446	.705	912	1906	16.2

Three-Point Field Goals: 1986-87, 1-for-1 (1.000). 1987-88, 1-for-2 (.500). Totals, 2-for-3 (.667).

NBA REGULAR SEASON RECORD

Sea.—Team	G.	Min.	FGA	FGM	Pct.	FTA	FTM	Pct.	—Rebounds— Off.	Def.	Tot.	Ast.	PF	Dq.	Stl.	Blk.	Pts.	Avg.
88-89—Portland	56	803	247	120	.486	69	40	.580	65	114	179	33	144	3	20	7	280	5.0
89-90—Portland	58	562	153	70	.458	50	28	.560	54	92	146	13	93	0	18	9	168	2.9
Totals	114	1365	400	190	.475	119	68	.571	119	206	325	46	237	3	38	16	448	3.9

NBA PLAYOFF RECORD

Sea.—Team	G.	Min.	FGA	FGM	Pct.	FTA	FTM	Pct.	—Rebounds— Off.	Def.	Tot.	Ast.	PF	Dq.	Stl.	Blk.	Pts.	Avg.
89-90—Portland	13	160	33	18	.545	8	6	.750	9	20	29	3	27	1	3	2	42	3.2

TORGEIR BRYN

Born August 8, 1964 at Oslo, Norway. Height 6:09. Weight 250.
Colleges—Mira Costa College, Oceanside, Calif., and
Southwest Texas State University, San Marcos, Tex.
Never drafted by an NBA franchise.

Signed by Los Angeles Clippers as a free agent, October 21, 1989.
Waived by Los Angeles Clippers, November 17, 1989.
Played in Continental Basketball Association with Quad City Thunder, San Jose Jammers and Tulsa Fast Breakers, 1989-90.

—COLLEGIATE RECORD—

Mira Costa

Year	G.	Min.	FGA	FGM	Pct.	FTA	FTM	Pct.	Reb.	Pts.	Avg.
85-86						Statistics Unavailable					
86-87						Statistics Unavailable					

Southwest Texas State

Year	G.	Min.	FGA	FGM	Pct.	FTA	FTM	Pct.	Reb.	Pts.	Avg.
87-88	31	916	350	169	.483	178	100	.730	232	468	15.1
88-89	30	....	386	203	.526	133	97	.729	271	503	16.8
SWT Totals	61	....	736	372	.505	311	227	.730	503	971	15.9

Three-Point Field Goals: 1987-88, 0-for-2. 1988-89, 0-for-1. Totals, 0-for-3.

CBA REGULAR SEASON RECORD

Sea.—Team	G.	Min.	—2-Point— FGM	FGA	Pct.	—3-Point— FGM	FGA	Pct.	FTM	FTA	Pct.	Reb.	Ast.	Pts.	Avg.
89-90—Q.C.-S.J.-Tul.	36	722	87	179	.486	0	0	.000	52	82	.634	171	42	226	6.3

NBA REGULAR SEASON RECORD

Sea.—Team	G.	Min.	FGA	FGM	Pct.	FTA	FTM	Pct.	—Rebounds— Off.	Def.	Tot.	Ast.	PF	Dq.	Stl.	Blk.	Pts.	Avg.
89-90—L.A. Clippers	3	10	2	0	.000	6	4	.667	0	2	2	0	5	0	2	1	4	1.3

STEVE BUCKNALL

Born March 17, 1966 at London, England. Height 6:06. Weight 215.
High School—Byfield, Mass., Gov. Dummer.
College—University of North Carolina, Chapel Hill, N.C.
Never drafted by an NBA franchise.

Signed by Los Angeles Lakers as a free agent, September 28, 1989.
Waived by Los Angeles Lakers, March 6, 1990.
Played in Continental Basketball Association with Tulsa Fast Breakers, 1989-90.

—COLLEGIATE RECORD—

Year	G.	Min.	FGA	FGM	Pct.	FTA	FTM	Pct.	Reb.	Pts.	Avg.
85-86	24	152	53	26	.491	17	7	.412	36	59	2.5
86-87	36	432	91	45	.495	59	42	.712	68	132	3.7
87-88	33	960	219	108	.493	94	75	.798	137	300	9.1
88-89	37	1061	333	154	.462	144	113	.785	151	483	13.1
Totals	130	2605	696	333	.478	314	237	.755	392	974	7.5

Three-Point Field Goals: 1986-87, 0-for-1. 1987-88, 9-for-19 (.474). 1988-89, 62-for-148 (.419). Totals, 71-for-168 (.423).

CBA REGULAR SEASON RECORD

			—2-Point—			—3-Point—									
Sea.—Team	G.	Min.	FGM	FGA	Pct.	FGM	FGA	Pct.	FTM	FTA	Pct.	Reb.	Ast.	Pts.	Avg.
89-90—Tulsa	4	40	8	16	.500	0	0	.000	4	7	.571	10	3	20	5.0

NBA REGULAR SEASON RECORD

									—Rebounds—									
Sea.—Team	G.	Min.	FGA	FGM	Pct.	FTA	FTM	Pct.	Off.	Def.	Tot.	Ast.	PF	Dq.	Stl.	Blk.	Pts.	Avg.
89-90—L.A. Lakers	18	75	33	9	.273	6	5	.833	5	2	7	10	10	0	2	1	23	1.3

Three-Point Field Goals: 1989-90, 0-for-1.

GREG EDWARD BUTLER

Born March 11, 1966 at Inglewood, Calif. Height 6:11. Weight 240.

High School—Rolling Hills Estates, Calif., Rolling Hills.

College—Stanford University, Stanford, Calif.

Drafted by New York on second round, 1988 (37th pick).

—COLLEGIATE RECORD—

Year	G.	Min.	FGA	FGM	Pct.	FTA	FTM	Pct.	Reb.	Pts.	Avg.
84-85	27	395	158	70	.443	40	24	.600	68	164	6.1
85-86	30	635	244	122	.500	61	45	.738	118	289	9.6
86-87	27	566	140	62	.443	56	38	.679	107	163	6.0
87-88	33	967	299	169	.565	114	83	.728	193	422	12.8
Totals	117	2563	841	423	.503	271	190	.701	486	1038	8.9

Three-Point Field Goals: 1986-87, 1-for-3 (.333). 1987-88, 1-for-1 (1.000). Totals, 2-for-4 (.500).

NBA REGULAR SEASON RECORD

									—Rebounds—									
Sea.—Team	G.	Min.	FGA	FGM	Pct.	FTA	FTM	Pct.	Off.	Def.	Tot.	Ast.	PF	Dq.	Stl.	Blk.	Pts.	Avg.
88-89—New York	33	140	48	20	.417	20	16	.800	9	19	28	2	28	0	1	2	56	1.7
89-90—New York	13	33	12	3	.250	2	0	.000	3	6	9	1	8	0	0	0	6	0.5
Totals	46	173	60	23	.383	22	16	.727	12	25	37	3	36	0	1	2	62	1.3

Three-Point Field Goals: 1988-89, 0-for-3.

MICHAEL JEROME CAGE

Born January 28, 1962 at West Memphis, Ark. Height 6:09. Weight 235.

High School—West Memphis, Ark.

College—San Diego State University, San Diego, Calif.

Drafted by Los Angeles Clippers on first round, 1984 (14th pick).

Traded by Los Angeles Clippers to Seattle for draft rights to Gary Grant and a 1989 1st round draft choice, June 28, 1988.

—COLLEGIATE RECORD—

Year	G.	Min.	FGA	FGM	Pct.	FTA	FTM	Pct.	Reb.	Pts.	Avg.
80-81	27	1031	206	115	.558	86	65	.756	355	295	10.9
81-82	29	1076	252	123	.488	109	72	.661	256	318	11.0
82-83	28	1070	335	191	.570	221	165	.747	354	547	19.5
83-84	28	1085	445	250	.562	251	186	.741	352	686	24.5
Totals	112	4262	1238	679	.548	667	488	.732	1317	1846	16.5

NBA REGULAR SEASON RECORD

									—Rebounds—									
Sea.—Team	G.	Min.	FGA	FGM	Pct.	FTA	FTM	Pct.	Off.	Def.	Tot.	Ast.	PF	Dq.	Stl.	Blk.	Pts.	Avg.
84-85—L.A. Clippers	75	1610	398	216	.543	137	101	.737	126	266	392	51	164	1	41	32	533	7.1
85-86—L.A. Clippers	78	1566	426	204	.479	174	113	.649	168	249	417	81	176	1	62	34	521	6.7
86-87—L.A. Clippers	80	2922	878	457	.521	467	341	.730	354	568	922	131	221	1	99	67	1255	15.7
87-88—L.A. Clippers	72	2660	766	360	.470	474	326	.688	371	567	938	110	194	1	91	58	1046	14.5
88-89—Seattle	80	2536	630	314	.498	265	197	.743	276	489	765	126	184	1	92	52	825	10.3
89-90—Seattle	82	2595	645	325	.504	212	148	.698	306	515	821	70	232	1	79	45	798	9.7
Totals	467	13889	3743	1876	.501	1729	1226	.709	1601	2654	4255	569	1171	6	464	288	4978	10.7

Three-Point Field Goals: 1985-86, 0-for-3. 1986-87, 0-for-3. 1987-88, 0-for-1. 1988-89, 0-for-4. Totals, 0-for-11.

NBA PLAYOFF RECORD

Sea.—Team	G.	Min.	FGA	FGM	Pct.	FTA	FTM	Pct.	—Rebounds— Off.	Def.	Tot.	Ast.	PF	Dq.	Stl.	Blk.	Pts.	Avg.
88-89—Seattle	8	175	40	24	.600	22	9	.409	22	24	46	5	14	0	7	3	57	7.1

Three-Point Field Goals: 1988-89, 0-for-1.

Led NBA in rebounding, 1988.

ADRIAN BERNARD CALDWELL

Born July 4, 1966 at Falls County, Tex. Height 6:08. Weight 265.

High School—Corpus Christi, Tex., West Oso.

Colleges—Navarro College, Corsicana, Tex.; Southern Methodist University, Dallas, Tex., and Lamar University, Beaumont, Tex.

Never drafted by an NBA franchise.

—COLLEGIATE RECORD—

Navarro

Year	G.	Min.	FGA	FGM	Pct.	FTA	FTM	Pct.	Reb.	Pts.	Avg.
84-85	Statistics Unavailable										
85-86	Statistics Unavailable										

Southern Methodist

Year	G.	Min.	FGA	FGM	Pct.	FTA	FTM	Pct.	Reb.	Pts.	Avg.
86-87	28	300	45	22	.489	44	15	.341	68	59	2.1

Lamar

Year	G.	Min.	FGA	FGM	Pct.	FTA	FTM	Pct.	Reb.	Pts.	Avg.
87-88	Did Not Play—Transfer Student										
88-89	26	839	266	151	.568	178	80	.449	260	382	14.7
Col. Totals	54	1139	311	173	.556	222	95	.428	328	441	8.2

NBA REGULAR SEASON RECORD

Sea.—Team	G.	Min.	FGA	FGM	Pct.	FTA	FTM	Pct.	—Rebounds— Off.	Def.	Tot.	Ast.	PF	Dq.	Stl.	Blk.	Pts.	Avg.
89-90—Houston	51	331	76	42	.553	28	13	.464	36	73	109	7	69	0	11	18	97	1.9

NBA PLAYOFF RECORD

Sea.—Team	G.	Min.	FGA	FGM	Pct.	FTA	FTM	Pct.	—Rebounds— Off.	Def.	Tot.	Ast.	PF	Dq.	Stl.	Blk.	Pts.	Avg.
89-90—Houston	1	1	0	0	....	0	0	....	0	0	0	0	0	0	0	0	0	0.0

ANTHONY CAMPBELL
(Tony)

Born May 7, 1962 at Teaneck, N. J. Height 6:07. Weight 215.

High School—Teaneck, N. J.

College—Ohio State University, Columbus, Ohio.

Drafted by Detroit on first round, 1984 (20th pick).

Signed by Washington as a Veteran Free Agent, October 8, 1987; Detroit agreed not to exercise its right of first refusal in exchange for a 1989 2nd round draft choice.

Waived by Washington, November 3, 1987; signed by Los Angeles Lakers as a free agent, March 30, 1988.

Signed by Minnesota as an unrestricted free agent, September 13, 1989.

Played in Continental Basketball Association with Albany Patroons, 1987-88.

—COLLEGIATE RECORD—

Year	G.	Min.	FGA	FGM	Pct.	FTA	FTM	Pct.	Reb.	Pts.	Avg.
80-81	14	55	24	10	.417	6	3	.500	9	23	1.6
81-82	31	986	356	151	.424	119	95	.798	154	397	12.8
82-83	30	1122	451	227	.503	144	115	.799	250	569	19.0
83-84	29	1095	392	201	.513	171	138	.807	215	540	18.6
Totals	104	3258	1223	589	.482	440	351	.798	628	1529	14.7

Three-Point Field Goals: 1982-83, 0-for-2.

CBA REGULAR SEASON RECORD

Sea.—Team	G.	Min.	—2-Point— FGM	FGA	Pct.	—3-Point— FGM	FGA	Pct.	FTM	FTA	Pct.	Reb.	Ast.	Pts.	Avg.
87-88—Albany	38	1133	332	513	.647	3	8	.375	229	266	.861	251	51	902	23.7

NBA REGULAR SEASON RECORD

Sea.—Team	G.	Min.	FGA	FGM	Pct.	FTA	FTM	Pct.	—Rebounds— Off.	Def.	Tot.	Ast.	PF	Dq.	Stl.	Blk.	Pts.	Avg.
84-85—Detroit	56	625	262	130	.496	70	56	.800	41	48	89	24	107	1	28	3	316	5.6
85-86—Detroit	82	1292	608	294	.484	73	58	.795	83	153	236	45	164	0	62	7	648	7.9
86-87—Detroit	40	332	145	57	.393	39	24	.615	21	37	58	19	40	0	12	1	138	3.5

TONY CAMPBELL

									—Rebounds—									
Sea.—Team	G.	Min.	FGA	FGM	Pct.	FTA	FTM	Pct.	Off.	Def.	Tot.	Ast.	PF	Dq.	Stl.	Blk.	Pts.	Avg.
87-88—L.A. Lakers	13	242	101	57	.564	39	28	.718	8	19	27	15	41	0	11	2	143	11.0
88-89—L.A. Lakers	63	787	345	158	.458	83	70	.843	53	77	130	47	108	0	37	6	388	6.2
89-90—Minnesota	82	3164	1581	723	.457	569	448	.787	209	242	451	213	260	7	111	31	1903	23.2
Totals	336	6442	3042	1419	.466	873	684	.784	415	576	991	363	720	8	261	50	3536	10.5

Three-Point Field Goals: 1984-85, 0-for-1. 1985-86, 2-for-9 (.222). 1986-87, 0-for-3. 1987-88, 1-for-3 (.333). 1988-89, 2-for-21 (.095). 1989-90, 9-for-54 (.167). Totals, 14-for-91 (.154).

NBA PLAYOFF RECORD

									—Rebounds—									
Sea.—Team	G.	Min.	FGA	FGM	Pct.	FTA	FTM	Pct.	Off.	Def.	Tot.	Ast.	PF	Dq.	Stl.	Blk.	Pts.	Avg.
84-85—Detroit	2	9	3	1	.333	0	0	.000	0	2	2	1	1	0	0	0	2	1.0
85-86—Detroit	2	16	10	4	.400	2	1	.500	0	2	2	0	5	0	0	0	9	4.5
86-87—Detroit	4	13	6	3	.500	2	2	1.000	0	5	5	0	1	0	0	0	9	2.3
87-88—L.A. Lakers	15	94	42	18	.429	16	11	.688	4	6	10	5	16	0	3	0	47	3.1
88-89—L.A. Lakers	9	106	31	19	.613	22	16	.727	4	8	12	6	26	1	3	0	56	6.2
Totals	32	238	92	45	.489	42	30	.714	8	23	31	12	49	1	6	0	123	3.8

Three-Point Field Goals: 1986-87, 1-for-1 (1.000). 1987-88, 0-for-1. 1988-89, 2-for-4 (.500). Totals, 3-for-6 (.500).

Member of NBA championship team, 1988. . . . Named to CBA All-Star First Team, 1988. . . . CBA Newcomer of the Year, 1988.

RICHARD PRESTON CARLISLE
(Rick)

Born October 27, 1959 at Ogdensburg, N. Y. Height 6:05. Weight 210.
High School—Lisbon, N. Y., Central.
Prep School—Worcester Academy, Worcester, Mass.
Colleges—University of Maine, Orono, Me., and University of Virginia, Charlottesville, Va.
Drafted by Boston on third round, 1984 (69th pick).

Waived by Boston, November 3, 1987; signed by New York as a free agent, November 30, 1987.
Signed by New Jersey as an unrestricted free agent, October 4, 1989.
Waived by New Jersey, December 1, 1989.
Played in Continental Basketball Association with Albany Patroons, 1987-88.

—COLLEGIATE RECORD—

Maine

Year	G.	Min.	FGA	FGM	Pct.	FTA	FTM	Pct.	Reb.	Pts.	Avg.
79-80	28	....	236	131	.555	97	83	.856	96	345	12.3
80-81	28	....	322	176	.547	126	102	.810	118	454	16.2
Maine Totals	56	....	558	307	.550	223	185	.830	214	799	14.3

Virginia

Year	G.	Min.	FGA	FGM	Pct.	FTA	FTM	Pct.	Reb.	Pts.	Avg.
81-82					Did Not Play—Transfer Student						
82-83	34	965	277	142	.513	104	87	.837	100	379	11.1
83-84	33	959	289	149	.516	96	67	.698	93	365	11.1
Va. Totals	67	1924	566	291	.514	200	154	.770	193	744	11.1
College Totals	123	....	1124	598	.532	443	339	.765	407	1543	12.5

Three-Point Field Goals: 1982-83, 8-for-12 (.750).

CBA REGULAR SEASON RECORD

			—2-Point—			—3-Point—									
Sea.—Team	G.	Min.	FGM	FGA	Pct.	FGM	FGA	Pct.	FTM	FTA	Pct.	Reb.	Ast.	Pts.	Avg.
87-88—Albany	6	172	38	74	.514	4	8	.500	16	19	.842	11	14	104	17.3

NBA REGULAR SEASON RECORD

									—Rebounds—									
Sea.—Team	G.	Min.	FGA	FGM	Pct.	FTA	FTM	Pct.	Off.	Def.	Tot.	Ast.	PF	Dq.	Stl.	Blk.	Pts.	Avg.
84-85—Boston	38	179	67	26	.388	17	15	.882	8	13	21	25	21	0	3	0	67	1.8
85-86—Boston	77	760	189	92	.487	23	15	.652	22	55	77	104	92	1	19	4	199	2.6
86-87—Boston	42	297	92	30	.326	20	15	.750	8	22	30	35	28	0	8	0	80	1.9
87-88—New York	26	204	67	29	.433	11	10	.909	6	7	13	32	39	1	11	4	74	2.8
89-90—New Jersey	5	21	7	1	.143	0	0	....	0	0	0	5	7	0	1	1	2	0.4
Totals	188	1461	422	178	.422	71	55	.775	44	97	141	201	187	2	42	9	422	2.2

Three-Point Field Goals: 1984-85, 0-for-2. 1985-86, 0-for-10. 1986-87, 5-for-16 (.313). 1987-88, 6-for-17 (.353). 1989-90, 0-for-3. Totals, 11-for-48 (.229).

NBA PLAYOFF RECORD

									—Rebounds—									
Sea.—Team	G.	Min.	FGA	FGM	Pct.	FTA	FTM	Pct.	Off.	Def.	Tot.	Ast.	PF	Dq.	Stl.	Blk.	Pts.	Avg.
85-86—Boston	10	54	15	8	.533	4	3	.750	3	2	5	8	9	0	2	0	19	1.9

								—Rebounds—									
Sea.—Team	G.	Min.	FGA	FGM	Pct.	FTA	FTM	Pct.	Off.	Def.	Tot.	Ast.	PF	Dq.	Stl.	Blk.	Pts.	Avg.
87-88—New York	2	8	4	1	.250	0	0	.000	1	1	2	0	1	0	1	0	2	1.0
Totals	12	62	19	9	.474	4	3	.750	4	3	7	8	10	0	3	0	21	1.8

Three-Point Field Goals: 1987-88, 0-for-2.

Member of NBA championship team, 1986.

ANTOINE LABOTTE CARR

Born July 23, 1961 at Oklahoma City, Okla. Height 6:09. Weight 235.
High School—Wichita, Kan., Wichita Heights.
College—Wichita State University, Wichita, Kan.
Drafted by Detroit on first round, 1983 (8th pick).

Draft rights traded by Detroit with Cliff Levingston and 1986 and 1987 2nd round draft choices to Atlanta for Dan Roundfield, June 18, 1984.

Traded by Atlanta with Sedric Toney and future considerations to Sacramento for Kenny Smith and Mike Williams, February 13, 1990.

Played in Italy, 1983-84.

—COLLEGIATE RECORD—

Year	G.	Min.	FGA	FGM	Pct.	FTA	FTM	Pct.	Reb.	Pts.	Avg.
79-80	29	818	355	178	.501	129	86	.667	171	442	15.2
80-81	33	1030	360	211	.586	132	101	.765	241	523	15.8
81-82	28	785	316	179	.566	115	91	.791	196	449	16.0
82-83	22	727	339	195	.575	136	104	.765	168	497	22.6
Totals	112	3360	1370	763	.557	512	382	.746	776	1911	17.1

Three-Point Field Goals: 1982-83, 3-for-5 (.600).

ITALIAN LEAGUE RECORD

Year	G.	Min.	FGA	FGM	Pct.	FTA	FTM	Pct.	Reb.	Pts.	Avg.
83-84—Milan	27	956	434	242	.558	137	86	.628	237	570	21.1

NBA REGULAR SEASON RECORD

									—Rebounds—									
Sea.—Team	G.	Min.	FGA	FGM	Pct.	FTA	FTM	Pct.	Off.	Def.	Tot.	Ast.	PF	Dq.	Stl.	Blk.	Pts.	Avg.
84-85—Atlanta	62	1195	375	198	.528	128	101	.789	79	153	232	80	219	4	29	78	499	8.0
85-86—Atlanta	17	258	93	49	.527	27	18	.667	16	36	52	14	51	1	7	15	116	6.8
86-87—Atlanta	65	695	265	134	.506	103	73	.709	60	96	156	34	146	1	14	48	342	5.3
87-88—Atlanta	80	1483	517	281	.544	182	142	.780	94	195	289	103	272	7	38	83	705	8.8
88-89—Atlanta	78	1488	471	226	.480	152	130	.855	106	168	274	91	221	0	31	62	582	7.5
89-90—Atl.-Sac.	77	1727	721	356	.494	298	237	.795	115	207	322	119	247	6	30	68	949	12.3
Totals	379	6846	2442	1244	.509	890	701	.788	470	855	1325	441	1156	19	149	354	3193	8.4

Three-Point Field Goals: 1984-85, 2-for-6 (.333). 1986-87, 1-for-3 (.333). 1987-88, 1-for-4 (.250). 1988-89, 0-for-1. 1989-90, 0-for-7. Totals, 4-for-21 (.190).

NBA PLAYOFF RECORD

									—Rebounds—									
Sea.—Team	G.	Min.	FGA	FGM	Pct.	FTA	FTM	Pct.	Off.	Def.	Tot.	Ast.	PF	Dq.	Stl.	Blk.	Pts.	Avg.
86-87—Atlanta	9	162	56	39	.696	32	26	.813	11	16	27	13	36	1	3	8	104	11.6
87-88—Atlanta	12	210	68	36	.529	14	9	.643	12	29	41	15	47	2	4	17	81	6.8
88-89—Atlanta	5	81	21	13	.619	11	8	.727	5	3	8	7	13	0	0	4	34	6.8
Totals	26	453	145	88	.607	57	43	.754	28	48	76	35	96	3	7	29	219	8.4

Three-Point Field Goals: 1988-89, 0-for-1.

Named to THE SPORTING NEWS All-America First Team, 1983.

JOSEPH BARRY CARROLL
(Joe Barry)

Born July 24, 1958 at Pine Bluff, Ark. Height 7:01. Weight 255.
High School—Denver, Colo., East.
College—Purdue University, West Lafayette, Ind.
Drafted by Golden State on first round, 1980 (1st pick).

Traded by Golden State with Eric Floyd to Houston for Ralph Sampson and Steve Harris, December 12, 1987.

Traded by Houston with Lester Conner to New Jersey for Tony Brown, Frank Johnson, Tim McCormick and Lorenzo Romar, November 2, 1988.

Traded by New Jersey to Denver for Michael Cutright and future considerations, February 21, 1990.

Played in Italy, 1984-85.

—COLLEGIATE RECORD—

Year	G.	Min.	FGA	FGM	Pct.	FTA	FTM	Pct.	Reb.	Pts.	Avg.
76-77	28	573	187	93	.497	54	34	.630	206	220	7.9

Year	G.	Min.	FGA	FGM	Pct.	FTA	FTM	Pct.	Reb.	Pts.	Avg.
77-78	27	855	312	163	.522	143	95	.664	288	421	15.6
78-79	35	1235	545	318	.583	253	162	.640	352	798	22.8
79-80	33	1168	558	301	.539	203	134	.660	302	736	22.3
Totals	123	3831	1602	875	.546	653	425	.651	1148	2175	17.7

ITALIAN LEAGUE RECORD

Year	G.	Min.	FGA	FGM	Pct.	FTA	FTM	Pct.	Reb.	Pts.	Avg.
84-85—Milan	25	875	472	249	.528	165	125	.758	277	623	24.9

NBA REGULAR SEASON RECORD

									—Rebounds—									
Sea.—Team	G.	Min.	FGA	FGM	Pct.	FTA	FTM	Pct.	Off.	Def.	Tot.	Ast.	PF	Dq.	Stl.	Blk.	Pts.	Avg.
80-81—Golden State	82	2919	1254	616	.491	440	315	.716	274	485	759	117	313	10	50	121	1547	18.9
81-82—Golden State	76	2627	1016	527	.519	323	235	.728	210	423	633	64	265	8	64	127	1289	17.0
82-83—Golden State	79	2988	1529	785	.513	469	337	.719	220	468	688	169	260	7	108	155	1907	24.1
83-84—Golden State	80	2962	1390	663	.477	433	313	.723	235	401	636	193	244	9	103	142	1639	20.5
85-86—Golden State	79	2801	1404	650	.463	501	377	.752	193	477	670	176	277	13	101	144	1677	21.2
86-87—Golden State	81	2724	1461	690	.472	432	340	.787	173	416	589	214	255	2	92	123	1720	21.2
87-88—G.S.-Hou.	77	2004	924	402	.435	225	172	.764	131	358	489	113	195	1	50	106	976	12.7
88-89—New Jersey	64	1996	810	363	.448	220	176	.800	118	355	473	105	193	2	71	81	902	14.1
89-90—N.J.-Den.	76	1721	759	312	.411	177	137	.774	133	310	443	97	192	4	47	115	761	10.0
Totals	694	22742	10547	5008	.475	3220	2402	.746	1687	3693	5380	1253	2194	56	686	1114	12418	17.9

Three-Point Field Goals: 1980-81, 0-for-2. 1981-82, 0-for-1. 1982-83, 0-for-3. 1983-84, 0-for-1. 1985-86, 0-for-2. 1987-88, 0-for-2. 1989-90, 0-for-2. Totals, 0-for-13.

NBA PLAYOFF RECORD

									—Rebounds—									
Sea.—Team	G.	Min.	FGA	FGM	Pct.	FTA	FTM	Pct.	Off.	Def.	Tot.	Ast.	PF	Dq.	Stl.	Blk.	Pts.	Avg.
86-87—Golden State	10	334	163	74	.454	51	41	.804	16	49	65	19	42	2	14	25	189	18.9
87-88—Houston	4	116	47	18	.383	10	8	.800	8	11	19	2	12	0	3	1	44	11.0
89-90—Denver	3	46	16	9	.563	2	2	1.000	1	8	9	3	6	0	1	5	20	6.7
Totals	17	496	226	101	.447	63	51	.810	25	68	93	24	60	2	18	31	253	14.9

Three-Point Field Goals: 1986-87, 0-for-1.

NBA ALL-STAR GAME RECORD

								—Rebounds—							
Season—Team	Min.	FGA	FGM	Pct.	FTA	FTM	Pct.	Off.	Def.	Tot.	Ast.	PF	Dq.	Stl.	Blk.	Pts.
1987—Golden State	18	7	1	.143	2	2	1.000	4	2	6	0	4	0	0	1	4

Named to NBA All-Rookie Team, 1981. . . . THE SPORTING NEWS All-America First Team, 1980.

JAMES WILLIAM CARTWRIGHT
(Bill)

Born July 30, 1957 at Lodi, Calif. Height 7:01. Weight 245.
High School—Elk Grove, Calif.
College—University of San Francisco, San Francisco, Calif.
Drafted by New York on first round, 1979 (3rd pick).

Traded by New York with 1988 1st and 3rd round draft choices to Chicago for Charles Oakley and 1988 1st and 3rd round draft choices, June 27, 1988.
Missed entire 1984-85 season due to injury.

—COLLEGIATE RECORD—

Year	G.	Min.	FGA	FGM	Pct.	FTA	FTM	Pct.	Reb.	Pts.	Avg.
75-76	30	845	285	151	.530	98	72	.735	207	374	12.5
76-77	31	969	426	241	.566	161	118	.733	262	600	19.4
77-78	21	712	252	168	.667	131	96	.733	213	432	20.6
78-79	29	1020	443	268	.605	237	174	.734	455	710	24.5
Totals	111	3546	1406	828	.589	627	460	.734	1137	2116	19.1

NBA REGULAR SEASON RECORD

									—Rebounds—									
Sea.—Team	G.	Min.	FGA	FGM	Pct.	FTA	FTM	Pct.	Off.	Def.	Tot.	Ast.	PF	Dq.	Stl.	Blk.	Pts.	Avg.
79-80—New York	82	3150	1215	665	.547	566	451	.797	194	532	726	165	279	2	48	101	1781	21.7
80-81—New York	82	2925	1118	619	.554	518	408	.788	161	452	613	111	259	2	48	83	1646	20.1
81-82—New York	72	2060	694	390	.562	337	257	.763	116	305	421	87	208	2	48	65	1037	14.4
82-83—New York	82	2468	804	455	.566	511	380	.744	185	405	590	136	315	7	41	127	1290	15.7
83-84—New York	77	2487	808	453	.561	502	404	.805	195	454	649	107	262	4	44	97	1310	17.0
85-86—New York	2	36	7	3	.429	10	6	.600	2	8	10	5	6	0	1	1	12	6.0
86-87—New York	58	1989	631	335	.531	438	346	.790	132	313	445	96	188	2	40	26	1016	17.5
87-88—New York	82	1676	528	287	.544	426	340	.798	127	257	384	85	234	4	43	43	914	11.1
88-89—Chicago	78	2333	768	365	.475	308	236	.766	152	369	521	90	234	2	21	41	966	12.4
89-90—Chicago	71	2160	598	292	.488	280	227	.811	137	328	465	145	243	6	38	34	811	11.4
Totals	686	21284	7171	3864	.539	3896	3055	.784	1401	3423	4824	1027	2228	31	372	618	10783	15.7

Three-Point Field Goals: 1980-81, 0-for-1. 1983-84, 0-for-1. Totals, 0-for-2.

NBA PLAYOFF RECORD

									—Rebounds—									
Sea.—Team	G.	Min.	FGA	FGM	Pct.	FTA	FTM	Pct.	Off.	Def.	Tot.	Ast.	PF	Dq.	Stl.	Blk.	Pts.	Avg.
80-81—New York	2	49	17	6	.353	12	8	.667	4	9	13	1	7	0	1	1	20	10.0
82-83—New York	6	172	43	25	.581	22	17	.773	9	25	34	4	25	0	3	7	67	11.2
83-84—New York	12	398	126	70	.556	80	69	.863	27	72	99	5	44	0	2	14	209	17.4
87-88—New York	4	76	18	9	.500	15	11	.733	8	11	19	6	12	0	0	3	29	7.3
88-89—Chicago	17	583	148	72	.486	80	56	.700	33	88	121	20	70	1	9	12	200	11.8
89-90—Chicago	16	462	121	50	.413	43	29	.674	25	50	75	16	52	0	5	4	129	8.1
Totals	57	1740	473	232	.490	252	190	.754	106	255	361	52	210	1	20	41	654	11.5

NBA ALL-STAR GAME RECORD

								—Rebounds—								
Season—Team	Min.	FGA	FGM	Pct.	FTA	FTM	Pct.	Off.	Def.	Tot.	Ast.	PF	Dq.	Stl.	Blk.	Pts.
1980—New York	14	8	4	.500	0	0	.000	1	2	3	1	1	0	0	0	8

Named to NBA All-Rookie Team, 1980. . . . THE SPORTING NEWS All-America First Team, 1979.

TERRY DEWAYNE CATLEDGE

Born August 22, 1963 at Houston, Miss. Height 6:08. Weight 230.
High School—Houston, Miss.
Colleges—Itawamba Junior College, Fulton, Miss., and University of South Alabama, Mobile, Ala.
Drafted by Philadelphia on first round, 1985 (21st pick).

Traded by Philadelphia with Moses Malone and 1986 and 1988 1st round draft choices to Washington for Jeff Ruland and Cliff Robinson, June 16, 1986.
Selected from Washington by Orlando in NBA expansion draft, June 15, 1989.

—COLLEGIATE RECORD—

Itawamba

Year	G.	Min.	FGA	FGM	Pct.	FTA	FTM	Pct.	Reb.	Pts.	Avg.
81-82			Transferred before basketball season.								

South Alabama

Year	G.	Min.	FGA	FGM	Pct.	FTA	FTM	Pct.	Reb.	Pts.	Avg.
81-82			Did Not Play—Transfer Student								
82-83	28	911	387	216	.558	171	119	.696	278	551	19.7
83-84	30	1032	373	220	.590	219	157	.717	332	597	19.9
84-85	28	1038	536	285	.532	250	148	.592	322	718	25.6
Totals	86	2981	1296	721	.556	640	424	.663	932	1866	21.7

NBA REGULAR SEASON RECORD

									—Rebounds—									
Sea.—Team	G.	Min.	FGA	FGM	Pct.	FTA	FTM	Pct.	Off.	Def.	Tot.	Ast.	PF	Dq.	Stl.	Blk.	Pts.	Avg.
85-86—Philadelphia	64	1092	431	202	.469	139	90	.647	107	165	272	21	127	0	31	8	494	7.7
86-87—Washington	78	2149	835	413	.495	335	199	.594	248	312	560	56	195	1	43	14	1025	13.1
87-88—Washington	70	1610	585	296	.506	235	154	.655	180	217	397	63	172	0	33	9	746	10.7
88-89—Washington	79	2077	681	334	.490	254	153	.602	230	342	572	75	250	5	46	25	822	10.4
89-90—Orlando	74	2462	1152	546	.474	486	341	.702	271	292	563	72	201	0	36	17	1435	19.4
Totals	365	9390	3684	1791	.486	1449	937	.647	1036	1328	2364	287	945	6	189	73	4522	12.4

Three-Point Field Goals: 1985-86, 0-for-4. 1986-87, 0-for-4. 1987-88, 0-for-2. 1988-89, 1-for-5 (.200). 1989-90, 2-for-8 (.250). Totals, 3-for-23 (.130).

NBA PLAYOFF RECORD

									—Rebounds—									
Sea.—Team	G.	Min.	FGA	FGM	Pct.	FTA	FTM	Pct.	Off.	Def.	Tot.	Ast.	PF	Dq.	Stl.	Blk.	Pts.	Avg.
85-86—Philadelphia	11	293	117	46	.393	38	22	.579	37	38	75	5	34	0	6	8	114	10.4
86-87—Washington	3	98	41	23	.561	17	9	.529	7	18	25	0	5	0	3	1	55	18.3
87-88—Washington	5	45	11	4	.364	4	3	.750	2	4	6	2	9	0	0	0	11	2.2
Totals	19	436	169	73	.432	59	34	.576	46	60	106	7	48	0	9	9	180	9.5

Three-Point Field Goals: 1987-88, 0-for-1.

THOMAS DOANE CHAMBERS
(Tom)

Born June 21, 1959 at Ogden, Utah. Height 6:10. Weight 230.
High School—Boulder, Colo., Fairview.
College—University of Utah, Salt Lake City, Utah.
Drafted by San Diego on first round, 1981 (8th pick).

Traded by San Diego with Al Wood, a 1987 2nd round draft choice and a future 3rd round draft choice to Seattle for James Donaldson, Greg Kelser, Mark Radford, a 1984 1st round draft choice and a 1985 2nd round draft choice, August 18, 1983.

Signed by Phoenix as an unrestricted free agent, July 5, 1988.

—COLLEGIATE RECORD—

Year	G.	Min.	FGA	FGM	Pct.	FTA	FTM	Pct.	Reb.	Pts.	Avg.
77-78	28	355	139	69	.496	64	40	.625	104	178	6.4
78-79	30	853	379	206	.544	127	69	.543	266	481	16.0
79-80	28	792	359	195	.543	129	92	.713	244	482	17.2
80-81	30	959	372	221	.594	155	115	.742	262	557	18.6
Totals	116	2959	1249	691	.553	475	316	.665	876	1698	14.6

NBA REGULAR SEASON RECORD

									—Rebounds—									
Sea.—Team	G.	Min.	FGA	FGM	Pct.	FTA	FTM	Pct.	Off.	Def.	Tot.	Ast.	PF	Dq.	Stl.	Blk.	Pts.	Avg.
81-82—San Diego	81	2682	1056	554	.525	458	284	.620	211	350	561	146	341	17	58	46	1392	17.2
82-83—San Diego	79	2665	1099	519	.472	488	353	.723	218	301	519	192	333	15	79	57	1391	17.6
83-84—Seattle	82	2570	1110	554	.499	469	375	.800	219	313	532	133	309	8	47	51	1483	18.1
84-85—Seattle	81	2923	1302	629	.483	571	475	.832	164	415	579	209	312	4	70	57	1739	21.5
85-86—Seattle	66	2019	928	432	.466	414	346	.836	126	305	431	132	248	6	55	37	1223	18.5
86-87—Seattle	82	3018	1446	660	.456	630	535	.849	163	382	545	245	307	9	81	50	1909	23.3
87-88—Seattle	82	2680	1364	611	.448	519	419	.807	135	355	490	212	297	4	87	53	1674	20.4
88-89—Phoenix	81	3002	1643	774	.471	598	509	.851	143	541	684	231	271	2	87	55	2085	25.7
89-90—Phoenix	81	3046	1617	810	.501	647	557	.861	121	450	571	190	260	1	88	47	2201	27.2
Totals	715	24605	11565	5543	.479	4794	3853	.804	1500	3412	4912	1690	2678	66	652	453	15097	21.1

Three-Point Field Goals: 1981-82, 0-for-2. 1982-83, 0-for-8. 1983-84, 0-for-12. 1984-85, 6-for-22 (.273). 1985-86, 13-for-48 (.271). 1986-87, 54-for-145 (.372). 1987-88, 33-for-109 (.303). 1988-89, 28-for-86 (.326). 1989-90, 24-for-86 (.279). Totals, 158-for-518 (.305).

NBA PLAYOFF RECORD

									—Rebounds—									
Sea.—Team	G.	Min.	FGA	FGM	Pct.	FTA	FTM	Pct.	Off.	Def.	Tot.	Ast.	PF	Dq.	Stl.	Blk.	Pts.	Avg.
83-84—Seattle	5	191	59	28	.475	18	12	.667	4	29	33	8	23	0	5	3	68	13.6
86-87—Seattle	14	498	263	118	.449	99	80	.808	32	58	90	32	51	0	12	13	322	23.0
87-88—Seattle	5	168	91	50	.549	35	29	.829	8	23	31	11	24	1	3	1	129	25.8
88-89—Phoenix	12	495	257	118	.459	78	67	.859	22	109	131	46	44	0	13	15	312	26.0
89-90—Phoenix	16	612	275	117	.425	132	116	.879	20	87	107	31	54	0	7	7	355	22.2
Totals	52	1964	945	431	.456	362	304	.840	86	306	392	128	196	1	40	39	1186	22.8

Three-Point Field Goals: 1983-84, 0-for-1. 1986-87, 6-for-17 (.353). 1987-88, 0-for-2. 1988-89, 9-for-22 (.409). 1989-90, 5-for-19 (.263). Totals, 20-for-62 (.323).

NBA ALL-STAR GAME RECORD

								—Rebounds—								
Season—Team	Min.	FGA	FGM	Pct.	FTA	FTM	Pct.	Off.	Def.	Tot.	Ast.	PF	Dq.	Stl.	Blk.	Pts.
1987—Seattle	29	25	13	.520	9	6	.667	3	1	4	2	5	0	4	0	34
1989—Phoenix	16	8	4	.500	6	6	1.000	2	3	5	1	3	0	0	0	14
1990—Phoenix	21	12	8	.667	7	5	.714	2	1	3	1	0	0	1	0	21
Totals	66	45	25	.556	22	17	.773	7	5	12	4	8	0	5	0	69

Three-Point Field Goals: 1987, 2-for-3 (.667). 1990, 0-for-1. Totals, 2-for-4 (.500).

Named to All-NBA Second Team, 1989 and 1990. . . . NBA All-Star Game MVP, 1987.

REX EVERETT CHAPMAN

Born October 5, 1967 at Bowling Green, Ky. Height 6:04. Weight 185.

High School—Owensboro, Ky., Apollo.

College—University of Kentucky, Lexington, Ky.

Drafted by Charlotte on first round as an undergraduate, 1988 (8th pick).

—COLLEGIATE RECORD—

Year	G.	Min.	FGA	FGM	Pct.	FTA	FTM	Pct.	Reb.	Pts.	Avg.
86-87	29	962	390	173	.444	68	50	.735	66	464	16.0
87-88	32	1108	461	231	.501	102	81	.794	93	609	19.0
Totals	61	2070	851	404	.475	170	131	.771	159	1073	17.6

Three-Point Field Goals: 1986-87, 68-for-176 (.386). 1987-88, 66-for-159 (.415). Totals, 134-for-335 (.400).

NBA REGULAR SEASON RECORD

									—Rebounds—									
Sea.—Team	G.	Min.	FGA	FGM	Pct.	FTA	FTM	Pct.	Off.	Def.	Tot.	Ast.	PF	Dq.	Stl.	Blk.	Pts.	Avg.
88-89—Charlotte	75	2219	1271	526	.414	195	155	.795	74	113	187	176	167	1	70	25	1267	16.9
89-90—Charlotte	54	1762	924	377	.408	192	144	.750	52	127	179	132	113	0	46	6	945	17.5
Totals	129	3981	2195	903	.411	387	299	.773	126	240	366	308	280	1	116	31	2212	17.1

Three-Point Field Goals: 1988-89, 60-for-191 (.314). 1989-90, 47-for-142 (.331). Totals, 107-for-333 (.321).

Named to NBA All-Rookie Second Team, 1989. . . . Son of Wayne Chapman, who played for Kentucky, Denver and Indiana in the ABA, 1968-69 through 1971-72.

MAURICE CHEEKS

MAURICE EDWARD CHEEKS

Born September 8, 1956 at Chicago, Ill. Height 6:01. Weight 180.
High School—Chicago, Ill., DuSable.
College—West Texas State University, Canyon, Tex.
Drafted by Philadelphia on second round, 1978 (36th pick).

Traded by Philadelphia with Christian Welp and David Wingate to San Antonio for Johnny Dawkins and Jay Vincent, August 28, 1989.

Traded by San Antonio to New York for Rod Strickland, February 21, 1990.

—COLLEGIATE RECORD—

Year	G.	Min.	FGA	FGM	Pct.	FTA	FTM	Pct.	Reb.	Pts.	Avg.
74-75	26	....	75	35	.467	53	31	.585	56	101	3.9
75-76	23	767	170	102	.600	84	52	.619	91	256	11.1
76-77	30	1095	246	149	.606	169	119	.704	119	417	13.9
77-78	27	941	319	174	.545	147	105	.714	152	453	16.8
Totals	106	....	810	460	.568	453	307	.678	418	1227	11.6

NBA REGULAR SEASON RECORD

									—Rebounds—									
Sea.—Team	G.	Min.	FGA	FGM	Pct.	FTA	FTM	Pct.	Off.	Def.	Tot.	Ast.	PF	Dq.	Stl.	Blk.	Pts.	Avg.
78-79—Philadelphia	82	2409	572	292	.510	140	101	.721	63	191	254	431	198	2	174	12	685	8.4
79-80—Philadelphia	79	2623	661	357	.540	231	180	.779	75	199	274	556	197	1	183	32	898	11.4
80-81—Philadelphia	81	2415	581	310	.534	178	140	.787	67	178	245	560	231	1	193	39	763	9.4
81-82—Philadelphia	79	2498	676	352	.521	220	171	.777	51	197	248	667	247	0	209	33	881	11.2
82-83—Philadelphia	79	2465	745	404	.542	240	181	.754	53	156	209	543	182	0	184	31	990	12.5
83-84—Philadelphia	75	2494	702	386	.550	232	170	.733	44	161	205	478	196	1	171	20	950	12.7
84-85—Philadelphia	78	2616	741	422	.570	199	175	.879	54	163	217	497	184	0	169	24	1025	13.1
85-86—Philadelphia	82	3270	913	490	.537	335	282	.842	55	180	235	753	160	0	207	27	1266	15.4
86-87—Philadelphia	68	2624	788	415	.527	292	227	.777	47	168	215	538	109	0	180	15	1061	15.6
87-88—Philadelphia	79	2871	865	428	.495	275	227	.825	59	194	253	635	116	0	167	22	1086	13.7
88-89—Philadelphia	71	2298	696	336	.483	195	151	.774	39	144	183	554	114	0	105	17	824	11.6
89-90—S.A.-N.Y.	81	2519	609	307	.504	202	171	.847	50	190	240	453	78	0	124	10	789	9.7
Totals	934	31102	8549	4499	.526	2739	2176	.794	657	2121	2778	6665	2012	5	2066	282	11218	12.0

Three-Point Field Goals: 1979-80, 4-for-9 (.444). 1980-81, 3-for-8 (.375). 1981-82, 6-for-22 (.273). 1982-83, 1-for-6 (.167). 1983-84, 8-for-20 (.400). 1984-85, 6-for-26 (.231). 1985-86, 4-for-17 (.235). 1986-87, 4-for-17 (.235). 1987-88, 3-for-22 (.136). 1988-89, 1-for-13 (.077). 1989-90, 4-for-16 (.250). Totals, 44-for-176 (.250).

NBA PLAYOFF RECORD

									—Rebounds—									
Sea.—Team	G.	Min.	FGA	FGM	Pct.	FTA	FTM	Pct.	Off.	Def.	Tot.	Ast.	PF	Dq.	Stl.	Blk.	Pts.	Avg.
78-79—Philadelphia	9	330	121	66	.545	56	37	.661	13	22	35	63	29	0	37	4	169	18.8
79-80—Philadelphia	18	675	174	89	.511	41	29	.707	22	52	74	111	43	0	45	4	208	11.6
80-81—Philadelphia	16	513	125	68	.544	42	32	.762	4	47	51	116	55	1	40	12	168	10.5
81-82—Philadelphia	21	765	265	125	.472	65	50	.769	15	47	62	172	58	0	48	6	301	14.3
82-83—Philadelphia	13	483	165	83	.503	64	45	.703	11	28	39	91	23	0	26	2	212	16.3
83-84—Philadelphia	5	171	67	35	.522	15	13	.867	2	10	12	19	18	0	13	0	83	16.6
84-85—Philadelphia	13	483	153	81	.529	42	36	.857	12	34	46	67	29	0	31	5	198	15.2
85-86—Philadelphia	12	519	182	94	.516	73	62	.849	13	43	56	85	18	0	13	3	250	20.8
86-87—Philadelphia	5	210	66	35	.530	21	18	.857	1	12	13	44	14	0	9	4	88	17.6
88-89—Philadelphia	3	128	41	21	.512	13	11	.846	3	8	11	39	4	0	7	1	53	17.7
89-90—New York	10	388	104	50	.481	31	28	.903	12	27	39	85	21	0	17	2	128	12.8
Totals	125	4665	1463	747	.511	463	361	.780	108	330	438	892	312	1	286	43	1858	14.9

Three-Point Field Goals: 1979-80, 1-for-5 (.200). 1980-81, 0-for-3. 1981-82, 1-for-9 (.111). 1982-83, 1-for-2 (.500). 1983-84, 0-for-1. 1984-85, 0-for-5. 1985-86, 0-for-7. 1986-87, 0-for-1. 1988-89, 0-for-1. 1989-90, 0-for-4. Totals, 3-for-38 (.079).

NBA ALL-STAR GAME RECORD

								—Rebounds—							
Season—Team	Min.	FGA	FGM	Pct.	FTA	FTM	Pct.	Off.	Def.	Tot.	Ast.	PF	Dq.	Stl.	Blk.	Pts.
1983—Philadelphia	18	8	3	.375	0	0	.000	0	1	1	1	0	0	0	0	6
1986—Philadelphia	14	6	3	.500	0	0	.000	0	0	0	2	0	0	2	0	6
1987—Philadelphia	8	2	1	.500	2	2	1.000	0	0	0	0	1	0	1	0	4
1988—Philadelphia	4	0	0	.000	0	0	.000	0	2	2	1	1	0	0	0	0
Totals	44	16	7	.438	2	2	1.000	0	3	3	4	2	0	3	0	16

Named to NBA All-Defensive First Team, 1983, 1984, 1985, 1986. . . . All-Defensive Second Team, 1987. . . . Member of NBA championship team, 1983. . . . NBA all-time steals leader.

DERRICK JOSEPH CHIEVOUS

Born July 3, 1967 at New York, N.Y. Height 6:07. Weight 205.
High School—Flushing, N.Y., Holy Cross.
College—University of Missouri, Columbia, Mo.
Drafted by Houston on first round, 1988 (16th pick).

Traded by Houston to Cleveland for three future 2nd round draft choices and cash, February 21, 1990.

—COLLEGIATE RECORD—

Year	G.	Min.	FGA	FGM	Pct.	FTA	FTM	Pct.	Reb.	Pts.	Avg.
84-85	32	1019	278	142	.511	168	134	.798	170	418	13.1
85-86	34	1091	433	227	.524	232	186	.802	262	640	18.8
86-87	34	1215	522	282	.540	302	244	.808	291	821	24.1
87-88	30	943	477	242	.507	261	200	.766	256	701	23.4
Totals	130	4268	1710	893	.522	963	764	.793	979	2580	19.8

Three-Point Field Goals: 1986-87, 13-for-33 (.394). 1987-88, 17-for-33 (.515). Totals, 30-for-66 (.455).

NBA REGULAR SEASON RECORD

									—Rebounds—									
Sea.—Team	G.	Min.	FGA	FGM	Pct.	FTA	FTM	Pct.	Off.	Def.	Tot.	Ast.	PF	Dq.	Stl.	Blk.	Pts.	Avg.
88-89—Houston	81	1539	634	277	.437	244	191	.783	114	142	256	77	161	1	48	11	750	9.3
89-90—Hou.-Cle.	55	591	220	105	.477	111	80	.721	35	55	90	31	70	0	26	5	293	5.3
Totals	136	2130	854	382	.447	355	271	.763	149	197	346	108	231	1	74	16	1043	7.7

Three-Point Field Goals: 1988-89, 5-for-24 (.208). 1989-90, 3-for-9 (.333). Totals, 8-for-33 (.242).

NBA PLAYOFF RECORD

									—Rebounds—									
Sea.—Team	G.	Min.	FGA	FGM	Pct.	FTA	FTM	Pct.	Off.	Def.	Tot.	Ast.	PF	Dq.	Stl.	Blk.	Pts.	Avg.
88-89—Houston	4	40	17	5	.294	10	8	.800	5	1	6	2	7	0	1	1	18	4.5
89-90—Cleveland	3	28	10	6	.600	9	7	.778	2	1	3	2	2	0	1	0	19	6.3
Totals	7	68	27	11	.407	19	15	.789	7	2	9	4	9	0	2	1	37	5.3

BEN COLEMAN

Born November 14, 1961 at Minneapolis, Minn. Height 6:09. Weight 235.

High School—Minneapolis, Minn., North.

Colleges—University of Minnesota, Minneapolis, Minn., and University of Maryland, College Park, Md.

Drafted by Chicago on second round, 1984 (37th pick).

Draft rights traded by Chicago with draft rights to Ken Johnson to Portland for draft rights to Mike Smrek, June 18, 1985.

Waived by Portland, November 12, 1985; signed by New Jersey as a free agent, September 22, 1986.

Traded by New Jersey with Mike Gminski to Philadelphia for Roy Hinson, Tim McCormick and a 1989 2nd round draft choice, January 16, 1988.

Waived by Philadelphia, October 9, 1989; signed by Milwaukee as a free agent, October 18, 1989.

Played in Italy during 1984-85 and 1985-86 seasons.

—COLLEGIATE RECORD—

Minnesota

Year	G.	Min.	FGA	FGM	Pct.	FTA	FTM	Pct.	Reb.	Pts.	Avg.
79-80	17	....	38	14	.369	8	3	.375	21	31	1.8
80-81	23	....	190	85	.447	35	23	.657	118	193	8.4
Minn. Totals	40	....	228	99	.434	43	26	.605	139	224	5.6

Maryland

Year	G.	Min.	FGA	FGM	Pct.	FTA	FTM	Pct.	Reb.	Pts.	Avg.
81-82					Did Not Play—Transfer Student						
82-83	30	995	319	192	.571	138	90	.652	242	454	15.1
83-84	32	1094	319	194	.608	144	103	.715	269	491	15.3
Md. Totals	62	2089	638	376	.589	282	193	.684	511	945	15.2
Col. Totals	102	....	866	475	.548	325	219	.674	650	1169	11.5

ITALIAN LEAGUE RECORD

Year	G.	Min.	FGA	FGM	Pct.	FTA	FTM	Pct.	Reb.	Pts.	Avg.
84-85—Trieste	30	1127	540	329	.609	147	111	.755	328	772	25.7
85-86—Trieste	22	812	354	207	.585	103	67	.650	240	484	22.0

NBA REGULAR SEASON RECORD

									—Rebounds—									
Sea.—Team	G.	Min.	FGA	FGM	Pct.	FTA	FTM	Pct.	Off.	Def.	Tot.	Ast.	PF	Dq.	Stl.	Blk.	Pts.	Avg.
86-87—New Jersey	68	1029	313	182	.581	121	88	.727	99	189	288	37	200	7	32	31	452	6.6
87-88—N.J.-Phil.	70	1498	453	226	.499	185	141	.762	116	234	350	62	230	5	43	41	593	8.5
88-89—Philadelphia	58	703	241	117	.485	77	61	.792	49	128	177	17	120	0	10	18	295	5.1
89-90—Milwaukee	22	305	97	46	.474	41	34	.829	31	56	87	12	54	0	7	7	126	5.7
Totals	218	3535	1104	571	.517	424	324	.764	295	607	902	128	604	12	92	97	1466	6.7

Three-Point Field Goals: 1986-87, 0-for-1. 1987-88, 0-for-3. 1989-90, 0-for-1. Totals, 0-for-5.

NBA PLAYOFF RECORD

									—Rebounds—									
Sea.—Team	G.	Min.	FGA	FGM	Pct.	FTA	FTM	Pct.	Off.	Def.	Tot.	Ast.	PF	Dq.	Stl.	Blk.	Pts.	Avg.
88-89—Philadelphia	3	23	8	6	.750	2	2	1.000	2	3	5	0	8	0	1	0	14	4.7

STEVE COLTER

Born July 24, 1962 at Phoenix, Ariz. Height 6:03. Weight 175.
High School—Phoenix, Ariz., Union.
College—New Mexico State University, Las Cruces, N. M.
Drafted by Portland on second round, 1984 (33rd pick).

Traded by Portland to Chicago for draft rights to Larry Krystkowiak and 1987 and 1992 2nd round draft choices, June 17, 1986.

Traded by Chicago with a future 2nd round draft choice to Philadelphia for Sedale Threatt, December 31, 1986.

Waived by Philadelphia, December 3, 1987; signed by Washington as a free agent, December 22, 1987.

Waived by Washington, December 29, 1987; re-signed by Washington, January 1, 1988, to the first of consecutive 10-day contracts that expired, January 20, 1988.

Re-signed by Washington, January 21, 1988, for remainder of season.

Re-signed by Washington, July 25, 1988.

—COLLEGIATE RECORD—

Year	G.	Min.	FGA	FGM	Pct.	FTA	FTM	Pct.	Reb.	Pts.	Avg.
80-81	22	233	47	18	.383	41	28	.683	37	64	2.9
81-82	28	822	194	94	.485	87	66	.759	100	254	9.1
82-83	29	1079	329	166	.505	179	135	.754	137	469	16.2
83-84	28	1120	438	219	.500	138	108	.783	137	546	19.5
Totals	107	3254	1008	497	.493	445	337	.757	411	1333	12.5

Three-Point Field Goals: 1982-83, 2-for-6 (.333).

NBA REGULAR SEASON RECORD

									—Rebounds—									
Sea.—Team	G.	Min.	FGA	FGM	Pct.	FTA	FTM	Pct.	Off.	Def.	Tot.	Ast.	PF	Dq.	Stl.	Blk.	Pts.	Avg.
84-85—Portland	78	1462	477	216	.453	130	98	.754	40	110	150	243	142	0	75	9	556	7.1
85-86—Portland	81	1868	597	272	.456	164	135	.823	41	136	177	257	188	0	113	10	706	8.7
86-87—Chi.-Phil.	70	1322	397	169	.426	107	82	.766	23	85	108	210	99	0	56	12	424	6.1
87-88—Phil.-Wash.	68	1513	441	203	.460	95	75	.789	58	115	173	261	132	0	62	14	484	7.1
88-89—Washington	80	1425	457	203	.444	167	125	.749	62	120	182	225	158	0	69	14	534	6.7
89-90—Washington	73	977	297	142	.478	95	77	.811	55	121	176	148	98	0	47	10	361	4.9
Totals	450	8567	2666	1205	.452	758	592	.781	279	687	966	1344	817	0	422	69	3065	6.8

Three-Point Field Goals: 1984-85, 26-for-74 (.351). 1985-86, 27-for-83 (.325). 1986-87, 4-for-17 (.235). 1987-88, 3-for-10 (.300). 1988-89, 3-for-25 (.120). 1989-90, 0-for-5. Totals, 63-for-214 (.294).

NBA PLAYOFF RECORD

									—Rebounds—									
Sea.—Team	G.	Min.	FGA	FGM	Pct.	FTA	FTM	Pct.	Off.	Def.	Tot.	Ast.	PF	Dq.	Stl.	Blk.	Pts.	Avg.
84-85—Portland	9	166	75	36	.480	8	5	.625	4	12	16	37	24	1	5	0	80	8.9
85-86—Portland	4	104	26	12	.462	2	2	1.000	3	12	15	23	13	0	5	1	26	6.5
86-87—Philadelphia	2	8	2	1	.500	0	0	.000	0	0	0	2	1	0	0	0	2	1.0
87-88—Washington	5	86	31	14	.452	7	4	.571	5	10	15	13	9	0	3	3	32	6.4
Totals	20	364	134	63	.470	17	11	.647	12	34	46	75	47	1	13	4	140	7.0

Three-Point Field Goals: 1984-85, 3-for-11 (.273). 1985-86, 0-for-1. Totals, 3-for-12 (.250).

LESTER ALLEN CONNER

Born September 17, 1959 at Memphis, Tenn. Height 6:04. Weight 185.
High School—Oakland, Calif., Fremont.
Colleges—Los Medanos College, Antioch, Calif.; Chabot College, Hayward, Calif., and Oregon State University, Corvallis, Ore.
Drafted by Golden State on first round, 1982 (14th pick).

Signed by Houston as a Veteran Free Agent, October 9, 1987; Golden State agreed not to exercise its right of first refusal in exchange for a 1988 2nd round draft choice.

Traded by Houston with Joe Barry Carroll to New Jersey for Tony Brown, Frank Johnson, Tim McCormick and Lorenzo Romar, November 2, 1988.

—COLLEGIATE RECORD—

Los Medanos

Year	G.	Min.	FGA	FGM	Pct.	FTA	FTM	Pct.	Reb.	Pts.	Avg.
78-79	31	....	...	...	....	...	...	....	....	781	25.2

Chabot

Year	G.	Min.	FGA	FGM	Pct.	FTA	FTM	Pct.	Reb.	Pts.	Avg.
79-80	35	1179	549	319	.581	217	158	.728	215	796	22.7
JC Totals	66	....	...	...	....	...	...	....	....	1577	23.9

Oregon State

Year	G.	Min.	FGA	FGM	Pct.	FTA	FTM	Pct.	Reb.	Pts.	Avg.
80-81	28	790	141	68	.482	91	61	.670	119	197	7.0
81-82	30	1106	292	151	.517	196	146	.745	163	448	14.9
Totals	58	1896	433	219	.506	287	207	.721	282	645	11.1

NBA REGULAR SEASON RECORD

Sea.—Team	G.	Min.	FGA	FGM	Pct.	FTA	FTM	Pct.	—Rebounds— Off.	Def.	Tot.	Ast.	PF	Dq.	Stl.	Blk.	Pts.	Avg.
82-83—Golden State	75	1416	303	145	.479	113	79	.699	69	152	221	253	141	1	116	7	369	4.9
83-84—Golden State	82	2573	730	360	.493	259	186	.718	132	173	305	401	176	1	162	12	907	11.1
84-85—Golden State	79	2258	546	246	.451	192	144	.750	87	159	246	369	136	1	161	13	640	8.1
85-86—Golden State	36	413	136	51	.375	54	40	.741	25	37	62	43	23	0	24	1	144	4.0
87-88—Houston	52	399	108	50	.463	41	32	.780	20	18	38	59	31	0	38	1	132	2.5
88-89—New Jersey	82	2532	676	309	.457	269	212	.788	100	255	355	604	132	1	181	5	843	10.3
89-90—New Jersey	82	2355	573	237	.414	214	172	.804	90	175	265	385	182	0	172	8	648	7.9
Totals	488	11946	3072	1398	.455	1142	865	.757	523	969	1492	2114	821	4	854	47	3683	7.5

Three-Point Field Goals: 1982-83, 0-for-4. 1983-84, 1-for-6 (.167). 1984-85, 4-for-20 (.200). 1985-86, 2-for-7 (.286). 1987-88, 0-for-7. 1988-89, 13-for-37 (.351). 1989-90, 2-for-13 (.154). Totals, 22-for-94 (.234).

NBA PLAYOFF RECORD

Sea.—Team	G.	Min.	FGA	FGM	Pct.	FTA	FTM	Pct.	—Rebounds— Off.	Def.	Tot.	Ast.	PF	Dq.	Stl.	Blk.	Pts.	Avg.
87-88—Houston	1	1	0	0	.000	2	2	1.000	0	1	1	1	0	0	1	0	2	2.0

ARTIS WAYNE COOPER

(Known by middle name.)

Born November 16, 1956 at Milan, Ga. Height 6:10. Weight 220.

High School—McRae, Ga., Telfair County.

College—University of New Orleans, New Orleans, La.

Drafted by Golden State on second round, 1978 (40th pick).

Traded by Golden State with a 1981 2nd round draft choice to Utah for Bernard King, September 11, 1980.
Traded by Utah with Allan Bristow to Dallas for Bill Robinzine, August 20, 1981.
Traded by Dallas with a 1985 1st round draft choice to Portland for Kelvin Ransey, June 28, 1982.
Traded by Portland with Lafayette Lever, Calvin Natt, a 1984 2nd round draft choice and a 1985 1st round draft choice to Denver for Kiki Vandeweghe, June 7, 1984.
Signed by Portland as an unrestricted free agent, July 24, 1989.

—COLLEGIATE RECORD—

Year	G.	Min.	FGA	FGM	Pct.	FTA	FTM	Pct.	Reb.	Pts.	Avg.
74-75	17	....	33	16	.485	4	3	.750	52	35	2.1
75-76	26	....	278	140	.504	47	34	.723	244	314	12.1
76-77	28	....	368	166	.451	55	38	.691	284	370	13.2
77-78	27	....	377	202	.536	111	86	.775	343	490	18.1
Totals	98	....	1056	524	.496	217	161	.742	923	1209	12.3

NBA REGULAR SEASON RECORD

Sea.—Team	G.	Min.	FGA	FGM	Pct.	FTA	FTM	Pct.	—Rebounds— Off.	Def.	Tot.	Ast.	PF	Dq.	Stl.	Blk.	Pts.	Avg.
78-79—Golden State	65	795	293	128	.437	61	41	.672	90	190	280	21	118	0	7	44	297	4.6
79-80—Golden State	79	1781	750	367	.489	181	136	.751	202	305	507	42	246	5	20	79	871	11.0
80-81—Utah	71	1420	471	213	.452	90	62	.689	166	274	440	52	219	8	18	51	489	6.9
81-82—Dallas	76	1818	669	281	.420	160	119	.744	200	350	550	115	285	10	37	106	682	9.0
82-83—Portland	80	2099	723	320	.443	197	135	.685	214	397	611	116	318	5	27	136	775	9.7
83-84—Portland	81	1662	663	304	.459	230	185	.804	176	300	476	76	247	2	26	106	793	9.8
84-85—Denver	80	2031	856	404	.472	235	161	.685	229	402	631	86	304	2	28	197	969	12.1
85-86—Denver	78	2112	906	422	.466	219	174	.795	190	420	610	81	315	6	42	227	1021	13.1
86-87—Denver	69	1561	524	235	.448	109	79	.725	162	311	473	68	257	5	13	101	549	8.0
87-88—Denver	45	865	270	118	.437	67	50	.746	98	172	270	30	145	3	12	94	286	6.4
88-89—Denver	79	1864	444	220	.495	106	79	.745	212	407	619	78	302	7	36	211	520	6.6
89-90—Portland	79	1176	304	138	.454	39	25	.641	118	221	339	44	211	2	18	95	301	3.8
Totals	882	19184	6873	3150	.458	1694	1246	.736	2057	3749	5806	809	2967	55	284	1447	7553	8.6

Three-Point Field Goals: 1979-80, 1-for-4 (.250). 1980-81, 1-for-3 (.333). 1981-82, 1-for-8 (.125). 1982-83, 0-for-5. 1983-84, 0-for-7. 1984-85, 0-for-2. 1985-86, 3-for-7 (.429). 1986-87, 0-for-3. 1987-88, 0-for-1. 1988-89, 1-for-4 (.250). 1989-90, 0-for-3. Totals, 7-for-47 (.149).

NBA PLAYOFF RECORD

Sea.—Team	G.	Min.	FGA	FGM	Pct.	FTA	FTM	Pct.	—Rebounds— Off.	Def.	Tot.	Ast.	PF	Dq.	Stl.	Blk.	Pts.	Avg.
82-83—Portland	7	228	74	36	.486	17	15	.882	24	32	56	9	33	3	2	8	87	12.4
83-84—Portland	5	104	27	10	.370	8	4	.500	11	9	20	4	14	0	1	4	24	4.8
84-85—Denver	15	321	143	67	.469	40	30	.750	34	59	93	20	52	0	8	36	164	10.9
85-86—Denver	8	154	56	24	.429	22	15	.682	11	29	40	7	31	2	2	5	63	7.9
86-87—Denver	3	41	12	5	.417	2	2	1.000	6	11	17	2	9	0	0	1	12	4.0
87-88—Denver	9	96	23	8	.348	2	2	1.000	16	17	33	6	19	0	3	8	18	2.0
88-89—Denver	3	44	12	6	.500	0	0	......	4	9	13	2	10	0	1	2	12	4.0
89-90—Portland	18	248	47	19	.404	19	10	.526	25	46	71	5	40	0	5	29	48	2.7
Totals	68	1236	394	175	.444	110	78	.709	131	212	343	55	208	5	22	93	428	6.3

Three-Point Field Goals: 1985-86, 0-for-1.

MICHAEL JEROME COOPER

Born April 15, 1956 at Los Angeles, Calif. Height 6:07. Weight 176.

High School—Pasadena, Calif.

Colleges—Pasadena City College, Pasadena, Calif., and University of New Mexico, Albuquerque, N. M.

Drafted by Los Angeles on third round, 1978 (60th pick).

—COLLEGIATE RECORD—

Pasadena City

Year	G.	Min.	FGA	FGM	Pct.	FTA	FTM	Pct.	Reb.	Pts.	Avg.
74-75	23	....	336	177	.527	65	38	.585	91	392	17.0
75-76	28	....	473	261	.552	129	102	.791	230	624	22.3
JC Totals	51	....	809	438	.541	194	140	.722	321	1016	19.9

New Mexico

Year	G.	Min.	FGA	FGM	Pct.	FTA	FTM	Pct.	Reb.	Pts.	Avg.
76-77	30	957	333	171	.514	140	112	.800	150	454	15.1
77-78	28	830	387	189	.488	111	73	.658	158	451	16.1
Totals	58	1787	720	360	.500	251	185	.737	308	905	15.6

NBA REGULAR SEASON RECORD

									—Rebounds—									
Sea.—Team	G.	Min.	FGA	FGM	Pct.	FTA	FTM	Pct.	Off.	Def.	Tot.	Ast.	PF	Dq.	Stl.	Blk.	Pts.	Avg.
78-79—Los Angeles	3	7	6	3	.500	0	0	.000	0	0	0	0	1	0	1	0	6	2.0
79-80—Los Angeles	82	1973	578	303	.524	143	111	.776	101	128	229	221	215	3	86	38	722	8.8
80-81—Los Angeles	81	2625	654	321	.491	149	117	.785	121	215	336	332	249	4	133	78	763	9.4
81-82—Los Angeles	76	2197	741	383	.517	171	139	.813	84	185	269	230	216	1	120	61	907	11.9
82-83—Los Angeles	82	2148	497	266	.535	130	102	.785	82	192	274	315	208	0	115	50	639	7.8
83-84—Los Angeles	82	2387	549	273	.497	185	155	.838	53	209	262	482	267	3	113	67	739	9.0
84-85—L.A. Lakers	82	2189	593	276	.465	133	115	.865	56	199	255	429	208	0	93	49	702	8.6
85-86—L.A. Lakers	82	2269	606	274	.452	170	147	.865	44	200	244	466	238	2	89	43	758	9.2
86-87—L.A. Lakers	82	2253	736	322	.438	148	126	.851	58	196	254	373	199	1	78	43	859	10.5
87-88—L.A. Lakers	61	1793	482	189	.392	113	97	.858	50	178	228	289	136	1	66	26	532	8.7
88-89—L.A. Lakers	80	1943	494	213	.431	93	81	.871	33	158	191	314	186	0	72	32	587	7.3
89-90—L.A. Lakers	80	1851	493	191	.387	94	83	.883	59	168	227	215	206	1	67	36	515	6.4
Totals	873	23635	6429	3014	.469	1529	1273	.833	741	2028	2769	3666	2329	16	1033	523	7729	8.9

Three-Point Field Goals: 1979-80, 5-for-20 (.250). 1980-81, 4-for-19 (.211). 1981-82, 2-for-17 (.118). 1982-83, 5-for-21 (.238). 1983-84, 38-for-121 (.314). 1984-85, 35-for-123 (.285). 1985-86, 63-for-163 (.387). 1986-87, 89-for-231 (.385). 1987-88, 57-for-178 (.320). 1988-89, 80-for-210 (.381). 1989-90, 50-for-157 (.318). Totals, 428-for-1260 (.340).

NBA PLAYOFF RECORD

									—Rebounds—									
Sea.—Team	G.	Min.	FGA	FGM	Pct.	FTA	FTM	Pct.	Off.	Def.	Tot.	Ast.	PF	Dq.	Stl.	Blk.	Pts.	Avg.
79-80—Los Angeles	16	464	140	57	.407	36	31	.861	28	31	59	58	54	0	24	11	145	9.1
80-81—Los Angeles	3	102	20	11	.550	14	10	.714	2	8	10	7	7	0	6	0	32	10.7
81-82—Los Angeles	14	383	124	70	.565	34	25	.735	19	42	61	62	47	0	24	11	166	11.9
82-83—Los Angeles	15	453	114	53	.465	41	34	.829	12	47	59	44	54	1	26	6	141	9.4
83-84—Los Angeles	21	723	191	88	.461	62	50	.806	20	62	82	119	80	1	24	20	238	11.3
84-85—L.A. Lakers	19	501	126	71	.563	52	48	.923	12	64	76	93	46	0	21	9	198	10.4
85-86—L.A. Lakers	14	421	115	54	.470	11	9	.818	16	30	46	68	24	0	18	4	136	9.7
86-87—L.A. Lakers	18	522	159	77	.484	54	46	.852	8	51	59	90	46	0	25	14	234	13.0
87-88—L.A. Lakers	24	588	131	54	.412	27	20	.741	15	43	58	66	57	0	19	9	153	6.4
88-89—L.A. Lakers	15	414	89	37	.416	24	20	.833	9	31	40	71	38	0	9	8	115	7.7
89-90—L.A. Lakers	9	173	35	10	.286	0	0	....	11	13	24	25	21	0	7	4	23	2.6
Totals	168	4744	1244	582	.468	355	293	.825	152	422	574	703	474	2	203	96	1581	9.4

Three-Point Field Goals: 1979-80, 0-for-2. 1980-81, 0-for-3. 1981-82, 1-for-2 (.500). 1982-83, 1-for-7 (.143). 1983-84, 12-for-36 (.333). 1984-85, 8-for-26 (.308). 1985-86, 19-for-41 (.463). 1986-87, 34-for-70 (.486). 1987-88, 25-for-62 (.403). 1988-89, 21-for-55 (.382). 1989-90, 3-for-12 (.250). Totals, 124-for-316 (.392).

Named NBA Defensive Player of the Year, 1987. . . . NBA All-Defensive First Team, 1982, 1984, 1985, 1987, 1988 . . . . NBA All-Defensive Second Team, 1981, 1983, 1986. . . . Member of NBA championship teams, 1980, 1982, 1985, 1987, 1988. . . . Shares championship series game record for most three-point field goals made, 6, vs. Boston, June 4, 1987.

LANARD COPELAND

Born July 16, 1965 at Atlanta, Ga. Height 6:06. Weight 190.

High School—Atlanta, Ga., Booker T. Washington (did not play high school basketball).

College—Georgia State University, Atlanta, Ga.

Never drafted by an NBA franchise.

Signed by Philadelphia as a free agent, August 11, 1989.

—COLLEGIATE RECORD—

Year	G.	Min.	FGA	FGM	Pct.	FTA	FTM	Pct.	Reb.	Pts.	Avg.
85-86	6	42	15	7	.467	11	8	.727	9	22	2.7
86-87	27	563	217	99	.456	39	25	.641	108	226	8.4
87-88	28	654	290	119	.410	35	25	.714	116	307	11.0
88-89	28	779	398	171	.430	75	51	.680	113	428	15.3
Totals	89	2038	920	396	.430	160	109	.681	346	983	11.0

Three-Point Field Goals: 1986-87, 3-for-9 (.333). 1987-88, 44-for-111 (.396). 1988-89, 35-for-111 (.315). Totals, 82-for-213 (.355).

NBA REGULAR SEASON RECORD

									—Rebounds—									
Sea.—Team	G.	Min.	FGA	FGM	Pct.	FTA	FTM	Pct.	Off.	Def.	Tot.	Ast.	PF	Dq.	Stl.	Blk.	Pts.	Avg.
89-90—Philadelphia	23	110	68	31	.456	14	11	.786	4	6	10	9	12	0	1	1	74	3.2

Three-Point Field Goals: 1989-90, 1-for-5 (.200).

NBA PLAYOFF RECORD

									—Rebounds—									
Sea.—Team	G.	Min.	FGA	FGM	Pct.	FTA	FTM	Pct.	Off.	Def.	Tot.	Ast.	PF	Dq.	Stl.	Blk.	Pts.	Avg.
89-90—Philadelphia	4	9	6	2	.333	0	0	....	0	1	1	0	1	0	0	0	4	1.0

TYRONE KENNEDY CORBIN

Born December 31, 1962 at Columbia, S. C. Height 6:06. Weight 222.
High School—Columbia, S. C., A. C. Flora.
College—DePaul University, Chicago, Ill.
Drafted by San Antonio on second round, 1985 (35th pick).

Waived by San Antonio, January 21, 1987; signed by Cleveland as a free agent, January 24, 1987.
Traded by Cleveland with Kevin Johnson, Mark West, 1988 1st and 2nd round draft choices and a 1989 2nd round draft choice to Phoenix for Larry Nance, Mike Sanders and a 1988 1st round draft choice, February 25, 1988.
Selected from Phoenix by Minnesota in NBA expansion draft, June 15, 1989.

—COLLEGIATE RECORD—

Year	G.	Min.	FGA	FGM	Pct.	FTA	FTM	Pct.	Reb.	Pts.	Avg.
81-82	28	602	103	43	.417	78	56	.718	172	142	5.1
82-83	33	1060	263	124	.471	132	102	.773	262	350	10.6
83-84	30	1070	316	166	.525	125	93	.744	223	425	14.2
84-85	29	1004	354	189	.534	102	83	.814	236	461	15.8
Totals	120	3736	1036	522	.504	437	334	.764	893	1378	11.5

NBA REGULAR SEASON RECORD

									—Rebounds—									
Sea.—Team	G.	Min.	FGA	FGM	Pct.	FTA	FTM	Pct.	Off.	Def.	Tot.	Ast.	PF	Dq.	Stl.	Blk.	Pts.	Avg.
85-86—San Antonio	16	174	64	27	.422	14	10	.714	11	14	25	11	21	0	11	2	64	4.0
86-87—S.A.-Clev.	63	1170	381	156	.409	124	91	.734	88	127	215	97	129	0	55	5	404	6.4
87-88—Clev.-Phoe.	84	1739	525	257	.490	138	110	.797	127	223	350	115	181	2	72	18	625	7.4
88-89—Phoenix	77	1655	454	245	.540	179	141	.788	176	222	398	118	222	2	82	13	631	8.2
89-90—Minnesota	82	3011	1083	521	.481	209	161	.770	219	385	604	216	288	5	175	41	1203	14.7
Totals	322	7749	2507	1206	.481	664	513	.773	621	971	1592	557	841	9	395	79	2927	9.1

Three-Point Field Goals: 1985-86, 0-for-1. 1986-87, 1-for-4 (.250). 1987-88, 1-for-6 (.167). 1988-89, 0-for-2. 1989-90, 0-for-11. Totals, 2-for-24 (.083).

NBA PLAYOFF RECORD

									—Rebounds—									
Sea.—Team	G.	Min.	FGA	FGM	Pct.	FTA	FTM	Pct.	Off.	Def.	Tot.	Ast.	PF	Dq.	Stl.	Blk.	Pts.	Avg.
85-86—San Antonio	1	14	4	0	.000	0	0	.000	0	1	1	1	0	0	0	0	0	0.0
88-89—Phoenix	12	310	86	45	.523	25	19	.760	43	42	85	26	37	0	24	4	109	9.1
Totals	13	324	90	45	.500	25	19	.760	43	43	86	27	37	0	24	4	109	8.4

DAVID JOHN CORZINE
(Dave)

Born April 25, 1956 at Arlington Heights, Ill. Height 6:11. Weight 265.
High School—Arlington Heights, Ill., Hersey.
College—DePaul University, Chicago, Ill.
Drafted by Washington on first round, 1978 (18th pick).

Traded by Washington to San Antonio for 1981 and 1982 2nd round draft choices, September 26, 1980.
Traded by San Antonio with Mark Olberding and cash to Chicago for Artis Gilmore, July 22, 1982.
Traded by Chicago to Orlando for 1990 and 1992 2nd round draft choices, June 27, 1989.

—COLLEGIATE RECORD—

Year	G.	Min.	FGA	FGM	Pct.	FTA	FTM	Pct.	Reb.	Pts.	Avg.
74-75	25	....	309	134	.434	56	36	.643	216	304	12.2
75-76	29	....	386	181	.469	124	88	.710	256	450	15.5
76-77	27	....	448	219	.489	97	74	.763	339	512	19.0
77-78	30	....	462	255	.552	152	120	.789	340	630	21.0
Totals	111	....	1605	789	.492	429	318	.741	1151	1896	17.1

NBA REGULAR SEASON RECORD

									—Rebounds—									
Sea.—Team	G.	Min.	FGA	FGM	Pct.	FTA	FTM	Pct.	Off.	Def.	Tot.	Ast.	PF	Dq.	Stl.	Blk.	Pts.	Avg.
78-79—Washington	59	532	118	63	.534	63	49	.778	52	95	147	49	67	0	10	14	175	3.0
79-80—Washington	78	826	216	90	.417	68	45	.662	104	166	270	63	120	1	9	31	225	2.9
80-81—San Antonio	82	1960	747	366	.490	175	125	.714	228	408	636	117	212	0	42	99	857	10.5
81-82—San Antonio	82	2189	648	336	.519	213	159	.746	211	418	629	130	235	3	33	126	832	10.1
82-83—Chicago	82	2496	920	457	.497	322	232	.720	243	474	717	154	242	4	47	109	1146	14.0
83-84—Chicago	82	2674	824	385	.467	275	231	.840	169	406	575	202	227	3	58	120	1004	12.2
84-85—Chicago	82	2062	568	276	.486	200	149	.745	130	292	422	140	189	2	32	64	701	8.5
85-86—Chicago	67	1709	519	255	.491	171	127	.743	132	301	433	150	133	0	28	53	640	9.6
86-87—Chicago	82	2287	619	294	.475	129	95	.736	199	341	540	209	202	1	38	87	683	8.3
87-88—Chicago	80	2328	715	344	.481	153	115	.752	170	357	527	154	149	1	36	95	804	10.1
88-89—Chicago	81	1483	440	203	.461	96	71	.740	92	223	315	103	134	0	29	45	479	5.9
89-90—Orlando	6	79	29	11	.379	2	0	.000	7	11	18	2	7	0	2	0	22	3.7
Totals	863	20625	6363	3080	.484	1867	1398	.749	1737	3492	5229	1473	1917	15	364	843	7568	8.8

Three-Point Field Goals: 1980-81, 0-for-3. 1981-82, 1-for-4 (.250). 1982-83, 0-for-2. 1983-84, 3-for-9 (.333). 1984-85, 0-for-1. 1985-86, 3-for-12 (.250). 1986-87, 0-for-5. 1987-88, 1-for-9 (.111). 1988-89, 2-for-8 (.250). Totals, 10-for-53 (.189).

NBA PLAYOFF RECORD

									—Rebounds—									
Sea.—Team	G.	Min.	FGA	FGM	Pct.	FTA	FTM	Pct.	Off.	Def.	Tot.	Ast.	PF	Dq.	Stl.	Blk.	Pts.	Avg.
78-79—Washington	12	63	15	4	.267	0	0	.000	12	13	25	5	9	0	2	0	8	0.7
79-80—Washington	2	9	5	4	.800	2	2	1.000	2	1	3	0	2	0	0	0	10	5.0
80-81—San Antonio	7	161	55	27	.491	13	9	.692	12	36	48	16	15	0	4	8	63	9.0
81-82—San Antonio	9	258	106	49	.462	34	24	.706	38	47	85	17	30	0	6	9	122	13.6
84-85—Chicago	4	77	21	14	.667	6	5	.833	9	13	22	3	14	0	2	1	33	8.3
85-86—Chicago	3	103	29	16	.552	4	4	1.000	6	21	27	6	12	0	1	2	36	12.0
86-87—Chicago	3	122	22	10	.455	9	7	.778	7	14	21	7	6	0	1	3	27	9.0
87-88—Chicago	10	308	76	27	.355	13	7	.538	15	42	57	8	21	0	3	8	61	6.1
88-89—Chicago	16	219	64	27	.422	17	11	.647	14	27	41	9	27	0	4	6	65	4.1
Totals	66	1320	393	178	.453	98	69	.704	115	214	329	71	136	0	23	37	425	6.4

PATRICK MICHAEL CUMMINGS
(Pat)

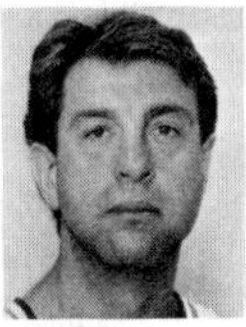

Born July 11, 1956 at Johnstown, Pa. Height 6:09. Weight 235.
High School—Johnstown, Pa.
College—University of Cincinnati, Cincinnati, O.
Drafted by Milwaukee on third round as junior eligible, 1978 (59th pick).

Traded by Milwaukee to Dallas for a 1982 2nd round draft choice, June 28, 1982.

Signed by New York as a Veteran Free Agent, June 27, 1984; Dallas agreed not to exercise its right of first refusal in exchange for a 1985 3rd round draft choice and a 1986 2nd round draft choice.

Became free agent, August 1, 1988; signed by Miami as a free agent, August 29, 1988.

Waived by Miami, March 1, 1990.

—COLLEGIATE RECORD—

Year	G.	Min.	FGA	FGM	Pct.	FTA	FTM	Pct.	Reb.	Pts.	Avg.
74-75	18	458	190	111	.584	39	29	.744	131	251	13.9
75-76	31	810	291	163	.560	57	37	.649	210	363	11.7
76-77					Did Not Play—Broken Foot						
77-78	27	854	330	212	.642	87	63	.724	206	487	18.0
78-79	27	1013	490	270	.551	147	121	.823	304	661	24.5
Totals	103	3135	1301	756	.581	330	250	.758	851	1762	17.1

NBA REGULAR SEASON RECORD

									—Rebounds—									
Sea.—Team	G.	Min.	FGA	FGM	Pct.	FTA	FTM	Pct.	Off.	Def.	Tot.	Ast.	PF	Dq.	Stl.	Blk.	Pts.	Avg.
79-80—Milwaukee	71	900	370	187	.505	123	94	.764	81	157	238	53	141	0	22	17	468	6.6
80-81—Milwaukee	74	1084	460	248	.539	140	99	.707	97	195	292	62	192	4	31	19	595	8.0
81-82—Milwaukee	78	1132	430	219	.509	91	67	.736	61	184	245	99	227	6	22	8	505	6.5
82-83—Dallas	81	2317	878	433	.493	196	148	.755	225	443	668	144	296	9	57	35	1014	12.5
83-84—Dallas	80	2492	915	452	.494	190	141	.742	151	507	658	158	282	2	64	23	1045	13.1
84-85—New York	63	2069	797	410	.514	227	177	.780	139	379	518	109	247	6	50	17	997	15.8
85-86—New York	31	1007	408	195	.478	139	97	.698	92	188	280	47	136	7	27	12	487	15.7
86-87—New York	49	1056	382	172	.450	110	79	.718	123	189	312	38	145	2	26	7	423	8.6
87-88—New York	62	946	307	140	.456	80	59	.738	82	153	235	37	143	0	20	10	339	5.5

Sea.—Team	G.	Min.	FGA	FGM	Pct.	FTA	FTM	Pct.	Rebounds— Off.	Def.	Tot.	Ast.	PF	Dq.	Stl.	Blk.	Pts.	Avg.
88-89—Miami	53	1096	394	197	.500	97	72	.742	84	197	281	47	160	3	29	18	466	8.8
89-90—Miami	37	391	159	77	.484	37	21	.568	28	65	93	13	60	1	12	4	175	4.7
Totals	679	14490	5500	2730	.496	1430	1054	.737	1163	2657	3820	807	2029	40	360	171	6514	9.6

Three-Point Field Goals: 1980-81, 0-for-2. 1981-82, 0-for-2. 1982-83, 0-for-1. 1983-84, 0-for-2. 1984-85, 0-for-4. 1985-86, 0-for-2. 1987-88, 0-for-1. 1988-89, 0-for-2. Totals, 0-for-16.

NBA PLAYOFF RECORD

Sea.—Team	G.	Min.	FGA	FGM	Pct.	FTA	FTM	Pct.	Rebounds— Off.	Def.	Tot.	Ast.	PF	Dq.	Stl.	Blk.	Pts.	Avg.
79-80—Milwaukee	6	57	17	11	.647	6	5	.833	4	12	16	2	9	0	1	0	27	4.5
80-81—Milwaukee	5	25	11	3	.273	4	3	.750	3	3	6	0	2	0	1	0	9	1.8
81-82—Milwaukee	6	44	11	4	.364	2	1	.500	3	8	11	2	7	0	0	2	9	1.5
83-84—Dallas	10	300	115	47	.409	15	14	.933	26	46	72	15	30	0	4	2	108	10.8
87-88—New York	3	28	5	2	.400	4	3	.750	2	5	7	3	11	0	0	0	7	2.3
Totals	30	454	159	67	.421	31	26	.839	38	74	112	22	59	0	6	4	160	5.3

ROBERT TERRELL CUMMINGS
(Terry)

Born March 15, 1961 at Chicago, Ill. Height 6:09. Weight 235.

High School—Chicago, Ill., Carver.

College—DePaul University, Chicago, Ill.

Drafted by San Diego on first round as an undergraduate, 1982 (2nd pick).

Traded by Los Angeles Clippers with Craig Hodges and Ricky Pierce to Milwaukee for Marques Johnson, Harvey Catchings, Junior Bridgeman and cash, September 29, 1984.

Traded by Milwaukee with future considerations to San Antonio for Alvin Robertson, Greg Anderson and future considerations, May 28, 1989.

—COLLEGIATE RECORD—

Year	G.	Min.	FGA	FGM	Pct.	FTA	FTM	Pct.	Reb.	Pts.	Avg.
79-80	28	....	303	154	.508	107	89	.832	263	397	14.2
80-81	29	994	303	151	.498	100	75	.750	260	377	13.0
81-82	28	1031	430	244	.567	180	136	.756	334	624	22.3
Totals	85	2025	1036	549	.530	387	300	.775	857	1398	16.4

NBA REGULAR SEASON RECORD

Sea.—Team	G.	Min.	FGA	FGM	Pct.	FTA	FTM	Pct.	Rebounds— Off.	Def.	Tot.	Ast.	PF	Dq.	Stl.	Blk.	Pts.	Avg.
82-83—San Diego	70	2531	1309	684	.523	412	292	.709	303	441	744	177	294	10	129	62	1660	23.7
83-84—San Diego	81	2907	1491	737	.494	528	380	.720	323	454	777	139	298	6	92	57	1854	22.9
84-85—Milwaukee	79	2722	1532	759	.495	463	343	.741	244	472	716	228	264	4	117	67	1861	23.6
85-86—Milwaukee	82	2669	1438	681	.474	404	265	.656	222	472	694	193	283	4	121	51	1627	19.8
86-87—Milwaukee	82	2770	1426	729	.511	376	249	.662	214	486	700	229	296	3	129	81	1707	20.8
87-88—Milwaukee	76	2629	1392	675	.485	406	270	.665	184	369	553	181	274	6	78	46	1621	21.3
88-89—Milwaukee	80	2824	1563	730	.467	460	362	.787	281	369	650	198	265	5	106	72	1829	22.9
89-90—San Antonio	81	2821	1532	728	.475	440	343	.780	226	451	677	219	286	1	110	52	1818	22.4
Totals	631	21873	11683	5723	.490	3489	2504	.718	1997	3514	5511	1564	2260	39	882	488	13977	22.2

Three-Point Field Goals: 1982-83, 0-for-1. 1983-84, 0-for-3. 1984-85, 0-for-1. 1985-86, 0-for-2. 1986-87, 0-for-3. 1987-88, 1-for-3 (.333). 1988-89, 7-for-15 (.467). 1989-90, 19-for-59 (.322). Totals, 27-for-87 (.310).

NBA PLAYOFF RECORD

Sea.—Team	G.	Min.	FGA	FGM	Pct.	FTA	FTM	Pct.	Rebounds— Off.	Def.	Tot.	Ast.	PF	Dq.	Stl.	Blk.	Pts.	Avg.
84-85—Milwaukee	8	311	149	86	.577	58	48	.828	21	49	70	20	33	1	12	7	220	27.5
85-86—Milwaukee	14	510	253	130	.514	62	43	.694	33	105	138	42	52	0	20	16	303	21.6
86-87—Milwaukee	12	443	215	105	.488	83	57	.687	29	66	95	28	51	1	12	13	267	22.3
87-88—Milwaukee	5	193	89	50	.562	44	29	.659	12	27	39	13	16	0	9	3	129	25.8
88-89—Milwaukee	5	124	69	25	.362	16	14	.875	19	14	33	7	16	0	3	0	64	12.8
89-90—San Antonio	10	375	195	103	.528	52	42	.808	31	63	94	22	39	0	7	4	249	24.9
Totals	54	1956	970	499	.514	315	233	.740	145	324	469	132	207	2	63	43	1232	22.8

Three-Point Field Goals: 1984-85, 0-for-1. 1988-89, 0-for-1. 1989-90, 1-for-5 (.200). Totals, 1-for-7 (.143).

NBA ALL-STAR GAME RECORD

Season—Team	Min.	FGA	FGM	Pct.	FTA	FTM	Pct.	Rebounds— Off.	Def.	Tot.	Ast.	PF	Dq.	Stl.	Blk.	Pts.
1985—Milwaukee	16	17	7	.412	4	3	.750	4	3	7	0	1	0	0	1	17
1989—Milwaukee	19	9	4	.444	2	2	1.000	2	3	5	1	4	0	3	1	10
Totals	35	26	11	.423	6	5	.833	6	6	12	1	5	0	3	2	27

Named to All-NBA Second Team, 1985.... All-NBA Third Team, 1989.... NBA Rookie of the Year, 1983.... NBA All-Rookie Team, 1983.... THE SPORTING NEWS All-America First Team, 1982.

WARDELL STEPHEN CURRY
(Dell)

Born June 25, 1964 at Harrisonburg, Va. Height 6:05. Weight 195.

High School—Fort Defiance, Va.

College—Virginia Polytechnic Institute and State University, Blacksburg, Va.

Drafted by Utah on first round, 1986 (15th pick).

Traded by Utah with Kent Benson and future 2nd round draft considerations to Cleveland for Darryl Dawkins, Mel Turpin and future 2nd round draft considerations, October 8, 1987.

Selected from Cleveland by Charlotte in NBA expansion draft, June 23, 1988.

—COLLEGIATE RECORD—

Year	G.	Min.	FGA	FGM	Pct.	FTA	FTM	Pct.	Reb.	Pts.	Avg.
82-83	32	1024	417	198	.475	80	68	.850	95	464	14.5
83-84	35	1166	561	293	.522	116	88	.759	143	674	19.3
84-85	29	968	467	225	.482	99	75	.758	169	529	18.2
85-86	30	1117	577	305	.529	142	112	.789	203	722	24.1
Totals	126	4275	2022	1021	.505	437	343	.785	610	2389	19.0

Three-Point Field Goals: 1984-85, 4-for-7 (.571).

NBA REGULAR SEASON RECORD

									—Rebounds—									
Sea.—Team	G.	Min.	FGA	FGM	Pct.	FTA	FTM	Pct.	Off.	Def.	Tot.	Ast.	PF	Dq.	Stl.	Blk.	Pts.	Avg.
86-87—Utah	67	636	326	139	.426	38	30	.789	30	48	78	58	86	0	27	4	325	4.9
87-88—Cleveland	79	1499	742	340	.458	101	79	.782	43	123	166	149	128	0	94	22	787	10.0
88-89—Charlotte	48	813	521	256	.491	46	40	.870	26	78	104	50	68	0	42	4	571	11.9
89-90—Charlotte	67	1860	990	461	.466	104	96	.923	31	137	168	159	148	0	98	26	1070	16.0
Totals	261	4808	2579	1196	.464	289	245	.848	130	386	516	416	430	0	261	56	2753	10.5

Three-Point Field Goals: 1986-87, 17-for-60 (.283). 1987-88, 28-for-81 (.346). 1988-89, 19-for-55 (.345). 1989-90, 52-for-147 (.354). Totals, 116-for-343 (.338).

NBA PLAYOFF RECORD

									—Rebounds—									
Sea.—Team	G.	Min.	FGA	FGM	Pct.	FTA	FTM	Pct.	Off.	Def.	Tot.	Ast.	PF	Dq.	Stl.	Blk.	Pts.	Avg.
86-87—Utah	2	4	3	0	.000	1	0	.000	0	0	0	0	1	0	0	0	0	0.0
87-88—Cleveland	2	17	4	1	.250	0	0	.000	1	0	1	2	1	0	0	1	2	1.0
Totals	4	21	7	1	.143	0	0	.000	1	0	1	2	2	0	0	1	2	0.5

Three-Point Field Goals: 1986-87, 0-for-1. 1987-88, 0-for-1. Totals, 0-for-2.

Named to THE SPORTING NEWS All-America Second Team, 1986.

QUINTIN DAILEY

Born January 22, 1961 at Baltimore, Md. Height 6:03. Weight 180.

High School—Baltimore, Md., Cardinal Gibbons.

College—University of San Francisco, San Francisco, Calif.

Drafted by Chicago on first round as an undergraduate, 1982 (7th pick).

Signed by Los Angeles Clippers as a free agent, December 29, 1986; Chicago waived its right of first refusal.

Signed by Los Angeles Lakers as an unrestricted free agent, September 12, 1989.

Waived by Los Angeles Lakers, October 13, 1989; signed by Seattle, February 2, 1990, to the first of consecutive 10-day contracts that expired, February 21, 1990.

Re-signed by Seattle, February 22, 1990, for remainder of season.

Played in Continental Basketball Association with Mississippi Jets, 1986-87, and Sioux Falls Skyforce, 1989-90.

—COLLEGIATE RECORD—

Year	G.	Min.	FGA	FGM	Pct.	FTA	FTM	Pct.	Reb.	Pts.	Avg.
79-80	29	....	292	154	.527	134	85	.634	107	393	13.6
80-81	31	....	467	267	.572	206	159	.772	170	693	22.4
81-82	30	1138	524	286	.546	232	183	.789	156	755	25.2
Totals	90	....	1283	707	.551	572	427	.747	433	1841	20.5

CBA REGULAR SEASON RECORD

			——2-Point——			——3-Point——									
Sea.—Team	G.	Min.	FGM	FGA	Pct.	FGM	FGA	Pct.	FTM	FTA	Pct.	Reb.	Ast.	Pts.	Avg.
86-87—Mississippi	8	220	54	99	.545	0	2	.000	35	47	.745	17	11	143	17.9
89-90—Sioux Falls	25	578	147	336	.438	2	6	.333	89	119	.748	80	71	389	15.6
Totals	33	798	201	435	.462	2	8	.250	124	166	.747	97	82	532	16.1

NBA REGULAR SEASON RECORD

Sea.—Team	G.	Min.	FGA	FGM	Pct.	FTA	FTM	Pct.	—Rebounds— Off.	Def.	Tot.	Ast.	PF	Dq.	Stl.	Blk.	Pts.	Avg.
82-83—Chicago	76	2081	1008	470	.466	282	206	.730	87	173	260	280	248	7	72	10	1151	15.1
83-84—Chicago	82	2449	1229	583	.474	396	321	.811	61	174	235	254	218	4	109	11	1491	18.2
84-85—Chicago	79	2101	1111	525	.473	251	205	.817	57	151	208	191	192	0	71	5	1262	16.0
85-86—Chicago	35	723	470	203	.432	198	163	.823	20	48	68	67	86	0	22	5	569	16.3
86-87—L.A. Clippers	49	924	491	200	.407	155	119	.768	34	49	83	79	113	4	43	8	520	10.6
87-88—L.A. Clippers	67	1282	755	328	.434	313	243	.776	62	92	154	109	128	1	69	4	901	13.4
88-89—L.A. Clippers	69	1722	964	448	.465	286	217	.759	69	135	204	154	152	0	90	6	1114	16.1
89-90—Seattle	30	491	240	97	.404	66	52	.788	18	33	51	34	63	0	12	0	247	8.2
Totals	487	11773	6268	2854	.455	1947	1526	.784	408	855	1263	1168	1200	16	488	49	7255	14.9

Three-Point Field Goals: 1982-83, 5-for-25 (.200). 1983-84, 4-for-32 (.125). 1984-85, 7-for-30 (.233). 1985-86, 0-for-8. 1986-87, 1-for-10 (.100). 1987-88, 2-for-12 (.167). 1988-89, 1-for-9 (.111). 1989-90, 1-for-5 (.200). Totals, 21-for-131 (.160).

NBA PLAYOFF RECORD

Sea.—Team	G.	Min.	FGA	FGM	Pct.	FTA	FTM	Pct.	—Rebounds— Off.	Def.	Tot.	Ast.	PF	Dq.	Stl.	Blk.	Pts.	Avg.
84-85—Chicago	4	129	62	26	.419	11	8	.727	5	8	13	11	9	0	4	0	61	15.3

Three-Point Field Goals: 1984-85, 1-for-7 (.143).

Named to NBA All-Rookie Team, 1983. . . . THE SPORTING NEWS All-America First Team, 1982.

ADRIAN DELANO DANTLEY

Born February 28, 1956 at Washington, D. C. Height 6:05. Weight 210.
High School—Hyattsville, Md., DeMatha.
College—University of Notre Dame, Ind.
Drafted by Buffalo on first round as hardship case, 1976 (6th pick).

Traded by Buffalo with Mike Bantom to Indiana for Billy Knight, September 1, 1977.
Traded by Indiana with Dave Robisch to Los Angeles for James Edwards, Earl Tatum and cash, December 13, 1977.
Traded by Los Angeles to Utah for Spencer Haywood, September 13, 1979.
Traded by Utah with 1987 and 1990 2nd round draft choices to Detroit for Kelly Tripucka and Kent Benson, August 21, 1986.
Traded by Detroit with a 1991 1st round draft choice to Dallas for Mark Aguirre, February 15, 1989.

—COLLEGIATE RECORD—

Year	G.	Min.	FGA	FGM	Pct.	FTA	FTM	Pct.	Reb.	Pts.	Avg.
73-74	28	795	339	189	.558	161	133	.826	255	511	18.3
74-75	29	1091	581	315	.542	314	253	.806	296	883	30.4
75-76	29	1056	510	300	.588	294	229	.779	292	829	28.6
Totals	86	2942	1430	804	.562	769	615	.800	843	2223	25.8

NBA REGULAR SEASON RECORD

Sea.—Team	G.	Min.	FGA	FGM	Pct.	FTA	FTM	Pct.	—Rebounds— Off.	Def.	Tot.	Ast.	PF	Dq.	Stl.	Blk.	Pts.	Avg.
76-77—Buffalo	77	2816	1046	544	.520	582	476	.818	251	336	587	144	215	2	91	15	1564	20.3
77-78—Ind.-L. A.	79	2933	1128	578	.512	680	541	.796	265	355	620	253	233	2	118	24	1697	21.5
78-79—Los Angeles	60	1775	733	374	.510	342	292	.854	131	211	342	138	162	0	63	12	1040	17.3
79-80—Utah	68	2674	1267	730	.576	526	443	.842	183	333	516	191	211	2	96	14	1903	28.0
80-81—Utah	80	3417	1627	909	.559	784	632	.806	192	317	509	322	245	1	109	18	2452	30.7
81-82—Utah	81	3222	1586	904	.570	818	648	.792	231	283	514	324	252	1	95	14	2457	30.3
82-83—Utah	22	887	402	233	.580	248	210	.847	58	82	140	105	62	2	20	0	676	30.7
83-84—Utah	79	2984	1438	802	.558	946	813	.859	179	269	448	310	201	0	61	4	2418	30.6
84-85—Utah	55	1971	964	512	.531	545	438	.804	148	175	323	186	133	0	57	8	1462	26.6
85-86—Utah	76	2744	1453	818	.563	796	630	.791	178	217	395	264	206	2	64	4	2267	29.8
86-87—Detroit	81	2736	1126	601	.534	664	539	.812	104	228	332	162	193	1	63	7	1742	21.5
87-88—Detroit	69	2144	863	444	.514	572	492	.860	84	143	227	171	144	0	39	10	1380	20.0
88-89—Det-Dal.	73	2422	954	470	.493	568	460	.810	117	200	317	171	186	1	43	13	1400	19.2
89-90—Dallas	45	1300	484	231	.477	254	200	.787	78	94	172	80	99	0	20	7	662	14.7
Totals	945	34025	15071	8150	.541	8325	6814	.818	2199	3243	5442	2821	2542	14	939	150	23120	24.5

Three-Point Field Goals: 1979-80, 0-for-2. 1980-81, 2-for-7 (.286). 1981-82, 1-for-3 (.333). 1983-84, 1-for-4 (.250). 1985-86, 1-for-11 (.091). 1986-87, 1-for-6 (.167). 1987-88, 0-for-2. 1988-89, 0-for-1. 1989-90, 0-for-2. Totals, 6-for-38 (.158).

NBA PLAYOFF RECORD

Sea.—Team	G.	Min.	FGA	FGM	Pct.	FTA	FTM	Pct.	—Rebounds— Off.	Def.	Tot.	Ast.	PF	Dq.	Stl.	Blk.	Pts.	Avg.
77-78—Los Angeles	3	104	35	20	.571	17	11	.647	9	16	25	11	9	0	5	3	51	17.0
78-79—Los Angeles	8	236	89	50	.562	52	41	.788	10	23	33	11	24	0	6	1	141	17.5
83-84—Utah	11	454	232	117	.504	139	120	.863	37	46	83	46	30	0	10	1	354	32.2
84-85—Utah	10	398	151	79	.523	122	95	.779	25	50	75	20	39	1	16	0	253	25.3
86-87—Detroit	15	500	206	111	.539	111	86	.775	29	39	68	35	36	0	13	0	308	20.5
87-88—Detroit	23	804	292	153	.524	178	140	.787	37	70	107	46	50	0	19	1	446	19.4
Totals	70	2496	1005	530	.527	619	493	.796	147	244	391	169	188	1	69	6	1553	22.2

Three-Point Field Goals: 1984-85, 0-for-1. 1987-88, 0-for-2. Totals, 0-for-3.

NBA ALL-STAR GAME RECORD

								—Rebounds—								
Season—Team	Min.	FGA	FGM	Pct.	FTA	FTM	Pct.	Off.	Def.	Tot.	Ast.	PF	Dq.	Stl.	Blk.	Pts.
1980—Utah	30	15	8	.533	8	7	.875	4	1	5	2	1	0	2	0	23
1981—Utah	21	9	3	.333	2	2	1.000	2	3	5	0	1	0	1	0	8
1982—Utah	21	8	6	.750	1	0	.000	1	1	2	0	2	0	0	0	12
1984—Utah	18	8	1	.125	0	0	.000	0	2	2	1	4	0	1	0	2
1985—Utah	23	6	2	.333	6	6	1.000	0	2	2	1	4	0	1	0	10
1986—Utah	17	8	3	.375	2	2	1.000	1	6	7	3	1	0	1	0	8
Totals	130	54	23	.426	19	17	.895	8	15	23	7	13	0	6	0	63

Named to All-NBA Second Team, 1981 and 1984. . . . NBA Rookie of the Year, 1977. . . . NBA All-Rookie Team, 1977. . . . Led NBA in scoring, 1981 and 1984. . . . NBA Comeback Player of the Year, 1984. . . . Shares NBA record for most free throws made in one game, 28, vs. Houston, January 4, 1984. . . . THE SPORTING NEWS All-America First Team, 1975 and 1976. . . . Member of U.S. Olympic team, 1976.

BRADLEY LEE DAUGHERTY
(Brad)

Born October 19, 1965 at Black Mountain, N.C. Height 7:01. Weight 263.
High School—Swannanoa, N.C., Charles D. Owen.
College—University of North Carolina, Chapel Hill, N.C.
Drafted by Cleveland on first round, 1986 (1st pick).

—COLLEGIATE RECORD—

Year	G.	Min.	FGA	FGM	Pct.	FTA	FTM	Pct.	Reb.	Pts.	Avg.
82-83	35	815	197	110	.558	101	67	.663	181	287	8.2
83-84	30	821	210	128	.610	87	59	.678	167	315	10.5
84-85	36	1250	381	238	.625	198	147	.742	349	623	17.3
85-86	34	1087	438	284	.648	174	119	.684	306	687	20.2
Totals	135	3973	1226	760	.620	560	392	.700	1003	1912	14.2

Three-Point Field Goals: 1982-83, 0-for-1.

NBA REGULAR SEASON RECORD

									—Rebounds—									
Sea.—Team	G.	Min.	FGA	FGM	Pct.	FTA	FTM	Pct.	Off.	Def.	Tot.	Ast.	PF	Dq.	Stl.	Blk.	Pts.	Avg.
86-87—Cleveland	80	2695	905	487	.538	401	279	.696	152	495	647	304	248	3	49	63	1253	15.7
87-88—Cleveland	79	2957	1081	551	.510	528	378	.716	151	514	665	333	235	2	48	56	1480	18.7
88-89—Cleveland	78	2821	1012	544	.538	524	386	.737	167	551	718	285	175	1	63	40	1475	18.9
89-90—Cleveland	41	1438	509	244	.479	287	202	.704	77	296	373	130	108	1	29	22	690	16.8
Totals	278	9911	3507	1826	.521	1740	1245	.716	547	1856	2403	1052	766	7	189	181	4898	17.6

Three-Point Field Goals: 1987-88, 0-for-2. 1988-89, 1-for-3 (.333). 1989-90, 0-for-2. Totals, 1-for-7 (.143).

NBA PLAYOFF RECORD

									—Rebounds—									
Sea.—Team	G.	Min.	FGA	FGM	Pct.	FTA	FTM	Pct.	Off.	Def.	Tot.	Ast.	PF	Dq.	Stl.	Blk.	Pts.	Avg.
87-88—Cleveland	5	204	63	29	.460	31	21	.677	10	36	46	16	11	0	2	7	79	15.8
88-89—Cleveland	5	167	47	17	.362	35	21	.600	12	34	46	12	18	0	6	5	55	11.0
89-90—Cleveland	5	186	70	41	.586	46	32	.696	4	44	48	20	12	0	2	4	114	22.8
Totals	15	557	180	87	.483	112	74	.661	26	114	140	48	41	0	10	16	248	16.5

Three-Point Field Goals: 1988-89, 0-for-1.

NBA ALL-STAR GAME RECORD

								—Rebounds—								
Season—Team	Min.	FGA	FGM	Pct.	FTA	FTM	Pct.	Off.	Def.	Tot.	Ast.	PF	Dq.	Stl.	Blk.	Pts.
1988—Cleveland	15	7	6	.857	0	0	.000	0	3	3	1	4	0	0	1	12
1989—Cleveland	15	3	0	.000	0	0	.000	2	1	3	0	0	0	1	0	0
Totals	30	10	6	.600	0	0	.000	2	4	6	1	4	0	1	1	12

Named to NBA All-Rookie Team, 1987. . . . THE SPORTING NEWS All-America Second Team, 1986. . . . Led NCAA Division I in field-goal percentage, 1986.

BRADLEY ERNEST DAVIS
(Brad)

Born December 17, 1955 at Monaca, Pa. Height 6:03. Weight 180.
High School—Monaca, Pa.
College—University of Maryland, College Park, Md.
Drafted by Los Angeles on first round as an undergraduate, 1977 (15th pick).

Waived by Los Angeles, October 27, 1978; signed by Indiana as a free agent, February 14, 1979.
Waived by Indiana, October 22, 1979; signed by Utah to two 10-day contracts that expired March 20, 1979.
Signed by Detroit as a free agent, July 9, 1980.
Waived by Detroit, October 8, 1980; signed by Dallas as a free agent, December 2, 1980.
Played in Western Basketball Association with Montana Sky, 1978-79.
Played in Continental Basketball Association with Anchorage Northern Knights, 1979-80 and 1980-81.

—COLLEGIATE RECORD—

Year	G.	Min.	FGA	FGM	Pct.	FTA	FTM	Pct.	Reb.	Pts.	Avg.
74-75	29	....	243	141	.580	100	82	.820	95	364	12.6
75-76	28	....	228	117	.513	116	92	.793	73	326	11.6
76-77	27	....	250	128	.512	102	80	.784	94	336	12.4
Totals	84	....	721	386	.535	318	254	.799	262	1026	12.2

WBA & CBA REGULAR SEASON RECORD

			—2-Point—			—3-Point—									
Sea.—Team	G.	Min.	FGM	FGA	Pct.	FGM	FGA	Pct.	FTM	FTA	Pct.	Reb.	Ast.	Pts.	Avg.
78-79—Montana WBA	34	1395	194	362	.536	3	16	.188	105	133	.789	119	224	502	14.8
79-80—Anchorage WBA	40	955	206	361	.571	0	8	.000	120	139	.863	158	291	532	13.3
80-81—Anchorage CBA	5	165	18	43	.418	0	5	.000	12	16	.750	18	41	48	9.6

NBA REGULAR SEASON RECORD

									—Rebounds—									
Sea.—Team	G.	Min.	FGA	FGM	Pct.	FTA	FTM	Pct.	Off.	Def.	Tot.	Ast.	PF	Dq.	Stl.	Blk.	Pts.	Avg.
77-78—Los Angeles	33	334	72	30	.417	29	22	.759	4	31	35	83	39	1	15	2	82	2.5
78-79—L.A.-Ind.	27	298	55	31	.564	23	16	.696	1	16	17	52	32	0	16	2	78	2.9
79-80—Ind.-Utah	18	268	63	35	.556	16	13	.813	4	13	17	50	28	0	13	1	83	4.6
80-81—Dallas	56	1686	410	230	.561	204	163	.799	29	122	151	385	156	2	52	11	626	11.2
81-82—Dallas	82	2614	771	397	.515	230	185	.804	35	191	226	509	218	5	73	6	993	12.1
82-83—Dallas	79	2323	628	359	.572	220	186	.845	34	164	198	565	176	2	80	11	915	11.6
83-84—Dallas	81	2665	651	345	.530	238	199	.836	41	146	187	561	218	4	94	13	896	11.1
84-85—Dallas	82	2539	614	310	.505	178	158	.888	39	154	193	581	219	1	91	10	825	10.1
85-86—Dallas	82	1971	502	267	.532	228	198	.868	26	120	146	467	174	2	57	15	764	9.3
86-87—Dallas	82	1582	436	199	.456	171	147	.860	27	87	114	373	159	0	63	10	577	7.0
87-88—Dallas	75	1480	415	208	.501	108	91	.843	18	84	102	303	149	0	51	18	537	7.2
88-89—Dallas	78	1395	379	183	.483	123	99	.805	14	94	108	242	151	0	48	18	497	6.4
89-90—Dallas	73	1292	365	179	.490	100	77	.770	12	81	93	242	151	2	47	9	470	6.4
Totals	848	20447	5361	2773	.517	1868	1554	.832	284	1303	1587	4413	1870	19	700	126	7343	8.7

Three-Point Field Goals: 1979-80, 0-for-1. 1980-81, 3-for-17 (.176). 1981-82, 14-for-49 (.286). 1982-83, 11-for-43 (.256). 1983-84, 7-for-38 (.184). 1984-85, 47-for-115 (.409). 1985-86, 32-for-89 (.360). 1986-87, 32-for-106 (.302). 1987-88, 30-for-74 (.405). 1988-89, 32-for-102 (.314). 1989-90, 35-for-104 (.337). Totals, 243-for-738 (.329).

NBA PLAYOFF RECORD

									—Rebounds—									
Sea.—Team	G.	Min.	FGA	FGM	Pct.	FTA	FTM	Pct.	Off.	Def.	Tot.	Ast.	PF	Dq.	Stl.	Blk.	Pts.	Avg.
83-84—Dallas	10	304	73	33	.452	19	15	.789	6	13	19	50	18	0	6	0	81	8.1
84-85—Dallas	4	113	26	13	.500	13	12	.923	1	7	8	22	11	0	4	1	41	10.3
85-86—Dallas	10	163	44	24	.545	24	19	.792	1	18	19	23	22	0	3	0	77	7.7
86-87—Dallas	4	75	23	13	.565	9	7	.778	2	7	9	17	4	0	0	0	33	8.3
87-88—Dallas	17	295	70	42	.600	26	24	.923	1	19	20	55	34	0	3	5	109	6.4
Totals	45	950	236	125	.530	91	77	.846	11	64	75	167	89	0	16	6	341	7.6

Three-Point Field Goals: 1983-84, 0-for-2. 1984-85, 3-for-8 (.375). 1985-86, 10-for-15 (.667). 1986-87, 0-for-2. 1987-88, 1-for-5 (.200). Totals, 14-for-32 (.438).

Named CBA Co-Newcomer of the Year, 1980. . . . CBA All-Star Second Team, 1980. . . . Member of CBA championship team, 1980.

CHARLES EDWARD DAVIS
(Charlie)

Born October 5, 1958 at Nashville, Tenn. Height 6:07. Weight 215.

High School—Nashville, Tenn., McGavock.

College—Vanderbilt University, Nashville, Tenn.

Drafted by Washington on second round, 1981 (35th pick).

Waived by Washington, November 6, 1984; signed by Milwaukee as a free agent, November 11, 1984.

Traded by Milwaukee with a 1989 2nd round draft choice to San Antonio for Larry Krystkowiak, November 18, 1987.

Waived by San Antonio, December 28, 1987; signed by Chicago as a free agent, September 27, 1988.

Played in Italy, 1986-87.

—COLLEGIATE RECORD—

Year	G.	Min.	FGA	FGM	Pct.	FTA	FTM	Pct.	Reb.	Pts.	Avg.
76-77	26	825	368	164	.446	94	71	.755	181	399	15.3
77-78	25	889	353	178	.504	87	63	.724	178	419	16.8
78-79	27	964	352	203	.577	130	96	.738	234	502	18.6
79-80	1	15	6	3	.500	0	0	.000	3	6	6.0
80-81	26	676	249	135	.542	99	79	.798	150	349	13.4
Totals	105	3369	1328	683	.514	410	309	.754	746	1675	16.0

(Granted extra year of eligibility because he was able to play only one game in 1979-80 because of tendinitis in left ankle.)

ITALIAN LEAGUE RECORD

Year	G.	Min.	FGA	FGM	Pct.	FTA	FTM	Pct.	Reb.	Pts.	Avg.
86-87—Scavolini	36	1112	374	209	.559	83	63	.759	189	631	17.5

NBA REGULAR SEASON RECORD

									Rebounds									
Sea.—Team	G.	Min.	FGA	FGM	Pct.	FTA	FTM	Pct.	Off.	Def.	Tot.	Ast.	PF	Dq.	Stl.	Blk.	Pts.	Avg.
81-82—Washington	54	575	184	88	.478	37	30	.811	54	79	133	31	89	0	10	13	206	3.8
82-83—Washington	74	1161	534	251	.470	89	56	.629	83	130	213	73	122	0	32	22	560	7.6
83-84—Washington	46	467	218	103	.472	39	24	.615	34	69	103	30	58	1	14	10	231	5.0
84-85—Wash.-Mil.	61	774	356	153	.430	62	51	.823	59	94	153	51	113	1	22	5	358	5.9
85-86—Milwaukee	57	873	397	188	.474	75	61	.813	60	110	170	55	113	1	26	7	440	7.7
87-88—Mil.-S.A.	21	226	115	48	.417	10	7	.700	16	25	41	20	29	0	2	4	104	5.0
88-89—Chicago	49	545	190	81	.426	26	19	.731	47	67	114	31	58	1	11	5	185	3.8
89-90—Chicago	53	429	158	58	.367	8	7	.875	25	56	81	18	52	0	10	8	130	2.5
Totals	415	5050	2152	970	.451	346	255	.737	378	630	1008	309	634	4	127	74	2214	5.3

Three-Point Field Goals: 1981-82, 0-for-2. 1982-83, 2-for-10 (.200). 1983-84, 1-for-9 (.111). 1984-85, 1-for-10 (.100). 1985-86, 3-for-24 (.125). 1987-88, 1-for-17 (.059). 1988-89, 4-for-15 (.267). 1989-90, 7-for-25 (.280). Totals, 19-for-112 (.170).

NBA PLAYOFF RECORD

									Rebounds									
Sea.—Team	G.	Min.	FGA	FGM	Pct.	FTA	FTM	Pct.	Off.	Def.	Tot.	Ast.	PF	Dq.	Stl.	Blk.	Pts.	Avg.
81-82—Washington	6	52	17	7	.412	2	2	1.000	1	4	5	3	6	0	1	1	16	2.7
83-84—Washington	3	17	12	7	.583	0	0	.000	1	2	3	0	0	0	0	0	14	4.7
84-85—Milwaukee	5	51	20	8	.400	4	3	.750	6	4	10	4	2	0	0	0	19	3.8
85-86—Milwaukee	12	145	58	21	.362	20	18	.900	9	16	25	6	28	1	4	0	60	5.0
88-89—Chicago	17	191	47	19	.404	9	7	.778	16	27	43	5	29	0	4	1	46	2.7
89-90—Chicago	6	20	7	2	.286	0	0	....	3	0	3	1	5	0	0	0	4	0.7
Totals	49	476	161	64	.398	35	30	.857	36	53	89	19	70	1	9	2	159	3.2

Three-Point Field Goals: 1981-82, 0-for-1. 1984-85, 0-for-2. 1985-86, 0-for-1. 1988-89, 1-for-6 (.167). 1989-90, 0-for-1. Totals, 1-for-11 (.091).

TERRY DAVIS

Born June 17, 1967 at Danville, Va. Height 6:09. Weight 225.
High School—Danville, Va.
College—Virginia Union University, Richmond, Va.
Never drafted by an NBA franchise.

—COLLEGIATE RECORD—

Year	G.	Min.	FGA	FGM	Pct.	FTA	FTM	Pct.	Reb.	Pts.	Avg.
85-86	27	....	91	42	.462	43	26	.605	116	110	4.1
86-87	32	....	259	135	.521	142	98	.690	360	368	11.5
87-88	31	....	454	257	.566	267	191	.715	338	705	22.7
88-89	31	1034	442	272	.615	217	148	.682	369	692	22.3
Totals	121	....	1246	706	.567	669	463	.692	1183	1875	15.5

Three-Point Field Goals: 1988-89, 0-for-1.

NBA REGULAR SEASON RECORD

									Rebounds									
Sea.—Team	G.	Min.	FGA	FGM	Pct.	FTA	FTM	Pct.	Off.	Def.	Tot.	Ast.	PF	Dq.	Stl.	Blk.	Pts.	Avg.
89-90—Miami	63	884	262	122	.466	87	54	.621	93	136	229	25	171	2	25	28	298	4.7

Three-Point Field Goals: 1989-90, 0-for-1.

WALTER PAUL DAVIS

Born September 9, 1954 at Pineville, N. C. Height 6:06. Weight 200.
High School—Pineville, N. C., South Mecklenberg.
Prep School—Hockessin, Del., Sanford.
College—University of North Carolina, Chapel Hill, N. C.
Drafted by Phoenix on first round, 1977 (5th pick).

Signed by Denver as an unrestricted free agent, July 6, 1988.

—COLLEGIATE RECORD—

Year	G.	Min.	FGA	FGM	Pct.	FTA	FTM	Pct.	Reb.	Pts.	Avg.
73-74	27	....	322	161	.500	82	65	.793	126	387	14.3
74-75	31	....	396	200	.505	130	98	.754	195	498	16.1
75-76	29	....	351	190	.541	130	101	.777	166	481	16.6
76-77	32	....	351	203	.578	117	91	.778	183	497	15.5
Totals	119	....	1420	754	.531	459	355	.773	670	1863	15.7

NBA REGULAR SEASON RECORD

									Rebounds									
Sea.—Team	G.	Min.	FGA	FGM	Pct.	FTA	FTM	Pct.	Off.	Def.	Tot.	Ast.	PF	Dq.	Stl.	Blk.	Pts.	Avg.
77-78—Phoenix	81	2590	1494	786	.526	466	387	.830	158	326	484	273	242	2	113	20	1959	24.2
78-79—Phoenix	79	2437	1362	764	.561	409	340	.831	111	262	373	339	250	5	147	26	1868	23.6

									—Rebounds—									
Sea.—Team	G.	Min.	FGA	FGM	Pct.	FTA	FTM	Pct.	Off.	Def.	Tot.	Ast.	PF	Dq.	Stl.	Blk.	Pts.	Avg.
79-80—Phoenix	75	2309	1166	657	.563	365	299	.819	75	197	272	337	202	2	114	19	1613	21.5
80-81—Phoenix	78	2182	1101	593	.539	250	209	.836	63	137	200	302	192	3	97	12	1402	18.0
81-82—Phoenix	55	1182	669	350	.523	111	91	.820	21	82	103	162	104	1	46	3	794	14.4
82-83—Phoenix	80	2491	1289	665	.516	225	184	.818	63	134	197	397	186	2	117	12	1521	19.0
83-84—Phoenix	78	2546	1274	652	.512	270	233	.863	38	164	202	429	202	0	107	12	1557	20.0
84-85—Phoenix	23	570	309	139	.450	73	64	.877	6	29	35	98	42	0	18	0	345	15.0
85-86—Phoenix	70	2239	1287	624	.485	305	257	.843	54	149	203	361	153	1	99	3	1523	21.8
86-87—Phoenix	79	2646	1515	779	.514	334	288	.862	90	154	244	364	184	1	96	5	1867	23.6
87-88—Phoenix	68	1951	1031	488	.473	231	205	.887	32	127	159	278	131	0	86	3	1217	17.9
88-89—Denver	81	1857	1076	536	.498	199	175	.879	41	110	151	190	187	1	72	5	1267	15.6
89-90—Denver	69	1635	1033	497	.481	227	207	.912	46	133	179	155	160	1	59	9	1207	17.5
Totals	916	26635	14606	7530	.516	3465	2939	.848	798	2004	2802	3685	2235	19	1171	129	18140	19.8

Three-Point Field Goals: 1979-80, 0-for-4. 1980-81, 7-for-17 (.412). 1981-82, 3-for-16 (.188). 1982-83, 7-for-23 (.304). 1983-84, 20-for-87 (.230). 1984-85, 3-for-10 (.300). 1985-86, 18-for-76 (.237). 1986-87, 21-for-81 (.259). 1987-88, 36-for-96 (.375). 1988-89, 20-for-69 (.290). 1989-90, 6-for-46 (.130). Totals, 141-for-525 (.269).

NBA PLAYOFF RECORD

									—Rebounds—									
Sea.—Team	G.	Min.	FGA	FGM	Pct.	FTA	FTM	Pct.	Off.	Def.	Tot.	Ast.	PF	Dq.	Stl.	Blk.	Pts.	Avg.
77-78—Phoenix	2	66	40	19	.475	16	12	.750	4	13	17	8	8	0	3	0	50	25.0
78-79—Phoenix	15	490	244	127	.520	96	78	.813	24	45	69	79	41	0	26	5	332	22.1
79-80—Phoenix	8	245	137	69	.504	38	28	.737	9	14	23	35	20	0	4	1	166	20.8
80-81—Phoenix	7	199	106	51	.481	17	10	.588	7	12	19	22	17	0	7	1	112	16.0
81-82—Phoenix	7	173	116	52	.448	24	22	.917	5	17	22	30	19	0	5	1	127	18.1
82-83—Phoenix	3	113	69	30	.435	21	17	.810	5	10	15	13	6	0	6	5	78	26.0
83-84—Phoenix	17	623	327	175	.535	78	70	.897	15	31	46	109	55	0	29	3	423	24.9
88-89—Denver	3	94	60	31	.517	15	15	1.000	2	3	5	4	11	0	3	0	77	25.7
89-90—Denver	3	70	45	18	.400	6	6	1.000	4	5	9	6	4	0	1	0	42	14.0
Totals	65	2073	1144	572	.500	311	258	.830	75	150	225	306	181	0	84	16	1407	21.6

Three-Point Field Goals: 1979-80, 0-for-3. 1980-81, 0-for-1. 1981-82, 1-for-3 (.333). 1982-83, 1-for-2 (.500). 1983-84, 3-for-11 (.273). 1988-89, 0-for-4. 1989-90, 0-for-1. Totals, 5-for-25 (.200).

NBA ALL-STAR GAME RECORD

								—Rebounds—								
Season—Team	Min.	FGA	FGM	Pct.	FTA	FTM	Pct.	Off.	Def.	Tot.	Ast.	PF	Dq.	Stl.	Blk.	Pts.
1978—Phoenix	15	6	3	.500	4	4	1.000	0	1	1	6	1	0	1	0	10
1979—Phoenix	19	9	4	.444	0	0	.000	1	3	4	4	0	0	1	0	8
1980—Phoenix	23	10	5	.500	2	2	1.000	2	2	4	2	2	0	4	0	12
1981—Phoenix	22	9	5	.556	2	2	1.000	1	6	7	1	2	0	0	0	12
1984—Phoenix	15	9	5	.556	0	0	.000	0	2	2	1	0	0	1	0	10
1987—Phoenix	15	12	3	.250	0	0	.000	2	0	2	1	0	0	0	0	7
Totals	109	55	25	.455	8	8	1.000	6	14	20	15	5	0	7	0	59

Three-Point Field Goals: 1987, 1-for-1 (1.000).

Named to All-NBA Second Team, 1978 and 1979. . . . NBA Rookie of the Year, 1978. . . . NBA All-Rookie Team, 1978. . . . Member of U. S. Olympic team, 1976.

JOHNNY EARL DAWKINS JR.

Born September 28, 1963 at Washington D.C. Height 6:02. Weight 165.

High School—Washington, D.C., Mackin.

College—Duke University, Durham, N.C.

Drafted by San Antonio on first round, 1986 (10th pick).

Traded by San Antonio with Jay Vincent to Philadelphia for Maurice Cheeks, Christian Welp and David Wingate, August 28, 1989.

—COLLEGIATE RECORD—

Year	G.	Min.	FGA	FGM	Pct.	FTA	FTM	Pct.	Reb.	Pts.	Avg.
82-83	28	1002	414	207	.500	107	73	.682	115	506	18.1
83-84	34	1306	547	263	.481	160	133	.831	138	659	19.4
84-85	31	1117	455	225	.495	166	132	.795	141	582	18.8
85-86	40	1324	603	331	.549	181	147	.812	142	809	20.2
Totals	133	4749	2019	1026	.508	614	485	.790	536	2556	19.2

Three-Point Field Goals: 1982-83, 19-for-54 (.352).

NBA REGULAR SEASON RECORD

									—Rebounds—									
Sea.—Team	G.	Min.	FGA	FGM	Pct.	FTA	FTM	Pct.	Off.	Def.	Tot.	Ast.	PF	Dq.	Stl.	Blk.	Pts.	Avg.
86-87—San Antonio	81	1682	764	334	.437	191	153	.801	56	113	169	290	118	0	67	3	835	10.3
87-88—San Antonio	65	2179	835	405	.485	221	198	.896	66	138	204	480	95	0	88	2	1027	15.8
88-89—San Antonio	32	1083	400	177	.443	112	100	.893	32	69	101	224	64	0	55	0	454	14.2
89-90—Philadelphia	81	2865	950	465	.489	244	210	.861	48	199	247	601	159	1	121	9	1162	14.3
Totals	259	7809	2949	1381	.468	768	661	.861	202	519	721	1595	436	1	331	14	3478	13.4

Three-Point Field Goals: 1986-87, 14-for-47 (.298). 1987-88, 19-for-61 (.311). 1988-89, 0-for-4. 1989-90, 22-for-66 (.333). Totals, 55-for-178 (.309).

VLADE DIVAC

NBA PLAYOFF RECORD

Sea.—Team	G.	Min.	FGA	FGM	Pct.	FTA	FTM	Pct.	—Rebounds— Off.	Def.	Tot.	Ast.	PF	Dq.	Stl.	Blk.	Pts.	Avg.
87-88—San Antonio	3	53	23	6	.261	4	3	.750	1	2	3	5	2	0	2	0	15	5.0
89-90—Philadelphia	10	386	115	53	.461	43	36	.837	5	17	22	93	22	0	17	2	142	14.2
Totals	13	439	138	59	.428	47	39	.830	6	19	25	98	24	0	19	2	157	12.1

Three-Point Field Goals: 1987-88, 0-for-2. 1989-90, 0-for-7. Totals, 0-for-9.

Named to THE SPORTING NEWS All-America First Team, 1986. . . . THE SPORTING NEWS All-America Second Team, 1985.

VINCENT JOSEPH DEL NEGRO
(Vinny)

Born August 9, 1966 at Springfield, Mass. Height 6:05. Weight 185.
High School—Suffield, Conn., Suffield Academy.
College—North Carolina State University, Raleigh, N.C.
Drafted by Sacramento on second round, 1988 (29th pick).

—COLLEGIATE RECORD—

Year	G.	Min.	FGA	FGM	Pct.	FTA	FTM	Pct.	Reb.	Pts.	Avg.
84-85	19	125	21	12	.571	23	15	.652	14	39	2.1
85-86	17	139	30	11	.367	11	7	.636	14	29	1.7
86-87	35	918	269	133	.494	71	63	.887	115	265	10.4
87-88	32	1093	363	187	.515	124	104	.839	158	509	15.9
Totals	103	2275	683	343	.502	229	189	.825	301	942	9.1

Three-Point Field Goals: 1986-87, 36-for-72 (.500). 1987-88, 31-for-78 (.397). Totals, 67-for-150 (.447).

NBA REGULAR SEASON RECORD

Sea.—Team	G.	Min.	FGA	FGM	Pct.	FTA	FTM	Pct.	—Rebounds— Off.	Def.	Tot.	Ast.	PF	Dq.	Stl.	Blk.	Pts.	Avg.
88-89—Sacramento	80	1556	503	239	.475	100	85	.850	48	123	171	206	160	2	65	14	569	7.1
89-90—Sacramento	76	1858	643	297	.462	155	135	.871	39	159	198	250	182	2	64	10	739	9.7
Totals	156	3414	1146	536	.468	255	220	.863	87	282	369	456	342	4	129	24	1308	8.4

Three-Point Field Goals: 1988-89, 6-for-20 (.300). 1989-90, 10-for-32 (.313). Totals, 16-for-52 (.308).

BYRON STEWART DINKINS

Born June 15, 1967 at Charlotte, N.C. Height 6:02. Weight 170.
High School—Charlotte, N.C., East Mecklenburg.
College—University of North Carolina at Charlotte, Charlotte, N.C.
Never drafted by an NBA franchise.

—COLLEGIATE RECORD—

Year	G.	Min.	FGA	FGM	Pct.	FTA	FTM	Pct.	Reb.	Pts.	Avg.
85-86	17	....	100	43	.430	12	9	.750	15	95	5.6
86-87	32	....	395	157	.397	92	64	.696	90	431	13.5
87-88	29	....	462	236	.511	137	100	.730	86	622	21.4
88-89	29	....	457	200	.438	112	73	.652	107	509	17.6
Totals	107	....	1414	636	.450	353	246	.697	298	1657	15.5

Three-Point Field Goals: 1986-87, 53-for-164 (.323). 1987-88, 50-for-111 (.450). 1988-89, 36-for-130 (.277). Totals, 139-for-405 (.343).

NBA REGULAR SEASON RECORD

Sea.—Team	G.	Min.	FGA	FGM	Pct.	FTA	FTM	Pct.	—Rebounds— Off.	Def.	Tot.	Ast.	PF	Dq.	Stl.	Blk.	Pts.	Avg.
89-90—Houston	33	362	109	44	.404	30	26	.867	13	27	40	75	30	0	19	2	115	3.5

Three-Point Field Goals: 1989-90, 1-for-9 (.111).

VLADE DIVAC

(Name pronounced VLA-day DEE-vatz)
Born February 2, 1968 at Belgrade, Yugoslavia. Height 6:11. Weight 243.
High School—Belgrade, Yugoslavia.
Did not attend college.
Drafted by Los Angeles Lakers on first round, 1989 (26th pick).

NBA REGULAR SEASON RECORD

Sea.—Team	G.	Min.	FGA	FGM	Pct.	FTA	FTM	Pct.	—Rebounds— Off.	Def.	Tot.	Ast.	PF	Dq.	Stl.	Blk.	Pts.	Avg.
89-90—L.A. Lakers	82	1611	549	274	.499	216	153	.708	167	345	512	75	240	2	79	114	701	8.5

Three-Point Field Goals: 1989-90, 0-for-5.

NBA PLAYOFF RECORD

								—Rebounds—									
Sea.—Team	G.	Min.	FGA	FGM	Pct.	FTA	FTM	Pct.	Off.	Def.	Tot.	Ast.	PF	Dq.	Stl.	Blk.	Pts.	Avg.
89-90—L.A. Lakers	9	175	44	32	.727	19	17	.895	16	32	48	10	27	1	8	15	82	9.1

Three-Point Field Goals: 1989-90, 1-for-2 (.500).

Named to NBA All-Rookie First Team, 1990.

JAMES LEE DONALDSON III

Born August 16, 1957 at Heacham, England. Height 7:02. Weight 278.
High School—Sacramento, Calif., Burbank.
College—Washington State University, Pullman, Wash.
Drafted by Seattle on fourth round, 1979 (73rd pick).

Traded by Seattle with Greg Kelser, Mark Radford, a 1984 1st round draft choice and a 1985 2nd round draft choice to San Diego for Tom Chambers, Al Wood, a 1987 2nd round draft choice and a 1984 3rd round draft choice, August 18, 1983.

Traded by Los Angeles Clippers to Dallas for Kurt Nimphius, November 25, 1985.

Played in Europe during 1979-80 season.

—COLLEGIATE RECORD—

Year	G.	Min.	FGA	FGM	Pct.	FTA	FTM	Pct.	Reb.	Pts.	Avg.
75-76	9	36	7	4	.571	3	2	.667	17	10	1.1
76-77	22	297	59	34	.576	19	6	.316	74	74	3.4
77-78	27	999	251	131	.522	121	79	.653	305	341	12.6
78-79	26	946	216	120	.556	98	53	.541	281	293	11.3
Totals	84	2278	533	289	.542	241	140	.581	677	718	8.5

NBA REGULAR SEASON RECORD

									—Rebounds—									
Sea.—Team	G.	Min.	FGA	FGM	Pct.	FTA	FTM	Pct.	Off.	Def.	Tot.	Ast.	PF	Dq.	Stl.	Blk.	Pts.	Avg.
80-81—Seattle	68	980	238	129	.542	170	101	.594	107	202	309	42	79	0	8	74	359	5.3
81-82—Seattle	82	1710	419	255	.609	240	151	.629	138	352	490	51	186	2	27	139	661	8.1
82-83—Seattle	82	1789	496	289	.583	218	150	.688	131	370	501	97	171	1	19	101	728	8.9
83-84—San Diego	82	2525	604	360	.596	327	249	.761	165	484	649	90	214	1	40	139	969	11.8
84-85—L.A. Clippers	82	2392	551	351	.637	303	227	.749	168	500	668	48	217	1	28	130	929	11.3
85-86—L.A.C.-Dal.	83	2682	459	256	.558	254	204	.803	171	624	795	96	189	0	28	139	716	8.6
86-87—Dallas	82	3028	531	311	.586	329	267	.812	295	678	973	63	191	0	51	136	889	10.8
87-88—Dallas	81	2523	380	212	.558	189	147	.778	247	508	755	66	175	2	40	104	571	7.0
88-89—Dallas	53	1746	337	193	.573	124	95	.766	158	412	570	38	111	0	24	81	481	9.1
89-90—Dallas	73	2265	479	258	.539	213	149	.700	155	475	630	57	129	0	22	47	665	9.1
Totals	768	21640	4494	2614	.582	2367	1740	.735	1735	4605	6340	648	1662	7	287	1090	6968	9.1

NBA PLAYOFF RECORD

									—Rebounds—									
Sea.—Team	G.	Min.	FGA	FGM	Pct.	FTA	FTM	Pct.	Off.	Def.	Tot.	Ast.	PF	Dq.	Stl.	Blk.	Pts.	Avg.
81-82—Seattle	8	189	43	18	.419	24	18	.750	25	49	74	7	16	0	2	5	54	6.8
82-83—Seattle	2	47	22	11	.500	3	2	.667	5	12	17	2	4	0	0	3	24	12.0
85-86—Dallas	10	410	48	36	.750	40	37	.925	30	87	117	10	26	0	6	12	109	10.9
86-87—Dallas	3	68	5	4	.800	9	8	.889	2	15	17	2	6	0	1	3	16	5.3
87-88—Dallas	17	499	104	68	.654	37	22	.595	47	99	146	12	41	0	7	15	158	9.3
89-90—Dallas	3	74	13	9	.692	5	4	.800	6	10	16	2	8	0	2	0	22	7.3
Totals	43	1287	235	146	.621	118	91	.771	115	272	387	35	101	0	18	38	383	8.9

NBA ALL-STAR GAME RECORD

								—Rebounds—								
Season—Team	Min.	FGA	FGM	Pct.	FTA	FTM	Pct.	Off.	Def.	Tot.	Ast.	PF	Dq.	Stl.	Blk.	Pts.
1988—Dallas	8	0	0	.000	2	2	1.000	1	5	6	1	2	0	0	2	2

Led NBA in field-goal percentage, 1985.

SHERMAN DOUGLAS

Born September 15, 1966 at Washington, D.C. Height 6:00. Weight 180.
High School—Washington, D.C., Spingarn.
College—Syracuse University, Syracuse, N.Y.
Drafted by Miami on second round, 1989 (28th pick).

—COLLEGIATE RECORD—

Year	G.	Min.	FGA	FGM	Pct.	FTA	FTM	Pct.	Reb.	Pts.	Avg.
85-86	27	307	93	57	.613	44	32	.727	33	146	5.4
86-87	38	1240	463	246	.531	203	151	.744	97	659	17.3
87-88	35	1195	428	222	.519	150	104	.693	76	562	16.1
88-89	38	1348	498	272	.546	174	110	.632	93	693	18.2
Totals	138	4090	1482	797	.538	571	397	.695	299	2060	14.9

(1986-87 minutes played are missing one game.)

Three-Point Field Goals: 1986-87, 16-for-49 (.327). 1987-88, 14-for-53 (.264). 1988-89, 39-for-106 (.368). Totals, 69-for-208 (.332).

NBA REGULAR SEASON RECORD

									—Rebounds—									
Sea.—Team	G.	Min.	FGA	FGM	Pct.	FTA	FTM	Pct.	Off.	Def.	Tot.	Ast.	PF	Dq.	Stl.	Blk.	Pts.	Avg.
89-90—Miami	81	2470	938	463	.494	326	224	.687	70	136	206	619	187	0	145	10	1155	14.3

Three-Point Field Goals: 1989-90, 5-for-31 (.161).

Named to NBA All-Rookie First Team, 1990.

TERRY LINNARD DOZIER

Born June 29, 1966 at Baltimore, Md. Height 6:09. Weight 210.
High School—Baltimore, Md., Dunbar.
College—University of South Carolina, Columbia, S.C.
Never drafted by an NBA franchise.

Signed by Charlotte as a free agent, September 28, 1989.
Waived by Charlotte, November 27, 1989.
Played in Continental Basketball Association with Quad City Thunder, 1989-90.

—COLLEGIATE RECORD—

Year	G.	Min.	FGA	FGM	Pct.	FTA	FTM	Pct.	Reb.	Pts.	Avg.
85-86	17	581	194	92	.474	64	50	.781	84	234	13.8
86-87	29	1090	388	188	.485	129	105	.814	156	492	17.0
87-88	28	905	307	153	.498	89	59	.663	119	374	13.4
88-89	30	966	284	127	.447	112	85	.759	128	345	11.5
Totals	104	3542	1173	560	.477	394	299	.759	487	1445	13.9

Three-Point Field Goals: 1986-87, 11-for-26 (.423). 1987-88, 9-for-30 (.300), 1988-89, 6-for-20 (.300). Totals, 26-for-76 (.342).

CBA REGULAR SEASON RECORD

			—2-Point—			—3-Point—									
Sea.—Team	G.	Min.	FGM	FGA	Pct.	FGM	FGA	Pct.	FTM	FTA	Pct.	Reb.	Ast.	Pts.	Avg.
89-90—Quad City	12	423	70	154	.455	0	0	.000	42	53	.792	91	19	182	15.2

NBA REGULAR SEASON RECORD

									—Rebounds—									
Sea.—Team	G.	Min.	FGA	FGM	Pct.	FTA	FTM	Pct.	Off.	Def.	Tot.	Ast.	PF	Dq.	Stl.	Blk.	Pts.	Avg.
89-90—Charlotte	9	92	27	9	.333	8	4	.500	7	8	15	3	10	0	6	2	22	2.4

Three-Point Field Goals: 1989-90, 0-for-1.

GREGORY ALAN DREILING
(Greg)

Born November 7, 1963 at Wichita, Kan. Height 7:01. Weight 250.
High School—Wichita, Kan., Kapaun-Mt. Carmel.
Colleges—Wichita State University, Wichita, Kan., and University of Kansas, Lawrence, Kan.
Drafted by Indiana on second round, 1986 (26th pick).

—COLLEGIATE RECORD—

Wichita State

Year	G.	Min.	FGA	FGM	Pct.	FTA	FTM	Pct.	Reb.	Pts.	Avg.
81-82	29	534	151	82	.543	93	70	.753	121	234	8.1

Kansas

Year	G.	Min.	FGA	FGM	Pct.	FTA	FTM	Pct.	Reb.	Pts.	Avg.
82-83				Did Not Play—Transfer Student							
83-84	32	742	228	121	.531	93	69	.742	153	311	9.7
84-85	34	987	300	173	.577	139	101	.727	235	447	13.1
85-86	39	1031	300	180	.600	128	91	.711	262	451	11.6
Kan. Totals	105	2760	828	474	.572	360	261	.725	650	1209	11.5
Col. Totals	134	3294	979	556	.568	453	331	.731	771	1443	10.8

NBA REGULAR SEASON RECORD

									—Rebounds—									
Sea.—Team	G.	Min.	FGA	FGM	Pct.	FTA	FTM	Pct.	Off.	Def.	Tot.	Ast.	PF	Dq.	Stl.	Blk.	Pts.	Avg.
86-87—Indiana	24	128	37	16	.432	12	10	.833	12	31	43	7	42	0	2	2	42	1.8
87-88—Indiana	20	74	17	8	.471	26	18	.692	3	14	17	5	19	0	2	4	34	1.7
88-89—Indiana	53	396	77	43	.558	64	43	.672	39	53	92	18	100	0	5	11	129	2.4
89-90—Indiana	49	307	53	20	.377	34	25	.735	21	66	87	8	69	0	4	14	65	1.3
Totals	146	905	184	87	.473	136	96	.706	75	164	239	38	230	0	13	31	270	1.8

LARRY DONNELL DREW

Born April 2, 1958 at Kansas City, Kan. Height 6:02. Weight 190.
High School—Kansas City, Kan., Wyandotte.
College—University of Missouri, Columbia, Mo.
Drafted by Detroit on first round, 1980 (17th pick).

Traded by Detroit to Kansas City for 1982 and 1984 2nd round draft choices, August 26, 1981.
Traded by Sacramento with Mike Woodson, a 1988 1st round draft choice and a 1989 2nd round draft choice to Los Angeles Clippers for Franklin Edwards and Derek Smith, August 19, 1986.
Signed by Los Angeles Lakers as a Veteran Free Agent, August 4, 1989.
Played in Italy, 1988-89.

—COLLEGIATE RECORD—

Year	G.	Min.	FGA	FGM	Pct.	FTA	FTM	Pct.	Reb.	Pts.	Avg.
76-77	28	....	175	75	.429	59	44	.746	77	194	6.9
77-78	30	1029	344	150	.436	105	80	.762	90	380	12.7
78-79	28	1037	366	181	.495	100	64	.640	73	426	15.2
79-80	31	1092	279	151	.541	121	99	.818	89	401	12.9
Totals	117	....	1164	557	.479	385	287	.745	329	1401	12.0

ITALIAN LEAGUE RECORD

Year	G.	Min.	FGA	FGM	Pct.	FTA	FTM	Pct.	Reb.	Pts.	Avg.
88-89—Scavolini	23	847	204	126	.618	117	99	.846	64	507	22.0

NBA REGULAR SEASON RECORD

									—Rebounds—									
Sea.—Team	G.	Min.	FGA	FGM	Pct.	FTA	FTM	Pct.	Off.	Def.	Tot.	Ast.	PF	Dq.	Stl.	Blk.	Pts.	Avg.
80-81—Detroit	76	1581	484	197	.407	133	106	.797	24	96	120	249	125	0	88	7	504	6.6
81-82—Kansas City	81	1973	757	358	.473	189	150	.794	30	116	149	419	150	0	110	1	874	10.8
82-83—Kansas City	75	2690	1218	599	.492	378	310	.820	44	163	207	610	207	1	126	10	1510	20.1
83-84—Kansas City	73	2363	1026	474	.462	313	243	.776	33	113	146	558	170	0	121	10	1194	16.4
84-85—Kansas City	72	2373	913	457	.501	194	154	.794	39	125	164	484	147	0	93	8	1075	14.9
85-86—Sacramento	75	1971	776	376	.485	161	128	.795	25	100	125	338	134	0	66	2	890	11.9
86-87—L.A. Clippers	60	1566	683	295	.432	166	139	.837	26	77	103	326	107	0	60	2	741	12.4
87-88—L.A. Clippers	74	2024	720	328	.456	108	83	.769	21	98	119	383	114	0	65	0	765	10.3
89-90—L.A. Lakers	80	1333	383	170	.444	60	46	.767	12	86	98	217	92	0	47	4	418	5.2
Totals	666	17874	6960	3254	.468	1702	1359	.798	254	977	1231	3584	1246	1	776	44	7971	12.0

Three-Point Field Goals: 1980-81, 4-for-17 (.235). 1981-82, 8-for-27 (.296). 1982-83, 2-for-16 (.125). 1983-84, 3-for-10 (.300). 1984-85, 7-for-28 (.250). 1985-86, 10-for-31 (.323). 1986-87, 12-for-72 (.167). 1987-88, 26-for-90 (.289). 1989-90, 32-for-81 (.395). Totals, 104-for-372 (.280).

NBA PLAYOFF RECORD

									—Rebounds—									
Sea.—Team	G.	Min.	FGA	FGM	Pct.	FTA	FTM	Pct.	Off.	Def.	Tot.	Ast.	PF	Dq.	Stl.	Blk.	Pts.	Avg.
83-84—Kansas City	3	70	19	7	.368	3	3	1.000	0	4	4	11	5	0	3	0	17	5.7
85-86—Sacramento	3	56	25	14	.560	2	2	1.000	0	1	1	14	2	0	5	0	31	10.3
89-90—L.A. Lakers	7	51	8	3	.375	6	5	.833	0	2	2	4	9	0	3	0	12	1.7
Totals	13	177	52	24	.462	11	10	.909	0	7	7	29	16	0	11	0	60	4.6

Three-Point Field Goals: 1985-86, 1-for-3 (.333). 1989-90, 1-for-4 (.250). Totals, 2-for-7 (.286).

CLYDE DREXLER

Born June 22, 1962 at New Orleans, La. Height 6:07. Weight 215.
High School—Houston, Tex., Sterling.
College—University of Houston, Houston, Tex.
Drafted by Portland on first round as an undergraduate, 1983 (14th pick).

—COLLEGIATE RECORD—

Year	G.	Min.	FGA	FGM	Pct.	FTA	FTM	Pct.	Reb.	Pts.	Avg.
80-81	30	992	303	153	.505	85	50	.588	314	356	11.9
81-82	32	1077	362	206	.569	120	73	.608	336	485	15.2
82-83	34	1186	440	236	.536	95	70	.737	298	542	15.9
Totals	96	3255	1105	595	.538	300	193	.643	948	1383	14.4

NBA REGULAR SEASON RECORD

									—Rebounds—									
Sea.—Team	G.	Min.	FGA	FGM	Pct.	FTA	FTM	Pct.	Off.	Def.	Tot.	Ast.	PF	Dq.	Stl.	Blk.	Pts.	Avg.
83-84—Portland	82	1408	559	252	.451	169	123	.728	112	123	235	153	209	2	107	29	628	7.7
84-85—Portland	80	2555	1161	573	.494	294	223	.759	217	259	476	441	265	3	177	68	1377	17.2
85-86—Portland	75	2576	1142	542	.475	381	293	.769	171	250	421	600	270	8	197	46	1389	18.5
86-87—Portland	82	3114	1408	707	.502	470	357	.760	227	291	518	566	281	7	204	71	1782	21.7
87-88—Portland	81	3060	1679	849	.506	587	476	.811	261	272	533	467	250	2	203	52	2185	27.0
88-89—Portland	78	3064	1672	829	.496	548	438	.799	289	326	615	450	269	2	213	54	2123	27.2

Sea.—Team	G.	Min.	FGA	FGM	Pct.	FTA	FTM	Pct.	—Rebounds— Off.	Def.	Tot.	Ast.	PF	Dq.	Stl.	Blk.	Pts.	Avg.
89-90—Portland	73	2683	1357	670	.494	430	333	.774	208	299	507	432	222	1	145	51	1703	23.3
Totals	551	18460	8978	4422	.493	2879	2243	.779	1485	1820	3305	3109	1766	25	1246	371	11187	20.3

Three-Point Field Goals: 1983-84, 1-for-4 (.250). 1984-85, 8-for-37 (.216). 1985-86, 12-for-60 (.200). 1986-87, 11-for-47 (.234). 1987-88, 11-for-52 (.212). 1988-89, 27-for-104 (.260). 1989-90, 30-for-106 (.283). Totals, 100-for-410 (.244).

NBA PLAYOFF RECORD

Sea.—Team	G.	Min.	FGA	FGM	Pct.	FTA	FTM	Pct.	—Rebounds— Off.	Def.	Tot.	Ast.	PF	Dq.	Stl.	Blk.	Pts.	Avg.
83-84—Portland	5	85	35	15	.429	7	6	.857	7	10	17	8	11	0	5	1	36	7.2
84-85—Portland	9	339	134	55	.410	45	38	844	27	28	55	83	37	0	23	9	150	16.7
85-86—Portland	4	145	57	26	.456	23	18	.783	9	16	25	26	19	1	6	3	72	18.0
86-87—Portland	4	153	79	36	.456	29	23	.793	16	14	30	15	16	1	7	3	96	24.0
87-88—Portland	4	170	83	32	.386	29	21	.724	12	16	28	21	14	0	12	2	88	22.0
88-89—Portland	3	128	71	35	.493	17	13	.765	13	7	20	25	11	0	6	2	83	27.7
89-90—Portland	21	853	390	172	.441	124	96	.774	63	88	151	150	72	2	53	18	449	21.4
Totals	50	1873	849	371	.437	274	215	.785	147	179	326	328	180	4	112	38	974	19.5

Three-Point Field Goals: 1983-84, 0-for-1. 1984-85, 2-for-7 (.286). 1985-86, 2 for-5 (.400). 1986-87, 1-for-4 (.250). 1987-88, 3-for-6 (.500). 1988-89, 0-for-2. 1989-90, 9-for-41 (.220). Totals, 17-for-66 (.258).

NBA ALL-STAR GAME RECORD

Season—Team	Min.	FGA	FGM	Pct.	FTA	FTM	Pct.	—Rebounds— Off.	Def.	Tot.	Ast.	PF	Dq.	Stl.	Blk.	Pts.
1986—Portland	15	7	5	.714	0	0	.000	0	4	4	4	3	0	3	1	10
1988—Portland	15	5	3	.600	6	6	1.000	2	3	5	0	3	0	1	0	12
1989—Portland	25	19	7	.368	0	0	.000	6	6	12	4	3	0	2	0	14
1990—Portland	19	6	2	.333	2	2	1.000	4	0	4	2	1	0	1	1	7
Totals	74	37	17	.459	8	8	1.000	12	13	25	10	10	0	7	2	43

Three-Point Field Goals: 1986, 0-for-1. 1988, 0-for-1. 1990, 1-for-1 (1.000). Totals, 1-for-3 (.333).

Named to All-NBA Second Team, 1988. . . . All-NBA Third Team, 1990.

KEVIN JEROME DUCKWORTH

Born April 1, 1964 at Harvey, Ill. Height 7:00. Weight 280.
High School—Dolton, Ill., Thornridge.
College—Eastern Illinois University, Charleston, Ill.
Drafted by San Antonio on second round, 1986 (33rd pick).

Traded by San Antonio to Portland for Walter Berry, December 18, 1986.

—COLLEGIATE RECORD—

Year	G.	Min.	FGA	FGM	Pct.	FTA	FTM	Pct.	Reb.	Pts.	Avg.
82-83	30	669	212	112	.528	95	64	.674	181	288	9.6
83-84	28	642	221	132	.597	89	61	.685	191	325	11.6
84-85	28	733	258	133	.516	99	65	.657	205	331	11.8
85-86	32	1023	396	250	.631	164	125	.762	290	625	19.5
Totals	118	3067	1087	627	.577	447	315	.705	867	1569	13.3

NBA REGULAR SEASON RECORD

Sea.—Team	G.	Min.	FGA	FGM	Pct.	FTA	FTM	Pct.	—Rebounds— Off.	Def.	Tot.	Ast.	PF	Dq.	Stl.	Blk.	Pts.	Avg.
86-87—S.A.-Port.	65	875	273	130	.476	134	92	.687	76	147	223	29	192	3	21	21	352	5.4
87-88—Portland	78	2223	907	450	.496	430	331	.770	224	352	576	66	280	5	31	32	1231	15.8
88-89—Portland	79	2662	1161	554	.477	428	324	.757	246	389	635	60	300	6	56	49	1432	18.1
89-90—Portland	82	2462	1146	548	.478	312	231	.740	184	325	509	91	271	2	36	34	1327	16.2
Totals	304	8222	3487	1682	.482	1304	978	.750	730	1213	1943	246	1043	16	144	136	4342	14.3

Three-Point Field Goals: 1986-87, 0-for-1. 1988-89, 0-for-2. Totals, 0-for-3.

NBA PLAYOFF RECORD

Sea.—Team	G.	Min.	FGA	FGM	Pct.	FTA	FTM	Pct.	—Rebounds— Off.	Def.	Tot.	Ast.	PF	Dq.	Stl.	Blk.	Pts.	Avg.
86-87—Portland	4	53	12	6	.500	5	2	.400	3	5	8	1	14	0	4	1	14	3.5
87-88—Portland	4	151	70	34	.486	23	18	.783	20	24	44	7	14	0	1	2	86	21.5
88-89—Portland	3	83	35	14	.400	11	6	.545	8	9	17	2	17	2	1	1	34	11.3
89-90—Portland	15	453	187	82	.439	46	33	.717	28	59	87	16	60	2	5	9	197	13.1
Totals	26	740	304	136	.447	85	59	.694	59	97	156	26	105	4	11	13	331	12.7

Three-Point Field Goals: 1987-88, 0-for-1.

NBA ALL-STAR GAME RECORD

Season—Team	Min.	FGA	FGM	Pct.	FTA	FTM	Pct.	—Rebounds— Off.	Def.	Tot.	Ast.	PF	Dq.	Stl.	Blk.	Pts.
1989—Portland	7	5	2	.400	2	1	.500	1	0	1	0	2	0	0	0	5

Named NBA Most Improved Player, 1988.

CHRISTOPHER GUILFORD DUDLEY
(Chris)

Born February 22, 1965 at Stamford, Conn. Height 6:11. Weight 235.
High School—Del Mar, Calif., Torrey Pines.
College—Yale University, New Haven, Conn.
Drafted by Cleveland on fourth round, 1987 (75th pick).

Traded by Cleveland to New Jersey for two future 2nd round draft choices, February 21, 1990.

—COLLEGIATE RECORD—

Year	G.	Min.	FGA	FGM	Pct.	FTA	FTM	Pct.	Reb.	Pts.	Avg.
83-84	26	498	97	45	.464	60	28	.467	132	118	4.5
84-85	26	795	294	131	.446	122	65	.533	266	327	12.6
85-86	26	756	317	171	.539	166	80	.482	256	422	16.2
86-87	24	749	290	165	.569	177	96	.542	320	426	17.8
Totals	102	2798	998	512	.513	525	269	.512	974	1293	12.7

NBA REGULAR SEASON RECORD

									—Rebounds—									
Sea.—Team	G.	Min.	FGA	FGM	Pct.	FTA	FTM	Pct.	Off.	Def.	Tot.	Ast.	PF	Dq.	Stl.	Blk.	Pts.	Avg.
87-88—Cleveland	55	513	137	65	.474	71	40	.563	74	70	144	23	87	2	13	19	170	3.1
88-89—Cleveland	61	544	168	73	.435	107	39	.364	72	85	157	21	82	0	9	23	185	3.0
89-90—Clev.-N.J.	64	1356	355	146	.411	182	58	.319	174	249	423	39	164	2	41	72	350	5.5
Totals	180	2413	660	284	.430	360	137	.381	320	404	724	83	333	4	63	114	705	3.9

Three-Point Field Goals: 1988-89, 0-for-1.

NBA PLAYOFF RECORD

									—Rebounds—									
Sea.—Team	G.	Min.	FGA	FGM	Pct.	FTA	FTM	Pct.	Off.	Def.	Tot.	Ast.	PF	Dq.	Stl.	Blk.	Pts.	Avg.
87-88—Cleveland	4	24	4	2	.500	2	1	.500	4	2	6	2	3	0	0	0	5	1.3
88-89—Cleveland	1	4	1	0	.000	0	0	....	0	0	0	0	1	0	0	0	0	0.0
Totals	5	28	5	2	.400	2	1	.500	4	2	6	2	4	0	0	0	5	1.0

JOE DUMARS III

Born May 24, 1963 at Shreveport, La. Height 6:03. Weight 190.
High School—Natchitoches, La., Central.
College—McNeese State University, Lake Charles, La.
Drafted by Detroit on first round, 1985 (18th pick).

—COLLEGIATE RECORD—

Year	G.	Min.	FGA	FGM	Pct.	FTA	FTM	Pct.	Reb.	Pts.	Avg.
81-82	29	....	464	206	.444	160	115	.719	64	527	18.2
82-83	29	....	487	212	.435	197	140	.711	128	569	19.6
83-84	31	....	586	276	.471	324	267	.824	164	819	26.4
84-85	27	....	501	248	.495	236	201	.852	132	697	25.8
Totals	116	....	2038	942	.462	917	723	.788	488	2612	22.5

Three-Point Field Goals: 1982-83, 5-for-8 (.625).

NBA REGULAR SEASON RECORD

									—Rebounds—									
Sea.—Team	G.	Min.	FGA	FGM	Pct.	FTA	FTM	Pct.	Off.	Def.	Tot.	Ast.	PF	Dq.	Stl.	Blk.	Pts.	Avg.
85-86—Detroit	82	1957	597	287	.481	238	190	.798	60	59	119	390	200	1	66	11	769	9.4
86-87—Detroit	79	2439	749	369	.493	246	184	.748	50	117	167	352	194	1	83	5	931	11.8
87-88—Detroit	82	2732	960	453	.472	308	251	.815	63	137	200	387	155	1	87	15	1161	14.2
88-89—Detroit	69	2408	903	456	.505	306	260	.850	57	115	172	390	103	1	63	5	1186	17.2
89-90—Detroit	75	2578	1058	508	.480	330	297	.900	60	152	212	368	129	1	63	2	1335	17.8
Totals	387	12114	4267	2073	.486	1428	1182	.828	290	580	870	1887	781	5	362	38	5382	13.9

Three-Point Field Goals: 1985-86, 5-for-16 (.313). 1986-87, 9-for-22 (.409). 1987-88, 4-for-19 (.211). 1988-89, 14-for-29 (.483). 1989-90, 22-for-55 (.400). Totals, 54-for-141 (.383).

NBA PLAYOFF RECORD

									—Rebounds—									
Sea.—Team	G.	Min.	FGA	FGM	Pct.	FTA	FTM	Pct.	Off.	Def.	Tot.	Ast.	PF	Dq.	Stl.	Blk.	Pts.	Avg.
85-86—Detroit	4	147	41	25	.610	15	10	.667	6	7	13	25	16	0	4	0	60	15.0
86-87—Detroit	15	473	145	78	.538	41	32	.780	8	11	19	72	26	0	12	1	190	12.7
87-88—Detroit	23	804	247	113	.457	63	56	.889	18	32	50	112	50	1	13	2	284	12.3
88-89—Detroit	17	620	233	106	.455	101	87	.861	11	33	44	96	31	0	12	1	300	17.6
89-90—Detroit	20	754	284	130	.458	113	99	.876	18	26	44	95	37	0	22	0	364	18.2
Totals	79	2798	950	452	.476	333	284	.853	61	109	170	400	160	1	63	4	1198	15.2

Three-Point Field Goals: 1986-87, 2-for-3 (.667). 1987-88, 2-for-6 (.333). 1988-89, 1-for-12 (.083). 1989-90, 5-for-19 (.263). Totals, 10-for-40 (.250).

JOE DUMARS

NBA ALL-STAR GAME RECORD

Season—Team	Min.	FGA	FGM	Pct.	FTA	FTM	Pct.	—Rebounds— Off.	Def.	Tot.	Ast.	PF	Dq.	Stl.	Blk.	Pts.
1990—Detroit	18	4	3	.750	2	1	.500	0	1	1	5	0	0	0	0	9

Three-Point Field Goals: 1990, 2-for-2 (1.000).

Named to All-NBA Third Team, 1990. . . . NBA All-Defensive First Team, 1989 and 1990. . . . Member of NBA championship teams, 1989 and 1990. . . . NBA Playoff MVP, 1989. . . . NBA All-Rookie Team, 1986. . . . THE SPORTING NEWS All-America Second Team, 1985.

THEODORE ROOSEVELT DUNN
(T. R.)

Born February 1, 1955 at Birmingham, Ala. Height 6:04. Weight 192.

High School—Birmingham, Ala., West End.

College—University of Alabama, University, Ala.

Drafted by Portland on second round, 1977 (41st pick).

Traded by Portland to Denver for a 1984 2nd round draft choice and other considerations, August 15, 1980.

Rights relinquished by Denver, July 6, 1988; signed by Phoenix, January 16, 1989, to the first of consecutive 10-day contracts that expired, February 4, 1989.

Re-signed by Phoenix, February 5, 1989, for remainder of season.

Signed by Denver as a free agent, November 6, 1989.

—COLLEGIATE RECORD—

Year	G.	Min.	FGA	FGM	Pct.	FTA	FTM	Pct.	Reb.	Pts.	Avg.
73-74	25	839	232	99	.427	58	38	.655	199	236	9.4
74-75	27	948	297	140	.471	70	51	.729	176	331	12.3
75-76	28	961	303	118	.389	59	37	.627	145	273	9.8
76-77	31	1094	353	173	.490	86	61	.709	220	407	13.1
Totals	111	3842	1185	530	.447	273	187	.685	740	1247	11.2

NBA REGULAR SEASON RECORD

Sea.—Team	G.	Min.	FGA	FGM	Pct.	FTA	FTM	Pct.	—Rebounds— Off.	Def.	Tot.	Ast.	PF	Dq.	Stl.	Blk.	Pts.	Avg.
77-78—Portland	63	768	240	100	.417	56	37	.661	63	84	147	45	74	0	46	8	237	3.8
78-79—Portland	80	1828	549	246	.448	158	122	.772	145	199	344	103	166	1	86	23	614	7.7
79-80—Portland	82	1841	551	240	.436	111	84	.757	132	192	324	147	145	1	102	31	564	6.9
80-81—Denver	82	1427	354	146	.412	121	79	.653	133	168	301	81	141	0	66	29	371	4.5
81-82—Denver	82	2519	504	258	.512	215	153	.712	211	348	559	188	210	1	135	36	669	8.2
82-83—Denver	82	2640	527	254	.482	163	119	.730	231	384	615	189	218	2	147	25	627	7.6
83-84—Denver	80	2705	370	174	.470	145	106	.731	195	379	574	228	233	5	173	32	454	5.7
84-85—Denver	81	2290	358	175	.489	116	84	.724	169	216	385	153	213	3	140	14	434	5.4
85-86—Denver	82	2401	379	172	.454	88	68	.773	143	234	377	171	228	1	155	16	412	5.0
86-87—Denver	81	1932	276	118	.428	55	36	.655	91	174	265	147	160	0	100	21	272	3.4
87-88—Denver	82	1534	156	70	.449	52	40	.769	110	130	240	87	152	0	101	11	180	2.2
88-89—Phoenix	34	321	35	12	.343	12	9	.750	30	30	60	25	35	0	12	1	33	1.0
89-90—Denver	65	657	97	44	.454	39	26	.667	56	82	138	43	67	1	41	4	114	1.8
Totals	976	22863	4396	2009	.457	1331	963	.724	1709	2620	4329	1607	2042	15	1304	251	4981	5.1

Three-Point Field Goals: 1979-80, 0-for-3. 1980-81, 0-for-2. 1981-82, 0-for-1. 1982-83, 0-for-1. 1983-84, 0-for-1. 1984-85, 0-for-2. 1985-86, 0-for-1. 1986-87, 0-for-2. 1987-88, 0-for-1. 1989-90, 0-for-2. Totals, 0-for-16.

NBA PLAYOFF RECORD

Sea.—Team	G.	Min.	FGA	FGM	Pct.	FTA	FTM	Pct.	—Rebounds— Off.	Def.	Tot.	Ast.	PF	Dq.	Stl.	Blk.	Pts.	Avg.
77-78—Portland	4	35	4	2	.500	0	0	.000	1	4	5	3	3	0	1	0	4	1.0
78-79—Portland	3	52	11	5	.455	0	0	.000	2	4	6	4	7	0	5	0	10	3.3
79-80—Portland	3	24	8	2	.250	2	2	1.000	1	3	4	4	3	0	1	0	6	2.0
81-82—Denver	3	81	13	6	.462	8	7	.875	10	8	18	10	11	0	8	1	19	6.3
82-83—Denver	8	300	41	18	.439	8	5	.625	27	51	78	20	21	0	12	3	41	5.1
83-84—Denver	5	178	25	14	.560	7	5	.714	20	19	39	8	19	0	10	4	33	6.6
84-85—Denver	15	371	65	27	.415	19	14	.737	27	33	60	34	45	0	24	3	68	4.5
85-86—Denver	10	276	46	20	.435	14	9	.643	22	31	53	13	34	1	16	0	49	4.9
86-87—Denver	3	22	4	1	.250	0	0	.000	1	2	3	2	3	0	1	1	2	0.7
87-88—Denver	11	185	20	11	.550	8	4	.500	11	18	29	3	20	0	8	0	26	2.4
88-89—Phoenix	8	79	7	3	.429	2	1	.500	7	8	15	1	11	0	5	0	7	0.9
89-90—Denver	3	31	0	0	....	0	0	....	1	6	7	2	3	0	4	1	0	0.0
Totals	76	1634	244	109	.447	68	47	.691	130	187	317	104	180	1	95	13	265	3.5

Named to NBA All-Defensive Second Team, 1983, 1984, 1985.

LEDELL EACKLES

Born November 24, 1966 at Baton Rouge, La. Height 6:05. Weight 220.

High School—Baton Rouge, La., Broadmoor.

Colleges—San Jacinto College, Pasadena, Tex.,
and University of New Orleans, New Orleans, La.

Drafted by Washington on second round, 1988 (36th pick).

—COLLEGIATE RECORD—

San Jacinto

Year	G.	Min.	FGA	FGM	Pct.	FTA	FTM	Pct.	Reb.	Pts.	Avg.
84-85	29	....	....	....	.550	....	....	.730	156	552	19.0
85-86	37	....	715	417	.583	229	173	.755	238	1007	27.2
JC Totals	56	....	....	....	....	....	....	....	394	1559	27.8

New Orleans

Year	G.	Min.	FGA	FGM	Pct.	FTA	FTM	Pct.	Reb.	Pts.	Avg.
86-87	28	902	554	239	.456	116	84	.724	114	632	22.6
87-88	31	982	512	260	.508	232	186	.802	153	726	23.4
Totals	59	1884	1036	499	.482	348	270	.776	267	1358	23.0

Three-Point Field Goals: 1986-87, 70-for-172 (.407). 1987-88, 20-for-84 (.238). Totals, 90-for-256 (.352).

NBA REGULAR SEASON RECORD

									—Rebounds—									
Sea.—Team	G.	Min.	FGA	FGM	Pct.	FTA	FTM	Pct.	Off.	Def.	Tot.	Ast.	PF	Dq.	Stl.	Blk.	Pts.	Avg.
88-89—Washington	80	1459	732	318	.434	346	272	.786	100	80	180	123	156	1	41	5	917	11.5
89-90—Washington	78	1696	940	413	.439	280	210	.750	74	101	175	182	157	0	50	4	1055	13.5
Totals	158	3155	1672	731	.437	626	482	.770	174	181	355	305	313	1	91	9	1972	12.5

Three-Point Field Goals: 1988-89, 9-for-40 (.225). 1989-90, 19-for-59 (.322). Totals, 28-for-99 (.283).

MARK E. EATON

Born January 24, 1957 at Westminister, Calif. Height 7:04. Weight 290.

High School—Westminster, Calif.

Colleges—Cypress College, Cypress, Calif., and University of California at Los Angeles, Los Angeles, Calif.

Drafted by Phoenix on fifth round, 1979 (107th pick). (Eligible for NBA draft because he was out of school three seasons between high school and college and his college class graduated in 1979.)

Drafted by Utah on fourth round, 1982 (72nd pick).

—COLLEGIATE RECORD—

Cypress

Year	G.	Min.	FGA	FGM	Pct.	FTA	FTM	Pct.	Reb.	Pts.	Avg.
78-79	35	....	319	202	.633	117	78	.667	381	482	13.8
79-80	25	....	289	167	.578	83	40	.482	218	374	15.0
JC Totals	60	....	608	369	.607	200	118	.590	599	856	14.3

UCLA

Year	G.	Min.	FGA	FGM	Pct.	FTA	FTM	Pct.	Reb.	Pts.	Avg.
80-81	19	155	37	17	.459	17	5	.294	49	39	2.1
81-82	11	41	12	5	.417	5	4	.800	22	14	1.3
Totals	30	196	49	22	.449	22	9	.409	71	53	1.8

NBA REGULAR SEASON RECORD

									—Rebounds—									
Sea.—Team	G.	Min.	FGA	FGM	Pct.	FTA	FTM	Pct.	Off.	Def.	Tot.	Ast.	PF	Dq.	Stl.	Blk.	Pts.	Avg.
82-83—Utah	81	1528	353	146	.414	90	59	.656	86	376	462	112	257	6	24	275	351	4.3
83-84—Utah	82	2139	416	194	.466	123	73	.593	148	447	595	113	303	4	25	351	461	5.6
84-85—Utah	82	2813	673	302	.449	267	190	.712	207	720	927	124	312	5	36	456	794	9.7
85-86—Utah	80	2551	589	277	.470	202	122	.604	172	503	675	101	282	5	33	369	676	8.5
86-87—Utah	79	2505	585	234	.400	213	140	.657	211	486	697	105	273	5	43	321	608	7.7
87-88—Utah	82	2731	541	226	.418	191	119	.623	230	487	717	55	320	8	41	304	571	7.0
88-89—Utah	82	2914	407	188	.462	200	132	.660	227	616	843	83	290	6	40	315	508	6.2
89-90—Utah	82	2281	300	158	.527	118	79	.669	171	430	601	39	238	3	33	201	395	4.8
Totals	650	19462	3864	1725	.446	1404	914	.651	1452	4065	5517	732	2275	42	275	2592	4364	6.7

Three-Point Field Goals: 1982-83, 0-for-1. 1983-84, 0-for-1. Totals, 0-for-2.

NBA PLAYOFF RECORD

									—Rebounds—									
Sea.—Team	G.	Min.	FGA	FGM	Pct.	FTA	FTM	Pct.	Off.	Def.	Tot.	Ast.	PF	Dq.	Stl.	Blk.	Pts.	Avg.
83-84—Utah	11	254	41	21	.512	17	8	.471	19	57	76	9	33	1	5	34	50	4.5
84-85—Utah	5	158	34	12	.353	7	5	.714	11	34	45	5	19	0	4	29	29	5.8
85-86—Utah	4	157	57	28	.491	3	2	.667	13	23	36	10	12	0	1	18	58	14.5
86-87—Utah	5	193	41	19	.463	25	16	.640	16	39	55	3	18	0	1	21	54	10.8
87-88—Utah	11	461	65	31	.477	36	23	.639	28	75	103	13	48	3	12	34	85	7.7
88-89—Utah	3	99	17	8	.471	11	9	.818	11	22	33	1	6	0	1	2	25	8.3
89-90—Utah	5	128	17	9	.529	5	1	.200	8	22	30	0	17	0	3	14	19	3.8
Totals	44	1450	272	128	.471	104	64	.615	106	272	378	41	153	4	27	152	320	7.3

NBA ALL-STAR GAME RECORD

								—Rebounds—							
Season—Team	Min.	FGA	FGM	Pct.	FTA	FTM	Pct.	Off.	Def.	Tot.	Ast.	PF	Dq.	Stl.	Blk.	Pts.
1989—Utah	9	0	0	.000	0	0	.000	0	5	5	0	1	0	0	2	0

Named NBA Defensive Player of the Year, 1985 and 1989.... NBA All-Defensive First Team, 1985, 1986, 1989.... NBA All-Defensive Second Team, 1987 and 1988.... Holds NBA record for most blocked shots in a season, 1985.... Holds NBA playoff game record for most blocked shots, 10, vs. Denver, April 26, 1985.... Led NBA in blocked shots, 1984, 1985, 1987, 1988.

JAMES FRANKLIN EDWARDS

Born November 22, 1955 at Seattle, Wash. Height 7:01. Weight 252.
High School—Seattle, Wash., Roosevelt.
College—University of Washington, Seattle, Wash.
Drafted by Los Angeles on third round, 1977 (46th pick).

Traded by Los Angeles with Earl Tatum and cash to Indiana for Adrian Dantley and Dave Robisch, December 13, 1977.

Signed by Cleveland as a Veteran Free Agent, May 25, 1981; Indiana agreed not to exercise its right of first refusal in exchange for 1981 and 1982 2nd round draft choices, June 8, 1981.

Traded by Cleveland to Phoenix for Jeff Cook, a 1983 3rd round draft choice and cash, February 7, 1983.

Traded by Phoenix to Detroit for Ron Moore and a 1991 2nd round draft choice, February 24, 1988.

—COLLEGIATE RECORD—

Year	G.	Min.	FGA	FGM	Pct.	FTA	FTM	Pct.	Reb.	Pts.	Avg.
73-74	25	....	160	68	.425	62	34	.548	115	170	6.8
74-75	26	575	264	125	.473	129	70	.543	198	320	12.3
75-76	28	811	392	205	.523	137	83	.606	200	493	17.6
76-77	27	940	404	223	.552	184	119	.647	282	565	20.9
Totals	106	....	1220	621	.509	512	306	.598	795	1548	14.6

NBA REGULAR SEASON RECORD

									—Rebounds—									
Sea.—Team	G.	Min.	FGA	FGM	Pct.	FTA	FTM	Pct.	Off.	Def.	Tot.	Ast.	PF	Dq.	Stl.	Blk.	Pts.	Avg.
77-78—LA-Ind.	83	2405	1093	495	.453	421	272	.646	197	418	615	85	322	12	53	78	1262	15.2
78-79—Indiana	82	2546	1065	534	.501	441	298	.676	179	514	693	92	363	16	60	109	1366	16.7
79-80—Indiana	82	2314	1032	528	.512	339	231	.681	179	399	578	127	324	12	55	104	1287	15.7
80-81—Indiana	81	2375	1004	511	.509	347	244	.703	191	380	571	212	304	7	32	128	1266	15.6
81-82—Cleveland	77	2539	1033	528	.511	339	232	.684	189	392	581	123	347	17	24	117	1288	16.7
82-83—Clev.-Phoe.	31	667	263	128	.487	108	69	.639	56	99	155	40	110	5	12	19	325	10.5
83-84—Phoenix	72	1897	817	438	.536	254	183	.720	108	240	348	184	254	3	23	30	1059	14.7
84-85—Phoenix	70	1787	766	384	.501	370	276	.746	95	292	387	153	237	5	26	52	1044	14.9
85-86—Phoenix	52	1314	587	318	.542	302	212	.702	79	222	301	74	200	5	23	29	848	16.3
86-87—Phoenix	14	304	110	57	.518	70	54	.771	20	40	60	19	42	1	6	7	168	12.0
87-88—Phoe.-Det.	69	1705	643	302	.470	321	210	.654	119	293	412	78	216	2	16	37	814	11.8
88-89—Detroit	76	1254	422	211	.500	194	133	.686	68	163	231	49	226	1	11	31	555	7.3
89-90—Detroit	82	2283	928	462	.498	354	265	.749	112	233	345	63	295	4	23	37	1189	14.5
Totals	871	23390	9763	4896	.501	3860	2679	.694	1592	3685	5277	1299	3240	90	364	778	12471	14.3

Three-Point Field Goals: 1979-80, 0-for-1. 1980-81, 0-for-3. 1981-82, 0-for-4. 1983-84, 0-for-1. 1984-85, 0-for-3. 1987-88, 0-for-1. 1988-89, 0-for-2. 1989-90, 0-for-3. Totals, 0-for-18.

NBA PLAYOFF RECORD

									—Rebounds—									
Sea.—Team	G.	Min.	FGA	FGM	Pct.	FTA	FTM	Pct.	Off.	Def.	Tot.	Ast.	PF	Dq.	Stl.	Blk.	Pts.	Avg.
80-81—Indiana	2	56	24	7	.292	0	0	.000	4	10	14	5	8	0	1	1	14	7.0
82-83—Phoenix	3	54	26	11	.423	6	6	1.000	6	12	18	4	7	0	1	1	28	9.3
83-84—Phoenix	17	463	189	93	.492	68	48	.706	22	69	91	27	62	3	4	11	234	13.8
87-88—Detroit	22	308	110	56	.509	41	27	.659	23	45	68	11	55	0	2	10	139	6.3
88-89—Detroit	17	317	85	40	.471	51	40	.784	11	25	36	12	53	0	1	8	120	7.1
89-90—Detroit	20	536	231	114	.494	96	58	.604	24	47	71	13	74	0	5	11	286	14.3
Totals	81	1734	665	321	.483	262	179	.683	90	208	298	72	259	3	14	42	821	10.1

Three-Point Field Goals: 1987-88, 0-for-1. 1988-89, 0-for-1. 1989-90, 0-for-1. Totals, 0-for-3.

Member of NBA championship teams, 1989 and 1990.

JAY CHARLES EDWARDS

Born January 3, 1969 at Muncie, Ind. Height 6:04. Weight 185.
High School—Marion, Ind.
College—Indiana University, Bloomington, Ind.
Drafted by Los Angeles Clippers on second round as an undergraduate, 1989 (33rd pick).

—COLLEGIATE RECORD—

Year	G.	Min.	FGA	FGM	Pct.	FTA	FTM	Pct.	Reb.	Pts.	Avg.
87-88	23	....	256	115	.449	76	69	.908	51	358	15.6
88-89	34	....	460	218	.474	198	163	.823	146	680	20.0
Totals	57	....	716	333	.465	274	232	.847	197	1038	18.2

Three-Point Field Goals: 1987-88, 59-for-110 (.536). 1988-89, 81-for-181 (.448). Totals, 140-for-291 (.481).

NBA REGULAR SEASON RECORD

Sea.—Team	G.	Min.	FGA	FGM	Pct.	FTA	FTM	Pct.	—Rebounds— Off.	Def.	Tot.	Ast.	PF	Dq.	Stl.	Blk.	Pts.	Avg.
89-90—L.A. Clippers	4	26	7	3	.429	3	1	.333	1	1	2	4	4	0	1	0	7	1.8

Three-Point Field Goals: 1989-90, 0-for-2.

Named to THE SPORTING NEWS All-America Second Team, 1989.

KEVIN EDWARDS

Born October 30, 1965 at Cleveland Heights, O. Height 6:03. Weight 200.

High School—Cleveland, O., St. Joseph.

Colleges—Lakeland Community College, Mentor, O., and DePaul University, Chicago, Ill.

Drafted by Miami on first round, 1988 (20th pick).

—COLLEGIATE RECORD—

Lakeland

Year	G.	Min.	FGA	FGM	Pct.	FTA	FTM	Pct.	Reb.	Pts.	Avg.
84-85	33	....	435	256	.589	144	103	.715	178	615	18.6
85-86	32	....	519	325	.626	159	121	.761	239	771	24.1
J.C. Totals	65	....	954	581	.609	303	224	.739	417	1386	21.3

DePaul

Year	G.	Min.	FGA	FGM	Pct.	FTA	FTM	Pct.	Reb.	Pts.	Avg.
86-87	31	1060	343	184	.536	78	63	.808	156	447	14.4
87-88	30	999	413	220	.533	106	83	.783	158	548	18.3
DePaul Totals	61	2059	756	404	.534	184	146	.793	314	995	16.3

Three-Point Field Goals: 1986-87, 16-for-36 (.444). 1987-88, 25-for-56 (.446). Totals, 41-for-92 (.446).

NBA REGULAR SEASON RECORD

Sea.—Team	G.	Min.	FGA	FGM	Pct.	FTA	FTM	Pct.	—Rebounds— Off.	Def.	Tot.	Ast.	PF	Dq.	Stl.	Blk.	Pts.	Avg.
88-89—Miami	79	2349	1105	470	.425	193	144	.746	85	177	262	349	154	0	139	27	1094	13.8
89-90—Miami	78	2211	959	395	.412	183	139	.760	77	205	282	252	149	1	125	33	938	12.0
Totals	157	4560	2064	865	.419	376	283	.753	162	382	544	601	303	1	264	60	2032	12.9

Three-Point Field Goals: 1988-89, 10-for-37 (.270). 1989-90, 9-for-30 (.300). Totals, 19-for-67 (.284).

Named to NBA All-Rookie Second Team, 1989.

THEODORE EDWARDS (Blue)

Born October 31, 1965 at Washington, D.C. Height 6:04. Weight 200.

High School—Snow Hill, N.C., Greene Central.

Colleges—Louisburg College, Louisburg, N.C., and East Carolina University, Greenville, N.C.

Drafted by Utah on first round, 1989 (21st pick).

—COLLEGIATE RECORD—

Louisburg

Year	G.	Min.	FGA	FGM	Pct.	FTA	FTM	Pct.	Reb.	Pts.	Avg.
84-85	29	....	....	....	.636	....	....	.645	177	515	17.5
85-86	31	....	....	....	.700	....	....	.658	187	690	22.3
Louis. Tot.	60	....	....	....	....	....	....	....	364	1205	20.1

East Carolina

Year	G.	Min.	FGA	FGM	Pct.	FTA	FTM	Pct.	Reb.	Pts.	Avg.
86-87	28	876	301	169	.561	88	65	.739	158	404	14.4
87-88			Did Not Play—Disciplinary Reasons								
88-89	29	987	539	297	.551	204	154	.755	201	773	26.7
ECU Totals	57	1863	840	466	.555	292	219	.750	359	1177	20.6

Three-Point Field Goals: 1986-87, 1-for-4 (.250). 1988-89, 25-for-51 (.490). Totals, 26-for-55 (.473).

NBA REGULAR SEASON RECORD

Sea.—Team	G.	Min.	FGA	FGM	Pct.	FTA	FTM	Pct.	—Rebounds— Off.	Def.	Tot.	Ast.	PF	Dq.	Stl.	Blk.	Pts.	Avg.
89-90—Utah	82	1889	564	286	.507	203	146	.719	69	182	251	145	280	2	76	36	727	8.9

Three-Point Field Goals: 1989-90, 9-for-30 (.300).

NBA PLAYOFF RECORD

Sea.—Team	G.	Min.	FGA	FGM	Pct.	FTA	FTM	Pct.	—Rebounds— Off.	Def.	Tot.	Ast.	PF	Dq.	Stl.	Blk.	Pts.	Avg.
89-90—Utah	5	94	26	14	.538	8	7	.875	8	10	18	8	16	0	7	2	36	7.2

Three-Point Field Goals: 1989-90, 1-for-3 (.333).
Named to NBA All-Rookie Second Team, 1990.

JOEL CRAIG EHLO

(Known by middle name.)
Born August 11, 1961 at Lubbock, Tex. Height 6:07. Weight 200.
High School—Lubbock, Tex., Monterey.
Colleges—Odessa College, Odessa, Tex., and
Washington State University, Pullman, Wash.
Drafted by Houston on third round, 1983 (48th pick).

Waived by Houston, October 30, 1986; signed by Cleveland as a free agent, January 13, 1987.
Played in Continental Basketball Association with Mississippi Jets, 1986-87.

—COLLEGIATE RECORD—

Odessa

Year	G.	Min.	FGA	FGM	Pct.	FTA	FTM	Pct.	Reb.	Pts.	Avg.
79-80	28	...	300	146	.487	84	60	.714	142	352	12.6
80-81	30	...	482	241	.500	180	139	.772	204	621	20.7
JC Totals	58	...	782	387	.495	264	199	.754	346	973	16.8

Washington State

Year	G.	Min.	FGA	FGM	Pct.	FTA	FTM	Pct.	Reb.	Pts.	Avg.
81-82	30	592	119	57	.479	65	39	.600	65	153	5.1
82-83	30	911	265	145	.547	109	69	.633	97	359	12.0
Totals	60	1503	384	202	.526	174	108	.621	162	512	8.5

CBA REGULAR SEASON RECORD

			—2-Point—			—3-Point—									
Sea.—Team	G.	Min.	FGM	FGA	Pct.	FGM	FGA	Pct.	FTM	FTA	Pct.	Reb.	Ast.	Pts.	Avg.
86-87—Mississippi	6	144	20	31	.645	1	1	1.000	20	30	.667	22	20	63	10.5

NBA REGULAR SEASON RECORD

									—Rebounds—									
Sea.—Team	G.	Min.	FGA	FGM	Pct.	FTA	FTM	Pct.	Off.	Def.	Tot.	Ast.	PF	Dq.	Stl.	Blk.	Pts.	Avg.
83-84—Houston	7	63	27	11	.407	1	1	1.000	4	5	9	6	13	0	3	0	23	3.3
84-85—Houston	45	189	69	34	.493	30	19	.633	8	17	25	26	26	0	11	3	87	1.9
85-86—Houston	36	199	84	36	.429	29	23	.793	17	29	46	29	22	0	11	4	98	2.7
86-87—Cleveland	44	890	239	99	.414	99	70	.707	55	106	161	92	80	0	40	30	273	6.2
87-88—Cleveland	79	1709	485	226	.466	132	89	.674	86	188	274	206	182	0	82	30	563	7.1
88-89—Cleveland	82	1867	524	249	.475	117	71	.607	100	195	295	266	161	0	110	19	608	7.4
89-90—Cleveland	81	2894	940	436	.464	185	126	.681	147	292	439	371	226	2	126	23	1102	13.6
Totals	374	7811	2368	1091	.461	593	399	.673	417	832	1249	996	710	2	383	109	2754	7.4

Three-Point Field Goals: 1984-85, 0-for-3. 1985-86, 3-for-9 (.333). 1986-87, 5-for-29 (.172). 1987-88, 22-for-64 (.344). 1988-89, 39-for-100 (.390). 1989-90, 104-for-248 (.419). Totals, 173-for-453 (.382).

NBA PLAYOFF RECORD

									—Rebounds—									
Sea.—Team	G.	Min.	FGA	FGM	Pct.	FTA	FTM	Pct.	Off.	Def.	Tot.	Ast.	PF	Dq.	Stl.	Blk.	Pts.	Avg.
84-85—Houston	3	6	1	1	1.000	2	2	1.000	0	0	0	0	3	0	4	0	4	1.3
85-86—Houston	10	38	16	8	.500	5	4	.800	1	2	3	6	4	0	4	1	20	2.0
87-88—Cleveland	5	128	40	17	.425	16	10	.625	3	15	18	17	14	0	5	0	44	8.8
88-89—Cleveland	4	97	39	17	.436	11	9	.818	2	4	6	13	10	0	3	1	48	12.0
89-90—Cleveland	5	196	62	26	.419	19	12	.632	7	25	32	32	18	0	6	0	69	13.8
Totals	27	465	158	69	.437	53	37	.698	13	46	59	68	49	0	22	2	185	6.9

Three-Point Field Goals: 1985-86, 0-for-1. 1987-88, 0-for-8. 1988-89, 5-for-13 (.385). 1989-90, 5-for-15 (.333). Totals, 10-for-37 (.270).

SEAN MICHAEL ELLIOTT

Born February 2, 1968 at Tucson, Ariz. Height 6:08. Weight 205.
High School—Tucson, Ariz., Cholla.
College—University of Arizona, Tucson, Ariz.
Drafted by San Antonio on first round, 1989 (3rd pick).

—COLLEGIATE RECORD—

Year	G.	Min.	FGA	FGM	Pct.	FTA	FTM	Pct.	Reb.	Pts.	Avg.
85-86	32	1079	385	187	.486	167	125	.749	171	499	15.6
86-87	30	1046	410	209	.510	165	127	.770	181	578	19.3
87-88	38	1249	461	263	.570	222	176	.793	219	743	19.6
88-89	33	1125	494	237	.480	232	195	.841	237	735	22.3
Totals	133	4499	1750	896	.512	786	623	.793	808	2555	19.2

Three-Point Field Goals: 1986-87, 33-for-89 (.371). 1987-88, 41-for-87 (.471). 1988-89, 66-for-151 (.437). Totals, 140-for-327 (.428).

NBA REGULAR SEASON RECORD

									—Rebounds—									
Sea.—Team	G.	Min.	FGA	FGM	Pct.	FTA	FTM	Pct.	Off.	Def.	Tot.	Ast.	PF	Dq.	Stl.	Blk.	Pts.	Avg.
89-90—San Antonio	81	2032	647	311	.481	216	187	.866	127	170	297	154	172	0	45	14	810	10.0

Three-Point Field Goals: 1989-90, 1-for-9 (.111).

NBA PLAYOFF RECORD

									—Rebounds—									
Sea.—Team	G.	Min.	FGA	FGM	Pct.	FTA	FTM	Pct.	Off.	Def.	Tot.	Ast.	PF	Dq.	Stl.	Blk.	Pts.	Avg.
89-90—San Antonio	10	291	96	53	.552	29	21	.724	11	30	41	18	37	0	9	6	127	12.7

Three-Point Field Goals: 1989-90, 0-for-1.

Named to NBA All-Rookie Second Team, 1990. . . . THE SPORTING NEWS All-America First Team, 1988 and 1989.

DALE ELLIS

Born August 6, 1960 at Marietta, Ga. Height 6:07. Weight 215.
High School—Marietta, Ga.
College—University of Tennessee, Knoxville, Tenn.
Drafted by Dallas on first round, 1983 (9th pick).

Traded by Dallas to Seattle for Al Wood, July 23, 1986.

—COLLEGIATE RECORD—

Year	G.	Min.	FGA	FGM	Pct.	FTA	FTM	Pct.	Reb.	Pts.	Avg.
79-80	27	573	182	81	.445	40	31	.775	96	193	7.1
80-81	29	1057	360	215	.597	111	83	.748	185	513	17.7
81-82	30	1134	393	257	.654	152	121	.796	189	635	21.2
82-83	32	1179	464	279	.601	221	166	.751	209	724	22.6
Totals	118	4943	1399	832	.595	523	401	.767	679	2065	17.5

NBA REGULAR SEASON RECORD

									—Rebounds—									
Sea.—Team	G.	Min.	FGA	FGM	Pct.	FTA	FTM	Pct.	Off.	Def.	Tot.	Ast.	PF	Dq.	Stl.	Blk.	Pts.	Avg.
83-84—Dallas	67	1059	493	225	.456	121	87	.719	106	144	250	56	118	0	41	9	549	8.2
84-85—Dallas	72	1314	603	274	.454	104	77	.740	100	138	238	56	131	1	46	7	667	9.3
85-86—Dallas	72	1086	470	193	.411	82	59	.720	86	82	168	37	78	0	40	9	508	7.1
86-87—Seattle	82	3073	1520	785	.516	489	385	.787	187	260	447	238	267	2	104	32	2041	24.9
87-88—Seattle	75	2790	1519	764	.503	395	303	.767	167	173	340	197	221	1	74	11	1938	25.8
88-89—Seattle	82	3190	1710	857	.501	462	377	.816	156	186	342	164	197	0	108	22	2253	27.5
89-90—Seattle	55	2033	1011	502	.497	236	193	.818	90	148	238	110	124	3	59	7	1293	23.5
Totals	505	14545	7326	3600	.491	1889	1481	.784	892	1131	2023	858	1136	7	472	97	9249	18.3

Three-Point Field Goals: 1983-84, 12-for-29 (.414). 1984-85, 42-for-109 (.385). 1985-86, 63-for-173 (.364). 1986-87, 86-for-240 (.358). 1987-88, 107-for-259 (.413). 1988-89, 162-for-339 (.478). 1989-90, 96-for-256 (.375). Totals, 568-for-1405 (.404).

NBA PLAYOFF RECORD

									—Rebounds—									
Sea.—Team	G.	Min.	FGA	FGM	Pct.	FTA	FTM	Pct.	Off.	Def.	Tot.	Ast.	PF	Dq.	Stl.	Blk.	Pts.	Avg.
83-84—Dallas	8	178	80	26	.325	8	6	.750	19	23	42	4	17	0	10	2	59	7.4
84-85—Dallas	4	68	23	10	.435	2	1	.500	4	3	7	3	3	0	4	0	23	5.8
85-86—Dallas	7	67	22	9	.409	5	5	1.000	3	4	7	2	6	0	2	2	30	4.3
86-87—Seattle	14	530	304	148	.487	54	44	.815	37	53	90	37	54	1	10	6	353	25.2
87-88—Seattle	5	172	83	40	.482	29	21	.724	11	12	23	15	17	0	3	2	104	20.8
88-89—Seattle	8	304	160	72	.450	33	24	.727	14	18	32	10	19	1	11	1	183	22.9
Totals	46	1319	672	305	.454	131	101	.771	88	113	201	71	116	2	40	13	752	16.3

Three-Point Field Goals: 1983-84, 1-for-12 (.083). 1984-85, 2-for-5 (.400). 1985-86, 7-for-12 (.583). 1986-87, 13-for-36 (.361). 1987-88, 3-for-12 (.250). 1988-89, 15-for-37 (.405). Totals, 41-for-114 (.360).

NBA ALL-STAR GAME RECORD

								—Rebounds—								
Season—Team	Min.	FGA	FGM	Pct.	FTA	FTM	Pct.	Off.	Def.	Tot.	Ast.	PF	Dq.	Stl.	Blk.	Pts.
1989—Seattle	26	16	12	.750	2	2	1.000	3	3	6	2	2	0	0	0	27

Three-Point Field Goals: 1989, 1-for-1 (1.000).

Named to All-NBA Third Team, 1989. . . . NBA Most Improved Player, 1987. . . . Holds NBA record for most minutes played in one game, 69, vs. Milwaukee, November 9, 1989 (5 ot). . . . THE SPORTING NEWS All-America First Team, 1983.

—DID YOU KNOW—

That Utah's John Stockton has dished out over 1,000 assists in each of the last three years? No other player in NBA history has more than one 1,000-assist season.

PERVIS ELLISON

Born April 3, 1967 at Savannah, Ga. Height 6:09. Weight 210.
High School—Savannah, Ga.
College—University of Louisville, Louisville, Ky.
Drafted by Sacramento on first round, 1989 (1st pick).

Traded by Sacramento to Washington in three-way deal that sent Jeff Malone from Washington to Utah and Bob Hansen, Eric Leckner and 1990 1st and 2nd round draft choices from Utah to Sacramento, June 25, 1990. Utah also received a 1990 2nd round draft choice and Sacramento also received a 1991 2nd round draft choice.

—COLLEGIATE RECORD—

Year	G.	Min.	FGA	FGM	Pct.	FTA	FTM	Pct.	Reb.	Pts.	Avg.
85-86	39	1194	379	210	.554	132	90	.682	318	510	13.1
86-87	31	952	347	185	.533	139	100	.719	270	470	15.2
87-88	35	1175	391	235	.601	211	146	.692	291	617	17.6
88-89	31	1014	369	227	.615	141	92	.652	270	546	17.6
Totals	136	4335	1486	857	.577	623	428	.687	1149	2143	15.8

Three-Point Field Goals: 1987-88, 1-for-2 (.500). 1988-89, 0-for-1. Totals, 1-for-3 (.333).

NBA REGULAR SEASON RECORD

									—Rebounds—									
Sea.—Team	G.	Min.	FGA	FGM	Pct.	FTA	FTM	Pct.	Off.	Def.	Tot.	Ast.	PF	Dq.	Stl.	Blk.	Pts.	Avg.
89-90—Sacramento	34	866	251	111	.442	78	49	.628	64	132	196	65	132	4	16	57	271	8.0

Three-Point Field Goals: 1989-90, 0-for-2.

Member of NCAA Division I championship team, 1986. . . . Named Outstanding Player in NCAA Division I tournament, 1986. . . . THE SPORTING NEWS All-America Second Team, 1989.

ALEXANDER ENGLISH
(Alex)

Born January 5, 1954 at Columbia, S. C. Height 6:07. Weight 190.
High School—Columbia, S. C., Dreher.
College—University of South Carolina, Columbia, S. C.
Drafted by Milwaukee on second round, 1976 (23rd pick).

Signed by Indiana as a Veteran Free Agent, June 8, 1978; Milwaukee waived its right of first refusal in exchange for a 1979 1st round draft choice, October 3, 1978.
Traded by Indiana with a 1980 1st round draft choice to Denver for George McGinnis, February 1, 1980.

—COLLEGIATE RECORD—

Year	G.	Min.	FGA	FGM	Pct.	FTA	FTM	Pct.	Reb.	Pts.	Avg.
72-73	29	1037	368	189	.514	70	44	.629	306	422	14.6
73-74	27	1007	395	209	.529	112	75	.670	237	493	18.3
74-75	28	1024	359	199	.554	77	49	.636	244	447	16.0
75-76	27	1045	468	258	.551	134	94	.701	277	610	22.6
Totals	111	4113	1590	855	.538	393	262	.667	1064	1972	17.8

NBA REGULAR SEASON RECORD

									—Rebounds—									
Sea.—Team	G.	Min.	FGA	FGM	Pct.	FTA	FTM	Pct.	Off.	Def.	Tot.	Ast.	PF	Dq.	Stl.	Blk.	Pts.	Avg.
76-77—Milwaukee	60	648	277	132	.477	60	46	.767	68	100	168	25	78	0	17	18	310	5.2
77-78—Milwaukee	82	1552	633	343	.542	143	104	.727	144	251	395	129	178	1	41	55	790	9.6
78-79—Indiana	81	2696	1102	563	.511	230	173	.752	253	402	655	271	214	3	70	78	1299	16.0
79-80—Ind.-Den.	78	2401	1113	553	.501	266	210	.789	269	336	605	224	206	0	73	62	1318	16.9
80-81—Denver	81	3093	1555	768	.494	459	390	.850	273	373	646	290	255	2	106	100	1929	23.8
81-82—Denver	82	3015	1553	855	.551	443	372	.840	210	348	558	433	261	2	87	120	2082	25.4
82-83—Denver	82	2988	1857	959	.516	490	406	.829	263	338	601	397	235	1	116	126	2326	28.4
83-84—Denver	82	2870	1714	907	.529	427	352	.824	216	248	464	406	252	3	83	95	2167	26.4
84-85—Denver	81	2924	1812	939	.518	462	383	.829	203	255	458	344	259	1	101	46	2262	27.9
85-86—Denver	81	3024	1888	951	.504	593	511	.862	192	213	405	320	235	1	73	29	2414	29.8
86-87—Denver	82	3085	1920	965	.503	487	411	.844	146	198	344	422	216	0	73	21	2345	28.6
87-88—Denver	80	2818	1704	843	.495	379	314	.828	166	207	373	377	193	1	70	23	2000	25.0
88-89—Denver	82	2990	1881	924	.491	379	325	.858	148	178	326	383	174	0	66	12	2175	26.5
89-90—Denver	80	2211	1293	635	.491	183	161	.880	119	167	286	225	130	0	51	23	1433	17.9
Totals	1114	36315	20302	10337	.509	5001	4158	.831	2670	3614	6284	4246	2886	15	1027	808	24850	22.3

Three-Point Field Goals: 1979-80, 2-for-6 (.333). 1980-81, 3-for-5 (.600). 1981-82, 0-for-8. 1982-83, 2-for-12 (.167). 1983-84, 1-for-7 (.143). 1984-85, 1-for-5 (.200). 1985-86, 1-for-5 (.200). 1986-87, 4-for-15 (.267). 1987-88, 0-for-6. 1988-89, 2-for-8 (.250). 1989-90, 2-for-5 (.400). Totals, 18-for-82 (.220).

ALEX ENGLISH

NBA PLAYOFF RECORD

Sea.—Team	G.	Min.	FGA	FGM	Pct.	FTA	FTM	Pct.	—Rebounds— Off.	Def.	Tot.	Ast.	PF	Dq.	Stl.	Blk.	Pts.	Avg.
77-78—Milwaukee	9	208	78	48	.615	32	25	.781	16	26	42	13	20	0	6	7	121	13.4
81-82—Denver	3	118	55	26	.473	7	6	.857	8	15	23	17	6	0	3	3	58	19.3
82-83—Denver	7	270	150	67	.447	53	47	.887	20	24	44	42	21	0	4	7	181	25.9
83-84—Denver	5	203	102	60	.588	28	25	.893	16	24	40	28	17	0	3	2	145	29.0
84-85—Denver	14	536	304	163	.536	109	97	.890	36	56	92	63	40	1	17	5	423	30.2
85-86—Denver	10	394	229	106	.463	71	61	.859	18	17	35	52	29	0	4	4	273	27.3
86-87—Denver	3	76	49	25	.510	7	6	.857	10	4	14	10	9	1	0	0	56	18.7
87-88—Denver	11	438	255	116	.455	43	35	.814	31	28	59	48	34	0	7	3	267	24.3
88-89—Denver	3	108	62	32	.516	16	14	.875	8	5	13	11	6	0	1	0	78	26.0
89-90—Denver	3	76	44	25	.568	11	9	.818	3	6	9	9	6	0	2	1	59	19.7
Totals	68	2427	1328	668	.503	377	325	.862	166	205	371	293	188	2	47	32	1661	24.4

Three-Point Field Goals: 1982-83, 0-for-2. 1983-84, 0-for-1. 1984-85, 0-for-1. 1985-86, 0-for-1. 1987-88, 0-for-3. Totals, 0-for-8.

NBA ALL-STAR GAME RECORD

Season—Team	Min.	FGA	FGM	Pct.	FTA	FTM	Pct.	—Rebounds— Off.	Def.	Tot.	Ast.	PF	Dq.	Stl.	Blk.	Pts.
1982—Denver	12	6	2	.333	0	0	.000	2	3	5	1	2	0	1	0	4
1983—Denver	23	14	7	.500	1	0	.000	2	2	4	0	2	0	1	2	14
1984—Denver	19	8	6	.750	1	1	1.000	0	0	0	2	2	0	1	1	13
1985—Denver	14	3	0	.000	0	0	.000	1	1	2	1	1	0	0	0	0
1986—Denver	16	12	8	.667	0	0	.000	1	0	1	2	0	0	0	1	16
1987—Denver	13	6	0	.000	0	0	.000	0	0	0	1	1	0	0	0	0
1988—Denver	22	10	5	.500	0	0	.000	2	1	3	4	0	0	1	0	10
1989—Denver	29	13	8	.615	0	0	.000	1	2	3	4	0	0	2	0	16
Totals	148	72	36	.500	2	1	.500	9	9	18	15	8	0	6	4	73

Named to All-NBA Second Team, 1982, 1983, 1986. . . . Led NBA in scoring, 1983.

PATRICK ALOYSIUS EWING

Born August 5, 1962 at Kingston, Jamaica. Height 7:00. Weight 240.

High School—Cambridge, Mass., Rindge & Latin.

College—Georgetown University, Washington, D.C.

Drafted by New York on first round, 1985 (1st pick).

—COLLEGIATE RECORD—

Year	G.	Min.	FGA	FGM	Pct.	FTA	FTM	Pct.	Reb.	Pts.	Avg.
81-82	37	1064	290	183	.631	167	103	.617	279	469	12.7
82-83	32	1024	372	212	.570	224	141	.629	325	565	17.7
83-84	37	1179	368	242	.658	189	124	.656	371	608	16.4
84-85	37	1132	352	220	.625	160	102	.638	341	542	14.6
Totals	143	4399	1382	857	.620	740	470	.635	1316	2184	15.3

NBA REGULAR SEASON RECORD

Sea.—Team	G.	Min.	FGA	FGM	Pct.	FTA	FTM	Pct.	—Rebounds— Off.	Def.	Tot.	Ast.	PF	Dq.	Stl.	Blk.	Pts.	Avg.
85-86—New York	50	1771	814	386	.474	306	226	.739	124	327	451	102	191	7	54	103	998	20.0
86-87—New York	63	2206	1053	530	.503	415	296	.713	157	398	555	104	248	5	89	147	1356	21.5
87-88—New York	82	2546	1183	656	.555	476	341	.716	245	431	676	125	332	5	104	245	1653	20.2
88-89—New York	80	2896	1282	727	.567	484	361	.746	213	527	740	188	311	5	117	281	1815	22.7
89-90—New York	82	3165	1673	922	.551	648	502	.775	235	658	893	182	325	7	78	327	2347	28.6
Totals	357	12584	6005	3221	.536	2329	1726	.741	974	2341	3315	701	1407	29	442	1103	8169	22.9

Three-Point Field Goals: 1985-86, 0-for-5. 1986-87, 0-for-7. 1987-88, 0-for-3. 1988-89, 0-for-6. 1989-90, 1-for-4 (.250). Totals, 1-for-25 (.040).

NBA PLAYOFF RECORD

Sea.—Team	G.	Min.	FGA	FGM	Pct.	FTA	FTM	Pct.	—Rebounds— Off.	Def.	Tot.	Ast.	PF	Dq.	Stl.	Blk.	Pts.	Avg.
87-88—New York	4	153	57	28	.491	22	19	.864	16	35	51	10	17	0	6	13	75	18.8
88-89—New York	9	340	144	70	.486	52	39	.750	23	67	90	20	35	0	9	18	179	19.9
89-90—New York	10	395	219	114	.521	79	65	.823	21	84	105	31	41	0	13	20	294	29.4
Totals	23	888	420	212	.505	153	123	.804	60	186	246	61	93	0	28	51	548	23.8

Three-Point Field Goals: 1987-88, 0-for-1. 1989-90, 1-for-2 (.500). Totals, 1-for-3 (.333).

NBA ALL-STAR GAME RECORD

Season—Team	Min.	FGA	FGM	Pct.	FTA	FTM	Pct.	—Rebounds— Off.	Def.	Tot.	Ast.	PF	Dq.	Stl.	Blk.	Pts.
1986—New York						Did Not Play—Injured										
1988—New York	16	8	4	.500	1	1	1.000	1	5	6	0	1	0	0	1	9
1989—New York	17	8	2	.250	4	0	.000	1	5	6	2	2	0	1	2	4
1990—New York	27	9	5	.556	2	2	1.000	1	9	10	1	5	0	1	5	12
Totals	60	25	11	.440	7	3	.429	3	19	22	3	8	0	2	8	25

Named to All-NBA First Team, 1990. . . . All-NBA Second Team, 1988 and 1989. . . . NBA All-Defensive Second

Team, 1988 and 1989. . . . NBA Rookie of the Year, 1986. . . . NBA All-Rookie Team, 1986. . . . Member of NCAA Division I championship team, 1984. . . . Named NCAA Division I Tournament Most Outstanding Player, 1984. . . . Member of U.S. Olympic team, 1984. . . . THE SPORTING NEWS College Player of the Year, 1985. . . . THE SPORTING NEWS All-America First Team, 1985. . . . THE SPORTING NEWS All-America Second Team, 1983 and 1984.

JAMES HUBERT FARMER III
(Jim)

Born September 23, 1964 at Dothan, Ala. Height 6:04. Weight 203.
High School—Dothan, Ala., Houston Academy.
College—University of Alabama, University, Ala.
Drafted by Dallas on first round, 1987 (20th pick).

Waived by Dallas, November 3, 1988; signed by Utah as a free agent, January 4, 1989.
Selected from Utah by Orlando in NBA expansion draft, June 15, 1989.
Signed by Minnesota as a free agent, August 30, 1989.
Waived by Minnesota, October 20, 1989; signed by Seattle, January 22, 1990, to the first of consecutive 10-day contracts that expired, February 10, 1990.
Re-signed by Seattle, February 12, 1990, for remainder of season.
Played in Continental Basketball Association with Pensacola Tornados, 1989-90.

—COLLEGIATE RECORD—

Year	G.	Min.	FGA	FGM	Pct.	FTA	FTM	Pct.	Reb.	Pts.	Avg.
82-83					Redshirted						
83-84	12	59	24	7	.292	13	7	.538	6	21	1.8
84-85	33	700	186	82	.441	65	45	.692	71	209	6.3
85-86	33	1101	326	168	.515	114	85	.746	154	421	12.8
86-87	33	1084	421	196	.466	133	118	.887	159	546	16.5
Totals	111	2944	957	453	.473	325	255	.785	390	1197	10.8

Three-Point Field Goals: 1986-87, 36-for-93 (.387).

CBA REGULAR SEASON RECORD

Sea.—Team	G.	Min.	2-Point FGM	FGA	Pct.	3-Point FGM	FGA	Pct.	FTM	FTA	Pct.	Reb.	Ast.	Pts.	Avg.
89-90—Pensacola	23	529	102	207	.493	20	58	.345	83	100	.830	51	39	347	15.1

NBA REGULAR SEASON RECORD

Sea.—Team	G.	Min.	FGA	FGM	Pct.	FTA	FTM	Pct.	Rebounds Off.	Def.	Tot.	Ast.	PF	Dq.	Stl.	Blk.	Pts.	Avg.
87-88—Dallas	30	157	69	26	.377	10	9	.900	9	9	18	16	18	0	3	1	61	2.0
88-89—Utah	37	412	142	57	.401	41	29	.707	22	33	55	28	41	0	9	0	152	4.1
89-90—Seattle	38	400	203	89	.438	80	57	.713	17	26	43	25	44	0	17	1	243	6.4
Totals	105	969	414	172	.415	131	95	.725	48	68	116	69	103	0	29	2	456	4.3

Three-Point Field Goals: 1987-88, 0-for-6. 1988-89, 9-for-20 (.450). 1989-90, 8-for-27 (.296). Totals, 17-for-53 (.321).

NBA PLAYOFF RECORD

Sea.—Team	G.	Min.	FGA	FGM	Pct.	FTA	FTM	Pct.	Rebounds Off.	Def.	Tot.	Ast.	PF	Dq.	Stl.	Blk.	Pts.	Avg.
87-88—Dallas	3	11	6	2	.333	0	0	.000	3	1	4	1	2	0	0	0	4	1.3
88-89—Utah	2	3	2	0	.000	0	0	....	0	0	0	0	0	0	0	0	0	0.0
Totals	5	14	8	2	.250	0	0	....	3	1	4	1	2	0	0	0	4	0.8

Three-Point Field Goals: 1988-89, 0-for-1.

DUANE FERRELL

Born February 28, 1965 at Baltimore, Md. Height 6:07. Weight 210.
High School—Towson, Md., Calvert Hall.
College—Georgia Institute of Technology, Atlanta, Ga.
Never drafted by an NBA franchise.

Signed by Atlanta as a free agent, October 6, 1988.
Waived by Atlanta, November 2, 1989; re-signed by Atlanta, February 23, 1990, to the first of consecutive 10-day contracts that expired, March 14, 1990.
Re-signed by Atlanta, March 15, 1990, for remainder of season.
Played in Continental Basketball Association with Topeka Sizzlers, 1989-90.

—COLLEGIATE RECORD—

Year	G.	Min.	FGA	FGM	Pct.	FTA	FTM	Pct.	Reb.	Pts.	Avg.
84-85	32	802	232	117	.504	98	56	.571	131	290	9.1
85-86	34	1068	289	172	.595	91	69	.758	168	413	12.1
86-87	29	1058	387	201	.519	138	112	.812	170	520	17.9
87-88	32	1051	432	230	.532	175	131	.749	211	595	18.6
Totals	127	3979	1340	720	.537	502	368	.733	680	1818	14.3

Three-Point Field Goals: 1986-87, 6-for-15 (.400). 1987-88, 4-for-14 (.286). Totals, 10-for-29 (.345).

CBA REGULAR SEASON RECORD

Sea.—Team	G.	Min.	2-Point FGM	2-Point FGA	2-Point Pct.	3-Point FGM	3-Point FGA	3-Point Pct.	FTM	FTA	Pct.	Reb.	Ast.	Pts.	Avg.
89-90—Topeka	40	1546	372	683	.545	5	16	.313	212	276	.768	252	95	971	24.3

NBA REGULAR SEASON RECORD

Sea.—Team	G.	Min.	FGA	FGM	Pct.	FTA	FTM	Pct.	Rebounds Off.	Rebounds Def.	Rebounds Tot.	Ast.	PF	Dq.	Stl.	Blk.	Pts.	Avg.
88-89—Atlanta	41	231	83	35	.422	44	30	.682	19	22	41	10	33	0	7	6	100	2.4
89-90—Atlanta	14	29	14	5	.357	6	2	.333	3	4	7	2	3	0	1	0	12	0.9
Totals	55	260	97	40	.412	50	32	.640	22	26	48	12	36	0	8	6	112	2.0

Three-Point Field Goals: 1989-90, 0-for-1.

VERN FLEMING

Born February 4, 1961 at New York, N.Y. Height 6:05. Weight 195.

High School—Long Island City, N. Y., Mater Christi.

College—University of Georgia, Athens, Ga.

Drafted by Indiana on first round, 1984 (18th pick).

—COLLEGIATE RECORD—

Year	G.	Min.	FGA	FGM	Pct.	FTA	FTM	Pct.	Reb.	Pts.	Avg.
80-81	30	1082	225	108	.480	122	85	.697	80	301	10.0
81-82	31	1079	236	117	.496	114	73	.640	120	307	9.9
82-83	34	1130	424	227	.535	169	121	.716	158	575	16.9
83-84	30	1030	493	248	.503	130	98	.754	120	594	19.8
Totals	125	4321	1378	700	.508	535	377	.705	478	1777	14.2

NBA REGULAR SEASON RECORD

Sea.—Team	G.	Min.	FGA	FGM	Pct.	FTA	FTM	Pct.	Rebounds Off.	Rebounds Def.	Rebounds Tot.	Ast.	PF	Dq.	Stl.	Blk.	Pts.	Avg.
84-85—Indiana	80	2486	922	433	.470	339	260	.767	148	175	323	247	232	4	99	8	1126	14.1
85-86—Indiana	80	2870	862	436	.506	353	263	.745	102	284	386	505	230	3	131	5	1136	14.2
86-87—Indiana	82	2549	727	370	.509	302	238	.788	109	225	334	473	222	3	109	18	980	12.0
87-88—Indiana	80	2733	845	442	.523	283	227	.802	106	258	364	568	225	0	115	11	1111	13.9
88-89—Indiana	76	2552	814	419	.515	304	243	.799	85	225	310	494	212	4	77	12	1084	14.3
89-90—Indiana	82	2876	919	467	.508	294	230	.782	118	204	322	610	213	1	92	10	1176	14.3
Totals	480	16066	5089	2567	.504	1875	1461	.779	668	1371	2039	2897	1334	15	623	64	6613	13.8

Three-Point Field Goals: 1984-85, 0-for-4. 1985-86, 1-for-6 (.167). 1986-87, 2-for-10 (.200). 1987-88, 0-for-13. 1988-89, 3-for-23 (.130). 1989-90, 12-for-34 (.353). Totals, 18-for-90 (.200).

NBA PLAYOFF RECORD

Sea.—Team	G.	Min.	FGA	FGM	Pct.	FTA	FTM	Pct.	Rebounds Off.	Rebounds Def.	Rebounds Tot.	Ast.	PF	Dq.	Stl.	Blk.	Pts.	Avg.
86-87—Indiana	4	141	36	13	.361	30	23	.767	9	17	26	24	15	1	4	1	49	12.3
89-90—Indiana	3	113	34	16	.471	9	8	.889	4	9	13	18	6	0	2	1	40	13.3
Totals	7	254	70	29	.414	39	31	.795	13	26	39	42	21	1	6	2	89	12.7

Three-Point Field Goals: 1986-87, 0-for-1. 1989-90, 0-for-2. Totals, 0-for-3.

Member of U.S. Olympic team, 1984.

ERIC A. FLOYD
(Sleepy)

Born March 6, 1960 at Gastonia, N.C. Height 6:03. Weight 175.

High School—Gastonia, N. C., Hunter Huss.

College—Georgetown University, Washington, D. C.

Drafted by New Jersey on first round, 1982 (13th pick).

Traded by New Jersey with Mickey Johnson to Golden State for Micheal Ray Richardson, February 6, 1983.

Traded by Golden State with Joe Barry Carroll to Houston for Ralph Sampson and Steve Harris, December 12, 1987.

—COLLEGIATE RECORD—

Year	G.	Min.	FGA	FGM	Pct.	FTA	FTM	Pct.	Reb.	Pts.	Avg.
78-79	29	975	388	177	.456	155	126	.813	119	480	16.6
79-80	32	1052	444	246	.554	140	106	.757	98	598	18.7
80-81	32	1115	508	237	.467	165	133	.806	133	607	19.0
81-82	37	1200	494	249	.504	168	121	.720	127	619	16.7
Totals	130	4342	1834	909	.496	628	486	.774	477	2304	17.7

NBA REGULAR SEASON RECORD

Sea.—Team	G.	Min.	FGA	FGM	Pct.	FTA	FTM	Pct.	—Rebounds— Off.	Def.	Tot.	Ast.	PF	Dq.	Stl.	Blk.	Pts.	Avg.
82-83—N.J.-G.S.	76	1248	527	226	.429	180	150	.833	56	81	137	138	134	3	58	17	612	8.1
83-84—Golden State	77	2555	1045	484	.463	386	315	.816	87	184	271	269	216	0	103	31	1291	16.8
84-85—Golden State	82	2873	1372	610	.445	415	336	.810	62	140	202	406	226	1	134	41	1598	19.5
85-86—Golden State	82	2764	1007	510	.506	441	351	.796	76	221	297	746	199	2	157	16	1410	17.2
86-87—Golden State	82	3064	1030	503	.488	537	462	.860	56	212	268	848	199	1	146	18	1541	18.8
87-88—G.S.-Hou.	77	2514	969	420	.433	354	301	.850	77	219	296	544	190	1	95	12	1155	15.0
88-89—Houston	82	2788	893	396	.443	309	261	.845	48	258	306	709	196	1	124	11	1162	14.2
89-90—Houston	82	2630	803	362	.451	232	187	.806	46	152	198	600	159	0	94	11	1000	12.2
Totals	640	20436	7646	3511	.459	2854	2363	.828	508	1467	1975	4260	1519	9	911	157	9769	15.3

Three-Point Field Goals: 1982-83, 10-for-25 (.400). 1983-84, 8-for-45 (.178). 1984-85, 42-for-143 (.294). 1985-86, 39-for-119 (.328). 1986-87, 73-for-190 (.384). 1987-88, 14-for-72 (.194). 1988-89, 109-for-292 (.373). 1989-90, 89-for-234 (.380). Totals, 384-for-1120 (.343).

NBA PLAYOFF RECORD

Sea.—Team	G.	Min.	FGA	FGM	Pct.	FTA	FTM	Pct.	—Rebounds— Off.	Def.	Tot.	Ast.	PF	Dq.	Stl.	Blk.	Pts.	Avg.
86-87—Golden State	10	414	152	77	.507	51	47	.922	9	21	30	102	24	0	18	2	214	21.4
87-88—Houston	4	154	61	26	.426	22	19	.864	3	4	7	34	10	0	8	0	75	18.8
88-89—Houston	4	160	46	22	.478	14	10	.714	3	15	18	26	10	0	8	1	62	15.5
89-90—Houston	4	172	64	30	.469	17	11	.647	7	8	15	41	5	0	5	1	74	18.5
Totals	22	900	323	155	.480	104	87	.837	22	48	70	203	49	0	39	4	425	19.3

Three-Point Field Goals: 1986-87, 13-for-28 (.464). 1987-88, 4-for-8 (.500). 1988-89, 8-for-15 (.533). 1989-90, 3-for-12 (.250). Totals, 28-for-63 (.444).

NBA ALL-STAR GAME RECORD

Season—Team	Min.	FGA	FGM	Pct.	FTA	FTM	Pct.	—Rebounds— Off.	Def.	Tot.	Ast.	PF	Dq.	Stl.	Blk.	Pts.
1987—Golden State	19	7	4	.571	7	5	.714	2	3	5	1	2	0	1	0	14

Three-Point Field Goals: 1987, 1-for-3 (.333).

Holds NBA playoff game records for most points in one half, 39, and in one quarter, 29, vs. Los Angeles Lakers, May 10, 1987. . . . Named to THE SPORTING NEWS All-America Second Team, 1982.

TELLIS JOSEPH FRANK JR.

Born April 26, 1965 at Gary, Ind. Height 6:10. Weight 225.
High School—Gary, Ind., Lew Wallace.
College—Western Kentucky University, Bowling Green, Ky.
Drafted by Golden State on first round, 1987 (14th pick).

Traded by Golden State to Miami for a 1992 2nd round draft choice, October 2, 1989.

—COLLEGIATE RECORD—

Year	G.	Min.	FGA	FGM	Pct.	FTA	FTM	Pct.	Reb.	Pts.	Avg.
83-84	27	....	121	42	.347	36	22	.611	92	106	3.9
84-85	27	....	213	93	.437	62	41	.661	134	227	8.4
85-86	30	....	212	109	.514	111	88	.793	157	306	10.2
86-87	38	....	542	281	.518	175	122	.697	281	684	18.0
Totals	122	....	1088	525	.483	384	273	.711	664	1323	10.8

NBA REGULAR SEASON RECORD

Sea.—Team	G.	Min.	FGA	FGM	Pct.	FTA	FTM	Pct.	—Rebounds— Off.	Def.	Tot.	Ast.	PF	Dq.	Stl.	Blk.	Pts.	Avg.
87-88—Golden State	78	1597	565	242	.428	207	150	.725	95	235	330	111	267	5	53	23	634	8.1
88-89—Golden State	32	245	91	34	.374	51	39	.765	26	35	61	15	59	1	14	6	107	3.3
89-90—Miami	77	1762	607	278	.458	234	179	.765	151	234	385	85	282	6	51	27	735	9.5
Totals	187	3604	1263	554	.439	492	368	.748	272	504	776	211	608	12	118	56	1476	7.9

Three-Point Field Goals: 1987-88, 0-for-1. 1988-89, 0-for-1. Totals, 0-for-2.

COREY YASUTO GAINES

Born June 1, 1965 at Los Angeles, Calif. Height 6:04. Weight 195.
High School—Playa del Ray, Calif., St. Bernard.
Colleges—University of California at Los Angeles, Los Angeles, Calif., and Loyola Marymount University, Los Angeles, Calif.
Drafted by Seattle on third round, 1988 (65th pick).

Waived by Seattle, October 31, 1988; signed by New Jersey, February 7, 1989, to the first of consecutive 10-day contracts that expired, February 26, 1989.
Re-signed by New Jersey, February 27, 1989, for remainder of season.

Signed by Denver as a free agent, October 2, 1989.
Waived by Denver, October 31, 1989; signed by Philadelphia, January 1, 1990, to the first of consecutive 10-day contracts that expired, January 20, 1990.
Played in Continental Basketball Association with Quad City Thunder, 1988-89, and Omaha Racers, 1989-90.

—COLLEGIATE RECORD—

UCLA

Year	G.	Min.	FGA	FGM	Pct.	FTA	FTM	Pct.	Reb.	Pts.	Avg.
83-84	24	273	50	23	.460	40	32	.800	20	78	3.3
84-85	32	519	98	48	.490	49	31	.633	37	127	4.0
85-86	22	378	108	53	.491	40	25	.625	37	131	6.0
UCLA Totals	78	1170	256	124	.484	129	88	.682	94	336	4.3

Loyola Marymount

Year	G.	Min.	FGA	FGM	Pct.	FTA	FTM	Pct.	Reb.	Pts.	Avg.
87-88	31	853	363	188	.518	180	122	.678	68	540	17.4
College Totals	109	2023	619	312	.504	309	210	.680	162	876	8.0

Three-Point Field Goals: 1987-88, 42-for-83 (.506).

CBA REGULAR SEASON RECORD

			—2-Point—			—3-Point—									
Sea.—Team	G.	Min.	FGM	FGA	Pct.	FGM	FGA	Pct.	FTM	FTA	Pct.	Reb.	Ast.	Pts.	Avg.
88-89—Quad City	24	806	53	128	.414	34	91	.374	41	63	.651	43	216	249	10.4
89-90—Omaha	48	1835	263	558	.471	32	99	.323	214	280	.764	140	556	836	17.4
Totals	72	2641	316	686	.461	66	190	.347	255	343	.743	183	772	1085	15.1

NBA REGULAR SEASON RECORD

									—Rebounds—									
Sea.—Team	G.	Min.	FGA	FGM	Pct.	FTA	FTM	Pct.	Off.	Def.	Tot.	Ast.	PF	Dq.	Stl.	Blk.	Pts.	Avg.
88-89—New Jersey	32	337	64	27	.422	16	12	.750	3	16	19	67	27	0	15	1	67	2.1
89-90—Philadelphia	9	81	12	4	.333	4	1	.250	1	4	5	26	11	0	4	0	10	1.1
Totals	41	418	76	31	.408	20	13	.650	4	20	24	93	38	0	19	1	77	1.9

Three-Point Field Goals: 1988-89, 1-for-5 (.200). 1989-90, 1-for-2 (.500). Totals, 2-for-7 (.286).

KEVIN DOUGLAS GAMBLE

Born November 13, 1965 at Springfield, Ill. Height 6:05. Weight 215.
High School—Springfield, Ill., Lanphier.
Colleges—Lincoln College, Lincoln, Ill., and University of Iowa, Iowa City, Ia.
Drafted by Portland on third round, 1987 (63rd pick).

Waived by Portland, December 9, 1987; signed by Boston as a free agent, December 15, 1988.
Played in Continental Basketball Association with Quad City Thunder, 1987-88 and 1988-89.

—COLLEGIATE RECORD—

Lincoln

Year	G.	Min.	FGA	FGM	Pct.	FTA	FTM	Pct.	Reb.	Pts.	Avg.
83-84	30	....	469	262	.559	148	115	.777	276	639	21.3
84-85	31	....	461	267	.579	126	103	.817	301	637	20.5
J.C. Totals	61	....	930	529	.569	274	218	.796	577	1276	20.9

Iowa

Year	G.	Min.	FGA	FGM	Pct.	FTA	FTM	Pct.	Reb.	Pts.	Avg.
85-86	30	260	76	36	.474	10	7	.700	52	79	2.6
86-87	35	867	298	162	.544	99	69	.697	158	418	11.9
Iowa Totals	65	1127	374	198	.529	109	76	.697	210	497	7.6

Three-Point Field Goals: 1986-87, 35-for-76 (.329).

CBA REGULAR SEASON RECORD

			—2-Point—			—3-Point—									
Sea.—Team	G.	Min.	FGM	FGA	Pct.	FGM	FGA	Pct.	FTM	FTA	Pct.	Reb.	Ast.	Pts.	Avg.
87-88—Quad City	40	1450	299	565	.529	31	75	.413	151	184	.821	237	149	842	21.1
88-89—Quad City	12	490	107	203	.527	3	20	.150	110	129	.853	66	48	333	27.8
Totals	52	1940	406	768	.529	34	95	.358	261	313	.834	303	197	1175	22.6

NBA REGULAR SEASON RECORD

									—Rebounds—									
Sea.—Team	G.	Min.	FGA	FGM	Pct.	FTA	FTM	Pct.	Off.	Def.	Tot.	Ast.	PF	Dq.	Stl.	Blk.	Pts.	Avg.
87-88—Portland	9	19	3	0	.000	0	0	.000	2	1	3	1	2	0	2	0	0	0.0
88-89—Boston	44	375	136	75	.551	55	35	.636	11	31	42	34	40	0	14	3	187	4.3
89-90—Boston	71	990	301	137	.455	107	85	.794	42	70	112	119	77	1	28	8	362	5.1
Totals	124	1384	440	212	.482	162	120	.741	55	102	157	154	119	1	44	11	549	4.4

Three-Point Field Goals: 1987-88, 0-for-1. 1988-89, 2-for-11 (.182). 1989-90, 3-for-18 (.167). Totals, 5-for-30 (.167).

NBA PLAYOFF RECORD

Sea.—Team	G.	Min.	FGA	FGM	Pct.	FTA	FTM	Pct.	Rebounds Off.	Def.	Tot.	Ast.	PF	Dq.	Stl.	Blk.	Pts.	Avg.
88-89—Boston	1	29	11	4	.364	2	0	.000	1	0	1	2	1	0	1	0	8	8.0
89-90—Boston	3	8	5	3	.600	0	0	....	1	0	1	2	1	0	0	0	6	2.0
Totals	4	37	16	7	.438	2	0	.000	2	0	2	4	2	0	1	0	14	3.5

Three-Point Field Goals: 1988-89, 0-for-1.

WINSTON KINNARD GARLAND

Born December 19, 1964 at Gary, Ind. Height 6:02. Weight 170.

High School—Gary, Ind., Roosevelt.

Colleges—Southeastern Community College, West Burlington, Ia., and Southwest Missouri State University, Springfield, Mo.

Drafted by Milwaukee on second round, 1987 (40th pick).

Waived by Milwaukee, November 4, 1987; signed by Golden State as a free agent, November 25, 1987.
Waived by Golden State, December 9, 1987; re-signed by Golden State, December 14, 1987.
Traded by Golden State to Los Angeles Clippers for two future 2nd round draft choices, February 22, 1990.
Played in Continental Basketball Association with Pensacola Tornados, 1987-88.

—COLLEGIATE RECORD—

Southeastern

Year	G.	Min.	FGA	FGM	Pct.	FTA	FTM	Pct.	Reb.	Pts.	Avg.
83-84	34	1053	450	233	.518	134	112	.836	150	578	17.0
84-85	30	1006	401	207	.516	156	133	.853	107	547	18.2
J. C. Totals	64	2059	851	440	.517	290	245	.845	257	1125	17.6

Southwest Missouri State

Year	G.	Min.	FGA	FGM	Pct.	FTA	FTM	Pct.	Reb.	Pts.	Avg.
85-86	32	1006	445	205	.461	153	118	.771	116	528	16.5
86-87	34	1119	545	274	.503	153	115	.752	85	720	21.2
Totals	66	2231	990	479	.484	306	233	.761	201	1248	18.9

Three-Point Field Goals: 1986-87, 57-for-113 (.504).

CBA REGULAR SEASON RECORD

Sea.—Team	G.	Min.	2-Point FGM	FGA	Pct.	3-Point FGM	FGA	Pct.	FTM	FTA	Pct.	Reb.	Ast.	Pts.	Avg.
87-88—Pensacola	4	60	17	34	.500	0	1	.000	10	11	.909	7	5	44	11.0

NBA REGULAR SEASON RECORD

Sea.—Team	G.	Min.	FGA	FGM	Pct.	FTA	FTM	Pct.	Rebounds Off.	Def.	Tot.	Ast.	PF	Dq.	Stl.	Blk.	Pts.	Avg.
87-88—Golden State	67	2122	775	340	.439	157	138	.879	68	159	227	429	188	2	116	7	831	12.4
88-89—Golden State	79	2661	1074	466	.434	251	203	.809	101	227	328	505	216	2	175	14	1145	14.5
89-90—G.S.-L.A.C.	79	1762	573	230	.401	122	102	.836	51	163	214	303	152	1	78	10	574	7.3
Totals	225	6545	2422	1036	.428	530	443	.836	220	549	769	1237	556	5	369	31	2550	11.3

Three-Point Field Goals: 1987-88, 13-for-39 (.333). 1988-89, 10-for-43 (.233). 1989-90, 12-for-36 (.333). Totals, 35-for-118 (.297).

NBA PLAYOFF RECORD

Sea.—Team	G.	Min.	FGA	FGM	Pct.	FTA	FTM	Pct.	Rebounds Off.	Def.	Tot.	Ast.	PF	Dq.	Stl.	Blk.	Pts.	Avg.
88-89—Golden State	8	270	98	41	.418	28	24	.857	14	19	33	29	31	1	13	2	107	13.4

Three-Point Field Goals: 1988-89, 1-for-3 (.333).

THOMAS S. GARRICK
(Tom)

Born July 7, 1966 at West Warwick, R.I. Height 6:02. Weight 185.

High School—West Warwick, R.I.

College—University of Rhode Island, Kingston, R.I.

Drafted by Los Angeles Clippers on second round, 1988 (45th pick).

Waived by Los Angeles Clippers, November 14, 1988; re-signed by Los Angeles Clippers as a free agent, November 17, 1988.

—COLLEGIATE RECORD—

Year	G.	Min.	FGA	FGM	Pct.	FTA	FTM	Pct.	Reb.	Pts.	Avg.
84-85	28	739	114	54	.474	78	58	.744	102	166	5.9
85-86	27	623	135	65	.481	66	49	.742	76	179	6.6
86-87	30	1037	421	192	.456	132	108	.818	129	510	17.0
87-88	35	1241	561	273	.487	174	138	.793	143	718	20.5
Totals	120	3640	1231	584	.474	450	353	.784	450	1573	13.1

Three-Point Field Goals: 1986-87, 18-for-55 (.327). 1987-88, 34-for-62 (.548). Totals, 52-for-117 (.444).

NBA REGULAR SEASON RECORD

Sea.—Team	G.	Min.	FGA	FGM	Pct.	FTA	FTM	Pct.	—Rebounds— Off.	Def.	Tot.	Ast.	PF	Dq.	Stl.	Blk.	Pts.	Avg.
88-89—L.A. Clippers	71	1499	359	176	.490	127	102	.803	37	119	156	243	141	1	78	9	454	6.4
89-90—L.A. Clippers	73	1721	421	208	.494	114	88	.772	34	128	162	289	151	4	90	7	508	7.0
Totals	144	3220	780	384	.492	241	190	.788	71	247	318	532	292	5	168	16	962	6.7

Three-Point Field Goals: 1988-89, 0-for-13. 1989-90, 4-for-21 (.190). Totals, 4-for-34 (.118).

KENNETH CLAY GATTISON
(Kenny)

Born May 23, 1964 at Wilmington, N.C. Height 6.08. Weight 225.
High School—Wilmington, N.C., New Hanover.
College—Old Dominion University, Norfolk, Va.
Drafted by Phoenix on third round, 1986 (55th pick).

Waived by Phoenix, September 21, 1989; signed by Charlotte as a free agent, September 26, 1989.
Waived by Charlotte, October 18, 1989; re-signed by Charlotte as a free agent, December 2, 1989.
Played in Continental Basketball Association with Quad City Thunder, 1989-90.
Played in Italy, 1988-89.

—COLLEGIATE RECORD—

Year	G.	Min.	FGA	FGM	Pct.	FTA	FTM	Pct.	Reb.	Pts.	Avg.
82-83	29	705	187	94	.503	78	55	.705	218	243	8.4
83-84	31	916	257	127	.494	137	89	.650	219	343	11.1
84-85	31	890	357	192	.538	187	114	.610	285	498	16.1
85-86	31	1008	342	218	.637	153	103	.673	241	539	17.4
Totals	122	3519	1143	631	.552	555	361	.650	963	1623	13.3

ITALIAN LEAGUE RECORD

Year	G.	Min.	FGA	FGM	Pct.	FTA	FTM	Pct.	Reb.	Pts.	Avg.
88-89—Jolly	21	769	235	147	.626	109	73	.670	202	367	17.5

CBA REGULAR SEASON RECORD

Sea.—Team	G.	Min.	—2-Point— FGM	FGA	Pct.	—3-Point— FGM	FGA	Pct.	FTM	FTA	Pct.	Reb.	Ast.	Pts.	Avg.
89-90—Quad City	7	277	55	99	.556	0	1	.000	51	61	.836	81	15	161	23.0

NBA REGULAR SEASON RECORD

Sea.—Team	G.	Min.	FGA	FGM	Pct.	FTA	FTM	Pct.	—Rebounds— Off.	Def.	Tot.	Ast.	PF	Dq.	Stl.	Blk.	Pts.	Avg.
86-87—Phoenix	77	1104	311	148	.476	171	108	.632	87	183	270	36	178	1	24	33	404	5.2
88-89—Phoenix	2	9	1	0	.000	2	1	.500	0	1	1	0	2	0	0	0	1	0.5
89-90—Charlotte	63	941	269	148	.550	110	75	.682	75	122	197	39	150	1	35	31	372	5.9
Totals	142	2054	581	296	.509	283	184	.650	162	306	468	75	330	2	59	64	777	5.5

Three-Point Field Goals: 1988-89, 0-for-3. 1989-90, 1-for-1 (1.000). Totals, 1-for-4 (.250).

DERRICK EUGENE GERVIN

Born March 28, 1963 at Detroit, Mich. Height 6:08. Weight 200.
High School—Detroit, Mich., King.
College—University of Texas at San Antonio, San Antonio, Tex.
Drafted by Philadelphia on fourth round as an undergraduate, 1985 (90th pick).

Signed by Los Angeles Clippers as a free agent, August 15, 1989.

Waived by Los Angeles Clippers, October 24, 1989; signed by New Jersey, February 12, 1990, to the first of consecutive 10-day contracts that expired, March 3, 1990.

Re-signed by New Jersey, March 5, 1990, for remainder of season.

Played in Continental Basketball Association with Evansville Thunder, 1985-86, and Santa Barbara Islanders, 1989-90.

Did not play basketball, 1986-87.

Played in Spain, 1987-88.

Played in Italy, 1988-89.

—COLLEGIATE RECORD—

Year	G.	Min.	FGA	FGM	Pct.	FTA	FTM	Pct.	Reb.	Pts.	Avg.
82-83	25	....	268	140	.522	92	67	.728	177	347	13.9
83-84	27	....	438	239	.546	194	148	.763	239	626	23.2
84-85	28	....	483	272	.563	213	174	.817	268	718	25.6
Totals	80	....	1189	651	.548	499	389	.780	684	1691	21.1

CBA REGULAR SEASON RECORD

			2-Point			3-Point									
Sea.—Team	G.	Min.	FGM	FGA	Pct.	FGM	FGA	Pct.	FTM	FTA	Pct.	Reb.	Ast.	Pts.	Avg.
85-86—Evansville	1	5	0	1	.000	0	0	.000	0	0	.000	1	0	0	0.0
89-90—Santa Barbara	40	1422	509	934	.545	2	18	.111	243	320	.759	349	67	1267	31.7
Totals	41	1427	509	935	.544	2	18	.111	243	320	.759	350	67	1267	30.9

NBA REGULAR SEASON RECORD

									—Rebounds—									
Sea.—Team	G.	Min.	FGA	FGM	Pct.	FTA	FTM	Pct.	Off.	Def.	Tot.	Ast.	PF	Dq.	Stl.	Blk.	Pts.	Avg.
89-90—New Jersey	21	339	197	93	.472	89	65	.730	29	36	65	8	47	0	20	7	251	12.0

Three-Point Field Goals: 1989-90, 0-for-3.

Brother of George Gervin, guard with Virginia Squires, 1973-74, San Antonio Spurs, 1974-85, and Chicago Bulls, 1985-86. . . . Named to CBA All-Star First Team, 1990. . . . Led CBA in scoring, 1990.

ARMON LOUIS GILLIAM

Born May 28, 1964 at Pittsburgh, Pa. Height 6:09. Weight 245.

High School—Bethel Park, Pa.

Colleges—Independence Junior College, Independence, Kan., and University of Nevada at Las Vegas, Las Vegas, Nev.

Drafted by Phoenix on first round, 1987 (2nd pick).

Traded by Phoenix to Charlotte for Kurt Rambis and two future 2nd round draft choices, December 13, 1989.

—COLLEGIATE RECORD—

Independence

Year	G.	Min.	FGA	FGM	Pct.	FTA	FTM	Pct.	Reb.	Pts.	Avg.
82-83	38	....	422	262	.621	185	117	.632	314	641	16.9

Nevada-Las Vegas

Year	G.	Min.	FGA	FGM	Pct.	FTA	FTM	Pct.	Reb.	Pts.	Avg.
83-84				Did Not Play—Redshirted							
84-85	31	800	219	136	.621	150	98	.653	212	370	11.9
85-86	37	1243	418	221	.529	190	140	.737	315	582	15.7
86-87	39	1259	598	359	.600	254	185	.728	363	903	23.2
UNLV Totals	107	3302	1235	716	.580	594	423	.712	890	1855	17.3

NBA REGULAR SEASON RECORD

									—Rebounds—									
Sea.—Team	G.	Min.	FGA	FGM	Pct.	FTA	FTM	Pct.	Off.	Def.	Tot.	Ast.	PF	Dq.	Stl.	Blk.	Pts.	Avg.
87-88—Phoenix	55	1807	720	342	.475	193	131	.679	134	300	434	72	143	1	58	29	815	14.8
88-89—Phoenix	74	2120	930	468	.503	323	240	.743	165	376	541	52	176	2	54	27	1176	15.9
89-90—Phoe.-Char.	76	2426	940	484	.515	419	303	.723	211	388	599	99	212	4	69	51	1271	16.7
Totals	205	6353	2590	1294	.500	935	674	.721	510	1064	1574	223	531	7	181	107	3262	15.9

Three-Point Field Goals: 1989-90, 0-for-2.

NBA PLAYOFF RECORD

									—Rebounds—									
Sea.—Team	G.	Min.	FGA	FGM	Pct.	FTA	FTM	Pct.	Off.	Def.	Tot.	Ast.	PF	Dq.	Stl.	Blk.	Pts.	Avg.
88-89—Phoenix	9	126	51	27	.529	22	19	.864	18	27	45	2	11	0	1	2	73	8.1

Named to NBA All-Rookie Team, 1988. . . . THE SPORTING NEWS All-America Second Team, 1987.

MICHAEL THOMAS GMINSKI
(Mike)

Born August 3, 1959 at Monroe, Conn. Height 6:11. Weight 260.

High School—Monroe, Conn., Masuk.

College—Duke University, Durham, N. C.

Drafted by New Jersey on first round, 1980 (7th pick).

Traded by New Jersey with Ben Coleman to Philadelphia for Roy Hinson, Tim McCormick and a 1989 2nd round draft choice, January 16, 1988.

—COLLEGIATE RECORD—

Year	G.	Min.	FGA	FGM	Pct.	FTA	FTM	Pct.	Reb.	Pts.	Avg.
76-77	27	....	340	175	.515	91	64	.703	289	414	15.3
77-78	32	....	450	246	.547	176	148	.841	319	640	20.0
78-79	30	....	420	218	.519	177	129	.729	275	565	18.8
79-80	33	1192	487	262	.538	214	180	.841	359	704	21.3
Totals	122	....	1697	901	.531	658	521	.792	1242	2323	19.0

NBA REGULAR SEASON RECORD

Sea.—Team	G.	Min.	FGA	FGM	Pct.	FTA	FTM	Pct.	—Rebounds— Off.	Def.	Tot.	Ast.	PF	Dq.	Stl.	Blk.	Pts.	Avg.
80-81—New Jersey	56	1579	688	291	.423	202	155	.767	137	282	419	72	127	1	54	100	737	13.2
81-82—New Jersey	64	740	270	119	.441	118	97	.822	70	116	186	41	69	0	17	48	335	5.2
82-83—New Jersey	80	1255	426	213	.500	225	175	.778	154	228	382	61	118	0	35	116	601	7.5
83-84—New Jersey	82	1655	462	237	.513	184	147	.799	161	272	433	92	162	0	37	70	621	7.6
84-85—New Jersey	81	2418	818	380	.465	328	276	.841	229	404	633	158	135	0	38	92	1036	12.8
85-86—New Jersey	81	2525	949	491	.517	393	351	.893	206	462	668	133	163	0	56	71	1333	16.5
86-87—New Jersey	72	2272	947	433	.457	370	313	.846	192	438	630	99	159	0	52	69	1179	16.4
87-88—N.J.-Phil.	81	2961	1126	505	.448	392	355	.906	245	569	814	139	176	0	64	118	1365	16.9
88-89—Philadelphia	82	2739	1166	556	.477	341	297	.871	213	556	769	138	142	0	46	106	1409	17.2
89-90—Philadelphia	81	2659	1002	458	.457	235	193	.821	196	491	687	128	136	0	43	102	1112	13.7
Totals	760	20803	7854	3683	.469	2788	2359	.846	1803	3818	5621	1061	1387	1	442	892	9728	12.8

Three-Point Field Goals: 1980-81, 0-for-1. 1982-83, 0-for-1. 1983-84, 0-for-3. 1984-85, 0-for-1. 1985-86, 0-for-1. 1987-88, 0-for-2. 1988-89, 0-for-6. 1989-90, 3-for-17 (.176). Totals, 3-for-32 (.094).

NBA PLAYOFF RECORD

Sea.—Team	G.	Min.	FGA	FGM	Pct.	FTA	FTM	Pct.	—Rebounds— Off.	Def.	Tot.	Ast.	PF	Dq.	Stl.	Blk.	Pts.	Avg.
81-82—New Jersey	1	10	3	2	.667	2	1	.500	0	2	2	0	2	0	0	0	5	5.0
82-83—New Jersey	2	29	9	6	.667	4	3	.750	4	5	9	1	2	0	0	4	15	7.5
83-84—New Jersey	11	223	50	29	.580	52	36	.692	22	33	55	6	17	0	7	15	94	8.5
84-85—New Jersey	3	81	33	18	.545	6	6	1.000	4	15	19	4	5	0	3	5	42	14.0
85-86—New Jersey	3	109	43	16	.372	27	26	.963	11	19	30	5	11	0	4	2	58	19.3
88-89—Philadelphia	3	118	48	19	.396	16	11	.688	6	17	23	2	8	0	0	8	49	16.3
89-90—Philadelphia	10	342	117	57	.487	15	14	.933	8	46	54	11	27	0	8	23	128	12.8
Totals	33	912	303	147	.485	122	97	.795	55	137	192	29	72	0	22	57	391	11.8

Three-Point Field Goals: 1989-90, 0-for-5.

Named to THE SPORTING NEWS All-America Second Team, 1979 and 1980.

GARY GRANT

Born April 21, 1965 at Parson, Kan. Height 6:03. Weight 195.

High School—Canton, O., McKinley.

College—University of Michigan, Ann Arbor, Mich.

Drafted by Seattle on first round, 1988 (15th pick).

Draft rights traded by Seattle with a 1989 1st round draft choice to Los Angeles Clippers for Michael Cage, June 28, 1988.

—COLLEGIATE RECORD—

Year	G.	Min.	FGA	FGM	Pct.	FTA	FTM	Pct.	Reb.	Pts.	Avg.
84-85	30	950	307	169	.550	60	49	.817	76	387	12.9
85-86	33	1010	348	172	.494	78	58	.744	104	402	12.2
86-87	32	....	533	286	.537	142	111	.782	159	716	22.4
87-88	34	....	508	269	.530	167	135	.808	116	717	21.1
Totals	129	....	1696	896	.528	447	353	.790	455	2222	17.2

Three-Point Field Goals: 1986-87, 33-for-68 (.485). 1987-88, 44-for-99 (.444). Totals, 77-for-167 (.461).

NBA REGULAR SEASON RECORD

Sea.—Team	G.	Min.	FGA	FGM	Pct.	FTA	FTM	Pct.	—Rebounds— Off.	Def.	Tot.	Ast.	PF	Dq.	Stl.	Blk.	Pts.	Avg.
88-89—L.A. Clippers	71	1924	830	361	.435	162	119	.735	80	158	238	506	170	1	144	9	846	11.9
89-90—L.A. Clippers	44	1529	517	241	.466	113	88	.779	59	136	195	442	120	1	108	5	575	13.1
Totals	115	3453	1347	602	.447	275	207	.753	139	294	433	948	290	2	252	14	1421	12.4

Three-Point Field Goals: 1988-89, 5-for-22 (.227). 1989-90, 5-for-21 (.238). Totals, 10-for-43 (.233).

Named to THE SPORTING NEWS All-America Second Team, 1988.

GREGORY ALAN GRANT
(Greg)

Born August 29, 1966 at Trenton, N.J. Height 5:07. Weight 140.

High School—Trenton, N.J., Central.

Colleges—Morris Brown College, Atlanta, Ga., and Trenton State College, Trenton, N.J.

Drafted by Phoenix on second round, 1989 (52nd pick).

—COLLEGIATE RECORD—

Morris Brown

Year	G.	Min.	FGA	FGM	Pct.	FTA	FTM	Pct.	Reb.	Pts.	Avg.
85-86	Statistics Unavailable										

Trenton State

Year	G.	Min.	FGA	FGM	Pct.	FTA	FTM	Pct.	Reb.	Pts.	Avg.
86-87	26	....	543	263	.484	220	171	.777	104	740	28.5
87-88	27	912	537	302	.562	204	171	.838	69	827	30.6
88-89	32	1077	742	387	.522	239	194	.812	75	1044	32.6
T.S. Totals	85	....	1822	952	.523	663	536	.808	248	2611	30.7

Three-Point Field Goals: 1986-87, 43-for-83 (.518). 1987-88, 52-for-105 (.495). 1988-89, 76-for-186 (.409). Totals, 171-for-374 (.457).

NBA REGULAR SEASON RECORD

									—Rebounds—									
Sea.—Team	G.	Min.	FGA	FGM	Pct.	FTA	FTM	Pct.	Off.	Def.	Tot.	Ast.	PF	Dq.	Stl.	Blk.	Pts.	Avg.
89-90—Phoenix	67	678	216	83	.384	59	39	.661	16	43	59	168	58	0	36	1	208	3.1

Three-Point Field Goals: 1989-90, 3-for-16 (.188).

NBA PLAYOFF RECORD

									—Rebounds—									
Sea.—Team	G.	Min.	FGA	FGM	Pct.	FTA	FTM	Pct.	Off.	Def.	Tot.	Ast.	PF	Dq.	Stl.	Blk.	Pts.	Avg.
89-90—Phoenix	7	47	20	9	.450	0	0	....	2	4	6	10	2	0	2	0	19	2.7

Three-Point Field Goals: 1989-90, 1-for-3 (.333).

Led NCAA Division III in scoring, 1989. . . . Named Outstanding Player in NCAA Division III tournament, 1989.

HARVEY GRANT

Born July 4, 1965 at Augusta, Ga. Height 6:08. Weight 200.

High School—Sparta, Ga., Hancock Central.

Colleges—Clemson University, Clemson, S.C.; Independence Junior College, Independence, Kan., and University of Oklahoma, Norman, Okla.

Drafted by Washington on first round, 1988 (12th pick).

—COLLEGIATE RECORD—

Clemson

Year	G.	Min.	FGA	FGM	Pct.	FTA	FTM	Pct.	Reb.	Pts.	Avg.
83-84				Did Not Play—Red Shirted							
84-85	28	418	121	60	.496	41	24	.585	126	144	5.1

Independence

Year	G.	Min.	FGA	FGM	Pct.	FTA	FTM	Pct.	Reb.	Pts.	Avg.
85-86	33	....	580	340	.586	82	58	.707	388	738	22.4

Oklahoma

Year	G.	Min.	FGA	FGM	Pct.	FTA	FTM	Pct.	Reb.	Pts.	Avg.
86-87	34	1165	427	228	.534	163	119	.730	338	575	16.9
87-88	39	1339	640	350	.547	155	113	.729	365	816	20.9
Okla. Totals	73	2504	1067	578	.542	318	232	.730	703	1391	19.1
College Totals	101	2922	1188	638	.537	359	256	.713	829	1535	15.2

Three-Point Field Goals: 1986-87, 0-for-1. 1987-88, 3-for-14 (.214). Totals, 3-for-15 (.200).

NBA REGULAR SEASON RECORD

									—Rebounds—									
Sea.—Team	G.	Min.	FGA	FGM	Pct.	FTA	FTM	Pct.	Off.	Def.	Tot.	Ast.	PF	Dq.	Stl.	Blk.	Pts.	Avg.
88-89—Washington	71	1193	390	181	.464	57	34	.596	75	88	163	79	147	2	35	29	396	5.6
89-90—Washington	81	1846	601	284	.473	137	96	.701	138	204	342	131	194	1	52	43	664	8.2
Totals	152	3039	991	465	.469	194	130	.670	213	292	505	210	341	3	87	72	1060	7.0

Three-Point Field Goals: 1988-89, 0-for-1. 1989-90, 0-for-8. Totals, 0-for-9.

Twin brother of Chicago Bulls forward Horace Grant.

HORACE JUNIOR GRANT

Born July 4, 1965 at Augusta, Ga. Height 6:10. Weight 220.

High School—Sparta, Ga., Hancock Central.

College—Clemson University, Clemson, S.C.

Drafted by Chicago on first round, 1987 (10th pick).

—COLLEGIATE RECORD—

Year	G.	Min.	FGA	FGM	Pct.	FTA	FTM	Pct.	Reb.	Pts.	Avg.
83-84	28	551	120	64	.533	43	32	.744	129	160	5.7
84-85	29	703	238	132	.555	102	65	.637	196	329	11.3
85-86	34	1099	356	208	.584	193	140	.725	357	556	16.4
86-87	31	1010	390	256	.656	195	138	.708	299	651	21.0
Totals	122	3363	1104	660	.598	533	375	.704	981	1696	13.9

Three-Point Field Goals: 1986-87, 1-for-2 (.500).

NBA REGULAR SEASON RECORD

									—Rebounds—									
Sea.—Team	G.	Min.	FGA	FGM	Pct.	FTA	FTM	Pct.	Off.	Def.	Tot.	Ast.	PF	Dq.	Stl.	Blk.	Pts.	Avg.
87-88—Chicago	81	1827	507	254	.501	182	114	.626	155	292	447	89	221	3	51	53	622	7.7
88-89—Chicago	79	2809	781	405	.519	199	140	.704	240	441	681	168	251	1	86	62	950	12.0
89-90—Chicago	80	2753	853	446	.523	256	179	.699	236	393	629	227	230	1	92	84	1071	13.4
Totals	240	7389	2141	1105	.516	637	433	.680	631	1126	1757	484	702	5	229	199	2643	11.0

Three-Point Field Goals: 1987-88, 0-for-2. 1988-89, 0-for-5. Totals, 0-for-7.

NBA PLAYOFF RECORD

									—Rebounds—									
Sea.—Team	G.	Min.	FGA	FGM	Pct.	FTA	FTM	Pct.	Off.	Def.	Tot.	Ast.	PF	Dq.	Stl.	Blk.	Pts.	Avg.
87-88—Chicago	10	299	81	46	.568	15	9	.600	25	45	70	16	35	2	14	2	101	10.1
88-89—Chicago	17	625	139	72	.518	50	40	.800	53	114	167	35	68	2	11	16	184	10.8
89-90—Chicago	16	616	159	81	.509	53	33	.623	73	86	159	40	51	1	18	18	195	12.2
Totals	43	1540	379	199	.525	118	82	.695	151	245	396	91	154	5	43	36	480	11.2

Three-Point Field Goals: 1987-88, 0-for-1. 1989-90, 0-for-2. Totals, 0-for-3.

Twin brother of Washington Bullets forward Harvey Grant.

STUART ALLAN GRAY

Born May 27, 1963 in the Panama Canal Zone. Height 7:00. Weight 245.
High School—Granada Hills, Calif., Kennedy.
College—University of California at Los Angeles, Los Angeles, Calif.
Drafted by Indiana on second round as an undergraduate, 1984 (29th pick).

Traded by Indiana to Charlotte for draft rights to Dyron Nix, June 27, 1989.
Traded by Charlotte to New York for a 1991 2nd round draft choice, February 22, 1990.

—COLLEGIATE RECORD—

Year	G.	Min.	FGA	FGM	Pct.	FTA	FTM	Pct.	Reb.	Pts.	Avg.
81-82	27	589	111	57	.514	44	19	.432	129	133	4.9
82-83	23	570	134	78	.582	45	20	.444	158	176	7.7
83-84	28	860	177	107	.605	90	62	.689	220	276	9.9
Totals	78	2019	422	242	.573	179	101	.564	507	585	7.5

NBA REGULAR SEASON RECORD

									—Rebounds—									
Sea.—Team	G.	Min.	FGA	FGM	Pct.	FTA	FTM	Pct.	Off.	Def.	Tot.	Ast.	PF	Dq.	Stl.	Blk.	Pts.	Avg.
84-85—Indiana	52	391	92	35	.380	47	32	.681	29	94	123	15	82	1	9	14	102	2.0
85-86—Indiana	67	423	108	54	.500	74	47	.635	45	73	118	15	94	0	8	11	155	2.3
86-87—Indiana	55	456	101	41	.406	39	28	.718	39	90	129	26	93	0	10	28	110	2.0
87-88—Indiana	74	807	193	90	.466	73	44	.603	70	180	250	44	152	1	11	32	224	3.0
88-89—Indiana	72	783	153	72	.471	64	44	.688	84	161	245	29	128	0	11	21	188	2.6
89-90—Char.-N.Y.	58	560	99	42	.424	47	32	.681	40	105	145	19	90	0	15	26	116	2.0
Totals	378	3420	746	334	.448	344	227	.660	307	703	1010	148	639	2	64	132	895	2.4

Three-Point Field Goals: 1987-88, 0-for-1. 1988-89, 0-for-1. 1989-90, 0-for-5. Totals, 0-for-7.

NBA PLAYOFF RECORD

									—Rebounds—									
Sea.—Team	G.	Min.	FGA	FGM	Pct.	FTA	FTM	Pct.	Off.	Def.	Tot.	Ast.	PF	Dq.	Stl.	Blk.	Pts.	Avg.
86-87—Indiana	3	14	1	0	.000	4	2	.500	2	5	7	0	3	0	0	0	2	0.7
89-90—New York	4	12	5	2	.400	0	0	....	3	5	8	0	3	0	1	0	4	1.0
Totals	7	26	6	2	.333	4	2	.500	5	10	15	0	6	0	1	0	6	0.9

JEFFREY GRAYER
(Jeff)

Born December 17, 1965 at Flint, Mich. Height 6:05. Weight 200.
High School—Flint, Mich., Northwestern.
College—Iowa State University, Ames, Iowa.
Drafted by Milwaukee on first round, 1988 (13th pick).

—COLLEGIATE RECORD—

Year	G.	Min.	FGA	FGM	Pct.	FTA	FTM	Pct.	Reb.	Pts.	Avg.
84-85	33	1119	289	153	.529	147	96	.653	213	402	12.2
85-86	33	1159	514	281	.547	194	122	.629	208	684	20.7
86-87	27	995	452	228	.504	192	142	.740	189	605	22.4
87-88	32	1165	597	312	.523	235	167	.711	300	811	25.3
Totals	125	4438	1852	974	.526	768	527	.686	910	2502	20.0

Three-Point Field Goals: 1986-87, 7-for-21 (.333). 1987-88, 20-for-61 (.328). Totals, 27-for-82 (.329).

NBA REGULAR SEASON RECORD

									—Rebounds—									
Sea.—Team	G.	Min.	FGA	FGM	Pct.	FTA	FTM	Pct.	Off.	Def.	Tot.	Ast.	PF	Dq.	Stl.	Blk.	Pts.	Avg.
88-89—Milwaukee	11	200	73	32	.438	20	17	.850	14	21	35	22	15	0	10	1	81	7.4
89-90—Milwaukee	71	1427	487	224	.460	152	99	.651	94	123	217	107	125	0	48	10	548	7.7
Totals	82	1627	560	256	.457	172	116	.674	108	144	252	129	140	0	58	11	629	7.7

Three-Point Field Goals: 1988-89, 0-for-2. 1989-90, 1-for-8 (.125). Totals, 1-for-10 (.100).

NBA PLAYOFF RECORD

									—Rebounds—									
Sea.—Team	G.	Min.	FGA	FGM	Pct.	FTA	FTM	Pct.	Off.	Def.	Tot.	Ast.	PF	Dq.	Stl.	Blk.	Pts.	Avg.
89-90—Milwaukee	4	12	0	0	....	0	0	....	0	2	2	1	1	0	0	0	0	0.0

Member of U.S. Olympic team, 1988.

A. C. GREEN JR.

Born October 4, 1963 at Portland, Ore. Height 6:09. Weight 224.

High School—Portland, Ore., Benson.

College—Oregon State University, Corvallis, Ore.

Drafted by Los Angeles Lakers on first round, 1985 (23rd pick).

—COLLEGIATE RECORD—

Year	G.	Min.	FGA	FGM	Pct.	FTA	FTM	Pct.	Reb.	Pts.	Avg.
81-82	30	895	161	99	.615	100	61	.610	158	259	8.6
82-83	31	1113	290	162	.559	161	111	.689	235	435	14.0
83-84	23	853	204	134	.657	183	141	.770	201	409	17.8
84-85	31	1191	362	217	.599	231	157	.680	286	591	19.1
Totals	115	4052	1017	612	.602	675	470	.696	880	1694	14.7

NBA REGULAR SEASON RECORD

									—Rebounds—									
Sea.—Team	G.	Min.	FGA	FGM	Pct.	FTA	FTM	Pct.	Off.	Def.	Tot.	Ast.	PF	Dq.	Stl.	Blk.	Pts.	Avg.
85-86—L.A. Lakers	82	1542	388	209	.539	167	102	.611	160	221	381	54	229	2	49	49	521	6.4
86-87—L.A. Lakers	79	2240	587	316	.538	282	220	.780	210	405	615	84	171	0	70	80	852	10.8
87-88—L.A. Lakers	82	2636	640	322	.503	379	293	.773	245	465	710	93	204	0	87	45	937	11.4
88-89—L.A. Lakers	82	2510	758	401	.529	359	282	.786	258	481	739	103	172	0	94	55	1088	13.3
89-90—L.A. Lakers	82	2709	806	385	.478	370	278	.751	262	450	712	90	207	0	66	50	1061	12.9
Totals	407	11637	3179	1633	.514	1557	1175	.755	1135	2022	3157	424	983	2	366	279	4459	11.0

Three-Point Field Goals: 1985-86, 1-for-6 (.167). 1986-87, 0-for-5. 1987-88, 0-for-2. 1988-89, 4-for-17 (.235). 1989-90, 13-for-46 (.283). Totals, 18-for-76 (.237).

NBA PLAYOFF RECORD

									—Rebounds—									
Sea.—Team	G.	Min.	FGA	FGM	Pct.	FTA	FTM	Pct.	Off.	Def.	Tot.	Ast.	PF	Dq.	Stl.	Blk.	Pts.	Avg.
85-86—L.A. Lakers	9	106	17	9	.529	9	4	.444	3	13	16	0	13	0	1	3	22	2.4
86-87—L.A. Lakers	18	505	130	71	.546	87	65	.747	54	88	142	11	47	0	9	8	207	11.5
87-88—L.A. Lakers	24	726	169	92	.544	73	55	.753	57	118	175	20	61	0	11	12	239	10.0
88-89—L.A. Lakers	15	502	114	47	.412	76	58	.763	38	99	137	18	37	1	16	6	152	10.1
89-90—L.A. Lakers	9	252	79	41	.519	32	24	.750	34	47	81	9	22	0	5	4	106	11.8
Totals	75	2091	509	260	.511	277	206	.744	186	365	551	58	180	1	42	33	726	9.7

Three-Point Field Goals: 1988-89, 0-for-3.

NBA ALL-STAR GAME RECORD

								—Rebounds—							
Season—Team	Min.	FGA	FGM	Pct.	FTA	FTM	Pct.	Off.	Def.	Tot.	Ast.	PF	Dq.	Stl.	Blk.	Pts.
1990—L.A. Lakers	12	3	0	.000	0	0	....	0	3	3	1	1	0	0	1	0

Named to NBA All-Defensive Second Team, 1989. . . . Member of NBA championship teams, 1987 and 1988.

RICKEY GREEN

Born August 18, 1954 at Chicago, Ill. Height 6:00. Weight 172.

High School—Chicago, Ill., Hirsch.

Colleges—Vincennes University, Vincennes, Ind., and University of Michigan, Ann Arbor, Mich.

Drafted by Golden State on first round, 1977 (16th pick).

Traded by Golden State to Detroit for a 1980 2nd round draft choice, October 9, 1978.
Waived by Detroit, December 11, 1978; signed by Chicago as a free agent, August 12, 1980.
Waived by Chicago, October 8, 1980; signed by Utah as a free agent, December 2, 1980.
Selected from Utah by Charlotte in NBA expansion draft, June 23, 1988.

Waived by Charlotte, February 22, 1989; signed by Milwaukee as a free agent, March 1, 1989.
Signed by Indiana as an unrestricted free agent, 1989.
Played in Continental Basketball Association with Hawaii and Billings Volcanos, 1979-80 and 1980-81.

—COLLEGIATE RECORD—

Vincennes

Year	G.	Min.	FGA	FGM	Pct.	FTA	FTM	Pct.	Reb.	Pts.	Avg.
73-74	36	....	633	254	.401	163	114	.699	237	622	17.3
74-75	32	....	600	302	.503	105	69	.657	208	673	21.0
JC Totals	68	....	1233	556	.451	268	183	.683	445	1295	19.0

Michigan

Year	G.	Min.	FGA	FGM	Pct.	FTA	FTM	Pct.	Reb.	Pts.	Avg.
75-76	32	....	542	266	.491	135	106	.785	117	638	19.9
76-77	28	....	464	224	.483	128	98	.766	81	546	19.5
Totals	60	....	1006	490	.487	263	204	.776	198	1184	19.7

CBA REGULAR SEASON RECORD

			—2-Point—			—3-Point—									
Sea.—Team	G.	Min.	FGM	FGA	Pct.	FGM	FGA	Pct.	FTM	FTA	Pct.	Reb.	Ast.	Pts.	Avg.
79-80—Hawaii	44	1753	408	824	.495	3	17	.176	155	205	.756	188	345	980	22.3
80-81—Billings	5	197	47	95	.494	0	1	.000	19	24	.791	22	32	113	22.6
Totals	49	1950	455	919	.495	3	18	.167	174	229	.760	210	377	1093	22.3

NBA REGULAR SEASON RECORD

									—Rebounds—									
Sea.—Team	G.	Min.	FGA	FGM	Pct.	FTA	FTM	Pct.	Off.	Def.	Tot.	Ast.	PF	Dq.	Stl.	Blk.	Pts.	Avg.
77-78—Golden State	76	1098	375	143	.381	90	54	.600	49	67	116	149	95	0	58	1	340	4.5
78-79—Detroit	27	431	177	67	.379	67	45	.672	15	25	40	63	37	0	25	1	179	6.6
80-81—Utah	47	1307	366	176	.481	97	70	.722	30	86	116	235	123	2	75	1	422	9.0
81-82—Utah	81	2822	1015	500	.493	264	202	.765	85	158	243	630	183	0	185	9	1202	14.8
82-83—Utah	78	2783	942	464	.493	232	185	.797	62	161	223	697	154	0	220	4	1115	14.3
83-84—Utah	81	2768	904	439	.486	234	192	.821	56	174	230	748	155	1	215	13	1072	13.2
84-85—Utah	77	2431	798	381	.477	267	232	.869	37	152	189	597	131	0	132	3	1000	13.0
85-86—Utah	80	2012	758	357	.471	250	213	.852	32	103	135	411	130	0	106	6	932	11.7
86-87—Utah	81	2090	644	301	.467	208	172	.827	38	125	163	541	108	0	110	2	781	9.6
87-88—Utah	81	1116	370	157	.424	83	75	.904	14	66	80	300	83	0	57	1	393	4.9
88-89—Char.-Milw.	63	871	264	129	.489	33	30	.909	11	58	69	187	35	0	40	2	291	4.6
89-90—Indiana	69	927	231	100	.433	51	43	.843	9	45	54	182	60	0	51	1	244	3.5
Totals	841	20656	6844	3214	.470	1876	1513	.807	438	1220	1658	4740	1294	3	1274	44	7971	9.5

Three-Point Field Goals: 1980-81, 0-for-1. 1981-82, 0-for-8. 1982-83, 2-for-13 (.154). 1983-84, 2-for-17 (.118). 1984-85, 6-for-20 (.300). 1985-86, 5-for-29 (.172). 1986-87, 7-for-19 (.368). 1987-88, 4-for-19 (.211). 1988-89, 3-for-11 (.273). 1989-90, 1-for-11 (.091). Totals, 30-for-148 (.203).

NBA PLAYOFF RECORD

									—Rebounds—									
Sea.—Team	G.	Min.	FGA	FGM	Pct.	FTA	FTM	Pct.	Off.	Def.	Tot.	Ast.	PF	Dq.	Stl.	Blk.	Pts.	Avg.
83-84—Utah	11	404	151	64	.424	43	32	.744	9	25	34	104	17	0	19	4	161	14.6
84-85—Utah	10	302	106	57	.538	38	35	.921	10	20	30	75	23	0	12	0	150	15.0
85-86—Utah	4	119	43	21	.488	11	10	.909	0	9	9	38	1	0	2	0	53	13.3
86-87—Utah	4	72	23	11	.478	6	5	.833	1	7	8	25	5	0	2	0	27	6.8
87-88—Utah	7	38	8	2	.250	0	0	.000	0	1	1	9	2	0	2	0	4	0.6
88-89—Milwaukee	8	110	29	12	.414	4	4	1.000	3	10	13	18	9	0	5	0	29	3.6
89-90—Indiana	3	31	7	1	.143	0	0	......	0	1	1	3	5	0	1	0	2	0.7
Totals	47	1076	367	168	.458	102	86	.843	23	73	96	272	62	0	43	4	426	9.1

Three-Point Field Goals: 1983-84, 1-for-4 (.250). 1984-85, 1-for-7 (.143). 1985-86, 1-for-2 (.500). 1986-87, 0-for-1. 1988-89, 1-for-2 (.500). Totals, 4-for-16 (.250).

NBA ALL-STAR GAME RECORD

								—Rebounds—							
Season—Team	Min.	FGA	FGM	Pct.	FTA	FTM	Pct.	Off.	Def.	Tot.	Ast.	PF	Dq.	Stl.	Blk.	Pts.
1984—Utah	19	8	3	.375	0	0	.000	0	0	0	11	1	0	1	0	6

Led NBA in steals, 1984. . . . Named to THE SPORTING NEWS All-America First Team, 1977.

SIDNEY GREEN

Born January 4, 1961 at Brooklyn, N. Y. Height 6:09. Weight 220.
High School—Brooklyn, N. Y., Jefferson.
College—University of Nevada at Las Vegas, Las Vegas, Nev.
Drafted by Chicago on first round, 1983 (5th pick).

Traded by Chicago to Detroit for Earl Cureton and a 1987 2nd round draft choice, August 21, 1986.
Traded by Detroit to New York for Ron Moore and a 1988 2nd round draft choice, October 29, 1987.
Selected from New York by Orlando in NBA expansion draft, June 15, 1989.

—COLLEGIATE RECORD—

Year	G.	Min.	FGA	FGM	Pct.	FTA	FTM	Pct.	Reb.	Pts.	Avg.
79-80	32	1024	388	201	.518	132	96	.727	354	498	15.6
80-81	26	817	297	153	.515	120	85	.708	284	391	15.0
81-82	30	963	374	200	.535	130	100	.769	270	500	16.7
82-83	31	1120	491	269	.548	203	142	.700	368	684	22.1
Totals	119	3924	1550	823	.531	585	423	.723	1276	2073	17.4

Three-Point Field Goals: 1982-83, 4-for-12 (.333).

NBA REGULAR SEASON RECORD

									—Rebounds—									
Sea.—Team	G.	Min.	FGA	FGM	Pct.	FTA	FTM	Pct.	Off.	Def.	Tot.	Ast.	PF	Dq.	Stl.	Blk.	Pts.	Avg.
83-84—Chicago	49	667	228	100	.439	77	55	.714	58	116	174	25	128	1	18	17	255	5.2
84-85—Chicago	48	740	250	108	.432	98	79	.806	72	174	246	29	102	0	11	11	295	6.1
85-86—Chicago	80	2307	875	407	.465	335	262	.782	208	450	658	139	292	5	70	37	1076	13.5
86-87—Detroit	80	1792	542	256	.472	177	119	.672	196	457	653	62	197	0	41	50	631	7.9
87-88—New York	82	2049	585	258	.441	190	126	.663	221	421	642	93	318	9	65	32	642	7.8
88-89—New York	82	1277	422	194	.460	170	129	.759	157	237	394	76	172	0	47	18	517	6.3
89-90—Orlando	73	1860	667	312	.468	209	136	.651	166	422	588	99	231	4	50	26	761	10.4
Totals	494	10692	3569	1635	.458	1256	906	.721	1078	2277	3355	523	1440	19	302	191	4177	8.5

Three-Point Field Goals: 1984-85, 0-for-4, 1985-86, 0-for-8. 1986-87, 0-for-2. 1987-88, 0-for-2. 1988-89, 0-for-3. 1989-90, 1-for-3 (.333). Totals, 1-for-22 (.045).

NBA PLAYOFF RECORD

									—Rebounds—									
Sea.—Team	G.	Min.	FGA	FGM	Pct.	FTA	FTM	Pct.	Off.	Def.	Tot.	Ast.	PF	Dq.	Stl.	Blk.	Pts.	Avg.
84-85—Chicago	3	54	24	12	.500	11	7	.636	10	5	15	2	8	0	0	1	31	10.3
85-86—Chicago	3	53	20	6	.300	12	6	.500	7	5	12	0	9	0	1	1	18	6.0
86-87—Detroit	9	42	10	6	.600	6	5	.833	3	6	9	1	2	0	1	2	17	1.9
87-88—New York	4	93	17	8	.471	0	0	.000	8	25	33	7	14	0	0	1	16	4.0
88-89—New York	9	128	30	13	.433	14	10	.714	14	22	36	5	23	0	2	1	36	4.0
Totals	28	370	101	45	.446	43	28	.651	42	63	105	15	56	0	4	6	118	4.2

Named to THE SPORTING NEWS All-America Second Team, 1983.

DAVID KASIM GREENWOOD
(Dave)

Born May 27, 1957 at Lynwood, Calif. Height 6:09. Weight 225.
High School—Los Angeles, Calif., Verbum Dei.
College—University of California at Los Angeles, Los Angeles, Calif.
Drafted by Chicago on first round, 1979 (2nd pick).

Traded by Chicago to San Antonio for George Gervin, October 24, 1985.
Traded by San Antonio with Darwin Cook to Denver for Jay Vincent and Calvin Natt, January 26, 1989.
Signed by Detroit as an unrestricted free agent, October 6, 1989.

—COLLEGIATE RECORD—

Year	G.	Min.	FGA	FGM	Pct.	FTA	FTM	Pct.	Reb.	Pts.	Avg.
75-76	31	403	122	62	.508	35	28	.800	114	152	4.9
76-77	29	979	395	202	.511	112	80	.714	280	484	16.7
77-78	28	978	364	196	.538	133	97	.729	319	489	17.5
78-79	30	1069	421	247	.587	126	102	.810	309	596	19.9
Totals	118	3439	1302	707	.543	406	307	.756	1022	1721	14.6

NBA REGULAR SEASON RECORD

									—Rebounds—									
Sea.—Team	G.	Min.	FGA	FGM	Pct.	FTA	FTM	Pct.	Off.	Def.	Tot.	Ast.	PF	Dq.	Stl.	Blk.	Pts.	Avg.
79-80—Chicago	82	2791	1051	498	.474	416	337	.810	223	550	773	182	313	8	60	129	1334	16.3
80-81—Chicago	82	2710	989	481	.486	290	217	.748	243	481	724	218	282	5	77	124	1179	14.4
81-82—Chicago	82	2914	1014	480	.473	291	240	.825	192	594	786	262	292	1	70	93	1200	14.6
82-83—Chicago	79	2355	686	312	.455	233	165	.708	217	548	765	151	261	5	54	90	789	10.0
83-84—Chicago	78	2718	753	369	.490	289	213	.737	214	572	786	139	265	9	67	72	951	12.2
84-85—Chicago	61	1523	332	152	.458	94	67	.713	108	280	388	78	190	1	34	21	371	6.1
85-86—San Antonio	68	1910	388	198	.510	184	142	.772	151	380	531	90	207	3	37	52	538	7.9
86-87—San Antonio	79	2587	655	336	.513	307	241	.785	256	527	783	237	248	3	71	50	916	11.6
87-88—San Antonio	45	1236	328	151	.460	111	83	.748	92	208	300	97	134	2	33	22	385	8.6
88-89—S.A.-Den.	67	1403	395	167	.423	176	132	.750	140	262	402	96	201	5	47	52	466	7.0
89-90—Detroit	37	205	52	22	.423	29	16	.552	24	54	78	12	40	0	4	9	60	1.6
Totals	760	22352	6643	3166	.477	2420	1853	.766	1860	4456	6316	1562	2433	42	554	714	8189	10.8

Three-Point Field Goals: 1979-80, 1-for-7 (.143). 1980-81, 0-for-2. 1981-82, 0-for-3. 1982-83, 0-for-4. 1983-84, 0-for-1. 1984-85, 0-for-1. 1985-86, 0-for-1. 1986-87, 3-for-6 (.500). 1987-88, 0-for-2. Totals, 4-for-27 (.148).

NBA PLAYOFF RECORD

									—Rebounds—									
Sea.—Team	G.	Min.	FGA	FGM	Pct.	FTA	FTM	Pct.	Off.	Def.	Tot.	Ast.	PF	Dq.	Stl.	Blk.	Pts.	Avg.
80-81—Chicago	6	212	87	51	.586	12	5	.417	16	28	44	11	26	0	9	5	107	17.8
84-85—Chicago	4	139	28	15	.536	10	8	.800	10	21	31	5	14	0	6	4	38	9.5
85-86—San Antonio	3	101	23	12	.522	8	6	.750	1	17	18	3	12	0	3	1	30	10.0
88-89—Denver	3	34	6	2	.333	2	1	.500	2	9	11	1	7	0	1	1	5	1.7
89-90—Detroit	5	47	4	2	.500	4	1	.250	2	7	9	0	11	0	2	0	5	1.0
Totals	21	533	148	82	.554	36	21	.583	31	82	113	20	70	0	21	11	185	8.8

Three-Point Field Goals: 1980-81, 0-for-2.

Named to NBA All-Rookie Team, 1980. . . . Member of NBA championship team, 1990. . . . THE SPORTING NEWS All-America Second Team, 1979.

DARRELL STEVEN GRIFFITH

Born June 16, 1958 at Louisville, Ky. Height 6:04. Weight 195.

High School—Louisville, Ky., Male.

College—University of Louisville, Louisville, Ky.

Drafted by Utah on first round, 1980 (2nd pick).

Missed entire 1985-86 season due to injury.

—COLLEGIATE RECORD—

Year	G.	Min.	FGA	FGM	Pct.	FTA	FTM	Pct.	Reb.	Pts.	Avg.
76-77	28	652	299	150	.502	93	59	.634	109	359	12.8
77-78	30	996	460	240	.522	110	78	.709	162	558	18.6
78-79	32	1001	487	242	.497	151	107	.709	140	591	18.5
79-80	36	1246	631	349	.553	178	127	.713	174	825	22.9
Totals	126	3895	1877	981	.523	532	371	.697	585	2333	18.5

NBA REGULAR SEASON RECORD

									—Rebounds—									
Sea.—Team	G.	Min.	FGA	FGM	Pct.	FTA	FTM	Pct.	Off.	Def.	Tot.	Ast.	PF	Dq.	Stl.	Blk.	Pts.	Avg.
80-81—Utah	81	2867	1544	716	.464	320	229	.716	79	209	288	194	219	0	106	40	1671	20.6
81-82—Utah	80	2597	1429	689	.482	271	189	.697	128	177	305	187	213	0	95	34	1582	19.8
82-83—Utah	77	2787	1554	752	.484	246	167	.679	100	204	304	270	184	0	138	33	1709	22.2
83-84—Utah	82	2650	1423	697	.490	217	151	.696	95	243	338	283	202	1	114	23	1636	20.0
84-85—Utah	78	2776	1593	728	.457	298	216	.725	124	220	344	243	178	1	133	30	1764	22.6
86-87—Utah	76	1843	1038	463	.446	212	149	.703	81	146	227	129	167	0	97	29	1142	150
87-88—Utah	52	1052	585	251	.429	92	59	.641	36	91	127	91	102	0	52	5	589	11.3
88-89—Utah	82	2382	1045	466	.446	182	142	.780	77	253	330	130	175	0	86	22	1135	13.8
89-90—Utah	82	1444	649	301	.464	78	51	.654	43	123	166	63	149	0	68	19	733	8.9
Totals	690	20398	10860	5063	.466	1916	1353	.706	763	1666	2429	1590	1589	2	889	235	11961	17.3

Three-Point Field Goals: 1980-81, 10-for-52 (.192). 1981-82, 15-for-52 (.288). 1982-83, 38-for-132 (.288). 1983-84, 91-for-252 (.361). 1984-85, 92-for-257 (.358). 1986-87, 67-for-200 (.335). 1987-88, 28-for-102 (.275). 1988-89, 61-for-196 (.311). 1989-90, 80-for-215 (.372). Totals, 482-for-1458 (.331).

NBA PLAYOFF RECORD

									—Rebounds—									
Sea.—Team	G.	Min.	FGA	FGM	Pct.	FTA	FTM	Pct.	Off.	Def.	Tot.	Ast.	PF	Dq.	Stl.	Blk.	Pts.	Avg.
83-84—Utah	11	417	183	81	.443	48	33	.688	16	49	65	41	24	0	19	2	211	19.2
84-85—Utah	10	340	158	72	.456	25	18	.720	6	23	29	25	21	0	12	5	175	17.5
86-87—Utah	5	104	65	24	.369	19	14	.737	5	7	12	8	5	0	6	2	68	13.6
88-89—Utah	3	71	49	20	.408	0	0	....	3	9	12	0	7	0	4	1	46	15.3
89-90—Utah	5	97	42	19	.452	5	4	.800	6	15	21	3	3	0	6	1	47	9.4
Totals	34	1029	497	216	.435	97	69	.711	36	103	139	77	60	0	47	11	547	16.1

Three-Point Field Goals: 1983-84, 16-for-45 (.356). 1984-85, 13-for-36 (.361). 1986-87, 6-for-15 (.400). 1988-89, 6-for-19 (.316). 1989-90, 5-for-9 (.556). Totals, 46-for-124 (.371).

Named NBA Rookie of the Year, 1981. . . . NBA All-Rookie Team, 1981. . . . Led NBA in three-point field goal percentage, 1984 and 1985. . . . THE SPORTING NEWS College Player of the Year, 1980. . . . THE SPORTING NEWS All-America First Team, 1979 and 1980. . . . THE SPORTING NEWS All-America Second Team, 1978. . . . NCAA Division I Tournament Most Outstanding Player, 1980. . . . Member of NCAA Division I championship team, 1980.

SCOTT RICHARD HAFFNER

Born February 2, 1966 at Terre Haute, Ind. Height 6:03. Weight 180.

High School—Noblesville, Ind.

Colleges—University of Illinois, Champaign, Ill., and University of Evansville, Evansville, Ind.

Drafted by Miami on second round, 1989 (45th pick).

—COLLEGIATE RECORD—

Illinois

Year	G.	Min.	FGA	FGM	Pct.	FTA	FTM	Pct.	Reb.	Pts.	Avg.
84-85	29	201	62	20	.323	16	9	.563	16	49	1.7

Evansville

Year	G.	Min.	FGA	FGM	Pct.	FTA	FTM	Pct.	Reb.	Pts.	Avg.
85-86	Did Not Play—Transfer Student										
86-87	27	1010	382	165	.432	88	80	.909	90	483	17.9
87-88	29	1017	313	144	.460	96	81	.844	96	443	15.3
88-89	31	1124	489	263	.538	151	136	.901	137	760	24.5
Evan. Totals	87	3151	1184	572	.483	335	297	.887	323	1686	19.4
Col. Totals	116	3352	1246	592	.475	351	306	.872	339	1735	15.0

Three-Point Field Goals: 1986-87, 73-for-192 (.380). 1987-88, 74-for-163 (.454). 1988-89, 98-for-214 (.458). Totals, 245-for-569 (.431).

NBA REGULAR SEASON RECORD

									—Rebounds—									
Sea.—Team	G.	Min.	FGA	FGM	Pct.	FTA	FTM	Pct.	Off.	Def.	Tot.	Ast.	PF	Dq.	Stl.	Blk.	Pts.	Avg.
89-90—Miami	43	559	217	88	.406	25	17	.680	7	44	51	80	53	0	13	2	196	4.6

Three-Point Field Goals: 1989-90, 3-for-21 (.143).

JACK KEVIN HALEY

Born January 27, 1964 at Long Beach, Calif. Height 6:10. Weight 240.

High School—Huntington Beach, Calif.

Colleges—Golden West College, Huntington Beach, Calif., and University of California at Los Angeles, Los Angeles, Calif.

Drafted by Chicago on fourth round, 1987 (79th pick).

Waived by Chicago, December 18, 1989; claimed off waivers by New Jersey, December 20, 1989.

—COLLEGIATE RECORD—

Golden West

Year	G.	Min.	FGA	FGM	Pct.	FTA	FTM	Pct.	Reb.	Pts.	Avg.
82-83	Did Not Play										
83-84	Statistics Unavailable										

UCLA

Year	G.	Min.	FGA	FGM	Pct.	FTA	FTM	Pct.	Reb.	Pts.	Avg.
84-85	25	125	22	9	.409	17	7	.412	42	25	1.0
85-86	29	709	108	41	.380	61	44	.721	183	126	4.3
86-87	32	740	122	57	.467	84	52	.619	151	166	5.2
Totals	86	1574	252	107	.425	162	103	.636	376	317	3.7

NBA REGULAR SEASON RECORD

									—Rebounds—									
Sea.—Team	G.	Min.	FGA	FGM	Pct.	FTA	FTM	Pct.	Off.	Def.	Tot.	Ast.	PF	Dq.	Stl.	Blk.	Pts.	Avg.
88-89—Chicago	51	289	78	37	.474	46	36	.783	21	50	71	10	56	0	11	0	110	2.2
89-90—Chi.-N.J.	67	1084	347	138	.398	125	85	.680	115	185	300	26	170	1	18	12	361	5.4
Totals	118	1373	425	175	.412	171	121	.708	136	235	371	36	226	1	29	12	471	4.0

Three-Point Field Goals: 1989-90, 0-for-1.

NBA PLAYOFF RECORD

									—Rebounds—									
Sea.—Team	G.	Min.	FGA	FGM	Pct.	FTA	FTM	Pct.	Off.	Def.	Tot.	Ast.	PF	Dq.	Stl.	Blk.	Pts.	Avg.
88-89—Chicago	5	7	3	2	.667	2	1	.500	0	1	1	1	2	0	0	0	5	1.0

TOM EDWARD HAMMONDS

Born March 27, 1967 at Fort Walton, Fla. Height 6:09. Weight 215.

High School—Crestview, Fla.

College—Georgia Institute of Technology, Atlanta, Ga.

Drafted by Washington on first round, 1989 (9th pick).

—COLLEGIATE RECORD—

Year	G.	Min.	FGA	FGM	Pct.	FTA	FTM	Pct.	Reb.	Pts.	Avg.
85-86	34	1112	276	168	.609	98	80	.816	219	416	12.2
86-87	29	1088	362	206	.569	74	59	.797	208	471	16.2
87-88	30	1076	403	229	.568	132	109	.826	216	567	18.9
88-89	30	1111	465	250	.538	163	126	.773	242	627	20.9
Totals	123	4387	1506	853	.566	467	374	.801	885	2081	16.9

Three-Point Field Goals: 1988-89, 1-for-3 (.333).

NBA REGULAR SEASON RECORD

Sea.—Team	G.	Min.	FGA	FGM	Pct.	FTA	FTM	Pct.	—Rebounds— Off.	Def.	Tot.	Ast.	PF	Dq.	Stl.	Blk.	Pts.	Avg.
89-90—Washington	61	805	295	129	.437	98	63	.643	61	107	168	51	98	0	11	14	321	5.3

Three-Point Field Goals: 1989-90, 0-for-1.

ROBERT LOUIS HANSEN II
(Bob)

Born January 18, 1961 at Des Moines, Iowa. Height 6:06. Weight 200.
High School—Des Moines, Iowa, Dowling.
College—University of Iowa, Iowa City, Iowa.
Drafted by Utah on third round, 1983 (54th pick).

Traded by Utah with Eric Leckner and 1990 1st and 2nd round draft choices to Sacramento in three-way deal that sent Jeff Malone from Washington to Utah and Pervis Ellison from Sacramento to Washington, June 25, 1990. Utah also received a 1990 2nd round draft choice and Sacramento also received a 1991 2nd round draft choice.

—COLLEGIATE RECORD—

Year	G.	Min.	FGA	FGM	Pct.	FTA	FTM	Pct.	Reb.	Pts.	Avg.
79-80	33	....	167	71	.425	73	43	.589	67	185	5.6
80-81	22	....	156	70	.449	53	45	.849	75	185	8.4
81-82	25	....	237	117	.494	93	65	.699	102	299	12.0
82-83	31	....	378	184	.487	129	98	.760	166	476	15.4
Totals	111	....	938	442	.471	388	251	.647	410	1145	10.3

Three-Point Field Goals: 1982-83, 10-for-20 (.500).

NBA REGULAR SEASON RECORD

Sea.—Team	G.	Min.	FGA	FGM	Pct.	FTA	FTM	Pct.	—Rebounds— Off.	Def.	Tot.	Ast.	PF	Dq.	Stl.	Blk.	Pts.	Avg.
83-84—Utah	55	419	145	65	.448	28	18	.643	13	35	48	44	62	0	15	4	148	2.7
84-85—Utah	54	646	225	110	.489	72	40	.556	20	50	70	75	88	0	25	1	261	4.8
85-86—Utah	82	2032	628	299	.476	132	95	.720	82	162	244	193	205	1	74	9	710	8.7
86-87—Utah	72	1453	601	272	.453	179	136	.760	84	119	203	102	146	0	44	6	696	9.7
87-88—Utah	81	1796	611	316	.517	152	113	.743	64	123	187	175	193	2	65	5	777	9.6
88-89—Utah	46	964	300	140	.467	75	42	.560	29	99	128	50	105	0	37	6	341	7.4
89-90—Utah	81	2174	568	265	.467	64	33	.516	66	163	229	149	194	2	52	11	617	7.6
Totals	471	9484	3078	1467	.477	702	477	.679	358	751	1109	788	993	5	312	42	3550	7.5

Three-Point Field Goals: 1983-84, 0-for-8. 1984-85, 1-for-7 (.143). 1985-86, 17-for-50 (.340). 1986-87, 16-for-45 (.356). 1987-88, 32-for-97 (.330). 1988-89, 19-for-54 (.352). 1989-90, 54-for-154 (.351). Totals, 139-for-415 (.335).

NBA PLAYOFF RECORD

Sea.—Team	G.	Min.	FGA	FGM	Pct.	FTA	FTM	Pct.	—Rebounds— Off.	Def.	Tot.	Ast.	PF	Dq.	Stl.	Blk.	Pts.	Avg.
83-84—Utah	4	18	7	2	.286	2	1	.500	2	5	7	2	4	0	0	0	7	1.8
84-85—Utah	8	34	8	2	.250	8	5	.625	1	3	4	6	6	0	3	0	9	1.1
85-86—Utah	4	140	37	27	.730	9	8	.889	10	8	18	11	16	0	3	1	64	16.0
86-87—Utah	5	142	49	21	.429	20	17	.850	3	12	15	11	14	0	1	1	61	12.2
87-88—Utah	11	408	135	67	.496	22	16	.727	8	31	39	32	42	1	7	0	169	15.4
88-89—Utah	3	123	35	11	.314	10	8	.800	5	12	17	4	15	0	1	2	33	11.0
89-90—Utah	5	145	43	21	.488	4	1	.250	7	7	14	5	14	0	3	0	50	10.0
Totals	40	1010	314	151	.481	75	56	.747	36	78	114	71	111	1	18	4	393	9.8

Three-Point Field Goals: 1983-84, 2-for-3 (.667). 1985-86, 2-for-3 (.667). 1986-87, 2-for-5 (.400). 1987-88, 19-for-36 (.528). 1988-89, 3-for-9 (.333). 1989-90, 7-for-14 (.500). Totals, 35-for-70 (.500).

WILLIAM HENRY HANZLIK
(Bill)

Born December 6, 1957 at Middletown, O. Height 6:07. Weight 200.
High Schools—Lake Oswego, Ore. (Junior) and
Beloit, Wis., Memorial (Senior).
College—University of Notre Dame, Notre Dame, Ind.
Drafted by Seattle on first round, 1980 (20th pick).

Traded by Seattle to Denver to complete deal for David Thompson, July 20, 1982. Seattle's earlier trade of the rights to free agent Wally Walker and a 1982 1st round draft choice for Thompson was nullified when Walker's rights were ruled non-transferable by an arbitrator.

—COLLEGIATE RECORD—

Year	G.	Min.	FGA	FGM	Pct.	FTA	FTM	Pct.	Reb.	Pts.	Avg.
76-77	28	274	91	38	.418	55	39	.709	51	115	4.1

TIM HARDAWAY

Year	G.	Min.	FGA	FGM	Pct.	FTA	FTM	Pct.	Reb.	Pts.	Avg.
77-78	30	307	78	40	.513	38	30	.789	57	110	3.7
78-79	29	654	164	95	.579	77	63	.818	84	253	8.7
79-80	22	603	135	61	.452	60	44	.733	74	166	7.5
Totals	109	1838	468	234	.500	230	176	.765	266	644	5.9

NBA REGULAR SEASON RECORD

									—Rebounds—									
Sea.—Team	G.	Min.	FGA	FGM	Pct.	FTA	FTM	Pct.	Off.	Def.	Tot.	Ast.	PF	Dq.	Stl.	Blk.	Pts.	Avg.
80-81—Seattle	74	1259	289	138	.478	150	119	.793	67	86	153	111	168	1	58	20	396	5.4
81-82—Seattle	81	1974	357	167	.468	176	138	.784	99	167	266	183	250	3	81	30	472	5.8
82-83—Denver	82	1547	437	187	.428	160	125	.781	80	156	236	268	220	0	75	15	500	6.1
83-84—Denver	80	1469	306	132	.431	207	167	.807	66	139	205	252	255	6	68	19	434	5.4
84-85—Denver	80	1673	522	220	.421	238	180	.756	88	119	207	210	291	5	84	26	621	7.8
85-86—Denver	79	1982	741	331	.447	405	318	.785	88	176	264	316	277	2	107	16	988	12.5
86-87—Denver	73	1990	746	307	.412	402	316	.786	79	177	256	280	245	3	87	28	952	13.0
87-88—Denver	77	1334	287	109	.380	163	129	.791	39	132	171	166	185	1	64	17	350	4.5
88-89—Denver	41	701	151	66	.437	87	68	.782	18	75	93	86	82	1	25	5	201	4.9
89-90—Denver	81	1605	396	179	.452	183	136	.743	67	140	207	186	249	7	78	29	500	6.2
Totals	748	15534	4232	1836	.434	2171	1696	.781	691	1367	2058	2058	2222	29	727	205	5414	7.2

Three-Point Field Goals: 1980-81, 1-for-5 (.200). 1981-82, 0-for-4. 1982-83, 1-for-7 (.143). 1983-84, 3-for-12 (.250). 1984-85, 1-for-15 (.067). 1985-86, 8-for-41 (.195). 1986-87, 22-for-80 (.275). 1987-88, 3-for-16 (.188). 1988-89, 1-for-5 (.200). 1989-90, 6-for-31 (.194). Totals, 46-for-216 (.213).

NBA PLAYOFF RECORD

									—Rebounds—									
Sea.—Team	G.	Min.	FGA	FGM	Pct.	FTA	FTM	Pct.	Off.	Def.	Tot.	Ast.	PF	Dq.	Stl.	Blk.	Pts.	Avg.
81-82—Seattle	8	203	34	16	.471	22	20	.909	10	22	32	20	26	1	6	5	52	6.5
82-83—Denver	8	157	50	20	.400	17	14	.824	3	22	25	21	26	0	6	5	54	6.8
83-84—Denver	5	82	19	11	.579	6	6	1.000	3	5	8	21	16	0	3	0	28	5.6
84-85—Denver	15	310	92	45	.489	41	30	.732	24	22	46	33	57	2	14	6	120	8.0
85-86—Denver	6	102	28	15	.536	16	13	.813	2	4	6	19	12	0	1	1	44	7.3
86-87—Denver	3	76	25	8	.320	15	9	.600	0	6	6	7	6	0	4	0	25	8.3
87-88—Denver	11	212	56	20	.357	26	18	.692	11	18	29	26	40	1	5	9	58	5.3
88-89—Denver	3	106	33	14	.424	12	7	.583	6	14	20	9	13	0	5	1	38	12.7
89-90—Denver	3	79	17	5	.294	10	10	1.000	5	5	10	11	13	1	5	2	21	7.0
Totals	62	1327	354	154	.435	165	127	.770	64	118	182	167	209	5	49	29	440	7.1

Three-Point Field Goals: 1981-82, 0-for-1. 1982-83, 0-for-2. 1983-84, 0-for-2. 1984-85, 0-for-1. 1985-86, 1-for-1 (1.000). 1986-87, 0-for-2. 1987-88, 0-for-8. 1988-89, 3-for-6 (.500). 1989-90, 1-for-3 (.333). Totals, 5-for-26 (.192).

Named to NBA All-Defensive Second Team, 1986.... Member of U. S. Olympic team, 1980.

TIMOTHY DUANE HARDAWAY
(Tim)

Born September 12, 1966 at Chicago, Ill. Height 6:00. Weight 175.
High School—Chicago, Ill., Carver.
College—University of Texas at El Paso, El Paso, Tex.
Drafted by Golden State on first round, 1989 (14th pick).

—COLLEGIATE RECORD—

Year	G.	Min.	FGA	FGM	Pct.	FTA	FTM	Pct.	Reb.	Pts.	Avg.
85-86	28	435	71	37	.521	63	41	.651	35	115	4.1
86-87	31	922	245	120	.490	101	67	.663	62	310	10.0
87-88	32	1036	354	159	.449	130	98	.754	93	434	13.6
88-89	33	1182	509	255	.501	228	169	.741	131	727	22.0
Totals	124	3575	1179	571	.484	522	375	.718	321	1586	12.8

Three-Point Field Goals: 1986-87, 3-for-12 (.250). 1987-88, 18-for-53 (.340). 1988-89, 48-for-131 (.366). Totals, 69-for-196 (.352).

NBA REGULAR SEASON RECORD

									—Rebounds—									
Sea.—Team	G.	Min.	FGA	FGM	Pct.	FTA	FTM	Pct.	Off.	Def.	Tot.	Ast.	PF	Dq.	Stl.	Blk.	Pts.	Avg.
89-90—Golden State	79	2663	985	464	.471	276	211	.764	57	253	310	689	232	6	165	12	1162	14.7

Three-Point Field Goals: 1989-90, 23-for-84 (.274).

Named to NBA All-Rookie First Team, 1990.

DEREK RICARDO HARPER

Born October 13, 1961 at Elberton, Ga. Height 6:04. Weight 203.
High School—West Palm Beach, Fla., North Shore.
College—University of Illinois, Champaign, Ill.
Drafted by Dallas on first round as an undergraduate, 1983 (11th pick).

—COLLEGIATE RECORD—

Year	G.	Min.	FGA	FGM	Pct.	FTA	FTM	Pct.	Reb.	Pts.	Avg.
80-81	29	934	252	104	.413	46	33	.717	75	241	8.3
81-82	29	1059	230	105	.457	45	34	.756	133	244	8.4
82-83	32	1182	369	198	.537	123	83	.675	112	492	15.4
Totals	90	3175	851	407	.478	214	150	.701	320	977	10.9

Three-Point Field Goals: 1982-83, 13-for-24 (.542).

NBA REGULAR SEASON RECORD

Sea.—Team	G.	Min.	FGA	FGM	Pct.	FTA	FTM	Pct.	—Rebounds— Off.	Def.	Tot.	Ast.	PF	Dq.	Stl.	Blk.	Pts.	Avg.
83-84—Dallas	82	1712	451	200	.443	98	66	.673	53	119	172	239	143	0	95	21	469	5.7
84-85—Dallas	82	2218	633	329	.520	154	111	.721	47	152	199	360	194	1	144	37	790	9.6
85-86—Dallas	79	2150	730	390	.534	229	171	.747	75	151	226	416	166	1	153	23	963	12.2
86-87—Dallas	77	2556	993	497	.501	234	160	.684	51	148	199	609	195	0	167	25	1230	16.0
87-88—Dallas	82	3032	1167	536	.459	344	261	.759	71	175	246	634	164	0	168	35	1393	17.0
88-89—Dallas	81	2968	1127	538	.477	284	229	.806	46	182	228	570	219	3	172	41	1404	17.3
89-90—Dallas	82	3007	1161	567	.488	315	250	.794	54	190	244	609	224	1	187	26	1473	18.0
Totals	565	17643	6262	3057	.488	1658	1248	.753	397	1117	1514	3437	1305	6	1086	208	7722	13.7

Three-Point Field Goals: 1983-84, 3-for-26 (.115). 1984-85, 21-for-61 (.344). 1985-86, 12-for-51 (.235). 1986-87, 76-for-212 (.358). 1987-88, 60-for-192 (.313). 1988-89, 99-for-278 (.356). 1989-90, 89-for-240 (.371). Totals, 360-for-1060 (.340).

NBA PLAYOFF RECORD

Sea.—Team	G.	Min.	FGA	FGM	Pct.	FTA	FTM	Pct.	—Rebounds— Off.	Def.	Tot.	Ast.	PF	Dq.	Stl.	Blk.	Pts.	Avg.
83-84—Dallas	10	226	54	21	.389	7	5	.714	8	12	20	28	16	0	11	2	50	5.0
84-85—Dallas	4	132	21	10	.476	7	5	.714	1	11	12	20	12	0	6	1	26	6.5
85-86—Dallas	10	348	107	57	.533	16	12	.750	13	6	19	76	27	0	23	0	134	13.4
86-87—Dallas	4	123	40	20	.500	30	24	.800	2	10	12	27	7	0	7	0	66	16.5
87-88—Dallas	17	602	202	89	.441	59	43	.729	11	32	43	121	44	0	32	5	230	13.5
89-90—Dallas	3	119	48	21	.438	16	11	.688	2	6	8	23	13	0	4	0	58	19.3
Totals	48	1550	472	218	.462	135	100	.741	37	77	114	295	119	0	83	8	564	11.8

Three-Point Field Goals: 1983-84, 3-for-8 (.375). 1984-85, 1-for-3 (.333). 1985-86, 8-for-14 (.571). 1986-87, 2-for-9 (.222). 1987-88, 9-for-36 (.250). 1989-90, 5-for-16 (.313). Totals, 28-for-86 (.326).

Named to NBA All-Defensive Second Team, 1987 and 1990.

RONALD HARPER
(Ron)

Born January 20, 1964 at Dayton, O. Height 6:06. Weight 198.

High School—Dayton, O., Kiser.

College—Miami University, Oxford, O.

Drafted by Cleveland on first round, 1986 (8th pick).

Traded by Cleveland with 1990 and 1992 1st round draft choices and a 1991 2nd round draft choice to Los Angeles Clippers for Reggie Williams and the draft rights to Danny Ferry, November 16, 1989.

—COLLEGIATE RECORD—

Year	G.	Min.	FGA	FGM	Pct.	FTA	FTM	Pct.	Reb.	Pts.	Avg.
82-83	28	887	298	148	.497	95	64	.674	195	360	12.9
83-84	30	989	367	197	.537	165	94	.570	229	448	16.3
84-85	31	1144	577	312	.541	224	148	.661	333	772	24.9
85-86	31	1144	572	312	.545	200	133	.665	362	757	24.4
Totals	120	4164	1814	969	.534	684	439	.642	1119	2377	19.8

NBA REGULAR SEASON RECORD

Sea.—Team	G.	Min.	FGA	FGM	Pct.	FTA	FTM	Pct.	—Rebounds— Off.	Def.	Tot.	Ast.	PF	Dq.	Stl.	Blk.	Pts.	Avg.
86-87—Cleveland	82	3064	1614	734	.455	564	386	.684	169	223	392	394	247	3	209	84	1874	22.9
87-88—Cleveland	57	1830	732	340	.464	278	196	.705	64	159	223	281	157	3	122	52	879	15.4
88-89—Cleveland	82	2851	1149	587	.511	430	323	.751	122	287	409	434	224	1	185	74	1526	18.6
89-90—Clev.-L.A.C.	35	1367	637	301	.473	231	182	.788	74	132	206	182	105	1	81	41	798	22.8
Totals	256	9112	4132	1962	.475	1503	1087	.723	429	801	1230	1291	733	8	597	251	5077	19.8

Three-Point Field Goals: 1986-87, 20-for-94 (.213). 1987-88, 3-for-20 (.150). 1988-89, 29-for-116 (.250). 1989-90, 14-for-51 (.275). Totals, 66-for-281 (.235).

NBA PLAYOFF RECORD

Sea.—Team	G.	Min.	FGA	FGM	Pct.	FTA	FTM	Pct.	—Rebounds— Off.	Def.	Tot.	Ast.	PF	Dq.	Stl.	Blk.	Pts.	Avg.
87-88—Cleveland	4	134	63	30	.476	16	11	.688	4	16	20	15	9	0	11	4	71	17.8
88-89—Cleveland	5	189	69	39	.565	26	20	.769	7	14	21	20	20	1	11	4	98	19.6
Totals	9	323	132	69	.523	42	31	.738	11	30	41	35	29	1	22	8	169	18.8

Three-Point Field Goals: 1987-88, 0-for-2. 1988-89, 0-for-2. Totals, 0-for-4.

Named to NBA All-Rookie Team, 1987. . . . THE SPORTING NEWS All-America Second Team, 1986.

STEVEN DWAYNE HARRIS
(Steve)

Born October 15, 1963 at Kansas City, Mo. Height 6:05. Weight 195.
High School—Blue Springs, Mo.
College—University of Tulsa, Tulsa, Okla.
Drafted by Houston on first round, 1985 (19th pick).

Traded by Houston with Ralph Sampson to Golden State for Joe Barry Carroll and Eric Floyd, December 12, 1987.
Waived by Golden State, November 3, 1988; signed by Detroit, December 30, 1988, to the first of consecutive 10-day contracts that expired, January 18, 1989.
Signed by Los Angeles Clippers, February 27, 1990, to a 10-day contract that expired, March 8, 1990.
Re-signed by Los Angeles Clippers, March 10, 1990, for remainder of season.
Played in Continental Basketball Association with Albany Patroons, 1988-89, and Columbus Horizon, 1989-90.

—COLLEGIATE RECORD—

Year	G.	Min.	FGA	FGM	Pct.	FTA	FTM	Pct.	Reb.	Pts.	Avg.
81-82	29	587	239	137	.531	67	57	.851	60	311	10.7
82-83	31	1119	443	233	.526	119	104	.874	130	574	18.5
83-84	31	1043	468	271	.579	142	113	.796	104	655	21.1
84-85	31	1069	499	273	.547	215	186	.865	134	732	23.6
Totals	122	3818	1649	904	.548	543	460	.847	428	2272	18.6

Three-Point Field Goals: 1982-83, 4-for-12 (.333).

CBA REGULAR SEASON RECORD

			—2-Point—			—3-Point—									
Sea.—Team	G.	Min.	FGM	FGA	Pct.	FGM	FGA	Pct.	FTM	FTA	Pct.	Reb.	Ast.	Pts.	Avg.
88-89—Albany	10	211	37	83	.446	0	0	.000	11	16	.688	39	15	85	8.5
89-90—Columbus	47	1719	523	962	.544	7	21	.333	131	153	.856	256	113	1198	25.5
Totals	57	1930	560	1045	.536	7	21	.333	142	169	.840	295	128	1283	22.5

NBA REGULAR SEASON RECORD

									—Rebounds—									
Sea.—Team	G.	Min.	FGA	FGM	Pct.	FTA	FTM	Pct.	Off.	Def.	Tot.	Ast.	PF	Dq.	Stl.	Blk.	Pts.	Avg.
85-86—Houston	57	482	233	103	.442	54	50	.926	25	32	57	50	55	0	21	4	257	4.5
86-87—Houston	74	1174	599	251	.419	130	111	.854	71	99	170	100	111	1	37	16	613	8.3
87-88—Hou.-G.S.	58	1084	487	223	.458	113	89	.788	53	73	126	87	89	0	50	8	535	9.2
88-89—Detroit	3	7	4	1	.250	2	2	1.000	0	2	2	0	1	0	1	0	4	1.3
89-90—L.A. Clippers	15	93	40	14	.350	4	3	.750	5	5	10	1	9	0	7	1	31	2.1
Totals	207	2840	1363	592	.434	303	255	.842	154	211	365	238	265	1	116	29	1440	7.0

Three-Point Field Goals: 1985-86, 1-for-5 (.200). 1986-87, 0-for-8. 1987-88, 0-for-7. Totals, 1-for-20 (.050).

NBA PLAYOFF RECORD

									—Rebounds—									
Sea.—Team	G.	Min.	FGA	FGM	Pct.	FTA	FTM	Pct.	Off.	Def.	Tot.	Ast.	PF	Dq.	Stl.	Blk.	Pts.	Avg.
85-86—Houston	15	83	29	14	.483	5	2	.400	5	5	10	2	3	0	4	3	30	2.0
86-87—Houston	9	91	43	16	.372	6	5	.833	3	4	7	5	15	0	3	0	37	4.1
Totals	24	174	72	30	.417	11	7	.636	8	9	17	7	18	0	7	3	67	2.8

Three-Point Field Goals: 1986-87, 0-for-1.

SCOTT ALAN HASTINGS

Born June 3, 1960 at Independence, Kan. Height 6:10. Weight 235.
High School—Independence, Kan.
College—University of Arkansas, Fayetteville, Ark.
Drafted by New York on second round, 1982 (29th pick).

Traded by New York with cash to Atlanta for Rory Sparrow, February 12, 1983.
Selected from Atlanta by Miami in NBA expansion draft, June 23, 1988.
Signed by Detroit as an unrestricted free agent, July 15, 1989.

—COLLEGIATE RECORD—

Year	G.	Min.	FGA	FGM	Pct.	FTA	FTM	Pct.	Reb.	Pts.	Avg.
78-79	30	753	191	97	.508	74	54	.730	138	248	8.3
79-80	29	1033	322	172	.534	160	125	.781	194	469	16.2
80-81	32	1054	341	192	.563	189	139	.735	173	523	16.3
81-82	29	1040	369	204	.553	177	131	.740	175	539	18.6
Totals	120	3880	1223	665	.544	600	449	.748	680	1779	14.8

NBA REGULAR SEASON RECORD

									—Rebounds—									
Sea.—Team	G.	Min.	FGA	FGM	Pct.	FTA	FTM	Pct.	Off.	Def.	Tot.	Ast.	PF	Dq.	Stl.	Blk.	Pts.	Avg.
82-83—N.Y.-Atl.	31	140	38	13	.342	20	11	.550	15	26	41	3	34	0	6	1	37	1.2

									Rebounds									
Sea.—Team	G.	Min.	FGA	FGM	Pct.	FTA	FTM	Pct.	Off.	Def.	Tot.	Ast.	PF	Dq.	Stl.	Blk.	Pts.	Avg.
83-84—Atlanta	68	1135	237	111	.468	104	82	.788	96	174	270	46	220	7	40	36	305	4.5
84-85—Atlanta	64	825	188	89	.473	81	63	.778	59	100	159	46	135	1	24	23	241	3.8
85-86—Atlanta	62	650	159	65	.409	70	60	.857	44	80	124	26	118	2	14	8	193	3.1
86-87—Atlanta	40	256	68	23	.338	29	23	.793	16	54	70	13	35	0	10	7	71	1.8
87-88—Atlanta	55	403	82	40	.488	27	25	.926	27	70	97	16	67	1	8	10	110	2.0
88-89—Miami	75	1206	328	143	.436	107	91	.850	72	159	231	59	203	5	32	42	386	5.1
89-90—Detroit	40	166	33	10	.303	22	19	.864	7	25	32	8	31	0	3	3	42	1.1
Totals	435	4781	1133	494	.436	460	374	.813	336	688	1024	217	843	16	137	130	1385	3.2

Three-Point Field Goals: 1982-83, 0-for-3. 1983-84, 1-for-4 (.250). 1985-86, 3-for-4 (.750). 1986-87, 2-for-12 (.167). 1987-88, 5-for-12 (.417). 1988-89, 9-for-28 (.321). 1989-90, 3-for-12 (.250). Totals, 23-for-75 (.307).

NBA PLAYOFF RECORD

									Rebounds									
Sea.—Team	G.	Min.	FGA	FGM	Pct.	FTA	FTM	Pct.	Off.	Def.	Tot.	Ast.	PF	Dq.	Stl.	Blk.	Pts.	Avg.
83-84—Atlanta	5	32	9	2	.222	4	3	.750	2	6	8	1	4	0	1	0	7	1.4
85-86—Atlanta	9	49	14	11	.786	11	5	.455	3	7	10	2	11	0	2	0	28	3.1
86-87—Atlanta	4	21	3	2	.667	2	2	1.000	1	5	6	0	5	0	1	1	6	1.5
87-88—Atlanta	11	103	14	9	.643	8	8	1.000	7	10	17	3	21	1	3	1	26	2.4
89-90—Detroit	5	16	4	1	.250	0	0	....	0	0	0	0	4	0	1	0	2	0.4
Totals	34	221	44	25	.568	25	18	.720	13	28	41	6	45	1	8	2	69	2.0

Three-Point Field Goals: 1985-86, 1-for-4 (.250). 1987-88, 0-for-1. 1989-90, 0-for-3. Totals, 1-for-8 (.125).

Member of NBA championship team, 1990.

HERSEY R. HAWKINS JR.

Born September 29, 1965 at Chicago, Ill. Height 6:03. Weight 190.
High School—Chicago, Ill., Westinghouse.
College—Bradley University, Peoria, Ill.
Drafted by Los Angeles Clippers on first round, 1988 (6th pick).

Draft rights traded with a 1989 1st round draft choice by Los Angeles Clippers to Philadelphia for draft rights to Charles Smith, June 28, 1988.

—COLLEGIATE RECORD—

Year	G.	Min.	FGA	FGM	Pct.	FTA	FTM	Pct.	Reb.	Pts.	Avg.
84-85	30	1121	308	179	.581	105	81	.771	182	439	14.6
85-86	35	1291	461	250	.542	203	156	.768	200	656	18.7
86-87	29	1102	552	294	.533	213	169	.793	195	788	27.2
87-88	31	1202	720	377	.524	335	284	.848	241	1125	36.3
Totals	125	4716	2041	1100	.539	856	690	.806	818	3008	24.1

Three-Point Field Goals: 1986-87, 31-for-108 (.287). 1987-88, 87-for-221 (.394). Totals, 118-for-329 (.359).

NBA REGULAR SEASON RECORD

									Rebounds									
Sea.—Team	G.	Min.	FGA	FGM	Pct.	FTA	FTM	Pct.	Off.	Def.	Tot.	Ast.	PF	Dq.	Stl.	Blk.	Pts.	Avg.
88-89—Philadelphia	79	2577	971	442	.455	290	241	.831	51	174	225	239	184	0	120	37	1196	15.1
89-90—Philadelphia	82	2856	1136	522	.460	436	387	.888	85	219	304	261	217	2	130	28	1515	18.5
Totals	161	5433	2107	964	.458	726	628	.865	136	393	529	500	401	2	250	65	2711	16.8

Three-Point Field Goals: 1988-89, 71-for-166 (.428). 1989-90, 84-for-200 (.420). Totals, 155-for-366 (.423).

NBA PLAYOFF RECORD

									Rebounds									
Sea.—Team	G.	Min.	FGA	FGM	Pct.	FTA	FTM	Pct.	Off.	Def.	Tot.	Ast.	PF	Dq.	Stl.	Blk.	Pts.	Avg.
88-89—Philadelphia	3	72	24	3	.125	2	2	1.000	1	4	5	4	6	0	3	1	8	2.7
89-90—Philadelphia	10	415	163	81	.497	63	59	.937	8	23	31	36	25	0	12	7	235	23.5
Totals	13	487	187	84	.449	65	61	.938	9	27	36	40	31	0	15	8	243	18.7

Three-Point Field Goals: 1988-89, 0-for-5. 1989-90, 14-for-36 (.389). Totals, 14-for-41 (.341).

Named to NBA All-Rookie First Team, 1989. . . . Led NCAA Division I in scoring, 1988. . . . Named THE SPORTING NEWS College Player of the Year, 1988. . . . THE SPORTING NEWS All-America First Team, 1988.

JEROME McKINLEY HENDERSON
(Gerald)

Born January 16, 1956 at Richmond, Va. Height 6:02. Weight 180.
High School—Richmond, Va., Huguenot.
College—Virginia Commonwealth University, Richmond, Va.
Drafted by San Antonio on third round, 1978 (64th pick).

Waived by San Antonio, September 20, 1978; signed by Boston as a free agent, June 25, 1979.

Traded by Boston to Seattle for a 1986 1st round draft choice, October 16, 1984.

Traded by Seattle to New York for a 1990 2nd round draft choice and the right to exchange 1987 1st round draft choices, November 12, 1986.

Waived by New York, November 14, 1987; signed by Philadelphia as a free agent, December 3, 1987.

Waived by Milwaukee, November 27, 1989; signed by Detroit as an unrestricted free agent, December 6, 1989.

Played in Western Basketball Association with Tucson Gunners, 1978-79.

—COLLEGIATE RECORD—

Year	G.	Min.	FGA	FGM	Pct.	FTA	FTM	Pct.	Reb.	Pts.	Avg.
74-75	25	....	182	73	.401	39	21	.538	64	167	6.7
75-76	25	....	395	196	.496	43	27	.628	71	419	16.8
76-77	25	903	465	228	.490	81	50	.617	102	506	20.2
77-78	28	939	377	185	.491	121	80	.661	94	450	16.1
Totals	103	....	1419	682	.481	284	178	.627	331	1542	15.0

WBA REGULAR SEASON RECORD

			—2-Point—			—3-Point—									
Sea.—Team	G.	Min.	FGM	FGA	Pct.	FGM	FGA	Pct.	FTM	FTA	Pct.	Reb.	Ast.	Pts.	Avg.
78-79—Tucson	48	1288	239	447	.535	1	7	.143	124	173	.717	138	140	605	12.6

NBA REGULAR SEASON RECORD

									—Rebounds—										
Sea.—Team	G.	Min.	FGA	FGM	Pct.	FTA	FTM	Pct.	Off.	Def.	Tot.	Ast.	PF	Dq.	Stl.	Blk.	Pts.	Avg.
79-80—Boston	76	1061	382	191	.500	129	89	.690	37	46	83	147	96	0	45	15	473	6.2
80-81—Boston	82	1608	579	261	.451	157	113	.720	43	89	132	213	177	0	79	12	636	7.8
81-82—Boston	82	1844	705	353	.501	172	125	.727	47	105	152	252	199	3	82	11	833	10.2
82-83—Boston	82	1551	618	286	.463	133	96	.722	57	67	124	195	190	6	95	3	671	8.2
83-84—Boston	78	2088	718	376	.524	177	136	.768	68	79	147	300	209	1	117	14	908	11.6
84-85—Seattle	79	2648	891	427	.479	255	199	.780	71	119	190	559	196	1	140	9	1062	13.4
85-86—Seattle	82	2568	900	434	.482	223	185	.830	89	98	187	487	230	2	138	12	1071	13.1
86-87—Sea.-N.Y.	74	2045	674	298	.442	230	190	.826	50	125	175	471	208	1	101	11	805	10.9
87-88—N.Y.-Phil.	75	1505	453	194	.428	170	138	.812	27	80	107	231	187	0	69	5	595	7.9
88-89—Philadelphia	65	986	348	144	.414	127	104	.819	17	51	68	140	121	1	42	3	425	6.5
89-90—Milw.-Det.	57	464	109	53	.486	15	12	.800	11	32	43	74	50	0	16	2	135	2.4
Totals	832	18368	6377	3017	.473	1788	1387	.776	517	891	1408	3069	1863	15	924	97	7614	9.2

Three-Point Field Goals: 1979-80, 2-for-6 (.333). 1980-81, 1-for-16 (.063). 1981-82, 2-for-12 (.167). 1982-83, 3-for-16 (.188). 1983-84, 20-for-57 (.351). 1984-85, 9-for-38 (.237). 1985-86, 18-for-52 (.346). 1986-87, 19-for-77 (.247). 1987-88, 69-for-163 (.423). 1988-89, 33-for-107 (.308). 1989-90, 17-for-38 (.447). Totals, 193-for-582 (.332).

NBA PLAYOFF RECORD

									—Rebounds—									
Sea.—Team	G.	Min.	FGA	FGM	Pct.	FTA	FTM	Pct.	Off.	Def.	Tot.	Ast.	PF	Dq.	Stl.	Blk.	Pts.	Avg.
79-80—Boston	9	101	37	15	.405	20	12	.600	4	6	10	12	8	0	4	0	42	4.7
80-81—Boston	16	228	86	41	.477	12	10	.833	10	15	25	26	24	0	10	3	92	5.8
81-82—Boston	12	310	93	38	.409	35	24	.686	12	13	25	48	30	0	14	2	100	8.3
82-83—Boston	7	187	85	35	.412	7	6	.857	8	6	14	31	25	1	11	1	76	10.9
83-84—Boston	23	616	237	115	.485	75	54	.720	23	29	52	97	78	0	34	1	287	12.5
88-89—Philadelphia	3	69	25	10	.400	6	2	.333	3	4	7	5	10	0	2	0	24	8.0
89-90—Detroit	8	19	5	1	.200	0	0	....	2	1	3	4	3	0	2	0	2	0.3
Totals	78	1530	568	255	.449	155	108	.697	62	74	136	223	178	1	77	7	623	8.0

Three-Point Field Goals: 1979-80, 0-for-2. 1980-81, 0-for-1. 1981-82, 0-for-2. 1982-83, 0-for-3. 1983-84, 3-for-11 (.273). 1988-89, 2-for-7 (.286). 1989-90, 0-for-3. Totals, 5-for-29 (.172).

Member of NBA championship teams, 1981, 1984, 1990.

MIKE HIGGINS

Born February 17, 1967 at Grand Island, Neb. Height 6:09. Weight 220.

High School—Greeley, Colo., West.

College—University of Northern Colorado, Greeley, Colo.

Never drafted by an NBA franchise.

Signed by Los Angeles Lakers as a free agent, September 1, 1989.

Waived by Los Angeles Lakers, December 13, 1989; signed by Denver, December 29, 1989, to the first of consecutive 10-day contracts that expired, January 17, 1990.

Played in Continental Basketball Association with Rapid City Thrillers, 1989-90.

—COLLEGIATE RECORD—

Year	G.	Min.	FGA	FGM	Pct.	FTA	FTM	Pct.	Reb.	Pts.	Avg.
85-86	28	766	227	140	.617	118	70	.593	177	350	12.5
86-87	28	867	265	156	.589	177	129	.729	193	442	15.8
87-88	28	885	314	218	.694	184	133	.723	248	569	20.3
88-89	30	998	422	274	.649	281	203	.722	335	751	25.0
Totals	114	3516	1228	788	.642	760	535	.704	953	2112	18.5

Three-Point Field Goals: 1986-87, 1-for-1 (1.000).

CBA REGULAR SEASON RECORD

Sea.—Team	G.	Min.	2-Point FGM	2-Point FGA	2-Point Pct.	3-Point FGM	3-Point FGA	3-Point Pct.	FTM	FTA	Pct.	Reb.	Ast.	Pts.	Avg.
89-90—Rapid City	20	597	69	119	.580	0	2	.000	72	101	.713	148	44	210	10.5

NBA REGULAR SEASON RECORD

Sea.—Team	G.	Min.	FGA	FGM	Pct.	FTA	FTM	Pct.	Rebounds Off.	Rebounds Def.	Rebounds Tot.	Ast.	PF	Dq.	Stl.	Blk.	Pts.	Avg.
89-90—L.A.L.-Den.	11	50	8	3	.375	10	8	.800	2	2	4	3	5	0	2	2	14	1.3

RODERICK DWAYNE HIGGINS
(Rod)

Born January 31, 1960 at Monroe, La. Height 6:07. Weight 205.

High School—Harvey, Ill., Thornton.

College—Fresno State University, Fresno, Calif.

Drafted by Chicago on second round, 1982 (31st pick).

Waived by Chicago, October 24, 1985; signed by Seattle as a free agent, November 4, 1985.

Waived by Seattle, December 17, 1985; signed by San Antonio, January 15, 2986, to the first of consecutive 10-day contracts that expired, February 3, 1986.

Signed by New Jersey, February 21, 1986, to a 10-day contract that expired, March 2, 1986.

Signed by Chicago, March 14, 1986, to a 10-day contract that expired, March 23, 1986.

Re-signed by Chicago, March 24, 1986; released, March 27, 1986.

Signed by Golden State as a free agent, October 2, 1986.

Played in Continental Basketball Association with Tampa Bay Thrillers, 1985-86.

—COLLEGIATE RECORD—

Year	G.	Min.	FGA	FGM	Pct.	FTA	FTM	Pct.	Reb.	Pts.	Avg.
78-79	22	....	153	79	.516	66	49	.742	127	207	9.4
79-80	24	....	235	119	.506	86	72	.837	136	310	12.9
80-81	29	941	319	178	.558	108	92	.852	158	448	15.4
81-82	29	1025	335	178	.531	105	81	.771	182	437	15.1
Totals	104	....	1042	554	.532	365	294	.805	603	1402	13.5

CBA REGULAR SEASON RECORD

Sea.—Team	G.	Min.	2-Point FGM	2-Point FGA	2-Point Pct.	3-Point FGM	3-Point FGA	3-Point Pct.	FTM	FTA	Pct.	Reb.	Ast.	Pts.	Avg.
85-86—Tampa Bay	11	422	105	190	.553	4	10	.400	92	115	.800	85	30	314	28.5

NBA REGULAR SEASON RECORD

Sea.—Team	G.	Min.	FGA	FGM	Pct.	FTA	FTM	Pct.	Rebounds Off.	Rebounds Def.	Rebounds Tot.	Ast.	PF	Dq.	Stl.	Blk.	Pts.	Avg.
82-83—Chicago	82	2196	698	313	.448	264	209	.792	159	207	366	175	248	3	66	65	848	10.3
83-84—Chicago	78	1577	432	193	.447	156	113	.724	87	119	206	116	161	0	49	29	500	6.4
84-85—Chicago	68	942	270	119	.441	90	60	.667	55	92	147	73	91	0	21	13	308	4.5
85-86—Se-SA-NJ-Ch	30	332	106	39	.368	27	19	.704	14	37	51	24	49	0	9	11	98	3.3
86-87—Golden State	73	1497	412	214	.519	240	200	.833	72	165	237	96	145	0	40	21	631	8.6
87-88—Golden State	68	2188	725	381	.526	322	273	.848	94	199	293	188	188	2	70	31	1054	15.5
88-89—Golden State	81	1887	633	301	.476	229	188	.821	111	265	376	160	172	2	39	42	856	10.6
89-90—Golden State	82	1993	632	304	.481	285	234	.821	120	302	422	129	184	0	47	53	909	11.1
Totals	562	12612	3908	1864	.477	1613	1296	.803	712	1386	2098	961	1238	7	341	265	5204	9.3

Three-Point Field Goals: 1982-83, 13-for-41 (.317). 1983-84, 1-for-22 (.045). 1984-85, 10-for-37 (.270). 1985-86, 1-for-9 (.111). 1986-87, 3-for-17 (.176). 1987-88, 19-for-39 (.487). 1988-89, 66-for-168 (.393). 1989-90, 67-for-193 (.347). Totals, 180-for-526 (.342).

NBA PLAYOFF RECORD

Sea.—Team	G.	Min.	FGA	FGM	Pct.	FTA	FTM	Pct.	Rebounds Off.	Rebounds Def.	Rebounds Tot.	Ast.	PF	Dq.	Stl.	Blk.	Pts.	Avg.
84-85—Chicago	1	1	0	0	.000	0	0	.000	0	0	0	0	0	0	0	0	0	0.0
86-87—Golden State	10	177	46	18	.391	9	6	.667	5	16	21	12	20	0	11	6	43	4.3
88-89—Golden State	8	267	82	40	.488	34	29	.853	23	36	59	20	19	0	13	7	119	14.9
Totals	19	445	128	58	.453	43	35	.814	28	52	80	32	39	0	24	13	162	8.5

Three-Point Field Goals: 1986-87, 1-for-1 (1.000). 1988-89, 10-for-35 (.286). Totals, 11-for-36 (.306).

Only NBA player ever to play for four teams in one season, 1985-86. . . . CBA Playoff MVP, 1986. . . . Member of CBA championship team, 1986.

ROY MANUS HINSON

Born May 2, 1961 at Trenton, N. J. Height 6:09. Weight 220.

High School—Somerset, N. J., Franklin Township.

College—Rutgers University, New Brunswick, N. J.

Drafted by Cleveland on first round, 1983 (20th pick).

Traded by Cleveland with other considerations to Philadelphia for a 1986 1st round draft choice, June 16, 1986.

Traded by Philadelphia with Tim McCormick and a 1989 2nd round draft choice to New Jersey for Ben Coleman and Mike Gminski, January 16, 1988.

—COLLEGIATE RECORD—

Year	G.	Min.	FGA	FGM	Pct.	FTA	FTM	Pct.	Reb.	Pts.	Avg.
79-80	28	796	228	115	.504	76	42	.553	157	272	9.7
80-81	30	952	309	150	.485	98	59	.602	218	359	12.0
81-82	30	1015	316	153	.484	119	70	.588	215	376	12.5
82-83	31	1048	377	199	.528	184	118	.641	268	516	16.6
Totals	119	3811	1230	617	.502	477	289	.606	858	1523	12.8

NBA REGULAR SEASON RECORD

									—Rebounds—									
Sea.—Team	G.	Min.	FGA	FGM	Pct.	FTA	FTM	Pct.	Off.	Def.	Tot.	Ast.	PF	Dq.	Stl.	Blk.	Pts.	Avg.
83-84—Cleveland	80	1858	371	184	.496	117	69	.590	175	324	499	69	306	11	31	145	437	5.5
84-85—Cleveland	76	2344	925	465	.503	376	271	.721	186	410	596	68	311	13	51	173	1201	15.8
85-86—Cleveland	82	2834	1167	621	.532	506	364	.719	167	472	639	102	316	7	62	112	1606	19.6
86-87—Philadelphia	76	2489	823	393	.478	360	273	.758	150	338	488	60	281	4	45	161	1059	13.9
87-88—Phil.-N.J.	77	2592	930	453	.487	351	272	.775	159	358	517	99	275	6	69	140	1178	15.3
88-89—New Jersey	82	2542	1027	495	.482	420	318	.757	152	370	522	71	268	3	34	121	1308	16.0
89-90—New Jersey	25	793	286	145	.507	99	86	.869	61	111	172	22	87	0	14	27	376	15.0
Totals	498	15452	5529	2756	.498	2229	1653	.742	1050	2383	3433	491	1874	44	306	879	7165	14.4

Three-Point Field Goals: 1984-85, 0-for-3. 1985-86, 0-for-4. 1986-87, 0-for-1. 1987-88, 0-for-2. 1988-89, 0-for-2. Totals, 0-for-12.

NBA PLAYOFF RECORD

									—Rebounds—									
Sea.—Team	G.	Min.	FGA	FGM	Pct.	FTA	FTM	Pct.	Off.	Def.	Tot.	Ast.	PF	Dq.	Stl.	Blk.	Pts.	Avg.
84-85—Cleveland	4	120	48	26	.542	23	15	652	10	20	30	3	18	1	3	9	67	16.8
86-87—Philadelphia	5	159	52	31	.596	38	24	.632	6	17	23	3	18	0	4	10	86	17.2
Totals	9	279	100	57	.570	61	39	.639	16	37	53	6	36	1	7	19	153	17.0

CRAIG ANTHONY HODGES

Born June 27, 1960 at Park Forest, Ill. Height 6:02. Weight 190.

High School—Park Forest, Ill., Rich East.

College—California State University at Long Beach, Long Beach, Calif.

Drafted by San Diego on third round, 1982 (48th pick).

Traded by Los Angeles Clippers with Terry Cummings and Ricky Pierce to Milwaukee for Marques Johnson, Harvey Catchings, Junior Bridgeman and cash, September 29, 1984.

Traded by Milwaukee with a 1988 2nd round draft choice to Phoenix for Jay Humphries, February 25, 1988.

Traded by Phoenix to Chicago for Ed Nealy and a 1989 2nd round draft choice, December 14, 1988.

—COLLEGIATE RECORD—

Year	G.	Min.	FGA	FGM	Pct.	FTA	FTM	Pct.	Reb.	Pts.	Avg.
78-79	28	801	234	122	.521	49	38	.776	56	282	10.1
79-80	33	1148	361	180	.499	68	57	.838	70	417	12.6
80-81	26	755	275	127	.462	55	33	.600	67	287	11.0
81-82	28	1005	444	211	.475	92	68	.739	89	490	17.5
Totals	115	3709	1314	640	.487	264	196	.742	282	1476	12.8

NBA REGULAR SEASON RECORD

									—Rebounds—									
Sea.—Team	G.	Min.	FGA	FGM	Pct.	FTA	FTM	Pct.	Off.	Def.	Tot.	Ast.	PF	Dq.	Stl.	Blk.	Pts.	Avg.
82-83—San Diego	76	2022	704	318	.452	130	94	.723	53	69	122	275	192	3	82	4	750	9.9
83-84—San Diego	76	1571	573	258	.450	88	66	.750	22	64	86	116	166	2	58	1	592	7.8
84-85—Milwaukee	82	2496	733	359	.490	130	106	.815	74	112	186	349	262	8	96	1	871	10.6
85-86—Milwaukee	66	1739	568	284	.500	86	75	.872	39	78	117	229	157	3	74	2	716	10.8
86-87—Milwaukee	78	2147	682	315	.462	147	131	.891	48	92	140	240	189	3	76	7	846	10.8
87-88—Mil.-Phoe.	66	1445	523	242	.463	71	59	.831	19	59	78	153	118	1	46	2	629	9.5
88-89—Phoe.-Chi.	59	1204	430	203	.472	57	48	.842	23	66	89	146	90	0	43	4	529	9.0
89-90—Chicago	63	1055	331	145	.438	33	30	.909	11	42	53	110	87	1	30	2	407	6.5
Totals	566	13679	4544	2124	.467	742	609	.821	289	582	871	1618	1261	21	505	23	5340	9.4

Three-Point Field Goals: 1982-83, 20-for-90 (.222). 1983-84, 10-for-46 (.217). 1984-85, 47-for-135 (.348). 1985-86, 73-for-162 (.451). 1986-87, 85-for-228 (.373). 1987-88, 86-for-175 (.491). 1988-89, 75-for-180 (.417). 1989-90, 87-for-181 (.481). Totals, 483-for-1197 (.404).

NBA PLAYOFF RECORD

									—Rebounds—									
Sea.—Team	G.	Min.	FGA	FGM	Pct.	FTA	FTM	Pct.	Off.	Def.	Tot.	Ast.	PF	Dq.	Stl.	Blk.	Pts.	Avg.
84-85—Milwaukee	8	216	77	28	.364	5	4	.800	2	11	13	26	29	2	12	1	64	8.0
85-86—Milwaukee	14	460	145	74	.510	34	27	.794	9	16	25	63	44	1	32	2	189	13.5
86-87—Milwaukee	12	226	77	40	.519	11	10	.909	11	11	22	20	16	0	9	2	95	7.9
88-89—Chicago	17	554	177	73	.412	14	10	.714	8	17	25	62	55	1	22	3	191	11.2
89-90—Chicago	16	254	74	28	.378	4	3	.750	6	12	18	17	31	1	4	0	71	4.4
Totals	67	1710	550	243	.442	68	54	.794	36	67	103	188	175	5	79	8	610	9.1

Three-Point Field Goals: 1984-85, 4-for-23 (.174). 1985-86, 14-for-31 (.452). 1986-87, 5-for-17 (.294). 1988-89, 35-for-88 (.398). 1989-90, 12-for-41 (.293). Totals, 70-for-200 (.350).

Led NBA in three-point field goal percentage, 1986 and 1988.

MICHAEL DAVID HOLTON

Born August 4, 1961 at Seattle, Wash. Height 6:04. Weight 185.
High School—Pasadena, Calif., Pasadena.
College—University of California at Los Angeles, Los Angeles, Calif.
Drafted by Golden State on third round, 1983 (53rd pick).

Waived by Golden State, October 5, 1983; signed by Phoenix as a free agent, September 24, 1984.
Waived by Phoenix, November 4, 1985; signed by Chicago as a free agent, February 12, 1986.
Signed by Portland as a Veteran Free Agent, August 7, 1986; Chicago agreed not to exercise its right of first refusal in exchange for a 1992 2nd round draft choice.
Selected from Portland by Charlotte in NBA expansion draft, June 23, 1988.
Played in Continental Basketball Association with Puerto Rico Coquis, 1983-84, and Tampa Bay Thrillers and Florida Stingers, 1985-86.

—COLLEGIATE RECORD—

Year	G.	Min.	FGA	FGM	Pct.	FTA	FTM	Pct.	Reb.	Pts.	Avg.
79-80	32	802	105	55	.524	73	54	.740	78	164	5.1
80-81	27	734	161	79	.491	67	53	.791	75	211	7.8
81-82	27	677	154	75	.487	65	46	.708	64	196	7.3
82-83	29	721	161	88	.547	75	64	.853	78	240	8.3
Totals	115	2934	581	297	.511	280	217	.775	295	811	7.1

CBA REGULAR SEASON RECORD

			2-Point			3-Point									
Sea.—Team	G.	Min.	FGM	FGA	Pct.	FGM	FGA	Pct.	FTM	FTA	Pct.	Reb.	Ast.	Pts.	Avg.
83-84—Puerto Rico	44	1646	293	574	.510	6	23	.261	207	250	.828	149	198	811	18.4
85-86—Tampa Bay-Florida	29	1095	202	365	.553	7	30	.233	133	154	.863	85	193	558	19.2
Totals	73	2741	495	939	.527	13	53	.245	340	404	.841	234	391	1369	18.8

NBA REGULAR SEASON RECORD

									—Rebounds—									
Sea.—Team	G.	Min.	FGA	FGM	Pct.	FTA	FTM	Pct.	Off.	Def.	Tot.	Ast.	PF	Dq.	Stl.	Blk.	Pts.	Avg.
84-85—Phoenix	74	1761	576	257	.446	118	96	.814	30	102	132	198	141	0	59	6	624	8.4
85-86—Phoe.-Chi.	28	512	175	77	.440	44	28	.636	11	22	33	55	47	1	25	0	183	6.5
86-87—Portland	58	479	171	70	.409	55	44	.800	9	29	38	73	51	0	16	2	191	3.3
87-88—Portland	82	1279	353	163	.462	129	107	.829	50	99	149	211	154	0	41	10	436	5.3
88-89—Charlotte	67	1696	504	215	.427	143	120	.839	30	75	105	424	165	0	66	12	553	8.3
89-90—Charlotte	16	109	26	14	.538	2	1	.500	1	1	2	16	19	0	1	0	29	1.8
Totals	325	5836	1805	796	.441	491	396	.807	131	328	459	977	577	1	208	30	2016	6.2

Three-Point Field Goals: 1984-85, 14-for-45 (.311). 1985-86, 1-for-12 (.083). 1986-87, 7-for-23 (.304). 1987-88, 3-for-15 (.200). 1988-89, 3-for-14 (.214). Totals, 28-for-109 (.257).

NBA PLAYOFF RECORD

									—Rebounds—									
Sea.—Team	G.	Min.	FGA	FGM	Pct.	FTA	FTM	Pct.	Off.	Def.	Tot.	Ast.	PF	Dq.	Stl.	Blk.	Pts.	Avg.
84-85—Phoenix	3	55	19	9	.474	4	4	1.000	0	2	2	9	8	0	0	0	22	7.3
86-87—Portland	2	9	2	1	.500	0	0	.000	0	1	1	0	1	0	0	0	2	1.0
87-88—Portland	4	34	13	3	.231	0	0	.000	1	4	5	6	6	0	2	0	6	1.5
Totals	9	98	34	13	.382	4	4	1.000	1	7	8	15	15	0	2	0	30	3.3

Three-Point Field Goals: 1984-85, 0-for-4. 1987-88, 0-for-1. Totals, 0-for-5.

DAVID DIRK HOPPEN
(Dave)

Born March 13, 1964 at Omaha, Neb. Height 6:11. Weight 235.
High School—Omaha, Neb., Benson.
College—University of Nebraska, Lincoln, Neb.
Drafted by Atlanta on third round, 1986 (65th pick).

Waived by Atlanta, December 29, 1987; signed by Milwaukee, January 12, 1988, to a 10-day contract that expired, January 21, 1988.
Signed by Golden State as a free agent, January 22, 1988.
Selected from Golden State by Charlotte in NBA expansion draft, June 23, 1988.
Missed entire 1986-87 season due to injury.
Played in Continental Basketball Association with Topeka Sizzlers, 1987-88.
Played in Italy, 1987-88.

—COLLEGIATE RECORD—

Year	G.	Min.	FGA	FGM	Pct.	FTA	FTM	Pct.	Reb.	Pts.	Avg.
82-83	32	829	311	163	.524	159	119	.748	161	445	13.9
83-84	30	1058	367	220	.599	208	158	.760	207	598	19.9
84-85	30	1155	418	270	.646	210	164	.781	258	704	23.5
85-86	19	669	245	151	.616	147	118	.803	147	420	22.1
Totals	111	3711	1341	804	.600	724	559	.772	773	2167	19.5

ITALIAN LEAGUE RECORD

Year	G.	Min.	FGA	FGM	Pct.	FTA	FTM	Pct.	Reb.	Pts.	Avg.
87-88—Biklim Rimini	2	73	20	9	.450	10	6	.600	18	24	12.0

CBA REGULAR SEASON RECORD

			—2-Point—			—3-Point—									
Sea.—Team	G.	Min.	FGM	FGA	Pct.	FGM	FGA	Pct.	FTM	FTA	Pct.	Reb.	Ast.	Pts.	Avg.
87-88—Topeka	6	204	33	51	.647	0	0	.000	26	33	.788	65	11	92	15.3

NBA REGULAR SEASON RECORD

									—Rebounds—									
Sea.—Team	G.	Min.	FGA	FGM	Pct.	FTA	FTM	Pct.	Off.	Def.	Tot.	Ast.	PF	Dq.	Stl.	Blk.	Pts.	Avg.
87-88—Mil.-G.S.	39	642	183	84	.459	62	54	.871	58	116	174	32	87	1	13	6	222	5.7
88-89—Charlotte	77	1419	353	199	.564	139	101	.727	123	261	384	57	239	4	25	21	500	6.5
89-90—Charlotte	10	135	41	16	.390	10	8	.800	19	17	36	6	26	0	2	1	40	4.0
Totals	126	2196	577	299	.518	211	163	.773	200	394	594	95	352	5	40	28	762	6.0

Three-Point Field Goals: 1987-88, 0-for-1. 1988-89, 1-for-2 (.500). Totals, 1-for-3 (.333).

DENNIS HOPSON

Born April 22, 1965 at Toledo, O. Height 6:05. Weight 200.
High School—Toledo, O., Bowsher.
College—Ohio State University, Columbus, O.
Drafted by New Jersey on first round, 1987 (3rd pick).

Traded by New Jersey to Chicago for a 1990 1st round draft choice and 1991 and 1992 2nd round draft choices, June 26, 1990.

—COLLEGIATE RECORD—

Year	G.	Min.	FGA	FGM	Pct.	FTA	FTM	Pct.	Reb.	Pts.	Avg.
83-84	29	541	133	63	.474	35	29	.829	108	155	5.3
84-85	30	764	243	120	.494	72	53	.736	142	293	9.8
85-86	33	1148	505	275	.545	180	140	.778	193	690	20.9
86-87	33	1158	653	338	.518	264	215	.814	269	958	29.0
Totals	125	3611	1534	796	.519	551	437	.793	712	2096	16.8

Three-Point Field Goals: 1986-87, 67-for-160 (.419).

NBA REGULAR SEASON RECORD

									—Rebounds—									
Sea.—Team	G.	Min.	FGA	FGM	Pct.	FTA	FTM	Pct.	Off.	Def.	Tot.	Ast.	PF	Dq.	Stl.	Blk.	Pts.	Avg.
87-88—New Jersey	61	1365	549	222	.404	177	131	.740	63	80	143	118	145	0	57	25	587	9.6
88-89—New Jersey	62	1551	714	299	.419	219	186	.849	91	111	202	103	150	0	70	30	788	12.7
89-90—New Jersey	79	2551	1093	474	.434	342	271	.792	113	166	279	151	183	1	100	51	1251	15.8
Totals	202	5467	2356	995	.422	738	588	.797	267	357	624	372	478	1	227	106	2626	13.0

Three-Point Field Goals: 1987-88, 12-for-45 (.267). 1988-89, 4-for-27 (.148). 1989-90, 32-for-101 (.317). Totals, 48-for-173 (.277).

Named to THE SPORTING NEWS All-America First Team, 1987.

ALFREDO WILLIAM HORFORD
(Tito)

Born January 19, 1966 at LaRomana, Dominican Republic. Height 7:01. Weight 245.
High School—Houston, Tex., Marian Christian.
Colleges—Louisiana State University, Baton Rouge, La.,
and University of Miami, Coral Gables, Fla.
Drafted by Milwaukee on second round as an undergraduate, 1988 (39th pick).

—COLLEGIATE RECORD—

Louisiana State

Year	G.	Min.	FGA	FGM	Pct.	FTA	FTM	Pct.	Reb.	Pts.	Avg.
85-86	Did Not Play—Left School Before Basketball Season										

Miami (Fla.)

Year	G.	Min.	FGA	FGM	Pct.	FTA	FTM	Pct.	Reb.	Pts.	Avg.
85-86				Did Not Play—Transfer Student							
86-87	25	803	287	137	.477	152	84	.533	241	358	14.3
87-88	30	963	326	176	.540	126	73	.579	271	425	14.2
Totals	55	1766	613	313	.511	278	157	.565	512	783	14.2

NBA REGULAR SEASON RECORD

										—Rebounds—								
Sea.—Team	G.	Min.	FGA	FGM	Pct.	FTA	FTM	Pct.	Off.	Def.	Tot.	Ast.	PF	Dq.	Stl.	Blk.	Pts.	Avg.
88-89—Milwaukee	25	112	46	15	.326	19	12	.632	9	13	22	3	14	0	1	7	42	1.7
89-90—Milwaukee	35	236	62	18	.290	24	15	.625	19	40	59	2	33	0	5	16	51	1.5
Totals	60	348	108	33	.306	43	27	.628	28	53	81	5	47	0	6	23	93	1.6

NBA PLAYOFF RECORD

										—Rebounds—								
Sea.—Team	G.	Min.	FGA	FGM	Pct.	FTA	FTM	Pct.	Off.	Def.	Tot.	Ast.	PF	Dq.	Stl.	Blk.	Pts.	Avg.
89-90—Milwaukee	2	2	1	1	1.000	0	0	....	0	0	0	0	0	0	0	0	2	1.0

JEFFREY JOHN HORNACEK
(Jeff)

Born May 3, 1963 at Elmhurst, Ill. Height 6:04. Weight 190.
High School—LaGrange, Ill., Lyons.
College—Iowa State University, Ames, Ia.
Drafted by Phoenix on second round, 1986 (46th pick).

—COLLEGIATE RECORD—

Year	G.	Min.	FGA	FGM	Pct.	FTA	FTM	Pct.	Reb.	Pts.	Avg.
81-82					Did Not Play—Redshirted						
82-83	27	583	135	57	.422	45	32	.711	62	146	5.4
83-84	29	1065	208	104	.500	105	83	.790	101	291	10.0
84-85	34	1224	330	172	.521	96	81	.844	122	425	12.5
85-86	33	1229	370	177	.478	125	97	.776	127	451	13.7
Totals	123	4101	1043	510	.489	371	293	.790	412	1313	10.7

NBA REGULAR SEASON RECORD

										—Rebounds—								
Sea.—Team	G.	Min.	FGA	FGM	Pct.	FTA	FTM	Pct.	Off.	Def.	Tot.	Ast.	PF	Dq.	Stl.	Blk.	Pts.	Avg.
86-87—Phoenix	80	1561	350	159	.454	121	94	.777	41	143	184	361	130	0	70	5	424	5.3
87-88—Phoenix	82	2243	605	306	.506	185	152	.822	71	191	262	540	151	0	107	10	781	9.5
88-89—Phoenix	78	2487	889	440	.495	178	147	.826	75	191	266	465	188	0	129	8	1054	13.5
89-90—Phoenix	67	2278	901	483	.536	202	173	.856	86	227	313	337	144	2	117	14	1179	17.6
Totals	307	8569	2745	1388	.506	686	566	.825	273	752	1025	1703	613	2	423	37	3438	11.2

Three-Point Field Goals: 1986-87, 12-for-43 (.279). 1987-88, 17-for-58 (.293). 1988-89, 27-for-81 (.333). 1989-90, 40-for-98 (.408). Totals, 96-for-280 (.343).

NBA PLAYOFF RECORD

										—Rebounds—								
Sea.—Team	G.	Min.	FGA	FGM	Pct.	FTA	FTM	Pct.	Off.	Def.	Tot.	Ast.	PF	Dq.	Stl.	Blk.	Pts.	Avg.
88-89—Phoenix	12	374	149	74	.497	25	21	.840	25	44	69	62	34	0	16	3	169	14.1
89-90—Phoenix	16	583	219	112	.511	73	68	.932	13	49	62	73	43	1	24	0	298	18.6
Total	28	957	368	186	.505	98	89	.908	38	93	131	135	77	1	40	3	467	16.7

Three-Point Field Goals: 1988-89, 0-for-7. 1989-90, 6-for-24 (.250). Totals, 6-for-31 (.194).

ED HORTON

Born December 17, 1967 at Springfield, Ill. Height 6:08. Weight 230.
High School—Springfield, Ill., Lanphier.
College—University of Iowa, Iowa City, Ia.
Drafted by Washington on second round, 1989 (39th pick).

—COLLEGIATE RECORD—

Year	G.	Min.	FGA	FGM	Pct.	FTA	FTM	Pct.	Reb.	Pts.	Avg.
85-86	30	382	104	44	.423	50	22	.440	117	110	3.7
86-87	35	707	228	106	.465	104	61	.587	197	273	7.8
87-88	34	794	301	160	.532	117	65	.556	213	385	11.3
88-89	33	1054	453	250	.552	181	103	.569	350	604	18.3
Totals	132	2937	1086	560	.516	452	251	.555	877	1372	10.4

Three-Point Field Goals: 1987-88, 0-for-2. 1988-89, 1-for-6 (.167). Totals, 1-for-8 (.125).

NBA REGULAR SEASON RECORD

									—Rebounds—									
Sea.—Team	G.	Min.	FGA	FGM	Pct.	FTA	FTM	Pct.	Off.	Def.	Tot.	Ast.	PF	Dq.	Stl.	Blk.	Pts.	Avg.
89-90—Washington	45	374	162	80	.494	69	42	.609	59	49	108	19	63	1	9	5	202	4.5

Three-Point Field Goals: 1989-90, 0-for-4.

EDDIE HUGHES

Born May 26, 1960 at Greenville, Miss. Height 5:10. Weight 165.

High School—Chicago, Ill., Austin.

College—Colorado State University, Fort Collins, Colo.

Drafted by San Diego on seventh round, 1982 (140th pick).

Waived by Utah, October 27, 1982; signed by Denver as a free agent, August 1, 1985.
Waived by Denver, October 3, 1985; signed by Utah as a free agent, October 3, 1986.
Waived by Utah, October 27, 1986; re-signed by Utah as a free agent, October 8, 1987.
Waived by Utah, November 3, 1987; re-signed by Utah as a free agent, March 23, 1988.
Waived by Utah, October 21, 1988; signed by Denver as a free agent, November 4, 1988.
Waived by Denver, December 27, 1988; re-signed by Denver, January 12, 1989, to a 10-day contract that expired, January 21, 1989.
Signed by Denver as a free agent, September 27, 1989.
Waived by Denver, March 22, 1990.
Played in Continental Basketball Association with Wyoming Wildcatters and Maine Lumberjacks, 1982-83; Bay State Bombardiers and Albuquerque Silvers, 1983-84; Albuquerque Silvers, 1984-85; LaCrosse Catbirds, 1985-86, and Pensacola Tornados, 1986-87.

—COLLEGIATE RECORD—

Year	G.	Min.	FGA	FGM	Pct.	FTA	FTM	Pct.	Reb.	Pts.	Avg.
78-79	27	....	342	175	.512	89	66	.742	77	416	15.4
79-80	27	1033	293	149	.509	77	55	.714	90	353	13.1
80-81	26	935	295	140	.475	98	66	.673	79	346	13.3
81-82	26	831	224	102	.455	62	41	.661	102	245	9.4
Totals	106	....	1154	566	.490	326	228	.699	348	1360	12.8

CBA REGULAR SEASON RECORD

			—2-Point—			—3-Point—									
Sea.—Team	G.	Min.	FGM	FGA	Pct.	FGM	FGA	Pct.	FTM	FTA	Pct.	Reb.	Ast.	Pts.	Avg.
82-83—Wyoming-Maine	42	1483	197	420	.469	38	99	.384	79	116	.681	122	304	587	14.0
83-84—Bay St.-Albu.	43	1448	185	344	.537	48	118	.407	116	154	.753	130	230	630	14.7
84-85—Albuquerque	48	1826	162	296	.547	68	153	.444	112	145	.772	135	293	640	13.3
85-86—LaCrosse	47	1620	163	354	.460	50	153	.327	151	210	.719	120	261	627	13.3
86-87—Pensacola	48	1539	143	360	.397	45	119	.378	123	154	.798	104	298	544	11.3
Totals	228	7916	850	1774	.479	249	642	.388	581	779	.745	611	1386	3028	13.3

NBA REGULAR SEASON RECORD

									—Rebounds—									
Sea.—Team	G.	Min.	FGA	FGM	Pct.	FTA	FTM	Pct.	Off.	Def.	Tot.	Ast.	PF	Dq.	Stl.	Blk.	Pts.	Avg.
87-88—Utah	11	42	13	5	.385	6	6	1.000	3	1	4	8	5	0	0	0	17	1.5
88-89—Denver	26	224	64	28	.438	12	7	.583	6	13	19	35	30	0	17	2	70	2.7
89-90—Denver	60	892	202	83	.411	34	23	.676	15	55	70	116	87	0	48	1	209	3.5
Totals	97	1158	279	116	.416	52	36	.692	24	69	93	159	122	0	65	3	296	3.1

Three-Point Field Goals: 1987-88, 1-for-6 (.167). 1988-89, 7-for-22 (.318). 1989-90, 20-for-49 (.408). Totals, 28-for-77 (.364).

NBA PLAYOFF RECORD

									—Rebounds—									
Sea.—Team	G.	Min.	FGA	FGM	Pct.	FTA	FTM	Pct.	Off.	Def.	Tot.	Ast.	PF	Dq.	Stl.	Blk.	Pts.	Avg.
87-88—Utah	7	16	7	2	.286	0	0	.000	0	0	0	1	1	0	1	0	5	0.7

Three-Point Field Goals: 1987-88, 1-for-3 (.333).

Named to CBA All-Defensive First Team, 1984.

JOHN JAY HUMPHRIES

(Known by middle name.)

Born October 17, 1962 at Los Angeles, Calif. Height 6:03. Weight 185.

High School—Inglewood, Calif.

College—University of Colorado, Boulder, Colo.

Drafted by Phoenix on first round, 1984 (13th pick).

Traded by Phoenix to Milwaukee for Craig Hodges and a 1988 2nd round draft choice, February 25, 1988.

—COLLEGIATE RECORD—

Year	G.	Min.	FGA	FGM	Pct.	FTA	FTM	Pct.	Reb.	Pts.	Avg.
80-81	28	762	143	74	.517	47	31	.660	59	179	6.4
81-82	27	948	242	113	.467	83	53	.639	71	279	10.3
82-83	28	1034	339	170	.501	95	60	.632	91	400	14.3

Year	G.	Min.	FGA	FGM	Pct.	FTA	FTM	Pct.	Reb.	Pts.	Avg.
83-84	29	1120	334	170	.509	137	108	.788	94	448	15.4
Totals	112	3864	1058	527	.498	362	252	.696	315	1306	11.7

NBA REGULAR SEASON RECORD

Sea.—Team	G.	Min.	FGA	FGM	Pct.	FTA	FTM	Pct.	—Rebounds— Off.	Def.	Tot.	Ast.	PF	Dq.	Stl.	Blk.	Pts.	Avg.
84-85—Phoenix	80	2062	626	279	.446	170	141	.829	32	132	164	350	209	2	107	8	703	8.8
85-86—Phoenix	82	2733	735	352	.479	257	197	.767	56	204	260	526	222	1	132	9	905	11.0
86-87—Phoenix	82	2579	753	359	.477	260	200	.769	62	198	260	632	239	1	112	9	923	11.3
87-88—Phoe-Mil.	68	1809	538	284	.528	153	112	.732	49	125	174	395	177	1	81	5	683	10.0
88-89—Milwaukee	73	2220	714	345	.483	158	129	.816	70	119	189	405	187	1	142	5	844	11.6
89-90—Milwaukee	81	2818	1005	496	.494	285	224	.786	80	189	269	472	253	2	156	11	1237	15.3
Totals	466	14221	4371	2115	.484	1283	1003	.782	349	967	1316	2780	1287	8	730	47	5295	11.4

Three-Point Field Goals: 1984-85, 4-for-20 (.200). 1985-86, 4-for-29 (.138). 1986-87, 5-for-27 (.185). 1987-88, 3-for-18 (.167). 1988-89, 25-for-94 (.266). 1989-90, 21-for-70 (.300). Totals, 62-for-258 (.240).

NBA PLAYOFF RECORD

Sea.—Team	G.	Min.	FGA	FGM	Pct.	FTA	FTM	Pct.	—Rebounds— Off.	Def.	Tot.	Ast.	PF	Dq.	Stl.	Blk.	Pts.	Avg.
84-85—Phoenix	3	90	31	20	.645	12	9	.750	1	4	5	16	12	0	2	0	49	16.3
87-88—Milwaukee	2	18	5	0	.000	0	0	.000	1	2	3	1	6	0	1	0	0	0.0
88-89—Milwaukee	9	323	99	49	.495	34	30	.882	8	19	27	70	29	0	8	0	131	14.6
89-90—Milwaukee	3	79	15	8	.533	13	10	.769	1	4	5	19	6	0	3	0	27	9.0
Totals	17	510	150	77	.513	59	49	.831	11	29	40	106	53	0	14	0	207	12.2

Three-Point Field Goals: 1988-89, 3-for-18 (.167). 1989-90, 1-for-3 (.333). Totals, 4-for-21 (.190).

BYRON EDWARD IRVIN

Born December 2, 1966 at LaGrange, Ill. Height 6:06. Weight 195.
High School—Chicago, Ill., Julian.
Colleges—University of Arkansas, Fayetteville, Ark., and University of Missouri, Columbia, Mo.
Drafted by Portland on first round, 1989 (22nd pick).

Traded by Portland with a 1991 1st round draft choice and a 1992 2nd round draft choice to Sacramento for Danny Ainge, August 1, 1990.

—COLLEGIATE RECORD—

Arkansas

Year	G.	Min.	FGA	FGM	Pct.	FTA	FTM	Pct.	Reb.	Pts.	Avg.
84-85	33	512	155	74	.477	52	30	.577	58	178	5.4
85-86	28	658	239	107	.448	89	63	.708	79	277	9.9
Ark. Totals	61	1170	394	181	.459	141	93	.660	137	455	7.5

Missouri

Year	G.	Min.	FGA	FGM	Pct.	FTA	FTM	Pct.	Reb.	Pts.	Avg.
86-87			Did Not Play—Transfer Student								
87-88	30	805	257	132	.514	124	89	.718	104	388	12.9
88-89	36	1166	427	227	.532	259	214	.826	168	708	19.7
Mo. Totals	66	1971	684	359	.525	383	303	.791	272	1096	16.6
Col. Totals	127	3141	1078	540	.501	524	396	.756	409	1551	12.2

Three-Point Field Goals: 1987-88, 35-for-89 (.393). 1988-89, 40-for-115 (.348). Totals, 75-for-204 (.368).

NBA REGULAR SEASON RECORD

Sea.—Team	G.	Min.	FGA	FGM	Pct.	FTA	FTM	Pct.	—Rebounds— Off.	Def.	Tot.	Ast.	PF	Dq.	Stl.	Blk.	Pts.	Avg.
89-90—Portland	50	488	203	96	.473	91	61	.670	30	44	74	47	40	0	28	1	258	5.2

Three-Point Field Goals: 1989-90, 5-for-14 (.357).

NBA PLAYOFF RECORD

Sea.—Team	G.	Min.	FGA	FGM	Pct.	FTA	FTM	Pct.	—Rebounds— Off.	Def.	Tot.	Ast.	PF	Dq.	Stl.	Blk.	Pts.	Avg.
89-90—Portland	4	47	22	5	.227	6	5	.833	4	4	8	5	7	0	2	0	15	3.8

Cousin of Atlanta Hawks guard Glenn (Doc) Rivers.

JAREN JACKSON

Born October 27, 1967 at New Orleans, La. Height 6:04. Weight 190.
High School—New Orleans, La., Walter Cohen.
College—Georgetown University, Washington, D.C.
Never drafted by an NBA franchise.

Signed by New Jersey as a free agent, October 3, 1989.
Waived by New Jersey, February 27, 1990.

—COLLEGIATE RECORD—

Year	G.	Min.	FGA	FGM	Pct.	FTA	FTM	Pct.	Reb.	Pts.	Avg.
85-86	32	283	97	42	.433	22	18	.818	49	102	3.2
86-87	34	387	148	68	.459	52	37	.712	69	193	5.7
87-88	30	558	243	100	.412	56	42	.750	88	262	8.7
88-89	34	923	357	161	.451	90	59	.656	176	417	12.3
Totals	130	2151	845	371	.439	220	156	.709	382	974	7.5

Three-Point Field Goals: 1986-87, 20-for-48 (.417). 1987-88, 20-for-73 (.274). 1988-89, 36-for-87 (.414). Totals, 76-for-208 (.365).

NBA REGULAR SEASON RECORD

									—Rebounds—									
Sea.—Team	G.	Min.	FGA	FGM	Pct.	FTA	FTM	Pct.	Off.	Def.	Tot.	Ast.	PF	Dq.	Stl.	Blk.	Pts.	Avg.
89-90—New Jersey	28	160	69	25	.362	21	17	.810	16	8	24	13	16	0	13	1	67	2.4

Three-Point Field Goals: 1989-90, 0-for-3.

MARK A. JACKSON

Born April 1, 1965 at Brooklyn, N.Y. Height 6:03. Weight 205.
High School—Brooklyn, N.Y., Bishop Loughlin.
College—St. John's University, Jamaica, N.Y.
Drafted by New York on first round, 1987 (18th pick).

—COLLEGIATE RECORD—

Year	G.	Min.	FGA	FGM	Pct.	FTA	FTM	Pct.	Reb.	Pts.	Avg.
83-84	30	855	106	61	.575	77	53	.688	59	175	5.8
84-85	35	601	101	57	.564	91	66	.725	44	180	5.1
85-86	36	1340	316	151	.478	142	105	.739	125	407	11.3
86-87	30	1184	389	196	.504	155	125	.806	110	566	18.9
Totals	131	3980	912	465	.510	465	349	.751	338	1328	10.1

Three-Point Field Goals: 1986-87, 49-for-117 (.419).

NBA REGULAR SEASON RECORD

									—Rebounds—									
Sea.—Team	G.	Min.	FGA	FGM	Pct.	FTA	FTM	Pct.	Off.	Def.	Tot.	Ast.	PF	Dq.	Stl.	Blk.	Pts.	Avg.
87-88—New York	82	3249	1013	438	.432	266	206	.774	120	276	396	868	244	2	205	6	1114	13.6
88-89—New York	72	2477	1025	479	.467	258	180	.698	106	235	341	619	163	1	139	7	1219	16.9
89-90—New York	82	2428	749	327	.437	165	120	.727	106	212	318	604	121	0	109	4	809	9.9
Totals	236	8154	2787	1244	.446	689	506	.734	332	723	1055	2091	528	3	453	17	3142	13.3

Three-Point Field Goals: 1987-88, 32-for-126 (.254). 1988-89, 81-for-240 (.338). 1989-90, 35-for-131 (.267). Totals, 148-for-497 (.298).

NBA PLAYOFF RECORD

									—Rebounds—									
Sea.—Team	G.	Min.	FGA	FGM	Pct.	FTA	FTM	Pct.	Off.	Def.	Tot.	Ast.	PF	Dq.	Stl.	Blk.	Pts.	Avg.
87-88—New York	4	171	60	22	.367	11	8	.727	6	13	19	39	13	0	10	0	57	14.3
88-89—New York	9	336	100	51	.510	28	19	.679	7	24	31	91	9	0	10	3	132	14.7
89-90—New York	9	81	31	13	.419	11	8	.727	1	4	5	21	5	0	2	0	34	3.8
Totals	22	588	191	86	.450	50	35	.700	14	41	55	151	27	0	22	3	223	10.1

Three-Point Field Goals: 1987-88, 5-for-12 (.417). 1988-89, 11-for-28 (.393). 1989-90, 0-for-2. Totals, 16-for-42 (.381).

NBA ALL-STAR GAME RECORD

								—Rebounds—								
Season—Team	Min.	FGA	FGM	Pct.	FTA	FTM	Pct.	Off.	Def.	Tot.	Ast.	PF	Dq.	Stl.	Blk.	Pts.
1989—New York	16	5	3	.600	4	2	.500	1	1	2	4	1	0	1	1	9

Three-Point Field Goals: 1989, 1-for-1 (1.000).

Named NBA Rookie of the Year, 1988. . . . NBA All-Rookie Team, 1988. . . . Led NCAA Division I in assists, 1986. . . . THE SPORTING NEWS All-America Second Team, 1987.

MICHAEL JACKSON

Born July 13, 1964 at Fairfax, Va. Height 6:02. Weight 185.
High School—Reston, Va., South Lakes.
College—Georgetown University, Washington, D. C.
Drafted by New York on second round, 1986 (47th pick).

Waived by New York, October 28, 1986; signed by Sacramento as a free agent, October 8, 1987.

Waived by Sacramento, December 19, 1988; re-signed by Sacramento, February 7, 1989, to a 10-day contract that expired, February 16, 1989.

—COLLEGIATE RECORD—

Year	G.	Min.	FGA	FGM	Pct.	FTA	FTM	Pct.	Reb.	Pts.	Avg.
82-83	32	858	278	128	.460	137	114	.832	51	370	11.6
83-84	31	833	226	115	.509	103	84	.816	52	314	10.1

Year	G.	Min.	FGA	FGM	Pct.	FTA	FTM	Pct.	Reb.	Pts.	Avg.
84-85	36	980	234	104	.444	75	55	.733	58	263	7.3
85-86	32	947	260	130	.500	95	77	.811	64	337	10.5
Totals	131	3618	998	477	.478	410	330	.805	225	1284	9.8

NBA REGULAR SEASON RECORD

								—Rebounds—									
Sea.—Team	G.	Min.	FGA	FGM	Pct.	FTA	FTM	Pct.	Off.	Def.	Tot.	Ast.	PF	Dq.	Stl.	Blk.	Pts.	Avg.
87-88—Sacramento	58	760	171	64	.374	32	23	.719	17	42	59	179	81	0	20	5	157	2.7
88-89—Sacramento	14	70	24	9	.375	2	1	.500	1	3	4	11	12	0	3	0	21	1.5
89-90—Sacramento	17	58	11	3	.273	6	3	.500	2	5	7	8	3	0	5	0	10	0.6
Totals	89	888	206	76	.369	40	27	.675	20	50	70	198	96	0	28	5	188	2.1

Three-Point Field Goals: 1987-88, 6-for-25 (.240). 1988-89, 2-for-6 (.333). 1989-90, 1-for-2 (.500). Totals, 9-for-33 (.273).

Member of NCAA Division I championship team, 1984.

ALFONSO JOHNSON JR.
(Buck)

Born January 3, 1964 at Birmingham, Ala. Height 6:07. Weight 200.
High School—Birmingham, Ala., Hayes.
College—University of Alabama, University, Ala.
Drafted by Houston on first round, 1986 (20th pick).

—COLLEGIATE RECORD—

Year	G.	Min.	FGA	FGM	Pct.	FTA	FTM	Pct.	Reb.	Pts.	Avg.
82-83	32	834	217	104	.479	88	56	.636	144	264	8.3
83-84	28	1042	356	183	.514	152	111	.730	237	477	17.0
84-85	33	1172	373	209	.560	156	111	.712	310	529	16.0
85-86	29	1082	407	235	.577	155	129	.832	242	599	20.7
Totals	122	4130	1353	731	.540	551	407	.739	933	1869	15.3

NBA REGULAR SEASON RECORD

									—Rebounds—									
Sea.—Team	G.	Min.	FGA	FGM	Pct.	FTA	FTM	Pct.	Off.	Def.	Tot.	Ast.	PF	Dq.	Stl.	Blk.	Pts.	Avg.
86-87—Houston	60	520	201	94	.468	58	40	.690	38	50	88	40	81	0	17	15	228	3.8
87-88—Houston	70	879	298	155	.520	91	67	.736	77	91	168	49	127	0	30	26	378	5.4
88-89—Houston	67	1850	515	270	.524	134	101	.754	114	172	286	126	213	4	64	35	642	9.6
89-90—Houston	82	2832	1019	504	.495	270	205	.759	113	268	381	252	321	8	104	62	1215	14.8
Totals	279	6081	2033	1023	.503	553	413	.747	342	581	923	467	742	12	215	138	2463	8.8

Three-Point Field Goals: 1986-87, 0-for-1. 1987-88, 1-for-8 (.125). 1988-89, 1-for-9 (.111). 1989-90, 2-for-17 (.118). Totals, 4-for-35 (.114).

NBA PLAYOFF RECORD

									—Rebounds—									
Sea.—Team	G.	Min.	FGA	FGM	Pct.	FTA	FTM	Pct.	Off.	Def.	Tot.	Ast.	PF	Dq.	Stl.	Blk.	Pts.	Avg.
86-87—Houston	5	10	6	2	.333	0	0	.000	0	0	0	0	1	0	0	0	4	0.8
87-88—Houston	4	20	3	2	.667	2	1	.500	2	2	4	0	1	0	1	0	5	1.3
88-89—Houston	4	118	40	19	.475	14	8	.571	6	8	14	12	15	0	3	2	46	11.5
89-90—Houston	4	148	48	20	.417	13	11	.846	8	8	16	9	16	0	6	2	51	12.8
Totals	17	296	97	43	.443	29	20	.690	16	18	34	21	33	0	10	4	106	6.2

Three-Point Field Goals: 1988-89, 0-for-1. 1989-90, 0-for-1. Totals, 0-for-2.

AVERY JOHNSON

Born March 25, 1965 at New Orleans, La. Height 5:11. Weight 175.
High School—New Orleans, La., St. Augustine.
Colleges—New Mexico Junior College, Hobbs, N.M., Cameron University, Lawton, Okla., and Southern University, Baton Rouge, La.
Never drafted by an NBA franchise.

Signed by Seattle as a free agent, August 2, 1988.

—COLLEGIATE RECORD—

New Mexico J.C.

Year	G.	Min.	FGA	FGM	Pct.	FTA	FTM	Pct.	Reb.	Pts.	Avg.
83-84	Statistics Unavailable										

Cameron

Year	G.	Min.	FGA	FGM	Pct.	FTA	FTM	Pct.	Reb.	Pts.	Avg.
84-85	33	....	106	54	.509	55	34	.618	31	142	4.3

Southern

Year	G.	Min.	FGA	FGM	Pct.	FTA	FTM	Pct.	Reb.	Pts.	Avg.
85-86			Did Not Play—Transfer Student								
86-87	31	1111	196	86	.439	65	40	.615	73	219	7.1
87-88	30	1145	257	138	.537	64	44	.688	84	342	11.4
Sou. Totals	61	2256	453	224	.494	129	84	.651	157	561	9.2
Col. Totals	94	....	559	278	.497	184	118	.641	188	703	7.5

Three-Point Field Goals: 1986-87, 7-for-24 (.292). 1987-88, 22-for-47 (.468). Totals, 29-for-71 (.408).

NBA REGULAR SEASON RECORD

									—Rebounds—									
Sea.—Team	G.	Min.	FGA	FGM	Pct.	FTA	FTM	Pct.	Off.	Def.	Tot.	Ast.	PF	Dq.	Stl.	Blk.	Pts.	Avg.
88-89—Seattle	43	291	83	29	.349	16	9	.563	11	13	24	73	34	0	21	3	68	1.6
89-90—Seattle	53	575	142	55	.387	40	29	.725	21	22	43	162	55	0	26	1	140	2.6
Totals	96	866	225	84	.373	56	38	.679	32	35	67	235	89	0	47	4	208	2.2

Three-Point Field Goals: 1988-89, 1-for-9 (.111). 1989-90, 1-for-4 (.250). Totals, 2-for-13 (.154).

NBA PLAYOFF RECORD

									—Rebounds—									
Sea.—Team	G.	Min.	FGA	FGM	Pct.	FTA	FTM	Pct.	Off.	Def.	Tot.	Ast.	PF	Dq.	Stl.	Blk.	Pts.	Avg.
88-89—Seattle	6	31	12	5	.417	2	1	.500	2	2	4	5	1	0	4	0	11	1.8

Three-Point Field Goals: 1988-89, 0-for-4.

Led NCAA Division I in assists, 1987 and 1988.

CLARENCE STEPHEN JOHNSON
(Steve)

Born November 3, 1957 at Akron, O. Height 6:10. Weight 240.

High School—San Bernardino, Calif., San Gorgonio.

College—Oregon State University, Corvallis, Ore.

Drafted by Kansas City on first round, 1981 (7th pick).

Traded by Kansas City with a 1984 2nd round draft choice and two 1985 2nd round draft choices to Chicago for Reggie Theus, February 15, 1984.

Traded by Chicago with a 1985 2nd round draft choice to San Antonio for Gene Banks, June 18, 1985.

Traded by San Antonio to Portland for Mychal Thompson and draft rights to Larry Krystkowiak, June 19, 1986.

Selected from Portland by Minnesota in NBA expansion draft, June 15, 1989.

Traded by Minnesota with a 1991 2nd round draft choice to Seattle for Brad Sellers, February 22, 1990.

—COLLEGIATE RECORD—

Year	G.	Min.	FGA	FGM	Pct.	FTA	FTM	Pct.	Reb.	Pts.	Avg.
76-77	28	616	267	159	.596	91	61	.670	156	379	13.5
77-78	3	62	45	26	.578	13	8	.615	29	60	20.0
78-79	27	724	298	197	.661	169	104	.615	178	498	18.4
79-80	30	711	297	211	.710	145	87	.600	207	509	17.0
80-81	28	716	315	235	.746	174	119	.684	215	589	21.0
Totals	116	2829	1222	828	.678	592	379	.640	785	2035	17.5

(Suffered broken left foot in 1977-78 season; granted extra year of eligibility).

NBA REGULAR SEASON RECORD

									—Rebounds—									
Sea.—Team	G.	Min.	FGA	FGM	Pct.	FTA	FTM	Pct.	Off.	Def.	Tot.	Ast.	PF	Dq.	Stl.	Blk.	Pts.	Avg.
81-82—Kansas City	78	1741	644	395	.613	330	212	.642	152	307	459	91	372	25	39	89	1002	12.8
82-83—Kansas City	79	1544	595	371	.624	324	186	.574	140	258	398	95	323	9	40	83	928	11.7
83-84—K.C.-Chi.	81	1487	540	302	.559	287	165	.575	162	256	418	81	307	15	37	69	769	9.5
84-85—Chicago	74	1659	516	281	.545	252	181	.718	146	291	437	64	265	7	37	62	743	10.0
85-86—San Antonio	71	1828	573	362	.632	373	259	.694	143	319	462	95	291	13	44	66	983	13.8
86-87—Portland	79	2345	889	494	.556	490	342	.698	194	372	566	155	340	16	49	76	1330	16.8
87-88—Portland	43	1050	488	258	.529	249	146	.586	84	158	242	57	151	4	17	32	662	15.4
88-89—Portland	72	1477	565	296	.524	245	129	.527	135	223	358	105	254	3	20	44	721	10.0
89-90—Min.-Sea.	25	259	92	48	.522	35	21	.600	19	34	53	17	56	0	3	5	117	4.7
Totals	602	13390	4902	2807	.573	2585	1641	.635	1175	2218	3393	760	2359	92	286	526	7255	12.1

Three-Point Field Goals: 1984-85, 0-for-3. 1987-88, 0-for-1. Totals, 0-for-4.

NBA PLAYOFF RECORD

									—Rebounds—									
Sea.—Team	G.	Min.	FGA	FGM	Pct.	FTA	FTM	Pct.	Off.	Def.	Tot.	Ast.	PF	Dq.	Stl.	Blk.	Pts.	Avg.
84-85—Chicago	3	22	7	2	.286	2	2	1.000	3	2	5	2	4	0	0	0	6	2.0
85-86—San Antonio	3	53	15	5	.333	11	5	.455	2	4	6	2	14	1	0	1	15	5.0
86-87—Portland	4	137	61	28	.459	43	27	.628	17	23	40	2	15	0	2	1	83	20.8
88-89—Portland	3	34	8	2	.250	3	3	1.000	1	5	6	0	7	0	2	0	7	2.3
Totals	13	246	91	37	.407	59	37	.627	23	34	57	6	40	1	4	2	111	8.5

NBA ALL-STAR GAME RECORD

Season—Team	Min.	FGA	FGM	Pct.	FTA	FTM	Pct.	—Rebounds— Off.	Def.	Tot.	Ast.	PF	Dq.	Stl.	Blk.	Pts.
1988—Portland							Did Not Play—Injured									

Led NBA in field-goal percentage, 1986. . . . Named to THE SPORTING NEWS All-America Second Team, 1981. . . . Holds NCAA record for career field-goal percentage. . . . Led NCAA in field-goal percentage, 1980 and 1981.

DENNIS WAYNE JOHNSON

Born September 18, 1954 at San Pedro, Calif. Height 6:04. Weight 202.

High School—Compton, Calif., Dominguez.

Colleges—Los Angeles Harbor Junior College, Wilmington, Calif., and Pepperdine University, Malibu, Calif.

Drafted by Seattle on second round as hardship case, 1976 (29th pick).

Traded by Seattle to Phoenix for Paul Westphal, June 4, 1980.

Traded by Phoenix with 1983 1st and 3rd round draft choices to Boston for Rick Robey and two 1983 2nd round draft choices, June 27, 1983.

—COLLEGIATE RECORD—

Los Angeles Harbor JC

Year	G.	Min.	FGA	FGM	Pct.	FTA	FTM	Pct.	Reb.	Pts.	Avg.
73-74	...	699	191	103	.539	82	45	.549	230	251	.....
74-75	28	967	....	....	....	....	...	....	336	511	18.3
JC Totals	...	1166	....	....	....	...	...	....	566	762	....

Pepperdine

Year	G.	Min.	FGA	FGM	Pct.	FTA	FTM	Pct.	Reb.	Pts.	Avg.
75-76	27	930	378	181	.479	112	63	.563	156	425	15.7

NBA REGULAR SEASON RECORD

Sea.—Team	G.	Min.	FGA	FGM	Pct.	FTA	FTM	Pct.	—Rebounds— Off.	Def.	Tot.	Ast.	PF	Dq.	Stl.	Blk.	Pts.	Avg.
76-77—Seattle	81	1667	566	285	.504	287	179	.624	161	141	302	123	221	3	123	57	749	9.2
77-78—Seattle	81	2209	881	367	.417	406	297	.732	152	142	294	230	213	2	118	51	1031	12.7
78-79—Seattle	80	2717	1110	482	.434	392	306	.781	146	228	374	280	209	2	100	97	1270	15.9
79-80—Seattle	81	2937	1361	574	.422	487	380	.780	173	241	414	332	267	6	144	82	1540	19.0
80-81—Phoenix	79	2615	1220	532	.436	501	411	.820	160	203	363	291	244	2	136	61	1486	18.8
81-82—Phoenix	80	2937	1228	577	.470	495	399	.806	142	268	410	369	253	6	105	55	1561	19.5
82-83—Phoenix	77	2551	861	398	.462	369	292	.791	92	243	335	388	204	1	97	39	1093	14.2
83-84—Boston	80	2665	878	384	.437	330	281	.852	87	193	280	338	251	6	93	57	1053	13.2
84-85—Boston	80	2976	1066	493	.462	306	261	.853	91	226	317	543	224	2	96	39	1254	15.7
85-86—Boston	78	2732	1060	482	.455	297	243	.818	69	199	268	456	206	3	110	35	1213	15.6
86-87—Boston	79	2933	953	423	.444	251	209	.833	45	216	261	594	201	0	87	38	1062	13.4
87-88—Boston	77	2670	803	352	.438	298	255	.856	62	178	240	598	204	0	93	29	971	12.6
88-89—Boston	72	2309	638	277	.434	195	160	.821	31	159	190	472	211	3	94	21	721	10.0
89-90—Boston	75	2036	475	206	.434	140	118	.843	48	153	201	485	179	2	81	14	531	7.1
Totals	1100	35954	13100	5832	.445	4754	3791	.797	1459	2790	4249	5499	3087	38	1477	675	15535	14.1

Three-Point Field Goals: 1979-80, 12-for-58 (.207). 1980-81, 11-for-51 (.216). 1981-82, 8-for-42 (.190). 1982-83, 5-for-31 (.161). 1983-84, 4-for-32 (.125). 1984-85, 7-for-26 (.269). 1985-86, 6-for-42 (.143). 1986-87, 7-for-62 (.113). 1987-88, 12-for-46 (.261). 1988-89, 7-for-50 (.140). 1989-90, 1-for-24 (.042). Totals, 80-for-464 (.172).

NBA PLAYOFF RECORD

Sea.—Team	G.	Min.	FGA	FGM	Pct.	FTA	FTM	Pct.	—Rebounds— Off.	Def.	Tot.	Ast.	PF	Dq.	Stl.	Blk.	Pts.	Avg.
77-78—Seattle	22	827	294	121	.412	159	112	.704	47	54	101	72	63	0	23	23	354	16.1
78-79—Seattle	17	691	302	136	.450	109	84	.771	44	60	104	69	63	0	28	26	356	20.9
79-80—Seattle	15	582	244	100	.410	62	52	.839	25	39	64	57	48	2	27	10	257	17.1
80-81—Phoenix	7	267	110	52	.473	42	32	.762	7	26	33	20	18	0	9	9	137	19.6
81-82—Phoenix	7	271	132	63	.477	39	30	.769	13	18	31	32	28	2	15	4	156	22.3
82-83—Phoenix	3	108	48	22	.458	12	10	.833	6	17	23	17	9	0	5	2	54	18.0
83-84—Boston	22	808	319	129	.404	120	104	.867	30	49	79	97	75	1	25	7	365	16.6
84-85—Boston	21	848	319	142	.445	93	80	.860	24	60	84	154	66	0	31	9	364	17.3
85-86—Boston	18	715	245	109	.445	84	67	.798	23	53	76	107	58	2	39	5	291	16.2
86-87—Boston	23	964	361	168	.465	113	96	.850	24	67	91	205	71	0	16	8	435	18.9
87-88—Boston	17	702	210	91	.433	103	82	.796	15	62	77	139	51	0	24	8	270	15.9
88-89—Boston	3	59	15	4	.267	0	0	....	2	2	4	9	8	0	3	0	8	2.7
89-90—Boston	5	162	62	30	.484	7	7	1.000	2	12	14	28	17	1	2	2	69	13.8
Totals	180	7004	2661	1167	.439	943	756	.802	262	519	781	1006	575	8	247	113	3116	17.3

Three-Point Field Goals: 1979-80, 5-for-15 (.333). 1980-81, 1-for-5 (.200). 1981-82, 0-for-3. 1982-83, 0-for-1. 1983-84, 3-for-7 (.429). 1984-85, 0-for-14. 1985-86, 6-for-16 (.375). 1986-87, 3-for-26 (.115). 1987-88, 6-for-16 (.375). 1989-90, 2-for-6 (.333). Totals, 26-for-109 (.239).

MAGIC JOHNSON

NBA ALL-STAR GAME RECORD

Season—Team	Min.	FGA	FGM	Pct.	FTA	FTM	Pct.	—Rebounds— Off.	Def.	Tot.	Ast.	PF	Dq.	Stl.	Blk.	Pts.
1979—Seattle	27	7	5	.714	2	2	1.000	1	0	1	3	3	0	0	1	12
1980—Seattle	20	13	7	.538	6	5	.833	2	2	4	1	3	0	2	1	19
1981—Phoenix	24	8	5	.625	10	9	.900	1	1	2	1	1	0	3	0	19
1982—Phoenix	15	2	0	.000	2	1	.500	2	3	5	1	1	0	0	2	1
1985—Boston	12	7	3	.429	2	2	1.000	1	5	6	3	2	0	0	0	8
Totals	98	37	20	.541	22	19	.864	7	11	18	9	10	0	5	4	59

Named to All-NBA First Team, 1981. . . . All-NBA Second Team, 1980. . . . NBA All-Defensive First Team, 1979, 1980, 1981, 1982, 1983, 1987. . . . NBA All-Defensive Second Team, 1984, 1985, 1986. . . . NBA Playoff MVP, 1979. . . . Member of NBA championship teams, 1979, 1984, 1986. . . . Shares NBA record for most free throws made in one half of championship series game, 12, vs. Los Angeles, June 12, 1984.

EARVIN JOHNSON JR.
(Magic)

Born August 14, 1959 at Lansing, Mich. Height 6:09. Weight 220.

High School—Lansing, Mich., Everett.

College—Michigan State University, East Lansing, Mich.

Drafted by Los Angeles on first round as an undergraduate, 1979 (1st pick).

—COLLEGIATE RECORD—

Year	G.	Min.	FGA	FGM	Pct.	FTA	FTM	Pct.	Reb.	Pts.	Avg.
77-78	30	....	382	175	.458	205	161	.785	237	511	17.0
78-79	32	1159	370	173	.468	240	202	.842	234	548	17.1
Totals	62	....	752	348	.463	445	363	.816	471	1059	17.1

NBA REGULAR SEASON RECORD

Sea.—Team	G.	Min.	FGA	FGM	Pct.	FTA	FTM	Pct.	—Rebounds— Off.	Def.	Tot.	Ast.	PF	Dq.	Stl.	Blk.	Pts.	Avg.
79-80—Los Angeles	77	2795	949	503	.530	462	374	.810	166	430	596	563	218	1	187	41	1387	18.0
80-81—Los Angeles	37	1371	587	312	.532	225	171	.760	101	219	320	317	100	0	127	27	798	21.6
81-82—Los Angeles	78	2991	1036	556	.537	433	329	.760	252	499	751	743	223	1	208	34	1447	18.6
82-83—Los Angeles	79	2907	933	511	.548	380	304	.800	214	469	683	829	200	1	176	47	1326	16.8
83-84—Los Angeles	67	2567	780	441	.565	358	290	.810	99	392	491	875	169	1	150	49	1178	17.6
84-85—L.A. Lakers	77	2781	899	504	.561	464	391	.843	90	386	476	968	155	0	113	25	1406	18.3
85-86—L.A. Lakers	72	2578	918	483	.526	434	378	.871	85	341	426	907	133	0	113	16	1354	18.8
86-87—L.A. Lakers	80	2904	1308	683	.522	631	535	.848	122	382	504	977	168	0	138	36	1909	23.9
87-88—L.A. Lakers	72	2637	996	490	.492	489	417	.853	88	361	449	858	147	0	114	13	1408	19.6
88-89—L.A. Lakers	77	2886	1137	579	.509	563	513	.911	111	496	607	988	172	0	138	22	1730	22.5
89-90—L.A. Lakers	79	2937	1138	546	.480	637	567	.890	128	394	522	907	167	1	132	34	1765	22.3
Totals	795	29354	10681	5608	.525	5076	4269	.841	1456	4369	5825	8932	1852	5	1596	344	15708	19.8

Three-Point Field Goals: 1979-80, 7-for-31 (.226). 1980-81, 3-for-17 (.176). 1981-82, 6-for-29 (.207). 1982-83, 0-for-21. 1983-84, 6-for-29 (.207). 1984-85, 7-for-37 (.189). 1985-86, 10-for-43 (.233). 1986-87, 8-for-39 (.205). 1987-88, 11-for-56 (.196). 1988-89, 59-for-188 (.314). 1989-90, 106-for-276 (.384). Totals, 223-for-766 (.291).

NBA PLAYOFF RECORD

Sea.—Team	G.	Min.	FGA	FGM	Pct.	FTA	FTM	Pct.	—Rebounds— Off.	Def.	Tot.	Ast.	PF	Dq.	Stl.	Blk.	Pts.	Avg.
79-80—Los Angeles	16	658	199	103	.518	106	85	.802	52	116	168	151	47	1	49	6	293	18.3
80-81—Los Angeles	3	127	49	19	.388	20	13	.650	8	33	41	21	14	1	8	3	51	17.0
81-82—Los Angeles	14	562	157	83	529	93	77	.828	54	104	158	130	50	0	40	3	243	17.4
82-83—Los Angeles	15	643	206	100	.485	81	68	.840	51	77	128	192	49	0	34	12	268	17.9
83-84—Los Angeles	21	837	274	151	.551	100	80	.800	26	113	139	284	71	0	42	20	382	18.2
84-85—L.A. Lakers	19	687	226	116	.513	118	100	.847	19	115	134	289	48	0	32	4	333	17.5
85-86—L.A. Lakers	14	541	205	110	.537	107	82	.766	21	79	100	211	43	0	27	1	302	21.6
86-87—L.A. Lakers	18	666	271	146	.539	118	98	.831	28	111	139	219	37	0	31	7	392	21.8
87-88—L.A. Lakers	24	965	329	169	.514	155	132	.852	32	98	130	303	61	0	34	4	477	19.9
88-89—L.A. Lakers	14	518	174	85	.489	86	78	.907	15	68	83	165	30	1	27	3	258	18.4
89-90—L.A. Lakers	9	376	155	76	.490	79	70	.886	12	45	57	115	28	0	11	1	227	25.2
Totals	167	6580	2245	1158	.516	1063	883	.831	318	959	1277	2080	478	3	335	64	3226	19.3

Three-Point Field Goals: 1979-80, 2-for-8 (.250). 1981-82, 0-for-4. 1982-83, 0-for-11. 1983-84, 0-for-7. 1984-85, 1-for-7 (.143). 1985-86, 0-for-11. 1986-87, 2-for-10 (.200). 1987-88, 7-for-14 (.500). 1988-89, 10-for-35 (.286). 1989-90, 5-for-25 (.200). Totals, 27-for-132 (.205).

NBA ALL-STAR GAME RECORD

Season—Team	Min.	FGA	FGM	Pct.	FTA	FTM	Pct.	—Rebounds— Off.	Def.	Tot.	Ast.	PF	Dq.	Stl.	Blk.	Pts.
1980—Los Angeles	24	8	5	.625	2	2	1.000	2	0	2	4	3	0	3	2	12
1982—Los Angeles	23	9	5	.556	7	6	.857	3	1	4	7	5	0	0	0	16
1983—Los Angeles	33	16	7	.438	4	3	.750	3	2	5	16	2	0	5	0	17
1984—Los Angeles	37	13	6	.462	2	2	1.000	4	5	9	22	3	0	3	2	15
1985—L.A. Lakers	31	14	7	.500	8	7	.875	2	3	5	15	2	0	1	0	21
1986—L.A. Lakers	28	3	1	.333	4	4	1.000	0	4	4	15	4	0	1	0	6

Season—Team	Min.	FGA	FGM	Pct.	FTA	FTM	Pct.	—Rebounds— Off.	Def.	Tot.	Ast.	PF	Dq.	Stl.	Blk.	Pts.
1987—L.A. Lakers..	34	10	4	.400	2	1	.500	1	6	7	13	2	0	4	0	9
1988—L.A. Lakers..	39	15	4	.267	9	9	1.000	1	5	6	19	2	0	2	2	17
1989—L.A. Lakers..	Did Not Play—Injured															
1990—L.A. Lakers..	25	15	9	.600	0	0	......	1	5	6	4	1	0	0	1	22
Totals	274	103	48	.466	38	34	.895	17	31	48	115	24	0	19	7	135

Three-Point Field Goals: 1980, 0-for-1. 1983, 0-for-2. 1984, 1-for-3 (.333). 1986, 0-for-1. 1988, 0-for-1. 1990, 4-for-6 (.667). Totals, 5-for-13 (.385).

NBA Most Valuable Player, 1987, 1989, 1990. . . . Named to All-NBA First Team, 1983, 1984, 1985, 1986, 1987, 1988, 1989, 1990. . . . All-NBA Second Team, 1982. . . . NBA All-Rookie Team, 1980. . . . NBA Playoff MVP, 1980, 1982, 1987. . . . Recipient of Schick Pivotal Player Award, 1984. . . . Member of NBA championship teams, 1980, 1982, 1985, 1987, 1988. . . . Holds all-time NBA playoff record for most assists. . . . Shares NBA playoff game record for most assists, 24, vs. Phoenix, May 15, 1984, and most assists in one half, 15, vs. Portland, May 3, 1985. . . . Holds NBA championship series game records for most assists, 21, vs. Boston, June 3, 1984, most assists in one half, 14, vs. Detroit, June 19, 1988, and shares record for most assists in one quarter, 8, vs. Boston, June 3, 1984. . . . Holds NBA All-Star Game records for career assists and assists in one game, 22, 1984. . . . Led NBA in steals, 1981 and 1982. . . . Led NBA in assists, 1983, 1984, 1986, 1987. . . . Led NBA in free-throw percentage, 1989. . . . Named to THE SPORTING NEWS All-America First Team, 1979. . . . NCAA Division I Tournament Most Outstanding Player, 1979. . . . Member of NCAA championship team, 1979.

EDWARD A. JOHNSON
(Eddie)

Born May 1, 1959 at Chicago, Ill. Height 6:07. Weight 215.
High School—Chicago, Ill., Westinghouse.
College—University of Illinois, Champaign, Ill.
Drafted by Kansas City on second round, 1981 (29th pick).

Traded by Sacramento to Phoenix for Ed Pinckney and a 1988 2nd round draft choice, June 21, 1987.

—COLLEGIATE RECORD—

Year	G.	Min.	FGA	FGM	Pct.	FTA	FTM	Pct.	Reb.	Pts.	Avg.
77-78	27	469	234	100	.427	27	20	.741	84	220	8.1
78-79	30	786	405	168	.415	49	26	.531	170	362	12.1
79-80	35	1215	576	266	.462	119	78	.655	310	610	17.4
80-81	29	1009	443	219	.494	82	62	.756	267	500	17.2
Totals	121	3479	1658	753	.454	277	186	.671	831	1692	14.0

NBA REGULAR SEASON RECORD

Sea.—Team	G.	Min.	FGA	FGM	Pct.	FTA	FTM	Pct.	—Rebounds— Off.	Def.	Tot.	Ast.	PF	Dq.	Stl.	Blk.	Pts.	Avg.
81-82—Kansas City	74	1517	643	295	.459	149	99	.664	128	194	322	109	210	6	50	14	690	9.3
82-83—Kansas City	82	2933	1370	677	.494	317	247	.779	191	310	501	216	259	3	70	20	1621	19.8
83-84—Kansas City	82	2920	1552	753	.485	331	268	.810	165	290	455	296	266	4	76	21	1794	21.9
84-85—Kansas City	82	3029	1565	769	.491	373	325	.871	151	256	407	273	237	2	83	22	1876	22.9
85-86—Sacramento	82	2514	1311	623	.475	343	280	.816	173	246	419	214	237	0	54	17	1530	18.7
86-87—Sacramento	81	2457	1309	606	.463	322	267	.829	146	207	353	251	218	4	42	19	1516	18.7
87-88—Phoenix	73	2177	1110	533	.480	240	204	.850	121	197	318	180	190	0	33	9	1294	17.7
88-89—Phoenix	70	2043	1224	608	.497	250	217	.868	91	215	306	162	198	0	47	7	1504	21.5
89-90—Phoenix	64	1811	907	411	.453	205	188	.917	69	177	246	107	174	4	32	10	1080	16.9
Totals	690	21401	10991	5275	.480	2530	2095	.828	1235	2092	3327	1808	1989	23	487	139	12905	18.7

Three-Point Field Goals: 1981-82, 1-for-11 (.091). 1982-83, 20-for-71 (.282). 1983-84, 20-for-64 (.313). 1984-85, 13-for-54 (.241). 1985-86, 4-for-20 (.200). 1986-87, 37-for-118 (314). 1987-88, 24-for-94 (.255). 1988-89, 71-for-172 (.413). 1989-90, 70-for-184 (.380). Totals, 260-for-788 (.330).

NBA PLAYOFF RECORD

Sea.—Team	G.	Min.	FGA	FGM	Pct.	FTA	FTM	Pct.	—Rebounds— Off.	Def.	Tot.	Ast.	PF	Dq.	Stl.	Blk.	Pts.	Avg.
83-84—Kansas City	3	107	48	21	.438	7	7	1.000	4	6	10	12	8	0	3	1	51	17.0
85-86—Sacramento	3	96	55	24	.436	9	8	.889	10	11	21	4	7	0	3	1	56	18.7
88-89—Phoenix	12	392	206	85	.413	39	30	.769	28	59	87	25	41	1	12	2	213	17.8
89-90—Phoenix	16	337	160	72	.450	47	37	.787	15	42	57	17	40	0	10	4	196	12.3
Totals	34	932	469	202	.431	102	82	.804	57	118	175	58	96	1	28	8	516	15.2

Three-Point Field Goals: 1983-84, 2-for-5 (.400). 1985-86, 0-for-3. 1988-89, 13-for-38 (.342). 1989-90, 15-for-38 (.395). Totals, 30-for-84 (.357).

Recipient of NBA Sixth Man Award, 1989.

ERIC JOHNSON

Born February 7, 1966 at Brooklyn, N.Y. Height 6:02. Weight 205.
High School—Brooklyn, N.Y., Franklin Roosevelt.
Colleges—Baylor University, Waco, Tex., and University of Nebraska, Lincoln, Neb.
Never drafted by an NBA franchise.

Signed by Utah as a free agent, September 28, 1989.

—COLLEGIATE RECORD—

Baylor

Year	G.	Min.	FGA	FGM	Pct.	FTA	FTM	Pct.	Reb.	Pts.	Avg.
84-85	28	677	260	103	.396	79	53	.671	74	259	9.3
85-86	18	....	189	69	.365	30	19	.633	53	157	8.7
Bay. Totals	46	....	449	172	.383	109	72	.661	127	416	9.0

Nebraska

Year	G.	Min.	FGA	FGM	Pct.	FTA	FTM	Pct.	Reb.	Pts.	Avg.
86-87	Did Not Play—Transfer Student										
87-88	31	889	254	110	.433	59	44	.746	110	274	8.8
88-89	32	996	288	126	.438	121	94	.777	121	373	11.7
Neb. Totals	63	1885	542	236	.435	180	138	.767	231	647	10.3
Col. Totals	109	....	991	408	.412	289	210	.727	358	1063	9.8

Three-Point Field Goals: 1987-88, 10-for-34 (.294). 1988-89, 27-for-74 (.365). Totals, 37-for-108 (.343).

NBA REGULAR SEASON RECORD

									—Rebounds—									
Sea.—Team	G.	Min.	FGA	FGM	Pct.	FTA	FTM	Pct.	Off.	Def.	Tot.	Ast.	PF	Dq.	Stl.	Blk.	Pts.	Avg.
89-90—Utah	48	272	84	20	.238	17	13	.765	8	20	28	64	49	1	17	2	54	1.1

Three-Point Field Goals: 1989-90, 1-for-6 (.167).

NBA PLAYOFF RECORD

									—Rebounds—									
Sea.—Team	G.	Min.	FGA	FGM	Pct.	FTA	FTM	Pct.	Off.	Def.	Tot.	Ast.	PF	Dq.	Stl.	Blk.	Pts.	Avg.
89-90—Utah	1	3	0	0	....	0	0	....	0	0	0	0	0	0	0	0	0	0.0

Brother of Detroit Pistons guard Vinnie Johnson.

KEVIN MAURICE JOHNSON

Born March 4, 1966 at Sacramento, Calif. Height 6:02. Weight 188.
High School—Sacramento, Calif., Sacramento.
College—University of California, Berkeley, Calif.
Drafted by Cleveland on first round, 1987 (7th pick).

Traded by Cleveland with Tyrone Corbin, Mark West, 1988 1st and 2nd round draft choices and a 1989 2nd round draft choice to Phoenix for Larry Nance, Mike Sanders and a 1988 2nd round draft choice, February 25, 1988.

—COLLEGIATE RECORD—

Year	G.	Min.	FGA	FGM	Pct.	FTA	FTM	Pct.	Reb.	Pts.	Avg.
83-84	28	....	192	98	.510	104	75	.721	83	271	9.7
84-85	27	....	282	127	.450	142	94	.662	104	348	12.9
85-86	29	....	335	164	.490	151	123	.815	104	451	15.6
86-87	34	....	450	212	.471	138	113	.819	132	585	17.2
Totals	118	....	1259	601	.477	535	405	.757	423	1655	14.0

Three-Point Field Goals: 1986-87, 48-for-124 (.387).

NBA REGULAR SEASON RECORD

									—Rebounds—									
Sea.—Team	G.	Min.	FGA	FGM	Pct.	FTA	FTM	Pct.	Off.	Def.	Tot.	Ast.	PF	Dq.	Stl.	Blk.	Pts.	Avg.
87-88—Clev.-Phoe.	80	1917	596	275	.461	211	177	.839	36	155	191	437	155	1	103	24	732	9.2
88-89—Phoenix	81	3179	1128	570	.505	576	508	.882	46	294	340	991	226	1	135	24	1650	20.4
89-90—Phoenix	74	2782	1159	578	.499	598	501	.838	42	228	270	846	143	0	95	14	1665	22.5
Totals	235	7878	2883	1423	.494	1385	1186	.856	124	677	801	2274	524	2	333	62	4047	17.2

Three-Point Field Goals: 1987-88, 5-for-24 (.208). 1988-89, 2-for-22 (.091). 1989-90, 8-for-41 (.195). Totals, 15-for-87 (.172).

NBA PLAYOFF RECORD

									—Rebounds—									
Sea.—Team	G.	Min.	FGA	FGM	Pct.	FTA	FTM	Pct.	Off.	Def.	Tot.	Ast.	PF	Dq.	Stl.	Blk.	Pts.	Avg.
88-89—Phoenix	12	494	182	90	.495	110	102	.927	12	39	51	147	28	0	19	5	285	23.0
89-90—Phoenix	16	582	257	123	.479	112	92	.821	9	44	53	170	28	0	25	0	340	21.3
Totals	28	1076	439	213	.485	222	194	.874	21	83	104	317	56	0	44	5	625	22.3

Three-Point Field Goals: 1988-89, 3-for-10 (.300). 1989-90, 2-for-11 (.182). Totals, 5-for-21 (.238).

NBA ALL-STAR GAME RECORD

								—Rebounds—								
Season—Team	Min.	FGA	FGM	Pct.	FTA	FTM	Pct.	Off.	Def.	Tot.	Ast.	PF	Dq.	Stl.	Blk.	Pts.
1990—Phoenix	14	1	1	1.000	0	0	....	0	0	0	4	2	0	0	0	2

RECORD AS BASEBALL PLAYER

Year Club	League	Pos.	G.	AB.	R.	H.	2B.	3B.	HR.	RBI.	B.A.	PO.	A.	E.	F.A.
1986—Modesto	Calif.	SS	2	2	1	0	0	0	0	0	.000	1	2	1	.750

Named to All-NBA Second Team, 1989 and 1990. . . . NBA Most Improved Player, 1989. . . . Drafted by Oakland Athletics in 23rd round of free-agent draft, June 2, 1986.

MARQUES KEVIN JOHNSON

Born February 8, 1956 at Nachitoches, La. Height 6:07. Weight 224.
High School—Los Angeles, Calif., Crenshaw.
College—University of California at Los Angeles, Los Angeles, Calif.
Drafted by Milwaukee on first round, 1977 (3rd pick).

Traded by Milwaukee with Harvey Catchings, Junior Bridgeman and cash to Los Angeles Clippers for Terry Cummings, Craig Hodges and Ricky Pierce, September 29, 1984.
Signed by Golden State as an unrestricted free agent, October 7, 1989.
Waived by Golden State, November 29, 1989.
Missed entire 1987-88 season due to injury.

—COLLEGIATE RECORD—

Year	G.	Min.	FGA	FGM	Pct.	FTA	FTM	Pct.	Reb.	Pts.	Avg.
73-74	27	....	131	83	.634	38	28	.737	90	194	7.2
74-75	29	....	254	138	.543	86	59	.686	205	335	11.6
75-76	32	1165	413	223	.540	140	106	.757	301	552	17.3
76-77	27	1004	413	244	.591	145	90	.621	301	578	21.4
Totals	115	....	1211	688	.568	409	283	.692	897	1659	14.4

NBA REGULAR SEASON RECORD

									—Rebounds—									
Sea.—Team	G.	Min.	FGA	FGM	Pct.	FTA	FTM	Pct.	Off.	Def.	Tot.	Ast.	PF	Dq.	Stl.	Blk.	Pts.	Avg.
77-78—Milwaukee	80	2765	1204	628	.522	409	301	.736	292	555	847	190	221	3	92	103	1557	19.5
78-79—Milwaukee	77	2779	1491	820	.550	437	332	.760	212	374	586	234	186	1	116	89	1972	25.6
79-80—Milwaukee	77	2686	1267	689	.544	368	291	.791	217	349	566	273	173	0	100	70	1671	21.7
80-81—Milwaukee	76	2542	1153	636	.552	381	269	.706	225	293	518	346	196	1	115	41	1541	20.3
81-82—Milwaukee	60	1900	760	404	.532	260	182	.700	153	211	364	213	142	1	59	35	990	16.5
82-83—Milwaukee	80	2853	1420	723	.509	359	264	.735	196	366	562	363	211	0	100	56	1714	21.4
83-84—Milwaukee	74	2715	1288	646	.502	340	241	.709	173	307	480	315	194	1	115	45	1535	20.7
84-85—L.A. Clippers	72	2448	1094	494	.452	260	190	.731	184	244	428	248	193	2	72	30	1181	16.4
85-86—L.A. Clippers	75	2605	1201	613	.510	392	298	.760	156	260	416	283	214	2	107	50	1525	20.3
86-87—L.A. Clippers	10	302	155	68	.439	42	30	.714	9	24	33	28	24	0	12	5	166	16.6
89-90—Golden State	10	99	32	12	.375	17	14	.824	8	9	17	9	12	0	0	1	40	4.0
Totals	691	23694	11065	5733	.518	3265	2412	.739	1825	2992	4817	2502	1766	11	888	525	13892	20.1

Three-Point Field Goals: 1979-80, 2-for-9 (.222). 1980-81, 0-for-9. 1981-82, 0-for-4. 1982-83, 4-for-20 (.200). 1983-84, 2-for-13 (.154). 1984-85, 3-for-13 (.231). 1985-86, 1-for-15 (.067). 1986-87, 0-for-6. 1989-90, 2-for-3 (.667). Totals, 14-for-92 (.152).

NBA PLAYOFF RECORD

									—Rebounds—									
Sea.—Team	G.	Min.	FGA	FGM	Pct.	FTA	FTM	Pct.	Off.	Def.	Tot.	Ast.	PF	Dq.	Stl.	Blk.	Pts.	Avg.
77-78—Milwaukee	9	321	153	84	.549	64	48	.750	35	77	112	31	25	0	10	17	216	24.0
79-80—Milwaukee	7	303	128	54	.422	40	30	.750	17	31	48	20	20	0	5	6	139	19.9
80-81—Milwaukee	7	266	135	75	.556	32	23	.719	41	25	66	34	14	0	10	7	173	24.7
81-82—Milwaukee	6	235	100	44	.440	42	24	.571	23	21	44	20	25	0	6	2	113	18.8
82-83—Milwaukee	9	382	175	85	.486	43	28	.651	28	44	72	38	22	0	8	7	198	22.0
83-84—Milwaukee	16	605	273	129	.473	90	65	.722	29	56	85	55	50	0	17	6	324	20.3
Totals	54	2112	964	471	.489	311	218	.701	173	254	427	198	156	0	56	45	1163	21.5

Three-Point Field Goals: 1979-80, 1-for-3 (.333). 1980-81, 0-for-1. 1981-82, 1-for-4 (.250). 1982-83, 0-for-1. 1983-84, 1-for-4 (.250). Totals, 3-for-13 (.231).

NBA ALL-STAR GAME RECORD

								—Rebounds—								
Season—Team	Min.	FGA	FGM	Pct.	FTA	FTM	Pct.	Off.	Def.	Tot.	Ast.	PF	Dq.	Stl.	Blk.	Pts.
1979—Milwaukee	20	11	3	.273	6	4	.667	3	3	6	2	1	0	0	0	10
1980—Milwaukee	34	6	1	.167	2	2	1.000	1	3	4	1	2	0	1	1	4
1981—Milwaukee	19	2	1	.500	6	5	.833	1	3	4	2	2	0	0	0	7
1983—Milwaukee	20	10	3	.300	2	1	.500	2	0	2	2	1	0	0	1	7
1986—L.A. Clippers	13	6	3	.500	0	0	.000	2	1	3	2	3	0	0	0	6
Totals	106	35	11	.314	16	12	.750	9	10	19	9	9	0	1	2	34

Named to All-NBA First Team, 1979. . . . All-NBA Second Team, 1980 and 1981. . . . NBA All-Rookie Team, 1978. . . . NBA Comeback Player of the Year, 1986. . . . THE SPORTING NEWS College Player of the Year, 1977. . . . THE SPORTING NEWS All-America First Team, 1977. . . . Member of NCAA Division I championship team, 1975.

—DID YOU KNOW—

That the Detroit Pistons hadn't won a game at Portland's Memorial Coliseum since October 1974 before sweeping the Trail Blazers in three straight last spring to win their second straight league title?

VINCENT JOHNSON
(Vinnie)

Born September 1, 1956 at Brooklyn, N. Y. Height 6:02. Weight 200.
High School—Brooklyn, N. Y., Franklin Roosevelt.
Colleges—McLennan Community College, Waco, Tex., and Baylor University, Waco, Tex.
Drafted by Seattle on first round, 1979 (7th pick).

Traded by Seattle to Detroit for Greg Kelser, November 23, 1981.

—COLLEGIATE RECORD—

McLennan CC

Year	G.	Min.	FGA	FGM	Pct.	FTA	FTM	Pct.	Reb.	Pts.	Avg.
75-76	35	....	...	398	....	...	169	....	....	965	27.6
76-77	31	....	...	382	....	...	152	....	....	916	29.5
JC Totals	66	....	....	780	....	...	321	....	....	1881	28.5

Baylor

Year	G.	Min.	FGA	FGM	Pct.	FTA	FTM	Pct.	Reb.	Pts.	Avg.
77-78	25	....	481	241	.501	141	93	.660	140	575	23.0
78-79	26	....	502	262	.522	170	132	.776	128	656	25.2
Totals	51	....	983	503	.512	311	225	.723	268	1231	24.1

NBA REGULAR SEASON RECORD

									—Rebounds—									
Sea.—Team	G.	Min.	FGA	FGM	Pct.	FTA	FTM	Pct.	Off.	Def.	Tot.	Ast.	PF	Dq.	Stl.	Blk.	Pts.	Avg.
79-80—Seattle	38	325	115	45	.391	39	31	.795	19	36	55	54	40	0	19	4	121	3.2
80-81—Seattle	81	2311	785	419	.534	270	214	.793	193	173	366	341	198	0	78	20	1053	13.0
81-82—Sea.-Det.	74	1295	444	217	.489	142	107	.754	82	77	159	171	101	0	56	25	544	7.4
82-83—Detroit	82	2511	1013	520	.513	315	245	.778	167	186	353	301	263	2	93	49	1296	15.8
83-84—Detroit	82	1909	901	426	.473	275	207	.753	130	107	237	271	196	1	44	19	1063	13.0
84-85—Detroit	82	2093	942	428	.454	247	190	.769	134	118	252	325	205	2	71	20	1051	12.8
85-86—Detroit	79	1978	996	465	.467	214	165	.771	119	107	226	269	180	2	80	23	1097	13.9
86-87—Detroit	78	2166	1154	533	.462	201	158	.786	123	134	257	300	159	0	92	16	1228	15.7
87-88—Detroit	82	1935	959	425	.443	217	147	.677	90	141	231	267	164	0	58	18	1002	12.2
88-89—Detroit	82	2073	996	462	.464	263	193	.734	109	146	255	242	155	0	74	17	1130	13.8
89-90—Detroit	82	1972	775	334	.431	196	131	.668	108	148	256	255	143	0	71	13	804	9.8
Totals	842	20568	9080	4274	.471	2379	1788	.752	1274	1373	2647	2796	1804	7	736	224	10389	12.3

Three-Point Field Goals: 1979-80, 0-for-1. 1980-81, 1-for-5 (.200). 1981-82, 3-for-12 (.250). 1982-83, 11-for-40 (.275). 1983-84, 4-for-19 (.211). 1984-85, 5-for-27 (.185). 1985-86, 2-for-13 (.154). 1986-87, 4-for-14 (.286). 1987-88, 5-for-24 (.208). 1988-89, 13-for-44 (.295). 1989-90, 5-for-34 (.147). Totals, 53-for-233 (.227).

NBA PLAYOFF RECORD

									—Rebounds—									
Sea.—Team	G.	Min.	FGA	FGM	Pct.	FTA	FTM	Pct.	Off.	Def.	Tot.	Ast.	PF	Dq.	Stl.	Blk.	Pts.	Avg.
79-80—Seattle	5	12	3	1	.333	0	0	.000	0	2	2	2	1	0	1	0	2	0.4
83-84—Detroit	5	132	46	17	.370	19	17	.895	5	9	14	12	9	0	1	1	51	10.2
84-85—Detroit	9	235	103	53	.515	28	22	.786	15	12	27	29	24	0	6	1	128	14.2
85-86—Detroit	4	85	49	22	.449	13	7	.538	8	9	17	11	9	0	3	0	51	12.8
86-87—Detroit	15	388	207	95	.459	36	31	.861	20	24	44	62	33	0	9	4	221	14.7
87-88—Detroit	23	477	239	101	.423	50	33	.660	35	40	75	43	48	0	17	4	236	10.3
88-89—Detroit	17	372	200	91	.455	62	47	.758	16	29	45	43	32	0	4	3	239	14.1
89-90—Detroit	20	463	184	85	.462	43	34	.791	28	28	56	54	38	0	8	4	206	10.3
Totals	98	2164	1031	465	.451	251	191	.761	127	153	280	256	194	0	49	17	1134	11.6

Three-Point Field Goals: 1983-84, 0-for-1. 1984-85, 0-for-3. 1985-86, 0-for-1. 1986-87, 0-for-2. 1987-88, 1-for-7 (.143). 1988-89, 10-for-24 (.417). 1989-90, 2-for-7 (.286). Totals, 13-for-45 (.289).

Member of NBA championship teams, 1989 and 1990.

NATE JOHNSTON

Born December 18, 1966 at Birmingham, Ala. Height 6:08. Weight 210.
High School—Belle Glade, Fla.
College—University of Tampa, Tampa, Fla.
Drafted by Miami on third round, 1988 (59th pick).

Waived by Miami, October 24, 1988; signed by Portland as a free agent, August 22, 1989.
Waived by Portland, October 31, 1989; signed by Utah as a free agent, November 10, 1989.
Waived by Utah, December 15, 1989; signed by Portland, January 8, 1990, to the first of consecutive 10-day contracts that expired, January 27, 1990.
Re-signed by Portland, January 29, 1990, for remainder of season.
Played in Continental Basketball Association with Quad City Thunder, 1988-89 and 1989-90.

—COLLEGIATE RECORD—

Year	G.	Min.	FGA	FGM	Pct.	FTA	FTM	Pct.	Reb.	Pts.	Avg.
84-85	31	954	203	99	.488	126	90	.714	165	288	9.3
85-86	30	984	327	170	.520	120	90	.750	362	430	14.3
86-87	32	966	389	180	.463	168	124	.738	228	512	16.0
87-88	32	1022	485	234	.482	158	121	.766	248	629	19.7
Totals	125	3926	1404	683	.486	572	425	.743	1003	1859	14.9

Three-Point Field Goals: 1986-87, 28-for-86 (.326). 1987-88, 40-for-112 (.357). Totals, 68-for-198 (.343).

CBA REGULAR SEASON RECORD

			—2-Point—			—3-Point—									
Sea.—Team	G.	Min.	FGM	FGA	Pct.	FGM	FGA	Pct.	FTM	FTA	Pct.	Reb.	Ast.	Pts.	Avg.
88-89—Quad City	53	1055	184	399	.461	34	107	.318	107	136	.787	257	75	577	10.9
89-90—Quad City	10	241	44	92	.478	1	1	1.000	24	35	.686	65	11	115	11.5
Totals	63	1296	228	491	.464	35	108	.324	131	171	.766	322	86	692	11.0

NBA REGULAR SEASON RECORD

									—Rebounds—									
Sea.—Team	G.	Min.	FGA	FGM	Pct.	FTA	FTM	Pct.	Off.	Def.	Tot.	Ast.	PF	Dq.	Stl.	Blk.	Pts.	Avg.
89-90—Utah-Port.	21	87	48	18	.375	13	9	.692	13	10	23	1	11	1	3	8	46	2.2

Three-Point Field Goals: 1989-90, 1-for-4 (.250).

NBA PLAYOFF RECORD

									—Rebounds—									
Sea.—Team	G.	Min.	FGA	FGM	Pct.	FTA	FTM	Pct.	Off.	Def.	Tot.	Ast.	PF	Dq.	Stl.	Blk.	Pts.	Avg.
89-90—Portland	3	19	11	6	.545	1	1	1.000	2	4	6	1	5	0	1	1	13	4.3

ANTHONY HAMILTON JONES

Born September 13, 1962 at Washington, D.C. Height 6:06. Weight 195.

High School—Washington, D.C., Dunbar.

Colleges—Georgetown University, Washington, D.C., and University of Nevada-Las Vegas, Las Vegas, Nev.

Drafted by Washington on first round, 1986 (21st pick).

Waived by Washington, December 23, 1986; signed by San Antonio as a free agent, December 29, 1986.

Waived by San Antonio, November 3, 1987; signed by Chicago as a free agent, September 27, 1988.

Waived by Chicago, November 21, 1988; signed by Dallas, January 22, 1989, to the first of consecutive 10-day contracts that expired, February 10, 1989.

Re-signed by Dallas, February 14, 1989, for remainder of season.

Played in Continental Basketball Association with Pensacola Tornados, 1987-88 and 1988-89.

—COLLEGIATE RECORD—

Georgetown

Year	G.	Min.	FGA	FGM	Pct.	FTA	FTM	Pct.	Reb.	Pts.	Avg.
81-82	37	643	207	102	.493	73	44	.603	104	248	6.7
82-83	25	504	163	86	.528	42	15	.357	88	187	7.5
G'town Totals	62	1147	370	188	.508	115	59	.513	192	435	7.0

Nevada-Las Vegas

Year	G.	Min.	FGA	FGM	Pct.	FTA	FTM	Pct.	Reb.	Pts.	Avg.
83-84					Transfer Student—Did Not Play						
84-85	31	976	364	182	.500	67	40	.597	136	414	13.4
85-86	38	1259	543	277	.510	118	89	.754	207	684	18.0
UNLV Totals	69	2235	907	459	.506	185	129	.697	343	1098	15.9
Totals	131	3382	1277	647	.507	300	188	.627	535	1533	11.7

Three-Point Field Goals: 1984-85, 10-for-32 (.313). 1985-86, 41-for 92 (.446). Totals, 51-for-124 (.411).

CBA REGULAR SEASON RECORD

			—2-Point—			—3-Point—									
Sea.—Team	G.	Min.	FGM	FGA	Pct.	FGM	FGA	Pct.	FTM	FTA	Pct.	Reb.	Ast.	Pts.	Avg.
87-88—Pensacola	41	1494	286	572	.500	43	101	.426	228	286	.797	217	101	929	22.6
88-89—Pensacola	15	587	118	234	.504	21	64	.328	73	98	.745	88	25	372	24.8
Totals	56	2081	404	806	.501	64	165	.388	301	384	.784	305	126	1301	23.2

NBA REGULAR SEASON RECORD

									—Rebounds—									
Sea.—Team	G.	Min.	FGA	FGM	Pct.	FTA	FTM	Pct.	Off.	Def.	Tot.	Ast.	PF	Dq.	Stl.	Blk.	Pts.	Avg.
86-87—Wash.-S.A.	65	858	322	133	.413	65	50	.769	40	64	104	73	79	0	42	19	323	5.0
88-89—Chi.-Dallas	33	196	79	29	.367	16	14	.875	14	14	28	17	20	0	11	3	76	2.3
89-90—Dallas	66	650	194	72	.371	69	47	.681	33	49	82	29	77	0	32	16	195	3.0
Totals	164	1704	595	234	.393	150	111	.740	87	127	214	119	176	0	85	38	594	3.6

Three-Point Field Goals: 1986-87, 7-for-20 (.350). 1988-89, 4-for-16 (.250). 1989-90, 4-for-13 (.308). Totals, 15-for-49 (.306).

NBA PLAYOFF RECORD

									—Rebounds—									
Sea.—Team	G.	Min.	FGA	FGM	Pct.	FTA	FTM	Pct.	Off.	Def.	Tot.	Ast.	PF	Dq.	Stl.	Blk.	Pts.	Avg.
89-90—Dallas	1	3	0	0	....	0	0	....	0	0	0	0	0	0	0	0	0	0.0

CALDWELL JONES

Born August 4, 1950 at McGehee, Ark. Height 6:11. Weight 225.
High School—Rohwer, Ark., Desha Central.
College—Albany State College, Albany, Ga.
Drafted by Philadelphia on second round, 1973 (32nd pick).

Selected by Virginia on third round of ABA draft, 1973.
Signed by San Diego; Larry Miller sent by San Diego to Virginia as compensation, October 29, 1973.
Signed by Philadelphia (for future services), February 25, 1975.
Purchased by Kentucky from disbanded San Diego franchise, November 14, 1975.
Traded by Kentucky to St. Louis for Maurice Lucas, December 17, 1975.
Traded by Philadelphia with a 1983 1st round draft choice to Houston for Moses Malone, September 15, 1982.
Traded by Houston to Chicago for Mitchell Wiggins and 1985 2nd and 3rd round draft choices, August 10, 1984.
Signed by Portland as a Veteran Free Agent, October 1, 1985; Chicago agreed not to exercise its right of first refusal in exchange for a 1987 2nd round draft choice.
Signed by San Antonio as an unrestricted free agent, July 20, 1989.

—COLLEGIATE RECORD—

Year	G.	Min.	FGA	FGM	Pct.	FTA	FTM	Pct.	Reb.	Pts.	Avg.
69-70†	25	....	367	185	.504	108	80	.741	440	450	18.0
70-71	27	....	437	206	.471	137	76	.555	576	488	18.1
71-72	28	....	539	288	.534	219	156	.712	567	732	26.1
72-73	29	....	470	238	.506	134	91	.679	633	567	19.6
Varsity Totals	109	....	1813	917	.506	598	403	.674	2216	2237	20.5

ABA REGULAR SEASON RECORD

			2-Point			3-Point									
Sea.—Team	G.	Min.	FGM	FGA	Pct.	FGM	FGA	Pct.	FTM	FTA	Pct.	Reb.	Ast.	Pts.	Avg.
73-74—San Diego	79	2929	505	1083	.466	2	8	.250	171	230	.743	1095	144	1187	15.0
74-75—San Diego	76	3004	603	1229	.491	3	11	.273	264	335	.788	1074	162	1479	19.5
75-76—SD-Ky-St.L.	76	2674	423	893	.474	0	7	.000	140	186	.753	853	147	986	13.0
Totals	231	8607	1531	3205	.478	5	26	.192	575	751	.766	3022	453	3652	15.8

ABA PLAYOFF RECORD

			2-Point			3-Point									
Sea.—Team	G.	Min.	FGM	FGA	Pct.	FGM	FGA	Pct.	FTM	FTA	Pct.	Reb.	Ast.	Pts.	Avg.
73-74—San Diego	6	277	36	88	.409	0	0	.000	11	16	.688	94	15	83	13.8

ABA ALL-STAR GAME RECORD

		2-Point			3-Point									
Sea.—Team	Min.	FGM	FGA	Pct.	FGM	FGA	Pct.	FTM	FTA	Pct.	Reb.	Ast.	Pts.	Avg.
1975—San Diego	15	2	4	.500	0	0	.000	1	1	1.000	4	0	5	5.0

NBA REGULAR SEASON RECORD

									—Rebounds—									
Sea.—Team	G.	Min.	FGA	FGM	Pct.	FTA	FTM	Pct.	Off.	Def.	Tot.	Ast.	PF	Dq.	Stl.	Blk.	Pts.	Avg.
76-77—Philadelphia	82	2023	424	215	.507	116	64	.552	190	476	666	92	301	3	43	200	494	6.0
77-78—Philadelphia	80	1636	359	169	.471	153	96	.627	165	405	570	92	281	4	26	127	434	5.4
78-79—Philadelphia	78	2171	637	302	.474	162	121	.747	177	570	747	151	303	10	39	157	725	9.3
79-80—Philadelphia	80	2771	532	232	.436	178	124	.697	219	731	950	164	298	5	43	162	588	7.4
80-81—Philadelphia	81	2639	485	218	.449	193	148	.767	200	613	813	122	271	2	53	134	584	7.2
81-82—Philadelphia	81	2446	465	231	.497	219	179	.817	164	544	708	100	301	3	38	146	641	7.9
82-83—Houston	82	2440	677	307	.453	206	162	.786	222	446	668	138	278	2	46	131	776	9.5
83-84—Houston	81	2506	633	318	.502	196	164	.837	168	414	582	156	335	7	46	80	801	9.9
84-85—Chicago	42	885	115	53	.461	47	36	.766	49	162	211	34	125	3	12	31	142	3.4
85-86—Portland	80	1437	254	126	.496	150	124	.827	105	250	355	74	244	2	38	61	376	4.7
86-87—Portland	78	1578	224	111	.496	124	97	.782	114	341	455	64	227	5	23	77	319	4.1
87-88—Portland	79	1778	263	128	.487	106	78	.736	105	303	408	81	251	0	29	99	334	4.2
88-89—Portland	72	1279	183	77	.421	61	48	.787	88	212	300	59	166	0	24	85	202	2.8
89-90—San Antonio	72	885	144	67	.465	54	38	.704	76	154	230	20	146	2	20	27	173	2.4
Totals	1068	26474	5395	2554	.473	1965	1479	.753	2042	5621	7663	1347	3527	48	480	1517	6589	6.2

Three-Point Field Goals: 1979-80, 0-for-2. 1981-82, 0-for-3. 1982-83, 0-for-2. 1983-84, 1-for-3 (.333). 1984-85, 0-for-2. 1985-86, 0-for-7. 1986-87, 0-for-2. 1987-88, 0-for-4. 1988-89, 0-for-1. 1989-90, 1-for-5 (.200). Totals, 2-for-31 (.065).

NBA PLAYOFF RECORD

									—Rebounds—									
Sea.—Team	G.	Min.	FGA	FGM	Pct.	FTA	FTM	Pct.	Off.	Def.	Tot.	Ast.	PF	Dq.	Stl.	Blk.	Pts.	Avg.
76-77—Philadelphia	19	513	73	37	.507	30	18	.600	38	112	150	20	81	4	9	40	92	4.8
77-78—Philadelphia	10	301	56	28	.500	10	8	.800	22	84	106	14	36	2	5	30	64	6.4
78-79—Philadelphia	9	320	89	43	.483	36	28	.778	37	84	121	21	36	0	4	22	114	12.7
79-80—Philadelphia	18	639	129	58	.450	52	42	.808	50	135	185	34	75	1	13	37	158	8.8
80-81—Philadelphia	16	580	95	54	.568	42	31	.738	37	118	155	27	53	0	7	31	139	8.7
81-82—Philadelphia	21	679	160	74	.463	41	35	.854	52	137	189	19	77	1	11	40	183	8.7
84-85—Chicago	2	18	6	5	.833	0	0	.000	1	4	5	0	7	1	0	1	10	5.0
85-86—Portland	4	73	17	6	.353	4	2	.500	9	10	19	3	13	0	0	2	14	3.5
86-87—Portland	4	129	12	5	.417	6	5	.833	9	22	31	6	15	0	0	6	15	3.8
87-88—Portland	4	98	16	6	.375	2	1	.500	4	13	17	1	17	0	2	8	13	3.3

Sea.—Team	G.	Min.	FGA	FGM	Pct.	FTA	FTM	Pct.	Rebounds Off.	Def.	Tot.	Ast.	PF	Dq.	Stl.	Blk.	Pts.	Avg.
88-89—Portland	3	50	3	2	.667	0	0	.000	2	6	8	0	6	0	0	3	4	1.3
89-90—San Antonio	9	66	9	4	.444	1	0	.000	6	7	13	2	10	0	0	3	8	0.9
Totals	119	3466	665	322	.484	224	170	.759	267	732	999	147	426	9	51	223	814	6.8

Three-Point Field Goals: 1979-80, 0-for-3. 1984-85, 0-for-1. Totals, 0-for-4.

COMBINED ABA AND NBA REGULAR SEASON RECORDS

Sea.—Team	G.	Min.	FGA	FGM	Pct.	FTA	FTM	Pct.	Rebounds Off.	Def.	Tot.	Ast.	PF	Dq.	Stl.	Blk.	Pts.	Avg.
Totals	1299	35081	8626	4090	.474	2716	2054	.756	2921	7764	10685	1800	4436	48	685	2297	10241	7.9

Named to NBA All-Defensive First Team, 1981 and 1982. . . . Shares ABA record for most blocked shots in one game, 12, vs. Carolina, January 6, 1974. . . . Led ABA in blocked shots, 1974 and 1975. . . . Brother of Washington Bullets forward-center Charles Jones.

CHARLES JONES

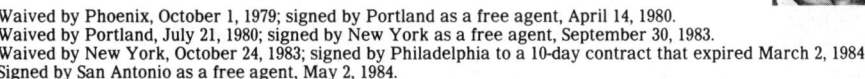

Born April 3, 1957 at McGehee, Ark. Height 6:09. Weight 215.

High School—McGehee, Ark., Delta.

College—Albany State College, Albany, Ga.

Drafted by Phoenix on eighth round, 1979 (165th pick).

Waived by Phoenix, October 1, 1979; signed by Portland as a free agent, April 14, 1980.
Waived by Portland, July 21, 1980; signed by New York as a free agent, September 30, 1983.
Waived by New York, October 24, 1983; signed by Philadelphia to a 10-day contract that expired March 2, 1984.
Signed by San Antonio as a free agent, May 2, 1984.
Waived by San Antonio, September 11, 1984; signed by Chicago as a free agent, September 20, 1984.
Waived by Chicago, November 16, 1984; signed by Washington as a free agent, February 14, 1985.
Played in Continental Basketball Association with Maine Lumberjacks during 1979-80 and 1982-83 seasons, with Bay State Bombardiers during 1983-84 season and with Tampa Bay Thrillers during 1984-85 season.
Played in France during 1980-81 season.
Played in Italy during 1981-82 season.

—COLLEGIATE RECORD—

Year	G.	Min.	FGA	FGM	Pct.	FTA	FTM	Pct.	Reb.	Pts.	Avg.
75-76	24	....	206	106	.515	35	16	.457	198	228	9.5
76-77	27	....	284	136	.479	84	39	.464	374	311	11.5
77-78	27	....	276	148	.536	100	68	.680	368	364	13.5
78-79	29	....	352	182	.517	97	66	.680	438	430	14.8
Totals	107	....	1118	572	.512	316	189	.598	1378	1333	12.5

CBA REGULAR SEASON RECORD

Sea.—Team	G.	Min.	2-Point FGM	FGA	Pct.	3-Point FGM	FGA	Pct.	FTM	FTA	Pct.	Reb.	Ast.	Pts.	Avg.
79-80—Maine	39	1606	222	459	.484	0	2	.000	60	94	.619	506	70	504	12.9
82-83—Maine	24	914	105	215	.488	0	1	.000	70	89	.786	223	35	280	11.7
83-84—Bay State	37	1365	149	297	.501	0	1	.000	94	139	.676	293	73	392	10.6
84-85—Tampa Bay	24	802	80	154	.519	0	1	.000	38	53	.716	227	38	198	8.3
Totals	124	4687	556	1125	.494	0	5	.000	262	760	.560	1249	216	1374	11.1

ITALIAN LEAGUE RECORD

Year	G.	Min.	FGA	FGM	Pct.	FTA	FTM	Pct.	Reb.	Pts.	Avg.
81-82—S. Benedetto	38	1458	398	215	.540	114	73	.640	429	503	13.2

NBA REGULAR SEASON RECORD

Sea.—Team	G.	Min.	FGA	FGM	Pct.	FTA	FTM	Pct.	Rebounds Off.	Def.	Tot.	Ast.	PF	Dq.	Stl.	Blk.	Pts.	Avg.
83-84—Philadelphia	1	3	1	0	.000	4	1	.250	0	0	0	0	1	0	0	0	1	1.0
84-85—Chi.-Wash.	31	667	127	67	.528	58	40	.690	71	113	184	26	107	3	22	79	174	5.6
85-86—Washington	81	1609	254	129	.508	86	54	.628	122	199	321	76	235	2	57	133	312	3.9
86-87—Washington	79	1609	249	118	.474	76	48	.632	144	212	356	80	252	2	67	165	284	3.6
87-88—Washington	69	1313	177	72	.407	75	53	.707	106	219	325	59	226	5	53	113	197	2.9
88-89—Washington	53	1154	125	60	.480	25	16	.640	77	180	257	42	187	4	39	76	136	2.6
89-90—Washington	81	2240	185	94	.508	105	68	.648	145	359	504	139	296	10	50	197	256	3.2
Totals	395	8595	1118	540	.483	429	280	.653	665	1282	1947	422	1304	26	288	763	1360	3.4

Three-Point Field Goals: 1985-86, 0-for-2. 1986-87, 0-for-1. 1987-88, 0-for-1. 1988-89, 0-for-1. Totals, 0-for-5.

NBA PLAYOFF RECORD

Sea.—Team	G.	Min.	FGA	FGM	Pct.	FTA	FTM	Pct.	Rebounds Off.	Def.	Tot.	Ast.	PF	Dq.	Stl.	Blk.	Pts.	Avg.
84-85—Washington	4	110	19	10	.526	16	9	.563	11	15	26	3	16	0	3	10	29	7.3
85-86—Washington	5	72	11	4	.364	4	4	1.000	6	3	9	3	13	0	2	2	12	2.4
86-87—Washington	3	56	5	3	.600	0	0	.000	1	7	8	3	9	0	2	5	6	2.0
87-88—Washington	5	95	5	1	.200	2	1	.500	5	12	17	2	18	0	2	4	3	0.6
Totals	17	333	40	18	.450	22	14	.636	23	37	60	11	56	0	9	21	50	2.9

Led CBA in blocked shots, 1980, 1983 and 1984. . . . Named to CBA All-Star Second Team, 1984. . . . CBA

All-Defensive First Team, 1983 and 1984.... CBA All-Defensive Second Team, 1985.... Brother of former ABA and NBA forward-center Caldwell Jones.

MICHAEL JEFFREY JORDAN

Born February 17, 1963 at Brooklyn, N. Y. Height 6:06. Weight 198.

High School—Wilmington, N. C., Laney.

College—University of North Carolina, Chapel Hill, N. C.

Drafted by Chicago on first round as an undergraduate, 1984 (3rd pick).

—COLLEGIATE RECORD—

Year	G.	Min.	FGA	FGM	Pct.	FTA	FTM	Pct.	Reb.	Pts.	Avg.
81-82	34	....	358	191	.534	108	78	.722	149	460	13.5
82-83	36	....	527	182	.535	167	123	.737	197	721	20.0
83-84	31	....	448	247	.551	145	113	.779	163	607	19.6
Totals	101	....	1333	720	.540	420	314	.748	509	1788	17.7

Three-Point Field Goals: 1982-83, 34-for-76 (.447).

NBA REGULAR SEASON RECORD

									—Rebounds—									
Sea.—Team	G.	Min.	FGA	FGM	Pct.	FTA	FTM	Pct.	Off.	Def.	Tot.	Ast.	PF	Dq.	Stl.	Blk.	Pts.	Avg.
84-85—Chicago	82	3144	1625	837	.515	746	630	.845	167	367	534	481	285	4	196	69	2313	28.2
85-86—Chicago	18	451	328	150	.457	125	105	.840	23	41	64	53	46	0	37	21	408	22.7
86-87—Chicago	82	3281	2279	1098	.482	972	833	.857	166	264	430	377	237	0	236	125	3041	37.1
87-88—Chicago	82	3311	1998	1069	.535	860	723	.841	139	310	449	485	270	2	259	131	2868	35.0
88-89—Chicago	81	3255	1795	966	.538	793	674	.850	149	503	652	650	247	2	234	65	2633	32.5
89-90—Chicago	82	3197	1964	1034	.526	699	593	.848	143	422	565	519	241	0	227	54	2753	33.6
Totals	427	16639	9989	5154	.516	4195	3558	.848	787	1907	2694	2565	1326	8	1189	465	14016	32.8

Three-Point Field Goals: 1984-85, 9-for-52 (.173). 1985-86, 3-for-18 (.167). 1986-87, 12-for-66 (.182). 1987-88, 7-for-53 (.132). 1988-89, 27-for-98 (.276). 1989-90, 92-for-245 (.376). Totals, 150-for-532 (.282).

NBA PLAYOFF RECORD

									—Rebounds—									
Sea.—Team	G.	Min.	FGA	FGM	Pct.	FTA	FTM	Pct.	Off.	Def.	Tot.	Ast.	PF	Dq.	Stl.	Blk.	Pts.	Avg.
84-85—Chicago	4	171	78	34	.436	58	48	.828	7	16	23	34	15	0	11	4	117	29.3
85-86—Chicago	3	135	95	48	.505	39	34	.872	5	14	19	17	13	1	7	4	131	43.7
86-87—Chicago	3	128	84	35	.417	39	35	.897	7	14	21	18	11	0	6	7	107	35.7
87-88—Chicago	10	427	260	138	.531	99	86	.869	23	48	71	47	38	1	24	11	363	36.3
88-89—Chicago	17	718	390	199	.510	229	183	.799	26	93	119	130	65	1	42	13	591	34.8
89-90—Chicago	16	674	426	219	.514	159	133	.836	24	91	115	109	54	0	45	14	587	36.7
Totals	53	2253	1333	673	.505	623	519	.833	92	276	368	355	196	3	135	53	1896	35.8

Three-Point Field Goals: 1984-85, 1-for-8 (.125). 1985-86, 1-for-1 (1.000). 1986-87, 2-for-5 (.400). 1987-88, 1-for-3 (.333). 1988-89, 10-for-35 (.286). 1989-90, 16-for-50 (.320). Totals, 31-for-102 (.304).

NBA ALL-STAR GAME RECORD

								—Rebounds—								
Season—Team	Min.	FGA	FGM	Pct.	FTA	FTM	Pct.	Off.	Def.	Tot.	Ast.	PF	Dq.	Stl.	Blk.	Pts.
1985—Chicago	22	9	2	.222	4	3	.750	3	3	6	2	4	0	3	1	7
1986—Chicago							Did Not Play—Injured									
1987—Chicago	28	12	5	.417	2	1	.500	0	0	0	4	2	0	2	0	11
1988—Chicago	29	23	17	.739	6	6	1.000	3	5	8	3	5	0	4	4	40
1989—Chicago	33	23	13	.565	4	2	.500	1	1	2	3	1	0	5	0	28
1990—Chicago	29	17	8	.471	0	0	....	1	4	5	2	1	0	5	1	17
Totals	141	84	45	.536	16	12	.750	8	13	21	14	13	0	19	6	103

Three-Point Field Goals: 1985, 0-for-1. 1987, 0-for-1. 1989, 0-for-1. 1990, 1-for-1 (1.000). Totals, 1-for-4 (.250).

NBA Most Valuable Player, 1988.... Named to All-NBA First Team, 1987, 1988, 1989, 1990.... All-NBA Second Team, 1985.... NBA Defensive Player of the Year, 1988.... NBA All-Defensive First Team, 1988, 1989, 1990.... NBA All-Star Game MVP, 1988.... NBA Rookie of the Year, 1985.... NBA All-Rookie Team, 1985.... Recipient of Schick Pivotal Player Award, 1985 and 1989.... Led NBA in scoring, 1987, 1988, 1989, 1990.... Led NBA in steals, 1988 and 1990.... Holds NBA playoff game record for most points, 63, vs. Boston, April 20, 1986.... Member of NCAA Division I championship team, 1982.... Member of U.S. Olympic Team, 1984.... Named THE SPORTING NEWS College Player of the Year, 1983 and 1984.... THE SPORTING NEWS All-America First Team, 1983 and 1984.

SHAWN T. KEMP

Born November 26, 1969 at Elkhart, Ind. Height 6:10. Weight 230.

High School—Elkhart, Ind., Concord.

Colleges—University of Kentucky, Lexington, Ky.,
and Trinity Valley Community College, Athens, Tex.

Drafted by Seattle on first round as an undergraduate, 1989 (17th pick).

—COLLEGIATE RECORD—

Kentucky

Year	G.	Min.	FGA	FGM	Pct.	FTA	FTM	Pct.	Reb.	Pts.	Avg.
88-89	Did Not Play—Left School Before Basketball Season										

Trinity Valley CC

Year	G.	Min.	FGA	FGM	Pct.	FTA	FTM	Pct.	Reb.	Pts.	Avg.
88-89	Did Not Play										

NBA REGULAR SEASON RECORD

								—Rebounds—									
Sea.—Team	G.	Min.	FGA	FGM	Pct.	FTA	FTM	Pct.	Off.	Def.	Tot.	Ast.	PF	Dq.	Stl.	Blk.	Pts.	Avg.
89-90—Seattle	81	1120	424	203	.479	159	117	.736	146	200	346	26	204	5	47	70	525	6.5

Three-Point Field Goals: 1989-90, 2-for-12 (.167).

TIMOTHY JOSEPH KEMPTON
(Tim)

Born January 25, 1964 at Jamaica, N.Y. Height 6.10. Weight 245.
High School—Oyster Bay, N.Y., St. Dominic.
College—University of Notre Dame, South Bend, Ind.
Drafted by Los Angeles Clippers on sixth round, 1986 (124th pick).

Became free agent, July 1, 1988; signed by Charlotte as a free agent, August 17, 1988.
Traded by Charlotte to Denver for a 1991 2nd round draft choice, September 11, 1989.
Played in Italy, 1988-89.

—COLLEGIATE RECORD—

Year	G.	Min.	FGA	FGM	Pct.	FTA	FTM	Pct.	Reb.	Pts.	Avg.
82-83	27	739	168	101	.601	113	83	.735	159	285	10.6
83-84	26	775	165	78	.473	148	113	.764	165	269	10.3
84-85	27	671	141	62	.440	87	68	.782	130	192	7.1
85-86	27	617	127	69	.543	58	43	.741	143	181	6.5
Totals	108	2802	601	310	.516	406	307	.756	597	927	8.6

ITALIAN LEAGUE RECORD

Year	G.	Min.	FGA	FGM	Pct.	FTA	FTM	Pct.	Reb.	Pts.	Avg.
88-89—Wuber	33	1229	462	252	.545	188	127	.676	298	631	19.1

NBA REGULAR SEASON RECORD

									—Rebounds—									
Sea.—Team	G.	Min.	FGA	FGM	Pct.	FTA	FTM	Pct.	Off.	Def.	Tot.	Ast.	PF	Dq.	Stl.	Blk.	Pts.	Avg.
86-87—L.A. Clippers	66	936	206	97	.471	137	95	.693	70	124	194	53	162	6	38	12	289	4.4
88-89—Charlotte	79	1341	335	171	.510	207	142	.686	91	213	304	102	215	3	41	14	484	6.1
89-90—Denver	71	1061	312	153	.490	114	77	.675	51	167	218	118	144	2	30	9	383	5.4
Totals	216	3338	853	421	.494	458	314	.686	212	504	716	273	521	11	109	35	1156	5.4

Three-Point Field Goals: 1986-87, 0-for-1. 1988-89, 0-for-1. 1989-90, 0-for-1. Totals, 0-for-3.

NBA PLAYOFF RECORD

									—Rebounds—									
Sea.—Team	G.	Min.	FGA	FGM	Pct.	FTA	FTM	Pct.	Off.	Def.	Tot.	Ast.	PF	Dq.	Stl.	Blk.	Pts.	Avg.
89-90—Denver	3	32	9	7	.778	4	4	1.000	1	4	5	4	8	0	0	0	18	6.0

STEPHEN DOUGLAS KERR
(Steve)

Born September 27, 1965 at Beirut, Lebanon. Height 6:03. Weight 175.
High School—Pacific Palisades, Calif.
College—University of Arizona, Tucson, Ariz.
Drafted by Phoenix on second round, 1988 (50th pick).

Traded by Phoenix to Cleveland for a 1993 2nd round draft choice, September 5, 1989.

—COLLEGIATE RECORD—

Year	G.	Min.	FGA	FGM	Pct.	FTA	FTM	Pct.	Reb.	Pts.	Avg.
83-84	28	633	157	81	.516	52	36	.692	33	198	7.1
84-85	31	1036	222	126	.568	71	57	.803	73	309	10.0
85-86	32	1228	361	195	.540	79	71	.899	101	461	14.4
86-87	Did Not Play—Knee Injury										
87-88	38	1239	270	151	.559	74	61	.824	76	477	12.6
Totals	129	4136	1010	553	.548	276	225	.815	283	1445	11.2

Three-Point Field Goals: 1987-88, 114-for-199 (.573).

STEVE KERR

NBA REGULAR SEASON RECORD

									—Rebounds—									
Sea.—Team	G.	Min.	FGA	FGM	Pct.	FTA	FTM	Pct.	Off.	Def.	Tot.	Ast.	PF	Dq.	Stl.	Blk.	Pts.	Avg.
88-89—Phoenix	26	157	46	20	.435	9	6	.667	3	14	17	24	12	0	7	0	54	2.1
89-90—Cleveland	78	1664	432	192	.444	73	63	.863	12	86	98	248	59	0	45	7	520	6.7
Totals	104	1821	478	212	.444	82	69	.841	15	100	115	272	71	0	52	7	574	5.5

Three-Point Field Goals: 1988-89, 8-for-17 (.471). 1989-90, 73-for-144 (.507). Totals, 81-for-161 (.503).

NBA PLAYOFF RECORD

									—Rebounds—									
Sea.—Team	G.	Min.	FGA	FGM	Pct.	FTA	FTM	Pct.	Off.	Def.	Tot.	Ast.	PF	Dq.	Stl.	Blk.	Pts.	Avg.
89-90—Cleveland	5	73	14	4	.286	0	0	....	1	5	6	10	6	0	4	0	8	1.6

Three-Point Field Goals: 1989-90, 0-for-3.

Led NBA in three-point field-goal percentage, 1990.

JEROME KERSEY

Born June 26, 1962 at Clarksville, Va. Height 6:07. Weight 222.

High School—Clarksville, Va., Bluestone.

College—Longwood College, Farmville, Va.

Drafted by Portland on second round, 1984 (46th pick).

—COLLEGIATE RECORD—

Year	G.	Min.	FGA	FGM	Pct.	FTA	FTM	Pct.	Reb.	Pts.	Avg.
80-81	28	....	313	197	.629	133	78	.586	249	472	16.9
81-82	23	....	282	165	.585	98	62	.633	260	392	17.0
82-83	25	....	257	144	.560	125	76	.608	270	364	14.6
83-84	27	....	411	214	.521	165	100	.606	383	528	19.6
Totals	103	....	1263	720	.570	521	316	.607	1162	1756	17.0

NBA REGULAR SEASON RECORD

									—Rebounds—									
Sea.—Team	G.	Min.	FGA	FGM	Pct.	FTA	FTM	Pct.	Off.	Def.	Tot.	Ast.	PF	Dq.	Stl.	Blk.	Pts.	Avg.
84-85—Portland	77	958	372	178	.478	181	117	.646	95	111	206	63	147	1	49	29	473	6.1
85-86—Portland	79	1217	470	258	.549	229	156	.681	137	156	293	83	208	2	85	32	672	8.5
86-87—Portland	82	2088	733	373	.509	364	262	.720	201	295	496	194	328	5	122	77	1009	12.3
87-88—Portland	79	2888	1225	611	.499	396	291	.735	211	446	657	243	302	8	127	65	1516	19.2
88-89—Portland	76	2716	1137	533	.469	372	258	.694	246	383	629	243	277	6	137	84	1330	17.5
89-90—Portland	82	2843	1085	519	.478	390	269	.690	251	439	690	188	304	7	121	63	1310	16.0
Totals	475	12710	5022	2472	.492	1932	1353	.700	1141	1830	2971	1014	1566	29	641	350	6310	13.3

Three-Point Field Goals: 1984-85, 0-for-3. 1985-86, 0-for-6. 1986-87, 1-for-23 (.043). 1987-88, 3-for-15 (.200). 1988-89, 6-for-21 (.286). 1989-90, 3-for-20 (.150). Totals, 13-for-88 (.148).

NBA PLAYOFF RECORD

									—Rebounds—									
Sea.—Team	G.	Min.	FGA	FGM	Pct.	FTA	FTM	Pct.	Off.	Def.	Tot.	Ast.	PF	Dq.	Stl.	Blk.	Pts.	Avg.
84-85—Portland	8	60	31	16	.516	8	6	.750	5	4	9	6	11	0	7	2	38	4.8
85-86—Portland	4	56	22	9	.409	4	4	1.000	7	8	15	4	13	0	1	4	22	5.5
86-87—Portland	4	60	25	10	.400	4	4	1.000	6	13	19	3	13	0	5	1	24	6.0
87-88—Portland	4	127	65	32	.492	21	15	.714	17	13	30	9	17	1	7	4	79	19.8
88-89—Portland	3	117	47	23	.489	19	15	.789	11	13	24	7	12	0	10	1	61	20.3
89-90—Portland	21	831	361	166	.460	144	103	.715	66	108	174	45	87	2	34	20	435	20.7
Totals	44	1251	551	256	.465	200	147	.735	112	159	271	74	153	3	64	32	659	15.0

Three-Point Field Goals: 1985-86, 0-for-1. 1987-88, 0-for-1. 1988-89, 0-for-2. 1989-90, 0-for-3. Totals, 0-for-7.

Led NCAA Division II in rebounding, 1984.

RANDOLPH KEYS

Born April 19, 1966 at Collins, Miss. Height 6:07. Weight 195.

High School—Collins, Miss.

College—University of Southern Mississippi, Hattiesburg, Miss.

Drafted by Cleveland on first round, 1988 (22nd pick).

Traded by Cleveland to Charlotte for a future 2nd round draft choice, February 22, 1990.

—COLLEGIATE RECORD—

Year	G.	Min.	FGA	FGM	Pct.	FTA	FTM	Pct.	Reb.	Pts.	Avg.
84-85	28	396	112	51	.455	36	26	.722	70	128	4.6
85-86	29	923	366	184	.503	72	42	.583	164	410	14.1
86-87	34	1142	525	243	.463	85	60	.706	268	558	16.4
87-88	30	978	455	216	.475	102	78	.765	221	530	17.7
Totals	121	3439	1458	694	.476	295	206	.698	723	1626	13.4

Three-Point Field Goals: 1986-87, 12-for-51 (.235). 1987-88, 20-for-58 (.345). Totals, 32-for-109 (.294).

NBA REGULAR SEASON RECORD

										—Rebounds—								
Sea.—Team	G.	Min.	FGA	FGM	Pct.	FTA	FTM	Pct.	Off.	Def.	Tot.	Ast.	PF	Dq.	Stl.	Blk.	Pts.	Avg.
88-89—Cleveland	42	331	172	74	.430	29	20	.690	23	33	56	19	51	0	12	6	169	4.0
89-90—Clev.-Char.	80	1615	678	293	.432	140	101	.721	100	153	253	88	224	1	68	8	701	8.8
Totals	122	1946	850	367	.432	169	121	.716	123	186	309	107	275	1	80	14	870	7.1

Three-Point Field Goals: 1988-89, 1-for-10 (.100). 1989-90, 14-for-43 (.326). Totals, 15-for-53 (.283).

NBA PLAYOFF RECORD

										—Rebounds—								
Sea.—Team	G.	Min.	FGA	FGM	Pct.	FTA	FTM	Pct.	Off.	Def.	Tot.	Ast.	PF	Dq.	Stl.	Blk.	Pts.	Avg.
88-89—Cleveland	1	12	3	0	.000	0	0	—	0	3	3	1	1	0	0	0	0	0.0

Three-Point Field Goals: 1988-89, 0-for-1.

STAN KIMBROUGH

Born April 24, 1966 at Tuscaloosa, Ala. Height 5:11. Weight 155.

High School—Cleveland, O., St. Joseph's.

Colleges—University of Central Florida, Orlando, Fla., and Xavier University, Cincinnati, O.

Never drafted by an NBA franchise.

Signed by Detroit as a free agent, September 18, 1989.
Waived by Detroit, December 6, 1989.
Played in Continental Basketball Association with Grand Rapids Hoops, 1989-90.

—COLLEGIATE RECORD—

Central Florida

Year	G.	Min.	FGA	FGM	Pct.	FTA	FTM	Pct.	Reb.	Pts.	Avg.
84-85	28	1047	417	207	.496	124	93	.750	94	507	18.1

Xavier

Year	G.	Min.	FGA	FGM	Pct.	FTA	FTM	Pct.	Reb.	Pts.	Avg.
85-86	Did Not Play—Transfer Student										
86-87	32	1159	429	195	.455	115	82	.713	112	511	16.0
87-88	30	969	329	177	.538	98	80	.816	91	465	15.5
88-89	33	1178	477	234	.491	109	82	.752	89	620	18.8
Xav. Totals	95	3306	1235	606	.491	322	244	.758	292	1596	16.8
Col. Totals	123	4353	1652	813	.492	446	337	.756	386	2103	17.1

Three-Point Field Goals: 1986-87, 39-for-98 (.398). 1987-88, 31-for-74 (.419). 1988-89, 70-for-168 (.417). Totals, 140-for-340 (.412).

CBA REGULAR SEASON RECORD

			—2-Point—			—3-Point—									
Sea.—Team	G.	Min.	FGM	FGA	Pct.	FGM	FGA	Pct.	FTM	FTA	Pct.	Reb.	Ast.	Pts.	Avg.
89-90—Grand Rapids	40	1211	143	285	.502	22	73	.301	77	93	.828	143	204	429	10.7

NBA REGULAR SEASON RECORD

										—Rebounds—								
Sea.—Team	G.	Min.	FGA	FGM	Pct.	FTA	FTM	Pct.	Off.	Def.	Tot.	Ast.	PF	Dq.	Stl.	Blk.	Pts.	Avg.
89-90—Detroit	10	50	16	7	.438	2	2	1.000	4	3	7	5	4	0	4	0	16	1.6

BERNARD KING

Born December 4, 1956 at Brooklyn, N. Y. Height 6:07. Weight 205.

High School—Brooklyn, N. Y., Fort Hamilton.

College—University of Tennessee, Knoxville, Tenn.

Drafted by New Jersey on first round as an undergraduate, 1977 (7th pick).

Traded by New Jersey with John Gianelli and Jim Boylan to Utah for Rich Kelley, October 2, 1979.
Traded by Utah to Golden State for Wayne Cooper and a 1981 2nd round draft choice, September 11, 1980.
Signed by New York as a Veteran Free Agent, September 28, 1982; Golden State matched offer and traded King to New York for Micheal Ray Richardson and a 1984 5th round draft choice, October 22, 1982.
Signed by Washington as a free agent, October 16, 1987.
Missed entire 1985-86 season due to injury.

—COLLEGIATE RECORD—

Year	G.	Min.	FGA	FGM	Pct.	FTA	FTM	Pct.	Reb.	Pts.	Avg.
74-75	25	....	439	273	.622	147	115	.782	308	661	26.4
75-76	25	....	454	260	.573	163	109	.669	325	629	25.2
76-77	26	....	481	278	.578	163	116	.712	371	672	25.8
Totals	76	....	1374	811	.590	473	340	.719	1004	1962	25.8

NBA REGULAR SEASON RECORD

Sea.—Team	G.	Min.	FGA	FGM	Pct.	FTA	FTM	Pct.	—Rebounds— Off.	Def.	Tot.	Ast.	PF	Dq.	Stl.	Blk.	Pts.	Avg.
77-78—New Jersey	79	3092	1665	798	.479	462	313	.677	265	486	751	193	302	5	122	36	1909	24.2
78-79—New Jersey	82	2859	1359	710	.522	619	349	.564	251	418	669	295	326	10	118	39	1769	21.6
79-80—Utah	19	419	137	71	.518	63	34	.540	24	64	88	52	66	3	7	4	176	9.3
80-81—Golden State	81	2914	1244	731	.588	437	307	.703	178	373	551	287	304	5	72	34	1771	21.9
81-82—Golden State	79	2861	1307	740	.566	499	352	.705	140	329	469	282	285	6	78	23	1833	23.2
82-83—New York	68	2207	1142	603	.528	388	280	.722	99	227	326	195	233	5	90	13	1486	21.9
83-84—New York	77	2667	1391	795	.572	561	437	.779	123	271	394	164	273	2	75	17	2027	26.3
84-85—New York	55	2063	1303	691	.530	552	426	.772	114	203	317	204	191	3	71	15	1809	32.9
86-87—New York	6	214	105	52	.495	43	32	.744	13	19	32	19	14	0	2	0	136	22.7
87-88—Washington	69	2044	938	470	.501	324	247	.762	86	194	280	192	202	3	49	10	1188	17.2
88-89—Washington	81	2559	1371	654	.477	441	361	.819	133	251	384	294	219	1	64	13	1674	20.7
89-90—Washington	82	2687	1459	711	.487	513	412	.803	129	275	404	376	230	1	51	7	1837	22.4
Totals	778	26586	13421	7026	.524	4902	3550	.724	1555	3110	4665	2553	2645	44	799	211	17615	22.6

Three-Point Field Goals: 1980-81, 2-for-6 (.333). 1981-82, 1-for-5 (.200). 1982-83, 0-for-6. 1983-84, 0-for-4. 1984-85, 1-for-10 (.100). 1987-88, 1-for-6 (.167). 1988-89, 5-for-30 (.167). 1989-90, 3-for-23 (.130). Totals, 13-for-90 (.144).

NBA PLAYOFF RECORD

Sea.—Team	G.	Min.	FGA	FGM	Pct.	FTA	FTM	Pct.	—Rebounds— Off.	Def.	Tot.	Ast.	PF	Dq.	Stl.	Blk.	Pts.	Avg.
78-79—New Jersey	2	81	42	21	.500	24	10	.417	5	6	11	7	10	0	4	0	52	26.0
82-83—New York	6	184	97	56	.577	35	28	.800	8	16	24	13	16	0	2	0	141	23.5
83-84—New York	12	477	282	162	.574	123	93	.756	28	46	74	36	48	0	14	6	417	34.8
87-88—Washington	5	168	53	26	.491	21	17	.810	3	8	11	9	17	0	3	0	69	13.8
Totals	25	910	474	265	.559	203	148	.729	44	76	120	65	91	0	23	6	679	27.2

Three-Point Field Goals: 1982-83, 1-for-3 (.333). 1983-84, 0-for-1. Totals, 1-for-4 (.250).

NBA ALL-STAR GAME RECORD

Season—Team	Min.	FGA	FGM	Pct.	FTA	FTM	Pct.	—Rebounds— Off.	Def.	Tot.	Ast.	PF	Dq.	Stl.	Blk.	Pts.
1982—Golden State	14	7	2	.286	2	2	1.000	0	4	4	1	2	0	3	1	6
1984—New York	22	13	8	.615	5	2	.400	2	1	3	4	2	0	0	0	18
1985—New York	22	10	6	.600	2	1	.500	4	3	7	1	5	0	0	0	13
Totals	58	30	16	.533	9	5	.556	6	8	14	6	9	0	3	1	37

Named to All-NBA First Team, 1984 and 1985. . . . Named to All-NBA Second Team, 1982. . . . Led NBA in scoring, 1985. . . . NBA All-Rookie Team, 1978. . . . NBA Comeback Player of the Year, 1981. . . . Named to THE SPORTING NEWS All-America Second Team, 1977. . . . Led NCAA in field-goal percentage, 1975. . . . Brother of former NBA forward Albert King.

RONALD STACEY KING

(Known by middle name.)

Born January 29, 1967 at Lawton, Okla. Height 6:11. Weight 230.

High School—Lawton, Okla.

College—University of Oklahoma, Norman, Okla.

Drafted by Chicago on first round, 1989 (6th pick).

—COLLEGIATE RECORD—

Year	G.	Min.	FGA	FGM	Pct.	FTA	FTM	Pct.	Reb.	Pts.	Avg.
85-86	14	230	67	26	.388	43	32	.744	53	84	6.0
86-87	28	441	162	71	.438	87	54	.621	108	196	7.0
87-88	39	1212	621	337	.543	289	195	.675	332	869	22.3
88-89	33	1142	618	324	.524	294	211	.718	332	859	26.0
Totals	114	3025	1468	758	.516	713	492	.690	825	2008	17.6

Three-Point Field Goals: 1986-87, 0-for-1. 1987-88, 0-for-1. Totals, 0-for-2.

NBA REGULAR SEASON RECORD

Sea.—Team	G.	Min.	FGA	FGM	Pct.	FTA	FTM	Pct.	—Rebounds— Off.	Def.	Tot.	Ast.	PF	Dq.	Stl.	Blk.	Pts.	Avg.
89-90—Chicago	82	1777	530	267	.504	267	194	.727	169	215	384	87	215	0	38	58	728	8.9

Three-Point Field Goals: 1989-90, 0-for-1.

NBA PLAYOFF RECORD

Sea.—Team	G.	Min.	FGA	FGM	Pct.	FTA	FTM	Pct.	—Rebounds— Off.	Def.	Tot.	Ast.	PF	Dq.	Stl.	Blk.	Pts.	Avg.
89-90—Chicago	16	281	91	37	.407	47	36	.766	17	34	51	9	32	0	6	8	110	6.9

Three-Point Field Goals: 1989-90, 0-for-1.

Named to NBA All-Rookie Second Team, 1990. . . . THE SPORTING NEWS College Player of the Year, 1989. . . . THE SPORTING NEWS All-America First Team, 1989. . . . THE SPORTING NEWS All-America Second Team, 1988.

GREGORY FULLER KITE
(Greg)

Born August 5, 1961 at Houston, Tex. Height 6:11. Weight 250.
High School—Houston, Tex., Madison.
College—Brigham Young University, Provo, Utah.
Drafted by Boston on first round, 1983 (21st pick).

Waived by Boston, February 1, 1988; claimed off waivers by Los Angeles Clippers, February 3, 1988. Waived by Los Angeles Clippers, March 27, 1989; signed by Charlotte as a free agent, March 29, 1989. Signed by Sacramento as an unrestricted free agent, November 25, 1989.

—COLLEGIATE RECORD—

Year	G.	Min.	FGA	FGM	Pct.	FTA	FTM	Pct.	Reb.	Pts.	Avg.
79-80	21	192	48	14	.292	25	12	.480	86	40	1.9
80-81	32	1002	221	108	.489	101	50	.495	272	266	8.3
81-82	30	853	169	79	.467	65	29	.446	234	187	6.2
82-83	29	896	206	90	.437	77	44	.571	255	224	7.7
Totals	112	2943	644	291	.452	268	135	.504	847	717	6.4

NBA REGULAR SEASON RECORD

									—Rebounds—									
Sea.—Team	G.	Min.	FGA	FGM	Pct.	FTA	FTM	Pct.	Off.	Def.	Tot.	Ast.	PF	Dq.	Stl.	Blk.	Pts.	Avg.
83-84—Boston	35	197	66	30	.455	16	5	.313	27	35	62	7	42	0	1	5	65	1.9
84-85—Boston	55	424	88	33	.375	32	22	.688	38	51	89	17	84	3	3	10	88	1.6
85-86—Boston	64	464	91	34	.374	39	15	.385	35	93	128	17	81	1	3	28	83	1.3
86-87—Boston	74	745	110	47	.427	76	29	.382	61	108	169	27	148	2	17	46	123	1.7
87-88—Bos.-L.A.C.	53	1063	205	92	.449	79	40	.506	85	179	264	47	153	1	19	58	224	4.2
88-89—L.A.C.-Char.	70	942	151	65	.430	41	20	.488	81	162	243	36	161	1	27	54	150	2.1
89-90—Sacramento	71	1515	234	101	.432	54	27	.500	131	246	377	76	201	2	31	51	230	3.2
Totals	422	5350	945	402	.425	337	158	.469	458	874	1332	227	870	10	101	252	963	2.3

Three-Point Field Goals: 1985-86, 0-for-1. 1986-87, 0-for-1. 1987-88, 0-for-1. 1989-90, 1-for-1 (1.000). Totals, 1-for-4 (.250).

NBA PLAYOFF RECORD

									—Rebounds—									
Sea.—Team	G.	Min.	FGA	FGM	Pct.	FTA	FTM	Pct.	Off.	Def.	Tot.	Ast.	PF	Dq.	Stl.	Blk.	Pts.	Avg.
83-84—Boston	11	38	8	1	.125	6	5	.833	5	4	9	3	9	0	0	1	7	0.6
84-85—Boston	9	63	12	5	.417	2	1	.500	5	11	16	3	13	0	1	0	11	1.2
85-86—Boston	13	78	10	7	.700	7	4	.571	5	14	19	3	20	0	2	4	18	1.4
86-87—Boston	20	172	20	7	.350	7	3	.429	15	31	46	8	43	1	2	8	17	0.9
Totals	53	351	50	20	.400	22	13	.591	30	60	90	17	85	1	5	13	53	1.0

Member of NBA championship teams, 1984 and 1986.

JOSEPH WILLIAM KLEINE
(Joe)

Born January 4, 1962 at Colorado Springs, Colo. Height 6:11. Weight 271.
High School—Slater, Mo.
Colleges—University of Notre Dame, Notre Dame, Ind., and University of Arkansas, Fayetteville, Ark.
Drafted by Sacramento on first round, 1985 (6th pick).

Traded by Sacramento with Ed Pinckney to Boston for Brad Lohaus and Danny Ainge, February 23, 1989.

—COLLEGIATE RECORD—

Notre Dame

Year	G.	Min.	FGA	FGM	Pct.	FTA	FTM	Pct.	Reb.	Pts.	Avg.
80-81	29	291	50	32	.640	16	12	.750	71	76	2.6

Arkansas

Year	G.	Min.	FGA	FGM	Pct.	FTA	FTM	Pct.	Reb.	Pts.	Avg.
81-82			Did Not Play—Transfer Student								
82-83	30	950	307	165	.537	109	69	.633	219	399	13.3
83-84	32	1173	351	209	.595	211	163	.773	293	581	18.2
84-85	35	1289	484	294	.607	257	185	.720	294	773	22.1
Ark. Totals	97	3412	1142	668	.585	577	417	.723	806	1753	18.1
College Totals	126	3703	1192	700	.587	593	429	.723	877	1829	14.5

NBA REGULAR SEASON RECORD

									—Rebounds—									
Sea.—Team	G.	Min.	FGA	FGM	Pct.	FTA	FTM	Pct.	Off.	Def.	Tot.	Ast.	PF	Dq.	Stl.	Blk.	Pts.	Avg.
85-86—Sacramento	80	1180	344	160	.465	130	94	.723	113	260	373	46	224	1	24	34	414	5.2
86-87—Sacramento	79	1658	543	256	.471	140	110	.786	173	310	483	71	213	2	35	30	622	7.9
87-88—Sacramento	82	1999	686	324	.472	188	153	.814	179	400	579	93	228	1	28	59	801	9.8

Sea.—Team	G.	Min.	FGA	FGM	Pct.	FTA	FTM	Pct.	—Rebounds— Off.	Def.	Tot.	Ast.	PF	Dq.	Stl.	Blk.	Pts.	Avg.
88-89—Sac.-Bos.	75	1411	432	175	.405	152	134	.882	124	254	378	67	192	2	33	23	484	6.5
89-90—Boston	81	1365	367	176	.480	100	83	.830	117	238	355	46	170	0	15	27	435	5.4
Totals	397	7613	2372	1091	.460	710	574	.808	706	1462	2168	323	1027	6	135	173	2756	6.9

Three-Point Field Goals: 1986-87, 0-for-1. 1988-89, 0-for-2. 1989-90, 0-for-4. Totals, 0-for-7.

NBA PLAYOFF RECORD

Sea.—Team	G.	Min.	FGA	FGM	Pct.	FTA	FTM	Pct.	—Rebounds— Off.	Def.	Tot.	Ast.	PF	Dq.	Stl.	Blk.	Pts.	Avg.
85-86—Sacramento	3	45	13	5	.385	6	5	.833	8	6	14	1	8	0	1	1	15	5.0
88-89—Boston	3	65	11	6	.545	9	7	.778	4	13	17	2	9	0	0	1	19	6.3
89-90—Boston	5	79	17	13	.765	6	5	.833	3	11	14	2	12	0	2	3	31	6.2
Totals	11	189	41	24	.585	21	17	.810	15	30	45	5	29	0	3	5	65	5.9

Three-Point Field Goals: 1988-89, 0-for-1. 1989-90, 0-for-1. Totals, 0-for-2.

Member of U.S. Olympic team, 1984.

JON FRANCIS KONCAK

Born May 17, 1963 at Cedar Rapids, Ia. Height 7:00. Weight 260.
High School—Kansas City, Mo., Center.
College—Southern Methodist University, Dallas, Tex.
Drafted by Atlanta on first round, 1985 (5th pick).

—COLLEGIATE RECORD—

Year	G.	Min.	FGA	FGM	Pct.	FTA	FTM	Pct.	Reb.	Pts.	Avg.
81-82	27	745	232	107	.461	92	57	.620	155	271	10.0
82-83	30	980	334	176	.527	123	85	.691	282	437	14.6
83-84	33	1162	340	211	.621	145	88	.607	378	510	15.5
84-85	33	1084	370	219	.592	192	128	.667	354	566	17.2
Totals	123	3971	1276	713	.559	552	358	.649	1169	1784	14.5

NBA REGULAR SEASON RECORD

Sea.—Team	G.	Min.	FGA	FGM	Pct.	FTA	FTM	Pct.	—Rebounds— Off.	Def.	Tot.	Ast.	PF	Dq.	Stl.	Blk.	Pts.	Avg.
85-86—Atlanta	82	1695	519	263	.507	257	156	.607	171	296	467	55	296	10	37	69	682	8.3
86-87—Atlanta	82	1684	352	169	.480	191	125	.654	153	340	493	31	262	2	52	76	463	5.6
87-88—Atlanta	49	1073	203	98	.483	136	83	.610	103	230	333	19	161	1	36	56	279	5.7
88-89—Atlanta	74	1531	269	141	.524	114	63	.553	147	306	453	56	238	4	54	98	345	4.7
89-90—Atlanta	54	977	127	78	.614	79	42	.532	58	168	226	23	182	4	38	34	198	3.7
Totals	341	6960	1470	749	.510	777	469	.604	632	1340	1972	184	1139	21	217	333	1967	5.8

Three-Point Field Goals: 1985-86, 0-for-1. 1986-87, 0-for-1. 1987-88, 0-for-2. 1988-89, 0-for-3. 1989-90, 0-for-1. Totals, 0-for-8.

NBA PLAYOFF RECORD

Sea.—Team	G.	Min.	FGA	FGM	Pct.	FTA	FTM	Pct.	—Rebounds— Off.	Def.	Tot.	Ast.	PF	Dq.	Stl.	Blk.	Pts.	Avg.
85-86—Atlanta	9	193	29	14	.483	46	26	.565	11	23	34	5	27	2	6	10	54	6.0
86-87—Atlanta	8	86	13	7	.538	8	6	.750	5	20	25	3	24	0	3	4	20	2.5
88-89—Atlanta	5	192	29	18	.621	33	28	.848	16	32	48	4	23	1	2	8	64	12.8
Totals	22	471	71	39	.549	87	60	.690	32	75	107	12	74	3	11	22	138	6.3

Member of U.S. Olympic team, 1984. . . . Named to THE SPORTING NEWS All-America Second Team, 1985.

FRANCIS MILTON KORNET
(Frank)

Born January 27, 1967 at Lexington, Ky. Height 6:09. Weight 225.
High School—Lexington, Ky., Catholic.
College—Vanderbilt University, Nashville, Tenn.
Drafted by Milwaukee on second round, 1989 (30th pick).

—COLLEGIATE RECORD—

Year	G.	Min.	FGA	FGM	Pct.	FTA	FTM	Pct.	Reb.	Pts.	Avg.
85-86	26	425	102	51	.500	35	24	.686	95	126	4.8
86-87	27	246	45	20	.444	24	18	.750	61	59	2.2
87-88	31	691	171	86	.503	39	27	.692	133	199	6.4
88-89	33	1047	388	220	.567	184	112	.609	235	554	16.8
Totals	117	2409	706	377	.534	282	181	.642	524	938	8.0

Three-Point Field Goals: 1986-87, 1-for-1 (1.000). 1987-88, 0-for-1. 1988-89, 2-for-7 (.286). Totals, 3-for-9 (.333).

NBA REGULAR SEASON RECORD

									—Rebounds—									
Sea.—Team	G.	Min.	FGA	FGM	Pct.	FTA	FTM	Pct.	Off.	Def.	Tot.	Ast.	PF	Dq.	Stl.	Blk.	Pts.	Avg.
89-90—Milwaukee	57	438	114	42	.368	39	24	.615	25	46	71	21	54	0	14	3	113	2.0

Three-Point Field Goals: 1989-90, 5-for-20 (.250).

NBA PLAYOFF RECORD

									—Rebounds—									
Sea.—Team	G.	Min.	FGA	FGM	Pct.	FTA	FTM	Pct.	Off.	Def.	Tot.	Ast.	PF	Dq.	Stl.	Blk.	Pts.	Avg.
89-90—Milwaukee	2	4	1	0	.000	0	0	....	0	1	1	0	1	0	0	0	0	0.0

Three-Point Field Goals: 1989-90, 0-for-1.

LARRY BRETT KRYSTKOWIAK

Born September 23, 1964 at Missoula, Mont. Height 6:09. Weight 240.
High School—Missoula, Mont., Big Sky.
College—University of Montana, Missoula, Mont.
Drafted by Chicago on second round, 1986 (28th pick).

Draft rights traded by Chicago with 1987 and 1992 2nd round draft choices to Portland for Steve Colter, June 17, 1986.
Draft rights traded by Portland with Mychal Thompson to San Antonio for Steve Johnson, June 20, 1986.
Traded by San Antonio to Milwaukee for Charles Davis and a 1989 2nd round draft choice, November 18, 1987.
Played in Italy, 1987-88.

—COLLEGIATE RECORD—

Year	G.	Min.	FGA	FGM	Pct.	FTA	FTM	Pct.	Reb.	Pts.	Avg.
82-83	28	396	97	42	.433	77	53	.688	120	137	4.9
83-84	30	1068	338	185	.547	210	169	.805	315	539	18.0
84-85	30	1079	366	214	.585	243	204	.840	306	632	21.1
85-86	32	1118	446	258	.578	254	193	.760	364	709	22.2
Totals	120	3661	1247	699	.561	784	619	.790	1105	2017	16.8

ITALIAN LEAGUE RECORD

Year	G.	Min.	FGA	FGM	Pct.	FTA	FTM	Pct.	Reb.	Pts.	Avg.
87-88—Roberts	8	291	129	70	.543	52	46	.885	84	186	23.2

NBA REGULAR SEASON RECORD

									—Rebounds—									
Sea.—Team	G.	Min.	FGA	FGM	Pct.	FTA	FTM	Pct.	Off.	Def.	Tot.	Ast.	PF	Dq.	Stl.	Blk.	Pts.	Avg.
86-87—San Antonio	68	1004	373	170	.456	148	110	.743	77	162	239	85	141	1	22	12	451	6.6
87-88—Milwaukee	50	1050	266	128	.481	127	103	.811	88	143	231	50	137	0	18	8	359	7.2
88-89—Milwaukee	80	2472	766	362	.473	351	289	.823	198	412	610	107	219	0	93	9	1017	12.7
89-90—Milwaukee	16	381	118	43	.364	33	26	.788	16	60	76	25	41	0	10	2	112	7.0
Totals	214	4907	1523	703	.462	659	528	.801	379	777	1156	267	538	1	143	31	1939	9.1

Three-Point Field Goals: 1986-87, 1-for-12 (.083). 1987-88, 0-for-3. 1988-89, 4-for-12 (.333). 1989-90, 0-for-2. Totals, 5-for-29 (.172).

NBA PLAYOFF RECORD

									—Rebounds—									
Sea.—Team	G.	Min.	FGA	FGM	Pct.	FTA	FTM	Pct.	Off.	Def.	Tot.	Ast.	PF	Dq.	Stl.	Blk.	Pts.	Avg.
87-88—Milwaukee	5	163	29	13	.448	18	16	.889	13	21	34	7	17	0	4	0	42	8.4
88-89—Milwaukee	8	239	68	29	.426	31	27	.871	14	31	45	12	22	0	2	1	85	10.6
Totals	13	402	97	42	.433	49	43	.878	27	52	79	19	39	0	6	1	127	9.8

Three-Point Field Goals: 1988-89, 0-for-2.

WILLIAM LAIMBEER JR.
(Bill)

Born May 19, 1957 at Boston, Mass. Height 6:11. Weight 260.
High School—Palos Verdes, Calif.
Colleges—University of Notre Dame, Notre Dame, Ind., and Owens Technical College, Toledo, O.
Drafted by Cleveland on third round, 1979 (65th pick).

Traded by Cleveland with Kenny Carr to Detroit for Phil Hubbard, Paul Mokeski and 1982 1st and 2nd round draft choices, February 16, 1982.
Played in Italy during 1979-80 season.

—COLLEGIATE RECORD—

Notre Dame

Year	G.	Min.	FGA	FGM	Pct.	FTA	FTM	Pct.	Reb.	Pts.	Avg.
75-76	10	190	65	32	.492	23	18	.783	79	82	8.2

Owens Tech

Year	G.	Min.	FGA	FGM	Pct.	FTA	FTM	Pct.	Reb.	Pts.	Avg.
76-77	Did Not Play										

Notre Dame

Year	G.	Min.	FGA	FGM	Pct.	FTA	FTM	Pct.	Reb.	Pts.	Avg.
77-78	29	654	175	97	.554	62	42	.677	190	236	8.1
78-79	30	614	145	78	.538	50	35	.700	164	191	6.4
Totals	69	1458	385	207	.538	135	95	.704	433	509	7.4

ITALIAN LEAGUE RECORD

Year	G.	Min.	FGA	FGM	Pct.	FTA	FTM	Pct.	Reb.	Pts.	Avg.
79-80—Brescia	29	....	465	258	.555	124	97	.782	363	613	21.1

NBA REGULAR SEASON RECORD

									—Rebounds—									
Sea.—Team	G.	Min.	FGA	FGM	Pct.	FTA	FTM	Pct.	Off.	Def.	Tot.	Ast.	PF	Dq.	Stl.	Blk.	Pts.	Avg.
80-81—Cleveland	81	2460	670	337	.503	153	117	.765	266	427	693	216	332	14	56	78	791	9.8
81-82—Clev.-Det.	80	1829	536	265	.494	232	184	.793	234	383	.617	100	296	5	39	64	718	9.0
82-83—Detroit	82	2871	877	436	.497	310	245	.790	282	711	993	263	320	9	51	118	1119	13.6
83-84—Detroit	82	2864	1044	553	.530	365	316	.866	329	674	1003	149	273	4	49	84	1422	17.3
84-85—Detroit	82	2892	1177	595	.506	306	244	.797	295	718	1013	154	308	4	69	71	1438	17.5
85-86—Detroit	82	2891	1107	545	.492	319	266	.834	305	770	1075	146	291	4	59	65	1360	16.6
86-87—Detroit	82	2854	1010	506	.501	274	245	.894	243	712	955	151	283	4	72	69	1263	15.4
87-88—Detroit	82	2897	923	455	.493	214	187	.874	165	667	832	199	284	6	66	78	1110	13.5
88-89—Detroit	81	2640	900	449	.499	212	178	.840	138	638	776	177	259	2	51	100	1106	13.7
89-90—Detroit	81	2675	785	380	.484	192	164	.854	166	614	780	171	278	4	57	84	981	12.1
Totals	815	26873	9029	4521	.501	2577	2146	.833	2423	6314	8737	1726	2924	56	569	811	11308	13.9

Three-Point Field Goals: 1981-82, 4-for-13 (.308). 1982-83, 2-for-13 (.154). 1983-84, 0-for-11. 1984-85, 4-for-18 (.222). 1985-86, 4-for-14 (.286). 1986-87, 6-for-21 (.286). 1987-88, 13-for-39 (.333). 1988-89, 30-for-86 (.349). 1989-90, 57-for-158 (.361). Totals, 120-for-373 (.322).

NBA PLAYOFF RECORD

									—Rebounds—									
Sea.—Team	G.	Min.	FGA	FGM	Pct.	FTA	FTM	Pct.	Off.	Def.	Tot.	Ast.	PF	Dq.	Stl.	Blk.	Pts.	Avg.
83-84—Detroit	5	165	51	29	.569	20	18	.900	14	48	62	12	23	2	4	3	76	15.2
84-85—Detroit	9	325	107	48	.449	51	36	.706	36	60	96	15	32	1	7	7	132	14.7
85-86—Detroit	4	168	68	34	.500	23	21	.913	20	36	56	1	19	1	2	3	90	22.5
86-87—Detroit	15	543	163	84	.515	24	15	.625	30	126	156	37	53	2	15	12	184	12.3
87-88—Detroit	23	779	250	114	.456	45	40	.889	43	178	221	44	77	2	18	19	273	11.9
88-89—Detroit	17	497	142	66	.465	31	25	.806	26	114	140	31	55	1	6	8	172	10.1
89-90—Detroit	20	667	199	91	.457	29	25	.862	41	170	211	28	77	3	23	18	222	11.1
Totals	93	3144	980	466	.476	223	180	.807	210	732	942	168	336	12	75	70	1149	12.4

Three-Point Field Goals: 1984-85, 0-for-2. 1985-86, 1-for-1 (1.000). 1986-87, 1-for-5 (.200). 1987-88, 5-for-17 (.294). 1988-89, 15-for-42 (.357). 1989-90, 15-for-43 (.349). Totals, 37-for-110 (.336).

NBA ALL-STAR GAME RECORD

								—Rebounds—							
Season—Team	Min.	FGA	FGM	Pct.	FTA	FTM	Pct.	Off.	Def.	Tot.	Ast.	PF	Dq.	Stl.	Blk.	Pts.
1983—Detroit	6	1	1	1.000	0	0	.000	1	0	1	0	1	0	0	0	2
1984—Detroit	17	8	6	.750	1	1	1.000	1	4	5	0	3	0	1	2	13
1985—Detroit	11	4	2	.500	2	1	.500	1	2	3	1	1	0	0	0	5
1987—Detroit	11	7	4	.571	0	0	.000	0	2	2	1	2	0	1	0	8
Totals	45	20	13	.650	3	2	.667	3	8	11	2	7	0	2	2	28

Member of NBA championship teams, 1989 and 1990.... Led NBA in rebounding, 1986.... Shares championship series game record for most three-point field goals made, 6, vs. Portland, June 7, 1990.

JEROME LANE

Born December 4, 1966 at Akron, O. Height 6:06. Weight 230.

High School—Akron, O., St. Vincent-St. Mary.

College—University of Pittsburgh, Pittsburgh, Pa.

Drafted by Denver on first round as an undergraduate, 1988 (23rd pick).

—COLLEGIATE RECORD—

Year	G.	Min.	FGA	FGM	Pct.	FTA	FTM	Pct.	Reb.	Pts.	Avg.
85-86	29	711	202	95	.470	113	74	.655	148	264	9.1
86-87	33	1169	329	187	.568	230	114	.626	444	522	15.8
87-88	31	1090	300	154	.513	200	123	.615	378	431	13.9
Totals	93	2970	831	436	.525	543	341	.628	970	1217	13.1

Three-Point Field Goals: 1986-87, 4-for-8 (.500). 1987-88, 0-for-7. Totals, 4-for-15 (.267).

NBA REGULAR SEASON RECORD

									—Rebounds—									
Sea.—Team	G.	Min.	FGA	FGM	Pct.	FTA	FTM	Pct.	Off.	Def.	Tot.	Ast.	PF	Dq.	Stl.	Blk.	Pts.	Avg.
88-89—Denver	54	550	256	109	.426	112	43	.384	87	113	200	60	105	1	20	4	261	4.8

Sea.—Team	G.	Min.	FGA	FGM	Pct.	FTA	FTM	Pct.	—Rebounds— Off.	Def.	Tot.	Ast.	PF	Dq.	Stl.	Blk.	Pts.	Avg.
89-90—Denver	67	956	309	145	.469	120	44	.367	144	217	361	105	189	1	53	17	334	5.0
Totals	121	1506	565	254	.450	232	87	.375	231	330	561	165	294	2	73	21	595	4.9

Three-Point Field Goals: 1988-89, 0-for-7. 1989-90, 0-for-5. Totals, 0-for-12.

NBA PLAYOFF RECORD

Sea.—Team	G.	Min.	FGA	FGM	Pct.	FTA	FTM	Pct.	—Rebounds— Off.	Def.	Tot.	Ast.	PF	Dq.	Stl.	Blk.	Pts.	Avg.
88-89—Denver	2	21	7	2	.286	2	2	1.000	1	5	6	2	4	0	0	0	6	3.0
89-90—Denver	2	14	3	0	.000	2	1	.500	0	1	1	2	4	0	0	0	1	0.5
Totals	4	35	10	2	.200	4	3	.750	1	6	7	4	8	0	0	0	7	1.8

Three-Point Field Goals: 1988-89, 0-for-1.

Led NCAA Division I in rebounding, 1987.

ANDREW CHARLES LANG

Born June 28, 1966 at Pine Bluff, Ark. Height 6:11. Weight 250.
High School—Pine Bluff, Ark., Dollarway.
College—University of Arkansas, Fayetteville, Ark.
Drafted by Phoenix on second round, 1988 (28th pick).

—COLLEGIATE RECORD—

Year	G.	Min.	FGA	FGM	Pct.	FTA	FTM	Pct.	Reb.	Pts.	Avg.
84-85	33	467	84	34	.405	32	18	.563	67	86	2.6
85-86	26	694	189	88	.466	61	37	.607	168	213	8.2
86-87	32	722	204	102	.500	87	56	.644	240	260	8.1
87-88	30	743	239	126	.527	60	27	.450	218	279	9.3
Totals	121	2626	716	350	.489	230	138	.600	693	838	6.9

NBA REGULAR SEASON RECORD

Sea.—Team	G.	Min.	FGA	FGM	Pct.	FTA	FTM	Pct.	—Rebounds— Off.	Def.	Tot.	Ast.	PF	Dq.	Stl.	Blk.	Pts.	Avg.
88-89—Phoenix	62	526	117	60	.513	60	39	.650	54	93	147	9	112	1	17	48	159	2.6
89-90—Phoenix	74	1011	174	97	.557	98	64	.653	83	188	271	21	171	1	22	133	258	3.5
Totals	136	1537	291	157	.540	158	103	.652	137	281	418	30	283	2	39	181	417	3.1

NBA PLAYOFF RECORD

Sea.—Team	G.	Min.	FGA	FGM	Pct.	FTA	FTM	Pct.	—Rebounds— Off.	Def.	Tot.	Ast.	PF	Dq.	Stl.	Blk.	Pts.	Avg.
88-89—Phoenix	4	8	2	0	.000	0	0	.000	3	3	6	1	3	0	0	0	0	0.0
89-90—Phoenix	12	93	9	6	.667	7	4	.571	4	16	20	2	17	0	3	10	16	1.3
Totals	16	101	11	6	.545	7	4	.571	7	19	26	3	20	0	3	10	16	1.0

JEFFREY BRIAN LEBO
(Jeff)

Born October 5, 1966 at Carlisle, Pa. Height 6:02. Weight 180.
High School—Carlisle, Pa.
College—University of North Carolina, Chapel Hill, N. C.
Never drafted by an NBA franchise.

Signed by San Antonio as a free agent, September 29, 1989.
Waived by San Antonio, November 22, 1989.

—COLLEGIATE RECORD—

Year	G.	Min.	FGA	FGM	Pct.	FTA	FTM	Pct.	Reb.	Pts.	Avg.
85-86	34	893	253	130	.514	73	54	.740	84	314	9.2
86-87	34	1057	293	156	.532	93	79	.849	72	458	13.5
87-88	33	1115	275	120	.436	98	86	.878	87	404	12.2
88-89	32	983	274	118	.431	103	89	.864	84	391	12.2
Totals	133	4048	1095	524	.479	367	308	.839	327	1567	11.8

Three-Point Field Goals: 1986-87, 67-for-149 (.450). 1987-88, 78-for-168 (.464). 1988-89, 66-for-176 (.375). Totals, 211 for 493 (.428).

NBA REGULAR SEASON RECORD

Sea.—Team	G.	Min.	FGA	FGM	Pct.	FTA	FTM	Pct.	—Rebounds— Off.	Def.	Tot.	Ast.	PF	Dq.	Stl.	Blk.	Pts.	Avg.
89-90—San Antonio	4	32	7	2	.286	2	2	1.000	2	2	4	3	7	0	2	0	6	1.5

ERIC C. LECKNER

Born May 27, 1966 at Inglewood, Calif. Height 6.11. Weight 265.
High School—Manhattan Beach, Calif., Mira Costa.
College—University of Wyoming, Laramie, Wyo.
Drafted by Utah on first round, 1988 (17th pick).

Traded by Utah with Bob Hansen and 1990 1st and 2nd round draft choices to Sacramento in three-way deal that sent Jeff Malone from Washington to Utah and Pervis Ellison from Sacramento to Washington, June 25, 1990. Utah also received a 1990 2nd round draft choice and Sacramento also received a 1991 2nd round draft choice.

—COLLEGIATE RECORD—

Year	G.	Min.	FGA	FGM	Pct.	FTA	FTM	Pct.	Reb.	Pts.	Avg.
84-85	29	600	168	98	.583	78	48	.615	112	244	8.4
85-86	36	1113	392	228	.582	183	112	.612	207	568	15.8
86-87	34	1123	390	246	.631	201	142	.706	245	634	18.6
87-88	32	972	281	181	.644	172	130	.756	210	492	15.4
Totals	131	3808	1231	753	.612	634	432	.681	774	1938	14.8

NBA REGULAR SEASON RECORD

									—Rebounds—									
Sea.—Team	G.	Min.	FGA	FGM	Pct.	FTA	FTM	Pct.	Off.	Def.	Tot.	Ast.	PF	Dq.	Stl.	Blk.	Pts.	Avg.
88-89—Utah	75	779	220	120	.545	113	79	.699	48	151	199	16	174	1	8	22	319	4.3
89-90—Utah	77	764	222	125	.563	109	81	.743	48	144	192	19	157	0	15	23	331	4.3
Totals	152	1543	442	245	.554	222	160	.721	96	295	391	35	331	1	23	45	650	4.3

NBA PLAYOFF RECORD

									—Rebounds—									
Sea.—Team	G.	Min.	FGA	FGM	Pct.	FTA	FTM	Pct.	Off.	Def.	Tot.	Ast.	PF	Dq.	Stl.	Blk.	Pts.	Avg.
88-89—Utah	3	10	4	1	.250	0	0	.000	1	1	2	0	2	0	0	0	2	0.7
89-90—Utah	3	28	10	6	.600	9	5	.556	2	6	8	2	8	0	0	0	18	6.0
Totals	6	38	14	7	.500	9	5	.556	3	7	10	2	10	0	0	0	20	3.3

Three-Point Field Goals: 1989-90, 1-for-1 (1.000).

KEITH DEYWANE LEE

Born December 28, 1962 at West Memphis, Ark. Height 6:10. Weight 220.
High School—West Memphis, Ark.
College—Memphis State University, Memphis, Tenn.
Drafted by Chicago on first round, 1985 (11th pick).

Draft rights traded by Chicago with Ennis Whatley to Cleveland for draft rights to Charles Oakley and Calvin Duncan, June 18, 1985.
Traded by Cleveland with John Bagley to New Jersey for Darryl Dawkins and James Bailey, October 8, 1987.
Selected from New Jersey by Orlando in NBA expansion draft, June 15, 1989.
Missed entire 1987-88 season due to injury.

—COLLEGIATE RECORD—

Year	G.	Min.	FGA	FGM	Pct.	FTA	FTM	Pct.	Reb.	Pts.	Avg.
81-82	29	1041	370	199	.538	178	134	.753	320	532	18.3
82-83	31	1109	438	220	.502	172	141	.820	336	581	18.7
83-84	33	1139	453	245	.541	151	117	.775	357	607	18.4
84-85	35	1141	536	266	.496	200	156	.780	323	688	19.7
Totals	128	4430	1797	930	.518	701	548	.782	1336	2408	18.8

NBA REGULAR SEASON RECORD

									—Rebounds—									
Sea.—Team	G.	Min.	FGA	FGM	Pct.	FTA	FTM	Pct.	Off.	Def.	Tot.	Ast.	PF	Dq.	Stl.	Blk.	Pts.	Avg.
85-86—Cleveland	58	1197	380	177	.466	96	75	.781	116	235	351	67	204	9	29	37	431	7.4
86-87—Cleveland	67	870	374	170	.455	101	72	.713	93	158	251	69	147	0	25	40	412	6.1
88-89—New Jersey	57	840	258	109	.422	71	53	.746	73	186	259	42	138	1	20	33	271	4.8
Totals	182	2907	1012	456	.451	268	200	.746	282	579	861	178	489	10	74	110	1114	6.1

Three-Point Field Goals: 1985-86, 2-for-9 (.222). 1986-87, 0-for-1. 1988-89, 0-for-2. Totals, 2-for-12 (.167).

Named to THE SPORTING NEWS All-America First Team, 1983 and 1985.

TIM LEGLER

Born December 26, 1966 at Washington, D.C. Height 6:04. Weight 210.
High School—Richmond, Va., John Randolph Tucker.
College—La Salle University, Philadelphia, Pa.
Never drafted by an NBA franchise.

Signed by Phoenix, March 21, 1990, to the first of consecutive 10-day contracts that expired, April 9, 1990.
Signed by Minnesota as an unrestricted free agent, July 20, 1990.
Played in Continental Basketball Association with Rochester Flyers, 1988-89, and Omaha Racers, 1989-90.

—COLLEGIATE RECORD—

Year	G.	Min.	FGA	FGM	Pct.	FTA	FTM	Pct.	Reb.	Pts.	Avg.
84-85	26	....	147	69	.469	24	17	.708	72	155	6.0
85-86	28	....	315	158	.502	54	45	.833	110	361	12.9
86-87	33	....	487	233	.478	119	93	.782	147	616	18.7
87-88	34	....	414	203	.490	71	57	.803	139	567	16.7
Totals	121	....	1363	663	.486	268	212	.791	468	1699	14.0

Three-Point Field Goals: 1986-87, 57-for-141 (.404). 1987-88, 104-for-212 (.491). Totals, 161-for-353 (.456).

CBA REGULAR SEASON RECORD

			—2-Point—			—3-Point—									
Sea.—Team	G.	Min.	FGM	FGA	Pct.	FGM	FGA	Pct.	FTM	FTA	Pct.	Reb.	Ast.	Pts.	Avg.
88-89—Rochester	53	1504	223	452	.493	34	91	.374	119	151	.788	130	145	667	12.6
89-90—Omaha	40	1474	296	610	.485	41	88	.466	188	226	.832	165	178	903	22.6
Totals	93	2978	519	1062	.489	75	179	.419	307	377	.814	295	323	1570	16.9

NBA REGULAR SEASON RECORD

									—Rebounds—									
Sea.—Team	G.	Min.	FGA	FGM	Pct.	FTA	FTM	Pct.	Off.	Def.	Tot.	Ast.	PF	Dq.	Stl.	Blk.	Pts.	Avg.
89-90—Phoenix	11	83	29	11	.379	6	6	1.000	4	4	8	6	12	0	2	0	28	2.5

Three-Point Field Goals: 1989-90, 0-for-1.

GARY FRANCIS LEONARD

Born February 16, 1967 at Belleville, Ill. Height 7:01. Weight 265.
High School—Belleville, Ill., East.
College—University of Missouri, Columbia, Mo.
Drafted by Minnesota on second round, 1989 (34th pick).

—COLLEGIATE RECORD—

Year	G.	Min.	FGA	FGM	Pct.	FTA	FTM	Pct.	Reb.	Pts.	Avg.
85-86	34	685	141	67	.475	80	35	.438	123	169	5.0
86-87	32	416	113	60	.531	35	22	.629	99	142	4.4
87-88	29	339	94	59	.628	76	35	.461	100	153	5.3
88-89	37	776	270	160	.593	113	65	.575	205	385	10.4
Totals	132	2216	618	346	.560	304	157	.516	527	849	6.4

NBA REGULAR SEASON RECORD

									—Rebounds—									
Sea.—Team	G.	Min.	FGA	FGM	Pct.	FTA	FTM	Pct.	Off.	Def.	Tot.	Ast.	PF	Dq.	Stl.	Blk.	Pts.	Avg.
89-90—Minnesota	22	127	31	13	.419	14	6	.429	10	17	27	1	26	0	3	9	32	1.5

Three-Point Field Goals: 1989-90, 0-for-1.

JAMES ALLEN LES
(Jim)

Born August 18, 1963 at Niles, Ill. Height 5:11. Weight 165.
High School—Niles, Ill., Notre Dame.
Colleges—Cleveland State University, Cleveland, O., and Bradley University, Peoria, Ill.
Drafted by Atlanta on third round, 1986 (70th pick).

Waived by Atlanta, July, 1986; signed by Philadelphia as a free agent, September 9, 1986.
Waived by Philadelphia, December 8, 1986; re-signed by Philadelphia as a free agent, June 1, 1987.
Waived by Philadelphia, November 3, 1987; signed by Milwaukee as a free agent, October 19, 1988.
Waived by Milwaukee, October 20, 1988; signed by Utah as a free agent, October 25, 1988.
Waived by Utah, November 6, 1989; signed by Los Angeles Clippers, February 6, 1990, to the first of consecutive 10-day contracts that expired, February 27, 1990.
Played in Continental Basketball Association with Rochester Flyers, 1987-88, and Santa Barbara Islanders, 1989-90.
Missed entire 1986-87 season due to injury.

—COLLEGIATE RECORD—

Cleveland State

Year	G.	Min.	FGA	FGM	Pct.	FTA	FTM	Pct.	Reb.	Pts.	Avg.
81-82	27	....	152	71	.467	66	51	.773	67	193	7.1

Bradley

Year	G.	Min.	FGA	FGM	Pct.	FTA	FTM	Pct.	Reb.	Pts.	Avg.
82-83	Did Not Play—Transfer Student										
83-84	22	800	119	49	.412	58	41	.707	46	139	6.3
84-85	30	1126	215	107	.498	83	71	.855	100	285	9.5

Year	G.	Min.	FGA	FGM	Pct.	FTA	FTM	Pct.	Reb.	Pts.	Avg.
85-86	35	1278	408	198	.485	135	102	.756	120	498	14.2
Brad. Totals	87	3194	742	354	.477	276	214	.775	266	922	10.6
Col. Totals	114	....	894	425	.476	342	265	.775	333	1115	9.8

CBA REGULAR SEASON RECORD

			—2-Point—			—3-Point—									
Sea.—Team	G.	Min.	FGM	FGA	Pct.	FGM	FGA	Pct.	FTM	FTA	Pct.	Reb.	Ast.	Pts.	Avg.
87-88—Rochester	12	334	25	59	.423	10	25	.400	26	39	.666	25	81	106	8.8
89-90—Santa Barbara	20	594	89	187	.476	24	49	.490	89	100	.890	82	229	339	17.0
Totals	32	928	114	246	.463	34	74	.459	115	139	.827	107	310	445	13.9

NBA REGULAR SEASON RECORD

									—Rebounds—									
Sea.—Team	G.	Min.	FGA	FGM	Pct.	FTA	FTM	Pct.	Off.	Def.	Tot.	Ast.	PF	Dq.	Stl.	Blk.	Pts.	Avg.
88-89—Utah	82	781	133	40	.301	73	57	.781	23	64	87	215	88	0	27	5	138	1.7
89-90—Utah-L.A.C.	7	92	14	5	.357	17	13	.765	3	4	7	21	9	0	3	0	23	3.3
Totals	89	873	147	45	.306	90	70	.778	26	68	94	236	97	0	30	5	161	1.8

Three-Point Field Goals: 1988-89, 1-for-14 (.071). 1989-90, 0-for-1. Totals, 1-for-15 (.067).

NBA PLAYOFF RECORD

									—Rebounds—									
Sea.—Team	G.	Min.	FGA	FGM	Pct.	FTA	FTM	Pct.	Off.	Def.	Tot.	Ast.	PF	Dq.	Stl.	Blk.	Pts.	Avg.
88-89—Utah	3	5	0	0	.000	0	0	.000	0	0	0	1	2	0	0	0	0	0.0

CLIFFORD EARL LETT

Born December 23, 1965 at Pensacola, Fla. Height 6:03. Weight 170.
High School—Pensacola, Fla.
College—University of Florida, Gainesville, Fla.
Never drafted by an NBA franchise.

Signed by Charlotte as a free agent, August 16, 1989.
Waived by Charlotte, October 23, 1989; signed by Chicago, March 25, 1990, to the first of consecutive 10-day contracts that expired, April 13, 1990.
Played in Continental Basketball Association with Pensacola Tornados, 1989-90.

—COLLEGIATE RECORD—

Year	G.	Min.	FGA	FGM	Pct.	FTA	FTM	Pct.	Reb.	Pts.	Avg.
85-86	30	272	49	24	.490	23	13	.565	25	61	2.0
86-87	33	352	82	48	.585	22	17	.773	38	119	3.6
87-88	33	520	100	48	.480	67	38	.567	58	142	4.3
88-89	34	1274	298	137	.460	188	132	.702	142	445	13.1
Totals	130	2418	529	257	.486	300	200	.667	263	767	5.9

Three-Point Field Goals: 1986-87, 6-for-10 (.600). 1987-88, 8-for-21 (.381). 1988-89, 39-for-119 (.328). Totals, 53-for-150 (.353).

CBA REGULAR SEASON RECORD

			—2-Point—			—3-Point—									
Sea.—Team	G.	Min.	FGM	FGA	Pct.	FGM	FGA	Pct.	FTM	FTA	Pct.	Reb.	Ast.	Pts.	Avg.
89-90—Pensacola	55	2227	423	714	.592	31	97	.320	219	274	.799	242	215	1158	21.1

NBA REGULAR SEASON RECORD

									—Rebounds—									
Sea.—Team	G.	Min.	FGA	FGM	Pct.	FTA	FTM	Pct.	Off.	Def.	Tot.	Ast.	PF	Dq.	Stl.	Blk.	Pts.	Avg.
89-90—Chicago	4	28	8	2	.250	0	0	....	0	0	0	1	8	0	0	0	4	1.0

Named CBA Rookie of the Year, 1990.

LAFAYETTE LEVER
(Fat)

Born August 18, 1960 at Pine Bluff, Ark. Height 6:03. Weight 175.
High School—Tucson, Ariz., Pueblo.
College—Arizona State University, Tempe, Ariz.
Drafted by Portland on first round, 1982 (11th pick).

Traded by Portland with Calvin Natt, Wayne Cooper, a 1984 2nd round draft choice and a 1985 1st round draft choice to Denver for Kiki Vandeweghe, June 7, 1984.
Traded by Denver to Dallas for 1990 and 1991 1st round draft choices, June 21, 1990.

LAFAYETTE LEVER

—COLLEGIATE RECORD—

Year	G.	Min.	FGA	FGM	Pct.	FTA	FTM	Pct.	Reb.	Pts.	Avg.
78-79	29	377	92	38	.413	38	28	.737	44	104	3.6
79-80	29	974	220	98	.445	103	72	.699	125	268	9.2
80-81	28	1038	259	120	.463	116	84	.724	138	324	11.6
81-82	27	1032	357	162	.454	143	117	.818	146	441	16.3
Totals	113	3421	928	418	.450	400	301	.753	453	1137	10.1

NBA REGULAR SEASON RECORD

									—Rebounds—									
Sea.—Team	G.	Min.	FGA	FGM	Pct.	FTA	FTM	Pct.	Off.	Def.	Tot.	Ast.	PF	Dq.	Stl.	Blk.	Pts.	Avg.
82-83—Portland	81	2020	594	256	.431	159	116	.730	85	140	225	426	179	2	153	15	633	7.8
83-84—Portland	81	2010	701	313	.447	214	159	.743	96	122	218	372	178	1	135	31	788	9.7
84-85—Denver	82	2559	985	424	.430	256	197	.770	147	264	411	613	226	1	202	30	1051	12.8
85-86—Denver	78	2616	1061	468	.441	182	132	.725	136	284	420	584	204	3	178	15	1080	13.8
86-87—Denver	82	3054	1370	643	.469	312	244	.782	216	513	729	654	219	1	201	34	1552	18.9
87-88—Denver	82	3061	1360	643	.473	316	248	.785	203	462	665	639	214	0	223	21	1546	18.9
88-89—Denver	71	2745	1221	558	.457	344	270	.785	187	475	662	559	178	1	195	20	1409	19.8
89-90—Denver	79	2832	1283	568	.443	337	271	.804	230	504	734	517	172	1	168	13	1443	18.3
Totals	636	20897	8575	3873	.452	2120	1637	.772	1300	2764	4064	4364	1570	10	1455	179	9502	14.9

Three-Point Field Goals: 1982-83, 5-for-15 (.333). 1983-84, 3-for-15 (.200). 1984-85, 6-for-24 (.250). 1985-86, 12-for-38 (.316). 1986-87, 22-for-92 (.239). 1987-88, 12-for-57 (.211). 1988-89, 23-for-66 (.348). 1989-90, 36-for-87 (.414). Totals, 119-for-394 (.302).

NBA PLAYOFF RECORD

									—Rebounds—									
Sea.—Team	G.	Min.	FGA	FGM	Pct.	FTA	FTM	Pct.	Off.	Def.	Tot.	Ast.	PF	Dq.	Stl.	Blk.	Pts.	Avg.
82-83—Portland	7	134	42	19	.452	5	4	.800	3	11	14	31	13	0	7	0	42	6.0
83-84—Portland	5	75	30	8	.267	10	8	.800	10	5	15	9	6	0	4	0	26	5.2
84-85—Denver	11	342	122	49	.402	63	48	.762	23	48	71	93	33	0	26	2	146	13.3
85-86—Denver	10	347	131	59	.450	24	17	.708	15	33	48	53	33	0	20	2	143	14.3
86-87—Denver	3	99	50	19	.380	9	6	.667	5	13	18	22	7	0	7	0	46	15.3
87-88—Denver	7	273	98	45	.459	33	26	.788	16	49	65	49	15	0	13	4	119	17.0
88-89—Denver	2	58	24	9	.375	2	2	1.000	2	11	13	19	4	0	4	0	22	11.0
89-90—Denver	3	113	51	19	.373	14	13	.929	11	21	32	21	7	0	8	1	52	17.3
Totals	48	1441	548	227	.414	160	124	.775	85	191	276	297	118	0	89	9	596	12.4

Three-Point Field Goals: 1983-84, 2-for-3 (.667). 1984-85, 0-for-2. 1985-86, 8-for-14 (.571). 1986-87, 2-for-8 (.250). 1987-88, 3-for-7 (.429). 1988-89, 2-for-3 (.667). 1989-90, 1-for-7 (.143). Totals, 18-for-44 (.409).

NBA ALL-STAR GAME RECORD

								—Rebounds—								
Season—Team	Min.	FGA	FGM	Pct.	FTA	FTM	Pct.	Off.	Def.	Tot.	Ast.	PF	Dq.	Stl.	Blk.	Pts.
1988—Denver	31	14	7	.500	4	3	.750	0	4	4	3	4	0	0	0	17
1990—Denver	22	13	7	.538	2	2	1.000	0	3	3	2	0	0	2	0	16
Totals	53	27	14	.519	6	5	833	0	7	7	5	4	0	2	0	33

Three-Point Field Goals: 1990, 0-for-2.

Named to All-NBA Second Team, 1987. . . . NBA All-Defensive Second Team, 1988.

CLIFFORD EUGENE LEVINGSTON
(Cliff)

Born January 4, 1961 at San Diego, Calif. Height 6:08. Weight 220.

High School—San Diego, Calif., Morse.

College—Wichita State University, Wichita, Kan.

Drafted by Detroit on first round as an undergraduate, 1982 (9th pick).

Traded by Detroit with the draft rights to Antoine Carr and 1986 and 1987 2nd round draft choices to Atlanta for Dan Roundfield, June 18, 1984.

—COLLEGIATE RECORD—

Year	G.	Min.	FGA	FGM	Pct.	FTA	FTM	Pct.	Reb.	Pts.	Avg.
79-80	29	914	346	189	.546	127	79	.622	294	457	15.8
80-81	33	1108	452	246	.544	194	120	.619	376	612	18.5
81-82	29	902	312	162	.519	125	78	.624	295	402	13.9
Totals	91	2924	1110	597	.538	446	277	.621	965	1471	16.2

NBA REGULAR SEASON RECORD

									—Rebounds—									
Sea.—Team	G.	Min.	FGA	FGM	Pct.	FTA	FTM	Pct.	Off.	Def.	Tot.	Ast.	PF	Dq.	Stl.	Blk.	Pts.	Avg.
82-83—Detroit	62	879	270	131	.485	147	84	.571	104	128	232	52	125	2	23	36	346	5.6
83-84—Detroit	80	1746	436	229	.525	186	125	.672	234	311	545	109	281	7	44	78	583	7.3
84-85—Atlanta	74	2017	552	291	.527	222	145	.653	230	336	566	104	231	3	70	69	727	9.8
85-86—Atlanta	81	1945	551	294	.534	242	164	.678	193	341	534	72	260	5	76	39	752	9.3
86-87—Atlanta	82	1848	496	251	.506	212	155	.731	219	314	533	40	261	4	48	68	657	8.0
87-88—Atlanta	82	2135	564	314	.557	246	190	.772	228	276	504	71	287	5	52	84	819	10.0

Sea.—Team	G.	Min.	FGA	FGM	Pct.	FTA	FTM	Pct.	—Rebounds— Off.	Def.	Tot.	Ast.	PF	Dq.	Stl.	Blk.	Pts.	Avg.
88-89—Atlanta	80	2184	568	300	.528	191	133	.696	194	304	498	75	270	4	97	70	734	9.2
89-90—Atlanta	75	1706	424	216	.509	122	83	.680	113	206	319	80	216	2	55	41	516	6.9
Totals	616	14460	3861	2026	.525	1568	1079	.688	1515	2216	3731	603	1931	32	465	485	5134	8.3

Three-Point Field Goals: 1982-83, 0-for-1. 1983-84, 0-for-3. 1984-85, 0-for-2. 1985-86, 0-for-1. 1986-87, 0-for-3. 1987-88, 1-for-2 (.500). 1988-89, 1-for-5 (.200). 1989-90, 1-for-5 (.200). Totals, 3-for-22 (.136).

NBA PLAYOFF RECORD

Sea.—Team	G.	Min.	FGA	FGM	Pct.	FTA	FTM	Pct.	—Rebounds— Off.	Def.	Tot.	Ast.	PF	Dq.	Stl.	Blk.	Pts.	Avg.
83-84—Detroit	5	101	19	15	.789	16	10	.625	11	13	24	1	15	0	1	2	40	8.0
85-86—Atlanta	9	180	37	22	.595	9	7	.778	15	26	41	3	23	0	4	9	52	5.8
86-87—Atlanta	9	108	18	7	.389	18	14	.778	12	22	34	3	21	0	0	3	28	3.1
87-88—Atlanta	12	163	50	24	.480	16	12	.750	14	12	26	7	25	0	5	5	60	5.0
88-89—Atlanta	5	77	11	3	.273	10	9	.900	6	11	17	2	15	0	0	3	16	3.2
Totals	40	629	135	71	.526	69	52	.754	58	84	142	16	99	0	10	22	196	4.9

Three-Point Field Goals: 1985-86, 1-for-1 (1.000). 1986-87, 0-for-1. 1988-89, 1-for-1 (1.000). Totals, 2-for-3 (.667).

RALPH ADOLPHUS LEWIS

Born March 28, 1963 at Philadelphia, Pa. Height 6:06. Weight 200.

High School—Philadelphia, Pa., Frankford.

College—La Salle University, Philadelphia, Pa.

Drafted by Boston on sixth round, 1985 (139th pick).

Draft rights relinquished by Boston, September 30, 1986.
Signed by Detroit as a free agent, October 6, 1987.
Selected from Detroit by Charlotte in NBA expansion draft, June 23, 1988.
Waived by Charlotte, March 29, 1989; signed by Detroit, March 28, 1990, to the first of consecutive 10-day contracts that expired, April 17, 1990.
Waived by Detroit, April 10, 1990; signed by Charlotte, April 14, 1990, to a 10-day contract that expired, April 22, 1990.
Played in Continental Basketball Association with Bay State Bombardiers, 1985-86, Pensacola Tornados, 1986-87, and Sioux Falls Skyforce, 1989-90.

—COLLEGIATE RECORD—

Year	G.	Min.	FGA	FGM	Pct.	FTA	FTM	Pct.	Reb.	Pts.	Avg.
81-82	25	....	174	83	.477	100	61	.610	158	227	9.1
82-83	32	1071	339	156	.460	158	106	.671	259	418	13.1
83-84	31	....	404	237	.587	220	164	.745	281	638	20.6
84-85	28	....	360	201	.558	165	122	.739	268	524	18.7
Totals	116	....	1277	677	.530	643	453	.705	966	1807	15.6

CBA REGULAR SEASON RECORD

Sea.—Team	G.	Min.	—2-Point— FGM	FGA	Pct.	—3-Point— FGM	FGA	Pct.	FTM	FTA	Pct.	Reb.	Ast.	Pts.	Avg.
85-86—Bay State	38	444	74	151	.490	0	2	.000	41	74	.554	89	23	189	5.0
86-87—Pensacola	48	1742	353	684	.516	1	9	.111	296	388	.762	293	104	1005	20.9
89-90—Sioux Falls	55	2149	468	972	.481	2	15	.133	275	359	.766	375	190	1217	22.1
Totals	141	4335	895	1807	.495	3	26	.115	612	821	.745	757	317	2411	17.1

NBA REGULAR SEASON RECORD

Sea.—Team	G.	Min.	FGA	FGM	Pct.	FTA	FTM	Pct.	—Rebounds— Off.	Def.	Tot.	Ast.	PF	Dq.	Stl.	Blk.	Pts.	Avg.
87-88—Detroit	50	310	87	27	.310	48	29	.604	17	34	51	14	36	0	13	4	83	1.7
88-89—Charlotte	42	336	121	58	.479	39	19	.487	35	26	61	15	28	0	11	3	136	3.2
89-90—Det.-Char.	7	26	7	4	.571	2	2	1.000	4	2	6	0	3	0	1	0	10	1.4
Totals	99	672	215	89	.414	89	50	.562	56	62	118	29	67	0	25	7	229	2.3

Three-Point Field Goals: 1987-88, 0-for-1. 1988-89, 1-for-3 (.333). Totals, 1-for-4 (.250).

NBA PLAYOFF RECORD

Sea.—Team	G.	Min.	FGA	FGM	Pct.	FTA	FTM	Pct.	—Rebounds— Off.	Def.	Tot.	Ast.	PF	Dq.	Stl.	Blk.	Pts.	Avg.
1987-88—Detroit	10	17	6	2	.333	0	0	.000	3	5	8	1	2	0	0	0	4	0.4

Three-Point Field Goals: 1987-88, 0-for-1.

REGGIE LEWIS

Born November 21, 1965 at Baltimore, Md. Height 6:07. Weight 195.

High School—Baltimore, Md., Dunbar.

College—Northeastern University, Boston, Mass.

Drafted by Boston on first round, 1987 (22nd pick).

—COLLEGIATE RECORD—

Year	G.	Min.	FGA	FGM	Pct.	FTA	FTM	Pct.	Reb.	Pts.	Avg.
83-84	32	1030	447	236	.528	144	99	.688	198	571	17.8
84-85	31	1082	585	294	.503	213	159	.746	241	747	24.1
85-86	30	1118	559	265	.474	229	184	.803	279	714	23.8
86-87	29	957	507	248	.489	197	150	.761	246	676	23.3
Totals	122	4187	2098	1043	.497	783	592	.756	964	2708	22.2

Three-Point Field Goals: 1986-87, 30-for-91 (.330).

NBA REGULAR SEASON RECORD

									—Rebounds—									
Sea.—Team	G.	Min.	FGA	FGM	Pct.	FTA	FTM	Pct.	Off.	Def.	Tot.	Ast.	PF	Dq.	Stl.	Blk.	Pts.	Avg.
87-88—Boston	49	405	193	90	.466	57	40	.702	28	35	63	26	54	0	16	15	220	4.5
88-89—Boston	81	2657	1242	604	.486	361	284	.787	116	261	377	218	258	5	124	72	1495	18.5
89-90—Boston	79	2522	1089	540	.496	317	256	.808	109	238	347	225	216	2	88	63	1340	17.0
Totals	209	5584	2524	1234	.489	735	580	.789	253	534	787	469	528	7	228	150	3055	14.6

Three-Point Field Goals: 1987-88, 0-for-4. 1988-89, 3-for-22 (.136). 1989-90, 4-for-15 (.267). Totals, 7-for-41 (.171).

NBA PLAYOFF RECORD

									—Rebounds—									
Sea.—Team	G.	Min.	FGA	FGM	Pct.	FTA	FTM	Pct.	Off.	Def.	Tot.	Ast.	PF	Dq.	Stl.	Blk.	Pts.	Avg.
87-88—Boston	12	70	34	13	.382	5	3	.600	9	7	16	4	13	0	3	2	29	2.4
88-89—Boston	3	125	55	26	.473	13	9	.692	5	16	21	11	11	0	5	0	61	20.3
89-90—Boston	5	200	62	37	.597	35	27	.771	9	16	25	22	14	0	7	2	101	20.2
Totals	20	395	151	76	.503	53	39	.736	23	39	62	37	38	0	15	4	191	9.6

Three-Point Field Goals: 1987-88, 0-for-1. 1988-89, 0-for-2. 1989-90, 0-for-1. Totals, 0-for-4.

TODD SAMUEL LICHTI

Born January 8, 1967 at Walnut Creek, Calif. Height 6:04. Weight 205.
High School—Concord, Calif., Mt. Diablo.
College—Stanford University, Stanford, Calif.
Drafted by Denver on first round, 1989 (15th pick).

—COLLEGIATE RECORD—

Year	G.	Min.	FGA	FGM	Pct.	FTA	FTM	Pct.	Reb.	Pts.	Avg.
85-86	30	876	353	188	.533	172	140	.814	142	516	17.2
86-87	28	974	329	170	.517	152	123	.809	160	493	17.6
87-88	33	1140	406	222	.547	198	174	.879	184	664	20.1
88-89	33	1117	437	240	.549	173	147	.850	166	663	20.1
Totals	124	4107	1525	820	.538	695	584	.840	652	2336	18.8

Three-Point Field Goals: 1986-87, 30-for-63 (.476). 1987-88, 46-for-89 (.517). 1988-89, 36-for-83 (.434). Totals, 112-for-235 (.477).

NBA REGULAR SEASON RECORD

									—Rebounds—									
Sea.—Team	G.	Min.	FGA	FGM	Pct.	FTA	FTM	Pct.	Off.	Def.	Tot.	Ast.	PF	Dq.	Stl.	Blk.	Pts.	Avg.
89-90—Denver	79	1326	514	250	.486	174	130	.747	49	102	151	116	145	1	55	13	630	8.0

Three-Point Field Goals: 1989-90, 0-for-14.

NBA PLAYOFF RECORD

									—Rebounds—									
Sea.—Team	G.	Min.	FGA	FGM	Pct.	FTA	FTM	Pct.	Off.	Def.	Tot.	Ast.	PF	Dq.	Stl.	Blk.	Pts.	Avg.
89-90—Denver	3	70	29	15	.517	19	14	.737	5	13	18	9	6	0	1	0	44	14.7

Three-Point Field Goals: 1989-90, 0-for-1.

ALTON LAVELLE LISTER

Born October 1, 1958 at Dallas, Tex. Height 7:00. Weight 240.
High School—Dallas, Tex., Woodrow Wilson.
Colleges—San Jacinto College, Pasadena, Tex., and Arizona State University, Tempe, Ariz.
Drafted by Milwaukee on first round, 1981 (21st pick).

Traded by Milwaukee with 1987 and 1989 1st round draft choices to Seattle for Jack Sikma and 1987 and 1989 2nd round draft choices, July 1, 1986.
Traded by Seattle to Golden State for a 1990 1st round draft choice, August 7, 1989.

—COLLEGIATE RECORD—

San Jacinto

Year	G.	Min.	FGA	FGM	Pct.	FTA	FTM	Pct.	Reb.	Pts.	Avg.
76-77	40	....	....	....	....	....	....	....	640	680	17.0
77-78					Did Not Play—Redshirted						

Arizona State

Year	G.	Min.	FGA	FGM	Pct.	FTA	FTM	Pct.	Reb.	Pts.	Avg.
78-79	29	584	209	104	.498	84	47	.560	194	255	8.8
79-80	27	793	264	133	.504	104	58	.558	231	324	12.0
80-81	26	845	282	158	.560	123	85	.691	251	401	15.4
Totals	82	2222	755	395	.523	311	190	.611	676	980	12.0

NBA REGULAR SEASON RECORD

Sea.—Team	G.	Min.	FGA	FGM	Pct.	FTA	FTM	Pct.	—Rebounds— Off.	Def.	Tot.	Ast.	PF	Dq.	Stl.	Blk.	Pts.	Avg.
81-82—Milwaukee	80	1186	287	149	.519	123	64	.520	108	279	387	84	239	4	18	118	362	4.5
82-83—Milwaukee	80	1885	514	272	.529	242	130	.537	168	400	568	111	328	18	50	177	674	8.4
83-84—Milwaukee	82	1955	512	256	.500	182	114	.626	156	447	603	110	327	11	41	140	626	7.6
84-85—Milwaukee	81	2091	598	322	.538	262	154	.588	219	428	647	127	287	5	49	167	798	9.9
85-86—Milwaukee	81	1812	577	318	.551	266	160	.602	199	393	592	101	300	8	49	142	796	9.8
86-87—Seattle	75	2288	687	346	.504	265	179	.675	223	482	705	110	289	11	32	180	871	11.6
87-88—Seattle	82	1812	343	173	.504	188	114	.606	200	427	627	58	319	8	27	140	461	5.6
88-89—Seattle	82	1806	543	271	.499	178	115	.646	207	338	545	54	310	3	28	180	657	8.0
89-90—Golden State	3	40	8	4	.500	7	4	.571	5	3	8	2	8	0	1	0	12	4.0
Totals	646	14875	4069	2111	.519	1713	1034	.604	1485	3197	4682	757	2407	68	295	1244	5257	8.1

Three-Point Field Goals: 1984-85, 0-for-1. 1985-86, 0-for-2. 1986-87, 0-for-1. 1987-88, 1-for-2 (.500). 1989-90, 0-for-1. Totals, 1-for-7 (.143).

NBA PLAYOFF RECORD

Sea.—Team	G.	Min.	FGA	FGM	Pct.	FTA	FTM	Pct.	—Rebounds— Off.	Def.	Tot.	Ast.	PF	Dq.	Stl.	Blk.	Pts.	Avg.
81-82—Milwaukee	6	112	24	14	.583	7	5	.714	6	21	27	5	23	0	2	15	33	5.5
82-83—Milwaukee	9	206	63	27	.429	5	4	.800	21	40	61	11	30	1	9	15	58	6.4
83-84—Milwaukee	16	368	78	39	.500	48	30	.625	26	70	96	10	63	2	5	24	108	6.8
84-85—Milwaukee	8	203	60	27	.450	32	15	.469	27	35	62	15	36	1	6	15	69	8.6
85-86—Milwaukee	14	335	103	66	.641	58	35	.603	37	59	96	12	56	3	7	22	167	11.9
86-87—Seattle	9	206	50	20	.400	20	14	.700	29	27	56	7	37	3	7	13	54	6.0
87-88—Seattle	5	77	17	12	.706	5	4	.800	9	20	29	5	17	0	1	5	28	5.6
88-89—Seattle	8	160	39	17	.436	26	22	.846	13	25	38	2	28	0	2	21	56	7.0
Totals	75	1667	434	222	.512	201	129	.642	168	297	465	67	290	10	39	130	573	7.6

Three-Point Field Goals: 1982-83, 0-for-1. 1985-86, 0-for-1. Totals, 0-for-2.

Member of U.S. Olympic team, 1980.

LEWIS KEVIN LLOYD

Born February 22, 1959 at Philadelphia, Pa. Height 6:06. Weight 205.
High School—Philadelphia, Pa., Overbrook.
Colleges—New Mexico Military Institute, Roswell, N.M., and Drake University, Des Moines, Ia.
Drafted by Golden State on fourth round, 1981 (76th pick).

Signed by Houston as a Veteran Free Agent, August 29, 1983; Golden State agreed not to exercise its right of first refusal in exchange for a 1985 2nd round draft choice.

Disqualified from the NBA under rules of the league's Anti-Drug Program, January 13, 1987; reinstated by the NBA, September 8, 1989.

Waived by Houston, December 7, 1989; signed by Philadelphia, January 15, 1990, to a 10-day contract that expired, January 24, 1990.

Signed by Houston, February 27, 1990, to the first of consecutive 10-day contracts that expired, March 18, 1990.

Re-signed by Houston, March 20, 1990, for remainder of season.

Played in Continental Basketball Association with Cedar Rapids Silver Bullets, 1988-89.

—COLLEGIATE RECORD—

New Mexico Military

Year	G.	Min.	FGA	FGM	Pct.	FTA	FTM	Pct.	Reb.	Pts.	Avg.
77-78	22	....	411	244	.594	142	92	.648	295	580	26.4
78-79	30	....	580	377	.650	232	177	.763	377	931	31.0
JC Totals	52	....	991	621	.627	374	269	.719	672	1511	29.1

Drake

Year	G.	Min.	FGA	FGM	Pct.	FTA	FTM	Pct.	Reb.	Pts.	Avg.
79-80	27	1022	585	324	.554	236	167	.708	406	815	30.2
80-81	29	1044	548	298	.544	224	166	.741	291	762	26.3
Totals	56	2066	1133	622	.549	460	333	.724	697	1577	28.2

CBA REGULAR SEASON RECORD

Sea.—Team	G.	Min.	—2-Point— FGM	FGA	Pct.	—3-Point— FGM	FGA	Pct.	FTM	FTA	Pct.	Reb.	Ast.	Pts.	Avg.
88-89—Cedar Rapids	18	505	134	239	.561	3	9	.333	61	87	.701	118	43	338	18.8

NBA REGULAR SEASON RECORD

Sea.—Team	G.	Min.	FGA	FGM	Pct.	FTA	FTM	Pct.	—Rebounds— Off.	Def.	Tot.	Ast.	PF	Dq.	Stl.	Blk.	Pts.	Avg.
81-82—Golden State	16	95	45	25	.556	11	7	.636	9	7	16	6	20	0	5	1	57	3.6
82-83—Golden State	73	1350	566	293	.518	139	100	.719	77	183	260	130	109	0	61	31	687	9.4
83-84—Houston	82	2578	1182	610	.516	298	235	.789	128	167	295	321	211	4	102	44	1458	17.8
84-85—Houston	82	2128	869	457	.526	220	161	.732	98	133	231	280	196	1	73	28	1077	13.1
85-86—Houston	82	2444	1119	592	.529	236	199	.843	155	169	324	300	216	0	102	24	1386	16.9
86-87—Houston	32	688	310	165	.532	86	65	.756	13	35	48	90	69	0	19	5	396	12.4
89-90—Phil.-Hou.	21	123	53	30	.566	16	9	.563	8	10	18	11	12	0	3	0	69	3.3
Totals	388	9406	4144	2172	.524	1006	776	.771	488	704	1192	1138	833	5	365	133	5130	13.2

Three-Point Field Goals: 1982-83, 1-for-4 (.250). 1983-84, 3-for-13 (.231). 1984-85, 2-for-8 (.250). 1985-86, 3-for-14 (.214). 1986-87, 1-for-7 (.143). Totals, 10-for-46 (.217).

NBA PLAYOFF RECORD

Sea.—Team	G.	Min.	FGA	FGM	Pct.	FTA	FTM	Pct.	—Rebounds— Off.	Def.	Tot.	Ast.	PF	Dq.	Stl.	Blk.	Pts.	Avg.
84-85—Houston	5	174	77	38	.494	14	10	.714	15	14	29	25	12	0	7	8	86	17.2
85-86—Houston	20	589	241	116	.481	58	47	.810	34	32	66	86	47	0	16	6	281	14.1
Totals	25	763	318	154	.484	72	57	.792	49	46	95	111	59	0	23	14	367	14.7

Three-Point Field Goals: 1985-86, 2-for-5 (.400).

BRAD ALLEN LOHAUS

Born September 29, 1964 at New Ulm, Minn. Height 7:00. Weight 235.
High School—Phoenix, Ariz., Greenway.
College—University of Iowa, Iowa City, Ia.
Drafted by Boston on second round, 1987 (45th pick).

Traded by Boston with Danny Ainge to Sacramento for Joe Kleine and Ed Pinckney, February 23, 1989.
Selected from Sacramento by Minnesota in NBA expansion draft, June 15, 1989.
Traded by Minnesota to Milwaukee for Randy Breuer and a conditional exchange of 2nd round draft choices in 1991 or 1992, January 4, 1990.

—COLLEGIATE RECORD—

Year	G.	Min.	FGA	FGM	Pct.	FTA	FTM	Pct.	Reb.	Pts.	Avg.
82-83	20	....	29	9	.310	13	7	.538	11	26	1.3
83-84	28	626	193	78	.404	52	35	.673	146	191	6.8
84-85				Did Not Play—Redshirted							
85-86	32	407	102	44	.431	34	27	.794	101	115	3.6
86-87	35	943	276	149	.540	104	72	.692	268	395	11.3
Totals	115	....	600	280	.467	203	141	.695	526	727	6.3

Three-Point Field Goals: 1982-83, 1-for-1 (1.000). 1986-87, 25-for-72 (.347). Totals, 26-for-73 (.356).

NBA REGULAR SEASON RECORD

Sea.—Team	G.	Min.	FGA	FGM	Pct.	FTA	FTM	Pct.	—Rebounds— Off.	Def.	Tot.	Ast.	PF	Dq.	Stl.	Blk.	Pts.	Avg.
87-88—Boston	70	718	246	122	.496	62	50	.806	46	92	138	49	123	1	20	41	297	4.2
88-89—Bos.-Sac.	77	1214	486	210	.432	103	81	.786	84	172	256	66	161	1	30	56	502	6.5
89-90—Min.-Milw.	80	1943	663	305	.460	103	75	.728	98	300	398	168	211	3	58	88	732	9.2
Totals	227	3875	1395	637	.457	268	206	.769	228	564	792	283	495	5	108	185	1531	6.7

Three-Point Field Goals: 1987-88, 3-for-13 (.231). 1988-89, 1-for-11 (.091). 1989-90, 47-for-137 (.343). Totals, 51-for-161 (.317).

NBA PLAYOFF RECORD

Sea.—Team	G.	Min.	FGA	FGM	Pct.	FTA	FTM	Pct.	—Rebounds— Off.	Def.	Tot.	Ast.	PF	Dq.	Stl.	Blk.	Pts.	Avg.
87-88—Boston	9	26	11	8	.727	0	0	.000	1	3	4	0	4	0	0	1	16	1.8
89-90—Milwaukee	4	147	40	16	.400	0	0	....	4	23	27	5	17	1	8	9	38	9.5
Totals	13	173	51	24	.471	0	0	....	5	26	31	5	21	1	8	10	54	4.2

Three-Point Field Goals: 1987-88, 0-for-2. 1989-90, 6-for-16 (.375). Totals, 6-for-18 (.333).

GRANT ANDREW LONG

Born March 12, 1966 at Wayne, Mich. Height 6:08. Weight 225.
High School—Romulus, Mich.
College—Eastern Michigan University, Ypsilanti, Mich.
Drafted by Miami on second round, 1988 (33rd pick).

—COLLEGIATE RECORD—

Year	G.	Min.	FGA	FGM	Pct.	FTA	FTM	Pct.	Reb.	Pts.	Avg.
84-85	28	551	78	44	.564	46	28	.609	112	116	4.1
85-86	27	803	175	92	.526	73	47	.644	178	231	8.6

Year	G.	Min.	FGA	FGM	Pct.	FTA	FTM	Pct.	Reb.	Pts.	Avg.
86-87	29	879	308	169	.549	131	95	.725	260	433	14.9
87-88	30	1026	427	237	.555	281	215	.765	313	689	23.0
Totals	114	3259	988	542	.549	531	385	.725	863	1469	12.9

NBA REGULAR SEASON RECORD

Sea.—Team	G.	Min.	FGA	FGM	Pct.	FTA	FTM	Pct.	—Rebounds— Off.	Def.	Tot.	Ast.	PF	Dq.	Stl.	Blk.	Pts.	Avg.
88-89—Miami	82	2435	692	336	.486	406	304	.749	240	306	546	149	337	13	122	48	976	11.9
89-90—Miami	81	1856	532	257	.483	241	172	.714	156	246	402	96	300	11	91	38	686	8.5
Totals	163	4291	1224	593	.484	647	476	.736	396	552	948	245	637	24	213	86	1662	10.2

Three-Point Field Goals: 1988-89, 0-for-5. 1989-90, 0-for-3. Totals, 0-for-8.

Nephew of former NBA guard John Long.

JOHN EDDIE LONG

Born August 28, 1956 at Romulus, Mich. Height 6:05. Weight 195.
High School—Romulus, Mich.
College—University of Detroit, Detroit, Mich.
Drafted by Detroit on second round, 1978 (29th pick).

Traded by Detroit to Seattle for 1987 and 1991 2nd round draft choices, September 30, 1986.

Traded by Seattle with a future 2nd round draft choice to Indiana for Russ Schoene and Terence Stansbury, October 2, 1986.

Waived by Indiana, February 21, 1989; signed by Detroit as a free agent, February 23, 1989.

Signed by Dallas as an unrestricted free agent, October 3, 1989.

Waived by Dallas, October 31, 1989; signed by Atlanta, January 5, 1990, to the first of consecutive 10-day contracts that expired, January 24, 1990.

Re-signed by Atlanta, January 25, 1990, for remainder of season.

—COLLEGIATE RECORD—

Year	G.	Min.	FGA	FGM	Pct.	FTA	FTM	Pct.	Reb.	Pts.	Avg.
74-75	26	654	419	200	.477	58	45	.776	168	445	17.1
75-76	27	872	524	230	.439	95	72	.758	240	532	19.7
76-77	28	891	508	245	.482	102	78	.765	189	568	20.3
77-78	29	798	491	265	.540	114	92	.807	218	622	21.4
Totals	110	3215	1942	940	.484	369	287	.778	815	2167	19.7

NBA REGULAR SEASON RECORD

Sea.—Team	G.	Min.	FGA	FGM	Pct.	FTA	FTM	Pct.	—Rebounds— Off.	Def.	Tot.	Ast.	PF	Dq.	Stl.	Blk.	Pts.	Avg.
78-79—Detroit	82	2498	1240	581	.469	190	157	.826	127	139	266	121	224	1	102	19	1319	16.1
79-80—Detroit	69	2364	1164	588	.505	194	160	.825	152	185	337	206	221	4	129	26	1337	19.4
80-81—Detroit	59	1750	957	441	.461	184	160	.870	95	102	197	106	164	3	95	22	1044	17.7
81-82—Detroit	69	2211	1294	637	.492	275	238	.865	95	162	257	148	173	0	65	25	1514	21.9
82-83—Detroit	70	1485	692	312	.451	146	111	.760	56	124	180	105	130	1	44	12	737	10.5
83-84—Detroit	82	2514	1155	545	.472	275	243	.884	139	150	289	205	199	1	93	18	1334	16.3
84-85—Detroit	66	1820	885	431	.487	123	106	.862	81	109	190	130	139	0	71	14	973	14.7
85-86—Detroit	62	1176	548	264	.482	104	89	.856	47	51	98	82	92	0	41	13	620	10.0
86-87—Indiana	80	2265	1170	490	.419	246	219	.890	75	142	217	258	167	1	96	8	1218	15.2
87-88—Indiana	81	2022	879	417	.474	183	166	.907	72	157	229	173	164	1	84	11	1034	12.8
88-89—Ind.-Det.	68	919	359	147	.409	76	70	.921	18	59	77	80	84	1	29	3	372	5.5
89-90—Atlanta	48	1030	384	174	.453	55	46	.836	26	57	83	85	66	0	45	5	404	8.4
Totals	836	22054	10727	5027	.469	2051	1765	.861	983	1437	2420	1699	1823	13	894	176	11906	14.2

Three-Point Field Goals: 1979-80, 1-for-12 (083). 1980-81, 2-for-11 (.182). 1981-82, 2-for-15 (.133). 1982-83, 2-for-7 (.286). 1983-84, 1-for-5 (.200). 1984-85, 5-for-15 (.333). 1985-86, 3-for-16 (.188). 1986-87, 19-for-67 (.284). 1987-88, 34-for-77 (.442). 1988-89, 8-for-20 (.400). 1989-90, 10-for-29 (.345). Totals, 87-for-274 (.318).

NBA PLAYOFF RECORD

Sea.—Team	G.	Min.	FGA	FGM	Pct.	FTA	FTM	Pct.	—Rebounds— Off.	Def.	Tot.	Ast.	PF	Dq.	Stl.	Blk.	Pts.	Avg.
83-84—Detroit	5	149	55	20	.364	15	15	1.000	7	4	11	2	15	0	7	0	55	11.0
84-85—Detroit	9	255	105	48	.457	15	15	1.000	10	7	17	13	22	0	14	2	112	12.4
85-86—Detroit	1	13	5	2	.400	3	3	1.000	0	1	1	0	1	0	1	0	7	7.0
86-87—Indiana	4	109	52	16	.308	13	11	.846	2	4	6	9	16	0	6	0	44	11.0
88-89—Detroit	4	8	1	1	1.000	3	3	1.000	0	0	0	0	0	0	0	0	5	1.3
Totals	23	534	218	87	.399	49	47	.959	19	16	35	24	54	0	28	2	223	9.7

Three-Point Field Goals: 1983-84, 0-for-1. 1984-85, 1-for-4 (.250). 1986-87, 1-for-6 (.167). Totals, 2-for-11 (.182).

Member of NBA championship team, 1989. . . . Uncle of Grant Long, forward with Miami Heat.

—DID YOU KNOW—

That 53 players saw action in all 82 games during the 1989-90 season but only one—Portland rookie Cliff Robinson—did not start a single game?

SIDNEY ROCHELL LOWE

Born January 21, 1960 at Washington, D. C. Height 6:00. Weight 195.
High School—Hyattsville, Md., DeMatha.
College—North Carolina State University, Raleigh, N. C.
Drafted by Chicago on second round, 1983 (25th pick).

Draft rights traded by Chicago with a 1984 2nd round draft choice to Indiana for draft rights to Mitchell Wiggins, June 28, 1983.
Waived by Indiana, October 4, 1984; signed by Detroit as a free agent, October 12, 1984.
Waived by Detroit, November 11, 1984; signed by Atlanta as a free agent, November 28, 1984.
Waived by Atlanta, December 18, 1984; re-signed by Atlanta to a 10-day contract that expired, December 30, 1984.
Re-signed by Atlanta to a 10-day contract that expired, January 26, 1985.
Signed by Charlotte, March 27, 1989, to the first of consecutive 10-day contracts that expired, April 15, 1989.
Re-signed by Charlotte, April 16, 1989, for remainder of season.
Signed by Minnesota as a free agent, August 3, 1989.
Played in Continental Basketball Association with Tampa Bay Thrillers, 1984-85 and 1985-86; with Albany Patroons, 1987-88, and with Rapid City Thrillers, 1988-89.

—COLLEGIATE RECORD—

Year	G.	Min.	FGA	FGM	Pct.	FTA	FTM	Pct.	Reb.	Pts.	Avg.
79-80	28	....	97	43	.443	105	74	.705	53	160	5.7
80-81	24	....	148	67	.453	96	75	.781	80	209	8.7
81-82	32	....	188	97	.516	105	79	.752	85	273	8.5
82-83	36	....	295	136	.461	116	90	.776	134	406	11.3
Totals	120	....	728	343	.471	422	318	.754	352	1048	8.7

Three-Point Field Goals: 1982-83, 44-for-115 (.383).

CBA REGULAR SEASON RECORD

			—2-Point—			—3-Point—									
Sea.—Team	G.	Min.	FGM	FGA	Pct.	FGM	FGA	Pct.	FTM	FTA	Pct.	Reb.	Ast.	Pts.	Avg.
84-85—Tampa Bay	18	494	33	70	.471	1	6	.167	30	37	.810	42	152	99	5.5
85-86—Tampa Bay	43	1629	87	211	.412	3	13	.231	87	113	.769	158	406	270	6.2
87-88—Albany	50	1842	86	190	.452	8	26	.308	64	99	.646	140	437	260	5.2
88-89—Rapid City	8	271	15	45	.333	0	2	.000	11	16	.688	31	77	41	5.1
Totals	119	4236	221	516	.428	12	47	.255	192	265	.725	371	1072	670	5.6

NBA REGULAR SEASON RECORD

									—Rebounds—									
Sea.—Team	G.	Min.	FGA	FGM	Pct.	FTA	FTM	Pct.	Off.	Def.	Tot.	Ast.	PF	Dq.	Stl.	Blk.	Pts.	Avg.
83-84—Indiana	78	1238	259	107	.413	139	108	.777	30	92	122	269	112	0	93	5	324	4.2
84-85—Det.-Atl.	21	190	27	10	.370	8	8	1.000	4	12	16	50	28	0	11	0	28	1.3
88-89—Charlotte	14	250	25	8	.320	11	7	.636	6	28	34	93	28	0	14	0	23	1.6
89-90—Minnesota	80	1744	229	73	.319	54	39	.722	41	122	163	337	114	0	73	4	187	2.3
Totals	193	3422	540	198	.367	212	162	.764	81	254	335	749	282	0	191	9	562	2.9

Three-Point Field Goals: 1983-84, 2-for-18 (.111). 1984-85, 0-for-1. 1988-89, 0-for-2. 1989-90, 2-for-9 (.222). Totals, 4-for-30 (.133).

Named to CBA All-Star First Team, 1988. . . . CBA All-Defensive First Team, 1986 and 1988. . . . Led CBA in steals, 1988 . . . . Member of NCAA Division I championship team, 1983.

JOHN HARDING LUCAS JR.

Born October 31, 1953 at Durham, N. C. Height 6:03. Weight 185.
High School—Durham, N. C., Hillside.
College—University of Maryland, College Park, Md.
Drafted by Houston on first round, 1976 (1st pick).

Awarded from Houston with cash to Golden State as compensation for earlier signing of Veteran Free Agent Rick Barry, September 5, 1978.
Traded by Golden State to Washington for 1982 and 1984 2nd round draft choices, October 19, 1981.
Waived by Washington, January 25, 1983; signed by Cleveland as a free agent, August 29, 1983.
Waived by Cleveland, September 21, 1983; signed by San Antonio as a free agent, December 4, 1983.
Traded by San Antonio with a 1985 3rd round draft choice to Houston for James Bailey, a 1985 2nd round draft choice and cash, October 4, 1984.
Waived by Houston, December 10, 1984; re-signed by Houston, February 19, 1985.
Waived by Houston, March 14, 1986; signed by Milwaukee as a free agent, January 17, 1987.
Rights relinquished by Milwaukee, June 23, 1988; signed by Seattle as a free agent, September 19, 1988.
Signed by Houston as an unrestricted free agent, August 17, 1989.
Played in Continental Basketball Association with Lancaster Lightning, 1983-84.

—COLLEGIATE RECORD—

Year	G.	Min.	FGA	FGM	Pct.	FTA	FTM	Pct.	Reb.	Pts.	Avg.
72-73	30	....	353	190	.538	64	45	.703	83	425	14.2

Year	G.	Min.	FGA	FGM	Pct.	FTA	FTM	Pct.	Reb.	Pts.	Avg.
73-74	28	....	495	253	.511	77	58	.753	82	564	20.1
74-75	24	....	339	186	.549	116	97	.836	100	469	19.5
75-76	28	....	456	233	.511	117	91	.778	109	557	19.9
Totals	110	....	1643	862	.525	374	291	.778	374	2015	18.3

CBA REGULAR SEASON RECORD

			2-Point			3-Point									
Sea.—Team	G.	Min.	FGM	FGA	Pct.	FGM	FGA	Pct.	FTM	FTA	Pct.	Reb.	Ast.	Pts.	Avg.
83-84—Lancaster	2	48	11	17	.647	1	1	1.000	6	6	1.000	1	8	31	15.5

NBA REGULAR SEASON RECORD

									—Rebounds—									
Sea.—Team	G.	Min.	FGA	FGM	Pct.	FTA	FTM	Pct.	Off.	Def.	Tot.	Ast.	PF	Dq.	Stl.	Blk.	Pts.	Avg.
76-77—Houston	82	2531	814	388	.477	171	135	.789	55	164	219	463	174	0	125	19	911	11.1
77-78—Houston	82	2933	947	412	.435	250	193	.772	51	204	255	768	208	1	160	9	1017	12.4
78-79—Golden State	82	3095	1146	530	.462	321	264	.822	65	182	247	762	229	1	152	9	1324	16.1
79-80—Golden State	80	2763	830	388	.467	289	222	.768	61	159	220	602	196	2	138	3	1010	12.6
80-81—Golden State	66	1919	506	222	.439	145	107	.738	34	120	154	464	140	1	83	2	555	8.4
81-82—Washington	79	1940	618	263	.426	176	138	.784	40	126	166	551	105	0	95	6	666	8.4
82-83—Washington	35	386	131	62	.473	42	21	.500	8	21	29	102	18	0	25	1	145	4.1
83-84—San Antonio	63	1807	595	275	.462	157	120	.764	23	157	180	673	123	1	92	5	689	10.9
84-85—Houston	47	1158	446	206	.462	129	103	.798	21	64	85	318	78	0	62	2	536	11.4
85-86—Houston	65	2120	818	365	.446	298	231	.775	33	110	143	571	124	0	77	5	1006	15.5
86-87—Milwaukee	43	1358	624	285	.457	174	137	.787	29	96	125	290	82	0	71	6	753	17.5
87-88—Milwaukee	81	1766	631	281	.445	162	130	.802	29	130	159	392	102	1	88	3	743	9.2
88-89—Seattle	74	842	299	119	.398	77	54	.701	22	57	79	260	53	0	60	1	310	4.2
89-90—Houston	49	938	291	109	.375	55	42	.764	19	71	90	238	59	0	45	2	286	5.8
Totals	928	25556	8696	3905	.449	2446	1897	.776	490	1661	2151	6454	1691	7	1273	73	9951	10.7

Three-Point Field Goals: 1979-80, 12-for-42 (.286). 1980-81, 4-for-24 (.167). 1981-82, 2-for-22 (.091). 1982-83, 0-for-5. 1983-84, 19-for-69 (.275). 1984-85, 21-for-66 (.318). 1985-86, 45-for-146 (.308). 1986-87, 46-for-126 (.365). 1987-88, 51-for-151 (.338). 1988-89, 18-for-68 (.265). 1989-90, 26-for-87 (.299). Totals, 244-for-806 (.303).

NBA PLAYOFF RECORD

									—Rebounds—									
Sea.—Team	G.	Min.	FGA	FGM	Pct.	FTA	FTM	Pct.	Off.	Def.	Tot.	Ast.	PF	Dq.	Stl.	Blk.	Pts.	Avg.
76-77—Houston	12	430	139	75	.540	34	26	.765	4	29	33	83	33	1	24	4	176	14.7
81-82—Washington	7	74	26	14	.538	3	2	.667	0	8	8	20	6	0	3	1	31	4.4
84-85—Houston	5	152	80	26	.325	22	14	.636	7	14	21	27	14	0	6	0	68	13.6
86-87—Milwaukee	12	362	150	68	.453	48	39	.813	4	21	25	62	17	0	14	1	187	15.6
87-88—Milwaukee	5	80	27	10	.370	9	6	.667	5	3	8	19	5	0	5	0	29	5.8
88-89—Seattle	4	37	17	5	.294	2	1	.500	0	1	1	8	5	0	0	0	11	2.8
Totals	45	1135	439	198	.451	118	88	.746	20	76	96	219	80	1	52	6	502	11.2

Three-Point Field Goals: 1981-82, 1-for-3 (.333). 1984-85, 2-for-14 (.143). 1986-87, 12-for-36 (.333). 1987-88, 3-for-13 (.231). 1988-89, 0-for-3. Totals, 18-for-69 (.261).

Named to NBA All-Rookie Team, 1977. . . . Holds NBA record for most assists in one quarter, 14, vs. Denver, April 15, 1984. . . . Played World Team Tennis with Golden Gaters and New Orleans Nets, 1977 and 1978. . . . Named to THE SPORTING NEWS All-America First Team, 1975 and 1976. . . . THE SPORTING NEWS All-America Second Team, 1974.

DERRICK ALLEN MAHORN
(Ricky)

Born September 21, 1958 at Hartford, Conn. Height 6:10. Weight 255.

High School—Hartford, Conn., Weaver.

College—Hampton Institute, Hampton, Va.

Drafted by Washington on second round, 1980 (35th pick).

Traded by Washington with Mike Gibson to Detroit for Dan Roundfield, June 17, 1985.
Selected from Detroit by Minnesota in NBA expansion draft, June 15, 1989.
Traded by Minnesota to Philadelphia for a 1990 1st round draft choice and 1991 and 1992 2nd round draft choices, October 27, 1989.

—COLLEGIATE RECORD—

Year	G.	Min.	FGA	FGM	Pct.	FTA	FTM	Pct.	Reb.	Pts.	Avg.
76-77	28	....	159	65	.409	44	29	.659	168	159	5.7
77-78	30	....	570	291	.511	202	137	.678	377	719	24.0
78-79	30	....	489	274	.560	200	137	.685	430	685	22.8
79-80	31	1123	621	352	.567	220	151	.686	490	855	27.6
Totals	119	....	1839	982	.534	666	454	.682	1465	2418	20.3

NBA REGULAR SEASON RECORD

									—Rebounds—									
Sea.—Team	G.	Min.	FGA	FGM	Pct.	FTA	FTM	Pct.	Off.	Def.	Tot.	Ast.	PF	Dq.	Stl.	Blk.	Pts.	Avg.
80-81—Washington	52	696	219	111	.507	40	27	.675	67	148	215	25	134	3	21	44	249	4.8

									—Rebounds—									
Sea.—Team	G.	Min.	FGA	FGM	Pct.	FTA	FTM	Pct.	Off.	Def.	Tot.	Ast.	PF	Dq.	Stl.	Blk.	Pts.	Avg.
81-82—Washington	80	2664	816	414	.507	234	148	.632	149	555	704	150	349	12	57	138	976	12.2
82-83—Washington	82	3023	768	376	.490	254	146	.575	171	608	779	115	335	13	86	148	898	11.0
83-84—Washington	82	2701	605	307	.507	192	125	.651	169	569	738	131	358	14	62	123	739	9.0
84-85—Washington	77	2072	413	206	.499	104	71	.683	150	458	608	121	308	11	59	104	483	6.3
85-86—Detroit	80	1442	345	157	.455	119	81	.681	121	291	412	64	261	4	40	61	395	4.9
86-87—Detroit	63	1278	322	144	.447	117	96	.821	93	282	375	38	221	4	32	50	384	6.1
87-88—Detroit	67	1963	481	276	.574	217	164	.756	159	406	565	60	262	4	43	42	717	10.7
88-89—Detroit	72	1795	393	203	.517	155	116	.748	141	355	496	59	206	1	40	66	522	7.3
89-90—Philadelphia	75	2271	630	313	.497	256	183	.715	167	401	568	98	251	2	44	103	811	10.8
Totals	730	19905	4992	2507	.502	1688	1157	.685	1387	4073	5460	861	2685	68	484	879	6174	8.5

Three-Point Field Goals: 1981-82, 0-for-3. 1982-83, 0-for-3. 1985-86, 0-for-1. 1987-88, 1-for-2 (.500). 1988-89, 0-for-2. 1989-90, 2-for-9 (.222). Totals, 3-for-20 (.150).

NBA PLAYOFF RECORD

									—Rebounds—									
Sea.—Team	G.	Min.	FGA	FGM	Pct.	FTA	FTM	Pct.	Off.	Def.	Tot.	Ast.	PF	Dq.	Stl.	Blk.	Pts.	Avg.
81-82—Washington	7	242	73	32	.438	14	10	.714	14	47	61	13	30	1	10	5	74	10.6
83-84—Washington	4	154	25	15	.600	10	8	.800	7	36	43	6	19	0	1	6	38	9.5
84-85—Washington	4	41	8	4	.500	4	4	1.000	2	5	7	0	9	0	0	3	12	3.0
85-86—Detroit	4	61	13	5	.385	2	2	1.000	3	9	12	0	14	0	1	0	12	3.0
86-87—Detroit	15	483	109	59	.541	35	28	.800	42	100	142	5	60	1	6	11	146	9.7
87-88—Detroit	23	409	90	31	.344	19	13	.684	19	70	89	13	64	2	5	10	75	3.3
88-89—Detroit	17	360	69	40	.580	26	17	.654	30	57	87	7	59	1	9	13	97	5.7
89-90—Philadelphia	10	342	86	37	.430	26	20	.769	18	52	70	10	41	1	7	8	94	9.4
Totals	84	2092	473	223	.471	136	102	.750	135	376	511	54	296	6	39	56	548	6.5

Three-Point Field Goals: 1983-84, 0-for-1. 1986-87, 0-for-1. 1989-90, 0-for-1. Totals, 0-for-3.

Named to NBA All-Defensive Second Team, 1990. . . . Member of NBA championship team, 1989. . . . Led NCAA Division II in rebounding, 1980.

DANIEL LEWIS MAJERLE

Name pronounced MAR-lee.

(Dan)

Born September 9, 1965 at Traverse City, Mich. Height 6:06. Weight 220.

High School—Traverse City, Mich.

College—Central Michigan University, Mt. Pleasant, Mich.

Drafted by Phoenix on first round, 1988 (14th pick).

—COLLEGIATE RECORD—

Year	G.	Min.	FGA	FGM	Pct.	FTA	FTM	Pct.	Reb.	Pts.	Avg.
83-84				Did Not Play—Back Injury							
84-85	12	360	162	92	.568	67	39	.582	80	223	18.6
85-86	27	1002	433	228	.527	170	122	.718	212	578	21.4
86-87	23	824	344	191	.555	183	101	.552	196	485	21.1
87-88	32	1197	535	279	.521	242	156	.645	346	759	23.7
Totals	94	3383	1474	790	.536	662	418	.631	834	2045	21.8

Three-Point Field Goals: 1986-87, 2-for-8 (.250). 1987-88, 45-for-101 (.446). Totals, 47-for-109 (.431).

NBA REGULAR SEASON RECORD

									—Rebounds—									
Sea.—Team	G.	Min.	FGA	FGM	Pct.	FTA	FTM	Pct.	Off.	Def.	Tot.	Ast.	PF	Dq.	Stl.	Blk.	Pts.	Avg.
88-89—Phoenix	54	1354	432	181	.419	127	78	.614	62	147	209	130	139	1	63	14	467	8.6
89-90—Phoenix	73	2244	698	296	.424	260	198	.762	144	286	430	188	177	5	100	32	809	11.1
Totals	127	3598	1130	477	.422	387	276	.713	206	433	639	318	316	6	163	46	1276	10.0

Three-Point Field Goals: 1988-89, 27-for-82 (.329). 1989-90, 19-for-80 (.238). Totals, 46-for-162 (.284).

NBA PLAYOFF RECORD

									—Rebounds—									
Sea.—Team	G.	Min.	FGA	FGM	Pct.	FTA	FTM	Pct.	Off.	Def.	Tot.	Ast.	PF	Dq.	Stl.	Blk.	Pts.	Avg.
88-89—Phoenix	12	352	144	63	.438	48	38	.792	22	35	57	14	28	0	13	4	172	14.3
89-90—Phoenix	16	479	150	73	.487	65	51	.785	30	51	81	34	34	0	20	2	201	12.6
Totals	28	831	294	136	.463	113	89	.788	52	86	138	48	62	0	33	6	373	13.3

Three-Point Field Goals: 1988-89, 8-for-28 (.286). 1989-90, 4-for-12 (.333). Totals, 12-for-40 (.300).

Member of U.S. Olympic team, 1988.

JEFFREY NIGEL MALONE
(Jeff)

Born June 28, 1961 at Mobile, Ala. Height 6:04. Weight 205.

High School—Macon, Ga., Southwest.

College—Mississippi State University, Mississippi State, Miss.

Drafted by Washington on first round, 1983 (10th pick).

Traded by Washington to Utah in three-way deal that sent Pervis Ellison from Sacramento to Washington and Bob Hansen, Eric Leckner and 1990 1st and 2nd round draft choices from Utah to Sacramento, June 25, 1990. Utah also received a 1990 2nd round draft choice and Sacramento also received a 1991 2nd round draft choice.

—COLLEGIATE RECORD—

Year	G.	Min.	FGA	FGM	Pct.	FTA	FTM	Pct.	Reb.	Pts.	Avg.
79-80	27	781	303	139	.459	51	42	.824	90	320	11.9
80-81	27	999	447	219	.490	128	105	.820	113	543	20.1
81-82	27	1001	410	225	.549	70	52	.743	111	502	18.6
82-83	29	1070	608	323	.531	159	131	.824	106	777	26.8
Totals	110	3851	1768	906	.512	408	330	.809	420	2142	19.5

NBA REGULAR SEASON RECORD

									—Rebounds—										
Sea.—Team	G.	Min.	FGA	FGM	Pct.	FTA	FTM	Pct.	Off.	Def.	Tot.	Ast.	PF	Dq.	Stl.	Blk.	Pts.	Avg.
83-84—Washington	81	1976	918	408	.444	172	142	.826	57	98	155	151	162	1	23	13	982	12.1
84-85—Washington	76	2613	1213	605	.499	250	211	.844	60	146	206	184	176	1	52	9	1436	18.9
85-86—Washington	80	2992	1522	735	.483	371	322	.868	66	222	288	191	180	2	70	12	1795	22.4
86-87—Washington	80	2763	1509	689	.457	425	376	.885	50	168	218	298	154	0	75	13	1758	22.0
87-88—Washington	80	2655	1360	648	.476	380	335	.882	44	162	206	237	198	1	51	13	1641	20.5
88-89—Washington	76	2418	1410	677	.480	340	296	.871	55	124	179	219	155	0	39	14	1651	21.7
89-90—Washington	75	2567	1592	781	.491	293	257	.877	54	152	206	243	116	1	48	6	1820	24.3
Totals	548	17984	9524	4543	.477	2231	1939	.869	386	1072	1458	1523	1141	6	358	80	11083	20.2

Three-Point Field Goals: 1983-84, 24-for-74 (.324). 1984-85, 15-for-72 (.208). 1985-86, 3-for-17 (.176). 1986-87, 4-for-26 (.154). 1987-88, 10-for-24 (.417). 1988-89, 1-for-19 (.053). 1989-90, 1-for-6 (.167). Totals, 58-for-238 (.244).

NBA PLAYOFF RECORD

									—Rebounds—									
Sea.—Team	G.	Min.	FGA	FGM	Pct.	FTA	FTM	Pct.	Off.	Def.	Tot.	Ast.	PF	Dq.	Stl.	Blk.	Pts.	Avg.
83-84—Washington	4	71	26	12	.462	0	0	.000	2	3	5	2	6	0	1	0	24	6.0
84-85—Washington	4	126	56	27	.482	13	10	.769	3	3	6	8	14	1	5	0	65	16.3
85-86—Washington	5	197	103	42	.408	29	26	.897	4	12	16	17	13	0	7	3	110	22.0
86-87—Washington	3	105	46	17	.370	11	11	1.000	1	6	7	9	8	0	1	0	45	15.0
87-88—Washington	5	199	97	50	.515	37	28	.757	3	14	17	11	16	0	5	5	128	25.6
Totals	21	698	328	148	.451	90	75	.833	13	38	51	47	57	1	19	8	372	17.7

Three-Point Field Goals: 1983-84, 0-for-1. 1984-85, 1-for-3 (.333). 1985-86, 0-for-2. 1987-88, 0-for-1. Totals, 2-for-7 (.286).

NBA ALL-STAR GAME RECORD

								—Rebounds—								
Season—Team	Min.	FGA	FGM	Pct.	FTA	FTM	Pct.	Off.	Def.	Tot.	Ast.	PF	Dq.	Stl.	Blk.	Pts.
1986—Washington..	12	5	3	.600	0	0	.000	0	1	1	4	0	0	1	0	6
1987—Washington..	13	5	3	.600	0	0	.000	1	1	2	2	1	0	0	0	6
Totals	25	10	6	.600	0	0	.000	1	2	3	6	1	0	1	0	12

Three-Point Field Goals: 1987, 0-for-1.

Named to NBA All-Rookie Team, 1984. . . . Named to THE SPORTING NEWS All-America First Team, 1983.

KARL MALONE

Born July 24, 1963 at Summerfield, La. Height 6:09. Weight 256.

High School—Summerfield, La.

College—Louisiana Tech University, Ruston, La.

Drafted by Utah on first round as an undergraduate, 1985 (13th pick).

—COLLEGIATE RECORD—

Year	G.	Min.	FGA	FGM	Pct.	FTA	FTM	Pct.	Reb.	Pts.	Avg.
81-82			Did Not Play—Scholastically Ineligible								
82-83	28	....	373	217	.583	244	152	.623	289	586	20.9
83-84	32	....	382	220	.576	236	161	.682	282	601	18.8
84-85	32	....	399	216	.541	170	97	.571	288	529	16.5
Totals	92	....	1154	653	.566	650	410	.631	859	1716	18.7

NBA REGULAR SEASON RECORD

									—Rebounds—									
Sea.—Team	G.	Min.	FGA	FGM	Pct.	FTA	FTM	Pct.	Off.	Def.	Tot.	Ast.	PF	Dq.	Stl.	Blk.	Pts.	Avg.
85-86—Utah	81	2475	1016	504	.496	405	195	.481	174	544	718	236	295	2	105	44	1203	14.9
86-87—Utah	82	2857	1422	728	.512	540	323	.598	278	577	855	158	323	6	104	60	1779	21.7
87-88—Utah	82	3198	1650	858	.520	789	552	.700	277	709	986	199	296	2	117	50	2268	27.7
88-89—Utah	80	3126	1559	809	.519	918	703	.766	259	594	853	219	286	3	144	70	2326	29.1
89-90—Utah	82	3122	1627	914	.562	913	696	.762	232	679	911	226	259	1	121	50	2540	31.0
Totals	407	14778	7274	3813	.524	3565	2469	.693	1220	3103	4323	1038	1459	14	591	274	10116	24.9

Three-Point Field Goals: 1985-86, 0-for-2. 1986-87, 0-for-7. 1987-88, 0-for-5. 1988-89, 5-for-16 (.313). 1989-90, 16-for-43 (.372). Totals, 21-for-73 (.288).

KARL MALONE

NBA PLAYOFF RECORD

Sea.—Team	G.	Min.	FGA	FGM	Pct.	FTA	FTM	Pct.	—Rebounds— Off.	Def.	Tot.	Ast.	PF	Dq.	Stl.	Blk.	Pts.	Avg.
85-86—Utah	4	144	72	38	.528	26	11	.423	6	24	30	4	18	1	8	0	87	21.8
86-87—Utah	5	200	88	37	.420	36	26	.722	15	33	48	6	20	1	11	4	100	20.0
87-88—Utah	11	494	255	123	.482	112	81	.723	33	97	130	17	35	0	13	7	327	29.7
88-89—Utah	3	136	66	33	.500	32	26	.813	22	27	49	4	16	1	3	1	92	30.7
89-90—Utah	5	203	105	46	.438	45	34	.756	16	35	51	11	22	1	11	5	126	25.2
Totals	28	1177	586	277	.473	251	178	.709	92	216	308	42	111	4	46	17	732	26.1

Three-Point Field Goals: 1987-88, 0-for-1. 1989-90, 0-for-1. Totals, 0-for-2.

NBA ALL-STAR GAME RECORD

Season—Team	Min.	FGA	FGM	Pct.	FTA	FTM	Pct.	—Rebounds— Off.	Def.	Tot.	Ast.	PF	Dq.	Stl.	Blk.	Pts.
1988—Utah	33	19	9	.474	5	4	.800	4	6	10	2	4	0	2	0	22
1989—Utah	26	17	12	.706	6	4	.667	4	5	9	3	3	0	2	0	28
1990—Utah	Did Not Play—Injured															
Totals	59	36	21	.583	11	8	.727	8	11	19	5	7	0	4	0	50

Named to All-NBA First Team, 1989 and 1990. . . . Named to All-NBA Second Team, 1988. . . . NBA All-Defensive Second Team, 1988. . . . NBA All-Rookie Team, 1986. . . . NBA All-Star Game MVP, 1989.

MOSES EUGENE MALONE

Born March 23, 1955 at Petersburg, Va. Height 6:10. Weight 255.
High School—Petersburg, Va.
Did not attend college.

Selected as an undergraduate by Utah on third round of ABA draft, 1974.
Sold by Utah to St. Louis, December 2, 1975.
Selected by Portland NBA from St. Louis in ABA dispersal draft, August 5, 1976.
Traded by Portland to Buffalo for 1978 1st round draft choice, October 18, 1976.
Traded by Buffalo to Houston for 1977 and 1978 1st round draft choices, October 24, 1976.
Signed by Philadelphia as a Veteran Free Agent, September 2, 1982; Houston matched offer and traded Malone to Philadelphia for Caldwell Jones and a 1983 1st round draft choice, September 15, 1982.
Traded by Philadelphia with Terry Catledge and 1986 and 1988 1st round draft choices to Washington for Jeff Ruland and Cliff Robinson, June 16, 1986.
Signed by Atlanta as an unrestricted free agent, August 16, 1988.

ABA REGULAR SEASON RECORD

Sea.—Team	G.	Min.	—2-Point— FGM	FGA	Pct.	—3-Point— FGM	FGA	Pct.	FTM	FTA	Pct.	Reb.	Ast.	Pts.	Avg.
74-75—Utah	83	3205	591	1034	.572	0	1	.000	375	591	.635	1209	82	1557	18.8
75-76—St. Louis	43	1168	251	488	.514	0	2	.000	112	183	.612	413	58	614	14.3
Totals	126	4373	842	1522	.553	0	3	.000	487	774	.629	1622	140	2171	17.2

ABA PLAYOFF RECORD

Sea.—Team	G.	Min.	—2-Point— FGM	FGA	Pct.	—3-Point— FGM	FGA	Pct.	FTM	FTA	Pct.	Reb.	Ast.	Pts.	Avg.
74-75—Utah	6	235	51	80	.638	0	0	.000	34	51	.667	105	9	136	22.7

ABA ALL-STAR GAME RECORD

Sea.—Team	Min.	—2-Point— FGM	FGA	Pct.	—3-Point— FGM	FGA	Pct.	FTM	FTA	Pct.	Reb.	Ast.	Pts.	Avg.
1975—Utah	20	2	3	.667	0	0	.000	2	5	.400	10	0	6	6.0

NBA REGULAR SEASON RECORD

Sea.—Team	G.	Min.	FGA	FGM	Pct.	FTA	FTM	Pct.	—Rebounds— Off.	Def.	Tot.	Ast.	PF	Dq.	Stl.	Blk.	Pts.	Avg.
76-77—Buf-Hou	82	2506	810	389	.480	440	305	.693	437	635	1072	89	275	3	67	181	1083	13.2
77-78—Houston	59	2107	828	413	.499	443	318	.718	380	506	886	31	179	2	48	76	1144	19.4
78-79—Houston	82	3390	1325	716	.540	811	599	.739	587	857	1444	147	223	0	79	119	2031	24.8
79-80—Houston	82	3140	1549	778	.502	783	563	.719	573	617	1190	147	210	0	80	107	2119	25.8
80-81—Houston	80	3245	1545	806	.522	804	609	.757	474	706	1180	141	223	0	83	150	2222	27.8
81-82—Houston	81	3398	1822	945	.519	827	630	.762	558	630	1188	142	208	0	76	125	2520	31.1
82-83—Philadelphia	78	2922	1305	654	.501	788	600	.761	445	749	1194	101	206	0	89	157	1908	24.5
83-84—Philadelphia	71	2613	1101	532	.483	727	545	.750	352	598	950	96	188	0	71	110	1609	22.7
84-85—Philadelphia	79	2957	1284	602	.469	904	737	.815	385	646	1031	130	216	0	67	123	1941	24.6
85-86—Philadelphia	74	2706	1246	571	.458	784	617	.787	339	533	872	90	194	0	67	71	1759	23.8
86-87—Washington	73	2488	1311	595	.454	692	570	.824	340	484	824	120	139	0	59	92	1760	24.1
87-88—Washington	79	2692	1090	531	.487	689	543	.788	372	512	884	112	160	0	59	72	1607	20.3
88-89—Atlanta	81	2878	1096	538	.491	711	561	.789	386	570	956	112	154	0	79	100	1637	20.2
89-90—Atlanta	81	2735	1077	517	.480	631	493	.781	364	448	812	130	158	0	47	84	1528	18.9
Totals	1082	39777	17389	8587	.494	10034	7690	.766	5992	8491	14483	1588	2733	5	971	1567	24868	23.0

Three-Point Field Goals: 1979-80, 0-for-6. 1980-81, 1-for-3 (.333). 1981-82, 0-for-6. 1982-83, 0-for-1. 1983-84, 0-for-4. 1984-85, 0-for-2. 1985-86, 0-for-1. 1986-87, 0-for-11. 1987-88, 2-for-7 (.286). 1988-89, 0-for-12. 1989-90, 1-for-9 (.111). Totals, 4-for-62 (.065).

NBA PLAYOFF RECORD

Sea.—Team	G.	Min.	FGA	FGM	Pct.	FTA	FTM	Pct.	—Rebounds— Off.	Def.	Tot.	Ast.	PF	Dq.	Stl.	Blk.	Pts.	Avg.
76-77—Houston	12	518	162	81	.500	91	63	.692	84	119	203	7	42	0	13	21	225	18.8
78-79—Houston	2	78	41	18	.439	18	13	.722	25	16	41	2	5	0	1	8	49	24.5
79-80—Houston	7	275	138	74	.536	43	33	.767	42	55	97	7	18	0	4	16	181	25.9
80-81—Houston	21	955	432	207	.479	208	148	.711	125	180	305	35	54	0	13	34	562	26.8
81-82—Houston	3	136	67	29	.433	15	14	.933	28	23	51	10	8	0	2	2	72	24.0
82-83—Philadelphia	13	524	235	126	.536	120	86	.717	70	136	206	20	40	0	19	25	338	26.0
83-84—Philadelphia	5	212	83	38	.458	32	31	.969	20	49	69	7	15	0	3	11	107	21.4
84-85—Philadelphia	13	505	212	90	.425	103	82	.796	36	102	138	24	39	0	17	22	262	20.2
86-87—Washington	3	114	47	21	.447	21	20	.952	15	23	38	5	5	0	0	3	62	20.7
87-88—Washington	5	198	65	30	.462	40	33	.825	22	34	56	7	9	0	3	4	93	18.6
88-89—Atlanta	5	197	64	32	.500	51	40	.784	27	33	60	9	5	0	7	4	105	21.0
Totals	89	3712	1546	746	.483	742	563	.759	494	770	1264	133	240	0	82	150	2056	23.1

Three-Point Field Goals: 1979-80, 0-for-1. 1980-81, 0-for-2, 1982-83, 0-for-1. 1984-85, 0-for-1. 1987-88, 0-for-1. 1988-89, 1-for-1 (1.000). Totals, 1-for-7 (.143).

NBA ALL-STAR GAME RECORD

Season—Team	Min.	FGA	FGM	Pct.	FTA	FTM	Pct.	—Rebounds— Off.	Def.	Tot.	Ast.	PF	Dq.	Stl.	Blk.	Pts.
1978—Houston	14	1	1	1.000	4	2	.500	1	3	4	1	1	0	1	0	4
1979—Houston	17	2	2	1.000	5	4	.800	2	5	7	1	0	0	1	0	8
1980—Houston	31	12	7	.583	12	6	.500	6	6	12	2	4	0	1	2	20
1981—Houston	22	8	3	.375	4	2	.500	2	4	6	3	3	0	1	0	8
1982—Houston	20	11	5	.455	6	2	.333	5	6	11	0	2	0	1	1	12
1983—Philadelphia	24	8	3	.375	6	4	.667	2	6	8	3	1	0	0	1	10
1984—Philadelphia					Selected but did not play											
1985—Philadelphia	33	10	2	.200	6	3	.500	5	7	12	1	4	0	0	0	7
1986—Philadelphia	34	12	5	.417	9	6	.667	5	8	13	0	4	0	1	0	16
1987—Washington	35	19	11	.579	6	5	.833	7	11	18	2	4	0	2	1	27
1988—Washington	22	6	2	.333	6	3	.500	5	4	9	2	2	0	0	0	7
1989—Atlanta	19	3	9	.333	3	3	1.000	4	4	8	0	1	0	1	1	9
Totals	271	44	98	.449	40	67	.597	44	64	108	15	26	0	9	6	128

COMBINED ABA AND NBA REGULAR SEASON RECORDS

Sea.—Team	G.	Min.	FGA	FGM	Pct.	FTA	FTM	Pct.	—Rebounds— Off.	Def.	Tot.	Ast.	PF	Dq.	Stl.	Blk.	Pts.	Avg.
Totals	1208	44150	18914	9429	.499	10808	8177	.757	6643	9462	16105	1728	3134	5	1081	1723	27039	22.4

Named NBA Most Valuable Player, 1979, 1982, 1983. . . . All-NBA First Team, 1979, 1982, 1983, 1985. . . . All-NBA Second Team, 1980, 1981, 1984, 1987. . . . NBA All-Defensive First Team, 1983. . . . NBA All-Defensive Second Team, 1979. . . . NBA Playoff MVP, 1983. . . . Member of NBA championship team, 1983. . . . Led NBA in rebounding, 1979, 1981, 1982, 1983, 1984, 1985. . . . Named to ABA All-Rookie Team, 1975.

DANIEL RICARDO MANNING
(Danny)

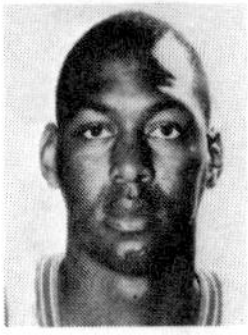

Born May 17, 1966 at Hattiesburg, Miss. Height 6:10. Weight 230.

High Schools—Greensboro, N.C., Page (Soph. and Jr.) and Lawrence, Kan.

College—University of Kansas, Lawrence, Kan.

Drafted by Los Angeles Clippers on first round, 1988 (1st pick).

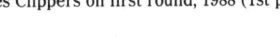

—COLLEGIATE RECORD—

Year	G.	Min.	FGA	FGM	Pct.	FTA	FTM	Pct.	Reb.	Pts.	Avg.
84-85	34	1120	369	209	.566	102	78	.765	258	496	14.6
85-86	39	1256	465	279	.600	127	95	.748	245	653	16.7
86-87	36	1249	562	347	.617	226	165	.730	342	860	23.9
87-88	38	1336	653	381	.583	233	171	.734	342	942	24.8
Totals	147	4961	2049	1216	.593	688	509	.740	1187	2951	20.1

Three-Point Field Goals: 1986-87, 1-for-3 (.333). 1987-88, 9-for-26 (.346). Totals, 10-for-29 (.345).

NBA REGULAR SEASON RECORD

Sea.—Team	G.	Min.	FGA	FGM	Pct.	FTA	FTM	Pct.	—Rebounds— Off.	Def.	Tot.	Ast.	PF	Dq.	Stl.	Blk.	Pts.	Avg.
88-89—L.A. Clippers	26	950	358	177	.494	103	79	.767	70	101	171	81	89	1	44	25	434	16.7
89-90—L.A. Clippers	71	2269	826	440	.533	370	274	.741	142	280	422	187	261	4	91	39	1154	16.3
Totals	97	3219	1184	617	.521	473	353	.746	212	381	593	268	350	5	135	64	1588	16.4

Three-Point Field Goals: 1988-89, 1-for-5 (.200). 1989-90, 0-for-5. Totals, 1-for-10 (.100).

Member of NCAA Division I championship team, 1988. . . . Named to THE SPORTING NEWS All-America First Team, 1987 and 1988. . . . Named Outstanding Player in NCAA Division I tournament, 1988. . . . Son of Ed Manning, currently an assistant coach with San Antonio Spurs and forward with Baltimore, Chicago and Portland of the NBA and Carolina, New York and Indiana of the ABA, 1967-68 through 1975-76.

ROY LANE MARBLE

Born December 13, 1966 at Flint, Mich. Height 6:06. Weight 190.
High School—Flint, Mich., Beecher.
College—University of Iowa, Iowa City, Ia.
Drafted by Atlanta on first round, 1989 (23rd pick).

—COLLEGIATE RECORD—

Year	G.	Min.	FGA	FGM	Pct.	FTA	FTM	Pct.	Reb.	Pts.	Avg.
85-86	32	930	300	157	.523	118	85	.720	157	399	12.5
86-87	35	1052	357	199	.557	173	118	.682	178	520	14.9
87-88	34	959	343	190	.554	190	141	.742	147	522	15.4
88-89	33	1031	459	241	.525	226	172	.761	186	675	20.5
Totals	134	3972	1459	787	.539	707	516	.730	668	2116	15.8

Three-Point Field Goals: 1986-87, 4-for-14 (.286). 1987-88, 1-for-9 (.111). 1988-89, 21-for-53 (.396). Totals, 26-for-76 (.342).

NBA REGULAR SEASON RECORD

									—Rebounds—									
Sea.—Team	G.	Min.	FGA	FGM	Pct.	FTA	FTM	Pct.	Off.	Def.	Tot.	Ast.	PF	Dq.	Stl.	Blk.	Pts.	Avg.
89-90—Atlanta	24	162	58	16	.276	29	19	.655	15	9	24	11	16	0	7	1	51	2.1

Three-Point Field Goals: 1989-90, 0-for-2.

SARUNAS MARCIULIONIS

(Name pronounced Shaw-ROON-iss Marsh-a-LOAN-iss)
Born June 13, 1964 at Kaunas, Lithuania. Height 6:05. Weight 200.
College—State University of Vilnius, Lithuania, Soviet Union.

Signed by Golden State as a free agent, June 23, 1989.

Played for Statbe and Zalgiris clubs, Lithuania, Soviet Union, and averaged 18.1 points per game for Soviet National Team in 1988 Olympics.

NBA REGULAR SEASON RECORD

									—Rebounds—									
Sea.—Team	G.	Min.	FGA	FGM	Pct.	FTA	FTM	Pct.	Off.	Def.	Tot.	Ast.	PF	Dq.	Stl.	Blk.	Pts.	Avg.
89-90—Golden State	75	1695	557	289	.519	403	317	.787	84	137	221	121	230	5	94	7	905	12.1

Three-Point Field Goals: 1989-90, 10-for-39 (.256).

JEFFERY ALLEN MARTIN
(Jeff)

Born January 14, 1967 at Cherry Valley, Ark. Height 6:05. Weight 195.
High School—Cherry Valley, Ark., Cross Country.
College—Murray State University, Murray, Ky.
Drafted by Los Angeles Clippers on second round, 1989 (31st pick).

—COLLEGIATE RECORD—

Year	G.	Min.	FGA	FGM	Pct.	FTA	FTM	Pct.	Reb.	Pts.	Avg.
85-86	29	918	271	128	.472	123	83	.675	157	339	11.7
86-87	28	1041	436	228	.523	158	123	.778	158	594	21.2
87-88	31	1162	545	304	.558	231	181	.784	204	806	26.0
88-89	29	1056	522	266	.510	186	148	.796	150	745	25.7
Totals	117	4177	1774	926	.522	698	535	.766	669	2484	21.2

Three-Point Field Goals: 1986-87, 15-for-37 (.405). 1987-88, 17-for-48 (.354). 1988-89, 65-for-131 (.496). Totals, 97-for-216 (.449).

NBA REGULAR SEASON RECORD

									—Rebounds—									
Sea.—Team	G.	Min.	FGA	FGM	Pct.	FTA	FTM	Pct.	Off.	Def.	Tot.	Ast.	PF	Dq.	Stl.	Blk.	Pts.	Avg.
89-90—L.A. Clippers	69	1351	414	170	.411	129	91	.705	78	81	159	44	97	0	41	16	433	6.3

Three-Point Field Goals: 1989-90, 2-for-15 (.133).

ANTHONY GEORGE DOUGLAS MASON

Born December 14, 1966 at Miami, Fla. Height 6:07. Weight 250.
High School—Springfield Gardens, N.Y.
College—Tennessee State University, Nashville, Tenn.
Drafted by Portland on third round, 1988 (53rd pick).

Draft rights relinquished by Portland, June 30, 1989; signed by New Jersey as a free agent, September 19, 1989.
Played in Turkey, 1988-89.

—COLLEGIATE RECORD—

Year	G.	Min.	FGA	FGM	Pct.	FTA	FTM	Pct.	Reb.	Pts.	Avg.
84-85	28	801	213	100	.469	122	79	.648	148	279	10.0
85-86	28	913	427	206	.482	130	93	.715	192	505	18.0
86-87	27	951	449	201	.448	135	89	.659	262	508	18.8
87-88	28	1064	608	276	.454	247	191	.773	292	783	28.0
Totals	111	3729	1697	783	.461	634	452	.713	894	2075	18.7

Three-Point Field Goals: 1986-87, 17-for-49 (.347). 1987-88, 40-for-81 (.494). Totals, 57-for-130 (.438).

NBA REGULAR SEASON RECORD

									—Rebounds—									
Sea.—Team	G.	Min.	FGA	FGM	Pct.	FTA	FTM	Pct.	Off.	Def.	Tot.	Ast.	PF	Dq.	Stl.	Blk.	Pts.	Avg.
89-90—New Jersey	21	108	40	14	.350	15	9	.600	11	23	34	7	20	0	2	2	37	1.8

WES JOEL MATTHEWS

Born August 24, 1959 at Sarasota, Fla. Height 6:01. Weight 170.

High School—Bridgeport, Conn., Harding.

College—University of Wisconsin, Madison, Wis.

Drafted by Washington on first round as an undergraduate, 1980 (14th pick).

Traded by Washington to Atlanta for Don Collins, January 17, 1981.
Traded by Atlanta with Kevin Figaro to San Diego for a conditional 2nd round draft choice, October 6, 1983.
Waived by San Diego, October 17, 1983; signed by Atlanta to a 10-day contract that expired, March 5, 1984.
Signed by Philadelphia, March 22, 1984, to the first of consecutive 10-day contracts that expired, April 11, 1984.
Signed by Chicago as a free agent, October 26, 1984; Chicago relinquished its right of first refusal, July 1, 1985.
Signed by San Antonio as a free agent, October 23, 1985.
Waived by San Antonio, October 9, 1986; signed by Los Angeles Lakers as a free agent, October 13, 1986.
Signed by Atlanta, January 6, 1990, to a 10-day contract that expired, January 15, 1990.
Played in Continental Basketball Association with Ohio Mixers, 1983-84, and Tulsa Fast Breakers, 1989-90.

—COLLEGIATE RECORD—

Year	G.	Min.	FGA	FGM	Pct.	FTA	FTM	Pct.	Reb.	Pts.	Avg.
77-78	14	408	197	83	.421	52	37	.712	47	203	14.5
78-79	27	986	417	195	.468	139	109	.784	69	499	18.5
79-80	28	955	412	211	.512	143	127	.888	73	549	19.6
Totals	69	2349	1026	489	.477	334	273	.817	189	1251	18.1

CBA REGULAR SEASON RECORD

			—2-Point—			—3-Point—									
Sea.—Team	G.	Min.	FGM	FGA	Pct.	FGM	FGA	Pct.	FTM	FTA	Pct.	Reb.	Ast.	Pts.	Avg.
83-84—Ohio	8	235	69	121	.570	1	10	.100	28	37	.756	21	66	169	21.1
89-90—Tulsa	4	134	31	62	.500	4	14	.286	25	29	.862	19	25	99	24.8
Totals	12	369	100	183	.546	5	24	.208	53	66	.803	40	91	268	22.3

NBA REGULAR SEASON RECORD

									—Rebounds—									
Sea.—Team	G.	Min.	FGA	FGM	Pct.	FTA	FTM	Pct.	Off.	Def.	Tot.	Ast.	PF	Dq.	Stl.	Blk.	Pts.	Avg.
80-81—Wash.-Atl.	79	2266	779	385	.494	252	202	.802	46	93	139	411	242	2	107	17	977	12.4
81-82—Atlanta	47	837	298	131	.440	79	60	.759	19	39	58	139	129	3	53	2	324	6.9
82-83—Atlanta	64	1187	424	171	.403	112	86	.768	25	66	91	249	129	0	60	8	442	6.9
83-84—Atl.-Phil.	20	388	131	61	.466	36	27	.750	7	20	27	83	45	0	16	3	150	7.5
84-85—Chicago	78	1523	386	191	.495	85	59	.694	16	51	67	354	133	0	73	12	443	5.7
85-86—San Antonio	75	1853	603	320	.531	211	173	.820	30	101	131	476	168	1	87	32	817	10.9
86-87—L.A. Lakers	50	532	187	89	.476	36	29	.806	13	34	47	100	53	0	23	4	208	4.2
87-88—L.A. Lakers	51	706	248	114	.460	65	54	.831	16	50	66	138	65	0	25	3	289	5.7
89-90—Atlanta	1	13	3	1	.333	2	2	1.000	0	0	0	5	0	0	0	0	4	4.0
Totals	465	9305	3059	1463	.478	878	692	.788	172	454	626	1955	964	6	444	81	3654	7.9

Three-Point Field Goals: 1980-81, 5-for-21 (.238). 1981-82, 2-for-8 (.250). 1982-83, 14-for-48 (.292). 1983-84, 1-for-8 (.125). 1984-85, 2-for-16 (.125). 1985-86, 4-for-25 (.160). 1986-87, 1-for-3 (.333). 1987-88, 7-for-30 (.233). 1989-90, 0-for-1. Totals, 36-for-160 (.225).

NBA PLAYOFF RECORD

									—Rebounds—									
Sea.—Team	G.	Min.	FGA	FGM	Pct.	FTA	FTM	Pct.	Off.	Def.	Tot.	Ast.	PF	Dq.	Stl.	Blk.	Pts.	Avg.
81-82—Atlanta	2	28	10	2	.200	4	4	1.000	0	0	0	4	4	0	0	1	8	4.0
82-83—Atlanta	3	38	9	3	.333	5	4	.800	0	0	0	11	5	0	0	1	10	3.3
83-84—Philadelphia	4	23	8	4	.500	2	1	.500	0	0	0	4	4	0	1	0	10	2.5
84-85—Chicago	4	91	32	11	.344	9	7	.778	2	4	6	12	10	0	5	0	29	7.3
85-86—San Antonio	3	116	54	35	.648	8	6	.750	1	6	7	24	7	0	6	0	76	25.3
86-87—L.A. Lakers	12	61	23	11	.478	7	6	.857	0	4	4	9	9	0	1	0	28	2.3
87-88—L.A. Lakers	10	27	5	2	.400	10	8	.800	0	1	1	2	4	0	1	0	12	1.2
Totals	38	384	141	68	.482	45	36	.800	3	15	18	66	43	0	14	2	173	4.6

Three-Point Field Goals: 1982-83, 0-for-1. 1983-84, 1-for-2 (.500). 1984-85, 0-for-3. 1985-86, 0-for-1. 1986-87, 0-for-1. 1987-88, 0-for-1. Totals, 1-for-9 (.111).

Member of NBA championship teams, 1987 and 1988.

VERNON MAXWELL

Born September 12, 1965 at Gainesville, Fla. Height 6:04. Weight 180.
High School—Gainesville, Fla., Buchholz.
College—University of Florida, Gainesville, Fla.
Drafted by Denver on second round, 1988 (47th pick).

Draft rights traded by Denver to San Antonio for a 1989 2nd round draft choice, June 28, 1988.
Traded by San Antonio to Houston for cash, February 21, 1990.

—COLLEGIATE RECORD—

Year	G.	Min.	FGA	FGM	Pct.	FTA	FTM	Pct.	Reb.	Pts.	Avg.
84-85	30	752	366	163	.445	105	72	.686	72	398	13.3
85-86	33	1142	566	262	.463	177	124	.701	147	648	19.6
86-87	34	1086	548	266	.485	217	161	.742	125	738	21.7
87-88	33	1214	515	230	.447	207	148	.715	138	666	20.2
Totals	130	4194	1995	921	.462	706	505	.715	482	2450	18.8

Three-Point Field Goals: 1986-87, 45-for-128 (.352). 1987-88, 58-for-147 (.395). Totals, 103-for-255 (.404).

NBA REGULAR SEASON RECORD

									—Rebounds—									
Sea.—Team	G.	Min.	FGA	FGM	Pct.	FTA	FTM	Pct.	Off.	Def.	Tot.	Ast.	PF	Dq.	Stl.	Blk.	Pts.	Avg.
88-89—San Antonio	79	2065	827	357	.432	243	181	.745	49	153	202	301	136	0	86	8	927	11.7
89-90—S.A.-Hou.	79	1987	627	275	.439	211	136	.645	50	178	228	296	148	0	84	10	714	9.0
Totals	158	4052	1454	632	.435	454	317	.698	99	331	430	597	284	0	170	18	1641	10.4

Three-Point Field Goals: 1988-89, 32-for-129 (.248). 1989-90, 28-for-105 (.267). Totals, 60-for-234 (.256).

NBA PLAYOFF RECORD

									—Rebounds—									
Sea.—Team	G.	Min.	FGA	FGM	Pct.	FTA	FTM	Pct.	Off.	Def.	Tot.	Ast.	PF	Dq.	Stl.	Blk.	Pts.	Avg.
89-90—Houston	4	159	81	30	.370	21	11	.524	5	7	12	17	12	0	5	0	79	19.8

Three-Point Field Goals: 1989-90, 8-for-26 (.308).

ROBERT McCANN
(Bob)

Born April 22, 1964 at Morristown, N.J. Height 6:06. Weight 245.
High School—Morristown, N.J.
Colleges—Upsala College, East Orange, N.J., and
Morehead State University, Morehead, Ky.
Drafted by Milwaukee on second round, 1987 (32nd pick).

Waived by Milwaukee, November 4, 1987; signed by Dallas as a free agent, October 5, 1988.
Waived by Dallas, November 1, 1988; re-signed by Dallas, February 12, 1990, to the first of consecutive 10-day contracts that expired, March 3, 1990.
Re-signed by Dallas, March 5, 1990, for remainder of season.
Played in Continental Basketball Association with Charleston Gunners and Pensacola Tornados, 1988-89, and with Pensacola Tornados, 1989-90.

—COLLEGIATE RECORD—

Upsala

Year	G.	Min.	FGA	FGM	Pct.	FTA	FTM	Pct.	Reb.	Pts.	Avg.
82-83	26	....	236	112	.475	64	34	.531	208	258	9.9

Morehead State

Year	G.	Min.	FGA	FGM	Pct.	FTA	FTM	Pct.	Reb.	Pts.	Avg.
83-84					Did Not Play—Transfer Student						
84-85	27	911	383	188	.491	152	85	.559	263	461	17.1
85-86	27	803	320	171	.534	173	113	.653	282	455	16.9
86-87	28	872	376	206	.548	170	107	.629	317	520	18.6
M.S. Totals	82	2586	1079	565	.524	495	305	.616	862	1436	17.5
Col. Totals	108	....	1315	677	.515	559	339	.606	1070	1694	15.7

Three-Point Field Goals: 1986-87, 1-for-3 (.333).

CBA REGULAR SEASON RECORD

			—2-Point—			—3-Point—									
Sea.—Team	G.	Min.	FGM	FGA	Pct.	FGM	FGA	Pct.	FTM	FTA	Pct.	Reb.	Ast.	Pts.	Avg.
88-89—Char.-Pens.	43	1555	327	636	.514	0	5	.000	143	213	.671	356	97	797	18.5
89-90—Pensacola	43	1879	388	735	.528	1	7	.143	203	296	.686	374	138	982	22.8
Totals	86	3434	715	1371	.522	1	12	.083	346	509	.680	730	235	1779	20.7

NBA REGULAR SEASON RECORD

									—Rebounds—									
Sea.—Team	G.	Min.	FGA	FGM	Pct.	FTA	FTM	Pct.	Off.	Def.	Tot.	Ast.	PF	Dq.	Stl.	Blk.	Pts.	Avg.
89-90—Dallas	10	62	21	7	.333	14	12	.857	4	8	12	6	7	0	2	2	26	2.6

MELVIN LAMONT McCANTS
(Mel)

Born August 19, 1967 at Chicago, Ill. Height 6:09. Weight 240.
High School—Chicago, Ill., Mt. Carmel.
College—Purdue University, West Lafayette, Ind.
Never drafted by an NBA franchise.

Signed by Los Angeles Lakers as a free agent, October 2, 1989.

—COLLEGIATE RECORD—

Year	G.	Min.	FGA	FGM	Pct.	FTA	FTM	Pct.	Reb.	Pts.	Avg.
85-86	32	856	216	119	.551	132	82	.621	147	320	10.0
86-87	29	752	220	135	.614	134	80	.597	159	350	12.1
87-88	33	903	295	169	.573	195	132	.677	166	470	14.2
88-89	31	890	284	147	.518	180	120	.667	176	414	13.4
Totals	125	3401	1015	570	.562	641	414	.646	648	1554	12.4

NBA REGULAR SEASON RECORD

									—Rebounds—									
Sea.—Team	G.	Min.	FGA	FGM	Pct.	FTA	FTM	Pct.	Off.	Def.	Tot.	Ast.	PF	Dq.	Stl.	Blk.	Pts.	Avg.
89-90—L.A. Lakers	13	65	26	8	.308	8	6	.750	1	5	6	2	11	0	3	1	22	1.7

NBA PLAYOFF RECORD

									—Rebounds—									
Sea.—Team	G.	Min.	FGA	FGM	Pct.	FTA	FTM	Pct.	Off.	Def.	Tot.	Ast.	PF	Dq.	Stl.	Blk.	Pts.	Avg.
89-90—L.A. Lakers	2	5	0	0	....	0	0	....	0	0	0	0	1	0	0	0	0	0.0

GEORGE AARON McCLOUD

Born May 27, 1967 at Daytona Beach, Fla. Height 6:06. Weight 205.
High School—Daytona Beach, Fla., Mainland.
College—Florida State University, Tallahassee, Fla.
Drafted by Indiana on first round, 1989 (7th pick).

—COLLEGIATE RECORD—

Year	G.	Min.	FGA	FGM	Pct.	FTA	FTM	Pct.	Reb.	Pts.	Avg.
85-86	27	283	87	42	.483	49	31	.633	49	115	4.3
86-87	30	590	197	87	.442	68	42	.618	126	230	7.7
87-88	30	902	403	193	.479	112	88	.786	111	546	18.2
88-89	30	1067	462	207	.448	176	154	.875	109	683	22.8
Totals	117	2842	1149	529	.460	405	315	.778	395	1574	13.5

Three-Point Field Goals: 1986-87, 14-for-47 (.298). 1987-88, 72-for-159 (.453). 1988-89, 115-for-262 (.439). Totals, 201-for-468 (.429).

NBA REGULAR SEASON RECORD

									—Rebounds—									
Sea.—Team	G.	Min.	FGA	FGM	Pct.	FTA	FTM	Pct.	Off.	Def.	Tot.	Ast.	PF	Dq.	Stl.	Blk.	Pts.	Avg.
89-90—Indiana	44	413	144	45	.313	19	15	.789	12	30	42	45	56	0	19	3	118	2.7

Three-Point Field Goals: 1989-90, 13-for-40 (.325).

NBA PLAYOFF RECORD

									—Rebounds—									
Sea.—Team	G.	Min.	FGA	FGM	Pct.	FTA	FTM	Pct.	Off.	Def.	Tot.	Ast.	PF	Dq.	Stl.	Blk.	Pts.	Avg.
89-90—Indiana	1	4	2	1	.500	0	0	....	1	0	1	0	2	0	0	0	2	2.0

TIMOTHY DANIEL McCORMICK
(Tim)

Born March 10, 1962 at Detroit, Mich. Height 7:00. Weight 240.
High School—Clarkston, Mich.
College—University of Michigan, Ann Arbor, Mich.
Drafted by Cleveland on first round as an undergraduate, 1984 (12th pick).

Draft rights traded by Cleveland with Cliff Robinson and cash to Washington for draft rights to Melvin Turpin, June 19, 1984.

Draft rights traded by Washington with Ricky Sobers to Seattle for Gus Williams, June 19, 1984.

Traded by Seattle with Danny Vranes to Philadelphia for Clemon Johnson and a 1989 1st round draft choice, September 29, 1986.

Traded by Philadelphia with Roy Hinson and a 1989 2nd round draft choice to New Jersey for Mike Gminski and Ben Coleman, January 16, 1988.

Traded by New Jersey with Tony Brown, Frank Johnson and Lorenzo Romar to Houston for Joe Barry Carroll and Lester Conner, November 2, 1988.

—COLLEGIATE RECORD—

Year	G.	Min.	FGA	FGM	Pct.	FTA	FTM	Pct.	Reb.	Pts.	Avg.
80-81	30	524	106	54	.509	60	47	.783	106	155	5.2
81-82	Did Not Play—Knee Operations										
82-83	28	....	220	122	.555	134	109	.813	180	353	12.6
83-84	32	960	226	131	.580	186	124	.667	189	386	12.1
Totals	90	....	552	307	.556	380	280	.737	475	894	9.9

NBA REGULAR SEASON RECORD

									—Rebounds—									
Sea.—Team	G.	Min.	FGA	FGM	Pct.	FTA	FTM	Pct.	Off.	Def.	Tot.	Ast.	PF	Dq.	Stl.	Blk.	Pts.	Avg.
84-85—Seattle	78	1584	483	269	.557	263	188	.715	146	252	398	78	207	2	18	33	726	9.3
85-86—Seattle	77	1705	444	253	.570	244	174	.713	140	263	403	83	219	4	19	28	681	8.8
86-87—Philadelphia	81	2817	718	391	.545	349	251	.719	180	431	611	114	270	4	36	64	1033	12.8
87-88—Phil.-N.J.	70	2114	648	348	.537	215	145	.674	146	321	467	118	234	3	32	23	841	12.0
88-89—Houston	81	1257	351	169	.481	129	87	.674	87	174	261	54	193	0	18	24	425	5.2
89-90—Houston	18	116	29	10	.345	19	10	.526	8	19	27	3	24	0	3	1	30	1.7
Totals	405	9593	2673	1440	.539	1219	855	.701	707	1460	2167	450	1147	13	126	173	3736	9.2

Three-Point Field Goals: 1984-85, 0-for-1. 1985-86, 1-for-2 (.500). 1986-87, 0-for-4. 1987-88, 0-for-2. 1988-89, 0-for-4. Totals, 1-for-13 (.077).

NBA PLAYOFF RECORD

									—Rebounds—									
Sea.—Team	G.	Min.	FGA	FGM	Pct.	FTA	FTM	Pct.	Off.	Def.	Tot.	Ast.	PF	Dq.	Stl.	Blk.	Pts.	Avg.
86-87—Philadelphia	5	121	24	12	.500	4	4	1.000	7	24	31	6	19	0	1	2	28	5.6
88-89—Houston	4	53	13	7	.538	9	8	.889	2	11	13	0	9	0	3	2	22	5.5
89-90—Houston	3	21	3	1	.333	2	1	.500	1	7	8	0	5	0	0	0	3	1.0
Totals	12	195	40	20	.500	15	13	.867	10	42	52	6	33	0	4	4	53	4.4

Three-Point Field Goals: 1988-89, 0-for-1.

RODNEY EARL McCRAY

Born August 29, 1961 at Mt. Vernon, N.Y. Height 6:08. Weight 235.

High School—Mt. Vernon, N.Y.

College—University of Louisville, Louisville, Ky.

Drafted by Houston on first round, 1983 (3rd pick).

Traded by Houston with Jim Petersen to Sacramento for Otis Thorpe, October 11, 1988.

Traded by Sacramento with 1990 and 1991 2nd round draft choices to Dallas for Bill Wennington and two 1990 1st round draft choices, June 26, 1990.

—COLLEGIATE RECORD—

Year	G.	Min.	FGA	FGM	Pct.	FTA	FTM	Pct.	Reb.	Pts.	Avg.
79-80	36	1178	197	107	.543	102	66	.647	269	280	7.8
80-81	30	917	194	114	.588	90	60	.667	222	288	9.6
81-82	33	961	196	112	.571	84	59	.702	234	283	8.6
82-83	36	1197	259	152	.587	124	92	.742	304	396	11.0
Totals	135	4253	846	485	.573	400	277	.693	1029	1247	9.2

NBA REGULAR SEASON RECORD

									—Rebounds—									
Sea.—Team	G.	Min.	FGA	FGM	Pct.	FTA	FTM	Pct.	Off.	Def.	Tot.	Ast.	PF	Dq.	Stl.	Blk.	Pts.	Avg.
83-84—Houston	79	2081	672	335	.499	249	182	.731	173	277	450	176	205	1	53	54	853	10.8
84-85—Houston	82	3001	890	476	.535	313	231	.738	201	338	539	355	215	2	90	75	1183	14.4
85-86—Houston	82	2610	629	338	.537	222	171	.770	159	361	520	292	197	2	50	58	847	10.3
86-87—Houston	81	3136	783	432	.552	393	306	.779	190	388	578	434	172	2	88	53	1170	14.4
87-88—Houston	81	2689	746	359	.481	367	288	.785	232	399	631	264	166	2	57	51	1006	12.4
88-89—Sacramento	68	2435	729	340	.466	234	169	.722	143	371	514	293	121	0	57	36	854	12.6
89-90—Sacramento	82	3238	1043	537	.515	348	273	.784	192	477	669	377	176	0	60	70	1358	16.6
Totals	555	19190	5492	2817	.513	2126	1620	.762	1290	2611	3901	2191	1252	9	455	397	7271	13.1

Three-Point Field Goals: 1983-84, 1-for-4 (.250). 1984-85, 0-for-6. 1985-86, 0-for-3. 1986-87, 0-for-9. 1987-88, 0-for-4. 1988-89, 5-for-22 (.227). 1989-90, 11-for-42 (.262). Totals, 17-for-90 (.189).

NBA PLAYOFF RECORD

									—Rebounds—									
Sea.—Team	G.	Min.	FGA	FGM	Pct.	FTA	FTM	Pct.	Off.	Def.	Tot.	Ast.	PF	Dq.	Stl.	Blk.	Pts.	Avg.
84-85—Houston	5	181	34	19	.559	23	15	.652	9	21	30	11	17	0	6	1	53	10.6
85-86—Houston	20	835	202	108	.535	58	43	.741	23	95	118	125	45	0	18	19	259	13.0
86-87—Houston	10	436	101	57	.564	54	43	.796	32	51	83	56	21	0	5	9	157	15.7
87-88—Houston	4	159	31	12	.387	12	8	.667	15	12	27	9	12	0	4	3	32	8.0
Totals	39	1611	368	196	.533	147	109	.741	79	179	258	201	95	0	33	32	501	12.8

Three-Point Field Goals: 1985-86, 0-for-3. 1986-87, 0-for-2. 1987-88, 0-for-1. Totals, 0-for-6.

Named to NBA All-Defensive First Team, 1988. . . . All-Defensive Second Team, 1987. . . . Member of U.S. Olympic team, 1980. . . . Member of NCAA Division I championship team, 1980. . . . Brother of former NBA forward Carlton (Scooter) McCray.

RODNEY McCRAY

XAVIER MAURICE McDANIEL

Born June 4, 1963 at Columbia, S.C. Height 6:07. Weight 205.
High School—Columbia, S.C., A.C. Flora.
College—Wichita State University, Wichita, Kan.
Drafted by Seattle on first round, 1985 (4th pick).

—COLLEGIATE RECORD—

Year	G.	Min.	FGA	FGM	Pct.	FTA	FTM	Pct.	Reb.	Pts.	Avg.
81-82	28	378	135	68	.504	43	27	.628	103	163	5.8
82-83	28	987	376	223	.593	148	80	.541	403	526	18.8
83-84	30	1130	445	251	.564	172	117	.680	393	619	20.6
84-85	31	1143	628	351	.559	224	142	.634	460	844	27.2
Totals	117	3638	1584	893	.564	587	366	.624	1359	2152	18.4

NBA REGULAR SEASON RECORD

									—Rebounds—									
Sea.—Team	G.	Min.	FGA	FGM	Pct.	FTA	FTM	Pct.	Off.	Def.	Tot.	Ast.	PF	Dq.	Stl.	Blk.	Pts.	Avg.
85-86—Seattle	82	2706	1176	576	.490	364	250	.687	307	348	655	193	305	8	101	37	1404	17.1
86-87—Seattle	82	3031	1583	806	.509	395	275	.696	338	367	705	207	300	4	115	52	1890	23.0
87-88—Seattle	78	2703	1407	687	.488	393	281	.715	206	312	518	263	230	2	96	52	1669	21.4
88-89—Seattle	82	2385	1385	677	.489	426	312	.732	177	256	433	134	231	0	84	40	1677	20.5
89-90—Seattle	69	2432	1233	611	.496	333	244	.733	165	282	447	171	231	2	73	36	1471	21.3
Totals	393	13257	6784	3357	.495	1911	1362	.713	1193	1565	2758	968	1297	16	469	217	8111	20.6

Three-Point Field Goals: 1985-86, 2-for-10 (.200). 1986-87, 3-for-14 (.214). 1987-88, 14-for-50 (.280). 1988-89, 11-for-36 (.306). 1989-90, 5-for-17 (.294). Totals, 35-for-127 (.276).

NBA PLAYOFF RECORD

									—Rebounds—									
Sea.—Team	G.	Min.	FGA	FGM	Pct.	FTA	FTM	Pct.	Off.	Def.	Tot.	Ast.	PF	Dq.	Stl.	Blk.	Pts.	Avg.
86-87—Seattle	14	528	254	124	.488	56	34	.607	52	65	117	42	63	2	21	9	284	20.3
87-88—Seattle	5	180	81	45	.556	24	12	.500	14	34	48	25	15	0	3	1	106	21.2
88-89—Seattle	8	281	144	58	.403	41	31	.756	24	43	67	22	30	0	2	5	150	18.8
Totals	27	989	479	227	.474	121	77	.636	90	142	232	89	108	2	26	15	540	20.0

Three-Point Field Goals: 1986-87, 2-for-10 (.200). 1987-88, 4-for-8 (.500). 1988-89, 3-for-9 (.333). Totals, 9-for-27 (.333).

NBA ALL-STAR GAME RECORD

								—Rebounds—							
Season—Team	Min.	FGA	FGM	Pct.	FTA	FTM	Pct.	Off.	Def.	Tot.	Ast.	PF	Dq.	Stl.	Blk.	Pts.
1988—Seattle	13	9	1	.111	0	0	.000	1	1	2	0	1	0	0	0	2

Named to NBA All-Rookie Team, 1986. . . . One of only two players in NCAA history to lead nation in both scoring and rebounding in same season, 1985. . . . Led NCAA Division I in scoring, 1985. . . . Led NCAA Division I in rebounding, 1983 and 1985.

MICHAEL RAY McGEE
(Mike)

Born July 29, 1959 at Tyler, Tex. Height 6:05. Weight 207.
High School—Omaha, Neb., North.
College—University of Michigan, Ann Arbor, Mich.
Drafted by Los Angeles on first round, 1981 (19th pick).

Traded by Los Angeles Lakers with draft rights to Ken Barlow to Atlanta for draft rights to Billy Thompson and Ron Kellogg, June 17, 1986.
Traded by Atlanta to Sacramento for 1991 and 1995 2nd round draft choices, December 14, 1987.
Traded by Sacramento to New Jersey for 1991 and 1996 2nd round draft choices, October 31, 1988.
Signed by Phoenix as an unrestricted free agent, March 26, 1990, for remainder of season.

—COLLEGIATE RECORD—

Year	G.	Min.	FGA	FGM	Pct.	FTA	FTM	Pct.	Reb.	Pts.	Avg.
77-78	27	....	439	217	.494	122	97	.795	132	531	19.7
78-79	27	....	454	207	.456	146	97	.664	150	511	18.9
79-80	30	....	584	277	.474	159	111	.698	130	665	22.2
80-81	30	1070	600	309	.515	169	114	.675	118	732	24.4
Totals	114	....	2077	1010	.486	596	419	.703	530	2439	21.4

NBA REGULAR SEASON RECORD

									—Rebounds—									
Sea.—Team	G.	Min.	FGA	FGM	Pct.	FTA	FTM	Pct.	Off.	Def.	Tot.	Ast.	PF	Dq.	Stl.	Blk.	Pts.	Avg.
81-82—Los Angeles	39	352	172	80	.465	53	31	.585	34	15	49	16	59	0	18	3	191	4.9
82-83—Los Angeles	39	381	163	69	.423	23	17	.739	33	20	53	26	50	1	11	5	156	4.0
83-84—Los Angeles	77	1425	584	347	.594	113	61	.540	117	76	193	81	176	0	49	6	757	9.8
84-85—L.A. Lakers	76	1170	612	329	.538	160	94	.588	97	68	165	71	147	1	39	7	774	10.2

Sea.—Team	G.	Min.	FGA	FGM	Pct.	FTA	FTM	Pct.	—Rebounds— Off.	Def.	Tot.	Ast.	PF	Dq.	Stl.	Blk.	Pts.	Avg.
85-86—L.A. Lakers	71	1213	544	252	.463	64	42	.656	51	89	140	83	131	0	53	7	587	8.3
86-87—Atlanta	76	1420	677	311	.459	137	80	.584	71	88	159	149	156	1	61	2	788	10.4
87-88—Atl.-Sac.	48	1003	530	223	.421	102	76	.745	55	73	128	71	81	0	52	6	575	12.0
88-89—New Jersey	80	2027	917	434	.473	144	77	.535	73	116	189	116	184	1	80	12	1038	13.0
89-90—Phoenix	14	280	87	42	.483	21	10	.476	11	25	36	16	28	0	8	1	102	7.3
Totals	520	9271	4286	2087	.487	817	488	.597	542	570	1112	629	1012	4	371	49	4968	9.6

Three-Point Field Goals: 1981-82, 0-for-4. 1982-83, 1-for-7 (.143). 1983-84, 2-for-13 (.154). 1984-85, 22-for-61 (.361). 1985-86, 41-for-114 (.360). 1986-87, 86-for-229 (.376). 1987-88, 53-for-160 (.331). 1988-89, 93-for-255 (.365). 1989-90, 8-for-23 (.348). Totals, 306-for-866 (.353).

NBA PLAYOFF RECORD

Sea.—Team	G.	Min.	FGA	FGM	Pct.	FTA	FTM	Pct.	—Rebounds— Off.	Def.	Tot.	Ast.	PF	Dq.	Stl.	Blk.	Pts.	Avg.
81-82—Los Angeles	4	10	13	6	.462	0	0	.000	3	0	3	0	1	0	0	0	12	3.0
82-83—Los Angeles	6	25	11	4	.364	4	3	.750	5	2	7	1	5	0	0	0	12	2.0
83-84—Los Angeles	17	370	157	90	.573	39	25	.641	22	12	34	23	52	0	11	1	211	12.4
84-85—L.A. Lakers	17	260	142	76	.535	42	29	.690	20	16	36	12	26	0	7	1	190	11.2
85-86—L.A. Lakers	6	28	18	8	.444	4	0	.000	3	2	5	2	3	0	0	0	16	2.7
86-87—Atlanta	8	101	39	10	256	10	5	.500	9	11	20	15	7	0	4	0	27	3.4
89-90—Phoenix	10	44	20	7	.350	4	1	.250	1	3	4	2	6	0	1	1	18	1.8
Totals	68	838	400	201	.503	103	63	.612	63	46	109	55	100	0	23	3	486	7.1

Three-Point Field Goals: 1981-82, 0-for-1. 1982-83, 1-for-1 (1.000). 1983-84, 6-for-17 (.353). 1984-85, 9-for-18 (.500). 1985-86, 0-for-3. 1986-87, 2-for-14 (.143). 1989-90, 3-for-7 (.429). Totals, 21-for-61 (.344).

Member of NBA championship teams, 1982 and 1985.

KEVIN EDWARD McHALE

Born December 19, 1957 at Hibbing, Minn. Height 6:10. Weight 225.
High School—Hibbing, Minn.
College—University of Minnesota, Minneapolis, Minn.
Drafted by Boston on first round, 1980 (3rd pick).

—COLLEGIATE RECORD—

Year	G.	Min.	FGA	FGM	Pct.	FTA	FTM	Pct.	Reb.	Pts.	Avg.
76-77	27	....	241	133	.552	77	58	.753	218	324	12.0
77-78	26	....	242	143	.591	77	54	.701	192	340	13.1
78.79	27	....	391	202	.517	96	79	.823	259	483	17.9
79-80	32	....	416	236	.567	107	85	.794	281	557	17.4
Totals	112	....	1290	714	.553	357	276	.773	950	1704	15.2

NBA REGULAR SEASON RECORD

Sea.—Team	G.	Min.	FGA	FGM	Pct.	FTA	FTM	Pct.	—Rebounds— Off.	Def.	Tot.	Ast.	PF	Dq.	Stl.	Blk.	Pts.	Avg.
80-81—Boston	82	1645	666	355	.533	159	108	.679	155	204	359	55	260	3	27	151	818	10.0
81-82—Boston	82	2332	875	465	.531	248	187	.754	191	365	556	91	264	1	30	185	1117	13.6
82-83—Boston	82	2345	893	483	.541	269	193	.717	215	338	553	104	241	3	34	192	1159	14.1
83-84—Boston	82	2577	1055	587	.556	439	336	.765	208	402	610	104	243	5	23	126	1511	18.4
84-85—Boston	79	2653	1062	605	.570	467	355	.760	229	483	712	141	234	3	28	120	1565	19.8
85-86—Boston	68	2397	978	561	.574	420	326	.776	171	380	551	181	192	2	29	134	1448	21.3
86-87—Boston	77	3060	1307	790	.604	512	428	.836	247	516	763	198	240	1	38	172	2008	26.1
87-88—Boston	64	2390	911	550	.604	434	346	.797	159	377	536	171	179	1	27	92	1446	22.6
88-89—Boston	78	2876	1211	661	.546	533	436	.818	223	414	637	172	223	2	26	97	1758	22.5
89-90—Boston	82	2722	1181	648	.549	440	393	.893	201	476	677	172	250	3	30	157	1712	20.9
Totals	776	24997	10139	5705	.563	3921	3108	.793	1999	3955	5954	1389	2326	24	292	1426	14542	18.7

Three-Point Field Goals: 1980-81, 0-for-2. 1982-83, 0-for-1. 1983-84, 1-for-3 (.333). 1984-85, 0-for-6. 1986-87, 0-for-4. 1988-89, 0-for-4. 1989-90, 23-for-69 (.333). Totals, 24-for-89 (.270).

NBA PLAYOFF RECORD

Sea.—Team	G.	Min.	FGA	FGM	Pct.	FTA	FTM	Pct.	—Rebounds— Off.	Def.	Tot.	Ast.	PF	Dq.	Stl.	Blk.	Pts.	Avg.
80-81—Boston	17	296	113	61	.540	36	23	.639	29	30	59	14	51	1	4	25	145	8.5
81-82—Boston	12	344	134	77	.575	53	40	.755	41	44	85	11	44	0	5	27	194	16.2
82-83—Boston	7	177	62	34	.548	18	10	.556	15	27	42	5	16	0	3	7	78	11.1
83-84—Boston	23	702	244	123	.504	121	94	.777	62	81	143	27	75	1	3	35	340	14.8
84-85—Boston	21	837	303	172	.568	150	121	.807	74	134	208	32	73	3	13	46	465	22.1
85-86—Boston	18	715	290	168	.579	141	112	.794	51	104	155	48	64	0	8	43	448	24.9
86-87—Boston	21	827	298	174	.584	126	96	.762	66	128	194	39	71	2	7	30	444	21.1
87-88—Boston	17	716	262	158	.603	137	115	.839	55	81	136	40	65	1	7	30	432	25.4
88-89—Boston	3	115	41	20	.488	23	17	.739	7	17	24	9	13	0	1	2	57	19.0
89-90—Boston	5	192	69	42	.609	29	25	.862	8	31	39	13	17	0	2	10	110	22.0
Totals	144	4921	1816	1029	.567	834	653	.783	408	677	1085	238	489	8	53	255	2713	18.8

Three-Point Field Goals: 1982-83, 0-for-1. 1983-84, 0-for-3. 1985-86, 0-for-1. 1987-88, 1-for-1 (1.000). 1989-90, 1-for-3 (.333). Totals, 2-for-9 (.222).

NBA ALL-STAR GAME RECORD

Season—Team	Min.	FGA	FGM	Pct.	FTA	FTM	Pct.	—Rebounds— Off.	Def.	Tot.	Ast.	PF	Dq.	Stl.	Blk.	Pts.
1984—Boston	11	7	3	.429	6	4	.667	2	3	5	0	1	0	0	0	10
1986—Boston	20	8	3	.375	2	2	1.000	3	7	10	2	4	0	0	4	8
1987—Boston	30	11	7	.636	2	2	1.000	4	3	7	2	5	0	0	4	16
1988—Boston	14	1	0	.000	2	2	1.000	0	1	1	1	2	0	0	2	2
1989—Boston	16	7	5	.714	0	0	.000	1	2	3	0	3	0	0	2	10
1990—Boston	20	11	6	.545	0	0	.000	2	6	8	1	4	0	0	0	13
Totals	111	45	24	.533	12	10	.833	12	22	34	6	19	0	0	12	59

Three-Point Field Goals: 1990, 1-for-1 (1.000).

Named to All-NBA First Team, 1987. . . . NBA All-Rookie Team, 1981. . . . Recipient of NBA Sixth Man Award, 1984 and 1985. . . . Member of NBA championship teams, 1981, 1984, 1986. . . . NBA All-Defensive First Team, 1986, 1987, 1988. . . . NBA All-Defensive Second Team, 1983, 1989, 1990. . . . Led NBA in field-goal percentage, 1987 and 1988.

DERRICK WAYNE McKEY

Born October 10, 1966 at Meridian, Miss. Height 6:09. Weight 210.

High School—Meridian, Miss.

College—University of Alabama, University, Ala.

Drafted by Seattle on first round as an undergraduate, 1987 (9th pick).

—COLLEGIATE RECORD—

Year	G.	Min.	FGA	FGM	Pct.	FTA	FTM	Pct.	Reb.	Pts.	Avg.
84-85	33	728	155	74	.477	33	20	.606	134	168	5.1
85-86	33	1117	280	178	.636	117	92	.786	262	448	13.6
86-87	33	1199	425	247	.581	116	100	.862	247	615	18.6
Totals	99	3044	860	499	.580	266	212	.797	643	1231	12.4

Three-Point Field Goals: 1986-87, 21-for-50 (.420).

NBA REGULAR SEASON RECORD

Sea.—Team	G.	Min.	FGA	FGM	Pct.	FTA	FTM	Pct.	—Rebounds— Off.	Def.	Tot.	Ast.	PF	Dq.	Stl.	Blk.	Pts.	Avg.
87-88—Seattle	82	1706	519	255	.491	224	173	.772	115	213	328	107	237	3	70	63	694	8.5
88-89—Seattle	82	2804	970	487	.502	375	301	.803	167	297	464	219	264	4	105	70	1305	15.9
89-90—Seattle	80	2748	949	468	.493	403	315	.782	170	319	489	187	247	2	87	81	1254	15.7
Totals	244	7258	2438	1210	.496	1002	789	.787	452	829	1281	513	748	9	262	214	3253	13.3

Three-Point Field Goals: 1987-88, 11-for-30 (.367). 1988-89, 30-for-89 (.337). 1989-90, 3-for-23 (.130). Totals, 44-for-142 (.310).

NBA PLAYOFF RECORD

Sea.—Team	G.	Min.	FGA	FGM	Pct.	FTA	FTM	Pct.	—Rebounds— Off.	Def.	Tot.	Ast.	PF	Dq.	Stl.	Blk.	Pts.	Avg.
87-88—Seattle	5	109	38	24	.632	17	10	.588	7	13	20	8	12	0	3	5	60	12.0
88-89—Seattle	8	286	89	44	.494	21	17	.810	21	31	52	18	33	1	6	15	106	13.3
Totals	13	395	127	68	.535	38	27	.711	28	44	72	26	45	1	9	20	166	12.8

Three-Point Field Goals: 1987-88, 2-for-6 (.333). 1988-89, 1-for-9 (.111). Totals, 3-for-15 (.200).

Named to NBA All-Rookie Team, 1988. . . . THE SPORTING NEWS All-America Second Team, 1987.

CARLTON B. McKINNEY

Born October 21, 1964 at San Diego, Calif. Height 6:05. Weight 190.

High School—Nixon, Tex.

Colleges—University of Tulsa, Tulsa, Okla., and Southern Methodist University, Dallas, Tex.

Never drafted by an NBA franchise.

Signed by Los Angeles Clippers as a free agent, August 15, 1989.

Waived by Los Angeles Clippers, November 29, 1989.

Played in Continental Basketball Association with Topeka Sizzlers, 1988-89, and Quad City Thunder and Santa Barbara Islanders, 1989-90.

—COLLEGIATE RECORD—

Tulsa

Year	G.	Min.	FGA	FGM	Pct.	FTA	FTM	Pct.	Reb.	Pts.	Avg.
83-84	21	309	100	43	.430	30	24	.800	47	110	5.2
84-85	31	470	173	81	.468	28	18	.643	52	180	5.8
Tulsa Totals	52	779	273	124	.454	58	42	.724	99	290	5.6

Southern Methodist

Year	G.	Min.	FGA	FGM	Pct.	FTA	FTM	Pct.	Reb.	Pts.	Avg.
85-86	Did Not Play—Transfer Student										
86-87	29	1011	417	193	.463	41	29	.707	164	444	15.3

Year	G.	Min.	FGA	FGM	Pct.	FTA	FTM	Pct.	Reb.	Pts.	Avg.
87-88	35	1197	483	243	.503	57	40	.702	128	561	16.0
SMU Totals	64	2208	900	436	.484	98	69	.704	292	1005	15.7
Col. Totals	116	2987	1173	560	.477	156	111	.712	391	1295	11.2

Three-Point Field Goals: 1986-87, 29-for-76 (.382). 1987-88, 35-for-84 (.417). Totals, 64-for-100 (.640).

CBA REGULAR SEASON RECORD

			—2-Point—			—3-Point—									
Sea.—Team	G.	Min.	FGM	FGA	Pct.	FGM	FGA	Pct.	FTM	FTA	Pct.	Reb.	Ast.	Pts.	Avg.
88-89—Topeka	41	1646	399	847	.471	31	92	.337	63	94	.670	219	111	954	23.3
89-90—Q.C.-S.B.	44	1127	322	661	.487	11	36	.306	48	59	.814	120	86	725	16.5
Totals	85	2773	721	1508	.478	42	128	.328	111	153	.725	339	197	1679	19.8

NBA REGULAR SEASON RECORD

									—Rebounds—									
Sea.—Team	G.	Min.	FGA	FGM	Pct.	FTA	FTM	Pct.	Off.	Def.	Tot.	Ast.	PF	Dq.	Stl.	Blk.	Pts.	Avg.
89-90—L.A. Clippers	7	104	32	8	.250	4	2	.500	4	8	12	7	15	1	6	1	18	2.6

Three-Point Field Goals: 1989-90, 0-for-1.

NATHANIEL McMILLAN
(Nate)

Born August 3, 1964 at Raleigh, N.C. Height 6:05. Weight 195.

High School—Raleigh, N.C., Enloe.

Colleges—Chowan College, Murfreesboro, N.C., and North Carolina State University, Raleigh, N.C.

Drafted by Seattle on second round, 1986 (30th pick).

—COLLEGIATE RECORD—

Chowan

Year	G.	Min.	FGA	FGM	Pct.	FTA	FTM	Pct.	Reb.	Pts.	Avg.
82-83	27	....	174	101	.580	92	64	.696	134	266	9.9
83-84	35	....	331	180	.544	130	100	.769	342	460	13.1
J.C. Totals	62	....	505	281	.556	222	164	.739	476	726	11.7

North Carolina State

Year	G.	Min.	FGA	FGM	Pct.	FTA	FTM	Pct.	Reb.	Pts.	Avg.
84-85	33	973	207	94	.454	95	64	.674	189	252	7.6
85-86	34	1208	262	127	.485	90	66	.733	155	320	9.4
N.C. St. Tot.	67	2181	469	221	.471	185	130	.703	344	572	8.5

NBA REGULAR SEASON RECORD

									—Rebounds—									
Sea.—Team	G.	Min.	FGA	FGM	Pct.	FTA	FTM	Pct.	Off.	Def.	Tot.	Ast.	PF	Dq.	Stl.	Blk.	Pts.	Avg.
86-87—Seattle	71	1972	301	143	.475	141	87	.617	101	230	331	583	238	4	125	45	373	5.3
87-88—Seattle	82	2453	496	235	.474	205	145	.707	117	221	338	702	238	1	169	47	624	7.6
88-89—Seattle	75	2341	485	199	.410	189	119	.630	143	245	388	696	236	3	156	42	532	7.1
89-90—Seattle	82	2338	438	207	.473	153	98	.641	127	276	403	598	289	7	140	37	523	6.4
Totals	310	9104	1720	784	.456	688	449	.653	488	972	1460	2579	1001	15	590	171	2052	6.6

Three-Point Field Goals: 1986-87, 0-for-7. 1987-88, 9-for-24 (.375). 1988-89, 15-for-70 (.214). 1989-90, 11-for-31 (.355). Totals, 35-for-132 (.265).

NBA PLAYOFF RECORD

									—Rebounds—									
Sea.—Team	G.	Min.	FGA	FGM	Pct.	FTA	FTM	Pct.	Off.	Def.	Tot.	Ast.	PF	Dq.	Stl.	Blk.	Pts.	Avg.
86-87—Seattle	14	356	62	27	.435	24	17	.708	13	41	54	112	42	1	14	10	71	5.1
87-88—Seattle	5	127	35	12	.343	14	9	.643	6	15	21	33	11	0	2	3	33	6.6
88-89—Seattle	8	200	40	19	.475	25	16	.640	9	16	25	63	21	0	10	5	54	6.8
Totals	27	683	137	58	.423	63	42	.667	28	72	100	208	74	1	26	18	158	5.9

Three-Point Field Goals: 1987-88, 0-for-1. 1988-89, 0-for-2. Totals, 0-for-3.

MARK ROBERT McNAMARA

Born June 8, 1959 at San Jose, Calif. Height 6:11. Weight 235.

High School—San Jose, Calif., Del Mar.

Colleges—Santa Clara University, Santa Clara, Calif., and University of California, Berkeley, Calif.

Drafted by Philadelphia on first round, 1982 (22nd pick).

Traded by Philadelphia to San Antonio for a 1986 2nd round draft choice, November 4, 1983.
Traded by San Antonio to Kansas City for Billy Knight, December 11, 1984.
Traded by Kansas City to Milwaukee for a 1986 4th round draft choice, August 9, 1985.

Waived by Milwaukee, October 22, 1985; signed by Philadelphia as a free agent, March 4, 1987.
Rights relinquished by Philadelphia, August 5, 1988; signed by Los Angeles Lakers as a free agent, October 3, 1988.
Played in Italy, 1985-86.

—COLLEGIATE RECORD—

Santa Clara

Year	G.	Min.	FGA	FGM	Pct.	FTA	FTM	Pct.	Reb.	Pts.	Avg.
77-78	29	....	229	143	.624	98	46	.469	197	332	11.4
78-79	25	652	266	153	.575	123	71	.577	167	377	15.1
SC Totals	54	....	495	296	.598	221	117	.529	364	709	13.1

California

Year	G.	Min.	FGA	FGM	Pct.	FTA	FTM	Pct.	Reb.	Pts.	Avg.
79-80	Did Not Play—Transfer Student										
80-81	26	....	295	182	.617	168	84	.500	272	448	17.2
81-82	27	....	329	231	.702	242	131	.541	341	593	22.0
Cal Totals	53	....	624	413	.662	410	215	.524	613	1041	19.6
College Totals	107	....	1119	709	.634	631	332	.526	977	1750	16.4

ITALIAN LEAGUE RECORD

Year	G.	Min.	FGA	FGM	Pct.	FTA	FTM	Pct.	Reb.	Pts.	Avg.
85-86—Cortan	28	867	315	184	.584	113	63	.558	307	431	15.4

NBA REGULAR SEASON RECORD

									—Rebounds—									
Sea.—Team	G.	Min.	FGA	FGM	Pct.	FTA	FTM	Pct.	Off.	Def.	Tot.	Ast.	PF	Dq.	Stl.	Blk.	Pts.	Avg.
82-83—Philadelphia	36	182	64	29	.453	45	20	.444	34	42	76	7	42	1	3	3	78	2.2
83-84—San Antonio	70	1037	253	157	.621	157	74	.471	137	180	317	31	138	2	14	12	388	5.5
84-85—S.A.-K.C.	45	273	76	40	.526	62	32	.516	31	43	74	6	27	0	7	8	112	2.5
86-87—Philadelphia	11	113	30	14	.467	19	7	.368	17	19	36	2	17	0	1	0	35	3.2
87-88—Philadelphia	42	581	133	52	.391	66	48	.727	66	91	157	18	67	0	4	12	152	3.6
88-89—L.A. Lakers	39	318	64	32	.500	78	49	.628	38	62	100	10	51	0	4	3	113	2.9
89-90—L.A. Lakers	33	190	86	38	.442	40	26	.650	22	41	63	3	31	1	2	1	102	3.1
Totals	276	2694	706	362	.513	467	256	.548	345	478	823	77	373	4	35	39	980	3.6

NBA PLAYOFF RECORD

									—Rebounds—									
Sea.—Team	G.	Min.	FGA	FGM	Pct.	FTA	FTM	Pct.	Off.	Def.	Tot.	Ast.	PF	Dq.	Stl.	Blk.	Pts.	Avg.
82-83—Philadelphia	2	2	2	2	1.000	0	0	.000	0	1	1	0	0	0	0	0	4	2.0
86-87—Philadelphia	1	2	1	1	1.000	0	0	.000	0	1	1	0	0	0	0	0	2	2.0
88-89—L.A. Lakers	3	7	2	1	.500	2	1	.500	0	1	1	0	0	0	0	0	3	1.0
89-90—L.A. Lakers	2	5	4	1	.250	0	0	....	0	1	1	0	1	0	0	0	2	1.0
Totals	8	16	9	5	.556	2	1	.500	0	4	4	0	1	0	0	0	11	1.4

Member of NBA championship team, 1983. . . . Led NCAA Division I in field-goal percentage, 1982.

SCOTT MEENTS

Born January 4, 1964 at Kankakee, Ill. Height 6:10. Weight 225.
High School—Herscher, Ill.
College—University of Illinois, Champaign, Ill.
Drafted by Chicago on fourth round, 1986 (74th pick).

Waived by Chicago, October 26, 1987; signed by Los Angeles Lakers as a free agent, August 30, 1988.
Waived by Los Angeles Lakers, October 17, 1988; signed by Seattle as a free agent, September 27, 1989.
Played in Continental Basketball Association with Pensacola Tornados, 1987-88.
Played in Italy, 1986-87 and 1987-88.

—COLLEGIATE RECORD—

Year	G.	Min.	FGA	FGM	Pct.	FTA	FTM	Pct.	Reb.	Pts.	Avg.
82-83	29	237	73	34	.466	17	13	.765	35	81	2.8
83-84	28	465	134	61	.455	33	23	.697	91	145	5.2
84-85	35	652	175	84	.480	37	25	.676	111	193	5.5
85-86	32	507	148	77	.520	30	24	.800	89	178	5.6
Totals	124	1861	530	256	.483	117	85	.726	326	597	4.8

ITALIAN LEAGUE RECORD

Year	G.	Min.	FGA	FGM	Pct.	FTA	FTM	Pct.	Reb.	Pts.	Avg.
86-87—Citrosil	11	337	119	58	.487	33	22	.667	75	141	12.8
87-88—Seagafredo	18	654	255	133	.522	53	33	.623	155	299	16.6

CBA REGULAR SEASON RECORD

			—2-Point—			—3-Point—									
Sea.—Team	G.	Min.	FGM	FGA	Pct.	FGM	FGA	Pct.	FTM	FTA	Pct.	Reb.	Ast.	Pts.	Avg.
87-88—Pensacola	8	186	20	47	.426	1	3	.333	20	24	.833	52	4	63	7.8

NBA REGULAR SEASON RECORD

Sea.—Team	G.	Min.	FGA	FGM	Pct.	FTA	FTM	Pct.	Rebounds Off.	Rebounds Def.	Rebounds Tot.	Ast.	PF	Dq.	Stl.	Blk.	Pts.	Avg.
89-90—Seattle	26	148	44	19	.432	23	17	.739	7	23	30	7	12	0	4	3	55	2.1

REGINALD WAYNE MILLER
(Reggie)

Born August 24, 1965 at Riverside, Calif. Height 6:07. Weight 190.

High School—Riverside, Calif., Poly.

College—University of California at Los Angeles, Los Angeles, Calif.

Drafted by Indiana on first round, 1987 (11th pick).

—COLLEGIATE RECORD—

Year	G.	Min.	FGA	FGM	Pct.	FTA	FTM	Pct.	Reb.	Pts.	Avg.
83-84	28	384	110	56	.509	28	18	.643	42	130	4.6
84-85	33	1174	347	192	.553	148	119	.804	141	503	15.2
85-86	29	1112	493	274	.556	229	202	.882	153	750	25.9
86-87	32	1166	455	247	.543	179	149	.832	173	712	22.3
Totals	122	3836	1405	769	.547	584	488	.836	509	2095	17.2

Three-Point Field Goals: 1986-87, 69-for-157 (.439).

NBA REGULAR SEASON RECORD

Sea.—Team	G.	Min.	FGA	FGM	Pct.	FTA	FTM	Pct.	Rebounds Off.	Rebounds Def.	Rebounds Tot.	Ast.	PF	Dq.	Stl.	Blk.	Pts.	Avg.
87-88—Indiana	82	1840	627	306	.488	186	149	.801	95	95	190	132	157	0	53	19	822	10.0
88-89—Indiana	74	2536	831	398	.479	340	287	.844	73	219	292	227	170	2	93	29	1181	16.0
89-90—Indiana	82	3192	1287	661	.514	627	544	.868	95	200	295	311	175	1	110	18	2016	24.6
Totals	238	7568	2745	1365	.497	1153	980	.850	263	514	777	670	502	3	256	66	4019	16.9

Three-Point Field Goals: 1987-88, 61-for-172 (.355). 1988-89, 98-for-244 (.402). 1989-90, 150-for-362 (.414). Totals, 309-for-778 (.397).

NBA PLAYOFF RECORD

Sea.—Team	G.	Min.	FGA	FGM	Pct.	FTA	FTM	Pct.	Rebounds Off.	Rebounds Def.	Rebounds Tot.	Ast.	PF	Dq.	Stl.	Blk.	Pts.	Avg.
89-90—Indiana	3	125	35	20	.571	21	19	.905	1	11	12	6	6	0	3	0	62	20.7

Three-Point Field Goals: 1989-90, 3-for-7 (.429).

NBA ALL-STAR GAME RECORD

Season—Team	Min.	FGA	FGM	Pct.	FTA	FTM	Pct.	Rebounds Off.	Rebounds Def.	Rebounds Tot.	Ast.	PF	Dq.	Stl.	Blk.	Pts.
1990—Indiana	14	3	2	.667	0	0	....	0	1	1	3	1	0	1	0	4

Three-Point Field Goals: 1990, 0-for-1.

Brother of former pro baseball player Darrell Miller and former Southern Cal basketball player Cheryl Miller.

SAMUEL E. MITCHELL JR.
(Sam)

Born September 2, 1963 at Columbus, Ga. Height 6:06. Weight 215.

High School—Columbus, Ga.

College—Mercer University, Macon, Ga.

Drafted by Houston on third round, 1985 (54th pick).

Waived by Houston, October 22, 1985; re-signed by Houston as a free agent, October 7, 1986.
Waived by Houston, October 28, 1986; signed by Minnesota as a free agent, July 23, 1989.
Played in Continental Basketball Association with Wisconsin Flyers, 1985-86, and with Wisconsin Flyers and Rapid City Thrillers, 1986-87.
Played in France, 1987-88 and 1988-89.

—COLLEGIATE RECORD—

Year	G.	Min.	FGA	FGM	Pct.	FTA	FTM	Pct.	Reb.	Pts.	Avg.
81-82	27	....	155	77	.497	53	38	.717	100	192	7.1
82-83	28	964	343	178	.519	134	105	.784	164	461	16.5
83-84	26	935	432	219	.507	155	121	.781	184	559	21.5
84-85	31	1157	570	294	.516	248	186	.750	255	774	25.0
Totals	112	....	1500	768	.512	590	450	.763	703	1986	17.7

CBA REGULAR SEASON RECORD

Sea.—Team	G.	Min.	2-Point FGM	2-Point FGA	2-Point Pct.	3-Point FGM	3-Point FGA	3-Point Pct.	FTM	FTA	Pct.	Reb.	Ast.	Pts.	Avg.
85-86—Wisconsin	13	450	106	235	.451	1	3	.333	55	83	.662	95	16	270	20.8
86-87—Wis.-R.C.	42	1370	250	542	.461	3	12	.250	154	210	.733	256	31	663	15.8
Totals	55	1820	356	777	.458	4	15	.267	209	293	.713	351	47	933	17.0

NBA REGULAR SEASON RECORD

Sea.—Team	G.	Min.	FGA	FGM	Pct.	FTA	FTM	Pct.	—Rebounds— Off.	Def.	Tot.	Ast.	PF	Dq.	Stl.	Blk.	Pts.	Avg.
89-90—Minnesota	80	2414	834	372	.446	349	268	.768	180	282	462	89	301	7	66	54	1012	12.7

Three-Point Field Goals: 1989-90, 0-for-9.

PAUL KEEN MOKESKI

Born January 3, 1957 at Spokane, Wash. Height 7:00. Weight 255.
High School—Encino, Calif., Crespi Carmelite.
College—University of Kansas, Lawrence, Kan.
Drafted by Houston on second round, 1979 (42nd pick).

Traded by Houston to Detroit for a 1982 2nd round draft choice, October 7, 1980.
Traded by Detroit with Phil Hubbard and 1982 1st and 2nd round draft choices to Cleveland for Kenny Carr and Bill Laimbeer, February 16, 1982.
Waived by Cleveland, December 20, 1982; signed by Milwaukee as a free agent, December 24, 1982.
Signed by Cleveland as an unrestricted free agent, September 26, 1989.

—COLLEGIATE RECORD—

Year	G.	Min.	FGA	FGM	Pct.	FTA	FTM	Pct.	Reb.	Pts.	Avg.
75-76	18	474	170	82	.482	37	27	.730	115	191	10.6
76-77	14	250	96	38	.396	16	10	.625	86	86	6.1
77-78	28	653	220	114	.518	54	31	.574	237	259	9.3
78-79	29	974	323	161	.498	120	87	.725	242	409	14.1
Totals	89	2351	809	395	.488	227	155	.683	680	945	10.6

NBA REGULAR SEASON RECORD

Sea.—Team	G.	Min.	FGA	FGM	Pct.	FTA	FTM	Pct.	—Rebounds— Off.	Def.	Tot.	Ast.	PF	Dq.	Stl.	Blk.	Pts.	Avg.
79-80—Houston	12	113	33	11	.333	9	7	.778	14	15	29	2	24	0	1	6	29	2.4
80-81—Detroit	80	1815	458	224	.489	200	120	.600	141	277	418	135	267	7	38	73	568	7.1
81-82—Det.-Clev.	67	868	193	84	.435	63	48	.762	59	149	208	35	171	2	33	40	216	3.2
82-83—Clev.-Milw.	73	1128	260	119	.458	68	50	.735	76	184	260	49	223	9	21	44	288	3.9
83-84—Milwaukee	68	838	213	102	.479	72	50	.694	51	115	166	44	168	1	11	29	255	3.8
84-85—Milwaukee	79	1586	429	205	.478	116	81	.698	107	303	410	99	266	6	28	35	491	6.2
85-86—Milwaukee	45	521	139	59	.424	34	25	.735	36	103	139	30	92	1	6	6	143	3.2
86-87—Milwaukee	62	626	129	52	.403	64	46	.719	45	93	138	22	126	0	18	13	150	2.4
87-88—Milwaukee	60	848	210	100	.476	72	51	.708	70	151	221	22	194	5	27	29	251	4.2
88-89—Milwaukee	74	690	164	59	.360	51	40	.784	63	124	187	36	153	0	29	21	165	2.2
89-90—Cleveland	38	449	150	63	.420	36	25	.694	27	72	99	17	76	0	8	10	151	4.0
Totals	658	9482	2378	1078	.453	785	543	.692	689	1586	2275	491	1760	31	220	306	2707	4.1

Three-Point Field Goals: 1980-81, 0-for-1. 1981-82, 0-for-3. 1982-83, 0-for-1. 1983-84, 1-for-3 (.333). 1984-85, 0-for-2. 1986-87, 0-for-1. 1987-88, 0-for-4. 1988-89, 7-for-26 (.269). 1989-90, 0-for-1. Totals, 8-for-42 (.190).

NBA PLAYOFF RECORD

Sea.—Team	G.	Min.	FGA	FGM	Pct.	FTA	FTM	Pct.	—Rebounds— Off.	Def.	Tot.	Ast.	PF	Dq.	Stl.	Blk.	Pts.	Avg.
82-83—Milwaukee	4	12	4	2	.500	0	0	.000	1	1	2	1	1	0	1	0	4	1.0
83-84—Milwaukee	16	322	63	34	.540	45	30	.667	20	68	88	6	62	0	9	11	98	6.1
84-85—Milwaukee	8	154	36	16	.444	12	12	1.000	8	26	34	12	28	1	2	4	44	5.5
85-86—Milwaukee	14	101	27	14	.519	9	6	.667	5	19	24	8	27	1	6	3	34	2.4
86-87—Milwaukee	12	107	22	8	.364	15	12	.800	12	17	29	2	22	1	3	2	28	2.3
87-88—Milwaukee	4	40	14	5	.357	6	4	.667	5	4	9	0	4	0	3	2	14	3.5
88-89—Milwaukee	5	61	14	8	.571	8	6	.750	8	9	17	3	16	0	0	0	23	4.6
89-90—Cleveland	3	10	2	1	.500	2	2	1.000	0	2	2	0	2	0	1	1	4	1.3
Totals	66	807	182	88	.484	97	72	.742	59	146	205	32	162	3	25	23	249	3.8

Three-Point Field Goals: 1983-84, 0-for-2. 1986-87, 0-for-1. 1988-89, 1-for-1 (1.000). Totals, 1-for-4 (.250).

JOHN BRIAN MOORE
(Johnny)

Born March 3, 1958 at Altoona, Pa. Height 6:03. Weight 185.
High School—Altoona, Pa.
College—University of Texas, Austin, Tex.
Drafted by Seattle on second round, 1979 (43rd pick).

Draft rights sold by Seattle to San Antonio, June 26, 1979.
Waived by San Antonio, October 12, 1979; re-signed by San Antonio, March 9, 1980.
Waived by San Antonio, November 19, 1987; signed by New Jersey as a free agent, December 3, 1987.
Waived by New Jersey, December 15, 1987; signed by San Antonio as a free agent, November 22, 1989.
Played in Continental Basketball Association with Tulsa Fast Breakers, 1989-90.

—COLLEGIATE RECORD—

Year	G.	Min.	FGA	FGM	Pct.	FTA	FTM	Pct.	Reb.	Pts.	Avg.
75-76	26	....	353	154	.436	61	45	.738	61	353	13.6
76-77	26	....	387	168	.434	97	78	.804	97	414	15.9
77-78	31	....	344	168	.488	110	81	.736	159	417	13.5
78-79	29	....	254	119	.469	88	57	.648	129	295	10.2
Totals	112	....	1338	609	.455	356	261	.733	446	1479	13.2

CBA REGULAR SEASON RECORD

			2-Point			3-Point									
Sea.—Team	G.	Min.	FGM	FGA	Pct.	FGM	FGA	Pct.	FTM	FTA	Pct.	Reb.	Ast.	Pts.	Avg.
89-90—Tulsa	4	108	16	32	.500	3	6	.500	4	5	.800	13	28	45	11.3

NBA REGULAR SEASON RECORD

									—Rebounds—									
Sea.—Team	G.	Min.	FGA	FGM	Pct.	FTA	FTM	Pct.	Off.	Def.	Tot.	Ast.	PF	Dq.	Stl.	Blk.	Pts.	Avg.
80-81—San Antonio	82	1578	520	249	.479	172	105	.610	58	138	196	373	178	0	120	22	604	7.4
81-82—San Antonio	79	2294	667	309	.463	182	122	.670	62	213	275	762	254	6	163	12	741	9.4
82-83—San Antonio	77	2552	841	394	.468	199	148	.744	65	212	277	753	247	2	194	32	941	12.2
83-84—San Antonio	59	1650	518	231	.446	139	105	.755	37	141	178	566	168	2	123	20	595	10.1
84-85—San Antonio	82	2689	910	416	.457	248	189	.762	94	284	378	816	247	3	229	18	1046	12.8
85-86—San Antonio	28	856	303	150	.495	86	59	.686	25	61	86	252	78	0	70	6	363	13.0
86-87—San Antonio	55	1234	448	198	.442	70	56	.800	32	68	100	250	97	0	83	3	474	8.6
87-88—S.A.-N.J.	5	61	10	4	.400	0	0	.000	2	4	6	12	1	0	3	0	8	1.6
89-90—San Antonio	53	516	126	47	.373	27	16	.593	16	36	52	82	55	0	32	3	118	2.2
Totals	520	13430	4343	1998	.460	1123	800	.712	391	1157	1548	3866	1325	13	1017	116	4890	9.4

Three-Point Field Goals: 1980-81, 1-for-19 (.053). 1981-82, 1-for-21 (.048). 1982-83, 5-for-22 (.277). 1983-84, 28-for-87 (.322). 1984-85, 25-for-89 (.281). 1985-86, 4-for-22 (.182). 1986-87, 22-for-79 (.278). 1987-88, 0-for-1. 1989-90, 8-for-34 (.235). Totals, 94-for-374 (.251).

NBA PLAYOFF RECORD

									—Rebounds—									
Sea.—Team	G.	Min.	FGA	FGM	Pct.	FTA	FTM	Pct.	Off.	Def.	Tot.	Ast.	PF	Dq.	Stl.	Blk.	Pts.	Avg.
80-81—San Antonio	7	124	37	18	.486	8	6	.750	8	5	13	27	14	0	10	1	42	6.0
81-82—San Antonio	9	292	82	39	.476	27	16	.593	9	22	31	93	38	0	15	6	94	10.4
82-83—San Antonio	11	414	197	105	.533	35	28	.800	8	39	47	161	41	0	28	3	247	22.5
84-85—San Antonio	5	168	54	25	.463	23	15	.652	13	17	30	42	17	0	10	2	66	13.2
89-90—San Antonio	9	86	24	6	.250	8	4	.500	3	8	11	21	11	0	7	1	16	1.8
Totals	41	1084	394	193	.490	101	69	.683	41	91	132	344	121	0	70	13	465	11.3

Three-Point Field Goals: 1980-81, 0-for-3. 1981-82, 0-for-3. 1982-83, 9-for-17 (.529). 1984-85, 1-for-3 (.333). 1989-90, 0-for-6. Totals, 10-for-32 (.313).

Led NBA in assists, 1982.

CHRISTOPHER VERNARD MORRIS
(Chris)

Born January 20, 1966 at Atlanta, Ga. Height 6:08. Weight 210.
High School—Atlanta, Ga., Douglass.
College—Auburn University, Auburn University, Ala.
Drafted by New Jersey on first round, 1988 (4th pick).

—COLLEGIATE RECORD—

Year	G.	Min.	FGA	FGM	Pct.	FTA	FTM	Pct.	Reb.	Pts.	Avg.
84-85	34	1032	325	155	.477	71	44	.620	169	354	10.4
85-86	33	1023	256	128	.500	103	69	.670	171	325	9.8
86-87	31	985	304	170	.559	97	69	.711	225	418	13.5
87-88	30	1018	501	241	.481	132	105	.795	295	620	20.7
Totals	128	4058	1386	694	.501	403	287	.712	860	1717	13.4

Three-Point Field Goals: 1986-87, 9-for-27 (.333). 1987-88, 33-for-97 (.340). Totals, 42-for-124 (.339).

NBA REGULAR SEASON RECORD

									—Rebounds—									
Sea.—Team	G.	Min.	FGA	FGM	Pct.	FTA	FTM	Pct.	Off.	Def.	Tot.	Ast.	PF	Dq.	Stl.	Blk.	Pts.	Avg.
88-89—New Jersey	76	2096	905	414	.457	254	182	.717	188	209	397	119	250	4	102	60	1074	14.1
89-90—New Jersey	80	2449	1065	449	.422	316	228	.722	194	228	422	143	219	1	130	79	1187	14.8
Totals	156	4545	1970	863	.438	570	410	.719	382	437	819	262	469	5	232	139	2261	14.5

Three-Point Field Goals: 1988-89, 64-for-175 (.366). 1989-90, 61-for-193 (.316). Totals, 125-for-368 (.340).

Named to NBA All-Rookie Second Team, 1989.

—DID YOU KNOW—

That the 1968-69 Boston Celtics are the only NBA championship team that failed to qualify for postseason play the following year?

MICHAEL FITZGERALD MORRISON
(Mike)

Born August 16, 1967 at Washington, D.C. Height 6:04. Weight 195.
High School—Hyattsville, Md., Northwestern.
College—Loyola College, Baltimore, Md.
Drafted by Phoenix on second round, 1989 (51st pick).

—COLLEGIATE RECORD—

Year	G.	Min.	FGA	FGM	Pct.	FTA	FTM	Pct.	Reb.	Pts.	Avg.
85-86	21	277	109	49	.450	22	13	.591	28	111	5.3
86-87	26	539	282	112	.397	75	50	.667	76	309	11.9
87-88	30	1039	522	239	.458	187	144	.770	110	666	22.2
88-89	28	878	456	226	.496	169	126	.746	151	611	21.8
Totals	105	2733	1369	626	.457	453	333	.735	365	1697	16.2

Three-Point Field Goals: 1986-87, 35-for-89 (.393). 1987-88, 44-for-136 (.324). 1988-89, 33-for-96 (.344). Totals, 112-for-321 (.349).

NBA REGULAR SEASON RECORD

									—Rebounds—									
Sea.—Team	G.	Min.	FGA	FGM	Pct.	FTA	FTM	Pct.	Off.	Def.	Tot.	Ast.	PF	Dq.	Stl.	Blk.	Pts.	Avg.
89-90—Phoenix	36	153	68	23	.338	30	24	.800	7	13	20	11	20	0	2	0	72	2.0

Three-Point Field Goals: 1989-90, 2-for-7 (.286).

JOHN MORTON JR.

Born May 18, 1967 at Bronx, N.Y. Height 6:03. Weight 180.
High School—Bronx, N.Y., Walton.
College—Seton Hall University, South Orange, N.J.
Drafted by Cleveland on first round, 1989 (25th pick).

—COLLEGIATE RECORD—

Year	G.	Min.	FGA	FGM	Pct.	FTA	FTM	Pct.	Reb.	Pts.	Avg.
85-86	31	611	186	82	.441	107	68	.636	47	232	7.5
86-87	27	734	199	90	.452	137	100	.730	70	282	10.4
87-88	35	1008	321	156	.486	157	132	.841	67	449	12.8
88-89	38	1082	482	210	.436	194	159	.820	129	658	17.3
Totals	131	3435	1188	538	.453	595	459	.771	313	1621	12.4

Three-Point Field Goals: 1986-87, 2-for-14 (.143). 1987-88, 5-for-17 (.294). 1988-89, 79-for-189 (.418). Totals, 86-for-220 (.391).

NBA REGULAR SEASON RECORD

									—Rebounds—									
Sea.—Team	G.	Min.	FGA	FGM	Pct.	FTA	FTM	Pct.	Off.	Def.	Tot.	Ast.	PF	Dq.	Stl.	Blk.	Pts.	Avg.
89-90—Cleveland	37	402	161	48	.298	62	43	.694	7	25	32	67	30	0	18	4	146	3.9

Three-Point Field Goals: 1989-90, 7-for-30 (.233).

NBA PLAYOFF RECORD

									—Rebounds—									
Sea.—Team	G.	Min.	FGA	FGM	Pct.	FTA	FTM	Pct.	Off.	Def.	Tot.	Ast.	PF	Dq.	Stl.	Blk.	Pts.	Avg.
89-90—Cleveland	2	9	5	2	.400	2	2	1.000	0	0	0	0	1	0	0	0	6	3.0

CHRISTOPHER PAUL MULLIN
(Chris)

Born July 30, 1963 at New York, N.Y. Height, 6:07. Weight 215.
High School—Brooklyn, N.Y., Xaverian.
College—St. John's University, Jamaica, N.Y.
Drafted by Golden State on first round, 1985 (7th pick).

—COLLEGIATE RECORD—

Year	G.	Min.	FGA	FGM	Pct.	FTA	FTM	Pct.	Reb.	Pts.	Avg.
81-82	30	1061	328	175	.534	187	148	.791	97	498	16.6
82-83	33	1210	395	228	.577	197	173	.878	123	629	19.1
83-84	27	1070	394	225	.571	187	169	.904	120	619	22.9
84-85	35	1327	482	251	.521	233	192	.824	169	694	19.8
Totals	125	4668	1599	879	.550	804	682	.848	509	2440	19.5

NBA REGULAR SEASON RECORD

Sea.—Team	G.	Min.	FGA	FGM	Pct.	FTA	FTM	Pct.	—Rebounds— Off.	Def.	Tot.	Ast.	PF	Dq.	Stl.	Blk.	Pts.	Avg.
85-86—Golden State	55	1391	620	287	.463	211	189	.896	42	73	115	105	130	1	70	23	768	14.0
86-87—Golden State	82	2377	928	477	.514	326	269	.825	39	142	181	261	217	1	98	36	1242	15.1
87-88—Golden State	60	2033	926	470	.508	270	239	.885	58	147	205	290	136	3	113	32	1213	20.2
88-89—Golden State	82	3093	1630	830	.509	553	493	.892	152	331	483	415	178	1	176	39	2176	26.5
89-90—Golden State	78	2830	1272	682	.536	568	505	.889	130	333	463	319	142	1	123	45	1956	25.1
Totals	357	11724	5376	2746	.511	1928	1695	.879	421	1026	1447	1390	803	7	580	175	7355	20.6

Three-Point Field Goals: 1985-86, 5-for-27 (.185). 1986-87, 19-for-63 (.302). 1987-88, 34-for-97 (.351). 1988-89, 23-for-100 (.230). 1989-90, 87-for-234 (.372). Totals, 168-for-521 (.322).

NBA PLAYOFF RECORD

Sea.—Team	G.	Min.	FGA	FGM	Pct.	FTA	FTM	Pct.	—Rebounds— Off.	Def.	Tot.	Ast.	PF	Dq.	Stl.	Blk.	Pts.	Avg.
86-87—Golden State	10	262	98	49	.500	16	12	.750	2	13	15	23	31	0	9	2	113	11.3
88-89—Golden State	8	341	163	88	.540	67	58	.866	11	36	47	36	19	0	14	11	235	29.4
Totals	18	603	261	137	.525	83	70	.843	13	49	62	59	50	0	23	13	348	19.3

Three-Point Field Goals: 1986-87, 3-for-4 (.750). 1988-89, 1-for-8 (.125). Totals, 4-for-12 (.333).

NBA ALL-STAR GAME RECORD

Season—Team	Min.	FGA	FGM	Pct.	FTA	FTM	Pct.	—Rebounds— Off.	Def.	Tot.	Ast.	PF	Dq.	Stl.	Blk.	Pts.
1989—Golden State	14	4	1	.250	2	2	1.000	2	0	2	2	0	0	0	0	4
1990—Golden State	16	5	1	.200	2	1	.500	1	2	3	1	0	0	2	1	3
Totals	30	9	2	.222	4	3	.750	3	2	5	3	0	0	2	1	7

Named to All-NBA Second Team, 1989. . . . All-NBA Third Team, 1990. . . . Member of U.S. Olympic team, 1984. . . . Named to THE SPORTING NEWS All-America First Team, 1985. . . . THE SPORTING NEWS All-America Second Team, 1984.

TOD JAMES MURPHY

Born December 24, 1963 at Long Beach, Calif. Height 6:09. Weight 220.

High School—Lakewood, Calif.

College—University of California at Irvine, Irvine, Calif.

Drafted by Seattle on third round, 1986 (53rd pick).

Draft rights relinquished by Seattle, September 17, 1987; signed by Los Angeles Clippers as a free agent, October 6, 1987.

Waived by Los Angeles Clippers, November 9, 1987; signed by Minnesota as a free agent, August 16, 1989.

Played in Continental Basketball Association with Albany Patroons, 1987-88.

—COLLEGIATE RECORD—

Year	G.	Min.	FGA	FGM	Pct.	FTA	FTM	Pct.	Reb.	Pts.	Avg.
82-83	28	704	172	89	.517	93	66	.710	150	244	8.7
83-84	29	872	268	154	.575	135	110	.815	203	418	14.4
84-85	30	1047	340	190	.559	153	130	.850	268	511	17.0
85-86	30	1116	378	211	.558	244	182	.746	216	605	20.2
Totals	117	3739	1158	644	.556	625	488	.781	837	1778	15.2

Three-Point Field Goals: 1984-85, 1-for-3 (.333). 1985-86, 1-for-1 (1.000). Totals, 2-for-4 (.500).

CBA REGULAR SEASON RECORD

Sea.—Team	G.	Min.	—2-Point— FGM	FGA	Pct.	—3-Point— FGM	FGA	Pct.	FTM	FTA	Pct.	Reb.	Ast.	Pts.	Avg.
87-88—Albany	32	751	104	175	.594	0	2	.000	98	120	.817	214	28	306	9.6

NBA REGULAR SEASON RECORD

Sea.—Team	G.	Min.	FGA	FGM	Pct.	FTA	FTM	Pct.	—Rebounds— Off.	Def.	Tot.	Ast.	PF	Dq.	Stl.	Blk.	Pts.	Avg.
87-88—L.A. Clippers	1	19	1	1	1.000	4	3	.750	1	1	2	2	2	0	1	0	5	5.0
89-90—Minnesota	82	2493	552	260	.471	203	144	.709	207	357	564	106	229	2	76	60	680	8.3
Totals	83	2512	553	261	.472	207	147	.710	208	358	566	108	231	2	77	60	685	8.3

Three-Point Field Goals: 1989-90, 16-for-43 (.372).

CBA Playoff MVP, 1988.

PETER E. MYERS
(Pete)

Born September 15, 1963 at Mobile, Ala. Height 6:06. Weight 180.

High School—Mobile, Ala., Williamson.

Colleges—Faulkner State Junior College, Bay Minette, Ala., and University of Arkansas at Little Rock, Little Rock, Ark.

Drafted by Chicago on sixth round, 1986 (120th pick).

Waived by Chicago, November 3, 1987; signed by San Antonio as a free agent, January 29, 1988.
Traded by San Antonio to Philadelphia for Albert King, August 24, 1988.
Waived by Philadelphia, December 15, 1988; signed by New York as a free agent, December 20, 1988.
Waived by New York, February 23, 1990; claimed off waivers by New Jersey, February 27, 1990.
Played in Continental Basketball Association with Rockford Lightning, 1987-88.

—COLLEGIATE RECORD—

Faulkner State

Year	G.	Min.	FGA	FGM	Pct.	FTA	FTM	Pct.	Reb.	Pts.	Avg.
81-82	26	....	199	109	.548	140	104	.743	132	322	12.4
82-83	26	....	249	144	.578	169	106	.627	196	394	15.2
J.C. Totals	52	....	448	253	.565	309	210	.680	328	716	13.8

Arkansas-Little Rock

Year	G.	Min.	FGA	FGM	Pct.	FTA	FTM	Pct.	Reb.	Pts.	Avg.
83-84						Did Not Play					
84-85	30	....	359	162	.451	167	120	.719	213	444	14.8
85-86	34	1142	429	229	.534	261	195	.747	270	653	19.2
Ark.-LR Totals	64	....	788	391	.496	428	315	.736	483	1097	17.1

CBA REGULAR SEASON RECORD

			—2-Point—			—3-Point—									
Sea.—Team	G.	Min.	FGM	FGA	Pct.	FGM	FGA	Pct.	FTM	FTA	Pct.	Reb.	Ast.	Pts.	Avg.
87-88—Rockford	28	1134	206	380	.542	10	26	.385	146	199	.734	103	147	588	21.0

NBA REGULAR SEASON RECORD

									—Rebounds—									
Sea.—Team	G.	Min.	FGA	FGM	Pct.	FTA	FTM	Pct.	Off.	Def.	Tot.	Ast.	PF	Dq.	Stl.	Blk.	Pts.	Avg.
86-87—Chicago	29	155	52	19	.365	43	28	.651	8	9	17	21	25	0	14	2	66	2.3
87-88—San Antonio	22	328	95	43	.453	39	26	.667	11	26	37	48	30	0	17	6	112	5.1
88-89—Phil.-N.Y.	33	270	73	31	.425	48	33	.688	15	18	33	48	44	0	20	2	95	2.9
89-90—N.Y.-N.J.	52	751	225	89	.396	100	66	.660	33	63	96	135	109	0	35	11	244	4.7
Totals	136	1504	445	182	.409	230	153	.665	67	116	183	252	208	0	86	21	517	3.8

Three-Point Field Goals: 1986-87, 0-for-6. 1987-88, 0-for-4. 1988-89, 0-for-2. 1989-90, 0-for-7. Totals, 0-for-19.

NBA PLAYOFF RECORD

									—Rebounds—									
Sea.—Team	G.	Min.	FGA	FGM	Pct.	FTA	FTM	Pct.	Off.	Def.	Tot.	Ast.	PF	Dq.	Stl.	Blk.	Pts.	Avg.
86-87—Chicago	1	1	1	0	.000	0	0	.000	0	0	0	0	0	0	0	0	0	0.0
88-89—New York	4	14	0	0	.000	6	4	.667	1	2	3	1	2	0	0	1	4	1.0
Totals	5	15	1	0	.000	6	4	.667	1	2	3	1	2	0	0	1	4	0.8

Named to CBA All-Star Second Team, 1988.

LARRY DONELL NANCE

Born February 12, 1959 at Anderson, S. C. Height 6:10. Weight 215.

High School—Anderson, S. C., McDuffie.

College—Clemson University, Clemson, S. C.

Drafted by Phoenix on first round, 1981 (20th pick).

Traded by Phoenix with Mike Sanders and a 1988 1st round draft choice to Cleveland for Tyrone Corbin, Kevin Johnson, Mark West, 1988 1st and 2nd round draft choices and a 1989 2nd round draft choice, February 25, 1988.

—COLLEGIATE RECORD—

Year	G.	Min.	FGA	FGM	Pct.	FTA	FTM	Pct.	Reb.	Pts.	Avg.
77-78	25	273	75	35	.467	17	8	.471	78	78	3.1
78-79	29	837	264	137	.519	77	49	.636	210	323	11.1
79-80	32	961	338	174	.515	164	98	.598	259	446	13.9
80-81	31	887	360	207	.575	116	80	.690	237	494	15.9
Totals	117	2958	1037	553	.533	374	235	.628	834	1341	11.5

NBA REGULAR SEASON RECORD

									—Rebounds—									
Sea.—Team	G.	Min.	FGA	FGM	Pct.	FTA	FTM	Pct.	Off.	Def.	Tot.	Ast.	PF	Dq.	Stl.	Blk.	Pts.	Avg.
81-82—Phoenix	80	1186	436	227	.521	117	75	.641	95	161	256	82	169	2	42	71	529	6.6
82-83—Phoenix	82	2914	1069	588	.550	287	193	.672	239	471	710	197	254	4	99	217	1370	16.7
83-84—Phoenix	82	2899	1044	601	.576	352	249	.707	227	451	678	214	274	5	86	174	1451	17.7
84-85—Phoenix	61	2202	877	515	.587	254	180	.709	195	341	536	159	185	2	88	104	1211	19.9
85-86—Phoenix	73	2484	1001	582	.581	444	310	.698	169	449	618	240	247	6	70	130	1474	20.2
86-87—Phoenix	69	2569	1062	585	.551	493	381	.773	188	411	599	233	223	4	86	148	1552	22.5
87-88—Phoe.-Clev.	67	2383	920	487	.529	390	304	.779	193	414	607	207	242	10	63	159	1280	19.1
88-89—Cleveland	73	2526	920	496	.539	334	267	.799	156	425	581	159	186	0	57	206	1259	17.2
89-90—Cleveland	62	2065	807	412	.511	239	186	.778	162	354	516	161	185	3	54	122	1011	16.3
Totals	649	21228	8136	4493	.552	2910	2145	.737	1624	3477	5101	1652	1965	36	645	1331	11137	17.2

Three-Point Field Goals: 1981-82, 0-for-1. 1982-83, 1-for-3 (.333). 1983-84, 0-for-7. 1984-85, 1-for-2 (.500). 1985-86, 0-for-8. 1986-87, 1-for-5 (.200). 1987-88, 2-for-6 (.333). 1988-89, 0-for-4. 1989-90, 1-for-1 (1.000). Totals, 6-for-37 (.162).

NBA PLAYOFF RECORD

Sea.—Team	G.	Min.	FGA	FGM	Pct.	FTA	FTM	Pct.	—Rebounds— Off.	Def.	Tot.	Ast.	PF	Dq.	Stl.	Blk.	Pts.	Avg.
81-82—Phoenix	7	128	41	25	.610	8	4	.500	13	19	32	7	15	1	10	11	54	7.7
82-83—Phoenix	3	103	35	14	.400	10	8	.800	10	15	25	3	12	1	3	6	36	12.0
83-84—Phoenix	17	633	200	118	.590	76	51	.671	51	97	148	40	59	1	16	34	287	16.9
87-88—Cleveland	5	200	64	34	.531	18	16	.889	10	26	36	18	13	0	2	11	84	16.8
88-89—Cleveland	5	195	69	38	.551	32	21	.656	16	23	39	16	12	0	3	12	97	19.4
89-90—Cleveland	5	159	45	26	.578	12	9	.750	4	20	24	12	20	0	3	10	61	12.2
Totals	42	1418	454	255	.562	156	109	.699	104	200	304	96	131	3	37	84	619	14.7

NBA ALL-STAR GAME RECORD

Season—Team	Min.	FGA	FGM	Pct.	FTA	FTM	Pct.	—Rebounds— Off.	Def.	Tot.	Ast.	PF	Dq.	Stl.	Blk.	Pts.
1985—Phoenix	15	8	7	.875	2	2	1.000	1	4	5	0	5	0	0	2	16
1989—Cleveland	17	9	5	.556	0	0	.000	3	3	6	1	1	0	1	1	10
Totals	32	17	12	.706	2	2	1.000	4	7	11	1	6	0	1	3	26

Named to NBA All-Defensive First Team, 1989.

CALVIN LEON NATT

Born January 8, 1957 at Monroe, La. Height 6:06. Weight 220.

High School—Bastrop, La.

College—Northeast Louisiana University, Monroe, La.

Drafted by New Jersey on first round, 1979 (8th pick).

Traded by New Jersey to Portland for Maurice Lucas and 1980 and 1981 1st round draft choices, February 8, 1980.

Traded by Portland with Lafayette Lever, Wayne Cooper, a 1984 2nd round draft choice and a 1985 1st round draft choice to Denver for Kiki Vandeweghe, June 7, 1984.

Traded by Denver with Jay Vincent to San Antonio for David Greenwood and Darwin Cook, January 26, 1989.

Waived by San Antonio, February 21, 1989; signed by Indiana as a free agent, October 9, 1989.

—COLLEGIATE RECORD—

Year	G.	Min.	FGA	FGM	Pct.	FTA	FTM	Pct.	Reb.	Pts.	Avg.
75-76	25	....	371	207	.558	129	102	.791	274	516	20.6
76-77	27	....	493	307	.623	226	168	.743	340	782	29.0
77-78	27	....	401	220	.549	186	136	.731	356	576	21.3
78-79	29	....	506	283	.559	178	141	.792	315	707	24.4
Totals	108	....	1771	1017	.574	719	547	.761	1285	2581	23.9

NBA REGULAR SEASON RECORD

Sea.—Team	G.	Min.	FGA	FGM	Pct.	FTA	FTM	Pct.	—Rebounds— Off.	Def.	Tot.	Ast.	PF	Dq.	Stl.	Blk.	Pts.	Avg.
79-80—N.J.-Port.	78	2857	1298	622	.479	419	306	.730	239	452	691	169	205	1	102	34	1553	19.9
80-81—Portland	74	2111	794	395	.497	283	200	.707	149	282	431	159	188	2	73	18	994	13.4
81-82—Portland	75	2599	894	515	.576	392	294	.750	193	420	613	150	175	1	62	36	1326	17.7
82-83—Portland	80	2879	1187	644	.543	428	339	.792	214	385	599	171	184	2	63	29	1630	20.4
83-84—Portland	79	2638	857	500	.583	345	275	.797	166	310	476	179	218	3	69	22	1277	16.2
84-85—Denver	78	2657	1255	685	.546	564	447	.793	209	401	610	238	182	1	75	33	1817	23.3
85-86—Denver	69	2007	930	469	.504	347	278	.801	125	311	436	164	143	0	58	13	1218	17.7
86-87—Denver	1	20	10	4	.400	2	2	1.000	2	3	5	2	2	0	1	0	10	10.0
87-88—Denver	27	533	208	102	.490	73	54	.740	35	61	96	47	43	0	13	3	258	9.6
88-89—Den.-S.A.	24	353	116	47	.405	79	57	.722	28	50	78	18	32	0	8	3	151	6.3
89-90—Indiana	14	164	31	20	.645	22	17	.773	10	25	35	9	14	0	1	0	57	4.1
Totals	599	18818	7580	4003	.528	2954	2269	.768	1370	2700	4070	1306	1386	10	525	191	10291	17.2

Three-Point Field Goals: 1979-80, 3-for-9 (.333). 1980-81, 4-for-8 (.500). 1981-82, 2-for-8 (.250). 1982-83, 3-for-20 (.150). 1983-84, 2-for-17 (.118). 1984-85, 0-for-3. 1985-86, 2-for-6 (.333). 1987-88, 0-for-1. 1988-89, 0-for-1. Totals, 16-for-73 (.219).

NBA PLAYOFF RECORD

Sea.—Team	G.	Min.	FGA	FGM	Pct.	FTA	FTM	Pct.	—Rebounds— Off.	Def.	Tot.	Ast.	PF	Dq.	Stl.	Blk.	Pts.	Avg.
79-80—Portland	3	125	48	21	.438	10	6	.600	9	15	24	2	7	0	2	1	48	16.0
80-81—Portland	3	95	31	14	.452	8	4	.500	6	14	20	1	4	0	1	1	32	10.7
82-83—Portland	7	274	102	50	.490	48	31	.646	22	42	64	11	14	0	8	1	132	18.9
83-84—Portland	5	195	72	37	.514	36	25	.694	11	27	38	9	10	0	6	1	99	19.8
84-85—Denver	15	508	238	131	.550	89	72	.809	31	68	99	57	35	0	8	5	334	22.3
85-86—Denver	10	293	142	66	.465	59	46	.780	17	62	79	28	25	0	2	3	179	17.9
89-90—Indiana	2	14	3	1	.333	0	0	......	1	1	2	1	5	0	0	0	2	1.0
Totals	45	1504	636	320	.503	250	184	.736	97	229	326	109	100	0	27	12	826	18.4

Three-Point Field Goals: 1979-80, 0-for-2. 1982-83, 1-for-2 (.500). 1983-84, 0-for-3. 1985-86, 1-for-2 (.500). Totals, 2-for-9 (.222).

NBA ALL-STAR GAME RECORD

Season—Team	Min.	FGA	FGM	Pct.	FTA	FTM	Pct.	—Rebounds— Off.	Def.	Tot.	Ast.	PF	Dq.	Stl.	Blk.	Pts.
1985—Denver	11	3	1	.333	2	1	.500	0	3	3	1	1	0	0	0	3

Named to NBA All-Rookie Team, 1980.... THE SPORTING NEWS All-America Second Team, 1979.

EDDIE CARL NEALY
(Ed)

Born February 19, 1960 at Pittsburg, Kan. Height 6:07. Weight 240.
High School—Bonner Springs, Kan.
College—Kansas State University, Manhattan, Kan.
Drafted by Kansas City on eighth round, 1982 (166th pick).

Waived by Kansas City, July 10, 1984; re-signed by Kansas City as a free agent, July 20, 1984.
Waived by Kansas City, October 24, 1984; re-signed by Kansas City as a free agent, February 27, 1985.
Waived by Kansas City, October 21, 1985; signed by San Antonio as a free agent, July 15, 1986.
Became free agent, July 1, 1988; signed by Chicago as a free agent, September 27, 1988.
Traded by Chicago with a 1989 2nd round draft choice to Phoenix for Craig Hodges, December 14, 1988.
Traded by Phoenix to Chicago for a 1996 2nd round draft choice, October 5, 1989.
Signed by Phoenix as a Veteran Free Agent, July 23, 1990.
Played in Continental Basketball Association with Sarasota Stingers, 1984-85, and Tampa Bay Thrillers, 1985-86.

—COLLEGIATE RECORD—

Year	G.	Min.	FGA	FGM	Pct.	FTA	FTM	Pct.	Reb.	Pts.	Avg.
78-79	28	....	266	115	.432	71	56	.789	230	286	10.2
79-80	31	....	242	114	.471	105	76	.724	272	304	9.8
80-81	33	....	289	152	.526	82	59	.720	301	363	11.0
81-82	31	....	243	138	.568	122	75	.615	268	351	11.3
Totals	123	....	1040	519	.499	380	266	.700	1071	1304	10.6

CBA REGULAR SEASON RECORD

			—2-Point—			—3-Point—									
Sea.—Team	G.	Min.	FGM	FGA	Pct.	FGM	FGA	Pct.	FTM	FTA	Pct.	Reb.	Ast.	Pts.	Avg.
84-85—Sarasota	39	1350	156	267	.584	1	2	.500	113	142	.795	371	53	428	11.0
85-86—Tampa Bay	29	926	91	169	.538	0	1	.000	59	79	.746	309	34	241	8.3
Totals	68	2276	247	436	.566	1	3	.333	172	221	.778	680	87	669	9.8

NBA REGULAR SEASON RECORD

									—Rebounds—									
Sea.—Team	G.	Min.	FGA	FGM	Pct.	FTA	FTM	Pct.	Off.	Def.	Tot.	Ast.	PF	Dq.	Stl.	Blk.	Pts.	Avg.
82-83—Kansas City	82	1643	247	147	.595	114	70	.614	170	315	485	62	247	4	68	12	364	4.4
83-84—Kansas City	71	960	126	63	.500	60	48	.800	73	149	222	50	138	1	41	9	174	2.5
84-85—Kansas City	22	225	44	26	.591	19	10	.526	15	29	44	18	26	0	3	1	62	2.8
86-87—San Antonio	60	980	192	84	.438	69	51	.739	96	188	284	83	144	1	40	11	223	3.7
87-88—San Antonio	68	837	109	50	.459	63	41	.651	82	140	222	49	94	0	29	5	142	2.1
88-89—Chi.-Phoe.	43	258	36	13	.361	9	4	.444	22	56	78	14	45	0	7	1	30	0.7
89-90—Chicago	46	503	70	37	.529	41	30	.732	46	92	138	28	67	0	16	4	104	2.3
Totals	392	5406	824	420	.510	375	254	.677	504	969	1473	304	761	6	204	43	1099	2.8

Three-Point Field Goals: 1986-87, 4-for-31 (.129). 1987-88, 1-for-2 (.500). 1988-89, 0-for-2. 1989-90, 0-for-2. Totals, 5-for-37 (.135).

NBA PLAYOFF RECORD

									—Rebounds—									
Sea.—Team	G.	Min.	FGA	FGM	Pct.	FTA	FTM	Pct.	Off.	Def.	Tot.	Ast.	PF	Dq.	Stl.	Blk.	Pts.	Avg.
83-84—Kansas City	2	19	2	2	1.000	2	2	1.000	2	4	6	2	1	0	0	0	6	3.0
87-88—San Antonio	2	36	4	2	.500	0	0	.000	3	4	7	4	6	0	1	0	4	2.0
88-89—Phoenix	4	6	3	1	.333	0	0	.000	1	2	3	0	0	0	0	0	2	0.5
89-90—Chicago	15	228	36	17	.472	21	13	.619	16	36	52	5	45	1	10	1	47	3.1
Totals	23	289	45	22	.489	23	15	.652	22	46	68	11	52	1	11	1	59	2.6

Three-Point Field Goals: 1989-90, 0-for-1.

CHARLES GOODRICH NEVITT
(Chuck)

Born June 13, 1959 at Cortez, Colo. Height 7:05. Weight 237.
High School—Marietta, Ga., Sprayberry.
College—North Carolina State University, Raleigh, N. C.
Drafted by Houston on third round, 1982 (63rd pick).

Waived by Houston and claimed by Milwaukee on waivers, October 22, 1982.
Waived by Milwaukee, October 28, 1982; signed by Houston as a free agent, June 1, 1983.
Waived by Houston, November 29, 1983; signed by Los Angeles Lakers as a free agent, September 15, 1984.
Waived by Los Angeles Lakers, November 6, 1984; re-signed by Los Angeles Lakers, March 5, 1985, to the first of consecutive 10-day contracts that expired, March 24, 1985.
Re-signed by Los Angeles Lakers, March 25, 1985.
Waived by Los Angeles Lakers, November 22, 1985; signed by Detroit as a free agent, November 29, 1985.
Rights relinquished by Detroit, July 25, 1988; signed by San Antonio as a free agent, September 27, 1988.
Waived by San Antonio, October 24, 1988; signed by Houston as a free agent, October 26, 1988.
Waived by Houston, January 11, 1990.
Played in Continental Basketball Association with Rapid City Thrillers, 1989-90.

—COLLEGIATE RECORD—

Year	G.	Min.	FGA	FGM	Pct.	FTA	FTM	Pct.	Reb.	Pts.	Avg.
77-78					Did Not Play—Injured						
78-79	19	....	20	10	.500	15	4	.267	25	24	1.3
79-80	19	....	23	14	.609	10	2	.200	34	30	1.6
80-81	21	....	26	15	.577	23	10	.435	24	40	1.9
81-82	31	....	119	70	.588	57	32	.561	137	172	5.5
Totals	90	....	188	109	.580	105	48	.457	220	266	3.0

CBA REGULAR SEASON RECORD

			—2-Point—			—3-Point—									
Sea.—Team	G.	Min.	FGM	FGA	Pct.	FGM	FGA	Pct.	FTM	FTA	Pct.	Reb.	Ast.	Pts.	Avg.
89-90—Rapid City	6	125	14	29	.483	0	0	....	9	10	.900	46	6	37	6.2

NBA REGULAR SEASON RECORD

									—Rebounds—									
Sea.—Team	G.	Min.	FGA	FGM	Pct.	FTA	FTM	Pct.	Off.	Def.	Tot.	Ast.	PF	Dq.	Stl.	Blk.	Pts.	Avg.
82-83—Houston	6	64	15	11	.733	4	1	.250	6	11	17	0	14	0	1	12	23	3.8
84-85—L.A. Lakers	11	59	17	5	.294	8	2	.250	5	15	20	3	20	0	0	15	12	1.1
85-86—L.A.L.-Det.	29	126	43	15	.349	26	19	.731	13	19	32	7	35	0	4	19	49	1.7
86-87—Detroit	41	267	63	31	.492	24	14	.583	36	47	83	4	73	0	7	30	76	1.9
87-88—Detroit	17	63	21	7	.333	6	3	.500	4	14	18	0	12	0	1	5	17	1.0
88-89—Houston	43	228	62	27	.435	16	11	.688	17	47	64	3	51	1	5	29	65	1.5
89-90—Houston	3	9	2	2	1.000	0	0	......	0	3	3	1	3	0	0	1	4	1.3
Totals	150	816	223	98	.439	84	50	.595	81	156	237	18	208	1	18	111	246	1.6

NBA PLAYOFF RECORD

									—Rebounds—									
Sea.—Team	G.	Min.	FGA	FGM	Pct.	FTA	FTM	Pct.	Off.	Def.	Tot.	Ast.	PF	Dq.	Stl.	Blk.	Pts.	Avg.
84-85—L.A. Lakers	7	37	9	3	.333	8	4	.500	3	3	6	1	11	0	4	6	10	1.4
85-86—Detroit	1	1	0	0	.000	0	0	.000	0	0	0	0	0	0	0	0	0	0.0
86-87—Detroit	3	10	5	1	.200	2	2	1.000	1	5	6	0	1	0	0	3	4	1.3
87-88—Detroit	3	4	2	1	.500	0	0	.000	2	1	3	0	1	0	0	0	2	0.7
88-89—Houston	2	3	0	0	.000	0	0	.000	0	1	1	0	0	0	0	0	0	0.0
Totals	16	55	16	5	.313	10	6	.600	6	10	16	1	13	0	4	9	16	1.0

Member of NBA championship team, 1985.

JOHN SYLVESTER NEWMAN JR.

Born November 28, 1963 at Danville, Va. Height 6:07. Weight 190.
High School—Danville, Va., George Washington.
College—University of Richmond, Richmond, Va.
Drafted by Cleveland on second round, 1986 (29th pick).

Waived by Cleveland, November 5, 1987; signed by New York as a free agent, November 12, 1987.
Signed by Charlotte as a free agent, July 28, 1990.

—COLLEGIATE RECORD—

Year	G.	Min.	FGA	FGM	Pct.	FTA	FTM	Pct.	Reb.	Pts.	Avg.
82-83	28	763	259	137	.528	96	69	.718	87	343	12.3
83-84	32	1189	517	273	.528	197	155	.786	196	701	21.9
84-85	32	1128	490	270	.551	181	140	.773	166	680	21.3
85-86	30	1123	489	253	.517	172	153	.895	219	659	22.0
Totals	122	4203	1755	933	.532	646	517	.800	668	2383	19.5

NBA REGULAR SEASON RECORD

									—Rebounds—									
Sea.—Team	G.	Min.	FGA	FGM	Pct.	FTA	FTM	Pct.	Off.	Def.	Tot.	Ast.	PF	Dq.	Stl.	Blk.	Pts.	Avg.
86-87—Cleveland	59	630	275	113	.411	76	66	.868	36	34	70	27	67	0	20	7	293	5.0
87-88—New York	77	1589	620	270	.435	246	207	.841	87	72	159	62	204	5	72	11	773	10.0
88-89—New York	81	2336	957	455	.475	351	286	.815	93	113	206	162	259	4	111	23	1293	16.0
89-90—New York	80	2277	786	374	.476	299	239	.799	60	131	191	180	254	3	95	22	1032	12.9
Totals	297	6832	2638	1212	.459	972	798	.821	276	350	626	431	784	12	298	63	3391	11.4

Three-Point Field Goals: 1986-87, 1-for-22 (.045). 1987-88, 26-for-93 (.280). 1988-89, 97-for-287 (.338). 1989-90, 45-for-142 (.317). Totals, 169-for-544 (.311).

NBA PLAYOFF RECORD

									—Rebounds—									
Sea.—Team	G.	Min.	FGA	FGM	Pct.	FTA	FTM	Pct.	Off.	Def.	Tot.	Ast.	PF	Dq.	Stl.	Blk.	Pts.	Avg.
87-88—New York	4	113	68	31	.456	16	14	.875	8	3	11	7	16	0	6	1	76	19.0
88-89—New York	9	258	107	50	.467	49	38	.776	13	12	25	17	27	1	8	1	145	16.1
89-90—New York	10	231	85	38	.447	49	37	.755	11	10	21	10	41	1	9	3	117	11.7
Totals	23	602	260	119	.458	114	89	.781	32	25	57	34	84	2	23	5	338	14.7

Three-Point Field Goals: 1987-88, 0-for-9. 1988-89, 7-for-28 (.250). 1989-90, 4-for-10 (.400). Totals, 11-for-47 (.234).

KURT ALLEN NIMPHIUS

Born March 13, 1958 at Milwaukee, Wis. Height 6:11. Weight 225.
High School—South Milwaukee, Wis.
College—Arizona State University, Tempe, Ariz.
Drafted by Denver on third round, 1980 (47th pick).

Waived by Denver and signed same day by Dallas as a free agent, September 2, 1981.
Traded by Dallas to Los Angeles Clippers for James Donaldson, November 25, 1985.
Traded by Los Angeles Clippers to Detroit for 1987 1st and 2nd round draft choices, January 29, 1987.
Signed by San Antonio as a Veteran Free Agent, October 27, 1987; Detroit agreed not to exercise its right of first refusal in exchange for a 1988 2nd round draft choice.
Signed by Philadelphia as an unrestricted free agent, October 23, 1989.
Played in Continental Basketball Association with Alberta Dusters, 1980-81.
Played in Italy, 1980-81.

—COLLEGIATE RECORD—

Year	G.	Min.	FGA	FGM	Pct.	FTA	FTM	Pct.	Reb.	Pts.	Avg.
76-77†	3	....	....	28	....	14	10	.714	44	66	22.0
76-77	18	76	19	10	.526	12	7	.583	28	27	1.5
77-78	27	670	176	98	.557	53	34	.642	166	230	8.5
78-79	30	576	180	105	.583	90	59	.656	150	269	9.0
79-80	29	977	304	185	.609	155	110	.710	277	480	16.6
Varsity Totals	104	2299	679	398	.586	310	210	.677	621	1006	9.7

ITALIAN LEAGUE RECORD

Year	G.	Min.	FGA	FGM	Pct.	FTA	FTM	Pct.	Reb.	Pts.	Avg.
80-81—Rodrigo	10	367	158	83	.525	29	21	.724	105	187	18.7

CBA REGULAR SEASON RECORD

			—2-Point—			—3-Point—									
Sea.—Team	G.	Min.	FGM	FGA	Pct.	FGM	FGA	Pct.	FTM	FTA	Pct.	Reb.	Ast.	Pts.	Avg.
80-81—Alberta	18	498	92	181	.508	0	1	.000	53	67	.791	156	20	237	13.2

NBA REGULAR SEASON RECORD

									—Rebounds—										
Sea.—Team	G.	Min.	FGA	FGM	Pct.	FTA	FTM	Pct.	Off.	Def.	Tot.	Ast.	PF	Dq.	Stl.	Blk.	Pts.	Avg.
81-82—Dallas	63	1085	297	137	.461	108	63	.583	92	203	295	61	190	5	17	82	337	5.3
82-83—Dallas	81	1515	355	174	.490	140	77	.550	157	247	404	115	287	11	24	111	426	5.3
83-84—Dallas	82	2284	523	272	.520	162	101	.623	182	331	513	176	283	5	41	144	646	7.9
84-85—Dallas	82	2010	434	196	.452	140	108	.771	136	272	408	183	262	4	30	126	500	6.1
85-86—Dal.-L.A.C.	80	2226	694	351	.506	262	194	.740	152	301	453	62	267	8	33	105	896	11.2
86-87—L.A.C.-Det.	66	1088	330	155	.470	120	81	.675	80	107	187	25	156	1	20	54	391	5.9
87-88—San Antonio	72	919	257	128	.498	83	60	.723	62	91	153	53	141	2	22	56	316	4.4
89-90—Philadelphia	38	314	91	38	.418	30	14	.467	22	39	61	6	45	0	4	18	90	2.4
Totals	564	11441	2981	1451	.487	1045	698	.668	883	1591	2474	681	1631	36	191	696	3602	6.4

Three-Point Field Goals: 1982-83, 1-for-1 (1.000). 1983-84, 1-for-4 (.250). 1984-85, 0-for-6. 1985-86, 0-for-3. 1986-87, 0-for-4. 1987-88, 0-for-1. 1989-90, 0-for-1. Totals, 2-for-20 (.100).

NBA PLAYOFF RECORD

									—Rebounds—										
Sea.—Team	G.	Min.	FGA	FGM	Pct.	FTA	FTM	Pct.	Off.	Def.	Tot.	Ast.	PF	Dq.	Stl.	Blk.	Pts.	Avg.
83-84—Dallas	10	178	33	14	.424	17	14	.824	20	33	53	13	24	0	0	14	42	4.2
84-85—Dallas	4	50	6	3	.500	0	0	.000	3	3	6	3	10	0	1	1	6	1.5
86-87—Detroit	4	30	9	3	.333	4	2	.500	5	5	10	0	10	0	0	2	8	2.0
87-88—San Antonio	3	30	10	5	.500	2	2	1.000	3	5	8	2	7	0	0	1	12	4.0
89-90—Philadelphia	4	18	7	1	.143	0	0	....	3	1	4	0	1	0	1	1	2	0.5
Totals	25	306	65	26	.400	23	18	.783	34	47	81	18	52	0	2	19	70	2.8

DYRON PATRICK NIX

Born February 11, 1967 at Meridian, Miss. Height 6:07. Weight 210.
High School—Fort Walton Beach, Fla.
College—University of Tennessee, Knoxville, Tenn.
Drafted by Charlotte on second round, 1989 (29th pick).

Draft rights traded by Charlotte to Indiana for Stuart Gray, June 27, 1989.

—COLLEGIATE RECORD—

Year	G.	Min.	FGA	FGM	Pct.	FTA	FTM	Pct.	Reb.	Pts.	Avg.
85-86	25	585	150	71	.473	51	34	.667	108	176	7.0
86-87	29	1039	283	153	.541	161	102	.634	294	408	14.1
87-88	29	1039	460	235	.511	227	173	.762	261	644	22.2
88-89	30	1078	492	254	.516	144	103	.715	281	649	21.6
Totals	113	3741	1385	713	.515	583	412	.707	944	1877	16.6

Three-Point Field Goals: 1986-87, 0-for-2. 1987-88, 1-for-7 (.143). 1988-89, 38-for-103 (.369). Totals, 39-for-112 (.348).

NBA REGULAR SEASON RECORD

Sea.—Team	G.	Min.	FGA	FGM	Pct.	FTA	FTM	Pct.	Off.	Def.	Tot.	Ast.	PF	Dq.	Stl.	Blk.	Pts.	Avg.
									—Rebounds—									
89-90—Indiana	20	109	39	14	.359	16	11	.688	8	18	26	5	15	0	3	1	39	2.0

KENNETH DARNEL NORMAN
(Snake)

(Known as Ken Colliers in high school.)

Born September 5, 1964 at Chicago, Ill. Height 6:08. Weight 215.

High School—Chicago, Ill., Crane.

Colleges—Wabash Valley College, Mt. Carmel, Ill., and University of Illinois, Champaign, Ill.

Drafted by Los Angeles Clippers on first round, 1987 (19th pick).

—COLLEGIATE RECORD—

Wabash Valley

Year	G.	Min.	FGA	FGM	Pct.	FTA	FTM	Pct.	Reb.	Pts.	Avg.
82-83	35	....	499	302	.605	165	111	.673	362	715	20.4

Illinois

Year	G.	Min.	FGA	FGM	Pct.	FTA	FTM	Pct.	Reb.	Pts.	Avg.
83-84					Did Not Play—Redshirted						
84-85	29	462	136	86	.632	83	55	.663	107	227	7.8
85-86	32	1015	337	216	.641	116	93	.802	226	525	16.4
86-87	31	1112	443	256	.578	176	128	.727	303	641	20.7
Ill. Totals	92	2589	916	558	.609	375	276	.736	636	1393	15.1

Three-Point Field Goals: 1986-87, 1-for-4 (.250).

NBA REGULAR SEASON RECORD

Sea.—Team	G.	Min.	FGA	FGM	Pct.	FTA	FTM	Pct.	Off.	Def.	Tot.	Ast.	PF	Dq.	Stl.	Blk.	Pts.	Avg.
									—Rebounds—									
87-88—L.A. Clippers	66	1435	500	241	.482	170	87	.512	100	163	263	78	123	0	44	34	569	8.6
88-89—L.A. Clippers	80	3020	1271	638	.502	270	170	.630	245	422	667	277	223	2	106	66	1450	18.1
89-90—L.A. Clippers	70	2334	949	484	.510	242	153	.632	143	327	470	160	196	0	78	59	1128	16.1
Totals	216	6789	2720	1363	.501	682	410	.601	488	912	1400	515	542	2	228	159	3147	14.6

Three-Point Field Goals: 1987-88, 0-for-10. 1988-89, 4-for-21 (.190). 1989-90, 7-for-16 (.438). Totals, 11-for-47 (.234).

Named to THE SPORTING NEWS All-America Second Team, 1987. . . . Half-brother of former NFL wide receiver Bobby Duckworth.

CHARLES OAKLEY

Born December 18, 1963 at Cleveland, O. Height 6:09. Weight 245.

High School—Cleveland, O., John Hay.

College—Virginia Union University, Richmond, Va.

Drafted by Cleveland on first round, 1985 (9th pick).

Draft rights traded by Cleveland with draft rights to Calvin Duncan to Chicago for Ennis Whatley and draft rights to Keith Lee, June 18, 1985.

Traded by Chicago with 1988 1st and 3rd round draft choices to New York for Bill Cartwright and 1988 1st and 3rd round draft choices, June 27, 1988.

—COLLEGIATE RECORD—

Year	G.	Min.	FGA	FGM	Pct.	FTA	FTM	Pct.	Reb.	Pts.	Avg.
81-82	28	....	....	....	.620	....	....	.610	349	444	15.9
82-83	28	....	378	220	.582	170	100	.588	365	540	19.3
83-84	30	....	418	256	.612	224	139	.621	393	651	21.7
84-85	31	....	453	283	.625	266	178	.669	535	744	24.0

NBA REGULAR SEASON RECORD

Sea.—Team	G.	Min.	FGA	FGM	Pct.	FTA	FTM	Pct.	Off.	Def.	Tot.	Ast.	PF	Dq.	Stl.	Blk.	Pts.	Avg.
									—Rebounds—									
85-86—Chicago	77	1772	541	281	.519	269	178	.662	255	409	664	133	250	9	68	30	740	9.6
86-87—Chicago	82	2980	1052	468	.445	357	245	.686	299	775	1074	296	315	4	85	36	1192	14.5
87-88—Chicago	82	2816	776	375	.483	359	261	.727	326	740	1066	248	272	2	68	28	1014	12.4
88-89—New York	82	2604	835	426	.510	255	197	.773	343	518	861	187	270	1	104	14	1061	12.9
89-90—New York	61	2196	641	336	.524	285	217	.761	258	469	727	146	220	3	64	16	889	14.6
Totals	384	12368	3845	1886	.491	1525	1098	.720	1481	2911	4392	1010	1327	19	389	124	4896	12.8

Three-Point Field Goals: 1985-86, 0-for-3. 1986-87, 11-for-30 (.367). 1987-88, 3-for-12 (.250). 1988-89, 12-for-48 (.250). 1989-90, 0-for-3. Totals, 26-for-96 (.271).

NBA PLAYOFF RECORD

										—Rebounds—								
Sea.—Team	G.	Min.	FGA	FGM	Pct.	FTA	FTM	Pct.	Off.	Def.	Tot.	Ast.	PF	Dq.	Stl.	Blk.	Pts.	Avg.
85-86—Chicago	3	88	21	11	.524	13	8	.615	10	20	30	3	13	0	6	2	30	10.0
86-87—Chicago	3	129	50	19	.380	24	20	.833	17	29	46	6	13	0	4	1	60	20.0
87-88—Chicago	10	373	91	40	.440	24	21	.875	39	89	128	32	33	0	6	4	101	10.1
88-89—New York	9	299	73	35	.479	24	16	.667	43	58	101	11	31	1	12	1	87	9.7
89-90—New York	10	336	84	43	.512	52	34	.654	39	71	110	27	33	1	11	2	121	12.1
Totals	35	1225	319	148	.464	137	99	.723	148	267	415	79	123	2	39	10	399	11.4

Three-Point Field Goals: 1986-87, 2-for-4 (.500). 1987-88, 0-for-2. 1988-89, 1-for-2 (.500). 1989-90, 1-for-1 (1.000). Totals, 4-for-9 (.444).

Named to NBA All-Rookie Team, 1986. . . . Led NCAA Division II in rebounding, 1985.

AKEEM ABDUL OLAJUWON

Born January 21, 1963 at Lagos, Nigeria. Height 6:10. Weight 250.

High School—Lagos, Nigeria, Moslem Teachers College.

College—University of Houston, Houston, Tex.

Drafted by Houston on first round as an undergraduate, 1984 (1st pick).

—COLLEGIATE RECORD—

Year	G.	Min.	FGA	FGM	Pct.	FTA	FTM	Pct.	Reb.	Pts.	Avg.
80-81					Did Not Play						
81-82	29	529	150	91	.607	103	58	.563	179	240	8.3
82-83	34	932	314	192	.612	148	88	.595	388	472	13.9
83-84	37	1260	369	249	.675	232	122	.526	500	620	16.8
Totals	100	2721	833	532	.639	483	168	.555	1067	1332	13.3

NBA REGULAR SEASON RECORD

										—Rebounds—								
Sea.—Team	G.	Min.	FGA	FGM	Pct.	FTA	FTM	Pct.	Off.	Def.	Tot.	Ast.	PF	Dq.	Stl.	Blk.	Pts.	Avg.
84-85—Houston	82	2914	1258	677	.538	551	338	.613	440	534	974	111	344	10	99	220	1692	20.6
85-86—Houston	68	2467	1188	625	.526	538	347	.645	333	448	781	137	271	9	134	231	1597	23.5
86-87—Houston	75	2760	1332	677	.508	570	400	.702	315	543	858	220	294	8	140	254	1755	23.4
87-88—Houston	79	2825	1385	712	.514	548	381	.695	302	657	959	163	324	7	162	214	1805	22.8
88-89—Houston	82	3024	1556	790	.508	652	454	.696	338	767	1105	149	329	10	213	282	2034	24.8
89-90—Houston	82	3124	1609	806	.501	536	382	.713	299	850	1149	234	314	6	174	376	1995	24.3
Totals	468	17114	8328	4287	.515	3395	2302	.678	2027	3799	5826	1014	1876	50	922	1577	10878	23.2

Three-Point Field Goals: 1986-87, 1-for-5 (.200). 1987-88, 0-for-4. 1988-89, 0-for-10. 1989-90, 1-for-6 (.167). Totals, 2-for-25 (.080).

NBA PLAYOFF RECORD

										—Rebounds—								
Sea.—Team	G.	Min.	FGA	FGM	Pct.	FTA	FTM	Pct.	Off.	Def.	Tot.	Ast.	PF	Dq.	Stl.	Blk.	Pts.	Avg.
84-85—Houston	5	187	88	42	.477	46	22	.478	33	32	65	7	22	0	7	13	106	21.2
85-86—Houston	20	766	387	205	.530	199	127	.638	101	135	236	39	87	3	40	69	537	26.9
86-87—Houston	10	389	179	110	.615	97	72	.742	39	74	113	25	44	1	13	43	292	29.2
87-88—Houston	4	162	98	56	.571	43	38	.884	20	47	67	7	14	0	9	11	150	37.5
88-89—Houston	4	162	81	42	.519	25	17	.680	14	38	52	12	17	0	10	11	101	25.3
89-90—Houston	4	161	70	31	.443	17	12	.706	15	31	46	8	19	0	10	23	74	18.5
Totals	47	1827	903	486	.538	427	288	.674	222	357	579	98	203	4	89	170	1260	26.8

Three-Point Field Goals: 1985-86, 0-for-1. 1986-87, 0-for-1. 1987-88, 0-for-1. Totals, 0-for-3.

NBA ALL-STAR GAME RECORD

								—Rebounds—							
Season—Team	Min.	FGA	FGM	Pct.	FTA	FTM	Pct.	Off.	Def.	Tot.	Ast.	PF	Dq.	Stl.	Blk.	Pts.
1985—Houston	15	2	2	1.000	6	2	.333	2	3	5	1	1	0	0	2	6
1986—Houston	15	8	1	.125	2	1	.500	1	4	5	0	3	0	1	2	3
1987—Houston	26	6	2	.333	8	6	.750	4	9	13	2	6	1	0	3	10
1988—Houston	28	13	8	.615	7	5	.714	7	2	9	2	3	0	2	2	21
1989—Houston	25	12	5	.417	3	2	.667	4	3	7	3	2	0	3	2	12
1990—Houston	31	14	2	.143	10	4	.400	9	7	16	2	1	0	1	1	8
Totals	140	55	20	.364	36	20	.556	27	28	55	10	16	1	7	12	60

Named to All-NBA First Team, 1987, 1988, 1989. . . . All-NBA Second Team, 1986 and 1990. . . . NBA All-Rookie Team, 1985. . . . NBA All-Defensive First Team, 1987, 1988, 1990. . . . NBA All-Defensive Second Team, 1985. . . . Led NBA in rebounding, 1989 and 1990. . . . Led NBA in blocked shots, 1990. . . . NCAA Division I Tournament Most Outstanding Player, 1983. . . . THE SPORTING NEWS All-America First Team, 1984. . . . Led NCAA Division I in field-goal percentage, rebounding and blocked shots, 1984.

—DID YOU KNOW—

That Steve Alford's father, Sam, was former NBA guard Jerry Sichting's high school coach in Martinsville, Ind.?

JAWANN OLDHAM

Born July 4, 1957 at Chicago, Ill. Height 7:00. Weight 215.
High School—Seattle, Wash., Cleveland.
College—Seattle University, Seattle, Wash.
Drafted by Denver on second round, 1980 (41st pick).

Waived by Denver, October 21, 1980; signed by Houston as a free agent, August 28, 1981.
Waived by Houston, October 26, 1982; signed by Chicago as a free agent, February 16, 1983.
Traded by Chicago to New York for a 1987 1st round draft choice and a future 2nd round draft choice, October 30, 1986.
Traded by New York to Sacramento for a 1988 2nd round draft choice, October 15, 1987.
Waived by Sacramento, November 2, 1989; signed by Orlando, February 23, 1990, to a 10-day contract that expired, March 4, 1990.
Signed by Los Angeles Lakers, March 5, 1990, to the first of consecutive 10-day contracts that expired, March 24, 1990.
Missed entire 1988-89 season due to injury.
Played in Continental Basketball Association with Montana Golden Nuggets, 1980-81, and Santa Barbara Islanders, 1989-90.

—COLLEGIATE RECORD—

Year	G.	Min.	FGA	FGM	Pct.	FTA	FTM	Pct.	Reb.	Pts.	Avg.
76-77	27	....	300	145	.483	51	31	.608	212	321	11.9
77-78	25	....	282	140	.496	74	32	.432	205	312	12.5
78-79	24	....	367	194	.529	73	42	.575	262	430	17.9
79-80	27	....	333	188	.565	143	81	.566	282	457	16.9
Totals	103	....	1282	667	.520	341	186	.545	961	1520	14.8

CBA REGULAR SEASON RECORD

			2-Point			3-Point									
Sea.—Team	G.	Min.	FGM	FGA	Pct.	FGM	FGA	Pct.	FTM	FTA	Pct.	Reb.	Ast.	Pts.	Avg.
80-81—Montana	7	172	36	83	.433	0	0	.000	7	15	.466	57	3	79	11.3
89-90—Santa Barbara	16	356	34	74	.459	0	0	.000	18	37	.486	108	11	86	5.4
Totals	23	528	70	157	.446	0	0	.000	25	52	.481	165	14	165	7.2

NBA REGULAR SEASON RECORD

									—Rebounds—									
Sea.—Team	G.	Min.	FGA	FGM	Pct.	FTA	FTM	Pct.	Off.	Def.	Tot.	Ast.	PF	Dq.	Stl.	Blk.	Pts.	Avg.
80-81—Denver	4	21	6	2	.333	0	0	.000	3	2	5	0	3	0	0	2	4	1.0
81-82—Houston	22	124	36	13	.361	14	8	.571	7	17	24	3	8	0	2	10	34	1.5
82-83—Chicago	16	171	58	31	.534	22	12	.545	18	29	47	5	30	1	5	13	74	4.6
83-84—Chicago	64	870	218	110	.505	66	39	.591	75	158	233	33	139	2	15	76	259	4.0
84-85—Chicago	63	993	192	89	.464	50	34	.680	79	157	236	31	166	3	11	127	212	3.4
85-86—Chicago	52	1276	323	167	.517	91	53	.582	112	194	306	37	206	6	28	134	387	7.4
86-87—New York	44	776	174	71	.408	57	31	.544	51	128	179	19	95	1	22	71	173	3.9
87-88—Sacramento	54	946	250	119	.476	87	59	.678	82	222	304	33	143	2	12	110	297	5.5
89-90—Orl.-L.A.L.	6	45	6	3	.500	7	3	.429	4	12	16	1	9	0	2	3	9	1.5
Totals	325	5222	1263	605	.479	394	239	.607	431	919	1350	162	819	15	97	546	1449	4.5

Three-Point Field Goals: 1984-85, 0-for-1. 1985-86, 0-for-1. 1986-87, 0-for-1. Totals, 0-for-3.

NBA PLAYOFF RECORD

									—Rebounds—									
Sea.—Team	G.	Min.	FGA	FGM	Pct.	FTA	FTM	Pct.	Off.	Def.	Tot.	Ast.	PF	Dq.	Stl.	Blk.	Pts.	Avg.
84-85—Chicago	4	91	15	7	.467	0	0	.000	8	14	22	3	19	1	6	7	14	3.5
85-86—Chicago	1	4	1	0	.000	0	0	.000	1	1	2	0	0	0	0	0	0	0.0
Totals	5	95	16	7	.438	0	0	.000	9	15	24	3	19	1	6	7	14	2.8

JOSE RAFAEL ORTIZ

Born October 25, 1963 at Albonito, Puerto Rico. Height 6:10. Weight 225.
High School—Cayey, Puerto Rico, Benjamin Harrison.
College—Oregon State University, Corvallis, Ore.
Graduated from high school in 1981; played with San German in Puerto Rico Superior League prior to enrolling at Oregon State in January, 1985.
Drafted by Utah on first round, 1987 (15th pick).

Waived by Utah, February 5, 1990.
Played in Spain, 1987-88.

—COLLEGIATE RECORD—

Year	G.	Min.	FGA	FGM	Pct.	FTA	FTM	Pct.	Reb.	Pts.	Avg.
84-85					Did Not Play						
85-86	22	765	266	137	.515	131	87	.664	188	361	16.4
86-87	30	1100	425	248	.584	236	171	.725	262	668	22.3
Totals	52	1865	681	385	.557	367	258	.703	450	1029	19.8

Three-Point Field Goals: 1986-87, 1-for-2 (.500).

NBA REGULAR SEASON RECORD

Sea.—Team	G.	Min.	FGA	FGM	Pct.	FTA	FTM	Pct.	—Rebounds— Off.	Def.	Tot.	Ast.	PF	Dq.	Stl.	Blk.	Pts.	Avg.
88-89—Utah	51	327	125	55	.440	52	31	.596	30	28	58	11	40	0	8	7	141	2.8
89-90—Utah	13	64	42	19	.452	5	3	.600	8	7	15	7	15	0	2	1	42	3.2
Totals	64	391	167	74	.443	57	34	.596	38	35	73	18	55	0	10	8	183	2.9

Three-Point Field Goals: 1988-89, 0-for-1. 1989-90, 1-for-2 (.500). Totals, 1-for-3 (.333).

ROBERT L. PARISH

Born August 30, 1953 at Shreveport, La. Height 7:00. Weight 230.

High School—Shreveport, La., Woodlawn.

College—Centenary College, Shreveport, La.

Drafted by Golden State on first round, 1976 (8th pick).

Traded by Golden State with a 1980 1st round draft choice to Boston for two 1980 1st round draft choices, June 9, 1980.

—COLLEGIATE RECORD—

Year	G.	Min.	FGA	FGM	Pct.	FTA	FTM	Pct.	Reb.	Pts.	Avg.
72-73	27	885	492	285	.579	82	50	.610	505	620	23.0
73-74	25	841	428	224	.523	78	49	.628	382	497	19.9
74-75	29	900	423	237	.560	112	74	.660	447	548	18.9
75-76	27	939	489	288	.589	134	93	.694	486	669	24.8
Totals	108	3565	1832	1034	.564	406	266	.655	1820	2334	21.6

NBA REGULAR SEASON RECORD

Sea.—Team	G.	Min.	FGA	FGM	Pct.	FTA	FTM	Pct.	—Rebounds— Off.	Def.	Tot.	Ast.	PF	Dq.	Stl.	Blk.	Pts.	Avg.
76-77—Golden State	77	1384	573	288	.503	171	121	.708	201	342	543	74	224	7	55	94	697	9.1
77-78—Golden State	82	1969	911	430	.472	264	165	.625	211	469	680	95	291	10	79	123	1025	12.5
78-79—Golden State	76	2411	1110	554	.499	281	196	.698	265	651	916	115	303	10	100	217	1304	17.2
79-80—Golden State	72	2119	1006	510	.507	284	203	.715	247	536	783	122	248	6	58	115	1223	17.0
80-81—Boston	82	2298	1166	635	.545	397	282	.710	245	532	777	144	310	9	81	214	1552	18.9
81-82—Boston	80	2534	1235	669	.542	355	252	.710	288	578	866	140	267	5	68	192	1590	19.9
82-83—Boston	78	2459	1125	619	.550	388	271	.698	260	567	827	141	222	4	79	148	1509	19.3
83-84—Boston	80	2867	1140	623	.546	368	274	.745	243	614	857	139	266	7	55	116	1520	19.0
84-85—Boston	79	2850	1016	551	.542	393	292	.743	263	577	840	125	223	2	56	101	1394	17.6
85-86—Boston	81	2567	966	530	.549	335	245	.731	246	524	770	145	215	3	65	116	1305	16.1
86-87—Boston	80	2995	1057	588	.556	309	227	.735	254	597	851	173	266	5	64	144	1403	17.5
87-88—Boston	74	2312	750	442	.589	241	177	.734	173	455	628	115	198	5	55	84	1061	14.3
88-89—Boston	80	2840	1045	596	.570	409	294	.719	342	654	996	175	209	2	79	116	1486	18.6
89-90—Boston	79	2396	871	505	.580	312	233	.747	259	537	796	103	189	2	38	69	1243	15.7
Totals	1100	34001	13971	7540	.540	4507	3232	.717	3497	7633	11130	1806	3431	77	932	1849	18312	16.6

Three-Point Field Goals: 1979-80, 0-for-1. 1980-81, 0-for-1. 1982-83, 0-for-1. 1986-87, 0-for-1. 1987-88, 0-for-1. Totals, 0-for-5.

NBA PLAYOFF RECORD

Sea.—Team	G.	Min.	FGA	FGM	Pct.	FTA	FTM	Pct.	—Rebounds— Off.	Def.	Tot.	Ast.	PF	Dq.	Stl.	Blk.	Pts.	Avg.
76-77—Golden State	10	239	108	52	.481	26	17	.654	43	60	103	11	42	1	7	11	121	12.1
80-81—Boston	17	492	219	108	.493	58	39	.672	50	96	146	19	74	2	21	39	255	15.0
81-82—Boston	12	426	209	102	.488	75	51	.680	43	92	135	18	47	1	5	48	255	21.3
82-83—Boston	7	249	89	43	.483	20	17	.850	21	53	74	9	18	0	5	9	103	14.7
83-84—Boston	23	869	291	139	.478	99	64	.646	76	172	248	27	100	6	23	41	342	14.9
84-85—Boston	21	803	276	136	.493	111	87	.784	57	162	219	31	68	0	21	34	359	17.1
85-86—Boston	18	591	225	106	.471	89	58	.652	52	106	158	25	47	1	9	30	270	15.0
86-87—Boston	21	734	263	149	.567	103	79	.767	59	139	198	28	79	4	18	35	377	18.0
87-88—Boston	17	626	188	100	.532	61	50	.820	51	117	168	21	42	0	11	19	250	14.7
88-89—Boston	3	112	44	20	.455	9	7	.778	6	20	26	6	5	0	4	2	47	15.7
89-90—Boston	5	170	54	31	.574	18	17	.944	23	27	50	13	21	0	5	7	79	15.8
Totals	154	5311	1966	986	.502	669	486	.726	481	1044	1525	208	543	15	129	275	2458	16.0

Three-Point Field Goals, 1986-87, 0-for-1.

NBA ALL-STAR GAME RECORD

Season—Team	Min.	FGA	FGM	Pct.	FTA	FTM	Pct.	—Rebounds— Off.	Def.	Tot.	Ast.	PF	Dq.	Stl.	Blk.	Pts.
1981—Boston	25	18	5	.278	6	6	1.000	6	4	10	2	3	0	0	2	16
1982—Boston	20	12	9	.750	4	3	.750	0	7	7	1	2	0	0	2	21
1983—Boston	18	6	5	.833	4	3	.750	0	3	3	0	2	0	1	1	13
1984—Boston	28	11	5	.455	4	2	.500	4	11	15	2	1	0	3	0	12
1985—Boston	10	5	2	.400	0	0	.000	3	3	6	1	0	0	0	0	4
1986—Boston	7	0	0	.000	2	0	.000	0	1	1	0	0	0	0	1	0
1987—Boston	8	3	2	.667	0	0	.000	0	3	3	0	1	0	0	1	4
1990—Boston	21	11	7	.636	1	0	.000	2	2	4	2	4	0	0	1	14
Totals	137	66	35	.530	21	14	.667	15	34	49	8	13	0	4	8	84

Named to All-NBA Second Team, 1982. . . . All-NBA Third Team, 1989. . . . Member of NBA championship teams, 1981, 1984, 1986. . . . Named to THE SPORTING NEWS All-America First Team, 1976.

ZARKO PASPALJ

Born March 27, 1966 at Pljevlja, Montenegro, Yugoslavia. Height 6:09. Weight 215.

Never drafted by an NBA franchise.

Signed by San Antonio as a free agent, July 28, 1989.
Waived by San Antonio, April 22, 1990.
Played for Partizan Belgrade club team and Yugoslavian National Team.

NBA REGULAR SEASON RECORD

Sea.—Team	G.	Min.	FGA	FGM	Pct.	FTA	FTM	Pct.	—Rebounds— Off.	Def.	Tot.	Ast.	PF	Dq.	Stl.	Blk.	Pts.	Avg.
89-90—San Antonio	28	181	79	27	.342	22	18	.818	15	15	30	10	37	0	3	7	72	2.6

Three-Point Field Goals: 1989-90, 0-for-1.

JAMES JOSEPH PAXSON JR.
(Jim)

Born July 9, 1957 at Kettering, O. Height 6:06. Weight 210.

High School—Kettering, O., Alter.

College—University of Dayton, Dayton, O.

Drafted by Portland on first round, 1979 (12th pick).

Traded by Portland to Boston for Jerry Sichting and future considerations, February 23, 1988.

—COLLEGIATE RECORD—

Year	G.	Min.	FGA	FGM	Pct.	FTA	FTM	Pct.	Reb.	Pts.	Avg.
75-76	27	1061	308	149	.484	73	55	.753	127	353	13.1
76-77	27	1012	401	219	.546	87	69	.793	157	507	18.8
77-78	29	1066	399	208	.521	115	89	.774	96	505	17.4
78-79	25	929	449	236	.526	134	108	.806	104	580	23.2
Totals	108	4068	1557	812	.521	409	321	.785	484	1945	18.0

NBA REGULAR SEASON RECORD

Sea.—Team	G.	Min.	FGA	FGM	Pct.	FTA	FTM	Pct.	—Rebounds— Off.	Def.	Tot.	Ast.	PF	Dq.	Stl.	Blk.	Pts.	Avg.
79-80—Portland	72	1270	460	189	.411	90	64	.711	25	84	109	144	97	0	48	5	443	6.2
80-81—Portland	79	2701	1092	585	.536	248	182	.734	74	137	211	299	172	1	140	9	1354	17.1
81-82—Portland	82	2756	1258	662	.526	287	220	.767	75	146	221	276	159	0	129	12	1552	18.9
82-83—Portland	81	2740	1323	682	.515	478	388	.812	68	106	174	231	160	0	140	17	1756	21.7
83-84—Portland	81	2686	1322	680	.514	410	345	.841	68	105	173	251	165	0	122	10	1722	21.3
84-85—Portland	68	2253	988	508	.514	248	196	.790	69	153	222	264	115	0	101	5	1218	17.9
85-86—Portland	75	1931	792	372	.470	244	217	.889	42	106	148	278	156	3	94	5	981	13.1
86-87—Portland	72	1798	733	337	.460	216	174	.806	41	98	139	237	134	0	76	12	874	12.1
87-88—Port.-Bos.	45	801	298	137	.460	79	68	.861	15	30	45	76	73	0	30	5	347	7.7
88-89—Boston	57	1138	445	202	.454	103	84	.816	18	56	74	107	96	0	38	8	492	8.6
89-90—Boston	72	1283	422	191	.453	90	73	.811	24	53	77	137	115	0	33	5	460	6.4
Totals	784	21357	9134	4545	.498	2493	2011	.807	519	1074	1593	2300	1442	4	951	93	11199	14.3

Three-Point Field Goals: 1979-80, 1-for-22 (.045). 1980-81, 2-for-30 (.067). 1981-82, 8-for-35 (.229). 1982-83, 4-for-25 (.160). 1983-84, 17-for-59 (.288). 1984-85, 6-for-39 (.154). 1985-86, 20-for-62 (.323). 1986-87, 26-for-98 (.265). 1987-88, 5-for-21 (.238). 1988-89, 4-for-24 (.167). 1989-90, 5-for-20 (.250). Totals, 98-for-435 (.225).

NBA PLAYOFF RECORD

Sea.—Team	G.	Min.	FGA	FGM	Pct.	FTA	FTM	Pct.	—Rebounds— Off.	Def.	Tot.	Ast.	PF	Dq.	Stl.	Blk.	Pts.	Avg.
79-80—Portland	3	44	16	5	.313	6	6	1.000	0	4	4	3	2	0	2	1	16	5.3
80-81—Portland	1	4	3	0	.000	0	0	.000	0	0	0	0	0	0	0	0	0	0.0
82-83—Portland	7	260	116	68	.586	33	25	.758	4	11	15	18	11	0	9	1	163	23.3
83-84—Portland	5	172	78	40	.513	40	33	.825	11	8	19	12	13	0	2	0	114	22.8
84-85—Portland	9	212	101	47	.465	24	19	.792	6	14	20	21	16	0	6	0	116	12.9
85-86—Portland	4	71	37	14	.378	15	12	.800	1	3	4	15	12	1	3	0	42	10.5
86-87—Portland	4	94	32	13	.406	9	8	.889	4	5	9	13	8	0	5	0	34	8.5
87-88—Boston	15	188	59	17	.288	20	16	.800	1	8	9	11	18	0	6	2	50	3.3
89-90—Boston	5	62	16	8	.500	4	3	.750	0	0	0	7	1	0	5	0	19	3.8
Totals	53	1107	458	212	.463	151	122	.808	27	53	80	100	81	1	38	4	554	10.5

Three-Point Field Goals: 1982-83, 2-for-4 (.500). 1983-84, 1-for-5 (.200). 1984-85, 3-for-10 (.300). 1985-86, 2-for-6 (.333). 1986-87, 0-for-2. 1987-88, 0-for-2. 1989-90, 0-for-1. Totals, 8-for-30 (.267).

NBA ALL-STAR GAME RECORD

Season—Team	Min.	FGA	FGM	Pct.	FTA	FTM	Pct.	—Rebounds— Off.	Def.	Tot.	Ast.	PF	Dq.	Stl.	Blk.	Pts.
1983—Portland	17	7	5	.714	2	1	.500	0	0	0	1	0	0	2	0	11
1984—Portland	14	9	5	.556	0	0	.000	1	2	3	2	0	0	0	0	10
Totals	31	16	10	.625	2	1	.500	1	2	3	3	0	0	2	0	21

Named to All-NBA Second Team, 1984. . . . Son of Jim Paxson Sr., forward with Minneapolis Lakers (1956-57) and Cincinnati Royals (1957-58) and brother of Chicago Bulls guard John Paxson.

JOHN MacBETH PAXSON

Born September 29, 1960 at Dayton, O. Height 6:02. Weight 185.
High School—Kettering, O., Archbishop Alter.
College—University of Notre Dame, Notre Dame, Ind.
Drafted by San Antonio on first round, 1983 (19th pick).

Signed by Chicago as a Veteran Free Agent, October 29, 1985; San Antonio relinquished its right of first refusal in exchange for cash.

—COLLEGIATE RECORD—

Year	G.	Min.	FGA	FGM	Pct.	FTA	FTM	Pct.	Reb.	Pts.	Avg.
79-80	27	459	87	42	.483	55	41	.745	34	125	4.6
80-81	29	1062	218	113	.518	89	61	.685	53	287	9.9
81-82	27	1055	346	185	.535	93	72	.774	55	442	16.4
82-83	29	1082	411	219	.533	100	74	.740	63	512	17.7
Totals	112	3658	1062	559	.526	337	248	.736	205	1366	12.2

NBA REGULAR SEASON RECORD

									—Rebounds—									
Sea.—Team	G.	Min.	FGA	FGM	Pct.	FTA	FTM	Pct.	Off.	Def.	Tot.	Ast.	PF	Dq.	Stl.	Blk.	Pts.	Avg.
83-84—San Antonio	49	458	137	61	.445	26	16	.615	4	29	33	149	47	0	10	2	142	2.9
84-85—San Antonio	78	1259	385	196	.509	100	84	.840	19	49	68	215	117	0	45	3	486	6.2
85-86—Chicago	75	1570	328	153	.466	92	74	.804	18	76	94	274	172	2	55	2	395	5.3
86-87—Chicago	82	2689	793	386	.487	131	106	.809	22	117	139	467	207	1	66	8	930	11.3
87-88—Chicago	81	1888	582	287	.493	45	33	.733	16	88	104	303	154	2	49	1	640	7.9
88-89—Chicago	78	1738	513	246	.480	36	31	.861	13	81	94	308	162	1	53	6	567	7.3
89-90—Chicago	82	2365	708	365	.516	68	56	.824	27	92	119	335	176	1	83	6	819	10.0
Totals	525	11967	3446	1694	.492	498	400	.803	119	532	651	2051	1035	7	361	28	3979	7.6

Three-Point Field Goals: 1983-84, 4-for-22 (.182). 1984-85, 10-for-34 (.294). 1985-86, 15-for-51 (.294). 1986-87, 52-for-140 (.371). 1987-88, 33-for-95 (.347). 1988-89, 44-for-133 (.331). 1989-90, 33-for-92 (.359). Totals, 191-for-567 (.337).

NBA PLAYOFF RECORD

									—Rebounds—									
Sea.—Team	G.	Min.	FGA	FGM	Pct.	FTA	FTM	Pct.	Off.	Def.	Tot.	Ast.	PF	Dq.	Stl.	Blk.	Pts.	Avg.
84-85—San Antonio	5	114	42	21	.500	9	7	.778	0	5	5	21	9	0	5	0	51	10.2
85-86—Chicago	3	80	15	7	.467	17	13	.765	0	0	0	5	9	0	3	0	27	9.0
86-87—Chicago	3	87	22	11	.500	1	1	1.000	0	3	3	11	9	0	2	0	26	8.7
87-88—Chicago	10	165	53	20	.377	4	4	1.000	0	4	4	30	24	1	1	1	46	4.6
88-89—Chicago	16	302	78	37	.474	16	14	.875	2	8	10	34	35	1	12	0	93	5.8
89-90—Chicago	15	395	87	37	.425	14	14	1.000	2	20	22	54	42	3	9	0	92	6.1
Totals	52	1143	297	133	.448	61	53	.869	4	40	44	155	128	5	32	1	335	6.4

Three-Point Field Goals: 1984-85, 2-for-9 (.222). 1986-87, 3-for-7 (.429). 1987-88, 2-for-12 (.167). 1988-89, 5-for-19 (.263). 1989-90, 4-for-9 (.444). Totals, 16-for-56 (.286).

Son of Jim Paxson Sr., forward with Minneapolis Lakers (1956-57) and Cincinnati Royals (1957-58) and brother of Boston Celtics guard Jim Paxson Jr. . . . Named to THE SPORTING NEWS All-America Second Team, 1983.

KENNETH VICTOR PAYNE
(Kenny)

Born November 25, 1966 at Laurel, Miss. Height 6:08. Weight 195.
High School—Laurel, Miss., Northeast Jones.
College—University of Louisville, Louisville, Ky.
Drafted by Philadelphia on first round, 1989 (19th pick).

—COLLEGIATE RECORD—

Year	G.	Min.	FGA	FGM	Pct.	FTA	FTM	Pct.	Reb.	Pts.	Avg.
85-86	34	303	119	52	.437	22	17	.773	58	121	3.6
86-87	26	320	123	43	.350	23	16	.696	66	108	4.2
87-88	35	1035	325	156	.480	38	29	.763	164	375	10.7
88-89	33	987	386	196	.508	50	42	.840	188	479	14.5
Totals	128	2645	953	447	.469	133	104	.782	476	1083	8.5

Three-Point Field Goals: 1986-87, 6-for-24 (.250). 1987-88, 34-for-83 (.410). 1988-89, 45-for-105 (.429). Totals, 85-for-212 (.401).

NBA REGULAR SEASON RECORD

									—Rebounds—									
Sea.—Team	G.	Min.	FGA	FGM	Pct.	FTA	FTM	Pct.	Off.	Def.	Tot.	Ast.	PF	Dq.	Stl.	Blk.	Pts.	Avg.
89-90—Philadelphia	35	216	108	47	.435	18	16	.889	11	15	26	10	37	0	7	6	114	3.3

Three-Point Field Goals: 1989-90, 4-for-10 (.400).

NBA PLAYOFF RECORD

									—Rebounds—									
Sea.—Team	G.	Min.	FGA	FGM	Pct.	FTA	FTM	Pct.	Off.	Def.	Tot.	Ast.	PF	Dq.	Stl.	Blk.	Pts.	Avg.
89-90—Philadelphia	3	10	5	2	.400	2	2	1.000	1	1	2	0	3	0	0	0	6	2.0

Three-Point Field Goals: 1989-90, 0-for-2.

Member of NCAA Division I championship team, 1986.

WILLIAM EDWARD PERDUE
(Will)

Born August 29, 1965 at Melbourne, Fla. Height 7:00. Weight 240.

High School—Merritt Island, Fla.

College—Vanderbilt University, Nashville, Tenn.

Drafted by Chicago on first round, 1988 (11th pick).

—COLLEGIATE RECORD—

Year	G.	Min.	FGA	FGM	Pct.	FTA	FTM	Pct.	Reb.	Pts.	Avg.
83-84	17	111	45	21	.467	9	4	.444	38	46	2.7
84-85	Did Not Play—Red Shirted										
85-86	22	181	53	31	.585	32	14	.438	61	76	3.5
86-87	34	1033	389	233	.599	204	126	.618	295	592	17.4
87-88	31	1013	369	234	.624	147	99	.673	314	567	18.3
Totals	104	2338	856	519	.606	392	243	.620	708	1281	12.3

NBA REGULAR SEASON RECORD

									—Rebounds—									
Sea.—Team	G.	Min.	FGA	FGM	Pct.	FTA	FTM	Pct.	Off.	Def.	Tot.	Ast.	PF	Dq.	Stl.	Blk.	Pts.	Avg.
88-89—Chicago	30	190	72	29	.403	14	8	.571	18	27	45	11	38	0	4	6	66	2.2
89-90—Chicago	77	884	268	111	.414	104	72	.692	88	126	214	46	150	0	19	26	294	3.8
Totals	107	1074	340	140	.412	118	80	.678	106	153	259	57	188	0	23	32	360	3.4

Three-Point Field Goals: 1989-90, 0-for-5.

NBA PLAYOFF RECORD

									—Rebounds—									
Sea.—Team	G.	Min.	FGA	FGM	Pct.	FTA	FTM	Pct.	Off.	Def.	Tot.	Ast.	PF	Dq.	Stl.	Blk.	Pts.	Avg.
88-89—Chicago	3	22	9	6	.667	3	2	.667	3	3	6	2	4	0	0	0	14	4.7
89-90—Chicago	13	78	28	13	.464	18	13	.722	7	12	19	2	13	0	0	5	40	3.1
Totals	16	100	37	19	.514	21	15	.714	10	15	25	4	17	0	0	5	54	3.4

Three-Point Field Goals: 1988-89, 0-for-1. 1989-90, 1-for-2 (.500). Totals, 1-for-3 (.333).

SAMUEL BRUCE PERKINS
(Sam)

Born June 14, 1961 at Brooklyn, N. Y. Height 6:09. Weight 235.

High School—Latham, N. Y., Shaker.

College—University of North Carolina, Chapel Hill, N. C.

Drafted by Dallas on first round, 1984 (4th pick).

Signed by Los Angeles Lakers as an unrestricted free agent, August 6, 1990.

—COLLEGIATE RECORD—

Year	G.	Min.	FGA	FGM	Pct.	FTA	FTM	Pct.	Reb.	Pts.	Avg.
80-81	37	....	318	199	.626	205	152	.741	289	550	14.9
81-82	32	....	301	174	.578	142	109	.768	250	457	14.3
82-83	35	....	414	218	.527	177	145	.819	330	593	16.9
83-84	31	....	331	195	.589	181	155	.856	298	545	17.6
Totals	135	....	1364	786	.576	705	561	.796	1167	2145	15.9

Three-Point Field Goals: 1982-83, 12-for-28 (.429).

NBA REGULAR SEASON RECORD

									—Rebounds—									
Sea.—Team	G.	Min.	FGA	FGM	Pct.	FTA	FTM	Pct.	Off.	Def.	Tot.	Ast.	PF	Dq.	Stl.	Blk.	Pts.	Avg.
84-85—Dallas	82	2317	736	347	.471	244	200	.820	189	416	605	135	236	1	63	63	903	11.0
85-86—Dallas	80	2626	910	458	.503	377	307	.814	195	490	685	153	212	2	75	94	1234	15.4
86-87—Dallas	80	2687	957	461	.482	296	245	.828	197	419	616	146	269	6	109	77	1186	14.8
87-88—Dallas	75	2499	876	394	.450	332	273	.822	201	400	601	118	227	2	74	54	1066	14.2
88-89—Dallas	78	2860	959	445	.464	329	274	.833	235	453	688	127	224	1	76	92	1171	15.0
89-90—Dallas	76	2668	883	435	.493	424	330	.778	209	363	572	175	225	4	88	64	1206	15.9
Totals	471	15657	5321	2540	.477	2002	1629	.814	1226	2541	3767	854	1393	16	485	444	6766	14.4

Three-Point Field Goals: 1984-85, 9-for-36 (.250). 1985-86, 11-for-33 (.333). 1986-87, 19-for-54 (.352). 1987-88, 5-for-30 (.167). 1988-89, 7-for-38 (.184). 1989-90, 6-for-28 (.214). Totals, 57-for-219 (.260).

NBA PLAYOFF RECORD

Sea.—Team	G.	Min.	FGA	FGM	Pct.	FTA	FTM	Pct.	—Rebounds— Off.	Def.	Tot.	Ast.	PF	Dq.	Stl.	Blk.	Pts.	Avg.
84-85—Dallas	4	169	49	24	.490	34	26	.765	16	35	51	11	13	1	2	1	75	18.8
85-86—Dallas	10	347	133	57	.429	43	33	.767	30	53	83	24	32	0	9	14	149	14.9
86-87—Dallas	4	133	52	26	.500	23	16	.696	12	22	34	5	16	0	4	1	68	17.0
87-88—Dallas	17	572	195	88	.451	66	53	.803	39	73	112	31	51	1	25	17	230	13.5
89-90—Dallas	3	118	36	16	.444	17	13	.765	10	12	22	8	17	2	3	2	45	15.0
Totals	38	1339	465	211	.454	183	141	.770	107	195	302	79	129	4	43	35	567	14.9

Three-Point Field Goals: 1984-85, 1-for-4 (.250). 1985-86, 2-for-8 (.250). 1986-87, 0-for-4. 1987-88, 1-for-7 (.143). 1989-90, 0-for-1. Totals, 4-for-24 (.167).

Named to NBA All-Rookie Team, 1985. . . . Member of NCAA Division I championship team, 1982. . . . Member of U.S. Olympic team, 1984. . . . Named to THE SPORTING NEWS All-America First Team, 1984. . . . Named to THE SPORTING NEWS All-America Second Team, 1982 and 1983.

TIMOTHY D. PERRY
(Tim)

Born June 4, 1965 at Freehold, N.J. Height 6:09. Weight 220.
High School—Freehold, N.J.
College—Temple University, Philadelphia, Pa.
Drafted by Phoenix on first round, 1988 (7th pick).

—COLLEGIATE RECORD—

Year	G.	Min.	FGA	FGM	Pct.	FTA	FTM	Pct.	Reb.	Pts.	Avg.
84-85	30	621	70	29	.414	20	10	.500	118	68	2.3
85-86	31	1101	249	141	.566	134	77	.575	293	359	11.6
86-87	36	1271	350	180	.514	166	103	.620	310	463	12.9
87-88	33	1103	347	203	.585	113	72	.637	264	478	14.5
Totals	130	4096	1016	553	.544	433	262	.605	985	1368	10.5

NBA REGULAR SEASON RECORD

Sea.—Team	G.	Min.	FGA	FGM	Pct.	FTA	FTM	Pct.	—Rebounds— Off.	Def.	Tot.	Ast.	PF	Dq.	Stl.	Blk.	Pts.	Avg.
88-89—Phoenix	62	614	201	108	.537	65	40	.615	61	71	132	18	47	0	19	32	257	4.1
89-90—Phoenix	60	612	195	100	.513	90	53	.589	79	73	152	17	76	0	21	22	254	4.2
Totals	122	1226	396	208	.525	155	93	.600	140	144	284	35	123	0	40	54	511	4.2

Three-Point Field Goals: 1988-89, 1-for-4 (.250). 1989-90, 1-for-1 (1.000). Totals, 2-for-5 (.400).

NBA PLAYOFF RECORD

Sea.—Team	G.	Min.	FGA	FGM	Pct.	FTA	FTM	Pct.	—Rebounds— Off.	Def.	Tot.	Ast.	PF	Dq.	Stl.	Blk.	Pts.	Avg.
88-89—Phoenix	4	17	4	2	.500	2	0	.000	1	1	2	0	1	0	2	1	4	1.0
89-90—Phoenix	11	100	25	13	.520	18	8	.444	10	11	21	2	19	0	3	6	34	3.1
Totals	15	117	29	15	.517	20	8	.400	11	12	23	2	20	0	5	7	38	2.5

CHUCK CONNORS PERSON

Born June 27, 1964 at Brantley, Ala. Height 6:08. Weight 225.
High School—Brantley, Ala.
College—Auburn University, Auburn, Ala.
Drafted by Indiana on first round, 1986 (4th pick).

—COLLEGIATE RECORD—

Year	G.	Min.	FGA	FGM	Pct.	FTA	FTM	Pct.	Reb.	Pts.	Avg.
82-83	28	636	218	118	.541	33	25	.758	128	261	9.3
83-84	31	1079	470	255	.543	114	83	.728	249	593	19.1
84-85	34	1240	614	334	.544	107	79	.738	303	747	22.0
85-86	33	1178	597	310	.519	112	90	.804	260	710	21.5
Totals	126	4133	1899	1017	.536	366	277	.757	940	2311	18.3

NBA REGULAR SEASON RECORD

Sea.—Team	G.	Min.	FGA	FGM	Pct.	FTA	FTM	Pct.	—Rebounds— Off.	Def.	Tot.	Ast.	PF	Dq.	Stl.	Blk.	Pts.	Avg.
86-87—Indiana	82	2956	1358	635	.468	297	222	.747	168	509	677	295	310	4	90	16	1541	18.8
87-88—Indiana	79	2807	1252	575	.459	197	132	.670	171	365	536	309	266	4	73	8	1341	17.0
88-89—Indiana	80	3012	1453	711	.489	307	243	.792	144	372	516	289	280	12	83	18	1728	21.6
89-90—Indiana	77	2714	1242	605	.487	270	211	.781	126	319	445	230	217	1	53	20	1515	19.7
Totals	318	11489	5305	2526	.476	1071	808	.754	609	1565	2174	1123	1073	21	299	62	6125	19.3

Three-Point Field Goals: 1986-87, 49-for-138 (.355). 1987-88, 59-for-177 (.333). 1988-89, 63-for-205 (.307). 1989-90, 94-for-253 (.372). Totals, 265-for-773 (.343).

NBA PLAYOFF RECORD

Sea.—Team	G.	Min.	FGA	FGM	Pct.	FTA	FTM	Pct.	—Rebounds— Off.	Def.	Tot.	Ast.	PF	Dq.	Stl.	Blk.	Pts.	Avg.
86-87—Indiana	4	159	74	38	.514	39	30	.769	6	27	33	20	14	0	5	2	108	27.0
89-90—Indiana	3	123	45	17	.378	12	5	.417	6	14	20	12	11	0	1	0	40	13.3
Totals	7	282	119	55	.462	51	35	.686	12	41	53	32	25	0	6	2	148	21.1

Three-Point Field Goals: 1986-87, 2-for-8 (.250). 1989-90, 1-for-10 (.100). Totals, 3-for-18 (.167).

Named NBA Rookie of the Year, 1987. . . . NBA All-Rookie Team, 1987. . . . THE SPORTING NEWS All-America Second Team, 1985 and 1986.

JAMES RICHARD PETERSEN
(Jim)

Born February 22, 1962 at Minneapolis, Minn. Height 6:10. Weight 235.
High School—St. Louis Park, Minn.
College—University of Minnesota, Minneapolis, Minn.
Drafted by Houston on third round, 1984 (51st pick).

Traded by Houston with Rodney McCray to Sacramento for Otis Thorpe, October 11, 1988.
Traded by Sacramento to Golden State for Ralph Sampson, September 27, 1989.

—COLLEGIATE RECORD—

Year	G.	Min.	FGA	FGM	Pct.	FTA	FTM	Pct.	Reb.	Pts.	Avg.
80-81	22	....	26	13	.500	4	1	.250	22	27	1.2
81-82	21	....	52	24	.462	22	14	.636	43	62	3.0
82-83	29	....	149	82	.550	28	18	.643	155	182	6.3
83-84	24	....	180	115	.639	54	39	.722	166	269	11.2
Totals	96	....	407	234	.575	108	72	.667	386	540	5.6

NBA REGULAR SEASON RECORD

Sea.—Team	G.	Min.	FGA	FGM	Pct.	FTA	FTM	Pct.	—Rebounds— Off.	Def.	Tot.	Ast.	PF	Dq.	Stl.	Blk.	Pts.	Avg.
84-85—Houston	60	714	144	70	.486	66	50	.758	44	103	147	29	125	1	14	32	190	3.2
85-86—Houston	82	1664	411	196	.477	160	113	.706	149	247	396	85	231	2	38	54	505	6.2
86-87—Houston	82	2403	755	386	.511	209	152	.727	177	380	557	127	268	5	43	102	924	11.3
87-88—Houston	69	1793	488	249	.510	153	114	.745	145	291	436	106	203	3	36	40	613	8.9
88-89—Sacramento	66	1633	606	278	.459	154	115	.747	121	292	413	81	236	8	47	68	671	10.2
89-90—Golden State	43	592	141	60	.426	73	52	.712	49	111	160	23	103	0	17	20	172	4.0
Totals	402	8799	2545	1239	.487	815	596	.731	685	1424	2109	451	1166	19	195	316	3075	7.6

Three-Point Field Goals: 1985-86, 0-for-3. 1986-87, 0-for-4. 1987-88, 1-for-6 (.167). 1988-89, 0-for-8. 1989-90, 0-for-1. Totals, 1-for-22 (.045).

NBA PLAYOFF RECORD

Sea.—Team	G.	Min.	FGA	FGM	Pct.	FTA	FTM	Pct.	—Rebounds— Off.	Def.	Tot.	Ast.	PF	Dq.	Stl.	Blk.	Pts.	Avg.
84-85—Houston	3	8	1	1	1.000	0	0	.000	1	1	2	1	2	0	0	0	2	0.7
85-86—Houston	20	378	108	44	.407	33	23	.697	47	64	111	21	58	1	9	9	111	5.6
86-87—Houston	10	187	51	28	.549	18	12	.667	14	32	46	6	26	1	5	2	68	6.8
87-88—Houston	4	98	23	12	.522	12	7	.583	7	14	21	6	11	1	1	2	31	7.8
Totals	37	671	183	85	.464	63	42	.667	69	111	180	34	97	3	15	13	212	5.7

DRAZEN PETROVIC

Born October 22, 1964 at Sibenik, Yugoslavia. Height 6:05. Weight 195.
College—University of Zagreb, Zagreb, Yugoslavia.
Drafted by Portland on third round, 1986 (60th pick).

NBA REGULAR SEASON RECORD

Sea.—Team	G.	Min.	FGA	FGM	Pct.	FTA	FTM	Pct.	—Rebounds— Off.	Def.	Tot.	Ast.	PF	Dq.	Stl.	Blk.	Pts.	Avg.
89-90—Portland	77	967	427	207	.485	160	135	.844	50	61	111	116	134	0	23	2	583	7.6

Three-Point Field Goals: 1989-90, 34-for-74 (.459).

NBA PLAYOFF RECORD

Sea.—Team	G.	Min.	FGA	FGM	Pct.	FTA	FTM	Pct.	—Rebounds— Off.	Def.	Tot.	Ast.	PF	Dq.	Stl.	Blk.	Pts.	Avg.
89-90—Portland	20	253	109	48	.440	36	21	.583	10	22	32	20	37	0	6	0	122	6.1

Three-Point Field Goals: 1989-90, 5-for-16 (.313).

RICKY PIERCE

RICKY CHARLES PIERCE

Born August 19, 1959 at Dallas, Tex. Height 6:04. Weight 222.
High School—Garland Tex., South Garland.
Colleges—Walla Walla Community College, Walla Walla, Wash., and Rice University, Houston, Tex.
Drafted by Detroit on first round, 1982 (18th pick).

Traded by Detroit to San Diego for 1986 and 1987 2nd round draft choices, October 17, 1983.
Traded by Los Angeles Clippers with Terry Cummings and Craig Hodges to Milwaukee for Marques Johnson, Harvey Catchings, Junior Bridgeman and cash, September 29, 1984.

—COLLEGIATE RECORD—

Walla Walla CC

Year	G.	Min.	FGA	FGM	Pct.	FTA	FTM	Pct.	Reb.	Pts.	Avg.
78-79	..	....	...	...	....	...	...	....	....	....	19.0

Rice

Year	G.	Min.	FGA	FGM	Pct.	FTA	FTM	Pct.	Reb.	Pts.	Avg.
79-80	26	878	421	202	.480	131	94	.718	214	498	19.2
80-81	26	901	444	230	.518	119	84	.706	181	544	20.9
81-82	30	1104	614	314	.511	223	177	.794	226	805	26.8
Totals	82	2883	1479	746	.504	473	355	.751	621	1847	22.5

NBA REGULAR SEASON RECORD

									—Rebounds—									
Sea.—Team	G.	Min.	FGA	FGM	Pct.	FTA	FTM	Pct.	Off.	Def.	Tot.	Ast.	PF	Dq.	Stl.	Blk.	Pts.	Avg.
82-83—Detroit	39	265	88	33	.375	32	18	.563	15	20	35	14	42	0	8	4	85	2.2
83-84—San Diego	69	1280	570	268	.470	173	149	.861	59	76	135	60	143	1	27	13	685	9.9
84-85—Milwaukee	44	882	307	165	.537	124	102	.823	49	68	117	94	117	0	34	5	433	9.8
85-86—Milwaukee	81	2147	798	429	.538	310	266	.858	94	137	231	177	252	6	83	6	1127	13.9
86-87—Milwaukee	79	2505	1077	575	.534	440	387	.880	117	149	266	144	222	0	64	24	1540	19.5
87-88—Milwaukee	37	965	486	248	.510	122	107	.877	30	53	83	73	94	0	21	7	606	16.4
88-89—Milwaukee	75	2078	1018	527	.518	297	255	.859	82	115	197	156	193	1	77	19	1317	17.6
89-90—Milwaukee	59	1709	987	503	.510	366	307	.839	64	103	167	133	158	2	50	7	1359	23.0
Totals	483	11831	5331	2748	.515	1864	1591	.854	510	721	1231	851	1221	10	364	85	7152	14.8

Three-Point Field Goals: 1982-83, 1-for-7 (.143). 1983-84, 0-for-9. 1984-85, 1-for-4 (.250). 1985-86, 3-for-23 (.130). 1986-87, 3-for-28 (.107). 1987-88, 3-for-14 (.214). 1988-89, 8-for-36 (.222). 1989-90, 46-for-133 (.346). Totals, 65-for-254 (.256).

NBA PLAYOFF RECORD

									—Rebounds—									
Sea.—Team	G.	Min.	FGA	FGM	Pct.	FTA	FTM	Pct.	Off.	Def.	Tot.	Ast.	PF	Dq.	Stl.	Blk.	Pts.	Avg.
84-85—Milwaukee	8	198	73	36	.493	9	7	.778	8	10	18	15	26	0	3	1	79	9.9
85-86—Milwaukee	13	322	113	52	.460	45	40	.889	20	16	36	20	42	0	8	3	144	11.1
86-87—Milwaukee	12	317	142	68	.479	67	55	.821	12	16	28	16	39	0	10	5	191	15.9
87-88—Milwaukee	5	105	53	25	.472	9	8	.889	6	8	14	9	9	0	1	2	59	11.8
88-89—Milwaukee	9	292	141	77	.546	47	41	.872	5	20	25	25	31	1	11	2	201	22.3
89-90—Milwaukee	4	122	60	28	.467	31	28	.903	6	3	9	6	14	0	5	0	89	22.3
Totals	51	1356	582	286	.491	208	179	.861	57	73	130	91	161	1	38	13	763	15.0

Three-Point Field Goals: 1984-85, 0-for-2. 1985-86, 0-for-2. 1987-88, 1-for-5 (.200). 1988-89, 6-for-8 (.750). 1989-90, 5-for-10 (.500). Totals, 12-for-27 (.444).

Recipient of NBA Sixth Man Award, 1987 and 1990.

EDWARD LEWIS PINCKNEY (Ed)

Born March 27, 1963 at Bronx, N.Y. Height 6:09. Weight 215.
High School—Bronx, N.Y., Adlai Stevenson.
College—Villanova University, Villanova, Pa.
Drafted by Phoenix on first round, 1985 (10th pick).

Traded by Phoenix with a 1988 2nd round draft choice to Sacramento for Eddie Johnson, June 21, 1987.
Traded by Sacramento with Joe Kleine to Boston for Danny Ainge and Brad Lohaus, February 23, 1989.

—COLLEGIATE RECORD—

Year	G.	Min.	FGA	FGM	Pct.	FTA	FTM	Pct.	Reb.	Pts.	Avg.
81-82	32	1083	264	169	.640	161	115	.714	249	453	14.2
82-83	31	1029	227	129	.568	171	130	.760	301	388	12.5
83-84	31	1068	268	162	.604	222	154	.694	246	478	15.4
84-85	35	1186	295	177	.600	263	192	.730	311	546	15.6
Totals	129	4366	1054	637	.604	817	591	.723	1107	1865	14.5

NBA REGULAR SEASON RECORD

Sea.—Team	G.	Min.	FGA	FGM	Pct.	FTA	FTM	Pct.	—Rebounds— Off.	Def.	Tot.	Ast.	PF	Dq.	Stl.	Blk.	Pts.	Avg.
85-86—Phoenix	80	1602	457	255	.558	254	171	.673	95	213	308	90	190	3	71	37	681	8.5
86-87—Phoenix	80	2250	497	290	.584	348	257	.739	179	401	580	116	196	1	86	54	837	10.5
87-88—Sacramento	79	1177	343	179	.522	178	133	.747	94	136	230	66	118	0	39	32	491	6.2
88-89—Sac.-Bos.	80	2012	622	319	.513	350	280	.800	166	283	449	118	202	2	83	66	918	11.5
89-90—Boston	77	1082	249	135	.542	119	92	.773	93	132	225	68	126	1	34	42	362	4.7
Totals	396	8123	2168	1178	.543	1249	933	.747	627	1165	1792	458	832	7	313	231	3289	8.3

Three-Point Field Goals: 1985-86, 0-for-2. 1986-87, 0-for-2. 1987-88, 0-for-2. 1988-89, 0-for-6. 1989-90, 0-for-1. Totals, 0-for-13.

NBA PLAYOFF RECORD

Sea.—Team	G.	Min.	FGA	FGM	Pct.	FTA	FTM	Pct.	—Rebounds— Off.	Def.	Tot.	Ast.	PF	Dq.	Stl.	Blk.	Pts.	Avg.
88-89—Boston	3	45	12	3	.250	2	2	1.000	2	3	5	1	7	0	1	1	8	2.7
89-90—Boston	4	25	7	6	.857	9	7	.778	2	4	6	0	3	0	0	0	19	4.8
Totals	7	70	19	9	.474	11	9	.818	4	7	11	1	10	0	1	1	27	3.9

Member of NCAA Division I championship team, 1985. . . . Named NCAA Division I Tournament Most Outstanding Player, 1985.

SCOTTIE PIPPEN

Born September 25, 1965 at Hamburg, Ark. Height 6:07. Weight 210.

High School—Hamburg, Ark.

College—University of Central Arkansas, Conway, Ark.

Drafted by Seattle on first round, 1987 (5th pick).

Draft rights traded by Seattle to Chicago for draft rights to Olden Polynice, a 1988 or 1989 2nd round draft choice and the option to exchange 1989 1st round draft choices, June 22, 1987.

—COLLEGIATE RECORD—

Year	G.	Min.	FGA	FGM	Pct.	FTA	FTM	Pct.	Reb.	Pts.	Avg.
83-84	20	....	79	36	.456	19	13	.684	59	85	4.3
84-85	19	....	250	141	.564	102	69	.676	175	351	18.5
85-86	29	....	412	229	.556	169	116	.686	266	574	19.8
86-87	25	....	390	231	.592	146	105	.719	249	590	23.6
Totals	93	....	1131	637	.563	436	303	.695	749	1600	17.2

Three-Point Field Goals: 1986-87, 23-for-40 (.575).

NBA REGULAR SEASON RECORD

Sea.—Team	G.	Min.	FGA	FGM	Pct.	FTA	FTM	Pct.	—Rebounds— Off.	Def.	Tot.	Ast.	PF	Dq.	Stl.	Blk.	Pts.	Avg.
87-88—Chicago	79	1650	564	261	.463	172	99	.576	115	183	298	169	214	3	91	52	625	7.9
88-89—Chicago	73	2413	867	413	.476	301	201	.668	138	307	445	256	261	8	139	61	1048	14.4
89-90—Chicago	82	3148	1150	562	.489	295	199	.675	150	397	547	444	298	6	211	101	1351	16.5
Totals	234	7211	2581	1236	.479	768	499	.650	403	887	1290	869	773	17	441	214	3024	12.9

Three-Point Field Goals: 1987-88, 4-for-23 (.174). 1988-89, 21-for-77 (.273). 1989-90, 28-for-112 (.250). Totals, 53-for-212 (.250).

NBA PLAYOFF RECORD

Sea.—Team	G.	Min.	FGA	FGM	Pct.	FTA	FTM	Pct.	—Rebounds— Off.	Def.	Tot.	Ast.	PF	Dq.	Stl.	Blk.	Pts.	Avg.
87-88—Chicago	10	294	99	46	.465	7	5	.714	24	28	52	24	33	1	8	8	100	10.0
88-89—Chicago	17	619	182	84	.462	50	32	.640	34	95	129	67	63	2	23	16	222	13.1
89-90—Chicago	15	612	210	104	.495	100	71	.710	33	75	108	83	62	0	31	19	289	19.3
Totals	42	1525	491	234	.477	157	108	.688	91	198	289	174	158	3	62	43	611	14.5

Three-Point Field Goals: 1987-88, 3-for-6 (.500). 1988-89, 22-for-56 (.393). 1989-90, 10-for-31 (.323). Totals, 35-for-93 (.376).

NBA ALL-STAR GAME RECORD

Season—Team	Min.	FGA	FGM	Pct.	FTA	FTM	Pct.	—Rebounds— Off.	Def.	Tot.	Ast.	PF	Dq.	Stl.	Blk.	Pts.
1990—Chicago	12	4	2	.500	0	0	....	0	1	1	0	1	0	1	1	4

Three-Point Field Goals: 1990, 0-for-1.

OLDEN POLYNICE

Born November 21, 1964 at Port-Au-Prince, Haiti. Height 7:00. Weight 242.

High School—Bronx, N.Y., All Hallows.

College—University of Virginia, Charlottesville, Va.

Drafted by Chicago on first round as an undergraduate, 1987 (8th pick).

Draft rights traded with a 1988 or 1989 2nd round draft choice and the option to exchange 1989 1st round draft choices by Chicago to Seattle for the draft rights to Scottie Pippen, June 22, 1987.

Played in Italy during 1986-87 season.

—COLLEGIATE RECORD—

Year	G.	Min.	FGA	FGM	Pct.	FTA	FTM	Pct.	Reb.	Pts.	Avg.
83-84	33	866	178	98	.551	97	57	.588	184	253	7.7
84-85	32	1095	267	161	.603	157	94	.599	243	416	13.0
85-86	30	1074	320	183	.572	182	116	.637	240	482	16.1
Totals	95	3035	765	442	.578	436	267	.612	667	1151	12.1

ITALIAN LEAGUE RECORD

Year	G.	Min.	FGA	FGM	Pct.	FTA	FTM	Pct.	Reb.	Pts.	Avg.
86-87—Rimini	30	968	378	214	.566	137	82	.599	330	518	17.3

NBA REGULAR SEASON RECORD

									—Rebounds—									
Sea.—Team	G.	Min.	FGA	FGM	Pct.	FTA	FTM	Pct.	Off.	Def.	Tot.	Ast.	PF	Dq.	Stl.	Blk.	Pts.	Avg.
87-88—Seattle	82	1080	254	118	.465	158	101	.639	122	208	330	33	215	1	32	26	337	4.1
88-89—Seattle	80	835	180	91	.506	86	51	.593	98	108	206	21	164	0	37	30	233	2.9
89-90—Seattle	79	1085	289	156	.540	99	47	.475	128	172	300	15	187	0	25	21	360	4.6
Totals	241	3000	723	365	.505	343	199	.580	348	488	836	69	566	1	94	77	930	3.9

Three-Point Field Goals: 1987-88, 0-for-2. 1988-89, 0-for-2. 1989-90, 1-for-2 (.500). Totals, 1-for-6 (.167).

NBA PLAYOFF RECORD

									—Rebounds—									
Sea.—Team	G.	Min.	FGA	FGM	Pct.	FTA	FTM	Pct.	Off.	Def.	Tot.	Ast.	PF	Dq.	Stl.	Blk.	Pts.	Avg.
87-88—Seattle	5	44	11	5	.455	2	0	.000	2	6	8	0	6	0	3	0	10	2.0
88-89—Seattle	8	162	41	25	.610	13	7	.538	27	35	62	1	32	1	6	4	57	7.1
Totals	13	206	52	30	.577	15	7	.467	29	41	70	1	38	1	9	4	67	5.2

TERRY PORTER

Born April 8, 1963 at Milwaukee, Wis. Height 6:03. Weight 195.

High School—Milwaukee, Wis., South Division.

College—University of Wisconsin at Stevens Point, Stevens Point, Wisc.

Drafted by Portland on first round, 1985 (24th pick).

—COLLEGIATE RECORD—

Year	G.	Min.	FGA	FGM	Pct.	FTA	FTM	Pct.	Reb.	Pts.	Avg.
81-82	25	273	57	21	.368	13	9	.692	13	51	2.0
82-83	30	949	229	140	.611	89	62	.697	117	342	11.4
83-84	32	1040	392	244	.622	135	112	.830	165	600	18.8
84-85	30	1042	405	233	.575	151	126	.834	155	592	19.7
Totals	117	3304	1083	638	.589	388	309	.796	450	1585	13.5

NBA REGULAR SEASON RECORD

									—Rebounds—									
Sea.—Team	G.	Min.	FGA	FGM	Pct.	FTA	FTM	Pct.	Off.	Def.	Tot.	Ast.	PF	Dq.	Stl.	Blk.	Pts.	Avg.
85-86—Portland	79	1214	447	212	.474	155	125	.806	35	82	117	198	136	0	81	1	562	7.1
86-87—Portland	80	2714	770	376	.488	334	280	.838	70	267	337	715	192	0	159	9	1045	13.1
87-88—Portland	82	2991	890	462	.519	324	274	.846	65	313	378	831	204	1	150	16	1222	14.9
88-89—Portland	81	3102	1146	540	.471	324	272	.840	85	282	367	770	187	1	146	8	1431	17.7
89-90—Portland	80	2781	969	448	.462	472	421	.892	59	213	272	726	150	0	151	4	1406	17.6
Totals	402	12802	4222	2038	.483	1609	1372	.853	314	1157	1471	3240	869	2	687	38	5666	14.1

Three-Point Field Goals: 1985-86, 13-for-42 (.310). 1986-87, 13-for-60 (.217). 1987-88, 24-for-69 (.348). 1988-89, 72-for-219 (.361). 1989-90, 89-for-238 (.374). Totals, 218-for-628 (.347).

NBA PLAYOFF RECORD

									—Rebounds—									
Sea.—Team	G.	Min.	FGA	FGM	Pct.	FTA	FTM	Pct.	Off.	Def.	Tot.	Ast.	PF	Dq.	Stl.	Blk.	Pts.	Avg.
85-86—Portland	4	68	27	12	.444	4	2	.500	1	4	5	12	10	0	3	2	27	6.8
86-87—Portland	4	150	50	24	.480	20	18	.900	1	18	19	40	14	0	10	2	68	17.0
87-88—Portland	4	149	52	29	.558	13	9	.692	4	10	14	28	13	0	10	0	68	17.0
88-89—Portland	3	124	52	26	.500	12	10	.833	6	10	16	25	8	0	1	1	66	22.0
89-90—Portland	21	815	274	127	.464	165	139	.842	9	52	61	155	51	1	28	3	433	20.6
Totals	36	1306	455	218	.479	214	178	.832	21	94	115	260	96	1	52	8	662	18.4

Three-Point Field Goals: 1985-86, 1-for-6 (.167). 1986-87, 2-for-5 (.400). 1987-88, 1-for-3 (.333). 1988-89, 4-for-11 (.364). 1989-90, 40-for-102 (.392). Totals, 48-for-127 (.378).

—DID YOU KNOW—

That only five active coaches—Chuck Daly, Bill Fitch, Phil Jackson, K.C. Jones and Lenny Wilkens—have winning career records in NBA playoff competition?

PAUL MATTHEW PRESSEY

Born December 24, 1958 at Richmond, Va. Height 6:05. Weight 200.

High School—Richmond, Va., George Wythe.

Colleges—Western Texas College, Snyder, Tex., and University of Tulsa, Tulsa, Okla.

Drafted by Milwaukee on first round, 1982 (20th pick).

Traded by Milwaukee to San Antonio for Frank Brickowski, August 1, 1990.

—COLLEGIATE RECORD—

Western Texas

Year	G.	Min.	FGA	FGM	Pct.	FTA	FTM	Pct.	Reb.	Pts.	Avg.
78-79	33	....	286	191	.668	103	78	.757	262	460	13.9
79-80	37	....	327	213	.651	122	93	.762	291	519	14.0
J.C. Totals	70	....	613	404	.659	225	171	.760	553	979	14.0

Tulsa

Year	G.	Min.	FGA	FGM	Pct.	FTA	FTM	Pct.	Reb.	Pts.	Avg.
80-81	33	1050	288	137	.476	114	66	.579	178	340	10.3
81-82	30	973	275	154	.560	131	87	.664	192	395	13.2
Totals	63	2023	563	291	.517	245	153	.624	370	735	11.7

NBA REGULAR SEASON RECORD

									—Rebounds—									
Sea.—Team	G.	Min.	FGA	FGM	Pct.	FTA	FTM	Pct.	Off.	Def.	Tot.	Ast.	PF	Dq.	Stl.	Blk.	Pts.	Avg.
82-83—Milwaukee	79	1528	466	213	.457	176	105	.597	83	198	281	207	174	2	99	47	532	6.7
83-84—Milwaukee	81	1730	528	276	.523	200	120	.600	102	180	282	252	241	6	86	50	674	8.3
84-85—Milwaukee	80	2876	928	480	.517	418	317	.758	149	280	429	543	258	4	129	56	1284	16.1
85-86—Milwaukee	80	2704	843	411	.488	392	316	.806	127	272	399	623	247	4	168	71	1146	14.3
86-87—Milwaukee	61	2057	616	294	.477	328	242	.738	98	198	296	441	213	4	110	47	846	13.9
87-88—Milwaukee	75	2484	702	345	.491	357	285	.798	130	245	375	523	233	6	112	34	983	13.1
88-89—Milwaukee	67	2170	648	307	.474	241	187	.776	73	189	262	439	221	2	119	44	813	12.1
89-90—Milwaukee	57	1400	506	239	.472	190	144	.758	59	113	172	244	149	3	71	23	628	11.0
Totals	580	16949	5237	2565	.490	2302	1716	.745	821	1675	2496	3272	1736	31	894	372	6906	11.9

Three-Point Field Goals: 1982-83, 1-for-9 (.111). 1983-84, 2-for-9 (.222). 1984-85, 7-for-20 (.350). 1985-86, 8-for-44 (.182). 1986-87, 16-for-55 (.291). 1987-88, 8-for-39 (.205). 1988-89, 12-for-55 (.218). 1989-90, 6-for-43 (.140). Totals, 60-for-274 (.219).

NBA PLAYOFF RECORD

									—Rebounds—									
Sea.—Team	G.	Min.	FGA	FGM	Pct.	FTA	FTM	Pct.	Off.	Def.	Tot.	Ast.	PF	Dq.	Stl.	Blk.	Pts.	Avg.
82-83—Milwaukee	9	150	47	19	.404	20	8	.400	14	19	33	14	23	0	9	6	46	5.1
83-84—Milwaukee	16	351	100	52	.520	56	38	.679	17	42	59	50	53	1	22	9	142	8.9
84-85—Milwaukee	8	296	88	45	.511	38	31	.816	15	33	48	61	27	1	18	5	122	15.3
85-86—Milwaukee	14	530	157	76	.484	88	67	.761	19	41	60	110	48	0	18	13	225	16.1
86-87—Milwaukee	12	465	146	68	.466	46	34	.739	28	34	62	103	51	3	28	8	171	14.3
87-88—Milwaukee	5	178	50	23	.460	30	23	.767	6	13	19	33	21	0	4	3	70	14.0
89-90—Milwaukee	4	129	44	19	.432	26	21	.808	8	13	21	30	14	0	6	1	59	14.8
Totals	68	2099	632	302	.478	304	222	.730	107	195	302	401	237	5	105	45	835	12.3

Three-Point Field Goals: 1982-83, 0-for-1. 1983-84, 0-for-3. 1984-85, 1-for-3 (.333). 1985-86, 6-for-18 (.333). 1986-87, 1-for-8 (.125). 1987-88, 1-for-3 (.333). 1989-90, 0-for-3. Totals, 9-for-39 (.231).

Named to NBA All-Defensive First Team, 1985 and 1986. . . . NBA All-Defensive Second Team, 1987.

HAROLD PRESSLEY

Born July 14, 1963 at Bronx, N.Y. Height 6:08. Weight 210.

High School—Uncasville, Conn., St. Bernard.

College—Villanova University, Villanova, Pa.

Drafted by Sacramento on first round, 1986 (17th pick).

—COLLEGIATE RECORD—

Year	G.	Min.	FGA	FGM	Pct.	FTA	FTM	Pct.	Reb.	Pts.	Avg.
82-83	32	681	170	66	.388	24	11	.458	143	143	4.5
83-84	31	1126	303	156	.515	118	78	.661	221	390	12.6
84-85	35	1191	340	166	.488	135	87	.644	278	419	12.0
85-86	37	1288	442	224	.507	224	172	.768	374	620	16.8
Totals	135	4286	1255	612	.488	501	348	.695	1016	1572	11.6

NBA REGULAR SEASON RECORD

									—Rebounds—									
Sea.—Team	G.	Min.	FGA	FGM	Pct.	FTA	FTM	Pct.	Off.	Def.	Tot.	Ast.	PF	Dq.	Stl.	Blk.	Pts.	Avg.
86-87—Sacramento	67	913	317	134	.423	48	35	.729	68	108	176	120	96	1	40	21	310	4.6
87-88—Sacramento	80	2029	702	318	.453	130	103	.792	139	230	369	185	211	4	84	55	775	9.7
88-89—Sacramento	80	2257	873	383	.439	123	96	.780	216	269	485	174	215	1	93	76	981	12.3
89-90—Sacramento	72	1603	566	240	.424	141	110	.780	94	215	309	149	148	0	58	36	636	8.8
Totals	299	6802	2458	1075	.437	442	344	.778	517	822	1339	628	670	6	275	188	2702	9.0

Three-Point Field Goals: 1986-87, 7-for-28 (.250). 1987-88, 36-for-110 (.327). 1988-89, 119-for-295 (.403). 1989-90, 46-for-148 (.311). Totals, 208-for-581 (.358).

Member of NCAA Division I championship team, 1985.

WILLIAM MARK PRICE

(Known by middle name.)

Born February 16, 1964 at Bartlesville, Okla. Height 6:01. Weight 170.
High School—Enid, Okla.
College—Georgia Institute of Technology, Atlanta, Ga.
Drafted by Dallas on second round, 1986 (25th pick).

Draft rights traded by Dallas to Cleveland for a 1989 2nd round draft choice and cash, June 17, 1986.

—COLLEGIATE RECORD—

Year	G.	Min.	FGA	FGM	Pct.	FTA	FTM	Pct.	Reb.	Pts.	Avg.
82-83	28	1020	462	201	.435	106	93	.877	105	568	20.3
83-84	29	1078	375	191	.509	85	70	.824	61	452	15.6
84-85	35	1302	462	223	.483	163	137	.840	71	583	16.7
85-86	34	1204	441	233	.528	145	124	.855	94	590	17.4
Totals	126	4604	1740	848	.487	499	424	.850	331	2193	17.4

Three-Point Field Goals: 1982-83, 73-for-166 (.440).

NBA REGULAR SEASON RECORD

									—Rebounds—									
Sea.—Team	G.	Min.	FGA	FGM	Pct.	FTA	FTM	Pct.	Off.	Def.	Tot.	Ast.	PF	Dq.	Stl.	Blk.	Pts.	Avg.
86-87—Cleveland	67	1217	424	173	.408	114	95	.833	33	84	117	202	75	1	43	4	464	6.9
87-88—Cleveland	80	2626	974	493	.506	252	221	.877	54	126	180	480	119	1	99	12	1279	16.0
88-89—Cleveland	75	2728	1006	529	.526	292	263	.901	48	178	226	631	98	0	115	7	1414	18.9
89-90—Cleveland	73	2706	1066	489	.459	338	300	.888	66	185	251	666	89	0	114	5	1430	19.6
Totals	295	9277	3470	1684	.485	996	879	.883	201	573	774	1979	381	2	371	28	4587	15.5

Three-Point Field Goals: 1986-87, 23-for-70 (.329). 1987-88, 72-for-148 (.486). 1988-89, 93-for-211 (.441). 1989-90, 152-for-374 (.406). Totals, 340-for-803 (.423).

NBA PLAYOFF RECORD

									—Rebounds—									
Sea.—Team	G.	Min.	FGA	FGM	Pct.	FTA	FTM	Pct.	Off.	Def.	Tot.	Ast.	PF	Dq.	Stl.	Blk.	Pts.	Avg.
87-88—Cleveland	5	205	67	38	.567	25	24	.960	3	15	18	38	11	1	3	0	105	21.0
88-89—Cleveland	4	158	57	22	.386	15	14	.933	4	9	13	22	3	0	3	0	64	16.0
89-90—Cleveland	5	192	61	32	.525	30	30	1.000	0	14	14	44	9	0	9	1	100	20.0
Totals	14	555	185	92	.497	70	68	.971	7	38	45	104	23	1	15	1	269	19.2

Three-Point Field Goals: 1987-88, 5-for-12 (.417). 1988-89, 6-for-16 (.375). 1989-90, 6-for-17 (.353). Totals, 17-for-45 (.378).

NBA ALL-STAR GAME RECORD

								—Rebounds—								
Season—Team	Min.	FGA	FGM	Pct.	FTA	FTM	Pct.	Off.	Def.	Tot.	Ast.	PF	Dq.	Stl.	Blk.	Pts.
1989—Cleveland	20	9	3	.333	2	2	1.000	1	2	3	1	2	0	2	0	9

Three-Point Field Goals: 1989, 1-for-4 (.250).

Named to All-NBA Third Team, 1989.

BRIAN RALPH QUINNETT

Born May 30, 1966 at Pullman, Wash. Height 6:08. Weight 235.
High School—Cheney, Wash.
College—Washington State University, Pullman, Wash.
Drafted by New York on second round, 1989 (50th pick).

—COLLEGIATE RECORD—

Year	G.	Min.	FGA	FGM	Pct.	FTA	FTM	Pct.	Reb.	Pts.	Avg.
84-85	24	517	133	63	.474	21	16	.762	77	142	5.9
85-86	31	815	250	122	.488	49	29	.592	138	273	8.8
86-87	28	944	373	186	.499	75	53	.707	145	462	16.5
87-88	1	29	16	6	.375	4	3	.750	8	15	15.0
88-89	28	917	437	210	.481	105	76	.724	164	516	18.4
Totals	112	3222	1209	587	.486	254	177	.697	532	1408	12.6

(Suffered broken foot, November, 1987; granted additional year of eligibility.)

Three-Point Field Goals: 1986-87, 37-for-94 (.394). 1987-88, 0-for-1. 1988-89, 20-for-55 (.364). Totals, 57-for-150 (.380).

NBA REGULAR SEASON RECORD

									—Rebounds—									
Sea.—Team	G.	Min.	FGA	FGM	Pct.	FTA	FTM	Pct.	Off.	Def.	Tot.	Ast.	PF	Dq.	Stl.	Blk.	Pts.	Avg.
89-90—New York	31	193	58	19	.328	3	2	.667	9	19	28	11	27	0	3	4	40	1.3

Three-Point Field Goals: 1989-90, 0-for-2.

NBA PLAYOFF RECORD

Sea.—Team	G.	Min.	FGA	FGM	Pct.	FTA	FTM	Pct.	—Rebounds— Off.	Def.	Tot.	Ast.	PF	Dq.	Stl.	Blk.	Pts.	Avg.
89-90—New York	3	16	4	2	.500	0	0	....	5	3	8	2	2	0	0	0	5	1.7

Three-Point Field Goals: 1989-90, 1-for-1 (1.000).

DARRELL KURT RAMBIS

(Known by middle name.)

Born February 25, 1958 at Cupertino, Calif. Height 6:08. Weight 213.
High School—Cupertino, Calif.
College—University of Santa Clara, Santa Clara, Calif.
Drafted by New York on third round, 1980 (58th pick).

Waived by New York, September 18, 1980; re-signed by New York to 10-day contract that expired January 30, 1981.
Signed by Los Angeles as a free agent, September 13, 1981.
Signed by Charlotte as an unrestricted free agent, July 28, 1988.
Traded by Charlotte with two future 2nd round draft choices to Phoenix for Armon Gilliam, December 13, 1989.
Played in Greece during 1980-81 season.

—COLLEGIATE RECORD—

Year	G.	Min.	FGA	FGM	Pct.	FTA	FTM	Pct.	Reb.	Pts.	Avg.
76-77	27	....	317	167	.527	125	70	.560	313	404	15.0
77-78	27	....	268	136	.507	143	99	.692	231	371	13.7
78-79	27	763	336	172	.512	109	78	.716	226	422	15.6
79-80	27	860	395	211	.534	168	107	.637	267	529	19.6
Totals	108	....	1316	686	.521	545	354	.650	1037	1726	16.0

NBA REGULAR SEASON RECORD

Sea.—Team	G.	Min.	FGA	FGM	Pct.	FTA	FTM	Pct.	—Rebounds— Off.	Def.	Tot.	Ast.	PF	Dq.	Stl.	Blk.	Pts.	Avg.
81-82—Los Angeles	64	1131	228	118	.518	117	59	.504	116	232	348	56	167	2	60	76	295	4.6
82-83—Los Angeles	78	1806	413	235	.569	166	114	.687	164	367	531	90	233	2	105	63	584	7.5
83-84—Los Angeles	47	743	113	63	.558	66	42	.636	82	184	266	34	108	0	30	14	168	3.6
84-85—L.A. Lakers	82	1617	327	181	.554	103	68	.660	164	364	528	69	211	0	82	47	430	5.2
85-86—L.A. Lakers	74	1573	269	160	.595	122	88	.721	156	361	517	69	198	0	66	33	408	5.5
86-87—L.A. Lakers	78	1514	313	163	.521	157	120	.764	159	294	453	63	201	1	74	41	446	5.7
87-88—L.A. Lakers	70	845	186	102	.548	93	73	.785	103	165	268	54	103	0	39	13	277	4.0
88-89—Charlotte	75	2233	627	325	.518	248	182	.734	269	434	703	159	208	4	100	57	832	11.1
89-90—Char.-Phoe.	74	1904	373	190	.509	127	82	.646	156	369	525	135	208	0	100	37	462	6.2
Totals	642	13366	2849	1537	.539	1199	828	.691	1369	2770	4139	729	1637	9	656	381	3902	6.1

Three-Point Field Goals: 1981-82, 0-for-1. 1982-83, 0-for-2. 1988-89, 0-for-3. 1989-90, 0-for-3. Totals, 0-for-9.

NBA PLAYOFF RECORD

Sea.—Team	G.	Min.	FGA	FGM	Pct.	FTA	FTM	Pct.	—Rebounds— Off.	Def.	Tot.	Ast.	PF	Dq.	Stl.	Blk.	Pts.	Avg.
81-82—Los Angeles	14	279	64	33	.516	26	16	.615	32	54	86	11	47	0	8	12	82	5.9
82-83—Los Angeles	15	377	79	45	.570	35	23	.657	27	63	90	19	51	0	13	16	113	7.5
83-84—Los Angeles	21	428	92	60	.652	33	21	.636	33	88	121	14	57	0	10	10	141	6.7
84-85—L.A. Lakers	19	375	81	48	.593	28	19	.679	42	87	129	17	52	0	18	9	115	6.1
85-86—L.A. Lakers	14	267	45	27	.600	18	13	.722	26	57	83	14	39	0	10	7	67	4.8
86-87—L.A. Lakers	17	215	41	24	.585	34	31	.912	16	51	67	9	42	0	8	3	79	4.6
87-88—L.A. Lakers	19	186	34	21	.618	13	9	.692	13	38	51	9	28	0	5	2	51	2.7
89-90—Phoenix	16	385	54	24	.444	28	19	.679	39	84	123	22	51	0	8	8	67	4.2
Totals	135	2512	490	282	.576	215	151	.702	228	522	750	115	367	0	80	67	715	5.3

Three-Point Field Goals: 1989-90, 0-for-1.

Member of NBA championship teams, 1982, 1985, 1987, 1988.

BLAIR ALLEN RASMUSSEN

Born November 13, 1962 at Auburn, Wash. Height 7:00. Weight 260.
High School—Auburn, Wash.
College—University of Oregon, Eugene, Ore.
Drafted by Denver on first round, 1985 (15th pick).

—COLLEGIATE RECORD—

Year	G.	Min.	FGA	FGM	Pct.	FTA	FTM	Pct.	Reb.	Pts.	Avg.
81-82	27	521	141	67	.475	53	39	.736	129	173	6.4
82-83	27	819	296	160	.540	116	80	.690	146	400	14.8
83-84	29	1017	377	196	.520	112	90	.804	176	482	16.6
84-85	31	1081	381	195	.512	151	109	.722	222	499	16.1
Totals	114	3438	1195	618	.517	432	318	.736	673	1554	13.6

NBA REGULAR SEASON RECORD

Sea.—Team	G.	Min.	FGA	FGM	Pct.	FTA	FTM	Pct.	—Rebounds— Off.	Def.	Tot.	Ast.	PF	Dq.	Stl.	Blk.	Pts.	Avg.
85-86—Denver	48	330	150	61	.407	39	31	.795	37	60	97	16	63	0	3	10	153	3.2
86-87—Denver	74	1421	570	268	.470	231	169	.732	183	282	465	60	224	6	24	58	705	9.5
87-88—Denver	79	1779	884	435	.492	170	132	.776	130	307	437	78	241	2	22	81	1002	12.7
88-89—Denver	77	1308	577	257	.445	81	69	.852	105	182	287	49	194	2	29	41	583	7.6
89-90—Denver	81	1995	895	445	.497	134	111	.828	174	420	594	82	300	10	40	104	1001	12.4
Totals	359	6833	3076	1466	.477	655	512	.782	629	1251	1880	285	1022	20	118	294	3444	9.6

Three-Point Field Goals: 1989-90, 0-for-1.

NBA PLAYOFF RECORD

Sea.—Team	G.	Min.	FGA	FGM	Pct.	FTA	FTM	Pct.	—Rebounds— Off.	Def.	Tot.	Ast.	PF	Dq.	Stl.	Blk.	Pts.	Avg.
85-86—Denver	10	175	96	39	.406	41	33	.805	27	33	60	10	28	1	5	9	111	11.1
86-87—Denver	3	92	45	22	.489	10	5	.500	8	15	23	7	12	0	2	2	49	16.3
87-88—Denver	11	277	127	60	.472	20	18	.900	25	46	71	7	33	0	1	12	138	12.5
88-89—Denver	2	4	0	0	......	0	0	......	0	0	0	0	1	0	0	0	0	0.0
89-90—Denver	3	84	48	19	.396	10	9	.900	8	18	26	1	10	0	2	4	47	15.7
Totals	29	632	316	140	.443	81	65	.802	68	112	180	25	84	1	10	27	345	11.9

HERMAN REID JR.
(J.R.)

Born March 31, 1968 at Virginia Beach, Va. Height 6:09. Weight 255.
High School—Virginia Beach, Va., Kempsville.
College—University of North Carolina, Chapel Hill, N.C.
Drafted by Charlotte on first round as an undergraduate, 1989 (5th pick).

—COLLEGIATE RECORD—

Year	G.	Min.	FGA	FGM	Pct.	FTA	FTM	Pct.	Reb.	Pts.	Avg.
86-87	36	1030	339	198	.584	202	132	.653	268	528	14.7
87-88	33	1042	366	222	.607	222	151	.680	293	595	18.0
88-89	27	716	267	164	.614	151	101	.669	170	429	15.9
Totals	96	2788	972	584	.601	575	384	.668	731	1552	16.2

NBA REGULAR SEASON RECORD

Sea.—Team	G.	Min.	FGA	FGM	Pct.	FTA	FTM	Pct.	—Rebounds— Off.	Def.	Tot.	Ast.	PF	Dq.	Stl.	Blk.	Pts.	Avg.
89-90—Charlotte	82	2757	814	358	.440	289	192	.664	199	492	691	101	292	7	92	54	908	11.1

Three-Point Field Goals: 1989-90, 0-for-5.

Named to NBA All-Rookie Second Team, 1990. . . . Member of 1988 U.S. Olympic team. . . . Named to THE SPORTING NEWS All-America Second Team, 1988.

ROBERT KEITH REID

Born August 30, 1955 at Atlanta, Ga. Height 6:08. Weight 215.
High School—Schertz, Tex., Samuel Clemens.
College—St. Mary's University, San Antonio, Tex.
Drafted by Houston on second round, 1977 (40th pick).

Traded by Houston to Charlotte for Bernard Thompson and a 1990 2nd round draft choice, July 18, 1988.
Traded by Charlotte to Portland for Richard Anderson, October 17, 1989.
Waived by Portland, December 7, 1989; signed by Charlotte as a free agent, December 13, 1989.
Sat out 1982-83 season for religious reasons.

—COLLEGIATE RECORD—

Year	G.	Min.	FGA	FGM	Pct.	FTA	FTM	Pct.	Reb.	Pts.	Avg.
73-74	19	....	30	14	.467	21	11	.524	14	39	2.1
74-75	33	....	368	197	.535	73	53	.726	286	447	13.5
75-76	28	....	458	237	.517	85	74	.871	288	548	19.6
76-77	29	....	405	196	.484	115	83	.722	244	475	16.4
Totals	109	...	1261	644	.511	294	221	.752	832	1509	13.8

NBA REGULAR SEASON RECORD

Sea.—Team	G.	Min.	FGA	FGM	Pct.	FTA	FTM	Pct.	—Rebounds— Off.	Def.	Tot.	Ast.	PF	Dq.	Stl.	Blk.	Pts.	Avg.
77-78—Houston	80	1849	574	261	.455	96	63	.656	111	248	359	121	277	8	67	51	585	7.3
78-79—Houston	82	2259	777	382	.492	186	131	.704	129	354	483	230	302	7	75	48	895	10.9
79-80—Houston	76	2304	861	419	.487	208	153	.736	140	301	441	244	281	2	132	57	991	13.0
80-81—Houston	82	2963	1113	536	.482	303	229	.756	164	419	583	344	325	4	163	66	1301	15.9
81-82—Houston	77	2913	958	437	.456	214	160	.748	175	336	511	314	297	2	115	48	1035	13.4
83-84—Houston	64	1936	857	406	.474	123	81	.659	97	244	341	217	243	5	88	30	895	14.0

Sea.—Team	G.	Min.	FGA	FGM	Pct.	FTA	FTM	Pct.	—Rebounds— Off.	Def.	Tot.	Ast.	PF	Dq.	Stl.	Blk.	Pts.	Avg.
84-85—Houston	82	1763	648	312	.481	126	88	.698	81	192	273	171	196	1	48	22	713	8.7
85-86—Houston	82	2157	881	409	.464	214	162	.757	67	234	301	222	231	3	91	16	986	12.0
86-87—Houston	75	2594	1006	420	.417	177	136	.768	47	242	289	323	232	2	75	21	1029	13.7
87-88—Houston	62	980	356	165	.463	63	50	.794	38	87	125	67	118	0	27	5	393	6.3
88-89—Charlotte	82	2152	1214	519	.428	196	152	.776	82	220	302	153	235	2	53	20	1207	14.7
89-90—Port.-Char.	72	1202	447	175	.391	86	54	.628	34	117	151	90	153	0	38	16	414	5.8
Totals	916	25072	9692	4441	.458	1992	1459	.732	1165	2994	4159	2496	2890	36	972	400	10444	11.4

Three-Point Field Goals: 1979-80, 0-for-3. 1980-81, 0-for-4. 1981-82, 1-for-10 (.100). 1983-84, 2-for-8 (.250). 1984-85, 1-for-16 (.063). 1985-86, 6-for-33 (.182). 1986-87, 53-for-162 (.327). 1987-88, 13-for-34 (.382). 1988-89, 17-for-52 (.327). 1989-90, 10-for-32 (.313). Totals, 103-for-354 (.291).

NBA PLAYOFF RECORD

Sea.—Team	G.	Min.	FGA	FGM	Pct.	FTA	FTM	Pct.	—Rebounds— Off.	Def.	Tot.	Ast.	PF	Dq.	Stl.	Blk.	Pts.	Avg.
78-79—Houston	2	45	17	7	.412	9	6	.667	5	4	9	2	7	0	1	2	20	10.0
79-80—Houston	7	266	102	52	.510	26	22	.846	14	41	55	26	28	0	6	7	126	18.0
80-81—Houston	21	868	303	139	.459	92	61	.663	56	86	142	98	80	2	50	24	339	16.1
81-82—Houston	3	115	31	15	.484	5	4	.800	9	17	26	9	10	0	5	2	34	11.3
84-85—Houston	5	87	45	19	.422	0	0	.000	3	14	17	5	22	0	4	2	38	7.6
85-86—Houston	20	773	288	124	.431	59	47	.797	13	70	83	137	74	1	27	1	298	14.9
86-87—Houston	10	431	155	56	.361	23	15	.652	6	30	36	48	36	0	10	3	129	12.9
87-88—Houston	4	114	33	15	.455	3	2	.667	3	12	15	8	13	0	2	0	35	8.8
Totals	72	2699	974	427	.438	217	157	.724	109	274	383	333	270	3	105	41	1019	14.2

Three-Point Field Goals: 1979-80, 0-for-1. 1980-81, 0-for-2. 1984-85, 0-for-4. 1985-86, 3-for-21 (.143). 1986-87, 2-for-17 (.118). 1987-88, 3-for-7 (.429). Totals, 8-for-52 (.154).

JERRY REYNOLDS

Born December 23, 1962 at Brooklyn, N.Y. Height 6:08. Weight 200.

High School—Brooklyn, N.Y., Alexander Hamilton.

Colleges—Madison Area Technical College, Madison, Wisc., and Louisiana State University, Baton Rouge, La.

Drafted by Milwaukee on first round as an undergraduate, 1985 (22nd pick).

Traded by Milwaukee to Seattle for a 1990 2nd round draft choice, October 4, 1988.
Selected from Seattle by Orlando in NBA expansion draft, June 15, 1989.

—COLLEGIATE RECORD—

Madison Tech

Year	G.	Min.	FGA	FGM	Pct.	FTA	FTM	Pct.	Reb.	Pts.	Avg.
81-82					Did Not Play						

Louisiana State

Year	G.	Min.	FGA	FGM	Pct.	FTA	FTM	Pct.	Reb.	Pts.	Avg.
82-83	32	888	236	126	.534	142	88	.620	198	340	10.6
83-84	29	899	307	162	.528	158	85	.538	239	409	14.1
84-85	29	803	255	128	.502	107	64	.598	176	320	11.0
Totals	90	2590	798	416	.521	407	237	.582	613	1069	11.9

NBA REGULAR SEASON RECORD

Sea.—Team	G.	Min.	FGA	FGM	Pct.	FTA	FTM	Pct.	—Rebounds— Off.	Def.	Tot.	Ast.	PF	Dq.	Stl.	Blk.	Pts.	Avg.
85-86—Milwaukee	55	508	162	72	.444	104	58	.558	37	43	80	86	57	0	43	19	203	3.7
86-87—Milwaukee	58	963	356	140	.393	184	118	.641	72	101	173	106	91	0	50	30	404	7.0
87-88—Milwaukee	62	1161	419	188	.449	154	119	.773	70	90	160	104	97	0	74	32	498	8.0
88-89—Seattle	56	737	357	149	.417	167	127	.760	49	51	100	62	58	0	53	26	428	7.6
89-90—Orlando	67	1817	741	309	.417	322	239	.742	91	232	323	180	162	1	93	64	858	12.8
Totals	298	5186	2035	858	.422	931	661	.710	319	517	836	538	465	1	313	171	2391	8.0

Three-Point Field Goals: 1985-86, 1-for-2 (.500). 1986-87, 6-for-18 (.333). 1987-88, 3-for-7 (.429). 1988-89, 3-for-15 (.200). 1989-90, 1-for-14 (.071). Totals, 14-for-56 (.250).

NBA PLAYOFF RECORD

Sea.—Team	G.	Min.	FGA	FGM	Pct.	FTA	FTM	Pct.	—Rebounds— Off.	Def.	Tot.	Ast.	PF	Dq.	Stl.	Blk.	Pts.	Avg.
85-86—Milwaukee	7	40	17	7	.412	11	6	.545	3	6	9	4	5	0	4	3	20	2.9
86-87—Milwaukee	4	5	3	1	.333	2	1	.500	1	0	1	2	0	0	3	0	3	0.8
87-88—Milwaukee	3	12	6	4	.667	0	0	.000	0	1	1	1	1	0	0	0	8	2.7
88-89—Seattle	4	40	22	7	.318	10	7	.700	1	4	5	1	6	0	2	6	22	5.5
Totals	18	97	48	19	.396	23	14	.609	5	11	16	8	12	0	9	9	53	2.9

Three-Point Field Goals: 1985-86, 0-for-1. 1986-87, 0-for-1. 1988-89, 1-for-4 (.250). Totals, 1-for-6 (.167).

GLEN A. RICE

Born May 28, 1967 at Flint, Mich. Height 6:07. Weight 215.
High School—Flint, Mich., Northwestern.
College—University of Michigan, Ann Arbor, Mich.
Drafted by Miami on first round, 1989 (4th pick).

—COLLEGIATE RECORD—

Year	G.	Min.	FGA	FGM	Pct.	FTA	FTM	Pct.	Reb.	Pts.	Avg.
85-86	32	520	191	105	.550	25	15	.600	97	225	7.0
86-87	32	....	402	226	.562	108	85	.787	294	540	16.9
87-88	33	....	539	308	.571	98	79	.806	236	728	22.1
88-89	37	....	629	363	.577	149	124	.832	232	949	25.6
Totals	134	....	1761	1002	.569	380	303	.797	859	2442	18.2

Three-Point Field Goals: 1986-87, 3-for-12 (.250). 1987-88, 33-for-77 (.429). 1988-89, 99-for-192 (.516). Totals, 135-for-281 (.480).

NBA REGULAR SEASON RECORD

									—Rebounds—									
Sea.—Team	G.	Min.	FGA	FGM	Pct.	FTA	FTM	Pct.	Off.	Def.	Tot.	Ast.	PF	Dq.	Stl.	Blk.	Pts.	Avg.
89-90—Miami	77	2311	1071	470	.439	124	91	.734	100	252	352	138	198	1	67	27	1048	13.6

Three-Point Field Goals: 1989-90, 17-for-69 (.246).

Named to NBA All-Rookie Second Team, 1990. . . . Member of NCAA Division I championship team, 1989. . . . Named to THE SPORTING NEWS All-America Second Team, 1989. . . . Outstanding Player in NCAA Division I tournament, 1989.

JEROME RICHARDSON JR.
(Pooh)

Born May 14, 1966 at Philadelphia, Pa. Height 6:01. Weight 180.
High School—Philadelphia, Pa., Ben Franklin.
College—University of California at Los Angeles, Los Angeles, Calif.
Drafted by Minnesota on first round, 1989 (10th pick).

—COLLEGIATE RECORD—

Year	G.	Min.	FGA	FGM	Pct.	FTA	FTM	Pct.	Reb.	Pts.	Avg.
85-86	29	983	260	128	.492	74	51	.689	131	307	10.6
86-87	32	1112	273	144	.527	79	46	.582	163	336	10.5
87-88	30	1035	302	142	.470	93	62	.667	153	348	11.6
88-89	31	1167	335	186	.555	89	50	.562	118	470	15.2
Totals	122	4297	1170	600	.513	335	209	.624	565	1461	12.0

Three-Point Field Goals: 1986-87, 2-for-8 (.250). 1987-88, 2-for-7 (.286). 1988-89, 48-for-97 (.493). Totals, 52-for-112 (.464).

NBA REGULAR SEASON RECORD

									—Rebounds—									
Sea.—Team	G.	Min.	FGA	FGM	Pct.	FTA	FTM	Pct.	Off.	Def.	Tot.	Ast.	PF	Dq.	Stl.	Blk.	Pts.	Avg.
89-90—Minnesota	82	2581	925	426	.461	107	63	.589	55	162	217	554	143	0	133	25	938	11.4

Three-Point Field Goals: 1989-90, 23-for-83 (.277).

Named to NBA All-Rookie First Team, 1990.

MITCHELL JAMES RICHMOND
(Mitch)

Born June 30, 1965 at Fort Lauderdale, Fla. Height 6:05. Weight 215.
High School—Fort Lauderdale, Fla., Boyd Anderson.
Colleges—Moberly Area Junior College, Moberly, Mo., and Kansas State University, Manhattan, Kan.
Drafted by Golden State on first round, 1988 (5th pick).

—COLLEGIATE RECORD—

Moberly

Year	G.	Min.	FGA	FGM	Pct.	FTA	FTM	Pct.	Reb.	Pts.	Avg.
84-85	40	....	375	180	.480	85	55	.647	185	415	10.4
85-86	38	....	506	242	.478	180	124	.689	251	608	16.0
J.C. Totals	78	....	881	422	.479	265	179	.675	436	1023	13.1

Kansas State

Year	G.	Min.	FGA	FGM	Pct.	FTA	FTM	Pct.	Reb.	Pts.	Avg.
86-87	30	964	450	201	.447	155	118	.761	170	559	18.6
87-88	34	1200	521	268	.514	240	186	.775	213	768	22.6
K.S. Totals	64	2164	971	469	.483	395	304	.770	383	1327	20.7

Three-Point Field Goals: 1986-87, 39-for-108 (.361). 1987-88, 46-for-98 (.469). Totals, 85-for-206 (.412).

NBA REGULAR SEASON RECORD

Sea.—Team	G.	Min.	FGA	FGM	Pct.	FTA	FTM	Pct.	—Rebounds— Off.	Def.	Tot.	Ast.	PF	Dq.	Stl.	Blk.	Pts.	Avg.
88-89—Golden State	79	2717	1386	649	.468	506	410	.810	158	310	468	334	223	5	82	13	1741	22.0
89-90—Golden State	78	2799	1287	640	.497	469	406	.866	98	262	360	223	210	3	98	24	1720	22.1
Totals	157	5516	2673	1289	.482	975	816	.837	256	572	828	557	433	8	180	37	3461	22.0

Three-Point Field Goals: 1988-89, 33-for-90 (.367). 1989-90, 34-for-95 (.358). Totals, 67-for-185 (.362).

NBA PLAYOFF RECORD

Sea.—Team	G.	Min.	FGA	FGM	Pct.	FTA	FTM	Pct.	—Rebounds— Off.	Def.	Tot.	Ast.	PF	Dq.	Stl.	Blk.	Pts.	Avg.
88-89—Golden State	8	314	135	62	.459	38	34	.895	10	48	58	35	25	0	14	1	161	20.1

Three-Point Field Goals: 1988-89, 3-for-16 (.188).

Named NBA Rookie of the Year, 1989. . . . NBA All-Rookie First Team, 1989. . . . THE SPORTING NEWS All-America Second Team, 1988.

DAVID LEE RIVERS

Born January 20, 1965 at Jersey City, N.J. Height 6:00. Weight 180.

High School—Jersey City, N.J., St. Anthony's.

College—University of Notre Dame, Notre Dame, Ind.

Drafted by Los Angeles Lakers on first round, 1988 (25th pick).

Selected from Los Angeles Lakers by Minnesota in NBA expansion draft, June 15, 1989.
Waived by Minnesota, November 2, 1989; signed by Los Angeles Clippers as a free agent, November 14, 1989.

—COLLEGIATE RECORD—

Year	G.	Min.	FGA	FGM	Pct.	FTA	FTM	Pct.	Reb.	Pts.	Avg.
84-85	30	1068	398	168	.422	173	138	.798	78	474	15.8
85-86	28	930	353	159	.450	186	149	.801	84	467	16.7
86-87	32	1179	380	172	.453	159	134	.843	116	501	15.7
87-88	28	1027	462	205	.444	199	162	.814	115	616	22.0
Totals	118	4204	1593	704	.442	717	583	.813	393	2058	17.4

Three-Point Field Goals: 1986-87, 23-for-60 (.383). 1987-88, 44-for-105 (.419). Totals, 67-for-165 (.406).

NBA REGULAR SEASON RECORD

Sea.—Team	G.	Min.	FGA	FGM	Pct.	FTA	FTM	Pct.	—Rebounds— Off.	Def.	Tot.	Ast.	PF	Dq.	Stl.	Blk.	Pts.	Avg.
88-89—L.A. Lakers	47	440	122	49	.402	42	35	.833	13	30	43	106	50	0	23	9	134	2.9
89-90—L.A. Clippers	52	724	197	80	.406	78	59	.756	30	55	85	155	53	0	31	0	219	4.2
Totals	99	1164	319	129	.404	120	94	.783	43	85	128	261	103	0	54	9	353	3.6

Three-Point Field Goals: 1988-89, 1-for-6 (.167). 1989-90, 0-for-5. Totals, 1-for-11 (.091).

NBA PLAYOFF RECORD

Sea.—Team	G.	Min.	FGA	FGM	Pct.	FTA	FTM	Pct.	—Rebounds— Off.	Def.	Tot.	Ast.	PF	Dq.	Stl.	Blk.	Pts.	Avg.
88-89—L.A. Lakers	6	33	12	4	.333	8	7	.875	1	3	4	6	6	0	0	0	15	2.5

Three-Point Field Goals: 1988-89, 0-for-2.

GLENN ANTON RIVERS
(Doc)

Born October 13, 1961 at Maywood, Ill. Height 6:04. Weight 185.

High School—Maywood, Ill., Proviso East.

College—Marquette University, Milwaukee, Wis.

Drafted by Atlanta on second round as an undergraduate, 1983 (31st pick).

—COLLEGIATE RECORD—

Year	G.	Min.	FGA	FGM	Pct.	FTA	FTM	Pct.	Reb.	Pts.	Avg.
80-81	31	....	329	182	.553	119	70	.588	99	434	14.0
81-82	29	....	382	173	.453	108	70	.648	99	416	14.3
82-83	29	....	373	163	.437	95	58	.611	94	384	13.2
Totals	89	....	1084	518	.478	322	198	.615	292	1234	13.9

NBA REGULAR SEASON RECORD

Sea.—Team	G.	Min.	FGA	FGM	Pct.	FTA	FTM	Pct.	—Rebounds— Off.	Def.	Tot.	Ast.	PF	Dq.	Stl.	Blk.	Pts.	Avg.
83-84—Atlanta	81	1938	541	250	.462	325	255	.785	72	148	220	314	286	8	127	30	757	9.3
84-85—Atlanta	69	2126	701	334	.476	378	291	.770	66	148	214	410	250	7	163	53	974	14.1
85-86—Atlanta	53	1571	464	220	.474	283	172	.608	49	113	162	443	185	2	120	13	612	11.5
86-87—Atlanta	82	2590	758	342	.451	441	365	.828	83	216	299	823	287	5	171	30	1053	12.8
87-88—Atlanta	80	2502	890	403	.453	421	319	.758	83	283	366	747	272	3	140	41	1134	14.2

Sea.—Team	G.	Min.	FGA	FGM	Pct.	FTA	FTM	Pct.	Off.	Def.	Tot.	Ast.	PF	Dq.	Stl.	Blk.	Pts.	Avg.
									—Rebounds—									
88-89—Atlanta	76	2462	816	371	.455	287	247	.861	89	197	286	525	263	6	181	40	1032	13.6
89-90—Atlanta	48	1526	480	218	.454	170	138	.812	47	153	200	264	151	2	116	22	598	12.5
Totals	489	14715	4650	2138	.460	2305	1787	.775	489	1258	1747	3526	1694	33	1018	229	6160	12.6

Three-Point Field Goals: 1983-84, 2-for-12 (.167). 1984-85, 15-for-36 (.417). 1985-86, 0-for-16. 1986-87, 4-for-21 (.190). 1987-88, 9-for-33 (.273). 1988-89, 43-for-124 (.347). 1989-90, 24-for-66 (.364). Totals, 97-for-308 (.315).

NBA PLAYOFF RECORD

Sea.—Team	G.	Min.	FGA	FGM	Pct.	FTA	FTM	Pct.	Off.	Def.	Tot.	Ast.	PF	Dq.	Stl.	Blk.	Pts.	Avg.
									—Rebounds—									
83-84—Atlanta	5	130	32	16	.500	41	36	.878	7	3	10	16	16	0	12	4	68	13.6
85-86—Atlanta	9	262	92	40	.435	42	31	.738	10	32	42	78	38	2	18	0	114	12.7
86-87—Atlanta	8	245	47	18	.383	52	26	.500	6	21	27	90	32	0	9	3	62	7.8
87-88—Atlanta	12	409	139	71	.511	43	39	.907	8	51	59	115	40	1	25	2	188	15.7
88-89—Atlanta	5	191	57	22	.386	24	17	.708	4	20	24	34	22	2	7	2	67	13.4
Totals	39	1237	367	167	.455	202	149	.738	35	127	162	333	148	5	71	11	499	12.8

Three-Point Field Goals: 1983-84, 0-for-3. 1985-86, 3-for-6 (.500). 1987-88, 7-for-22 (.318). 1988-89, 6-for-19 (.316). Totals, 16-for-50 (.320).

NBA ALL-STAR GAME RECORD

Season—Team	Min.	FGA	FGM	Pct.	FTA	FTM	Pct.	Off.	Def.	Tot.	Ast.	PF	Dq.	Stl.	Blk.	Pts.
								—Rebounds—								
1988—Atlanta	16	4	2	.500	11	5	.455	0	3	3	6	3	0	0	0	9

Shares NBA playoff game record for most assists in one half, 15, vs. Boston, May 16, 1988. . . . Nephew of former NBA forward Jim Brewer. . . . Cousin of former major league outfielder Ken Singleton and Portland Trail Blazers guard Byron Irvin.

FREDERICK CLARK ROBERTS
(Fred)

Born August 14, 1960 at Provo, Utah. Height 6:10. Weight 220.
High School—Riverton, Utah, Bingham.
College—Brigham Young University, Provo, Utah.
Drafted by Milwaukee on second round, 1982 (27th pick).

Draft rights traded by Milwaukee with Mickey Johnson to New Jersey for Phil Ford and a 1983 2nd round draft choice, November 10, 1982.

Draft rights traded by New Jersey with a 1983 2nd round draft choice and cash to San Antonio in exchange for the Spurs' relinquishing their rights to Coach Stan Albeck, June 7, 1983.

Traded by San Antonio to Utah for 1986 and 1988 2nd round draft choices, December 18, 1984.

Traded by Utah to Boston for a 1987 3rd round draft choice, September 25, 1986.

Selected from Boston by Miami in NBA expansion draft, June 23, 1988.

Traded by Miami to Milwaukee for a 1988 2nd round draft choice, June 23, 1988.

Played in Italy during 1982-83 season.

—COLLEGIATE RECORD—

Year	G.	Min.	FGA	FGM	Pct.	FTA	FTM	Pct.	Reb.	Pts.	Avg.
78-79	28	861	291	158	.543	106	83	.783	191	399	14.3
79-80	29	891	257	151	.588	98	71	.724	177	373	12.9
80-81	32	1188	373	216	.579	220	171	.777	255	603	18.8
81-82	30	1118	338	162	.479	178	142	.798	215	466	15.5
Totals	119	4058	1259	687	.546	602	467	.776	838	1841	15.5

ITALIAN LEAGUE RECORD

Year	G.	Min.	FGA	FGM	Pct.	FTA	FTM	Pct.	Reb.	Pts.	Avg.
82-83—Fort. Bologna	30	1114	462	233	.504	148	106	.716	258	572	19.1

NBA REGULAR SEASON RECORD

Sea.—Team	G.	Min.	FGA	FGM	Pct.	FTA	FTM	Pct.	Off.	Def.	Tot.	Ast.	PF	Dq.	Stl.	Blk.	Pts.	Avg.
									—Rebounds—									
83-84—San Antonio	79	1531	399	214	.536	172	144	.837	102	202	304	98	219	4	52	38	573	7.3
84-85—S.A.-Utah	74	1178	418	208	.498	182	150	.824	78	108	186	87	141	0	28	22	567	7.7
85-86—Utah	58	469	167	74	.443	87	67	.770	31	49	80	27	72	0	8	6	216	3.7
86-87—Boston	73	1079	270	139	.515	153	124	.810	54	136	190	62	129	1	22	20	402	5.5
87-88—Boston	74	1032	330	161	.488	165	128	.776	60	102	162	81	118	0	16	15	450	6.1
88-89—Milwaukee	71	1251	319	155	.486	129	104	.806	68	141	209	66	126	0	36	23	417	5.9
89-90—Milwaukee	82	2235	666	330	.495	249	195	.783	107	204	311	147	210	5	56	25	857	10.5
Totals	511	8775	2569	1281	.499	1137	912	.802	500	942	1442	568	1015	10	218	149	3482	6.8

Three-Point Field Goals: 1983-84, 1-for-4 (.250). 1984-85, 1-for-1. 1985-86, 1-for-2 (.500). 1986-87, 0-for-3. 1987-88, 0-for-6. 1988-89, 3-for-14 (.214). 1989-90, 2-for-11 (.182). Totals, 8-for-41 (.195).

NBA PLAYOFF RECORD

Sea.—Team	G.	Min.	FGA	FGM	Pct.	FTA	FTM	Pct.	—Rebounds— Off.	Def.	Tot.	Ast.	PF	Dq.	Stl.	Blk.	Pts.	Avg.
84-85—Utah	10	130	43	19	.442	20	16	.800	6	11	17	9	16	0	7	3	54	5.4
85-86—Utah	4	31	15	7	.467	9	8	.889	4	3	7	3	5	0	0	0	22	5.5
86-87—Boston	20	265	59	30	.508	44	31	.705	15	18	33	12	47	0	6	3	91	4.6
87-88—Boston	15	100	21	11	.524	11	7	.636	8	8	16	3	20	1	3	0	29	1.9
88-89—Milwaukee	9	345	100	49	.490	40	34	.850	11	28	39	20	29	1	5	4	132	14.7
89-90—Milwaukee	4	79	20	13	.650	16	13	.813	5	3	8	3	9	0	0	1	39	9.8
Totals	62	950	258	129	.500	140	109	.779	49	71	120	50	126	2	21	11	367	5.9

Three-Point Field Goals: 1988-89, 0-for-3. 1989-90, 0-for-1. Totals, 0-for-4.

ALVIN CYRRALE ROBERTSON

Born July 22, 1962 at Barberton, O. Height 6:04. Weight 190.

High School—Barberton, O.

Colleges—Crowder Junior College, Neosho, Mo., and University of Arkansas, Fayetteville, Ark.

Drafted by San Antonio on first round, 1984 (7th pick).

Traded by San Antonio with Greg Anderson and future considerations to Milwaukee for Terry Cummings and future considerations, May 28, 1989.

—COLLEGIATE RECORD—

Crowder JC

Year	G.	Min.	FGA	FGM	Pct.	FTA	FTM	Pct.	Reb.	Pts.	Avg.
80-81	34	....	470	269	.572	112	73	.652	284	611	18.0

Arkansas

Year	G.	Min.	FGA	FGM	Pct.	FTA	FTM	Pct.	Reb.	Pts.	Avg.
81-82	28	495	159	84	.528	58	35	.603	62	203	7.3
82-83	28	915	294	161	.548	115	76	.661	137	398	14.2
83-84	32	1109	375	187	.499	182	122	.670	175	496	15.5
Ark. Totals	88	2519	828	432	.522	355	233	.656	374	1097	12.5

NBA REGULAR SEASON RECORD

Sea.—Team	G.	Min.	FGA	FGM	Pct.	FTA	FTM	Pct.	—Rebounds— Off.	Def.	Tot.	Ast.	PF	Dq.	Stl.	Blk.	Pts.	Avg.
84-85—San Antonio	79	1685	600	299	.498	169	124	.734	116	149	265	275	217	1	127	24	726	9.2
85-86—San Antonio	82	2878	1093	562	.514	327	260	.795	184	332	516	448	296	4	301	40	1392	17.0
86-87—San Antonio	81	2697	1264	589	.466	324	244	.753	186	238	424	421	264	2	260	35	1435	17.7
87-88—San Antonio	82	2978	1408	655	.465	365	273	.748	165	333	498	557	300	4	243	69	1610	19.6
88-89—San Antonio	65	2287	962	465	.483	253	183	.723	157	227	384	393	259	6	197	36	1122	17.3
89-90—Milwaukee	81	2599	946	476	.503	266	197	.741	230	329	559	445	280	2	207	17	1153	14.2
Totals	470	15124	6273	3046	.486	1704	1281	.752	1038	1608	2646	2539	1616	19	1335	221	7438	15.8

Three-Point Field Goals: 1984-85, 4-for-11 (.364). 1985-86, 8-for-29 (.276). 1986-87, 13-for-48 (.271). 1987-88, 27-for-95 (.284). 1988-89, 9-for-45 (.200). 1989-90, 4-for-26 (.154). Totals, 65-for-254 (.256).

NBA PLAYOFF RECORD

Sea.—Team	G.	Min.	FGA	FGM	Pct.	FTA	FTM	Pct.	—Rebounds— Off.	Def.	Tot.	Ast.	PF	Dq.	Stl.	Blk.	Pts.	Avg.
85-86—San Antonio	3	98	29	8	.276	13	11	.846	5	9	14	19	10	0	7	1	27	9.0
87-88—San Antonio	3	119	53	30	.566	9	7	.778	5	9	14	28	15	1	12	1	70	23.3
89-90—Milwaukee	4	155	67	35	.522	34	24	.706	10	13	23	19	16	0	9	0	94	23.5
Totals	10	372	149	73	.490	56	42	.750	20	31	51	66	41	1	28	2	191	19.1

Three-Point Field Goals: 1987-88, 3-for-7 (.429). 1989-90, 0-for-1. Totals, 3-for-8 (.375).

NBA ALL-STAR GAME RECORD

Season—Team	Min.	FGA	FGM	Pct.	FTA	FTM	Pct.	—Rebounds— Off.	Def.	Tot.	Ast.	PF	Dq.	Stl.	Blk.	Pts.
1986—San Antonio..	20	6	2	.333	0	0	.000	1	8	9	5	1	0	0	0	4
1987—San Antonio..	16	5	2	.400	2	2	1.000	2	0	2	1	1	0	0	0	6
1988—San Antonio..	12	3	1	.333	0	0	.000	0	0	0	1	1	0	2	0	2
Totals	48	14	5	.357	2	2	1.000	3	8	11	7	3	0	2	0	12

Named to All-NBA Second Team, 1986. . . . NBA All-Defensive First Team, 1987. . . . NBA All-Defensive Second Team, 1986, 1988, 1989, 1990. . . . NBA Defensive Player of the Year, 1986. . . . NBA Most Improved Player, 1986. . . . Holds NBA record for most steals in a season, 1986. . . . Led NBA in steals, 1986 and 1987. . . . Member of U.S. Olympic team, 1984.

CLIFFORD RALPH ROBINSON
(Cliff)

Born December 16, 1966 at Buffalo, N.Y. Height 6:11. Weight 225.

High School—Buffalo, N.Y., Riverside.

College—University of Connecticut, Storrs, Conn.

Drafted by Portland on second round, 1989 (36th pick).

—COLLEGIATE RECORD—

Year	G.	Min.	FGA	FGM	Pct.	FTA	FTM	Pct.	Reb.	Pts.	Avg.
85-86	28	442	164	60	.366	59	36	.610	88	156	5.6
86-87	16	556	255	107	.420	121	69	.570	119	289	18.1
87-88	34	1079	463	222	.479	238	156	.655	233	600	17.6
88-89	31	974	500	235	.470	212	145	.684	228	619	20.0
Totals	109	3051	1382	624	.452	630	406	.644	668	1664	15.3

Three-Point Field Goals: 1986-87, 6-for-18 (.333). 1988-89, 4-for-12 (.333). Totals, 10-for-30 (.333).

NBA REGULAR SEASON RECORD

									—Rebounds—									
Sea.—Team	G.	Min.	FGA	FGM	Pct.	FTA	FTM	Pct.	Off.	Def.	Tot.	Ast.	PF	Dq.	Stl.	Blk.	Pts.	Avg.
89-90—Portland	82	1565	751	298	.397	251	138	.550	110	198	308	72	226	4	53	53	746	9.1

Three-Point Field Goals: 1989-90, 12-for-44 (.273).

NBA PLAYOFF RECORD

									—Rebounds—									
Sea.—Team	G.	Min.	FGA	FGM	Pct.	FTA	FTM	Pct.	Off.	Def.	Tot.	Ast.	PF	Dq.	Stl.	Blk.	Pts.	Avg.
89-90—Portland	21	391	151	54	.358	52	29	.558	32	55	87	23	71	1	19	24	137	6.5

Three-Point Field Goals: 1989-90, 0-for-4.

DAVID MAURICE ROBINSON

Born August 6, 1965 at Key West, Fla. Height 7:01. Weight 235.
High School—Manassas, Va., Osbourn Park.
College—United States Naval Academy, Annapolis, Md.
Drafted by San Antonio on first round, 1987 (1st pick).

In military service, 1987-88 and 1988-89 seasons.

—COLLEGIATE RECORD—

Year	G.	Min.	FGA	FGM	Pct.	FTA	FTM	Pct.	Reb.	Pts.	Avg.
83-84	28	....	138	86	.623	73	42	.575	111	214	7.6
84-85	32	....	469	302	.644	243	152	.626	370	756	23.6
85-86	35	....	484	294	.607	331	208	.628	455	796	22.7
86-87	32	....	592	350	.591	317	202	.637	378	903	28.2
Totals	127	....	1683	1032	.613	964	604	.627	1314	2669	21.0

Three-Point Field Goals: 1986-87, 1-for-1 (1.000).

NBA REGULAR SEASON RECORD

									—Rebounds—									
Sea.—Team	G.	Min.	FGA	FGM	Pct.	FTA	FTM	Pct.	Off.	Def.	Tot.	Ast.	PF	Dq.	Stl.	Blk.	Pts.	Avg.
89-90—San Antonio	82	3002	1300	690	.531	837	613	.732	303	680	983	164	259	3	138	319	1993	24.3

Three-Point Field Goals: 1989-90, 0-for-2.

NBA PLAYOFF RECORD

									—Rebounds—									
Sea.—Team	G.	Min.	FGA	FGM	Pct.	FTA	FTM	Pct.	Off.	Def.	Tot.	Ast.	PF	Dq.	Stl.	Blk.	Pts.	Avg.
89-90—San Antonio	10	375	167	89	.533	96	65	.677	36	84	120	23	35	1	11	40	243	24.3

NBA ALL-STAR GAME RECORD

								—Rebounds—								
Season—Team	Min.	FGA	FGM	Pct.	FTA	FTM	Pct.	Off.	Def.	Tot.	Ast.	PF	Dq.	Stl.	Blk.	Pts.
1990—San Antonio..	25	12	7	.583	2	1	.500	2	8	10	1	1	0	2	1	15

Named to All-NBA Third Team, 1990. . . . NBA All-Defensive Second Team, 1990. . . . NBA Rookie of the Year, 1990. . . . NBA All-Rookie First Team, 1990. . . . Recipient of Schick Pivotal Player Award, 1990. . . . Led NCAA Division I in rebounding and blocked shots, 1986. . . . Named to THE SPORTING NEWS All-America First Team, 1986 and 1987. . . . THE SPORTING NEWS College Player of the Year, 1987.

DENNIS KEITH RODMAN
(Worm)

Born May 13, 1961 at Trenton, N.J. Height 6:08. Weight 210.
High School—Dallas, Tex., South Oak Cliff.
(Did not play high school basketball.)
Colleges—Cooke County Junior College, Gainesville, Tex., and Southeastern Oklahoma State University, Durant, Okla.
Drafted by Detroit on second round, 1986 (27th pick).

—COLLEGIATE RECORD—

Cooke County

Year	G.	Min.	FGA	FGM	Pct.	FTA	FTM	Pct.	Reb.	Pts.	Avg.
82-83	16	....	185	114	.616	91	53	.582	212	281	17.6

Southeastern Oklahoma

Year	G.	Min.	FGA	FGM	Pct.	FTA	FTM	Pct.	Reb.	Pts.	Avg.
83-84	30	....	490	303	.618	264	173	.655	392	779	26.0
84-85	32	....	545	353	.648	267	151	.566	510	857	26.8
85-86	34	....	515	332	.645	252	165	.655	605	829	24.4
Totals	96	....	1550	988	.637	783	489	.625	1507	2465	25.7

NBA REGULAR SEASON RECORD

Sea.—Team	G.	Min.	FGA	FGM	Pct.	FTA	FTM	Pct.	—Rebounds— Off.	Def.	Tot.	Ast.	PF	Dq.	Stl.	Blk.	Pts.	Avg.
86-87—Detroit	77	1155	391	213	.545	126	74	.587	163	169	332	56	166	1	38	48	500	6.5
87-88—Detroit	82	2147	709	398	.561	284	152	.535	318	397	715	110	273	5	75	45	953	11.6
88-89—Detroit	82	2208	531	316	.595	155	97	.626	327	445	772	99	292	4	55	76	735	9.0
89-90—Detroit	82	2377	496	288	.581	217	142	.654	336	456	792	72	276	2	52	60	719	8.8
Totals	323	7887	2127	1215	.571	782	465	.595	1144	1467	2611	337	1007	12	220	229	2907	9.0

Three-Point Field Goals: 1986-87, 0-for-1. 1987-88, 5-for-17 (.294). 1988-89, 6-for-26 (.231). 1989-90, 1-for-9 (.111). Totals, 12-for-53 (.226).

NBA PLAYOFF RECORD

Sea.—Team	G.	Min.	FGA	FGM	Pct.	FTA	FTM	Pct.	—Rebounds— Off.	Def.	Tot.	Ast.	PF	Dq.	Stl.	Blk.	Pts.	Avg.
86-87—Detroit	15	245	74	40	.541	32	18	.563	32	39	71	3	48	0	6	17	98	6.5
87-88—Detroit	23	474	136	71	.522	54	22	.407	51	85	136	21	87	1	14	14	164	7.1
88-89—Detroit	17	409	70	37	.529	35	24	.686	56	114	170	16	58	0	6	12	98	5.8
89-90—Detroit	19	560	95	54	.568	35	18	.514	55	106	161	17	62	1	9	13	126	6.6
Totals	74	1688	375	202	.539	156	82	.526	194	344	538	57	255	2	35	56	486	6.6

Three-Point Field Goals: 1987-88, 0-for-2. 1988-89, 0-for-4. Totals, 0-for-6.

NBA ALL-STAR GAME RECORD

Season—Team	Min.	FGA	FGM	Pct.	FTA	FTM	Pct.	—Rebounds— Off.	Def.	Tot.	Ast.	PF	Dq.	Stl.	Blk.	Pts.
1990—Detroit	11	4	2	.500	0	0	....	3	1	4	1	1	0	0	1	4

Named NBA Defensive Player of the Year, 1990. . . . NBA All-Defensive First Team, 1989 and 1990. . . . Member of NBA championship teams, 1989 and 1990. . . . Led NBA in field-goal percentage, 1989. . . . Led NAIA in rebounding, 1985 and 1986.

WAYNE MONTE ROLLINS
(Tree)

Born June 16, 1955 at Winter Haven, Fla. Height 7:01. Weight 240.
High School—Cordele, Ga., Crisp County.
College—Clemson University, Clemson, S. C.
Drafted by Atlanta on first round, 1977 (14th pick).

Signed by Cleveland as an unrestricted free agent, August 2, 1988.

—COLLEGIATE RECORD—

Year	G.	Min.	FGA	FGM	Pct.	FTA	FTM	Pct.	Reb.	Pts.	Avg.
73-74	26	....	265	144	.543	54	34	.630	316	322	12.4
74-75	28	....	326	162	.497	67	40	.597	328	364	13.0
75-76	28	....	313	170	.543	76	43	.566	308	383	13.7
76-77	28	....	288	167	.580	95	60	.632	359	394	14.1
Totals	110	....	1192	643	.539	292	177	.606	1311	1463	13.3

NBA REGULAR SEASON RECORD

Sea.—Team	G.	Min.	FGA	FGM	Pct.	FTA	FTM	Pct.	—Rebounds— Off.	Def.	Tot.	Ast.	PF	Dq.	Stl.	Blk.	Pts.	Avg.
77-78—Atlanta	80	1795	520	253	.487	148	104	.703	179	373	552	79	326	16	57	218	610	7.6
78-79—Atlanta	81	1900	555	297	.535	141	89	.631	219	369	588	49	328	19	46	254	683	8.4
79-80—Atlanta	82	2123	514	287	.558	220	157	.714	283	491	774	76	322	12	54	244	731	8.9
80-81—Atlanta	40	1044	210	116	.552	57	46	.807	102	184	286	35	151	7	29	117	278	7.0
81-82—Atlanta	79	2018	346	202	.584	129	79	.612	168	443	611	59	285	4	35	224	483	6.1
82-83—Atlanta	80	2472	512	261	.510	135	98	.726	210	533	743	75	294	7	49	343	620	7.8
83-84—Atlanta	77	2351	529	274	.518	190	118	.621	200	393	593	62	297	9	35	277	666	8.6
84-85—Atlanta	70	1750	339	186	.549	93	67	.720	113	329	442	52	213	6	35	167	439	6.3
85-86—Atlanta	74	1781	347	173	.499	90	69	.767	131	327	458	41	239	5	38	167	415	5.6
86-87—Atlanta	74	1764	313	171	.546	87	63	.724	155	333	488	22	240	1	43	140	405	5.4
87-88—Atlanta	76	1765	260	133	.512	80	70	.875	142	317	459	20	229	2	31	132	336	4.4
88-89—Cleveland	60	583	138	62	.449	19	12	.632	38	101	139	19	89	0	11	38	136	2.3
89-90—Cleveland	48	674	125	57	.456	16	11	.688	58	95	153	24	83	3	13	53	125	2.6
Totals	922	22020	4708	2472	.525	1405	983	.700	1998	4288	6286	613	3096	91	476	2374	5927	6.4

Three-Point Field Goals: 1980-81, 0-for-1. 1982-83, 0-for-1. 1985-86, 0-for-1. 1988-89, 0-for-1. 1989-90, 0-for-1. Totals, 0-for-5.

NBA PLAYOFF RECORD

									—Rebounds—									
Sea.—Team	G.	Min.	FGA	FGM	Pct.	FTA	FTM	Pct.	Off.	Def.	Tot.	Ast.	PF	Dq.	Stl.	Blk.	Pts.	Avg.
77-78—Atlanta	2	51	12	7	.583	8	2	.250	3	6	9	1	8	1	1	4	16	8.0
78-79—Atlanta	9	212	51	21	.412	13	9	.692	19	52	71	5	29	1	3	24	51	5.7
79-80—Atlanta	5	134	31	18	.581	10	6	.600	18	20	38	3	25	3	2	14	42	8.4
81-82—Atlanta	2	65	6	2	.333	4	3	.750	5	3	8	2	8	1	0	6	7	3.5
82-83—Atlanta	3	118	27	13	.481	9	3	.333	10	20	30	3	12	1	1	10	29	9.7
83-84—Atlanta	5	152	25	10	.400	8	5	.625	10	24	34	1	23	1	2	10	25	5.0
85-86—Atlanta	9	248	47	26	.553	11	7	.636	18	60	78	3	32	2	2	15	59	6.6
86-87—Atlanta	9	221	28	15	.536	14	10	.714	19	34	53	3	33	0	3	16	40	4.4
87-88—Atlanta	12	333	36	20	.556	15	13	.867	23	48	71	6	46	0	10	19	53	4.4
88-89—Cleveland	5	74	8	6	.750	5	3	.600	5	11	16	1	10	0	3	7	15	3.0
89-90—Cleveland	3	38	3	1	.333	8	6	.750	0	8	8	1	7	0	2	1	8	2.7
Totals	64	1646	274	139	.507	105	67	.638	130	286	416	29	233	10	29	126	345	5.4

Named to NBA All-Defensive First Team, 1984. . . . NBA All-Defensive Second Team, 1983. . . . Led NBA in blocked shots, 1983.

DOUGLAS KEITH ROTH
(Doug)

Born August 24, 1967 at Knoxville, Tenn. Height 6:11. Weight 255.

High School—Knoxville, Tenn., Karns.

College—University of Tennessee, Knoxville, Tenn.

Drafted by Washington on second round, 1989 (41st pick).

—COLLEGIATE RECORD—

Year	G.	Min.	FGA	FGM	Pct.	FTA	FTM	Pct.	Reb.	Pts.	Avg.
85-86	26	366	97	38	.392	13	11	.846	57	87	3.3
86-87	29	879	247	120	.486	48	32	.667	201	280	9.7
87-88	29	582	200	84	.420	36	22	.611	141	199	6.9
88-89	30	820	239	127	.531	56	32	.571	243	297	9.9
Totals	114	2647	783	369	.471	153	97	.634	642	863	7.6

Three-Point Field Goals: 1986-87, 8-for-14 (.571). 1987-88, 9-for-25 (.360). 1988-89, 11-for-31 (.355). Totals, 28-for-70 (.400).

NBA REGULAR SEASON RECORD

									—Rebounds—									
Sea.—Team	G.	Min.	FGA	FGM	Pct.	FTA	FTM	Pct.	Off.	Def.	Tot.	Ast.	PF	Dq.	Stl.	Blk.	Pts.	Avg.
89-90—Washington	42	412	86	37	.430	14	7	.500	44	76	120	20	70	1	8	13	81	1.9

Three-Point Field Goals: 1989-90, 0-for-1.

SCOTT EDWARD ROTH

Born June 3, 1963 at Cleveland, O. Height 6:08. Weight 212.

High School—Brecksville, O.

College—University of Wisconsin, Madison, Wis.

Drafted by San Antonio on fourth round, 1985 (82nd pick).

Draft rights relinquished by San Antonio, June 2, 1987; signed by Utah as a free agent, February 25, 1988.
Waived by Utah, December 13, 1988; signed by San Antonio, January 4, 1989, to a 10-day contract that expired, January 13, 1989.
Re-signed by San Antonio, January 13, 1989, for remainder of season.
Selected from San Antonio by Minnesota in NBA expansion draft, June 15, 1989.
Played with EFES Pilsen Beer Co. in Istanbul, Turkey, 1985-86 and 1986-87.
Played in Continental Basketball Association with Albany Patroons, 1987-88.

—COLLEGIATE RECORD—

Year	G.	Min.	FGA	FGM	Pct.	FTA	FTM	Pct.	Reb.	Pts.	Avg.
81-82	25	330	102	47	.461	18	10	.556	47	104	4.2
82-83	28	710	156	59	.378	60	43	.717	94	162	5.8
83-84	28	973	304	151	.497	96	76	.792	83	378	13.5
84-85	28	927	365	198	.542	156	117	.750	86	513	18.3
Totals	109	2940	927	455	.491	330	246	.745	310	1157	10.6

Three-Point Field Goals: 1982-83, 1-for-5 (.200).

CBA REGULAR SEASON RECORD

			—2-Point—			—3-Point—									
Sea.—Team	G.	Min.	FGM	FGA	Pct.	FGM	FGA	Pct.	FTM	FTA	Pct.	Reb.	Ast.	Pts.	Avg.
87-88—Albany	47	1571	318	601	.529	13	26	.500	243	320	.759	220	107	918	19.5

NBA REGULAR SEASON RECORD

Sea.—Team	G.	Min.	FGA	FGM	Pct.	FTA	FTM	Pct.	—Rebounds— Off.	Def.	Tot.	Ast.	PF	Dq.	Stl.	Blk.	Pts.	Avg.
87-88—Utah	26	201	74	30	.405	30	22	.733	7	21	28	16	37	0	12	0	84	3.2
88-89—Utah-S.A.	63	536	167	59	.353	87	60	.690	20	44	64	55	69	0	24	5	181	2.9
89-90—Minnesota	71	1061	420	159	.379	201	150	.746	34	78	112	115	144	1	51	6	486	6.8
Totals	160	1798	661	248	.375	318	232	.730	61	143	204	186	250	1	87	11	751	4.7

Three-Point Field Goals: 1987-88, 2-for-11 (.182). 1988-89, 3-for-16 (.188). 1989-90, 18-for-52 (.346). Totals, 23-for-79 (.291).

NBA PLAYOFF RECORD

Sea.—Team	G.	Min.	FGA	FGM	Pct.	FTA	FTM	Pct.	—Rebounds— Off.	Def.	Tot.	Ast.	PF	Dq.	Stl.	Blk.	Pts.	Avg.
87-88—Utah	6	10	3	1	.333	0	0	.000	0	0	0	0	0	0	2	0	2	0.3

JAMES ROWINSKI
(Jim)

Born January 4, 1961 at Long Island, N.Y. Height 6:08. Weight 255.
High School—Syosset, N.Y.
College—Purdue University, West Lafayette, Ind.
Drafted by Utah on fourth round, 1984 (86th pick).

Waived by Utah, September, 1984; signed by Detroit, March 6, 1989, to the first of consecutive 10-day contracts that expired, March 25, 1989.

Signed by Philadelphia as a free agent, April 20, 1989.

Waived by Philadelphia, November 2, 1989; signed by Miami, March 8, 1990, for remainder of season.

Played in Continental Basketball Association with Topeka Sizzlers, 1988-89 and 1989-90.

Played in Europe, 1984-85, 1985-86, 1986-87 and 1987-88 seasons.

—COLLEGIATE RECORD—

Year	G.	Min.	FGA	FGM	Pct.	FTA	FTM	Pct.	Reb.	Pts.	Avg.
80-81	6	11	6	4	.667	3	0	.000	9	8	1.3
81-82	5	73	16	7	.438	9	3	.333	19	17	3.4
82-83	25	276	59	35	.593	31	11	.355	61	81	3.2
83-84	29	1045	312	156	.500	162	124	.765	194	436	15.0
Totals	65	1405	393	202	.514	205	138	.673	283	542	8.3

CBA REGULAR SEASON RECORD

Sea.—Team	G.	Min.	—2-Point— FGM	FGA	Pct.	—3-Point— FGM	FGA	Pct.	FTM	FTA	Pct.	Reb.	Ast.	Pts.	Avg.
88-89—Topeka	42	1568	285	602	.473	0	1	.000	284	373	.761	441	59	854	20.3
89-90—Topeka	45	1839	421	831	.507	0	0	.000	280	377	.743	457	75	1122	24.9
Totals	87	3407	706	1433	.493	0	1	.000	564	750	.752	898	134	1976	22.7

NBA REGULAR SEASON RECORD

Sea.—Team	G.	Min.	FGA	FGM	Pct.	FTA	FTM	Pct.	—Rebounds— Off.	Def.	Tot.	Ast.	PF	Dq.	Stl.	Blk.	Pts.	Avg.
88-89—Det.-Phil.	9	15	4	1	.250	6	5	.833	1	4	5	0	0	0	0	0	7	0.8
89-90—Miami	14	112	32	14	.438	26	22	.846	17	12	29	5	19	0	1	2	50	3.6
Totals	23	127	36	15	.417	32	27	.844	18	16	34	5	19	0	1	2	57	2.5

BRIAN MAURICE ROWSOM

Born October 23, 1965 at Newark, N.J. Height 6:09. Weight 220.
High School—Columbia, N.C.
College—University of North Carolina at Wilmington, Wilmington, N.C.
Drafted by Indiana on second round, 1987 (34th pick).

Waived by Indiana, December 8, 1987; signed by Charlotte as a free agent, October 6, 1988.

—COLLEGIATE RECORD—

Year	G.	Min.	FGA	FGM	Pct.	FTA	FTM	Pct.	Reb.	Pts.	Avg.
83-84	28	....	150	85	.567	69	47	.681	135	217	7.8
84-85	28	939	381	212	.556	126	90	.714	260	514	18.4
85-86	29	1056	418	224	.536	181	142	.785	275	590	20.3
86-87	30	1077	492	254	.516	194	144	.742	345	653	21.8
Totals	115	....	1441	775	.538	570	423	.742	1015	1974	17.2

Three-Point Field Goals: 1986-87, 1-for-4 (.250).

NBA REGULAR SEASON RECORD

Sea.—Team	G.	Min.	FGA	FGM	Pct.	FTA	FTM	Pct.	—Rebounds— Off.	Def.	Tot.	Ast.	PF	Dq.	Stl.	Blk.	Pts.	Avg.
87-88—Indiana	4	16	6	0	.000	6	6	1.000	1	4	5	1	3	0	1	0	6	1.5
88-89—Charlotte	34	517	162	80	.494	81	65	.802	56	81	137	24	69	1	10	12	226	6.6
89-90—Charlotte	44	559	179	78	.436	83	68	.819	44	87	131	22	58	0	18	11	225	5.1
Totals	82	1092	347	158	.455	170	139	.818	101	172	273	47	130	1	29	23	457	5.6

Three-Point Field Goals: 1988-89, 1-for-1 (1.000). 1989-90, 1-for-2 (.500). Totals, 2-for-3 (.667).

DONALD ADAM ROYAL

Born May 2, 1966 at New Orleans, La. Height 6:08. Weight 210.
High School—New Orleans, La., Augustine.
College—University of Notre Dame, Notre Dame, Ind.
Drafted by Cleveland on third round, 1987 (52nd pick).

Waived by Cleveland, October 23, 1987; signed by Minnesota as a free agent, September 12, 1989.
Played in Continental Basketball Association with Pensacola Tornados, 1987-88, and Cedar Rapids Silver Bullets, 1988-89.

—COLLEGIATE RECORD—

Year	G.	Min.	FGA	FGM	Pct.	FTA	FTM	Pct.	Reb.	Pts.	Avg.
83-84	31	405	64	38	.594	45	28	.622	72	104	3.4
84-85	30	848	151	75	.497	156	122	.782	164	272	9.1
85-86	28	777	151	88	.583	158	121	.766	138	297	10.6
86-87	28	1028	229	132	.576	217	178	.820	196	442	15.8
Totals	117	3058	595	333	.560	576	449	.780	570	1115	9.5

CBA REGULAR SEASON RECORD

Sea.—Team	G.	Min.	—2-Point— FGM	FGA	Pct.	—3-Point— FGM	FGA	Pct.	FTM	FTA	Pct.	Reb.	Ast.	Pts.	Avg.
87-88—Pensacola	48	904	122	233	524	0	1	.000	104	141	.738	158	44	348	7.3
88-89—Cedar Rapids	53	1206	216	438	.493	0	2	.000	266	359	.741	252	98	698	13.2
Totals	101	2110	338	671	.504	0	3	.000	370	500	.740	410	142	1046	10.4

NBA REGULAR SEASON RECORD

Sea.—Team	G.	Min.	FGA	FGM	Pct.	FTA	FTM	Pct.	—Rebounds— Off.	Def.	Tot.	Ast.	PF	Dq.	Stl.	Blk.	Pts.	Avg.
89-90—Minnesota	66	746	255	117	.459	197	153	.777	69	68	137	43	107	0	32	8	387	5.9

Three-Point Field Goals: 1989-90, 0-for-1.

EDWARD DELANEY RUDD

(Known by middle name.)
Born November 8, 1962 at Halifax, N.C. Height 6:02. Weight 180.
High School—Enfield, N.C., Eastman.
College—Wake Forest University, Winston-Salem, N.C.
Drafted by Utah on fourth round, 1985 (83rd pick).

Waived by Utah, October 21, 1985; signed by Milwaukee as a free agent, October 6, 1989.
Waived by Milwaukee, November 2, 1989; signed by Utah as a free agent, November 6, 1989.
Played in Continental Basketball Association with Bay State Bombardiers and Maine Windjammers, 1985-86.

—COLLEGIATE RECORD—

Year	G.	Min.	FGA	FGM	Pct.	FTA	FTM	Pct.	Reb.	Pts.	Avg.
81-82	22	150	30	10	.333	10	5	.500	4	25	1.1
82-83	32	1004	324	171	.528	69	53	.768	63	408	12.8
83-84	31	1011	328	170	.518	85	73	.859	55	413	13.3
84-85	29	1000	452	210	.465	77	63	.818	74	483	16.7
Totals	114	3165	1134	561	.495	241	194	.805	196	1329	11.7

Three-Point Field Goals: 1982-83, 13-for-29 (.448).

CBA REGULAR SEASON RECORD

Sea.—Team	G.	Min.	—2-Point— FGM	FGA	Pct.	—3-Point— FGM	FGA	Pct.	FTM	FTA	Pct.	Reb.	Ast.	Pts.	Avg.
85-86—B.S.-Maine	9	122	15	43	.348	0	1	.000	6	9	.667	10	23	36	4.0

NBA REGULAR SEASON RECORD

Sea.—Team	G.	Min.	FGA	FGM	Pct.	FTA	FTM	Pct.	—Rebounds— Off.	Def.	Tot.	Ast.	PF	Dq.	Stl.	Blk.	Pts.	Avg.
89-90—Utah	77	850	259	111	.429	53	35	.660	12	43	55	177	81	0	22	1	273	3.5

Three-Point Field Goals: 1989-90, 16-for-56 (.286).

NBA PLAYOFF RECORD

Sea.—Team	G.	Min.	FGA	FGM	Pct.	FTA	FTM	Pct.	—Rebounds— Off.	Def.	Tot.	Ast.	PF	Dq.	Stl.	Blk.	Pts.	Avg.
89-90—Utah	5	45	23	8	.348	2	1	.500	1	2	3	13	10	0	1	0	18	3.6

Three-Point Field Goals: 1989-90, 1-for-7 (.143).

JOHN THOMAS SALLEY

Born May 16, 1964 at Brooklyn, N.Y. Height 6:11. Weight 230.
High School—Brooklyn, N.Y., Canarsie.
College—Georgia Institute of Technology, Atlanta, Ga.
Drafted by Detroit on first round, 1986 (11th pick).

—COLLEGIATE RECORD—

Year	G.	Min.	FGA	FGM	Pct.	FTA	FTM	Pct.	Reb.	Pts.	Avg.
82-83	27	829	207	104	.502	160	102	.638	153	310	11.5
83-84	29	992	214	126	.589	132	89	.674	167	341	11.8
84-85	35	1231	308	193	.627	165	105	.636	250	491	14.0
85-86	34	1145	284	172	.606	170	101	.594	228	445	13.1
Totals	125	4197	1013	595	.587	627	397	.633	798	1587	12.7

NBA REGULAR SEASON RECORD

Sea.—Team	G.	Min.	FGA	FGM	Pct.	FTA	FTM	Pct.	—Rebounds— Off.	Def.	Tot.	Ast.	PF	Dq.	Stl.	Blk.	Pts.	Avg.
86-87—Detroit	82	1463	290	163	.562	171	105	.614	108	188	296	54	256	5	44	125	431	5.3
87-88—Detroit	82	2003	456	258	.566	261	185	.709	166	236	402	113	294	4	53	137	701	8.5
88-89—Detroit	67	1458	333	166	.498	195	135	.692	134	201	335	75	197	3	40	72	467	7.0
89-90—Detroit	82	1914	408	209	.512	244	174	.713	154	285	439	67	282	7	51	153	593	7.2
Totals	313	6838	1487	796	.535	871	599	.688	562	910	1472	309	1029	19	188	487	2192	7.0

Three-Point Field Goals: 1986-87, 0-for-1. 1988-89, 0-for-2. 1989-90, 1-for-4 (.250). Totals, 1-for-7 (.143).

NBA PLAYOFF RECORD

Sea.—Team	G.	Min.	FGA	FGM	Pct.	FTA	FTM	Pct.	—Rebounds— Off.	Def.	Tot.	Ast.	PF	Dq.	Stl.	Blk.	Pts.	Avg.
86-87—Detroit	15	311	66	33	.500	42	27	.643	30	42	72	11	60	1	3	17	93	6.2
87-88—Detroit	23	623	104	56	.538	69	49	.710	64	91	155	21	88	2	15	37	161	7.0
88-89—Detroit	17	392	99	58	.586	54	36	.667	34	45	79	9	58	0	9	25	152	8.9
89-90—Detroit	20	547	122	58	.475	98	74	.755	57	60	117	20	76	2	9	33	190	9.5
Totals	75	1873	391	205	.524	263	186	.707	185	238	423	61	282	5	36	112	596	7.9

Three-Point Field Goals: 1987-88, 0-for-1.

Member of NBA championship teams, 1989 and 1990.

RALPH LEE SAMPSON

Born July 7, 1960 at Harrisonburg, Va. Height 7:04. Weight 230.
High School—Harrisonburg, Va.
College—University of Virginia, Charlottesville, Va.
Drafted by Houston on first round, 1983 (1st pick).

Traded by Houston with Steve Harris to Golden State for Joe Barry Carroll and Eric Floyd, December 12, 1987.
Traded by Golden State to Sacramento for Jim Petersen, September 27, 1989.

—COLLEGIATE RECORD—

Year	G.	Min.	FGA	FGM	Pct.	FTA	FTM	Pct.	Reb.	Pts.	Avg.
79-80	34	1017	404	221	.547	94	66	.702	381	508	14.9
80-81	33	1056	413	230	.557	198	125	.631	378	585	17.7
81-82	32	1002	353	198	.561	179	110	.615	366	506	15.8
82-83	33	995	414	250	.604	179	126	.704	386	629	19.1
Totals	132	4070	1584	899	.568	650	427	.457	1511	2228	16.9

NBA REGULAR SEASON RECORD

Sea.—Team	G.	Min.	FGA	FGM	Pct.	FTA	FTM	Pct.	—Rebounds— Off.	Def.	Tot.	Ast.	PF	Dq.	Stl.	Blk.	Pts.	Avg.
83-84—Houston	82	2693	1369	716	.523	434	287	.661	293	620	913	163	339	16	70	197	1720	21.0
84-85—Houston	82	3086	1499	753	.502	448	303	.676	227	626	853	224	306	10	81	168	1809	22.1
85-86—Houston	79	2864	1280	624	.488	376	241	.641	258	621	879	283	308	12	99	129	1491	18.9
86-87—Houston	43	1326	566	277	.489	189	118	.624	88	284	372	120	169	6	40	58	672	15.6
87-88—Hou.-G.S.	48	1663	682	299	.438	196	149	.760	140	322	462	122	164	3	41	88	749	15.6
88-89—Golden State	61	1086	365	164	.449	95	62	.653	105	202	307	77	170	3	31	65	393	6.4
89-90—Sacramento	26	417	129	48	.372	23	12	.522	11	73	84	28	66	1	14	22	109	4.2
Totals	421	13135	5890	2881	.489	1761	1172	.666	1122	2748	3870	1017	1522	51	376	727	6943	16.5

Three-Point Field Goals: 1983-84, 1-for-4 (.250). 1984-85, 0-for-6. 1985-86, 2-for-15 (.133). 1986-87, 0-for-3. 1987-88, 2-for-11 (.182). 1988-89, 3-for-8 (.375). 1989-90, 1-for-4 (.250). Totals, 9-for-51 (.176).

NBA PLAYOFF RECORD

Sea.—Team	G.	Min.	FGA	FGM	Pct.	FTA	FTM	Pct.	—Rebounds— Off.	Def.	Tot.	Ast.	PF	Dq.	Stl.	Blk.	Pts.	Avg.
84-85—Houston	5	193	100	43	.430	37	19	.514	25	58	83	7	23	2	2	8	106	21.2
85-86—Houston	20	741	301	156	.518	118	86	.729	66	149	215	80	79	1	30	35	399	20.0
86-87—Houston	10	330	146	75	.514	43	35	.814	27	61	88	21	47	1	2	12	186	18.6
88-89—Golden State	3	43	22	9	.409	4	2	.500	6	8	14	1	8	0	1	2	20	6.7
Totals	38	1307	569	283	.497	202	142	.703	124	276	400	109	157	4	35	57	711	18.7

Three-Point Field Goals: 1984-85, 1-for-1 (1.000). 1985-86, 1-for-1 (1.000). 1986-87, 1-for-2 (.500). 1988-89, 0-for-4. Totals, 3-for-8 (.375).

NBA ALL-STAR GAME RECORD

Season—Team	Min.	FGA	FGM	Pct.	FTA	FTM	Pct.	—Rebounds— Off.	Def.	Tot.	Ast.	PF	Dq.	Stl.	Blk.	Pts.
1984—Houston	16	7	4	.571	2	1	.500	1	4	5	0	4	0	0	0	9
1985—Houston	29	15	10	.667	6	4	.667	3	7	10	1	5	0	0	1	24
1986—Houston	21	11	7	.636	2	2	1.000	1	3	4	1	4	0	0	0	16
Totals	66	33	21	.636	10	7	.700	5	14	19	2	13	0	0	1	49

Named to All-NBA Second Team, 1985. . . . NBA All-Star Game MVP, 1985. . . . NBA Rookie of the Year, 1984. . . . NBA All-Rookie Team, 1984. . . . THE SPORTING NEWS College Player of the Year, 1982. . . . THE SPORTING NEWS All-America First Team, 1981, 1982, 1983.

JEFFERY RAYNARD SANDERS
(Jeff)

Born January 14, 1966 at Augusta, Ga. Height 6:08. Weight 225.
High School—Augusta, Ga., T.W. Josey.
College—Georgia Southern College, Statesboro, Ga.
Drafted by Chicago on first round, 1989 (20th pick).

—COLLEGIATE RECORD—

Year	G.	Min.	FGA	FGM	Pct.	FTA	FTM	Pct.	Reb.	Pts.	Avg.
85-86	28	725	193	106	.549	94	57	.606	180	269	9.6
86-87	31	986	288	150	.521	88	58	.659	202	358	11.5
87-88	31	1092	419	231	.551	135	98	.726	255	560	18.1
88-89	29	1031	515	279	.542	159	116	.730	256	674	23.2
Totals	119	3834	1415	766	.541	476	329	.691	893	1861	15.6

NBA REGULAR SEASON RECORD

Sea.—Team	G.	Min.	FGA	FGM	Pct.	FTA	FTM	Pct.	—Rebounds— Off.	Def.	Tot.	Ast.	PF	Dq.	Stl.	Blk.	Pts.	Avg.
89-90—Chicago	31	182	40	13	.325	4	2	.500	17	22	39	9	27	0	4	4	28	0.9

NBA PLAYOFF RECORD

Sea.—Team	G.	Min.	FGA	FGM	Pct.	FTA	FTM	Pct.	—Rebounds— Off.	Def.	Tot.	Ast.	PF	Dq.	Stl.	Blk.	Pts.	Avg.
89-90—Chicago	3	3	1	1	1.000	0	0	....	0	0	0	0	0	0	0	0	2	0.7

MICHAEL ANTHONY SANDERS
(Mike)

Born May 7, 1960 at Vidalia, La. Height 6:06. Weight 215.
High School—DeRidder, La.
College—University of California at Los Angeles, Los Angeles, Calif.
Drafted by Kansas City on fourth round, 1982 (74th pick).

Waived by Kansas City, October 4, 1982; signed by San Antonio as a free agent, February 9, 1983.
Waived by San Antonio, October 17, 1983; signed by Phoenix as a free agent, December 19, 1983.
Traded by Phoenix with Larry Nance and a 1988 1st round draft choice to Cleveland for Tyrone Corbin, Kevin Johnson, Mark West, 1988 1st and 2nd round draft choices and a 1989 2nd round draft choice, February 25, 1988.
Signed by Indiana as an unrestricted free agent, September 8, 1989.
Played in Continental Basketball Association with Montana Golden Nuggets, 1982-83, and Sarasota Stingers, 1983-84.

—COLLEGIATE RECORD—

Year	G.	Min.	FGA	FGM	Pct.	FTA	FTM	Pct.	Reb.	Pts.	Avg.
78-79	23	138	38	16	.421	16	11	.688	35	43	1.9
79-80	32	805	248	142	.573	96	76	.792	190	360	11.3
80-81	27	814	287	161	.561	124	95	.766	179	417	15.4
81-82	27	943	299	150	.502	116	90	.776	173	390	14.4
Totals	109	2700	872	469	.538	352	272	.773	577	1210	11.1

CBA REGULAR SEASON RECORD

			—2-Point—			—3-Point—									
Sea.—Team	G.	Min.	FGM	FGA	Pct.	FGM	FGA	Pct.	FTM	FTA	Pct.	Reb.	Ast.	Pts.	Avg.
82-83—Montana	30	1036	273	473	.577	0	0	....	123	149	.825	247	42	669	22.3
83-84—Sarasota	7	295	69	126	.547	0	1	.000	56	65	.861	52	8	194	27.7
Totals	37	1331	342	599	.571	0	1	.000	179	214	.836	299	50	863	23.3

NBA REGULAR SEASON RECORD

									—Rebounds—									
Sea.—Team	G.	Min.	FGA	FGM	Pct.	FTA	FTM	Pct.	Off.	Def.	Tot.	Ast.	PF	Dq.	Stl.	Blk.	Pts.	Avg.
82-83—San Antonio	26	393	157	76	.484	43	31	.721	31	63	94	19	57	0	18	6	183	7.0
83-84—Phoenix	50	586	203	97	.478	42	29	.690	40	63	103	44	101	0	23	12	223	4.5
84-85—Phoenix	21	418	175	85	.486	59	45	.763	38	51	89	29	59	0	23	4	215	10.2
85-86—Phoenix	82	1644	676	347	.513	257	208	.809	104	169	273	150	236	3	76	31	905	11.0
86-87—Phoenix	82	1655	722	357	.494	183	143	.781	101	170	271	126	210	1	61	23	859	10.5
87-88—Phoe.-Clev.	59	883	303	153	.505	76	59	.776	38	71	109	56	131	1	31	9	365	6.2
88-89—Cleveland	82	2102	733	332	.453	135	97	.719	98	209	307	133	230	2	89	32	764	9.3
89-90—Indiana	82	1531	479	225	.470	75	55	.733	78	152	230	89	220	1	43	23	510	6.2
Totals	484	9212	3448	1672	.485	870	667	.767	528	948	1476	646	1244	8	364	140	4024	8.3

Three-Point Field Goals: 1982-83, 0-for-2. 1985-86, 3-for-15 (.200). 1986-87, 2-for-17 (.118). 1987-88, 0-for-1. 1988-89, 3-for-10 (.300). 1989-90, 5-for-14 (.357). Totals, 13-for-59 (.220).

NBA PLAYOFF RECORD

									—Rebounds—									
Sea.—Team	G.	Min.	FGA	FGM	Pct.	FTA	FTM	Pct.	Off.	Def.	Tot.	Ast.	PF	Dq.	Stl.	Blk.	Pts.	Avg.
82-83—San Antonio	6	25	13	7	.538	0	0	.000	2	7	9	4	3	0	0	0	14	2.3
83-84—Phoenix	15	152	46	22	.478	17	16	.941	10	10	20	7	31	0	6	4	60	4.0
84-85—Phoenix	3	91	37	22	.595	10	8	.800	8	7	15	10	8	0	5	0	52	17.3
87-88—Cleveland	5	134	52	28	.538	10	8	.800	11	14	25	7	21	0	3	2	64	12.8
88-89—Cleveland	5	87	30	15	.500	5	3	.600	6	10	16	4	11	0	2	1	33	6.6
89-90—Indiana	3	24	11	5	.455	0	0	....	5	1	6	2	4	0	0	0	11	3.7
Totals	37	513	189	99	.524	42	35	.833	42	49	91	34	78	0	16	7	234	6.3

Three-Point Field Goals: 1987-88, 0-for-1. 1989-90, 1-for-1 (1.000). Totals, 1-for-2 (.500).

Named to CBA All-Star First Team, 1983. . . . CBA All-Defensive Second Team, 1983. . . . CBA Rookie of the Year, 1983.

DANIEL LESLIE SCHAYES
(Dan)

Born May 10, 1959 at Syracuse, N. Y. Height 6:11. Weight 260.
High School—DeWitt, N. Y., Jamesville-DeWitt.
College—Syracuse University, Syracuse, N. Y.
Drafted by Utah on first round, 1981 (13th pick).

Traded by Utah with other considerations to Denver for Rich Kelley, February 7, 1983.
Traded by Denver to Milwaukee for draft rights to Terry Mills, August 1, 1990.

—COLLEGIATE RECORD—

Year	G.	Min.	FGA	FGM	Pct.	FTA	FTM	Pct.	Reb.	Pts.	Avg.
77-78	24	....	69	39	.565	45	34	.756	96	112	4.7
78-79	29	....	117	62	.530	66	55	.833	121	179	6.2
79-80	30	....	116	59	.509	78	60	.769	134	178	5.9
80-81	34	....	285	165	.579	202	166	.822	284	496	14.6
Totals	117	....	587	325	.554	391	315	.806	635	965	8.2

NBA REGULAR SEASON RECORD

									—Rebounds—									
Sea.—Team	G.	Min.	FGA	FGM	Pct.	FTA	FTM	Pct.	Off.	Def.	Tot.	Ast.	PF	Dq.	Stl.	Blk.	Pts.	Avg.
81-82—Utah	82	1623	524	252	.481	185	140	.757	131	296	427	146	292	4	46	72	644	7.9
82-83—Utah-Den.	82	2284	749	342	.457	295	228	.773	200	435	635	205	325	8	54	98	912	11.1
83-84—Denver	82	1420	371	183	.493	272	215	.790	145	288	433	91	308	5	32	60	581	7.1
84-85—Denver	56	542	129	60	.465	97	79	.814	48	96	144	38	98	2	20	25	199	3.6
85-86—Denver	80	1654	440	221	.502	278	216	.777	154	285	439	79	298	7	42	63	658	8.2
86-87—Denver	76	1556	405	210	.519	294	229	.779	120	260	380	85	266	5	20	74	649	8.5
87-88—Denver	81	2166	668	361	.540	487	407	.836	200	462	662	106	323	9	62	92	1129	13.9
88-89—Denver	76	1918	607	317	.522	402	332	.826	142	358	500	105	320	8	42	81	969	12.8
89-90—Denver	53	1194	330	163	.494	264	225	.852	117	225	342	61	200	7	41	45	551	10.4
Totals	668	14357	4223	2109	.499	2574	2071	.805	1257	2705	3962	916	2430	55	359	610	6292	9.4

Three-Point Field Goals: 1981-82, 0-for-1. 1982-83, 0-for-1. 1983-84, 0-for-2. 1985-86, 0-for-1. 1987-88, 0-for-2. 1988-89, 3-for-9 (.333). 1989-90, 0-for-4. Totals, 3-for-20 (.150).

NBA PLAYOFF RECORD

									—Rebounds—									
Sea.—Team	G.	Min.	FGA	FGM	Pct.	FTA	FTM	Pct.	Off.	Def.	Tot.	Ast.	PF	Dq.	Stl.	Blk.	Pts.	Avg.
82-83—Denver	8	163	43	21	.488	15	15	1.000	11	29	40	14	25	0	2	5	57	7.1
83-84—Denver	5	81	18	11	.611	8	6	.750	3	21	24	4	20	0	4	3	28	5.6

										—Rebounds—								
Sea.—Team	G.	Min.	FGA	FGM	Pct.	FTA	FTM	Pct.	Off.	Def.	Tot.	Ast.	PF	Dq.	Stl.	Blk.	Pts.	Avg.
84-85—Denver	9	118	26	11	.423	20	14	.700	8	22	30	12	22	0	3	4	36	4.0
85-86—Denver	10	295	86	46	.535	30	24	.800	34	48	82	9	37	1	4	17	116	11.6
86-87—Denver	3	75	17	12	.706	9	6	.667	6	11	17	2	10	0	1	2	30	10.0
87-88—Denver	11	314	88	55	.625	83	70	.843	30	49	79	18	46	1	3	10	180	16.4
88-89—Denver	2	36	7	1	.143	8	6	.750	2	9	11	1	4	0	1	1	8	4.0
Totals	48	1082	285	157	.551	173	141	.815	94	189	283	60	164	2	18	42	455	9.5

Son of Dolph Schayes, former NBA forward, former NBA Supervisor of Referees and a member of the Naismith Memorial Basketball Hall of Fame.

DETLEF SCHREMPF

Born January 21, 1963 at Leverkusen, West Germany. Height 6:10. Weight 214.
High School—Centralia, Wash.
College—University of Washington, Seattle, Wash.
Drafted by Dallas on first round, 1985 (8th pick).

Traded by Dallas with a 1990 or 1991 2nd round draft choice to Indiana for Herb Williams, February 21, 1989.

—COLLEGIATE RECORD—

Year	G.	Min.	FGA	FGM	Pct.	FTA	FTM	Pct.	Reb.	Pts.	Avg.
81-82	28	314	73	33	.452	47	26	.553	56	92	3.3
82-83	31	958	266	124	.466	113	81	.717	211	329	10.6
83-84	31	1186	362	195	.539	178	131	.736	230	521	16.8
84-85	32	1180	342	191	.558	175	125	.714	255	507	15.8
Totals	122	3638	1043	543	.521	513	363	.708	752	1449	11.9

NBA REGULAR SEASON RECORD

										—Rebounds—								
Sea.—Team	G.	Min.	FGA	FGM	Pct.	FTA	FTM	Pct.	Off.	Def.	Tot.	Ast.	PF	Dq.	Stl.	Blk.	Pts.	Avg.
85-86—Dallas	64	969	315	142	.451	152	110	.724	70	128	198	88	166	1	23	10	397	6.2
86-87—Dallas	81	1711	561	265	.472	260	193	.742	87	216	303	161	224	2	50	16	756	9.3
87-88—Dallas	82	1587	539	246	.456	266	201	.756	102	177	279	159	189	0	42	32	698	8.5
88-89—Dal.-Ind.	69	1850	578	274	.474	350	273	.780	126	269	395	179	220	3	53	19	828	12.0
89-90—Indiana	78	2573	822	424	.516	490	402	.820	149	471	620	247	271	6	59	16	1267	16.2
Totals	374	8690	2815	1351	.480	1518	1179	.777	534	1261	1795	834	1070	12	227	93	3946	10.6

Three-Point Field Goals: 1985-86, 3-for-7 (.429). 1986-87, 33-for-69 (.478). 1987-88, 5-for-32 (.156). 1988-89, 7-for-35 (.200). 1989-90, 17-for-48 (.354). Totals, 65-for-191 (.340).

NBA PLAYOFF RECORD

										—Rebounds—								
Sea.—Team	G.	Min.	FGA	FGM	Pct.	FTA	FTM	Pct.	Off.	Def.	Tot.	Ast.	PF	Dq.	Stl.	Blk.	Pts.	Avg.
85-86—Dallas	10	120	28	13	.464	17	11	.647	7	16	23	14	24	0	2	1	37	3.7
86-87—Dallas	4	97	35	13	.371	11	5	.455	4	8	12	6	13	0	3	2	31	7.8
87-88—Dallas	15	274	86	40	.465	51	36	.706	25	30	55	24	29	0	8	7	117	7.8
89-90—Indiana	3	125	47	23	.489	16	15	.938	5	17	22	5	13	0	2	1	61	20.3
Totals	32	616	196	89	.454	95	67	.705	41	71	112	49	79	0	15	11	246	7.7

Three-Point Field Goals: 1985-86, 0-for-1. 1986-87, 0-for-3. 1987-88, 1-for-3 (.333). 1989-90, 0-for-3. Totals, 1-for-10 (.100).

Member of West German Olympic team, 1984. . . . Named to THE SPORTING NEWS All-America Second Team, 1985.

BYRON ANTOM SCOTT

Born March 28, 1961 at Ogden, Utah. Height 6:04. Weight 195.
High School—Inglewood, Calif., Morningside.
College—Arizona State University, Tempe, Ariz.
Drafted by San Diego on first round as an undergraduate, 1983 (4th pick).

Draft rights traded by San Diego with Swen Nater to Los Angeles for Norm Nixon and Eddie Jordan and 1986 and 1987 2nd round draft choices, October 10, 1983.

—COLLEGIATE RECORD—

Year	G.	Min.	FGA	FGM	Pct.	FTA	FTM	Pct.	Reb.	Pts.	Avg.
79-80	29	936	332	166	.500	86	63	.733	79	395	13.6
80-81	28	1003	390	197	.505	101	70	.693	106	464	16.6
81-82	Did Not Play—Academic and Personal Reasons										
82-83	33	1206	552	283	.513	188	147	.782	177	713	21.6
Totals	90	3145	1274	646	.507	375	280	.747	362	1572	17.5

NBA REGULAR SEASON RECORD

Sea.—Team	G.	Min.	FGA	FGM	Pct.	FTA	FTM	Pct.	—Rebounds— Off.	Def.	Tot.	Ast.	PF	Dq.	Stl.	Blk.	Pts.	Avg.
83-84—Los Angeles	74	1637	690	334	.484	139	112	.806	50	114	164	177	174	0	81	19	788	10.6
84-85—L.A. Lakers	81	2305	1003	541	.539	228	187	.820	57	153	210	244	197	1	100	17	1295	16.0
85-86—L.A. Lakers	76	2190	989	507	.513	176	138	.784	55	134	189	164	167	0	85	15	1174	15.4
86-87—L.A. Lakers	82	2729	1134	554	.489	251	224	.892	63	223	286	281	163	0	125	18	1397	17.0
87-88—L.A. Lakers	81	3048	1348	710	.527	317	272	.858	76	257	333	335	204	2	155	27	1754	21.7
88-89—L.A. Lakers	74	2605	1198	588	.491	226	195	.863	72	230	302	231	181	1	114	27	1448	19.6
89-90—L.A. Lakers	77	2593	1005	472	.470	209	160	.766	51	191	242	274	180	2	77	31	1197	15.5
Totals	545	17107	7367	3706	.503	1546	1288	.833	424	1302	1726	1706	1266	6	737	154	9053	16.6

Three-Point Field Goals: 1983-84, 8-for-34 (.235). 1984-85, 26-for-60 (.433). 1985-86, 22-for-61 (.361). 1986-87, 65-for-149 (.436). 1987-88, 62-for-179 (.346). 1988-89, 77-for-193 (.399). 1989-90, 93-for-220 (.423). Totals, 353-for-896 (.394).

NBA PLAYOFF RECORD

Sea.—Team	G.	Min.	FGA	FGM	Pct.	FTA	FTM	Pct.	—Rebounds— Off.	Def.	Tot.	Ast.	PF	Dq.	Stl.	Blk.	Pts.	Avg.
83-84—Los Angeles	20	404	161	74	.460	35	21	.600	11	26	37	34	39	1	18	2	171	8.6
84-85—L.A. Lakers	19	585	267	138	.517	44	35	.795	16	36	52	50	47	0	41	4	321	16.9
85-86—L.A. Lakers	14	470	181	90	.497	42	38	.905	15	40	55	42	38	0	19	2	224	16.0
86-87—L.A. Lakers	18	608	210	103	.490	67	53	.791	20	42	62	57	52	0	19	4	266	14.8
87-88—L.A. Lakers	24	897	357	178	.499	104	90	.865	26	74	100	60	65	0	34	5	470	19.6
88-89—L.A. Lakers	11	402	160	79	.494	55	46	.836	10	35	45	25	31	0	18	2	219	19.9
89-90—L.A. Lakers	9	325	106	49	.462	13	10	.769	7	30	37	23	32	1	20	3	121	13.4
Totals	115	3691	1442	711	.493	360	293	.814	105	283	388	291	304	2	169	22	1792	15.6

Three-Point Field Goals: 1983-84, 2-for-10 (.200). 1984-85, 10-for-21 (.476). 1985-86, 6-for-17 (.353). 1986-87, 7-for-34 (.206). 1987-88, 24-for-55 (.436). 1988-89, 15-for-39 (.385). 1989-90, 13-for-34 (.382). Totals, 77-for-210 (.367).

Named to NBA All-Rookie Team, 1984. . . . Member of NBA championship teams, 1985, 1987, 1988. . . . Led NBA in three-point field goal percentage, 1985.

RONY F. SEIKALY

Born May 10, 1965 at Athens, Greece. Height 6:11. Weight 230.

High School—Athens, Greece, American School.

College—Syracuse University, Syracuse, N.Y.

Drafted by Miami on first round, 1988 (9th pick).

—COLLEGIATE RECORD—

Year	G.	Min.	FGA	FGM	Pct.	FTA	FTM	Pct.	Reb.	Pts.	Avg.
84-85	31	775	177	96	.542	104	58	.558	198	250	8.1
85-86	32	875	223	122	.547	142	80	.563	250	324	10.1
86-87	38	*1032	380	216	.568	235	141	.600	311	573	15.1
87-88	35	1084	385	218	.566	234	133	.568	335	569	16.3
Totals	136	*3766	1165	652	.560	715	412	.576	1094	1716	12.6

*Missing one game.

Three-Point Field Goal: 1986-87, 0-for-1.

NBA REGULAR SEASON RECORD

Sea.—Team	G.	Min.	FGA	FGM	Pct.	FTA	FTM	Pct.	—Rebounds— Off.	Def.	Tot.	Ast.	PF	Dq.	Stl.	Blk.	Pts.	Avg.
88-89—Miami	78	1962	744	333	.448	354	181	.511	204	345	549	55	258	8	46	96	848	10.9
89-90—Miami	74	2409	968	486	.502	431	256	.594	253	513	766	78	258	8	78	124	1228	16.6
Totals	152	4371	1712	819	.478	785	437	.557	457	858	1315	133	516	16	124	220	2076	13.7

Three-Point Field Goals: 1988-89, 1-for-4 (.250). 1989-90, 0-for-1. Totals, 1-for-5 (.200).

Named NBA Most Improved Player, 1990.

BRADLEY DONN SELLERS
(Brad)

Born December 17, 1962 at Warrensville Heights, O. Height 7:00. Weight 227.

High School—Warrensville Heights, O.

Colleges—University of Wisconsin, Madison, Wisc., and Ohio State University, Columbus, O.

Drafted by Chicago on first round, 1986 (9th pick).

Traded by Chicago to Seattle for a 1989 1st round draft choice, June 26, 1989.
Traded by Seattle to Minnesota for Steve Johnson and a 1991 2nd round draft choice, February 22, 1990.

—COLLEGIATE RECORD—

Wisconsin

Year	G.	Min.	FGA	FGM	Pct.	FTA	FTM	Pct.	Reb.	Pts.	Avg.
81-82	27	964	351	167	.476	67	44	.657	254	378	14.0
82-83	28	1009	372	189	.508	99	82	.828	219	460	16.4
Wisc. Totals	55	1973	723	356	.492	166	126	.759	473	838	15.2

Ohio State

Year	G.	Min.	FGA	FGM	Pct.	FTA	FTM	Pct.	Reb.	Pts.	Avg.
83-84	Did Not Play—Transfer Student										
84-85	30	979	354	186	.525	125	97	.776	264	469	15.6
85-86	33	1234	492	234	.476	226	185	.819	416	653	19.8
Ohio St. Totals	63	2213	846	420	.496	351	282	.803	680	1122	17.8
Totals	118	4186	1569	776	.495	517	408	.789	1153	1960	16.6

Three-Point Field Goals: 1982-83, 0-for-1.

NBA REGULAR SEASON RECORD

									—Rebounds—									
Sea.—Team	G.	Min.	FGA	FGM	Pct.	FTA	FTM	Pct.	Off.	Def.	Tot.	Ast.	PF	Dq.	Stl.	Blk.	Pts.	Avg.
86-87—Chicago	80	1751	606	276	.455	173	126	.728	155	218	373	102	194	1	44	68	680	8.5
87-88—Chicago	82	2212	714	326	.457	157	124	.790	107	143	250	141	174	0	34	66	777	9.5
88-89—Chicago	80	1732	476	231	.485	101	86	.851	85	142	227	99	176	2	35	69	551	6.9
89-90—Sea.-Min.	59	700	254	103	.406	73	58	.795	39	50	89	33	74	1	17	22	264	4.5
Totals	301	6395	2050	936	.457	504	394	.782	386	553	939	375	618	4	130	225	2272	7.5

Three-Point Field Goals: 1986-87, 2-for-10 (.200). 1987-88, 1-for-7 (.143). 1988-89, 3-for-6 (.500). 1989-90, 0-for-5. Totals, 6-for-28 (.214).

NBA PLAYOFF RECORD

									—Rebounds—									
Sea.—Team	G.	Min.	FGA	FGM	Pct.	FTA	FTM	Pct.	Off.	Def.	Tot.	Ast.	PF	Dq.	Stl.	Blk.	Pts.	Avg.
86-87—Chicago	3	68	19	6	.316	3	3	1.000	2	5	7	3	8	0	0	1	15	5.0
87-88—Chicago	10	144	43	15	.349	17	15	.882	10	11	21	8	18	0	2	5	45	4.5
88-89—Chicago	13	177	58	22	.379	12	10	.833	15	16	31	15	21	0	3	4	54	4.2
Totals	26	389	120	43	.358	32	28	.875	27	32	59	26	47	0	5	10	114	4.4

CHARLES EDWARD SHACKLEFORD

Born April 22, 1966 at Kinston, N.C. Height 6:10. Weight 225.

High School—Kinston, N.C.

College—North Carolina State University, Raleigh, N.C.

Drafted by New Jersey on second round as an undergraduate, 1988 (32nd pick).

—COLLEGIATE RECORD—

Year	G.	Min.	FGA	FGM	Pct.	FTA	FTM	Pct.	Reb.	Pts.	Avg.
85-86	29	876	244	128	.525	68	42	.618	178	298	10.3
86-87	34	1079	429	204	.476	127	66	.520	260	474	13.9
87-88	31	942	416	224	.538	115	68	.591	297	516	16.6
Totals	94	2897	1089	556	.511	310	176	.568	735	1288	13.7

Three-Point Field Goals: 1986-87, 0-for-1.

NBA REGULAR SEASON RECORD

									—Rebounds—									
Sea.—Team	G.	Min.	FGA	FGM	Pct.	FTA	FTM	Pct.	Off.	Def.	Tot.	Ast.	PF	Dq.	Stl.	Blk.	Pts.	Avg.
88-89—New Jersey	60	484	168	83	.494	42	21	.500	50	103	153	21	71	0	15	18	187	3.1
89-90—New Jersey	70	1557	535	247	.462	115	79	.687	180	299	479	56	183	1	40	35	573	8.2
Totals	130	2041	703	330	.469	157	100	.637	230	402	632	77	254	1	55	53	760	5.8

Three-Point Field Goals: 1988-89, 0-for-1. 1989-90, 0-for-1. Totals, 0-for-2.

JOHN PAUL SHASKY

Born July 31, 1964 at Birmingham, Mich. Height 6:11. Weight 240.

High School—Birmingham, Mich., Brother Rice.

College—University of Minnesota, Minneapolis, Minn.

Drafted by Utah on third round, 1986 (61st pick).

Draft rights relinquished by Utah, July 14, 1988; signed by Miami as a free agent, September 30, 1988.
Waived by Miami, October 31, 1989; signed by Golden State as a free agent, December 4, 1989.
Waived by Golden State, February 27, 1990.
Played in France and Spain, 1986-87, and in Italy, 1987-88.
Played in Continental Basketball Association with Rapid City Thrillers, 1987-88.

—COLLEGIATE RECORD—

Year	G.	Min.	FGA	FGM	Pct.	FTA	FTM	Pct.	Reb.	Pts.	Avg.
82-83	26	....	46	23	.500	23	10	.435	43	56	2.2
83-84	28	....	145	70	.483	67	44	.657	155	184	6.6
84-85	28	....	268	152	.567	110	77	.700	190	381	13.6
85-86	30	1069	334	175	.524	152	101	.664	210	451	15.0
Totals	112	....	793	420	.530	352	232	.659	598	1072	9.6

ITALIAN LEAGUE RECORD

Year	G.	Min.	FGA	FGM	Pct.	FTA	FTM	Pct.	Reb.	Pts.	Avg.
87-88—Brescia............	8	291	104	64	.615	45	31	.689	81	159	7.4

CBA REGULAR SEASON RECORD

			—2-Point—			—3-Point—									
Sea.—Team	G.	Min.	FGM	FGA	Pct.	FGM	FGA	Pct.	FTM	FTA	Pct.	Reb.	Ast.	Pts.	Avg.
87-88—Rapid City..................	33	608	98	175	.560	0	0	.000	64	104	.615	182	29	260	7.8

NBA REGULAR SEASON RECORD

									—Rebounds—									
Sea.—Team	G.	Min.	FGA	FGM	Pct.	FTA	FTM	Pct.	Off.	Def.	Tot.	Ast.	PF	Dq.	Stl.	Blk.	Pts.	Avg.
88-89—Miami	65	944	248	121	.488	167	115	.689	96	136	232	22	94	0	14	13	357	5.5
89-90—Golden State	14	51	14	4	.286	6	2	.333	4	9	13	1	10	0	1	2	10	0.7
Totals................	79	995	262	125	.477	173	117	.676	100	145	245	23	104	0	15	15	367	4.6

Three-Point Field Goals: 1988-89, 0-for-2.

BRIAN K. SHAW

Born March 22, 1966 at Oakland, Calif. Height 6:06. Weight 190.
High School—Oakland, Calif., Bishop O'Dowd.
Colleges—St. Mary's College, Moraga, Calif., and University of California at Santa Barbara, Santa Barbara, Calif.
Drafted by Boston on first round, 1988 (24th pick).

Played in Italy, 1989-90.

—COLLEGIATE RECORD—

St. Mary's

Year	G.	Min.	FGA	FGM	Pct.	FTA	FTM	Pct.	Reb.	Pts.	Avg.
83-84..............................	14	129	36	13	.361	19	14	.737	12	40	2.9
84-85..............................	27	976	246	99	.402	76	55	.724	144	253	9.4
St. M. Tot...............	41	1105	282	112	.397	95	69	.726	156	293	7.1

California-Santa Barbara

Year	G.	Min.	FGA	FGM	Pct.	FTA	FTM	Pct.	Reb.	Pts.	Avg.
85-86..............................			Did Not Play—Transfer Student								
86-87..............................	29	1013	288	125	.434	66	47	.712	224	315	10.9
87-88..............................	30	1073	324	151	.466	96	71	.740	260	399	13.3
UCSB Totals..........	59	2086	612	276	.451	162	118	.728	484	714	12.1
College Totals.......	100	3191	894	388	.434	257	187	.728	640	1007	10.1

Three-Point Field Goals: 1986-87, 18-for-42 (.429). 1987-88, 26-for-74 (.351). Totals, 44-for-116 (.379).

ITALIAN LEAGUE RECORD

Year	G.	Min.	FGA	FGM	Pct.	FTA	FTM	Pct.	Reb.	Pts.	Avg.
89-90—Il Messaggero.	30	1144	418	244	.584	139	111	.799	274	749	25.0

Three-Point Field Goals: 1989-90, 50-for-140 (.357).

NBA REGULAR SEASON RECORD

									—Rebounds—									
Sea.—Team	G.	Min.	FGA	FGM	Pct.	FTA	FTM	Pct.	Off.	Def.	Tot.	Ast.	PF	Dq.	Stl.	Blk.	Pts.	Avg.
88-89—Boston	82	2301	686	297	.433	132	109	.826	119	257	376	.472	211	1	78	27	703	8.6

Three-Point Field Goals: 1988-89, 0-for-13.

NBA PLAYOFF RECORD

									—Rebounds—									
Sea.—Team	G.	Min.	FGA	FGM	Pct.	FTA	FTM	Pct.	Off.	Def.	Tot.	Ast.	PF	Dq.	Stl.	Blk.	Pts.	Avg.
88-89—Boston	3	124	43	22	.512	9	7	.778	2	15	17	19	11	0	3	0	51	17.0

Three-Point Field Goals: 1988-89, 0-for-1.

Named to NBA All-Rookie Second Team, 1989.

PURVIS SHORT

Born July 2, 1957 at Hattiesburg, Miss. Height 6:07. Weight 220.
High School—Hattiesburg, Miss., Blair.
College—Jackson State University, Jackson, Miss.
Drafted by Golden State on first round, 1978 (5th pick).

Traded by Golden State to Houston for Dave Feitl and a future 1st round draft choice, November 5, 1987.
Signed by New Jersey as an unrestricted free agent, September 20, 1989.

—COLLEGIATE RECORD—

Year	G.	Min.	FGA	FGM	Pct.	FTA	FTM	Pct.	Reb.	Pts.	Avg.
74-75	28	....	325	190	.585	66	44	.667	218	424	15.1
75-76	28	....	635	324	.510	91	66	.725	283	714	25.5
76-77	26	....	541	288	.532	92	70	.761	218	646	24.8
77-78	22	....	535	285	.532	111	80	.721	250	650	29.5
Totals	104	....	2036	1087	.534	360	260	.722	969	2434	23.4

NBA REGULAR SEASON RECORD

									—Rebounds—									
Sea.—Team	G.	Min.	FGA	FGM	Pct.	FTA	FTM	Pct.	Off.	Def.	Tot.	Ast.	PF	Dq.	Stl.	Blk.	Pts.	Avg.
78-79—Golden State	75	1703	771	369	.479	85	57	.671	127	220	347	97	233	6	54	12	795	10.6
79-80—Golden State	62	1636	916	461	.503	165	134	.812	119	197	316	123	186	4	63	9	1056	17.0
80-81—Golden State	79	2309	1157	549	.475	205	168	.820	151	240	391	249	244	3	78	19	1269	16.1
81-82—Golden State	76	1782	935	456	.488	221	177	.801	123	143	266	209	220	3	65	10	1095	14.4
82-83—Golden State	67	2397	1209	589	.487	308	255	.828	145	209	354	228	242	3	94	14	1437	21.4
83-84—Golden State	79	2945	1509	714	.473	445	353	.793	184	254	438	246	252	2	103	11	1803	22.8
84-85—Golden State	78	3081	1780	819	.460	613	501	.817	157	241	398	234	255	4	116	27	2186	28.0
85-86—Golden State	64	2427	1313	633	.482	406	351	.865	126	203	329	237	229	5	92	22	1632	25.5
86-87—Golden State	34	950	501	240	.479	160	137	.856	55	82	137	86	103	1	45	7	621	18.3
87-88—Houston	81	1949	986	474	.481	240	206	.858	71	151	222	162	197	0	58	14	1159	14.3
88-89—Houston	65	1157	480	198	.413	89	77	.865	65	114	179	107	116	1	44	13	482	7.4
89-90—New Jersey	82	2213	950	432	.455	237	198	.835	101	147	248	145	202	2	66	20	1072	13.1
Totals	842	24549	12507	5934	.474	3174	2614	.824	1424	2201	3625	2123	2479	34	878	178	14607	17.3

Three-Point Field Goals: 1979-80, 0-for-6. 1980-81, 3-for-17 (.176). 1981-82, 6-for-28 (.214). 1982-83, 4-for-15 (.267). 1983-84, 22-for-72 (.306). 1984-85, 47-for-150 (.313). 1985-86, 15-for-49 (.306). 1986-87, 4-for-17 (.253). 1987-88, 5-for-21 (.238). 1988-89, 9-for-33 (.273). 1989-90, 10-for-35 (.286). Totals, 125-for-443 (.282).

NBA PLAYOFF RECORD

									—Rebounds—									
Sea.—Team	G.	Min.	FGA	FGM	Pct.	FTA	FTM	Pct.	Off.	Def.	Tot.	Ast.	PF	Dq.	Stl.	Blk.	Pts.	Avg.
86-87—Golden State	10	253	123	57	.463	36	32	.889	12	21	33	27	34	0	12	2	146	14.6
87-88—Houston	4	71	26	7	.269	8	8	1.000	4	5	9	1	8	0	1	0	22	5.5
88-89—Houston	4	37	21	8	.381	5	3	.600	7	3	10	2	7	0	0	0	19	4.8
Totals	18	361	170	72	.424	49	43	.878	23	29	52	30	49	0	13	2	187	10.4

Three-Point Field Goals: 1986-87, 0-for-2. 1987-88, 0-for-1. 1988-89, 0-for-2. Totals, 0-for-5.

Brother of Eugene Short, forward with Seattle SuperSonics and New York Knickerbockers, 1975-76.

DEXTER WAYNE SHOUSE

Born March 23, 1963 at Terre Haute, Ind. Height 6:02. Weight 200.

High School—Terre Haute, Ind., North.

Colleges—Panola Junior College, Carthage, Tex., and University of South Alabama, Mobile, Ala.

Drafted by Los Angeles Lakers on fourth round, 1985 (94th pick).

Waived by Los Angeles Lakers, October 16, 1985; signed by Atlanta as a free agent, October 6, 1988.
Waived by Atlanta, October 24, 1988; signed by Philadelphia as a free agent, November 27, 1989.
Waived by Philadelphia, December 7, 1989.

Played in Continental Basketball Association with Kansas City Sizzlers and Baltimore Lightning, 1985-86, and Tulsa Fast Breakers, 1988-89 and 1989-90.

—COLLEGIATE RECORD—

Panola

Year	G.	Min.	FGA	FGM	Pct.	FTA	FTM	Pct.	Reb.	Pts.	Avg.
81-82					Statistics Unavailable						
Year	G.	Min.	FGA	FGM	Pct.	FTA	FTM	Pct.	Reb.	Pts.	Avg.
82-83					Statistics Unavailable						

South Alabama

Year	G.	Min.	FGA	FGM	Pct.	FTA	FTM	Pct.	Reb.	Pts.	Avg.
83-84	30	929	307	138	.450	85	70	.824	61	346	11.5
84-85	28	963	339	170	.501	78	60	.769	85	400	14.3
Totals	58	1892	646	308	.477	163	130	.798	146	746	12.9

CBA REGULAR SEASON RECORD

			—2-Point—			—3-Point—									
Sea.—Team	G.	Min.	FGM	FGA	Pct.	FGM	FGA	Pct.	FTM	FTA	Pct.	Reb.	Ast.	Pts.	Avg.
85-86—K.C.-Bal.	40	1001	224	433	.517	4	19	.211	71	94	.755	107	137	531	13.3
88-89—Tulsa	46	1341	308	674	.457	41	119	.345	274	316	.867	207	172	1013	22.0
89-90—Tulsa	24	841	205	373	.550	38	104	.365	88	107	.822	86	92	612	25.5
Totals	110	3183	737	1480	.498	83	242	.343	433	517	.838	400	401	2156	19.6

NBA REGULAR SEASON RECORD

Sea.—Team	G.	Min.	FGA	FGM	Pct.	FTA	FTM	Pct.	—Rebounds— Off.	Def.	Tot.	Ast.	PF	Dq.	Stl.	Blk.	Pts.	Avg.
89-90—Philadelphia	3	18	4	0	.000	0	0	....	0	0	0	2	2	0	1	1	0	0.0

Three-Point Field Goals: 1989-90, 0-for-1.

Named CBA Playoff MVP, 1989.

JERRY LEE SICHTING

Born November 29, 1956 at Martinsville, Ind. Height 6:01. Weight 180.

High School—Martinsville, Ind.

College—Purdue University, West Lafayette, Ind.

Drafted by Golden State on fourth round, 1979 (82nd pick).

Waived by Golden State, October 4, 1979; signed by Indiana as a free agent, October 9, 1980.
Traded by Indiana to Boston for a 1990 2nd round draft choice, October 3, 1985.
Traded by Boston with future considerations to Portland for Jim Paxson, February 23, 1988.
Waived by Portland, July 24, 1989; signed by Charlotte as a free agent, September 11, 1989.
Waived by Charlotte, February 23, 1990; signed by Milwaukee, February 27, 1990, to a 10-day contract that expired, March 8, 1990.

—COLLEGIATE RECORD—

Year	G.	Min.	FGA	FGM	Pct.	FTA	FTM	Pct.	Reb.	Pts.	Avg.
75-76	27	436	123	67	.545	38	31	.816	42	165	6.1
76-77	28	536	131	71	.542	69	61	.884	36	203	7.3
77-78	27	975	233	120	.515	90	78	.867	67	318	11.8
78-79	35	1202	367	186	.507	118	103	.873	97	475	13.6
Totals	117	3149	854	444	.520	315	273	.867	242	1161	9.9

NBA REGULAR SEASON RECORD

Sea.—Team	G.	Min.	FGA	FGM	Pct.	FTA	FTM	Pct.	—Rebounds— Off.	Def.	Tot.	Ast.	PF	Dq.	Stl.	Blk.	Pts.	Avg.
80-81—Indiana	47	450	95	34	.358	32	25	.781	11	32	43	70	38	0	23	1	93	2.0
81-82—Indiana	51	800	194	91	.469	38	29	.763	14	41	55	117	63	0	33	1	212	4.2
82-83—Indiana	78	2435	661	316	.478	107	92	.860	33	122	155	433	185	0	104	2	727	9.3
83-84—Indiana	80	2497	746	397	.532	135	117	.867	44	127	171	457	179	0	90	8	917	11.5
84-85—Indiana	70	1808	624	325	.521	128	112	.875	24	90	114	264	116	0	47	4	771	11.0
85-86—Boston	82	1596	412	235	.570	66	61	.924	27	77	104	188	118	0	50	0	537	6.5
86-87—Boston	78	1566	398	202	.508	42	37	.881	22	69	91	187	124	0	40	1	448	5.7
87-88—Bos.-Port.	52	694	172	93	.541	23	17	.739	9	27	36	93	60	0	21	0	213	4.1
88-89—Portland	25	390	104	46	.442	8	7	.875	9	20	29	59	17	0	15	0	102	4.1
89-90—Char.-Milw.	35	496	125	50	.400	22	18	.818	3	16	19	94	40	0	16	2	121	3.5
Totals	598	12732	3531	1789	.507	601	515	.857	196	621	817	1962	940	0	439	19	4141	6.9

Three-Point Field Goals: 1980-81, 0-for-5. 1981-82, 1-for-9 (.111). 1982-83, 3-for-18 (.167). 1983-84, 6-for-20 (.300). 1984-85, 9-for-37 (.243). 1985-86, 6-for-16 (.375). 1986-87, 7-for-26 (.269). 1987-88, 10-for-22 (.455). 1988-89, 3-for-12 (.250). 1989-90, 3-for-12 (.250). Totals, 48-for-177 (.271).

NBA PLAYOFF RECORD

Sea.—Team	G.	Min.	FGA	FGM	Pct.	FTA	FTM	Pct.	—Rebounds— Off.	Def.	Tot.	Ast.	PF	Dq.	Stl.	Blk.	Pts.	Avg.
80-81—Indiana	1	1	0	0	.000	0	0	.000	0	0	0	0	0	0	1	0	0	0.0
85-86—Boston	18	274	61	27	.443	7	3	.429	5	11	16	40	18	0	5	0	57	3.2
86-87—Boston	23	338	82	35	.427	10	8	.800	5	15	20	33	36	0	9	0	79	3.4
87-88—Portland	4	31	7	2	.286	0	0	.000	1	1	2	5	4	0	1	0	4	1.0
88-89—Portland	1	11	3	0	.000	0	0	.000	0	1	1	1	1	0	0	0	0	0.0
Totals	47	655	153	64	.418	17	11	.647	11	28	39	79	59	0	16	0	140	3.0

Three-Point Field Goals: 1985-86, 0-for-1. 1986-87, 1-for-6 (.167). Totals, 1-for-7 (.143).

Member of NBA championship team, 1986.

JACK WAYNE SIKMA

Born November 14, 1955 at Kankakee, Ill. Height 7:00. Weight 250.

High School—St. Anne, Ill.

College—Illinois Wesleyan University, Bloomington, Ill.

Drafted by Seattle on first round, 1977 (8th pick).

Traded by Seattle with 1987 and 1989 2nd round draft choices to Milwaukee for Alton Lister and 1987 and 1989 1st round draft choices, July 1, 1986.

—COLLEGIATE RECORD—

Year	G.	Min.	FGA	FGM	Pct.	FTA	FTM	Pct.	Reb.	Pts.	Avg.
73-74	21	....	306	148	.484	37	28	.757	223	324	15.4
74-75	30	....	537	265	.493	112	80	.714	415	610	20.3

Year	G.	Min.	FGA	FGM	Pct.	FTA	FTM	Pct.	Reb.	Pts.	Avg.
75-76	25	....	385	204	.530	126	93	.738	290	501	20.0
76-77	31	....	302	324	.528	235	189	.804	477	837	27.0
Totals	107	....	1530	941	.514	510	390	.765	1405	2272	21.2

NBA REGULAR SEASON RECORD

									—Rebounds—									
Sea.—Team	G.	Min.	FGA	FGM	Pct.	FTA	FTM	Pct.	Off.	Def.	Tot.	Ast.	PF	Dq.	Stl.	Blk.	Pts.	Avg.
77-78—Seattle	82	2238	752	342	.455	247	192	.777	196	482	678	134	300	6	68	40	876	10.7
78-79—Seattle	82	2958	1034	476	.460	404	329	.814	232	781	1013	261	295	4	82	67	1281	15.6
79-80—Seattle	82	2793	989	470	.475	292	235	.805	198	710	908	279	232	5	68	77	1175	14.3
80-81—Seattle	82	2920	1311	595	.454	413	340	.823	184	668	852	248	282	5	78	93	1530	18.7
81-82—Seattle	82	3049	1212	581	.479	523	447	.855	223	815	1038	277	268	5	102	107	1611	19.6
82-83—Seattle	75	2564	1043	484	.464	478	400	.837	213	645	858	233	263	4	87	65	1368	18.2
83-84—Seattle	82	2993	1155	576	.499	480	411	.856	225	686	911	327	301	6	95	92	1563	19.1
84-85—Seattle	68	2402	943	461	.489	393	335	.852	164	559	723	285	239	1	83	91	1259	18.5
85-86—Seattle	80	2790	1100	508	.462	411	355	.864	146	602	748	301	293	4	92	73	1371	17.1
86-87—Milwaukee	82	2536	842	390	.463	313	265	.847	208	614	822	203	328	14	88	90	1045	12.7
87-88—Milwaukee	82	2923	1058	514	.486	348	321	.922	195	514	709	279	316	11	93	80	1352	16.5
88-89—Milwaukee	80	2587	835	360	.431	294	266	.905	141	482	623	289	300	6	85	61	1068	13.4
89-90—Milwaukee	71	2250	827	344	.416	260	230	.885	109	383	492	229	244	5	76	48	986	13.9
Totals	1030	35003	13101	6101	.466	4856	4126	.850	2434	7941	10375	3345	3661	76	1097	984	16485	16.0

Three-Point Field Goals: 1979-80, 0-for-1. 1980-81, 0-for-5. 1981-82, 2-for-13 (.154). 1982-83, 0-for-8. 1983-84, 0-for-2. 1984-85, 2-for-10 (.200). 1985-86, 0-for-13. 1986-87, 0-for-2. 1987-88, 3-for-14 (.214). 1988-89, 82-for-216 (.380). 1989-90, 68-for-199 (.342). Totals, 157-for-483 (.325).

NBA PLAYOFF RECORD

									—Rebounds—									
Sea.—Team	G.	Min.	FGA	FGM	Pct.	FTA	FTM	Pct.	Off.	Def.	Tot.	Ast.	PF	Dq.	Stl.	Blk.	Pts.	Avg.
77-78—Seattle	22	701	247	115	.466	91	71	.780	50	128	178	27	101	7	18	11	301	13.7
78-79—Seattle	17	655	224	103	.460	61	48	.787	39	160	199	43	70	2	16	24	254	14.9
79-80—Seattle	15	534	163	65	.399	54	46	.852	30	96	126	55	55	1	17	5	176	11.7
81-82—Seattle	8	315	128	57	.445	58	50	.862	21	76	97	24	34	1	9	8	164	20.5
82-83—Seattle	2	75	31	11	.355	12	8	.667	6	20	26	11	7	0	2	2	30	15.0
83-84—Seattle	5	193	98	49	.500	14	12	.857	11	40	51	5	22	1	3	7	110	22.0
86-87—Milwaukee	12	426	150	73	.487	49	48	.980	33	97	130	23	56	3	15	10	194	16.2
87-88—Milwaukee	5	190	76	35	.461	30	25	.833	24	38	62	13	23	0	2	4	95	19.0
88-89—Milwaukee	9	301	94	37	.394	28	23	.821	9	41	50	30	41	2	8	4	105	11.7
89-90—Milwaukee	4	117	23	6	.261	8	6	.750	0	14	14	7	19	0	2	4	20	5.0
Totals	99	3507	1234	551	.447	405	337	.832	223	710	933	238	428	17	92	79	1449	14.6

Three-Point Field Goals: 1979-80, 0-for-2. 1982-83, 0-for-1. 1983-84, 0-for-1. 1986-87, 0-for-1. 1987-88, 0-for-3. 1988-89, 8-for-28 (.286). 1989-90, 2-for-7 (.286). Totals, 10-for-43 (.233).

NBA ALL-STAR GAME RECORD

								—Rebounds—								
Season—Team	Min.	FGA	FGM	Pct.	FTA	FTM	Pct.	Off.	Def.	Tot.	Ast.	PF	Dq.	Stl.	Blk.	Pts.
1979—Seattle	18	5	4	.800	0	0	.000	1	3	4	0	1	0	0	0	8
1980—Seattle	28	10	4	.400	0	0	.000	2	6	8	4	5	0	2	3	8
1981—Seattle	21	5	2	.400	2	2	1.000	1	3	4	4	5	0	1	1	6
1982—Seattle	21	11	5	.455	0	0	.000	2	7	9	1	2	0	2	1	10
1983—Seattle	17	6	4	.667	0	0	.000	1	2	3	1	2	0	1	1	5
1984—Seattle	30	12	5	.417	6	5	.833	5	7	12	1	4	0	3	0	15
1985—Seattle	12	2	0	.000	0	0	.000	0	2	2	0	1	0	0	1	0
Totals	147	51	24	.471	8	7	.875	12	30	42	11	20	0	9	7	52

Three-Point Field Goals: 1980, 0-for-1. 1981, 0-for-1. 1983, 0-for-1. Totals, 0-for-3.

Named to NBA All-Defensive Second Team, 1982. . . . NBA All-Rookie Team, 1978. . . . Member of NBA championship team, 1979. . . . Led NBA in free-throw percentage, 1988.

SCOTT ALLEN SKILES

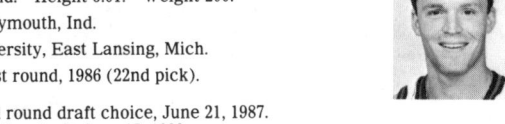

Born March 5, 1964 at LaPorte, Ind. Height 6:01. Weight 200.

High School—Plymouth, Ind.

College—Michigan State University, East Lansing, Mich.

Drafted by Milwaukee on first round, 1986 (22nd pick).

Traded by Milwaukee to Indiana for a future 2nd round draft choice, June 21, 1987.
Selected from Indiana by Orlando in NBA expansion draft, June 15, 1989.

—COLLEGIATE RECORD—

Year	G.	Min.	FGA	FGM	Pct.	FTA	FTM	Pct.	Reb.	Pts.	Avg.
82-83	30	1023	286	141	.493	83	69	.831	63	376	12.5
83-84	28	983	319	153	.480	119	99	.832	62	405	14.5
84-85	29	1107	420	212	.505	114	90	.790	93	514	17.7
85-86	31	1172	598	331	.554	209	188	.900	135	850	27.4
Totals	118	4285	1623	837	.516	525	446	.850	353	2145	18.2

Three-Point Field Goals: 1982-83, 25-for-50 (.500).

NBA REGULAR SEASON RECORD

									—Rebounds—									
Sea.—Team	G.	Min.	FGA	FGM	Pct.	FTA	FTM	Pct.	Off.	Def.	Tot.	Ast.	PF	Dq.	Stl.	Blk.	Pts.	Avg.
86-87—Milwaukee	13	205	62	18	.290	12	10	.833	6	20	26	45	18	0	5	1	49	3.8
87-88—Indiana	51	760	209	86	.411	54	45	.833	11	55	66	180	97	0	22	3	223	4.4
88-89—Indiana	80	1571	442	198	.448	144	130	.903	21	128	149	390	151	1	64	2	546	6.8
89-90—Orlando	70	1460	464	190	.409	119	104	.874	23	136	159	334	126	0	36	4	536	7.7
Totals	214	3996	1177	492	.418	329	289	.878	61	339	400	949	392	1	127	10	1354	6.3

Three-Point Field Goals: 1986-87, 3-for-14 (.214). 1987-88, 6-for-20 (.300). 1988-89, 20-for-67 (.267). 1989-90, 52-for-132 (.394). Totals, 81-for-241 (.336).

Named to THE SPORTING NEWS All-America First Team, 1986.

CHARLES DANIEL SMITH

Born July 16, 1965 at Bridgeport, Conn. Height 6:10. Weight 230.
High School—Bridgeport, Conn., Harding.
College—University of Pittsburgh, Pittsburgh, Pa.
Drafted by Philadelphia on first round, 1988 (3rd pick).

Draft rights traded by Philadelphia to Los Angeles Clippers for draft rights to Hersey Hawkins and a 1989 1st round draft choice, June 28, 1988.

—COLLEGIATE RECORD—

Year	G.	Min.	FGA	FGM	Pct.	FTA	FTM	Pct.	Reb.	Pts.	Avg.
84-85	29	956	301	151	.502	175	133	.760	231	435	15.0
85-86	29	1077	408	165	.404	172	131	.762	235	461	15.9
86-87	33	1050	327	180	.550	275	202	.735	282	562	17.0
87-88	31	1020	378	211	.558	212	162	.764	239	587	18.9
Totals	122	4103	1414	707	.500	834	628	.753	987	2045	16.8

Three-Point Field Goals: 1987-88, 3-for-11 (.273).

NBA REGULAR SEASON RECORD

									—Rebounds—									
Sea.—Team	G.	Min.	FGA	FGM	Pct.	FTA	FTM	Pct.	Off.	Def.	Tot.	Ast.	PF	Dq.	Stl.	Blk.	Pts.	Avg.
88-89—L.A. Clippers	71	2161	878	435	.495	393	285	.725	173	292	465	103	273	6	68	89	1155	16.3
89-90—L.A. Clippers	78	2732	1145	595	.520	572	454	.794	177	347	524	114	294	6	86	119	1645	21.1
Totals	149	4893	2023	1030	.509	965	739	.766	350	639	989	217	567	12	154	208	2800	18.8

Three-Point Field Goals: 1988-89, 0-for-3. 1989-90, 1-for-12 (.083). Totals, 1-for-15 (.067).

Named to NBA All-Rookie First Team, 1989. . . . Member of U.S. Olympic team, 1988.

CHARLES SMITH IV

Born November 29, 1967 at Washington, D.C. Height 6:01. Weight 160.
High School—Washington, D.C., All Saints.
College—Georgetown University, Washington, D.C.
Never drafted by an NBA franchise.

Signed by Boston as a free agent, September 27, 1989.

—COLLEGIATE RECORD—

Year	G.	Min.	FGA	FGM	Pct.	FTA	FTM	Pct.	Reb.	Pts.	Avg.
85-86	30	243	59	28	.475	45	34	.756	30	90	3.0
86-87	33	514	193	81	.420	62	40	.645	49	221	6.7
87-88	30	870	405	173	.427	100	77	.770	100	470	15.7
88-89	33	1111	446	222	498	175	137	.783	118	617	18.7
Totals	126	2738	1103	504	.457	382	288	.754	297	1398	11.1

Three-Point Field Goals: 1986-87, 19-for-50 (.380). 1987-88, 47-for-136 (.346). 1988-89, 36-for-89 (.404). Totals, 102-for-275 (.371).

NBA REGULAR SEASON RECORD

									—Rebounds—									
Sea.—Team	G.	Min.	FGA	FGM	Pct.	FTA	FTM	Pct.	Off.	Def.	Tot.	Ast.	PF	Dq.	Stl.	Blk.	Pts.	Avg.
89-90—Boston	60	519	133	59	.444	76	53	.697	14	55	69	103	75	0	35	3	171	2.9

Three-Point Field Goals: 1989-90, 0-for-7.

NBA PLAYOFF RECORD

									—Rebounds—									
Sea.—Team	G.	Min.	FGA	FGM	Pct.	FTA	FTM	Pct.	Off.	Def.	Tot.	Ast.	PF	Dq.	Stl.	Blk.	Pts.	Avg.
89-90—Boston	3	9	2	1	.500	0	0	....	1	0	1	3	0	0	1	0	2	0.7

Member of U.S. Olympic team, 1988. . . . Named to THE SPORTING NEWS All-America Second Team, 1989.

DEREK ERVIN SMITH

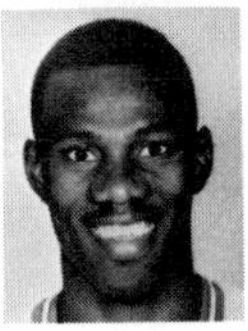

Born November 1, 1961 at Hogansville, Ga. Height 6:06. Weight 218.
High School—Hogansville, Ga.
College—University of Louisville, Louisville, Ky.
Drafted by Golden State on second round, 1982 (35th pick).

Waived by Golden State, September 8, 1983; signed by San Diego as a free agent, September 13, 1983.
Traded by Los Angeles Clippers with Junior Bridgeman and Franklin Edwards to Sacramento for Larry Drew, Mike Woodson, a 1988 1st round draft choice and a 1989 2nd round draft choice, August 19, 1986.
Waived by Sacramento, February 7, 1989; signed by Philadelphia as a free agent, February 13, 1989.

—COLLEGIATE RECORD—

Year	G.	Min.	FGA	FGM	Pct.	FTA	FTM	Pct.	Reb.	Pts.	Avg.
78-79	32	622	185	117	.632	123	79	.642	153	313	9.8
79-80	36	1222	372	213	.573	150	105	.700	299	531	14.8
80-81	30	964	348	188	.540	135	89	.659	233	465	15.5
81-82	33	950	346	204	.590	162	109	.673	199	517	15.7
Totals	131	3758	1251	722	.577	570	382	.670	884	1826	13.9

NBA REGULAR SEASON RECORD

									—Rebounds—									
Sea.—Team	G.	Min.	FGA	FGM	Pct.	FTA	FTM	Pct.	Off.	Def.	Tot.	Ast.	PF	Dq.	Stl.	Blk.	Pts.	Avg.
82-83—Golden State	27	154	51	21	.412	25	17	.680	10	28	38	2	40	0	0	4	59	2.2
83-84—San Diego	61	1297	436	238	.546	163	123	.755	54	116	170	82	165	2	33	22	600	9.8
84-85—L.A. Clippers	80	2762	1271	682	.537	504	400	.794	174	253	427	216	317	8	77	52	1767	22.1
85-86—L.A. Clippers	11	339	181	100	.552	84	58	.690	20	21	41	31	35	2	9	13	259	23.5
86-87—Sacramento	52	1658	757	338	.447	228	178	.781	60	122	182	204	184	3	46	23	863	16.6
87-88—Sacramento	35	899	364	174	.478	113	87	.770	35	68	103	89	108	2	21	17	443	12.7
88-89—Sac.-Phil.	65	1295	496	216	.435	188	129	.686	61	106	167	128	164	4	43	23	568	8.7
89-90—Philadelphia	75	1405	514	261	.508	186	130	.699	62	110	172	109	198	2	35	20	668	8.9
Totals	406	9809	4070	2030	.499	1491	1122	.753	476	824	1300	861	1211	23	264	174	5227	12.9

Three-Point Field Goals: 1982-83, 0-for-2. 1983-84, 1-for-6 (.167). 1984-85, 3-for-19 (.158). 1985-86, 1-for-2 (.500). 1986-87, 9-for-33 (.273). 1987-88, 8-for-23 (.348). 1988-89, 7-for-31 (.226). 1989-90, 16-for-36 (.444). Totals, 45-for-152 (.296).

NBA PLAYOFF RECORD

									—Rebounds—									
Sea.—Team	G.	Min.	FGA	FGM	Pct.	FTA	FTM	Pct.	Off.	Def.	Tot.	Ast.	PF	Dq.	Stl.	Blk.	Pts.	Avg.
88-89—Philadelphia	3	48	14	9	.643	2	1	.500	2	5	7	3	9	0	1	0	19	6.3
89-90—Philadelphia	1	15	8	5	.625	2	1	.500	0	0	0	1	3	0	1	0	11	11.0
Totals	4	63	22	14	.636	4	2	.500	2	5	7	4	12	0	2	0	30	7.5

Three-Point Field Goals: 1989-90, 0-for-1.

Member of NCAA Division I championship team, 1980.

KENNY SMITH

Born March 8, 1965 at Queens, N.Y. Height 6:03. Weight 170.
High School—Jamaica, N.Y., Archbishop Molloy.
College—University of North Carolina, Chapel Hill, N.C.
Drafted by Sacramento on first round, 1987 (6th pick).

Traded by Sacramento with Mike Williams to Atlanta for Antoine Carr, Sedric Toney and future draft considerations, February 13, 1990.

—COLLEGIATE RECORD—

Year	G.	Min.	FGA	FGM	Pct.	FTA	FTM	Pct.	Reb.	Pts.	Avg.
83-84	23	667	160	83	.519	55	44	.800	40	210	9.1
84-85	36	1350	334	173	.518	114	98	.860	92	444	12.3
85-86	34	1109	318	164	.516	99	80	.808	75	408	12.0
86-87	34	1092	414	208	.502	88	71	.807	76	574	16.9
Totals	127	4218	1226	628	.512	356	293	.823	283	1636	12.9

Three-Point Field Goals: 1986-87, 87-for-213 (.408).

NBA REGULAR SEASON RECORD

									—Rebounds—									
Sea.—Team	G.	Min.	FGA	FGM	Pct.	FTA	FTM	Pct.	Off.	Def.	Tot.	Ast.	PF	Dq.	Stl.	Blk.	Pts.	Avg.
87-88—Sacramento	61	2170	694	331	.477	204	167	.819	40	98	138	434	140	1	92	8	841	13.8
88-89—Sacramento	81	3145	1183	547	.462	357	263	.737	49	177	226	621	173	0	102	7	1403	17.3
89-90—Sac.-Atl.	79	2421	811	378	.466	196	161	.821	18	139	157	445	143	0	79	8	943	11.9
Totals	221	7736	2688	1256	.467	757	591	.781	107	414	521	1500	456	1	273	23	3187	14.4

Three-Point Field Goals: 1987-88, 12-for-39 (.308). 1988-89, 46-for-128 (.359). 1989-90, 26-for-83 (.313). Totals, 84-for-250 (.336).

Named to NBA All-Rookie Team, 1988. . . . THE SPORTING NEWS All-America First Team, 1987.

LARRY SMITH

Born January 18, 1958 at Rolling Fork, Miss. Height 6:08. Weight 235.
High School—Hollandale, Miss., Simmons.
College—Alcorn State University, Lorman, Miss.
Drafted by Golden State on second round, 1980 (24th pick).

Signed by Houston as an unrestricted free agent, July 11, 1989.

—COLLEGIATE RECORD—

Year	G.	Min.	FGA	FGM	Pct.	FTA	FTM	Pct.	Reb.	Pts.	Avg.
76-77	34	....	402	212	.526	124	74	.596	222	498	14.6
77-78	22	....	231	137	.593	74	45	.608	222	319	14.5
78-79	29	....	360	216	.600	142	81	.570	398	513	17.7
79-80	26	849	342	198	.579	182	126	.692	392	522	20.1
Totals	111	....	1335	763	.572	522	326	.625	1234	1852	16.7

NBA REGULAR SEASON RECORD

									—Rebounds—									
Sea.—Team	G.	Min.	FGA	FGM	Pct.	FTA	FTM	Pct.	Off.	Def.	Tot.	Ast.	PF	Dq.	Stl.	Blk.	Pts.	Avg.
80-81—Golden State	82	2578	594	304	.512	301	177	.588	433	561	994	93	316	10	70	63	785	9.6
81-82—Golden State	74	2213	412	220	.534	159	88	.553	279	534	813	83	291	7	65	54	528	7.1
82-83—Golden State	49	1433	306	180	.588	99	53	.535	209	276	485	46	186	5	36	20	413	8.4
83-84—Golden State	75	2091	436	244	.560	168	94	.560	282	390	672	72	274	6	61	22	582	7.8
84-85—Golden State	80	2497	690	366	.530	256	155	.605	405	464	869	96	285	5	78	54	887	11.1
85-86—Golden State	77	2441	586	314	.536	227	112	.493	384	472	856	95	286	7	62	50	740	9.6
86-87—Golden State	80	2374	544	297	.546	197	113	.574	366	551	917	95	295	7	71	56	707	8.8
87-88—Golden State	20	499	123	58	.472	27	11	.407	79	103	182	25	63	1	12	11	127	6.4
88-89—Golden State	80	1897	397	219	.552	58	18	.310	272	380	652	118	248	2	61	54	456	5.7
89-90—Houston	74	1300	213	101	.474	55	20	.364	180	272	452	69	203	3	56	28	222	3.0
Totals	691	19323	4301	2303	.535	1547	841	.544	2889	4003	6892	792	2447	53	572	412	5447	7.9

Three-Point Field Goals: 1981-82, 0-for-1. 1985-86, 0-for-1. 1986-87, 0-for-1. 1987-88, 0-for-1. 1989-90, 0-for-2. Totals, 0-for-6.

NBA PLAYOFF RECORD

									—Rebounds—									
Sea.—Team	G.	Min.	FGA	FGM	Pct.	FTA	FTM	Pct.	Off.	Def.	Tot.	Ast.	PF	Dq.	Stl.	Blk.	Pts.	Avg.
86-87—Golden State	10	329	81	43	.531	24	17	.708	61	76	137	17	39	0	12	6	103	10.3
88-89—Golden State	8	148	16	4	.250	0	0	.000	17	23	40	16	24	0	6	11	8	1.0
89-90—Houston	4	73	8	6	.750	0	0	....	7	6	13	5	11	0	4	0	12	3.0
Totals	22	550	105	53	.505	24	17	.708	85	105	190	38	74	0	22	17	123	5.6

Named to NBA All-Rookie Team, 1981. . . . Led NCAA Division I in rebounding, 1980.

MICHAEL JOHN SMITH

Born May 19, 1965 at Rochester, N.Y. Height 6:10. Weight 225.
High School—Hacienda Heights, Calif., Los Altos.
College—Brigham Young University, Provo, Utah.
Drafted by Boston on first round, 1989 (13th pick).

—COLLEGIATE RECORD—

Year	G.	Min.	FGA	FGM	Pct.	FTA	FTM	Pct.	Reb.	Pts.	Avg.
83-84	29	....	218	99	.454	45	34	.756	153	232	8.0
84-85				On Mormon Mission							
85-86				On Mormon Mission							
86-87	32	....	497	253	.509	114	103	.904	273	643	20.1
87-88	32	....	489	248	.507	159	134	.843	248	679	21.2
88-89	29	....	545	286	.525	173	160	.925	248	765	26.4
Totals	122	....	1749	886	.507	491	431	.878	922	2319	19.0

Three-Point Field Goals: 1986-87, 34-for-70 (.486). 1987-88, 49-for-113 (.434). 1988-89, 33-for-87 (.379). Totals, 116-for-270 (.430).

NBA REGULAR SEASON RECORD

									—Rebounds—									
Sea.—Team	G.	Min.	FGA	FGM	Pct.	FTA	FTM	Pct.	Off.	Def.	Tot.	Ast.	PF	Dq.	Stl.	Blk.	Pts.	Avg.
89-90—Boston	65	620	286	136	.476	64	53	.828	40	60	100	79	51	0	9	1	327	5.0

Three-Point Field Goals: 1989-90, 2-for-28 (.071).

NBA PLAYOFF RECORD

									—Rebounds—									
Sea.—Team	G.	Min.	FGA	FGM	Pct.	FTA	FTM	Pct.	Off.	Def.	Tot.	Ast.	PF	Dq.	Stl.	Blk.	Pts.	Avg.
89-90—Boston	4	16	8	5	.625	7	7	1.000	0	0	0	0	1	0	1	0	17	4.3

Three-Point Field Goals: 1989-90, 0-for-2.

Led NCAA Division I in free-throw percentage, 1989.

OTIS FITZGERALD SMITH

Born January 30, 1964 at Jacksonville, Fla. Height 6:05. Weight 210.
High School—Jacksonville, Fla., Forrest.
College—Jacksonville University, Jacksonville, Fla.
Drafted by Denver on second round, 1986 (41st pick).

Traded by Denver to Golden State for cash, December 22, 1987.
Selected from Golden State by Orlando in NBA expansion draft, June 15, 1989.

—COLLEGIATE RECORD—

Year	G.	Min.	FGA	FGM	Pct.	FTA	FTM	Pct.	Reb.	Pts.	Avg.
82-83	29	979	362	171	.472	102	70	.686	251	414	14.3
83-84	28	1095	375	183	.488	120	87	.725	215	453	16.2
84-85	29	1025	313	151	.482	99	73	.737	197	375	12.9
85-86	31	1164	387	180	.465	149	113	.758	248	473	15.3
Totals	117	4263	1437	685	.477	470	343	.730	911	1715	14.7

Three-Point Field Goals: 1982-83, 2-for-7 (.286).

NBA REGULAR SEASON RECORD

									—Rebounds—									
Sea.—Team	G.	Min.	FGA	FGM	Pct.	FTA	FTM	Pct.	Off.	Def.	Tot.	Ast.	PF	Dq.	Stl.	Blk.	Pts.	Avg.
86-87—Denver	28	168	79	33	.418	21	12	.571	17	17	34	22	30	0	1	1	78	2.8
87-88—Den.-G.S.	72	1549	662	325	.491	229	178	.777	126	121	247	155	160	0	91	42	841	11.7
88-89—Golden State	80	1597	715	311	.435	218	174	.798	128	202	330	140	165	1	88	40	803	10.0
89-90—Orlando	65	1644	708	348	.492	222	169	.761	117	183	300	147	174	0	76	57	875	13.5
Totals	245	4958	2164	1017	.470	690	533	.772	388	523	911	464	529	1	256	140	2597	10.6

Three-Point Field Goals: 1986-87, 0-for-2. 1987-88, 13-for-41 (.317). 1988-89, 7-for-37 (.189). 1989-90, 10-for-40 (.250). Totals, 30-for-120 (.250).

NBA PLAYOFF RECORD

									—Rebounds—									
Sea.—Team	G.	Min.	FGA	FGM	Pct.	FTA	FTM	Pct.	Off.	Def.	Tot.	Ast.	PF	Dq.	Stl.	Blk.	Pts.	Avg.
86-87—Denver	3	19	6	2	.333	9	6	.667	1	4	5	4	1	0	0	2	10	3.3
88-89—Golden State	4	49	24	9	.375	2	1	.500	6	7	13	6	5	0	2	1	19	4.8
Totals	7	68	30	11	.367	11	7	.636	7	11	18	10	6	0	2	3	29	4.1

RIK SMITS

Born August 23, 1966 at Eindhoven, Holland. Height 7:04. Weight 250.
High School—Eindhoven, Holland, Almonta.
College—Marist College, Poughkeepsie, N.Y.
Drafted by Indiana on first round, 1988 (2nd pick).

—COLLEGIATE RECORD—

Year	G.	Min.	FGA	FGM	Pct.	FTA	FTM	Pct.	Reb.	Pts.	Avg.
84-85	29	776	233	132	.567	104	60	.577	162	324	11.2
85-86	30	870	347	216	.622	144	98	.681	242	530	17.7
86-87	21	634	258	157	.609	151	109	.722	171	423	20.1
87-88	27	861	403	251	.623	226	166	.735	236	668	24.7
Totals	107	3141	1241	756	.609	625	433	.693	811	1945	18.2

Three-Point Field Goals: 1987-88, 0-for-2.

NBA REGULAR SEASON RECORD

									—Rebounds—									
Sea.—Team	G.	Min.	FGA	FGM	Pct.	FTA	FTM	Pct.	Off.	Def.	Tot.	Ast.	PF	Dq.	Stl.	Blk.	Pts.	Avg.
88-89—Indiana	82	2041	746	386	.517	255	184	.722	185	315	500	70	310	14	37	151	956	11.7
89-90—Indiana	82	2404	967	515	.533	297	241	.811	135	377	512	142	328	11	45	169	1271	15.5
Totals	164	4445	1713	901	.526	552	425	.770	320	692	1012	212	638	25	82	320	2227	13.6

Three-Point Field Goals: 1988-89, 0-for-1. 1989-90, 0-for-1. Totals, 0-for-2.

NBA PLAYOFF RECORD

									—Rebounds—									
Sea.—Team	G.	Min.	FGA	FGM	Pct.	FTA	FTM	Pct.	Off.	Def.	Tot.	Ast.	PF	Dq.	Stl.	Blk.	Pts.	Avg.
89-90—Indiana	3	96	28	14	.500	11	9	.818	4	12	16	3	12	0	2	4	37	12.3

Named to NBA All-Rookie First Team, 1989.

—DID YOU KNOW—

That Jim Luisi, a member of the 1953-54 Baltimore Bullets, played the part of Lt. Chapman in "The Rockford Files" television series?

MICHAEL FRANK SMREK
(Mike)

Born August 31, 1962 at Welland, Ontario. Height 7:00. Weight 260.
High School—Port Robinson, Ontario, Eastdale.
College—Canisius College, Buffalo, N.Y.
Drafted by Portland on second round, 1985 (25th pick).

Draft rights traded by Portland to Chicago for draft rights to Ben Coleman and Ken Johnson, June 18, 1985.
Waived by Chicago, October 30, 1986; signed by Los Angeles Lakers as a free agent, November 7, 1986.
Traded by Los Angeles Lakers to San Antonio for a 1990 2nd round draft choice, November 2, 1988.
Rights relinquished by San Antonio, July 19, 1989; signed by Golden State, February 27, 1990, for remainder of season.

—COLLEGIATE RECORD—

Year	G.	Min.	FGA	FGM	Pct.	FTA	FTM	Pct.	Reb.	Pts.	Avg.
81-82	22	311	54	24	.444	14	7	.500	68	55	2.5
82-83	28	560	106	49	.462	52	27	.519	131	125	4.5
83-84	30	829	242	153	.632	96	56	.583	175	362	12.1
84-85	28	812	286	172	.601	148	97	.655	192	441	15.8
Totals	108	2512	688	398	.578	310	187	.603	566	983	9.1

NBA REGULAR SEASON RECORD

									—Rebounds—									
Sea.—Team	G.	Min.	FGA	FGM	Pct.	FTA	FTM	Pct.	Off.	Def.	Tot.	Ast.	PF	Dq.	Stl.	Blk.	Pts.	Avg.
85-86—Chicago	38	408	122	46	.377	29	16	.552	46	64	110	19	95	0	6	23	108	2.8
86-87—L.A. Lakers	35	233	60	30	.500	25	16	.640	13	24	37	5	70	1	4	13	76	2.2
87-88—L.A. Lakers	48	421	103	44	.427	66	44	.667	27	58	85	8	105	3	7	42	132	2.8
88-89—San Antonio	43	623	153	72	.471	76	49	.645	42	87	129	12	102	2	13	58	193	4.5
89-90—Golden State	13	107	24	10	.417	6	1	.167	11	23	34	1	18	0	4	11	21	1.6
Totals	177	1792	462	202	.437	202	126	.624	139	256	395	45	390	6	34	147	530	3.0

Three-Point Field Goals: 1985-86, 0-for-2.

NBA PLAYOFF RECORD

									—Rebounds—									
Sea.—Team	G.	Min.	FGA	FGM	Pct.	FTA	FTM	Pct.	Off.	Def.	Tot.	Ast.	PF	Dq.	Stl.	Blk.	Pts.	Avg.
85-86—Chicago	3	5	1	0	.000	0	0	.000	0	0	0	0	2	0	0	1	0	0.0
86-87—L.A. Lakers	10	33	10	2	.200	6	4	.667	3	4	7	0	15	0	0	6	8	0.8
87-88—L.A. Lakers	8	34	5	1	.200	3	1	.333	1	5	6	0	4	0	1	3	3	0.4
Totals	21	72	16	3	.188	9	5	.556	4	9	13	0	21	0	1	10	11	0.5

Member of NBA championship teams, 1987 and 1988.

RORY DARNELL SPARROW

Born June 12, 1958 at Suffolk, Va. Height 6:02. Weight 175.
High School—Paterson, N. J., Eastside.
College—Villanova University, Villanova, Pa.
Drafted by New Jersey on fourth round, 1980 (75th pick).

Waived by New Jersey, October 7, 1980; re-signed by New Jersey to a 10-day contract that expired, December 29, 1980.
Re-signed by New Jersey as a free agent, February 18, 1981.
Traded by New Jersey to Atlanta for a 1982 4th round draft choice, August 12, 1981.
Traded by Atlanta to New York for Scott Hastings and cash, February 12, 1983.
Traded by New York to Chicago for a 1988 2nd round draft choice, November 12, 1987.
Rights relinquished by Chicago, September 22, 1988; signed by Miami as a free agent, November 3, 1988.
Traded by Miami to Sacramento for draft rights to Bimbo Coles, June 27, 1990.
Played in Continental Basketball Association with Scranton Aces, 1980-81.

—COLLEGIATE RECORD—

Year	G.	Min.	FGA	FGM	Pct.	FTA	FTM	Pct.	Reb.	Pts.	Avg.
76-77	33	....	193	99	.513	42	34	.810	69	232	7.0
77-78	32	1036	213	109	.512	79	57	.722	74	275	8.6
78-79	28	877	282	145	.514	61	50	.820	60	340	12.1
79-80	31	937	243	136	.560	77	64	.831	75	336	10.8
Totals	124	....	931	489	.525	259	205	.792	278	1183	9.5

CBA REGULAR SEASON RECORD

			—2-Point—			—3-Point—									
Sea.—Team	G.	Min.	FGM	FGA	Pct.	FGM	FGA	Pct.	FTM	FTA	Pct.	Reb.	Ast.	Pts.	Avg.
80-81—Scranton	20	827	196	388	.505	2	8	.250	83	107	.775	82	180	481	24.1

NBA REGULAR SEASON RECORD

Sea.—Team	G.	Min.	FGA	FGM	Pct.	FTA	FTM	Pct.	—Rebounds— Off.	Def.	Tot.	Ast.	PF	Dq.	Stl.	Blk.	Pts.	Avg.
80-81—New Jersey	15	212	63	22	.349	16	12	.750	7	11	18	32	15	0	13	3	56	3.7
81-82—Atlanta	82	2610	730	366	.501	148	124	.838	53	171	224	424	240	2	87	13	857	10.5
82-83—Atl.-N.Y.	81	2428	810	392	.484	199	147	.739	61	169	230	397	255	4	107	5	936	11.6
83-84—New York	79	2436	738	350	.474	131	108	.824	48	141	189	539	230	4	100	8	818	10.4
84-85—New York	79	2292	662	326	.492	141	122	.865	38	131	169	557	200	2	81	9	781	9.9
85-86—New York	74	2344	723	345	.477	127	101	.795	50	120	170	472	182	1	85	14	796	10.8
86-87—New York	80	1951	590	263	.446	89	71	.798	29	86	115	432	160	0	67	6	608	7.6
87-88—N.Y.-Chi.	58	1044	293	117	.399	33	24	.727	15	57	72	167	79	1	41	3	260	4.5
88-89—Miami	80	2613	982	444	.452	107	94	.879	55	161	216	429	168	0	103	17	1000	12.5
89-90—Miami	82	1756	510	210	.412	77	59	.766	37	101	138	298	140	0	49	4	487	5.9
Totals	710	19686	6101	2835	.465	1068	862	.807	393	1148	1541	3747	1669	14	733	82	6599	9.3

Three-Point Field Goals: 1981-82, 1-for-15 (.067). 1982-83, 5-for-22 (.227). 1983-84, 10-for-39 (.256). 1984-85, 7-for-31 (.226). 1985-86, 5-for-20 (.250). 1986-87, 11-for-42 (.262). 1987-88, 2-for-13 (.154). 1988-89, 18-for-74 (.243). 1989-90, 8-for-40 (.200). Totals, 67-for-296 (.226).

NBA PLAYOFF RECORD

Sea.—Team	G.	Min.	FGA	FGM	Pct.	FTA	FTM	Pct.	—Rebounds— Off.	Def.	Tot.	Ast.	PF	Dq.	Stl.	Blk.	Pts.	Avg.
81-82—Atlanta	2	69	12	5	.417	4	4	1.000	2	6	8	11	7	0	2	0	14	7.0
82-83—New York	6	202	71	30	.423	21	17	.810	3	10	13	42	18	1	7	0	78	13.0
83-84—New York	12	389	121	54	.446	30	24	.800	10	16	26	86	41	2	12	1	134	11.2
87-88—Chicago	7	106	32	10	.313	6	4	.667	0	3	3	18	11	0	4	0	26	3.7
Totals	27	766	236	99	.419	61	49	.803	15	35	50	157	77	3	25	1	252	9.3

Three-Point Field Goals: 1981-82, 0-for-1. 1982-83, 1-for-5 (.200). 1983-84, 2-for-6 (.333). 1987-88, 2-for-4 (.500). Totals, 5-for-16 (.313).

JOHN HOUSTON STOCKTON

Born March 26, 1962 at Spokane, Wash. Height 6:01. Weight 175.
High School—Spokane, Wash., Gonzaga Prep.
College—Gonzaga University, Spokane, Wash.
Drafted by Utah on first round, 1984 (16th pick).

—COLLEGIATE RECORD—

Year	G.	Min.	FGA	FGM	Pct.	FTA	FTM	Pct.	Reb.	Pts.	Avg.
80-81	25	235	45	26	.578	35	26	.743	11	78	3.1
81-82	27	1054	203	117	.576	102	69	.676	67	303	11.2
82-83	27	1036	274	142	.518	115	91	.791	87	375	13.9
83-84	28	1053	397	229	.577	182	126	.692	66	584	20.9
Totals	107	3378	919	514	.559	434	312	.719	231	1340	12.5

NBA REGULAR SEASON RECORD

Sea.—Team	G.	Min.	FGA	FGM	Pct.	FTA	FTM	Pct.	—Rebounds— Off.	Def.	Tot.	Ast.	PF	Dq.	Stl.	Blk.	Pts.	Avg.
84-85—Utah	82	1490	333	157	.471	193	142	.736	26	79	105	415	203	3	109	11	458	5.6
85-86—Utah	82	1935	466	228	.489	205	172	.839	33	146	179	610	227	2	157	10	630	7.7
86-87—Utah	82	1858	463	231	.499	229	179	.782	32	119	151	670	224	1	177	14	648	7.9
87-88—Utah	82	2842	791	454	.574	324	272	.840	54	183	237	1128	247	5	242	16	1204	14.7
88-89—Utah	82	3171	923	497	.538	452	390	.863	83	165	248	1118	241	3	263	14	1400	17.1
89-90—Utah	78	2915	918	472	.514	432	354	.819	57	149	206	1134	233	3	207	18	1345	17.2
Totals	488	14211	3894	2039	.524	1835	1509	.822	285	841	1126	5075	1375	17	1155	83	5685	11.6

Three-Point Field Goals: 1984-85, 2-for-11 (.182). 1985-86, 2-for-15 (.133). 1986-87, 7-for-38 (.184). 1987-88, 24-for-67 (.358). 1988-89, 16-for-66 (.242). 1989-90, 47-for-113 (.416). Totals, 98-for-310 (.316).

NBA PLAYOFF RECORD

Sea.—Team	G.	Min.	FGA	FGM	Pct.	FTA	FTM	Pct.	—Rebounds— Off.	Def.	Tot.	Ast.	PF	Dq.	Stl.	Blk.	Pts.	Avg.
84-85—Utah	10	186	45	21	.467	35	26	.743	7	21	28	43	30	0	11	2	68	6.8
85-86—Utah	4	73	17	9	.529	9	8	.889	3	3	6	14	10	0	5	0	27	6.8
86-87—Utah	5	157	29	18	.621	13	10	.769	2	9	11	40	18	0	15	1	50	10.0
87-88—Utah	11	478	134	68	.507	91	75	.824	14	31	45	163	36	0	37	3	215	19.5
88-89—Utah	3	139	59	30	.508	21	19	.905	2	8	10	41	15	0	11	5	82	27.3
89-90—Utah	5	194	69	29	.420	20	16	.800	4	12	16	75	20	0	6	0	75	15.0
Totals	38	1227	353	175	.496	189	154	.815	32	84	116	376	129	0	85	11	517	13.6

Three-Point Field Goals: 1984-85, 0-for-2. 1985-86, 1-for-1 (1.000). 1986-87, 4-for-5 (.800). 1987-88, 4-for-14 (.286). 1988-89, 3-for-4 (.750). 1989-90, 1-for-13 (.077). Totals, 13-for-39 (.333).

NBA ALL-STAR GAME RECORD

Season—Team	Min.	FGA	FGM	Pct.	FTA	FTM	Pct.	—Rebounds— Off.	Def.	Tot.	Ast.	PF	Dq.	Stl.	Blk.	Pts.
1989—Utah	32	6	5	.833	0	0	.000	0	2	2	17	4	0	5	0	11
1990—Utah	15	4	1	.250	0	0	....	0	0	0	6	1	0	1	1	2
Totals	47	10	6	.600	0	0	....	0	2	2	23	5	0	6	1	13

JOHN STOCKTON

Three-Point Field Goals: 1989, 1-for-1 (1.000). 1990, 0-for-1. Totals, 1-for-2 (.500).

Named to All-NBA Second Team, 1988, 1989, 1990. . . . NBA All-Defensive Second Team, 1989. . . . Holds NBA record for most assists in one season, 1990. . . . Led NBA in assists, 1988, 1989, 1990. . . . Led NBA in steals, 1989. . . . Shares NBA playoff game record for most assists, 24, vs. L.A. Lakers, May 17, 1988.

GREGORY LEWIS STOKES
(Greg)

Born August 5, 1963 at New Haven, Conn. Height 6:10. Weight 220.

High School—Hamilton, Ohio.

College—University of Iowa, Iowa City, Ia.

Drafted by Philadelphia on second round, 1985 (33rd pick).

Signed by Sacramento as an unrestricted free agent, October 2, 1989.
Waived by Sacramento, December 18, 1989.
Played in Italy, 1986-87, 1987-88 and 1988-89.

—COLLEGIATE RECORD—

Year	G.	Min.	FGA	FGM	Pct.	FTA	FTM	Pct.	Reb.	Pts.	Avg.
81-82	29	....	128	61	.477	77	43	.558	123	165	5.7
82-83	31	....	403	219	.543	173	110	.636	223	548	17.7
83-84	28	1013	284	163	.574	134	91	.679	193	417	14.9
84-85	32	1148	479	262	.547	170	114	.671	268	638	19.9
Totals	120	....	1294	705	.545	554	358	.646	807	1768	14.7

ITALIAN LEAGUE RECORD

Year	G.	Min.	FGA	FGM	Pct.	FTA	FTM	Pct.	Reb.	Pts.	Avg.
86-87—Dietor	32	1134	501	279	.557	171	113	.661	272	671	21.0
87-88—Dietor	25	745	262	149	.569	106	61	.764	198	385	15.4
88-89—Vis. Cantu	16	494	168	92	.548	64	48	.750	118	235	14.7

NBA REGULAR SEASON RECORD

									—Rebounds—									
Sea.—Team	G.	Min.	FGA	FGM	Pct.	FTA	FTM	Pct.	Off.	Def.	Tot.	Ast.	PF	Dq.	Stl.	Blk.	Pts.	Avg.
85-86—Philadelphia	31	350	119	56	.471	21	14	.667	27	30	57	17	56	0	14	11	126	4.1
89-90—Sacramento	11	34	9	1	.111	2	2	1.000	2	3	5	0	8	0	0	0	4	0.4
Totals	42	384	128	57	.445	23	16	.696	29	33	62	17	64	0	14	11	130	3.1

Three-Point Field Goals: 1985-86, 0-for-1.

NBA PLAYOFF RECORD

									—Rebounds—									
Sea.—Team	G.	Min.	FGA	FGM	Pct.	FTA	FTM	Pct.	Off.	Def.	Tot.	Ast.	PF	Dq.	Stl.	Blk.	Pts.	Avg.
85-86—Philadelphia	7	90	28	8	.286	13	11	.846	6	7	13	4	12	0	2	6	27	3.9

RODNEY STRICKLAND
(Rod)

Born July 11, 1966 at Bronx, N.Y. Height 6:03. Weight 175.

High Schools—Bronx, N.Y., Harry S Truman (Jr.) and
Mouth of Wilson, Va., Oak Hill (Sr.).

College—DePaul University, Chicago, Ill.

Drafted by New York on first round as an undergraduate, 1988 (19th pick).

Traded by New York to San Antonio for Maurice Cheeks, February 21, 1990.

—COLLEGIATE RECORD—

Year	G.	Min.	FGA	FGM	Pct.	FTA	FTM	Pct.	Reb.	Pts.	Avg.
85-86	31	1063	354	176	.497	126	85	.675	84	437	14.1
86-87	30	980	323	188	.582	175	106	.606	113	490	16.3
87-88	26	837	392	207	.528	137	83	.606	98	521	20.0
Totals	87	2880	1069	571	.534	438	274	.626	295	1448	16.6

Three-Point Field Goals: 1986-87, 8-for-15 (.533). 1987-88, 24-for-54 (.444). Totals, 32-for-69 (.464).

NBA REGULAR SEASON RECORD

									—Rebounds—									
Sea.—Team	G.	Min.	FGA	FGM	Pct.	FTA	FTM	Pct.	Off.	Def.	Tot.	Ast.	PF	Dq.	Stl.	Blk.	Pts.	Avg.
88-89—New York	81	1358	567	265	.467	231	172	.745	51	109	160	319	142	2	98	3	721	8.9
89-90—N.Y.-S.A.	82	2140	756	343	.454	278	174	.626	90	169	259	468	160	3	127	14	868	10.6
Totals	163	3498	1323	608	.460	509	346	.680	141	278	419	787	302	5	225	17	1589	9.7

Three-Point Field Goals: 1988-89, 19-for-59 (.322). 1989-90, 8-for-30 (.267). Totals, 27-for-89 (.303).

NBA PLAYOFF RECORD

Sea.—Team	G.	Min.	FGA	FGM	Pct.	FTA	FTM	Pct.	—Rebounds— Off.	Def.	Tot.	Ast.	PF	Dq.	Stl.	Blk.	Pts.	Avg.
88-89—New York	9	111	49	22	.449	17	9	.529	6	7	13	25	21	0	4	1	54	6.0
89-90—San Antonio	10	384	127	54	.425	27	15	.556	22	31	53	112	30	2	14	0	123	12.3
Totals	19	495	176	76	.432	44	24	.545	28	38	66	137	51	2	18	1	177	9.3

Three-Point Field Goals: 1988-89, 1-for-1 (1.000). 1989-90, 0-for-7. Totals, 1-for-8 (.125).

Named to NBA All-Rookie Second Team, 1989. . . . THE SPORTING NEWS All-America First Team, 1988.

JON THOMAS SUNDVOLD

Born July 2, 1961 at Sioux Falls, S. D. Height 6:02. Weight 170.

High School—Blue Springs, Mo.

College—University of Missouri, Columbia, Mo.

Drafted by Seattle on first round, 1983 (16th pick).

Traded by Seattle to San Antonio for a 1986 2nd round draft choice, October 23, 1985.
Selected from San Antonio by Miami in NBA expansion draft, June 23, 1988.

—COLLEGIATE RECORD—

Year	G.	Min.	FGA	FGM	Pct.	FTA	FTM	Pct.	Reb.	Pts.	Avg.
79-80	31	790	169	76	.450	59	44	.746	52	196	6.3
80-81	32	1134	350	178	.509	99	85	.859	54	441	13.8
81-82	31	1062	307	149	.485	93	81	.871	66	379	12.2
82-83	34	1303	447	225	.503	151	131	.868	82	581	17.1
Totals	128	4289	1273	628	.493	402	341	.848	254	1597	12.5

NBA REGULAR SEASON RECORD

Sea.—Team	G.	Min.	FGA	FGM	Pct.	FTA	FTM	Pct.	—Rebounds— Off.	Def.	Tot.	Ast.	PF	Dq.	Stl.	Blk.	Pts.	Avg.
83-84—Seattle	73	1284	488	217	.445	72	64	.889	23	68	91	239	81	0	29	1	507	6.9
84-85—Seattle	73	1150	400	170	.425	59	48	.814	17	53	70	206	87	0	36	1	400	5.5
85-86—San Antonio	70	1150	476	220	.462	48	39	.813	22	58	80	261	110	0	34	0	500	7.1
86-87—San Antonio	76	1765	751	365	.486	84	70	.833	20	78	98	315	109	1	35	0	850	11.2
87-88—San Antonio	52	1024	379	176	.464	48	43	.896	14	34	48	183	54	0	27	2	421	8.1
88-89—Miami	68	1338	675	307	.455	57	47	.825	18	69	87	137	78	0	27	1	709	10.4
89-90—Miami	63	867	363	148	.408	52	44	.846	15	56	71	102	69	0	25	0	384	6.1
Totals	475	8578	3532	1603	.454	420	355	.845	129	416	545	1443	588	1	213	5	3771	7.9

Three-Point Field Goals: 1983-84, 9-for-37 (.243). 1984-85, 12-for-38 (.316). 1985-86, 21-for-60 (.350). 1986-87, 50-for-149 (.336). 1987-88, 26-for-64 (.406). 1988-89, 48-for-92 (.522). 1989-90, 44-for-100 (.440). Totals, 210-for-540 (.389).

NBA PLAYOFF RECORD

Sea.—Team	G.	Min.	FGA	FGM	Pct.	FTA	FTM	Pct.	—Rebounds— Off.	Def.	Tot.	Ast.	PF	Dq.	Stl.	Blk.	Pts.	Avg.
83-84—Seattle	3	22	8	3	.375	2	2	1.000	1	1	2	5	1	0	0	0	8	2.7
85-86—San Antonio	3	43	18	7	.389	1	1	1.000	0	1	1	5	1	0	0	0	16	5.3
87-88—San Antonio	3	90	30	15	.500	3	2	.667	1	3	4	15	3	0	4	0	35	11.7
Totals	9	155	56	25	.446	6	5	.833	2	5	7	25	5	0	4	0	59	6.6

Three-Point Field Goals: 1983-84, 0-for-3. 1985-86, 1-for-6 (.167). 1987-88, 3-for-9 (.333). Totals, 4-for-18 (.222).

Led NBA in three-point field goal percentage, 1989.

ROY JAMES TARPLEY JR.

Born November 28, 1964 at New York, N.Y. Height 6:11. Weight 240.

High School—Detroit, Mich., Cooley.

College—University of Michigan, Ann Arbor, Mich.

Drafted by Dallas on first round, 1986 (7th pick).

—COLLEGIATE RECORD—

Year	G.	Min.	FGA	FGM	Pct.	FTA	FTM	Pct.	Reb.	Pts.	Avg.
82-83	26	....	86	35	.407	38	22	.579	83	92	3.5
83-84	33	932	315	166	.527	102	81	.794	266	413	12.5
84-85	30	1018	425	223	.525	160	124	.775	313	570	19.0
85-86	33	1045	379	205	.541	143	116	.811	291	526	15.9
Totals	122	....	1205	629	.522	443	343	.774	953	1601	13.1

NBA REGULAR SEASON RECORD

Sea.—Team	G.	Min.	FGA	FGM	Pct.	FTA	FTM	Pct.	—Rebounds— Off.	Def.	Tot.	Ast.	PF	Dq.	Stl.	Blk.	Pts.	Avg.
86-87—Dallas	75	1405	499	233	.467	139	94	.676	180	353	533	52	232	3	56	79	561	7.5
87-88—Dallas	81	2307	888	444	.500	277	205	.740	360	599	959	86	313	8	103	86	1093	13.5
88-89—Dallas	19	591	242	131	.541	96	66	.688	77	141	218	17	70	2	28	30	328	17.3

									—Rebounds—									
Sea.—Team	G.	Min.	FGA	FGM	Pct.	FTA	FTM	Pct.	Off.	Def.	Tot.	Ast.	PF	Dq.	Stl.	Blk.	Pts.	Avg.
89-90—Dallas	45	1648	696	314	.451	172	130	.756	189	400	589	67	160	0	79	70	758	16.8
Totals	220	5951	2325	1122	.483	684	495	.724	806	1493	2299	222	775	13	266	265	2740	12.5

Three-Point Field Goals: 1986-87, 1-for-3 (.333). 1987-88, 0-for-5. 1988-89, 0-for-1. 1989-90, 0-for-6. Totals, 1-for-15 (.067).

NBA PLAYOFF RECORD

									—Rebounds—									
Sea.—Team	G.	Min.	FGA	FGM	Pct.	FTA	FTM	Pct.	Off.	Def.	Tot.	Ast.	PF	Dq.	Stl.	Blk.	Pts.	Avg.
86-87—Dallas	4	114	48	24	.500	7	5	.714	18	24	42	1	18	1	1	7	53	13.3
87-88—Dallas	17	563	241	125	.519	73	54	.740	88	131	219	30	69	3	21	26	304	17.9
89-90—Dallas	3	129	46	22	.478	12	6	.500	9	37	46	1	12	0	7	10	50	16.7
Totals	24	806	335	171	.510	92	65	.707	115	192	307	32	99	4	29	43	407	17.0

Three-Point Field Goals: 1987-88, 0-for-3. 1989-90, 0-for-1. Totals, 0-for-4.

Recipient of NBA Sixth Man Award, 1988. . . . Named to NBA All-Rookie Team, 1987.

CORNELIUS F. TAYLOR
(Jay)

Born October 3, 1967 at Aurora, Ill. Height 6:03. Weight 190.

High School—Aurora, Ill., East.

College—Eastern Illinois University, Charleston, Ill.

Never drafted by an NBA franchise.

Signed by New Jersey as a free agent, August 1, 1989.
Waived by New Jersey, December 20, 1989.
Played in Continental Basketball Association with Wichita Falls Texans, 1989-90.

—COLLEGIATE RECORD—

Year	G.	Min.	FGA	FGM	Pct.	FTA	FTM	Pct.	Reb.	Pts.	Avg.
85-86	29	649	207	94	.454	66	48	.727	80	236	8.1
86-87	27	796	293	146	.498	132	99	.750	138	398	14.7
87-88	27	883	355	203	.572	154	114	.740	111	544	20.1
88-89	32	1042	536	271	.506	201	150	.746	170	748	23.4
Totals	115	3370	1391	714	.513	553	411	.743	499	1926	16.7

Three-Point Field Goals: 1986-87, 7-for-30 (.233). 1987-88, 24-for-54 (.444). 1988-90, 56-for-148 (.378). Totals, 87-for-232 (.375).

CBA REGULAR SEASON RECORD

			—2-Point—			—3-Point—									
Sea.—Team	G.	Min.	FGM	FGA	Pct.	FGM	FGA	Pct.	FTM	FTA	Pct.	Reb.	Ast.	Pts.	Avg.
89-90—Wichita Falls	16	444	103	187	.551	13	44	.295	43	58	.741	48	54	288	18.0

NBA REGULAR SEASON RECORD

									—Rebounds—									
Sea.—Team	G.	Min.	FGA	FGM	Pct.	FTA	FTM	Pct.	Off.	Def.	Tot.	Ast.	PF	Dq.	Stl.	Blk.	Pts.	Avg.
89-90—New Jersey	17	114	52	21	.404	9	6	.667	5	6	11	5	9	0	5	3	51	3.0

Three-Point Field Goals: 1989-90, 3-for-13 (.231).

LEONARD CHESTER TAYLOR JR.

Born May 2, 1966 at Los Angeles, Calif. Height 6:08. Weight 220.

High School—Playa del Ray, Calif., St. Bernard's.

College—University of California, Berkeley, Calif.

Never drafted by an NBA franchise.

Signed by Golden State as a free agent, August 1, 1989.
Waived by Golden State, December 12, 1989.
Played in Continental Basketball Association with San Jose Jammers, 1989-90.

—COLLEGIATE RECORD—

Year	G.	Min.	FGA	FGM	Pct.	FTA	FTM	Pct.	Reb.	Pts.	Avg.
84-85	28	....	235	125	.532	134	97	.724	171	347	12.4
85-86	29	....	257	131	.510	117	84	.718	220	346	11.9
86-87	14	....	147	87	.592	114	92	.807	123	266	19.0
87-88	Did Not Play—broken foot.										
88-89	33	1134	429	233	.543	206	166	.806	270	648	19.6
Totals	104	....	1068	576	.593	571	439	.769	784	1607	15.5

Three-Point Field Goals: 1988-89, 16-for-41 (.390).

CBA REGULAR SEASON RECORD

			—2-Point—			—3-Point—									
Sea.—Team	G.	Min.	FGM	FGA	Pct.	FGM	FGA	Pct.	FTM	FTA	Pct.	Reb.	Ast.	Pts.	Avg.
89-90—San Jose	35	833	128	257	.498	3	10	.300	82	99	.828	222	35	347	9.9

NBA REGULAR SEASON RECORD

Sea.—Team	G.	Min.	FGA	FGM	Pct.	FTA	FTM	Pct.	Rebounds Off.	Def.	Tot.	Ast.	PF	Dq.	Stl.	Blk.	Pts.	Avg.
89-90—Golden State	10	37	6	0	.000	16	11	.688	4	8	12	1	4	0	0	0	11	1.1

Three-Point Field Goals: 1989-90, 0-for-1.

TERRY MICHAEL TEAGLE

Born April 10, 1960 at Broaddus, Tex. Height 6:05. Weight 195.
High School—Broaddus, Tex.
College—Baylor University, Waco, Tex.
Drafted by Houston on first round, 1982 (16th pick).

Waived by Houston, October 23, 1984; signed by Detroit as a free agent, November 7, 1984.
Waived by Detroit, November 20, 1984; signed by Golden State as a free agent, March 11, 1985.
Played in Continental Basketball Association with Detroit Spirits, 1984-85.

—COLLEGIATE RECORD—

Year	G.	Min.	FGA	FGM	Pct.	FTA	FTM	Pct.	Reb.	Pts.	Avg.
78-79	28	....	310	164	.529	113	80	.708	183	408	14.6
79-80	27	....	440	239	.543	171	142	.830	222	620	23.0
80-81	27	....	399	214	.536	151	111	.735	190	539	20.0
81-82	28	....	479	259	.541	144	104	.722	210	622	22.2
Totals	110	....	1628	876	.538	579	437	.755	805	2189	19.9

CBA REGULAR SEASON RECORD

Sea.—Team	G.	Min.	2-Point FGM	FGA	Pct.	3-Point FGM	FGA	Pct.	FTM	FTA	Pct.	Reb.	Ast.	Pts.	Avg.
84-85—Detroit	40	1146	294	532	.552	2	14	.143	187	222	.842	171	67	781	19.5

NBA REGULAR SEASON RECORD

Sea.—Team	G.	Min.	FGA	FGM	Pct.	FTA	FTM	Pct.	Rebounds Off.	Def.	Tot.	Ast.	PF	Dq.	Stl.	Blk.	Pts.	Avg.
82-83—Houston	73	1708	776	332	.428	125	87	.696	74	120	194	150	171	0	53	18	761	10.4
83-84—Houston	68	616	315	148	.470	44	37	.841	28	50	78	63	81	1	13	4	340	5.0
84-85—Det.-G.S.	21	349	137	74	.540	35	25	.714	22	21	43	14	36	0	13	5	175	8.3
85-86—Golden State	82	2158	958	475	.496	265	211	.796	96	139	235	115	241	2	71	34	1165	14.2
86-87—Golden State	82	1650	808	370	.458	234	182	.778	68	107	175	105	190	0	68	13	922	11.2
87-88—Golden State	47	958	546	248	.454	121	97	.802	41	40	81	61	95	0	32	4	594	12.6
88-89—Golden State	66	1569	859	409	.476	225	182	.809	110	153	263	96	173	2	79	17	1002	15.2
89-90—Golden State	82	2376	1122	538	.480	294	244	.830	114	253	367	155	231	3	91	15	1323	16.1
Totals	521	11384	5521	2594	.470	1343	1065	.793	553	883	1436	759	1218	8	420	110	6282	12.1

Three-Point Field Goals: 1982-83, 10-for-29 (.345). 1983-84, 7-for-27 (.259). 1984-85, 2-for-4 (.500). 1985-86, 4-for-25 (.160). 1986-87, 0-for-10. 1987-88, 1-for-9 (.111). 1988-89, 2-for-12 (.167). 1989-90, 3-for-14 (.214). Totals, 29-for-130 (.223).

NBA PLAYOFF RECORD

Sea.—Team	G.	Min.	FGA	FGM	Pct.	FTA	FTM	Pct.	Rebounds Off.	Def.	Tot.	Ast.	PF	Dq.	Stl.	Blk.	Pts.	Avg.
86-87—Golden State	10	233	124	57	.460	38	30	.789	13	7	20	13	27	0	8	1	144	14.4
88-89—Golden State	8	240	141	70	.496	22	18	.818	15	22	37	10	27	0	8	3	158	19.8
Totals	18	473	265	127	.479	60	48	.800	28	29	57	23	54	0	16	4	302	16.8

Three-Point Field Goals: 1986-87, 0-for-2. 1988-89, 0-for-2. Totals, 0-for-4.

REGGIE WAYNE THEUS

Born October 13, 1957 at Inglewood, Calif. Height 6:07. Weight 213.
High School—Inglewood, Calif.
College—University of Nevada at Las Vegas, Las Vegas, Nev.
Drafted by Chicago on first round as an undergraduate, 1978 (9th pick).

Traded by Chicago to Kansas City for Steve Johnson, a 1984 2nd round draft choice and two 1985 2nd round draft choices, February 15, 1984.

Traded by Sacramento with a 1988 3rd round draft choice and future considerations to Atlanta for Randy Wittman and a 1988 1st round draft choice, June 27, 1988.

Selected from Atlanta by Orlando in NBA expansion draft, June 15, 1989.

Traded by Orlando to New Jersey for 1993 and 1995 2nd round draft choices, June 25, 1990.

—COLLEGIATE RECORD—

Year	G.	Min.	FGA	FGM	Pct.	FTA	FTM	Pct.	Reb.	Pts.	Avg.
75-76	31	....	163	68	.417	60	48	.800	53	184	5.9
76-77	32	....	358	178	.497	132	108	.818	145	464	14.5
77-78	28	....	389	181	.465	207	167	.807	191	529	18.9
Totals	91	....	910	427	.469	399	323	.810	389	1177	12.9

NBA REGULAR SEASON RECORD

									—Rebounds—									
Sea.—Team	G.	Min.	FGA	FGM	Pct.	FTA	FTM	Pct.	Off.	Def.	Tot.	Ast.	PF	Dq.	Stl.	Blk.	Pts.	Avg.
78-79—Chicago	82	2753	1119	537	.480	347	264	.761	92	136	228	429	270	2	93	18	1338	16.3
79-80—Chicago	82	3029	1172	566	.483	597	500	.838	143	186	329	515	262	4	114	20	1660	20.2
80-81—Chicago	82	2820	1097	543	.495	550	445	.809	124	163	287	426	258	1	122	20	1549	18.9
81-82—Chicago	82	2838	1194	560	.469	449	363	.808	115	197	312	476	243	1	87	16	1508	18.4
82-83—Chicago	82	2856	1567	749	.478	542	434	.801	91	209	300	484	281	6	143	17	1953	23.8
83-84—Chi.-K.C.	61	1498	625	262	.419	281	214	.762	50	79	129	352	171	3	50	12	745	12.2
84-85—Kansas City	82	2543	1029	501	.487	387	334	.863	106	164	270	656	250	0	95	18	1341	16.4
85-86—Sacramento	82	2919	1137	546	.480	490	405	.827	73	231	304	788	231	3	112	20	1503	18.3
86-87—Sacramento	79	2872	1223	577	.472	495	429	.867	86	180	266	692	208	3	78	16	1600	20.3
87-88—Sacramento	73	2653	1318	619	.470	385	320	.831	72	160	232	463	173	0	59	16	1574	21.6
88-89—Atlanta	82	2517	1067	497	.466	335	285	.851	86	156	242	387	236	0	108	16	1296	15.8
89-90—Orlando	76	2350	1178	517	.439	443	378	.853	75	146	221	407	194	1	60	12	1438	18.9
Totals	945	31648	13726	6474	.472	5301	4371	.825	1113	2007	3120	6075	2777	24	1121	201	17505	18.5

Three-Point Field Goals: 1979-80, 28-for-105 (.267). 1980-81, 18-for-90 (.200). 1981-82, 25-for-100 (.250). 1982-83, 21-for-91 (.231). 1983-84, 7-for-42 (.167). 1984-85, 5-for-38 (.132). 1985-86, 6-for-35 (.171). 1986-87, 17-for-78 (.218). 1987-88, 16-for-59 (.271). 1988-89, 17-for-58 (.293). 1989-90, 26-for-105 (.248). Totals, 186-for-801 (.232).

NBA PLAYOFF RECORD

									—Rebounds—									
Sea.—Team	G.	Min.	FGA	FGM	Pct.	FTA	FTM	Pct.	Off.	Def.	Tot.	Ast.	PF	Dq.	Stl.	Blk.	Pts.	Avg.
80-81—Chicago	6	232	90	40	.444	43	37	.860	7	14	21	38	22	0	9	0	119	19.8
83-84—Kansas City	3	81	43	17	.395	10	9	.900	4	7	11	16	9	0	5	0	43	14.3
85-86—Sacramento	3	102	46	18	.391	12	9	.750	3	5	8	19	9	0	3	2	45	15.0
88-89—Atlanta	5	127	38	14	.368	12	9	.750	3	4	7	24	18	1	1	0	37	7.4
Totals	17	542	217	89	.410	77	64	.831	17	30	47	97	58	1	18	2	244	14.4

Three-Point Field Goals: 1980-81, 2-for-9 (.222). 1983-84, 0-for-3. 1985-86, 0-for-1. 1988-89, 0-for-2. Totals, 2-for-15 (.133).

NBA ALL-STAR GAME RECORD

								—Rebounds—							
Season—Team	Min.	FGA	FGM	Pct.	FTA	FTM	Pct.	Off.	Def.	Tot.	Ast.	PF	Dq.	Stl.	Blk.	Pts.
1981—Chicago	19	7	4	.571	0	0	.000	0	1	1	3	0	0	2	0	8
1983—Chicago	8	5	0	.000	0	0	.000	1	0	1	1	1	0	0	0	0
Totals	27	12	4	.333	0	0	.000	1	1	2	4	1	0	2	0	8

Named to NBA All-Rookie Team, 1979.

ISIAH LORD THOMAS III

Born April 30, 1961 at Chicago, Ill. Height 6:01. Weight 185.

High School—Westchester, Ill., St. Joseph's.

College—Indiana University, Bloomington, Ind.

Drafted by Detroit on first round as an undergraduate, 1981 (2nd pick).

—COLLEGIATE RECORD—

Year	G.	Min.	FGA	FGM	Pct.	FTA	FTM	Pct.	Reb.	Pts.	Avg.
79-80	29	....	302	154	.510	149	115	.772	116	423	14.6
80-81	34	....	383	212	.554	163	121	.742	105	545	16.0
Totals	63	....	685	366	.534	312	236	.756	221	968	15.4

NBA REGULAR SEASON RECORD

									—Rebounds—									
Sea.—Team	G.	Min.	FGA	FGM	Pct.	FTA	FTM	Pct.	Off.	Def.	Tot.	Ast.	PF	Dq.	Stl.	Blk.	Pts.	Avg.
81-82—Detroit	72	2433	1068	453	.424	429	302	.704	57	152	209	565	253	2	150	17	1225	17.0
82-83—Detroit	81	3093	1537	725	.472	518	368	.710	105	223	328	634	318	8	199	29	1854	22.9
83-84—Detroit	82	3007	1448	669	.462	529	388	.733	103	224	327	914	324	8	204	33	1748	21.3
84-85—Detroit	81	3089	1410	646	.458	493	399	.809	114	247	361	1123	288	8	187	25	1720	21.2
85-86—Detroit	77	2790	1248	609	.488	462	365	.790	83	194	277	830	245	9	171	20	1609	20.9
86-87—Detroit	81	3013	1353	626	.463	521	400	.768	82	237	319	813	251	5	153	20	1671	20.6
87-88—Detroit	81	2927	1341	621	.463	394	305	.774	64	214	278	678	217	0	141	17	1577	19.5
88-89—Detroit	80	2924	1227	569	.464	351	287	.818	49	224	273	663	209	0	133	20	1458	18.2
89-90—Detroit	81	2993	1322	579	.438	377	292	.775	74	234	308	765	206	0	139	19	1492	18.4
Totals	716	26269	11954	5497	.460	4074	3106	.762	731	1949	2680	6985	2311	40	1477	200	14354	20.0

Three-Point Field Goals: 1981-82, 17-for-59 (.288). 1982-83, 36-for-125 (.288). 1983-84, 22-for-65 (.338). 1984-85, 29-for-113 (.257). 1985-86, 26-for-84 (.310). 1986-87, 19-for-98 (.194). 1987-88, 30-for-97 (.309). 1988-89, 33-for-121 (.273). 1989-90, 42-for-136 (.309). Totals, 254-for-898 (.283).

NBA PLAYOFF RECORD

									—Rebounds—									
Sea.—Team	G.	Min.	FGA	FGM	Pct.	FTA	FTM	Pct.	Off.	Def.	Tot.	Ast.	PF	Dq.	Stl.	Blk.	Pts.	Avg.
83-84—Detroit	5	198	83	39	.470	35	27	.771	7	12	19	55	22	1	13	6	107	21.4
84-85—Detroit	9	355	166	83	.500	62	47	.758	11	36	47	101	39	2	19	4	219	24.3
85-86—Detroit	4	163	91	41	.451	36	24	.667	8	14	22	48	17	0	9	3	106	26.5
86-87—Detroit	15	562	297	134	.451	110	83	.755	21	46	67	130	51	1	39	4	361	24.1

								—Rebounds—										
Sea.—Team	G.	Min.	FGA	FGM	Pct.	FTA	FTM	Pct.	Off.	Def.	Tot.	Ast.	PF	Dq.	Stl.	Blk.	Pts.	Avg.
87-88—Detroit	23	911	419	183	.437	151	125	.828	26	81	107	201	71	2	66	8	504	21.9
88-89—Detroit	17	633	279	115	.412	96	71	.740	24	49	73	141	39	0	27	4	309	18.2
89-90—Detroit	20	758	320	148	.463	102	81	.794	21	88	109	163	65	1	43	7	409	20.5
Totals	93	3580	1655	743	.449	592	458	.774	118	326	444	839	304	7	216	36	2015	21.7

Three-Point Field Goals: 1983-84, 2-for-6 (.333). 1984-85, 6-for-15 (.400). 1985-86, 0-for-5. 1986-87, 10-for-33 (.303). 1987-88, 13-for-44 (.295). 1988-89, 8-for-30 (.267). 1989-90, 32-for-68 (.471). Totals, 71-for-201 (.353).

NBA ALL-STAR GAME RECORD

								—Rebounds—								
Season—Team	Min.	FGA	FGM	Pct.	FTA	FTM	Pct.	Off.	Def.	Tot.	Ast.	PF	Dq.	Stl.	Blk.	Pts.
1982—Detroit	17	7	5	.714	4	2	.500	1	0	1	4	1	0	3	0	12
1983—Detroit	29	14	9	.643	1	1	1.000	3	1	4	7	0	0	4	0	19
1984—Detroit	39	17	9	.529	3	3	1.000	3	2	5	15	4	0	4	0	21
1985—Detroit	25	14	9	.643	1	1	1.000	1	1	2	5	2	0	2	0	22
1986—Detroit	36	19	11	.579	9	8	.889	0	1	1	10	2	0	5	0	30
1987—Detroit	24	6	4	.667	9	8	.889	2	1	3	9	3	0	0	0	16
1988—Detroit	28	10	4	.400	0	0	.000	1	1	2	15	1	0	1	0	8
1989—Detroit	33	13	7	.538	6	4	.667	1	1	2	14	2	0	4	0	19
1990—Detroit	27	12	7	.583	0	0	....	1	3	4	9	0	0	3	0	15
Totals	258	112	65	.580	33	27	.818	12	12	24	88	15	0	26	0	162

Three-Point Field Goals: 1984, 0-for-2. 1985, 3-for-4 (.750). 1986, 0-for-1. 1989, 1-for-3 (.333). 1990, 1-for-1 (1.000). Totals, 5-for-11 (.455).

Named to All-NBA First Team, 1984, 1985, 1986. . . . All-NBA Second Team, 1983 and 1987. . . . NBA All-Rookie Team, 1982. . . . NBA All-Star Game MVP, 1984 and 1986. . . . Member of NBA championship teams, 1989 and 1990. . . . NBA Playoff MVP, 1990. . . . Holds NBA championship series record for most points in one quarter, 25, vs. L.A. Lakers, June 19, 1988. . . . Led NBA in assists, 1985. . . . Named to THE SPORTING NEWS All-America First Team, 1981. . . . NCAA Division I Tournament Most Outstanding Player, 1981. . . . Member of NCAA Division I championship team, 1981. . . . Member of U.S. Olympic team, 1980.

LaSALLE THOMPSON III

Born June 23, 1961 at Cincinnati, O. Height 6:10. Weight 253.
High School—Cincinnati, O., Withrow.
College—University of Texas, Austin, Tex.
Drafted by Kansas City on first round as an undergraduate, 1982 (5th pick).

Traded by Sacramento with Randy Wittman to Indiana for Wayman Tisdale and a 1990 or 1991 2nd round draft choice, February 20, 1989.

—COLLEGIATE RECORD—

Year	G.	Min.	FGA	FGM	Pct.	FTA	FTM	Pct.	Reb.	Pts.	Avg.
79-80	30	971	274	153	.558	103	77	.748	292	383	12.8
80-81	30	1106	411	235	.572	147	107	.728	370	577	19.2
81-82	27	1042	371	196	.528	164	111	.677	365	503	18.6
Totals	87	3119	1056	584	.553	414	295	.713	1027	1463	16.8

NBA REGULAR SEASON RECORD

									—Rebounds—									
Sea.—Team	G.	Min.	FGA	FGM	Pct.	FTA	FTM	Pct.	Off.	Def.	Tot.	Ast.	PF	Dq.	Stl.	Blk.	Pts.	Avg.
82-83—Kansas City	71	987	287	147	.512	137	89	.650	133	242	375	33	186	1	40	61	383	5.4
83-84—Kansas City	80	1915	637	333	.523	223	160	.717	260	449	709	86	327	8	71	145	826	10.3
84-85—Kansas City	82	2458	695	369	.531	315	227	.721	274	580	854	130	328	4	98	128	965	11.8
85-86—Sacramento	80	2377	794	411	.518	276	202	.732	252	518	770	168	295	8	71	109	1024	12.8
86-87—Sacramento	82	2166	752	362	.481	255	188	.737	237	450	687	122	290	6	69	126	912	11.1
87-88—Sacramento	69	1257	456	215	.471	164	118	.720	138	289	427	68	217	1	54	73	550	8.0
88-89—Sac.-Ind.	76	2329	850	416	.489	281	227	.808	224	494	718	81	285	12	79	94	1059	13.9
89-90—Indiana	82	2126	471	223	.473	134	107	.799	175	455	630	106	313	11	65	71	554	6.8
Totals	622	15615	4942	2476	.501	1785	1318	.738	1693	3477	5170	794	2241	51	547	807	6273	10.1

Three-Point Field Goals: 1982-83, 0-for-1. 1985-86, 0-for-1. 1986-87, 0-for-5. 1987-88, 2-for-5 (.400). 1988-89, 0-for-1. 1989-90, 1-for-5 (.200). Totals, 3-for-18 (.167).

NBA PLAYOFF RECORD

									—Rebounds—									
Sea.—Team	G.	Min.	FGA	FGM	Pct.	FTA	FTM	Pct.	Off.	Def.	Tot.	Ast.	PF	Dq.	Stl.	Blk.	Pts.	Avg.
83-84—Kansas City	3	93	40	18	.450	11	9	.818	11	19	30	4	14	0	3	4	45	15.0
85-86—Sacramento	3	99	32	11	.344	12	7	.583	14	21	35	2	8	0	2	6	29	9.7
89-90—Indiana	3	54	15	7	.467	4	4	1.000	6	9	15	2	13	0	0	1	18	6.0
Totals	9	246	87	36	.414	27	20	.741	31	49	80	8	35	0	5	11	92	10.2

Led NCAA Division I in rebounding, 1982.

MYCHAL GEORGE THOMPSON

Born January 30, 1955 at Nassau, Bahamas. Height 6:10. Weight 235.
High School—Miami, Fla., Jackson.
College—University of Minnesota, Minneapolis, Minn.
Drafted by Portland on first round, 1978 (1st pick).

Traded by Portland with draft rights to Larry Krystkowiak to San Antonio for Steve Johnson, June 19, 1986.
Traded by San Antonio to Los Angeles Lakers for Frank Brickowski, Petur Gudmundsson, a 1987 1st round draft choice, a 1990 2nd round draft choice and cash, February 13, 1987.
Missed entire 1979-80 season due to injury.

—COLLEGIATE RECORD—

Year	G.	Min.	FGA	FGM	Pct.	FTA	FTM	Pct.	Reb.	Pts.	Avg.
74-75	23	....	215	114	.530	78	59	.756	176	287	12.5
75-76	25	....	461	264	.573	171	119	.696	312	647	25.9
76-77	27	....	414	251	.606	132	93	.705	240	595	22.0
77-78	21	....	362	194	.536	119	75	.630	228	463	22.0
Totals	96	....	1452	823	.567	500	346	.692	956	1992	20.8

NBA REGULAR SEASON RECORD

									—Rebounds—									
Sea.—Team	G.	Min.	FGA	FGM	Pct.	FTA	FTM	Pct.	Off.	Def.	Tot.	Ast.	PF	Dq.	Stl.	Blk.	Pts.	Avg.
78-79—Portland	73	2144	938	460	.490	269	154	.572	198	406	604	176	270	10	67	134	1074	14.7
80-81—Portland	79	2790	1151	569	.494	323	207	.641	223	463	686	284	260	5	62	170	1345	17.0
81-82—Portland	79	3129	1303	681	.523	446	280	.628	258	663	921	329	233	2	69	107	1642	20.8
82-83—Portland	80	3017	1033	505	.489	401	249	.621	183	570	753	380	213	1	68	110	1259	15.7
83-84—Portland	79	2648	929	487	.524	399	266	.667	235	453	688	308	237	2	84	108	1240	15.7
84-85—Portland	79	2616	1111	572	.515	449	307	.684	211	407	618	205	216	0	78	104	1451	18.4
85-86—Portland	82	2569	1011	503	.498	309	198	.641	181	427	608	176	267	5	76	35	1204	14.7
86-87—S.A.-L.A.L.	82	1890	797	359	.450	297	219	.737	138	274	412	115	202	1	45	71	938	11.4
87-88—L.A. Lakers	80	2007	722	370	.512	292	185	.634	198	291	489	66	251	1	38	79	925	11.6
88-89—L.A. Lakers	80	1994	521	291	.559	230	156	.678	157	310	467	48	224	0	58	59	738	9.2
89-90—L.A. Lakers	70	1883	562	281	.500	204	144	.706	173	304	477	43	207	0	33	73	706	10.1
Totals	863	26687	10078	5078	.504	3619	2365	.653	2155	4568	6723	2120	2580	27	678	1050	12522	14.5

Three-Point Field Goals: 1980-81, 0-for-1. 1982-83, 0-for-1. 1983-84, 0-for-2. 1986-87, 1-for-2 (.500). 1987-88, 0-for-3. 1988-89, 0-for-1. Totals, 1-for-10 (.100).

NBA PLAYOFF RECORD

									—Rebounds—									
Sea.—Team	G.	Min.	FGA	FGM	Pct.	FTA	FTM	Pct.	Off.	Def.	Tot.	Ast.	PF	Dq.	Stl.	Blk.	Pts.	Avg.
78-79—Portland	3	121	54	27	.500	10	5	.500	9	22	31	6	11	0	2	5	59	19.7
80-81—Portland	3	132	51	31	.608	18	13	.722	5	18	23	4	10	0	3	9	75	25.0
82-83—Portland	7	284	85	40	.471	38	25	.658	16	40	56	39	24	0	6	8	105	15.0
83-84—Portland	4	121	44	22	.500	22	17	.773	9	20	29	15	11	0	5	3	61	15.3
84-85—Portland	9	250	102	50	.490	49	33	.673	25	47	72	14	32	2	7	12	133	14.8
85-86—Portland	4	140	54	31	.574	26	14	.538	11	22	33	14	13	0	1	3	76	19.0
86-87—L.A. Lakers	18	401	137	62	.453	50	34	.680	29	59	88	9	50	0	7	17	158	8.8
87-88—L.A. Lakers	24	615	191	98	.513	62	36	.581	63	107	170	12	70	1	17	21	232	9.7
88-89—L.A. Lakers	15	377	128	65	.508	60	41	.683	39	38	77	11	52	1	6	12	171	11.4
89-90—L.A. Lakers	9	225	44	21	.477	26	16	.615	15	24	39	2	26	0	2	13	58	6.4
Totals	96	2666	890	447	.502	361	234	.648	221	397	618	126	299	4	56	103	1128	11.8

Named to NBA All-Rookie Team, 1979. . . . Member of NBA championship teams, 1987 and 1988. . . . THE SPORTING NEWS All-America First Team, 1978. . . . THE SPORTING NEWS All-America Second Team, 1977.

WILLIAM STANSBURY THOMPSON
(Billy)

Born December 1, 1963 at Camden, N.J. Height 6:07. Weight 220.
High School—Camden, N.J.
College—University of Louisville, Louisville, Ky.
Drafted by Atlanta on first round, 1986 (19th pick).

Draft rights traded by Atlanta with draft rights to Ron Kellogg to Los Angeles Lakers for Mike McGee and draft rights to Ken Barlow, June 17, 1986.
Selected from Los Angeles Lakers by Miami in NBA expansion draft, June 23, 1988.

—COLLEGIATE RECORD—

Year	G.	Min.	FGA	FGM	Pct.	FTA	FTM	Pct.	Reb.	Pts.	Avg.
82-83	36	710	213	104	.488	81	53	.654	140	261	7.3
83-84	31	877	209	106	.507	98	72	.735	173	284	9.2
84-85	37	1262	427	220	.515	158	118	.747	311	558	15.1
85-86	39	1216	384	221	.576	196	140	.714	304	582	14.9
Totals	143	4065	1233	651	.528	533	383	.719	928	1685	11.8

NBA REGULAR SEASON RECORD

Sea.—Team	G.	Min.	FGA	FGM	Pct.	FTA	FTM	Pct.	—Rebounds— Off.	Def.	Tot.	Ast.	PF	Dq.	Stl.	Blk.	Pts.	Avg.
86-87—L.A. Lakers	59	762	261	142	.544	74	48	.649	69	102	171	60	148	1	15	30	332	5.6
87-88—L.A. Lakers	9	38	13	3	.231	10	8	.800	2	7	9	1	11	0	1	0	14	1.6
88-89—Miami	79	2273	716	349	.487	224	156	.696	241	331	572	176	260	8	56	105	854	10.8
89-90—Miami	79	2142	727	375	.516	185	115	.622	238	313	551	166	237	1	54	89	867	11.0
Totals	226	5215	1717	869	.506	493	327	.663	550	753	1303	403	656	10	126	224	2067	9.1

Three-Point Field Goals: 1986-87, 0-for-1. 1988-89, 0-for-4. 1989-90, 2-for-4 (.500). Totals, 2-for-9 (.222).

NBA PLAYOFF RECORD

Sea.—Team	G.	Min.	FGA	FGM	Pct.	FTA	FTM	Pct.	—Rebounds— Off.	Def.	Tot.	Ast.	PF	Dq.	Stl.	Blk.	Pts.	Avg.
86-87—L.A. Lakers	3	27	11	6	.545	2	2	1.000	3	3	6	2	2	0	4	0	14	4.7

Member of NBA championship teams, 1987 and 1988. . . . Member of NCAA Division I championship team, 1986.

ROBERT GEORGE THORNTON
(Bob)

Born July 10, 1962 at Los Angeles, Calif. Height 6:10. Weight 225.

High School—Mission Viejo, Calif.

Colleges—Saddleback Community College, Mission Viejo, Calif., and University of California at Irvine, Irvine, Calif.

Drafted by New York on fourth round, 1984 (87th pick).

Waived by New York, December 16, 1987; signed by Philadelphia as a free agent, December 19, 1987.
Played in Spanish National League with Madrid Caja, 1984-85.

—COLLEGIATE RECORD—

Saddleback

Year	G.	Min.	FGA	FGM	Pct.	FTA	FTM	Pct.	Reb.	Pts.	Avg.
80-81	28	....	136	70	.515	50	31	.620	149	171	6.1

California-Irvine

Year	G.	Min.	FGA	FGM	Pct.	FTA	FTM	Pct.	Reb.	Pts.	Avg.
81-82	29	452	88	44	.500	45	33	.733	93	121	4.2
82-83	27	639	216	125	.579	117	75	.641	161	325	12.0
83-84	29	817	236	151	.640	118	65	.551	236	367	12.7
Totals	85	1908	540	320	.593	280	173	.618	490	813	9.6

NBA REGULAR SEASON RECORD

Sea.—Team	G.	Min.	FGA	FGM	Pct.	FTA	FTM	Pct.	—Rebounds— Off.	Def.	Tot.	Ast.	PF	Dq.	Stl.	Blk.	Pts.	Avg.
85-86—New York	71	1323	274	125	.456	162	86	.531	113	177	290	43	209	5	30	7	336	4.7
86-87—New York	33	282	67	29	.433	20	13	.650	18	38	56	8	48	0	4	3	71	2.2
87-88—N.Y.-Phil.	48	593	130	65	.500	55	34	.618	46	66	112	15	103	1	11	3	164	3.4
88-89—Philadelphia	54	449	111	47	.423	60	32	.533	36	56	92	15	87	0	8	7	127	2.4
89-90—Philadelphia	56	592	112	48	.429	51	26	.510	45	88	133	17	105	1	20	12	123	2.2
Totals	262	3239	694	314	.452	348	191	.549	258	425	683	98	552	7	73	32	821	3.1

Three-Point Field Goals: 1986-87, 0-for-1. 1987-88, 0-for-2. 1988-89, 1-for-3 (.333). 1989-90, 1-for-3 (.333). Totals, 2-for-9 (.222).

NBA PLAYOFF RECORD

Sea.—Team	G.	Min.	FGA	FGM	Pct.	FTA	FTM	Pct.	—Rebounds— Off.	Def.	Tot.	Ast.	PF	Dq.	Stl.	Blk.	Pts.	Avg.
89-90—Philadelphia	9	89	18	7	.389	10	5	.500	11	4	15	4	22	0	2	1	19	2.1

OTIS THORPE

Born August 5, 1962 at Boynton Beach, Fla. Height 6:11. Weight 236.

High School—Lake Worth, Fla.

College—Providence College, Providence, R.I.

Drafted by Kansas City on first round, 1984 (9th pick).

Traded by Sacramento to Houston for Rodney McCray and Jim Petersen, October 11, 1988.

—COLLEGIATE RECORD—

Year	G.	Min.	FGA	FGM	Pct.	FTA	FTM	Pct.	Reb.	Pts.	Avg.
80-81	26	668	194	100	.515	76	50	.658	137	250	9.6
81-82	27	942	283	153	.541	115	74	.643	216	380	14.1
82-83	31	1041	321	204	.636	138	91	.659	249	499	16.1
83-84	29	1051	288	167	.580	248	162	.653	300	496	17.1
Totals	113	3702	1086	624	.575	577	377	.653	902	1625	14.4

NBA REGULAR SEASON RECORD

									—Rebounds—									
Sea.—Team	G.	Min.	FGA	FGM	Pct.	FTA	FTM	Pct.	Off.	Def.	Tot.	Ast.	PF	Dq.	Stl.	Blk.	Pts.	Avg.
84-85—Kansas City	82	1918	685	411	.600	371	230	620	187	369	556	111	256	2	34	37	1052	12.8
85-86—Sacramento	75	1675	492	289	.587	248	164	.661	137	283	420	84	233	3	35	34	742	9.9
86-87—Sacramento	82	2956	1050	567	.540	543	413	.761	259	560	819	201	292	11	46	60	1547	18.9
87-88—Sacramento	82	3072	1226	622	.507	609	460	.755	279	558	837	266	264	3	62	56	1704	20.8
88-89—Houston	82	3135	961	521	.542	450	328	.729	272	515	787	202	259	6	82	37	1370	16.7
89-90—Houston	82	2947	998	547	.548	446	307	.688	258	476	734	261	270	5	66	24	1401	17.1
Totals	485	15703	5412	2957	.546	2667	1902	.713	1392	2761	4153	1125	1574	30	325	248	7816	16.1

Three-Point Field Goals: 1984-85, 0-for-2. 1986-87, 0-for-3. 1987-88, 0-for-6. 1988-89, 0-for-2. 1989-90, 0-for-10. Totals, 0-for-23.

NBA PLAYOFF RECORD

									—Rebounds—									
Sea.—Team	G.	Min.	FGA	FGM	Pct.	FTA	FTM	Pct.	Off.	Def.	Tot.	Ast.	PF	Dq.	Stl.	Blk.	Pts.	Avg.
85-86—Sacramento	3	35	13	3	.231	13	6	.462	8	4	12	0	4	0	0	1	12	4.0
88-89—Houston	4	152	37	24	.649	21	16	.762	6	14	20	12	17	1	5	1	64	16.0
89-90—Houston	4	164	45	27	.600	38	26	.684	14	19	33	7	12	0	5	0	80	20.0
Totals	11	351	95	54	.568	72	48	.667	28	37	65	19	33	1	10	2	156	14.2

SEDALE EUGENE THREATT

Born September 10, 1961, at Atlanta, Ga. Height 6:02. Weight 177.

High School—Atlanta, Ga., Therrell.

College—West Virginia Institute of Technology, Montgomery, W. Va.

Drafted by Philadelphia on sixth round, 1983 (139th pick).

Traded by Philadelphia to Chicago for Steve Colter and a future 2nd round draft choice, December 31, 1986.
Traded by Chicago to Seattle for Sam Vincent, February 25, 1988.

—COLLEGIATE RECORD—

Year	G.	Min.	FGA	FGM	Pct.	FTA	FTM	Pct.	Reb.	Pts.	Avg.
79-80	28	....	424	204	.481	126	90	.714	97	498	17.8
80-81	31	....	524	237	.452	104	74	.712	122	548	17.7
81-82	34	....	598	299	.500	214	156	.729	118	754	22.2
82-83	27	951	510	284	.557	164	120	.732	104	688	25.5
Totals	120	....	2056	1024	.498	608	440	.724	441	2488	20.7

NBA REGULAR SEASON RECORD

									—Rebounds—									
Sea.—Team	G.	Min.	FGA	FGM	Pct.	FTA	FTM	Pct.	Off.	Def.	Tot.	Ast.	PF	Dq.	Stl.	Blk.	Pts.	Avg.
83-84—Philadelphia	45	464	148	62	.419	28	23	.821	17	23	40	41	65	1	13	2	148	3.3
84-85—Philadelphia	82	1304	416	188	.452	90	66	.733	21	78	99	175	171	2	80	16	446	5.4
85-86—Philadelphia	70	1754	684	310	.453	90	75	.833	21	100	121	193	157	1	93	5	696	9.9
86-87—Phil.-Chi.	68	1446	534	239	.448	119	95	.798	26	82	108	259	164	0	74	13	580	8.5
87-88—Chi.-Sea.	71	1055	425	216	.508	71	57	.803	23	65	88	160	100	0	60	8	492	6.9
88-89—Seattle	63	1220	476	235	.494	77	63	.818	31	86	117	238	155	0	83	4	544	8.6
89-90—Seattle	65	1481	599	303	.506	157	130	.828	43	72	115	216	164	0	65	8	744	11.4
Totals	464	8724	3282	1553	.473	632	509	.805	182	506	688	1282	976	4	468	56	3650	7.9

Three-Point Field Goals: 1983-84, 1-for-8 (.125). 1984-85, 4-for-22 (.182). 1985-86, 1-for-24 (.042). 1986-87, 7-for-32 (.219). 1987-88, 3-for-27 (.111). 1988-89, 11-for-30 (.367). 1989-90, 8-for-32 (.250). Totals, 35-for-175 (.200).

NBA PLAYOFF RECORD

									—Rebounds—									
Sea.—Team	G.	Min.	FGA	FGM	Pct.	FTA	FTM	Pct.	Off.	Def.	Tot.	Ast.	PF	Dq.	Stl.	Blk.	Pts.	Avg.
83-84—Philadelphia	3	6	3	1	.333	0	0	.000	1	1	2	1	0	0	1	0	2	0.7
84-85—Philadelphia	4	28	7	2	.286	0	0	.000	1	0	1	5	2	0	1	0	4	1.0
85-86—Philadelphia	12	312	143	67	.469	33	26	.788	6	19	25	42	35	0	23	2	160	13.3
86-87—Chicago	3	70	17	8	.471	4	4	1.000	2	3	5	16	11	0	1	0	20	6.7
87-88—Seattle	5	80	34	14	.412	4	4	1.000	2	9	11	11	7	0	1	0	32	6.4
88-89—Seattle	8	201	82	39	.476	20	17	.850	3	10	13	49	22	0	17	0	96	12.0
Totals	35	697	286	131	.458	61	51	.836	15	42	57	124	77	0	44	2	314	9.0

Three-Point Field Goals: 1983-84, 0-for-2. 1985-86, 0-for-2. 1987-88, 0-for-1. 1988-89, 1-for-4 (.250). Totals, 1-for-9 (.111).

WAYMAN LAWRENCE TISDALE

Born June 9, 1964 at Tulsa, Okla. Height 6:09. Weight 240.

High School—Tulsa, Okla., Washington.

College—University of Oklahoma, Norman, Okla.

Drafted by Indiana on first round as an undergraduate, 1985 (2nd pick).

Traded by Indiana with a 1990 or 1991 2nd round draft choice to Sacramento for LaSalle Thompson and Randy Wittman, February 20, 1989.

—COLLEGIATE RECORD—

Year	G.	Min.	FGA	FGM	Pct.	FTA	FTM	Pct.	Reb.	Pts.	Avg.
82-83	33	1138	583	338	.580	211	134	.635	341	810	24.5
83-84	34	1232	639	369	.577	283	181	.640	329	919	27.0
84-85	37	1283	640	370	.578	273	192	.703	378	932	25.2
Totals	104	3653	1862	1077	.578	767	507	.661	1048	2661	25.6

NBA REGULAR SEASON RECORD

									—Rebounds—									
Sea.—Team	G.	Min.	FGA	FGM	Pct.	FTA	FTM	Pct.	Off.	Def.	Tot.	Ast.	PF	Dq.	Stl.	Blk.	Pts.	Avg.
85-86—Indiana	81	2277	1002	516	.515	234	160	.684	191	393	584	79	290	3	32	44	1192	14.7
86-87—Indiana	81	2159	892	458	.513	364	258	.709	217	258	475	117	293	9	50	26	1174	14.5
87-88—Indiana	79	2378	998	511	.512	314	246	.783	168	323	491	103	274	5	54	34	1268	16.1
88-89—Ind.-Sac.	79	2434	1036	532	.514	410	317	.773	187	422	609	128	290	7	55	52	1381	17.5
89-90—Sacramento	79	2937	1383	726	.525	391	306	.783	185	410	595	108	251	3	54	54	1758	22.3
Totals	399	12185	5311	2743	.516	1713	1287	.751	948	1806	2754	535	1398	27	245	210	6773	17.0

Three-Point Field Goals: 1985-86, 0-for-2. 1986-87, 0-for-2. 1987-88, 0-for-2. 1988-89, 0-for-4. 1989-90, 0-for-6. Totals, 0-for-16.

NBA PLAYOFF RECORD

									—Rebounds—									
Sea.—Team	G.	Min.	FGA	FGM	Pct.	FTA	FTM	Pct.	Off.	Def.	Tot.	Ast.	PF	Dq.	Stl.	Blk.	Pts.	Avg.
86-87—Indiana	4	108	31	19	.613	23	13	.565	5	11	16	9	17	1	1	0	51	12.8

Member of U.S. Olympic team, 1984. . . . Named to THE SPORTING NEWS All-America First Team, 1984 and 1985. . . . THE SPORTING NEWS All-America Second Team, 1983.

BYRON THOMAS TOLBERT
(Tom)

Born October 16, 1965 at Long Beach, Calif. Height 6:07. Weight 240.

High School—Lakewood, Calif.

Colleges—University of California at Irvine, Irvine, Calif; Cerritos College, Norwalk, Calif., and University of Arizona, Tucson, Ariz.

Drafted by Charlotte on second round, 1988 (34th pick).

Waived by Charlotte, December 30, 1988; signed by Golden State as a free agent, October 5, 1989.
Waived by Golden State, November 2, 1989; re-signed by Golden State as a free agent, November 9, 1989.

—COLLEGIATE RECORD—

California-Irvine

Year	G.	Min.	FGA	FGM	Pct.	FTA	FTM	Pct.	Reb.	Pts.	Avg.
83-84	4	15	4	3	.750	0	0	.000	1	6	1.5
84-85	6	53	19	6	.316	5	4	.800	12	16	2.7
UCI Totals	10	68	23	9	.391	5	4	.800	13	22	2.2

Cerritos

Year	G.	Min.	FGA	FGM	Pct.	FTA	FTM	Pct.	Reb.	Pts.	Avg.
85-86	32	....	354	217	.613	125	85	.680	251	519	16.2

Arizona

Year	G.	Min.	FGA	FGM	Pct.	FTA	FTM	Pct.	Reb.	Pts.	Avg.
86-87	30	803	305	156	.511	139	98	.705	186	418	13.9
87-88	38	1034	351	192	.547	186	151	.812	220	536	14.1
Ariz. Totals	68	1837	656	348	.530	325	249	.766	406	954	14.0
College Totals	78	1905	679	357	.526	330	253	.767	419	976	12.5

(Suffered shoulder injury in 1983-84 season; granted extra year of eligibility.)

Three-Point Field Goals: 1986-87, 8-for-18 (.444). 1987-88, 1-for-2 (.500). Totals. 9-for-20 (.450).

NBA REGULAR SEASON RECORD

									—Rebounds—									
Sea.—Team	G.	Min.	FGA	FGM	Pct.	FTA	FTM	Pct.	Off.	Def.	Tot.	Ast.	PF	Dq.	Stl.	Blk.	Pts.	Avg.
88-89—Charlotte	14	117	37	17	.459	12	6	.500	7	14	21	7	20	0	2	4	40	2.9
89-90—Golden State	70	1347	442	218	.493	241	175	.726	122	241	363	58	191	0	23	25	616	8.8
Totals	84	1464	479	235	.491	253	181	.715	129	255	384	65	211	0	25	29	656	7.8

Three-Point Field Goals: 1988-89, 0-for3. 1989-90, 5-for-18 (.278). Totals, 5-for-21 (.238).

—DID YOU KNOW—

That San Antonio's 35-game improvement from a 21-61 record in 1988-89 to 56-26 in 1989-90 was the largest single-season turnaround in NBA history? The Boston Celtics had improved 32 games a decade earlier following the arrival of Larry Bird.

SEDRIC ANDRE TONEY

Born April 13, 1962 at Columbus, Miss. Height 6:02. Weight 178.

High School—Dayton, O., Wilbur Wright.

Colleges—Phillips Business College, Miss.; Western Nebraska Community College, Scottsbluff, Neb., and University of Dayton, Dayton, O.

Drafted by Atlanta on third round, 1985 (59th pick).

Waived by Atlanta, November 4, 1985; signed by Phoenix as a free agent, March 29, 1986.
Waived by Phoenix, October 23, 1986; signed by Denver as a free agent, October 7, 1987.
Waived by Denver, October 29, 1987; signed by New York, March 13, 1988, to a 10-day contract that expired, March 22, 1988.
Re-signed by New York, March 23, 1988, for remainder of season.
Selected from New York by Charlotte in NBA expansion draft, June 23, 1988.
Rights relinquished by Charlotte, October 17, 1988; signed by Indiana, February 2, 1989, to a 10-day contract that expired, February 11, 1989.
Signed by Atlanta as a free agent, September 29, 1989.
Traded by Atlanta with Antoine Carr and future draft considerations to Sacramento for Kenny Smith and Mike Williams, February 13, 1990.
Played in Continental Basketball Association with Cincinnati Slammers, 1985-86, and LaCrosse Catbirds and Cincinnati Slammers, 1986-87.

—COLLEGIATE RECORD—

Phillips Business College

Year	G.	Min.	FGA	FGM	Pct.	FTA	FTM	Pct.	Reb.	Pts.	Avg.
80-81	Statistics Unavailable										

Year	G.	Min.	FGA	FGM	Pct.	FTA	FTM	Pct.	Reb.	Pts.	Avg.
81-82	Did Not Play College Basketball										

Western Nebraska

Year	G.	Min.	FGA	FGM	Pct.	FTA	FTM	Pct.	Reb.	Pts.	Avg.
82-83	34	....	....	....	....	....	....	....	....	612	18.0

Dayton

Year	G.	Min.	FGA	FGM	Pct.	FTA	FTM	Pct.	Reb.	Pts.	Avg.
83-84	32	963	295	150	.508	108	72	.667	79	372	11.6
84-85	27	834	274	130	.474	115	90	.783	78	350	13.0
Totals	59	1797	569	280	.492	223	162	.726	157	722	12.3

CBA REGULAR SEASON RECORD

			—2-Point—			—3-Point—									
Sea.—Team	G.	Min.	FGM	FGA	Pct.	FGM	FGA	Pct.	FTM	FTA	Pct.	Reb.	Ast.	Pts.	Avg.
85-86—Cincinnati	48	989	169	337	.501	1	4	.250	146	186	.784	63	138	487	10.1
86-87—LaCrosse-Cincinnati	32	605	78	181	.430	7	27	.259	64	89	.719	39	96	241	7.5
Totals	80	1594	247	518	.476	8	31	.258	210	275	.763	102	234	728	9.1

NBA REGULAR SEASON RECORD

									—Rebounds—									
Sea.—Team	G.	Min.	FGA	FGM	Pct.	FTA	FTM	Pct.	Off.	Def.	Tot.	Ast.	PF	Dq.	Stl.	Blk.	Pts.	Avg.
85-86—Atl.-Phoe.	13	230	66	28	.424	31	21	.677	3	22	25	26	24	0	6	0	80	6.2
87-88—New York	21	139	48	21	.438	11	10	.909	3	5	8	24	20	0	9	1	57	2.7
88-89—Indiana	2	9	5	1	.200	1	0	.000	1	1	2	0	1	0	0	0	2	1.0
89-90—Atl.-Sac.	64	968	250	87	.348	83	67	.807	14	46	60	174	106	1	33	0	264	4.1
Totals	100	1346	369	137	.371	126	98	.778	21	74	95	224	151	1	48	1	403	4.0

Three-Point Field Goals: 1985-86, 3-for-10 (.300). 1987-88, 5-for-14 (.357). 1988-89, 0-for-3. 1989-90, 23-for-63 (.365). Totals, 31-for-90 (.344).

NBA PLAYOFF RECORD

									—Rebounds—									
Sea.—Team	G.	Min.	FGA	FGM	Pct.	FTA	FTM	Pct.	Off.	Def.	Tot.	Ast.	PF	Dq.	Stl.	Blk.	Pts.	Avg.
87-88—New York	3	15	6	3	.500	2	2	1.000	0	0	0	2	4	0	1	0	11	3.7

Three-Point Field Goals: 1987-88, 3-for-6 (.500).

PETER KELLY TRIPUCKA

(Known by middle name.)

Born February 16, 1959 at Glen Ridge, N. J. Height 6:06. Weight 225.

High School—Bloomfield, N. J.

College—University of Notre Dame, Notre Dame, Ind.

Drafted by Detroit on first round, 1981 (12th pick).

Traded by Detroit with Kent Benson to Utah for Adrian Dantley and 1987 and 1990 2nd round draft choices, August 21, 1986.
Traded by Utah to Charlotte for Mike Brown, June 23, 1988.

—COLLEGIATE RECORD—

Year	G.	Min.	FGA	FGM	Pct.	FTA	FTM	Pct.	Reb.	Pts.	Avg.
77-78	31	643	247	141	.571	108	80	.741	161	362	11.7
78-79	29	807	277	143	.516	151	129	.854	125	415	14.3
79-80	23	691	270	150	.556	151	115	.762	151	415	18.0
80-81	29	919	354	195	.551	168	137	.815	169	527	18.2
Totals	112	3060	1148	629	.548	578	461	.798	606	1719	15.3

NBA REGULAR SEASON RECORD

									—Rebounds—									
Sea.—Team	G.	Min.	FGA	FGM	Pct.	FTA	FTM	Pct.	Off.	Def.	Tot.	Ast.	PF	Dq.	Stl.	Blk.	Pts.	Avg.
81-82—Detroit	82	3077	1281	636	.496	621	495	.797	219	224	443	270	241	0	89	16	1772	21.6
82-83—Detroit	58	2252	1156	565	.489	464	392	.845	126	138	264	237	157	0	67	20	1536	26.5
83-84—Detroit	76	2493	1296	595	.459	523	426	.815	119	187	306	228	190	0	65	17	1618	21.3
84-85—Detroit	55	1675	831	396	.477	288	255	.885	66	152	218	135	118	1	49	14	1049	19.1
85-86—Detroit	81	2626	1236	615	.498	444	380	.856	116	232	348	265	167	0	93	10	1622	20.0
86-87—Utah	79	1865	621	291	.469	226	197	.872	54	188	242	243	147	0	85	11	798	10.1
87-88—Utah	49	976	303	139	.459	68	59	.868	30	87	117	105	68	1	34	4	368	7.5
88-89—Charlotte	71	2302	1215	568	.467	508	440	.866	79	188	267	224	196	0	88	16	1606	22.6
89-90—Charlotte	79	2404	1029	442	.430	351	310	.883	82	240	322	224	220	1	75	16	1232	15.6
Totals	630	19670	8968	4247	.474	3493	2954	.846	891	1636	2527	1931	1504	3	645	124	11601	18.4

Three-Point Field Goals: 1981-82, 5-for-22 (.227). 1982-83, 14-for-37 (.378). 1983-84, 2-for-17 (.118). 1984-85, 2-for-5 (.400). 1985-86, 12-for-25 (.480). 1986-87, 19-for-52 (.365). 1987-88, 31-for-74 (.419). 1988-89, 30-for-84 (.357). 1989-90, 38-for-104 (.365). Totals, 153-for-420 (.364).

NBA PLAYOFF RECORD

									—Rebounds—									
Sea.—Team	G.	Min.	FGA	FGM	Pct.	FTA	FTM	Pct.	Off.	Def.	Tot.	Ast.	PF	Dq.	Stl.	Blk.	Pts.	Avg.
83-84—Detroit	5	208	102	48	.471	51	41	.804	10	13	23	15	22	1	11	0	137	27.4
84-85—Detroit	9	288	118	49	.415	40	35	.875	19	20	39	29	22	0	4	3	133	14.8
85-86—Detroit	4	175	71	33	.465	23	21	.913	10	13	23	9	14	1	3	2	87	21.8
86-87—Utah	5	70	20	14	.700	4	4	1.000	1	6	7	3	6	0	4	0	32	6.4
87-88—Utah	2	9	3	1	.333	0	0	.000	1	0	1	1	1	0	0	0	2	1.0
Totals	25	750	314	145	.462	118	101	.856	41	52	93	57	65	2	22	5	391	15.6

Three-Point Field Goals: 1983-84, 0-for-1. 1984-85, 0-for-1. 1986-87, 0-for-3. Totals, 0-for-5.

NBA ALL-STAR GAME RECORD

								—Rebounds—								
Season—Team	Min.	FGA	FGM	Pct.	FTA	FTM	Pct.	Off.	Def.	Tot.	Ast.	PF	Dq.	Stl.	Blk.	Pts.
1982—Detroit	15	7	3	.429	0	0	.000	0	1	1	2	0	0	0	0	6
1984—Detroit	6	0	0	.000	2	1	.500	0	0	0	2	1	0	1	0	1
Totals	21	7	3	.429	2	1	.500	0	1	1	4	1	0	1	0	7

Named to NBA All-Rookie Team, 1982.

KELVIN TRENT TUCKER

(Known by middle name.)

Born December 20, 1959 at Tarboro, N. C. Height 6:05. Weight 193.

High School—Flint, Mich., Northwestern.

College—University of Minnesota, Minneapolis, Minn.

Drafted by New York on first round, 1982 (6th pick).

—COLLEGIATE RECORD—

Year	G.	Min.	FGA	FGM	Pct.	FTA	FTM	Pct.	Reb.	Pts.	Avg.
78-79	25	....	239	114	.477	32	19	.594	85	247	9.9
79-80	32	....	310	152	.490	46	34	.739	103	338	10.6
80-81	29	....	362	187	.517	69	56	.812	102	430	14.8
81-82	29	....	353	178	.504	90	74	.822	103	430	14.8
Totals	115	....	1264	631	.499	237	183	.772	393	1445	12.6

NBA REGULAR SEASON RECORD

									—Rebounds—									
Sea.—Team	G.	Min.	FGA	FGM	Pct.	FTA	FTM	Pct.	Off.	Def.	Tot.	Ast.	PF	Dq.	Stl.	Blk.	Pts.	Avg.
82-83—New York	78	1830	647	299	.462	64	43	.672	75	141	216	195	235	1	56	6	655	8.4
83-84—New York	63	1228	450	225	.500	33	25	.758	43	87	130	138	124	0	63	8	481	7.6
84-85—New York	77	1819	606	293	.483	48	38	.792	74	114	188	199	195	0	75	15	653	8.5
85-86—New York	77	1788	740	349	.472	100	79	.790	70	99	169	192	167	0	65	8	818	10.6
86-87—New York	70	1691	691	325	.470	101	77	.762	49	86	135	166	169	1	116	13	795	11.4
87-88—New York	71	1248	455	193	.424	71	51	.718	32	87	119	117	158	3	53	6	506	7.1
88-89—New York	81	1824	579	263	.454	55	43	.782	55	121	176	132	163	0	88	6	687	8.5
89-90—New York	81	1725	606	253	.417	86	66	.767	57	117	174	173	159	0	74	8	667	8.2
Totals	598	13153	4774	2200	.461	558	422	.756	455	852	1307	1312	1370	5	590	70	5262	8.8

Three-Point Field Goals: 1982-83, 14-for-30 (.467). 1983-84, 6-for-16 (.375). 1984-85, 29-for-72 (.403). 1985-86, 41-for-91 (.451). 1986-87, 68-for-161 (.422). 1987-88, 69-for-167 (.413). 1988-89, 118-for-296 (.399). 1989-90, 95-for-245 (.388). Totals, 440-for-1078 (.408).

NBA PLAYOFF RECORD

									—Rebounds—									
Sea.—Team	G.	Min.	FGA	FGM	Pct.	FTA	FTM	Pct.	Off.	Def.	Tot.	Ast.	PF	Dq.	Stl.	Blk.	Pts.	Avg.
82-83—New York	6	85	15	9	.600	10	7	.700	2	7	9	5	7	0	2	0	26	4.3
83-84—New York	12	254	84	42	.500	10	6	.600	6	12	18	27	32	0	11	3	91	7.6
87-88—New York	4	71	19	8	.421	4	3	.750	0	2	2	4	4	0	3	0	25	6.3
88-89—New York	9	159	58	27	.466	4	2	.500	9	10	19	14	20	0	10	2	71	7.9
89-90—New York	10	178	55	22	.400	6	6	1.000	5	9	14	20	19	0	10	0	60	6.0
Totals	41	747	231	108	.468	34	24	.706	22	40	62	70	82	0	36	5	273	6.7

Three-Point Field Goals: 1982-83, 1-for-2 (.500). 1983-84, 1-for-5 (.200). 1987-88, 6-for-13 (.462). 1988-89, 15-for-32 (.469). 1989-90, 10-for-27 (.370). Totals, 33-for-79 (.418).

Named to THE SPORTING NEWS All-America First Team, 1982.

ANDRE TURNER

Born December 13, 1964 at Memphis, Tenn. Height 5:11. Weight 160.

High School—Memphis, Tenn., Mitchell.

College—Memphis State University, Memphis, Tenn.

Drafted by Los Angeles Lakers on third round, 1986 (69th pick).

Waived by Los Angeles Lakers, October 28, 1986; signed by Boston as a free agent, November 6, 1986.

Waived by Boston, November 25, 1986; signed by Houston as a free agent, October 9, 1987.

Selected from Houston by Miami in NBA expansion draft, June 23, 1988.

Waived by Miami, November 3, 1988; signed by Milwaukee, January 3, 1989, to a 10-day contract that expired, January 12, 1989.

Signed by Charlotte as a free agent, October 5, 1989.

Waived by Charlotte, October 31, 1989; claimed off waivers by Los Angeles Clippers, November 1, 1989.

Waived by Los Angeles Clippers, November 14, 1989; signed by Charlotte as a free agent, November 23, 1989.

Waived by Charlotte, December 13, 1989.

Played in Continental Basketball Association with Rockford Lightning and LaCrosse Catbirds, 1986-87, and with LaCrosse Catbirds, 1988-89 and 1989-90.

—COLLEGIATE RECORD—

Year	G.	Min.	FGA	FGM	Pct.	FTA	FTM	Pct.	Reb.	Pts.	Avg.
82-83	31	1006	245	127	.518	67	54	.806	35	308	9.9
83-84	33	1052	234	107	.457	87	58	.667	45	272	8.2
84-85	34	1157	309	154	.498	112	80	.714	79	388	11.4
85-86	34	1137	410	196	.478	96	82	.854	67	474	13.9
Totals	132	4352	1198	584	.487	362	274	.757	226	1442	10.9

CBA REGULAR SEASON RECORD

			—2-Point—			—3-Point—									
Sea.—Team	G.	Min.	FGM	FGA	Pct.	FGM	FGA	Pct.	FTM	FTA	Pct.	Reb.	Ast.	Pts.	Avg.
86-87—Rock.-LaCrosse	47	1329	228	475	.480	5	35	.143	117	142	.824	110	240	588	12.5
88-89—LaCrosse	38	1378	222	474	.468	19	84	.226	169	204	.828	102	220	670	17.6
89-90—LaCrosse	34	1343	255	509	.501	13	50	.260	151	182	.830	115	308	700	20.6
Totals	119	4050	705	1458	.484	37	169	.219	437	528	.828	327	768	1958	16.5

NBA REGULAR SEASON RECORD

									—Rebounds—									
Sea.—Team	G.	Min.	FGA	FGM	Pct.	FTA	FTM	Pct.	Off.	Def.	Tot.	Ast.	PF	Dq.	Stl.	Blk.	Pts.	Avg.
86-87—Boston	3	18	5	2	.400	0	0	.000	1	1	2	1	1	0	0	0	4	1.3
87-88—Houston	12	99	34	12	.353	14	10	.714	4	4	8	23	13	0	7	1	35	2.9
88-89—Milwaukee	4	13	6	3	.500	0	0	.000	0	3	3	0	2	0	2	0	6	1.5
89-90—L.A.C.-Char.	11	115	38	11	.289	4	4	1.000	4	4	8	23	6	0	8	0	26	2.4
Totals	30	245	83	28	.337	18	14	.778	9	12	21	47	22	0	17	1	71	2.4

Three-Point Field Goals: 1986-87, 0-for-1. 1987-88, 1-for-7 (.143). 1989-90, 0-for-2. Totals, 1-for-10 (.100).

HENRY TURNER

Born August 18, 1966 at Oakland, Calif. Height 6:07. Weight 205.

High School—Oakland, Calif., Fremont.

College—California State University at Fullerton, Fullerton, Calif.

Never drafted by an NBA franchise.

Signed by Sacramento as a free agent, September 10, 1989.

Played in Continental Basketball Association with Rochester Flyers, 1988-89.

—COLLEGIATE RECORD—

Year	G.	Min.	FGA	FGM	Pct.	FTA	FTM	Pct.	Reb.	Pts.	Avg.
84-85	25	198	56	23	.411	28	17	.607	53	63	2.5
85-86	32	978	275	137	.498	115	69	.600	199	343	10.7
86-87	30	1010	417	177	.424	116	81	.698	180	456	15.2
87-88	27	902	351	176	.501	154	111	.721	198	467	17.3
Totals	114	3088	1099	513	.467	413	278	.673	630	1329	11.7

Three-Point Field Goals: 1986-87, 21-for-53 (.396). 1987-88, 4-for-14 (.286). Totals, 25-for-67 (.373).

CBA REGULAR SEASON RECORD

			—2-Point—			—3-Point—									
Sea.—Team	G.	Min.	FGM	FGA	Pct.	FGM	FGA	Pct.	FTM	FTA	Pct.	Reb.	Ast.	Pts.	Avg.
88-89—Rochester	52	1354	284	579	.491	8	36	.222	119	189	.630	280	105	711	13.7

NBA REGULAR SEASON RECORD

								—Rebounds—									
Sea.—Team	G.	Min.	FGA	FGM	Pct.	FTA	FTM	Pct.	Off.	Def.	Tot.	Ast.	PF	Dq.	Stl.	Blk.	Pts.	Avg.
89-90—Sacramento	36	315	122	58	.475	65	40	.615	22	28	50	22	40	0	17	7	156	4.3

Three-Point Field Goals: 1989-90, 0-for-3.

JEFFREY STEVEN TURNER
(Jeff)

Born April 9, 1962 at Bangor, Maine. Height 6:09. Weight 240.
High School—Brandon, Fla.
College—Vanderbilt University, Nashville, Tenn.
Drafted by New Jersey on first round, 1984 (17th pick).

Signed by Orlando as an unrestricted free agent, July 11, 1989.
Played in Italy, 1987-88 and 1988-89 seasons.

—COLLEGIATE RECORD—

Year	G.	Min.	FGA	FGM	Pct.	FTA	FTM	Pct.	Reb.	Pts.	Avg.
80-81	28	586	96	40	.417	31	20	.645	84	100	3.6
81-82	27	772	189	99	.524	71	52	.732	145	250	9.3
82-83	33	1008	366	180	.492	98	75	.765	182	435	13.2
83-84	29	953	375	200	.533	102	86	.843	213	486	16.8
Totals	117	3319	1026	519	.506	302	233	.772	624	1271	10.9

ITALIAN LEAGUE RECORD

Year	G.	Min.	FGA	FGM	Pct.	FTA	FTM	Pct.	Reb.	Pts.	Avg.
87-88—Arexons Cantu	35	1271	216	417	.518	137	150	.913	187	641	18.3
88-89—Vis. Cantu	33	1104	186	318	.585	124	148	.838	249	562	17.0

NBA REGULAR SEASON RECORD

									—Rebounds—									
Sea.—Team	G.	Min.	FGA	FGM	Pct.	FTA	FTM	Pct.	Off.	Def.	Tot.	Ast.	PF	Dq.	Stl.	Blk.	Pts.	Avg.
84-85—New Jersey	72	1429	377	171	.454	92	79	.859	88	130	218	108	243	8	29	7	421	5.8
85-86—New Jersey	53	650	171	84	.491	78	58	.744	45	92	137	14	125	4	21	3	226	4.3
86-87—New Jersey	76	1003	325	151	.465	104	76	.731	80	117	197	60	200	6	33	13	378	5.0
89-90—Orlando	60	1105	308	132	.429	54	42	.778	52	175	227	53	161	4	23	12	308	5.1
Totals	261	4187	1181	538	.456	328	255	.777	265	514	779	235	729	22	106	35	1333	5.1

Three-Point Field Goals: 1984-85, 0-for-3. 1985-86, 0-for-1. 1986-87, 0-for-1. 1989-90, 2-for-10 (.200). Totals, 2-for-15 (.133).

NBA PLAYOFF RECORD

									—Rebounds—									
Sea.—Team	G.	Min.	FGA	FGM	Pct.	FTA	FTM	Pct.	Off.	Def.	Tot.	Ast.	PF	Dq.	Stl.	Blk.	Pts.	Avg.
84-85—New Jersey	3	21	5	2	.400	0	0	.000	2	2	4	2	6	0	0	0	4	1.3
85-86—New Jersey	3	18	3	1	.333	1	1	1.000	0	3	3	3	7	0	0	0	3	1.0
Totals	6	39	8	3	.375	1	1	1.000	2	5	7	5	13	0	0	0	7	1.2

Member of U.S. Olympic team, 1984.

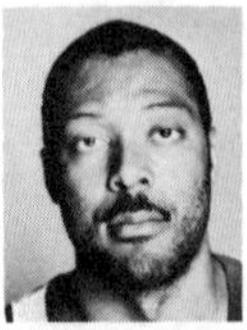

MELVIN HARRISON TURPIN

Born December 28, 1960 at Lexington, Ky. Height 6:11. Weight 240.
High School—Lexington, Ky., Bryan Station.
Prep School—Fork Union Military Academy, Fork Union, Va.
College—University of Kentucky, Lexington, Ky.
Drafted by Washington on first round, 1984 (6th pick).

Draft rights traded by Washington to Cleveland for Cliff Robinson, the draft rights to Tim McCormick and cash, June 19, 1984.

Traded by Cleveland with Darryl Dawkins and future 2nd round draft considerations to Utah for Kent Benson, Dell Curry and future 2nd round draft considerations, October 8, 1987.

Waived by Utah, September 9, 1988; signed by Washington as a free agent, August 8, 1989.

Waived by Washington, July 24, 1990.

Played in Spain, 1988-89.

—COLLEGIATE RECORD—

Year	G.	Min.	FGA	FGM	Pct.	FTA	FTM	Pct.	Reb.	Pts.	Avg.
80-81	28	380	95	50	.526	44	31	.705	106	131	4.7
81-82	30	912	275	160	.582	106	72	.679	212	392	13.1
82-83	31	962	311	192	.617	125	84	.672	195	468	15.1
83-84	34	1071	378	224	.593	94	70	.745	217	518	15.2
Totals	123	3325	1059	626	.591	369	257	.696	730	1509	12.3

NBA REGULAR SEASON RECORD

									—Rebounds—									
Sea.—Team	G.	Min.	FGA	FGM	Pct.	FTA	FTM	Pct.	Off.	Def.	Tot.	Ast.	PF	Dq.	Stl.	Blk.	Pts.	Avg.
84-85—Cleveland	79	1949	711	363	.511	139	109	.784	155	297	452	36	211	3	38	87	835	10.6
85-86—Cleveland	80	2292	838	456	.544	228	185	.811	182	374	556	55	260	6	65	106	1097	13.7
86-87—Cleveland	64	801	366	169	.462	77	55	.714	62	128	190	33	90	1	11	40	393	6.1
87-88—Utah	79	1011	389	199	.512	98	71	.724	88	148	236	32	157	2	26	68	470	5.9
89-90—Washington	59	818	209	110	.526	71	56	.789	88	133	221	27	135	0	15	47	276	4.7
Totals	361	6871	2513	1297	.516	613	476	.777	575	1080	1655	183	853	12	155	348	3071	8.5

Three-Point Field Goals: 1985-86, 0-for-4. 1987-88, 1-for-3 (.333). 1989-90, 0-for-2. Totals, 1-for-9 (.111).

NBA PLAYOFF RECORD

									—Rebounds—									
Sea.—Team	G.	Min.	FGA	FGM	Pct.	FTA	FTM	Pct.	Off.	Def.	Tot.	Ast.	PF	Dq.	Stl.	Blk.	Pts.	Avg.
84-85—Cleveland	4	45	19	12	.632	2	1	.500	3	5	8	0	3	0	4	1	25	6.3
87-88—Utah	7	31	9	3	.333	2	2	1.000	3	3	6	2	5	0	1	4	8	1.1
Totals	11	76	28	15	.536	4	3	.750	6	8	14	2	8	0	5	5	33	3.0

KELVIN UPSHAW

Born January 24, 1963 at Chicago, Ill. Height 6:02. Weight 180.

High School—Chicago, Ill., Marshall.

Colleges—Northeastern Oklahoma A&M College, Miami, Okla., and University of Utah, Salt Lake City, Utah.

Never drafted by an NBA franchise.

Signed by Miami, January 11, 1989, to the first of consecutive 10-day contracts that expired, January 30, 1989.

Signed by Boston, March 9, 1989, to the first of consecutive 10-day contracts that expired, March 28, 1989.

Re-signed by Boston, March 28, 1989.

Waived by Boston, November 17, 1989; re-signed by Boston as a free agent, November 24, 1989.

Waived by Boston, December 26, 1989; signed by Dallas, January 6, 1990, to the first of consecutive 10-day contracts that expired, January 21, 1990.

Signed by Golden State, February 28, 1990, for remainder of season.

Played in Continental Basketball Association with Mississippi Jets, 1986-87; Mississippi Jets and Rapid City Thrillers, 1987-88, and Albany Patroons, 1988-89.

—COLLEGIATE RECORD—

Northeastern Oklahoma A&M

Year	G.	Min.	FGA	FGM	Pct.	FTA	FTM	Pct.	Reb.	Pts.	Avg.
81-82	31	....	527	257	.488	114	84	.737	91	598	19.3

Utah

Year	G.	Min.	FGA	FGM	Pct.	FTA	FTM	Pct.	Reb.	Pts.	Avg.
83-84	30	982	333	172	.517	113	94	.832	91	438	14.6
84-85	28	889	396	199	.503	112	88	.786	100	486	17.4
85-86	26	621	238	116	.487	88	73	.830	58	305	11.7
Utah Totals	84	2492	967	487	.504	313	255	.815	249	1229	14.6

CBA REGULAR SEASON RECORD

			—2-Point—			—3-Point—									
Sea.—Team	G.	Min.	FGM	FGA	Pct.	FGM	FGA	Pct.	FTM	FTA	Pct.	Reb.	Ast.	Pts.	Avg.
86-87—Mississippi	46	1132	195	387	.503	4	18	.222	87	112	.776	97	181	489	10.6
87-88—Miss.-Rapid C.	45	1540	335	688	.486	4	22	.182	201	249	.807	153	252	883	19.6
88-89—Albany	40	1242	216	440	.491	12	31	.387	132	157	.841	105	238	600	15.0
Totals	131	3914	746	1515	.492	20	71	.282	420	518	.811	355	671	1972	15.1

NBA REGULAR SEASON RECORD

									—Rebounds—									
Sea.—Team	G.	Min.	FGA	FGM	Pct.	FTA	FTM	Pct.	Off.	Def.	Tot.	Ast.	PF	Dq.	Stl.	Blk.	Pts.	Avg.
88-89—Mia.-Bos.	32	617	212	99	.467	26	18	.692	10	39	49	117	80	1	26	3	219	6.8
89-90—Bos.-Dal.—G.S.	40	387	146	64	.438	37	28	.757	9	32	41	54	53	0	27	1	160	4.0
Totals	72	1004	358	163	.455	63	46	.730	19	71	90	171	133	1	53	4	379	5.3

Three-Point Field Goals: 1988-89, 3-for-15 (.200). 1989-90, 4-for-15 (.267). Totals, 7-for-30 (.233).

NBA PLAYOFF RECORD

Sea.—Team	G.	Min.	FGA	FGM	Pct.	FTA	FTM	Pct.	—Rebounds— Off.	Def.	Tot.	Ast.	PF	Dq.	Stl.	Blk.	Pts.	Avg.
88-89—Boston	3	24	12	5	.417	0	0	.000	0	2	2	5	4	0	1	0	10	3.3

Named to CBA All-Star Second Team, 1989. . . . CBA All-Defensive Second Team, 1987.

ERNEST MAURICE VANDEWEGHE
(Kiki)

Born August 1, 1958 at Weisbaden, Germany. Height 6:08. Weight 220.
High School—Pacific Palisades, Calif., Palisades.
College—University of California at Los Angeles, Los Angeles, Calif.
Drafted by Dallas on first round, 1980 (11th pick).

Traded by Dallas with a 1986 1st round draft choice to Denver for 1981 and 1985 1st round draft choices, December 3, 1980.

Traded by Denver to Portland for Lafayette Lever, Calvin Natt, Wayne Cooper, a 1985 1st round draft choice and a 1984 2nd round draft choice, June 7, 1984.

Traded by Portland to New York for a 1989 1st round draft choice, February 23, 1989.

—COLLEGIATE RECORD—

Year	G.	Min.	FGA	FGM	Pct.	FTA	FTM	Pct.	Reb.	Pts.	Avg.
76-77	23	230	70	35	.500	17	12	.706	41	82	3.6
77-78	28	592	184	101	.549	67	46	.687	123	248	8.9
78-79	30	916	267	166	.622	117	95	.812	189	427	14.2
79-80	32	1081	420	234	.557	196	155	.791	216	623	19.5
Totals	113	2819	941	536	.570	397	308	.776	569	1380	12.2

NBA REGULAR SEASON RECORD

Sea.—Team	G.	Min.	FGA	FGM	Pct.	FTA	FTM	Pct.	—Rebounds— Off.	Def.	Tot.	Ast.	PF	Dq.	Stl.	Blk.	Pts.	Avg.
80-81—Denver	51	1376	537	229	.426	159	130	.818	86	184	270	94	116	0	29	24	588	11.5
81-82—Denver	82	2775	1260	706	.560	405	347	.857	149	312	461	247	217	1	52	29	1760	21.5
82-83—Denver	82	2909	1537	841	.547	559	489	.875	124	313	437	203	198	0	66	38	2186	26.7
83-84—Denver	78	2734	1603	895	.558	580	494	.852	84	289	373	238	187	1	53	50	2295	29.4
84-85—Portland	72	2502	1158	618	.534	412	369	.896	74	154	228	106	116	0	37	22	1616	22.4
85-86—Portland	79	2791	1332	719	.540	602	523	.869	92	124	216	187	161	0	54	17	1962	24.8
86-87—Portland	79	3029	1545	808	.523	527	467	.886	86	165	251	220	137	0	52	17	2122	26.9
87-88—Portland	37	1038	557	283	.508	181	159	.878	36	73	109	71	68	0	21	7	747	20.2
88-89—Port.-N.Y.	45	934	426	200	.469	89	80	.899	26	45	71	69	78	0	19	11	499	11.1
89-90—New York	22	563	231	102	.442	48	44	.917	15	38	53	41	28	0	15	3	258	11.7
Totals	627	20651	10186	5401	.530	3562	3102	.871	772	1697	2469	1476	1306	2	398	218	14033	22.4

Three-Point Field Goals: 1980-81, 0-for-7. 1981-82, 1-for-13 (.077). 1982-83, 15-for-51 (.294). 1983-84, 11-for-30 (.367). 1984-85, 11-for-33 (.333). 1985-86, 1-for-8 (.125). 1986-87, 39-for-81 (.481). 1987-88, 22-for-58 (.379). 1988-89, 19-for-48 (.396). 1989-90, 10-for-19 (.526). Totals, 129-for-348 (.371).

NBA PLAYOFF RECORD

Sea.—Team	G.	Min.	FGA	FGM	Pct.	FTA	FTM	Pct.	—Rebounds— Off.	Def.	Tot.	Ast.	PF	Dq.	Stl.	Blk.	Pts.	Avg.
81-82—Denver	3	109	43	25	.581	18	18	1.000	4	14	18	9	7	0	2	4	68	22.7
82-83—Denver	8	317	160	87	.544	50	40	.800	6	46	52	32	16	0	4	7	214	26.8
83-84—Denver	5	180	96	49	.510	28	27	.964	6	17	23	20	14	1	9	5	127	25.4
84-85—Portland	9	311	158	85	.538	33	31	.939	14	13	27	17	23	0	8	3	202	22.4
85-86—Portland	4	149	69	40	.580	32	32	1.000	2	3	5	8	12	0	2	2	112	28.0
86-87—Portland	4	174	71	38	.535	26	22	.846	5	8	13	11	10	0	1	1	99	24.8
87-88—Portland	4	72	40	11	.275	9	9	1.000	3	10	13	7	8	0	1	0	31	7.8
88-89—New York	9	159	49	25	.510	21	20	.952	2	9	11	7	10	0	3	2	73	8.1
89-90—New York	10	236	74	31	.419	10	8	.800	7	5	12	14	14	0	5	2	76	7.6
Totals	56	1707	760	391	.514	227	207	.912	49	125	174	125	114	1	35	26	1002	17.9

Three-Point Field Goals: 1982-83, 0-for-4. 1983-84, 2-for-5 (.400). 1984-85, 1-for-7 (.143). 1985-86, 0-for-2. 1986-87, 1-for-4 (.250). 1987-88, 0-for-5. 1988-89, 3-for-8 (.375). 1989-90, 6-for-13 (.462). Totals, 13-for-48 (.271).

NBA ALL-STAR GAME RECORD

Season—Team	Min.	FGA	FGM	Pct.	FTA	FTM	Pct.	—Rebounds— Off.	Def.	Tot.	Ast.	PF	Dq.	Stl.	Blk.	Pts.
1983—Denver	14	4	3	.750	2	1	.500	0	3	3	1	0	0	1	0	7
1984—Denver	26	13	7	.538	0	0	.000	1	2	3	1	2	0	0	0	14
Totals	40	17	10	.588	2	1	.500	1	5	6	2	2	0	1	0	21

Led NBA in three-point field goal percentage, 1987. . . . Son of former NBA forward-guard Ernie Vandeweghe and nephew of former NBA forward-center Mel Hutchins.

—DID YOU KNOW—

That Michael Jordan would have to be shut out in his next 13 postseason games to relinquish his spot as the player with the highest scoring average (35.8) in NBA playoff history?

JAMES SAMUEL VINCENT
(Sam)

Born May 18, 1963 at Lansing, Mich. Height 6:02. Weight 185.
High School—Lansing, Mich., Eastern.
College—Michigan State University, Lansing, Mich.
Drafted by Boston on first round, 1985 (20th pick).

Traded by Boston with Scott Wedman to Seattle for a 1989 2nd round draft choice, October 16, 1987.
Traded by Seattle to Chicago for Sedale Threatt, February 25, 1988.
Selected from Chicago by Orlando in NBA expansion draft, June 15, 1989.

—COLLEGIATE RECORD—

Year	G.	Min.	FGA	FGM	Pct.	FTA	FTM	Pct.	Reb.	Pts.	Avg.
81-82	28	965	282	130	.461	91	68	.747	78	328	11.7
82-83	30	1066	401	180	.449	172	133	.773	79	498	16.6
83-84	23	740	261	130	.498	122	99	.811	62	359	15.6
84-85	29	1093	450	245	.544	208	176	.846	112	666	23.0
Totals	110	3864	1394	685	.491	593	476	.803	331	1851	16.8

Three-Point Field Goals: 1982-83, 5-for-11 (.455).

NBA REGULAR SEASON RECORD

									—Rebounds—									
Sea.—Team	G.	Min.	FGA	FGM	Pct.	FTA	FTM	Pct.	Off.	Def.	Tot.	Ast.	PF	Dq.	Stl.	Blk.	Pts.	Avg.
85-86—Boston	57	432	162	59	.364	70	65	.929	11	37	48	69	59	0	17	4	184	3.2
86-87—Boston	46	374	136	60	.441	55	51	.927	5	22	27	59	33	0	13	1	171	3.7
87-88—Sea.-Chi.	72	1501	461	210	.456	167	145	.868	35	117	152	381	145	0	55	16	573	8.0
88-89—Chicago	70	1703	566	274	.484	129	106	.822	34	156	190	335	124	0	53	10	656	9.4
89-90—Orlando	63	1657	564	258	.457	214	188	.879	37	157	194	354	108	1	65	20	705	11.2
Totals	308	5667	1889	861	.456	635	555	.874	122	489	611	1198	469	1	203	51	2289	7.4

Three-Point Field Goals: 1985-86, 1-for-4 (.250). 1987-88, 8-for-21 (.381). 1988-89, 2-for-17 (.118). 1989-90, 1-for-14 (.071). Totals, 12-for-56 (.214).

NBA PLAYOFF RECORD

									—Rebounds—									
Sea.—Team	G.	Min.	FGA	FGM	Pct.	FTA	FTM	Pct.	Off.	Def.	Tot.	Ast.	PF	Dq.	Stl.	Blk.	Pts.	Avg.
85-86—Boston	9	41	28	8	.286	6	6	1.000	1	6	7	5	9	0	2	0	22	2.4
86-87—Boston	17	141	56	23	.411	35	27	.771	3	9	12	19	13	0	3	2	74	4.4
87-88—Chicago	10	251	110	41	.373	25	20	.800	6	13	19	44	23	0	8	1	102	10.2
88-89—Chicago	16	113	33	10	.303	12	9	.750	4	4	8	19	9	0	3	1	29	1.8
Totals	52	546	227	82	.361	78	62	.795	14	32	46	87	54	0	16	4	227	4.4

Three-Point Field Goals: 1985-86, 0-for-1. 1986-87, 1-for-2 (.500). 1987-88, 0-for-3. 1988-89, 0-for-2. Totals, 1-for-8 (.125).

Member of NBA championship team, 1986. . . . Named to THE SPORTING NEWS All-America First Team, 1985. . . . Brother of Los Angeles Lakers forward Jay Vincent.

JAY FLETCHER VINCENT

Born June 10, 1959 at Kalamazoo, Mich. Height 6:07. Weight 220.
High School—Lansing, Mich., Eastern.
College—Michigan State University, East Lansing, Mich.
Drafted by Dallas on second round, 1981 (24th pick).

Traded by Dallas to Washington for a 1990 1st round draft choice, September 3, 1986.
Traded by Washington with Michael Adams to Denver for Mark Alarie and Darrell Walker, November 2, 1987.
Traded by Denver with Calvin Natt to San Antonio for David Greenwood and Darwin Cook, January 26, 1989.
Traded by San Antonio with Johnny Dawkins to Philadelphia for Maurice Cheeks, Christian Welp and David Wingate, August 28, 1989.
Waived by Philadelphia, December 14, 1989; signed by Los Angeles Lakers as a free agent, December 24, 1989.

—COLLEGIATE RECORD—

Year	G.	Min.	FGA	FGM	Pct.	FTA	FTM	Pct.	Reb.	Pts.	Avg.
77-78	29	....	239	137	.573	86	55	.640	110	329	11.3
78-79	31	939	343	170	.496	93	54	.581	161	394	12.7
79-80	27	965	451	233	.517	161	116	.720	209	582	21.6
80-81	27	1001	522	259	.496	141	91	.645	229	609	22.6
Totals	114	....	1555	799	.514	481	316	.657	709	1914	16.8

NBA REGULAR SEASON RECORD

									—Rebounds—									
Sea.—Team	G.	Min.	FGA	FGM	Pct.	FTA	FTM	Pct.	Off.	Def.	Tot.	Ast.	PF	Dq.	Stl.	Blk.	Pts.	Avg.
81-82—Dallas	81	2626	1448	719	.497	409	293	.716	182	383	565	176	308	8	89	22	1732	21.4
82-83—Dallas	81	2726	1272	622	.489	343	269	.784	217	375	592	212	295	4	70	45	1513	18.7

Sea.—Team	G.	Min.	FGA	FGM	Pct.	FTA	FTM	Pct.	—Rebounds— Off.	Def.	Tot.	Ast.	PF	Dq.	Stl.	Blk.	Pts.	Avg.
83-84—Dallas	61	1421	579	252	.435	215	168	.781	81	166	247	114	159	1	30	10	672	11.0
84-85—Dallas	79	2543	1138	545	.479	420	351	.836	185	519	704	169	226	0	48	22	1441	18.2
85-86—Dallas	80	1994	919	442	.481	274	222	.810	107	261	368	180	193	2	66	21	1106	13.8
86-87—Washington	51	1386	613	274	.447	169	130	.769	69	141	210	85	127	0	40	17	678	13.3
87-88—Denver	73	1755	958	446	.466	287	231	.805	80	229	309	143	198	1	46	26	1124	15.4
88-89—Den.-S.A.	29	646	257	104	.405	60	40	.667	38	72	110	27	63	0	6	4	249	8.6
89-90—Phil.-L.A.L.	41	459	183	86	.470	49	41	.837	20	42	62	18	52	0	18	5	214	5.2
Totals	576	15556	7367	3490	.474	2226	1745	.784	979	2188	3167	1124	1621	16	413	171	8729	15.2

Three-Point Field Goals: 1981-82, 1-for-4 (.250). 1982-83, 0-for-3. 1983-84, 0-for-1. 1984-85, 0-for-4. 1985-86, 0-for-3. 1986-87, 0-for-3. 1987-88, 1-for-4 (.250). 1988-89, 1-for-3 (.333). 1989-90, 1-for-2 (.500). Totals, 4-for-27 (.148).

NBA PLAYOFF RECORD

Sea.—Team	G.	Min.	FGA	FGM	Pct.	FTA	FTM	Pct.	—Rebounds— Off.	Def.	Tot.	Ast.	PF	Dq.	Stl.	Blk.	Pts.	Avg.
83-84—Dallas	10	353	124	48	.387	62	56	.903	29	41	70	19	36	1	7	1	152	15.2
84-85—Dallas	4	134	56	20	.357	29	22	.759	9	13	22	3	16	0	6	3	62	15.5
85-86—Dallas	10	204	99	38	.384	34	30	.882	15	24	39	15	19	0	4	1	106	10.6
86-87—Washington	3	72	30	11	.367	9	8	.889	2	7	9	3	10	0	2	0	30	10.0
87-88—Denver	8	200	104	53	.510	40	34	.850	10	27	37	6	25	0	5	4	140	17.5
89-90—L.A. Lakers	3	8	2	0	.000	0	0	....	0	0	0	0	1	0	0	0	0	0.0
Totals	38	971	415	170	.410	174	150	.862	65	112	177	46	107	1	24	9	490	12.9

Three-Point Field Goals: 1983-84, 0-for-1. 1987-88, 0-for-1. Totals, 0-for-2.

Named to NBA All-Rookie Team, 1982.... Member of NCAA Division I championship team, 1979.... Brother of Orlando Magic guard Sam Vincent.

GARY ANTHONY VOCE

Born November 24, 1965 in Jamaica. Height 6:09. Weight 250.

High School—Bronx, N.Y., Tolentine.

College—University of Notre Dame, Notre Dame, Ind.

Never drafted by an NBA franchise.

Signed by Cleveland as a free agent, October 5, 1989.
Waived by Cleveland, November 15, 1989.
Played in Continental Basketball Association with Rapid City Thrillers and Tulsa Fast Breakers (playoffs only), 1988-89.

—COLLEGIATE RECORD—

Year	G.	Min.	FGA	FGM	Pct.	FTA	FTM	Pct.	Reb.	Pts.	Avg.
84-85	27	185	41	25	.610	19	10	.526	64	60	2.2
85-86	22	188	44	24	.545	24	15	.625	57	63	2.9
86-87	32	903	103	54	.524	57	43	.754	200	151	4.7
87-88	27	877	216	118	.546	98	79	.806	210	315	11.7
Totals	108	2153	404	221	.547	198	147	.742	531	589	5.5

Three-Point Field Goals: 1987-88, 0-for-1.

CBA REGULAR SEASON RECORD

Sea.—Team	G.	Min.	—2-Point— FGM	FGA	Pct.	—3-Point— FGM	FGA	Pct.	FTM	FTA	Pct.	Reb.	Ast.	Pts.	Avg.
88-89—Rapid City	3	10	0	4	.000	0	0	.000	2	2	1.000	2	0	2	0.7

NBA REGULAR SEASON RECORD

Sea.—Team	G.	Min.	FGA	FGM	Pct.	FTA	FTM	Pct.	—Rebounds— Off.	Def.	Tot.	Ast.	PF	Dq.	Stl.	Blk.	Pts.	Avg.
89-90—Cleveland	1	4	3	1	.333	0	0	....	2	0	2	0	0	0	0	0	2	2.0

ALEXANDER VOLKOV

Born March 29, 1964 at Omsk, Soviet Union. Height 6:10. Weight 218.

Drafted by Atlanta on sixth round, 1986 (134th pick).

NBA REGULAR SEASON RECORD

Sea.—Team	G.	Min.	FGA	FGM	Pct.	FTA	FTM	Pct.	—Rebounds— Off.	Def.	Tot.	Ast.	PF	Dq.	Stl.	Blk.	Pts.	Avg.
89-90—Atlanta	72	937	284	137	.482	120	70	.583	52	67	119	83	166	3	36	22	357	5.0

Three-Point Field Goals: 1989-90, 13-for-34 (.382).

MARK A. WADE

Born October 15, 1965 at Torrance, Calif. Height 5:11. Weight 160.

High School—Los Angeles, Calif., Banning.

Colleges—University of Oklahoma, Norman, Okla.; El Camino College, Torrance, Calif., and University of Nevada at Las Vegas, Las Vegas, Nev.

Never drafted by an NBA franchise.

Signed by Golden State, March 30, 1988, to the first of consecutive 10-day contracts that expired, April 18, 1988.
Re-signed by Golden State, April 20, 1988, for remainder of season.
Signed by Dallas, April 9, 1990, to a 10-day contract that expired, April 18, 1990.
Played in Continental Basketball Association with Quad City Thunder and Pensacola Tornados, 1987-88, and Pensacola Tornados, 1988-89 and 1989-90.

—COLLEGIATE RECORD—

Year	G.	Min.	FGA	FGM	Pct.	FTA	FTM	Pct.	Reb.	Pts.	Avg.
Oklahoma											
83-84	6	45	8	3	.375	7	6	.857	5	12	2.0
El Camino											
84-85	35	....	154	85	.552	78	56	.718	82	226	6.5
Nevada-Las Vegas											
85-86	38	1054	65	28	.431	73	50	.685	81	106	2.8
86-87	38	1169	142	60	.423	49	38	.776	103	180	4.7
UNLV Totals	76	2223	207	88	.425	122	88	.721	184	286	3.8
College Totals	82	2268	215	91	.423	129	94	.729	189	298	3.6

Three-Point Field Goals: 1985-86, 0-for-5. 1986-87, 22-for-60 (.367). Totals, 22-for-65 (.338).

CBA REGULAR SEASON RECORD

			2-Point			3-Point									
Sea.—Team	G.	Min.	FGM	FGA	Pct.	FGM	FGA	Pct.	FTM	FTA	Pct.	Reb.	Ast.	Pts.	Avg.
87-88—Quad City-Pen.	37	1459	62	168	.369	33	80	.413	54	73	.740	127	417	277	7.5
88-89—Pensacola	54	2515	139	307	.453	85	248	.343	125	181	.691	193	626	658	12.2
89-90—Pensacola	56	2493	187	441	.424	92	232	.397	110	151	.728	202	613	760	13.6
Totals	147	6467	388	916	.424	210	560	.375	289	405	.714	522	1656	1695	11.5

NBA REGULAR SEASON RECORD

									—Rebounds—									
Sea.—Team	G.	Min.	FGA	FGM	Pct.	FTA	FTM	Pct.	Off.	Def.	Tot.	Ast.	PF	Dq.	Stl.	Blk.	Pts.	Avg.
87-88—Golden State	11	123	20	3	.150	4	2	.500	3	12	15	34	13	0	7	1	8	0.7
89-90—Dallas	1	3	0	0	....	0	0	....	0	0	0	2	0	0	0	0	0	0.0
Totals	12	126	20	3	.150	4	2	.500	3	12	15	36	13	0	7	1	8	0.7

Three-Point Field Goals: 1987-88, 0-for-2.

DARRELL WALKER

Born March 9, 1961 at Chicago, Ill. Height 6:04. Weight 180.

High School—Chicago, Ill., Corliss.

Colleges—Westark Community College, Fort Smith, Ark., and University of Arkansas, Fayetteville, Ark.

Drafted by New York on first round, 1983 (12th pick).

Traded by New York to Denver for a 1987 1st round draft choice, October 2, 1986.
Traded by Denver with Mark Alarie to Washington for Michael Adams and Jay Vincent, November 2, 1987.

—COLLEGIATE RECORD—

Year	G.	Min.	FGA	FGM	Pct.	FTA	FTM	Pct.	Reb.	Pts.	Avg.
Westark CC											
79-80	37	1332	472	255	.540	178	117	.657	259	627	16.9
Arkansas											
80-81	31	926	269	137	.509	125	75	.600	139	349	11.3
81-82	29	1039	316	162	.513	161	106	.658	152	430	14.8
82-83	30	1105	374	197	.527	238	152	.639	172	546	18.2
Totals	90	3070	959	496	.517	524	333	.635	463	1325	14.7

NBA REGULAR SEASON RECORD

									—Rebounds—									
Sea.—Team	G.	Min.	FGA	FGM	Pct.	FTA	FTM	Pct.	Off.	Def.	Tot.	Ast.	PF	Dq.	Stl.	Blk.	Pts.	Avg.
83-84—New York	82	1324	518	216	.417	263	208	.791	74	93	167	284	202	1	127	15	644	7.9
84-85—New York	82	2489	989	430	.435	347	243	.700	128	150	278	408	244	2	167	21	1103	13.5
85-86—New York	81	2023	753	324	.430	277	190	.686	100	120	220	337	216	1	146	36	838	10.3
86-87—Denver	81	2020	742	358	.482	365	272	.745	157	170	327	282	229	0	120	37	988	12.2
87-88—Washington	52	940	291	114	.392	105	82	.781	43	84	127	100	105	2	62	10	310	6.0
88-89—Washington	79	2565	681	286	.420	184	142	.772	135	372	507	496	215	2	155	23	714	9.0
89-90—Washington	81	2883	696	316	.454	201	138	.687	173	541	714	652	220	1	139	30	772	9.5
Totals	538	14244	4670	2044	.438	1742	1275	.732	810	1530	2340	2559	1431	9	916	172	5369	10.0

Three-Point Field Goals: 1983-84, 4-for-15 (.267). 1984-85, 0-for-17. 1985-86, 0-for-10. 1986-87, 0-for-4. 1987-88, 0-for-6. 1988-89, 0-for-9. 1989-90, 2-for-21 (.095). Totals, 6-for-82 (.073).

NBA PLAYOFF RECORD

Sea.—Team	G.	Min.	FGA	FGM	Pct.	FTA	FTM	Pct.	—Rebounds— Off.	Def.	Tot.	Ast.	PF	Dq.	Stl.	Blk.	Pts.	Avg.
83-84—New York	12	195	73	27	.370	46	28	.609	20	15	35	20	29	0	24	2	82	6.8
86-87—Denver	3	68	34	11	.324	7	4	.571	3	7	10	5	4	0	2	0	26	8.7
87-88—Washington	5	155	54	22	.407	16	11	.688	9	15	24	14	18	0	7	4	55	11.0
Totals	20	418	161	60	.373	69	43	.623	32	37	69	39	51	0	33	6	163	8.2

Three-Point Field Goals: 1987-88, 0-for-1.

Named to NBA All-Rookie Team, 1984.

KENNETH WALKER
(Kenny)

Born August 18, 1964 at Roberta, Ga. Height 6:08. Weight 217.

High School—Roberta, Ga., Crawford County.

College—University of Kentucky, Lexington, Ky.

Drafted by New York on first round, 1986 (5th pick).

—COLLEGIATE RECORD—

Year	G.	Min.	FGA	FGM	Pct.	FTA	FTM	Pct.	Reb.	Pts.	Avg.
82-83	31	599	144	88	.611	77	51	.662	151	227	7.3
83-84	34	1087	308	171	.555	109	80	.734	200	422	12.4
84-85	31	1139	440	246	.559	284	218	.768	315	710	22.9
85-86	36	1254	447	260	.582	263	201	.764	276	721	20.0
Totals	132	4079	1339	765	.571	733	550	.750	942	2080	15.8

NBA REGULAR SEASON RECORD

Sea.—Team	G.	Min.	FGA	FGM	Pct.	FTA	FTM	Pct.	—Rebounds— Off.	Def.	Tot.	Ast.	PF	Dq.	Stl.	Blk.	Pts.	Avg.
86-87—New York	68	1719	581	285	.491	185	140	.757	118	220	338	75	236	7	49	49	710	10.4
87-88—New York	82	2139	728	344	.473	178	138	.775	192	197	389	86	290	5	63	59	826	10.1
88-89—New York	79	1163	356	174	.489	85	66	.776	101	129	230	36	190	1	41	45	419	5.3
89-90—New York	68	1595	384	204	.531	173	125	.723	131	212	343	49	178	1	33	52	535	7.9
Totals	297	6616	2049	1007	.491	621	469	.755	542	758	1300	246	894	14	186	205	2490	8.4

Three-Point Field Goals: 1986-87, 0-for-4. 1987-88, 0-for-1. 1988-89, 5-for-20 (.250). 1989-90, 2-for-5 (.400). Totals, 7-for-30 (.233).

NBA PLAYOFF RECORD

Sea.—Team	G.	Min.	FGA	FGM	Pct.	FTA	FTM	Pct.	—Rebounds— Off.	Def.	Tot.	Ast.	PF	Dq.	Stl.	Blk.	Pts.	Avg.
87-88—New York	4	80	24	8	.333	2	2	1.000	3	6	9	5	11	0	2	3	18	4.5
88-89—New York	9	90	13	3	.231	19	14	.737	5	11	16	2	22	0	1	3	20	2.2
89-90—New York	10	154	29	16	.552	14	9	.643	7	18	25	6	22	0	0	4	41	4.1
Totals	23	324	66	27	.409	35	25	.714	15	35	50	13	55	0	3	10	79	3.4

Three-Point Field Goals: 1989-90, 0-for-1.

Named to THE SPORTING NEWS All-America Second Team, 1986.

ANTHONY JEROME WEBB
(Spud)

Born July 13, 1963 at Dallas, Tex. Height 5:07. Weight 135.

High School—Dallas, Tex., Wilmer-Hutchins.

Colleges—Midland College, Midland, Tex., and North Carolina State University, Raleigh, N.C.

Drafted by Detroit on fourth round, 1985 (87th pick).

Draft rights relinquished by Detroit, September 24, 1985; signed by Atlanta as a free agent, September 26, 1985.

—COLLEGIATE RECORD—

Midland

Year	G.	Min.	FGA	FGM	Pct.	FTA	FTM	Pct.	Reb.	Pts.	Avg.
81-82	38	....	538	277	.515	301	235	.781	77	789	20.8
82-83	35	....	440	196	.445	155	120	.774	106	512	14.6
J.C. Totals	73	....	978	473	.484	456	355	.779	183	1301	17.8

North Carolina State

Year	G.	Min.	FGA	FGM	Pct.	FTA	FTM	Pct.	Reb.	Pts.	Avg.
83-84	33	980	279	128	.459	88	67	.761	59	323	9.8
84-85	33	919	291	140	.481	113	86	.761	66	366	11.1
N.C. St. Totals	66	1899	570	268	.470	201	153	.761	125	689	10.4

NBA REGULAR SEASON RECORD

									—Rebounds—									
Sea.—Team	G.	Min.	FGA	FGM	Pct.	FTA	FTM	Pct.	Off.	Def.	Tot.	Ast.	PF	Dq.	Stl.	Blk.	Pts.	Avg.
85-86—Atlanta	79	1229	412	199	.483	275	216	.785	27	96	123	337	164	1	82	5	616	7.8
86-87—Atlanta	33	532	162	71	.438	105	80	.762	6	54	60	167	65	1	34	2	223	6.8
87-88—Atlanta	82	1347	402	191	.475	131	107	.817	16	130	146	337	125	0	63	11	490	6.0
88-89—Atlanta	81	1219	290	133	.459	60	52	.867	21	102	123	284	104	0	70	6	319	3.9
89-90—Atlanta	82	2184	616	294	.477	186	162	.871	38	163	201	477	185	0	105	12	751	9.2
Totals	357	6511	1882	888	.472	757	617	.815	108	545	653	1602	643	2	354	36	2399	6.7

Three-Point Field Goals: 1985-86, 2-for-11 (.182). 1986-87, 1-for-6 (.167). 1987-88, 1-for-19 (.053). 1988-89, 1-for-22 (.045). 1989-90, 1-for-19 (.053). Totals, 6-for-77 (.078).

NBA PLAYOFF RECORD

									—Rebounds—									
Sea.—Team	G.	Min.	FGA	FGM	Pct.	FTA	FTM	Pct.	Off.	Def.	Tot.	Ast.	PF	Dq.	Stl.	Blk.	Pts.	Avg.
85-86—Atlanta	9	183	81	42	.519	33	26	.788	6	25	31	65	13	0	4	1	110	12.2
86-87—Atlanta	8	122	19	9	.474	17	13	.765	1	7	8	38	10	0	6	0	31	3.9
87-88—Atlanta	12	211	81	35	.432	37	34	.919	4	16	20	56	22	0	9	0	106	8.8
88-89—Atlanta	5	55	11	3	.273	2	2	1.000	0	4	4	15	6	0	4	0	8	1.6
Totals	34	571	192	89	.464	89	75	.843	11	52	63	174	51	0	23	1	255	7.5

Three-Point Field Goals: 1985-86, 0-for-2. 1986-87, 0-for-1. 1987-88, 2-for-8 (.250). Totals, 2-for-11 (.182).

CHRISTIAN ANSGAR WELP
(Chris)

Born January 2, 1964 at Delmenhorst, West Germany. Height 7:00. Weight 245.

High School—Silverdale, Wash., Olympia.

College—University of Washington, Seattle, Wash.

Drafted by Philadelphia on first round, 1987 (16th pick).

Traded by Philadelphia with Maurice Cheeks and David Wingate to San Antonio for Johnny Dawkins and Jay Vincent, August 28, 1989.

Traded by San Antonio to Golden State for Uwe Blab, February 22, 1990.

—COLLEGIATE RECORD—

Year	G.	Min.	FGA	FGM	Pct.	FTA	FTM	Pct.	Reb.	Pts.	Avg.
83-84	31	947	237	135	.570	89	58	.652	192	328	10.6
84-85	32	971	294	170	.578	108	75	.694	225	415	13.0
85-86	31	1053	436	234	.537	177	133	.751	263	601	19.4
86-87	35	1143	473	281	.594	226	167	.739	315	729	20.8
Totals	129	4114	1440	820	.569	600	433	.722	995	2073	16.1

NBA REGULAR SEASON RECORD

									—Rebounds—									
Sea.—Team	G.	Min.	FGA	FGM	Pct.	FTA	FTM	Pct.	Off.	Def.	Tot.	Ast.	PF	Dq.	Stl.	Blk.	Pts.	Avg.
87-88—Philadelphia	10	132	31	18	.581	18	12	.667	11	13	24	5	25	0	5	5	48	4.8
88-89—Philadelphia	72	843	222	99	.446	73	48	.658	59	134	193	29	176	0	23	41	246	3.4
89-90—S.A.-G.S.	27	198	61	23	.377	25	19	.760	18	30	48	9	58	0	6	8	65	2.4
Totals	109	1173	314	140	.446	116	79	.681	88	177	265	43	259	0	34	54	359	3.3

Three-Point Field Goals: 1988-89, 0-for-1.

NBA PLAYOFF RECORD

									—Rebounds—									
Sea.—Team	G.	Min.	FGA	FGM	Pct.	FTA	FTM	Pct.	Off.	Def.	Tot.	Ast.	PF	Dq.	Stl.	Blk.	Pts.	Avg.
88-89—Philadelphia	3	22	3	1	.333	2	0	.000	0	7	7	0	7	0	0	0	2	0.7

Member of West German Olympic team, 1984.

WILLIAM PERCEY WENNINGTON
(Bill)

Born April 26, 1963 at Montreal, Can. Height 7:00. Weight 245.

High School—Brookville, N.Y., Long Island Lutheran.

College—St. John's University, Jamaica, N.Y.

Drafted by Dallas on first round, 1985 (16th pick).

Traded by Dallas with two 1990 1st round draft choices to Sacramento for Rodney McCray and 1990 and 1991 2nd round draft choices, June 26, 1990.

—COLLEGIATE RECORD—

Year	G.	Min.	FGA	FGM	Pct.	FTA	FTM	Pct.	Reb.	Pts.	Avg.
81-82	30	505	85	37	.435	34	23	.676	126	97	3.2
82-83	33	656	114	69	.605	63	44	.698	146	182	5.5

Year	G.	Min.	FGA	FGM	Pct.	FTA	FTM	Pct.	Reb.	Pts.	Avg.
83-84	26	735	209	124	.593	83	56	.675	148	304	11.7
84-85	35	1099	279	168	.602	125	102	.816	224	438	12.5
Totals	124	2995	687	398	.579	305	225	.738	644	1021	8.2

NBA REGULAR SEASON RECORD

									—Rebounds—									
Sea.—Team	G.	Min.	FGA	FGM	Pct.	FTA	FTM	Pct.	Off.	Def.	Tot.	Ast.	PF	Dq.	Stl.	Blk.	Pts.	Avg.
85-86—Dallas	56	562	153	72	.471	62	45	.726	32	100	132	21	83	0	11	22	189	3.4
86-87—Dallas	58	560	132	56	.424	60	45	.750	53	76	129	24	95	0	13	10	157	2.7
87-88—Dallas	30	125	49	25	.510	19	12	.632	14	25	39	4	33	0	5	9	63	2.1
88-89—Dallas	65	1074	275	119	.433	82	61	.744	82	204	286	46	211	3	16	35	300	4.6
89-90—Dallas	60	814	234	105	.449	75	60	.800	64	134	198	41	144	2	20	21	270	4.5
Totals	269	3135	843	377	.447	298	223	.748	245	539	784	136	566	5	65	97	979	3.6

Three-Point Field Goals: 1985-86, 0-for-4. 1986-87, 0-for-2. 1987-88, 1-for-2 (.500). 1988-89, 1-for-9 (.111). 1989-90, 0-for-4. Totals, 2-for-21 (.095).

NBA PLAYOFF RECORD

									—Rebounds—									
Sea.—Team	G.	Min.	FGA	FGM	Pct.	FTA	FTM	Pct.	Off.	Def.	Tot.	Ast.	PF	Dq.	Stl.	Blk.	Pts.	Avg.
85-86—Dallas	6	18	6	2	.333	2	2	1.000	4	1	5	0	4	0	0	0	7	1.2
86-87—Dallas	4	47	12	6	.500	5	3	.600	4	6	10	4	9	0	0	3	15	3.8
87-88—Dallas	6	14	4	0	.000	0	0	.000	3	1	4	1	5	0	1	0	0	0.0
89-90—Dallas	3	25	5	1	.200	0	0	....	0	3	3	1	5	0	0	1	2	0.7
Totals	19	104	27	9	.333	7	5	.714	11	11	22	6	23	0	1	4	24	1.3

Three-Point Field Goals: 1986-87, 1-for-1 (1.000).

Member of Canadian Olympic team, 1984.

JEFFERY DOUGLAS WEST
(Doug)

Born May 27, 1967 at Altoona, Pa. Height 6:07. Weight 205.

High School—Altoona, Pa.

College—Villanova University, Villanova, Pa.

Drafted by Minnesota on second round, 1989 (38th pick).

—COLLEGIATE RECORD—

Year	G.	Min.	FGA	FGM	Pct.	FTA	FTM	Pct.	Reb.	Pts.	Avg.
85-86	37	995	307	158	.515	88	60	.682	136	376	10.2
86-87	31	1022	376	180	.479	129	94	.729	151	470	15.2
87-88	37	1281	433	215	.497	127	92	.724	181	583	15.8
88-89	33	1137	488	226	.463	125	90	.720	162	608	18.4
Totals	138	4435	1604	779	.486	469	336	.716	630	2037	14.8

Three-Point Field Goals: 1986-87, 16-for-43 (.372). 1987-88, 61-for-143 (.427). 1988-89, 66-for-177 (.373). Totals, 143-for-363 (.394).

NBA REGULAR SEASON RECORD

									—Rebounds—									
Sea.—Team	G.	Min.	FGA	FGM	Pct.	FTA	FTM	Pct.	Off.	Def.	Tot.	Ast.	PF	Dq.	Stl.	Blk.	Pts.	Avg.
89-90—Minnesota	52	378	135	53	.393	32	26	.813	24	46	70	18	61	0	10	6	135	2.6

Three-Point Field Goals: 1989-90, 3-for-11 (.273).

MARK ANDRE WEST

Born November 5, 1960 at Fort Campbell, Ky. Height 6:10. Weight 246.

High School—Petersburg, Va.

College—Old Dominion University, Norfolk, Va.

Drafted by Dallas on second round, 1983 (30th pick).

Waived by Dallas, October 23, 1984; signed by Milwaukee as a free agent, November 6, 1984.

Waived by Milwaukee, November 12, 1984; signed by Cleveland as a free agent, November 23, 1984.

Traded by Cleveland with Tyrone Corbin, Kevin Johnson, 1988 1st and 2nd round draft choices and a 1989 2nd round draft choice to Phoenix for Larry Nance, Mike Sanders and a 1988 1st round draft choice, February 25, 1988.

—COLLEGIATE RECORD—

Year	G.	Min.	FGA	FGM	Pct.	FTA	FTM	Pct.	Reb.	Pts.	Avg.
79-80	30	679	141	67	.475	27	10	.370	212	144	4.8
80-81	28	845	243	128	.527	83	48	.578	287	304	10.9
81-82	30	1007	323	197	.610	147	78	.531	300	472	15.7
82-83	29	1005	297	169	.569	163	80	.491	314	418	14.4
Totals	117	3536	1004	561	.559	420	216	.514	1113	1338	11.4

NBA REGULAR SEASON RECORD

Sea.—Team	G.	Min.	FGA	FGM	Pct.	FTA	FTM	Pct.	—Rebounds— Off.	Def.	Tot.	Ast.	PF	Dq.	Stl.	Blk.	Pts.	Avg.
83-84—Dallas	34	202	42	15	.357	22	7	.318	19	27	46	13	55	0	1	15	37	1.1
84-85—Mil.-Clev.	66	888	194	106	.546	87	43	.494	90	161	251	15	197	7	13	49	255	3.9
85-86—Cleveland	67	1172	209	113	.541	103	54	.524	97	225	322	20	235	6	27	62	280	4.2
86-87—Cleveland	78	1333	385	209	.543	173	89	.514	126	213	339	41	229	5	22	81	507	6.5
87-88—Clev.-Phoe.	83	2098	573	316	.551	285	170	.596	165	358	523	74	265	4	47	147	802	9.7
88-89—Phoenix	82	2019	372	243	.653	202	108	.535	167	384	551	39	273	4	35	187	594	7.2
89-90—Phoenix	82	2399	530	331	.625	288	199	.691	212	516	728	45	277	5	36	184	861	10.5
Totals	492	10111	2305	1333	.578	1160	670	.578	876	1884	2760	247	1531	31	181	725	3336	6.8

Three-Point Field Goals: 1984-85, 0-for-1. 1986-87, 0-for-2. 1987-88, 0-for-1. Totals, 0-for-4.

NBA PLAYOFF RECORD

Sea.—Team	G.	Min.	FGA	FGM	Pct.	FTA	FTM	Pct.	—Rebounds— Off.	Def.	Tot.	Ast.	PF	Dq.	Stl.	Blk.	Pts.	Avg.
83-84—Dallas	4	32	9	5	.556	3	2	.667	0	7	7	3	11	1	0	3	12	3.0
84-85—Cleveland	4	68	5	3	.600	5	2	.400	5	13	18	4	19	0	2	0	8	2.0
88-89—Phoenix	12	227	50	32	.640	14	10	.714	21	32	53	6	36	1	7	19	74	6.2
89-90—Phoenix	16	544	130	75	.577	50	27	.540	53	111	164	5	73	3	4	41	177	11.1
Totals	36	871	194	115	.593	72	41	.569	79	163	242	18	139	5	13	63	271	7.5

Led NBA in field-goal percentage, 1990. . . . Led NCAA Division I in blocked shots, 1981 and 1982.

RANDY WHITE

Born November 4, 1967 at Shreveport, La. Height 6:08. Weight 255.

High School—Shreveport, La., Huntington.

College—Louisiana Tech University, Ruston, La.

Drafted by Dallas on first round, 1989 (8th pick).

—COLLEGIATE RECORD—

Year	G.	Min.	FGA	FGM	Pct.	FTA	FTM	Pct.	Reb.	Pts.	Avg.
85-86	34	697	221	115	.520	123	82	.667	156	312	9.2
86-87	30	782	252	145	.575	130	88	.677	196	379	12.6
87-88	31	1009	354	226	.638	189	121	.640	359	578	18.6
88-89	32	1026	408	245	.600	229	171	.747	337	678	21.2
Totals	127	3514	1235	731	.592	671	462	.689	1048	1947	15.3

Three-Point Field Goals: 1986-87, 1-for-1 (1.000). 1987-88, 5-for-15 (.333). 1988-89, 17-for-38 (.447). Totals, 23-for-54 (.426).

NBA REGULAR SEASON RECORD

Sea.—Team	G.	Min.	FGA	FGM	Pct.	FTA	FTM	Pct.	—Rebounds— Off.	Def.	Tot.	Ast.	PF	Dq.	Stl.	Blk.	Pts.	Avg.
89-90—Dallas	55	707	252	93	.369	89	50	.562	78	95	173	21	124	0	24	6	237	4.3

Three-Point Field Goals: 1989-90, 1-for-14 (.071).

NBA PLAYOFF RECORD

Sea.—Team	G.	Min.	FGA	FGM	Pct.	FTA	FTM	Pct.	—Rebounds— Off.	Def.	Tot.	Ast.	PF	Dq.	Stl.	Blk.	Pts.	Avg.
89-90—Dallas	1	2	0	0	....	0	0	....	0	0	0	0	0	0	0	0	0	0.0

MITCHELL WIGGINS

Born September 28, 1959 at Lenoir County, N.C. Height 6:04. Weight 185.

High School—La Grange, N.C., North Lenoir.

Colleges—Truett-McConnell College, Cleveland, Ga.; Clemson University, Clemson, S.C., and Florida State University, Tallahassee, Fla.

Drafted by Indiana on first round, 1983 (23rd pick).

Draft rights traded by Indiana to Chicago for draft rights to Sidney Lowe and a 1984 2nd round draft choice, June 28, 1983.

Traded by Chicago with 1985 2nd and 3rd round draft choices to Houston for Caldwell Jones, August 10, 1984.

Disqualified from the NBA under rules of the league's Anti-Drug Program, January 13, 1987; reinstated by the NBA, July 27, 1989.

Played in Continental Basketball Association with Mississippi Jets, 1986-87, and Quad City Thunder, 1987-88.

—COLLEGIATE RECORD—

Truett-McConnell

Year	G.	Min.	FGA	FGM	Pct.	FTA	FTM	Pct.	Reb.	Pts.	Avg.
78-79											25.2

Clemson

Year	G.	Min.	FGA	FGM	Pct.	FTA	FTM	Pct.	Reb.	Pts.	Avg.
79-80	32	537	162	76	.469	45	25	.556	96	177	5.5

Florida State

Year	G.	Min.	FGA	FGM	Pct.	FTA	FTM	Pct.	Reb.	Pts.	Avg.
80-81	Did Not Play—Transfer Student										
81-82	22	808	388	223	.574	102	77	755	213	523	23.8
82-83	24	873	410	216	.527	147	112	.762	196	544	22.7
FSU Totals	46	1681	798	439	.550	249	189	.759	409	1067	23.2
College Totals	78	2218	960	515	.536	294	214	.728	505	1244	15.9

CBA REGULAR SEASON RECORD

Sea.—Team	G.	Min.	2-Point FGM	2-Point FGA	2-Point Pct.	3-Point FGM	3-Point FGA	3-Point Pct.	FTM	FTA	Pct.	Reb.	Ast.	Pts.	Avg.
86-87—Mississippi	6	175	55	128	.430	0	3	.000	16	22	.727	38	24	126	21.0
87-88—Quad City	5	204	53	116	.456	0	3	.000	30	40	.750	41	15	136	27.2
Totals	11	379	108	244	.442	0	6	.000	46	62	.741	79	39	262	23.8

NBA REGULAR SEASON RECORD

Sea.—Team	G.	Min.	FGA	FGM	Pct.	FTA	FTM	Pct.	Rebounds Off.	Rebounds Def.	Rebounds Tot.	Ast.	PF	Dq.	Stl.	Blk.	Pts.	Avg.
83-84—Chicago	82	2123	890	399	.448	287	213	.742	138	190	328	187	278	8	106	11	1018	12.4
84-85—Houston	82	1575	657	318	.484	131	96	.733	110	125	235	119	195	1	83	13	738	9.0
85-86—Houston	78	1198	489	222	.454	118	86	.729	87	72	159	101	155	1	59	5	531	6.8
86-87—Houston	32	788	350	153	.437	65	49	.754	74	59	133	76	82	1	44	3	355	11.1
89-90—Houston	66	1852	853	416	.488	237	192	.810	133	153	286	104	165	0	85	1	1024	15.5
Totals	340	7536	3239	1508	.466	838	636	.759	542	599	1141	587	875	11	377	33	3666	10.8

Three-Point Field Goals: 1983-84, 7-for-29 (.241). 1984-85, 6-for-23 (.261). 1985-86, 1-for-12 (.083). 1986-87, 0-for-5. 1989-90, 0-for-3. Totals, 14-for-72 (.194).

NBA PLAYOFF RECORD

Sea.—Team	G.	Min.	FGA	FGM	Pct.	FTA	FTM	Pct.	Rebounds Off.	Rebounds Def.	Rebounds Tot.	Ast.	PF	Dq.	Stl.	Blk.	Pts.	Avg.
84-85—Houston	5	45	18	9	.500	0	0	.000	3	1	4	1	6	0	4	0	18	3.6
85-86—Houston	20	443	179	89	.497	28	21	.750	38	38	76	31	44	0	14	3	199	10.0
89-90—Houston	4	51	15	7	.467	3	2	.667	4	9	13	2	5	0	1	0	16	4.0
Totals	29	539	212	105	.495	31	23	.742	45	48	93	34	55	0	19	3	233	8.0

Three-Point Field Goals: 1985-86, 0-for-3.

MORLON DAVID WILEY

Born September 24, 1966 at New Orleans, La. Height 6:04. Weight 185.
High School—Long Beach, Calif., Poly.
College—California State University at Long Beach, Long Beach, Calif.
Drafted by Dallas on second round, 1988 (46th pick).

Selected from Dallas by Orlando in NBA expansion draft, June 15, 1989.

—COLLEGIATE RECORD—

Year	G.	Min.	FGA	FGM	Pct.	FTA	FTM	Pct.	Reb.	Pts.	Avg.
84-85	27	641	152	58	.382	32	24	.750	50	157	5.8
85-86	29	802	299	137	.458	68	54	.794	76	338	11.7
86-87	28	783	324	125	.386	80	64	.800	80	357	12.8
87-88	29	977	425	218	.513	111	85	.766	116	578	19.9
Totals	113	3203	1200	538	.448	291	227	.780	322	1430	12.7

Three-Point Field Goals: 1984-85, 17-for-41 (.415). 1985-86, 10-for-39 (.256). 1986-87, 43-for-109 (.394). 1987-88, 57-for-137 (.416). Totals, 127-for-326 (.390).

NBA REGULAR SEASON RECORD

Sea.—Team	G.	Min.	FGA	FGM	Pct.	FTA	FTM	Pct.	Rebounds Off.	Rebounds Def.	Rebounds Tot.	Ast.	PF	Dq.	Stl.	Blk.	Pts.	Avg.
88-89—Dallas	51	408	114	46	.404	16	13	.813	13	34	47	76	61	0	25	6	111	2.2
89-90—Orlando	40	638	208	92	.442	38	28	.737	13	39	52	114	65	0	45	3	229	5.7
Totals	91	1046	322	138	.429	54	41	.759	26	73	99	190	126	0	70	9	340	3.7

Three-Point Field Goals: 1988-89, 6-for-24 (.250). 1989-90, 17-for-46 (.370). Totals, 23-for-70 (.329).

Brother of Michael Wiley, forward with San Antonio Spurs and San Diego Clippers, 1980-81 and 1981-82.

EDDIE LEE WILKINS

Born May 7, 1962 at Cartersville, Ga. Height 6:10. Weight 220.
High School—Cartersville, Ga., Cass.
College—Gardner-Webb College, Boiling Springs, N. C.
Drafted by New York on sixth round, 1984 (133rd pick).

Missed entire 1985-86 season due to injury.

Played in Continental Basketball Association with Rockford Lightning, 1986-87, and Savannah Spirits and Quad City Thunder, 1987-88.

—COLLEGIATE RECORD—

Year	G.	Min.	FGA	FGM	Pct.	FTA	FTM	Pct.	Reb.	Pts.	Avg.
80-81	36	....	296	166	.561	163	104	.638	242	436	12.1
81-82	29	....	350	217	.620	211	142	.673	257	576	19.9
82-83	32	....	463	295	.637	284	203	.715	340	793	24.8
83-84	29	....	376	214	.569	209	128	.612	264	556	19.2
Totals	126	....	1485	892	.601	867	577	.666	1103	2361	18.7

CBA REGULAR SEASON RECORD

			2-Point			3-Point									
Sea.—Team	G.	Min.	FGM	FGA	Pct.	FGM	FGA	Pct.	FTM	FTA	Pct.	Reb.	Ast.	Pts.	Avg.
86-87—Rockford	4	126	31	48	.646	0	1	.000	7	18	.389	32	3	69	17.3
87-88—Sav.-Quad City	54	1880	484	838	.578	0	4	.000	262	392	.668	498	31	1230	22.8
Totals	58	2006	515	886	.581	0	5	.000	269	410	.656	530	34	1299	22.4

NBA REGULAR SEASON RECORD

									—Rebounds—									
Sea.—Team	G.	Min.	FGA	FGM	Pct.	FTA	FTM	Pct.	Off.	Def.	Tot.	Ast.	PF	Dq.	Stl.	Blk.	Pts.	Avg.
84-85—New York	54	917	233	116	.498	122	66	.541	86	176	262	16	155	3	21	16	298	5.5
86-87—New York	24	454	127	56	.441	58	27	.466	45	62	107	6	67	1	9	2	139	5.8
88-89—New York	71	584	245	114	.465	111	61	.550	72	76	148	7	110	1	10	16	289	4.1
89-90—New York	79	972	310	141	.455	147	89	.605	114	151	265	16	152	1	18	18	371	4.7
Totals	228	2927	915	427	.467	438	243	.555	317	465	782	45	484	6	58	52	1097	4.8

Three-Point Field Goals: 1984-85, 0-for-2. 1986-87, 0-for-1. 1988-89, 0-for-1. 1989-90, 0-for-2. Totals, 0-for-6.

NBA PLAYOFF RECORD

									—Rebounds—									
Sea.—Team	G.	Min.	FGA	FGM	Pct.	FTA	FTM	Pct.	Off.	Def.	Tot.	Ast.	PF	Dq.	Stl.	Blk.	Pts.	Avg.
88-89—New York	7	26	11	5	.455	10	5	.500	5	6	11	0	3	0	0	0	15	2.1
89-90—New York	7	54	18	9	.500	11	6	.545	5	6	11	0	7	0	2	0	24	3.4
Totals	14	80	29	14	.483	21	11	.524	10	12	22	0	10	0	2	0	39	2.8

GERALD BERNARD WILKINS

Born September 11, 1963 at Atlanta, Ga. Height 6:06. Weight 195.

High School—Atlanta, Ga., Mays Academy.

Colleges—Moberly Area Junior College, Moberly, Mo., and University of Tennessee-Chattanooga, Chattanooga, Tenn.

Drafted by New York on second round, 1985 (47th pick).

—COLLEGIATE RECORD—

Moberly

Year	G.	Min.	FGA	FGM	Pct.	FTA	FTM	Pct.	Reb.	Pts.	Avg.
81-82	39	1340	566	312	.551	126	97	.770	229	721	18.5

Tennessee-Chattanooga

Year	G.	Min.	FGA	FGM	Pct.	FTA	FTM	Pct.	Reb.	Pts.	Avg.
82-83	30	....	350	169	.483	62	41	.661	113	379	12.6
83-84	23	737	297	161	.542	105	73	.695	92	398	17.3
84-85	32	1188	532	276	.519	190	120	.632	147	672	21.0
UTC Totals	85	....	1179	606	.514	357	234	.655	352	1449	17.0

Three-Point Field Goals: 1982-83, 0-for-2. 1983-84, 3-for-10 (.300). Totals, 3-for-12 (.250).

NBA REGULAR SEASON RECORD

									—Rebounds—									
Sea.—Team	G.	Min.	FGA	FGM	Pct.	FTA	FTM	Pct.	Off.	Def.	Tot.	Ast.	PF	Dq.	Stl.	Blk.	Pts.	Avg.
85-86—New York	81	2025	934	437	.468	237	132	.557	92	116	208	161	155	0	68	9	1013	12.5
86-87—New York	80	2758	1302	633	.486	335	235	.701	120	174	294	354	165	0	88	18	1527	19.1
87-88—New York	81	2703	1324	591	.446	243	191	.786	106	164	270	326	183	1	90	22	1412	17.4
88-89—New York	81	2414	1025	462	.451	246	186	.756	95	149	244	274	166	1	115	22	1161	14.3
89-90—New York	82	2609	1032	472	.457	259	208	.803	133	238	371	330	188	0	95	21	1191	14.5
Totals	405	12509	5617	2595	.462	1320	952	.721	546	841	1387	1445	857	2	456	92	6304	15.6

Three-Point Field Goals: 1985-86, 7-for-25 (.280). 1986-87, 26-for-74 (.351). 1987-88, 39-for-129 (.302). 1988-89, 51-for-172 (.297). 1989-90, 39-for-125 (.312). Totals, 162-for-525 (.309).

NBA PLAYOFF RECORD

									—Rebounds—									
Sea.—Team	G.	Min.	FGA	FGM	Pct.	FTA	FTM	Pct.	Off.	Def.	Tot.	Ast.	PF	Dq.	Stl.	Blk.	Pts.	Avg.
87-88—New York	4	149	69	33	.478	14	12	.857	1	7	8	19	12	0	4	0	80	20.0
88-89—New York	9	290	131	63	.481	23	18	.783	9	24	33	42	27	1	12	3	145	16.1
89-90—New York	10	319	137	63	.460	22	18	.818	14	22	36	52	23	0	14	1	146	14.6
Totals	23	758	337	159	.472	59	48	.814	24	53	77	113	62	1	30	4	371	16.1

Three-Point Field Goals: 1987-88, 2-for-4 (.500). 1988-89, 1-for-10 (.100). 1989-90, 2-for-8 (.250). Totals, 5-for-22 (.227).

Brother of Atlanta Hawks forward Dominique Wilkins.

JACQUES DOMINIQUE WILKINS

(Known by middle name.)

Born January 12, 1960 at Paris, France. Height 6:08. Weight 200.
High School—Washington, N. C.
College—University of Georgia, Athens, Ga.
Drafted by Utah on first round as an undergraduate, 1982 (3rd pick).

Draft rights traded by Utah to Atlanta for John Drew, Freeman Williams and cash, September 2, 1982.

—COLLEGIATE RECORD—

Year	G.	Min.	FGA	FGM	Pct.	FTA	FTM	Pct.	Reb.	Pts.	Avg.
79-80	16	508	257	135	.525	37	27	.730	104	297	18.6
80-81	31	1157	582	310	.533	149	112	.752	234	732	23.6
81-82	31	1083	526	278	.529	160	103	.644	250	659	21.3
Totals	78	2748	1365	723	.530	346	242	.699	588	1688	21.6

NBA REGULAR SEASON RECORD

									—Rebounds—									
Sea.—Team	G.	Min.	FGA	FGM	Pct.	FTA	FTM	Pct.	Off.	Def.	Tot.	Ast.	PF	Dq.	Stl.	Blk.	Pts.	Avg.
82-83—Atlanta	82	2697	1220	601	.493	337	230	.682	226	252	478	129	210	1	84	63	1434	17.5
83-84—Atlanta	81	2961	1429	684	.479	496	382	.770	254	328	582	126	197	1	117	87	1750	21.6
84-85—Atlanta	81	3023	1891	853	.451	603	486	.806	226	331	557	200	170	0	135	54	2217	27.4
85-86—Atlanta	78	3049	1897	888	.468	705	577	.818	261	357	618	206	170	0	138	49	2366	30.3
86-87—Atlanta	79	2969	1787	828	.463	742	607	.818	210	284	494	261	149	0	117	51	2294	29.0
87-88—Atlanta	78	2948	1957	909	.464	655	541	.826	211	291	502	224	162	0	103	47	2397	30.7
88-89—Atlanta	80	2997	1756	814	.464	524	442	.844	256	297	553	211	138	0	117	52	2099	26.2
89-90—Atlanta	80	2888	1672	810	.484	569	459	.807	217	304	521	200	141	0	126	47	2138	26.7
Totals	639	23532	13609	6387	.469	4631	3724	.804	1861	2444	4305	1557	1337	2	937	450	16695	26.1

Three-Point Field Goals: 1982-83, 2-for-11 (.182). 1983-84, 0-for-11. 1984-85, 25-for-81 (.309). 1985-86, 13-for-70 (.186). 1986-87, 31-for-106 (.292). 1987-88, 38-for-129 (.295). 1988-89, 29-for-105 (.276). 1989-90, 59-for-183 (.322). Totals, 197-for-696 (.283).

NBA PLAYOFF RECORD

									—Rebounds—									
Sea.—Team	G.	Min.	FGA	FGM	Pct.	FTA	FTM	Pct.	Off.	Def.	Tot.	Ast.	PF	Dq.	Stl.	Blk.	Pts.	Avg.
82-83—Atlanta	3	109	42	17	.405	14	12	.887	8	7	15	1	9	0	2	1	47	15.7
83-84—Atlanta	5	197	84	35	.417	31	26	.839	21	20	41	11	13	0	12	1	96	19.2
85-86—Atlanta	9	360	217	94	.433	79	68	.861	20	34	54	25	24	0	9	2	257	28.6
86-87—Atlanta	9	360	210	86	.410	74	66	.892	27	43	70	25	25	0	16	8	241	26.8
87-88—Atlanta	12	473	300	137	.457	125	96	.768	37	40	77	34	24	0	16	6	374	31.2
88-89—Atlanta	5	212	116	52	.448	38	27	.711	10	17	27	17	5	0	4	8	136	27.2
Totals	43	1711	969	421	.434	361	295	.817	123	161	284	113	100	0	59	26	1151	26.8

Three-Point Field Goals: 1982-83, 1-for-1 (1.000). 1983-84, 0-for-1. 1985-86, 1-for-5 (.200). 1986-87, 3-for-10 (.300). 1987-88, 4-for-18 (.222). 1988-89, 5-for-17 (.294). Totals, 14-for-52 (.269).

NBA ALL-STAR GAME RECORD

								—Rebounds—								
Season—Team	Min.	FGA	FGM	Pct.	FTA	FTM	Pct.	Off.	Def.	Tot.	Ast.	PF	Dq.	Stl.	Blk.	Pts.
1986—Atlanta	17	15	6	.400	2	1	.500	2	1	3	2	2	0	0	1	13
1987—Atlanta	24	9	3	.333	7	4	.571	3	2	5	1	2	0	0	1	10
1988—Atlanta	30	22	12	.545	6	5	.833	1	4	5	0	3	0	0	1	29
1989—Atlanta	15	8	3	.375	3	3	1.000	1	1	2	0	0	0	3	0	9
1990—Atlanta	16	10	5	.500	2	2	1.000	0	0	0	4	1	0	1	0	13
Totals	102	64	29	.453	20	15	.750	7	8	15	7	8	0	4	3	74

Three-Point Field Goals: 1990, 1-for-1 (1.000).

Named to All-NBA First Team, 1986. . . . All-NBA Second Team, 1987 and 1988. . . . All-NBA Third Team, 1989. . . . NBA All-Rookie Team, 1983. . . . Led NBA in scoring, 1986. . . . THE SPORTING NEWS All-America Second Team, 1981 and 1982. . . . Brother of New York Knicks forward Gerald Wilkins.

CHARLES LINWOOD WILLIAMS
(Buck)

Born March 8, 1960 at Rocky Mount, N. C. Height 6:08. Weight 225.
High School—Rocky Mount, N. C.
College—University of Maryland, College Park, Md.
Drafted by New Jersey on first round as an undergraduate, 1981 (3rd pick).

Traded by New Jersey to Portland for Sam Bowie and a 1989 1st round draft choice, June 24, 1989.

—COLLEGIATE RECORD—

Year	G.	Min.	FGA	FGM	Pct.	FTA	FTM	Pct.	Reb.	Pts.	Avg.
78-79	30	....	206	120	.583	109	60	.550	323	300	10.0

Year	G.	Min.	FGA	FGM	Pct.	FTA	FTM	Pct.	Reb.	Pts.	Avg.
79-80	24	....	236	143	.606	128	85	.664	242	371	15.5
80-81	31	1080	283	183	.647	182	116	.637	363	482	15.5
Totals	85	....	725	446	.615	419	261	.623	928	1153	13.6

NBA REGULAR SEASON RECORD

									—Rebounds—									
Sea.—Team	G.	Min.	FGA	FGM	Pct.	FTA	FTM	Pct.	Off.	Def.	Tot.	Ast.	PF	Dq.	Stl.	Blk.	Pts.	Avg.
81-82—New Jersey	82	2825	881	513	.582	388	242	.624	347	658	1005	107	285	5	84	84	1268	15.5
82-83—New Jersey	82	2961	912	536	.588	523	324	.620	365	662	1027	125	270	4	91	110	1396	17.0
83-84—New Jersey	81	3003	926	495	.535	498	284	.570	355	645	1000	130	298	3	81	125	1274	15.7
84-85—New Jersey	82	3182	1089	577	.530	538	336	.625	323	682	1005	167	293	7	63	110	1491	18.2
85-86—New Jersey	82	3070	956	500	.523	445	301	.676	329	657	986	131	294	9	73	96	1301	15.9
86-87—New Jersey	82	2976	936	521	.557	588	430	.731	322	701	1023	129	315	8	78	91	1472	18.0
87-88—New Jersey	70	2637	832	466	.560	518	346	.668	298	536	834	109	266	5	68	44	1279	18.3
88-89—New Jersey	74	2446	702	373	.531	320	213	.666	249	447	696	78	223	0	61	36	959	13.0
89-90—Portland	82	2801	754	413	.548	408	288	.706	250	550	800	116	285	4	69	39	1114	13.6
Totals	717	25901	7988	4394	.550	4226	2764	.654	2838	5538	8376	1092	2529	45	668	735	11554	16.1

Three-Point Field Goals: 1981-82, 0-for-1. 1982-83, 0-for-4. 1983-84, 0-for-4. 1984-85, 1-for-4 (.250). 1985-86, 0-for-2. 1986-87, 0-for-1. 1987-88, 1-for-1 (1.000). 1988-89, 0-for-3. 1989-90, 0-for-1. Totals, 2-for-21 (.095).

NBA PLAYOFF RECORD

									—Rebounds—									
Sea.—Team	G.	Min.	FGA	FGM	Pct.	FTA	FTM	Pct.	Off.	Def.	Tot.	Ast.	PF	Dq.	Stl.	Blk.	Pts.	Avg.
81-82—New Jersey	2	79	26	14	.538	15	7	.467	11	10	21	3	7	0	1	2	35	17.5
82-83—New Jersey	2	85	22	11	.500	20	16	.800	9	14	23	4	12	2	2	2	38	19.0
83-84—New Jersey	11	473	130	63	.485	81	45	.556	57	98	155	16	44	2	15	17	171	15.5
84-85—New Jersey	3	123	40	26	.650	30	22	.733	14	18	32	1	12	0	3	5	74	24.7
85-86—New Jersey	3	126	29	21	.724	26	20	.769	12	19	31	2	15	1	6	1	62	20.7
89-90—Portland	21	776	199	101	.508	105	71	.676	67	126	193	39	74	1	13	6	273	13.0
Totals	42	1662	446	236	.529	277	181	.653	170	285	455	65	164	6	40	33	653	15.5

NBA ALL-STAR GAME RECORD

								—Rebounds—								
Season—Team	Min.	FGA	FGM	Pct.	FTA	FTM	Pct.	Off.	Def.	Tot.	Ast.	PF	Dq.	Stl.	Blk.	Pts.
1982—New Jersey	22	7	2	.286	2	0	.000	1	9	10	1	3	0	0	2	4
1983—New Jersey	19	4	3	.750	4	2	.500	3	4	7	1	0	0	1	0	8
1986—New Jersey	20	8	5	.625	5	3	.600	3	4	7	4	0	0	0	0	13
Totals	61	19	10	.526	11	5	.455	7	17	24	6	3	0	1	2	25

Named to All-NBA Second Team, 1983. . . . NBA All-Defensive First Team, 1990. . . . NBA All-Defensive Second Team, 1988. . . . NBA Rookie of the Year, 1982. . . . NBA All-Rookie Team, 1982. . . . Member of U.S. Olympic team, 1980.

HERBERT L. WILLIAMS
(Herb)

Born February 16, 1958 at Columbus, O. Height 6:11. Weight 242.
High School—Columbus, O., Marion Franklin.
College—Ohio State University, Columbus, O.
Drafted by Indiana on first round, 1981 (14th pick).

Traded by Indiana to Dallas for Detlef Schrempf and a 1990 or 1991 2nd round draft choice, February 21, 1989.

—COLLEGIATE RECORD—

Year	G.	Min.	FGA	FGM	Pct.	FTA	FTM	Pct.	Reb.	Pts.	Avg.
77-78	27	992	407	196	.482	91	60	.659	308	452	16.7
78-79	31	1212	483	253	.524	166	111	.669	325	617	19.9
79-80	29	1069	415	206	.496	147	97	.660	263	509	17.6
80-81	27	1020	368	179	.486	109	75	.688	215	433	16.0
Totals	114	4293	1673	834	.499	513	343	.669	1111	2011	17.6

NBA REGULAR SEASON RECORD

									—Rebounds—									
Sea.—Team	G.	Min.	FGA	FGM	Pct.	FTA	FTM	Pct.	Off.	Def.	Tot.	Ast.	PF	Dq.	Stl.	Blk.	Pts.	Avg.
81-82—Indiana	82	2277	854	407	.477	188	126	.670	175	430	605	139	200	0	53	178	942	11.5
82-83—Indiana	78	2513	1163	580	.499	220	155	.705	151	432	583	262	230	4	54	171	1315	16.9
83-84—Indiana	69	2279	860	411	.478	295	207	.702	154	400	554	215	193	4	60	108	1029	14.9
84-85—Indiana	75	2557	1211	575	.475	341	224	.657	154	480	634	252	218	1	54	134	1375	18.3
85-86—Indiana	78	2770	1275	627	.492	403	294	.730	172	538	710	174	244	2	50	184	1549	19.9
86-87—Indiana	74	2526	939	451	.480	269	199	.740	143	400	543	174	255	9	59	93	1101	14.9
87-88—Indiana	75	1966	732	311	.425	171	126	.737	116	353	469	98	244	1	37	146	748	10.0
88-89—Ind.-Dal.	76	2470	739	322	.436	194	133	.686	135	458	593	124	236	5	46	134	777	10.2
89-90—Dallas	81	2199	665	295	.444	159	108	.679	76	315	391	119	243	4	51	106	700	8.6
Totals	688	21557	8438	3979	.472	2240	1572	.702	1276	3806	5082	1557	2063	30	464	1254	9536	13.9

Three-Point Field Goals: 1981-82, 2-for-7 (.286). 1982-83, 0-for-7. 1983-84, 0-for-4. 1984-85, 1-for-9 (.111). 1985-86, 1-for-12 (.083). 1986-87, 0-for-9. 1987-88, 0-for-6. 1988-89, 0-for-5. 1989-90, 2-for-9 (.222). Totals, 6-for-68 (.088).

NBA PLAYOFF RECORD

									—Rebounds—									
Sea.—Team	G.	Min.	FGA	FGM	Pct.	FTA	FTM	Pct.	Off.	Def.	Tot.	Ast.	PF	Dq.	Stl.	Blk.	Pts.	Avg.
86-87—Indiana	4	134	34	20	.588	13	7	.538	3	17	20	7	12	0	0	1	47	11.8
89-90—Dallas	3	81	23	14	.609	16	13	.813	4	9	13	5	16	1	1	2	41	13.7
Totals	7	215	57	34	.596	29	20	.690	7	26	33	12	28	1	1	3	88	12.6

JOHN WILLIAMS
(Hot Rod)

Born August 9, 1961 at Sorrento, La. Height 6:11. Weight 230.

High School—Sorrento, La., St. Amant.

College—Tulane University, New Orleans, La.

Drafted by Cleveland on second round, 1985 (45th pick).

—COLLEGIATE RECORD—

Year	G.	Min.	FGA	FGM	Pct.	FTA	FTM	Pct.	Reb.	Pts.	Avg.
81-82	28	932	279	163	.584	133	88	.662	202	414	14.8
82-83	31	996	317	151	.476	118	83	.703	166	385	12.4
83-84	28	1038	355	202	.569	184	140	.761	222	544	19.4
84-85	28	1006	334	189	.566	155	120	.774	219	498	17.8
Totals	115	3972	1285	705	.549	590	431	.731	809	1841	16.0

NBA REGULAR SEASON RECORD

									—Rebounds—									
Sea.—Team	G.	Min.	FGA	FGM	Pct.	FTA	FTM	Pct.	Off.	Def.	Tot.	Ast.	PF	Dq.	Stl.	Blk.	Pts.	Avg.
86-87—Cleveland	80	2714	897	435	.485	400	298	.745	222	407	629	154	197	0	58	167	1168	14.6
87-88—Cleveland	77	2106	663	316	.477	279	211	.756	159	347	506	103	203	2	61	145	843	10.9
88-89—Cleveland	82	2125	700	356	.509	314	235	.748	173	304	477	108	188	1	77	134	948	11.6
89-90—Cleveland	82	2776	1070	528	.493	440	325	.739	220	443	663	168	214	2	86	167	1381	16.8
Totals	321	9721	3330	1635	.491	1433	1069	.746	774	1501	2275	533	802	5	282	613	4340	13.5

Three-Point Field Goals: 1986-87, 0-for-1. 1987-88, 0-for-1. 1988-89, 1-for-4 (.250). Totals, 1-for-6 (.167).

NBA PLAYOFF RECORD

									—Rebounds—									
Sea.—Team	G.	Min.	FGA	FGM	Pct.	FTA	FTM	Pct.	Off.	Def.	Tot.	Ast.	PF	Dq.	Stl.	Blk.	Pts.	Avg.
87-88—Cleveland	5	133	40	20	.500	13	6	.462	13	16	29	4	13	0	3	7	46	9.2
88-89—Cleveland	5	161	45	21	.467	18	13	.722	7	27	34	10	12	0	2	7	55	11.0
89-90—Cleveland	5	174	70	39	.557	22	17	.773	14	32	46	11	23	1	2	5	95	19.0
Totals	15	468	155	80	.516	53	36	.679	34	75	109	25	48	1	7	19	196	13.1

Named to NBA All-Rookie Team, 1987.

JOHN SAM WILLIAMS

Born October 26, 1966 at Los Angeles, Calif. Height 6:09. Weight 235.

High School—Los Angeles, Calif., Crenshaw.

College—Louisiana State University, Baton Rouge, La.

Drafted by Washington on first round as an undergraduate, 1986 (12th pick).

—COLLEGIATE RECORD—

Year	G.	Min.	FGA	FGM	Pct.	FTA	FTM	Pct.	Reb.	Pts.	Avg.
84-85	29	935	305	163	.534	81	62	.765	190	388	13.4
85-86	37	1277	540	269	.498	155	120	.774	313	658	17.8
Totals	66	2212	845	432	.511	236	182	.771	503	1046	15.8

NBA REGULAR SEASON RECORD

									—Rebounds—									
Sea.—Team	G.	Min.	FGA	FGM	Pct.	FTA	FTM	Pct.	Off.	Def.	Tot.	Ast.	PF	Dq.	Stl.	Blk.	Pts.	Avg.
86-87—Washington	78	1773	624	283	.454	223	144	.646	130	236	366	191	173	1	129	30	718	9.2
87-88—Washington	82	2428	910	427	.469	256	188	.734	127	317	444	232	217	3	117	34	1047	12.8
88-89—Washington	82	2413	940	438	.466	290	225	.776	158	415	573	356	213	1	142	70	1120	13.7
89-90—Washington	18	632	274	130	.474	84	65	.774	27	109	136	84	33	0	21	9	327	18.2
Totals	260	7246	2748	1278	.465	853	622	.729	442	1077	1519	863	636	5	409	143	3212	12.4

Three-Point Field Goals: 1986-87, 8-for-36 (.222). 1987-88, 5-for-38 (.132). 1988-89, 19-for-71 (.268). 1989-90, 2-for-18 (.111). Totals, 34-for-163 (.209).

NBA PLAYOFF RECORD

									—Rebounds—									
Sea.—Team	G.	Min.	FGA	FGM	Pct.	FTA	FTM	Pct.	Off.	Def.	Tot.	Ast.	PF	Dq.	Stl.	Blk.	Pts.	Avg.
86-87—Washington	3	49	14	8	.571	7	4	.571	4	7	11	2	3	0	2	0	20	6.7
87-88—Washington	5	185	48	23	.479	32	19	.594	11	18	29	21	18	1	8	4	65	13.0
Totals	8	234	62	31	.500	39	23	.590	15	25	40	23	21	1	10	4	85	10.6

Three-Point Field Goals: 1986-87, 0-for-1. 1987-88, 0-for-1. Totals, 0-for-2.

MICHAEL DOUGLAS WILLIAMS

Born July 23, 1966 at Dallas, Tex. Height 6:02. Weight 175.
High School—Dallas, Tex., David Carter.
College—Baylor University, Waco, Tex.
Drafted by Detroit on second round, 1988 (48th pick).

Traded by Detroit with draft rights to Kenny Battle to Phoenix for draft rights to Anthony Cook, June 27, 1989.
Waived by Phoenix, December 12, 1989; signed by Dallas as a free agent, December 14, 1989.
Waived by Dallas, December 26, 1989; signed by Charlotte, March 13, 1990, to the first of consecutive 10-day contracts that expired, April 1, 1990.
Re-signed by Charlotte, April 2, 1990, for remainder of season.
Played in Continental Basketball Association with Rapid City Thrillers, 1989-90.

—COLLEGIATE RECORD—

Year	G.	Min.	FGA	FGM	Pct.	FTA	FTM	Pct.	Reb.	Pts.	Avg.
84-85	28	787	306	149	.487	140	111	.793	66	409	14.6
85-86	22	.000	225	104	.462	98	79	.806	63	287	13.0
86-87	31	1112	396	188	.475	192	137	.714	94	534	17.2
87-88	34	1262	428	216	.505	231	161	.697	108	625	18.4
Totals	115	....	1355	657	.485	661	488	.738	331	1855	16.1

Three-Point Field Goals: 1986-87, 21-for-67 (.313). 1987-88, 32-for-85 (.376). Totals, 53-for-152 (.349).

CBA REGULAR SEASON RECORD

			—2-Point—			—3-Point—									
Sea.—Team	G.	Min.	FGM	FGA	Pct.	FGM	FGA	Pct.	FTM	FTA	Pct.	Reb.	Ast.	Pts.	Avg.
89-90—Rapid City	23	817	152	265	.574	0	7	.000	119	146	.815	94	184	423	18.4

NBA REGULAR SEASON RECORD

									—Rebounds—									
Sea.—Team	G.	Min.	FGA	FGM	Pct.	FTA	FTM	Pct.	Off.	Def.	Tot.	Ast.	PF	Dq.	Stl.	Blk.	Pts.	Avg.
88-89—Detroit	49	358	129	47	.364	47	31	.660	9	18	27	70	44	0	13	3	127	2.6
89-90—Phoe.-Char.	28	329	119	60	.504	46	36	.783	12	20	32	81	39	0	22	1	156	5.6
Totals	77	687	248	107	.431	93	67	.720	21	38	59	151	83	0	35	4	283	3.7

Three-Point Field Goals: 1988-89, 2-for-9 (.222). 1989-90, 0-for-3. Totals, 2-for-12 (.167).

NBA PLAYOFF RECORD

									—Rebounds—									
Sea.—Team	G.	Min.	FGA	FGM	Pct.	FTA	FTM	Pct.	Off.	Def.	Tot.	Ast.	PF	Dq.	Stl.	Blk.	Pts.	Avg.
88-89—Detroit	4	6	0	0	.000	2	2	1.000	1	1	2	2	1	0	1	0	2	0.5

Member of NBA championship team, 1989.

MICHAEL GEORGE WILLIAMS
(Mike)

Born August 14, 1963 at Chicago, Ill. Height 6:08. Weight 255.
High School—Chicago, Ill., DeLaSalle.
Colleges—University of Cincinnati, Cincinnati, O., and Bradley University, Peoria, Ill.
Drafted by Golden State on third round, 1986 (51st pick).

Waived by Golden State, October 10, 1986; signed by Washington as a free agent, September 7, 1988.
Waived by Washington, October 10, 1988; signed by Sacramento as a free agent, December 18, 1989.
Traded by Sacramento with Kenny Smith to Atlanta for Antoine Carr, Sedric Toney and future draft considerations, February 13, 1990.
Waived by Atlanta, March 15, 1990.
Played in Continental Basketball Association with LaCrosse Catbirds, 1988-89 and 1989-90.

—COLLEGIATE RECORD—

Cincinnati

Year	G.	Min.	FGA	FGM	Pct.	FTA	FTM	Pct.	Reb.	Pts.	Avg.
81-82	26	753	218	105	.482	83	50	.602	192	260	10.0
82-83	11	316	121	62	.512	35	23	.657	86	147	13.4
Cin. Totals	37	1069	339	167	.493	118	73	.619	278	407	11.0

Bradley

Year	G.	Min.	FGA	FGM	Pct.	FTA	FTM	Pct.	Reb.	Pts.	Avg.
83-84					Did Not Play—Transfer Student						
84-85	30	879	256	137	.535	126	79	.627	193	353	11.8
85-86	35	1065	326	199	.610	164	92	.561	250	490	14.0
Brad. Totals	65	1944	582	336	.577	290	171	.590	443	843	13.0
Totals	102	3013	921	503	.546	408	244	.598	721	1250	12.3

CBA REGULAR SEASON RECORD

Sea.—Team	G.	Min.	2-Point FGM	2-Point FGA	2-Point Pct.	3-Point FGM	3-Point FGA	3-Point Pct.	FTM	FTA	Pct.	Reb.	Ast.	Pts.	Avg.
88-89—LaCrosse	8	56	2	13	.154	0	0	.000	0	2	.000	18	0	4	0.5
89-90—LaCrosse	13	370	67	118	.568	0	0	.000	28	47	.596	122	17	162	12.5
Totals	21	426	69	131	.527	0	0	.000	28	49	.571	140	17	166	7.9

NBA REGULAR SEASON RECORD

Sea.—Team	G.	Min.	FGA	FGM	Pct.	FTA	FTM	Pct.	Rebounds Off.	Rebounds Def.	Rebounds Tot.	Ast.	PF	Dq.	Stl.	Blk.	Pts.	Avg.
89-90—Sac.-Atl.	21	102	18	6	.333	6	3	.500	5	18	23	2	30	0	3	7	15	0.7

Three-Point Field Goals: 1989-90, 0-for-1.

REGGIE WILLIAMS

Born March 5, 1964 at Baltimore, Md. Height 6:07. Weight 190.
High School—Baltimore, Md., Dunbar.
College—Georgetown University, Washington, D.C.
Drafted by Los Angeles Clippers on first round, 1987 (4th pick).

Traded by Los Angeles Clippers with draft rights to Danny Ferry to Cleveland for Ron Harper, 1990 and 1992 1st round draft choices and a 1991 2nd round draft choice, November 16, 1989.

Waived by Cleveland, February 26, 1990; signed by San Antonio, March 5, 1990, for remainder of season.

—COLLEGIATE RECORD—

Year	G.	Min.	FGA	FGM	Pct.	FTA	FTM	Pct.	Reb.	Pts.	Avg.
83-84	37	764	300	130	.433	99	76	.768	131	336	9.1
84-85	35	1043	332	168	.506	106	80	.755	200	416	11.9
85-86	32	1013	430	227	.528	149	109	.732	261	563	17.6
86-87	34	1205	589	284	.482	194	156	.804	294	802	23.6
Totals	138	4025	1651	809	.490	548	421	.768	886	2117	15.3

Three-Point Field Goals: 1986-87, 78-for-202 (.386).

NBA REGULAR SEASON RECORD

Sea.—Team	G.	Min.	FGA	FGM	Pct.	FTA	FTM	Pct.	Rebounds Off.	Rebounds Def.	Rebounds Tot.	Ast.	PF	Dq.	Stl.	Blk.	Pts.	Avg.
87-88—L.A. Clippers	35	857	427	152	.356	66	48	.727	55	63	118	58	108	1	29	21	365	10.4
88-89—L.A. Clippers	63	1303	594	260	.438	122	92	.754	70	109	179	103	181	1	81	29	642	10.2
89-90—LAC-Cle-SA	47	743	338	131	.388	68	52	.765	28	55	83	53	102	2	32	14	320	6.8
Totals	145	2903	1359	543	.400	256	192	.750	153	227	380	214	391	4	142	64	1327	9.2

Three-Point Field Goals: 1987-88, 13-for-58 (.224). 1988-89, 30-for-104 (.288). 1989-90, 6-for-37 (.162). Totals, 49-for-199 (.246).

NBA PLAYOFF RECORD

Sea.—Team	G.	Min.	FGA	FGM	Pct.	FTA	FTM	Pct.	Rebounds Off.	Rebounds Def.	Rebounds Tot.	Ast.	PF	Dq.	Stl.	Blk.	Pts.	Avg.
89-90—San Antonio	9	49	27	9	.333	2	2	1.000	5	6	11	3	8	0	2	0	20	2.2

Three-Point Field Goals: 1989-90, 0-for-2.

Member of NCAA Division I championship team, 1984. . . . Named to THE SPORTING NEWS All-America First Team, 1987.

KEVIN ANDRE WILLIS

Born September 6, 1962 at Los Angeles, Calif. Height 7:00. Weight 235.
High School—Detroit, Mich., Pershing.
Colleges—Jackson Community College, Jackson, Mich., and
Michigan State University, East Lansing, Mich.
Drafted by Atlanta on first round, 1984 (11th pick).

Missed entire 1988-89 season due to injury.

—COLLEGIATE RECORD—

Jackson CC

Year	G.	Min.	FGA	FGM	Pct.	FTA	FTM	Pct.	Reb.	Pts.	Avg.
80-81	....	....	....	....	....	....	....	....	....	....	19.0

Michigan State

Year	G.	Min.	FGA	FGM	Pct.	FTA	FTM	Pct.	Reb.	Pts.	Avg.
81-82	27	518	154	73	.474	30	17	.567	113	163	6.0
82-83	27	865	272	162	.596	70	36	.514	258	360	13.3
83-84	25	738	240	118	.492	59	39	.661	192	275	11.0
MSU Totals	79	2121	666	353	.530	159	92	.579	563	798	10.1

Three-Point Field Goals: 1982-83, 0-for-1.

NBA REGULAR SEASON RECORD

									—Rebounds—								
Sea.—Team	G.	Min.	FGA	FGM	Pct.	FTA	FTM	Pct.	Off.	Def.	Tot.	Ast.	PF	Dq.	Stl.	Blk.	Pts.	Avg.
84-85—Atlanta	82	1785	690	322	.467	181	119	.657	177	345	522	36	226	4	31	49	765	9.3
85-86—Atlanta	82	2300	511	419	.517	263	172	.654	243	461	704	45	294	6	66	44	1010	12.3
86-87—Atlanta	81	2626	1003	538	.536	320	227	.709	321	528	849	62	313	4	65	61	1304	16.1
87-88—Atlanta	75	2091	687	356	.518	245	159	.649	235	312	547	28	240	2	68	42	871	11.6
89-90—Atlanta	81	2273	805	418	.519	246	168	.683	253	392	645	57	259	4	63	47	1006	12.4
Totals	401	11075	3996	2053	.514	1255	845	.673	1229	2038	3267	228	1332	20	293	243	4956	12.4

Three-Point Field Goals: 1984-85, 2-for-9 (.222). 1985-86, 0-for-6. 1986-87, 1-for-4 (.250). 1987-88, 0-for-2. 1989-90, 2-for-7 (.286). Totals, 5-for-28 (.179).

NBA PLAYOFF RECORD

									—Rebounds—								
Sea.—Team	G.	Min.	FGA	FGM	Pct.	FTA	FTM	Pct.	Off.	Def.	Tot.	Ast.	PF	Dq.	Stl.	Blk.	Pts.	Avg.
85-86—Atlanta	9	280	98	55	.561	23	15	.652	31	34	65	5	38	2	7	8	125	13.9
86-87—Atlanta	9	356	115	60	.522	31	21	.677	33	50	83	6	33	0	9	7	141	15.7
87-88—Atlanta	12	462	138	80	.580	50	34	.680	36	72	108	11	51	1	10	10	194	16.2
Totals	30	1098	351	195	.556	104	70	.673	100	156	256	22	122	3	26	25	460	15.3

Three-Point Field Goals: 1987-88, 0-for-1.

DAVID WINGATE

Born December 15, 1963 at Baltimore, Md. Height 6:05. Weight 185.
High School—Baltimore, Md., Dunbar.
College—Georgetown University, Washington, D.C.
Drafted by Philadelphia on second round, 1986 (44th pick).

Traded by Philadelphia with Maurice Cheeks and Christian Welp to San Antonio for Johnny Dawkins and Jay Vincent, August 28, 1989.

—COLLEGIATE RECORD—

Year	G.	Min.	FGA	FGM	Pct.	FTA	FTM	Pct.	Reb.	Pts.	Avg.
82-83	32	855	335	149	.445	124	87	.702	95	385	12.0
83-84	37	1005	370	161	.435	129	93	.721	135	415	11.2
84-85	38	1128	395	191	.484	132	91	.689	135	473	12.4
85-86	32	956	394	196	.497	155	117	.755	129	509	15.9
Totals	139	3944	1494	697	.467	540	388	.719	494	1782	12.8

NBA REGULAR SEASON RECORD

									—Rebounds—								
Sea.—Team	G.	Min.	FGA	FGM	Pct.	FTA	FTM	Pct.	Off.	Def.	Tot.	Ast.	PF	Dq.	Stl.	Blk.	Pts.	Avg.
86-87—Philadelphia	77	1612	602	259	.430	201	149	.741	70	86	156	155	169	1	93	19	680	8.8
87-88—Philadelphia	61	1419	545	218	.400	132	99	.750	44	57	101	119	125	0	47	22	545	8.9
88-89—Philadelphia	33	372	115	54	.470	34	27	.794	12	25	37	73	43	0	9	2	137	4.2
89-90—San Antonio	78	1856	491	220	.448	112	87	.777	62	133	195	208	154	2	89	18	527	6.8
Totals	249	5259	1753	751	.428	479	362	.756	188	301	489	555	491	3	238	61	1889	7.6

Three-Point Field Goals: 1986-87, 13-for-52 (.250). 1987-88, 10-for-40 (.250). 1988-89, 2-for-6 (.333). 1989-90, 0-for-13. Totals, 25-for-111 (.225).

NBA PLAYOFF RECORD

									—Rebounds—								
Sea.—Team	G.	Min.	FGA	FGM	Pct.	FTA	FTM	Pct.	Off.	Def.	Tot.	Ast.	PF	Dq.	Stl.	Blk.	Pts.	Avg.
86-87—Philadelphia	5	90	37	15	.405	14	9	.643	5	7	12	9	11	1	5	1	41	8.2
89-90—San Antonio	10	293	77	40	.519	12	9	.750	9	28	37	38	34	1	18	3	91	9.1
Totals	15	383	114	55	.482	26	18	.692	14	35	49	47	45	2	23	4	132	8.8

Three-Point Field Goals: 1986-87, 2-for-2 (1.000). 1989-90, 2-for-3 (.667). Totals, 4-for-5 (.800).

Member of NCAA Division I championship team, 1984.

RANDY SCOTT WITTMAN

Born October 28, 1959 at Indianapolis, Ind. Height 6:06. Weight 210.
High School—Indianapolis, Ind., Ben Davis.
College—Indiana University, Bloomington, Ind.
Drafted by Washington on first round, 1983 (22nd pick).

Draft rights traded by Washington to Atlanta for Tom McMillen and a 1984 2nd round draft choice, July 5, 1983.
Traded by Atlanta with a 1988 1st round draft choice to Sacramento for Reggie Theus, a 1988 3rd round draft choice and future considerations, June 27, 1988.
Traded by Sacramento with LaSalle Thompson to Indiana for Wayman Tisdale and a 1990 or 1991 2nd round draft choice, February 20, 1989.

—COLLEGIATE RECORD—

Year	G.	Min.	FGA	FGM	Pct.	FTA	FTM	Pct.	Reb.	Pts.	Avg.
78-79	34	....	190	101	.532	53	39	.736	90	241	7.1
79-80	5	....	28	13	.464	4	3	.750	7	29	5.8
80-81	35	....	286	155	.542	69	53	.768	79	363	10.4
81-82	29	....	299	144	.482	78	59	.756	94	347	12.0
82-83	30	....	435	236	.543	108	89	.824	135	569	19.0
Totals	133	....	1238	649	.524	312	243	.779	405	1549	11.6

Three-Point Field Goals: 1982-83, 8-for-18 (.444).
(Suffered stress fracture of right ankle in 1979-80 season; granted extra year of eligibility.)

NBA REGULAR SEASON RECORD

									—Rebounds—									
Sea.—Team	G.	Min.	FGA	FGM	Pct.	FTA	FTM	Pct.	Off.	Def.	Tot.	Ast.	PF	Dq.	Stl.	Blk.	Pts.	Avg.
83-84—Atlanta	78	1071	318	160	.503	46	28	.609	14	57	71	71	82	0	17	0	350	4.5
84-85—Atlanta	41	1168	352	187	.531	41	30	.732	16	57	73	125	58	0	28	7	406	9.9
85-86—Atlanta	81	2760	881	467	.530	135	104	.770	51	119	170	306	118	0	81	14	1043	12.9
86-87—Atlanta	71	2049	792	398	.503	127	100	.787	30	94	124	211	107	0	39	16	900	12.7
87-88—Atlanta	82	2412	787	376	.478	89	71	.798	39	131	170	302	117	0	50	18	823	10.0
88-89—Sac.-Ind.	64	1120	286	130	.455	41	28	.683	26	54	80	111	43	0	23	2	291	4.5
89-90—Indiana	61	544	122	62	.508	6	5	.833	4	26	30	39	21	0	7	4	130	2.1
Totals	478	11124	3538	1780	.503	485	366	.755	180	538	718	1165	546	0	245	61	3943	8.2

Three-Point Field Goals: 1983-84, 2-for-5 (.400). 1984-85, 2-for-7 (.286). 1985-86, 5-for-16 (.313). 1986-87, 4-for-12 (.333). 1988-89, 3-for-6 (.500). 1989-90, 1-for-2 (.500). Totals, 17-for-48 (.354).

NBA PLAYOFF RECORD

									—Rebounds—									
Sea.—Team	G.	Min.	FGA	FGM	Pct.	FTA	FTM	Pct.	Off.	Def.	Tot.	Ast.	PF	Dq.	Stl.	Blk.	Pts.	Avg.
83-84—Atlanta	5	96	37	20	.541	0	0	.000	5	4	9	11	5	0	1	0	40	8.0
85-86—Atlanta	9	348	135	71	.526	26	18	.692	4	20	24	30	16	0	10	1	160	17.8
86-87—Atlanta	9	300	121	67	.554	17	14	.824	3	15	18	30	22	0	4	4	148	16.4
87-88—Atlanta	12	344	122	66	.541	7	5	.714	9	17	26	43	24	0	7	1	137	11.4
89-90—Indiana	2	11	1	0	.000	0	0	....	0	1	1	0	0	0	0	0	0	0.0
Totals	37	1099	416	224	.538	50	37	.740	21	57	78	114	67	0	22	6	485	13.1

Three-Point Field Goals: 1985-86, 0-for-2.

Member of NCAA Division I championship team, 1981.

JOSEPH JAMES WOLF
(Joe)

Born December 17, 1964 at Kohler, Wis. Height 6:11. Weight 230.
High School—Kohler, Wis.
College—University of North Carolina, Chapel Hill, N.C.
Drafted by Los Angeles Clippers on first round, 1987 (13th pick).

—COLLEGIATE RECORD—

Year	G.	Min.	FGA	FGM	Pct.	FTA	FTM	Pct.	Reb.	Pts.	Avg.
83-84	30	412	79	38	.481	33	25	.758	85	101	3.4
84-85	30	914	198	112	.566	64	50	.781	158	274	9.1
85-86	34	854	280	149	.532	59	42	.712	224	340	10.0
86-87	34	1005	371	212	.571	87	69	.793	240	516	15.2
Totals	128	3185	928	511	.551	243	186	.765	707	1231	9.6

Three-Point Field Goals: 1986-87, 23-for-40 (.575).

NBA REGULAR SEASON RECORD

									—Rebounds—									
Sea.—Team	G.	Min.	FGA	FGM	Pct.	FTA	FTM	Pct.	Off.	Def.	Tot.	Ast.	PF	Dq.	Stl.	Blk.	Pts.	Avg.
87-88—L.A. Clippers	42	1137	334	136	.407	54	45	.833	51	136	187	98	139	8	38	16	320	7.6
88-89—L.A. Clippers	66	1450	402	170	.423	64	44	.688	83	188	271	113	152	1	32	16	386	5.8
89-90—L.A. Clippers	77	1325	392	155	.395	71	55	.775	63	169	232	62	129	0	30	24	370	4.8
Totals	185	3912	1128	461	.409	189	144	.762	197	493	690	273	420	9	100	56	1076	5.8

Three-Point Field Goals: 1987-88, 3-for-15 (.200). 1988-89, 2-for-14 (.143). 1989-90, 5-for-25 (.200). Totals, 10-for-54 (.185).

OSIE LEON WOOD III
(Known by middle name.)

Born March 25, 1962 at Columbia, S.C. Height 6:03. Weight 185.
High School—Santa Monica, Calif., St. Monica.
Colleges—University of Arizona, Tucson, Ariz., and
California State University at Fullerton, Fullerton, Calif.
Drafted by Philadelphia on first round, 1984 (10th pick).

Traded by Philadelphia to Washington for Kenny Green, January 10, 1986.

Traded by Washington to New Jersey for Mike O'Koren, October 30, 1986.
Waived by New Jersey, November 5, 1987; signed by San Antonio as a free agent, November 12, 1987.
Waived by San Antonio, February 17, 1988; signed by Atlanta, March 4, 1988, to the first of consecutive 10-day contracts that expired, March 24, 1988.
Re-signed by Atlanta, March 25, 1988, for remainder of season.
Signed by New Jersey, February 12, 1990, to the first of consecutive 10-day contracts that expired, March 3, 1990.
Re-signed by New Jersey, March 5, 1990, for remainder of season.
Played in Continental Basketball Association with Santa Barbara Islanders, 1989-90.

—COLLEGIATE RECORD—

Year	G.	Min.	FGA	FGM	Pct.	FTA	FTM	Pct.	Reb.	Pts.	Avg.
79-80	25	221	111	43	.387	26	19	.731	6	105	4.2

Cal State-Fullerton

Year	G.	Min.	FGA	FGM	Pct.	FTA	FTM	Pct.	Reb.	Pts.	Avg.
80-81	Did Not Play—Transfer Student										
81-82	32	1263	448	222	.496	229	187	.817	57	631	19.7
82-83	29	1076	378	178	.471	180	142	.789	72	526	18.1
83-84	30	1170	540	254	.470	257	211	.821	78	719	24.0
CSF Totals	91	3509	1366	654	.479	666	540	.811	207	1876	20.6
College Totals	116	3730	1477	697	.472	692	559	.808	213	1981	17.1

Three-Point Field Goals: 1982-83, 28-for-63 (.444).

CBA REGULAR SEASON RECORD

			—2-Point—			—3-Point—									
Sea.—Team	G.	Min.	FGM	FGA	Pct.	FGM	FGA	Pct.	FTM	FTA	Pct.	Reb.	Ast.	Pts.	Avg.
89-90—Santa Barbara	40	1648	134	289	.464	68	173	.393	153	184	.832	97	432	625	15.6

NBA REGULAR SEASON RECORD

									—Rebounds—									
Sea.—Team	G.	Min.	FGA	FGM	Pct.	FTA	FTM	Pct.	Off.	Def.	Tot.	Ast.	PF	Dq.	Stl.	Blk.	Pts.	Avg.
84-85—Philadelphia	38	269	134	50	.373	26	18	.692	3	15	18	45	17	0	8	0	122	3.2
85-86—Phil.-Wash.	68	1198	466	184	.395	155	123	.794	25	65	90	182	70	0	34	0	532	7.8
86-87—New Jersey	76	1733	501	187	.373	154	123	.799	23	97	120	370	126	0	48	3	557	7.3
87-88—S.A.-Atl.	52	909	312	136	.436	99	76	.768	17	40	57	174	50	0	26	1	400	7.7
89-90—New Jersey	28	200	49	16	.327	16	14	.875	1	11	12	47	16	0	6	0	50	1.8
Totals	262	4309	1462	573	.392	450	354	.787	69	228	297	818	279	0	122	4	1661	6.3

Three-Point Field Goals: 1984-85, 4-for-30 (.133). 1985-86, 41-for-114 (.360). 1986-87, 60-for-200 (.300). 1987-88, 52-for-127 (.409). 1989-90, 4-for-21 (.190). Totals, 161-for-492 (.327).

NBA PLAYOFF RECORD

									—Rebounds—									
Sea.—Team	G.	Min.	FGA	FGM	Pct.	FTA	FTM	Pct.	Off.	Def.	Tot.	Ast.	PF	Dq.	Stl.	Blk.	Pts.	Avg.
84-85—Philadelphia	5	15	9	4	.444	8	6	.750	0	1	1	2	0	0	0	0	14	2.8
85-86—Washington	1	2	5	1	.200	2	2	1.000	0	0	0	0	0	0	0	0	5	5.0
87-88—Atlanta	4	4	1	1	1.000	0	0	.000	0	0	0	1	0	0	0	0	3	0.8
Totals	10	21	15	6	.400	10	8	.800	0	1	1	3	0	0	0	0	22	2.2

Three-Point Field Goals: 1984-85, 0-for-1. 1985-86, 1-for-1 (1.000). 1987-88, 1-for-1 (1.000). Totals, 2-for-3 (.667).

Member of U.S. Olympic team, 1984. . . . Named to THE SPORTING NEWS All-America First Team, 1984.

MICHAEL WOODSON
(Mike)

Born March 24, 1958 at Indianapolis, Ind. Height 6:05. Weight 198.
High School—Indianapolis, Ind., Broad Ripple.
College—Indiana University, Bloomington, Ind.
Drafted by New York on first round, 1980 (12th pick).

Traded by New York to New Jersey for Mike Newlin, June 10, 1981.
Traded by New Jersey with a 1982 1st round draft choice to Kansas City for Sam Lacey, November 12, 1981.
Traded by Sacramento with Larry Drew, a 1988 1st round draft choice and a 1989 2nd round draft choice to Los Angeles Clippers for Junior Bridgeman, Franklin Edwards and Derek Smith, August 19, 1986.
Signed by Houston as an unrestricted free agent, July 19, 1988.

—COLLEGIATE RECORD—

Year	G.	Min.	FGA	FGM	Pct.	FTA	FTM	Pct.	Reb.	Pts.	Avg.
76-77	27	....	407	212	.521	96	76	.792	182	500	18.5
77-78	29	....	462	242	.524	121	93	.769	157	577	19.9
78-79	34	....	532	265	.498	241	184	.763	193	714	21.0
79-80	14	....	225	102	.453	79	66	.835	49	270	19.3
Totals	104	....	1626	821	.505	537	419	.780	581	2061	19.8

NBA REGULAR SEASON RECORD

									—Rebounds—									
Sea.—Team	G.	Min.	FGA	FGM	Pct.	FTA	FTM	Pct.	Off.	Def.	Tot.	Ast.	PF	Dq.	Stl.	Blk.	Pts.	Avg.
80-81—New York	81	949	373	165	.442	64	49	.766	33	64	97	75	95	0	36	12	380	4.7
81-82—N.J.-K.C.	83	2331	1069	538	.503	286	221	.773	102	145	247	222	220	3	142	35	1304	15.7

										—Rebounds—								
Sea.—Team	G.	Min.	FGA	FGM	Pct.	FTA	FTM	Pct.	Off.	Def.	Tot.	Ast.	PF	Dq.	Stl.	Blk.	Pts.	Avg.
82-83—Kansas City	81	2426	1154	584	.506	377	298	.790	84	164	248	254	203	0	137	59	1473	18.2
83-84—Kansas City	71	1838	816	389	.477	302	247	.818	62	113	175	175	174	2	83	28	1027	14.5
84-85—Kansas City	78	1998	1068	530	.496	330	264	.800	69	129	198	143	216	1	117	28	1329	17.0
85-86—Sacramento	81	2417	1073	510	.475	289	242	.837	94	132	226	197	215	1	92	37	1264	15.6
86-87—L.A. Clippers	74	2126	1130	494	.437	290	240	.828	68	94	162	196	201	1	100	16	1262	17.1
87-88—L.A. Clippers	80	2534	1263	562	.445	341	296	.868	64	126	190	273	210	1	109	26	1438	18.0
88-89—Houston	81	2259	936	410	.438	237	195	.823	51	143	194	206	195	1	89	18	1046	12.9
89-90—Houston	61	972	405	160	.395	86	62	.721	25	63	88	66	100	1	42	11	394	6.5
Totals	771	19850	9287	4342	.468	2602	2114	.812	652	1173	1825	1807	1829	11	947	270	10917	14.2

Three-Point Field Goals: 1980-81, 1-for-5 (.200). 1981-82, 7-for-25 (.280). 1982-83, 7-for-33 (.212). 1983-84, 2-for-8 (.250). 1984-85, 5-for-21 (.238). 1985-86, 2-for-13 (.154). 1986-87, 34-for-123 (.276). 1987-88, 18-for-78 (.231). 1988-89, 31-for-89 (.348). 1989-90, 12-for-41 (.293). Totals, 119-for-436 (.273).

NBA PLAYOFF RECORD

										—Rebounds—								
Sea.—Team	G.	Min.	FGA	FGM	Pct.	FTA	FTM	Pct.	Off.	Def.	Tot.	Ast.	PF	Dq.	Stl.	Blk.	Pts.	Avg.
80-81—New York	2	8	3	1	.333	2	2	1.000	2	0	2	0	3	0	0	0	4	2.0
83-84—Kansas City	3	87	44	18	.409	15	13	.867	4	4	8	9	11	0	2	0	49	16.3
85-86—Sacramento	3	110	49	22	.449	12	12	1.000	7	4	11	5	13	0	4	2	56	18.7
88-89—Houston	4	137	49	17	.347	12	10	.833	4	5	9	18	7	0	4	2	47	11.8
89-90—Houston	1	6	3	1	.333	0	0	....	0	0	0	2	1	0	0	0	2	2.0
Totals	13	348	148	59	.399	41	37	.902	17	13	30	34	35	0	10	4	158	12.2

Three-Point Field Goals: 1983-84, 0-for-1. 1985-86, 0-for-2. 1988-89, 3-for-9 (.333). 1989-90, 0-for-1. Totals, 3-for-13 (.231).

ORLANDO VERNADA WOOLRIDGE

Born December 16, 1959 at Bernice, La. Height 6:09. Weight 215.

High Schools—Pelican, La., All Saints (Freshman, Sophomore and Junior) and Mansfield, La. (Senior).

College—University of Notre Dame, Notre Dame, Ind.

Drafted by Chicago on first round, 1981 (6th pick).

Signed by New Jersey as a Veteran Free Agent, October 2, 1986; Chicago agreed not to exercise its right of first refusal in exchange for a 1987 1st round draft choice and 1988 and 1990 2nd round draft choices.

Signed by Los Angeles Lakers as an unrestricted free agent, August 10, 1988.

Traded by Los Angeles Lakers to Denver for 1993 and 1995 2nd round draft choices, August 3, 1990.

—COLLEGIATE RECORD—

Year	G.	Min.	FGA	FGM	Pct.	FTA	FTM	Pct.	Reb.	Pts.	Avg.
77-78	24	230	78	41	.526	33	16	.485	51	98	4.1
78-79	30	752	253	145	.573	56	41	.732	145	331	11.0
79-80	27	835	212	124	.585	117	81	.692	186	329	12.2
80-81	28	924	240	156	.650	135	90	.667	168	402	14.4
Totals	109	2741	783	466	.595	341	228	.669	550	1160	10.6

NBA REGULAR SEASON RECORD

										—Rebounds—								
Sea.—Team	G.	Min.	FGA	FGM	Pct.	FTA	FTM	Pct.	Off.	Def.	Tot.	Ast.	PF	Dq.	Stl.	Blk.	Pts.	Avg.
81-82—Chicago	75	1188	394	202	.513	206	144	.699	82	145	227	81	152	1	23	24	548	7.3
82-83—Chicago	57	1627	622	361	.580	340	217	.638	122	176	298	97	177	1	38	44	939	16.5
83-84—Chicago	75	2544	1086	570	.525	424	303	.715	130	239	369	136	253	6	71	60	1444	19.3
84-85—Chicago	77	2816	1225	679	.554	521	409	.785	158	277	435	135	185	0	58	38	1767	22.9
85-86—Chicago	70	2248	1090	540	.495	462	364	.788	150	200	350	213	186	2	49	47	1448	20.7
86-87—New Jersey	75	2638	1067	556	.521	564	438	.777	118	249	367	261	243	4	54	86	1551	20.7
87-88—New Jersey	19	622	247	110	.445	130	92	.708	31	60	91	71	73	2	13	20	312	16.4
88-89—L.A. Lakers	74	1491	494	231	.468	343	253	.738	81	189	270	58	130	0	30	65	715	9.7
89-90—L.A. Lakers	62	1421	550	306	.556	240	176	.733	49	136	185	96	160	2	39	46	788	12.7
Totals	584	16595	6775	3555	.525	3230	2396	.742	921	1671	2592	1148	1559	18	375	430	9512	16.3

Three-Point Field Goals: 1981-82, 0-for-3. 1982-83, 0-for-3. 1983-84, 1-for-2 (.500). 1984-85, 0-for-5. 1985-86, 4-for-23 (.174). 1986-87, 1-for-8 (.125). 1987-88, 0-for-2. 1988-89, 0-for-1. 1989-90, 0-for-5. Totals, 6-for-52 (.115).

NBA PLAYOFF RECORD

										—Rebounds—								
Sea.—Team	G.	Min.	FGA	FGM	Pct.	FTA	FTM	Pct.	Off.	Def.	Tot.	Ast.	PF	Dq.	Stl.	Blk.	Pts.	Avg.
84-85—Chicago	4	167	68	34	.500	18	14	.778	6	7	13	8	19	1	6	1	82	20.5
85-86—Chicago	3	135	62	25	.403	15	13	.867	6	8	14	4	12	0	3	1	63	21.0
88-89—L.A. Lakers	15	276	75	39	.520	62	44	.710	20	50	70	17	35	0	2	15	122	8.1
89-90—L.A. Lakers	9	199	70	40	.571	37	26	.703	6	17	23	10	25	1	8	8	106	11.8
Totals	31	777	275	138	.502	132	97	.735	38	82	120	39	91	2	19	25	373	12.0

Three-Point Field Goals: 1985-86, 0-for-1. 1989-90, 0-for-1. Totals, 0-for-2.

Named to THE SPORTING NEWS All-America Second Team, 1981.

HAYWOODE WILVON WORKMAN

Born January 23, 1966 at Charlotte, N.C. Height 6:02. Weight 180.
High School—Charlotte, N.C., Myers Park.
Colleges—Winston-Salem State University, Winston-Salem, N.C., and Oral Roberts University, Tulsa, Okla.
Drafted by Atlanta on second round, 1989 (49th pick).

Waived by Atlanta, November 2, 1989; re-signed by Atlanta, February 26, 1990, to the first of consecutive 10-day contracts that expired, February 15, 1990.

Played in Continental Basketball Association with Topeka Sizzlers, 1989-90.

—COLLEGIATE RECORD—

Winston-Salem

Year	G.	Min.	FGA	FGM	Pct.	FTA	FTM	Pct.	Reb.	Pts.	Avg.
84-85	25	....	223	102	.457	90	53	.589	75	257	10.3

Oral Roberts

Year	G.	Min.	FGA	FGM	Pct.	FTA	FTM	Pct.	Reb.	Pts.	Avg.
85-86					Did Not Play—Transfer Student						
86-87	28	1086	342	125	.366	152	121	.796	93	387	13.8
87-88	29	988	496	206	.415	143	108	.755	174	562	19.4
88-89	28	980	424	205	.483	135	110	.815	171	557	19.9
ORU Totals	85	3054	1262	536	.425	430	339	.788	438	1506	13.7
Col. Totals	110	....	1485	638	.430	520	392	.754	513	1763	16.0

Three-Point Field Goals: 1986-87, 16-for-56 (.286). 1987-88, 42-for-149 (.282). 1988-89, 37-for-101 (.366). Totals, 95-for-306 (.310).

CBA REGULAR SEASON RECORD

			2-Point			3-Point									
Sea.—Team	G.	Min.	FGM	FGA	Pct.	FGM	FGA	Pct.	FTM	FTA	Pct.	Reb.	Ast.	Pts.	Avg.
89-90—Topeka	46	1513	243	496	.490	40	154	.260	179	218	.821	200	213	785	17.1

NBA REGULAR SEASON RECORD

									—Rebounds—									
Sea.—Team	G.	Min.	FGA	FGM	Pct.	FTA	FTM	Pct.	Off.	Def.	Tot.	Ast.	PF	Dq.	Stl.	Blk.	Pts.	Avg.
89-90—Atlanta	6	16	3	2	.667	2	2	1.000	0	3	3	2	3	0	3	0	6	1.0

JAMES AGER WORTHY

Born February 27, 1961 at Gastonia, N. C. Height 6:09. Weight 225.
High School—Gastonia, N. C., Ashbrook.
College—University of North Carolina, Chapel Hill, N. C.
Drafted by Los Angeles on first round as an undergraduate, 1982 (1st pick).

—COLLEGIATE RECORD—

Year	G.	Min.	FGA	FGM	Pct.	FTA	FTM	Pct.	Reb.	Pts.	Avg.
79-80	14	....	126	74	.587	45	27	.600	104	175	12.5
80-81	36	....	416	208	.500	150	96	.640	301	512	14.2
81-82	34	....	354	203	.573	187	126	.674	215	532	15.6
Totals	84	....	896	485	.541	382	249	.652	620	1219	14.5

NBA REGULAR SEASON RECORD

									—Rebounds—									
Sea.—Team	G.	Min.	FGA	FGM	Pct.	FTA	FTM	Pct.	Off.	Def.	Tot.	Ast.	PF	Dq.	Stl.	Blk.	Pts.	Avg.
82-83—Los Angeles	77	1970	772	447	.579	221	138	.624	157	242	399	132	221	2	91	64	1033	13.4
83-84—Los Angeles	82	2415	890	495	.556	257	195	.759	157	358	515	207	244	5	77	70	1185	14.5
84-85—L.A. Lakers	80	2696	1066	610	.572	245	190	.776	169	342	511	201	196	0	87	67	1410	17.6
85-86—L.A. Lakers	75	2454	1086	629	.579	314	242	.771	136	251	387	201	195	0	82	77	1500	20.0
86-87—L.A. Lakers	82	2819	1207	651	.539	389	292	.751	158	308	466	226	206	0	108	83	1594	19.4
87-88—L.A. Lakers	75	2655	1161	617	.531	304	242	.796	129	245	374	289	175	1	72	55	1478	19.7
88-89—L.A. Lakers	81	2960	1282	702	.548	321	251	.782	169	320	489	288	175	0	108	56	1657	20.5
89-90—L.A. Lakers	80	2960	1298	711	.548	317	248	.782	160	318	478	288	190	0	99	49	1685	21.1
Totals	632	20929	8762	4862	.555	2368	1798	.759	1235	2384	3619	1832	1602	8	724	521	11542	18.3

Three-Point Field Goals: 1982-83, 1-for-4 (.250). 1983-84, 0-for-6. 1984-85, 0-for-7. 1985-86, 0-for-13. 1986-87, 0-for-13. 1987-88, 2-for-16 (.125). 1988-89, 2-for-23 (.087). 1989-90, 15-for-49 (.306). Totals, 20-for-131 (.153).

NBA PLAYOFF RECORD

									—Rebounds—									
Sea.—Team	G.	Min.	FGA	FGM	Pct.	FTA	FTM	Pct.	Off.	Def.	Tot.	Ast.	PF	Dq.	Stl.	Blk.	Pts.	Avg.
83-84—Los Angeles	21	708	274	164	.599	69	42	.609	36	69	105	56	57	0	27	11	371	17.7
84-85—L.A. Lakers	19	626	267	166	.622	111	75	.676	35	61	96	41	53	1	17	13	408	21.5
85-86—L.A. Lakers	14	539	217	121	.558	47	32	.681	22	43	65	45	43	0	16	10	274	19.6
86-87—L.A. Lakers	18	681	298	176	.591	97	73	.753	31	70	101	63	42	1	28	22	425	23.6
87-88—L.A. Lakers	24	896	390	204	.523	128	97	.758	53	86	139	106	58	0	33	19	506	21.1
88-89—L.A. Lakers	15	600	270	153	.567	80	63	.788	37	64	101	42	36	0	18	16	372	24.8
89-90—L.A. Lakers	9	366	181	90	.497	43	36	.837	11	39	50	27	18	0	14	3	218	24.2
Totals	120	4416	1897	1074	.566	575	418	.727	225	432	657	380	307	2	153	94	2574	21.5

Three-Point Field Goals: 1983-84, 1-for-2 (.500). 1984-85, 1-for-2 (.500). 1985-86, 0-for-4. 1986-87, 0-for-2. 1987-88, 1-for-9 (.111). 1988-89, 3-for-8 (.375). 1989-90, 2-for-8 (.250). Totals, 8-for-35 (.229).

NBA ALL-STAR GAME RECORD

								—Rebounds—								
Season—Team	Min.	FGA	FGM	Pct.	FTA	FTM	Pct.	Off.	Def.	Tot.	Ast.	PF	Dq.	Stl.	Blk.	Pts.
1986—L.A. Lakers..	28	19	10	.526	0	0	.000	2	1	3	2	3	0	0	2	20
1987—L.A. Lakers..	29	14	10	.714	2	2	1.000	6	2	8	3	3	0	1	0	22
1988—L.A. Lakers..	13	8	2	.250	1	0	.000	1	2	3	1	1	0	0	1	4
1989—L.A. Lakers..	18	7	4	.571	0	0	.000	0	2	2	2	0	0	2	0	8
1990—L.A. Lakers..	19	11	1	.091	0	0	—	3	1	4	0	1	0	1	0	2
Totals	107	59	27	.458	3	2	.667	12	8	20	8	8	0	4	3	56

Three-Point Field Goals: 1986, 0-for-2. 1989, 0-for-1. Totals, 0-for-3.

Named to All-NBA Third Team, 1990. . . . NBA All-Rookie Team, 1983. . . . Member of NBA championship teams, 1985, 1987, 1988. . . . NBA Playoff MVP, 1988. . . . THE SPORTING NEWS All-America First Team, 1982. . . . NCAA Division I Tournament Most Outstanding Player, 1982. . . . Member of NCAA Division I championship team, 1982.

DANNY YOUNG

Born July 26, 1962 at Raleigh, N.C. Height 6:04. Weight 175.

High School—Raleigh, N.C., Enloe.

College—Wake Forest University, Winston-Salem, N.C.

Drafted by Seattle on second round, 1984 (39th pick).

Waived by Seattle, November 13, 1984; re-signed by Seattle as a free agent, August 9, 1985.
Waived by Seattle, October 31, 1988; signed by Portland as a free agent, November 2, 1988.
Played in Continental Basketball Association with Wyoming Wildcatters, 1984-85.

—COLLEGIATE RECORD—

Year	G.	Min.	FGA	FGM	Pct.	FTA	FTM	Pct.	Reb.	Pts.	Avg.
80-81	29	491	117	58	.496	48	33	.688	38	149	5.1
81-82	30	946	254	129	.508	84	60	.714	74	318	10.6
82-83	31	999	315	144	.457	115	82	.713	66	397	12.8
83-84	32	1043	272	124	.456	82	58	.707	59	306	9.6
Totals	122	3479	958	455	.475	329	233	.708	237	1170	9.6

Three-Point Field Goals: 1982-83, 27-for-73 (.370).

CBA REGULAR SEASON RECORD

			—2-Point—			—3-Point—									
Sea.—Team	G.	Min.	FGM	FGA	Pct.	FGM	FGA	Pct.	FTM	FTA	Pct.	Reb.	Ast.	Pts.	Avg.
84-85—Wyoming	26	489	77	156	.493	4	12	.333	59	61	.967	34	95	225	8.7

NBA REGULAR SEASON RECORD

									—Rebounds—									
Sea.—Team	G.	Min.	FGA	FGM	Pct.	FTA	FTM	Pct.	Off.	Def.	Tot.	Ast.	PF	Dq.	Stl.	Blk.	Pts.	Avg.
84-85—Seattle	3	26	10	2	.200	0	0	.000	0	3	3	2	2	0	3	0	4	1.3
85-86—Seattle	82	1901	449	227	.506	106	90	.849	29	91	120	303	113	0	110	9	568	6.9
86-87—Seattle	73	1482	288	132	.458	71	59	.831	23	90	113	353	72	0	74	3	352	4.8
87-88—Seattle	77	949	218	89	.408	53	43	.811	18	57	75	218	69	0	52	2	243	3.2
88-89—Portland	48	952	250	115	.460	64	50	.781	17	57	74	123	50	0	55	3	297	6.2
89-90—Portland	82	1393	328	138	.421	112	91	.813	29	93	122	231	84	0	82	4	383	4.7
Totals	365	6703	1543	703	.456	406	333	.820	116	391	507	1230	390	0	376	21	1847	5.1

Three-Point Field Goals: 1984-85, 0-for-1. 1985-86, 24-for-74 (.324). 1986-87, 29-for-79 (.367). 1987-88, 22-for-77 (.286). 1988-89, 17-for-50 (.340). 1989-90, 16-for-59 (.271). Totals, 108-for-340 (.318).

NBA PLAYOFF RECORD

									—Rebounds—									
Sea.—Team	G.	Min.	FGA	FGM	Pct.	FTA	FTM	Pct.	Off.	Def.	Tot.	Ast.	PF	Dq.	Stl.	Blk.	Pts.	Avg.
86-87—Seattle	14	208	52	21	.404	10	10	1.000	4	12	16	48	21	1	15	0	57	4.1
87-88—Seattle	5	95	21	11	.524	10	10	1.000	3	7	10	19	7	0	2	2	32	6.4
88-89—Portland	3	66	26	12	.462	2	1	.500	2	6	8	12	2	0	1	0	28	9.3
89-90—Portland	21	294	72	28	.389	27	19	.704	11	19	30	32	29	0	14	2	86	4.1
Totals	43	663	171	72	.421	49	40	.816	20	44	64	111	59	1	32	4	203	4.7

Three-Point Field Goals: 1986-87, 5-for-16 (.313). 1987-88, 0-for-3. 1988-89, 3-for-8 (.375). 1989-90, 11-for-29 (.379). Totals, 19-for-56 (.339).

MICHAEL WAYNE YOUNG

Born January 2, 1961 at Houston, Tex. Height 6:07. Weight 220.

High School—Houston, Tex., Yates.

College—University of Houston, Houston, Tex.

Drafted by Boston on first round, 1984 (24th pick).

Waived by Boston, October 25, 1984; signed by Phoenix as a free agent, November 27, 1984.

Waived by Phoenix, December 10, 1984; signed by Houston as a free agent, September 26, 1985.
Waived by Houston, October 22, 1985; signed by Philadelphia as a free agent, April 4, 1986.
Waived by Philadelphia, November 19, 1987; signed by Los Angeles Clippers as a free agent, September 6, 1989.
Played in Continental Basketball Association with Detroit Spirits, 1984-85 and 1985-86.

—COLLEGIATE RECORD—

Year	G.	Min.	FGA	FGM	Pct.	FTA	FTM	Pct.	Reb.	Pts.	Avg.
80-81	30	1049	319	157	.492	84	47	.560	190	361	12.0
81-82	33	979	358	158	.441	64	44	.688	179	360	10.9
82-83	34	1116	519	266	.513	88	56	.636	195	588	17.3
83-84	37	1354	637	319	.501	149	96	.644	231	734	19.8
Totals	134	4498	1833	900	.491	385	243	.631	795	2043	15.2

CBA REGULAR SEASON RECORD

			—2-Point—			—3-Point—									
Sea.—Team	G.	Min.	FGM	FGA	Pct.	FGM	FGA	Pct.	FTM	FTA	Pct.	Reb.	Ast.	Pts.	Avg.
84-85—Detroit	43	1308	313	586	.534	9	31	.290	79	119	.663	256	85	732	17.0
85-86—Detroit	48	1778	533	993	.536	5	25	.200	204	274	.744	411	105	1285	26.8
Totals	91	3086	846	1579	.535	14	56	.250	283	393	.720	667	190	2017	22.2

NBA REGULAR SEASON RECORD

									—Rebounds—									
Sea.—Team	G.	Min.	FGA	FGM	Pct.	FTA	FTM	Pct.	Off.	Def.	Tot.	Ast.	PF	Dq.	Stl.	Blk.	Pts.	Avg.
84-85—Phoenix	2	11	6	2	.333	0	0	.000	1	1	2	0	0	0	0	0	4	2.0
85-86—Philadelphia	2	2	2	0	.000	0	0	.000	0	0	0	0	0	0	0	0	0	0.0
89-90—L.A. Clippers	45	459	194	92	.474	38	27	.711	36	50	86	24	47	0	25	3	219	4.9
Totals	49	472	202	94	.465	38	27	.711	37	51	88	24	47	0	25	3	223	4.6

Three-Point Field Goals: 1984-85, 0-for-1. 1989-90, 8-for-26 (.308). Totals, 8-for-27 (.296).

NBA PLAYOFF RECORD

									—Rebounds—									
Sea.—Team	G.	Min.	FGA	FGM	Pct.	FTA	FTM	Pct.	Off.	Def.	Tot.	Ast.	PF	Dq.	Stl.	Blk.	Pts.	Avg.
85-86—Philadelphia	3	3	4	1	.250	0	0	.000	1	0	1	0	0	0	0	0	2	0.7

Named CBA Most Valuable Player, 1986. . . . CBA All-Star First Team, 1986. . . . THE SPORTING NEWS All-America Second Team, 1984.

Individual Career Highs

Regular Season

Player	FGM	FGA	FTM	FTA	Reb.	Ast.	Pts.
Mark Acres	8	11	6	10	15	4	19
Michael Adams	12	24	14	18	10	17	35
Mark Aguirre	21	40	14	20	15	17	49
Danny Ainge	20	29	13	13	11	15	45
Mark Alarie	10	18	6	6	13	5	22
Steve Alford	7	14	4	4	4	7	17
Randy Allen	7	13	3	5	7	2	14
Greg Anderson	13	19	11	15	21	6	31
Nick Anderson	12	20	8	13	13	6	29
Richard Anderson	11	20	8	10	14	8	23
Ron Anderson	15	26	12	12	15	8	36
Willie Anderson	18	26	12	14	12	12	36
Michael Ansley	11	23	9	11	16	4	26
B.J. Armstrong	9	16	5	5	4	9	20
John Bagley	16	21	10	12	11	19	35
Thurl Bailey	17	27	13	16	17	9	41
Ken Bannister	14	25	11	16	16	4	35
Charles Barkley	18	30	21	26	25	14	47
Dana Barros	11	22	8	8	6	10	28
John Battle	12	22	10	12	7	14	27
Kenny Battle	7	9	6	8	7	4	16
William Bedford	8	18	6	8	13	4	17
Benoit Benjamin	15	23	12	15	23	9	34
Winston Bennett	9	13	7	8	14	5	20
Walter Berry	14	24	15	21	14	8	31
Larry Bird	22	36	16	17	21	17	60
Uwe Blab	5	11	6	8	10	3	14
Rolando Blackman	19	32	22	23	11	10	46
Mookie Blaylock	11	20	8	8	11	9	24
Muggsy Bogues	10	17	7	8	7	19	22
Manute Bol	7	14	8	14	19	3	18
Anthony Bowie	12	18	6	8	8	5	24
Sam Bowie	11	26	14	18	20	7	31
Adrian Branch	12	22	7	10	7	4	28
Randy Breuer	14	28	12	17	17	6	40
Frank Brickowski	12	28	14	20	15	10	34
Scott Brooks	7	13	7	8	5	13	20
Tony Brown	11	19	11	14	11	9	29
Chucky Brown	12	17	8	8	9	3	30
Mike Brown	8	13	8	11	12	4	22
Raymond Brown	3	5	0	2	5	2	6
Stanley Brundy	6	6	3	7	7	2	12
Mark Bryant	7	12	5	6	15	4	17
Torgeir Bryn	0	2	4	6	2	0	4
Steve Bucknall	2	4	3	4	1	2	4
Greg Butler	3	7	3	4	3	1	7
Michael Cage	12	19	15	19	30	6	29
Adrian Caldwell	4	6	3	4	8	1	11
Tony Campbell	15	29	16	23	14	8	44
Rick Carlisle	9	12	3	4	5	7	21
Antoine Carr	10	23	14	18	12	8	32
Joe Barry Carroll	22	37	14	18	24	7	52
Bill Cartwright	16	26	19	19	18	8	38
Terry Catledge	18	29	14	19	20	4	49
Tom Chambers	22	32	18	22	18	9	60
Rex Chapman	17	32	13	13	9	7	38
Maurice Cheeks	15	23	11	14	10	21	32
Derrick Chievous	12	18	9	11	10	5	27
Ben Coleman	10	17	8	11	18	3	23
Steve Colter	14	21	12	14	10	12	35
Lester Conner	10	17	11	13	13	18	24
Wayne Cooper	13	22	12	14	19	7	32
Michael Cooper	13	22	10	11	13	17	31
Lanard Copeland	4	10	2	2	2	2	8
Tyrone Corbin	15	27	8	10	19	7	36
Dave Corzine	15	29	17	19	22	9	35

Player	FGM	FGA	FTM	FTA	Reb.	Ast.	Pts.
Pat Cummings	14	25	10	13	20	6	34
Terry Cummings	19	32	14	20	24	10	52
Dell Curry	14	26	6	8	8	8	31
Quintin Dailey	17	29	15	18	10	12	44
Adrian Dantley	24	36	28	31	19	11	57
Brad Daugherty	15	22	14	18	17	13	44
Brad Davis	14	17	11	14	8	17	32
Charles Davis	15	22	5	7	13	5	33
Terry Davis	9	16	3	6	16	3	18
Walter Davis	19	33	19	21	13	12	45
Johnny Dawkins	13	25	13	14	8	15	30
Vinny Del Negro	13	19	12	15	8	13	28
Byron Dinkins	4	9	4	6	4	12	12
Vlade Divac	10	15	7	10	14	5	25
James Donaldson	12	17	13	17	27	7	29
Sherman Douglas	15	26	10	14	7	17	37
Terry Dozier	3	8	3	6	5	1	6
Greg Dreiling	5	7	7	10	7	3	12
Larry Drew	13	27	15	18	8	17	33
Clyde Drexler	20	33	15	17	16	16	50
Kevin Duckworth	14	27	12	16	18	5	32
Chris Dudley	7	16	5	18	20	4	15
Joe Dumars	18	26	18	19	10	14	42
Mike Dunleavy	19	30	12	15	7	17	48
T.R. Dunn	10	18	11	14	17	8	23
Ledell Eackles	17	33	11	14	8	7	40
Mark Eaton	8	18	10	12	25	7	20
Blue Edwards	9	15	7	10	8	6	22
James Edwards	16	29	18	19	18	7	39
Jay Edwards	2	2	1	2	1	3	5
Kevin Edwards	14	25	8	9	10	12	34
Craig Ehlo	11	23	8	11	14	12	31
Sean Elliott	12	17	8	8	10	6	24
Dale Ellis	20	39	17	19	12	9	53
Pervis Ellison	9	13	7	11	12	7	25
Alex English	24	37	17	19	20	16	54
Patrick Ewing	20	32	16	20	24	7	51
Jim Farmer	7	12	12	14	4	4	26
Duane Ferrell	5	10	6	9	3	2	16
Vern Fleming	12	23	14	18	13	17	30
Sleepy Floyd	15	26	14	17	13	19	41
Tellis Frank	11	22	8	11	15	6	24
Corey Gaines	7	9	3	5	2	11	18
Kevin Gamble	13	18	9	12	7	10	31
Winston Garland	12	23	10	12	12	16	31
Tom Garrick	10	14	8	9	8	18	23
Kenny Gattison	14	18	7	8	11	3	29
Derrick Gervin	8	20	9	11	11	2	25
Armon Gilliam	18	26	11	14	21	5	41
Mike Gminski	15	23	15	16	22	9	41
Gary Grant	13	23	9	10	11	21	31
Greg Grant	6	14	5	6	6	14	14
Harvey Grant	11	18	6	6	14	6	24
Horace Grant	11	19	13	14	18	9	25
Stuart Gray	6	10	7	8	16	3	15
Jeff Grayer	8	17	8	9	11	5	18
A.C. Green	13	23	17	21	18	5	33
Rickey Green	16	25	13	17	9	20	45
Sidney Green	16	27	13	14	23	8	36
David Greenwood	14	26	12	14	23	10	35
Darrell Griffith	19	32	11	12	13	10	41
Scott Haffner	7	18	5	6	4	7	14
Jack Haley	8	15	7	10	15	3	19
Tom Hammonds	7	16	5	7	10	5	17
Bobby Hansen	12	20	9	11	11	9	28
Bill Hanzlik	11	25	17	18	11	11	33
Tim Hardaway	12	20	8	11	10	19	28
Derek Harper	16	29	10	14	11	18	42
Ron Harper	19	29	15	19	16	12	40
Steve Harris	10	18	16	17	8	6	24
Scott Hastings	8	16	9	10	17	6	17
Hersey Hawkins	13	25	12	13	11	8	32

Player	FGM	FGA	FTM	FTA	Reb.	Ast.	Pts.
Gerald Henderson	12	20	9	12	9	17	31
Mike Higgins	1	3	4	4	2	1	6
Rod Higgins	15	20	14	14	12	9	41
Roy Hinson	14	26	17	20	18	5	39
Craig Hodges	13	23	8	8	9	12	29
Michael Holton	10	17	8	8	9	15	25
Dave Hoppen	7	14	6	6	14	4	17
Dennis Hopson	12	24	12	14	9	6	32
Tito Horford	5	10	4	4	7	1	10
Jeff Hornacek	13	25	7	8	12	18	32
Ed Horton	8	14	5	6	11	3	18
Eddie Hughes	6	9	6	6	6	7	17
Jay Humphries	13	23	12	15	10	16	30
Byron Irvin	10	15	8	11	7	6	23
Jaren Jackson	5	8	3	5	4	3	13
Mark Jackson	14	27	12	15	10	18	34
Michael Jackson	5	13	5	6	4	13	11
Buck Johnson	13	22	10	10	11	10	30
Avery Johnson	5	11	7	10	3	18	12
Steve Johnson	14	23	17	19	18	9	40
Dennis Johnson	14	29	16	18	12	17	39
Magic Johnson	18	36	19	22	18	24	46
Eddie A. Johnson	18	32	11	14	15	10	45
Eric Johnson	3	6	2	2	3	8	6
Kevin Johnson	16	28	23	24	13	21	44
Marques Johnson	18	32	14	18	18	11	40
Vinnie Johnson	15	25	11	12	11	15	35
Nate Johnston	4	7	3	4	5	1	8
Anthony Jones	10	17	5	6	7	5	24
Caldwell Jones	12	22	13	14	27	7	29
Charles Jones	7	13	6	9	14	7	17
Michael Jordan	24	43	26	27	18	17	69
Shawn Kemp	10	15	7	8	10	3	20
Tim Kempton	8	13	9	11	10	7	21
Steve Kerr	6	12	5	5	5	11	19
Jerome Kersey	15	26	15	16	20	10	36
Randolph Keys	11	20	5	8	9	5	22
Stan Kimbrough	2	4	2	2	2	2	4
Bernard King	20	34	22	26	18	14	60
Stacey King	10	14	10	13	14	6	24
Greg Kite	7	13	6	8	15	5	16
Joe Kleine	10	17	8	10	18	8	23
Jon Koncak	9	19	9	16	20	5	25
Frank Kornet	5	7	6	8	6	2	16
Larry Krystkowiak	11	18	15	17	18	7	31
Bill Laimbeer	16	27	12	13	24	11	35
Jerome Lane	8	15	4	10	16	7	18
Andrew Lang	8	13	6	9	15	2	21
Jeff Lebo	1	3	2	2	2	2	4
Eric Leckner	8	15	7	9	9	2	21
Keith Lee	8	15	9	9	17	7	25
Tim Legler	2	7	4	4	5	2	8
Gary Leonard	3	6	2	4	4	1	6
Jim Les	3	8	6	6	5	8	11
Clifford Lett	1	3	0	0	0	1	2
Lafayette Lever	16	28	13	14	22	23	38
Cliff Levingston	11	20	11	14	17	7	29
Ralph Lewis	7	11	5	7	6	3	17
Reggie Lewis	16	30	11	15	12	9	39
Todd Lichti	9	13	10	12	5	6	20
Alton Lister	13	17	8	12	21	6	30
Lewis Lloyd	16	26	12	14	13	12	38
Brad Lohaus	11	24	7	10	16	7	29
Grant Long	10	17	12	15	14	5	30
John Long	18	31	13	15	13	12	44
Sidney Lowe	10	14	5	8	8	17	22
John Lucas	15	26	11	15	11	24	35
Rick Mahorn	12	23	14	15	20	7	34
Dan Majerle	13	20	10	11	12	7	32
Jeff Malone	19	35	14	15	11	10	48
Karl Malone	22	34	20	24	22	9	61
Moses Malone	20	35	21	26	37	7	53

Player	FGM	FGA	FTM	FTA	Reb.	Ast.	Pts.
Danny Manning	14	22	11	15	15	9	39
Roy Marble	3	8	3	5	4	3	7
Sarunas Marciulionis	11	20	10	12	9	4	33
Jeff Martin	8	15	6	7	12	4	20
Anthony Mason	4	8	2	4	7	2	8
Wes Matthews	13	20	12	13	7	18	29
Vernon Maxwell	15	23	9	12	8	12	32
Bob McCann	2	6	4	4	3	2	8
Mel McCants	2	8	4	4	3	1	4
George McCloud	5	9	4	4	5	3	13
Tim McCormick	13	19	11	15	16	8	29
Rodney McCray	12	21	12	14	18	14	30
Xavier McDaniel	17	29	13	20	19	8	41
Mike McGee	18	30	9	12	10	12	41
Kevin McHale	22	30	15	19	18	10	56
Derrick McKey	15	25	13	14	17	7	34
Carlton McKinney	3	8	1	2	4	4	7
Nate McMillan	8	13	10	13	14	25	21
Mark McNamara	9	15	5	8	22	2	22
Scott Meents	4	5	4	6	4	2	10
Reggie Miller	15	28	15	17	10	10	44
Sam Mitchell	12	24	13	14	15	4	31
Paul Mokeski	9	16	9	10	13	6	21
Johnny Moore	12	22	10	12	11	20	30
Chris Morris	14	23	10	14	16	7	33
Mike Morrison	5	11	4	4	3	1	11
John Morton	4	15	8	12	5	9	14
Chris Mullin	16	27	17	19	18	14	47
Tod Murphy	10	18	8	10	20	4	24
Pete Myers	7	12	9	10	6	9	16
Larry Nance	19	29	13	18	21	11	45
Calvin Natt	16	29	16	22	19	8	39
Ed Nealy	9	15	8	10	16	5	23
Chuck Nevitt	5	6	4	4	10	2	12
Johnny Newman	12	22	14	14	9	7	35
Kurt Nimphius	11	20	9	10	15	10	26
Dyron Nix	2	7	4	6	7	2	8
Ken Norman	18	30	10	15	20	12	38
Charles Oakley	14	27	13	15	35	15	35
Akeem Olajuwon	21	34	14	20	25	10	52
Jawann Oldham	8	14	5	8	15	4	19
Jose Ortiz	7	9	4	6	6	4	15
Robert Parish	16	31	13	18	32	10	40
Zarko Paspalj	4	12	5	5	4	1	13
Jim Paxson	18	33	13	15	8	11	41
John Paxson	12	20	9	10	6	14	27
Kenny Payne	5	9	4	4	4	1	10
Will Perdue	5	10	8	12	8	3	14
Sam Perkins	19	29	11	15	20	7	45
Tim Perry	9	14	6	9	11	2	22
Chuck Person	19	32	12	13	18	10	47
Jim Petersen	11	19	12	16	16	6	28
Drazen Petrovic	11	19	9	10	5	6	24
Ricky Pierce	17	28	14	17	12	7	45
Ed Pinckney	11	17	12	15	17	6	27
Scottie Pippen	13	24	10	14	15	12	31
Olden Polynice	9	13	8	10	12	4	18
Terry Porter	14	24	14	15	13	19	40
Paul Pressey	13	23	17	19	15	16	30
Harold Pressley	12	25	14	14	15	8	31
Mark Price	13	24	18	20	11	20	37
Brian Quinnett	3	6	2	2	4	2	6
Kurt Rambis	11	16	8	12	22	8	23
Blair Rasmussen	16	28	10	11	16	5	35
J.R. Reid	10	22	9	12	20	4	25
Robert Reid	15	26	12	13	16	12	32
Jerry Reynolds	13	25	10	14	12	10	34
Glen Rice	13	26	7	7	13	6	28
Jerome Richardson	12	25	4	6	10	15	27
Mitch Richmond	17	28	16	19	12	11	47
David Rivers	5	11	5	8	8	10	15
Glenn Rivers	14	24	17	17	14	21	37

Player	FGM	FGA	FTM	FTA	Reb.	Ast.	Pts.
Fred Roberts	11	17	13	14	15	7	27
Alvin Robertson	17	29	14	15	16	17	41
Cliff R. Robinson	10	19	6	12	10	3	22
David Robinson	16	29	17	22	21	7	41
Dennis Rodman	13	17	9	12	21	5	32
Wayne Rollins	11	20	8	9	23	6	26
Doug Roth	4	6	2	2	13	3	8
Scott Roth	8	17	10	13	7	7	24
Jim Rowinski	3	6	7	9	7	1	11
Brian Rowsom	7	14	8	8	12	3	20
Donald Royal	8	16	11	13	11	4	23
Delaney Rudd	7	12	4	5	5	7	18
John Salley	10	15	11	12	13	5	28
Ralph Sampson	19	33	15	17	25	9	43
Jeff Sanders	2	4	2	4	7	2	6
Mike Sanders	14	20	11	14	13	7	30
Danny Schayes	12	23	18	18	24	11	37
Detlef Schrempf	11	18	13	14	19	10	29
Byron Scott	15	27	13	14	10	10	38
Rony Seikaly	15	23	13	19	22	6	40
Brad Sellers	14	25	9	12	13	8	32
Charles Shackleford	9	17	7	11	26	5	23
John Shasky	8	13	8	10	12	3	19
Brian Shaw	14	23	6	6	15	13	31
Purvis Short	24	38	18	20	15	14	59
Dexter Shouse	0	3	0	0	0	1	0
Jerry Sichting	12	18	10	11	7	16	29
Jack Sikma	15	28	21	23	25	10	39
Scott Skiles	9	18	10	10	12	17	23
Charles D. Smith (L.A.C.)	14	25	14	19	16	6	40
Charles E. Smith (Bos.)	5	12	6	8	7	9	12
Derek Smith	14	26	13	17	11	10	41
Kenny Smith	13	23	11	12	8	15	33
Larry Smith	11	19	9	14	31	6	25
Michael Smith	11	18	5	6	10	8	24
Otis Smith	14	24	12	12	16	8	33
Rik Smits	14	24	10	13	15	5	34
Mike Smrek	6	11	5	7	11	4	15
Rory Sparrow	13	23	11	12	10	17	30
John Stockton	14	22	15	16	9	27	34
Greg Stokes	1	4	2	2	2	0	2
Rod Strickland	10	18	8	12	10	17	22
Jon Sundvold	12	22	8	9	7	14	28
Roy Tarpley	15	25	11	13	25	7	35
Jay Taylor	3	7	4	4	2	1	8
Leonard Taylor	0	2	3	4	5	1	3
Terry Teagle	16	26	16	18	12	7	44
Reggie Theus	18	33	16	18	17	18	46
Isiah Thomas	19	34	16	20	12	25	47
LaSalle Thompson	13	20	13	14	22	8	31
Mychal Thompson	17	28	12	20	22	11	38
Billy Thompson	13	20	11	14	18	7	30
Bob Thornton	7	13	6	8	14	5	17
Otis Thorpe	15	27	14	19	26	11	37
Sedale Threatt	16	29	8	9	7	15	36
Wayman Tisdale	19	28	13	17	18	6	40
Tom Tolbert	10	14	10	12	15	4	27
Sedric Toney	7	11	7	10	5	11	22
Kelly Tripucka	19	30	20	22	14	11	56
Trent Tucker	13	21	8	10	9	11	34
Andre Turner	4	8	3	4	4	8	8
Henry Turner	6	9	7	9	6	5	16
Jeff Turner	8	14	5	8	10	5	18
Mel Turpin	13	23	14	15	17	4	32
Kelvin Upshaw	9	17	6	8	7	8	19
Kiki Vandeweghe	21	31	18	22	13	10	51
Sam Vincent	13	20	14	15	11	17	29
Jay Vincent	17	33	17	20	17	8	42
Gary Voce	1	3	0	0	2	0	2
Aleksandr Volkov	8	14	6	8	8	4	17
Mark Wade	1	4	2	4	4	10	4
Darrell Walker	14	25	13	16	16	17	39

Player	FGM	FGA	FTM	FTA	Reb.	Ast.	Pts.
Kenny Walker	11	19	11	14	13	5	26
Spud Webb	12	17	13	14	8	15	26
Chris Welp	5	9	8	10	6	2	18
Bill Wennington	8	14	8	8	12	5	21
Doug West	9	15	5	8	6	2	23
Mark West	11	17	12	14	24	5	27
Randy White	8	13	4	8	12	3	18
Mitchell Wiggins	15	26	12	12	10	9	34
Morlon Wiley	11	17	8	8	7	12	24
Eddie Wilkins	9	15	6	11	15	3	24
Gerald Wilkins	18	30	13	14	14	13	43
Dominique Wilkins	21	42	20	22	17	10	57
Buck Williams	14	22	18	19	27	7	35
Herb Williams	17	32	17	20	29	8	40
John Williams	13	23	13	15	18	7	33
John S. Williams	12	24	11	13	14	13	30
Michael D. Williams	6	11	9	10	4	9	17
Mike G. Williams	2	3	2	2	4	1	4
Reggie Williams	15	27	9	10	9	6	34
Kevin Willis	16	23	8	12	21	4	39
David Wingate	11	24	11	13	11	15	28
Randy Wittman	14	22	9	9	7	12	30
Joe Wolf	9	16	6	7	12	7	23
Leon Wood	10	20	10	12	7	13	30
Mike Woodson	22	28	12	15	11	10	48
Orlando Woolridge	18	28	14	19	16	10	44
Haywoode Workman	1	2	2	2	1	2	4
James Worthy	17	27	11	15	17	12	38
Danny Young	9	13	7	7	6	13	20
Michael Young	12	22	4	6	14	4	27

Playoffs

Player	FGM	FGA	FTM	FTA	Reb.	Ast.	Pts.
Mark Acres	3	5	4	4	7	1	10
Michael Adams	8	19	7	8	12	9	25
Mark Aguirre	19	30	11	12	17	10	39
Danny Ainge	12	22	7	9	10	14	30
Mark Alarie	4	7	2	2	3	1	8
Steve Alford	4	9	2	2	3	4	12
Greg Anderson	8	14	3	4	10	2	18
Richard Anderson	6	13	4	4	5	3	14
Ron Anderson	13	20	8	8	7	6	26
Willie Anderson	13	21	7	9	10	7	30
B.J. Armstrong	2	8	8	8	4	7	11
John Bagley	11	19	4	6	7	15	22
Thurl Bailey	15	29	12	15	14	6	39
Charles Barkley	15	25	15	21	22	12	39
John Battle	7	13	5	8	6	5	19
Kenny Battle	2	7	1	1	2	0	5
William Bedford	1	4	2	2	2	0	2
Winston Bennett	10	13	2	4	8	2	22
Walter Berry	12	18	9	10	8	3	27
Larry Bird	17	33	14	15	21	16	43
Uwe Blab	2	3	2	4	3	1	4
Rolando Blackman	19	33	13	14	10	11	43
Muggsy Bogues	0	0	0	0	0	2	0
Manute Bol	3	7	2	4	12	1	8
Anthony Bowie	0	1	0	0	0	0	0
Sam Bowie	6	14	6	12	20	5	15
Adrian Branch	1	5	3	4	4	6	10
Randy Breuer	9	14	7	8	12	3	21
Frank Brickowski	9	16	6	10	12	5	22
Scott Brooks	3	4	2	3	2	3	10
Tony Brown	3	4	2	2	4	2	7
Mike Brown	3	5	2	2	6	2	7
Raymond Brown	0	0	0	0	0	0	0
Mark Bryant	3	6	4	4	7	1	8
Michael Cage	7	10	2	6	10	1	16
Adrian Caldwell	0	0	0	0	0	0	0
Tony Campbell	6	12	5	7	4	2	15

Player	FGM	FGA	FTM	FTA	Reb.	Ast.	Pts.
Rick Carlisle	3	6	3	4	3	2	6
Antoine Carr	7	10	6	7	6	3	20
Joe Barry Carroll	10	19	8	10	11	4	24
Bill Cartwright	10	19	11	13	14	4	29
Terry Catledge	13	22	6	9	12	2	27
Tom Chambers	17	29	16	16	17	7	41
Maurice Cheeks	12	20	11	14	10	16	33
Derrick Chievous	5	7	6	8	3	2	13
Ben Coleman	5	7	2	2	2	0	12
Steve Colter	11	15	3	5	6	8	26
Lester Conner	0	0	2	2	1	1	2
Wayne Cooper	10	18	4	8	14	7	23
Michael Cooper	9	16	10	12	8	13	23
Lanard Copeland	1	3	0	0	1	0	2
Tyrone Corbin	8	12	6	7	14	4	16
Dave Corzine	9	17	6	7	15	7	23
Pat Cummings	8	16	4	4	14	3	16
Terry Cummings	16	26	13	16	18	6	41
Dell Curry	1	3	0	0	1	2	2
Quintin Dailey	12	20	4	4	5	5	25
Adrian Dantley	16	27	15	20	14	7	46
Brad Daugherty	12	19	11	12	17	9	34
Brad Davis	8	10	6	7	6	10	26
Charles Davis	4	12	5	6	9	3	13
Walter Davis	15	29	11	13	10	13	34
Johnny Dawkins	9	17	7	10	5	15	18
Vlade Divac	7	8	6	6	8	3	18
James Donaldson	8	12	9	10	20	3	18
Larry Drew	9	13	4	4	3	7	20
Clyde Drexler	14	27	12	15	13	14	35
Kevin Duckworth	14	21	9	11	16	4	33
Chris Dudley	1	1	1	2	4	2	2
Joe Dumars	15	23	13	17	7	11	35
Mike Dunleavy	11	22	6	6	4	10	28
T.R. Dunn	10	16	4	4	12	6	21
Mark Eaton	10	17	8	10	15	5	20
Blue Edwards	5	8	2	3	5	2	12
James Edwards	13	23	9	10	9	4	32
Craig Ehlo	9	18	5	7	10	9	25
Sean Elliott	9	15	5	7	8	3	21
Dale Ellis	18	30	8	11	14	6	43
Alex English	17	31	13	14	11	12	42
Patrick Ewing	18	34	17	18	20	10	45
Jim Farmer	1	3	0	0	2	1	2
Vern Fleming	9	14	9	11	11	8	19
Sleepy Floyd	18	26	13	14	8	18	51
Kevin Gamble	4	11	0	2	1	2	8
Winston Garland	6	15	6	7	7	8	18
Armon Gilliam	7	10	6	6	15	1	14
Mike Gminski	12	19	12	12	13	5	28
Greg Grant	4	7	0	0	3	3	9
Horace Grant	10	17	7	8	20	5	20
Stuart Gray	1	3	2	2	4	0	2
Jeff Grayer	0	0	0	0	2	1	0
A.C. Green	9	13	10	13	18	7	21
Rickey Green	12	24	8	10	10	16	32
Sidney Green	7	14	3	6	12	3	17
David Greenwood	11	18	5	6	13	3	24
Darrell Griffith	11	23	7	10	10	8	28
Jack Haley	1	2	1	2	1	1	3
Bobby Hansen	10	19	8	10	9	7	25
Bill Hanzlik	7	15	7	9	9	7	21
Derek Harper	12	21	9	12	6	16	35
Ron Harper	12	23	7	10	11	6	31
Steve Harris	6	12	4	5	3	2	12
Scott Hastings	4	5	4	5	4	2	10
Hersey Hawkins	14	26	11	11	6	8	39
Gerald Henderson	10	17	5	7	6	9	22
Rod Higgins	7	12	8	8	14	6	21
Roy Hinson	10	17	8	13	11	3	28
Craig Hodges	10	18	5	5	5	9	25
Michael Holton	5	7	4	4	3	5	10

Player	FGM	FGA	FTM	FTA	Reb.	Ast.	Pts.
Tito Horford	1	1	0	0	0	0	2
Jeff Hornacek	11	22	14	14	11	10	36
Eddie Hughes	1	2	0	0	0	1	3
Jay Humphries	9	15	7	8	6	15	21
Byron Irvin	3	11	4	4	6	3	10
Mark Jackson	11	24	9	11	7	16	28
Buck Johnson	6	15	6	6	6	6	16
Avery Johnson	3	5	1	2	2	2	6
Steve Johnson	9	18	11	16	12	2	29
Dennis Johnson	13	27	13	17	12	17	33
Magic Johnson	15	26	16	17	18	24	43
Eddie A. Johnson	13	25	9	10	11	6	35
Eric Johnson	0	0	0	0	0	0	0
Kevin Johnson	14	27	18	19	9	18	37
Marques Johnson	16	26	11	16	17	9	36
Vinnie Johnson	16	21	10	13	12	13	34
Nate Johnston	3	7	1	1	5	1	6
Anthony Jones	0	0	0	0	0	0	0
Caldwell Jones	8	15	8	11	26	5	24
Charles Jones	5	9	4	6	9	2	11
Michael Jordan	24	45	23	28	15	13	63
Tim Kempton	5	7	4	4	3	2	10
Steve Kerr	2	6	0	0	3	5	4
Jerome Kersey	14	23	11	15	16	5	33
Randolph Keys	0	3	0	0	3	1	0
Bernard King	19	35	12	15	12	5	46
Stacey King	9	15	7	8	9	2	21
Greg Kite	4	5	2	3	9	2	8
Joe Kleine	4	6	6	7	11	1	12
Jon Koncak	5	7	11	11	13	2	19
Frank Kornet	0	1	0	0	1	0	0
Larry Krystkowiak	8	15	14	16	13	5	22
Bill Laimbeer	10	23	13	13	19	6	31
Jerome Lane	2	5	2	2	3	2	4
Andrew Lang	3	4	2	5	10	2	8
Eric Leckner	3	7	3	4	6	2	8
Jim Les	0	0	0	0	0	1	0
Lafayette Lever	12	24	12	12	16	18	30
Cliff Levingston	6	9	6	8	9	2	17
Ralph Lewis	1	2	0	0	2	1	2
Reggie Lewis	10	21	8	10	9	9	23
Todd Lichti	9	15	7	7	13	8	22
Alton Lister	9	14	9	13	17	3	22
Lewis Lloyd	12	23	6	6	9	8	28
Brad Lohaus	6	14	0	0	8	2	15
John Long	9	17	7	7	5	3	20
John Lucas	12	20	10	12	10	14	30
Rick Mahorn	8	14	8	8	18	4	17
Dan Majerle	10	20	9	12	10	5	24
Jeff Malone	15	24	9	11	8	6	35
Karl Malone	17	29	17	22	22	4	38
Moses Malone	16	34	18	20	26	6	42
Wes Matthews	14	21	4	6	5	10	30
Vernon Maxwell	11	25	5	8	5	5	26
Mel McCants	0	0	0	0	0	0	0
George McCloud	1	2	0	0	1	0	2
Tim McCormick	5	7	3	4	9	3	12
Rodney McCray	10	19	10	10	12	11	24
Xavier McDaniel	20	29	8	12	17	8	42
Mike McGee	12	19	6	8	7	4	27
Kevin McHale	15	25	14	16	17	7	34
Derrick McKey	11	17	6	7	11	4	26
Nate McMillan	5	9	7	8	8	16	15
Mark McNamara	2	4	1	2	1	0	4
Reggie Miller	8	13	7	8	5	4	23
Paul Mokeski	7	10	6	8	12	6	17
Johnny Moore	16	24	8	10	10	20	39
John Morton	2	3	2	2	0	0	6
Chris Mullin	16	30	16	19	9	7	41
Pete Myers	0	1	4	6	3	1	4
Larry Nance	12	22	9	13	15	8	29
Calvin Natt	15	24	12	17	12	10	40

Player	FGM	FGA	FTM	FTA	Reb.	Ast.	Pts.
Ed Nealy	4	7	4	6	9	3	9
Chuck Nevitt	2	5	2	2	5	1	6
Johnny Newman	14	25	10	14	6	5	34
Kurt Nimphius	4	7	4	4	10	3	10
Charles Oakley	8	20	10	12	20	7	26
Akeem Olajuwon	19	33	13	20	26	6	49
Jawann Oldham	3	5	0	0	9	2	6
Robert Parish	14	25	11	15	19	6	33
Jim Paxson	13	21	8	12	6	5	32
John Paxson	7	16	11	15	3	9	23
Kenny Payne	2	4	2	2	1	0	4
Will Perdue	5	8	6	9	5	1	15
Sam Perkins	13	22	11	13	19	5	29
Tim Perry	6	7	5	9	5	1	17
Chuck Person	14	27	12	15	17	7	40
Jim Petersen	7	12	9	11	13	4	15
Drazen Petrovic	5	11	4	6	5	3	14
Ricky Pierce	13	21	14	17	7	5	35
Ed Pinckney	6	6	4	5	4	1	16
Scottie Pippen	13	20	11	13	12	13	32
Olden Polynice	5	7	5	5	11	1	13
Terry Porter	13	19	15	16	8	15	38
Paul Pressey	12	20	15	17	10	16	28
Mark Price	11	18	9	9	6	18	31
Brian Quinnett	1	2	0	0	7	2	3
Kurt Rambis	8	11	5	7	15	5	19
Blair Rasmussen	13	23	6	8	13	4	28
Robert Reid	12	25	11	14	14	17	33
Jerry Reynolds	4	10	5	6	4	2	14
Mitch Richmond	13	21	8	9	13	8	30
David Rivers	2	6	3	3	1	2	6
Glenn Rivers	10	17	15	16	13	22	32
Fred Roberts	12	19	9	11	6	5	33
Alvin Robertson	15	23	10	11	8	12	38
Cliff R. Robinson	8	13	4	9	8	3	20
David Robinson	11	21	9	15	16	6	31
Dennis Rodman	10	16	6	10	20	3	23
Wayne Rollins	8	14	6	10	17	3	18
Scott Roth	1	1	0	0	0	0	2
Delaney Rudd	2	7	1	2	1	6	6
John Salley	10	16	9	12	13	4	23
Ralph Sampson	13	25	10	14	24	10	33
Jeff Sanders	1	1	0	0	0	0	2
Mike Sanders	8	17	6	6	8	4	20
Danny Schayes	11	16	13	15	14	5	33
Detlef Schrempf	9	16	8	8	8	4	26
Byron Scott	14	24	9	12	8	7	35
Brad Sellers	8	14	8	8	7	3	22
Brian Shaw	8	16	4	4	8	8	20
Purvis Short	13	20	7	7	7	4	32
Jerry Sichting	5	11	2	2	4	8	12
Jack Sikma	12	24	14	15	21	8	33
Charles E. Smith (Bos.)	1	1	0	0	1	3	2
Derek Smith	5	8	1	2	3	1	11
Larry Smith	8	15	4	5	23	6	18
Michael Smith	4	5	4	4	0	0	9
Otis Smith	6	9	4	5	8	2	12
Rik Smits	9	10	5	6	7	2	23
Mike Smrek	1	4	4	6	2	0	4
Rory Sparrow	8	16	8	8	8	11	22
John Stockton	13	21	16	19	9	24	34
Rod Strickland	8	15	4	9	9	17	18
Jon Sundvold	6	11	2	2	2	7	14
Roy Tarpley	12	24	9	15	20	6	27
Terry Teagle	14	24	7	8	6	4	30
Reggie Theus	10	20	17	18	8	11	37
Isiah Thomas	18	33	13	17	12	16	43
LaSalle Thompson	9	19	5	6	17	2	23
Mychal Thompson	15	23	10	12	17	8	40
Billy Thompson	4	7	2	2	4	2	8
Bob Thornton	3	4	2	4	5	2	6
Otis Thorpe	8	14	11	14	9	4	27

Player	FGM	FGA	FTM	FTA	Reb.	Ast.	Pts.
Sedale Threatt	12	17	6	9	7	9	28
Wayman Tisdale	8	13	5	8	5	3	20
Sedric Toney	3	5	2	2	0	1	9
Kelly Tripucka	15	27	11	14	11	6	40
Trent Tucker	9	13	4	4	6	7	18
Jeff Turner	2	4	1	1	4	2	4
Mel Turpin	5	9	2	2	3	1	10
Kelvin Upshaw	4	7	0	0	1	2	8
Kiki Vandeweghe	17	24	12	12	14	7	37
Sam Vincent	11	17	9	11	4	14	31
Jay Vincent	10	20	10	14	11	5	28
Darrell Walker	8	17	7	10	9	7	20
Kenny Walker	4	12	7	10	6	2	9
Spud Webb	10	19	13	16	7	18	21
Chris Welp	1	2	0	2	4	0	2
Bill Wennington	4	7	2	3	5	2	10
Mark West	10	17	6	8	21	2	24
Randy White	0	0	0	0	0	0	0
Mitchell Wiggins	10	16	4	4	7	4	24
Eddie Wilkins	6	12	4	8	8	0	14
Gerald Wilkins	16	22	7	9	11	10	34
Dominique Wilkins	19	37	15	17	14	6	50
Buck Williams	12	17	11	16	18	5	28
Herb Williams	9	12	6	8	8	4	19
John Williams	10	17	5	8	13	3	23
John S. Williams	7	14	6	10	7	9	19
Michael D. Williams	0	0	2	2	2	1	2
Reggie Williams	3	13	1	1	5	1	7
Kevin Willis	12	19	8	10	14	3	27
David Wingate	6	14	5	6	8	6	16
Randy Wittman	16	25	9	12	7	8	35
Leon Wood	2	5	6	7	1	1	10
Mike Woodson	9	21	7	8	8	7	25
Orlando Woolridge	11	27	8	8	9	5	28
James Worthy	17	26	10	11	16	10	40
Danny Young	5	11	6	6	4	8	12

Promising Newcomers

ALAA ABDELNABY

Born June 24, 1968 at Cairo, Egypt. Height 6:10. Weight 240.
High School—Bloomfield, N.J.
College—Duke University, Durham, N.C.
Drafted by Portland on first round, 1990 (25th pick).

—COLLEGIATE RECORD—

Year	G.	Min.	FGA	FGM	Pct.	FTA	FTM	Pct.	Reb.	Pts.	Avg.
86-87	29	192	81	47	.580	23	12	.522	50	106	3.7
87-88	34	320	123	61	.496	63	44	.698	67	166	4.9
88-89	33	530	194	123	.634	67	47	.701	125	293	8.9
89-90	38	947	350	217	.620	178	138	.775	252	572	15.1
Totals	134	1989	748	448	.599	331	241	.728	494	1137	8.5

MILOS BABIC

(Name pronounced Me-losh Bob-itch.)
Born November 23, 1968 at Kraljevo, Yugoslavia. Height 7:00. Weight 240.
College—Tennessee Tech University, Cookeville, Tenn.
Drafted by Phoenix on second round, 1990 (50th pick).

Draft rights traded by Phoenix to Cleveland for draft rights to Stefano Rusconi, June 27, 1990.

—COLLEGIATE RECORD—

Year	G.	Min.	FGA	FGM	Pct.	FTA	FTM	Pct.	Reb.	Pts.	Avg.
86-87				Did Not Play—Ineligible							
87-88	25	650	224	103	.460	97	64	.660	170	270	10.8
88-89	30	899	322	161	.500	114	75	.658	244	399	13.3
89-90	25	591	259	122	.471	95	65	.684	183	309	12.4
Totals	80	2140	805	386	.480	306	204	.667	597	978	12.2

Three-Point Field Goals: 1988-89, 2-for-7 (.286).

STEPHEN DEAN BARDO
(Steve)

Born April 5, 1968 at Henderson, Ky. Height 6:05. Weight 190.
High School—Carbondale, Ill.
College—University of Illinois, Champaign, Ill.
Drafted by Atlanta on second round, 1990 (41st pick).

—COLLEGIATE RECORD—

Year	G.	Min.	FGA	FGM	Pct.	FTA	FTM	Pct.	Reb.	Pts.	Avg.
86-87	31	630	102	42	.412	50	34	.680	92	119	3.8
87-88	33	820	178	80	.449	87	53	.609	138	216	6.5
88-89	36	1000	212	94	.443	96	76	.792	144	293	8.1
89-90	29	944	225	99	.440	78	55	.705	178	281	9.7
Totals	129	3394	717	315	.439	311	218	.701	552	909	7.0

Three-Point Field Goals: 1986-87, 1-for-3 (.333). 1987-88, 3-for-8 (.375). 1988-89, 29-for-59 (.492). 1989-90, 28-for-64 (.438). Totals, 61-for-134 (.455).

LANCE BLANKS

Born September 9, 1966 at Del Rio, Tex. Height 6:04. Weight 190.
High School—Woodlands, Tex., McCullough.
Colleges—University of Virginia, Charlottesville, Va., and
University of Texas, Austin, Tex.
Drafted by Detroit on first round, 1990 (26th pick).

—COLLEGIATE RECORD—

Virginia

Year	G.	Min.	FGA	FGM	Pct.	FTA	FTM	Pct.	Reb.	Pts.	Avg.
85-86	14	103	32	14	.438	12	6	.500	15	34	2.4
86-87	24	145	25	13	.520	7	2	.286	18	29	1.2
Va. Totals	38	248	57	27	.474	19	8	.421	33	63	1.7

Texas

Year	G.	Min.	FGA	FGM	Pct.	FTA	FTM	Pct.	Reb.	Pts.	Avg.
87-88	Did Not Play—Transfer Student										
88-89	34	1295	527	237	.450	174	119	.684	191	671	19.7
89-90	32	1157	512	206	.402	202	161	.797	136	651	20.3
Tex. Totals	66	2452	1039	443	.426	376	280	.745	327	1322	20.0
Col. Totals	104	2700	1096	470	.429	395	288	.729	390	1385	13.3

Three-Point Field Goals: 1986-87, 1-for-4 (.250). 1988-89, 78-for-218 (.358). 1989-90, 78-for-214 (.364). Virginia Totals, 1-for-4 (.250). Texas Totals, 156-for-432 (.361). College Totals, 157-for-436 (.360).

Son of Sid Blanks, running back with Houston Oilers and Boston Patriots, 1964 and 1966 through 1970. . . . Cousin of Larvell Blanks, infielder with Atlanta Braves, Cleveland Indians and Texas Rangers, 1972 through 1980.

ANTHONY BONNER

Born June 8, 1968 at St. Louis, Mo. Height 6:08. Weight 215.
High School—St. Louis, Mo., Vashon.
College—St. Louis University, St. Louis, Mo.
Drafted by Sacramento on first round, 1990 (23rd pick).

—COLLEGIATE RECORD—

Year	G.	Min.	FGA	FGM	Pct.	FTA	FTM	Pct.	Reb.	Pts.	Avg.
86-87	35	1066	233	138	.592	127	84	.661	337	360	10.3
87-88	28	942	287	154	.537	129	77	.597	245	385	13.8
88-89	37	1246	407	228	.560	201	117	.582	386	573	15.5
89-90	33	....	508	254	.500	205	142	.693	456	654	19.8
Totals	133	....	1435	774	.539	662	420	.634	1424	1972	14.8

Three-Point Field Goals: 1989-90, 4-for-12 (.333).

Led NCAA Division I in rebounding, 1990.

DeCOVAN KADELL BROWN (Dee)

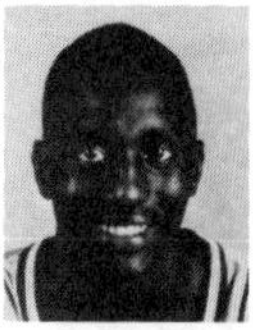

Born November 29, 1968 at Jacksonville, Fla. Height 6:01. Weight 160.
High School—Jacksonville, Fla., Bolles.
College—Jacksonville University, Jacksonville, Fla.
Drafted by Boston on first round, 1990 (19th pick).

—COLLEGIATE RECORD—

Year	G.	Min.	FGA	FGM	Pct.	FTA	FTM	Pct.	Reb.	Pts.	Avg.
86-87	21	186	65	28	.431	22	13	.431	28	71	3.4
87-88	28	764	239	108	.452	66	54	.818	125	282	10.1
88-89	30	1133	447	219	.490	131	108	.824	228	589	19.6
89-90	29	1052	466	231	.496	101	69	.683	192	561	19.3
Totals	108	3135	1217	586	.482	320	244	.763	573	1503	13.9

Three-Point Field Goals: 1986-87, 2-for-12 (.167). 1987-88, 12-for-45 (.267). 1988-89, 43-for-101 (.426). 1989-90, 30-for-80 (.375). Totals, 87-for-238 (.366).

JUDSON DONALD BUECHLER (Jud)

Born June 19, 1968 at San Diego, Calif. Height 6:06. Weight 220.
High School—Poway, Calif.
College—University of Arizona, Tucson, Ariz.
Drafted by Seattle on second round, 1990 (38th pick).

Draft rights traded by Seattle to New Jersey for New Jersey's agreement not to select Dennis Scott in the 1990 draft, June 27, 1990.

—COLLEGIATE RECORD—

Year	G.	Min.	FGA	FGM	Pct.	FTA	FTM	Pct.	Reb.	Pts.	Avg.
86-87	30	474	111	54	.486	28	16	.571	68	134	4.5
87-88	36	422	124	64	.516	58	38	.655	87	170	4.7
88-89	33	962	229	139	.607	103	84	.816	219	363	11.0
89-90	32	1072	338	182	.538	115	88	.765	264	477	14.9
Totals	131	2930	802	439	.547	304	226	.743	638	1144	8.7

Three-Point Field Goals: 1986-87, 10-for-25 (.400). 1987-88, 4-for-9 (.444). 1988-89, 1-for-5 (.200). 1989-90, 25-for-66 (.379). Totals, 40-for-105 (.381).

WILLIE RICARDO BURTON

Born May 26, 1968 at Detroit, Mich. Height 6:06. Weight 210.
High School—Detroit, Mich., DePorres.
College—University of Minnesota, Minneapolis, Minn.
Drafted by Miami on first round, 1990 (9th pick).

—COLLEGIATE RECORD—

Year	G.	Min.	FGA	FGM	Pct.	FTA	FTM	Pct.	Reb.	Pts.	Avg.
86-87	28	674	211	96	.455	74	48	.649	118	243	8.7
87-88	28	751	275	142	.516	136	97	.713	158	384	13.7
88-89	30	922	374	198	.529	172	137	.797	224	557	18.6
89-90	32	1001	405	210	.519	187	144	.770	205	616	19.3
Totals	118	3348	1265	646	.511	569	426	.749	705	1800	15.3

Three-Point Field Goals: 1986-87, 3-for-11 (.273). 1987-88, 3-for-10 (.300). 1988-89, 24-for-60 (.400). 1989-90, 52-for-136 (.382). Totals, 82-for-217 (.378).

ELDEN JEROME CAMPBELL

Born July 23, 1968 at Los Angeles, Calif. Height 6:11. Weight 215.
High School—Inglewood, Calif., Morningside.
College—Clemson University, Clemson, S.C.
Drafted by Los Angeles Lakers on first round, 1990 (27th pick).

—COLLEGIATE RECORD—

Year	G.	Min.	FGA	FGM	Pct.	FTA	FTM	Pct.	Reb.	Pts.	Avg.
86-87	31	534	193	107	.554	84	59	.702	126	273	8.8
87-88	28	808	345	217	.629	147	91	.619	207	525	18.8
88-89	29	814	373	205	.550	138	95	.688	222	507	17.5
89-90	35	1038	431	225	.522	207	124	.599	281	575	16.4
Totals	123	3194	1342	754	.562	576	369	.641	836	1880	15.3

Three-Point Field Goals: 1987-88, 0-for-4. 1988-89, 2-for-5 (.400). 1989-90, 1-for-1 (1.000). Totals, 3-for-10 (.300).

DUANE CAUSWELL

Born May 31, 1968 at Queens Village, N.Y. Height 7:00. Weight 240.
High School—Bayside, N.Y., Benjamin Cardozo.
College—Temple University, Philadelphia, Pa.
Drafted by Sacramento on first round, 1990 (18th pick).

—COLLEGIATE RECORD—

Year	G.	Min.	FGA	FGM	Pct.	FTA	FTM	Pct.	Reb.	Pts.	Avg.
86-87				Did Not Play—Red Shirted							
87-88	33	399	55	27	.491	30	13	.433	85	67	2.0
88-89	30	1081	249	128	.514	123	84	.683	267	340	11.3
89-90	12	416	107	52	.486	52	31	.596	99	135	11.3
Totals	75	1896	411	207	.504	205	128	.624	451	542	7.2

Three-Point Field Goals: 1988-89, 0-for-1.

CEDRIC Z. CEBALLOS

Born August 2, 1969 at Maui, Haw. Height 6:06. Weight 190.
High School—Compton, Calif., Dominguez.
Colleges—Ventura College, Ventura, Calif., and California State University at Fullerton, Fullerton, Calif.
Drafted by Phoenix on second round, 1990 (48th pick).

—COLLEGIATE RECORD—

Ventura

Year	G.	Min.	FGA	FGM	Pct.	FTA	FTM	Pct.	Reb.	Pts.	Avg.
86-87				Statistics Unavailable							
87-88				Statistics Unavailable							

Fullerton State

Year	G.	Min.	FGA	FGM	Pct.	FTA	FTM	Pct.	Reb.	Pts.	Avg.
88-89	29	986	545	241	.442	174	117	.672	256	615	21.2
89-90	29	1071	509	247	.485	215	144	.670	362	669	23.1
Ful. St. Totals	58	2057	1054	488	.463	389	261	.671	618	1284	22.1

Three-Point Field Goals: 1988-89, 16-for-58 (.276). 1989-90, 31-for-96 (.323). Fullerton State Totals, 47-for-154 (.305).

DERRICK COLEMAN

DERRICK COLEMAN

Born June 21, 1967 at Mobile, Ala. Height 6:10. Weight 230.
High School—Detroit, Mich., Northern.
College—Syracuse University, Syracuse, N.Y.
Drafted by New Jersey on first round, 1990 (1st pick).

—COLLEGIATE RECORD—

Year	G.	Min.	FGA	FGM	Pct.	FTA	FTM	Pct.	Reb.	Pts.	Avg.
86-87	38	1163	309	173	.560	156	107	.686	333	453	11.9
87-88	35	1133	300	176	.587	192	121	.630	384	474	13.5
88-89	37	1226	395	227	.575	247	171	.692	422	625	16.9
89-90	33	1166	352	194	.551	263	188	.715	398	591	17.9
Totals	143	4688	1356	770	.568	858	587	.684	1537	2143	15.0

(1986-87 minutes played are missing one game.)

Three-Point Field Goals: 1987-88, 1-for-6 (.167). 1988-89, 0-for-8. 1989-90, 15-for-41 (.366). Totals, 16-for-55 (.291).

Named to THE SPORTING NEWS All-America First Team, 1990.

VERNELL E. COLES (Bimbo)

Born April 22, 1968 at Covington, Va. Height 6:01. Weight 180.
High School—Lewisburg, W. Va., Greenbriar East.
College—Virginia Polytechnic Institute and State University, Blacksburg, Va.
Drafted by Sacramento on second round, 1990 (40th pick).

Draft rights traded by Sacramento to Miami for Rory Sparrow, June 27, 1990.

—COLLEGIATE RECORD—

Year	G.	Min.	FGA	FGM	Pct.	FTA	FTM	Pct.	Reb.	Pts.	Avg.
86-87	28	752	245	101	.412	109	78	.716	85	280	10.0
87-88	29	990	544	241	.443	270	200	.741	103	702	24.2
88-89	27	924	547	249	.455	200	157	.785	111	717	26.6
89-90	31	1147	693	280	.404	214	158	.738	147	785	25.3
Totals	115	3813	2029	871	.429	793	593	.748	446	2484	21.6

Three-Point Field Goals: 1986-87, 0-for-14. 1987-88, 20-for-62 (.323). 1988-89, 62-for-166 (.373). 1989-90, 67-for-218 (.307). Totals, 149-for-460 (.324).

Member of U.S. Olympic team, 1988.

ANTHONY LACQUISE COOK

Born May 19, 1967 at Los Angeles, Calif. Height 6:09. Weight 205.
High School—Van Nuys, Calif.
College—University of Arizona, Tucson, Ariz.
Drafted by Phoenix on first round, 1989 (24th pick).

Draft rights traded by Phoenix to Detroit for Michael Williams and draft rights to Kenny Battle, June 27, 1989.
Played in Greece, 1989-90.

—COLLEGIATE RECORD—

Year	G.	Min.	FGA	FGM	Pct.	FTA	FTM	Pct.	Reb.	Pts.	Avg.
85-86	32	833	146	73	.500	73	48	.658	137	194	6.1
86-87	30	969	246	118	.480	100	54	.540	217	290	9.7
87-88	38	1169	325	201	.618	176	126	.716	269	528	13.9
88-89	33	1066	377	237	.629	166	104	.627	238	578	17.5
Totals	133	4037	1094	629	.575	515	332	.645	861	1590	12.0

Three-Point Field Goals: 1987-88, 0-for-1. Totals, 0-for-2.

MICHAEL LANE CUTRIGHT

Born May 10, 1967 at Zwolle, La. Height 6:04. Weight 210.
High School—Zwolle, La.
College—McNeese State University, Lake Charles, La.
Drafted by Denver on second round, 1989 (42nd pick).

Traded by Denver with future draft considerations to New Jersey for Joe Barry Carroll, February 21, 1990.

—COLLEGIATE RECORD—

Year	G.	Min.	FGA	FGM	Pct.	FTA	FTM	Pct.	Reb.	Pts.	Avg.
85-86	32	724	270	124	.459	35	18	.514	98	266	8.3
86-87	25	750	352	153	.435	59	38	.644	98	394	15.8
87-88	29	921	414	169	.408	52	35	.673	103	432	14.9
88-89	30	1028	503	237	.471	110	87	.791	156	611	20.4
Totals	116	3423	1539	683	.444	256	178	.695	455	1703	14.7

Three-Point Field Goals: 1986-87, 50-for-143 (.350). 1987-88, 59-for-175 (.337). 1988-89, 50-for-143 (.350). Totals, 159-for-461 (.345).

ANTONIO LEE DAVIS

Born October 31, 1968 at Oakland, Calif. Height 6:09. Weight 215.
High School—Oakland, Calif., McClymonds.
College—University of Texas at El Paso, El Paso, Tex.
Drafted by Indiana on second round, 1990 (45th pick).

—COLLEGIATE RECORD—

Year	G.	Min.	FGA	FGM	Pct.	FTA	FTM	Pct.	Reb.	Pts.	Avg.
86-87	28	240	32	11	.344	30	13	.433	51	35	1.3
87-88	30	907	183	108	.590	115	63	.548	195	279	9.3
88-89	32	1014	298	162	.544	218	135	.619	255	459	14.3
89-90	32	991	228	119	.522	165	106	.642	243	344	10.8
Totals	122	3152	741	400	.540	528	317	.600	744	1117	9.2

Three-Point Field Goals: 1988-89, 0-for-1. 1989-90, 0-for-1. Totals, 0-for-2.

PATRICK WAYNE DURHAM
(Pat)

Born March 10, 1967 at Dallas, Tex. Height 6:07. Weight 210.
High School—Dallas, Tex., Wilmer-Hutchins.
College—Colorado State University, Fort Collins, Colo.
Drafted by Dallas on second round, 1989 (35th pick).

Played in Continental Basketball Association with Rapid City Thrillers, 1989-90.

—COLLEGIATE RECORD—

Year	G.	Min.	FGA	FGM	Pct.	FTA	FTM	Pct.	Reb.	Pts.	Avg.
85-86	28	499	146	64	.438	71	39	.549	101	167	6.0
86-87	29	1067	348	193	.555	206	140	.680	271	526	18.1
87-88	35	1287	505	252	.499	249	172	.691	228	676	19.3
88-89	33	1244	370	196	.530	290	218	.752	251	611	18.5
Totals	125	4097	1369	705	.515	816	569	.697	851	1980	15.8

Three-Point Field Goals: 1986-87, 0-for-2. 1987-88, 0-for-3. 1988-89, 1-for-4 (.250). Totals, 1-for-9 (.111).

CBA REGULAR SEASON RECORD

			2-Point			3-Point									
Sea.—Team	G.	Min.	FGM	FGA	Pct.	FGM	FGA	Pct.	FTM	FTA	Pct.	Reb.	Ast.	Pts.	Avg.
89-90—Rapid City	23	536	117	225	.520	0	1	.000	71	100	.710	137	25	305	13.3

ALBERT ENGLISH
(A.J.)

Born July 11, 1967 at Wilmington, Del. Height 6:05. Weight 175.
High School—Wilmington, Del., Howard.
College—Virginia Union University, Richmond, Va.
Drafted by Washington on second round, 1990 (37th pick).

—COLLEGIATE RECORD—

Year	G.	Min.	FGA	FGM	Pct.	FTA	FTM	Pct.	Reb.	Pts.	Avg.
86-87	31	....	235	105	.447	95	72	.758	90	305	9.8
87-88	29	....	365	172	.471	133	95	.714	137	474	16.3
88-89	30	....	417	210	.504	170	138	.812	120	616	20.5
89-90	30	....	672	333	.496	341	270	.792	154	1001	33.4
Totals	120	....	1689	820	.485	739	575	.778	501	2396	20.0

Three-Point Field Goals: 1986-87, 23-for-50 (.460). 1987-88, 35-for-79 (.443). 1988-89, 58-for-123 (.472). 1989-90, 65-for-144 (.451). Totals, 181-for-396 (.457).

Led NCAA Division II in scoring, 1990.

DANIEL JOHN WILLARD FERRY
(Danny)

Born October 17, 1966 at Hyattsville, Md. Height 6:10. Weight 230.
High School—Hyattsville, Md., DeMatha.
College—Duke University, Durham, N.C.
Drafted by Los Angeles Clippers on first round, 1989 (2nd pick).

Draft rights traded by Los Angeles Clippers with Reggie Williams to Cleveland for Ron Harper, 1990 and 1992 1st round draft choices and a 1991 2nd round draft choice, November 16, 1989.

Played in Italy, 1989-90.

—COLLEGIATE RECORD—

Year	G.	Min.	FGA	FGM	Pct.	FTA	FTM	Pct.	Reb.	Pts.	Avg.
85-86	40	912	198	91	.460	86	54	.628	221	236	5.9
86-87	33	1094	383	172	.449	109	92	.844	256	461	14.0
87-88	35	1138	519	247	.476	163	135	.828	266	667	19.1
88-89	35	1163	575	300	.522	193	146	.756	260	791	22.6
Totals	143	4307	1675	810	.484	551	427	.775	1003	2155	15.1

Three-Point Field Goals: 1986-87, 25-for-63 (.397). 1987-88, 38-for-109 (.349). 1988-89, 45-for-106 (.425). Totals, 108-for-278 (.388).

ITALIAN LEAGUE RECORD

Year	G.	Min.	FGA	FGM	Pct.	FTA	FTM	Pct.	Reb.	Pts.	Avg.
89-90—Il Messaggero.	30	1090	370	203	.549	168	125	.744	195	878	29.3

Three-Point Field Goals: 1989-90, 49-for-118 (.415).

Named to THE SPORTING NEWS All-America First Team, 1988 and 1989. . . . Son of Bob Ferry, former center-forward with St. Louis Hawks, Detroit Pistons and Baltimore Bullets, 1959-60 through 1968-69.

GREGORY CLINTON FOSTER
(Greg)

Born October 3, 1968 at Oakland, Calif. Height 7:00. Weight 250.
High School—Oakland, Calif., Skyline.
Colleges—University of California at Los Angeles, Los Angeles, Calif., and University of Texas at El Paso, El Paso, Tex.
Drafted by Washington on second round, 1990 (35th pick).

—COLLEGIATE RECORD—

UCLA

Year	G.	Min.	FGA	FGM	Pct.	FTA	FTM	Pct.	Reb.	Pts.	Avg.
86-87	31	441	88	44	.500	26	13	.500	76	101	3.3
87-88	11	292	74	39	.527	37	16	.432	61	94	8.5
UCLA Totals	42	733	162	83	.512	63	29	.460	137	195	4.6

Texas-El Paso

Year	G.	Min.	FGA	FGM	Pct.	FTA	FTM	Pct.	Reb.	Pts.	Avg.
88-89	26	728	242	117	.484	83	54	.651	189	288	11.1
89-90	32	837	286	133	.465	90	73	.811	198	339	10.6
UTEP Totals	58	1565	528	250	.473	173	127	.734	387	627	10.8
Col. Totals	100	2298	690	333	.483	236	156	.661	524	822	8.2

Three-Point Field Goals: 1988-89, 0-for-1. 1989-90, 0-for-2. Totals, 0-for-3.

TATE CLAUDE GEORGE

Born May 29, 1968 at Newark, N.J. Height 6:05. Weight 195.
High School—Scotch Plains, N.J., Union Catholic.
College—University of Connecticut, Storrs, Conn.
Drafted by New Jersey on first round, 1990 (22nd pick).

—COLLEGIATE RECORD—

Year	G.	Min.	FGA	FGM	Pct.	FTA	FTM	Pct.	Reb.	Pts.	Avg.
86-87	26	962	247	91	.368	89	69	.775	93	261	10.0
87-88	34	1111	230	115	.500	118	98	.831	99	337	9.9
88-89	31	863	178	77	.433	91	69	.758	104	225	7.3
89-90	37	1090	334	160	.479	121	88	.727	131	424	11.5
Totals	128	4026	989	443	.448	419	324	.773	427	1247	9.7

Three-Point Field Goals: 1986-87, 10-for-29 (.345), 1987-88, 9-for-23 (.391). 1988-89, 2-for-10 (.200). 1989-90, 16-for-53 (.302). Totals, 37-for-115 (.322).

KENDALL CEDRIC GILL

Born May 25, 1968 at Chicago, Ill. Height 6:05. Weight 195.
High School—Olympia Fields, Ill., Rich Central.
College—University of Illinois, Champaign, Ill.
Drafted by Charlotte on first round, 1990 (5th pick).

—COLLEGIATE RECORD—

Year	G.	Min.	FGA	FGM	Pct.	FTA	FTM	Pct.	Reb.	Pts.	Avg.
86-87	31	345	83	40	.482	53	34	.642	42	114	3.7
87-88	33	946	272	128	.471	89	67	.753	73	344	10.4
88-89	24	681	264	143	.542	58	46	.793	70	370	15.4
89-90	29	1000	422	211	.500	175	136	.777	143	581	20.0
Totals	117	2972	1041	522	.501	375	283	.755	328	1409	12.0

Three-Point Field Goals: 1986-87, 0-for-1. 1987-88, 21-for-69 (.304). 1988-89, 38-for-83 (.458). 1989-90, 23-for-66 (.348). Totals, 82-for-219 (.374).

Named to THE SPORTING NEWS All-America Third Team, 1990.

GERALD DAMON GLASS

Born November 12, 1967 at Greenwood, Miss. Height 6:05. Weight 240.
High School—Greenwood, Miss., Amanda Elzy.
Colleges—Delta State University, Cleveland, Miss., and University of Mississippi, University, Miss.
Drafted by Minnesota on first round, 1990 (20th pick).

—COLLEGIATE RECORD—

Delta State

Year	G.	Min.	FGA	FGM	Pct.	FTA	FTM	Pct.	Reb.	Pts.	Avg.
85-86	31	....	303	168	.554	72	52	.722	203	388	12.5
86-87	33	....	595	360	.605	191	134	.702	414	861	26.1
D. St. Totals	64	....	898	528	.588	263	186	.707	617	1249	19.5

Mississippi

Year	G.	Min.	FGA	FGM	Pct.	FTA	FTM	Pct.	Reb.	Pts.	Avg.
87-88	Did Not Play—Transfer Student										
88-89	30	1070	613	326	.532	201	148	.736	255	841	28.0
89-90	30	1108	580	284	.490	148	109	.736	229	723	24.1
Miss. Totals	60	2178	1193	610	.511	349	257	.736	484	1564	26.1
Col. Totals	124	....	2091	1138	.544	612	443	.724	1101	2813	22.7

Three-Point Field Goals: 1986-87, 7-for-27 (.259). 1988-89, 41-for-109 (.376). 1989-90, 46-for-122 (.377). Delta State Totals, 7-for-27 (.259). Mississippi Totals, 87-for-231 (.377). College Totals, 94-for-258 (.364).

PHILLIP TERRY HENDERSON
(Phil)

Born April 17, 1968 at Chicago, Ill. Height 6:04. Weight 180.
High School—Crete, Ill., Crete-Monee.
College—Duke University, Durham, N.C.
Drafted by Dallas on second round, 1990 (49th pick).

—COLLEGIATE RECORD—

Year	G.	Min.	FGA	FGM	Pct.	FTA	FTM	Pct.	Reb.	Pts.	Avg.
86-87	8	94	36	20	.556	15	9	.600	6	58	7.3
87-88	34	560	168	72	.429	60	44	.733	59	199	5.9
88-89	36	1066	318	167	.525	123	94	.764	124	457	12.7
89-90	37	1165	531	251	.473	122	102	.836	141	683	18.5
Totals	115	2885	1053	510	.484	320	249	.778	330	1397	12.1

Three-Point Field Goals: 1986-87, 9-for-13 (.692). 1987-88, 11-for-41 (.268). 1988-89, 29-for-75 (.387). 1989-90, 79-for-191 (.414). Totals, 128-for-320 (.400).

STEVEN MICHAEL HENSON
(Steve)

Born February 2, 1968 at Junction City, Kan. Height 6:01. Weight 180.
High School—McPherson, Kan.
College—Kansas State University, Manhattan, Kan.
Drafted by Milwaukee on second round, 1990 (44th pick).

—COLLEGIATE RECORD—

Year	G.	Min.	FGA	FGM	Pct.	FTA	FTM	Pct.	Reb.	Pts.	Avg.
86-87	31	950	190	75	.395	69	57	.826	63	233	7.5
87-88	34	1243	184	79	.429	120	111	.925	81	311	9.1
88-89	30	1123	413	192	.465	100	92	.920	81	555	18.5
89-90	32	1158	406	181	.446	112	101	.902	85	556	17.4
Totals	127	4474	1193	527	.442	401	361	.900	310	1655	13.0

Three-Point Field Goals: 1986-87, 26-for-64 (.406). 1987-88, 42-for-83 (.506). 1988-89, 79-for-177 (.446). 1989-90, 93-for-213 (.437). Totals, 240-for-537 (.447).

Led NCAA Division I in free-throw percentage, 1988.

CARL VICTOR HERRERA

Born December 14, 1966 in Trinidad. Height 6:09. Weight 220.

High School—Caracas, Venezuela, Simon Bolivar.

Colleges—Jacksonville College, Jacksonville, Tex., and University of Houston, Houston, Tex.

Drafted by Miami on second round, 1990 (30th pick).

Draft rights traded with draft rights to Dave Jamerson to Houston for draft rights to Alec Kessler, June 27, 1990.

—COLLEGIATE RECORD—

Jacksonville

Year	G.	Min.	FGA	FGM	Pct.	FTA	FTM	Pct.	Reb.	Pts.	Avg.
87-88				Statistics Unavailable							
88-89	28	....	459	261	.587	238	180	.756	....	713	25.5

Houston

Year	G.	Min.	FGA	FGM	Pct.	FTA	FTM	Pct.	Reb.	Pts.	Avg.
89-90	33	....	333	188	.565	214	172	.804	302	551	16.7

Three-Point Field Goals: 1988-89, 11-for-20 (.550). 1989-90, 3-for-8 (.375). Totals, 14-for-28 (.500).

SEAN MARIELLE HIGGINS

Born December 30, 1968 at Los Angeles, Calif. Height 6:09. Weight 205.

High School—Los Angeles, Calif., Fairfax.

College—University of Michigan, Ann Arbor, Mich.

Drafted by San Antonio on second round as an undergraduate, 1990 (54th pick).

—COLLEGIATE RECORD—

Year	G.	Min.	FGA	FGM	Pct.	FTA	FTM	Pct.	Reb.	Pts.	Avg.
87-88	12	228	96	48	.500	14	11	.786	38	117	9.8
88-89	34	782	312	158	.506	70	54	.771	107	421	12.4
89-90	26	728	302	142	.470	46	37	.804	93	364	14.0
Totals	72	1738	710	348	.490	130	102	.785	238	902	12.5

Three-Point Field Goals: 1987-88, 10-for-20 (.500). 1988-89, 51-for-110 (.464). 1989-90, 43-for-102 (.422). Totals, 104-for-232 (.448).

Member of NCAA Division I championship team, 1989. . . . Son of Earle Higgins, forward with Indiana Pacers, 1970-71.

TYRONE HILL

Born March 17, 1968 at Cincinnati, O. Height 6:10. Weight 240.

High School—Cincinnati, O., Withrow.

College—Xavier University, Cincinnati, O.

Drafted by Golden State on first round, 1990 (11th pick).

—COLLEGIATE RECORD—

Year	G.	Min.	FGA	FGM	Pct.	FTA	FTM	Pct.	Reb.	Pts.	Avg.
86-87	31	881	172	95	.552	125	84	.672	261	274	8.8
87-88	30	858	309	172	.557	153	114	.745	314	458	15.3
88-89	33	1094	388	235	.606	221	155	.701	403	625	18.9
89-90	32	1063	430	250	.581	222	146	.658	402	646	20.2
Totals	126	3896	1299	752	.579	721	499	.692	1380	2003	15.9

Three-Point Field Goals: 1989-90, 0-for-2.

CHRIS WAYNE JACKSON

Born March 9, 1969 at Gulfport, Miss. Height 6:01. Weight 170.

High School—Gulfport, Miss.

College—Louisiana State University, Baton Rouge, La.

Drafted by Denver on first round as an undergraduate, 1990 (3rd pick).

—COLLEGIATE RECORD—

Year	G.	Min.	FGA	FGM	Pct.	FTA	FTM	Pct.	Reb.	Pts.	Avg.
88-89	32	1180	739	359	.486	200	163	.815	108	965	30.2
89-90	32	1202	662	305	.461	210	191	.910	81	889	27.8
Totals	64	2382	1401	664	.474	410	354	.863	189	1854	29.0

Three-Point Field Goals: 1988-89, 84-for-216 (.389). 1989-90, 88-for-246 (.358). Totals, 172-for-462 (.372).

Named to THE SPORTING NEWS All-America First Team, 1989. . . . THE SPORTING NEWS All-America Second Team, 1990.

JOHN DAVID JAMERSON
(Dave)

Born August 13, 1967 at Clarksburg, W. Va. Height 6:05. Weight 190.
High School—Stow, O.
College—Ohio University, Athens, O.
Drafted by Miami on first round, 1990 (15th pick).

Draft rights traded by Miami with draft rights to Carl Herrera to Houston for draft rights to Alec Kessler, June 27, 1990.

—COLLEGIATE RECORD—

Year	G.	Min.	FGA	FGM	Pct.	FTA	FTM	Pct.	Reb.	Pts.	Avg.
85-86	28	668	294	169	.575	65	54	.831	85	392	14.0
86-87					Did Not Play—Knee Injury						
87-88	30	948	416	198	.476	87	74	.851	115	519	17.3
88-89	29	1034	413	200	.484	107	92	.860	136	551	19.0
89-90	28	1072	647	297	.459	177	149	.842	179	874	31.2
Totals	115	3722	1770	864	.488	436	369	.846	515	2336	20.3

Three-Point Field Goals: 1987-88, 49-for-122 (.402). 1988-89, 59-for-145 (.407). 1989-90, 131-for-303 (.432). Totals, 239-for-570 (.419).

LES JEPSEN

Born June 24, 1967 at Bowbells, N.D. Height 7:00. Weight 245.
High School—Bowbells, N.D.
College—University of Iowa, Iowa City, Ia.
Drafted by Golden State on second round, 1990 (28th pick).

—COLLEGIATE RECORD—

Year	G.	Min.	FGA	FGM	Pct.	FTA	FTM	Pct.	Reb.	Pts.	Avg.
85-86					Did Not Play—Red Shirted						
86-87	15	46	11	5	.455	9	5	.556	16	15	1.0
87-88	26	114	27	10	.370	30	14	.567	39	35	1.3
88-89	33	666	94	53	.564	53	33	.623	175	139	4.2
89-80	28	818	249	155	.622	173	107	.618	281	417	14.9
Totals	102	1644	381	223	.585	265	159	.600	511	606	5.9

Three-Point Field Goals: 1987-88, 1-for-1 (1.000). 1988-89, 0-for-2. 1989-90, 0-for-1. Totals, 1-for-4 (.250).

ALEC CHRISTOPHER KESSLER

Born January 13, 1967 at Minneapolis, Minn. Height 6:11. Weight 230.
High School—Roswell, Ga.
College—University of Georgia, Athens, Ga.
Drafted by Houston on first round, 1990 (12th pick).

Draft rights traded by Houston to Miami for draft rights to Dave Jamerson and Carl Herrera, June 27, 1990.

—COLLEGIATE RECORD—

Year	G.	Min.	FGA	FGM	Pct.	FTA	FTM	Pct.	Reb.	Pts.	Avg.
85-86					Did Not Play—Red Shirted						
86-87	28	421	89	55	.618	42	30	.714	95	140	5.0
87-88	35	1077	303	149	.492	183	144	.787	197	442	12.6
88-89	31	984	431	210	.487	232	176	.759	301	596	19.2
89-90	29	970	403	198	.491	263	199	.757	300	610	21.0
Totals	123	3452	1226	612	.499	720	549	.763	893	1788	14.5

Three-Point Field Goals: 1988-89, 0-for-1. 1989-90, 14-for-35 (.400). Totals, 14-for-36 (.389).

GREG KIMBLE
(Bo)

Born April 9, 1966 at Philadelphia, Pa. Height 6:04. Weight 200.

High School—Philadelphia, Pa., Dobbins Tech.

Colleges—University of Southern California, Los Angeles, Calif., and Loyola Marymount University, Los Angeles, Calif.

Drafted by Los Angeles Clippers on first round, 1990 (8th pick).

—COLLEGIATE RECORD—

Southern California

Year	G.	Min.	FGA	FGM	Pct.	FTA	FTM	Pct.	Reb.	Pts.	Avg.
85-86	28	694	297	138	.465	83	64	.771	101	340	12.1

Loyola Marymount

Year	G.	Min.	FGA	FGM	Pct.	FTA	FTM	Pct.	Reb.	Pts.	Avg.
86-87	Did Not Play—Transfer Student										
87-88	26	683	481	211	.439	103	81	.786	81	577	22.2
88-89	18	421	259	119	.459	41	31	.756	76	302	16.8
89-90	32	1053	763	404	.529	268	231	.862	247	1131	35.3
LMU Totals	76	2157	1503	734	.488	412	343	.833	404	2010	26.4
Col. Totals	104	2851	1800	872	.484	495	407	.822	505	2350	22.6

Three-Point Field Goals: 1987-88, 74-for-195 (.379). 1988-89, 33-for-94 (.351). 1989-90, 92-for-200 (.460). Totals, 199-for-489 (.407).

Led NCAA Division I in scoring, 1990. . . . Named to THE SPORTING NEWS All-America Third Team, 1990.

NEGELE OSCAR KNIGHT

Born March 6, 1967 at Detroit, Mich. Height 6:02. Weight 175.

High School—Detroit, Mich., St. Martin De Porres.

College—University of Dayton, Dayton, O.

Drafted by Phoenix on second round, 1990 (31st pick).

—COLLEGIATE RECORD—

Year	G.	Min.	FGA	FGM	Pct.	FTA	FTM	Pct.	Reb.	Pts.	Avg.
85-86	30	801	198	75	.379	94	63	.670	63	213	7.1
86-87	Did Not Play—Ankle Surgery										
87-88	31	1169	373	176	.472	136	97	.713	98	459	14.8
88-89	29	1024	306	145	.474	136	100	.735	96	403	13.9
89-90	32	1072	465	234	.503	240	192	.800	123	731	22.8
Totals	122	4066	1342	630	.469	606	452	.746	380	1806	14.8

Three-Point Field Goals: 1987-88, 10-for-36 (.286). 1988-89, 13-for-41 (.317). 1989-90, 71-for-144 (.493). Totals, 94-for-221 (.425).

MARCUS LIBERTY

Born October 27, 1968 at Chicago, Ill. Height 6:08. Weight 205.

High School—Chicago, Ill., King.

College—University of Illinois, Champaign, Ill.

Drafted by Denver on second round as an undergraduate, 1990 (42nd pick).

—COLLEGIATE RECORD—

Year	G.	Min.	FGA	FGM	Pct.	FTA	FTM	Pct.	Reb.	Pts.	Avg.
87-88	Did Not Play—Ineligible										
88-89	36	748	252	120	.476	73	57	.781	141	303	8.4
89-90	29	958	400	203	.508	135	103	.763	206	517	17.8
Totals	65	1706	652	323	.495	208	160	.769	347	820	12.6

Three-Point Field Goals: 1988-89, 6-for-12 (.500). 1989-90, 8-for-21 (.381). Totals, 14-for-33 (.424).

TONY ARNEL MASSENBURG

Born July 31, 1967 at Sussex, Va. Height 6:09. Weight 220.

High School—Sussex, Va., Central.

College—University of Maryland, College Park, Md.

Drafted by San Antonio on second round, 1990 (43rd pick).

—COLLEGIATE RECORD—

Year	G.	Min.	FGA	FGM	Pct.	FTA	FTM	Pct.	Reb.	Pts.	Avg.
85-86	29	349	56	28	.500	48	27	.563	60	83	2.9
86-87	Did Not Play										
87-88	23	616	179	93	.520	82	47	.573	122	233	10.1

Year	G.	Min.	FGA	FGM	Pct.	FTA	FTM	Pct.	Reb.	Pts.	Avg.
88-89	29	1001	358	197	.550	145	87	.600	226	481	16.6
89-90	31	973	408	206	.505	201	145	.721	314	557	18.0
Totals	112	2939	1001	524	.523	476	306	.643	722	1354	12.1

Three-Point Field Goals: 1988-89, 0-for-1. 1989-90, 0-for-2. Totals, 0-for-3.

TRAVIS CORTEZ MAYS

Born June 19, 1968 at Ocala, Fla. Height 6:02. Weight 190.

High School—Ocala, Fla., Vanguard.

College—University of Texas, Austin, Tex.

Drafted by Sacramento on first round, 1990 (14th pick).

—COLLEGIATE RECORD—

Year	G.	Min.	FGA	FGM	Pct.	FTA	FTM	Pct.	Reb.	Pts.	Avg.
86-87	30	890	239	101	.423	84	50	.595	112	258	8.6
87-88	28	1055	357	164	.459	166	128	.771	153	506	18.1
88-89	34	1210	564	253	.449	200	142	.710	161	743	21.9
89-90	32	1186	554	240	.433	243	197	.811	164	772	24.1
Totals	124	4341	1714	758	.442	693	517	.746	590	2279	18.4

Three-Point Field Goals: 1986-87, 6-for-26 (.231). 1987-88, 50-for-129 (.388). 1988-89, 95-for-257 (.370). 1989-90, 95-for-252 (.357). Totals, 246-for-664 (.370).

TERRY RICHARD MILLS

Born December 21, 1967 at Romulus, Mich. Height 6:10. Weight 240.

High School—Romulus, Mich.

College—University of Michigan, Ann Arbor, Mich.

Drafted by Milwaukee on first round, 1990 (16th pick).

Traded by Milwaukee to Denver for Danny Schayes, August 1, 1990.

—COLLEGIATE RECORD—

Year	G.	Min.	FGA	FGM	Pct.	FTA	FTM	Pct.	Reb.	Pts.	Avg.
86-87					Did Not Play—Ineligible						
87-88	34	884	341	181	.531	70	51	.729	216	413	12.1
88-89	37	999	319	180	.564	91	70	.769	218	430	11.6
89-90	31	961	405	237	.585	116	88	.759	247	562	18.1
Totals	102	2844	1065	598	.562	277	209	.755	681	1405	13.8

Three-Point Field Goals: 1987-88, 0-for-2. 1988-89, 0-for-2. Totals, 0-for-4.

Member of NCAA Division I championship team, 1989. . . . Nephew of John Long, guard with Detroit Pistons, Indiana Pacers and Atlanta Hawks, 1978-79 through 1989-90.

TERRAH JERROD MUSTAF

(Known by middle name.)

Born October 28, 1949 at Whiteville, N.C. Height 6:10. Weight 245.

High School—Hyattsville, Md., DeMatha.

College—University of Maryland, College Park, Md.

Drafted by New York on first round as an undergraduate, 1990 (17th pick).

—COLLEGIATE RECORD—

Year	G.	Min.	FGA	FGM	Pct.	FTA	FTM	Pct.	Reb.	Pts.	Avg.
88-89	26	847	302	157	.520	74	53	.716	202	371	14.3
89-90	33	1048	446	236	.529	164	127	.774	254	609	18.5
Totals	59	1895	746	393	.527	238	180	.756	456	980	16.6

Three-Point Field Goals: 1988-89, 4-for-16 (.250). 1989-90, 10-for-20 (.500). Totals, 14-for-36 (.389).

BRIAN DARNELL OLIVER

Born June 1, 1968 at Chicago, Ill. Height 6:04. Weight 210.

High School—Smyrna, Ga., Wills.

College—Georgia Institute of Technology, Atlanta, Ga.

Drafted by Philadelphia on second round, 1990 (32nd pick).

—COLLEGIATE RECORD—

Year	G.	Min.	FGA	FGM	Pct.	FTA	FTM	Pct.	Reb.	Pts.	Avg.
86-87	29	879	158	72	.456	75	54	.720	91	205	7.1
87-88	32	1106	310	157	.506	102	76	.745	139	403	12.6
88-89	32	1163	345	191	.554	135	106	.785	179	516	16.1
89-90	34	1277	504	260	.516	204	147	.721	204	724	21.3
Totals	127	4425	1317	680	.516	516	383	.742	613	1848	14.6

Three-Point Field Goals: 1986-87, 7-for-18 (.389). 1987-88, 13-for-38 (.342). 1988-89, 28-for-70 (.400). 1989-90, 57-for-147 (.388). Totals, 105-for-273 (.385).

WALTER SCOTT PALMER

Born October 23, 1968 at Ithaca, N.Y. Height 7:02. Weight 215.
High School—Arlington, Va., Washington & Lee.
College—Dartmouth College, Hanover, N.H.
Drafted by Utah on second round, 1990 (33rd pick).

—COLLEGIATE RECORD—

Year	G.	Min.	FGA	FGM	Pct.	FTA	FTM	Pct.	Reb.	Pts.	Avg.
86-87	10	60	15	9	.600	9	6	.667	19	24	2.4
87-88	26	463	125	66	.528	47	32	.681	123	164	6.3
88-89	26	540	200	121	.605	78	59	.756	158	301	11.6
89-90	25	565	290	149	.514	142	115	.810	162	414	16.6
Totals	87	1628	630	345	.548	276	212	.768	462	903	10.4

Three-Point Field Goals: 1989-90, 1-for-9 (.111).

GARY DWAYNE PAYTON

Born July 23, 1968 at Oakland, Calif. Height 6:04. Weight 180.
High School—Oakland, Calif., Skyline.
College—Oregon State University, Corvallis, Ore.
Drafted by Seattle on first round, 1990 (2nd pick).

—COLLEGIATE RECORD—

Year	G.	Min.	FGA	FGM	Pct.	FTA	FTM	Pct.	Reb.	Pts.	Avg.
86-87	30	1115	333	153	.460	82	55	.671	120	374	12.5
87-88	31	1178	368	180	.489	83	58	.699	103	449	14.5
88-89	30	1140	438	208	.475	155	105	.677	122	603	20.1
89-90	29	1095	571	288	.504	171	118	.690	135	746	25.7
Totals	120	4528	1710	829	.485	491	336	.684	480	2172	18.1

Three-Point Field Goals: 1986-87, 13-for-35 (.371). 1987-88, 31-for-78 (.397). 1988-89, 82-for-213 (.385). 1989-90, 52-for-156 (.333). Totals, 178-for-482 (.369).

Named to THE SPORTING NEWS All-America First Team, 1990.

KEVIN LEE PRITCHARD

Born July 17, 1967 at Bloomington, Ind. Height 6:03. Weight 180.
High School—Tulsa, Okla., Edison.
College—University of Kansas, Lawrence, Kan.
Drafted by Golden State on second round, 1990 (34th pick).

—COLLEGIATE RECORD—

Year	G.	Min.	FGA	FGM	Pct.	FTA	FTM	Pct.	Reb.	Pts.	Avg.
86-87	36	962	294	134	.456	54	41	.759	77	345	9.6
87-88	37	1100	296	144	.486	119	88	.739	95	393	10.6
88-89	31	944	306	155	.507	108	83	.769	76	448	14.5
89-90	35	976	337	177	.525	130	106	.815	89	506	14.5
Totals	139	3982	1233	610	.495	411	318	.774	337	1692	12.2

Three-Point Field Goals: 1986-87, 36-for-88 (.409). 1987-88, 17-for-54 (.315). 1988-89, 55-for-129 (.426). 1989-90, 46-for-108 (.426). Totals, 154-for-379 (.406).

Member of NCAA Division I championship team, 1988.

RUMEAL JAMES ROBINSON

Born November 13, 1966 in Jamaica. Height 6:02. Weight 195.
High School—Cambridge, Mass., Rindge-Latin.
College—University of Michigan, Ann Arbor, Mich.
Drafted by Atlanta on first round, 1990 (10th pick).

—COLLEGIATE RECORD—

Year	G.	Min.	FGA	FGM	Pct.	FTA	FTM	Pct.	Reb.	Pts.	Avg.
86-87				Did Not Play—Ineligible							
87-88	33	858	208	115	.553	126	84	.667	101	321	9.7
88-89	37	1110	357	199	.557	186	122	.656	125	550	14.9
89-90	30	1020	410	201	.490	185	125	.676	127	575	19.2
Totals	100	2988	975	515	.528	497	331	.666	353	1446	14.5

Three-Point Field Goals: 1987-88, 7-for-26 (.269). 1988-89, 30-for-64 (.469). 1989-90, 48-for-117 (.410). Totals, 85-for-207 (.411).

Member of NCAA Division I championship team, 1989. . . . Named to THE SPORTING NEWS All-America Third Team, 1990.

STEPHEN ROBERT SCHEFFLER (Steve)

Born September 3, 1967 at Grand Rapids, Mich. Height 6:09. Weight 250.
High School—Grand Rapids, Mich., Forest Hills Northern.
College—Purdue University, West Lafayette, Ind.
Drafted by Charlotte on second round, 1990 (39th pick).

—COLLEGIATE RECORD—

Year	G.	Min.	FGA	FGM	Pct.	FTA	FTM	Pct.	Reb.	Pts.	Avg.
86-87	16	73	16	9	.563	14	6	.429	24	24	1.5
87-88	33	548	113	80	.708	100	65	.650	144	225	6.8
88-89	31	830	219	146	.667	143	111	.776	187	403	13.0
89-90	30	996	248	173	.698	195	157	.805	183	503	16.8
Totals	110	2447	596	408	.685	452	339	.750	538	1155	10.5

Named to THE SPORTING NEWS All-America Second Team, 1990. . . . Brother of Tom Scheffler, forward with Portland Trail Blazers, 1984-85.

DWAYNE SCHINTZIUS

Born October 14, 1968 at Brandon, Fla. Height 7:01. Weight 260.
High School—Brandon, Fla.
College—University of Florida, Gainesville, Fla.
Drafted by San Antonio on first round, 1990 (24th pick).

—COLLEGIATE RECORD—

Year	G.	Min.	FGA	FGM	Pct.	FTA	FTM	Pct.	Reb.	Pts.	Avg.
86-87	34	931	366	161	.440	65	48	.738	206	370	10.9
87-88	35	1069	456	224	.491	74	54	.730	228	503	14.4
88-89	30	1120	422	220	.521	140	99	.707	290	541	18.0
89-90	11	355	163	90	.552	38	30	.789	105	210	19.1
Totals	110	3475	1407	695	.494	317	231	.729	829	1624	14.8

Three-Point Field Goals: 1987-88, 1-for-5 (.200). 1988-89, 2-for-6 (.333). 1989-90, 0-for-8. Totals, 3-for-19 (.158).

DENNIS EUGENE SCOTT

Born September 5, 1968 at Hagerstown, Md. Height 6:08. Weight 230.
High School—Oakton, Va., Flint Hill Prep.
College—Georgia Institute of Technology, Atlanta, Ga.
Drafted by Orlando on first round as an undergraduate, 1990 (4th pick).

—COLLEGIATE RECORD—

Year	G.	Min.	FGA	FGM	Pct.	FTA	FTM	Pct.	Reb.	Pts.	Avg.
87-88	32	1113	411	181	.440	55	36	.655	161	496	15.5
88-89	32	1205	512	227	.443	97	79	.814	131	649	20.3
89-90	35	1368	722	336	.465	203	161	.793	231	970	27.7
Totals	99	3686	1645	744	.452	355	276	.777	523	2115	21.4

Three-Point Field Goals: 1987-88, 98-for-208 (.471). 1988-89, 116-for-292 (.397). 1989-90, 137-for-331 (.414). Totals, 351-for-831 (.422).

Named THE SPORTING NEWS College Player of the Year, 1990. . . . Named to THE SPORTING NEWS All-America First Team, 1990.

ABDUL MOHAMMED SHAMSID-DEEN

Born August 1, 1968 at Staten Island, N.Y. Height 6:10. Weight 225.
High School—Staten Island, N.Y., Tottenville.
College—Providence College, Providence, R.I.
Drafted by Seattle on second round, 1990 (53rd pick).

—COLLEGIATE RECORD—

Year	G.	Min.	FGA	FGM	Pct.	FTA	FTM	Pct.	Reb.	Pts.	Avg.
86-87	33	330	80	45	.563	44	27	.614	84	117	3.5
87-88	20	277	93	37	.398	33	20	.606	64	94	4.7
88-89	29	490	123	71	.577	67	46	.687	104	188	6.5
89-90	29	673	191	97	.508	92	51	.554	212	245	8.4
Totals	111	1770	487	250	.513	236	144	.610	464	644	5.8

LIONEL J. SIMMONS

Born November 14, 1968 at Philadelphia, Pa. Height 6:07. Weight 220.
High School—Philadelphia, Pa., South Philadelphia.
College—La Salle University, Philadelphia, Pa.
Drafted by Sacramento on first round, 1990 (7th pick).

—COLLEGIATE RECORD—

Year	G.	Min.	FGA	FGM	Pct.	FTA	FTM	Pct.	Reb.	Pts.	Avg.
86-87	33	....	500	263	.526	186	142	.763	322	670	20.3
87-88	34	....	613	297	.485	259	196	.757	386	792	23.3
88-89	32	1245	716	349	.487	266	189	.711	365	908	28.4
89-90	32	1220	653	335	.513	221	146	.661	356	847	26.5
Totals	131	....	2482	1244	.501	932	673	.722	1429	3217	24.6

Three-Point Field Goals: 1986-87, 2-for-6 (.333). 1987-88, 2-for-8 (.250). 1988-89, 21-for-56 (.375). 1989-90, 31-for-65 (.477). Totals, 56-for-135 (.415).

Named to THE SPORTING NEWS All-America First Team, 1989. . . . THE SPORTING NEWS All-America Second Team, 1988 and 1990.

CHARLES ANTON SMITH
(Tony)

Born June 14, 1968 at Milwaukee, Wis. Height 6:03. Weight 185.
High School—Wauwatosa, Wis., East.
College—Marquette University, Milwaukee, Wis.
Drafted by Los Angeles Lakers on second round, 1990 (51st pick).

—COLLEGIATE RECORD—

Year	G.	Min.	FGA	FGM	Pct.	FTA	FTM	Pct.	Reb.	Pts.	Avg.
86-87	29	722	161	86	.534	81	61	.753	96	234	8.1
87-88	28	894	260	136	.523	119	88	.739	126	367	13.1
88-89	28	943	275	153	.556	115	84	.730	109	398	14.2
89-90	29	1131	485	240	.495	202	173	.856	137	689	23.8
Totals	114	3690	1181	615	.521	517	406	.785	468	1688	14.8

Three-Point Field Goals: 1986-87, 1-for-3 (.333). 1987-88, 7-for-19 (.368). 1988-89, 8-for-12 (.750). 1989-90, 36-for-87 (.414). Totals, 52-for-121 (.429).

FELTON LaFRANCE SPENCER

Born January 5, 1968 at Louisville, Ky. Height 7:00. Weight 265.
High School—Louisville, Ky., Eastern.
College—University of Louisville, Louisville, Ky.
Drafted by Minnesota on first round, 1990 (6th pick).

—COLLEGIATE RECORD—

Year	G.	Min.	FGA	FGM	Pct.	FTA	FTM	Pct.	Reb.	Pts.	Avg.
86-87	31	356	78	43	.551	65	32	.492	83	118	3.8
87-88	35	532	157	93	.592	114	73	.640	146	259	7.4
88-89	33	581	140	85	.607	135	99	.733	169	269	8.2
89-90	35	995	276	188	.681	204	146	.716	296	522	14.9
Totals	134	2464	651	409	.628	518	350	.676	694	1168	8.7

DEREK LAMAR STRONG

Born February 9, 1968 at Los Angeles, Calif. Height 6:08. Weight 228.
High School—Pacific Palisades, Calif.
College—Xavier University, Cincinnati, O.
Drafted by Philadelphia on second round, 1990 (47th pick).

—COLLEGIATE RECORD—

Year	G.	Min.	FGA	FGM	Pct.	FTA	FTM	Pct.	Reb.	Pts.	Avg.
86-87						Did Not Play					
87-88	30	668	197	112	.569	131	94	.718	213	318	10.6
88-89	33	983	264	163	.617	218	178	.817	264	504	15.3
89-90	33	981	274	146	.533	211	177	.839	328	469	14.2
Totals	96	2632	735	421	.573	560	449	.802	805	1291	13.4

LOY STEPHEN VAUGHT

Born February 27, 1967 at Grand Rapids, Mich. Height 6:09. Weight 230.
High School—Kentwood, Mich., East Kentwood.
College—University of Michigan, Ann Arbor, Mich.
Drafted by Los Angeles Clippers on first round, 1990 (13th pick).

—COLLEGIATE RECORD—

Year	G.	Min.	FGA	FGM	Pct.	FTA	FTM	Pct.	Reb.	Pts.	Avg.
86-87	32	416	122	68	.557	22	11	.500	125	147	4.6
87-88	34	748	243	151	.621	76	55	724	150	357	10.5
88-89	37	851	304	201	.661	81	63	.778	296	467	12.6
89-90	31	930	331	197	.595	107	86	.804	346	480	15.5
Totals	134	2945	1000	617	.617	286	215	.752	917	1451	10.8

Three-Point Field Goals: 1988-89, 2-for-5 (.400). 1989-90, 0-for-1. Totals, 2-for-6 (.333).

Member of NCAA Division I championship team, 1989.

JAYSON WILLIAMS

Born February 22, 1968 at Ritter, S.C. Height 6:09. Weight 240.
High School—Queens, N.Y., Christ The King.
College—St. John's University, Jamaica, N.Y.
Drafted by Phoenix on first round, 1990 (21st pick).

—COLLEGIATE RECORD—

Year	G.	Min.	FGA	FGM	Pct.	FTA	FTM	Pct.	Reb.	Pts.	Avg.
86-87				Did Not Play—Ineligible							
87-88	28	662	199	102	.513	120	72	.600	143	276	9.9
88-89	31	1036	412	236	.573	191	134	.702	246	606	19.5
89-90	13	377	131	70	.534	80	49	.613	101	190	14.6
Totals	72	2045	742	408	.550	391	255	.652	490	1072	14.9

Three-Point Field Goals: 1988-89, 0-for-2. 1989-90, 1-for-2 (.500). Totals, 1-for-4 (.250).

KENNETH RAY WILLIAMS
(Kenny)

Born June 9, 1969 at Elizabeth City, N.C. Height 6:09. Weight 215.
High Schools—Elizabeth City, N.C., Northeastern and Fork Union, Va., Fork Union Military Academy.
Colleges—Barton County Community College, Great Bend, Kan., and Elizabeth City State University, Elizabeth, N.C.

Drafted by Indiana on second round, 1990 (46th pick).

—COLLEGIATE RECORD—

Barton County

Year	G.	Min.	FGA	FGM	Pct.	FTA	FTM	Pct.	Reb.	Pts.	Avg.
88-89	31	....	...	...	....	...	...	...	278	636	20.5

Elizabeth City State

Year	G.	Min.	FGA	FGM	Pct.	FTA	FTM	Pct.	Reb.	Pts.	Avg.
89-90				Did Not Play							

TREVOR WILSON

Born March 16, 1968 at Los Angeles, Calif. Height 6:07. Weight 210.
High School—Reseda, Calif., Grover Cleveland.
College—University of California at Los Angeles, Los Angeles, Calif.
Drafted by Atlanta on second round, 1990 (36th pick).

—COLLEGIATE RECORD—

Year	G.	Min.	FGA	FGM	Pct.	FTA	FTM	Pct.	Reb.	Pts.	Avg.
86-87	32	576	146	65	.445	95	69	.726	152	199	6.2
87-88	30	1010	353	184	.521	153	95	.621	281	463	15.4
88-89	31	1066	451	226	.501	203	117	.576	269	570	18.4
89-90	33	1106	467	231	.495	203	103	.507	299	566	17.2
Totals	126	3758	1417	706	.498	654	384	.587	1001	1798	14.3

Three-Point Field Goals: 1987-88, 0-for-3. 1988-89, 1-for-6 (.167). 1989-90, 1-for-3 (.333). Totals, 2-for-12 (.167).

NBA Head Coaches

RICK ADELMAN
Portland Trail Blazers

Born June 16, 1946 at Lynwood, Calif. Height 6:02. Weight 180.
High School—Downey, Calif., St. Pius X.
College—Loyola University, Los Angeles, Calif.
Drafted by San Diego on seventh round, 1968 (79th pick).

Selected from San Diego by Portland in NBA expansion draft, May 11, 1970.
Traded by Portland to Chicago for cash and a 1974 2nd round draft choice, October 14, 1973.
Traded by Chicago to New Orleans for John Block, November 11, 1974.
Traded by New Orleans with Ollie Johnson to Kansas City-Omaha for Nate Williams, February 1, 1975.
Released by Kansas City, October 21, 1975.

—COLLEGIATE RECORD—

Year	G.	Min.	FGA	FGM	Pct.	FTA	FTM	Pct.	Reb.	Pts.	Avg.
64-65†	Statistics Unavailable										
65-66	26	....	376	149	.396	152	129	.849	113	427	16.4
66-67	25	....	349	151	.433	214	171	.799	124	473	18.9
67-68	25	....	420	177	.421	216	171	.792	127	525	21.0
Varsity Totals	76	....	1145	477	.417	582	471	.809	364	1425	18.8

NBA REGULAR SEASON RECORD

Sea.—Team	G.	Min.	FGA	FGM	Pct.	FTA	FTM	Pct.	Reb.	Ast.	PF	Disq.	Pts.	Avg.
68-69—San Diego	77	1448	449	177	.394	204	131	.642	216	238	158	1	485	6.3
69-70—San Diego	35	717	247	96	.389	91	68	.747	81	113	90	0	260	7.4
70-71—Portland	81	2303	895	378	.422	369	267	.724	282	380	214	2	1023	12.6
71-72—Portland	80	2445	753	329	.437	201	151	.751	229	413	209	2	808	10.1
72-73—Portland	76	1822	525	214	.408	102	73	.716	157	294	155	2	591	6.6

									—Rebounds—									
Sea.—Team	G.	Min.	FGA	FGM	Pct.	FTA	FTM	Pct.	Off.	Def.	Tot.	Ast.	PF	Dq.	Stl.	Blk.	Pts.	Avg.
73-74—Chicago	55	618	170	64	.376	76	54	.711	16	53	69	56	63	0	36	1	182	3.3
74-75—Chi-NO-KC-O	58	1074	291	123	.423	103	73	.709	25	70	95	112	101	1	70	8	319	5.5
Totals	462	10427	3330	1381	.415	1146	817	.713			1129	1606	990	8	106	9	3579	7.7

NBA PLAYOFF RECORD

Sea.—Team	G.	Min.	FGA	FGM	Pct.	FTA	FTM	Pct.	Reb.	Ast.	PF	Disq.	Pts.	Avg.
68-69—San Diego	6	187	53	24	.453	37	22	.595	15	29	18	0	70	11.7

									—Rebounds—									
Sea.—Team	G.	Min.	FGA	FGM	Pct.	FTA	FTM	Pct.	Off.	Def.	Tot.	Ast.	PF	Dq.	Stl.	Blk.	Pts.	Avg.
73-74—Chicago	9	108	34	16	.471	11	7	.636	1	9	10	7	5	0	7	0	39	4.3
74-75—KC-O	6	34	9	3	.333	8	6	.750	1	1	2	3	9	0	1	0	12	2.0
Totals	21	329	96	43	.448	56	35	.625			27	39	32	0	8	0	121	5.8

NBA COACHING RECORD

	Regular Season				Playoffs	
Sea. Club	W.	L.	Pct.	Pos.	W.	L.
1988-89—Portland	14	21	.400	5†	0	3
1989-90—Portland	59	23	.720	2†	12	9
Totals (2 seasons)	73	44	.624		12	12

†Pacific Division.

Assistant coach, Portland Trail Blazers, 1983-89.

RICHARD ADAM ADUBATO
(Name pronounced Ah-duh-bah-doe.)

(Richie)
Dallas Mavericks

Born November 23, 1937 at East Orange, N.J.
High School—East Orange, N.J.
College—William Paterson College, Wayne, N.J.

COLLEGIATE COACHING RECORD

Sea.	Club	Regular Season W.	L.	Pct.	Pos.
1972-73	—Upsala	15	9	.625	..
1973-74	—Upsala	17	10	.630	..
1974-75	—Upsala	18	11	.621	..
1975-76	—Upsala	20	9	.690	..
1976-77	—Upsala	11	14	.440	..
1977-78	—Upsala	19	9	.679	..
Totals (6 seasons)		100	62	.617	

Assistant coach, Upsala College, 1969-72.

NBA COACHING RECORD

Sea.	Club	Regular Season W.	L.	Pct.	Pos.	Playoffs W.	L.
1979-80	—Detroit	12	58	.171	..†	..	..
1989-90	—Dallas	42	29	.592	3‡	0	3
Totals (2 seasons)		54	87	.383		0	3

†Central Division. ‡Midwest Division.

Assistant coach, Detroit Pistons, 1978-79; New York Knicks, 1982-86, and Dallas Mavericks, 1986-89.
Scout, Atlanta Hawks, 1980-82.

LAWRENCE HARVEY BROWN
(Larry)
San Antonio Spurs

Born September 14, 1940 at Brooklyn, N. Y. Height 5:09. Weight 160.
High School—Long Beach, N. Y.
Prep School—Hargrave Military Academy, Chatham, Va.
College—University of North Carolina, Chapel Hill, N. C.

Signed by New Orleans ABA, 1967.
Traded by New Orleans with Doug Moe to Oakland for Steve Jones, Ron Franz and Barry Leibowitz, June 18, 1968.
Oakland franchise transferred to Washington, 1969.
Washington franchise transferred to Virginia, 1970.
Sold by Virginia to Denver, January 23, 1971.

—COLLEGIATE PLAYING RECORD—

Year	G.	Min.	FGA	FGM	Pct.	FTA	FTM	Pct.	Reb.	Pts.	Avg.
59-60†	15	....	....	88	....	143	100	.699	....	276	18.4
60-61	18	....	54	28	.519	34	25	.735	28	81	4.5
61-62	17	....	204	90	.441	127	101	.795	52	281	16.5
62-63	21	....	231	102	.442	122	95	.779	50	299	14.2
Varsity Totals	56	....	489	220	.450	283	221	.781	130	661	11.8

AMATEUR PLAYING RECORD

Akron (Ohio) Goodyears

Year	G.	Min.	FGA	FGM	Pct.	FTA	FTM	Pct.	Reb.	Pts.	Avg.
63-64	..	....	....	....	....	....	....	....	....	398	....
64-65	32	....	297	144	.485	167	139	.832	90	427	13.3

ABA REGULAR SEASON RECORD

Sea.—Team	G.	Min.	2-Point FGM	FGA	Pct.	3-Point FGM	FGA	Pct.	FTM	FTA	Pct.	Reb.	Ast.	Pts.	Avg.
67-68—New Orleans	78	2807	311	812	.383	19	89	.213	366	450	.813	249	506	1045	13.4
68-69—Oakland	77	2381	300	671	.447	8	35	.229	301	379	.794	235	544	925	12.0
69-70—Washington	82	2766	366	815	.449	10	39	.256	362	439	.825	246	580	1124	13.7
70-71—Virginia-Denver	63	1343	121	319	.379	6	21	.286	186	225	.827	109	330	446	7.1
71-72—Denver	76	2012	238	531	.448	5	25	.200	198	244	.811	166	549	689	9.1
Totals	376	11309	1336	3148	.424	48	209	.230	1413	1737	.813	1005	2509	4229	11.3

ABA PLAYOFF RECORD

Sea.—Team	G.	Min.	2-Point FGM	FGA	Pct.	3-Point FGM	FGA	Pct.	FTM	FTA	Pct.	Reb.	Ast.	Pts.	Avg.
67-68—New Orleans	17	696	86	194	.443	4	18	.222	100	122	.820	59	129	284	16.7
68-69—Oakland	16	534	74	170	.435	0	3	.000	76	90	.844	52	87	224	14.0
69-70—Washington	7	269	32	68	.471	1	5	.200	30	34	.882	35	68	97	13.9
71-72—Denver	7	211	21	47	.447	0	3	.000	23	24	.958	10	36	65	9.3
Totals	47	1710	213	479	.445	5	29	.172	229	270	.848	156	285	670	14.3

ABA ALL-STAR GAME RECORD

Sea.—Team	Min.	2-Point FGM	FGA	Pct.	3-Point FGM	FGA	Pct.	FTM	FTA	Pct.	Reb.	Ast.	Pts.	Avg.
1968—New Orleans	22	5	7	.714	2	2	1.000	1	1	1.000	3	5	17	17.0
1969—Oakland	25	1	6	.167	0	1	.000	3	5	.600	0	7	5	5.0
1970—Washington	15	0	2	.000	0	0	.000	3	3	1.000	3	3	3	3.0
Totals	62	6	15	.400	2	3	.667	7	9	.778	6	15	25	8.3

COLLEGIATE COACHING RECORD

	Regular Season			
Sea. Club	W.	L.	Pct.	Pos.
1979-80—UCLA	22	10	.688	4
1980-81—UCLA	20	7	.741	3
1983-84—Kansas	22	10	.688	
1984-85—Kansas	26	8	.765	
1985-86—Kansas	35	4	.897	
1986-87—Kansas	25	11	.694	
1987-88—Kansas	21	11	.656	
Totals (7 seasons)	171	61	.737	

Assistant coach at University of North Carolina, 1965-67.

ABA COACHING RECORD

	Regular Season				Playoffs	
Sea. Club	W.	L.	Pct.	Pos.	W.	L.
1972-73—Carolina	57	27	.679	1†	7	5
1973-74—Carolina	47	37	.560	3†	0	4
1974-75—Denver	65	19	.774	1‡	7	6
1975-76—Denver	60	24	.714	1	6	7
Totals (4 seasons)	229	107	.682		20	22

NBA COACHING RECORD

	Regular Season				Playoffs	
Sea. Club	W.	L.	Pct.	Pos.	W.	L.
1976-77—Denver	50	32	.610	1§	2	4
1977-78—Denver	48	34	.585	1§	6	7
1978-79—Denver	28	25	.528	2§	..	..
1981-82—New Jersey	44	38	.537	3x	0	2
1982-83—New Jersey	47	29	.618	..x	..	..
1988-89—San Antonio	21	61	.256	5§	..	..
1989-90—San Antonio	56	26	.683	1§	6	4
Totals (7 seasons)	294	245	.545		14	17

†Eastern Division. ‡Western Division. §Midwest Division. xAtlantic Division.

Named to ABA All-Star Second Team, 1968. . . . Led ABA in assists, 1968, 1969, 1970. . . . ABA All-Star Game MVP, 1968. . . . Member of ABA championship team, 1969. . . . Member of U.S. Olympic team, 1964. . . . ABA Coach of the Year, 1973, 1975, 1976. . . . Coach of NCAA Division I championship team, 1988.

DONALD CHANEY
(Don)
Houston Rockets

Born March 22, 1946 at Baton Rouge, La. Height 6:05. Weight 210.
High School—Baton Rouge, La., McKinley.
College—University of Houston, Houston, Tex.
Drafted by Boston on first round, 1968 (12th pick).

Signed by St. Louis ABA, September 27, 1974, for 1975-76 season.
Played out option with Boston, September 1, 1975; signed by Los Angeles as a free agent, September 22, 1976.
Traded by Los Angeles with Kermit Washington and a 1978 1st round draft choice to Boston for Charlie Scott, December 27, 1977.

—COLLEGIATE RECORD—

Year	G.	Min.	FGA	FGM	Pct.	FTA	FTM	Pct.	Reb.	Pts.	Avg.
64-65†	21	....	421	186	.442	123	84	.683	183	456	21.7
65-66	26	627	243	105	.432	38	21	.553	124	231	8.9
66-67	31	1038	448	197	.440	116	80	.690	160	474	15.3
67-68	33	1010	431	189	.439	84	50	.595	191	428	13.0
Varsity Totals	90	2675	1122	491	.438	238	151	.634	475	1133	12.6

ABA REGULAR SEASON RECORD

			—2-Point—			—3-Point—									
Sea.—Team	G.	Min.	FGM	FGA	Pct.	FGM	FGA	Pct.	FTM	FTA	Pct.	Reb.	Ast.	Pts.	Avg.
75-76—St. Louis	48	1475	190	453	.419	1	4	.250	64	82	.780	234	169	447	9.3

NBA REGULAR SEASON RECORD

									—Rebounds—									
Sea.—Team	G.	Min.	FGA	FGM	Pct.	FTA	FTM	Pct.	Off.	Def.	Tot.	Ast.	PF	Dq.	Stl.	Blk.	Pts.	Avg.
68-69—Boston	20	209	113	36	.319	20	8	.400			46	19	32	0			80	4.0
69-70—Boston	63	839	320	115	.359	109	82	.752			152	72	118	0			312	5.0
70-71—Boston	81	2289	766	348	.454	313	234	.748			463	235	288	11			930	11.5
71-72—Boston	79	2275	786	373	.475	255	197	.773			395	202	295	7			943	11.9
72-73—Boston	79	2488	859	414	.482	267	210	.787			449	221	276	6			1038	13.1
73-74—Boston	81	2258	750	348	.464	180	149	.828	210	168	378	176	247	7	83	62	845	10.4
74-75—Boston	82	2208	750	321	.428	165	133	.806	171	199	370	181	244	5	122	66	775	9.5
76-77—Los Angeles	81	2408	522	213	.408	94	70	.745	120	210	330	308	224	4	140	33	496	6.1
77-78—L.A.-Boston	51	835	269	104	.387	45	38	.844	40	76	116	66	107	0	44	13	246	4.8
78-79—Boston	65	1074	414	174	.420	42	36	.857	63	78	141	75	167	3	72	11	384	5.9

Sea.—Team	G.	Min.	FGA	FGM	Pct.	FTA	FTM	Pct.	—Rebounds— Off.	Def.	Tot.	Ast.	PF	Dq.	Stl.	Blk.	Pts.	Avg.
79-80—Boston	60	523	189	67	.354	42	32	.762	31	42	73	38	80	1	31	11	167	2.8
Totals	742	17406	5738	2513	.438	1532	1189	.776			2913	1593	2078	44	492	196	6216	8.4

Three-Point Field Goals: 1979-80, 1-for-6 (.167).

NBA PLAYOFF RECORD

Sea.—Team	G.	Min.	FGA	FGM	Pct.	FTA	FTM	Pct.	—Rebounds— Off.	Def.	Tot.	Ast.	PF	Dq.	Stl.	Blk.	Pts.	Avg.
68-69—Boston	7	25	6	1	.167	4	3	.750			4	0	7	0			5	0.7
71-72—Boston	11	271	81	41	.506	20	15	.750			39	22	39	0			97	8.8
72-73—Boston	12	288	82	39	.476	17	12	.706			40	25	41	1			90	7.5
73-74—Boston	18	545	141	65	.461	50	41	.820	37	40	77	40	64	0	24	9	171	9.5
74-75—Boston	11	294	105	48	.457	29	23	.793	24	14	38	21	46	2	21	5	119	10.8
76-77—Los Angeles	11	412	96	36	.375	22	16	.727	24	28	52	48	32	0	21	3	88	8.0
Totals	70	1835	511	230	.450	142	110	.775			250	156	229	3	66	17	570	8.1

NBA COACHING RECORD

Sea. Club	Regular Season W.	L.	Pct.	Pos.	Playoffs W.	L.
1984-85—L.A. Clippers......	9	12	.429	..		
1985-86—L.A. Clippers......	32	50	.390	3T†		
1986-87—L.A. Clippers......	12	70	.146	6†		
1988-89—Houston..............	45	37	.549	2‡	1	3
1989-90—Houston..............	41	41	.500	5‡	1	3
Totals (5 seasons)	139	210	.398		2	6

†Pacific Division. ‡Midwest Division.

Assistant coach, Detroit Pistons, 1980-83, Los Angeles Clippers, 1983-85, and Atlanta Hawks, 1987-88.

Member of NBA championship teams, 1969 and 1974. . . . Named to NBA All-Defensive Second Team, 1972, 1973, 1974, 1975, 1977.

CHARLES JOSEPH DALY
(Chuck)
Detroit Pistons

Born July 20, 1930 at St. Mary's, Pa. Height 6:02. Weight 180.

High School—Kane, Pa.

Colleges—St. Bonaventure University, Olean, N. Y.; Bloomsburg State College, Bloomsburg, Pa., and graduate work at Penn State University, University Park, Pa.

COLLEGIATE PLAYING RECORD

St. Bonaventure

Year	G.	Min.	FGA	FGM	Pct.	FTA	FTM	Pct.	Reb.	Pts.	Avg.
48-49†	Statistics Unavailable										

Bloomsburg State

Year	G.	Min.	FGA	FGM	Pct.	FTA	FTM	Pct.	Reb.	Pts.	Avg.
49-50	Did Not Play—Transfer Student										
50-51	16	....	...	...	....	...	...	....	....	215	13.4
51-52	16	....	...	...	....	...	...	....	....	203	12.7
Totals	32	....	...	...	....	...	...	....	....	418	13.1

COLLEGIATE COACHING RECORD

Sea. Club	Regular Season W.	L.	Pct.	Pos.
1969-70—Boston College ..	11	13	.458	..
1970-71—Boston College ..	15	11	.577	..
1971-72—Penn	25	3	.893	1
1972-73—Penn	21	7	.750	1
1973-74—Penn	21	6	.778	1
1974-75—Penn	23	5	.821	1
1975-76—Penn	17	9	.654	2
1976-77—Penn	18	8	.692	2
Tot. B. C. (2 sea.)............	26	24	.520	
Tot. Penn (6 sea.)............	125	38	.767	
Totals (8 seasons)	151	62	.709	

Assistant coach, Duke University, 1963 to 1969.

NOTE: Penn advanced to the NCAA championship tournament in 1972, 1973, 1974 and 1975.

NBA COACHING RECORD

Sea. Club	Regular Season W.	L.	Pct.	Pos.	Playoffs W.	L.
1981-82—Cleveland...........	9	32	.220	..	..	..
1983-84—Detroit................	49	33	.598	2†	2	3
1984-85—Detroit................	46	36	.561	2†	5	4
1985-86—Detroit................	46	36	.561	3†	1	3
1986-87—Detroit................	52	30	.634	2†	10	5
1987-88—Detroit................	54	28	.659	1†	14	9
1988-89—Detroit*..............	63	19	.768	1†	15	2
1989-90—Detroit*..............	59	23	.720	1†	15	5
Totals (8 seasons)	378	237	.615		62	31

*Won NBA championship. †Central Division.

Assistant coach, Philadelphia 76ers, 1978-82.

Coach of NBA championship teams, 1989 and 1990.

CHUCK DALY

MICHAEL JOSEPH DUNLEAVY
(Mike)
Los Angeles Lakers

Born March 21, 1954 at Brooklyn, N. Y. Height 6:03. Weight 180.
High School—Brooklyn, N. Y., Nazareth.
College—University of South Carolina, Columbia, S. C.
Drafted by Philadelphia on sixth round, 1976 (99th pick).

Waived by Philadelphia, November 14, 1977; signed by Houston as a free agent, March 10, 1978.

Signed by San Antonio as Veteran Free Agent, October 16, 1982; Houston agreed not to exercise its right of first refusal in exchange for a 1983 3rd round draft choice.

Signed by Milwaukee as Veteran Free Agent, March 8, 1984; San Antonio agreed not to exercise its right of first refusal in exchange for a 1984 4th round draft choice and cash.

Waived by Milwaukee, October 24, 1985; re-signed by Milwaukee, February 19, 1989, to a 10-day contract that expired, February 28, 1989.

Waived by Milwaukee, February 24, 1989; re-signed by Milwaukee as a free agent, December 10, 1989.

Waived by Milwaukee, December 15, 1989; re-signed by Milwaukee, March 2, 1990, to a 10-day contract.

Waived by Milwaukee, March 9, 1990.

Player-coach in All-America Basketball Alliance with Carolina Lightning, 1977-78.

—COLLEGIATE RECORD—

Year	G.	Min.	FGA	FGM	Pct.	FTA	FTM	Pct.	Reb.	Pts.	Avg.
72-73	29	803	236	122	.517	72	59	.819	60	303	10.4
73-74	27	983	369	167	.453	116	97	.836	85	431	16.0
74-75	28	1016	368	182	.495	119	91	.765	110	455	16.3
75-76	27	962	297	144	.485	139	109	.784	87	397	14.7
Totals	111	3764	1270	615	.484	446	356	.798	342	1586	14.3

AABA REGULAR SEASON RECORD

Sea.—Team	G.	Min.	2-Point FGM	2-Point FGA	2-Point Pct.	3-Point FGM	3-Point FGA	3-Point Pct.	FTM	FTA	Pct.	Reb.	Ast.	Pts.	Avg.
77-78—Carolina	10	332	66	123	.537	2	5	.400	53	60	.883	52	50	191	19.1

NBA REGULAR SEASON RECORD

Sea.—Team	G.	Min.	FGA	FGM	Pct.	FTA	FTM	Pct.	Rebounds Off.	Rebounds Def.	Rebounds Tot.	Ast.	PF	Dq.	Stl.	Blk.	Pts.	Avg.
76-77—Philadelphia	32	359	145	60	.414	45	34	.756	10	24	34	56	64	1	13	2	154	4.8
77-78—Phil.-Hous.	15	119	50	20	.400	18	13	.722	1	9	10	28	12	0	9	1	53	3.5
78-79—Houston	74	1486	425	215	.506	184	159	.864	28	100	128	324	168	2	56	5	589	8.0
79-80—Houston	51	1036	319	148	.464	134	111	.828	26	74	100	210	120	2	40	4	410	8.0
80-81—Houston	74	1609	632	310	.491	186	156	.839	28	90	118	268	165	1	64	2	777	10.5
81-82—Houston	70	1315	450	206	.458	106	75	.708	24	80	104	227	161	0	45	3	520	7.4
82-83—San Antonio	79	1619	510	213	.418	154	120	.779	18	116	134	437	210	1	74	4	613	7.8
83-84—Milwaukee	17	404	127	70	.551	40	32	.800	6	22	28	78	51	0	12	1	191	11.2
84-85—Milwaukee	19	433	135	64	.474	29	25	.862	6	25	31	85	55	1	15	3	169	8.9
88-89—Milwaukee	2	5	2	1	.500	0	0	.000	0	0	0	0	0	0	0	0	3	1.5
89-90—Milwaukee	5	43	14	4	.286	8	7	.875	0	2	2	10	7	0	1	0	17	3.4
Totals	438	8428	2809	1311	.467	904	732	.810	147	542	689	1723	1013	8	329	25	3496	8.0

Three-Point Field Goals: 1979-80, 3-for-20 (.150). 1980-81, 1-for-16 (.063). 1981-82, 33-for-86 (.384). 1982-83, 67-for-194 (.345). 1983-84, 19-for-45 (.422). 1984-85, 16-for-47 (.340). 1988-89, 1-for-2 (.500). 1989-90, 2-for-9 (.222). Totals, 142-for-419 (.339).

NBA PLAYOFF RECORD

Sea.—Team	G.	Min.	FGA	FGM	Pct.	FTA	FTM	Pct.	Rebounds Off.	Rebounds Def.	Rebounds Tot.	Ast.	PF	Dq.	Stl.	Blk.	Pts.	Avg.
76-77—Philadelphia	11	68	25	9	.360	5	4	.800	1	3	4	9	14	0	3	0	22	2.0
78-79—Houston	1	10	2	0	.000	0	0	.000	0	1	1	0	1	0	0	0	0	0.0
79-80—Houston	6	45	12	6	.500	6	5	.833	2	3	5	13	11	0	5	0	17	2.8
80-81—Houston	20	472	152	69	.454	38	33	.868	9	33	42	68	59	1	15	1	177	8.9
81-82—Houston	3	66	22	9	.409	6	5	.833	0	3	3	9	7	0	2	0	23	7.7
82-83—San Antonio	11	174	65	22	.338	13	9	.692	3	10	13	49	22	0	9	1	61	5.5
83-84—Milwaukee	15	393	129	59	.457	36	33	.917	10	25	35	46	59	2	17	0	169	11.3
Totals	67	1228	407	174	.428	104	89	.856	25	78	103	194	173	3	51	2	469	7.0

Three-Point Field Goals: 1979-80, 0-for-2. 1980-81, 6-for-15 (.400). 1981-82, 0-for-4. 1982-83, 8-for-30 (.267). 1983-84, 18-for-50 (.360). Totals, 32-for-101 (.317).

NBA COACHING RECORD

Assistant coach, Milwaukee Bucks, 1987-90.

Led NBA in three-point field-goal percentage, 1983.

—DID YOU KNOW—

That Michael Jordan's lowest scoring average against any opponent in 1989-90 (25 points) came against a team (Denver) that allowed more points than all teams except Golden State and Orlando?

WILLIAM CHARLES FITCH
(Bill)
New Jersey Nets

Born May 19, 1934 at Davenport, Iowa.
High School—Cedar Rapids, Iowa.
College—Coe College, Cedar Rapids, Iowa.

—COLLEGIATE PLAYING RECORD—

Year	G.	Min.	FGA	FGM	Pct.	FTA	FTM	Pct.	Reb.	Pts.	Avg.
50-51					Statistics Unavailable						
51-52	20	....	...	63	....	...	50	....	....	176	8.8
52-53	19	....	...	83	....	...	72	....	....	238	12.5
53-54	22	....	...	123	....	...	92	....	....	338	15.4

COLLEGIATE COACHING RECORD

Sea.	Club	Regular Season W.	L.	Pct.	Pos.
1958-59	Coe College	11	9	.550	6
1959-60	Coe College	12	9	.571	5T
1960-61	Coe College	10	12	.455	4T
1961-62	Coe College	11	10	.524	6T
1962-63	North Dakota	14	13	.519	
1963-64	North Dakota	10	16	.385	
1964-65	North Dakota	26	5	.839	
1965-66	North Dakota	24	5	.828	
1966-67	North Dakota	20	6	.769	
1967-68	Bowl. Green	18	7	.720	
1968-69	Minnesota	12	12	.500	5T
1969-70	Minnesota	13	11	.542	5
Totals (12 seasons)		181	115	.611	

NBA COACHING RECORD

Sea.	Club	Regular Season W.	L.	Pct.	Pos.	Playoffs W.	L.
1970-71	Cleveland	15	67	.183	4†	..	..
1971-72	Cleveland	23	59	.280	4†	..	..
1972-73	Cleveland	32	50	.390	4†	..	..
1973-74	Cleveland	29	53	.354	4†	..	..
1974-75	Cleveland	40	42	.488	3†	..	..
1975-76	Cleveland	49	33	.598	1†	6	7
1976-77	Cleveland	43	39	.524	4†	1	2
1977-78	Cleveland	43	39	.524	3†	0	2
1978-79	Cleveland	30	52	.366	4T†	..	..
1979-80	Boston	61	21	.744	1‡	5	4
1980-81	Boston*	62	20	.756	1T‡	12	5
1981-82	Boston	63	19	.768	1‡	7	5
1982-83	Boston	56	26	.683	2‡	2	5
1983-84	Houston	29	53	.354	6§	..	..
1984-85	Houston	48	34	.585	2§	2	3
1985-86	Houston	51	31	.622	1§	13	7
1986-87	Houston	42	40	.512	3§	5	5
1987-88	Houston	46	36	.561	4§	1	3
1989-90	New Jersey	17	65	.207	6‡	..	..
Totals (19 seasons)		779	779	.500		54	48

*Won NBA championship. †Central Division. ‡Atlantic Division. §Midwest Division.

Named NBA Coach of the Year, 1976 and 1980. . . . Coach of NBA championship team, 1981.

LOWELL FITZSIMMONS
(Cotton)
Phoenix Suns

Born October 7, 1931 at Hannibal, Mo.
High School—Bowling Green, Mo.
Colleges—Hannibal-LaGrange College, Hannibal, Mo., and Midwestern State University, Wichita Falls, Tex.

—COLLEGIATE PLAYING RECORD—

Hannibal-LaGrange

Year	G.	Min.	FGA	FGM	Pct.	FTA	FTM	Pct.	Reb.	Pts.	Avg.
52-53	33	....	...	...	....	...	...	....	....	838	25.4

Midwestern State

Year	G.	Min.	FGA	FGM	Pct.	FTA	FTM	Pct.	Reb.	Pts.	Avg.
53-54	27	....	161	53	.329	173	128	.740	....	234	8.7
54-55	27	....	258	118	.457	210	162	.771	....	398	14.7
55-56	28	....	319	148	.464	223	164	.735	....	460	16.4
Totals	82	....	738	319	.432	606	454	.749	....	1092	13.3

COLLEGIATE COACHING RECORD

Sea.	Club	Regular Season W.	L.	Pct.	Pos.
1958-59	Moberly J.C.	16	15	.516	..
1959-60	Moberly J.C.	19	8	.704	..
1960-61	Moberly J.C.	26	5	.839	..
1961-62	Moberly J.C.	26	9	.743	..
1962-63	Moberly J.C.	26	6	.813	..
1963-64	Moberly J.C.	24	5	.828	..
1964-65	Moberly J.C.	25	5	.833	..
1965-66	Moberly J.C.	29	5	.853	..
1966-67	Moberly J.C.	31	2	.939	..
1968-69	Kansas State	14	12	.538	2T*
1969-70	Kansas State	20	8	.714	1*
Totals (JC)		222	60	.787	
Totals (College)		34	20	.630	

Assistant coach at Kansas State, 1967-68. *Big Eight Conference.

NBA COACHING RECORD

Sea.	Club	Regular Season W.	L.	Pct.	Pos.	Playoffs W.	L.
1970-71	Phoenix	48	34	.585	3†	..	..
1971-72	Phoenix	49	33	.598	3†	..	..
1972-73	Atlanta	46	36	.561	2‡	2	4
1973-74	Atlanta	35	47	.427	2‡	..	..
1974-75	Atlanta	31	51	.378	4‡	..	..
1975-76	Atlanta	28	46	.378	5‡	..	..
1977-78	Buffalo	27	55	.329	4§	..	..
1978-79	Kansas City	48	34	.585	1†	1	4
1979-80	Kansas City	47	35	.573	2†	1	2
1980-81	Kansas City	40	42	.488	2T†	7	8
1981-82	Kansas City	30	52	.366	4†	..	..
1982-83	Kansas City	45	37	.549	2T†	..	..
1983-84	Kansas City	38	44	.463	3T†	0	3
1984-85	San Antonio	41	41	.500	4T†	2	3
1985-86	San Antonio	35	47	.427	6†	0	3
1988-89	Phoenix	55	27	.671	2x	7	5
1989-90	Phoenix	54	28	.659	3x	9	7
Totals (17 seasons)		697	689	.503		29	39

†Midwest Division. ‡Central Division. §Atlantic Division. xPacific Division.

NBA Coach of the Year, 1979 and 1989. . . . Father of Gary Fitzsimmons, Director of Player Personnel for Cleveland Cavaliers.

CHRISTOPHER JOSEPH FORD
(Chris)
Boston Celtics

Born January 11, 1949 at Atlantic City, N.J. Height 6:05. Weight 190.

High School—Absecon, N.J., Holy Spirit.

College—Villanova University, Villanova, Pa.

Drafted by Detroit on second round, 1972 (17th pick).

Traded by Detroit with a 1981 2nd round draft choice to Boston for Earl Tatum, October 19, 1978.

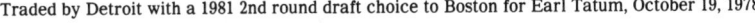

—COLLEGIATE RECORD—

Year	G.	Min.	FGA	FGM	Pct.	FTA	FTM	Pct.	Reb.	Pts.	Avg.
68-69	18	....	....	118	....	....	87	....	....	323	17.9
69-70	29	....	396	188	.475	124	89	.718	168	465	16.0
70-71	34	....	400	180	.450	176	108	.614	200	468	13.8
71-72	28	....	399	206	.516	146	88	.603	180	500	17.9
Varsity Totals	91	....	1195	574	.480	446	285	.639	548	1433	15.7

NBA REGULAR SEASON RECORD

Sea.—Team	G.	Min.	FGA	FGM	Pct.	FTA	FTM	Pct.	—Rebounds— Off.	Def.	Tot.	Ast.	PF	Dq.	Stl.	Blk.	Pts.	Avg.
72-73—Detroit	74	1537	434	208	.479	93	60	.645			266	194	133	1			476	6.4
73-74—Detroit	82	2059	595	264	.444	77	57	.740	109	195	304	279	159	1	148	14	585	7.1
74-75—Detroit	80	1962	435	206	.474	95	63	.663	93	176	269	230	187	0	113	26	475	5.9
75-76—Detroit	82	2198	707	301	.426	115	83	.722	80	211	291	272	222	0	178	24	685	8.4
76-77—Detroit	82	2539	918	437	.476	170	131	.771	96	174	270	337	192	1	179	26	1005	12.3
77-78—Detroit	82	2582	777	374	.481	154	113	.734	117	151	268	381	182	2	166	17	861	10.5
78-79—Det.-Bos.	81	2737	1142	538	.471	227	172	.758	124	150	274	374	209	3	115	25	1248	15.4
79-80—Boston	73	2115	709	330	.465	114	86	.754	77	104	181	215	178	0	111	27	816	11.2
80-81—Boston	82	2723	707	314	.444	87	64	.736	72	91	163	295	212	2	100	23	728	8.9
81-82—Boston	76	1591	450	188	.418	56	39	.696	52	56	108	142	143	0	42	10	435	5.7
Totals	794	22043	6874	3160	.460	1188	868	.731			2394	2719	1817	10	1152	191	7314	9.2

Three-Point Field Goals: 1979-80, 70-for-164 (.427). 1980-81, 36-for-109 (.330). 1981-82, 20-for-63 (.317). Totals, 126-for-336 (.375).

NBA PLAYOFF RECORD

Sea.—Team	G.	Min.	FGA	FGM	Pct.	FTA	FTM	Pct.	—Rebounds— Off.	Def.	Tot.	Ast.	PF	Dq.	Stl.	Blk.	Pts.	Avg.
73-74—Detroit	5	94	17	8	.471	6	4	.667	4	11	15	7	10	0	2	2	20	4.0
74-75—Detroit	3	82	11	6	.545	0	0	.000	2	11	13	10	8	0	1	0	12	4.0
75-76—Detroit	9	276	81	33	.407	15	12	.800	6	30	36	40	33	1	11	5	78	8.7
76-77—Detroit	3	101	44	18	.409	9	5	.556	8	11	19	12	11	0	7	0	41	13.7
79-80—Boston	9	279	79	34	.430	15	12	.800	9	16	25	21	35	1	14	6	82	9.1
80-81—Boston	17	507	146	66	.452	25	15	.600	13	32	45	46	47	0	14	1	154	9.1
81-82—Boston	12	138	42	20	.476	7	5	.714	6	9	15	15	15	0	1	3	47	3.9
Totals	58	1477	420	185	.440	77	53	.688	48	120	168	151	159	2	15	35	434	7.5

Three-Point Field Goals: 1979-80, 2-for-13 (.154). 1980-81, 7-for-25 (.280). 1981-82, 2-for-7 (.286). Totals, 11-for-45 (.244).

NBA COACHING RECORD

Assistant coach, Boston Celtics, 1983-90.

Member of NBA championship team, 1981.

—DID YOU KNOW—

That the Lakers' Pat Riley won his first NBA Coach of the Year award in 1989-90 but did not win any of the league's six Coach of the Month honors last year?

MATTHEW GEORGE GUOKAS JR.
(Matt)
Orlando Magic

Born February 25, 1944 at Philadelphia, Pa. Height 6:06. Weight 195.
High School—Philadelphia, Pa., St. Joseph's.
Colleges—University of Miami, Coral Gables, Fla., and St. Joseph's University, Philadelphia, Pa.
Drafted by Philadelphia on first round, 1966.

Traded by Philadelphia to Chicago for a draft choice, October 16, 1970.
Traded by Chicago with a draft choice to Cincinnati for Charlie Paulk, May 14, 1971.
Traded by Kansas City-Omaha to Houston for Jimmy Walker, October 29, 1973.
Traded by Houston with Jack Marin to Buffalo for Kevin Kunnert and Dave Wohl, February 1, 1974.
Traded by Buffalo with a draft choice to Chicago for Bob Weiss, September 4, 1974.
Traded by Chicago to Kansas City for draft choices, December 8, 1975.
Waived by Kansas City, July 29, 1976.

—COLLEGIATE RECORD—

Miami

Year	G.	Min.	FGA	FGM	Pct.	FTA	FTM	Pct.	Reb.	Pts.	Avg.
62-63	Freshman Team Statistics Unavailable										

St. Joseph's

Year	G.	Min.	FGA	FGM	Pct.	FTA	FTM	Pct.	Reb.	Pts.	Avg.
63-64	Did Not Play—Transfer Student										
64-65	29	....	342	157	.459	98	71	.724	195	385	13.3
65-66	29	....	413	207	.501	122	94	.770	72	508	17.5
Varsity Totals	58	....	755	364	.482	220	165	.750	267	893	15.4

NBA REGULAR SEASON RECORD

Sea.—Team	G.	Min.	FGA	FGM	Pct.	FTA	FTM	Pct.	Reb.	Ast.	PF	Disq.	Pts.	Avg.
66-67—Philadelphia	69	808	203	79	.389	81	49	.605	83	105	82	0	207	3.0
67-68—Philadelphia	82	1612	393	190	.483	152	118	.776	185	191	172	0	498	6.1
68-69—Philadelphia	72	838	216	92	.426	81	54	.667	94	104	121	1	238	3.3
69-70—Philadelphia	80	1558	416	189	.454	149	106	.711	216	222	201	0	484	6.1
70-71—Phil.-Chicago	79	2213	418	206	.493	138	101	.732	158	342	189	1	513	6.5
71-72—Cincinnati	61	1975	385	191	.496	83	64	.771	142	321	150	0	446	7.3
72-73—K.C.-Omaha	79	2846	565	322	.570	90	74	.822	245	403	190	0	718	9.1

									—Rebounds—									
Sea.—Team	G.	Min.	FGA	FGM	Pct.	FTA	FTM	Pct.	Off.	Def.	Tot.	Ast.	PF	Dq.	Stl.	Blk.	Pts.	Avg.
73-74—KC-O-Hou-Buf	75	1871	396	195	.492	60	39	.650	31	90	121	238	150	3	54	21	429	5.7
74-75—Chicago	82	2089	500	255	.510	103	78	.757	24	115	139	178	154	1	45	17	588	7.2
75-76—Chi.-K.C.	56	793	173	73	.422	27	18	.667	22	41	63	70	76	0	18	3	164	2.9
Totals	735	16603	3665	1792	.489	964	701	.727			1446	2174	1485	6	117	41	4285	5.8

NBA PLAYOFF RECORD

Sea.—Team	G.	Min.	FGA	FGM	Pct.	FTA	FTM	Pct.	Reb.	Ast.	PF	Disq.	Pts.	Avg.
66-67—Philadelphia	15	252	64	26	.406	17	13	.765	30	23	33	0	65	4.3
67-68—Philadelphia	13	327	79	30	.380	27	20	.741	43	30	39	0	80	6.2
68-69—Philadelphia	5	100	27	11	.407	5	4	.800	12	8	12	0	26	5.2
69-70—Philadelphia	2	23	8	6	.750	1	1	1.000	3	1	1	0	13	6.5
70-71—Chicago	6	83	14	8	.571	5	4	.800	8	12	8	0	20	3.3

									—Rebounds—									
Sea.—Team	G.	Min.	FGA	FGM	Pct.	FTA	FTM	Pct.	Off.	Def.	Tot.	Ast.	PF	Dq.	Stl.	Blk.	Pts.	Avg.
73-74—Buffalo	6	85	15	8	.533	4	3	.750	3	5	8	13	8	0	0	1	19	3.2
74-75—Chicago	13	202	35	12	.343	8	7	.875	4	10	14	11	20	0	7	1	31	2.4
Totals	60	1072	242	101	.417	67	52	.776			118	98	121	0	7	2	254	4.2

NBA COACHING RECORD

	Regular Season				Playoffs	
Sea. Club	W.	L.	Pct.	Pos.	W.	L.
1985-86—Philadelphia	54	28	.659	2†	6	6
1986-87—Philadelphia	45	37	.549	2†	2	3
1987-88—Philadelphia	20	23	.465	..†	..	..
1989-90—Orlando	18	64	.220	7‡	..	..
Totals (4 seasons)	137	152	.474		8	9

†Atlantic Division. ‡Central Division.

Assistant coach, Philadelphia 76ers, 1984.

Member of NBA championship team, 1967. . . . Son of Matt Guokas Sr., forward with Philadelphia Warriors, 1946-47.

DELMER HARRIS
(Del)
Milwaukee Bucks

Born June 18, 1937 at Orleans, Ind.
High School—Plainfield, Ind.
College—Milligan College, Milligan, Tenn.

—COLLEGIATE PLAYING RECORD—

Year	G.	Min.	FGA	FGM	Pct.	FTA	FTM	Pct.	Reb.	Pts.	Avg.
55-56	24	....	232	101	.435	126	89	.706	122	291	12.1
56-57	24	....	197	162	....	197	141	.716	165	465	19.4
57-58	22	....	272	167	.614	149	119	.799	144	453	20.6
58-59	21	....	346	136	.393	202	158	.782	338	430	20.5
Totals	91	....	1047	566	....	674	507	.752	769	1639	18.0

Note: Field-goal attempts for five games and rebounds for 13 games are unavailable.

COLLEGIATE COACHING RECORD

	Regular Season			
Sea. Club	W.	L.	Pct.	Pos.
1965-66—Earlham Col.	14	8	.636	....
1966-67—Earlham Col.	15	9	.625	4
1967-68—Earlham Col.	25	3	.893	1
1968-69—Earlham Col.	18	8	.692	2
1969-70—Earlham Col.	22	8	.733	1
1970-71—Earlham Col.	24	5	.828	1
1971-72—Earlham Col.	21	9	.700	1
1972-73—Earlham Col.	17	11	.607	3
1973-74—Earlham Col.	19	9	.679	3
Totals (9 seasons)	175	70	.714	

Assistant coach at Utah, 1975-76.

NBA COACHING RECORD

	Regular Season				Playoffs	
Sea. Club	W.	L.	Pct.	Pos.	W.	L.
1979-80—Houston	41	41	.500	2T†	2	5
1980-81—Houston	40	42	.488	2T‡	12	9
1981-82—Houston	46	36	.561	2T‡	1	2
1982-83—Houston	14	68	.171	6‡	..	..
1987-88—Milwaukee	42	40	.512	4T†	2	3
1988-89—Milwaukee	49	33	.598	4†	3	6
1989-90—Milwaukee	44	38	.537	3†	1	3
Totals (7 seasons)	276	298	.481		21	28

†Central Division. ‡Midwest Division.

Assistant coach, Milwaukee Bucks, 1986-87.

PHIL JACKSON
Chicago Bulls

Born September 17, 1945 at Deer Lodge, Mont. Height 6:08. Weight 230.
High School—Williston, N.D.
College—University of North Dakota, Grand Forks, N.D.
Drafted by New York on second round, 1967 (17th pick).

Traded by New York with a future draft choice to New Jersey for future draft choices, June 8, 1978.
Waived by New Jersey, October 11, 1978; re-signed by New Jersey, November 10, 1978.
Waived by New Jersey, October 12, 1979; re-signed by New Jersey, February 15, 1980.

—COLLEGIATE RECORD—

Year	G.	Min.	FGA	FGM	Pct.	FTA	FTM	Pct.	Reb.	Pts.	Avg.
63-64†	..	....	....	....	....	....	....	....	....	....	24.3
64-65	31	....	307	129	.420	156	107	.686	361	365	11.8
65-66	29	....	439	238	.542	203	155	.764	374	631	21.8
66-67	26	....	468	252	.539	278	208	.748	374	712	27.4
Varsity Totals	86	....	1214	619	.510	637	470	.738	1109	1708	19.9

†Eastern Division.

NBA REGULAR SEASON RECORD

Sea.—Team	G.	Min.	FGA	FGM	Pct.	FTA	FTM	Pct.	Reb.	Ast.	PF	Disq.	Pts.	Avg.
67-68—New York	75	1093	455	182	.400	168	99	.589	338	55	212	3	463	6.2
68-69—New York	47	924	294	126	.429	119	80	.672	246	43	168	6	332	7.1
69-70—New York	Did Not Play—Injured													
70-71—New York	80	1273	466	205	.440	228	167	.732	326	72	224	4	577	7.2
72-73—New York	80	1393	553	245	.443	195	154	.790	344	94	218	2	644	8.1

Sea.—Team	G.	Min.	FGA	FGM	Pct.	FTA	FTM	Pct.	—Rebounds— Off.	Def.	Tot.	Ast.	PF	Dq.	Stl.	Blk.	Pts.	Avg.
73-74—New York	82	2050	757	361	.477	246	191	.776	123	355	478	134	277	7	42	67	913	11.1
74-75—New York	78	2285	712	324	.455	253	193	.763	137	463	600	136	330	10	84	53	841	10.8
75-76—New York	80	1461	387	185	.478	150	110	.733	80	263	343	105	275	3	41	20	480	6.0
76-77—Knicks	76	1033	232	102	.440	71	51	.718	75	154	229	85	184	4	33	18	255	3.4
77-78—New York	63	654	115	55	.478	56	43	.768	29	81	110	46	106	0	31	15	153	2.4
78-79—New Jersey	59	1070	303	144	.475	105	86	.819	59	119	178	85	168	7	45	22	374	6.3
79-80—New Jersey	16	194	46	29	.630	10	7	.700	12	12	24	12	35	1	5	4	65	4.1
Totals	807	14201	4583	2076	.453	1734	1276	.736			3454	898	2366	51	281	199	5428	6.7

Three-Point Field Goals: 1979-80, 0-for-2.

NBA PLAYOFF RECORD

Sea.—Team	G.	Min.	FGA	FGM	Pct.	FTA	FTM	Pct.	Reb.	Ast.	PF	Disq.	Pts.	Avg.
67-68—New York	6	90	35	10	.286	5	4	.800	25	2	23	0	24	4.0
70-71—New York	5	30	14	4	.286	1	1	1.000	10	2	8	0	9	1.8
71-72—New York	16	320	120	57	.475	57	42	.737	82	15	51	1	156	9.8
72-73—New York	17	338	120	60	.500	38	28	.737	72	24	59	3	148	8.7

Sea.—Team	G.	Min.	FGA	FGM	Pct.	FTA	FTM	Pct.	—Rebounds— Off.	Def.	Tot.	Ast.	PF	Dq.	Stl.	Blk.	Pts.	Avg.
73-74—New York	12	297	116	54	.466	30	27	.900	15	42	57	15	40	0	10	5	135	11.3
74-75—New York	3	78	21	10	.476	8	7	.875	5	20	25	2	15	0	4	3	27	9.0
77-78—New York	6	50	8	4	.500	6	4	.667	4	6	10	3	11	0	3	0	12	2.0
78-79—New Jersey	2	20	3	1	.333	2	2	1.000	2	1	3	0	1	0	1	0	4	2.0
Totals	67	1223	437	200	.458	147	115	.782			284	63	208	4	18	8	515	7.7

CBA COACHING RECORD

Sea. Club	Regular Season W.	L.	Pct.	Pos.	Playoffs W.	L.
1982-83—Albany	16	28	.364	4†	..	..
1983-84—Albany	25	19	.568	2†	9	5
1984-85—Albany	34	14	.708	1†	5	5
1985-86—Albany	24	24	.500	4†	3	4
1986-87—Albany	26	22	.542	2T†	4	4
Totals (5 seasons)	115	107	.518		21	18

†Eastern Division.

NBA COACHING RECORD

Sea. Club	Regular Season W.	L.	Pct.	Pos.	Playoffs W.	L.
1989-90—Chicago	55	27	.671	2†	10	6

†Central Division.

Assistant coach, Chicago Bulls, 1987-89.

Named to NBA All-Rookie Team, 1973. . . . Member of NBA championship team, 1973. . . . CBA Coach of the Year, 1985. . . . Coach of CBA championship team, 1984.

STUART WAYNE JACKSON
(Stu)
New York Knickerbockers

Born December 11, 1955 at Reading, Pa. Height 6:05. Weight 220.

High School—Reading, Pa.

Colleges—University of Oregon, Eugene, Ore., and Seattle University, Seattle, Wash.

—COLLEGIATE RECORD—

Oregon

Year	G.	Min.	FGA	FGM	Pct.	FTA	FTM	Pct.	Reb.	Pts.	Avg.
73-74	25	473	116	57	.491	43	26	.605	75	140	5.6
74-75	30	871	380	169	.445	80	57	.713	182	395	13.2
75-76	29	770	281	137	.488	71	53	.746	125	327	11.3
76-77				Did Not Play—Injured							
Ore. Totals	84	2114	777	363	.462	194	136	.701	382	862	10.3

Seattle

Year	G.	Min.	FGA	FGM	Pct.	FTA	FTM	Pct.	Reb.	Pts.	Avg.
76-77				Did Not Play—Transfer Student							
77-78	16	....	155	79	.510	42	34	.810	69	192	12.0
Col. Totals	100	....	932	442	.474	236	170	.720	451	1054	10.5

—COLLEGIATE COACHING RECORD—

Graduate assistant coach, University of Oregon, 1981-82.

Assistant coach, University of Oregon, 1982-83; Washington State University, 1983-85, and associate coach, Providence College, 1985-87.

NBA COACHING RECORD

		Regular Season				Playoffs	
Sea.	Club	W.	L.	Pct.	Pos.	W.	L.
1989-90	New York..........	45	37	.549	3†	4	6

†Atlantic Division.

Assistant coach, New York Knicks, 1987-89.

K.C. JONES
Seattle SuperSonics

Born May 25, 1932 at Taylor, Tex. Height 6:01. Weight 200.

High School—San Francisco, Calif., Commerce.

College—University of San Francisco, San Francisco, Calif.

Drafted by Boston on second round, 1956.

In military service, 1956-57 and 1957-58; played at Fort Leonard Wood, Mo.; named to Amateur Athletic Union All-America team as a member of 1957-58 Fort Leonard Wood team.

Played in Eastern Basketball League with Hartford, 1967-68.

—COLLEGIATE RECORD—

Year	G.	Min.	FGA	FGM	Pct.	FTA	FTM	Pct.	Reb.	Pts.	Avg.
51-52	24	....	128	44	.344	64	46	.719	....	134	5.6
52-53	23	....	159	163	.396	149	81	.544	....	207	9.0
53-54	1	....	12	3	.250	2	2	1.000	3	8	8.0
54-55	29	....	293	105	.358	144	97	.674	148	307	10.6
55-56	25	....	208	76	.365	142	93	.655	130	245	9.8
Totals	102	....	800	291	.364	501	319	.637	....	901	8.8

(Jones underwent an appendectomy after one game of the 1953-54 season and was granted an extra year of eligibility by the University of San Francisco; however, he was ineligible for the 1955-56 NCAA tournament because he was playing his fifth season of college basketball.)

EBL REGULAR SEASON RECORD

Sea.—Team	G.	Min.	FGA	FGM	Pct.	FTA	FTM	Pct.	Reb.	Ast.	PF	Disq.	Pts.	Avg.
67-68—Hartford	6	....	....	15	....	18	9	.500	24	41	..	..	39	6.5

NBA REGULAR SEASON RECORD

Sea.—Team	G.	Min.	FGA	FGM	Pct.	FTA	FTM	Pct.	Reb.	Ast.	PF	Disq.	Pts.	Avg.
58-59—Boston	49	609	192	65	.339	68	41	.603	127	70	58	0	171	3.5
59-60—Boston	74	1274	414	169	.408	170	128	.752	199	189	109	1	466	6.3
60-61—Boston	78	1607	601	203	.337	320	186	.581	279	253	200	3	592	7.6
61-62—Boston	79	2023	707	289	.409	231	145	.628	291	339	204	2	723	9.1
62-63—Boston	79	1945	591	230	.389	177	112	.633	263	317	221	3	572	7.2
63-64—Boston	80	2424	722	283	.392	168	88	.524	372	407	253	0	654	8.2
64-65—Boston	78	2434	639	253	.396	227	143	.630	318	437	263	5	649	8.3
65-66—Boston	80	2710	619	240	.388	303	209	.690	304	503	243	4	689	8.6
66-67—Boston	78	2446	459	182	.397	189	110	.630	239	389	273	7	483	6.2
Totals	675	17472	4944	1914	.387	1853	1171	.632	2392	2904	1824	25	4999	7.4

NBA PLAYOFF RECORD

Sea.—Team	G.	Min.	FGA	FGM	Pct.	FTA	FTM	Pct.	Reb.	Ast.	PF	Disq.	Pts.	Avg.
58-59—Boston	8	75	20	5	.250	5	5	1.000	12	10	8	0	15	1.9
59-60—Boston	13	232	80	27	.337	22	17	.773	45	14	28	0	71	5.522
60-61—Boston	9	103	30	9	.300	14	7	.500	19	15	17	0	25	2.8
61-62—Boston	14	329	102	44	.431	53	38	.717	56	55	50	1	126	9.0
62-63—Boston	13	250	64	19	.297	30	21	.700	36	37	42	1	59	4.5
63-64—Boston	10	312	72	25	.347	25	13	.520	37	68	40	0	63	6.3
64-65—Boston	12	396	104	43	.413	45	35	.778	39	74	49	1	121	10.1
65-66—Boston	17	543	109	45	.413	57	39	.684	52	75	65	0	129	7.6
66-67—Boston	9	254	75	24	.320	18	11	.611	24	48	36	1	59	6.6
Totals	105	2494	656	241	.367	269	186	.691	320	396	335	4	668	6.4

COLLEGIATE COACHING RECORD

		Regular Season			
Sea.	Club	W.	L.	Pct.	Pos.
1967-68	Brandeis	11	10	.524	..
1968-69	Brandeis	14	10	.583	..
1969-70	Brandeis	10	12	.455	..
	Totals (3 seasons)	35	32	.522	

Assistant coach at Harvard, 1970-71.

ABA COACHING RECORD

		Regular Season				Playoffs	
Sea.	Club	W.	L.	Pct.	Pos.	W.	L.
1972-73	San Diego	30	54	.357	4†	0	4

†Western Division.

NBA COACHING RECORD

Sea.	Club	Regular Season W.	L.	Pct.	Pos.	Playoffs W.	L.
1973-74	Capital	47	35	.573	1†	3	4
1974-75	Washington	60	22	.732	1†	8	9
1975-76	Washington	48	34	.585	2†	3	4
1983-84	Boston*	62	20	.756	1‡	15	8
1984-85	Boston	63	19	.768	1‡	13	8
1985-86	Boston*	67	15	.817	1‡	15	3
1986-87	Boston	59	23	.720	1‡	13	10
1987-88	Boston	57	25	.695	1‡	9	8
Totals (8 seasons)		463	193	.706		79	54

*Won NBA championship. †Central Division. ‡Atlantic Division.

Assistant coach, Los Angeles Lakers, 1972; Milwaukee Bucks, 1977; Boston Celtics, 1978-83.

Elected to Naismith Memorial Basketball Hall of Fame, 1988. . . . Member of U.S. Olympic team, 1956. . . . Member of NCAA championship team, 1955. . . . Member of NBA championship teams, 1959, 1960, 1961, 1962, 1963, 1964, 1965, 1966. . . . Coach of NBA championship teams, 1984 and 1986. . . . Drafted by Los Angeles Rams in 30th round of 1955 National Football League draft.

EUGENE SCAPE LITTLES
(Gene)

Born July 29, 1943 at Washington, D.C. Height 6:01. Weight 165.
High School—Washington, D.C., McKinley.
College—High Point College, High Point, N.C.
Drafted by New York on fifth round, 1969 (68th pick).
Drafted by Carolina on seventh round of ABA draft, 1969.

Carolina franchise transferred to St. Louis, 1974.
Released by St. Louis ABA, October 15, 1974.
Signed as a free agent by Kentucky ABA, November 21, 1974.

—COLLEGIATE RECORD—

Year	G.	Min.	FGA	FGM	Pct.	FTA	FTM	Pct.	Reb.	Pts.	Avg.
65-66	20	....	326	162	.497	187	133	.711	97	457	22.9
66-67	22	....	386	197	.510	178	130	.730	135	524	23.8
67-68	25	....	428	206	.481	195	151	.774	218	563	22.5
69-69	31	....	524	266	.508	255	193	.757	287	725	23.4
Totals	98	....	1664	831	.499	815	607	.745	737	2269	23.2

ABA REGULAR SEASON RECORD

Sea.—Team	G.	Min.	2-Point FGM	FGA	Pct.	3-Point FGM	FGA	Pct.	FTM	FTA	Pct.	Reb.	Ast.	Pts.	Avg.
69-70—Carolina	82	2832	414	814	.509	0	3	.000	197	254	.776	415	282	1025	12.5
70-71—Carolina	70	1495	219	487	.450	4	14	.286	117	168	.696	205	173	567	8.1
71-72—Carolina	69	2006	273	579	.472	7	26	.269	178	237	.751	276	237	745	10.8
72-73—Carolina	84	2060	302	592	.510	8	30	.267	179	246	.728	262	245	807	9.6
73-74—Carolina	84	2017	290	603	.481	4	23	.174	115	161	.714	231	280	707	8.4
74-75—Kentucky	61	900	83	194	.428	2	8	.250	43	58	.741	86	119	215	3.5
Totals	450	11310	1581	3269	.484	25	104	.240	829	1124	.738	1475	1336	4066	9.0

ABA PLAYOFF RECORD

Sea.—Team	G.	Min.	2-Point FGM	FGA	Pct.	3-Point FGM	FGA	Pct.	FTM	FTA	Pct.	Reb.	Ast.	Pts.	Avg.
69-70—Carolina	4	133	18	33	.545	0	0	....	6	9	.667	18	14	42	10.5
72-73—Carolina	12	223	30	65	.462	0	2	.000	20	32	.625	36	16	80	6.7
73-74—Carolina	4	106	11	27	.407	4	7	.571	3	8	.375	11	18	37	9.3
74-75—Kentucky	8	30	2	9	.222	0	0	....	0	0	....	5	4	4	0.5
Totals	28	492	61	134	.455	4	9	.444	29	49	.592	20	52	163	5.8

COLLEGIATE COACHING RECORD

Sea.	Club	Regular Season W.	L.	Pct.	Pos.
1977-78	N.C. A&T	18	8	.692	1†
1978-79	N.C. A&T	18	7	.720	1†
Totals (2 seasons)		36	15	.706	

†Mid-Eastern Athletic Conference.

NBA COACHING RECORD

Sea.	Club	Regular Season W.	L.	Pct.	Pos.
1985-86	Cleveland	4	11	.267	..†
1989-90	Charlotte	11	31	.262	..‡
Totals (2 seasons)		15	42	.263	

†Central Division. ‡Midwest Division.

Assistant coach, Utah Jazz, 1979-82; Cleveland Cavaliers, 1982-86; Chicago Bulls, 1986-87, and Charlotte Hornets, 1988-90.

Named to ABA All-Rookie Team, 1970. . . . Member of ABA championship team, 1975. . . . Named to NAIA Basketball Hall of Fame, 1981.

JAMES F. LYNAM
(Jim)
Philadelphia 76ers

Born September 15, 1941 at Philadelphia, Pa. Height 5:08. Weight 160.
High School—Philadelphia, Pa., West Catholic.
College—St. Joseph's University, Philadelphia, Pa.

—COLLEGIATE PLAYING RECORD—

Year	G.	Min.	FGA	FGM	Pct.	FTA	FTM	Pct.	Reb.	Pts.	Avg.
59-60†	14	....	...	88	....	...	94	....	43	270	19.3
60-61	30	....	260	110	.423	143	118	.825	71	338	11.3
61-62	27	....	228	98	.430	140	111	.793	49	307	11.4
62-63	26	....	281	139	.495	131	89	.679	95	367	14.1
Varsity Totals	83	....	769	347	.451	414	318	.768	215	1012	12.2

COLLEGIATE COACHING RECORD

	Regular Season			
Sea. Club	W.	L.	Pct.	Pos.
1968-69—Fairfield	10	16	.385	..
1969-70—Fairfield	13	13	.500	..
1973-74—American U.	16	10	.615	..
1974-75—American U.	16	10	.615	..
1975-76—American U.	9	16	.360	..
1976-77—American U.	13	13	.500	..
1977-78—American U.	16	12	.571	..
1978-79—St. Joseph's	19	11	.633	..
1979-80—St. Joseph's	21	9	.700	..
1980-81—St. Joseph's	25	8	.758	..
Totals (10 seasons)	158	118	.572	

Assistant coach, St. Joseph's (Pa.), 1970 through 1973.
NOTE: St. Joseph's played in the NIT in 1979 and 1980 and the NCAA tournament in 1981.

NBA COACHING RECORD

	Regular Season				Playoffs	
Sea. Club	W.	L.	Pct.	Pos.	W.	L.
1983-84—San Diego	30	52	.366	6†		
1984-85—L.A. Clippers	22	39	.361	..†		
1987-88—Philadelphia	16	23	.410	..‡		
1988-89—Philadelphia	46	36	.561	2‡	0	3
1989-90—Philadelphia	53	29	.646	1‡	4	6
Totals (5 seasons)	167	179	.483		4	9

†Pacific Division. ‡Atlantic Division.
Assistant coach, Portland Trail Blazers, 1981-82, and Philadelphia 76ers, 1985-88.

DOUGLAS EDWIN MOE
(Doug)
Denver Nuggets

Born September 21, 1938 at Brooklyn, N. Y. Height 6:05. Weight 220.
High School—Brooklyn, N. Y., Erasmus Hall.
Prep School—Silver Springs, Md., Bullis.
Colleges—University of North Carolina, Chapel Hill, N. C.
and Elon College, Elon College, N. C.

Signed by New Orleans ABA, 1967.

Traded by New Orleans with Larry Brown to Oakland for Steve Jones, Ron Franz and Barry Leibowitz, June 18, 1968.

Traded by Oakland to Carolina in three-team deal that sent Stew Johnson from Carolina to Pittsburgh and Frank Card from Pittsburgh to Oakland, June 12, 1969.

Traded by Carolina to Washington for Gary Bradds and Ira Harge, July 24, 1970.

Washington franchise transferred to Virginia, 1970.

Played with Padua, Italy, during 1965-66 and 1966-67 seasons.

—COLLEGIATE PLAYING RECORD—

North Carolina

Year	G.	Min.	FGA	FGM	Pct.	FTA	FTM	Pct.	Reb.	Pts.	Avg.
57-58†					Statistics Unavailable						
58-59	25	....	265	106	.400	164	104	.634	179	316	12.6
59-60	12	....	144	60	.417	113	82	.726	135	202	16.8
60-61	23	....	401	163	.406	207	143	.691	321	469	20.4
Varsity Totals	60	....	810	329	.406	484	329	.680	635	987	16.5

ABA REGULAR SEASON RECORD

Sea.—Team	G.	Min.	2-Point FGM	2-Point FGA	2-Point Pct.	3-Point FGM	3-Point FGA	3-Point Pct.	FTM	FTA	Pct.	Reb.	Ast.	Pts.	Avg.
67-68—New Orleans	78	3113	662	1588	.417	3	22	.136	551	693	.795	795	202	1884	24.2
68-69—Oakland	75	2528	524	1213	.432	5	14	.357	360	444	.811	614	151	1423	19.0
69-70—Carolina	80	2671	527	1220	.432	8	34	.235	304	399	.762	437	425	1382	17.2
70-71—Virginia	78	2297	395	861	.459	2	10	.200	221	259	.853	473	270	1017	13.0
71-72—Virginia	67	1472	174	406	.429	1	9	.111	104	129	.806	241	149	455	6.8
Totals	378	12081	2282	5288	.432	19	89	.213	1540	1924	.800	2560	1197	6161	16.3

ABA PLAYOFF RECORD

Sea.—Team	G.	Min.	2-Point FGM	2-Point FGA	2-Point Pct.	3-Point FGM	3-Point FGA	3-Point Pct.	FTM	FTA	Pct.	Reb.	Ast.	Pts.	Avg.
67-68—New Orleans	17	715	140	335	.418	4	11	.364	107	149	.718	169	40	399	23.5
68-69—Oakland	16	593	115	280	.411	0	4	.000	87	111	.784	124	31	317	19.8
69-70—Carolina	4	168	25	72	.347	0	4	.000	12	16	.750	26	25	62	15.5
70-71—Virginia	12	421	89	174	.511	1	3	.333	31	41	.756	57	37	212	17.7
71-72—Virginia	11	245	37	84	.440	0	1	.000	22	25	.880	43	27	96	8.7
Totals	60	2142	406	945	.430	5	23	.217	259	342	.757	419	160	1086	18.1

ABA ALL-STAR GAME RECORD

Sea.—Team	Min.	2-Point FGM	2-Point FGA	2-Point Pct.	3-Point FGM	3-Point FGA	3-Point Pct.	FTM	FTA	Pct.	Reb.	Ast.	Pts.	Avg.
1968—New Orleans	29	7	12	.583	0	1	.000	3	5	.600	7	5	17	17.0
1969—Oakland	26	6	13	.462	0	0	.000	5	8	.625	6	6	17	17.0
1970—Carolina	36	0	5	.000	0	0	.000	2	3	.667	8	6	2	2.0
Totals	91	13	30	.433	0	1	.000	10	16	.625	21	17	36	12.0

NBA COACHING RECORD

Sea. Club	Regular Season W.	L.	Pct.	Pos.	Playoffs W.	L.
1976-77—San Antonio	44	38	.537	3†	0	2
1977-78—San Antonio	52	30	.634	1†	2	4
1978-79—San Antonio	48	34	.585	1†	7	7
1979-80—San Antonio	33	33	.500	2T†	..	..
1980-81—Denver	26	25	.510	4‡	..	..
1981-82—Denver	46	36	.561	2T‡	1	2
1982-83—Denver	45	37	.549	2T‡	3	5
1983-84—Denver	38	44	.463	3T‡	2	3
1984-85—Denver	52	30	.634	1‡	8	7
1985-86—Denver	47	35	.573	2‡	5	5
1986-87—Denver	37	45	.451	4‡	0	3
1987-88—Denver	54	28	.659	1‡	5	6
1988-89—Denver	44	38	.537	3‡	0	3
1989-90—Denver	43	39	.524	4‡	0	3
Totals (14 seasons)	609	492	.549		33	50

†Central Division. ‡Midwest Division.

Named NBA Coach of the Year, 1988. . . . ABA All-Star First Team, 1968. . . . ABA All-Star Second Team, 1969. . . . Member of ABA championship team, 1969. . . . Named to THE SPORTING NEWS All-America Second Team, 1959 and 1961.

JOHN RICHARD MOTTA
(Dick)
Sacramento Kings

Born September 3, 1931 at Medvale, Utah. Height 5:10. Weight 170.

High School—Jordan, Utah (did not play varsity basketball).

College—Utah State University, Logan, Utah (did not play basketball).

—COLLEGIATE COACHING RECORD—

Sea. Club	Regular Season W.	L.	Pct.	Pos.
1962-63—Weber State	22	4	.846	..
1963-64—Weber State	17	8	.680	2
1964-65—Weber State	22	3	.880	1
1965-66—Weber State	20	5	.800	1T

Sea. Club	Regular Season W.	L.	Pct.	Pos.
1966-67—Weber State	18	7	.720	3
1967-68—Weber State	21	6	.778	1
Totals (6 seasons)	120	33	.784	

NBA COACHING RECORD

		Regular Season				Playoffs	
Sea.	Club	W.	L.	Pct.	Pos.	W.	L.
1968-69	Chicago	33	49	.402	5†	..	..
1969-70	Chicago	39	43	.476	3T†	1	4
1970-71	Chicago	51	31	.622	2‡	3	4
1971-72	Chicago	57	25	.695	2‡	0	4
1972-73	Chicago	51	31	.622	2‡	3	4
1973-74	Chicago	54	28	.659	2‡	4	7
1974-75	Chicago	47	35	.573	1‡	7	6
1975-76	Chicago	24	58	.293	4‡	..	..
1976-77	Washington	48	34	.585	2§	4	5
1977-78	Washington	44	38	.537	2§	14	7
1978-79	Washington	54	28	.659	1x	9	10
1979-80	Washington	39	43	.476	3†	0	2
1980-81	Dallas	15	67	.183	6‡	..	..
1981-82	Dallas	28	54	.341	5‡	..	..
1982-83	Dallas	38	44	.463	4‡	..	..
1983-84	Dallas	43	39	.524	2‡	4	6
1984-85	Dallas	44	38	.537	3‡	1	3
1985-86	Dallas	44	38	.537	3‡	5	5
1986-87	Dallas	55	27	.671	1‡	1	3
1989-90	Sacramento	16	38	.296	7y	..	..
Totals (20 seasons)		824	788	.511		56	70

*Won NBA championship. †Western Division. ‡Midwest Division. §Central Division. xAtlantic Division. yPacific Division.

Named NBA Coach of the Year, 1971. . . . Coach of NBA championship team, 1978.

WILLIAM C. MUSSELMAN
(Bill)
Minnesota Timberwolves

Born August 13, 1940 at Wooster, O. Height 5:11. Weight 180.

High School—Wooster, O.

College—Wittenburg University, Springfield, O.

COLLEGIATE PLAYING RECORD

Played one season of college basketball (1958-59); statistics unavailable.

COLLEGIATE COACHING RECORD

Sea.	Club	W.	L.	Pct.	Pos.
1965-66	Ashland College	10	10	.500	..
1966-67	Ashland College	21	3	.875	..
1967-68	Ashland College	24	6	.800	..
1968-69	Ashland College	26	4	.867	..
1969-70	Ashland College	23	4	.852	..
1970-71	Ashland College	25	3	.893	..
1971-72	Minnesota	18	7	.720	1
1972-73	Minnesota	21	5	.808	2
1973-74	Minnesota	12	12	.500	6
1974-75	Minnesota	18	8	.692	3T
Totals Ashland		129	30	.811	
Totals Minnesota		69	32	.688	
Totals College		198	62	.762	

Assistant coach, Ashland (O.) College, 1964-65.

ABA COACHING RECORD

		Regular Season			
Sea.	Club	W.	L.	Pct.	Pos.
1975-76	San Diego	3	8	.273	..
1975-76	Virginia	4	22	.154	..
Totals (1 year)		7	30	.189	

WBA COACHING RECORD

		Regular Season				Playoffs	
Sea.	Club	W.	L.	Pct.	Pos.	W.	L.
1978-79	Reno	28	20	.583	3	8	5

CBA COACHING RECORD

		Regular Season				Playoffs	
Sea.	Club	W.	L.	Pct.	Pos.	W.	L.
1983-84	Sarasota	6	13	.316	..†	..	..
1984-85	Tampa Bay	35	13	.729	2†	10	5
1985-86	Tampa Bay	34	14	.708	1†	12	5
1986-87	Tampa Bay‡	34	14	.708	1†	12	1
1987-88	Albany	48	6	.889	1†	12	4
Totals (5 seasons)		157	60	.724		46	15

†Eastern Division.
‡Team relocated to Rapid City, S.D., at end of regular season.

NBA COACHING RECORD

Sea.	Club	Regular Season W.	L.	Pct.	Pos.
1980-81	—Cleveland	25	46	.352	5†
1981-82	—Cleveland	2	21	.087	6†
1989-90	—Minnesota	22	60	.268	6‡
Totals (3 seasons)		49	127	.278	

†Central Division. ‡Midwest Division.

Only man ever to coach in four professional basketball leagues. . . . Named CBA Coach of the Year, 1987 and 1988. . . . Coach of CBA championship teams, 1985, 1986, 1987, 1988.

DON ARVID NELSON
Golden State Warriors

Born May 15, 1940 at Muskegon, Mich. Height 6:06. Weight 210.

High School—Rock Island, Ill.

College—University of Iowa, Iowa City, Iowa.

Drafted by Chicago on third round, 1962 (19th pick).

Sold by Chicago (Baltimore) to Los Angeles, September 6, 1963.
Waived by Los Angeles, October 21, 1965; signed by Boston as a free agent, October 28, 1965.

—COLLEGIATE PLAYING RECORD—

Year	G.	Min.	FGA	FGM	Pct.	FTA	FTM	Pct.	Reb.	Pts.	Avg.
58-59†	(Freshman team did not play intercollegiate schedule.)										
59-60	24	....	320	140	.438	155	100	.645	241	380	15.8
60-61	24	....	377	197	.523	268	176	.657	258	570	23.8
61-62	24	....	348	193	.555	264	186	.705	285	572	23.8
Varsity Totals	72	....	1045	530	.507	687	462	.672	784	1522	21.1

NBA REGULAR SEASON RECORD

Sea.—Team	G.	Min.	FGA	FGM	Pct.	FTA	FTM	Pct.	Reb.	Ast.	PF	Disq.	Pts.	Avg.
62-63—Chicago	62	1071	293	129	.440	221	161	.729	279	72	136	3	419	6.8
63-64—Los Angeles	80	1406	323	135	.418	201	149	.741	323	76	181	1	419	5.2
64-65—Los Angeles	39	238	85	36	.424	26	20	.769	73	24	40	1	92	2.4
65-66—Boston	75	1765	618	271	.439	326	223	.684	403	79	187	1	765	10.2
66-67—Boston	79	1202	509	227	.446	190	141	.742	295	65	143	0	595	7.5
67-68—Boston	82	1498	632	312	.494	268	195	.728	431	103	178	1	819	10.0
68-69—Boston	82	1773	771	374	.485	259	201	.776	458	92	198	2	949	11.6
69-70—Boston	82	2224	920	461	.501	435	337	.775	601	148	238	3	1259	15.4
70-71—Boston	82	2254	881	412	.468	426	317	.744	565	153	232	2	1141	13.9
71-72—Boston	82	2086	811	389	.480	452	356	.788	453	192	220	3	1134	13.8
72-73—Boston	72	1425	649	309	.476	188	159	.846	315	102	155	1	777	10.8

									—Rebounds—								
Sea.—Team	G.	Min.	FGA	FGM	Pct.	FTA	FTM	Pct.	Off.	Def.	Tot.	Ast.	PF	Dq.	Stl.	Blk.	Pts.	Avg.
73-74—Boston	82	1748	717	364	.508	273	215	.788	90	255	345	162	189	1	19	13	943	11.5
74-75—Boston	79	2052	785	423	.539	318	263	.827	127	342	469	181	239	2	32	15	1109	14.0
75-76—Boston	75	943	379	175	.462	161	127	.789	56	126	182	77	115	0	14	7	477	6.4
Totals	1053	21685	8373	4017	.480	3744	2864	.765			5192	1526	2451	21	65	35	10898	10.3

NBA PLAYOFF RECORD

Sea.—Team	G.	Min.	FGA	FGM	Pct.	FTA	FTM	Pct.	Reb.	Ast.	PF	Disq.	Pts.	Avg.
63-64—Los Angeles	5	56	13	7	.538	3	3	1.000	13	2	11	1	17	3.4
64-65—Los Angeles	11	212	53	24	.453	25	19	.760	59	19	31	0	67	6.1
65-66—Boston	17	316	118	50	.424	52	42	.808	85	13	50	0	142	8.4
66-67—Boston	9	142	59	27	.458	17	10	.588	42	9	12	0	64	7.1
67-68—Boston	19	468	175	91	.520	74	55	.743	143	32	49	0	237	12.5
68-69—Boston	18	348	168	87	.518	60	50	.833	83	21	51	0	224	12.4
71-72—Boston	11	308	99	52	.525	48	41	.854	61	21	30	0	145	13.2
72-73—Boston	13	303	101	47	.465	56	49	.875	38	15	29	0	143	11.0

									—Rebounds—								
Sea.—Team	G.	Min.	FGA	FGM	Pct.	FTA	FTM	Pct.	Off.	Def.	Tot.	Ast.	PF	Dq.	Stl.	Blk.	Pts.	Avg.
73-74—Boston	18	467	164	82	.500	53	41	.774	25	72	97	35	54	2	8	3	205	11.4
74-75—Boston	11	274	117	66	.564	41	37	.902	18	27	45	26	36	1	2	2	169	15.4
75-76—Boston	18	315	108	52	.481	69	60	.870	17	36	53	17	46	1	3	2	164	9.1
Totals	150	3209	1175	585	.498	498	407	.817			719	210	399	5	13	7	1577	10.5

NBA COACHING RECORD

		Regular Season				Playoffs	
Sea.	Club	W.	L.	Pct.	Pos.	W.	L.
1976-77	—Milwaukee	27	37	.422	6†	...	...
1977-78	—Milwaukee	44	38	.537	2†	5	4
1978-79	—Milwaukee	38	44	.463	4†	...	...
1979-80	—Milwaukee	49	33	.598	1†	3	4
1980-81	—Milwaukee	60	22	.732	1‡	3	4
1981-82	—Milwaukee	55	27	.671	1‡	2	4
1982-83	—Milwaukee	51	31	.622	1‡	5	4
1983-84	—Milwaukee	50	32	.610	1‡	8	8
1984-85	—Milwaukee	59	23	.720	1‡	3	5
1985-86	—Milwaukee	57	25	.695	1‡	7	7
1986-87	—Milwaukee	50	32	.610	3‡	6	6
1988-89	—Golden State	43	39	.524	4§	4	4
1989-90	—Golden State	37	45	.451	5§	..	..
Totals (13 seasons)		620	428	.592		46	50

†Midwest Division. ‡Central Division. §Pacific Division.

Led NBA in field-goal percentage, 1975. . . . Member of NBA championship teams, 1966, 1968, 1969, 1974, 1976. . . . Named NBA Coach of the Year, 1983 and 1985.

RONALD ROTHSTEIN
(Ron)
Miami Heat

Born December 27, 1942 at Bronxville, N.Y. Height 5:08. Weight 165.

High School—Yonkers, N.Y., Roosevelt.

College—University of Rhode Island, Kingston, R.I.

—COLLEGIATE RECORD—

Year	G.	Min.	FGA	FGM	Pct.	FTA	FTM	Pct.	Reb.	Pts.	Avg.
60-61†					Statistics Unavailable						
61-62	25	....	85	37	.435	40	34	.850	35	108	4.3
62-63	26	....	138	45	.326	68	52	.765	68	142	5.5
63-64	24	....	107	48	.449	48	32	.667	75	128	5.3
Varsity Totals	75	....	330	130	.394	156	118	.756	178	378	5.0

NBA COACHING RECORD

	Regular Season			
Sea. Club	W.	L.	Pct.	Pos.
1988-89—Miami	15	67	.183	6†
1989-90—Miami	18	64	.220	5‡
Totals (2 seasons)	33	131	.201	

†Midwest Division.
‡Atlantic Division.

Assistant coach, Atlanta Hawks, 1983-86, and Detroit Pistons, 1986-88.

MICHAEL HAROLD SCHULER
(Mike)
Los Angeles Clippers

Born September 22, 1940 at Portsmouth, O. Height 5:11. Weight 165.

High School—Portsmouth, O.

College—Ohio University, Athens, O.

—COLLEGIATE RECORD—

Year	G.	Min.	FGA	FGM	Pct.	FTA	FTM	Pct.	Reb.	Pts.	Avg.
58-59†	11	....	...	9	....	4	3	.750	....	21	1.9
59-60	12	....	12	5	.417	2	0	.000	0	10	0.8
60-61	18	....	36	6	.167	3	3	1.000	12	15	0.8
61-62	8	....	13	3	.231	2	1	.500	5	7	0.9
Varsity Totals	38	....	61	14	.230	7	4	.571	17	32	0.8

COLLEGIATE COACHING RECORD

	Regular Season			
Sea. Club	W.	L.	Pct.	Pos.
1969-70—VMI	6	19	.240	
1970-71—VMI	1	25	.038	
1971-72—VMI	6	19	.240	
1977-78—Rice	4	22	.154	
1978-79—Rice	7	20	.259	
1979-80—Rice	7	19	.269	
1980-81—Rice	12	15	.444	
Totals VMI (3 seasons)	13	63	.171	
Totals Rice (4 seasons)	30	76	.283	
Totals (7 seasons)	43	139	.236	

Assistant coach, Army, 1965-66.
Assistant coach, Ohio University, 1966 through 1969.
Assistant coach, University of Virginia, 1972 through 1977.

NBA COACHING RECORD

	Regular Season				Playoffs	
Sea. Club	W.	L.	Pct.	Pos.	W.	L.
1986-87—Portland	49	33	.598	2†	1	3
1987-88—Portland	53	29	.646	2†	1	3
1988-89—Portland	25	22	.532	..†	..	..
Totals (3 seasons)	127	84	.602		2	6

†Pacific Division.

Assistant coach, New Jersey Nets, 1981-83; Milwaukee Bucks, 1983-86, and Golden State Warriors, 1989-90.

Named NBA Coach of the Year, 1987.

GERALD EUGENE SLOAN
(Jerry)
Utah Jazz

Born March 28, 1942 at McLeansboro, Ill. Height 6:05. Weight 200.
High School—McLeansboro, Ill.
Colleges—University of Illinois, Champaign, Ill. and Evansville College, Evansville, Ind.
Drafted by Baltimore on first round, 1965.

Selected from Baltimore by Chicago in NBA expansion draft, April 30, 1966.

—COLLEGIATE RECORD—

Illinois

Year	G.	Min.	FGA	FGM	Pct.	FTA	FTM	Pct.	Reb.	Pts.	Avg.
60-61	Dropped out of school prior to basketball season.										

Evansville

Year	G.	Min.	FGA	FGM	Pct.	FTA	FTM	Pct.	Reb.	Pts.	Avg.
61-62	Did Not Play—Transfer Student										
62-63	27	....	446	152	.341	151	103	.682	293	407	15.1
63-64	29	....	385	160	.416	114	84	.737	335	404	13.9
64-65	29	....	458	207	.452	126	95	.754	425	509	17.6
Totals	85	....	1289	519	.403	391	282	.721	1053	1320	15.5

NBA REGULAR SEASON RECORD

Sea.—Team	G.	Min.	FGA	FGM	Pct.	FTA	FTM	Pct.	Reb.	Ast.	PF	Disq.	Pts.	Avg.
65-66—Baltimore	59	952	289	120	.415	139	98	.705	230	110	176	7	338	5.7
66-67—Chicago	80	2942	1214	525	.432	427	340	.796	726	170	293	7	1390	17.4
67-68—Chicago	77	2454	959	369	.385	386	280	.749	591	229	291	11	1027	13.3
68-69—Chicago	78	2939	1179	488	.417	447	333	.745	619	276	313	6	1309	16.8
69-70—Chicago	53	1822	737	310	.421	318	207	.651	372	165	179	3	827	15.6
70-71—Chicago	80	3140	1342	592	.441	389	278	.715	701	281	289	5	1462	18.3
71-72—Chicago	82	3035	1206	535	.444	391	258	.660	691	211	309	8	1328	16.2
72-73—Chicago	69	2412	733	301	.411	133	94	.707	475	151	235	5	696	10.1

									—Rebounds—									
Sea.—Team	G.	Min.	FGA	FGM	Pct.	FTA	FTM	Pct.	Off.	Def.	Tot.	Ast.	PF	Dq.	Stl.	Blk.	Pts.	Avg.
73-74—Chicago	77	2860	921	412	.447	273	194	.711	150	406	556	149	273	3	183	10	1018	13.2
74-75—Chicago	78	2577	865	380	.439	258	193	.748	177	361	538	161	265	5	171	17	953	12.2
75-76—Chicago	22	617	210	84	.400	78	55	.705	40	76	116	22	77	1	27	5	223	10.1
Totals	755	25750	9646	4116	.427	3239	2339	.722			5615	1925	2700	61	381	32	10571	14.0

NBA PLAYOFF RECORD

Sea.—Team	G.	Min.	FGA	FGM	Pct.	FTA	FTM	Pct.	Reb.	Ast.	PF	Disq.	Pts.	Avg.
65-66—Baltimore	2	34	12	5	.417	4	3	.750	16	6	6	1	13	6.5
66-67—Chicago	3	71	31	12	.387	9	6	.667	10	1	7	0	30	10.0
67-68—Chicago	5	137	37	12	.324	25	19	.760	32	12	19	0	43	8.6
69-70—Chicago	5	190	74	29	.392	25	16	.640	39	11	18	0	74	14.8
70-71—Chicago	7	284	117	51	.436	23	17	.739	63	17	25	1	119	17.0
71-72—Chicago	4	170	64	26	.406	19	11	.579	35	10	18	1	63	15.8
72-73—Chicago	7	292	103	45	.437	19	14	.737	59	14	31	1	104	14.9

									—Rebounds—									
Sea.—Team	G.	Min.	FGA	FGM	Pct.	FTA	FTM	Pct.	Off.	Def.	Tot.	Ast.	PF	Dq.	Stl.	Blk.	Pts.	Avg.
73-74—Chicago	6	240	88	39	.443	29	22	.759	18	44	62	12	17	0	7	1	100	16.7
74-75—Chicago	13	470	163	75	.460	36	20	.556	24	72	96	26	46	0	20	0	170	13.1
Totals	52	1888	689	294	.427	189	128	.677			412	109	187	4	27	1	716	13.8

NBA ALL-STAR GAME RECORD

Season—Team	Min.	FGA	FGM	Pct.	FTA	FTM	Pct.	Reb.	Ast.	PF	Disq.	Pts.
1967—Chicago	22	9	4	.444	0	0	.000	4	4	5	0	8
1969—Chicago	18	8	2	.250	1	0	.000	3	0	5	0	4
Totals	40	17	6	.353	1	0	.000	7	4	10	0	12

NBA COACHING RECORD

	Regular Season				Playoffs	
Sea. Club	W.	L.	Pct.	Pos.	W.	L.
1979-80—Chicago	30	52	.366	†4	..	..
1980-81—Chicago	45	37	.549	‡2	2	4
1981-82—Chicago	19	32	.373	‡..	..	..
1988-89—Utah	40	25	.615	†1	0	3
1989-90—Utah	55	27	.671	†2	2	3
Totals (5 seasons)	189	173	.522		4	10

†Midwest Division. ‡Central Division.

Named to NBA All-Defensive First Team, 1969, 1972, 1974, 1975. . . . NBA All-Defensive Second Team, 1970 and 1971. . . . Named Outstanding Player in NCAA College Division Tournament, 1964 and 1965. . . . THE SPORTING NEWS All-America Second Team, 1965.

WESTLEY SISSEL UNSELD
(Wes)
Washington Bullets

Born March 14, 1946 at Louisville, Ky. Height 6:07. Weight 245.
High School—Louisville, Ky., Seneca.
College—University of Louisville, Louisville, Ky.
Drafted by Baltimore on first round, 1968 (2nd pick).

—COLLEGIATE RECORD—

Year	G.	Min.	FGA	FGM	Pct.	FTA	FTM	Pct.	Reb.	Pts.	Avg.
64-65†	14	....	312	214	.686	124	73	.589	331	501	35.8
65-66	26	....	374	195	.521	202	128	.634	505	518	19.9
66-67	28	....	374	201	.537	177	121	.684	533	523	18.7
67-68	28	....	382	234	.613	275	177	.644	513	645	23.0
Varsity Totals	82	....	1130	630	.558	654	426	.651	1551	1686	20.6

NBA REGULAR SEASON RECORD

Sea.—Team	G.	Min.	FGA	FGM	Pct.	FTA	FTM	Pct.	Reb.	Ast.	PF	Disq.	Pts.	Avg.
68-69—Baltimore	82	2970	897	427	.476	458	277	.605	1491	213	276	4	1131	13.8
69-70—Baltimore	82	3234	1015	526	.518	428	273	.638	1370	291	250	2	1325	16.2
70-71—Baltimore	74	2904	846	424	.501	303	199	.657	1253	293	235	2	1047	14.1
71-72—Baltimore	76	3171	822	409	.498	272	171	.629	1336	278	218	1	989	13.0
72-73—Baltimore	79	3085	854	421	.493	212	149	.703	1260	347	168	0	991	12.5

									—Rebounds—									
Sea.—Team	G.	Min.	FGA	FGM	Pct.	FTA	FTM	Pct.	Off.	Def.	Tot.	Ast.	PF	Dq.	Stl.	Blk.	Pts.	Avg.
73-74—Capital	56	1727	333	146	.438	55	36	.655	152	365	517	159	121	1	56	16	328	5.9
74-75—Washington	73	2904	544	273	.502	184	126	.685	318	759	1077	297	180	1	115	68	672	9.2
75-76—Washington	78	2922	567	318	.561	195	114	.585	271	765	1036	404	203	3	84	59	750	9.6
76-77—Washington	82	2860	551	270	.490	166	100	.602	243	634	877	363	253	5	87	45	640	7.8
77-78—Washington	80	2644	491	257	.523	173	93	.538	286	669	955	326	234	2	98	45	607	7.6
78-79—Washington	77	2406	600	346	.577	235	151	.643	274	556	830	315	204	2	71	37	843	10.9
79-80—Washington	82	2973	637	327	.513	209	139	.665	334	760	1094	366	249	5	65	61	794	9.7
80-81—Washington	63	2032	429	225	.524	86	55	.640	207	466	673	170	171	1	52	36	507	8.0
Totals	984	35832	8586	4369	.509	2976	1883	.633			13769	3822	2762	29	628	367	10624	10.8

Three-Point Field Goals: 1979-80, 1-for-2 (.500). 1980-81, 2-for-4 (.500). Totals, 3-for-6 (.500).

NBA PLAYOFF RECORD

Sea.—Team	G.	Min.	FGA	FGM	Pct.	FTA	FTM	Pct.	Reb.	Ast.	PF	Disq.	Pts.	Avg.
68-69—Baltimore	4	165	57	30	.526	19	15	.789	74	5	14	0	75	18.8
69-70—Baltimore	7	289	70	29	.414	19	15	.789	165	24	25	1	73	10.4
70-71—Baltimore	18	759	208	96	.462	81	46	.568	339	69	60	0	238	13.2
71-72—Baltimore	6	266	65	32	.492	19	10	.526	75	25	22	0	74	12.3
72-73—Baltimore	5	201	48	20	.417	19	9	.474	76	17	12	0	49	9.8

									—Rebounds—									
Sea.—Team	G.	Min.	FGA	FGM	Pct.	FTA	FTM	Pct.	Off.	Def.	Tot.	Ast.	PF	Dq.	Stl.	Blk.	Pts.	Avg.
73-74—Capital	7	297	63	31	.492	15	9	.600	22	63	85	27	15	0	4	1	71	10.1
74-75—Washington	17	734	130	71	.546	61	40	.656	65	211	276	64	39	0	15	20	182	10.7
75-76—Washington	7	310	39	18	.462	24	13	.542	26	59	85	28	19	0	6	4	49	7.0
76-77—Washington	9	368	54	30	.556	12	7	.583	24	81	105	44	32	0	8	6	67	7.4
77-78—Washington	18	677	134	71	.530	46	27	.587	72	144	216	79	62	2	17	7	169	9.4
78-79—Washington	19	736	158	78	.494	64	39	.609	90	163	253	64	66	2	17	14	195	10.3
79-80—Washington	2	87	14	7	.500	6	4	.667	7	21	28	7	5	0	0	3	18	9.0
Totals	119	4889	1040	513	.493	385	234	.608			1777	453	371	5	67	55	1260	10.6

Three-Point Field Goals: 1979-80, 0-for-1.

NBA ALL-STAR GAME RECORD

Season—Team	Min.	FGA	FGM	Pct.	FTA	FTM	Pct.	Reb.	Ast.	PF	Disq.	Pts.
1969—Baltimore	14	7	5	.714	3	1	.333	8	1	3	0	11
1971—Baltimore	21	9	4	.444	0	0	.000	10	2	2	0	8
1972—Baltimore	16	5	1	.200	0	0	.000	7	1	3	0	2
1973—Baltimore	11	4	2	.500	0	0	.000	5	1	0	0	4

								—Rebounds—							
Season—Team	Min.	FGA	FGM	Pct.	FTA	FTM	Pct.	Off.	Def.	Tot.	Ast.	PF	Dq.	Stl.	Blk.	Pts.
1975—Washington	15	3	2	.667	2	2	1.000	2	4	6	1	2	0	2	0	6
Totals	77	28	14	.500	5	3	.600			36	6	10	0			31

NBA COACHING RECORD

	Regular Season				Playoffs	
Sea. Club	W.	L.	Pct.	Pos.	W.	L.
1987-88—Washington	30	25	.545	T2†	2	3
1988-89—Washington	40	42	.488	4†	..	..
1989-90—Washington	31	51	.378	4†	..	..
Totals (3 seasons)	101	118	.461		2	3

†Atlantic Division.

Elected to Naismith Memorial Basketball Hall of Fame, 1987. . . . NBA Most Valuable Player, 1969. . . . NBA Rookie of the Year, 1969. . . . Named to All-NBA First Team, 1969. . . . NBA All-Rookie Team, 1969. . . . NBA Playoff MVP, 1978. . . . Member of NBA championship team, 1978. . . . Led NBA in rebounding, 1975. . . . Led NBA in field-goal percentage, 1976. . . . Named to THE SPORTING NEWS All-America Second Team, 1967 and 1968.

RICHARD VERSACE
(Dick)
Indiana Pacers

Born April 16, 1940 at Fort Bragg, N.C.

High School—Madison, Wisc., Edgewood.

College—University of Wisconsin, Madison, Wisc.
(Did not play college basketball.)

COLLEGIATE COACHING RECORD

	Regular Season			
Sea. Club	W.	L.	Pct.	Pos.
1978-79—Bradley	9	17	.346	8†
1979-80—Bradley	23	10	.697	1†
1980-81—Bradley	18	9	.667	4†
1981-82—Bradley	26	10	.722	1†
1982-83—Bradley	16	13	.552	5†
1983-84—Bradley	15	13	.536	5†
1984-85—Bradley	17	13	.567	4†
1985-86—Bradley	32	3	.914	1†
Totals (8 seasons)	156	88	.639	

†Missouri Valley Conference.

Assistant coach, St. Louis University, 1973-74; Michigan State University, 1974-76, and head coach, Jackson (Mich.) Community College, 1976-78.

NBA COACHING RECORD

	Regular Season				Playoffs	
Sea. Club	W.	L.	Pct.	Pos.	W.	L.
1988-89—Indiana	22	31	.415	6†	..	..
1989-90—Indiana	42	40	.512	T4†	0	3
Totals (2 seasons)	64	71	.474		0	3

†Central Division.

Assistant coach, Detroit Pistons, 1986-89.

Coach of NIT championship team, 1986.

ROBERT WEISS
(Bob)
Atlanta Hawks

Born May 7, 1942 at Easton, Pa. Height 6:03. Weight 185.

High School—Athens, Pa.

College—Pennsylvania State University, University Park, Pa.

Drafted by Philadelphia on third round, 1965 (25th pick).

Selected from Philadelphia by Seattle in expansion draft, May 1, 1967.
Selected from Seattle by Milwaukee in expansion draft, May 6, 1968.
Traded by Milwaukee with Bob Love to Chicago for Flynn Robinson, November 23, 1968.
Traded by Chicago to Buffalo for Matt Guokas and a draft choice, September 4, 1974.
Waived by Buffalo, September 29, 1976; signed by Washington as a free agent, November 15, 1976.
Played with Wilmington Blue Bombers in Eastern Basketball League, 1965-66 and 1966-67.

—COLLEGIATE RECORD—

Year	G.	Min.	FGA	FGM	Pct.	FTA	FTM	Pct.	Reb.	Pts.	Avg.
61-62†		Statistics Unavailable									
62-63	20	....	293	124	.424	81	57	.704	90	305	15.3
63-64	23	....	353	154	.436	105	84	.800	90	392	17.0
64-65	24	....	362	152	.420	117	90	.769	114	394	16.4
Varsity Totals	67	....	1008	430	.427	303	231	.762	294	1091	16.3

EBL REGULAR SEASON RECORD

			—2-Point—			—3-Point—									
Sea.—Team	G.	Min.	FGM	FGA	Pct.	FGM	FGA	Pct.	FTM	FTA	Pct.	Reb.	Ast.	Pts.	Avg.
65-66—Wilmington	19	....	56	...	....	....	....	....	32	44	.727	55	83	146	7.7
66-67—Wilmington	27	....	151	...	....	....	....	....	100	118	.847	103	238	403	14.9

NBA REGULAR SEASON RECORD

Sea.—Team	G.	Min.	FGA	FGM	Pct.	FTA	FTM	Pct.	Reb.	Ast.	PF	Disq.	Pts.	Avg.
65-66—Philadelphia	7	30	9	3	.333	0	0	.000	7	4	10	0	6	0.9
66-67—Philadelphia	6	29	10	5	.500	5	2	.400	3	10	8	0	12	2.0
67-68—Seattle	82	1614	686	295	.430	254	213	.839	150	342	137	0	803	9.8
68-69—Milw.-Chi.	77	1478	499	189	.379	160	128	.800	162	199	174	1	506	6.6
69-70—Chicago	82	2544	855	365	.427	253	213	.842	227	474	206	0	943	11.5

Sea.—Team	G.	Min.	FGA	FGM	Pct.	FTA	FTM	Pct.	Reb.	Ast.	PF	Disq.	Pts.	Avg.
70-71—Chicago	82	2237	659	278	.422	269	226	.840	189	387	216	1	782	9.5
71-72—Chicago	82	2450	832	358	.430	254	212	.835	170	377	212	1	928	11.3
72-73—Chicago	82	2086	655	279	.426	189	159	.841	148	295	151	1	717	8.7

									—Rebounds—									
Sea.—Team	G.	Min.	FGA	FGM	Pct.	FTA	FTM	Pct.	Off.	Def.	Tot.	Ast.	PF	Dq.	Stl.	Blk.	Pts.	Avg.
73-74—Chicago	79	1708	564	263	.466	170	142	.835	32	71	103	303	156	0	104	12	668	8.5
74-75—Buffalo	76	1338	261	102	.391	67	54	.806	21	83	104	260	146	0	82	19	258	3.4
75-76—Buffalo	66	995	183	89	.486	48	35	.729	13	53	66	150	94	0	48	14	213	3.2
76-77—Washington	62	768	133	62	.466	37	29	.784	15	54	69	130	66	0	53	7	153	2.5
Totals	783	7277	5346	2288	.428	1706	1413	.828			1398	2931	1576	4	287	52	5989	7.6

NBA PLAYOFF RECORD

Sea.—Team	G.	Min.	FGA	FGM	Pct.	FTA	FTM	Pct.	Reb.	Ast.	PF	Disq.	Pts.	Avg.
66-67—Philadelphia	1	4	3	2	.667	0	0	.000	2	2	1	0	4	4.0
69-70—Chicago	5	121	59	25	.424	10	8	.800	6	24	11	0	58	11.6
70-71—Chicago	7	250	92	42	.457	30	26	.867	18	57	19	0	110	15.7
71-72—Chicago	4	119	49	24	.490	8	7	.875	13	12	15	1	55	13.8
72-73—Chicago	7	175	79	34	.430	21	16	.762	16	15	20	0	84	12.0

									—Rebounds—									
Sea.—Team	G.	Min.	FGA	FGM	Pct.	FTA	FTM	Pct.	Off.	Def.	Tot.	Ast.	PF	Dq.	Stl.	Blk.	Pts.	Avg.
73-74—Chicago	11	251	74	23	.311	6	6	1.000	5	15	20	32	20	0	7	1	52	4.7
74-75—Buffalo	7	113	23	11	.478	12	8	.667	2	5	7	17	15	0	4	1	30	4.3
75-76—Buffalo	7	36	8	3	.375	3	2	.667	0	4	4	3	5	0	2	0	8	1.1
76-77—Washington	4	34	5	3	.600	1	0	.000	1	2	3	2	5	0	1	0	6	1.5
Totals	53	1103	392	167	.426	91	73	.802			89	164	111	1	14	2	407	7.7

NBA COACHING RECORD

	Regular Season				Playoffs	
Sea. Club	W.	L.	Pct.	Pos.	W.	L.
1986-87—San Antonio	28	54	.341	6†	..	..
1987-88—San Antonio	31	51	.378	5†	0	3
Totals (2 seasons)	59	105	.360		0	3

†Midwest Division.

Assistant coach, San Diego Clippers, 1977-79; Dallas Mavericks, 1980-86; and Orlando Magic, 1989-90.

Named to Eastern Basketball League All-Star First Team, 1967. . . . Led EBL in assists, 1967. . . . Member of NBA championship team, 1967.

LEONARD RANDOLPH WILKENS
(Lenny)
Cleveland Cavaliers

Born October 28, 1937 at Brooklyn, N. Y. Height 6:01. Weight 180.
High School—Brooklyn, N. Y., Boys.
College—Providence College, Providence, R. I.
Drafted by St. Louis on first round, 1960.

St. Louis franchise transferred to Atlanta, 1968.
Traded by Atlanta to Seattle for Walt Hazzard, October 12, 1968.
Traded by Seattle with Barry Clemens to Cleveland for Butch Beard, August 23, 1972.
Playing rights transferred from Cleveland to Portland, October 7, 1974.

—COLLEGIATE PLAYING RECORD—

Year	G.	Min.	FGA	FGM	Pct.	FTA	FTM	Pct.	Reb.	Pts.	Avg.
56-57†	23	....	....	....	....	....	....	....	....	488	21.2
57-58	24	....	....	137	.431	....	84	.651	190	358	14.9
58-59	27	....	....	167	.428	....	89	.618	188	423	15.7
59-60	29	....	362	157	.434	140	98	.700	205	412	14.2
Varsity Totals	80	....	....	461	....	....	271	....	583	1193	14.9

NBA REGULAR SEASON RECORD

Sea.—Team	G.	Min.	FGA	FGM	Pct.	FTA	FTM	Pct.	Reb.	Ast.	PF	Disq.	Pts.	Avg.
60-61—St. Louis	75	1898	783	333	.425	300	214	.713	335	212	215	5	880	11.7
61-62—St. Louis	20	870	364	140	.385	110	84	.764	131	116	63	0	364	18.2
62-63—St. Louis	75	2569	834	333	.399	319	222	.696	403	381	256	6	888	11.8
63-64—St. Louis	78	2526	808	334	.413	365	270	.740	335	359	287	7	938	12.0
64-65—St. Louis	78	2854	1048	434	.414	558	416	.746	365	431	283	7	1284	16.5
65-66—St. Louis	69	2692	954	411	.431	532	422	.793	322	429	248	4	1244	18.0
66-67—St. Louis	78	2974	1036	448	.432	583	459	.787	412	442	280	6	1355	17.4
67-68—St. Louis	82	3169	1246	546	.438	711	546	.768	438	679	255	3	1638	20.0
68-69—Seattle	82	3463	1462	644	.440	710	547	.770	511	674	294	8	1835	22.4
69-70—Seattle	75	2802	1066	448	.420	556	438	.788	378	683	212	5	1334	17.8
70-71—Seattle	71	2641	1125	471	.419	574	461	.803	319	654	201	3	1403	19.8
71-72—Seattle	80	2989	1027	479	.466	620	480	.774	338	766	209	4	1438	18.0
72-73—Cleveland	75	2973	1275	572	.449	476	394	.828	346	628	221	2	1538	20.5

Sea.—Team	G.	Min.	FGA	FGM	Pct.	FTA	FTM	Pct.	—Rebounds— Off.	Def.	Tot.	Ast.	PF	Dq.	Stl.	Blk.	Pts.	Avg.
73-74—Cleveland	74	2483	994	462	.465	361	289	.801	80	197	277	522	165	2	97	17	1213	16.4
74-75—Portland	65	1161	305	134	.439	198	152	.768	38	82	120	235	96	1	77	9	420	6.5
Totals	1077	38064	14327	6189	.432	6973	5394	.774			5030	7211	3285	63	174	26	17772	16.5

NBA PLAYOFF RECORD

Sea.—Team	G.	Min.	FGA	FGM	Pct.	FTA	FTM	Pct.	Reb.	Ast.	PF	Disq.	Pts.	Avg.
60-61—St. Louis	12	437	166	63	.380	58	44	.759	72	42	51	4	170	14.2
62-63—St. Louis	11	400	154	57	.370	49	37	.755	69	69	51	2	151	13.7
63-64—St. Louis	12	413	143	64	.448	58	44	.759	60	64	42	0	172	14.3
64-65—St. Louis	4	147	57	20	.351	29	24	.828	12	15	14	0	64	16.0
65-66—St. Louis	10	391	143	57	.399	83	57	.687	54	70	43	0	171	17.1
66-67—St. Louis	9	378	145	58	.400	90	77	.856	68	65	34	0	193	21.4
67-68—St. Louis	6	237	91	40	.440	40	30	.750	38	47	23	1	110	18.3
Totals	64	2403	899	359	.399	407	313	.769	373	372	258	7	1031	16.1

NBA ALL-STAR GAME RECORD

Season—Team	Min.	FGA	FGM	Pct.	FTA	FTM	Pct.	Reb.	Ast.	PF	Disq.	Pts.
1963—St. Louis	25	7	2	.286	1	0	.000	2	3	0	0	4
1964—St. Louis	14	5	1	.200	1	1	1.000	0	0	3	0	3
1965—St. Louis	20	6	2	.333	4	4	1.000	3	3	3	0	8
1967—St. Louis	16	6	2	.333	3	2	.667	2	6	2	0	6
1968—St. Louis	22	10	4	.400	8	6	.750	3	3	1	0	14
1969—Seattle	24	15	3	.200	5	4	.800	7	5	3	0	10
1970—Seattle	17	7	5	.714	3	2	.667	2	4	1	0	12
1971—Seattle	20	11	8	.727	5	5	1.000	1	1	1	0	21
1973—Cleveland	24	8	3	.375	2	1	.500	2	1	1	0	7
Totals (9 games)	182	75	30	.400	32	25	.781	22	26	15	0	85

NBA COACHING RECORD

Sea. Club	Regular Season W.	L.	Pct.	Pos.	Playoffs W.	L.
1969-70—Seattle	36	46	.439	5†	...	...
1970-71—Seattle	38	44	.463	4‡	...	...
1971-72—Seattle	47	35	.573	3‡	...	...
1974-75—Portland	38	44	.463	3‡	...	...
1975-76—Portland	37	45	.451	5‡	...	...
1977-78—Seattle	42	18	.700	3‡	13	9
1978-79—Seattle*	52	30	.634	1‡	12	5
1979-80—Seattle	56	26	.683	2‡	7	8
1980-81—Seattle	34	48	.415	6‡	...	...
1981-82—Seattle	52	30	.634	2‡	3	5
1982-83—Seattle	48	34	.585	3‡	0	2
1983-84—Seattle	42	40	.512	3‡	2	3
1984-85—Seattle	31	51	.378	4‡	..	..
1986-87—Cleveland	31	51	.378	6§	..	..
1987-88—Cleveland	42	40	.512	4T§	2	3
1988-89—Cleveland	57	25	.695	2§	2	3
1989-90—Cleveland	42	40	.512	T4§	2	3
Totals (17 seasons)	725	647	.528		43	41

*Won NBA Championship. †Western Division. ‡Pacific Division. §Central Division.

Elected to Naismith Memorial Basketball Hall of Fame, 1988. . . . NBA All-Star Game MVP, 1971. . . . Led NBA in assists, 1970. . . . Coach of NBA championship team, 1979. . . . Named to THE SPORTING NEWS All-America Second Team, 1960.

All-Time Greats

Included are coaches and non-active players who reached one or more of the following plateaus: 17,000 NBA or NBA/ABA points; 10,000 rebounds; 5,000 assists and 10,000 points; named to either the 25th or 35th NBA Anniversary All-Time Teams; NBA Most Valuable Player; four-time First, Second or Third Team All-NBA selection; six NBA All-Star Games; career scoring average of 23 points per game; 400 regular-season coaching victories in NBA with winning percentage of better than .500.

Players

KAREEM ABDUL-JABBAR

(Formerly known as Lew Alcindor.)

Born April 16, 1947 at New York, N. Y. Height 7:02. Weight 267.

High School—New York, N. Y., Power Memorial.

College—University of California at Los Angeles, Los Angeles, Calif.

Drafted by Milwaukee on first round, 1969 (1st pick).

Traded by Milwaukee with Walt Wesley to Los Angeles for Elmore Smith, Brian Winters, Dave Meyers and Junior Bridgeman, June 16, 1975.

—COLLEGIATE RECORD—

Year	G.	Min.	FGA	FGM	Pct.	FTA	FTM	Pct.	Reb.	Pts.	Avg.
65-66†	21	....	432	295	.683	179	106	.592	452	696	33.1
66-67	30	....	519	346	.667	274	178	.650	466	870	29.0
67-68	28	....	480	294	.613	237	146	.616	461	734	26.2
68-69	30	....	477	303	.635	188	115	.612	440	721	24.0
Varsity Totals	88	....	1476	943	.639	699	439	.628	1367	2325	26.4

NBA REGULAR SEASON RECORD

Sea.—Team	G.	Min.	FGA	FGM	Pct.	FTA	FTM	Pct.	Reb.	Ast.	PF	Disq.	Pts.	Avg.
69-70—Milwaukee	82	3534	1810	938	.518	743	485	.653	1190	337	283	8	2361	28.8
70-71—Milwaukee	82	3288	1843	1063	.577	681	470	.690	1311	272	264	4	2596	31.7
71-72—Milwaukee	81	3583	2019	1159	.574	732	504	.689	1346	370	235	1	2822	34.8
72-73—Milwaukee	76	3254	1772	982	.554	460	328	.713	1224	379	208	0	2292	30.2

									—Rebounds—									
Sea.—Team	G.	Min.	FGA	FGM	Pct.	FTA	FTM	Pct.	Off.	Def.	Tot.	Ast.	PF	Dq.	Stl.	Blk.	Pts.	Avg.
73-74—Milwaukee	81	3548	1759	948	.539	420	295	.702	287	891	1178	386	238	2	112	283	2191	27.0
74-75—Milwaukee	65	2747	1584	812	.513	426	325	.763	194	718	912	264	205	2	65	212	1949	30.0
75-76—Los Angeles	82	3379	1728	914	.529	636	447	.703	272	1111	1383	413	292	6	119	338	2275	27.7
76-77—Los Angeles	82	3016	1533	888	.579	536	376	.701	266	824	1090	319	262	4	101	261	2152	26.2
77-78—Los Angeles	62	2265	1205	663	.550	350	274	.783	186	615	801	269	182	1	103	185	1600	25.8
78-79—Los Angeles	80	3157	1347	777	.577	474	349	.736	207	818	1025	431	230	3	76	316	1903	23.8
79-80—Los Angeles	82	3143	1383	835	.604	476	364	.765	190	696	886	371	216	2	81	280	2034	24.8
80-81—Los Angeles	80	2976	1457	836	.574	552	423	.766	197	624	821	272	244	4	59	228	2095	26.2
81-82—Los Angeles	76	2677	1301	753	.579	442	312	.706	172	487	659	225	224	0	63	207	1818	23.9
82-83—Los Angeles	79	2554	1228	722	.588	371	278	.749	167	425	592	200	220	1	61	170	1722	21.8
83-84—Los Angeles	80	2622	1238	716	.578	394	285	.723	169	418	587	211	211	1	55	143	1717	21.5
84-85—L.A. Lakers	79	2630	1207	723	.599	395	289	.732	162	460	622	249	238	3	63	162	1735	22.0
85-86—L.A. Lakers	79	2629	1338	755	.564	439	336	.765	133	345	478	280	248	2	67	130	1846	23.4
86-87—L.A. Lakers	78	2441	993	560	.564	343	245	.714	152	371	523	203	245	2	49	97	1366	17.5
87-88—L.A. Lakers	80	2308	903	480	.532	269	205	.762	118	360	478	135	216	1	48	92	1165	14.6
88-89—L.A. Lakers	74	1695	659	313	.475	165	122	.739	103	231	334	74	196	1	38	85	748	10.1
Totals	1560	57446	28307	15837	.559	9304	6712	.721	2975	9394	17440	5660	4657	48	1160	3189	38387	24.6

Three-Point Field Goals: 1979-80, 0-for-1. 1980-81, 0-for-1. 1981-82, 0-for-3. 1982-83, 0-for-2. 1983-84, 0-for-1. 1984-85, 0-for-1. 1985-86, 0-for-2. 1986-87, 1-for-3 (.333). 1987-88, 0-for-1. 1988-89, 0-for-3. Totals, 1-for-18 (.056).

NBA PLAYOFF RECORD

Sea.—Team	G.	Min.	FGA	FGM	Pct.	FTA	FTM	Pct.	Reb.	Ast.	PF	Disq.	Pts.	Avg.
69-70—Milwaukee	10	435	245	139	.567	101	74	.733	168	41	25	1	352	35.2
70-71—Milwaukee	14	577	295	152	.515	101	68	.673	238	35	45	0	372	26.6
71-72—Milwaukee	11	510	318	139	.437	54	38	.704	200	56	35	0	316	28.7
72-73—Milwaukee	6	276	138	59	.428	35	19	.543	97	17	26	0	137	22.8

									—Rebounds—									
Sea.—Team	G.	Min.	FGA	FGM	Pct.	FTA	FTM	Pct.	Off.	Def.	Tot.	Ast.	PF	Dq.	Stl.	Blk.	Pts.	Avg.
73-74—Milwaukee	16	758	402	224	.557	91	67	.736	67	186	253	78	41	0	20	39	515	32.2
76-77—Los Angeles	11	467	242	147	.607	120	87	.725	51	144	195	45	42	0	19	38	381	34.6
77-78—Los Angeles	3	134	73	38	.521	9	5	.556	14	27	41	11	14	1	2	12	81	27.0
78-79—Los Angeles	8	367	152	88	.579	62	52	.839	18	83	101	38	26	0	8	33	228	28.5
79-80—Los Angeles	15	618	346	198	.572	105	83	.790	51	130	181	46	51	0	17	58	479	31.9
80-81—Los Angeles	3	134	65	30	.462	28	20	.714	13	37	50	12	14	0	3	8	80	26.7

Sea.—Team	G.	Min.	FGA	FGM	Pct.	FTA	FTM	Pct.	—Rebounds— Off.	Def.	Tot.	Ast.	PF	Dq.	Stl.	Blk.	Pts.	Avg.
81-82—Los Angeles	14	493	221	115	.520	87	55	.632	33	86	119	51	45	0	14	45	285	20.4
82-83—Los Angeles	15	588	287	163	.568	106	80	.755	25	90	115	42	61	1	17	55	406	27.1
83-84—Los Angeles	21	767	371	206	.555	120	90	.750	56	117	173	79	71	2	23	45	502	23.9
84-85—L.A. Lakers	19	610	300	168	.560	103	80	.777	50	104	154	76	67	1	23	36	416	21.9
85-86—L.A. Lakers	14	489	282	157	.557	61	48	.787	26	57	83	49	54	0	15	24	362	25.9
86-87—L.A. Lakers	18	559	234	124	.530	122	97	.795	39	84	123	36	56	0	8	35	345	19.2
87-88—L.A. Lakers	24	718	304	141	.464	71	56	.789	49	82	131	36	81	1	15	37	338	14.1
88-89—L.A. Lakers	15	351	147	68	.463	43	31	.721	13	46	59	19	43	0	5	11	167	11.1
Totals	237	8851	4422	2356	.533	1419	1050	.740	505	1273	2481	767	797	7	189	476	5762	24.3

Three-Point Field Goals: 1982-83, 0-for-1. 1986-87, 0-for-1. 1987-88, 0-for-2. 1988-89, 0-for-1. Totals, 0-for-4.

NBA ALL-STAR GAME RECORD

Season—Team	Min.	FGA	FGM	Pct.	FTA	FTM	Pct.	Reb.	Ast.	PF	Disq.	Pts.
1970—Milwaukee	18	8	4	.500	2	2	1.000	11	4	6	1	10
1971—Milwaukee	30	16	8	.500	4	3	.750	14	1	2	0	19
1972—Milwaukee	19	10	5	.500	2	2	1.000	7	2	0	0	12
1973—Milwaukee	Selected, Did Not Play.											

Season—Team	Min.	FGA	FGM	Pct.	FTA	FTM	Pct.	—Rebounds— Off.	Def.	Tot.	Ast.	PF	Dq.	Stl.	Blk.	Pts.
1974—Milwaukee	23	11	7	.636	0	0	.000	1	7	8	6	2	0	1	1	14
1975—Milwaukee	19	10	3	.300	2	1	.500	5	5	10	3	2	0	0	1	7
1976—Los Angeles	36	16	9	.563	4	4	1.000	2	13	15	3	3	0	0	3	22
1977—Los Angeles	23	14	8	.571	6	5	.833	3	1	4	2	1	0	0	1	21
1979—Los Angeles	28	12	5	.417	2	1	.500	1	7	8	3	4	0	1	1	11
1980—Los Angeles	30	17	6	.353	6	5	.833	5	11	16	9	5	0	0	6	17
1981—Los Angeles	23	9	6	.667	3	3	1.000	2	4	6	4	3	0	0	4	15
1982—Los Angeles	22	10	1	.100	0	0	.000	1	2	3	1	3	0	0	2	2
1983—Los Angeles	32	12	9	.750	3	2	.667	2	4	6	5	1	0	1	4	20
1984—Los Angeles	37	19	11	.579	4	3	.750	5	8	13	2	5	0	0	1	25
1985—L.A. Lakers	23	10	5	.500	2	1	.500	0	6	6	1	5	0	1	1	11
1986—L.A. Lakers	32	15	9	.600	4	3	.750	2	5	7	2	4	0	2	2	21
1987—L.A. Lakers	27	9	4	.444	2	2	1.000	2	6	8	3	5	0	0	2	10
1988—L.A. Lakers	14	9	4	.444	2	2	1.000	2	2	4	0	3	0	0	0	10
1989—L.A. Lakers	13	6	1	.167	2	2	1.000	0	3	3	0	3	0	0	2	4
Totals	449	213	105	.493	50	41	.820	33	84	149	51	57	1	6	31	251

Three-Point Field Goals: 1989, 0-for-1.

Named to NBA 35th Anniversary All-Time Team, 1980. . . . NBA Most Valuable Player, 1971, 1972, 1974, 1976, 1977, 1980. . . . All-NBA First Team, 1971, 1972, 1973, 1974, 1976, 1977, 1980, 1981, 1984, 1986. . . . All-NBA Second Team, 1970, 1978, 1979, 1983, 1985. . . . NBA All-Defensive First Team, 1974, 1975, 1979, 1980, 1981. . . . NBA All-Defensive Second Team, 1970, 1971, 1976, 1977, 1978, 1984. . . . NBA Rookie of the Year, 1970. . . . NBA All-Rookie Team, 1970. . . . NBA Playoff MVP, 1971 and 1985. . . . Member of NBA championship teams, 1971, 1980, 1982, 1985, 1987, 1988. . . . Led NBA in scoring, 1971 and 1972. . . . Led NBA in rebounding, 1976. . . . Led NBA in field-goal percentage, 1977. . . . Led NBA in blocked shots, 1975, 1976, 1979, 1980. . . . Holds NBA records for most seasons played, most games played and most minutes played. . . . Holds NBA records for most points, field goals made, field goals attempted, blocked shots and personal fouls. . . . Holds NBA playoff records for most seasons, games played, field goals attempted, field goals made, points and personal fouls. . . . Holds NBA All-Star Game records for most points, games played, most minutes played, field goals attempted, field goals made and personal fouls. . . . THE SPORTING NEWS College Player of the Year, 1967 and 1969. . . . THE SPORTING NEWS All-America First Team, 1967, 1968, 1969. . . . NCAA Tournament Most Outstanding Player, 1967, 1968, 1969. . . . Member of NCAA championship teams, 1967, 1968, 1969. . . . Led NCAA in field-goal percentage, 1967 and 1969.

NATHANIEL ARCHIBALD
(Tiny or Nate)

Born September 2, 1948 at New York, N. Y. Height 6:01. Weight 160.

High School—Bronx, N. Y., DeWitt Clinton.

Colleges—Arizona Western College, Yuma, Ariz., and University of Texas-El Paso, El Paso, Tex.

Drafted by Cincinnati on second round, 1970 (19th pick).

Traded by Kansas City to New York Nets for Brian Taylor, Jim Eakins and two 1st round draft choices (1977 and 1978), September 10, 1976.

Traded by New Jersey to Buffalo for George Johnson and a 1979 1st round draft choice, September 1, 1977.

Traded by San Diego with Marvin Barnes, Billy Knight and two 2nd round draft choices (1981 and 1983) to Boston for Kermit Washington, Kevin Kunnert, Sidney Wicks and the draft rights to Freeman Williams, August 4, 1978.

Waived by Boston, July 22, 1983; signed by Milwaukee as a free agent, August 1, 1983.

—COLLEGIATE RECORD—

Arizona Western

Year	G.	Min.	FGA	FGM	Pct.	FTA	FTM	Pct.	Reb.	Pts.	Avg.
66-67	27	....	....	303	....	....	190	....	....	796	29.5

Texas-El Paso

Year	G.	Min.	FGA	FGM	Pct.	FTA	FTM	Pct.	Reb.	Pts.	Avg.
67-68	23	....	281	131	.466	140	102	.729	81	364	15.8
68-69	25	....	374	199	.532	194	161	.830	69	559	22.4

Year	G.	Min.	FGA	FGM	Pct.	FTA	FTM	Pct.	Reb.	Pts.	Avg.
69-70	25	....	351	180	.512	225	176	.782	66	536	21.4
Totals	73	....	1006	510	.507	559	439	.785	216	1459	20.0

NBA REGULAR SEASON RECORD

Sea.—Team	G.	Min.	FGA	FGM	Pct.	FTA	FTM	Pct.	Reb.	Ast.	PF	Disq.	Pts.	Avg.
70-71—Cincinnati	82	2867	1095	486	.444	444	336	.757	242	450	218	2	1308	16.0
71-72—Cincinnati	76	3272	1511	734	.486	824	677	.822	222	701	198	3	2145	28.2
72-73—K.C.-Omaha	80	3681	2106	1028	.488	783	663	.847	223	910	207	2	2719	34.0

									—Rebounds—									
Sea.—Team	G.	Min.	FGA	FGM	Pct.	FTA	FTM	Pct.	Off.	Def.	Tot.	Ast.	PF	Dq.	Stl.	Blk.	Pts.	Avg.
73-74—KC-Omaha	35	1272	492	222	.451	211	173	.820	21	64	85	266	76	0	56	7	617	17.6
74-75—KC-Omaha	82	3244	1664	759	.456	748	652	.872	48	174	222	557	187	0	119	7	2170	26.5
75-76—Kan. City	78	3184	1583	717	.453	625	501	.802	67	146	213	615	169	0	126	15	1935	24.8
76-77—NY Nets	34	1277	560	250	.446	251	197	.785	22	58	80	254	77	1	59	11	697	20.5
77-78—Buffalo	Injured—Torn Achilles Tendon																	
78-79—Boston	69	1662	573	259	.452	307	242	.788	25	78	103	324	132	2	55	6	760	11.0
79-80—Boston	80	2864	794	383	.482	435	361	.830	59	138	197	671	218	2	106	10	1131	14.1
80-81—Boston	80	2820	766	382	.499	419	342	.816	36	140	176	618	201	1	75	18	1106	13.8
81-82—Boston	68	2167	652	308	.472	316	236	.747	25	91	116	541	131	1	52	3	858	12.6
82-83—Boston	66	1811	553	235	.425	296	220	.743	25	66	91	409	110	1	38	4	695	10.5
83-84—Milwaukee	46	1038	279	136	.487	101	64	.634	16	60	76	160	78	0	33	0	340	7.4
Totals	876	31159	12628	5899	.467	5760	4664	.810			2046	6476	2002	15	719	81	16481	18.8

Three-Point Field Goals: 1979-80, 4-for-18 (.222). 1980-81, 0-for-9. 1981-82, 6-for-16 (.375). 1982-83, 5-for-24 (.208). 1983-84, 4-for-18 (.222). Totals, 19-for-85 (.224).

NBA PLAYOFF RECORD

									—Rebounds—									
Sea.—Team	G.	Min.	FGA	FGM	Pct.	FTA	FTM	Pct.	Off.	Def.	Tot.	Ast.	PF	Dq.	Stl.	Blk.	Pts.	Avg.
74-75—KC-Omaha	6	242	118	43	.364	43	35	.814	2	9	11	32	18	0	4	0	121	20.2
79-80—Boston	9	332	89	45	.506	42	37	.881	3	8	11	71	28	1	10	0	128	14.2
80-81—Boston	17	630	211	95	.450	94	76	.809	6	22	28	107	39	0	13	0	266	15.6
81-82—Boston	8	277	70	30	.429	28	25	.893	1	16	17	52	21	0	5	2	85	10.6
82-83—Boston	7	161	68	22	.324	29	22	.759	3	7	10	44	12	0	2	0	67	9.6
Totals	47	1642	556	235	.423	236	195	.826	15	62	77	306	118	1	34	2	667	14.2

Three-Point Field Goals: 1979-80, 1-for-2 (.500). 1980-81, 0-for-5. 1981-82, 0-for-4. 1982-83, 1-for-6. (.167). Totals, 2-for-17 (.118).

NBA ALL-STAR GAME RECORD

								—Rebounds—								
Season—Team	Min.	FGA	FGM	Pct.	FTA	FTM	Pct.	Off.	Def.	Tot.	Ast.	PF	Dq.	Stl.	Blk.	Pts.
1973—K.C.-Omaha	27	12	6	.500	5	5	1.000			1	5	1	0			17
1975—K.C.-Omaha	36	15	10	.667	8	7	.875	1	1	2	6	2	0	3	1	27
1976—Kansas City	30	13	5	.385	3	3	1.000	2	3	5	7	0	0	2	0	13
1980—Boston	21	8	0	.000	3	2	.667	1	2	3	6	1	0	2	0	2
1981—Boston	25	7	4	.571	3	1	.333	0	5	5	9	3	0	3	0	9
1982—Boston	23	5	2	.400	2	2	1.000	1	1	2	7	3	0	1	0	6
Totals	162	60	27	.450	24	20	.833	5	13	18	40	10	0	11	1	74

Named to All-NBA First Team, 1973, 1975, 1976. . . . All-NBA Second Team, 1972 and 1981. . . . Member of NBA championship team, 1981. . . . Led NBA in scoring, 1973. . . . Led NBA in assists, 1973. . . . NBA All-Star Game MVP, 1981.

PAUL JOSEPH ARIZIN

Born April 9, 1928 at Philadelphia, Pa. Height 6:04. Weight 200.

High School—Philadelphia, Pa., La Salle (Did not play varsity basketball).

College—Villanova University, Villanova, Pa.

Drafted by Philadelphia on first round, 1950.

Played in Eastern Basketball League with Camden Bullets, 1962-63 through 1964-65.

—COLLEGIATE RECORD—

Year	G.	Min.	FGA	FGM	Pct.	FTA	FTM	Pct.	Reb.	Pts.	Avg.
46-47	Did Not Play										
47-48	24	....	...	101	....	...	65	....	...	267	11.1
48-49	27	....	...	210	....	233	174	.747	...	594	22.0
49-50	29	....	527	260	.493	277	215	.776	...	735	25.3
Totals	80	....	...	571	....	...	454	....	...	1596	20.0

NBA REGULAR SEASON RECORD

Sea.—Team	G.	Min.	FGA	FGM	Pct.	FTA	FTM	Pct.	Reb.	Ast.	PF	Disq.	Pts.	Avg.
50-51—Philadelphia	65	....	864	352	.407	526	417	.793	640	138	284	18	1121	17.2
51-51—Philadelphia	66	2939	1222	548	.448	707	578	.818	745	170	250	5	1674	25.4
52-53—Philadelphia	Did Not Play—Military Service													
53-54—Philadelphia	Did Not Play—Military Service													

Sea.—Team	G.	Min.	FGA	FGM	Pct.	FTA	FTM	Pct.	Reb.	Ast.	PF	Disq.	Pts.	Avg.
54-55—Philadelphia	72	2953	1325	529	.399	585	454	.776	675	210	270	5	1512	21.0
55-56—Philadelphia	72	2724	1378	617	.448	626	507	.810	539	189	282	11	1741	24.2
56-57—Philadelphia	71	2767	1451	613	.422	713	591	.829	561	150	274	13	1817	25.6
57-58—Philadelphia	68	2377	1229	483	.393	544	440	.809	503	135	235	7	1406	20.7
58-59—Philadelphia	70	2799	1466	632	.431	722	587	.813	637	119	264	7	1851	26.4
59-60—Philadelphia	72	2618	1400	593	.423	526	420	.798	621	165	263	6	1606	22.3
60-61—Philadelphia	79	2905	1529	650	.425	639	532	.832	681	188	335	11	1832	23.2
61-62—Philadelphia	78	2785	1490	611	.410	601	484	.805	527	201	307	18	1706	21.9
Totals	713	....	13354	5628	.421	6189	5010	.810	6129	1665	2764	101	16266	22.8

NBA PLAYOFF RECORD

Sea.—Team	G.	Min.	FGA	FGM	Pct.	FTA	FTM	Pct.	Reb.	Ast.	PF	Disq.	Pts.	Avg.
50-51—Philadelphia	2	....	27	14	.519	16	13	.813	20	3	10	1	41	20.5
51-52—Philadelphia	3	120	53	24	.453	33	29	.879	38	8	17	2	77	25.7
55-56—Philadelphia	10	409	229	103	.450	99	83	.838	84	29	31	1	289	28.9
56-57—Philadelphia	2	22	8	3	.375	5	3	.600	8	1	3	0	9	4.5
57-58—Philadelphia	8	309	169	66	.391	72	56	.778	62	16	26	1	188	23.5
59-60—Philadelphia	9	371	195	84	.431	79	69	.873	86	33	29	0	237	26.3
60-61—Philadelphia	3	125	67	22	.328	33	23	.697	26	12	17	2	67	22.3
61-62—Philadelphia	12	459	253	95	.375	102	88	.863	80	26	44	1	278	23.2
Totals	49	....	1001	411	.411	439	364	.829	404	128	177	8	1186	24.2

NBA ALL-STAR GAME RECORD

Season—Team	Min.	FGA	FGM	Pct.	FTA	FTM	Pct.	Reb.	Ast.	PF	Disq.	Pts.
1951—Philadelphia	..	12	7	.583	2	1	.500	7	0	2	0	15
1952—Philadelphia	32	13	9	.692	8	8	1.000	6	0	1	0	26
1955—Philadelphia	23	9	4	.444	2	1	.500	2	2	5	0	9
1956—Philadelphia	28	13	5	.385	5	3	.600	7	1	6	1	13
1957—Philadelphia	26	13	6	.462	2	1	.500	5	0	2	0	13
1958—Philadelphia	29	17	11	.647	2	2	1.000	8	2	3	0	24
1959—Philadelphia	30	15	4	.267	9	8	.889	8	0	2	0	16
1960—Philadelphia	Selected—Injured, Did Not Play											
1961—Philadelphia	17	12	6	.500	5	5	1.000	2	1	4	0	17
1962—Philadelphia	21	12	2	.167	0	0	.000	2	0	4	0	4
Totals (9 games)	...	116	54	.466	35	29	.829	47	6	29	1	137

EBL REGULAR SEASON RECORD

			—2-Point—			—3-Point—									
Sea.—Team	G.	Min.	FGM	FGA	Pct.	FGM	FGA	Pct.	FTM	FTA	Pct.	Reb.	Ast.	Pts.	Avg.
62-63—Camden	28	....	264	...	...	...	...	...	196	249	.787	203	42	724	27.4
63-64—Camden	27	....	261	...	...	...	...	...	174	218	.798	226	52	696	25.8
64-65—Camden	28	....	226	...	...	3	...	...	196	244	.803	164	50	657	23.5

Named to NBA 25th Anniversary All-Time Team, 1970. . . . Elected to Naismith Memorial Basketball Hall of Fame, 1977. . . . Named to All-NBA First Team, 1952, 1956, 1957. . . . All-NBA Second Team, 1959. . . . NBA All-Star Game MVP, 1952. . . . Member of NBA championship team, 1956. . . . Led NBA in field-goal percentage, 1952. . . . Led NBA in scoring, 1952 and 1957. . . . Eastern Basketball League MVP, 1963. . . . Named to EBL All-Star First Team, 1963, 1964. . . . EBL All-Star Second Team, 1965. . . . Led NCAA Division I in scoring, 1950. . . . THE SPORTING NEWS College Player of the Year, 1950. . . . Named to THE SPORTING NEWS All-America First Team, 1950.

RICHARD FRANCIS DENNIS BARRY, III
(Rick)

Born March 28, 1944 at Elizabeth, N. J. Height 6:07. Weight 220.

High School—Roselle Park, N. J.

College—University of Miami, Coral Gables, Fla.

Drafted by San Francisco on first round, 1965.

Signed as free agent by Oakland ABA for 1968-69 season (sat out option season with San Francisco NBA, 1967-68).
Oakland franchise transferred to Washington, 1969.
Washington franchise transferred to Virginia, 1970.
Traded by Virginia to New York for a 1st round draft choice and cash, August, 1970.
Returned to NBA with Golden State, 1972.
Signed by Houston as a Veteran Free Agent, June 17, 1978; Golden State waived its right of first refusal in exchange for John Lucas and cash.

—COLLEGIATE RECORD—

Year	G.	Min.	FGA	FGM	Pct.	FTA	FTM	Pct.	Reb.	Pts.	Avg.
61-62†	17	....		208			73			489	28.8
62-63	24	....	341	162	.475	158	131	.829	351	455	19.0
63-64	27	....	572	314	.549	287	242	.843	448	870	32.2
64-65	26	....	651	340	.522	341	293	.859	475	973	37.4
Varsity Totals	77	....	1564	816	.522	786	666	.847	1274	2298	29.8

ABA REGULAR SEASON RECORD

Sea.—Team	G.	Min.	2-Point FGM	2-Point FGA	2-Point Pct.	3-Point FGM	3-Point FGA	3-Point Pct.	FTM	FTA	Pct.	Reb.	Ast.	Pts.	Avg.
67-68	Did Not Play—Sat Out Option Year														
68-69—Oakland	35	1361	389	757	.514	3	10	.300	403	454	.888	329	136	1190	34.0
69-70—Washington	52	1849	509	907	.511	8	39	.205	400	463	.864	363	178	1442	27.7
70-71—New York	59	2502	613	1262	.486	19	86	.221	451	507	.890	401	294	1734	29.4
71-72—New York	80	3616	829	1732	.479	73	237	.308	641	730	.878	602	327	2518	31.5
Totals	226	9328	2340	4748	.493	103	374	.275	1895	2154	.880	1695	935	6884	30.5

ABA PLAYOFF RECORD

Sea.—Team	G.	Min.	2-Point FGM	2-Point FGA	2-Point Pct.	3-Point FGM	3-Point FGA	3-Point Pct.	FTM	FTA	Pct.	Reb.	Ast.	Pts.	Avg.
69-70—Washington	7	302	105	194	.541	3	9	.333	62	68	.912	70	23	281	40.1
70-71—New York	6	287	46	108	.426	14	27	.519	48	59	.814	66	17	202	33.7
71-72—New York	18	749	180	368	.489	23	66	.348	125	146	.856	117	69	554	30.7
Totals	31	1338	331	670	.494	40	102	.392	235	273	.861	253	109	1037	33.5

ABA ALL-STAR GAME RECORD

Sea.—Team	Min.	2-Point FGM	2-Point FGA	2-Point Pct.	3-Point FGM	3-Point FGA	3-Point Pct.	FTM	FTA	Pct.	Reb.	Ast.	Pts.	Avg.
68-69—Oakland	12	3	9	.333	0	0	.000	4	5	.800	3	1	10	10.0
69-70—Washington	27	7	12	.583	0	0	.000	2	2	1.000	7	7	16	16.0
70-71—New York	17	4	6	.667	0	0	.000	6	6	1.000	2	2	14	14.0
71-72—New York	26	2	10	.200	0	0	.000	0	1	.000	12	8	4	4.0
Totals	82	16	37	.432	0	0	.000	12	14	.857	24	18	44	11.0

NBA REGULAR SEASON RECORD

Sea.—Team	G.	Min.	FGA	FGM	Pct.	FTA	FTM	Pct.	Reb.	Ast.	PF	Disq.	Pts.	Avg.
65-66—San Fran.	80	2990	1698	745	.439	660	569	.862	850	173	297	2	2059	25.7
66-67—San Fran.	78	3175	2240	1011	.451	852	753	.884	714	282	258	1	2775	35.6
72-73—Golden St.	82	3075	1630	737	.452	397	358	.902	728	399	245	2	1832	22.3

Sea.—Team	G.	Min.	FGA	FGM	Pct.	FTA	FTM	Pct.	Rebounds Off.	Rebounds Def.	Rebounds Tot.	Ast.	PF	Dq.	Stl.	Blk.	Pts.	Avg.
73-74—Golden St.	80	2918	1746	796	.456	464	417	.899	103	437	540	484	265	4	169	40	2009	25.1
74-75—Golden St.	80	3235	2217	1028	.464	436	394	.904	92	364	456	492	225	0	228	33	2450	30.6
75-76—Golden St.	81	3122	1624	707	.435	311	287	.923	74	422	496	496	215	1	202	27	1701	21.0
76-77—Golden St.	79	2904	1551	682	.440	392	359	.916	73	349	422	475	194	2	172	58	1723	21.8
77-78—Golden St.	82	3024	1686	760	.451	409	378	.924	75	374	449	446	188	1	158	45	1898	23.1
78-79—Houston	80	2566	1000	461	.461	169	160	.947	40	237	277	502	195	0	95	38	1082	13.5
79-80—Houston	72	1816	771	325	.422	153	143	.935	53	183	236	268	182	0	80	28	866	12.0
Totals	794	28825	16163	7252	.449	4243	3818	.900			5168	4017	2264	13	1104	269	18395	23.2

Three-Point Field Goals: 1979-80, 73-for-221 (.330).

NBA PLAYOFF RECORD

Sea.—Team	G.	Min.	FGA	FGM	Pct.	FTA	FTM	Pct.	Reb.	Ast.	PF	Disq.	Pts.	Avg.
66-67—San Fran.	15	614	489	197	.403	157	127	.809	113	58	49	0	521	34.7
72-73—Golden St.	11	292	164	65	.396	55	50	.909	54	24	41	1	180	16.4

Sea.—Team	G.	Min.	FGA	FGM	Pct.	FTA	FTM	Pct.	Rebounds Off.	Rebounds Def.	Rebounds Tot.	Ast.	PF	Dq.	Stl.	Blk.	Pts.	Avg.
74-75—Golden St.	17	726	426	189	.444	110	101	.918	22	72	94	103	51	1	50	15	479	28.2
75-76—Golden St.	13	532	289	126	.436	68	60	.882	20	64	84	84	40	1	38	14	312	24.0
76-77—Golden St.	10	415	262	122	.466	44	40	.909	25	34	59	47	32	0	17	7	284	28.4
78-79—Houston	2	65	25	8	.320	8	8	1.000	2	6	8	9	8	0	0	2	24	12.0
79-80—Houston	6	79	33	12	.364	6	6	1.000	0	6	6	15	11	0	1	1	33	5.5
Totals	74	2723	1688	719	.426	448	392	.875			418	340	232	3	106	39	1833	24.8

Three-Point Field Goals: 1979-80, 3-for-12 (.250).

NBA ALL-STAR GAME RECORD

Season—Team	Min.	FGA	FGM	Pct.	FTA	FTM	Pct.	Reb.	Ast.	PF	Disq.	Pts.
1966—San Francisco	17	10	4	.400	4	2	.500	2	2	6	1	10
1967—San Francisco	34	27	16	.593	8	6	.750	6	3	5	0	38
1973—Golden State	Selected—Injured, Did Not Play											

Season—Team	Min.	FGA	FGM	Pct.	FTA	FTM	Pct.	Rebounds Off.	Rebounds Def.	Rebounds Tot.	Ast.	PF	Dq.	Stl.	Blk.	Pts.
1974—Golden St.	19	6	3	.500	2	2	1.000	1	3	4	3	3	0	1	0	8
1975—Golden St.	38	20	11	.550	0	0	.000	1	4	5	8	4	0	8	1	22
1976—Golden St.	28	15	6	.400	5	5	1.000	2	2	4	2	5	0	2	0	17
1977—Golden St.	29	16	7	.438	4	4	1.000	1	3	4	8	1	0	2	0	18
1978—Golden St.	30	17	7	.412	1	1	1.000	2	2	4	5	6	1	3	0	15
Totals	195	111	54	.486	24	20	.833			29	31	30	2	16	1	128

Elected to Naismith Memorial Basketball Hall of Fame, 1986. . . . Named to All-NBA First Team, 1966, 1967, 1974, 1975, 1976. . . . All-NBA Second Team, 1973. . . . NBA Rookie of the Year, 1966. . . . NBA All-Rookie Team, 1966. . . . NBA Playoff MVP, 1975. . . . Shares NBA record for most free throws made in one quarter, 14, vs. New York, December 6, 1966. . . . NBA all-time leader in free-throw percentage. . . . NBA All-Star Game MVP, 1967. . . . Holds NBA All-Star Game record for most field goals attempted in one game, 27, in 1967. . . . Shares NBA All-Star Game record for most free throws made in one half, 10, in 1967. . . . Holds NBA record for most field-goal attempts in championship series game, 48, and shares record for most field goals, 22, vs. Philadelphia, April 18, 1967. . . . Shares NBA record for most free throws made in one half of championship series game, 12, vs. Philadelphia, April 24, 1967. . . . Holds NBA record

for most field-goal attempts in one quarter of championship series game, 17, vs. Philadelphia, April 14, 1967. . . . Shares NBA record for most three-point field goals, 8, vs. Utah, February 9, 1980. . . . Member of NBA championship team, 1975. . . . Led NBA in scoring, 1967. . . . Led NBA in steals, 1975. . . . Led NBA in free-throw percentage, 1973, 1975, 1976, 1978, 1979, 1980. . . . ABA All-Star First Team, 1969, 1970, 1971, 1972. . . . Led ABA in scoring, 1969. . . . Led ABA in free-throw percentage, 1969, 1971, 1972. . . . Named to THE SPORTING NEWS All-America Second Team, 1965.

ELGIN GAY BAYLOR

Born September 16, 1934 at Washington, D. C. Height 6:05. Weight 225.

High Schools—Washington, D. C., Phelps Vocational (Fr.-Jr.) and Spingarn (Sr.).

Colleges—The College of Idaho, Caldwell, Idaho, and Seattle University, Seattle, Wash.

Drafted by Minneapolis on first round as junior eligible, 1958.

—COLLEGIATE RECORD—

College of Idaho

Year	G.	Min.	FGA	FGM	Pct.	FTA	FTM	Pct.	Reb.	Pts.	Avg.
54-55	26	....	651	332	.510	232	150	.647	492	814	31.3

Seattle

Year	G.	Min.	FGA	FGM	Pct.	FTA	FTM	Pct.	Reb.	Pts.	Avg.
55-56				Did Not Play—Transfer Student							
56-57	25	....	555	271	.488	251	201	.801	508	743	29.7
57-58	29	....	697	353	.506	308	237	.769	559	943	32.5
Totals	54	....	1252	624	.498	559	438	.784	1067	1686	31.2
College Totals	80	....	1903	956	.502	791	588	.743	1559	2500	31.3

NOTE: 1954-55 rebound figures are for 24 games. Baylor played for Westside Ford, an AAU team in Seattle, during 1955-56 season (averaged 34 points per game).

NBA REGULAR SEASON RECORD

Sea.—Team	G.	Min.	FGA	FGM	Pct.	FTA	FTM	Pct.	Reb.	Ast.	PF	Disq.	Pts.	Avg.
58-59—Minneapolis	70	2855	1482	605	.408	685	532	.777	1050	287	270	4	1742	24.9
59-60—Minneapolis	70	2873	1781	755	.424	770	564	.732	1150	243	234	2	2074	29.6
60-61—Los Angeles	73	3133	2166	931	.430	863	676	.783	1447	371	279	3	2538	34.8
61-62—Los Angeles	48	2129	1588	680	.428	631	476	.754	892	222	155	1	1836	38.3
62-63—Los Angeles	80	3370	2273	1029	.453	790	661	.837	1146	386	226	1	2719	34.0
63-64—Los Angeles	78	3164	1778	756	.425	586	471	.804	936	347	235	1	1983	25.4
64-65—Los Angeles	74	3056	1903	763	.401	610	483	.792	950	280	235	0	2009	27.1
65-66—Los Angeles	65	1975	1034	415	.401	337	249	.739	621	224	157	0	1079	16.6
66-67—Los Angeles	70	2706	1658	711	.429	541	440	.813	898	215	211	1	1862	26.6
67-68—Los Angeles	77	3029	1709	757	.443	621	488	.786	941	355	232	0	2002	26.0
68-69—Los Angeles	76	3064	1632	730	.447	567	421	.743	805	408	204	0	1881	24.8
69-70—Los Angeles	54	2213	1051	511	.486	357	276	.773	559	292	132	1	1298	24.0
70-71—Los Angeles	2	57	19	8	.421	6	4	.667	11	2	6	0	20	10.0
71-72—Los Angeles	9	239	97	42	.433	27	22	.815	57	18	20	0	106	11.8
Totals	846	33863	20171	8693	.431	7391	5763	.780	11463	3650	2596	14	23149	27.4

NBA PLAYOFF RECORD

Sea.—Team	G.	Min.	FGA	FGM	Pct.	FTA	FTM	Pct.	Reb.	Ast.	PF	Disq.	Pts.	Avg.
58-59—Minneapolis	13	556	303	122	.403	113	87	.770	156	43	52	0	331	25.5
59-60—Minneapolis	9	408	234	111	.474	94	79	.840	128	31	38	0	301	33.4
60-61—Los Angeles	12	540	362	170	.470	142	117	.824	183	55	44	1	457	38.1
61-62—Los Angeles	13	571	425	186	.428	168	130	.774	230	47	45	1	502	38.6
62-63—Los Angeles	13	562	362	160	.442	126	104	.825	177	58	58	0	424	32.6
63-64—Los Angeles	5	221	119	45	.378	40	31	.775	58	28	17	0	121	24.2
64-65—Los Angeles	1	5	2	0	.000	0	0	.000	0	1	0	0	0	0.0
65-66—Los Angeles	14	586	328	145	.442	105	85	.810	197	52	38	0	375	26.8
66-67—Los Angeles	3	121	76	28	.368	20	15	.750	39	9	6	0	71	23.7
67-68—Los Angeles	15	633	376	176	.468	112	76	.679	218	60	41	0	428	28.5
68-69—Los Angeles	18	640	278	107	.385	100	63	.630	166	74	56	0	277	15.4
69-70—Los Angeles	18	667	296	138	.466	81	60	.741	173	83	50	1	336	18.7
Totals	134	5510	3161	1388	.439	1101	847	.769	1725	541	445	3	3623	27.0

NBA ALL-STAR GAME RECORD

Season—Team	Min.	FGA	FGM	Pct.	FTA	FTM	Pct.	Reb.	Ast.	PF	Disq.	Pts.
1959—Minneapolis	32	20	10	.500	5	4	.800	11	1	3	0	24
1960—Minneapolis	28	18	10	.556	7	5	.714	13	3	4	0	25
1961—Los Angeles	27	11	3	.273	10	9	.900	10	4	5	0	15
1962—Los Angeles	37	23	10	.435	14	12	.857	9	4	2	0	32
1963—Los Angeles	36	15	4	.267	13	9	.692	14	7	0	0	17
1964—Los Angeles	29	15	5	.333	11	5	.455	8	5	1	0	15
1965—Los Angeles	27	13	5	.385	8	8	1.000	7	0	4	0	18
1967—Los Angeles	20	14	8	.571	4	4	1.000	5	5	2	0	20
1968—Los Angeles	27	13	8	.615	7	6	.857	6	1	5	0	22
1969—Los Angeles	32	13	5	.385	12	11	.917	9	5	2	0	21
1970—Los Angeles	26	9	2	.222	7	5	.714	7	3	3	0	9
Totals	321	164	70	.427	98	78	.796	99	38	31	0	218

ELGIN BAYLOR

NBA COACHING RECORD

Sea.	Club	Regular Season W.	L.	Pct.	Pos.
1974-75	—New Orleans......	0	1	.000	...†
1976-77	—New Orleans......	21	35	.375	5†
1977-78	—New Orleans......	39	43	.476	5†
1978-79	—New Orleans......	26	56	.317	6†
Totals (4 seasons)		86	135	.389	

†Central Division.

Named to NBA 35th Anniversary All-Time Team, 1980. . . . Elected to Naismith Memorial Basketball Hall of Fame, 1976. . . . Named to All-NBA First Team, 1959, 1960, 1961, 1962, 1963, 1964, 1965, 1967, 1968, 1969. . . . NBA Rookie of the Year, 1959. . . . Shares NBA record for most field goals in championship series game, 22, vs. Boston, April 14, 1962. . . . Holds NBA records for most points, 33, and most field-goal attempts, 25, in one half of championship series game, vs. Boston, April 14, 1962. . . . NBA All-Star Game co-MVP, 1959. . . . Holds NBA All-Star Game records for most career free throws made and most field goals attempted in one half, 15, in 1959. . . . Shares NBA All-Star Game records for most career free throws attempted and most free throws made in one game, 12, in 1962. . . . Led NCAA Division I in rebounding, 1957. . . . NCAA University Division tournament MVP, 1958. . . . Named to THE SPORTING NEWS All-America First Team, 1958.

WALTER JONES BELLAMY
(Walt)

Born July 24, 1939 at New Bern, N. C. Height 6:11. Weight 245.

High School—New Bern, N. C., J. T. Barber.

College—Indiana University, Bloomington, Ind.

Drafted by Chicago on first round, 1961.

Chicago franchise moved to Baltimore, 1963.
Traded by Baltimore to New York for John Green, John Egan, Jim Barnes and cash, November 2, 1965.
Traded by New York with Howard Komives to Detroit for Dave DeBusschere, December 19, 1968.
Traded by Detroit to Atlanta for a player to be designated, February 1, 1970. Detroit received John Arthurs from Milwaukee as part of deal.
Selected from Atlanta by New Orleans in expansion draft, May 20, 1974.
Waived by New Orleans, October 18, 1974.

—COLLEGIATE RECORD—

Year	G.	Min.	FGA	FGM	Pct.	FTA	FTM	Pct.	Reb.	Pts.	Avg.
57-58†	(Freshman team did not play intercollegiate schedule.)										
58-59	22	....	289	148	.512	141	86	.610	335	382	17.4
59-60	24	....	396	212	.535	161	113	.702	324	537	22.4
60-61	24	....	389	195	.501	204	132	.647	428	522	21.8
Varsity Totals	70	....	1074	555	.517	506	331	.654	1087	1441	20.6

NBA REGULAR SEASON RECORD

Sea.—Team	G.	Min.	FGA	FGM	Pct.	FTA	FTM	Pct.	Reb.	Ast.	PF	Disq.	Pts.	Avg.
61-62—Chicago	79	3344	1875	973	.519	853	549	.644	1500	210	281	6	2495	31.6
62-63—Chicago	80	3306	1595	840	.527	821	553	.674	1309	233	283	7	2233	27.9
63-64—Baltimore	80	3394	1582	811	.513	825	537	.651	1361	126	300	7	2159	27.0
64-65—Baltimore	80	3301	1441	733	.509	752	515	.685	1166	191	260	2	1981	24.8
65-66—Balt.-N.Y.	80	3352	1373	695	.506	689	430	.624	1254	235	294	9	1820	22.8
66-67—New York	79	3010	1084	565	.521	580	369	.637	1064	206	275	5	1499	19.0
67-68—New York	82	2695	944	511	.541	529	350	.662	961	164	259	3	1372	16.7
68-69—N.Y.-Det.	88	3159	1103	563	.510	618	401	.649	1101	176	320	5	1527	17.4
69-70—Det.-Atl.	79	2028	671	351	.523	373	215	.576	707	143	260	5	917	11.6
70-71—Atlanta	82	2908	879	433	.493	556	336	.604	1060	230	271	4	1202	14.7
71-72—Atlanta	82	3187	1089	593	.544	581	340	.585	1049	262	255	2	1526	18.6
72-73—Atlanta	74	2802	901	455	.505	526	283	.538	964	179	244	1	1193	16.1

Sea.—Team	G.	Min.	FGA	FGM	Pct.	FTA	FTM	Pct.	—Rebounds— Off.	Def.	Tot.	Ast.	PF	Dq.	Stl.	Blk.	Pts.	Avg.
73-74—Atlanta	77	2440	801	389	.486	383	233	.608	264	476	740	189	232	2	52	48	1011	13.1
74-75—N. O.	1	14	2	2	1.000	2	2	1.000	0	5	5	0	2	0	0	0	6	6.0
Totals	1043	38940	15340	7914	.516	8088	5113	.632			14241	2544	3536	58	52	48	20941	20.1

NBA PLAYOFF RECORD

Sea.—Team	G.	Min.	FGA	FGM	Pct.	FTA	FTM	Pct.	Reb.	Ast.	PF	Disq.	Pts.	Avg.
64-65—Baltimore	10	427	158	74	.468	92	61	.663	151	34	38	0	209	20.9
66-67—New York	4	157	54	28	.519	29	17	.586	66	12	15	0	73	18.3
67-68—New York	6	277	107	45	.421	48	30	.625	96	21	22	0	120	20.0
69-70—Atlanta	9	368	126	59	.468	46	33	.717	140	35	32	0	151	16.8
70-71—Atlanta	5	216	69	41	.594	29	22	.759	72	10	16	0	104	20.8
71-72—Atlanta	6	247	86	42	.488	43	27	.628	82	11	20	0	111	18.5
72-73—Atlanta	6	247	86	34	.395	31	14	.452	73	13	17	0	82	13.7
Totals	46	1939	686	323	.471	318	204	.642	680	136	160	0	850	18.5

NBA ALL-STAR GAME RECORD

Season—Team	Min.	FGA	FGM	Pct.	FTA	FTM	Pct.	Reb.	Ast.	PF	Disq.	Pts.
1962—Chicago	29	18	10	.556	8	3	.375	17	1	6	1	23
1963—Chicago	14	4	1	.250	2	0	.000	1	2	3	0	2
1964—Baltimore	23	11	4	.364	5	3	.600	7	0	3	0	11
1965—Baltimore	17	5	4	.800	4	4	1.000	5	1	3	0	12
Totals	83	38	19	.500	19	10	.526	30	4	15	1	48

Named NBA Rookie of the Year, 1962. . . . Led NBA in field-goal percentage, 1962. . . . Holds NBA record for most games played in one season, 1969. . . . Member of U.S. Olympic Team, 1960. . . . Named to THE SPORTING NEWS All-America Second Team, 1961.

DAVID BING
(Dave)

Born November 24, 1943 at Washington, D. C. Height 6:03. Weight 185.
High School—Washington, D. C., Spingarn.
College—Syracuse University, Syracuse, N. Y.
Drafted by Detroit on first round, 1966 (2nd pick).

Traded by Detroit with a 1977 1st round draft choice to Washington for Kevin Porter, August 28, 1975.
Waived by Washington, September 20, 1977; signed by Boston as a free agent, September 28, 1977.

—COLLEGIATE RECORD—

Year	G.	Min.	FGA	FGM	Pct.	FTA	FTM	Pct.	Reb.	Pts.	Avg.
62-63†	17	....	341	170	.499	131	97	.740	192	437	25.7
63-64	25	....	460	215	.467	172	126	.733	206	556	22.2
64-65	23	....	444	206	.464	162	121	.747	277	533	23.2
65-66	28	....	569	308	.541	222	178	.802	303	794	28.4
Varsity Totals	76	....	1473	729	.495	556	425	.764	786	1883	24.8

NBA REGULAR SEASON RECORD

Sea.—Team	G.	Min.	FGA	FGM	Pct.	FTA	FTM	Pct.	Reb.	Ast.	PF	Disq.	Pts.	Avg.
66-67—Detroit	80	2762	1522	664	.436	370	273	.738	359	330	217	2	1601	20.6
67-68—Detroit	79	3209	1893	835	.441	668	472	.707	373	509	254	2	2142	27.1
68-69—Detroit	77	3039	1594	678	.425	623	444	.713	382	546	256	3	1800	23.4
69-70—Detroit	70	2334	1295	575	.444	580	454	.783	299	418	196	0	1604	22.9
70-71—Detroit	82	3065	1710	799	.467	772	615	.797	364	408	228	4	2213	27.0
71-72—Detroit	45	1936	891	369	.414	354	278	.785	186	317	138	3	1016	22.6
72-73—Detroit	82	3361	1545	692	.448	560	456	.814	298	637	229	1	1840	22.4

									—Rebounds—									
Sea.—Team	G.	Min.	FGA	FGM	Pct.	FTA	FTM	Pct.	Off.	Def.	Tot.	Ast.	PF	Dq.	Stl.	Blk.	Pts.	Avg.
73-74—Detroit	81	3124	1336	582	.436	438	356	.813	108	173	281	555	216	1	109	17	1520	18.0
74-75—Detroit	79	3222	1333	578	.434	424	343	.809	86	200	286	610	222	3	116	26	1499	19.0
75-76—Wash.	82	2945	1113	497	.447	422	332	.787	94	143	237	492	262	0	118	23	1326	16.2
76-77—Wash.	64	1516	597	271	.454	176	136	.773	54	89	143	275	150	1	61	5	678	10.6
77-78—Boston	80	2256	940	422	.449	296	244	.824	76	136	212	300	247	2	79	18	1088	13.6
Totals	901	32769	15769	6962	.441	5683	4403	.775			3420	5397	2615	22	483	89	18327	20.3

NBA PLAYOFF RECORD

									—Rebounds—									
Sea.—Team	G.	Min.	FGA	FGM	Pct.	FTA	FTM	Pct.	Off.	Def.	Tot.	Ast.	PF	Dq.	Stl.	Blk.	Pts.	Avg.
67-68—Detroit	6	254	166	68	.410	45	33	.763			24	29	21	0			169	28.2
73-74—Detroit	7	312	131	55	.420	30	22	.733	6	20	26	42	20	0	3	1	132	18.9
74-75—Detroit	3	134	47	20	.426	13	8	.615	3	8	11	29	12	0	5	0	48	16.0
75-76—Wash.	7	209	76	34	.447	35	28	.800	6	12	18	28	18	0	7	2	96	13.7
76-77—Wash.	8	55	32	14	.438	4	4	1.000	3	3	6	5	5	0	0	1	32	4.0
Totals	31	964	452	191	.423	127	95	.748			85	133	76	0	15	4	477	15.4

NBA ALL-STAR GAME RECORD

Season—Team	Min.	FGA	FGM	Pct.	FTA	FTM	Pct.	Reb.	Ast.	PF	Disq.	Pts.
1968—Detroit	20	7	4	.571	1	1	1.000	2	4	3	0	9
1969—Detroit	13	3	1	.333	1	1	1.000	0	3	0	0	3
1971—Detroit	19	7	2	.286	0	0	.000	2	2	1	0	4
1973—Detroit	19	4	0	.000	2	2	1.000	3	0	1	0	2

								—Rebounds—								
Season—Team	Min.	FGA	FGM	Pct.	FTA	FTM	Pct.	Off.	Def.	Tot.	Ast.	PF	Dq.	Stl.	Blk.	Pts.
1974—Detroit	16	9	2	.222	1	1	1.000	1	5	6	2	1	0	0	0	5
1975—Detroit	12	2	0	.000	2	2	1.000	0	0	0	1	0	0	0	0	2
1976—Washington	26	11	7	.636	2	2	1.000	1	2	3	4	1	0	0	0	16
Totals	125	43	16	.372	9	9	1.000			16	16	7	0	0	0	41

Elected to Naismith Memorial Basketball Hall of Fame, 1989. . . . Named to All-NBA First Team, 1968 and 1971. . . . All-NBA Second Team, 1974. . . . NBA Rookie of the Year, 1967. . . . NBA All-Rookie Team, 1967. . . . Led NBA in scoring, 1968. . . . NBA All-Star Game MVP, 1976. . . . Named to THE SPORTING NEWS All-America First Team, 1965.

RONALD BRUCE BOONE

Born September 6, 1946 at Oklahoma City, Okla. Height 6:02. Weight 200.

High School—Omaha, Neb., Tech.

Colleges—Iowa Western Community College, Clarinda, Iowa, and Idaho State University, Pocatello, Idaho.

Drafted by Phoenix on eleventh round, 1968 (147th pick).

Selected by Dallas on eighth round of ABA draft, 1968.
Traded by Dallas with Glen Combs to Utah for Donnie Freeman and Wayne Hightower, January 8, 1971.
Sold by Utah to St. Louis, December 2, 1975.
Selected by Kansas City NBA from St. Louis for $250,000 in ABA dispersal draft, August 5, 1976.
Traded by Kansas City with a 1979 2nd round draft choice to Denver for Darnell Hillman and the draft rights to Mike Evans, June 26, 1978.
Traded by Denver with two 1979 2nd round draft choices to Los Angeles for Charlie Scott, June 26, 1978.
Traded by Los Angeles to Utah for a 1981 3rd round draft choice, October 25, 1979.
Waived by Utah, January 26, 1981.

Iowa Western CC

Year	G.	Min.	FGA	FGM	Pct.	FTA	FTM	Pct.	Reb.	Pts.	Avg.
64-65	9	....	....	....	....	....	....	....	....	227	25.2

Idaho State

Year	G.	Min.	FGA	FGM	Pct.	FTA	FTM	Pct.	Reb.	Pts.	Avg.
65-66	10	....	119	46	.387	26	17	.654	95	109	10.9
66-67	25	....	416	199	.478	215	160	.744	128	558	22.3
67-68	26	....	519	223	.430	159	108	.679	110	554	21.3
Totals	61	....	1054	468	.444	400	285	.713	333	1221	20.0

ABA REGULAR SEASON RECORD

			2-Point			3-Point									
Sea.—Team	G.	Min.	FGM	FGA	Pct.	FGM	FGA	Pct.	FTM	FTA	Pct.	Reb.	Ast.	Pts.	Avg.
68-69—Dallas	78	2682	518	1182	.438	2	15	.133	436	537	.812	394	279	1478	18.9
69-70—Dallas	84	2340	406	925	.439	17	55	.309	300	382	.785	366	272	1163	13.9
70-71—Dallas-Utah	86	2476	.561	1257	.446	49	138	.355	278	357	.779	564	256	1547	18.0
71-72—Utah	84	2040	391	897	.436	13	65	.200	271	341	.795	393	233	1092	13.0
72-73—Utah	84	2585	556	1096	.507	10	40	.250	415	479	.866	423	353	1557	18.5
73-74—Utah	84	3098	581	1162	.500	6	26	.231	300	343	.875	435	417	1480	17.6
74-75—Utah	84	3414	862	1743	.495	10	33	.303	363	422	.860	406	372	2117	25.2
75-76—Utah-St. Louis	78	2961	697	1424	.489	16	43	.372	277	318	.871	319	387	1719	22.0
Totals	662	21586	4572	9686	.472	123	415	.296	2640	3179	.830	3302	2569	12153	18.4

ABA PLAYOFF RECORD

			2-Point			3-Point									
Sea.—Team	G.	Min.	FGM	FGA	Pct.	FGM	FGA	Pct.	FTM	FTA	Pct.	Reb.	Ast.	Pts.	Avg.
68-69—Dallas	7	196	38	81	.469	0	4	.000	21	25	.840	22	27	97	13.9
69-70—Dallas	6	193	43	89	.483	3	8	.375	15	21	.714	27	27	110	18.3
70-71—Utah	18	569	104	229	.454	9	27	.333	74	86	.860	110	94	309	17.2
71-72—Utah	11	209	49	100	.490	1	5	.200	25	29	.862	24	26	126	11.5
72-73—Utah	10	360	68	132	.515	0	3	.000	33	34	.971	43	47	169	16.9
73-74—Utah	18	747	137	282	.486	0	7	.000	34	37	.919	108	109	308	17.1
74-75—Utah	6	219	54	127	.425	0	0	.000	34	38	.895	24	41	142	23.7
Totals	76	2493	493	1040	.474	13	54	.240	236	270	.874	358	371	1261	16.6

ABA ALL-STAR GAME RECORD

		2-Point			3-Point									
Sea.—Team	Min.	FGM	FGA	Pct.	FGM	FGA	Pct.	FTM	FTA	Pct.	Reb.	Ast.	Pts.	Avg.
1971—Utah	4	2	4	.500	0	0	.000	2	3	.667	2	0	6	6.0
1974—Utah	24	6	11	.545	1	2	.500	0	0	.000	3	5	15	15.0
1975—Utah	23	4	8	.500	0	0	.000	2	2	1.000	2	2	10	10.0
1976—St. Louis	16	5	11	.455	0	0	.000	0	0	.000	3	2	10	10.0
Totals	67	17	34	.500	1	2	.500	4	5	.800	10	9	41	10.3

NBA REGULAR SEASON RECORD

									—Rebounds—									
Sea.—Team	G.	Min.	FGA	FGM	Pct.	FTA	FTM	Pct.	Off.	Def.	Tot.	Ast.	PF	Dq.	Stl.	Blk.	Pts.	Avg.
76-77—Kan. City	82	3021	1577	747	.474	384	324	.844	128	193	321	338	258	1	119	19	1818	22.2
77-78—Kan. City	82	2653	1271	563	.443	377	322	.854	112	157	269	311	233	3	105	11	1448	17.7
78-79—Los Ang.	82	1583	569	259	.455	104	90	.865	53	92	145	154	171	1	66	11	608	7.4
79-80—L.A.-Utah	81	2392	915	405	.443	196	175	.893	54	173	227	309	232	3	97	3	1004	12.4
80-81—Utah	52	1146	371	160	.431	94	75	.798	17	67	84	161	126	0	33	8	406	7.8
Totals	379	10795	4703	2134	.454	1155	986	.854	364	682	1046	1273	1020	8	420	52	5284	13.9

Three-Point Field Goals: 1979-80, 19-for-50 (.380). 1980-81, 11-for-39 (.282). Totals, 30-for-89 (.337).

NBA PLAYOFF RECORD

									—Rebounds—									
Sea.—Team	G.	Min.	FGA	FGM	Pct.	FTA	FTM	Pct.	Off.	Def.	Tot.	Ast.	PF	Dq.	Stl.	Blk.	Pts.	Avg.
78-79—Los Ang.	8	226	77	37	.481	21	20	.952	7	8	15	14	28	0	9	0	94	11.8

Set professional basketball record by playing in 1,041 consecutive games. . . . Named to ABA All-Star First Team, 1975. . . . ABA All-Star Second Team, 1974. . . . ABA All-Rookie Team, 1969. . . . Member of ABA championship team, 1971.

BILL BRIDGES

Born April 4, 1939 at Hobbs, N. M. Height 6:06. Weight 235.
High School—Hobbs, N. M.
College—University of Kansas, Lawrence, Kan.
Drafted by Chicago on third round, 1961. (32nd pick).

Draft rights traded by Chicago (Baltimore) with Ralph Davis to St. Louis for Al Ferrari and Shellie McMillion, June 14, 1962.
Traded by Atlanta to Philadelphia for Jim Washington, November 19, 1971.
Traded by Philadelphia with Mel Counts to Los Angeles for Leroy Ellis and John Q. Trapp, November 2, 1972.
Waived by Los Angeles, December 6, 1974; signed by Golden State as a free agent, March 1, 1975.
Played in American Basketball League with Kansas City Steers, 1961-62 and 1962-63.

—COLLEGIATE RECORD—

Year	G.	Min.	FGA	FGM	Pct.	FTA	FTM	Pct.	Reb.	Pts.	Avg.
57-58†	(Freshman team did not play intercollegiate schedule)										
58-59	25	....	307	117	.381	129	74	.574	343	308	12.3
59-60	28	....	293	112	.382	142	94	.662	385	318	11.4
60-61	25	....	334	146	.437	155	110	.710	353	402	16.1
Varsity Totals	78	....	934	375	.401	426	278	.653	1081	1028	13.2

ABL REGULAR SEASON RECORD

			—2-Point—			—3-Point—									
Sea.—Team	G.	Min.	FGM	FGA	Pct.	FGM	FGA	Pct.	FTM	FTA	Pct.	Reb.	Ast.	Pts.	Avg.
61-62—Kan. City	79	3259	638	1400	.456	3	12	.250	412	587	.702	1059	181	1697	21.4
62-63—Kan. City	29	1185	312	606	.515	0	2	.000	225	289	.779	437	87	849	29.2

NBA REGULAR SEASON RECORD

Sea.—Team	G.	Min.	FGA	FGM	Pct.	FTA	FTM	Pct.	Reb.	Ast.	PF	Disq.	Pts.	Avg.
62-63—St. Louis	27	374	160	66	.413	51	32	.627	144	23	58	0	164	6.1
63-64—St. Louis	80	1949	675	268	.397	224	146	.652	680	181	269	6	682	8.5
64-65—St. Louis	79	2362	938	362	.386	275	186	.676	853	187	276	3	910	11.5
65-66—St. Louis	78	2677	927	377	.407	364	257	.706	951	208	333	11	1011	13.0
66-67—St. Louis	79	3130	1106	503	.455	523	367	.702	1190	222	325	12	1373	17.4
67-68—St. Louis	82	3197	1009	466	.462	484	347	.717	1102	253	366	12	1279	15.6
68-69—Atlanta	80	2930	775	351	.453	353	239	.677	1132	298	290	3	941	11.8
69-70—Atlanta	82	3269	932	443	.475	451	331	.734	1181	345	292	6	1217	14.8
70-71—Atlanta	82	3140	834	382	.458	330	211	.639	1233	240	317	7	975	11.9
71-72—Atl.-Phil.	78	2756	779	379	.487	316	222	.703	1051	198	269	6	980	12.6
72-73—Phil-LA	82	2867	722	333	.461	255	179	.702	904	219	296	3	845	10.3

									—Rebounds—									
Sea.—Team	G.	Min.	FGA	FGM	Pct.	FTA	FTM	Pct.	Off.	Def.	Tot.	Ast.	PF	Dq.	Stl.	Blk.	Pts.	Avg.
73-74—L.A.	65	1812	513	216	.421	164	116	.707	193	306	499	148	219	3	58	31	548	8.4
74-75—LA-GS	32	415	93	35	.376	34	17	.500	64	70	134	31	65	1	11	5	87	2.7
Totals	926	30878	9463	4181	.442	3824	2650	.693			11054	2553	3375	73	69	36	11012	11.9

NBA PLAYOFF RECORD

Sea.—Team	G.	Min.	FGA	FGM	Pct.	FTA	FTM	Pct.	Reb.	Ast.	PF	Disq.	Pts.	Avg.
62-63—St. Louis	11	204	96	41	.427	27	20	.741	86	9	31	0	102	9.3
63-64—St. Louis	12	240	83	26	.313	19	12	.632	84	24	40	0	64	5.3
64-65—St. Louis	4	145	59	21	.356	15	10	.667	67	9	19	1	52	13.0
65-66—St. Louis	10	421	170	86	.506	43	31	.721	149	28	47	2	203	20.3
66-67—St. Louis	9	369	128	48	.375	67	45	.672	169	22	36	2	141	15.7
67-68—St. Louis	6	216	75	38	.507	25	18	.720	77	14	23	0	94	15.7
68-69—Atlanta	11	442	156	69	.442	48	34	.708	178	37	48	2	172	15.6
69-70—Atlanta	9	381	110	44	.400	27	16	.593	154	29	37	1	104	11.6
70-71—Atlanta	5	229	58	23	.397	9	3	.333	104	5	17	0	49	9.8
72-73—Los Ang.	17	582	136	57	.419	49	38	.776	158	29	68	2	152	8.9

									—Rebounds—									
Sea.—Team	G.	Min.	FGA	FGM	Pct.	FTA	FTM	Pct.	Off.	Def.	Tot.	Ast.	PF	Dq.	Stl.	Blk.	Pts.	Avg.
73-74—L.A.	5	144	41	12	.293	13	6	.462	14	16	30	6	19	0	7	0	30	6.0
74-75—G.S.	14	148	23	10	.435	7	2	.286	13	36	49	7	23	0	9	4	22	1.6
Totals	113	3521	1135	475	.419	349	235	.673			1305	219	408	10	16	4	1185	10.5

NBA ALL-STAR GAME RECORD

Season—Team	Min.	FGA	FGM	Pct.	FTA	FTM	Pct.	Reb.	Ast.	PF	Disq.	Pts.
1967—St. Louis	17	5	4	.800	2	0	.000	3	3	1	0	8
1968—St. Louis	21	9	7	.778	4	1	.250	7	1	4	0	15
1970—Atlanta	15	2	2	1.000	5	1	.200	4	2	1	0	5
Totals	53	16	13	.813	11	2	.182	14	6	6	0	28

Named to NBA All-Defensive Second Team, 1969 and 1970. . . . Member of NBA championship team, 1975. . . . Named to ABL All-Star First Team, 1962. . . . Led ABL in scoring, 1963. . . . Led ABL in rebounding, 1962 and 1963. . . . Set ABL single-game scoring record with 55 points vs. Oakland, December 9, 1962. . . . Member of ABL championship team, 1963.

WILTON NORMAN CHAMBERLAIN
(Wilt)

Born August 21, 1936 at Philadelphia, Pa. Height 7:01. Weight 275.
High School—Philadelphia, Pa., Overbrook.
College—University of Kansas, Lawrence, Kan.
Drafted by Philadelphia on first round (territorial choice), 1959.

Philadelphia franchise moved to San Francisco, 1962.

Traded by San Francisco to Philadelphia for Paul Neumann, Connie Dierking, Lee Shaffer and cash, January 15, 1965.

Traded by Philadelphia to Los Angeles for Jerry Chambers, Archie Clark and Darrall Imhoff, July 9, 1968.

Played with Harlem Globetrotters during 1958-59 season.

—COLLEGIATE RECORD—

Year	G.	Min.	FGA	FGM	Pct.	FTA	FTM	Pct.	Reb.	Pts.	Avg.
55-56†	(Freshmen team did not play an intercollegiate schedule)										
56-57	27	....	588	275	.468	399	250	.627	510	800	29.6
57-58	21	....	482	228	.473	291	177	.608	367	633	30.1
Varsity Totals	48	....	1070	503	.470	690	427	.619	877	1433	29.9

NBA REGULAR SEASON RECORD

Sea.—Team	G.	Min.	FGA	FGM	Pct.	FTA	FTM	Pct.	Reb.	Ast.	PF	Disq.	Pts.	Avg.
59-60—Philadelphia	72	3338	2311	1065	.461	991	577	.582	1941	168	150	0	2707	37.6
60-61—Philadelphia	79	3773	2457	1251	.509	1054	531	.504	2149	148	130	0	3033	38.4
61-62—Philadelphia	80	3882	3159	1597	.505	1363	835	.613	2052	192	123	0	4029	50.4
62-63—San Francisco	80	3806	2770	1463	.528	1113	660	.593	1946	275	136	0	3586	44.8
63-64—San Francisco	80	3689	2298	1204	.524	1016	540	.531	1787	403	182	0	2948	36.9
64-65—S.F.-Phila.	73	3301	2083	1063	.510	880	408	.464	1673	250	146	0	2534	34.7
65-66—Philadelphia	79	3737	1990	1074	.540	976	501	.513	1943	414	171	0	2649	33.5
66-67—Philadelphia	81	3682	1150	785	.683	875	386	.441	1957	630	143	0	1956	24.1
67-68—Philadelphia	82	3836	1377	819	.595	932	354	.380	1952	702	160	0	1992	24.3
68-69—Los Angeles	81	3669	1099	641	.583	857	382	.446	1712	366	142	0	1664	20.5
69-70—Los Angeles	12	505	227	129	.568	157	70	.446	221	49	31	0	328	27.3
70-71—Los Angeles	82	3630	1226	668	.545	669	360	.538	1493	352	174	0	1696	20.7
71-72—Los Angeles	82	3469	764	496	.649	524	221	.422	1572	329	196	0	1213	14.8
72-73—Los Angeles	82	3542	586	426	.727	455	232	.510	1526	365	191	0	1084	13.2
Totals	1045	47859	23497	12681	.540	11862	6057	.511	23924	4643	2075	0	31419	30.1

NBA PLAYOFF RECORD

Sea.—Team	G.	Min.	FGA	FGM	Pct.	FTA	FTM	Pct.	Reb.	Ast.	PF	Disq.	Pts.	Avg.
59-60—Philadelphia	9	415	252	125	.496	110	49	.445	232	19	17	0	299	33.2
60-61—Philadelphia	3	144	96	45	.469	38	21	.553	69	6	10	0	111	37.0
61-62—Philadelphia	12	576	347	162	.467	151	96	.636	319	37	27	0	420	35.0
63-64—San Francisco	12	558	322	175	.543	139	66	.475	302	39	27	0	416	34.7
64-65—Philadelphia	11	536	232	123	.530	136	76	.559	299	48	29	0	322	29.3
65-66—Philadelphia	5	240	110	56	.509	68	28	.412	151	15	10	0	140	28.0
66-67—Philadelphia	15	718	228	132	.579	160	62	.388	437	135	37	0	326	21.7
67-68—Philadelphia	13	631	232	124	.534	158	60	.380	321	85	29	0	308	23.7
68-69—Los Angeles	18	832	176	96	.545	148	58	.392	444	46	56	0	250	13.9
69-70—Los Angeles	18	851	288	158	.549	202	82	.406	399	81	42	0	398	22.1
70-71—Los Angeles	12	554	187	85	.455	97	50	.515	242	53	33	0	220	18.3
71-72—Los Angeles	15	703	142	80	.563	122	60	.492	315	49	47	0	220	14.7
72-73—Los Angeles	17	801	116	64	.552	98	49	.500	383	60	48	0	177	10.4
Totals	160	7559	2728	1425	.522	1627	757	.465	3913	673	412	0	3607	22.5

NBA ALL-STAR GAME RECORD

Season—Team	Min.	FGA	FGM	Pct.	FTA	FTM	Pct.	Reb.	Ast.	PF	Disq.	Pts.
1960—Philadelphia	30	20	9	.450	7	5	.714	25	2	1	0	23
1961—Philadelphia	38	8	2	.250	15	8	.533	18	5	1	0	12
1962—Philadelphia	37	23	17	.739	16	8	.500	24	1	4	0	42
1963—San Francisco	35	11	7	.636	7	3	.429	19	0	2	0	17
1964—San Francisco	37	14	4	.286	14	11	.786	20	1	2	0	19
1965—San Francisco	31	15	9	.600	8	2	.250	16	1	4	0	20
1966—Philadelphia	25	11	8	.727	9	5	.556	9	3	2	0	21
1967—Philadelphia	39	7	6	.857	5	2	.400	22	4	1	0	14
1968—Philadelphia	25	4	3	.750	4	1	.250	7	6	2	0	7
1969—Los Angeles	27	3	2	.667	1	0	.000	12	2	2	0	4
1971—Los Angeles	18	1	1	1.000	0	0	.000	8	5	0	0	2
1972—Los Angeles	24	3	3	1.000	8	2	.250	10	3	2	0	8
1973—Los Angeles	22	2	1	.500	0	0	.000	7	3	0	0	2
Totals	.388	122	72	.590	94	47	.500	197	36	23	0	191

ABA COACHING RECORD

	Regular Season				Playoffs	
Sea. Club	W.	L.	Pct.	Pos.	W.	L.
1973-74—San Diego	37	47	.440	T4	2	4

WILT CHAMBERLAIN

Named to NBA 35th Anniversary All-Time Team, 1980. . . . Elected to Naismith Memorial Basketball Hall of Fame, 1978. . . . NBA Most Valuable Player, 1960, 1966, 1967, 1968. . . . Named to All-NBA First Team, 1960, 1961, 1962, 1964, 1966, 1967, 1968. . . . All-NBA Second Team, 1963, 1965, 1972. . . . NBA Rookie of the Year, 1960. . . . NBA All-Defensive First Team, 1972 and 1973. . . . NBA Playoff MVP, 1972. . . . Only NBA player ever to score over 4,000 points in a season. . . . Holds NBA single game records for most points, 100, most field-goals attempted, 63, most field-goals made, 36, and shares record for most free-throws made, 28, vs. New York at Hershey, Pa., March 2, 1962. . . . Holds NBA record for most consecutive field goals, 35, February 17-28, 1967. . . . Holds NBA single game record for most consecutive field goals, 18, vs. New York at Boston, November 27, 1963, and vs. Baltimore at Pittsburgh, February 24, 1967. . . . Holds NBA single game record for most free throws attempted, 34, vs. St. Louis, February 22, 1962. . . . Holds NBA single game record for most rebounds, 55, vs. Boston, November 24, 1960. . . . Holds NBA records for most points, 59, most field-goal attempts, 37, and most field-goals made, 22, in one half, vs. New York at Hershey, Pa., March 2, 1962. . . . Holds NBA record for most field-goals attempted in one quarter, 21, vs. New York at Hershey, Pa., March 2, 1962. . . . Holds NBA career records for most free-throw attempts, most rebounds and highest scoring average. . . . NBA all-time playoff leader in free-throw attempts. . . . Holds NBA playoff game record for most rebounds, 41, vs. Boston, April 5, 1967. . . . Shares NBA playoff game record for most field goals, 24, vs. Syracuse, March 14, 1960. . . . Holds NBA championship series game record for most rebounds in one half, 26, vs. San Francisco, April 16, 1967. . . . Shares NBA championship series record for most free-throw attempts in one quarter, 11, vs. San Francisco, April 16, 1967. . . . NBA All-Star Game MVP, 1960. . . . Holds NBA All-Star Game career records for most rebounds. . . . Holds NBA All-Star Game records for most points in one game, 42, in 1962; most field goals made in one game, 17, in 1962; most free throws attempted in one game, 16, in 1962; most points in one half, 23, in 1962, and most field goals made in one half, 10, in 1962. . . . Shares NBA All-Star Game record for most rebounds in one half, 16, in 1960. . . . Member of NBA championship teams, 1967 and 1972. . . . Led NBA in scoring, 1960, 1961, 1962, 1963, 1964, 1965, 1966. . . . Led NBA in rebounding, 1960, 1961, 1962, 1963, 1966, 1967, 1968, 1969, 1971, 1972, 1973. . . . Led NBA in field-goal percentage, 1961, 1963, 1965, 1966, 1967, 1968, 1969, 1972, 1973. . . . Led NBA in assists, 1968. . . . Named to THE SPORTING NEWS All-America First Team, 1958.

ROBERT JOSEPH COUSY
(Bob)

Born August 9, 1928 at New York, N. Y. Height 6:01. Weight 175.
High School—Queens, N. Y., Andrew Jackson.
College—Holy Cross College, Worcester, Mass.
Drafted by Tri-Cities on first round, 1950.

Traded by Tri-Cities to Chicago for Gene Vance, 1950.
NBA rights drawn out of a hat by Boston for $8,500 in dispersal of Chicago franchise, 1950.
Traded by Boston to Cincinnati for Bill Dinwiddie, November 18, 1969.

—COLLEGIATE RECORD—

Year	G.	Min.	FGA	FGM	Pct.	FTA	FTM	Pct.	Reb.	Pts.	Avg.
46-47	30	....	....	91	....	....	45	....	....	227	7.6
47-48	30	....	....	207	....	108	72	.667	....	486	16.2
48-49	27	....	....	195	....	134	90	.672	....	480	17.8
49-50	30	....	659	216	.328	199	150	.754	....	582	19.4
Totals	117	....	....	709	....	....	357	....	....	1775	15.2

NBA REGULAR SEASON RECORD

Sea.—Team	G.	Min.	FGA	FGM	Pct.	FTA	FTM	Pct.	Reb.	Ast.	PF	Disq.	Pts.	Avg.
50-51—Boston	69	....	1138	401	.352	365	276	.756	474	341	185	2	1078	15.6
51-52—Boston	66	2681	1388	512	.369	506	409	.808	421	441	190	5	1433	21.7
52-53—Boston	71	2945	1320	464	.352	587	479	.816	449	547	227	4	1407	19.8
53-54—Boston	72	2857	1262	486	.385	522	411	.787	394	518	201	3	1383	19.2
54-55—Boston	71	2747	1316	522	.397	570	460	.807	424	557	165	1	1504	21.2
55-56—Boston	72	2767	1223	440	.360	564	476	.844	492	642	206	2	1356	18.8
56-57—Boston	64	2364	1264	478	.378	442	363	.821	309	478	134	0	1319	20.6
57-58—Boston	65	2222	1262	445	.353	326	277	.850	322	463	136	1	1167	18.0
58-59—Boston	65	2403	1260	484	.384	385	329	.855	359	557	135	0	1297	20.0
59-60—Boston	75	2588	1481	568	.383	403	319	.791	352	715	146	2	1455	19.4
60-61—Boston	76	2468	1382	513	.371	452	352	.779	331	587	196	0	1378	18.1
61-62—Boston	75	2114	1181	462	.391	333	251	.754	261	584	135	0	1175	15.7
62-63—Boston	76	1975	988	392	.397	298	219	.735	193	515	175	0	1003	13.2
69-70—Cincinnati	7	34	3	1	.333	3	3	1.000	5	10	11	0	5	0.7
Totals	924	....	16468	6168	.375	5756	4624	.803	4786	6955	2242	20	16960	18.4

NBA PLAYOFF RECORD

Sea.—Team	G.	Min.	FGA	FGM	Pct.	FTA	FTM	Pct.	Reb.	Ast.	PF	Disq.	Pts.	Avg.
50-51—Boston	2	....	42	9	.214	12	10	.833	15	12	8	...	28	14.0
51-52—Boston	3	138	65	26	.400	44	41	.932	12	19	13	1	93	31.0
52-53—Boston	6	270	120	46	.383	73	61	.836	25	37	21	0	153	25.5
53-54—Boston	6	260	116	33	.284	75	60	.800	32	38	20	0	126	21.0
54-55—Boston	7	299	139	53	.381	48	46	.958	43	65	26	0	152	21.7
55-56—Boston	3	124	56	28	.500	25	23	.920	24	26	4	0	79	26.3
56-57—Boston	10	440	207	67	.324	91	68	.747	61	93	27	0	202	20.2
57-58—Boston	11	457	196	67	.342	75	64	.853	71	82	20	0	198	18.0
58-59—Boston	11	460	221	72	.326	94	70	.745	76	119	28	0	214	19.5
59-60—Boston	13	468	262	80	.305	51	39	.765	48	116	27	0	199	15.3
60-61—Boston	10	337	147	50	.340	88	67	.761	43	91	33	1	167	16.7
61-62—Boston	14	474	241	86	.357	76	52	.684	64	123	43	0	224	16.0
62-63—Boston	13	413	204	72	.353	47	39	.830	32	116	44	2	183	14.1
Totals	109	....	2016	689	.326	799	640	.801	546	937	314	4	2018	18.5

NBA ALL-STAR GAME RECORD

Season—Team	Min.	FGA	FGM	Pct.	FTA	FTM	Pct.	Reb.	Ast.	PF	Disq.	Pts.
1951—Boston	....	12	2	.167	5	4	.800	9	8	3	0	8
1952—Boston	33	14	4	.286	2	1	.500	4	13	3	0	9
1953—Boston	36	11	4	.364	7	7	1.000	5	3	1	0	15
1954—Boston	34	15	6	.400	8	8	1.000	11	4	1	0	20
1955—Boston	35	14	7	.500	7	6	.857	9	5	1	0	20
1956—Boston	24	8	2	.250	4	3	.750	7	2	6	1	7
1957—Boston	28	14	4	.286	2	2	1.000	5	7	0	0	10
1958—Boston	31	20	8	.400	6	4	.667	5	10	0	0	20
1959—Boston	32	8	4	.500	6	5	.833	5	4	0	0	13
1960—Boston	26	7	1	.143	0	0	.000	5	8	2	0	2
1961—Boston	33	11	2	.182	0	0	.000	3	8	6	1	4
1962—Boston	31	13	4	.308	4	3	.750	6	8	2	0	11
1963—Boston	25	11	4	.364	0	0	.000	4	6	2	0	8
Totals	....	158	52	.329	51	43	.843	78	86	27	2	147

COLLEGIATE COACHING RECORD

	Regular Season			
Sea. Club	W.	L.	Pct.	Pos.
1963-64—Boston College	10	11	.455	...
1964-65—Boston College	22	7	.759	...
1965-66—Boston College	21	5	.808	...
1966-67—Boston College	23	3	.885	...
1967-68—Boston College	17	8	.680	...
1968-69—Boston College	24	4	.857	
Totals (6 seasons)	117	38	.755	

NOTE: Cousy guided Boston College to NIT in 1965, 1966 and 1969 and to NCAA Tournament in 1967 and 1968.

NBA COACHING RECORD

	Regular Season			
Sea. Club	W.	L.	Pct.	Pos.
1969-70—Cincinnati	36	46	.439	5†
1970-71—Cincinnati	33	49	.402	3‡
1971-72—Cincinnati	30	52	.366	3‡
1972-73—K.C.-Omaha	36	46	.439	4§
1973-74—K.C.-Omaha	6	16	.375	...§
Totals (5 seasons)	141	209	.403	

†Eastern Division. ‡Central Division. §Midwest Division.

Elected to Naismith Memorial Basketball Hall of Fame, 1970. . . . Named to NBA 25th Anniversary All-Time Team, 1970, and 35th Anniversary All-Time Team, 1980. . . . NBA Most Valuable Player, 1957. . . . Named to All-NBA First Team, 1952, 1953, 1954, 1955, 1956, 1957, 1958, 1959, 1960, 1961. . . . All-NBA Second Team, 1962 and 1963. . . . Holds NBA record for most assists in one half, 19, vs. Minneapolis, February 27, 1959. . . . Holds NBA playoff game records for most free-throw attempts, 32, and most free throws made, 30, vs. Syracuse, March 21, 1953. . . . Holds NBA playoff game record for most points in an overtime period, 12, vs. Syracuse, March 17, 1954. . . . Shares NBA championship series record for most assists in one quarter, 8, vs. St. Louis, April 9, 1957. . . . NBA All-Star Game MVP, 1954 and 1957. . . . Member of NBA championship teams, 1957, 1959, 1960, 1961, 1962, 1963. . . . Led NBA in assists, 1953, 1954, 1955, 1956, 1957, 1958, 1959, 1960. . . . Named to THE SPORTING NEWS All-America First Team, 1950. . . . Named to THE SPORTING NEWS All-America Second Team, 1949. . . . Member of NCAA championship team, 1947. . . . Commissioner of American Soccer League, 1975 through mid-1980 season.

DAVID WILLIAM COWENS
(Dave)

Born October 25, 1948 at Newport, Ky. Height 6:09. Weight 230.

High School—Newport, Ky., Catholic.

College—Florida State University, Tallahassee, Fla.

Drafted by Boston on first round, 1970 (4th pick).

Traded by Boston to Milwaukee for Quinn Buckner, September 9, 1982.

—COLLEGIATE RECORD—

Year	G.	Min.	FGA	FGM	Pct.	FTA	FTM	Pct.	Reb.	Pts.	Avg.
66-67†	18	....	208	105	.505	90	49	.544	357	259	14.4
67-68	27	....	383	206	.538	131	96	.733	456	508	18.8
68-69	25	....	384	202	.526	164	104	.634	437	508	20.3
69-70	26	....	355	174	.490	169	115	.680	447	463	17.8
Varsity Totals	78	....	1122	582	.519	464	315	.679	1340	1479	19.0

NBA REGULAR SEASON RECORD

Sea.—Team	G.	Min.	FGA	FGM	Pct.	FTA	FTM	Pct.	Reb.	Ast.	PF	Disq.	Pts.	Avg.
70-71—Boston	81	3076	1302	550	.422	373	273	.732	1216	228	350	15	1373	17.0
71-72—Boston	79	3186	1357	657	.484	243	175	.720	1203	245	314	10	1489	18.8
72-73—Boston	82	3425	1637	740	.452	262	204	.779	1329	333	311	7	1684	20.5

Sea.—Team	G.	Min.	FGA	FGM	Pct.	FTA	FTM	Pct.	Rebounds Off.	Rebounds Def.	Rebounds Tot.	Ast.	PF	Dq.	Stl.	Blk.	Pts.	Avg.
73-74—Boston	80	3352	1475	645	.437	274	228	.832	264	993	1257	354	294	7	95	101	1518	19.0
74-75—Boston	65	2632	1199	569	.475	244	191	.783	229	729	958	296	243	7	87	73	1329	20.4
75-76—Boston	78	3101	1305	611	.468	340	257	.756	335	911	1246	325	314	10	94	71	1479	19.0
76-77—Boston	50	1888	756	328	.434	198	162	.818	147	550	697	248	181	7	46	49	818	16.4
77-78—Boston	77	3215	1220	598	.490	284	239	.842	248	830	1078	351	297	5	102	67	1435	18.6
78-79—Boston	68	2517	1010	488	.483	187	151	.807	152	500	652	242	263	16	76	51	1127	16.6
79-80—Boston	66	2159	932	422	.453	122	95	.779	126	408	534	206	216	2	69	61	940	14.2
82-83—Milwaukee	40	1014	306	136	.444	63	52	.825	73	201	274	82	137	4	30	15	324	8.1
Totals	766	29565	12499	5744	.460	2590	2027	.783			10444	2910	2920	90	599	488	13516	17.6

Three-Point Field Goals: 1979-80, 1-for-12 (.083). 1982-83, 0-for-2. Totals, 1-for-14 (.071).

NBA PLAYOFF RECORD

Sea.—Team	G.	Min.	FGA	FGM	Pct.	FTA	FTM	Pct.	Reb.	Ast.	PF	Disq.	Pts.	Avg.
71-72—Boston	11	441	156	71	.455	47	28	.596	152	33	50	2	170	15.5
72-73—Boston	13	598	273	129	.473	41	27	.659	216	48	54	2	285	21.9

Sea.—Team	G.	Min.	FGA	FGM	Pct.	FTA	FTM	Pct.	Rebounds Off.	Rebounds Def.	Rebounds Tot.	Ast.	PF	Dq.	Stl.	Blk.	Pts.	Avg.
73-74—Boston	18	772	370	161	.435	59	47	.797	60	180	240	66	85	2	21	17	369	20.5
74-75—Boston	11	479	236	101	.428	26	23	.885	49	132	181	46	50	2	18	6	225	20.5
75-76—Boston	18	798	341	156	.457	87	66	.759	87	209	296	83	85	4	22	13	378	21.0
76-77—Boston	9	379	148	66	.446	22	17	.773	29	105	134	36	37	3	8	13	149	16.6
79-80—Boston	9	301	103	49	.476	11	10	.909	18	48	66	21	37	0	9	7	108	12.0
Totals	89	3768	1627	733	.451	293	218	.744			1285	333	398	15	78	56	1684	18.9

Three-Point Field Goals: 1979-80, 0-for-2.

NBA ALL-STAR GAME RECORD

Season—Team	Min.	FGA	FGM	Pct.	FTA	FTM	Pct.	Reb.	Ast.	PF	Disq.	Pts.
1972—Boston	32	12	5	.417	5	4	.800	20	1	4	0	14
1973—Boston	30	15	7	.467	1	1	1.000	13	1	2	0	15

Season—Team	Min.	FGA	FGM	Pct.	FTA	FTM	Pct.	Rebounds Off.	Rebounds Def.	Rebounds Tot.	Ast.	PF	Dq.	Stl.	Blk.	Pts.
1974—Boston	26	10	5	.500	3	1	.333	6	6	12	1	3	0	0	1	11
1975—Boston	15	7	3	.429	0	0	.000	0	6	6	3	4	0	1	0	6
1976—Boston	23	13	6	.462	5	4	.800	8	8	16	1	3	0	1	0	16
1977—Boston	Selected—Injured, Did Not Play															
1978—Boston	28	9	7	.778	0	0	.000	6	8	14	5	5	0	2	0	14
Totals	154	66	33	.500	14	10	.714			81	12	21	0	4	1	76

NBA COACHING RECORD

Sea.	Club	Regular Season W.	L.	Pct.	Pos.
1978-79	Boston	27	41	.397	5†

†Atlantic Division.

CBA COACHING RECORD

Sea.	Club	Regular Season W.	L.	Pct.	Pos.
1984-85	Bay State	20	28	.417	6†

NBA Most Valuable Player, 1973. . . . Named to All-NBA Second Team, 1973, 1975, 1976. . . . NBA All-Defensive First Team, 1976. . . . NBA All-Defensive Second Team, 1975 and 1980. . . . NBA Co-Rookie of the Year, 1971. . . . NBA All-Rookie Team, 1971. . . . NBA All-Star Game MVP, 1973. . . . Member of NBA championship teams, 1974 and 1976. . . . Named to THE SPORTING NEWS All-America Second Team, 1970.

ROBERT EDRIS DAVIES
(Bob)

Born January 15, 1920 at Harrisburg, Pa. Height 6:01. Weight 175.

Died April 22, 1990.

High School—Harrisburg, Pa., John Harris.

Colleges—Franklin & Marshall College, Lancaster, Pa., and Seton Hall University, South Orange, N.J.

Signed as free agent by Rochester NBL, 1945.

In military service during 1942-43, 1943-44 and 1944-45 seasons.
Played with Great Lakes (Ill.) Naval Training Station during 1942-43 season.
Led team in scoring with 269 points (114 field goals and 41 free throws).
Played in American Basketball League with Brooklyn, 1943-44, and New York, 1944-45.

—COLLEGIATE RECORD—

Franklin & Marshall

Year	G.	Min.	FGA	FGM	Pct.	FTA	FTM	Pct.	Reb.	Pts.	Avg.
37-38†	Statistics Unavailable										

Seton Hall

Year	G.	Min.	FGA	FGM	Pct.	FTA	FTM	Pct.	Reb.	Pts.	Avg.
38-39†					Statistics Unavailable						
39-40	18	....	...	78	....	...	56	....	...	212	11.8
40-41	22	....	...	91	....	...	42	....	...	224	10.2
41-42	19	....	...	81	....	...	63	....	...	225	11.8
Varsity Totals	59	....	...	250	....	...	161	....	...	661	11.2

NBL AND NBA REGULAR SEASON RECORD

Sea.—Team	G.	Min.	FGA	FGM	Pct.	FTA	FTM	Pct.	Reb.	Ast.	PF	Disq.	Pts.	Avg.
45-46—Roch.-NBL	27	....	....	86	....	103	70	.680	....	....	85	..	242	9.0
46-47—Roch.-NBL	32	....	....	166	....	166	130	.783	....	....	90	..	462	14.4
47-48—Roch.-NBL	48	....	....	176	....	161	121	.752	....	....	111	..	473	9.9
48-49—Rochester	60	....	871	317	.364	348	270	.776	....	321	197	..	904	15.1
49-50—Rochester	64	....	887	317	.357	347	261	.752	....	294	187	..	895	14.0
50-51—Rochester	63	....	877	326	.372	381	303	.795	197	287	208	7	955	15.2
51-52—Rochester	65	2394	990	379	.383	379	294	.776	189	390	269	10	1052	16.2
52-53—Rochester	66	2216	880	339	.385	466	351	.753	195	280	261	7	1029	15.6
53-54—Rochester	72	2137	777	288	.371	433	311	.718	194	323	224	4	887	12.3
54-55—Rochester	72	1870	785	326	.415	293	220	.751	205	155	220	2	872	12.1
Totals	569	....	....	2720	....	3077	2331	.758	....	....	1852	...	7771	13.7

NBL AND NBA PLAYOFF RECORD

Sea.—Team	G.	Min.	FGA	FGM	Pct.	FTA	FTM	Pct.	Reb.	Ast.	PF	Disq.	Pts.	Avg.
45-46—Roch.-NBL	7	....	...	28	....	41	30	.732	....	....	13	..	86	12.3
46-47—Roch.-NBL	11	....	....	54	....	63	43	.683	....	....	30	..	151	13.7
47-48—Roch.-NBL	11	....	....	56	....	64	49	.766	....	....	26	..	161	14.6
48-49—Rochester	4	....	51	19	.373	13	10	.769	....	13	12	..	48	12.0
49-50—Rochester	2	....	17	4	.235	8	7	.875	....	9	11	..	15	7.5
50-51—Rochester	14	....	234	79	.338	80	64	.800	43	75	45	1	222	15.9
51-52—Rochester	6	233	92	37	.402	55	45	.818	13	28	18	0	119	19.8
52-53—Rochester	3	91	29	6	.207	20	14	.700	4	14	11	0	26	8.7
53-54—Rochester	6	172	52	17	.327	23	17	.739	12	14	16	0	51	8.5
54-55—Rochester	3	75	33	11	.333	4	3	.750	6	9	11	0	25	8.3
Totals	67	....	....	311	....	371	282	.752	....	....	193	..	904	13.5

NBA ALL-STAR GAME RECORD

Season—Team	Min.	FGA	FGM	Pct.	FTA	FTM	Pct.	Reb.	Ast.	PF	Disq.	Pts.
1951—Rochester	....	6	4	.667	5	5	1.000	5	5	3	0	13
1952—Rochester	27	11	4	.364	0	0	.000	0	5	4	0	8
1953—Rochester	17	7	3	.429	6	3	.500	3	2	2	0	9
1954—Rochester	31	16	8	.500	3	2	.667	5	5	4	0	18
Totals	....	40	19	.475	14	10	.714	13	17	13	0	48

COLLEGIATE COACHING RECORD

	Regular Season			
Sea. Club	W.	L.	Pct.	Pos.
1946-47—Seton Hall	24	3	.888	..
1955-56—Gettysburg	11	17	.393	..
1956-57—Gettysburg	7	18	.280	..

Named to NBA 25th Anniversary All-Time Team, 1970. . . . Elected to Naismith Memorial Basketball Hall of Fame, 1969. . . . All-NBA First Team, 1950, 1951, 1952. . . . All-NBA Second Team, 1953. . . . Led NBA in assists, 1949. . . . Member of NBA championship team, 1951. . . . NBL All-Star First Team, 1947. . . . NBL All-Star Second Team, 1948. . . . NBL Most Valuable Player, 1947. . . . Member of NBL championship team, 1946. . . . BAA All-Star First Team, 1949.

DAVID ALBERT DeBUSSCHERE
(Dave)

Born October 16, 1940 at Detroit, Mich. Height 6:06. Weight 235.
High School—Detroit, Mich., Austin Catholic.
College—University of Detroit, Detroit, Mich.
Drafted by Detroit on first round (territorial choice), 1962.

Traded by Detroit to New York for Walt Bellamy and Howard Komives, December 19, 1968.

—COLLEGIATE RECORD—

Year	G.	Min.	FGA	FGM	Pct.	FTA	FTM	Pct.	Reb.	Pts.	Avg.
58-59†	15	....	306	144	.471	101	68	.673	305	356	23.7
59-60	27	....	665	288	.433	196	115	.587	540	691	25.6
60-61	27	....	636	256	.403	155	86	.555	514	598	22.1
61-62	26	....	616	267	.433	242	162	.669	498	696	26.8
Varsity Totals	80	....	1917	811	.423	593	363	.612	1552	1985	24.8

NBA REGULAR SEASON RECORD

Sea.—Team	G.	Min.	FGA	FGM	Pct.	FTA	FTM	Pct.	Reb.	Ast.	PF	Disq.	Pts.	Avg.
62-63—Detroit	80	2352	944	406	.430	287	206	.718	694	207	247	2	1018	12.7
63-64—Detroit	15	304	133	52	.391	43	25	.581	105	23	32	1	129	8.6
64-65—Detroit	79	2769	1196	508	.425	437	306	.700	874	253	242	5	1322	16.7
65-66—Detroit	79	2696	1284	524	.408	378	249	.659	916	209	252	5	1297	16.4
66-67—Detroit	78	2897	1278	531	.415	512	361	.705	924	216	297	7	1423	18.2
67-68—Detroit	80	3125	1295	573	.442	435	289	.664	1081	181	304	3	1435	17.9
68-69—Det.-N. Y.	76	2943	1140	506	.444	328	229	.698	888	191	290	6	1241	16.3
69-70—New York	79	2627	1082	488	.451	256	176	.688	790	194	244	2	1152	14.6
70-71—New York	81	2891	1243	523	.421	312	217	.696	901	220	237	2	1263	15.6
71-72—New York	80	3072	1218	520	.427	265	193	.728	901	291	219	1	1233	15.4
72-73—New York	77	2827	1224	532	.435	260	194	.746	787	259	215	1	1258	16.3

								—Rebounds—									
Sea.—Team	G.	Min.	FGA	FGM	Pct.	FTA	FTM	Pct.	Off.	Def.	Tot.	Ast.	PF	Dq.	Stl.	Blk.	Pts.	Avg.
73-74—New York	71	2699	1212	559	.461	217	164	.756	134	623	757	253	222	2	67	39	1282	18.1
Totals	875	31202	13249	5722	.432	3730	2609	.699			9618	2497	2801	37			14053	16.1

NBA PLAYOFF RECORD

Sea.—Team	G.	Min.	FGA	FGM	Pct.	FTA	FTM	Pct.	Reb.	Ast.	PF	Disq.	Pts.	Avg.
62-63—Detroit	4	159	59	25	.424	44	30	.682	63	6	14	1	80	20.0
67-68—Detroit	6	263	106	45	.425	45	26	.578	97	13	23	0	116	19.3
68-69—New York	10	419	174	61	.351	50	41	.820	148	33	43	0	163	16.3
69-70—New York	19	701	309	130	.421	68	45	.662	220	46	63	1	305	16.1
70-71—New York	12	488	202	84	.416	44	29	.659	156	22	40	1	197	16.4
71-72—New York	16	616	242	109	.450	64	48	.750	193	37	51	2	266	16.6
72-73—New York	17	632	265	117	.442	40	31	.775	179	58	57	0	265	15.6

									—Rebounds—									
Sea.—Team	G.	Min.	FGA	FGM	Pct.	FTA	FTM	Pct.	Off.	Def.	Tot.	Ast.	PF	Dq.	Stl.	Blk.	Pts.	Avg.
73-74—New York	12	404	166	63	380	29	18	.621	25	74	99	38	36	0	7	4	144	12.0
Totals	96	3682	1523	634	416	384	268	.698			1155	253	327	5			1536	16.0

NBA ALL-STAR GAME RECORD

Season—Team	Min.	FGA	FGM	Pct.	FTA	FTM	Pct.	Reb.	Ast.	PF	Disq.	Pts.
1966—Detroit	22	14	1	.071	2	2	1.000	6	1	1	0	4
1967—Detroit	25	17	11	.647	0	0	.000	6	0	1	0	22
1968—Detroit	12	3	0	.000	0	0	.000	4	0	1	0	0
1970—New York	14	10	5	.500	0	0	.000	7	2	1	0	10
1971—New York	19	7	4	.571	0	0	.000	7	3	3	0	8
1972—New York	26	8	4	.500	0	0	.000	11	0	2	0	8
1973—New York	25	8	4	.500	2	1	.500	7	2	1	0	9

								—Rebounds—								
Season—Team	Min.	FGA	FGM	Pct.	FTA	FTM	Pct.	Off.	Def.	Tot.	Ast.	PF	Dq.	Stl.	Blk.	Pts.
1974—New York	24	14	8	.571	0	0	.000	2	1	3	3	2	0	1	0	16
Totals	167	81	37	.457	4	3	.750			51	11	12	0			77

NBA COACHING RECORD

	Regular Season			
Sea. Club	W.	L.	Pct.	Pos.
1964-65—Detroit	29	40	.420	4†
1965-66—Detroit	22	58	.275	5†
1966-67—Detroit	28	45	.384	5†
Totals (3 seasons)	79	143	.356	

†Western Division.

RECORD AS BASEBALL PLAYER

Led Pacific Coast League in games started with 34 in 1965.

Year Club	League	G.	IP.	W.	L.	Pct.	H.	R.	ER.	SO.	BB.	ERA.
1962—Chicago	American	12	18	0	0	.000	5	7	4	8	23	2.00
1962—Savannah	S. Atlantic	15	94	10	1	.909	62	35	26	93	53	2.49
1963—Chicago	American	24	84	3	4	.429	80	35	29	53	34	3.11
1964—Indianapolis	P. Coast	32	174	15	8	.652	173	88	76	126	66	3.93
1965—Indianapolis	P. Coast	35	*244	15	12	.556	*255	*120	99	176	66	3.65
Major League Totals		36	102	3	4	.429	85	42	33	126	66	3.93

Elected to Naismith Memorial Basketball Hall of Fame, 1982. . . . Named to All-NBA Second Team, 1969. . . . NBA All-Defensive First Team, 1969, 1970, 1971, 1972, 1973, 1974. . . . Holds NBA All-Star Game record for most field goals made in one quarter, 8, in 1967. . . . Member of NBA championship teams, 1970 and 1973. . . . Youngest coach (24) in NBA history. . . . ABA Commissioner during 1975-76 season.

JULIUS WINFIELD ERVING II
(Dr. J)

Born February 22, 1950 at Roosevelt, N. Y. Height 6:07. Weight 210.

High School—Roosevelt, N. Y.

College—University of Massachusetts, Amherst, Mass.

Drafted by Milwaukee on first round, 1972 (12th pick).

Signed as an undergraduate free agent by Virginia ABA, April 6, 1971.

Traded by Virginia with Willie Sojourner to New York for George Carter, draft rights to Kermit Washington and cash, August 1, 1973.

Entered NBA with New York Nets, 1976.

Sold by Nets to Philadelphia, October 20, 1976.

—COLLEGIATE RECORD—

Year	G.	Min.	FGA	FGM	Pct.	FTA	FTM	Pct.	Reb.	Pts.	Avg.
68-69†	15	....	216	112	.519	81	49	.605	214	273	18.2
69-70	25	969	468	238	.509	230	167	.726	522	643	25.7
70-71	27	1029	609	286	.470	206	155	.752	527	727	26.9
Varsity Totals	52	1998	1077	524	.487	436	322	.739	1049	1370	26.3

ABA REGULAR SEASON RECORD

			—2-Point—			—3-Point—									
Sea.—Team	G.	Min.	FGM	FGA	Pct.	FGM	FGA	Pct.	FTM	FTA	Pct.	Reb.	Ast.	Pts.	Avg.
1971-72—Virginia	84	3513	907	1810	.501	3	16	.188	467	627	.745	1319	335	2290	27.3
1972-73—Virginia	71	2993	889	1780	.499	5	24	.208	475	612	.776	867	298	2268	31.9
1973-74—New York	84	3398	897	1742	.515	17	43	.395	454	593	.766	899	434	2299	27.4
1974-75—New York	84	3402	885	1719	.515	29	87	.333	486	608	.799	914	462	2343	27.9
1975-76—New York	84	3244	915	1770	.517	34	103	.330	530	662	.801	925	423	2462	29.3
Totals	407	16550	4493	8821	.509	88	273	.322	2412	3102	.778	4924	1952	11662	28.7

ABA PLAYOFF RECORD

			—2-Point—			—3-Point—									
Sea.—Team	G.	Min.	FGM	FGA	Pct.	FGM	FGA	Pct.	FTM	FTA	Pct.	Reb.	Ast.	Pts.	Avg.
71-72—Virginia	11	504	146	280	521	1	4	.250	71	85	.835	224	72	366	33.3
72-73—Virginia	5	219	59	109	.541	0	3	.000	30	40	.750	45	16	148	29.6
73-74—New York	14	579	156	294	.531	5	11	.455	63	85	.741	135	67	390	27.9
74-75—New York	5	211	55	113	.487	0	8	.000	27	32	.844	49	28	137	27.4
75-76—New York	13	551	156	286	.545	4	14	.286	127	158	.804	164	64	451	34.7
Totals	48	2064	572	1082	.529	10	40	.250	318	400	.795	617	247	1492	31.1

ABA ALL-STAR GAME RECORD

		—2-Point—			—3-Point—									
Sea.—Team	Min.	FGM	FGA	Pct.	FGM	FGA	Pct.	FTM	FTA	Pct.	Reb.	Ast.	Pts.	Avg.
1972—Virginia	25	9	15	.600	0	0	.000	2	2	1.000	6	3	20	20.0
1973—Virginia	30	8	16	.500	0	0	.000	6	8	.750	5	1	22	22.0
1974—New York	27	6	15	.400	0	0	.000	2	2	1.000	11	8	14	14.0
1975—New York	27	5	11	.455	1	1	1.000	8	10	.800	7	7	21	21.0
1976—New York	25	9	12	.750	0	1	.000	5	7	.714	7	5	23	23.0
Totals	134	37	69	.536	1	2	.500	23	29	.793	36	24	100	20.0

NBA REGULAR SEASON RECORD

									—Rebounds—									
Sea.—Team	G.	Min.	FGA	FGM	Pct.	FTA	FTM	Pct.	Off.	Def.	Tot.	Ast.	PF	Dq.	Stl.	Blk.	Pts.	Avg.
76-77—Philadelphia	82	2940	1373	685	.499	515	400	.777	192	503	695	306	251	1	159	113	1770	21.6
77-78—Philadelphia	74	2429	1217	611	.502	362	306	.845	179	302	481	279	207	0	135	97	1528	20.6
78-79—Philadelphia	78	2802	1455	715	.491	501	373	.745	198	366	564	357	207	0	133	100	1803	23.1
79-80—Philadelphia	78	2812	1614	838	.519	534	420	.787	215	361	576	355	208	0	170	140	2100	26.9
80-81—Philadelphia	82	2874	1524	794	.521	536	422	.787	244	413	657	364	233	0	173	147	2014	24.6
81-82—Philadelphia	81	2789	1428	780	.546	539	411	.763	220	337	557	319	229	1	161	141	1974	24.4
82-83—Philadelphia	72	2421	1170	605	.517	435	330	.759	173	318	491	263	202	1	112	131	1542	21.4
83-84—Philadelphia	77	2683	1324	678	.512	483	364	.754	190	342	532	309	217	3	141	139	1727	22.4
84-85—Philadelphia	78	2535	1236	610	.494	442	338	.765	172	242	414	233	199	0	135	109	1561	20.0
85-86—Philadelphia	74	2474	1085	521	.480	368	289	.785	169	201	370	248	196	3	113	82	1340	18.1
86-87—Philadelphia	60	1918	850	400	.471	235	191	.813	115	149	264	191	137	0	76	94	1005	16.8
Totals	836	28677	14276	7237	.507	4950	3844	.777	2067	3534	5601	3224	2286	9	1508	1293	18364	22.0

Three-Point Field Goals: 1979-80, 4-for-20 (.200). 1980-81, 4-for-18 (.222). 1981-82, 3-for-11 (.273). 1982-83, 2-for-7 (.286). 1983-84, 7-for-21 (.333). 1984-85, 3-for-14 (.214). 1985-86, 9-for-32 (.281). 1986-87, 14-for-53 (.264). Totals, 46-for-176 (.261).

NBA PLAYOFF RECORD

									—Rebounds—									
Sea.—Team	G.	Min.	FGA	FGM	Pct.	FTA	FTM	Pct.	Off.	Def.	Tot.	Ast.	PF	Dq.	Stl.	Blk.	Pts.	Avg.
76-77—Philadelphia	19	758	390	204	.523	134	110	.821	41	81	122	85	45	0	41	23	518	27.3
77-78—Philadelphia	10	358	180	88	.489	56	42	.750	40	57	97	40	30	0	15	18	218	21.8
78-79—Philadelphia	9	372	172	89	.517	67	51	.761	29	41	70	53	22	0	18	17	229	25.4
79-80—Philadelphia	18	694	338	165	.488	136	108	.794	31	105	136	79	56	0	36	37	440	24.4
80-81—Philadelphia	16	592	301	143	.475	107	81	.757	52	62	114	54	54	0	22	41	367	22.9
81-82—Philadelphia	21	780	324	168	.519	165	124	.752	57	99	156	99	55	0	37	37	461	22.0
82-83—Philadelphia	13	493	211	95	.450	68	49	.721	32	67	99	44	42	1	15	27	239	18.4
83-84—Philadelphia	5	194	76	36	.474	22	19	.864	9	23	32	25	14	0	8	6	91	18.2
84-85—Philadelphia	13	434	187	84	.449	63	54	.857	29	44	73	48	34	0	25	11	222	17.1
85-86—Philadelphia	12	433	180	81	.450	65	48	.738	26	44	70	50	32	0	11	16	212	17.7
86-87—Philadelphia	5	180	82	34	.415	25	21	.840	14	11	25	17	19	0	7	6	91	18.2
Totals	141	5288	2441	1187	.486	908	707	.779	360	634	994	594	403	1	235	239	3088	21.9

Three-Point Field Goals: 1979-80, 2-for-9 (.222). 1980-81, 0-for-1. 1981-82, 1-for-6 (.167). 1982-83, 0-for-1. 1983-84, 0-for-1. 1984-85, 0-for-1. 1985-86, 2-for-11 (.182). Totals, 5-for-30 (.167).

NBA ALL-STAR GAME RECORD

								—Rebounds—								
Season—Team	Min.	FGA	FGM	Pct.	FTA	FTM	Pct.	Off.	Def.	Tot.	Ast.	PF	Dq.	Stl.	Blk.	Pts.
1977—Philadelphia	30	20	12	.600	6	6	1.000	5	7	12	3	2	0	4	1	30

Season—Team	Min.	FGA	FGM	Pct.	FTA	FTM	Pct.	—Rebounds— Off.	Def.	Tot.	Ast.	PF	Dq.	Stl.	Blk.	Pts.
1978—Philadelphia	27	14	3	.214	12	10	.833	2	6	8	3	1	0	0	1	16
1979—Philadelphia	39	22	10	.455	12	9	.750	6	2	8	5	4	0	2	0	29
1980—Philadelphia	20	12	4	.333	4	3	.750	2	3	5	2	5	0	2	1	11
1981—Philadelphia	29	15	6	.400	7	6	.857	3	0	3	2	2	0	2	1	18
1982—Philadelphia	32	16	7	.438	4	2	.500	3	5	8	2	4	0	1	2	16
1983—Philadelphia	28	19	11	.579	3	3	1.000	3	3	6	3	1	0	1	2	25
1984—Philadelphia	36	22	14	.636	8	6	.750	4	4	8	5	4	0	2	2	34
1985—Philadelphia	23	15	5	.333	2	2	1.000	2	2	4	3	3	0	1	0	12
1986—Philadelphia	19	10	4	.400	2	0	.000	1	3	4	2	2	0	2	0	8
1987—Philadelphia	33	13	9	.692	3	3	1.000	3	1	4	5	3	0	1	1	22
Totals	316	178	85	.478	63	50	.794	34	36	70	35	31	0	18	11	221

Three-Point Field Goals: 1987, 1-for-1 (1.000).

COMBINED ABA AND NBA REGULAR-SEASON RECORDS

	G.	Min.	FGA	FGM	Pct.	FTA	FTM	Pct.	—Rebounds— Off.	Def.	Tot.	Ast.	PF	Dq.	Stl.	Blk.	Pts.	Avg.
Totals	1243	45227	23370	11818	.506	8052	6256	.777	3689	6836	10525	5176	3494	na	2272	1941	30026	24.2

Named to NBA 35th Anniversary All-Time Team, 1980. . . . Named NBA Most Valuable Player, 1981. . . . Named to All-NBA First Team, 1978, 1980, 1981, 1982, 1983. . . . All-NBA Second Team, 1977 and 1984. . . . Member of NBA championship team, 1983. . . . NBA All-Star Game MVP, 1977 and 1983. . . . Holds NBA All-Star Game record for most free throws attempted in one quarter, 11, in 1978. . . . Shares NBA All-Star Game record for most free throws made in one quarter, 9, in 1978. . . . ABA Most Valuable Player, 1974 and 1976. . . . ABA co-MVP, 1975. . . . ABA All-Star First Team, 1973, 1974, 1975, 1976. . . . ABA All-Star Second Team, 1972. . . . ABA Playoff MVP, 1974 and 1976. . . . Member of ABA championship teams, 1974 and 1976. . . . ABA All-Defensive Team, 1976. . . . ABA All-Rookie Team, 1972. . . . Led ABA in scoring, 1973, 1974, 1976. . . . One of only seven players to average over 20 points and 20 rebounds per game during NCAA career.

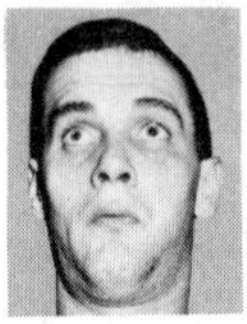

LAWRENCE MICHAEL FOUST
(Larry)

Born June 24, 1928 at Painesville, O. Height 6:09. Weight 250.

Died October 27, 1984.

High School—Philadelphia, Pa., South Catholic.

College—LaSalle College, Philadelphia, Pa.

Drafted by Chicago on first round, 1950.

Draft rights selected by Fort Wayne in dispersal of Chicago franchise, 1950.
Fort Wayne franchise transferred to Detroit, April, 1957.
Traded by Detroit with cash to Minneapolis for Walt Dukes, September 12, 1957.
Traded by Minneapolis to St. Louis for Charlie Share, cash and draft rights to Nick Mantis and Willie Merriweather, February 1, 1960.

—COLLEGIATE RECORD—

Year	G.	Min.	FGA	FGM	Pct.	FTA	FTM	Pct.	Reb.	Pts.	Avg.
46-47	26	....	...	103	....	...	49	....	....	255	9.8
47-48	24	....	...	157	....	...	87	....	....	401	16.7
48-49	28	....	...	177	....	164	99	.604	....	453	16.2
49-50	25	....	...	136	....	122	83	.680	....	355	14.2
Totals	103	....	...	573	....	...	318	....	....	1464	14.2

NBA REGULAR SEASON RECORD

Sea.—Team	G.	Min.	FGA	FGM	Pct.	FTA	FTM	Pct.	Reb.	Ast.	PF	Disq.	Pts.	Avg.
50-51—Ft. Wayne	68	....	944	327	.346	396	261	.659	681	90	247	6	915	13.5
51-52—Ft. Wayne	66	2615	989	390	.394	394	267	.678	880	200	245	10	1047	15.9
52-53—Ft. Wayne	67	2303	865	311	.360	465	336	.723	769	151	267	16	958	14.3
53-54—Ft. Wayne	72	2693	919	376	.409	475	338	.712	967	161	258	4	1090	15.1
54-55—Ft. Wayne	70	2264	818	398	.487	513	393	.766	700	118	264	9	1189	17.0
55-56—Ft. Wayne	72	2024	821	367	.447	555	432	.778	648	127	263	7	1166	16.2
56-57—Ft. Wayne	61	1533	617	243	.394	380	273	.718	555	71	221	7	759	12.4
57-58—Minn.	72	2200	982	391	.398	566	428	.756	876	108	299	11	1210	16.8
58-59—Minn.	72	1933	771	301	.390	366	280	.765	627	91	233	5	882	12.3
59-60—Minn.-StL.	72	1964	766	312	.407	320	253	.791	621	96	241	7	877	12.2
60-61—St. Louis	68	1208	489	194	.397	208	164	.788	389	77	165	0	552	8.1
61-62—St. Louis	57	1153	433	204	.471	178	145	.815	328	78	186	2	553	9.7
Totals	817	21880	9414	3814	.405	4816	3570	.741	8041	1368	2889	84	11198	13.7

NBA PLAYOFF RECORD

Sea.—Team	G.	Min.	FGA	FGM	Pct.	FTA	FTM	Pct.	Reb.	Ast.	PF	Disq.	Pts.	Avg.
50-51—Ft. Wayne	3	....	45	14	.311	10	8	.800	37	5	5	....	36	12.0
51-52—Ft. Wayne	2	77	23	12	.522	7	6	.857	30	5	8	1	30	15.0
52-53—Ft. Wayne	8	332	121	48	.397	68	57	.838	111	6	34	2	153	19.1
53-54—Ft. Wayne	4	129	41	11	.268	25	19	.760	38	7	21	2	41	10.3
54-55—Ft. Wayne	11	331	152	60	.395	73	52	.712	107	26	43	0	172	15.6
55-56—Ft. Wayne	10	289	130	49	.377	89	70	.787	127	14	38	2	168	16.8
56-57—Ft. Wayne	2	64	23	13	.565	23	19	.826	25	6	10	0	45	22.5
58-59—Minn.	13	404	134	56	.418	50	41	.820	136	12	47	2	153	11.8

Sea.—Team	G.	Min.	FGA	FGM	Pct.	FTA	FTM	Pct.	Reb.	Ast.	PF	Disq.	Pts.	Avg.
59-60—St. Louis	12	205	74	29	.391	25	20	.800	68	11	36	0	78	6.5
60-61—St. Louis	8	89	20	9	.450	14	8	.571	28	2	13	0	26	3.2
Totals	73	1920	763	301	.394	384	300	.781	707	94	255	9	902	12.4

NBA ALL-STAR GAME RECORD

Season—Team	Min.	FGA	FGM	Pct.	FTA	FTM	Pct.	Reb.	Ast.	PF	Disq.	Pts.
1951—Fort Wayne	..	6	1	.167	0	0	.000	5	2	3	0	2
1952—Fort Wayne					Selected—Injured, Did Not Play							
1953—Fort Wayne	18	7	5	.714	0	0	.000	6	0	4	0	10
1954—Fort Wayne	27	9	1	.111	1	1	1.000	15	0	1	0	3
1955—Fort Wayne	24	10	3	.300	1	1	1.000	7	1	1	0	7
1956—Fort Wayne	20	9	3	.333	4	3	.750	4	0	1	0	9
1958—Minneapolis	13	4	1	.250	8	8	1.000	3	0	3	0	10
1959—Minneapolis	16	9	3	.333	2	2	1.000	9	0	3	0	8
Totals	118	54	17	.315	16	15	.938	49	3	16	0	49

Named to All-NBA First Team, 1955. . . . All-NBA Second Team, 1952. . . . Led NBA in field-goal percentage, 1955. . . . Shared lead in NBA for rebounding, 1952. . . . Named to THE SPORTING NEWS All-America Fifth Team, 1950.

WALTER FRAZIER JR.
(Clyde)

Born March 29, 1945 at Atlanta, Ga. Height 6:04. Weight 205.
High School—Atlanta, Ga., David Howard.
College—Southern Illinois University, Carbondale, Ill.
Drafted by New York on first round, 1967 (5th pick).

Acquired from New York by Cleveland as compensation for anticipated signing of Veteran Free Agent Jim Cleamons, October 7, 1977.

Waived by Cleveland, October 19, 1979.

—COLLEGIATE RECORD—

Year	G.	Min.	FGA	FGM	Pct.	FTA	FTM	Pct.	Reb.	Pts.	Avg.
63-64†	14	....	225	133	.591	85	52	.612	129	318	22.7
64-65	24	....	353	161	.456	111	88	.793	221	410	17.1
65-66					Did Not Play—Ineligible						
66-67	26	....	397	192	.484	126	90	.714	310	474	18.2
Varsity Totals	50	....	750	353	.471	237	178	.751	531	884	17.7

NBA REGULAR SEASON RECORD

Sea.—Team	G.	Min.	FGA	FGM	Pct.	FTA	FTM	Pct.	Reb.	Ast.	PF	Disq.	Pts.	Avg.
67-68—New York	74	1588	568	256	.451	235	154	.655	313	305	199	2	666	9.0
68-69—New York	80	2949	1052	531	.505	457	341	.746	499	635	245	2	1403	17.5
69-70—New York	77	3040	1158	600	.518	547	409	.748	465	629	203	1	1609	20.9
70-71—New York	80	3455	1317	651	.494	557	434	.779	544	536	240	1	1736	21.7
71-72—New York	77	3126	1307	669	.512	557	450	.808	513	446	185	0	1788	23.2
72-73—New York	78	3181	1389	681	.490	350	286	.817	570	461	186	0	1648	21.1

									—Rebounds—									
Sea.—Team	G.	Min.	FGA	FGM	Pct.	FTA	FTM	Pct.	Off.	Def.	Tot.	Ast.	PF	Dq.	Stl.	Blk.	Pts.	Avg.
73-74—New York	80	3338	1429	674	.472	352	295	.838	120	416	536	551	212	2	161	15	1643	20.5
74-75—New York	78	3204	1391	672	.483	400	331	.828	90	375	465	474	205	2	190	14	1675	21.5
75-76—New York	59	2427	969	470	.485	226	186	.823	79	321	400	351	163	1	106	9	1126	19.1
76-77—Knicks	76	2687	1089	532	.489	336	259	.771	52	241	293	403	194	0	132	9	1323	17.4
77-78—Cleveland	51	1664	714	336	.471	180	153	.850	54	155	209	209	124	1	77	9	825	16.2
78-79—Cleveland	12	279	122	54	.443	27	21	.778	7	13	20	32	22	0	13	2	129	10.8
79-80—Cleveland	3	27	11	4	.364	2	2	1.000	1	2	3	8	2	0	2	1	10	3.3
Totals	825	30965	12516	6130	.490	4226	3321	.786			4830	5040	2180	12	681	59	15581	18.9

Three-Point Field Goals: 1979-80, 0-for-1.

NBA PLAYOFF RECORD

Sea.—Team	G.	Min.	FGA	FGM	Pct.	FTA	FTM	Pct.	Reb.	Ast.	PF	Disq.	Pts.	Avg.
67-68—New York	4	119	33	12	.364	18	14	.778	22	25	12	0	38	9.5
68-69—New York	10	415	177	89	.503	57	34	.596	74	91	30	0	212	21.2
69-70—New York	19	834	247	118	.478	89	68	.764	149	156	53	0	304	16.0
70-71—New York	12	501	204	108	.529	75	55	.733	70	54	45	0	271	22.6
71-72—New York	16	704	276	148	.536	125	92	.736	112	98	48	0	388	24.3
72-73—New York	17	765	292	150	.514	94	73	.777	124	106	52	1	373	21.9

									—Rebounds—									
Sea.—Team	G.	Min.	FGA	FGM	Pct.	FTA	FTM	Pct.	Off.	Def.	Tot.	Ast.	PF	Dq.	Stl.	Blk.	Pts.	Avg.
73-74—New York	12	491	225	113	.502	49	44	.898	21	74	95	48	41	1	21	4	270	22.5
74-75—New York	3	124	46	29	.630	16	13	.813	3	17	20	21	4	0	11	0	71	23.7
Totals	93	3953	1500	767	.511	523	393	.751			666	599	285	2	32	4	1927	20.7

NBA ALL-STAR GAME RECORD

Season—Team	Min.	FGA	FGM	Pct.	FTA	FTM	Pct.	Reb.	Ast.	PF	Disq.	Pts.
1970—New York	24	7	3	.429	2	1	.500	3	4	2	0	7
1971—New York	26	9	3	.333	0	0	.000	6	5	2	0	6
1972—New York	25	11	7	.636	2	1	.500	3	5	2	0	15
1973—New York	26	15	5	.333	0	0	.000	6	2	1	0	10

								—Rebounds—								
Season—Team	Min.	FGA	FGM	Pct.	FTA	FTM	Pct.	Off.	Def.	Tot.	Ast.	PF	Dq.	Stl.	Blk.	Pts.
1974—New York....	28	12	5	.417	2	2	1.000	1	1	2	5	1	0	3	0	12
1975—New York....	35	17	10	.588	11	10	.909	0	5	5	2	2	0	4	0	30
1976—New York....	19	7	2	.286	4	4	1.000	0	2	2	3	0	0	2	0	8
Totals...............	183	78	35	.449	21	18	.857			27	26	10	0	9	0	88

Elected to Naismith Memorial Basketball Hall of Fame, 1986.... Named to All-NBA First Team, 1970, 1972, 1974, 1975.... All-NBA Second Team, 1971 and 1973.... NBA All-Defensive First Team, 1969, 1970, 1971, 1972, 1973, 1974, 1975.... NBA All-Rookie Team, 1968.... NBA All-Star Game MVP, 1975.... Member of NBA championship teams, 1970 and 1973.... Named to THE SPORTING NEWS All-America Second Team, 1967.

JOSEPH E. FULKS
(Joe)

Born October 26, 1921 at Birmingham, Ky. Height 6:05. Weight 190.

Died March 21, 1976.

High Schools—Birmingham, Ky. (Fr.-Jr.), and Kuttawa, Ky. (Sr.).

College—Murray State College, Murray, Ky.

Signed by Philadelphia BAA, 1946.

—COLLEGIATE RECORD—

Year	G.	Min.	FGA	FGM	Pct.	FTA	FTM	Pct.	Reb.	Pts.	Avg.
41-42..............................	22	....	...	117	....	76	50	.658	....	284	12.9
42-43..............................	25	....	...	135	....	100	67	.670	....	337	13.5
Totals......................	47	....	...	252	....	176	117	.664	....	621	13.2

NOTE: In military service (Marines) during 1943-44, 1944-45 and 1945-46 seasons.

NBA REGULAR SEASON RECORD

Sea.—Team	G.	Min.	FGA	FGM	Pct.	FTA	FTM	Pct.	Reb.	Ast.	PF	Disq.	Pts.	Avg.
1946-47—Philadelphia	60	....	1557	475	.305	601	439	.730	....	25	199	..	1389	23.2
1947-48—Philadelphia	43	....	1258	326	.259	390	297	.762	....	26	162	..	949	22.1
1948-49—Philadelphia	60	....	1689	529	.313	638	502	.787	....	74	262	..	1560	26.0
1949-50—Philadelphia	68	....	1209	336	.278	421	293	.696	....	56	240	..	965	14.2
1950-51—Philadelphia	66	....	1358	429	.316	442	378	.855	523	117	247	8	1236	18.7
1951-52—Philadelphia	61	1904	1078	336	.312	303	250	.825	368	123	255	13	922	15.1
1952-53—Philadelphia	70	2085	960	332	.346	231	168	.727	387	138	319	20	832	11.9
1953-54—Philadelphia	61	501	229	61	.266	49	28	.571	101	28	90	0	150	2.5
Totals.........................	489	....	9338	2824	.302	3075	2355	.766	....	587	1774	..	8003	16.4

NBA PLAYOFF RECORD

Sea.—Team	G.	Min.	FGA	FGM	Pct.	FTA	FTM	Pct.	Reb.	Ast.	PF	Disq.	Pts.	Avg.
1946-47—Philadelphia	10	....	257	74	.288	94	74	.787	....	3	32	..	222	22.2
1947-48—Philadelphia	13	....	380	92	.242	121	98	.810	....	3	55	..	282	21.7
1948-49—Philadelphia	1	....	0	0	.000	0	0	.000	....	0	1	..	0	0.0
1949-50—Philadelphia	2	....	26	5	.192	10	5	.500	....	2	10	..	15	7.5
1950-51—Philadelphia	2	....	49	16	.327	27	20	.741	16	1	9	0	52	26.0
1951-52—Philadelphia	3	70	33	5	.152	9	7	.778	12	2	13	1	17	5.7
Totals.........................	31	....	745	192	.258	261	204	.782	....	11	120	..	588	19.0

NBA ALL-STAR GAME RECORD

Season—Team	Min.	FGA	FGM	Pct.	FTA	FTM	Pct.	Reb.	Ast.	PF	Disq.	Pts.
1951—Philadelphia............	....	15	6	.400	9	7	.778	7	3	5	0	19
1952—Philadelphia............	9	7	3	.429	1	0	.000	5	2	2	0	6
Totals............................	....	22	9	.409	10	7	.700	12	5	7	0	25

Named to NBA 25th Anniversary All-Time Team, 1970.... Elected to Naismith Memorial Basketball Hall of Fame, 1977.... Named to All-NBA First Team, 1947, 1948, 1949.... All-NBA Second Team, 1951.... Member of NBA championship team, 1947.... Led NBA in scoring, 1947.... Led NBA in free-throw percentage, 1951.

HARRY J. GALLATIN

Born April 26, 1927 at Roxana, Ill. Height 6:06. Weight 215.

High School—Roxana, Ill.

College—Northeast Missouri State Teachers College, Kirksville, Mo.

Drafted by New York on first round of BAA draft, 1948.

Traded by New York with Dick Atha and Nat Clifton to Detroit for Mel Hutchins and a 1st round draft choice, April 3, 1957.

—COLLEGIATE RECORD—

Year	G.	Min.	FGA	FGM	Pct.	FTA	FTM	Pct.	Reb.	Pts.	Avg.
46-47..............................	31	....	...	149	....	89	53	.596	....	351	11.3
47-48..............................	31	....	465	178	.383	162	109	.673	....	465	15.0
Totals......................	62	....	...	327	....	251	162	.645	....	816	13.2

NOTE: Played only two years of college basketball.

NBA REGULAR SEASON RECORD

Sea.—Team	G.	Min.	FGA	FGM	Pct.	FTA	FTM	Pct.	Reb.	Ast.	PF	Disq.	Pts.	Avg.
48-49—New York	52	....	479	157	.328	169	120	.710	....	63	127	....	434	8.3
49-50—New York	68	....	664	263	.396	366	277	.757	....	56	215	....	803	11.8
50-51—New York	66	....	705	293	.416	354	259	.732	800	180	244	4	845	12.8
51-52—New York	66	1931	527	233	.442	341	275	.807	661	115	223	5	741	11.2
52-53—New York	70	2333	635	282	.444	430	301	.700	916	126	224	6	865	12.4
53-54—New York	72	2690	639	258	.404	552	433	.784	1098	153	208	2	949	13.2
54-55—New York	72	2548	859	330	.384	483	393	.814	995	176	206	5	1053	14.6
55-56—New York	72	2378	834	322	.386	455	358	.787	740	168	220	6	1002	13.9
56-57—New York	72	1943	817	332	.406	519	415	.802	725	85	202	1	1079	15.0
57-58—Detroit	72	1990	898	340	.379	498	392	.787	749	86	217	5	1072	14.9
Totals	682	....	7057	2810	.398	4167	3223	.773	....	1208	2086	....	8843	13.0

NBA PLAYOFF RECORD

Sea.—Team	G.	Min.	FGA	FGM	Pct.	FTA	FTM	Pct.	Reb.	Ast.	PF	Disq.	Pts.	Avg.
48-49—New York	6	....	56	20	.357	39	32	.821	....	10	31	....	72	12.0
49-50—New York	5	....	52	20	.385	32	25	.781	....	6	23	....	65	13.0
50-51—New York	14	....	140	49	.350	87	67	.770	163	26	57	3	165	11.8
51-52—New York	14	471	122	50	.410	66	51	.773	134	19	45	1	151	10.8
52-53—New York	11	303	86	36	.419	59	44	.746	120	15	29	0	116	10.5
53-54—New York	4	151	35	16	.457	31	22	.710	61	6	12	0	54	13.5
54-55—New York	3	108	42	19	.452	22	17	.773	44	7	11	0	55	18.3
57-58—Detroit	7	182	87	32	.368	37	26	.703	70	11	27	1	90	12.9
Totals	64	....	620	242	.390	373	284	.762	....	100	235	....	768	12.0

NBA ALL-STAR GAME RECORD

Season—Team	Min.	FGA	FGM	Pct.	FTA	FTM	Pct.	Reb.	Ast.	PF	Disq.	Pts.
1951—New York	....	4	2	.500	1	1	1.000	5	2	4	0	5
1952—New York	22	5	3	.600	4	1	.250	9	3	3	0	7
1953—New York	19	4	1	.250	2	1	.500	3	2	1	0	3
1954—New York	28	2	0	.000	6	5	.833	18	3	0	0	5
1955—New York	36	7	4	.571	5	5	1.000	14	3	2	0	13
1956—New York	30	12	5	.417	7	6	.857	5	2	4	0	16
1957—New York	24	7	4	.571	2	0	.000	11	1	3	0	8
Totals (7 games)	....	41	19	.463	27	19	.704	65	16	17	0	57

COLLEGIATE COACHING RECORD

Sea. Club	Regular Season W.	L.	Pct.	Pos.
1958-59—So. Ill.-Carbon.	17	10	.630	2†
1959-60—So. Ill.-Carbon.	20	9	.690	1T†
1960-61—So. Ill.-Carbon.	21	6	.778	1†
1961-62—So. Ill.-Carbon.	21	10	.677	1†
1967-68—So. Ill.-Edwards.	5	5	.500	
1968-69—So. Ill.-Edwards.	7	10	.412	
1969-70—So. Ill.-Edwards.	7	16	.304	

†Interstate Intercollegiate Athletic Conference.

NBA COACHING RECORD

Sea. Club	Regular Season W.	L.	Pct.	Pos.	Playoffs W.	L.
1962-63—St. Louis	48	32	.600	2	6	5
1963-64—St. Louis	46	34	.575	2	6	6
1964-65—St. Louis	17	16	.515	...	..	..
1964-65—New York	19	23	.452	4	..	..
1965-66—New York	6	15	.286	...	..	..
Totals (4 years)	136	120	.531		12	11

Named to All-NBA First Team, 1954. . . . All-NBA Second Team, 1955. . . . Led NBA in rebounding, 1954. . . . NBA Coach of the Year, 1963. . . . Named to NAIA Basketball Hall of Fame, 1957.

GEORGE GERVIN
(Iceman)

Born April 27, 1952 at Detroit, Mich. Height 6:07. Weight 185.

High School—Detroit, Mich., Martin Luther King.

Colleges—Long Beach State, Long Beach, Calif., and Eastern Michigan University, Ypsilanti, Mich.

Drafted by Phoenix on third round, 1974 (40th pick).

Selected as an undergraduate by Virginia on first round of ABA special circumstance draft, 1973.
Sold by Virginia to San Antonio, January 30, 1974.
Entered NBA with San Antonio, 1976.
Traded by San Antonio to Chicago for David Greenwood, October 24, 1985.
Played in Continental Basketball Association with the Pontiac Capparells during 1972-73 season (averaged 37.4 points per game).

—COLLEGIATE RECORD—

Long Beach State

Year	G.	Min.	FGA	FGM	Pct.	FTA	FTM	Pct.	Reb.	Pts.	Avg.
69-70	Dropped out of school prior to basketball season.										

Eastern Michigan

Year	G.	Min.	FGA	FGM	Pct.	FTA	FTM	Pct.	Reb.	Pts.	Avg.
70-71	9	300	123	65	.528	39	28	.718	104	158	17.6
71-72	30	1098	571	339	.594	265	208	.785	458	886	29.5
Totals	39	1398	694	404	.582	304	236	.776	562	1044	26.8

ABA REGULAR SEASON RECORD

			2-Point			3-Point									
Sea.—Team	G.	Min.	FGM	FGA	Pct.	FGM	FGA	Pct.	FTM	FTA	Pct.	Reb.	Ast.	Pts.	Avg.
72-73—Virginia	30	689	155	315	.492	6	26	.231	96	118	.814	128	34	424	14.1
73-74—Va.-S.A.	74	2511	664	1370	.485	8	56	.143	378	464	.815	624	142	1730	23.4
74-75—San Antonio	84	3113	767	1600	.479	17	55	.309	380	458	.830	697	207	1965	23.4
75-76—San Antonio	81	2748	692	1359	.509	14	55	.255	342	399	.857	546	201	1768	21.8
Totals	269	9061	2278	4644	.491	45	192	.234	1196	1439	.831	1977	584	5887	21.9

ABA PLAYOFF RECORD

			2-Point			3-Point									
Sea.—Team	G.	Min.	FGM	FGA	Pct.	FGM	FGA	Pct.	FTM	FTA	Pct.	Reb.	Ast.	Pts.	Avg.
72-73—Virginia	5	200	33	72	.458	1	5	.200	23	34	.676	38	8	93	18.6
73-74—San Antonio	7	226	56	114	.491	1	1	1.000	29	31	.935	52	19	144	20.6
74-75—San Antonio	6	276	76	159	.478	3	12	.250	43	52	.827	84	8	204	34.0
75-76—San Antonio	7	288	67	125	.536	0	3	.000	56	69	.812	64	19	190	27.1
Totals	25	990	232	470	.494	5	21	.238	151	186	.812	238	54	631	25.2

ABA ALL-STAR GAME RECORD

		2-Point			3-Point									
Sea.—Team	Min.	FGM	FGA	Pct.	FGM	FGA	Pct.	FTM	FTA	Pct.	Reb.	Ast.	Pts.	Avg.
1974—Virginia	21	3	8	.375	0	1	.000	3	4	.750	5	3	9	9.0
1975—San Antonio	30	8	14	.571	0	1	.000	7	8	.875	6	3	23	23.0
1976—San Antonio	16	3	13	.231	0	0	.000	1	2	.500	6	1	8	8.0
Totals	67	14	35	.400	0	2	.000	11	14	.786	17	7	40	13.3

NBA REGULAR SEASON RECORD

									Rebounds									
Sea.—Team	G.	Min.	FGA	FGM	Pct.	FTA	FTM	Pct.	Off.	Def.	Tot.	Ast.	PF	Dq.	Stl.	Blk.	Pts.	Avg.
76-77—San Antonio	82	2705	1335	726	.544	532	443	.833	134	320	454	238	286	12	105	104	1895	23.1
77-78—San Antonio	82	2857	1611	864	.536	607	504	.830	118	302	420	302	255	3	136	110	2232	27.2
78-79—San Antonio	80	2888	1749	947	.541	570	471	.826	142	258	400	219	275	5	137	91	2365	29.6
79-80—San Antonio	78	2934	1940	1024	.528	593	505	.852	154	249	403	202	208	0	110	79	2585	33.1
80-81—San Antonio	82	2765	1729	850	.492	620	512	.826	126	293	419	260	212	4	94	56	2221	27.1
81-82—San Antonio	79	2817	1987	993	.500	642	555	.864	138	254	392	187	215	2	77	45	2551	32.3
82-83—San Antonio	78	2830	1553	757	.487	606	517	.853	111	246	357	264	243	5	88	67	2043	26.2
83-84—San Antonio	76	2584	1561	765	.490	507	427	.842	106	207	313	220	219	3	79	47	1967	25.9
84-85—San Antonio	72	2091	1182	600	.508	384	324	.844	79	155	234	178	208	2	66	48	1524	21.2
85-86—Chicago	82	2065	1100	519	.472	322	283	.879	78	137	215	144	210	4	49	23	1325	16.2
Totals	791	26536	15747	8045	.511	5383	4541	.844	1186	2421	3607	2214	2331	40	941	670	20708	26.2

Three-Point Field Goals: 1979-80, 32-for-102 (.314). 1980-81, 9-for-35 (.257). 1981-82, 10-for-36 (.278). 1982-83, 12-for-33 (.364). 1983-84, 10-for-24 (.417). 1984-85, 0-for-10. 1985-86, 4-for-19 (.211). Totals, 77-for-259 (.297).

NBA PLAYOFF RECORD

									Rebounds									
Sea.—Team	G.	Min.	FGA	FGM	Pct.	FTA	FTM	Pct.	Off.	Def.	Tot.	Ast.	PF	Dq.	Stl.	Blk.	Pts.	Avg.
76-77—San Antonio	2	62	44	19	.432	15	12	.800	5	6	11	3	9	1	1	2	50	25.0
77-78—San Antonio	6	227	142	78	.549	56	43	.768	11	23	34	19	23	0	6	16	199	33.2
78-79—San Antonio	14	513	295	158	.536	104	84	.808	33	49	82	35	51	1	27	14	400	28.6
79-80—San Antonio	3	122	74	37	.500	30	26	.867	9	11	20	12	8	0	5	3	100	33.3
80-81—San Antonio	7	274	154	77	.500	45	36	.800	9	26	35	24	19	1	5	5	190	27.1
81-82—San Antonio	9	373	228	103	.452	71	59	.831	19	47	66	41	36	1	10	4	265	29.4
82-83—San Antonio	11	437	208	108	.519	69	61	.884	21	53	74	37	39	1	12	4	277	25.2
84-85—San Antonio	5	183	79	42	.532	34	27	.794	3	15	18	14	19	0	3	3	111	22.2
85-86—Chicago	2	11	1	0	.000	0	0	.000	0	1	1	1	3	0	0	0	0	0.0
Totals	59	2202	1225	622	.508	424	348	.821	110	231	341	186	207	5	69	51	1592	27.0

Three-Point Field Goals: 1979-80, 0-for-2. 1980-81, 0-for-3. 1981-82, 0-for-3. 1982-83, 0-for-2. 1984-85, 0-for-3. Totals, 0-for-13.

NBA ALL-STAR GAME RECORD

								Rebounds								
Season—Team	Min.	FGA	FGM	Pct.	FTA	FTM	Pct.	Off.	Def.	Tot.	Ast.	PF	Dq.	Stl.	Blk.	Pts.
1977—San Antonio	12	6	0	.000	0	0	.000	0	1	1	0	1	0	0	1	0
1978—San Antonio	18	11	4	.364	3	1	.333	1	1	2	1	2	0	2	1	9
1979—San Antonio	34	16	8	.500	11	10	.909	2	4	6	2	4	0	1	1	26
1980—San Antonio	40	26	14	.538	9	6	.667	4	6	10	3	2	0	3	0	34
1981—San Antonio	24	9	5	.556	2	1	.500	1	2	3	0	3	0	2	1	11
1982—San Antonio	27	14	5	.357	2	2	1.000	1	5	6	1	3	0	3	3	12
1983—San Antonio	14	8	3	.375	2	2	1.000	0	0	0	3	3	0	2	0	9
1984—San Antonio	21	6	5	.833	3	3	1.000	0	2	2	1	5	0	0	1	13
1985—San Antonio	25	12	10	.833	4	3	.750	0	3	3	1	2	0	3	1	23
Totals	215	108	54	.500	36	28	.778	9	24	33	12	25	0	16	9	137

Named to All-NBA First Team, 1978, 1979, 1980, 1981, 1982 . . . . All-NBA Second Team, 1977 and 1983. . . . NBA All-Star Game MVP, 1980. . . . Holds NBA record for most points in one quarter, 33, against New Orleans, April 9,

1978. . . . Led NBA in scoring, 1978, 1979, 1980, 1982. . . . One of only two players in NBA history to win four scoring titles. . . . Named to ABA All-Star Second Team, 1975 and 1976.

ARTIS GILMORE

Born September 21, 1949 at Chipley, Fla. Height 7:02. Weight 265.

High Schools—Chipley, Fla., Roulhac and Dothan, Ala., Carver (Senior).

Colleges—Gardner-Webb Junior College, Boiling Springs, N.C., and Jacksonville University, Jacksonville, Fla.

Drafted by Chicago on seventh round, 1971 (117th pick).

Selected by Kentucky on first round of ABA draft, 1971.
Selected by Chicago NBA from Kentucky for $1,100,000 in ABA dispersal draft, August 5, 1976.
Traded by Chicago to San Antonio for Dave Corzine, Mark Olberding and cash, July 22, 1982.
Traded by San Antonio to Chicago for a 1988 2nd round draft choice, June 22, 1987.
Waived by Chicago, December 26, 1987; signed by Boston as a free agent, January 8, 1988.

—COLLEGIATE RECORD—

Gardner Webb JC

Year	G.	Min.	FGA	FGM	Pct.	FTA	FTM	Pct.	Reb.	Pts.	Avg.
67-68	31	....	...	296	....	...	121	....	....	713	23.0
68-69	36	....	...	326	....	...	140	....	....	792	22.0
JC Totals	67	....	....	622	....	....	261	....	....	1505	22.5

Jacksonville

Year	G.	Min.	FGA	FGM	Pct.	FTA	FTM	Pct.	Reb.	Pts.	Avg.
69-70	28	....	529	307	.580	202	128	.634	621	742	26.5
70-71	26	....	405	229	.565	188	112	.596	603	570	21.9
Totals	54	....	934	536	.574	390	240	.615	1224	1312	24.3

ABA REGULAR SEASON RECORD

			—2-Point—			—3-Point—									
Sea.—Team	G.	Min.	FGM	FGA	Pct.	FGM	FGA	Pct.	FTM	FTA	Pct.	Reb.	Ast.	Pts.	Avg.
71-72—Kentucky	84	3666	806	1348	.598	0	0	.000	391	605	.646	1491	230	2003	23.8
72-73—Kentucky	84	3502	686	1226	.560	1	2	.500	368	572	.643	1476	295	1743	20.9
73-74—Kentucky	84	3502	621	1257	.494	0	3	.000	326	489	.667	1538	329	1568	18.7
74-75—Kentucky	84	3493	783	1349	.580	1	2	.500	412	592	.696	1361	208	1081	23.6
75-76—Kentucky	84	3286	773	1401	.552	0	0	.000	521	764	.682	1303	211	2067	24.6
Totals	420	17449	3669	6581	.558	2	7	.286	2018	3022	.668	7169	1273	9362	22.3

ABA PLAYOFF RECORD

			—2-Point—			—3-Point—									
Sea.—Team	G.	Min.	FGM	FGA	Pct.	FGM	FGA	Pct.	FTM	FTA	Pct.	Reb.	Ast.	Pts.	Avg.
71-72—Kentucky	6	285	52	90	.577	0	0	.000	27	38	.711	106	25	131	21.8
72-73—Kentucky	19	780	142	261	.544	0	0	.000	77	123	.626	260	75	361	19.0
73-74—Kentucky	8	344	71	127	.559	0	0	.000	38	66	.576	149	28	180	22.5
74-75—Kentucky	15	679	132	245	.539	0	0	.000	98	127	.772	264	38	362	24.1
75-76—Kentucky	10	390	93	153	.608	0	0	.000	56	75	.747	152	19	242	24.2
Totals	58	2478	500	876	.571	0	0	.000	296	429	.690	931	185	1280	22.1

ABA ALL-STAR GAME RECORD

		—2-Point—			—3-Point—									
Sea.—Team	Min.	FGM	FGA	Pct.	FGM	FGA	Pct.	FTM	FTA	Pct.	Reb.	Ast.	Pts.	Avg.
1972—Kentucky	27	4	5	.800	0	0	.000	6	10	.600	10	2	14	14.0
1973—Kentucky	31	3	8	.375	0	0	.000	4	8	.500	16	0	10	10.0
1974—Kentucky	27	8	12	.667	0	0	.000	2	3	.667	13	1	18	18.0
1975—Kentucky	28	4	8	.500	0	0	.000	3	7	.429	13	2	11	11.0
1976—Kentucky	27	5	7	.714	0	0	.000	6	7	.857	7	1	14	14.0
Totals	140	24	40	.600	0	0	.000	21	35	.600	59	6	67	13.4

NBA REGULAR SEASON RECORD

									—Rebounds—								
Sea.—Team	G.	Min.	FGA	FGM	Pct.	FTA	FTM	Pct.	Off.	Def.	Tot.	Ast.	PF	Dq.	Stl.	Blk.	Pts.	Avg.
76-77—Chicago	82	2877	1091	570	.522	586	387	.660	313	757	1070	199	266	4	44	203	1527	18.6
77-78—Chicago	82	3067	1260	704	.559	669	471	.704	318	753	1071	263	261	4	42	181	1879	22.9
78-79—Chicago	82	3265	1310	753	.575	587	434	.739	293	750	1043	274	280	2	50	156	1940	23.7
79-80—Chicago	48	1568	513	305	.595	344	245	.712	108	324	432	133	167	5	29	59	855	17.8
80-81—Chicago	82	2832	816	547	.670	532	375	.705	220	608	828	172	295	2	47	198	1469	17.9
81-82—Chicago	82	2796	837	546	.652	552	424	.768	224	611	835	136	287	4	49	220	1517	18.5
82-83—San Antonio	82	2797	888	556	.626	496	367	.740	299	685	984	126	273	4	40	192	1479	18.0
83-84—San Antonio	64	2034	556	351	.631	390	280	.718	213	449	662	70	229	4	36	132	982	15.3
84-85—San Antonio	81	2756	854	532	.623	646	484	.749	231	615	846	131	306	4	40	173	1548	19.1
85-86—San Antonio	71	2395	684	423	.618	482	338	.701	166	434	600	102	239	3	39	108	1184	16.7
86-87—San Antonio	82	2405	580	346	.597	356	242	.680	185	394	579	150	235	2	39	95	934	11.4
87-88—Chi.-Bos.	71	893	181	99	.547	128	67	.523	69	142	211	21	148	0	15	30	265	3.7
Totals	909	29685	9570	5732	.599	5768	4114	.713	2639	6522	9161	1777	2986	38	470	1747	15579	17.1

Three-Point Field Goals: 1981-82, 1-for-1. 1982-83, 0-for-6. 1983-84, 0-for-3. 1984-85, 0-for-2. 1985-86, 0-for-1. Totals, 1-for-13 (.077).

NBA PLAYOFF RECORD

Sea.—Team	G.	Min.	FGA	FGM	Pct.	FTA	FTM	Pct.	—Rebounds— Off.	Def.	Tot.	Ast.	PF	Dq.	Stl.	Blk.	Pts.	Avg.
76-77—Chicago	3	126	40	19	.475	23	18	.783	15	24	39	6	9	0	3	8	56	18.7
80-81—Chicago	6	247	60	35	.583	55	38	.691	24	43	67	12	15	0	6	17	108	18.0
82-83—San Antonio	11	401	132	76	.576	46	32	.696	37	105	142	18	46	1	9	34	184	16.7
84-85—San Antonio	5	185	52	29	.558	45	31	.689	10	40	50	7	18	0	2	7	89	17.8
85-86—San Antonio	3	107	24	16	.667	14	8	.571	7	11	18	3	11	0	7	1	40	13.3
87-88—Boston	14	86	8	4	.500	14	7	.500	4	16	20	1	14	0	0	4	15	1.1
Totals	42	1152	316	179	.566	197	134	.680	97	239	336	47	113	1	27	71	492	11.7

NBA ALL-STAR GAME RECORD

Season—Team	Min.	FGA	FGM	Pct.	FTA	FTM	Pct.	—Rebounds— Off.	Def.	Tot.	Ast.	PF	Dq.	Stl.	Blk.	Pts.
1978—Chicago	13	4	2	.500	8	6	.750	0	2	2	0	1	0	1	2	10
1979—Chicago	15	4	3	.750	2	2	1.000	1	0	1	2	1	0	0	0	8
1981—Chicago	22	7	5	.714	2	1	.500	1	5	6	2	4	0	0	1	11
1982—Chicago	16	6	3	.500	1	1	1.000	1	2	3	2	4	0	0	1	7
1983—San Antonio	16	4	2	.500	2	1	.500	1	4	5	1	4	0	1	0	5
1986—San Antonio	13	4	3	.750	4	4	1.000	1	1	2	1	4	0	2	0	10
Totals	95	29	18	.621	19	15	.789	5	14	19	8	18	0	4	4	51

COMBINED ABA AND NBA REGULAR SEASON RECORDS

	G.	Min.	FGA	FGM	Pct.	FTA	FTM	Pct.	—Rebounds— Off.	Def.	Tot.	Ast.	PF	Dq.	Stl.	Blk.	Pts.	Avg.
Totals	1329	47134	16158	9403	.582	8790	6132	.698	4816	11514	16330	3050	4529	na	na	3178	24941	18.8

Named to NBA All-Defensive Second Team, 1978. . . . NBA all-time field-goal percentage leader. . . . Led NBA in field-goal percentage, 1981, 1982, 1983, 1984. . . . ABA All-Star First Team, 1972, 1973, 1974, 1975, 1976. . . . ABA Most Valuable Player and Rookie of the Year, 1972. . . . ABA All-Rookie Team, 1972. . . . ABA All-Defensive Team, 1973, 1974, 1975, 1976. . . . ABA All-Star Game MVP, 1974. . . . ABA Playoff MVP, 1975. . . . Member of ABA championship team, 1975. . . . Led ABA in rebounding, 1972, 1973, 1974, 1976. . . . Led ABA in field-goal percentage, 1972 and 1973. . . . Led ABA in blocked shots, 1973. . . . Named to THE SPORTING NEWS All-America First Team, 1971. . . . THE SPORTING NEWS All-America Second Team, 1970. . . . NCAA career leading rebounding average, 22.7. . . . Led NCAA in rebounding, 1970 and 1971. . . . One of only seven players to average over 20 points and 20 rebounds per game during NCAA career.

GAIL CHARLES GOODRICH

Born April 23, 1943 at Los Angeles, Calif. Height 6:01. Weight 175.
High School—Los Angeles, Calif., Polytechnic.
College—University of California at Los Angeles, Los Angeles, Calif.
Drafted by Los Angeles on first round (territorial choice), 1965.

Selected from Los Angeles by Phoenix in expansion draft, May 6, 1968.
Traded by Phoenix to Los Angeles for Mel Counts, May 20, 1970.
Played out option with Los Angeles; signed by New Orleans as a Veteran Free Agent, July 19, 1976. Los Angeles received two 1st round draft choices (1977 and 1979) and a 1980 2nd round draft choice as compensation. New Orleans received a 1977 2nd round draft choice to complete transaction, October 6, 1976.

—COLLEGIATE RECORD—

Year	G.	Min.	FGA	FGM	Pct.	FTA	FTM	Pct.	Reb.	Pts.	Avg.
61-62†	20	....	385	189	.491	155	110	.710	122	488	24.4
62-63	29	....	280	117	.418	103	66	.641	101	300	10.3
63-64	30	....	530	243	.458	225	160	.711	156	646	21.5
64-65	30	....	528	277	.525	265	190	.717	158	744	24.8
Varsity Totals	89	....	1338	637	.476	593	416	.702	415	1690	19.0

NBA REGULAR SEASON RECORD

Sea.—Team	G.	Min.	FGA	FGM	Pct.	FTA	FTM	Pct.	Reb.	Ast.	PF	Disq.	Pts.	Avg.
65-66—Los Ang.	65	1008	503	203	.404	149	103	.691	130	103	103	1	509	7.8
66-67—Los Ang.	77	1780	776	352	.454	337	253	.751	251	210	194	3	957	12.4
67-68—Los Ang.	79	2057	812	395	.486	392	302	.770	199	205	228	2	1092	13.8
68-69—Phoenix	81	3236	1746	718	.411	663	495	.747	437	518	253	3	1931	23.8
69-70—Phoenix	81	3234	1251	568	.454	604	488	.808	340	605	251	3	1624	20.0
70-71—Los Ang.	79	2808	1174	558	.475	343	264	.770	260	380	258	3	1380	17.5
71-72—Los Ang.	82	3040	1695	826	.487	559	475	.850	295	365	210	0	2127	25.9
72-73—Los Ang.	76	2697	1615	750	.464	374	314	.840	263	332	193	1	1814	23.9

Sea.—Team	G.	Min.	FGA	FGM	Pct.	FTA	FTM	Pct.	—Rebounds— Off.	Def.	Tot.	Ast.	PF	Dq.	Stl.	Blk.	Pts.	Avg.
73-74—L.A.	82	3061	1773	784	.442	588	508	.864	95	155	250	427	227	3	126	12	2076	25.3
74-75—L.A.	72	2668	1429	656	.459	378	318	.841	96	123	219	420	214	1	102	6	1630	22.6
75-76—L.A.	75	2646	1321	583	.441	346	293	.847	94	120	214	421	238	3	123	17	1459	19.5
76-77—N.O.	27	609	305	136	.446	85	68	.800	25	36	61	74	43	0	22	2	340	12.6
77-78—N.O.	81	2553	1050	520	.495	332	264	.795	75	102	177	388	186	0	82	22	1304	16.1
78-79—N.O.	74	2130	850	382	.449	204	174	.853	68	115	183	357	177	1	90	13	938	12.7
Totals	1031	33527	16300	7431	.456	5354	4319	.807			3279	4805	2775	24	545	72	19181	18.6

NBA PLAYOFF RECORD

Sea.—Team	G.	Min.	FGA	FGM	Pct.	FTA	FTM	Pct.	Reb.	Ast.	PF	Disq.	Pts.	Avg.
65-66—Los Ang.	11	290	92	43	.467	43	29	.674	42	33	35	0	115	10.5
66-67—Los Ang.	3	81	31	11	.355	18	11	.611	9	10	5	0	33	11.0
67-68—Los Ang.	10	100	47	23	.489	18	14	.778	14	14	10	0	60	6.0
69-70—Phoenix	7	265	118	56	.475	35	30	.857	32	38	21	0	142	20.3
70-71—Los Ang.	12	518	247	105	.425	113	95	.841	38	91	38	0	305	25.4
71-72—Los Ang.	15	575	292	130	.445	108	97	.898	38	50	50	0	357	23.8
72-73—Los Ang.	17	604	310	139	.448	79	62	.785	61	67	53	1	340	20.0

Sea.—Team	G.	Min.	FGA	FGM	Pct.	FTA	FTM	Pct.	—Rebounds— Off.	Def.	Tot.	Ast.	PF	Dq.	Stl.	Blk.	Pts.	Avg.
73-74—L.A.	5	189	90	35	.389	33	28	.848	7	9	16	30	7	0	7	1	98	19.6
Totals	80	2622	1227	542	.442	447	366	819			250	333	219	1			1450	18.1

NBA ALL-STAR GAME RECORD

Season—Team	Min.	FGA	FGM	Pct.	FTA	FTM	Pct.	Reb.	Ast.	PF	Disq.	Pts.
1969—Phoenix	6	4	2	.500	2	1	.500	1	1	1	0	5
1972—Los Angeles	14	7	2	.286	0	0	.000	1	2	2	0	4
1973—Los Angeles	16	7	1	.143	0	0	.000	2	1	2	0	2

Season—Team	Min.	FGA	FGM	Pct.	FTA	FTM	Pct.	—Rebounds— Off.	Def.	Tot.	Ast.	PF	Dq.	Stl.	Blk.	Pts.
1974—Los Angeles	26	16	9	.563	0	0	.000	1	3	4	6	2	0	1	0	18
1975—Los Angeles	15	4	2	.500	0	0	.000	0	1	1	4	1	0	0	0	4
Totals	77	38	16	.421	2	1	.500			9	14	8	0	1	0	33

Named to All-NBA First Team, 1974. . . . Member of NBA championship team, 1972. . . . Named to THE SPORTING NEWS All-America First Team, 1964. . . . Member of NCAA Division I championship teams, 1964 and 1965.

HAROLD EVERETT GREER
(Hal)

Born June 26, 1936 at Huntington, W. Va. Height 6:02. Weight 175.
High School—Huntington, W. Va., Douglass.
College—Marshall College, Huntington, W. Va.
Drafted by Syracuse on second round, 1958.

Syracuse franchise transferred to Philadelphia, 1963.

—COLLEGIATE RECORD—

Year	G.	Min.	FGA	FGM	Pct.	FTA	FTM	Pct.	Reb.	Pts.	Avg.
54-55†	..	....	....	...	...	....	....	...	...	...	18.0
55-56	23	....	213	128	.601	145	101	.697	153	357	15.5
56-57	24	....	329	167	.508	156	119	.763	332	453	18.9
57-58	24	....	432	236	.546	114	95	.833	280	567	23.6
Varsity Totals	71	....	974	531	.545	415	315	.759	765	1377	19.4

NBA REGULAR SEASON RECORD

Sea.—Team	G.	Min.	FGA	FGM	Pct.	FTA	FTM	Pct.	Reb.	Ast.	PF	Disq.	Pts.	Avg.
58-59—Syracuse	68	1625	679	308	.454	176	137	.778	196	101	189	1	753	11.1
59-60—Syracuse	70	1979	815	388	.476	189	148	.783	303	188	208	4	924	13.2
60-61—Syracuse	79	2763	1381	623	.451	394	305	.774	455	302	242	0	1551	19.6
61-62—Syracuse	71	2705	1442	644	.446	404	331	.819	524	313	252	2	1619	22.8
62-63—Syracuse	80	2631	1293	600	.464	434	362	.834	457	275	286	4	1562	19.5
63-64—Philadelphia	80	3157	1611	715	.444	525	435	.829	484	374	291	6	1865	23.3
64-65—Philadelphia	70	2600	1245	539	.433	413	335	.811	355	313	254	7	1413	20.2
65-66—Philadelphia	80	3326	1580	703	.445	514	413	.804	473	384	315	6	1819	22.7
66-67—Philadelphia	80	3086	1524	699	.459	466	367	.788	422	303	302	5	1765	22.1
67-68—Philadelphia	82	3263	1626	777	.478	549	422	.769	444	372	289	6	1976	24.1
68-69—Philadelphia	82	3311	1595	732	.459	543	432	.796	435	414	294	8	1896	23.1
69-70—Philadelphia	80	3024	1551	705	.455	432	352	.815	376	405	300	8	1762	22.0
70-71—Philadelphia	81	3060	1371	591	.431	405	326	.805	364	369	289	4	1508	18.6
71-72—Philadelphia	81	2410	866	389	.449	234	181	.774	271	316	268	10	959	11.8
72-73—Philadelphia	38	848	232	91	.392	39	32	.821	106	111	76	1	214	5.6
Totals	1122	39788	18811	8504	.452	5717	4578	.801	5665	4540	3855	72	21586	19.2

NBA PLAYOFF RECORD

Sea.—Team	G.	Min.	FGA	FGM	Pct.	FTA	FTM	Pct.	Reb.	Ast.	PF	Disq.	Pts.	Avg.
58-59—Syracuse	9	277	93	39	.419	32	26	.813	47	20	35	2	104	11.6
59-60—Syracuse	3	84	43	22	.512	4	3	.750	14	10	5	0	47	15.7
60-61—Syracuse	8	232	106	41	.387	40	33	.825	33	19	32	1	115	14.4
61-62—Syracuse	1	5	0	0	.000	0	0	.000	0	0	1	0	0	0.0
62-63—Syracuse	5	214	87	44	.506	35	29	.829	27	21	21	1	117	23.4
63-64—Philadelphia	5	211	95	37	.389	39	33	.846	28	30	19	1	107	21.4
64-65—Philadelphia	11	505	222	101	.455	87	69	.793	81	55	45	2	271	24.6
65-66—Philadelphia	5	226	91	32	.352	23	18	.783	36	21	21	0	82	16.4
66-67—Philadelphia	15	688	375	161	.429	118	94	.797	88	79	55	1	416	27.7

Sea.—Team	G.	Min.	FGA	FGM	Pct.	FTA	FTM	Pct.	Reb.	Ast.	PF	Disq.	Pts.	Avg.
67-68—Philadelphia	13	553	278	120	.432	111	95	.858	79	55	49	1	335	25.8
68-69—Philadelphia	5	204	81	26	.321	36	28	.778	30	23	23	0	80	16.0
69-70—Philadelphia	5	178	74	33	.446	13	11	.846	17	27	16	0	77	15.4
70-71—Philadelphia	7	265	112	49	.438	36	27	.750	25	33	35	4	125	17.9
Totals	92	3642	1657	705	.425	574	466	.812	505	393	357	13	1876	20.4

NBA ALL-STAR GAME RECORD

Season—Team	Min.	FGA	FGM	Pct.	FTA	FTM	Pct.	Reb.	Ast.	PF	Disq.	Pts.
1961—Syracuse	18	11	7	.636	0	0	.000	6	2	2	0	14
1962—Syracuse	24	14	3	.214	7	2	.286	10	9	3	0	8
1963—Syracuse	15	7	3	.429	0	0	.000	3	2	4	0	6
1964—Philadelphia	20	10	5	.500	4	3	.750	3	4	1	0	13
1965—Philadelphia	21	11	5	.455	4	3	.750	4	1	2	0	13
1966—Philadelphia	23	13	4	.308	1	1	1.000	5	1	4	0	9
1967—Philadelphia	31	16	5	.313	8	7	.875	4	1	5	0	17
1968—Philadelphia	17	8	8	1.000	7	5	.714	3	3	2	0	21
1969—Philadelphia	17	1	0	.000	5	4	.800	3	2	2	0	4
1970—Philadelphia	21	11	7	.636	1	1	1.000	4	3	4	0	15
Totals	207	102	47	.461	37	26	.703	45	28	29	0	120

CBA COACHING RECORD

		Regular Season				Playoffs	
Sea.	Club	W.	L.	Pct.	Pos.	W.	L.
1980-81	Phila. Kings	17	23	.425	3†	6	6

†Eastern Division.

Elected to Naismith Memorial Basketball Hall of Fame 1981. . . . Named to All-NBA Second Team, 1963, 1964, 1965, 1966, 1967, 1968, 1969. . . . NBA All-Star Game MVP, 1968. . . . Holds NBA All-Star Game record for most points in one quarter, 19, in 1968. . . . Member of NBA championship team, 1967.

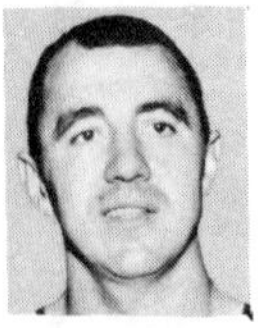

RICHARD V. GUERIN

Born May 29, 1932 at New York, N. Y. Height 6:04. Weight 210.

High School—Bronx, N. Y., Mt. St. Michael.

College—Iona College, New Rochelle, N. Y.

Drafted by New York on second round, 1954.

In military service, 1954-55 and 1955-56 seasons, played with Quantico Marines and Marine All-Star teams. Traded by New York to St. Louis for cash and a 2nd round draft choice, October 18, 1963.

—COLLEGIATE RECORD—

Year	G.	Min.	FGA	FGM	Pct.	FTA	FTM	Pct.	Reb.	Pts.	Avg.
50-51†	..	....	...	...	....	...	...	....	....	....	....
51-52	27	....	...	159	....	...	146	....	....	464	17.2
52-53	21	....	...	139	.491	...	114	.662	....	392	18.7
53-54	21	....	405	171	.422	249	177	.711	....	519	24.7
Varsity Totals	69	....	...	469	....	...	437	....	....	1375	19.9

NBA REGULAR SEASON RECORD

Sea.—Team	G.	Min.	FGA	FGM	Pct.	FTA	FTM	Pct.	Reb.	Ast.	PF	Disq.	Pts.	Avg.
56-57—New York	72	1793	699	257	.368	292	181	.620	334	182	186	3	695	9.7
57-58—New York	63	2368	973	344	.354	511	353	.691	489	317	202	3	1041	16.5
58-59—New York	71	2558	1046	443	.424	505	405	.802	518	364	255	1	1291	18.2
59-60—New York	74	2429	1379	579	.420	591	457	.773	505	468	242	3	1615	21.8
60-61—New York	79	3023	1545	612	.396	626	496	.792	628	503	310	3	1720	21.8
61-62—New York	78	3346	1897	839	.442	762	625	.820	501	539	299	3	2303	29.5
62-63—New York	79	2712	1380	596	.432	600	509	.848	331	348	228	2	1701	21.5
63-64—N.Y.-St.L.	80	2366	846	351	.415	424	347	.818	256	375	276	4	1049	13.1
64-65—St. Louis	57	1678	662	295	.446	301	231	.767	149	271	193	1	821	14.4
65-66—St. Louis	80	2363	998	414	.415	446	362	.812	314	388	256	4	1190	14.9
66-67—St. Louis	79	2275	904	394	.436	416	304	.731	192	345	247	2	1092	13.8
67-68—	Voluntarily Retired													
68-69—Atlanta	27	472	111	47	.423	74	57	.770	59	99	66	0	151	5.6
69-70—Atlanta	8	64	11	3	.273	1	1	1.000	2	12	9	0	7	0.9
Totals	847	27447	12451	5174	.416	5549	4328	.780	4278	4211	2769	29	14676	17.3

NBA PLAYOFF RECORD

Sea.—Team	G.	Min.	FGA	FGM	Pct.	FTA	FTM	Pct.	Reb.	Ast.	PF	Disq.	Pts.	Avg.
58-59—New York	2	77	35	9	.257	14	12	.857	18	15	11	1	30	15.0
63-64—St. Louis	12	428	169	75	.444	85	67	.788	50	49	54	1	217	18.1
64-65—St. Louis	4	125	65	25	.385	25	19	.760	8	21	14	0	69	17.3
65-66—St. Louis	10	399	159	72	.453	76	62	.816	37	79	41	0	206	20.6
66-67—St. Louis	9	228	86	36	.419	30	24	.800	23	39	23	0	96	10.7
68-69—Atlanta	3	32	4	1	.250	2	1	.500	5	7	8	0	3	1.0
69-70—Atlanta	2	56	21	13	.619	7	7	1.000	8	4	6	0	33	16.5
Totals	42	1345	539	231	.429	239	192	.803	149	214	157	2	654	15.6

NBA ALL-STAR GAME RECORD

Season—Team	Min.	FGA	FGM	Pct.	FTA	FTM	Pct.	Reb.	Ast.	PF	Disq.	Pts.
1958—New York	22	10	2	.200	4	3	.750	8	7	3	0	7
1959—New York	22	7	1	.143	5	3	.600	3	3	1	0	5
1960—New York	22	11	5	.455	2	2	1.000	4	4	4	0	12
1961—New York	15	8	3	.375	6	5	.833	0	2	1	0	11
1962—New York	27	17	10	.588	6	3	.500	3	1	6	1	23
1963—New York	14	3	2	.667	3	1	.333	1	1	2	0	5
Totals	122	56	23	.411	26	17	.654	19	18	17	0	63

NBA COACHING RECORD

	Regular Season				Playoffs	
Sea. Club	W.	L.	Pct.	Pos.	W.	L.
1964-65—St. Louis	28	19	.596	2	1	3
1965-66—St. Louis	36	44	.450	3	6	4
1966-67—St. Louis	39	42	.476	2	5	4
1967-68—St. Louis	56	26	.683	1	2	4
1968-69—Atlanta	48	34	.585	2	5	6
1969-70—Atlanta	48	34	.585	1	4	5
1970-71—Atlanta	36	46	.439	2	1	4
1971-72—Atlanta	36	46	.439	2	2	4
Totals (8 years)	327	291	.529		26	34

Named to All-NBA Second Team, 1959, 1960, 1962. . . . NBA Coach of the Year, 1968.

CLIFFORD OLDHAM HAGAN
(Cliff)

Born December 9, 1931 at Owensboro, Ky. Height 6:04. Weight 215.
High School—Owensboro, Ky.
College—University of Kentucky, Lexington, Ky.
Drafted by Boston on third round, 1953.

In military service, 1954-55 and 1955-56, played at Andrews Air Force Base.
Draft rights traded by Boston with Ed Macauley to St. Louis for 1st round draft choice, April 30, 1956.
Signed as player-coach by Dallas ABA, June, 1967.

—COLLEGIATE RECORD—

Year	G.	Min.	FGA	FGM	Pct.	FTA	FTM	Pct.	Reb.	Pts.	Avg.
49-50†	12	....	244	114	.467	58	42	.724	...	270	22.5
50-51	20	....	188	69	.367	61	45	.738	169	183	9.2
51-52	32	....	633	264	.417	235	164	.698	528	692	21.6
52-53	Did Not Play—Kentucky had no team										
53-54	25	....	514	234	.455	191	132	.691	338	600	24.0
Varsity Totals	77	....	1335	567	.425	487	341	.700	1035	1475	19.2

NBA REGULAR SEASON RECORD

Sea.—Team	G.	Min.	FGA	FGM	Pct.	FTA	FTM	Pct.	Reb.	Ast.	PF	Disq.	Pts.	Avg.
56-57—St. Louis	67	971	371	134	.361	145	100	.690	247	86	165	3	368	5.5
57-58—St. Louis	70	2190	1135	503	.443	501	385	.768	707	175	267	9	1391	19.9
58-59—St. Louis	72	2702	1417	646	.456	536	415	.774	783	245	275	10	1707	23.7
59-60—St. Louis	75	2798	1549	719	.464	524	421	.803	803	299	270	4	1859	24.8
60-61—St. Louis	78	2701	1490	661	.441	467	383	.820	718	381	286	9	1705	21.9
61-62—St. Louis	77	2784	1490	701	.470	439	362	.825	533	370	282	8	1764	22.9
62-63—St. Louis	79	1716	1055	491	.465	305	244	.800	341	191	221	2	1226	15.5
63-64—St. Louis	77	2279	1280	572	.447	331	269	.813	377	189	272	4	1413	18.4
64-65—St. Louis	77	1739	901	393	.436	268	214	.799	276	136	182	0	1000	13.0
65-66—St. Louis	74	1851	942	419	.445	206	176	.854	234	164	177	1	1014	13.7
Totals	746	21731	11630	5239	.450	3722	2969	.798	5019	2236	2397	50	13447	18.0

NBA PLAYOFF RECORD

Sea.—Team	G.	Min.	FGA	FGM	Pct.	FTA	FTM	Pct.	Reb.	Ast.	PF	Disq.	Pts.	Avg.
56-57—St. Louis	10	419	143	62	.434	63	46	.730	112	28	47	3	170	17.0
57-58—St. Louis	11	418	221	111	.502	99	83	.838	115	37	48	3	305	27.7
58-59—St. Louis	6	259	123	63	.512	54	45	.833	72	16	21	0	171	28.5
59-60—St. Louis	14	544	296	125	.422	109	89	.816	138	54	54	1	339	24.2
60-61—St. Louis	12	455	235	104	.442	69	56	.811	118	54	45	1	264	22.0
62-63—St. Louis	11	255	179	83	.464	53	37	.698	55	34	42	4	203	18.5
63-64—St. Louis	12	392	175	75	.429	54	45	.833	74	57	34	0	195	16.2
64-65—St. Louis	4	123	75	34	.453	12	6	.500	26	7	14	0	74	18.5
65-66—St. Louis	10	200	97	44	.454	27	25	.926	34	18	15	0	113	11.3
Totals	90	3065	1544	701	.454	540	432	.800	744	305	320	12	1834	20.4

NBA ALL-STAR GAME RECORD

Season—Team	Min.	FGA	FGM	Pct.	FTA	FTM	Pct.	Reb.	Ast.	PF	Disq.	Pts.
1958—St. Louis	Chosen—Injured, Did Not Play											
1959—St. Louis	22	12	6	.500	3	3	1.000	8	3	5	0	15
1960—St. Louis	21	9	1	.111	0	0	.000	3	2	1	0	2
1961—St. Louis	13	2	9	.000	2	2	1.000	2	0	1	0	2
1962—St. Louis	9	3	1	.333	0	0	.000	2	1	1	0	2
Totals	65	26	8	.308	5	5	1.000	15	6	8	0	21

ABA REGULAR SEASON RECORD

Sea.—Team	G.	Min.	2-Point FGM	2-Point FGA	2-Point Pct.	3-Point FGM	3-Point FGA	3-Point Pct.	FTM	FTA	Pct.	Reb.	Ast.	Pts.	Avg.
67-68—Dallas	56	1737	371	756	.491	0	3	.000	277	351	.789	334	276	1019	18.2
68-69—Dallas	35	579	132	258	.512	0	1	.000	123	144	.854	102	122	387	11.1
69-70—Dallas	3	27	8	12	.667	0	1	.000	1	2	.500	....	....	17	5.7
Totals	94	2343	511	1026	.498	0	5	.000	401	497	.807	436	398	1423	15.1

ABA PLAYOFF RECORD

Sea.—Team	G.	Min.	2-Point FGM	2-Point FGA	2-Point Pct.	3-Point FGM	3-Point FGA	3-Point Pct.	FTM	FTA	Pct.	Reb.	Ast.	Pts.	Avg.
67-68—Dallas	3	70	14	37	.378	0	0	.000	9	13	.692	13	9	37	12.3
68-69—Dallas	2	45	5	14	.357	0	0	.000	8	10	.800	6	14	18	9.0
Totals	5	115	19	51	.373	0	0	.000	17	23	.739	19	23	55	11.0

ABA ALL-STAR GAME RECORD

Sea.—Team	G.	Min.	2-Point FGM	2-Point FGA	2-Point Pct.	3-Point FGM	3-Point FGA	3-Point Pct.	FTM	FTA	Pct.	Reb.	Ast.	Pts.	Avg.
67-68—Dallas	1	24	4	11	.364	0	0	.000	2	2	1.000	0	5	10	10.0

ABA COACHING RECORD

Sea. Club	Regular Season W.	L.	Pct.	Pos.	Playoffs W.	L.
1967-68—Dallas	46	32	.590	2†	4	4
1968-69—Dallas	41	37	.526	4†	3	4
1969-70—Dallas	22	21	.512	..	..	..
Totals	109	90	.548		7	8

†Western Division.

Elected to Naismith Memorial Basketball Hall of Fame, 1977. . . . Member of NBA championship team, 1958. . . . Named to All-NBA Second Team, 1958 and 1959. . . . Member of NCAA championship team, 1951.

JOHN J. HAVLICEK
(Hondo)

Born April 8, 1940 at Martins Ferry, O. Height 6:05. Weight 205.
High School—Bridgeport, O.
College—Ohio State University, Columbus, O.
Drafted by Boston on first round, 1962.

—COLLEGIATE RECORD—

Year	G.	Min.	FGA	FGM	Pct.	FTA	FTM	Pct.	Reb.	Pts.	Avg.
58-59†	Freshman team did not play an intercollegiate schedule.										
59-60	28	....	312	144	.462	74	53	.716	205	341	12.2
60-61	28	....	321	173	.539	87	61	.701	244	407	14.5
61-62	28	....	377	196	.520	109	83	.761	271	475	17.0
Varsity Totals	84	....	1010	513	.508	270	197	.730	720	1223	14.6

NBA REGULAR SEASON RECORD

Sea.—Team	G.	Min.	FGA	FGM	Pct.	FTA	FTM	Pct.	Reb.	Ast.	PF	Disq.	Pts.	Avg.
62-63—Boston	80	2200	1085	483	.445	239	174	.728	534	179	189	2	1140	14.3
63-64—Boston	80	2587	1535	640	.417	422	315	.746	428	238	227	1	1595	19.9
64-65—Boston	75	2169	1420	570	.401	316	235	.744	371	199	200	2	1375	18.3
65-66—Boston	71	2175	1328	530	.399	349	274	.785	423	210	158	1	1334	18.8
66-67—Boston	81	2602	1540	684	.444	441	365	.828	532	278	210	0	1733	21.4
67-68—Boston	82	2921	1551	666	.429	453	368	.812	546	384	237	2	1700	20.7
68-69—Boston	82	3174	1709	692	.405	496	387	.780	570	441	247	0	1771	21.6
69-70—Boston	81	3369	1585	736	.464	578	488	.844	635	550	211	1	1960	24.2
70-71—Boston	81	3678	1982	892	.450	677	554	.818	730	607	200	0	2338	28.9
71-72—Boston	82	3698	1957	897	.458	549	458	.834	672	614	183	1	2252	27.5
72-73—Boston	80	3367	1704	766	.450	431	370	.858	567	529	195	1	1902	23.8

Sea.—Team	G.	Min.	FGA	FGM	Pct.	FTA	FTM	Pct.	Rebounds Off.	Rebounds Def.	Rebounds Tot.	Ast.	PF	Dq.	Stl.	Blk.	Pts.	Avg.
73-74—Boston	76	3091	1502	685	.456	416	346	.832	138	349	487	447	196	1	95	32	1716	22.6
74-75—Boston	82	3132	1411	642	.455	332	289	.870	154	330	484	432	231	2	110	16	1573	19.2
75-76—Boston	76	2598	1121	504	.450	333	281	.844	116	198	314	278	204	1	97	29	1289	17.0
76-77—Boston	79	2913	1283	580	.452	288	235	.816	109	273	382	400	208	4	84	18	1395	17.7
77-78—Boston	82	2797	1217	546	.449	269	230	.855	93	239	332	328	185	2	90	22	1322	16.1
Totals	1270	46471	23930	10513	.439	6589	5369	.815			8007	6114	3281	21	476	117	26395	20.8

NBA PLAYOFF RECORD

Sea.—Team	G.	Min.	FGA	FGM	Pct.	FTA	FTM	Pct.	Reb.	Ast.	PF	Disq.	Pts.	Avg.
62-63—Boston	11	254	125	56	.448	27	18	.667	53	17	28	1	130	11.8
63-64—Boston	10	289	159	61	.384	44	35	.795	43	32	26	0	157	15.7
64-65—Boston	12	405	250	88	.352	55	46	.836	88	29	44	1	222	18.5

JOHN HAVLICEK

Sea.—Team	G.	Min.	FGA	FGM	Pct.	FTA	FTM	Pct.	Reb.	Ast.	PF	Disq.	Pts.	Avg.
65-66—Boston	17	719	374	153	.409	113	95	.841	154	70	69	2	401	23.6
66-67—Boston	9	330	212	95	.448	71	57	.803	73	28	30	0	247	27.4
67-68—Boston	19	862	407	184	.452	151	125	.828	164	142	67	1	493	25.9
68-69—Boston	18	850	382	170	.445	138	118	.855	179	100	58	2	458	25.4
71-72—Boston	11	517	235	108	.460	99	85	.859	92	70	35	1	301	27.4
72-73—Boston	12	479	235	112	.477	74	61	.824	62	65	24	0	285	23.8

									—Rebounds—									
Sea.—Team	G.	Min.	FGA	FGM	Pct.	FTA	FTM	Pct.	Off.	Def.	Tot.	Ast.	PF	Dq.	Stl.	Blk.	Pts.	Avg.
73-74—Boston	18	811	411	199	.484	101	89	.881	28	88	116	108	43	0	24	6	487	27.1
74-75—Boston	11	464	192	83	.432	76	66	.868	18	39	57	51	38	1	16	1	232	21.1
75-76—Boston	15	505	180	80	.444	47	38	.809	18	38	56	51	22	0	12	5	198	13.2
76-77—Boston	9	375	167	62	.371	50	41	.820	15	34	49	62	33	0	8	4	165	18.3
Totals	172	6860	3329	1451	.436	1046	874	.836			1186	825	517	9	60	16	3776	22.0

NBA ALL-STAR GAME RECORD

Season—Team	Min.	FGA	FGM	Pct.	FTA	FTM	Pct.	Reb.	Ast.	PF	Disq.	Pts.
1966—Boston	25	16	6	.375	6	6	1.000	6	1	2	0	18
1967—Boston	17	14	7	.500	0	0	.000	2	1	1	0	14
1968—Boston	22	15	9	.600	11	8	.727	5	4	0	0	26
1969—Boston	31	14	6	.429	2	2	1.000	7	2	2	0	14
1970—Boston	29	15	7	.467	3	3	1.000	5	7	2	0	17
1971—Boston	24	12	6	.500	2	0	.000	3	2	3	0	12
1972—Boston	24	13	5	.385	5	5	1.000	3	2	2	0	15
1973—Boston	22	10	6	.600	5	2	.400	3	5	1	0	14

								—Rebounds—								
Season—Team	Min.	FGA	FGM	Pct.	FTA	FTM	Pct.	Off.	Def.	Tot.	Ast.	PF	Dq.	Stl.	Blk.	Pts.
1974—Boston	18	10	5	.500	2	0	.000	0	0	0	2	2	0	1	0	10
1975—Boston	31	12	7	.583	2	2	1.000	1	5	6	1	2	0	2	0	16
1976—Boston	21	10	3	.300	3	3	1.000	1	1	2	2	0	0	1	0	9
1977—Boston	17	5	2	.400	0	0	.000	0	1	1	1	1	0	0	0	4
1978—Boston	22	8	5	.625	0	0	.000	0	3	3	1	2	0	0	0	10
Totals	303	154	74	.481	41	31	.756			46	31	20	0	4	0	179

Elected to Naismith Memorial Basketball Hall of Fame, 1983. . . . Named to NBA 35th Anniversary All-Time Team, 1980. . . . All-NBA First Team, 1971, 1972, 1973, 1974. . . . All-NBA Second Team, 1964, 1966, 1968, 1969, 1970, 1975, 1976. . . . NBA All-Defensive First Team, 1972, 1973, 1974, 1975, 1976. . . . NBA All-Defensive Second Team, 1969, 1970, 1971. . . . NBA Playoff MVP, 1974. . . . Shares NBA playoff game record for most field goals made, 24, vs. Atlanta, April 1, 1973. . . . Holds NBA championship series record for most points in overtime period, 9, vs. Milwaukee, May 10, 1974. . . . Member of NBA championship teams, 1963, 1964, 1965, 1966, 1968, 1969, 1974, 1976. . . . Selected as wide receiver by Cleveland Browns on seventh round of 1962 National Football League draft. . . . Named to THE SPORTING NEWS All-America Second Team, 1962. . . . Member of NCAA championship team, 1960.

ELVIN ERNEST HAYES

Born November 17, 1945 at Rayville, La. Height 6:09. Weight 235.

High School—Rayville, La., Eula D. Britton.

College—University of Houston, Houston, Tex.

Drafted by San Diego on first round, 1968 (1st pick).

Traded by Houston to Baltimore for Jack Marin and future considerations, June 23, 1972.
Traded by Washington to Houston for 1981 and 1983 2nd round draft choices, June 8, 1981.

—COLLEGIATE RECORD—

Year	G.	Min.	FGA	FGM	Pct.	FTA	FTM	Pct.	Reb.	Pts.	Avg.
64-65†	21	......	478	217	.454	176	93	.528	500	527	25.1
65-66	29	946	570	323	.567	257	143	.556	490	789	27.2
66-67	31	1119	750	373	.497	227	135	.595	488	881	28.4
67-68	33	1270	945	519	.549	285	176	.618	624	1214	36.8
Varsity Totals	93	3335	2265	1215	.536	769	454	.590	1602	2884	31.0

NBA REGULAR SEASON RECORD

Sea.—Team	G.	Min.	FGA	FGM	Pct.	FTA	FTM	Pct.	Reb.	Ast.	PF	Disq.	Pts.	Avg.
68-69—San Diego	82	3695	2082	930	.447	746	467	.626	1406	113	266	2	2327	28.4
69-70—San Diego	82	3665	2020	914	.452	622	428	.688	1386	162	270	5	2256	27.5
70-71—San Diego	82	3633	2215	948	.428	676	454	.672	1362	186	225	1	2350	28.7
71-72—Houston	82	3461	1918	832	.434	615	399	.649	1197	270	233	1	2063	25.2
72-73—Baltimore	81	3347	1607	713	.444	434	291	.671	1177	127	232	3	1717	21.2

									—Rebounds—									
Sea.—Team	G.	Min.	FGA	FGM	Pct.	FTA	FTM	Pct.	Off.	Def.	Tot.	Ast.	PF	Dq.	Stl.	Blk.	Pts.	Avg.
73-74—Capital	81	3602	1627	689	.423	495	357	.721	354	1109	1463	163	252	1	86	240	1735	21.4
74-75—Washington	82	3465	1668	739	.443	534	409	.766	221	783	1004	206	238	0	158	187	1887	23.0
75-76—Washington	80	2975	1381	649	.470	457	287	.628	210	668	878	121	293	5	104	202	1585	19.8
76-77—Washington	82	3364	1516	760	.501	614	422	.687	289	740	1029	158	312	1	87	220	1942	23.7
77-78—Washington	81	3246	1409	636	.451	514	326	.634	335	740	1075	149	313	7	96	159	1598	19.7
78-79—Washington	82	3105	1477	720	.487	534	349	.654	312	682	994	143	308	5	75	190	1789	21.8
79-80—Washington	81	3183	1677	761	.454	478	334	.699	269	627	896	129	309	9	62	189	1859	23.0
80-81—Washington	81	2931	1296	584	.451	439	271	.617	235	554	789	98	300	6	68	171	1439	17.8

Sea.—Team	G.	Min.	FGA	FGM	Pct.	FTA	FTM	Pct.	—Rebounds— Off.	Def.	Tot.	Ast.	PF	Dq.	Stl.	Blk.	Pts.	Avg.
81-82—Houston	82	3032	1100	519	.472	422	280	.664	267	480	747	144	287	4	62	104	1318	16.1
82-83—Houston	81	2302	890	424	.476	287	196	.683	199	417	616	158	232	2	50	81	1046	12.9
83-84—Houston	81	994	389	158	.406	132	86	.652	87	173	260	71	123	1	16	28	402	5.0
Totals	1303	50000	24272	10976	.452	7999	5356	.670			16279	2398	4193	53	864	1771	27313	21.0

Three-Point Field Goals: 1979-80, 3-for-13 (.231). 1980-81, 0-for-10. 1981-82, 0-for-5. 1982-83, 2-for-4 (.500). 1983-84, 0-for-2. Totals, 5-for-34 (.147).

NBA PLAYOFF RECORD

Sea.—Team	G.	Min.	FGA	FGM	Pct.	FTA	FTM	Pct.	Reb.	Ast.	PF	Disq.	Pts.	Avg.
68-69—San Diego	6	278	114	60	.526	53	35	.660	83	5	21	0	155	25.8
72-73—Baltimore	5	228	105	53	.505	33	23	.697	57	5	16	0	129	25.8

Sea.—Team	G.	Min.	FGA	FGM	Pct.	FTA	FTM	Pct.	—Rebounds— Off.	Def.	Tot.	Ast.	PF	Dq.	Stl.	Blk.	Pts.	Avg.
73-74—Capital	7	323	143	76	.531	41	29	.707	31	80	111	21	23	0	5	15	181	25.9
74-75—Washington	17	751	372	174	.468	127	86	.677	46	140	186	37	70	3	26	39	434	25.5
75-76—Washington	7	305	122	54	.443	55	32	.582	16	72	88	10	24	0	5	28	140	20.0
76-77—Washington	9	405	173	74	.428	59	41	.695	29	93	122	17	39	0	10	22	189	21.0
77-78—Washington	21	868	385	189	.491	133	79	.594	103	176	279	43	86	2	32	52	457	21.8
78-79—Washington	19	786	396	170	.429	130	87	.669	94	172	266	38	79	3	17	52	427	22.5
79-80—Washington	2	92	41	16	.390	10	8	.800	10	12	22	6	8	0	0	4	40	20.0
81-82—Houston	3	124	50	17	.340	15	8	.533	7	23	30	3	12	0	2	10	42	14.0
Totals	96	4160	1901	883	.464	656	428	.652			1244	185	378	8	97	222	2194	22.9

NBA ALL-STAR GAME RECORD

Season—Team	Min.	FGA	FGM	Pct.	FTA	FTM	Pct.	Reb.	Ast.	PF	Disq.	Pts.
1969—San Diego	21	9	4	.444	3	3	1.000	5	0	4	0	11
1970—San Diego	35	21	9	.429	12	6	.500	15	1	1	0	24
1971—San Diego	19	13	4	.308	3	2	.667	4	2	1	0	10
1972—Houston	11	6	1	.167	2	2	1.000	2	0	2	0	4
1973—Baltimore	16	13	4	.308	2	2	1.000	12	0	0	0	10

Season—Team	Min.	FGA	FGM	Pct.	FTA	FTM	Pct.	—Rebounds— Off.	Def.	Tot.	Ast.	PF	Dq.	Stl.	Blk.	Pts.
1974—Capital	35	13	5	.385	3	2	.667	4	11	15	6	4	0	0	1	12
1975—Washington	17	6	2	.333	0	0	.000	0	5	5	2	1	0	1	0	4
1976—Washington	31	14	6	.429	2	0	.000	3	7	10	1	5	0	1	0	12
1977—Washington	11	6	6	1.000	0	0	.000	0	2	2	1	5	0	0	0	12
1978—Washington	11	7	1	.143	0	0	.000	3	1	4	0	4	0	1	0	2
1979—Washington	28	11	5	.455	5	3	.600	4	9	13	0	5	0	1	1	13
1980—Washington	29	10	5	.500	2	2	1.000	2	3	5	4	5	0	1	4	12
Totals	264	129	52	.403	34	22	.647			92	17	37	0	5	6	126

Elected to Naismith Memorial Basketball Hall of Fame, 1989. . . . Named to All-NBA First Team, 1975, 1977, 1979. . . . All-NBA Second Team, 1973, 1974, 1976. . . . NBA All-Rookie Team, 1969. . . . NBA All-Defensive Second Team, 1974 and 1975. . . . Led NBA in scoring, 1969. . . . Led NBA in rebounding, 1970 and 1974. . . . Member of NBA championship team, 1978. . . . THE SPORTING NEWS College Player of the Year, 1968. . . . Named to THE SPORTING NEWS All-America First Team, 1967 and 1968. . . . THE SPORTING NEWS All-America Second Team, 1966.

SPENCER HAYWOOD

Born April 22, 1949 at Silver City, Miss. Height 6:09. Weight 225.

High School—Detroit, Mich., Pershing.

Colleges—Trinidad State Junior College, Trinidad, Colo., and University of Detroit, Detroit, Mich.

Drafted by Buffalo on second round, 1971 (30th pick).

Signed as undergraduate free agent by Denver ABA, August 16, 1969.
Terminated contract with Denver ABA and signed by Seattle NBA, 1971.
Traded by Seattle to New York for cash and the option of Eugene Short or a future draft choice, October 24, 1975.
Traded by New York to New Orleans for Joe C. Meriweather, January 5, 1979.
Traded by Utah to Los Angeles for Adrian Dantley, September 13, 1979.
Waived by Los Angeles, August 19, 1980; signed by Washington as a free agent, October 24, 1981.
Waived by Washington, March 9, 1983.
Played in Italy during 1980-81 and 1981-82 seasons.

—COLLEGIATE RECORD—

Trinidad State JC

Year	G.	Min.	FGA	FGM	Pct.	FTA	FTM	Pct.	Reb.	Pts.	Avg.
67-68	30	......	675	358	.530	195	129	.662	663	845	28.2

Detroit

Year	G.	Min.	FGA	FGM	Pct.	FTA	FTM	Pct.	Reb.	Pts.	Avg.
68-69	24	......	508	288	.567	254	195	.768	530	771	32.1

ITALIAN LEAGUE RECORD

Year	G.	Min.	FGA	FGM	Pct.	FTA	FTM	Pct.	Reb.	Pts.	Avg.
80-81—Venezia	34	....	601	334	.556	179	132	.737	354	800	23.5
81-82—Carrera	5	175	100	63	.630	32	24	.750	37	150	30.0

ABA REGULAR SEASON RECORD

Sea.—Team	G.	Min.	2-Point FGM	2-Point FGA	2-Point Pct.	3-Point FGM	3-Point FGA	3-Point Pct.	FTM	FTA	Pct.	Reb.	Ast.	Pts.	Avg.
69-70—Denver	84	3808	986	1987	.496	0	11	.000	547	705	.776	1637	190	2519	30.0

NBA REGULAR SEASON RECORD

Sea.—Team	G.	Min.	FGA	FGM	Pct.	FTA	FTM	Pct.	Reb.	Ast.	PF	Disq.	Pts.	Avg.
70-71—Seattle	33	1162	579	260	.449	218	160	.733	396	48	84	1	680	20.6
71-72—Seattle	73	3167	1557	717	.461	586	480	.819	926	148	208	0	1914	26.2
72-73—Seattle	77	3259	1868	889	.476	564	473	.839	995	196	213	2	2251	29.2

									—Rebounds—									
Sea.—Team	G.	Min.	FGA	FGM	Pct.	FTA	FTM	Pct.	Off.	Def.	Tot.	Ast.	PF	Dq.	Stl.	Blk.	Pts.	Avg.
73-74—Seattle	75	3039	1520	694	.457	458	373	.814	318	689	1007	240	198	2	65	106	1761	23.5
74-75—Seattle	68	2529	1325	608	.459	381	309	.811	198	432	630	137	173	1	54	108	1525	22.4
75-76—New York	78	2892	1360	605	.445	448	339	.757	234	644	878	92	255	1	53	80	1549	19.9
76-77—Knicks	31	1021	449	202	.450	131	109	.832	77	203	280	50	72	0	14	29	513	16.5
77-78—New York	67	1765	852	412	.484	135	96	.711	141	301	442	126	188	1	37	72	920	13.7
78-79—N.Y.-N.O.	68	2361	1205	595	.494	292	231	.791	172	361	533	127	236	8	40	82	1421	20.9
79-80—Los Ang.	76	1544	591	288	.487	206	159	.772	132	214	346	93	197	2	35	57	736	9.7
81-82—Washington	76	2086	829	395	.476	260	219	.842	144	278	422	64	249	6	45	68	1009	13.3
82-83—Washington	38	775	312	125	.401	87	63	.724	77	106	183	30	94	2	12	27	313	8.2
Totals	760	25600	12447	5790	.465	3766	3011	.800			7038	1351	2167	26	355	629	14592	19.2

Three-Point Field Goals: 1979-80, 1-for-4 (.250). 1981-82, 0-for-3. 1982-83, 0-for-1. Totals, 1-for-8 (.125).

NBA PLAYOFF RECORD

									—Rebounds—									
Sea.—Team	G.	Min.	FGA	FGM	Pct.	FTA	FTM	Pct.	Off.	Def.	Tot.	Ast.	PF	Dq.	Stl.	Blk.	Pts.	Avg.
74-75—Seattle	9	337	131	47	.359	61	47	.770	20	61	81	18	29	0	7	11	141	15.7
77-78—New York	6	177	85	43	.506	11	11	1.000	19	23	42	12	24	1	2	5	97	16.2
79-80—Los Ang.	11	145	53	25	.472	16	13	.813	14	12	26	4	17	0	0	6	63	5.7
81-82—Washington	7	231	115	57	.496	35	26	.743	16	23	39	7	28	0	4	14	140	20.0
Totals	33	890	384	172	.448	123	97	.789	69	119	188	41	98	1	13	36	441	13.4

Three-Point Field Goals: 1979-80, 0-for-1.

NBA ALL-STAR GAME RECORD

Season—Team	Min.	FGA	FGM	Pct.	FTA	FTM	Pct.	Reb.	Ast.	PF	Disq.	Pts.
1972—Seattle	25	10	4	.400	4	3	.750	7	1	2	0	11
1973—Seattle	22	10	5	.500	2	2	1.000	10	0	5	0	12

								—Rebounds—								
Season—Team	Min.	FGA	FGM	Pct.	FTA	FTM	Pct.	Off.	Def.	Tot.	Ast.	PF	Dq.	Stl.	Blk.	Pts.
1974—Seattle	33	17	10	.588	3	3	1.000	2	9	11	5	5	0	0	3	23
1975—Seattle	17	9	1	.111	0	0	.000	1	2	3	0	1	0	0	0	2
Totals	97	46	20	.435	9	8	.889			31	6	13	0	0	3	48

Named to All-NBA First Team, 1972 and 1973. . . . All-NBA Second Team, 1974 and 1975. . . . Member of NBA championship team, 1980. . . . Named to ABA All-Star First Team, 1970. . . . ABA Most Valuable Player and Rookie of the Year, 1970. . . . ABA All-Star Game MVP, 1970. . . . Led ABA in scoring and rebounding, 1970. . . . Led NCAA in rebounding, 1969. . . . Member of U. S. Olympic team, 1968. . . . THE SPORTING NEWS All-America First Team, 1969.

BAILEY E. HOWELL

Born January 20, 1937 at Middleton, Tenn. Height 6:07. Weight 220.

High School—Middleton, Tenn.

College—Mississippi State University, Mississippi State, Miss.

Drafted by Detroit on first round, 1959.

Traded by Detroit with Bob Ferry, Don Ohl, Wally Jones and Les Hunter to Baltimore for Terry Dischinger, Don Kojis and Rod Thorn, June 18, 1964.

Traded by Baltimore to Boston for Mel Counts, September 1, 1966.

Selected from Boston by Buffalo in expansion draft, May 11, 1970.

Traded by Buffalo to Philadelphia for Bob Kauffman and cash or a draft choice, May 11, 1970.

—COLLEGIATE RECORD—

Year	G.	Min.	FGA	FGM	Pct.	FTA	FTM	Pct.	Reb.	Pts.	Avg.
55-56†					(Statistics unavailable)						
56-57	25	....	382	217	.568	285	213	.747	492	647	25.9
57-58	25	....	439	226	.515	315	243	.771	406	695	27.8
58-59	25	....	464	231	.498	292	226	.774	379	688	27.5
Varsity Totals	75	....	1285	674	.525	892	682	.765	1277	2030	27.1

NBA REGULAR SEASON RECORD

Sea.—Team	G.	Min.	FGA	FGM	Pct.	FTA	FTM	Pct.	Reb.	Ast.	PF	Disq.	Pts.	Avg.
59-60—Detroit	75	2346	1119	510	.456	422	312	.739	790	63	282	13	1332	17.8
60-61—Detroit	77	2752	1293	607	.469	798	601	.753	1111	196	297	10	1815	23.6
61-62—Detroit	79	2857	1193	553	.464	612	470	.768	996	186	317	10	1576	19.9
62-63—Detroit	79	2971	1235	637	.516	650	519	.798	910	232	301	9	1793	22.7

Sea.—Team	G.	Min.	FGA	FGM	Pct.	FTA	FTM	Pct.	Reb.	Ast.	PF	Disq.	Pts.	Avg.
63-64—Detroit	77	2700	1267	598	.472	581	470	.809	776	205	290	9	1666	21.6
64-65—Baltimore	80	2975	1040	515	.495	629	504	.801	869	208	345	10	1534	19.2
65-66—Baltimore	79	2328	986	481	.488	551	402	.730	773	155	306	12	1364	17.3
66-67—Boston	81	2503	1242	636	.512	471	349	.741	677	103	296	4	1621	20.0
67-68—Boston	82	2801	1336	643	.481	461	335	.727	805	133	285	4	1621	19.8
68-69—Boston	78	2527	1257	612	.487	426	313	.735	685	137	285	3	1537	19.7
69-70—Boston	82	2078	931	399	.429	308	235	.763	550	120	261	4	1033	12.6
70-71—Philadelphia	82	1589	686	324	.472	315	230	.730	441	115	234	2	878	10.7
Totals	951	30427	13585	6515	.480	6224	4740	.762	9383	1853	3499	90	17770	18.7

NBA PLAYOFF RECORD

Sea.—Team	G.	Min.	FGA	FGM	Pct.	FTA	FTM	Pct.	Reb.	Ast.	PF	Disq.	Pts.	Avg.
59-60—Detroit	2	72	41	14	.341	8	6	.750	17	3	8	0	34	17.0
60-61—Detroit	5	144	57	20	.351	23	16	.696	46	22	22	1	56	11.2
61-62—Detroit	10	378	163	69	.423	75	62	.827	96	23	48	3	200	20.0
62-63—Detroit	4	163	64	24	.375	27	23	.852	42	11	19	1	71	17.8
64-65—Baltimore	9	350	130	67	.515	70	53	.757	105	19	38	3	187	20.8
65-66—Baltimore	3	94	50	23	.460	11	8	.727	30	2	13	1	54	18.0
66-67—Boston	9	241	122	59	.484	30	20	.667	66	5	35	2	138	15.3
67-68—Boston	19	597	264	135	.511	107	74	.692	146	22	84	6	344	18.1
68-69—Boston	18	551	229	112	.489	64	46	.719	118	19	84	3	270	15.0
70-71—Philadelphia	7	122	45	19	.422	18	9	.500	31	4	25	1	47	6.7
Totals	86	2712	1165	542	.465	433	317	.732	697	130	376	21	1401	16.3

NBA ALL-STAR GAME RECORD

Season—Team	Min.	FGA	FGM	Pct.	FTA	FTM	Pct.	Reb.	Ast.	PF	Disq.	Pts.
1961—Detroit	16	10	5	.500	4	3	.750	3	3	4	0	13
1962—Detroit	8	2	1	.500	0	0	.000	0	1	1	0	2
1963—Detroit	11	3	2	.667	0	0	.000	1	1	2	0	4
1964—Detroit	6	3	1	.333	0	0	.000	2	0	0	0	2
1966—Baltimore	26	11	3	.273	2	1	.500	2	2	4	0	7
1967—Boston	14	4	1	.250	2	2	1.000	2	1	1	0	4
Totals	81	33	13	.394	8	6	.750	10	8	12	0	32

Named to All-NBA Second Team, 1963. . . . Member of NBA championship teams, 1968 and 1969. . . . Led NCAA major college division in field-goal percentage, 1957. . . . Named to THE SPORTING NEWS All-America First Team, 1959.

LOUIS C. HUDSON
(Lou)

Born July 11, 1944 at Greensboro, N. C. Height 6:05. Weight 210.
High School—Greensboro, N. C., Dudley.
College—University of Minnesota, Minneapolis, Minn.
Drafted by St. Louis on first round, 1966 (4th pick).

Traded by Atlanta to Los Angeles for Ollie Johnson, September 30, 1977.

—COLLEGIATE RECORD—

Year	G.	Min.	FGA	FGM	Pct.	FTA	FTM	Pct.	Reb.	Pts.	Avg.
62-63	(Freshman team did not play intercollegiate schedule.)										
63-64	24	....	435	191	.439	85	53	.624	191	435	18.1
64-65	24	....	463	231	.499	123	96	.780	247	558	23.3
65-66	17	....	303	143	.472	77	50	.649	138	336	19.8
Totals	65	....	1201	565	.470	285	199	.698	576	1329	20.4

NBA REGULAR SEASON RECORD

Sea.—Team	G.	Min.	FGA	FGM	Pct.	FTA	FTM	Pct.	Reb.	Ast.	PF	Disq.	Pts.	Avg.
66-67—St. Louis	80	2446	1328	620	.467	327	231	.706	435	95	277	3	1471	18.4
67-68—St. Louis	46	966	500	227	.454	164	120	.732	193	65	113	2	574	12.5
68-69—Atlanta	81	2869	1455	716	.492	435	338	.777	533	216	248	0	1770	21.9
69-70—Atlanta	80	3091	1564	830	.531	450	371	.824	373	276	225	1	2031	25.4
70-71—Atlanta	76	3113	1713	829	.484	502	381	.759	386	257	186	0	2039	26.8
71-72—Atlanta	77	3042	1540	775	.503	430	349	.812	385	309	225	0	1899	24.7
72-73—Atlanta	75	3027	1710	816	.477	481	397	.825	467	258	197	1	2029	27.1

									—Rebounds—										
Sea.—Team	G.	Min.	FGA	FGM	Pct.	FTA	FTM	Pct.	Off.	Def.	Tot.	Ast.	PF	Dq.	Stl.	Blk.	Pts.	Avg.
73-74—Atl.	65	2588	1356	678	.500	353	295	.836	126	224	350	216	205	3	160	29	1651	25.4
74-75—Atl.	11	380	225	97	.431	57	48	.842	14	33	47	40	33	1	13	2	242	22.0
75-76—Atl.	81	2558	1205	569	.472	291	237	.814	104	196	300	214	241	3	124	17	1375	17.0
76-77—Atl.	58	1745	905	413	.456	169	142	.840	48	81	129	155	160	2	67	19	968	16.7
77-78—L.A.	82	2283	992	493	.497	177	137	.774	80	108	188	193	196	0	94	14	1123	13.7
78-79—L.A.	78	1686	636	329	.517	124	110	.887	64	76	140	141	133	1	58	17	768	9.8
Totals	890	29794	15129	7392	.489	3960	3156	.797			3926	2432	2439	17	516	98	17940	20.2

NBA PLAYOFF RECORD

Sea.—Team	G.	Min.	FGA	FGM	Pct.	FTA	FTM	Pct.	Reb.	Ast.	PF	Disq.	Pts.	Avg.
66-67—St. Louis	9	317	179	77	.430	68	49	.723	48	15	35	1	203	22.6
67-68—St. Louis	6	181	99	44	.444	47	42	.894	43	14	21	0	130	21.7
68-69—Atlanta	11	424	216	101	.468	52	40	.769	59	32	43	1	242	22.0
69-70—Atlanta	9	360	187	78	.417	50	41	.820	40	33	34	2	197	21.9
70-71—Atlanta	5	213	108	49	.454	39	29	.744	35	15	19	0	127	25.4
71-72—Atlanta	6	266	139	63	.453	29	24	.828	33	21	13	0	150	25.0
72-73—Atlanta	6	255	166	76	.458	29	26	.897	47	17	16	0	178	29.7

Sea.—Team	G.	Min.	FGA	FGM	Pct.	FTA	FTM	Pct.	—Rebounds— Off.	Def.	Tot.	Ast.	PF	Dq.	Stl.	Blk.	Pts.	Avg.
77-78—L.A.	3	93	38	14	.368	8	7	.875	7	2	9	9	9	0	5	0	35	11.7
78-79—L.A.	6	90	32	17	.531	4	4	1.000	1	3	4	8	6	0	1	0	38	6.3
Totals	61	2199	1164	519	.446	326	262	.804			318	164	196	4	6	0	1300	21.3

NBA ALL-STAR GAME RECORD

Season—Team	Min.	FGA	FGM	Pct.	FTA	FTM	Pct.	Reb.	Ast.	PF	Disq.	Pts.
1969—Atlanta	20	13	6	.462	1	1	1.000	1	1	0	0	13
1970—Atlanta	18	12	5	.417	5	5	1.000	1	0	1	0	15
1971—Atlanta	17	13	6	.462	3	2	.667	3	1	3	0	14
1972—Atlanta	18	7	2	.286	2	2	1.000	3	3	3	0	6
1973—Atlanta	9	8	2	.250	2	2	1.000	2	0	2	0	6

Season—Team	Min.	FGA	FGM	Pct.	FTA	FTM	Pct.	—Rebounds— Off.	Def.	Tot.	Ast.	PF	Dq.	Stl.	Blk.	Pts.
1974—Atlanta	17	8	5	.625	2	2	1.000	1	2	3	1	2	0	0	1	12
Totals	99	61	26	.426	15	14	.933			13	6	11	0			66

Named to All-NBA Second Team, 1970. . . . NBA All-Rookie Team, 1967.

DANIEL PAUL ISSEL
(Dan)

Born October 25, 1948 at Batavia, Ill. Height 6:09. Weight 240.
High School—Batavia, Ill.
College—University of Kentucky, Lexington, Ky.
Drafted by Detroit on eighth round, 1970 (122nd pick).

Selected by Kentucky on first round of ABA draft, 1970.
Traded by Kentucky to Baltimore for Tom Owens and cash, September 19, 1975.
Traded by Baltimore to Denver for Dave Robisch and cash, October 8, 1975.
Entered NBA with Denver, 1976.

—COLLEGIATE RECORD—

Year	G.	Min.	FGA	FGM	Pct.	FTA	FTM	Pct.	Reb.	Pts.	Avg.
66-67†	20	....	332	168	.506	111	80	.721	355	416	20.8
67-68	27	836	390	171	.438	154	102	.662	328	444	16.4
68-69	28	1063	534	285	.534	232	176	.759	381	746	26.6
69-70	28	1044	667	369	.553	275	210	.764	369	948	33.9
Varsity Totals	83	2943	1591	825	.519	661	488	.738	1078	2138	25.8

ABA REGULAR SEASON RECORD

Sea.—Team	G.	Min.	—2-Point— FGM	FGA	Pct.	—3-Point— FGM	FGA	Pct.	FTM	FTA	Pct.	Reb.	Ast.	Pts.	Avg.
70-71—Kentucky	83	3274	938	1989	.472	0	5	.000	604	748	.807	1093	162	2480	29.9
71-72—Kentucky	83	3570	969	1990	.487	3	11	.273	591	753	.785	931	195	2538	30.6
72-73—Kentucky	84	3531	899	1742	.516	3	15	.200	485	635	.764	922	220	2292	27.3
73-74—Kentucky	83	3347	826	1709	.483	3	17	.176	457	581	.787	847	137	2118	25.5
74-75—Kentucky	83	2864	614	1298	.473	0	5	.000	237	321	.738	710	188	1465	17.7
75-76—Denver	84	2858	751	1468	.512	1	4	.250	425	521	.816	923	201	1930	23.0
Totals	500	19444	4997	10196	.490	10	57	.175	2799	3559	.787	5426	1103	12823	25.6

ABA PLAYOFF RECORD

Sea.—Team	G.	Min.	—2-Point— FGM	FGA	Pct.	—3-Point— FGM	FGA	Pct.	FTM	FTA	Pct.	Reb.	Ast.	Pts.	Avg.
70-71—Kentucky	19	670	207	408	.507	0	0	.000	123	141	.872	221	28	536	27.9
71-72—Kentucky	6	269	47	113	.416	0	1	.000	38	50	.760	54	5	132	22.0
72-73—Kentucky	19	821	197	392	.503	1	6	.167	124	156	.795	225	28	521	27.4
73-74—Kentucky	8	311	60	135	.444	0	0	.000	28	33	.848	87	14	148	18.5
74-75—Kentucky	15	578	122	261	.467	0	0	.000	60	74	.811	119	29	304	20.3
75-76—Denver	13	470	111	226	.491	0	1	.000	44	56	.786	156	32	266	20.5
Totals	80	3119	744	1535	.485	1	8	.125	417	510	.818	949	136	1907	23.8

ABA ALL-STAR GAME RECORD

Sea.—Team	Min.	—2-Point— FGM	FGA	Pct.	—3-Point— FGM	FGA	Pct.	FTM	FTA	Pct.	Reb.	Ast.	Pts.	Avg.
1971—Kentucky	34	8	15	.533	0	0	.000	5	8	.625	11	0	21	21.0
1972—Kentucky	23	9	13	.692	0	0	.000	3	4	.750	9	5	21	21.0
1973—Kentucky	29	6	14	.429	0	0	.000	2	2	1.000	7	4	14	14.0

Sea.—Team	Min.	2-Point FGM	FGA	Pct.	3-Point FGM	FGA	Pct.	FTM	FTA	Pct.	Reb.	Ast.	Pts.	Avg.
1974—Kentucky	26	10	15	.667	0	0	.000	1	1	1.000	4	1	21	21.0
1975—Kentucky	20	3	6	.500	0	0	.000	1	2	.500	7	1	7	7.0
1976—Denver	31	6	16	.375	0	0	.000	7	9	.778	9	5	19	19.0
Totals	163	42	79	.532	0	0	.000	19	26	.731	41	16	103	17.2

NBA REGULAR SEASON RECORD

Sea.—Team	G.	Min.	FGA	FGM	Pct.	FTA	FTM	Pct.	Rebounds Off.	Def.	Tot.	Ast.	PF	Dq.	Stl.	Blk.	Pts.	Avg.
76-77—Denver	79	2507	1282	660	.515	558	445	.797	211	485	696	177	246	7	91	29	1765	22.3
77-78—Denver	82	2851	1287	659	.512	547	428	.782	253	577	830	304	279	5	100	41	1746	21.3
78-79—Denver	81	2742	1030	532	.517	419	316	.754	240	498	738	255	233	6	61	46	1380	17.0
79-80—Denver	82	2938	1416	715	.505	667	517	.775	236	483	719	198	190	1	88	54	1951	23.8
80-81—Denver	80	2641	1220	614	.503	684	519	.759	229	447	676	158	249	6	83	53	1749	21.9
81-82—Denver	81	2472	1236	651	.527	655	546	.834	174	434	608	179	245	4	67	55	1852	22.9
82-83—Denver	80	2431	1296	661	.510	479	400	.835	151	445	596	223	227	0	83	43	1726	21.6
83-84—Denver	76	2076	1153	569	.493	428	364	.850	112	401	513	173	182	2	60	44	1506	19.8
84-85—Denver	77	1684	791	363	.459	319	257	.806	80	251	331	137	171	1	65	31	984	12.8
Totals	718	22342	10711	5424	.506	4756	3792	.797	1686	4021	5707	1804	2022	32	698	396	14659	20.4

Three-Point Field Goals: 1979-80, 4-for-12 (.333). 1980-81, 2-for-12 (.167). 1981-82, 4-for-6 (.667). 1982-83, 4-for-19 (.211). 1983-84, 4-for-19 (.211). 1984-85, 1-for-7 (.143). Totals, 19-for-75 (.253).

NBA PLAYOFF RECORD

Sea.—Team	G.	Min.	FGA	FGM	Pct.	FTA	FTM	Pct.	Rebounds Off.	Def.	Tot.	Ast.	PF	Dq.	Stl.	Blk.	Pts.	Avg.
76-77—Denver	6	222	96	49	.510	45	34	.756	18	40	58	17	20	0	5	4	132	22.0
77-78—Denver	13	460	212	103	.486	65	56	.862	41	93	134	53	43	1	7	3	262	20.2
78-79—Denver	3	109	45	24	.533	31	25	.806	7	21	28	10	15	0	0	0	73	24.3
81-82—Denver	3	103	60	32	.533	12	12	1.000	8	13	21	5	10	0	3	1	76	25.3
82-83—Denver	8	227	136	69	.507	29	25	.862	13	45	58	25	18	0	9	5	163	20.4
83-84—Denver	5	153	102	52	.510	39	32	.821	10	30	40	8	15	0	6	6	137	27.4
84-85—Denver	15	325	159	73	.459	48	39	.813	14	40	54	27	36	0	12	5	186	12.4
Totals	53	1599	810	402	.496	269	223	.829	111	282	393	145	157	1	42	24	1029	19.4

Three-Point Field Goals: 1982-83, 0-for-1. 1983-84, 1-for-2 (.500). 1984-85, 1-for-1 (1.000). Totals, 2-for-4 (.500).

NBA ALL-STAR GAME RECORD

Season—Team	Min.	FGA	FGM	Pct.	FTA	FTM	Pct.	Rebounds Off.	Def.	Tot.	Ast.	PF	Dq.	Stl.	Blk.	Pts.
1977—Denver	10	3	0	.000	0	0	.000	1	0	1	0	0	0	0	0	0

Named to ABA All-Star First Team, 1972. . . . ABA All-Star Second Team, 1971, 1973, 1974, 1976. . . . ABA Rookie of the Year, 1971. . . . ABA All-Rookie Team, 1971. . . . ABA All-Star Game MVP, 1972. . . . Member of ABA championship team, 1975. . . . Led ABA in scoring, 1971. . . . Set ABA record for most points in one season, 1972. . . . Named to THE SPORTING NEWS All-America First Team, 1970. . . . THE SPORTING NEWS All-America Second Team, 1969.

GUS JOHNSON JR.

Born December 13, 1938 at Akron, O. Height 6:06. Weight 235.

Died April 29, 1987.

High School—Akron, O., Central.

Colleges—University of Akron, Akron, O.; Boise Junior College, Boise, Idaho, and University of Idaho, Moscow, Ida.

Drafted by Baltimore on second round, 1963 (11th pick).

Traded by Baltimore to Phoenix for a 2nd round draft choice, April 10, 1972.
Waived by Phoenix NBA, December 1, 1972; signed by Indiana ABA as a free agent, December 15, 1972.

—COLLEGIATE RECORD—

Akron

Year	G.	Min.	FGA	FGM	Pct.	FTA	FTM	Pct.	Reb.	Pts.	Avg.
59-60	(Left school before start of basketball season.)										

Idaho

Year	G.	Min.	FGA	FGM	Pct.	FTA	FTM	Pct.	Reb.	Pts.	Avg.
62-63	23	....	438	188	.429	105	62	.590	466	438	19.0

NBA REGULAR SEASON RECORD

Sea.—Team	G.	Min.	FGA	FGM	Pct.	FTA	FTM	Pct.	Reb.	Ast.	PF	Disq.	Pts.	Avg.
63-64—Baltimore	78	2847	1329	571	.430	319	210	.658	1064	169	321	11	1352	17.3
64-65—Baltimore	76	2899	1379	577	.418	386	261	.676	988	270	258	4	1415	18.6
65-66—Baltimore	42	1284	661	273	.413	178	131	.736	546	114	136	3	677	16.1
66-67—Baltimore	73	2626	1377	620	.450	383	271	.708	855	194	281	7	1511	20.7
67-68—Baltimore	60	2271	1033	482	.467	270	180	.667	782	159	223	7	1144	19.1
68-69—Baltimore	49	1671	782	359	.459	223	160	.717	568	97	176	1	878	17.9
69-70—Baltimore	78	2919	1282	578	.451	272	197	.724	1086	264	269	6	1353	17.3
70-71—Baltimore	66	2538	1090	494	.453	290	214	.738	1128	192	227	4	1202	18.2
71-72—Baltimore	39	668	269	103	.383	63	43	.683	226	51	91	0	249	6.4
72-73—Phoenix	21	417	181	69	.381	36	25	.694	136	31	55	0	163	7.8
Totals	582	20140	9383	4126	.440	2420	1692	.699	7379	1541	2037	43	9944	17.1

NBA PLAYOFF RECORD

Sea.—Team	G.	Min.	FGA	FGM	Pct.	FTA	FTM	Pct.	Reb.	Ast.	PF	Disq.	Pts.	Avg.
64-65—Baltimore	10	377	173	62	.358	46	34	.739	111	34	38	1	158	15.8
65-66—Baltimore	1	8	4	1	.250	0	0	.000	0	0	1	0	2	2.0
69-70—Baltimore	7	298	111	51	.459	34	27	.794	80	9	20	0	129	18.4
70-71—Baltimore	11	365	128	54	.422	47	35	.745	114	30	34	0	143	13.0
71-72—Baltimore	5	77	30	9	.300	2	2	1.000	25	3	17	0	20	4.0
Totals	34	1125	446	177	.397	129	98	.760	330	76	110	1	452	13.3

NBA ALL-STAR GAME RECORD

Season—Team	Min.	FGA	FGM	Pct.	FTA	FTM	Pct.	Reb.	Ast.	PF	Disq.	Pts.
1965—Baltimore	25	13	7	.538	13	11	.846	8	2	2	0	25
1968—Baltimore	16	9	3	.333	2	1	.500	6	1	2	0	7
1969—Baltimore	18	10	4	.400	8	5	.625	10	0	3	0	13
1970—Baltimore	17	12	5	.417	0	0	.000	7	1	2	0	10
1971—Baltimore	23	12	5	.417	2	2	1.000	4	2	3	0	12
Totals	99	56	24	.429	25	19	.760	35	6	12	0	67

ABA REGULAR SEASON RECORD

			—2-Point—			—3-Point—									
Sea.—Team	G.	Min.	FGM	FGA	Pct.	FGM	FGA	Pct.	FTM	FTA	Pct.	Reb.	Ast.	Pts.	Avg.
72-73—Indiana	50	753	128	278	.460	4	21	.190	31	42	.738	245	62	299	6.0

ABA PLAYOFF RECORD

			—2-Point—			—3-Point—									
Sea.—Team	G.	Min.	FGM	FGA	Pct.	FGM	FGA	Pct.	FTM	FTA	Pct.	Reb.	Ast.	Pts.	Avg.
72-73—Indiana	17	184	15	56	.268	0	3	.000	3	4	.750	69	15	42	2.5

Named to All-NBA Second Team, 1965, 1966, 1970, 1971. . . . NBA All-Rookie Team, 1964. . . . NBA All-Defensive First Team, 1970 and 1971. . . . Member of ABA championship team, 1973.

DONALD NEIL JOHNSTON

(Known by middle name.)

Born February 4, 1929 at Chillicothe, O. Height 6:08. Weight 210.

Died September 27, 1978.

High School—Chillicothe, O.

College—Ohio State University, Columbus, O.

Signed by Philadelphia as a free agent, 1951.

Signed as player-coach by Pittsburgh, ABL, 1961.

—COLLEGIATE RECORD—

Year	G.	Min.	FGA	FGM	Pct.	FTA	FTM	Pct.	Reb.	Pts.	Avg.
46-47	7	....	....	5	....	8	3	.375	....	13	1.9
47-48	20	....	219	67	.306	87	46	.529	....	180	9.0
Totals	27	....	....	72	....	95	49	.516	....	193	7.1

(Signed pro baseball contract in 1948 and became ineligible for his final two years at Ohio State.)

NBA REGULAR SEASON RECORD

Sea.—Team	G.	Min.	FGA	FGM	Pct.	FTA	FTM	Pct.	Reb.	Ast.	PF	Disq.	Pts.	Avg.
51-52—Philadelphia	64	993	299	141	.472	151	100	.662	342	39	154	5	382	6.0
52-53—Philadelphia	70	3166	1114	504	.452	794	556	.700	976	197	248	6	1564	22.3
53-54—Philadelphia	72	3296	1317	591	.449	772	577	.747	797	203	259	7	1759	24.4
54-55—Philadelphia	72	2917	1184	521	.440	769	589	.766	1085	215	255	4	1631	22.7
55-56—Philadelphia	70	2594	1092	499	.457	685	549	.801	872	225	251	8	1547	22.1
56-57—Philadelphia	69	2531	1163	520	.447	648	535	.826	855	203	231	2	1575	22.8
57-58—Philadelphia	71	2408	1102	473	.429	540	442	.819	790	166	233	4	1388	19.5
58-59—Philadelphia	28	393	164	54	.329	88	69	.784	139	21	50	0	177	6.3
Totals	516	18298	7435	3303	.444	4447	3417	.768	5856	1269	1681	36	10023	19.4

NBA PLAYOFF RECORD

Sea.—Team	G.	Min.	FGA	FGM	Pct.	FTA	FTM	Pct.	Reb.	Ast.	PF	Disq.	Pts.	Avg.
51-52—Philadelphia	3	32	10	5	.500	8	6	.750	10	1	8	0	16	5.3
55-56—Philadelphia	10	397	169	69	.408	92	65	.707	143	51	41	0	203	20.3
56-57—Philadelphia	2	84	53	17	.321	6	4	.667	35	9	9	0	38	19.0
57-58—Philadelphia	8	189	78	30	.385	33	27	.818	69	14	18	0	87	10.9
Totals	23	702	310	121	.390	139	102	.734	257	75	76	0	344	15.0

—DID YOU KNOW—

That the Midwestern Collegiate Conference, which had five players selected in the 1990 NBA draft, had more players taken than the Big East (4), Southeastern (4), Pacific-10 (3), Southwest (3), Big Eight (2) and Metro (2) conferences?

NBA ALL-STAR GAME RECORD

Season—Team	Min.	FGA	FGM	Pct.	FTA	FTM	Pct.	Reb.	Ast.	PF	Disq.	Pts.
1953—Philadelphia	27	13	5	.385	2	1	.500	12	0	2	0	11
1954—Philadelphia	20	9	2	.222	4	2	.500	7	2	1	0	6
1955—Philadelphia	15	7	1	.143	1	1	1.000	6	1	0	0	3
1956—Philadelphia	25	9	5	.556	11	7	.636	10	1	3	0	17
1957—Philadelphia	23	12	8	.667	3	3	1.000	9	1	2	0	19
1958—Philadelpnia	22	13	6	.462	2	2	1.000	8	1	5	0	14
Totals	132	63	27	.429	23	16	.696	52	6	13	0	70

AMERICAN BASKETBALL LEAGUE PLAYING RECORD

Sea.—Team	G.	Min.	2-Point FGM	2-Point FGA	2-Point Pct.	3-Point FGM	3-Point FGA	3-Point Pct.	FTM	FTA	Pct.	Reb.	Ast.	Pts.	Avg.
61-62—Pittsburgh	5	106	37	15	.405	1	1	1.000	24	16	.667	18	10	49	9.8

ABL COACHING RECORD

Sea. Club	Regular Season W.	L.	Pct.	Pos.	Playoffs W.	L.
1961-62—Pittsburgh	41	40	.506	2†	0	1
1962-63—Pittsburgh	12	10	.545	3	..	..

NBA COACHING RECORD

Sea. Club	Regular Season W.	L.	Pct.	Pos.	Playoffs W.	L.
1959-60—Philadelphia	49	26	.653	2†	4	5
1960-61—Philadelphia	46	33	.582	2†	0	3
Totals (2 seasons)	95	59	.617		4	8

†Eastern Division.

EBL COACHING RECORD

Sea. Club	Regular Season W.	L.	Pct.	Pos.	Playoffs W.	L.
1964-65—Wilmington	12	16	.429	5	..	..
1965-66—Wilmington	20	8	.714	1†	4	2

†Eastern Division.

RECORD AS BASEBALL PLAYER

Year Club	League	G.	IP.	W.	L.	Pct.	H.	R.	ER.	SO.	BB.	ERA.
1949—Terre Haute	III	29	166	10	12	.455	159	85	58	129	73	3.14
1950—Terre Haute	III	28	168	11	12	.478	132	78	54	126	102	2.89
1951—Wilmington	Inter-State	27	115	3	9	.250	126	76	69	104	79	5.40

Elected to Naismith Memorial Basketball Hall of Fame, 1989. . . . Named to All-NBA First Team, 1953, 1954, 1955, 1956. . . . All-NBA Second Team, 1957. . . . Member of NBA championship team, 1956. . . . Led NBA in scoring, 1953, 1954, 1955. . . . Led NBA in rebounding, 1955. . . . Led NBA in field-goal percentage, 1953, 1956, 1957. . . . Played minor league baseball as a pitcher in the Philadelphia Phillies' organization, 1949 through 1951.

SAM JONES

Born June 24, 1933 at Wilmington, N. C. Height 6:04. Weight 205.
High School—Laurinburg, N. C., Institute.
College—North Carolina Central College, Durham, N. C.
Drafted by Boston on first round, 1957.

—COLLEGIATE RECORD—

Year	G.	Min.	FGA	FGM	Pct.	FTA	FTM	Pct.	Reb.	Pts.	Avg.
51-52	22	....	263	126	.479	78	48	.615	150	300	13.6
52-53	24	....	370	169	.457	180	115	.639	248	453	18.9
53-54	27	....	432	208	.481	137	98	.715	223	514	19.0
56-57	27	....	398	174	.437	202	155	.767	288	503	18.6
Totals	100	....	1463	677	.463	597	416	.697	909	1770	17.7

NOTE: In military service during 1954-55 and 1955-56 seasons.

NBA REGULAR SEASON RECORD

Sea.—Team	G.	Min.	FGA	FGM	Pct.	FTA	FTM	Pct.	Reb.	Ast.	PF	Disq.	Pts.	Avg.
57-58—Boston	56	594	233	100	.429	84	60	.714	160	37	42	0	260	4.6
58-59—Boston	71	1466	703	305	.434	196	151	.770	428	101	102	0	761	10.7
59-60—Boston	74	1512	782	355	.454	220	168	.764	375	125	101	1	878	11.9
60-61—Boston	78	2028	1069	480	.449	268	211	.787	421	217	148	1	1171	15.0
61-62—Boston	78	2388	1284	596	.464	297	243	.818	458	232	149	0	1435	18.4
62-63—Boston	76	2323	1305	621	.476	324	257	.793	396	241	162	1	1499	19.7
63-64—Boston	76	2381	1359	612	.450	318	249	.783	349	202	192	1	1473	19.4
64-65—Boston	80	2885	1818	821	.452	522	428	.820	411	223	176	0	2070	25.9
65-66—Boston	67	2155	1335	626	.469	407	325	.799	347	216	170	0	1577	23.2
66-67—Boston	72	2325	1406	638	.454	371	318	.857	338	217	191	1	1594	22.1
67-68—Boston	73	2408	1348	621	.461	376	311	.827	357	216	181	0	1553	21.3
68-69—Boston	70	1820	1103	496	.450	189	148	.783	265	182	121	0	1140	16.3
Totals	871	24285	13745	6271	.456	3572	2869	.803	4305	2209	1735	5	15411	17.7

NBA PLAYOFF RECORD

Sea.—Team	G.	Min.	FGA	FGM	Pct.	FTA	FTM	Pct.	Reb.	Ast.	PF	Disq.	Pts.	Avg.
57-58—Boston	8	75	22	10	.455	16	11	.688	24	4	7	0	31	3.9
58-59—Boston	11	192	108	40	.370	39	33	.846	63	17	14	0	113	10.3
59-60—Boston	13	197	117	45	.385	21	17	.809	41	18	15	0	107	8.2
60-61—Boston	10	258	112	50	.446	35	31	.886	54	22	22	0	131	13.1
61-62—Boston	14	504	277	123	.444	60	42	.700	99	44	30	0	288	20.6
62-63—Boston	13	450	248	120	.484	83	69	.831	81	32	42	1	309	23.8
63-64—Boston	10	356	180	91	.506	68	50	.735	47	23	24	0	232	23.2
64-65—Boston	12	495	294	135	.459	84	73	.869	55	30	39	1	343	28.6
65-66—Boston	17	602	343	154	.449	136	114	.838	86	53	65	1	422	24.8
66-67—Boston	9	326	207	95	.459	58	50	.862	46	28	30	1	240	26.7
67-68—Boston	19	685	367	162	.441	84	66	.786	64	50	58	0	390	20.5
68-69—Boston	18	514	296	124	.419	69	55	.797	58	37	45	1	303	16.8
Totals	154	4654	2571	1149	.447	753	611	.811	718	358	391	5	2909	18.9

NBA ALL-STAR GAME RECORD

Season—Team	Min.	FGA	FGM	Pct.	FTA	FTM	Pct.	Reb.	Ast.	PF	Disq.	Pts.
1962—Boston	14	8	1	.125	1	0	.000	1	0	1	0	2
1964—Boston	27	20	8	.400	0	0	.000	4	3	2	0	16
1965—Boston	24	12	2	.167	2	2	1.000	5	3	2	0	6
1966—Boston	22	11	5	.455	2	2	1.000	2	5	0	0	12
1968—Boston	15	5	2	.400	1	1	1.000	2	4	1	0	5
Totals	102	56	18	.321	6	5	.833	14	15	6	0	41

COLLEGIATE COACHING RECORD

	Regular Season			
Sea. Club	W.	L.	Pct.	Pos.
1969-70—Fed. City Col.	5	8	.385	...
1970-71—Fed. City Col.	12	9	.571	...
1971-72—Fed. City Col.	11	9	.550	...
1972-73—Fed. City Col.	11	13	.458	...
1973-74—N. C. Cent.	5	16	.238	†7

†Mid-Eastern Athletic Conference.
Assistant Coach, New Orleans NBA, 1974-75.

Elected to Naismith Memorial Basketball Hall of Fame, 1983. . . . Named to NBA 25th Anniversary All-Time Team, 1970. . . . All-NBA Second Team, 1965, 1966, 1967. . . . Member of NBA championship teams, 1959, 1960, 1961, 1962, 1963, 1964, 1965, 1966, 1968, 1969. . . . Elected to NAIA Basketball Hall of Fame, 1962.

JOHN G. KERR
(Red)

Born August 17, 1932 at Chicago, Ill. Height 6:09. Weight 230.
High School—Chicago, Ill., Tilden.
College—University of Illinois, Champaign, Ill.
Drafted by Syracuse on first round, 1954 (6th pick).

Syracuse franchise transferred to Philadelphia, 1963.
Traded by Philadelphia to Baltimore for Wally Jones, September 22, 1965; selected from Baltimore by Chicago Bulls in expansion draft, April 30, 1966.

—COLLEGIATE RECORD—

Year	G.	Min.	FGA	FGM	Pct.	FTA	FTM	Pct.	Reb.	Pts.	Avg.
50-51	(Freshman team did not play intercollegiate schedule.)										
51-52	26	....	365	143	.392	124	71	.573	....	357	13.7
52-53	22	....	397	153	.385	123	80	.650	....	386	17.5
53-54	22	....	520	210	.404	214	136	.636	....	556	25.3
Varsity Totals	70	....	1282	506	.395	461	287	.623	....	1299	18.6

NBA REGULAR SEASON RECORD

Sea.—Team	G.	Min.	FGA	FGM	Pct.	FTA	FTM	Pct.	Reb.	Ast.	PF	Disq.	Pts.	Avg.
54-55—Syracuse	72	1529	718	301	.419	223	152	.682	474	80	165	2	754	10.5
55-56—Syracuse	72	2114	935	377	.403	316	207	.655	607	84	168	3	961	13.3
56-57—Syracuse	72	2191	827	333	.403	313	225	.719	807	90	190	3	891	12.4
57-58—Syracuse	72	2384	1020	407	.399	422	280	.664	963	88	197	4	1094	15.2
58-59—Syracuse	72	2671	1139	502	.441	367	281	.766	1008	142	183	1	1285	17.8
59-60—Syracuse	75	2361	1111	436	.392	310	233	.752	913	168	207	4	1105	14.7
60-61—Syracuse	79	2676	1056	419	.397	299	218	.729	951	199	230	4	1056	13.4
61-62—Syracuse	80	2767	1220	541	.443	302	222	.735	1176	243	282	7	1304	16.3
62-63—Syracuse	80	2561	1069	507	.474	320	241	.753	1049	214	208	3	1255	15.7
63-64—Philadelphia	80	2938	1250	536	.429	357	268	.751	1018	275	187	2	1340	16.8
64-65—Philadelphia	80	1810	714	264	.370	181	126	.696	551	197	132	1	654	8.2
65-66—Baltimore	71	1770	692	286	.413	272	209	.768	586	225	148	0	781	11.0
Totals	905	27772	11751	4909	.418	3682	2662	.723	10103	2005	2297	34	12480	13.8

NBA PLAYOFF RECORD

Sea.—Team	G.	Min.	FGA	FGM	Pct.	FTA	FTM	Pct.	Reb.	Ast.	PF	Disq.	Pts.	Avg.
54-55—Syracuse	11	363	151	59	.391	61	34	.557	118	13	27	0	152	13.8
55-56—Syracuse	8	213	77	37	.481	33	15	.455	68	10	23	0	89	11.1
56-57—Syracuse	5	162	65	28	.431	29	20	.690	69	6	7	0	76	15.2
57-58—Syracuse	3	116	55	18	.327	18	14	.778	61	3	5	0	50	16.7
58-59—Syracuse	9	312	142	50	.352	33	30	.909	108	24	20	0	130	14.4
59-60—Syracuse	3	104	51	15	.294	12	11	.917	25	9	9	0	41	13.7
60-61—Syracuse	8	210	88	30	.341	23	16	.696	99	20	18	0	76	9.5
61-62—Syracuse	5	193	109	41	.376	8	6	.750	80	10	15	0	88	17.6
62-63—Syracuse	5	187	60	26	.433	21	16	.762	75	9	12	0	68	13.6
63-64—Philadelphia	5	185	83	40	.482	20	15	.750	69	16	12	0	95	19.0
64-65—Philadelphia	11	181	67	24	.358	21	15	.714	38	28	20	0	63	5.7
65-66—Baltimore	3	49	11	2	.182	2	1	.500	17	4	5	0	5	1.7
Totals	76	2275	959	370	.386	281	193	.687	827	152	173	0	933	12.3

NBA ALL-STAR GAME RECORD

Season—Team	Min.	FGA	FGM	Pct.	FTA	FTM	Pct.	Reb.	Ast.	PF	Disq.	Pts.
1956—Syracuse	16	4	2	.500	1	0	.000	8	0	2	0	4
1959—Syracuse	21	14	3	.214	2	1	.500	9	2	0	0	7
1963—Syracuse	11	4	0	.000	2	2	1.000	2	1	3	0	2
Totals	48	22	5	.227	5	3	.600	19	3	5	0	13

NBA COACHING RECORD

	Regular Season				Playoffs	
Sea. Club	W.	L.	Pct.	Pos.	W.	L.
1966-67—Chicago	33	48	.407	4†	0	3
1967-68—Chicago	29	53	.354	4†	1	4
1968-69—Phoenix	16	66	.195	7†	..	..
1969-70—Phoenix	15	23	.395	..†	..	..
Totals (4 years)	93	190	.329		1	7

†Western Division.

Named NBA Coach of the Year, 1967. . . . Member of NBA championship team, 1955.

ROBERT JERRY LANIER JR.
(Bob)

Born September 10, 1948 at Buffalo, N. Y. Height 6:11. Weight 265.
High School—Buffalo, N. Y., Bennett.
College—St. Bonaventure University, St. Bonaventure, N. Y.
Drafted by Detroit on first round, 1970 (1st pick).

Traded by Detroit to Milwaukee for Kent Benson and a 1980 1st round draft choice, February 4, 1980.

—COLLEGIATE RECORD—

Year	G.	Min.	FGA	FGM	Pct.	FTA	FTM	Pct.	Reb.	Pts.	Avg.
66-67†	15	....	....	....	....	....	....	....	....	450	30.0
67-68	25	....	466	272	.584	175	112	.640	390	656	26.2
68-69	24	....	460	270	.587	181	114	.630	374	654	27.3
69-70	26	....	549	308	.561	194	141	.727	416	757	29.1
Varsity Totals	75	....	1475	850	.576	550	367	.667	1180	2067	27.6

NBA REGULAR SEASON RECORD

Sea.—Team	G.	Min.	FGA	FGM	Pct.	FTA	FTM	Pct.	Reb.	Ast.	PF	Disq.	Pts.	Avg.
70-71—Detroit	82	2017	1108	504	.455	376	273	.726	665	146	272	4	1281	15.6
71-72—Detroit	80	3092	1690	834	.493	505	388	.768	1132	248	297	6	2056	25.7
72-73—Detroit	81	3150	1654	810	.490	397	307	.773	1205	260	278	4	1927	23.8

									—Rebounds—									
Sea.—Team	G.	Min.	FGA	FGM	Pct.	FTA	FTM	Pct.	Off.	Def.	Tot.	Ast.	PF	Dq.	Stl.	Blk.	Pts.	Avg.
73-74—Detroit	81	3047	1483	748	.504	409	326	.797	269	805	1074	343	273	7	110	247	1822	22.5
74-75—Detroit	76	2987	1433	731	.510	450	361	.802	225	689	914	350	237	1	75	172	1823	24.0
75-76—Detroit	64	2363	1017	541	.532	370	284	.768	217	529	746	217	203	2	79	86	1366	21.3
76-77—Detroit	64	2446	1269	678	.534	318	260	.818	200	545	745	214	174	0	70	126	1616	25.3
77-78—Detroit	63	2311	1159	622	.537	386	298	.772	197	518	715	216	185	2	82	93	1542	24.5
78-79—Detroit	53	1835	950	489	.515	367	275	.749	164	330	494	140	181	5	50	75	1253	23.6
79-80—Det.-Milw.	63	2131	867	466	.537	354	277	.782	152	400	552	184	200	3	74	89	1210	19.2
80-81—Milwaukee	67	1753	716	376	.525	277	208	.751	128	285	413	179	184	0	73	81	961	14.3
81-82—Milwaukee	74	1986	729	407	.558	242	182	.752	92	296	388	219	211	3	72	56	996	13.5
82-83—Milwaukee	39	978	332	163	.491	133	91	.684	58	142	200	105	125	2	34	24	417	10.7
83-84—Milwaukee	72	2007	685	392	.572	274	194	.708	141	314	455	186	228	8	58	51	978	13.6
Totals	959	32103	15092	7761	.514	4858	3724	.767			9698	3007	3048	47	777	1100	19248	20.1

Three-Point Field Goals: 1979-80, 1-for-6 (.167). 1980-81, 1-for-1. 1981-82, 0-for-2. 1982-83, 0-for-1. 1983-84, 0-for-3. Totals, 2-for-13 (.154).

NBA PLAYOFF RECORD

Sea.—Team	G.	Min.	FGA	FGM	Pct.	FTA	FTM	Pct.	—Rebounds— Off.	Def.	Tot.	Ast.	PF	Dq.	Stl.	Blk.	Pts.	Avg.
73-74—Detroit	7	303	152	77	.507	38	30	.789	26	81	107	21	28	1	4	14	184	26.3
74-75—Detroit	3	128	51	26	.510	12	9	.750	5	27	32	19	10	0	4	12	61	20.3
75-76—Detroit	9	359	172	95	.552	50	45	.900	39	75	114	30	34	1	8	21	235	26.1
76-77—Detroit	3	118	54	34	.630	19	16	.842	13	37	50	6	10	0	3	7	84	28.0
79-80—Milwaukee	7	256	101	52	.515	42	31	.738	17	48	65	31	23	0	7	8	135	19.3
80-81—Milwaukee	7	236	85	50	.588	32	23	.719	12	40	52	28	18	0	12	8	123	17.6
81-82—Milwaukee	6	212	80	41	.513	25	14	.560	18	27	45	22	21	2	8	5	96	16.0
82-83—Milwaukee	9	250	89	51	.573	35	21	.600	17	46	63	23	32	2	5	14	123	13.7
83-84—Milwaukee	16	499	171	82	.480	44	39	.886	32	85	117	55	57	1	11	10	203	12.7
Totals	67	2361	955	508	.532	297	228	.768	179	466	645	235	233	7	62	99	1244	18.6

Three-Point Field Goals: 1981-82, 0-for-1.

NBA ALL-STAR GAME RECORD

Season—Team	Min.	FGA	FGM	Pct.	FTA	FTM	Pct.	Reb.	Ast.	PF	Disq.	Pts.
1972—Detroit	5	2	0	.000	3	2	.667	3	0	0	0	2
1973—Detroit	12	9	5	.556	0	0	.000	6	0	1	0	10

Season—Team	Min.	FGA	FGM	Pct.	FTA	FTM	Pct.	—Rebounds— Off.	Def.	Tot.	Ast.	PF	Dq.	Stl.	Blk.	Pts.
1974—Detroit	26	15	11	.733	2	2	1.000	2	8	10	2	1	0	0	2	24
1975—Detroit	12	4	1	.250	0	0	.000	2	5	7	2	3	0	2	0	2
1977—Detroit	20	8	7	.875	3	3	1.000	5	5	10	4	3	0	1	1	17
1978—Detroit	4	0	0	.000	2	1	.500	2	0	2	0	0	0	0	0	1
1979—Detroit	31	10	5	.500	0	0	.000	1	3	4	4	4	0	1	1	10
1982—Milwaukee	11	7	3	.429	2	2	1.000	2	1	3	0	3	0	0	0	8
Totals	121	55	32	.582	12	10	.833			45	12	15	0	4	4	74

Named to NBA All-Rookie Team, 1971. . . . NBA All-Star Game MVP, 1974. . . . Named to THE SPORTING NEWS All-America First Team, 1970.

JERRY RAY LUCAS
(Luke)

Born March 30, 1940 at Middletown, O. Height 6:08. Weight 235.

High School—Middletown, O.

College—Ohio State University, Columbus, O.

Drafted by Cincinnati on first round (territorial choice), 1962.

Signed by Cleveland ABL, 1962; Cleveland dropped out of ABL prior to 1962-63 season; did not play pro basketball, 1962-63.

Traded by Cincinnati to San Francisco for Jim King and Bill Turner, October 25, 1969.
Traded by San Francisco to New York for Cazzie Russell, May 7, 1971.

—COLLEGIATE RECORD—

Year	G.	Min.	FGA	FGM	Pct.	FTA	FTM	Pct.	Reb.	Pts.	Avg.
58-59†	Freshman team did not play an intercollegiate schedule.										
59-60	27	....	444	283	.637	187	144	.770	442	710	26.3
60-61	27	....	411	256	.623	208	159	.764	470	671	24.9
61-62	28	....	388	237	.611	169	135	.799	499	609	21.8
Varsity Totals	82	....	1243	776	.624	564	438	.777	1411	1990	24.3

NBA REGULAR SEASON RECORD

Sea.—Team	G.	Min.	FGA	FGM	Pct.	FTA	FTM	Pct.	Reb.	Ast.	PF	Disq.	Pts.	Avg.
63-64—Cincinnati	79	3273	1035	545	.527	398	310	.779	1375	204	300	6	1400	17.7
64-65—Cincinnati	66	2864	1121	558	.498	366	298	.814	1321	157	214	1	1414	21.4
65-66—Cincinnati	79	3517	1523	690	.453	403	317	.787	1668	213	274	5	1697	21.5
66-67—Cincinnati	81	3558	1257	577	.459	359	284	.791	1547	268	280	2	1438	17.8
67-68—Cincinnati	82	3619	1361	707	.519	445	346	.778	1560	251	243	3	1760	21.4
68-69—Cincinnati	74	3075	1007	555	.551	327	247	.755	1360	306	206	0	1357	18.3
69-70—Cinn.-S.F.	67	2420	799	405	.507	255	200	.784	951	173	166	2	1010	15.1
70-71—San Fran.	80	3251	1250	623	.498	367	289	.787	1265	293	197	0	1535	19.2
71-72—New York	77	2926	1060	543	.512	249	197	.791	1011	318	218	1	1283	16.7
72-73—New York	71	2001	608	312	.513	100	80	.800	510	317	157	0	704	9.9

Sea.—Team	G.	Min.	FGA	FGM	Pct.	FTA	FTM	Pct.	—Rebounds— Off.	Def.	Tot.	Ast.	PF	Dq.	Stl.	Blk.	Pts.	Avg.
73-74—New York	73	1627	420	194	.462	96	67	.698	62	312	374	230	134	0	28	24	455	6.2
Totals	829	32131	11441	5709	.499	3365	2635	.783			12942	2730	2389	20			14053	17.0

NBA PLAYOFF RECORD

Sea.—Team	G.	Min.	FGA	FGM	Pct.	FTA	FTM	Pct.	Reb.	Ast.	PF	Disq.	Pts.	Avg.
63-64—Cincinnati	10	370	123	48	.390	37	26	.703	125	34	37	1	122	12.2
64-65—Cincinnati	4	195	75	38	.507	22	17	.773	84	9	12	0	93	23.3
65-66—Cincinnati	5	231	85	40	.471	35	27	.771	101	14	14	0	107	21.4
66-67—Cincinnati	4	183	55	24	.436	2	2	1.000	77	8	15	0	50	12.5

JERRY LUCAS

Sea.—Team	G.	Min.	FGA	FGM	Pct.	FTA	FTM	Pct.	Reb.	Ast.	PF	Disq.	Pts.	Avg.
70-71—San Fran.	5	171	77	39	.506	16	11	.688	50	16	14	0	89	17.8
71-72—New York	16	737	238	119	.500	71	59	.831	173	85	49	1	297	18.6
72-73—New York	17	368	112	54	.482	23	20	.870	85	39	47	0	128	7.5

									—Rebounds—									
Sea.—Team	G.	Min.	FGA	FGM	Pct.	FTA	FTM	Pct.	Off.	Def.	Tot.	Ast.	PF	Dq.	Stl.	Blk.	Pts.	Avg.
73-74—New York	11	115	21	5	.238	0	0	.000	6	16	22	9	9	0	4	0	10	0.9
Totals	72	2370	786	367	.467	206	162	.786			717	214	197	2			896	12.4

NBA ALL-STAR GAME RECORD

Season—Team	Min.	FGA	FGM	Pct.	FTA	FTM	Pct.	Reb.	Ast.	PF	Disq.	Pts.
1964—Cincinnati	36	6	3	.500	6	5	.833	8	0	5	0	11
1965—Cincinnati	35	19	12	.632	1	1	1.000	10	1	2	0	25
1966—Cincinnati	23	11	4	.364	2	2	1.000	19	0	2	0	10
1967—Cincinnati	22	5	3	.600	1	1	1.000	7	2	3	0	7
1968—Cincinnati	21	9	6	.667	4	4	1.000	5	4	3	0	16
1969—Cincinnati	17	5	2	.400	5	4	.800	6	1	3	0	8
1971—San Francisco	29	9	5	.556	2	2	1.000	9	4	2	0	12
Totals	183	64	35	.547	21	19	.905	64	12	20	0	89

Elected to Naismith Memorial Basketball Hall of Fame, 1979. . . . Named to All-NBA First Team, 1965, 1966, 1968. . . . All-NBA Second Team, 1964 and 1967. . . . NBA Rookie of the Year, 1964. . . . NBA All-Rookie Team, 1964. . . . Led NBA in field-goal percentage, 1964. . . . NBA All-Star Game MVP, 1965. . . . Member of NBA championship team, 1973. . . . THE SPORTING NEWS College Player of the Year, 1961 and 1962. . . . Named to THE SPORTING NEWS All-America First Team, 1960, 1961, 1962. . . . Member of NCAA championship team, 1960. . . . Member of U. S. Olympic team, 1960. . . . Led NCAA in rebounding, 1961 and 1962. . . . Led NCAA in field-goal percentage, 1960, 1961, 1962. . . . One of only seven players to average over 20 points and 20 rebounds per game in NCAA career.

CHARLES EDWARD MACAULEY JR.
(Easy Ed)

Born March 22, 1928 at St. Louis, Mo. Height 6:08. Weight 190.

High School—St. Louis, Mo., St. Louis University High.

College—St. Louis University, St. Louis, Mo.

Selected by St. Louis as a territorial choice (first round) in Basketball Association of America draft, 1949.

Drafted by Boston NBA from St. Louis NBA in dispersal draft, April 25, 1950.
Traded with draft rights to Cliff Hagan by Boston NBA to St. Louis NBA for a 1st round draft choice, April 29, 1956.

—COLLEGIATE RECORD—

Year	G.	Min.	FGA	FGM	Pct.	FTA	FTM	Pct.	Reb.	Pts.	Avg.
45-46	23	....	...	94	....	...	71	....	....	259	11.3
46-47	28	....	...	141	....	...	104	....	....	386	13.8
47-48	27	....	324	132	.407	159	104	.654	....	368	13.6
48-49	26	....	275	144	.524	153	116	.758	....	404	15.5
Totals	104	....	...	511	....	...	395	....	....	1417	13.6

NBA REGULAR SEASON RECORD

Sea.—Team	G.	Min.	FGA	FGM	Pct.	FTA	FTM	Pct.	Reb.	Ast.	PF	Disq.	Pts.	Avg.
49-50—St. Louis	67	....	882	351	.398	528	379	.718	....	200	221	....	1081	16.1
50-51—Boston	68	....	985	459	.466	614	466	.759	616	252	205	4	1384	20.4
51-52—Boston	66	2631	888	384	.432	621	496	.799	529	232	174	0	1264	19.2
52-53—Boston	69	2902	997	451	.452	667	500	.750	629	280	188	0	1402	20.3
53-54—Boston	71	2792	950	462	.486	554	420	.758	571	271	168	1	1344	18.9
54-55—Boston	71	2706	951	403	.424	558	442	.792	600	275	171	0	1248	17.6
55-56—Boston	71	2354	995	420	.422	504	400	.794	422	211	158	2	1240	17.5
56-57—St. Louis	72	2582	987	414	.419	479	359	.749	440	202	206	2	1187	16.5
57-58—St. Louis	72	1908	879	376	.428	369	267	.723	478	143	156	2	1019	14.2
58-59—St. Louis	14	196	75	22	.293	35	21	.600	40	13	20	1	65	4.6
Totals	641	....	8589	3742	.436	4929	3750	.761	....	2079	1667	12	11234	17.5

NBA PLAYOFF RECORD

Sea.—Team	G.	Min.	FGA	FGM	Pct.	FTA	FTM	Pct.	Reb.	Ast.	PF	Disq.	Pts.	Avg.
50-51—Boston	2	....	36	17	.472	16	10	.625	18	8	4	0	44	22.0
51-52—Boston	3	129	49	27	.551	19	16	.842	33	11	11	1	70	23.3
52-53—Boston	6	278	71	31	.437	54	39	.722	58	21	23	2	101	16.8
53-54—Boston	5	127	22	8	.364	13	9	.692	21	21	14	0	25	5.0
54-55—Boston	7	283	93	43	.462	54	41	.759	52	32	21	0	127	18.1
55-56—Boston	3	73	30	12	.400	11	7	.636	15	5	6	0	31	10.3
56-57—St. Louis	10	297	109	44	.404	74	54	.730	62	22	39	3	142	14.2
57-58—St. Louis	11	227	89	36	.404	50	36	.720	62	18	23	0	108	9.8
Totals	47	....	499	218	.437	291	212	.729	321	138	141	6	648	13.8

NBA ALL-STAR GAME RECORD

Season—Team	Min.	FGA	FGM	Pct.	FTA	FTM	Pct.	Reb.	Ast.	PF	Disq.	Pts.
1951—Boston	...	12	7	.583	7	6	.857	6	1	3	0	20
1952—Boston	28	7	3	.429	9	9	1.000	7	3	2	0	15
1953—Boston	35	12	5	.417	8	8	1.000	7	3	2	0	18
1954—Boston	25	11	4	.364	6	5	.833	1	3	2	0	13
1955—Boston	27	5	1	.200	5	4	.800	4	2	1	0	6
1956—Boston	20	9	1	.111	4	2	.500	2	3	3	0	4
1957—St. Louis	19	6	3	.500	2	1	.500	5	3	0	0	7
Totals	...	62	24	.387	41	35	.854	32	18	13	0	83

NBA COACHING RECORD

	Regular Season				Playoffs	
Sea. Club	W.	L.	Pct.	Pos.	W.	L.
1958-59—St. Louis	43	19	.694	1†	2	4
1959-60—St. Louis	46	29	.613	1†	7	7
Totals (2 seasons)	89	48	.650		9	11

†Western Division.

Elected to Naismith Memorial Basketball Hall of Fame, 1960. . . . Named to All-NBA First Team, 1951, 1952, 1953. . . . All-NBA Second Team, 1954. . . . NBA All-Star Game MVP, 1951. . . . Member of NBA championship team, 1958. . . . Led NBA in field-goal percentage, 1954. . . . Named to THE SPORTING NEWS All-America First Team, 1949. . . . Led NCAA in field-goal percentage, 1949.

PETER PRESS MARAVICH
(Pete)

Born June 22, 1947 at Aliquippa, Pa. Height 6:05. Weight 200.

Died January 5, 1988.

High Schools—Clemson, S. C., Daniels (Fr. and Soph.) and Raleigh, N. C., Needham Broughton (Jr. and Sr.).

Prep School—Salemburg, N. C., Edwards Military Institute.

College—Louisiana State University, Baton Rouge, La.

Drafted by Atlanta on first round, 1970 (3rd pick).

Traded by Atlanta to New Orleans for Dean Meminger, Bob Kauffman and four draft choices (1st round in 1974, 1st and 2nd in 1975, 2nd in 1976), May 3, 1974.

Waived by Utah, January 17, 1980; signed by Boston as a free agent, January 22, 1980.

Franchise moved from New Orleans to Utah, 1979.

—COLLEGIATE RECORD—

Year	G.	Min.	FGA	FGM	Pct.	FTA	FTM	Pct.	Reb.	Pts.	Avg.
66-67†	17	....	604	273	.452	234	195	.833	176	741	43.6
67-68	26	....	1022	432	.423	338	274	.811	195	1138	43.8
68-69	26	....	976	433	.444	378	282	.746	169	1148	44.2
69-70	31	....	1168	522	.447	436	337	.773	164	1381	44.5
Varsity Totals	83	....	3166	1387	.438	1152	893	.775	528	3667	44.2

NBA REGULAR SEASON RECORD

Sea.—Team	G.	Min.	FGA	FGM	Pct.	FTA	FTM	Pct.	Reb.	Ast.	PF	Disq.	Pts.	Avg.
70-71—Atlanta	81	2926	1613	738	.458	505	404	.800	298	355	238	1	1880	23.2
71-72—Atlanta	66	2302	1077	460	.427	438	355	.811	256	393	207	0	1275	19.3
72-73—Atlanta	79	3089	1788	789	.441	606	485	.800	346	546	245	1	2063	26.1

									—Rebounds—									
Sea.—Team	G.	Min.	FGA	FGM	Pct.	FTA	FTM	Pct.	Off.	Def.	Tot.	Ast.	PF	Dq.	Stl.	Blk.	Pts.	Avg.
73-74—Atlanta	76	2903	1791	819	.457	568	469	.826	98	276	374	396	261	4	111	13	2107	27.7
74-75—N. Orleans	79	2853	1562	655	.419	481	390	.811	93	329	422	488	227	4	120	18	1700	21.5
75-76—N. Orleans	62	2373	1316	604	.459	488	396	.811	46	254	300	332	197	3	87	23	1604	25.9
76-77—N. Orleans	73	3041	2047	886	.433	600	501	.835	90	284	374	392	191	1	84	22	2273	31.1
77-78—N. Orleans	50	2041	1253	556	.444	276	240	.870	49	129	178	335	116	1	101	8	1352	27.0
78-79—N. Orleans	49	1824	1035	436	.421	277	233	.841	33	88	121	243	104	2	60	18	1105	22.6
79-80—Utah-Bos.	43	964	543	244	.449	105	91	.867	17	61	78	83	79	1	24	6	589	13.7
Totals	658	24316	14025	6187	.441	4344	3564	.820			2747	3563	1865	18	587	108	15948	24.2

Three-Point Field Goals: 1979-80, 10-for-15 (.667).

NBA PLAYOFF RECORD

Sea.—Team	G.	Min.	FGA	FGM	Pct.	FTA	FTM	Pct.	Reb.	Ast.	PF	Disq.	Pts.	Avg.
70-71—Atlanta	5	199	122	46	.377	26	18	.692	26	24	14	0	110	22.0
71-72—Atlanta	6	219	121	54	.446	71	58	.817	32	28	24	0	166	27.7
72-73—Atlanta	6	234	155	65	.419	34	27	.794	29	40	24	1	157	26.2

									—Rebounds—									
Sea.—Team	G.	Min.	FGA	FGM	Pct.	FTA	FTM	Pct.	Off.	Def.	Tot.	Ast.	PF	Dq.	Stl.	Blk.	Pts.	Avg.
79-80—Boston	9	104	51	25	.490	3	2	.667	0	8	8	6	12	0	3	0	54	6.0
Totals	26	756	449	190	.423	134	105	.784			95	98	74	1	3	0	487	18.7

Three-Point Field Goals: 1979-80, 2-for-6 (.333).

NBA ALL-STAR GAME RECORD

Season—Team	Min.	FGA	FGM	Pct.	FTA	FTM	Pct.	—Rebounds— Off.	Def.	Tot.	Ast.	PF	Dq.	Stl.	Blk.	Pts.
1973—Atlanta	22	8	4	.500	0	0	.000			3	5	4	0			8
1974—Atlanta	22	15	4	.267	9	7	.778	1	2	3	4	2	0	0	0	15
1977—N. Orleans	21	13	5	.385	0	0	.000	0	0	0	4	1	0	4	0	10
1978—N. Orleans	Selected—Injured, Did Not Play															
1979—N. Orleans	14	8	5	.625	0	0	.000	0	2	2	2	1	0	0	0	10
Totals	79	44	18	.409	9	7	.778			8	15	8	0	4	0	43

Elected to Naismith Memorial Basketball Hall of Fame, 1986. . . . Named to All-NBA First Team, 1976 and 1977. . . . All-NBA Second Team, 1973 and 1978. . . . NBA All-Rookie Team, 1971. . . . Shares NBA record for most free-throw attempts in one quarter, 16, vs. Chicago, January 2, 1973. . . . Led NBA in scoring, 1977. . . . THE SPORTING NEWS College Player of the Year, 1970. . . . Named to THE SPORTING NEWS All-America First Team, 1968, 1969, 1970. . . . Led NCAA in scoring, 1968, 1969, 1970. . . . Holds the following NCAA career records: most points, highest scoring average, most games scoring at least 50 points (28), most field goals made, most field goals attempted, most free throws made (3-year career) and most free throws attempted (3-year career). . . . Holds the following NCAA season records: most points, highest scoring average, most games scoring at least 50 points (10 in 1970), most field goals made and most field goals attempted. . . . Holds NCAA record for most free throws made in one game, 30, vs. Oregon State in 31 attempts, December 22, 1969. . . . Son of former NBL and BAA guard and former college coach Press Maravich.

SLATER MARTIN
(Dugie)

Born October 22, 1925 at Houston, Tex. Height 5:10. Weight 170.

High School—Houston, Tex., Thomas Jefferson.

College—University of Texas, Austin, Tex.

Drafted by Minneapolis, 1949.

Drafted by Minneapolis in BAA draft, 1949 (BAA merged with NBL to form NBA later in 1949).

Traded by Minneapolis with Jerry Bird and a player to be named later to New York for Walter Dukes and draft rights to Burdette Haldorson, October 26, 1956.

Traded by New York to St. Louis for Willie Naulls, December 10, 1956.

—COLLEGIATE RECORD—

Year	G.	Min.	FGA	FGM	Pct.	FTA	FTM	Pct.	Reb.	Pts.	Avg.
43-44	14	....	...	75	....	...	34	....	....	184	13.2
44-45 and 45-46	Military Service										
46-47	27	....	...	109	....	...	37	....	....	255	9.4
47-48	25	....	...	126	....	85	65	.765	....	317	12.7
48-49	24	....	...	165	....	...	54	....	....	384	16.0
Totals	90	....	...	475	....	...	190	....	....	1140	12.7

NBA REGULAR SEASON RECORD

Sea.—Team	G.	Min.	FGA	FGM	Pct.	FTA	FTM	Pct.	Reb.	Ast.	PF	Disq.	Pts.	Avg.
49-50—Minneapolis	67	....	302	106	.351	93	59	.634	....	148	162	....	271	4.0
50-51—Minneapolis	68	....	627	227	.362	177	121	.684	246	235	199	3	575	8.5
51-52—Minneapolis	66	2480	632	237	.375	190	142	.747	228	249	226	9	616	9.3
52-53—Minneapolis	70	2556	634	260	.410	287	224	.780	186	250	246	4	744	10.6
53-54—Minneapolis	69	2472	654	254	.388	243	176	.724	166	253	198	3	684	9.9
54-55—Minneapolis	72	2784	919	350	.381	359	276	.769	260	427	221	7	976	13.6
55-56—Minneapolis	72	2838	863	309	.358	395	329	.833	260	445	202	2	947	13.2
56-57—N.Y.-St. L.	66	2401	736	244	.332	291	230	.790	288	269	193	1	718	10.9
57-58—St. Louis	60	2098	768	258	.336	276	206	.746	228	218	187	0	722	12.0
58-59—St. Louis	71	2504	706	245	.347	254	197	.776	253	336	230	8	687	9.4
59-60—St. Louis	64	1756	383	142	.371	155	113	.729	187	330	174	2	397	6.2
Totals	745	....	7224	2632	.364	2720	2073	.762	...	3160	2238	..	7337	9.8

NBA PLAYOFF RECORD

Sea.—Team	G.	Min.	FGA	FGM	Pct.	FTA	FTM	Pct.	Reb.	Ast.	PF	Disq.	Pts.	Avg.
49-50—Minneapolis	12	....	50	21	.420	24	14	.583	....	25	35	....	56	4.7
50-51—Minneapolis	7	....	51	18	.353	27	14	.519	42	25	20	....	50	7.1
51-52—Minneapolis	13	523	110	38	.345	56	41	.732	37	56	64	4	117	9.0
52-53—Minneapolis	12	453	103	41	.398	51	39	.765	31	43	49	1	121	10.1
53-54—Minneapolis	13	533	112	37	.330	70	52	.743	29	60	52	1	126	9.7
54-55—Minneapolis	7	315	94	28	.298	49	40	.816	28	31	23	0	96	13.7
55-56—Minneapolis	3	121	37	17	.459	24	20	.833	7	15	9	0	54	18.0
56-57—St. Louis	10	439	155	55	.355	74	56	.757	42	49	39	2	166	16.6
57-58—St. Louis	11	416	137	44	.321	63	39	.619	48	40	40	1	127	11.5
58-59—St. Louis	1	18	5	4	.800	0	0	.000	3	2	2	0	8	8.0
59-60—St. Louis	3	58	13	1	.077	4	1	.250	3	8	9	0	3	1.0
Totals	92	2876	867	304	.351	442	316	.715	270	354	342	9	924	10.0

NBA ALL-STAR GAME RECORD

Season—Team	Min.	FGA	FGM	Pct.	FTA	FTM	Pct.	Reb.	Ast.	PF	Disq.	Pts.
1953—Minneapolis	26	10	2	.200	1	1	1.000	2	1	2	0	5
1954—Minneapolis	23	5	1	.200	0	0	.000	0	3	3	0	2

Season—Team	Min.	FGA	FGM	Pct.	FTA	FTM	Pct.	Reb.	Ast.	PF	Disq.	Pts.
1955—Minneapolis	23	5	2	.400	2	1	.500	2	5	3	0	5
1956—Minneapolis	29	7	3	.429	3	3	1.000	1	7	5	0	9
1957—St. Louis	31	11	4	.364	0	0	.000	2	3	1	0	8
1958—St. Louis	26	9	2	.222	4	2	.500	2	8	3	0	6
1959—St. Louis	22	6	2	.333	2	1	.500	6	1	2	0	5
Totals	180	53	16	.302	12	8	.667	15	28	19	0	40

NBA COACHING RECORD

Sea.	Club	Regular Season W.	L.	Pct.	Pos.
1956-57	St. Louis	5	3	.625	..†

ABA COACHING RECORD

Sea.	Club	Regular Season W.	L.	Pct.	Pos.	Playoffs W.	L.
1967-68	Houston	29	49	.372	4†	0	3
1968-69	Houston	3	9	.250	...†	..	..
Totals (2 years)		32	58	.356		..	..

†Western Division.

Elected to Naismith Memorial Basketball Hall of Fame, 1981. . . . Named to All-NBA Second Team, 1954, 1956, 1957, 1958, 1959. . . . Member of NBA championship teams, 1950, 1952, 1953, 1954, 1958. . . . Named to THE SPORTING NEWS All-America Fifth Team, 1949.

ROBERT ALLEN McADOO
(Bob)

Born September 25, 1951 at Greensboro, N. C. Height 6:09. Weight 225.

High School—Greensboro, N. C., Ben Smith.

Colleges—Vincennes University, Vincennes, Ind., and University of North Carolina, Chapel Hill, N. C.

Drafted by Buffalo on first round as hardship case, 1972 (2nd pick).

Traded by Buffalo with Tom McMillen to New York Knicks for John Gianelli and cash, December 9, 1976.

Traded by New York to Boston for three 1979 1st round draft choices and a player to be named later, February 12, 1979. New York acquired Tom Barker to complete the deal, February 14, 1979.

Acquired from Boston by Detroit for two 1980 1st round draft choices to complete compensation for Boston's earlier signing of Veteran Free Agent M. L. Carr, September 6, 1979.

Waived by Detroit, March 11, 1981; signed by New Jersey as a free agent, March 13, 1981.

Traded by New Jersey to Los Angeles for a 1983 2nd round draft choice and cash, December 24, 1981.

Signed by Philadelphia as a Veteran Free Agent, January 31, 1986; Los Angeles Lakers relinquished their right of first refusal.

Played in Italy during 1986-87 season.

—COLLEGIATE RECORD—

Vincennes

Year	G.	Min.	FGA	FGM	Pct.	FTA	FTM	Pct.	Reb.	Pts.	Avg.
69-70	32	....	...	258	....	134	101	.754	320	617	19.3
70-71	27	....	...	273	....	164	129	.787	297	675	25.0
JC Totals	59	....	...	531	...	298	230	.772	617	1292	21.9

North Carolina

Year	G.	Min.	FGA	FGM	Pct.	FTA	FTM	Pct.	Reb.	Pts.	Avg.
71-72	31	....	471	243	.516	167	118	.707	312	604	19.5

NBA REGULAR SEASON RECORD

Sea.—Team	G.	Min.	FGA	FGM	Pct.	FTA	FTM	Pct.	—Rebounds— Off.	Def.	Tot.	Ast.	PF	Dq.	Stl.	Blk.	Pts.	Avg.
72-73—Buffalo	80	2562	1293	585	.452	350	271	.774			728	139	256	6			1441	18.0
73-74—Buffalo	74	3185	1647	901	.547	579	459	.793	281	836	1117	170	252	3	88	246	2261	30.6
74-75—Buffalo	82	3539	2138	1095	.512	796	641	.805	307	848	1155	179	278	3	92	174	2831	34.5
75-76—Buffalo	78	3328	1918	934	.487	734	559	.762	241	724	965	315	298	5	93	160	2427	31.1
76-77—Buf-Knicks	72	2798	1445	740	.512	516	381	.738	199	727	926	205	262	3	77	99	1861	25.8
77-78—New York	79	3182	1564	814	.520	645	469	.727	236	774	1010	298	297	6	105	126	2097	26.5
78-79—N.Y.-Bos.	60	2231	1127	596	.529	450	295	.656	130	390	520	168	189	3	74	67	1487	24.8
79-80—Detroit	58	2097	1025	492	.480	322	235	.730	100	367	467	200	178	3	73	65	1222	21.1
80-81—Det.-N.J.	16	321	157	68	.433	41	29	.707	17	50	67	30	38	0	17	13	165	10.3
81-82—Los Angeles	41	746	330	151	.458	126	90	.714	45	114	159	32	109	1	22	36	392	9.6
82-83—Los Angeles	47	1019	562	292	.520	163	119	.730	76	171	247	39	153	2	40	40	703	15.0
83-84—Los Angeles	70	1456	748	352	.471	264	212	.803	82	207	289	74	182	0	42	50	916	13.1
84-85—L.A. Lakers	66	1254	546	284	.520	162	122	.753	79	216	295	67	170	0	18	53	690	10.5
85-86—Philadelphia	29	609	251	116	.462	81	62	.765	25	78	103	35	64	0	10	18	294	10.1
Totals	852	28327	14751	7420	.503	5229	3944	.754			8048	1951	2726	35	751	1147	18787	22.1

Three-Point Field Goals: 1979-80, 3-for-24 (.125). 1980-81, 0-for-1. 1981-82, 0-for-5. 1982-83, 0-for-1. 1983-84, 0-for-5. 1984-85, 0-for-1. Totals, 3-for-37 (.081).

NBA PLAYOFF RECORD

Sea.—Team	G.	Min.	FGA	FGM	Pct.	FTA	FTM	Pct.	—Rebounds— Off.	Def.	Tot.	Ast.	PF	Dq.	Stl.	Blk.	Pts.	Avg.
73-74—Buffalo	6	271	159	76	.478	47	38	.809	14	68	82	9	25	1	6	13	190	31.7
74-75—Buffalo	7	327	216	104	.481	73	54	.740	25	69	94	10	29	1	6	19	262	37.4
75-76—Buffalo	9	406	215	97	.451	82	58	.707	31	97	128	29	37	3	7	18	252	28.0
77-78—New York	6	238	126	61	.484	35	21	.600	11	47	58	23	19	0	7	12	143	23.8
81-82—Los Angeles	14	388	179	101	.564	47	32	.681	21	74	95	22	43	2	10	21	234	16.7
82-83—Los Angeles	8	166	84	37	.440	14	11	.786	15	31	46	5	23	0	11	10	87	10.9
83-84—Los Angeles	20	447	215	111	.516	81	57	.704	30	78	108	12	63	0	12	27	279	14.0
84-85—L.A. Lakers	19	398	193	91	.472	47	35	.745	25	61	86	15	66	2	9	26	217	11.4
85-86—Philadelphia	5	73	36	20	.556	16	14	.875	8	6	14	2	13	0	4	5	54	10.8
Totals	94	2714	1423	698	.491	442	320	.724	180	531	711	127	318	9	72	151	1718	18.3

Three-Point Field Goals: 1982-83, 2-for-6 (.333). 1983-84, 0-for-1. 1984-85, 0-for-1. Totals, 2-for-8 (.250).

NBA ALL-STAR GAME RECORD

Season—Team	Min.	FGA	FGM	Pct.	FTA	FTM	Pct.	—Rebounds— Off.	Def.	Tot.	Ast.	PF	Dq.	Stl.	Blk.	Pts.
1974—Buffalo	13	4	3	.750	8	5	.625	1	2	3	1	4	0	0	1	11
1975—Buffalo	26	9	4	.444	3	3	1.000	4	2	6	2	4	0	0	0	11
1976—Buffalo	29	14	10	.714	4	2	.500	2	5	7	1	5	0	0	0	22
1977—Knicks	38	23	13	.565	4	4	1.000	3	7	10	2	3	0	3	1	30
1978—New York	20	14	7	.500	0	0	.000	3	1	4	0	2	0	1	0	14
Totals	126	64	37	.578	19	14	.737	13	17	30	6	18	0	4	2	88

Named NBA Most Valuable Player, 1975. . . . All-NBA First Team, 1975. . . . All-NBA Second Team, 1974. . . . NBA Rookie of the Year, 1973. . . . NBA All-Rookie Team, 1973. . . . Led NBA in scoring, 1974, 1975, 1976. . . . Led NBA in field-goal percentage, 1974. . . . Member of NBA championship teams, 1982 and 1985. . . . Named to THE SPORTING NEWS All-America First Team, 1972.

GEORGE McGINNIS

Born August 12, 1950 at Indianapolis, Ind. Height 6:08. Weight 235.

High School—Indianapolis, Ind., Washington.

College—Indiana University, Bloomington, Ind.

Drafted by Philadelphia on second round, 1973 (22nd pick).

Signed as an undergraduate free agent by Indiana ABA in lieu of a 1972 1st round draft choice, 1971.

Invoked proviso that he could buy his way out of contract with Indiana ABA; signed by Philadelphia NBA, July 10, 1975, after Commissioner Larry O'Brien revoked a contract McGinnis had signed with New York NBA, May 30, 1975.

Traded by Philadelphia to Denver for Bobby Jones and Ralph Simpson, August 16, 1978.

Traded by Denver to Indiana for Alex English and a 1980 1st round draft choice, February 1, 1980.

Waived by Indiana, October 27, 1982.

—COLLEGIATE RECORD—

Year	G.	Min.	FGA	FGM	Pct.	FTA	FTM	Pct.	Reb.	Pts.	Avg.
69-70†					Did Not Play—Ineligible						
70-71	24	....	615	283	.460	249	153	.614	352	719	30.0

ABA REGULAR SEASON RECORD

Sea.—Team	G.	Min.	—2-Point— FGM	FGA	Pct.	—3-Point— FGM	FGA	Pct.	FTM	FTA	Pct.	Reb.	Ast.	Pts.	Avg.
71-72—Indiana	78	2179	459	961	.478	6	38	.158	298	462	.645	711	137	1234	16.9
72-73—Indiana	82	3347	860	1723	.499	8	32	.250	517	778	.665	1022	205	2261	27.6
73-74—Indiana	80	3266	784	1652	.475	5	34	.147	488	715	.683	1197	267	2071	25.9
74-75—Indiana	79	3193	811	1759	.461	62	175	.354	545	753	.724	1126	495	2353	29.8
Totals	319	11985	2914	6095	.478	81	279	.290	1848	2708	.682	4056	1194	7919	24.8

ABA PLAYOFF RECORD

Sea.—Team	G.	Min.	—2-Point— FGM	FGA	Pct.	—3-Point— FGM	FGA	Pct.	FTM	FTA	Pct.	Reb.	Ast.	Pts.	Avg.
71-72—Indiana	20	633	102	246	.415	4	15	.267	94	150	.627	277	52	310	15.5
72-73—Indiana	18	732	161	352	.457	0	5	.000	109	149	732	222	39	431	23.9
73-74—Indiana	14	585	117	254	.461	2	7	.286	96	129	.744	166	47	336	24.0
74-75—Indiana	18	731	190	382	.497	23	73	.315	132	192	.688	286	148	581	32.3
Totals	70	2681	570	1234	.462	29	100	.290	431	620	.695	901	286	1658	23.7

ABA ALL-STAR GAME RECORD

Sea.—Team	Min.	—2-Point— FGM	FGA	Pct.	—3-Point— FGM	FGA	Pct.	FTM	FTA	Pct.	Reb.	Ast.	Pts.	Avg.
72-73—Indiana	34	10	14	.714	0	1	.000	3	6	.500	15	2	23	23.0
73-74—Indiana	30	7	21	.333	0	0	.000	0	0	.000	11	1	4	14.0
74-75—Indiana	32	6	13	.462	0	1	.000	6	11	.545	12	5	18	18.0
Totals	96	23	48	.479	0	2	.000	9	17	.529	38	8	55	18.3

NBA REGULAR SEASON RECORD

Sea.—Team	G.	Min.	FGA	FGM	Pct.	FTA	FTM	Pct.	—Rebounds— Off.	Def.	Tot.	Ast.	PF	Dq.	Stl.	Blk.	Pts.	Avg.
75-76—Philadelphia	77	2946	1552	647	.417	642	475	.740	260	707	967	359	334	13	198	41	1769	23.0
76-77—Philadelphia	79	2769	1439	659	.458	546	372	.681	324	587	911	302	299	4	163	37	1690	21.4
77-78—Philadelphia	78	2533	1270	588	.463	574	411	.716	282	528	810	294	287	6	137	27	1587	20.3
78-79—Denver	76	2552	1273	603	.474	765	509	.665	256	608	864	283	321	16	129	52	1715	22.6
79-80—Den.-Ind.	73	2208	886	400	.451	488	270	.553	222	477	699	333	303	12	101	23	1072	14.7
80-81—Indiana	69	1845	768	348	.453	385	207	.538	164	364	528	210	242	3	99	28	903	13.1
81-82—Indiana	76	1341	378	141	.373	159	72	.453	93	305	398	204	98	4	96	28	354	4.7
Totals	528	16194	7566	3386	.448	3559	2316	.651	1601	3576	5177	1985	1984	58	923	236	9090	17.2

Three-Point Field Goals: 1979-80, 2-for-15 (.133). 1980-81, 0-for-7. 1981-82, 0-for-3. Totals, 2-for-25 (.080).

NBA PLAYOFF RECORD

Sea.—Team	G.	Min.	FGA	FGM	Pct.	FTA	FTM	Pct.	—Rebounds— Off.	Def.	Tot.	Ast.	PF	Dq.	Stl.	Blk.	Pts.	Avg.
75-76—Philadelphia	3	120	61	29	.475	18	11	.611	9	32	41	12	14	1	1	4	69	23.0
76-77—Philadelphia	19	603	273	102	.374	114	65	.570	62	136	198	69	83	2	23	6	269	14.2
77-78—Philadelphia	10	273	125	53	.424	49	41	.837	24	54	78	30	40	1	15	1	147	14.7
80-81—Indiana	2	39	15	3	.200	8	4	.500	2	8	10	7	6	0	2	0	10	5.0
Totals	34	1035	474	187	.395	189	121	.640	97	230	327	118	143	4	41	11	495	14.6

NBA ALL-STAR GAME RECORD

Season—Team	Min.	FGA	FGM	Pct.	FTA	FTM	Pct.	—Rebounds— Off.	Def.	Tot.	Ast.	PF	Dq.	Stl.	Blk.	Pts.
1976—Philadelphia	19	9	4	.444	4	2	.500	1	6	7	2	2	0	0	0	10
1977—Philadelphia	26	9	2	.222	2	0	.000	5	2	7	2	3	0	4	0	4
1979—Denver	25	12	5	.417	11	6	.545	2	4	6	3	4	0	5	0	16
Totals	70	30	11	.367	17	8	.471	8	12	20	7	9	0	9	0	30

Named to All-NBA First Team, 1976.... All-NBA Second Team, 1977.... ABA Co-Most Valuable Player, 1975.... ABA All-Star First Team, 1974 and 1975.... ABA All-Star Second Team, 1973.... ABA All-Rookie Team, 1972.... ABA Playoff MVP, 1973.... Member of ABA championship teams, 1972 and 1973.... Led ABA in scoring, 1975.

RICHARD J. McGUIRE
(Dick)

Born January 25, 1926 at Huntington, N. Y. Height 6:00. Weight 180.

High School—New York, N. Y., LaSalle Academy.

Colleges—St. John's University, Brooklyn, N. Y., and Dartmouth College, Hanover, N. H.

Drafted by New York on first round, 1949.

Drafted by New York on first round of BAA draft, 1949 (BAA merged with NBL later that year to form the NBA). Traded by New York to Detroit for first-round draft choice, September, 1957.

—COLLEGIATE RECORD—

St. John's

Year	G.	Min.	FGA	FGM	Pct.	FTA	FTM	Pct.	Reb.	Pts.	Avg.
43-44	16	....	...	43	....	...	20	....	....	106	6.6

Dartmouth

Year	G.	Min.	FGA	FGM	Pct.	FTA	FTM	Pct.	Reb.	Pts.	Avg.
43-44	5	....	...	17	....	10	9	.900	....	43	8.6
44-45, 45-46						Military Service					

St. John's

Year	G.	Min.	FGA	FGM	Pct.	FTA	FTM	Pct.	Reb.	Pts.	Avg.
46-47	21	....	...	63	....	...	37	....	....	163	7.8
47-48	22	....	...	75	....	115	72	.626	....	222	10.1
48-49	25	....	...	121	....	125	72	.576	....	314	12.6

NBA REGULAR SEASON RECORD

Sea.—Team	G.	Min.	FGA	FGM	Pct.	FTA	FTM	Pct.	Reb.	Ast.	PF	Disq.	Pts.	Avg.
49-50—New York	68	....	563	190	.337	313	204	.652	....	386	160	....	584	8.6
50-51—New York	64	....	482	179	.371	276	179	.649	334	400	154	2	537	8.4
51-52—New York	64	2018	474	204	.430	290	183	.631	332	388	181	4	591	9.2
52-53—New York	61	1783	373	142	.381	269	153	.569	280	296	172	3	437	7.2
53-54—New York	68	2343	493	201	.408	345	220	.638	310	354	199	3	622	9.1
54-55—New York	71	2310	581	226	.389	303	195	.643	322	542	143	0	647	9.1
55-56—New York	62	1685	438	152	.347	193	121	.627	220	362	146	0	425	6.9
56-57—New York	72	1191	366	140	.383	163	105	.644	146	222	103	0	385	5.3
57-58—Detroit	69	2311	544	203	.373	225	150	.667	291	454	178	0	556	8.1
58-59—Detroit	71	2063	543	232	.427	258	191	.740	285	443	147	1	655	9.2
59-60—Detroit	68	1466	402	179	.445	201	124	.617	264	358	112	0	482	7.1
Totals	738	17170	5259	2048	.382	2836	1825	.644	2784	4205	1695	13	5921	8.0

NBA PLAYOFF RECORD

Sea.—Team	G.	Min.	FGA	FGM	Pct.	FTA	FTM	Pct.	Reb.	Ast.	PF	Disq.	Pts.	Avg.
49-50—New York	5	....	52	22	.423	26	19	.731	....	27	21	....	63	12.6
50-51—New York	14	....	80	25	.313	53	24	.453	83	78	50	1	74	5.3
51-52—New York	14	546	107	48	.449	86	49	.570	71	90	46	1	145	10.4
52-53—New York	11	360	59	24	.407	55	35	.636	63	70	25	0	83	7.5
53-54—New York	4	68	16	4	.250	5	3	.600	4	5	12	0	11	2.8
54-55—New York	3	75	19	6	.316	12	8	.667	9	12	7	0	20	6.7
57-58—Detroit	7	236	60	25	.417	24	17	.708	33	40	13	0	67	9.6
58-59—Detroit	3	109	32	20	.625	11	7	.636	17	19	10	0	47	15.7
59-60—Detroit	2	42	12	5	.417	3	1	.333	4	9	3	0	11	5.5
Totals	63	1436	437	179	.410	275	163	.593	284	350	187	2	521	8.3

NBA ALL-STAR GAME RECORD

Season—Team	Min.	FGA	FGM	Pct.	FTA	FTM	Pct.	Reb.	Ast.	PF	Disq.	Pts.
1951—New York	..	4	3	.750	0	0	.000	5	10	2	0	6
1952—New York	18	0	0	.000	3	1	.333	1	4	0	0	1
1954—New York	24	5	2	.400	0	0	.000	4	2	1	0	4
1955—New York	25	2	1	.500	2	1	.500	3	6	1	0	3
1956—New York	29	9	2	.222	5	2	.400	0	3	1	0	6
1958—Detroit	31	4	2	.500	0	0	.000	7	10	4	0	4
1959—Detroit	24	7	2	.286	2	1	.500	3	3	2	0	5
Totals	..	31	12	.387	12	5	.417	23	38	11	0	29

NBA COACHING RECORD

	Regular Season				Playoffs	
Sea. Club	W.	L.	Pct.	Pos.	W.	L.
1959-60—Detroit	17	24	.415	2†	0	2
1960-61—Detroit	34	45	.430	3†	2	3
1961-62—Detroit	37	43	.463	3†	5	5
1962-63—Detroit	34	46	.425	3†	1	3
1965-66—New York	24	35	.407	4‡	..	..
1966-67—New York	36	45	.444	4	‡1	3
1967-68—New York	15	22	.405	..‡	..	..
Totals (7 years)	197	260	.431		9	16

†Western Division. ‡Eastern Division.

Named to All-NBA Second Team, 1951. . . . Led NBA in assists, 1950. . . . Named to THE SPORTING NEWS All-America Second Team, 1944.

GEORGE LAWRENCE MIKAN JR.

Born June 18, 1924 at Joliet, Ill. Height 6:10. Weight 245.

High Schools—Joliet, Ill., Catholic (freshman, did not play basketball) and Chicago, Ill., Quigley Prep (sophomore, junior and senior).

College—DePaul University, Chicago, Ill.

Signed by Chicago of National Basketball League, March 16, 1946.

Chicago dropped out of National Basketball League and entered Professional Basketball League of America for 1947-48 season.

PBLA disbanded, November 13, 1947; Chicago was refused a franchise in the NBL and Mikan was awarded to Minneapolis at an NBL meeting, November 17, 1947. (Mikan scored 193 points in the eight PBLA games played by Chicago before the league folded, and led the league in total points and scoring average.)

Signed by Minneapolis NBL, November, 1947.

—COLLEGIATE RECORD—

Year	G.	Min.	FGA	FGM	Pct.	FTA	FTM	Pct.	Reb.	Pts.	Avg.
41-42†	..	....	...	...	....	...	...	....	....	....	....
42-43	24	....	...	97	....	111	77	.694	....	271	11.3
43-44	26	....	...	188	....	169	110	.655	....	486	18.7
44-45	24	....	...	218	....	199	122	.613	....	558	23.3
45-46	24	....	...	206	....	186	143	.769	....	555	23.1
Varsity Totals	98	....	...	709	....	665	454	.680	....	1870	19.1

NOTE: Mikan played five years at DePaul.

NBL AND NBA REGULAR SEASON PLAYING RECORD

Sea.—Team	G.	Min.	FGA	FGM	Pct.	FTA	FTM	Pct.	Reb.	Ast.	PF	Disq.	Pts.	Avg.
46-47—Chicago-NBL	25	....	....	147	....	164	119	.726	....	....	90	..	413	16.5
47-48—Minn.-NBL	56	....	....	406	....	500	383	.752	....	....	210	..	1195	21.3
48-49—Minneapolis	60	....	1403	583	.416	689	532	.772	....	218	260	..	1698	28.3
49-50—Minneapolis	68	....	1595	649	.407	728	567	.779	....	197	297	..	1865	27.4
50-51—Minneapolis	68	....	1584	678	.428	717	576	.803	958	208	308	14	1932	28.4
51-52—Minneapolis	64	2572	1414	545	.385	555	433	.780	866	194	286	14	1523	23.8
52-53—Minneapolis	70	2651	1252	500	.399	567	442	.780	1007	201	290	12	1442	20.6
53-54—Minneapolis	72	2362	1160	441	.380	546	424	.777	1028	174	268	4	1306	18.1
54-55—	Voluntarily Retired													
55-56—Minneapolis	37	765	375	148	.395	122	94	.770	308	53	153	6	390	10.5
Totals	520	....	....	4097	....	4588	3570	.778	....	....	2162	..	11764	22.6

NBL AND NBA PLAYOFF RECORD

Sea.—Team	G.	Min.	FGA	FGM	Pct.	FTA	FTM	Pct.	Reb.	Ast.	PF	Disq.	Pts.	Avg.
46-47—Chicago-NBL	11	....	....	72	....	104	73	.702	....	....	48	..	217	19.6
47-48—Minn.-NBL	10	....	....	88	....	97	68	.701	....	....	37	..	244	24.4
48-49—Minneapolis	10	....	227	103	.454	121	97	.802	....	21	44	..	303	30.3
49-50—Minneapolis	12	....	316	121	.383	170	134	.788	....	36	47	..	376	31.3
50-51—Minneapolis	7	....	152	62	.408	55	44	.800	74	9	25	1	168	24.0
51-52—Minneapolis	13	553	261	99	.379	138	109	.790	207	36	63	3	307	23.6
52-53—Minneapolis	12	463	213	78	.366	112	82	.732	185	23	56	5	238	19.8
53-54—Minneapolis	13	424	190	87	.458	96	78	.813	171	25	56	1	252	19.4
55-56—Minneapolis	3	60	35	13	.371	13	10	.769	28	5	14	0	36	12.0
Totals	91	....	....	723	....	906	695	.767	....	....	390	..	2141	23.5

NBA ALL-STAR GAME RECORD

Season—Team	Min.	FGA	FGM	Pct.	FTA	FTM	Pct.	Reb.	Ast.	PF	Disq.	Pts.
1951—Minneapolis	....	17	4	.235	6	4	.667	11	3	2	0	12
1952—Minneapolis	29	19	9	.474	9	8	.889	15	1	5	0	26
1953—Minneapolis	40	26	9	.346	4	4	1.000	16	2	2	0	22
1954—Minneapolis	31	18	6	.333	8	6	.750	9	1	5	0	18
Totals	....	80	28	.350	27	22	.815	51	7	14	0	78

NBA COACHING RECORD

		Regular Season			
Sea.	Club	W.	L.	Pct.	Pos.
1957-58	Minneapolis	9	30	.231	4†

†Western Division.

Elected to Naismith Memorial Basketball Hall of Fame, 1959. . . . Named to NBA 25th and 35th Anniversary All-Time Teams, 1970 and 1980. . . . All-NBA First Team, 1949, 1950, 1951, 1952, 1953, 1954. . . . Led NBA in scoring, 1949, 1950, 1952. . . . Led NBA in rebounding, 1953. . . . NBA All-Star Game MVP, 1953. . . . Member of NBA championship teams, 1949, 1950, 1952, 1953, 1954. . . . Member of NBL championship teams, 1947 and 1948. . . . Named to THE SPORTING NEWS All-America First Team, 1944 and 1945. . . . ABA Commissioner during 1968-69 season. . . . Brother of former NBA forward-center Ed Mikan and father of former NBA forward Larry Mikan.

ARILD VERNER AGERSKOV MIKKELSEN (Vern)

Born October 21, 1928 at Fresno, Calif. Height 6:07. Weight 230.

High School—Askov, Minn.

College—Hamline University, St. Paul, Minn.

Drafted by Minneapolis on first round, 1949.

—COLLEGIATE RECORD—

Year	G.	Min.	FGA	FGM	Pct.	FTA	FTM	Pct.	Reb.	Pts.	Avg.
45-46	Statistics Unavailable										
46-47	26	....	...	102	....	...	52	....	....	256	9.8
47-48	31	....	...	199	....	...	119	....	....	517	16.7
48-49	30	...	377	203	.538	177	113	.638	....	519	17.3

NBA REGULAR SEASON RECORD

Sea.—Team	G.	Min.	FGA	FGM	Pct.	FTA	FTM	Pct.	Reb.	Ast.	PF	Disq.	Pts.	Avg.
49-50—Minneapolis	68	....	722	288	.399	286	215	.752	....	123	222	...	791	11.6
50-51—Minneapolis	64	....	893	359	.402	275	186	.676	655	181	260	13	904	14.1
51-52—Minneapolis	66	2345	866	363	.419	372	283	.761	681	180	282	16	1009	15.3
52-53—Minneapolis	70	2465	868	378	.435	387	291	.752	654	148	289	14	1047	15.0
53-54—Minneapolis	72	2247	771	288	.374	298	221	.742	615	119	264	7	797	11.1
54-55—Minneapolis	71	2559	1043	440	.422	598	447	.747	722	145	319	14	1327	18.7
55-56—Minneapolis	72	2100	821	317	.386	408	328	.804	608	173	319	17	962	13.4
56-57—Minneapolis	72	2198	854	322	.377	424	342	.807	630	121	312	18	986	13.7
57-58—Minneapolis	72	2390	1070	439	.410	471	370	.786	805	166	299	20	1248	17.3
58-59—Minneapolis	72	2139	904	353	.390	355	286	.806	570	159	246	8	992	13.8
Totals	699	....	8812	3547	.403	3874	2969	.766	....	1515	2812	...	10063	14.4

NBA PLAYOFF RECORD

Sea.—Team	G.	Min.	FGA	FGM	Pct.	FTA	FTM	Pct.	Reb.	Ast.	PF	Disq.	Pts.	Avg.
49-50—Minneapolis	12	....	149	55	.369	60	46	.767	...	18	32	....	156	13.0
50-51—Minneapolis	7	....	96	39	.406	47	31	.660	67	17	35	3	109	15.6
51-52—Minneapolis	13	496	139	60	.432	64	53	.826	110	20	66	4	173	13.3
52-53—Minneapolis	12	400	133	44	.331	66	56	.848	104	24	59	3	144	12.0
53-54—Minneapolis	13	375	111	51	.459	36	31	.861	73	17	52	1	133	10.2
54-55—Minneapolis	7	209	85	30	.353	46	36	.783	78	13	36	4	96	13.7
55-56—Minneapolis	3	90	26	11	.423	20	18	.900	17	2	14	2	40	13.3
56-57—Minneapolis	5	162	83	33	.398	34	22	.647	43	17	29	4	88	17.6
58-59—Minneapolis	13	371	177	73	.412	73	56	.767	93	24	54	3	202	15.5
Totals	85	....	999	396	.396	446	349	.783	....	152	377	...	1141	13.4

NBA ALL-STAR GAME RECORD

Season—Team	Min.	FGA	FGM	Pct.	FTA	FTM	Pct.	Reb.	Ast.	PF	Disq.	Pts.
1951—Minneapolis	..	11	4	.364	4	3	.750	9	1	3	0	11
1952—Minneapolis	23	8	5	.625	2	2	1.000	10	0	2	0	12
1953—Minneapolis	19	13	3	.231	0	0	.000	6	3	3	0	6
1955—Minneapolis	25	15	7	.467	3	2	.667	9	1	5	0	16
1956—Minneapolis	22	13	5	.385	7	6	.857	9	2	4	0	16
1957—Minneapolis	21	10	3	.300	4	0	.000	9	1	3	0	6
Totals (6 games)	..	70	27	.386	20	13	.650	52	8	20	0	67

ABA COACHING RECORD

Sea.	Club	Regular Season W.	L.	Pct.	Pos.
1968-69	Minnesota	6	7	.462	...

Named to All-NBA Second Team, 1951, 1952, 1953, 1955. . . . Holds NBA record for most disqualifications. . . . Member of NBA championship team, 1950, 1952, 1953, 1954. . . . Led NCAA Division II in field-goal percentage, 1949. . . . Named to NAIA Basketball Hall of Fame, 1956. . . . THE SPORTING NEWS All-America Fourth Team, 1949.

SIDNEY A. MONCRIEF

Born September 21, 1957 at Little Rock, Ark. Height 6:03. Weight 183.

High School—Little Rock, Ark., Hall.

College—University of Arkansas, Fayetteville, Ark.

Drafted by Milwaukee on first round, 1979 (5th pick).

—COLLEGIATE RECORD—

Year	G.	Min.	FGA	FGM	Pct.	FTA	FTM	Pct.	Reb.	Pts.	Avg.
75-76	28	....	224	149	.665	77	56	.727	213	354	12.6
76-77	28	997	242	157	.649	171	117	.684	235	431	15.4
77-78	36	1293	354	209	.590	256	203	.793	278	621	17.3
78-79	30	1157	400	224	.560	248	212	.855	289	660	22.0
Totals	122	....	1220	739	.606	752	588	.782	1015	2066	16.9

NBA REGULAR SEASON RECORD

Sea.—Team	G.	Min.	FGA	FGM	Pct.	FTA	FTM	Pct.	—Rebounds— Off.	Def.	Tot.	Ast.	PF	Dq.	Stl.	Blk.	Pts.	Avg.
79-80—Milwaukee	77	1557	451	211	.468	292	232	.795	154	184	338	133	106	0	72	16	654	8.5
80-81—Milwaukee	80	2417	739	400	.541	398	320	.804	186	220	406	264	156	1	90	37	1122	14.0
81-82—Milwaukee	80	2980	1063	556	.523	573	468	.817	221	313	534	382	206	3	138	22	1581	19.8
82-83—Milwaukee	76	2710	1156	606	.524	604	499	.826	192	245	437	300	180	1	113	23	1712	22.5
83-84—Milwaukee	79	3075	1125	560	.498	624	529	.848	215	313	528	358	204	2	108	27	1654	20.9
84-85—Milwaukee	73	2734	1162	561	.483	548	454	.828	149	242	391	382	197	1	117	39	1585	21.7
85-86—Milwaukee	73	2567	962	470	.489	580	498	.859	115	219	334	357	178	1	103	18	1471	20.2
86-87—Milwaukee	39	992	324	158	.488	162	136	.840	57	70	127	121	73	0	27	10	460	11.8
87-88—Milwaukee	56	1428	444	217	.489	196	164	.837	58	122	180	204	109	0	41	12	603	10.8
88-89—Milwaukee	62	1594	532	261	.491	237	205	.865	46	126	172	188	114	1	65	13	752	12.1
Totals	695	22054	7958	4000	.503	4214	3505	.832	1393	2054	3447	2689	1523	10	874	217	11594	16.7

Three-Point Field Goals: 1979-80, 0-for-1. 1980-81, 2-for-9 (.222). 1981-82, 1-for-14 (.071). 1982-83, 1-for-10 (.100). 1983-84, 5-for-18 (.278). 1984-85, 9-for-33 (.273). 1985-86, 33-for-103 (.320). 1986-87, 8-for-31 (.258). 1987-88, 5-for-31 (.161). 1988-89, 25-for-73 (.342). Totals, 89-for-323 (.276).

NBA PLAYOFF RECORD

Sea.—Team	G.	Min.	FGA	FGM	Pct.	FTA	FTM	Pct.	—Rebounds— Off.	Def.	Tot.	Ast.	PF	Dq.	Stl.	Blk.	Pts.	Avg.
79-80—Milwaukee	7	182	51	30	.588	31	27	.871	17	14	31	11	14	0	5	1	87	12.4
80-81—Milwaukee	7	277	69	30	.435	51	38	.745	19	28	47	20	24	0	12	3	98	14.0
81-82—Milwaukee	6	252	74	31	.419	38	30	.789	15	15	30	24	22	1	9	2	92	15.3
82-83—Milwaukee	9	377	142	62	.437	61	46	.754	28	32	60	33	25	1	18	3	170	18.9
83-84—Milwaukee	16	618	191	99	.518	134	106	.791	44	67	111	68	54	1	28	9	305	19.1
84-85—Milwaukee	8	319	99	55	.556	75	70	.933	10	24	34	40	26	0	5	4	184	23.0
85-86—Milwaukee	9	327	122	52	.426	63	44	.698	15	26	41	44	30	0	5	5	152	16.9
86-87—Milwaukee	12	426	165	78	.473	90	73	.811	21	33	54	36	43	0	13	6	233	19.4
87-88—Milwaukee	5	173	50	24	.480	27	26	.963	6	13	19	26	14	0	3	1	75	15.0
88-89—Milwaukee	9	184	48	19	.396	16	15	.938	8	18	26	13	17	0	5	2	55	6.1
Totals	88	3135	1011	480	.475	586	475	.811	183	270	453	315	269	3	103	36	1451	16.5

Three-Point Field Goals: 1981-82, 0-for-1. 1982-83, 0-for-1. 1983-84, 1-for-4 (.250). 1984-85, 4-for-10 (.400). 1985-86, 4-for-14 (.286). 1986-87, 4-for-14 (.286). 1987-88, 1-for-1 (1.000). 1988-89, 2-for-7 (.286). Totals, 16-for-52 (.308).

NBA ALL-STAR GAME RECORD

Season—Team	Min.	FGA	FGM	Pct.	FTA	FTM	Pct.	—Rebounds— Off.	Def.	Tot.	Ast.	PF	Dq.	Stl.	Blk.	Pts.
1982—Milwaukee....	22	11	3	.273	2	0	.000	3	1	4	1	2	0	1	0	6
1983—Milwaukee....	23	14	8	.571	5	4	.800	3	2	5	4	1	0	6	1	20
1984—Milwaukee....	26	6	3	.500	2	2	1.000	1	4	5	2	3	0	5	0	8
1985—Milwaukee....	22	5	1	.200	6	6	1.000	2	3	5	4	1	0	0	0	8
1986—Milwaukee....	26	11	4	.364	7	7	1.000	3	0	3	1	0	0	0	1	16
Totals	119	47	19	.404	22	19	.864	12	10	22	12	7	0	12	2	58

Three-Point Field Goals: 1986, 1-for-1 (1.000).

Named to All-NBA First Team, 1983. . . . All-NBA Second Team, 1982, 1984, 1985, 1986. . . . NBA Defensive Player of the Year, 1983 and 1984. . . . NBA All-Defensive First Team, 1983, 1984, 1985, 1986. . . . NBA All-Defensive Second Team, 1982. . . . Named to THE SPORTING NEWS All-America Second Team, 1979. . . . Led NCAA in field-goal percentage, 1976.

EARL MONROE
(The Pearl)

Born November 21, 1944 at Philadelphia, Pa. Height 6:03. Weight 190.
High School—Philadelphia, Pa., Bartram.
College—Winston-Salem State University, Winston-Salem, N. C.
Drafted by Baltimore on first round, 1967 (2nd pick).

Traded by Baltimore to New York for Dave Stallworth, Mike Riordan and cash, November 10, 1971.

—COLLEGIATE RECORD—

Year	G.	Min.	FGA	FGM	Pct.	FTA	FTM	Pct.	Reb.	Pts.	Avg.
63-64	23	....	...	71	....	...	21	....	....	163	7.1
64-65	30	....	...	286	....	176	125	.710	211	697	23.2
65-66	25	....	519	292	.563	187	162	.866	167	746	29.8
66-67	32	....	839	509	.607	391	311	.795	218	1329	41.5
Totals	110	....	....	1158	....	....	619	....	.....	2935	26.7

NBA REGULAR SEASON RECORD

Sea.—Team	G.	Min.	FGA	FGM	Pct.	FTA	FTM	Pct.	Reb.	Ast.	PF	Disq.	Pts.	Avg.
67-68—Baltimore	82	3012	1637	742	.453	649	507	.781	465	349	282	3	1991	24.3
68-69—Baltimore	80	3075	1837	809	.440	582	447	.768	280	392	261	1	2065	25.8
69-70—Baltimore	82	3051	1557	695	.446	641	532	.830	257	402	258	3	1922	23.4
70-71—Baltimore	81	2843	1501	663	.442	506	406	.802	213	354	220	3	1732	21.4
71-72—Balt.-N.Y.	63	1337	662	287	.434	224	175	.781	100	142	139	1	749	11.9
72-73—New York	75	2370	1016	496	.488	208	171	.822	245	288	195	1	1163	15.5

Sea.—Team	G.	Min.	FGA	FGM	Pct.	FTA	FTM	Pct.	—Rebounds— Off.	Def.	Tot.	Ast.	PF	Dq.	Stl.	Blk.	Pts.	Avg.
73-74—New York	41	1194	513	240	.468	113	93	.823	22	99	121	110	97	0	34	19	573	14.0
74-75—New York	78	2814	1462	668	.457	359	297	.827	56	271	327	270	200	0	108	29	1633	20.9
75-76—New York	76	2889	1354	647	.478	356	280	.787	48	225	273	304	209	1	111	22	1574	20.7
76-77—Knicks	77	2656	1185	613	.517	366	307	.839	45	178	223	366	197	0	91	23	1533	19.9
77-78—New York	76	2369	1123	556	.495	291	242	.832	47	135	182	361	189	0	60	19	1354	17.8
78-79—New York	64	1393	699	329	.471	154	129	.838	26	48	74	189	123	0	48	6	787	12.3
79-80—New York	51	633	352	161	.457	64	56	.875	16	20	36	67	46	0	21	3	378	7.4
Totals	926	29636	14898	6906	.464	4513	3642	.807			2796	3594	2416	13	473	121	17454	18.8

NBA PLAYOFF RECORD

Sea.—Team	G.	Min.	FGA	FGM	Pct.	FTA	FTM	Pct.	Reb.	Ast.	PF	Disq.	Pts.	Avg.
68-69—Baltimore	4	171	114	44	.386	31	25	.806	21	16	10	0	113	28.3
69-70—Baltimore	7	299	154	74	.481	60	48	.800	23	28	23	0	196	28.0
70-71—Baltimore	18	671	356	145	.407	135	107	.793	64	74	56	0	397	22.1
71-72—New York	16	429	185	76	.411	57	45	.789	45	47	41	0	197	12.3
72-73—New York	16	504	211	111	.526	48	36	.750	51	51	39	0	258	16.1

Sea.—Team	G.	Min.	FGA	FGM	Pct.	FTA	FTM	Pct.	—Rebounds— Off.	Def.	Tot.	Ast.	PF	Dq.	Stl.	Blk.	Pts.	Avg.
73-74—New York	12	407	165	81	.491	55	47	.855	8	40	48	25	26	0	8	9	209	17.4
74-75—New York	3	89	45	12	.267	22	18	.818	1	8	9	6	6	0	4	2	42	14.0
77-78—New York	6	145	62	24	.389	18	11	.611	1	4	5	17	15	0	6	0	59	9.8
Totals	82	2715	1292	567	.439	426	337	.791			266	264	216	0	18	11	1471	17.9

NBA ALL-STAR GAME RECORD

Season—Team	Min.	FGA	FGM	Pct.	FTA	FTM	Pct.	Reb.	Ast.	PF	Disq.	Pts.
1969—Baltimore	27	15	6	.400	12	9	.750	4	4	4	0	21
1971—Baltimore	18	9	3	.333	0	0	.000	5	2	3	0	6

Season—Team	Min.	FGA	FGM	Pct.	FTA	FTM	Pct.	—Rebounds— Off.	Def.	Tot.	Ast.	PF	Dq.	Stl.	Blk.	Pts.
1975—New York	25	8	3	.375	5	3	.600	0	3	3	2	2	0	1	0	9
1977—Knicks	15	7	2	.286	0	0	.000	0	0	0	3	1	0	0	0	4
Totals	85	39	14	359	17	12	.706			12	11	10	0	1	0	40

Elected to Naismith Memorial Basketball Hall of Fame, 1989. . . . Named to All-NBA First Team, 1969. . . . NBA Rookie of the Year, 1968. . . . NBA All-Rookie Team, 1968. . . . Member of NBA championship team, 1973. . . . Holds NCAA Division II record for most points in a season, 1967. . . . Outstanding player in 1967 NCAA College Division tournament. . . . Member of NCAA College Division tournament championship team, 1967. . . . Named to THE SPORTING NEWS All-America First Team, 1966. . . . Named to NAIA Basketball Hall of Fame, 1975.

CALVIN JEROME MURPHY

Born May 9, 1948 at Norwalk, Conn. Height 5:09. Weight 165.
High School—Norwalk, Conn.
College—Niagara University, Niagara University, N. Y.
Drafted by San Diego on second round, 1970 (18th pick).

—COLLEGIATE RECORD—

Year	G.	Min.	FGA	FGM	Pct.	FTA	FTM	Pct.	Reb.	Pts.	Avg.
66-67†	19	....	719	364	.506	239	201	.841	102	929	48.9
67-68	24	....	772	337	.437	288	242	.840	118	916	38.2
68-69	24	....	700	294	.420	230	190	.826	87	778	32.4
69-70	29	....	692	316	.457	252	222	.881	103	854	29.4
Varsity Totals	77	....	2164	947	.438	770	654	.849	308	2548	33.1

NBA REGULAR SEASON RECORD

Sea.—Team	G.	Min.	FGA	FGM	Pct.	FTA	FTM	Pct.	Reb.	Ast.	PF	Disq.	Pts.	Avg.
70-71—San Diego	82	2020	1029	471	.458	434	356	.820	245	329	263	4	1298	15.8
71-72—Houston	82	2538	1255	571	.455	392	349	.890	258	393	298	6	1491	18.2
72-73—Houston	77	1697	820	381	.465	269	239	.888	149	262	211	3	1001	13.0

Sea.—Team	G.	Min.	FGA	FGM	Pct.	FTA	FTM	Pct.	—Rebounds— Off.	Def.	Tot.	Ast.	PF	Dq.	Stl.	Blk.	Pts.	Avg.
73-74—Houston	81	2922	1285	671	.522	357	310	.868	51	137	188	603	310	8	157	4	1652	20.4
74-75—Houston	78	2513	1152	557	.484	386	341	.883	52	121	173	381	281	8	128	4	1455	18.7
75-76—Houston	82	2995	1369	675	.493	410	372	.907	52	157	209	596	294	3	151	6	1722	21.0
76-77—Houston	82	2764	1216	596	.490	307	272	.886	54	118	172	386	281	6	144	8	1464	17.9
77-78—Houston	76	2900	1737	852	.491	267	245	.918	57	107	164	259	241	4	112	3	1949	25.6
78-79—Houston	82	2941	1424	707	.496	265	246	.928	78	95	173	351	288	5	117	6	1660	20.2
79-80—Houston	76	2676	1267	624	.493	302	271	.897	68	82	150	299	269	3	143	9	1520	20.0
80-81—Houston	76	2014	1074	528	.492	215	206	.958	33	54	87	222	209	0	111	6	1266	16.7
81-82—Houston	64	1204	648	277	.427	110	100	.909	20	41	61	163	142	0	43	1	655	10.2
82-83—Houston	64	1423	754	337	.447	150	138	.920	34	40	74	158	163	3	59	4	816	12.8
Totals	1002	30607	15030	7247	.482	3864	3445	.892			2103	4402	3250	53	1165	51	17949	17.9

Three-Point Field Goals: 1979-80, 1-for-25 (.040). 1980-81, 4-for-17 (.235). 1981-82, 1-for-16 (.063). 1982-83, 4-for-14 (.286). Totals, 10-for-72 (.139).

NBA PLAYOFF RECORD

Sea.—Team	G.	Min.	FGA	FGM	Pct.	FTA	FTM	Pct.	—Rebounds— Off.	Def.	Tot.	Ast.	PF	Dq.	Stl.	Blk.	Pts.	Avg.
74-75—Houston	8	305	156	72	.462	57	51	.895	9	10	19	45	36	2	14	1	195	24.4
76-77—Houston	12	420	213	102	.479	30	28	.933	7	12	19	75	47	1	19	2	232	19.3
78-79—Houston	2	73	31	9	.290	9	8	.889	2	1	3	6	9	0	8	1	26	13.0
79-80—Houston	7	265	108	58	.537	13	13	1.000	4	6	10	26	29	1	11	0	131	18.7
80-81—Houston	19	540	287	142	.495	60	58	.967	7	17	24	57	69	0	26	0	344	18.1
81-82—Houston	3	57	22	5	.227	8	7	.875	2	1	3	4	7	0	1	0	17	5.7
Totals	51	1660	817	388	.475	177	165	.932	31	47	78	213	197	4	79	4	945	18.5

Three-Point Field Goals: 1979-80, 2-for-4 (.500). 1980-81, 2-for-7 (.286). 1981-82, 0-for-3. Totals, 4-for-14 (.286).

NBA ALL-STAR GAME RECORD

Season—Team	Min.	FGA	FGM	Pct.	FTA	FTM	Pct.	—Rebounds— Off.	Def.	Tot.	Ast.	PF	Dq.	Stl.	Blk.	Pts.
1979—Houston	15	5	3	.600	0	0	.000	0	0	1	5	4	0	2	0	6

Three-Point Field Goals: 1979-80, 2-for-4 (.500). 1980-81, 2-for-7 (.286). Totals, 4-for-11 (.364).

—DID YOU KNOW—

That the Los Angeles Lakers lost only four games at home during the 1989-90 season? The New Jersey Nets, on the other hand, won just four games away from home all season.

Named to NBA All-Rookie Team, 1971. . . . Holds NBA records for highest free-throw percentage in one season, 1981, and most consecutive free throws made, 78, December 27, 1980 through February 28, 1981. . . . Led NBA in free-throw percentage, 1981 and 1983. . . . Named to THE SPORTING NEWS All-America Second Team, 1969 and 1970.

ROBERT LEE PETTIT JR.
(Bob)

Born December 12, 1932 at Baton Rouge, La. Height 6:09. Weight 215.
High School—Baton Rouge, La.
College—Louisiana State University, Baton Rouge, La.
Drafted by Milwaukee on first round, 1954.

Milwaukee franchise transferred to St. Louis, 1955.

—COLLEGIATE RECORD—

Year	G.	Min.	FGA	FGM	Pct.	FTA	FTM	Pct.	Reb.	Pts.	Avg.
50-51†	10	....	...	...	....	...	...	....	...	270	27.0
51-52	23	....	549	237	.432	192	115	.599	315	589	25.6
52-53	21	....	394	193	.490	215	133	.619	263	519	24.7
53-54	25	....	573	281	.490	308	223	.724	432	785	31.4
Varsity Totals	69	....	1516	711	.469	715	471	.659	1010	1893	27.4

NBA REGULAR SEASON RECORD

Sea.—Team	G.	Min.	FGA	FGM	Pct.	FTA	FTM	Pct.	Reb.	Ast.	PF	Disq.	Pts.	Avg.
54-55—Milwaukee	72	2659	1279	520	.407	567	426	.751	994	229	258	5	1466	20.4
55-56—St. Louis	72	2794	1507	646	.429	757	557	.736	1164	189	202	1	1849	25.7
56-57—St. Louis	71	2491	1477	613	.415	684	529	.773	1037	133	181	1	1755	24.7
57-58—St. Louis	70	2528	1418	581	.410	744	557	.745	1216	157	222	6	1719	24.6
58-59—St. Louis	72	2873	1640	719	.438	879	667	.758	1182	221	200	3	2105	29.2
59-60—St. Louis	72	2896	1526	669	.438	722	544	.753	1221	257	204	0	1882	26.1
60-61—St. Louis	76	3027	1720	769	.447	804	582	.724	1540	262	217	1	2120	27.9
61-62—St. Louis	78	3282	1928	867	.450	901	695	.771	1459	289	296	4	2429	31.1
62-63—St. Louis	79	3090	1746	778	.446	885	685	.774	1191	245	282	9	2241	28.4
63-64—St. Louis	80	3296	1708	791	.463	771	608	.789	1224	259	300	3	2190	27.4
64-65—St. Louis	50	1754	923	396	.429	405	332	.820	621	128	167	0	1124	22.5
Totals	792	30690	16872	7349	.436	8119	6182	.761	12849	2369	2529	33	20880	26.4

NBA PLAYOFF RECORD

Sea.—Team	G.	Min.	FGA	FGM	Pct.	FTA	FTM	Pct.	Reb.	Ast.	PF	Disq.	Pts.	Avg.
55-56—St. Louis	8	274	128	47	.367	70	59	.843	84	18	20	0	153	19.1
56-57—St. Louis	10	430	237	98	.414	133	102	.767	168	25	33	0	298	29.8
57-58—St. Louis	11	430	230	90	.391	118	86	.729	181	20	31	0	266	24.2
58-59—St. Louis	6	257	137	58	.423	65	51	.785	75	14	20	0	167	27.8
59-60—St. Louis	14	576	292	129	.442	142	107	.753	221	52	43	1	365	26.1
60-61—St. Louis	12	526	284	117	.412	144	109	.757	211	38	42	0	343	28.6
62-63—St. Louis	11	463	259	119	.459	144	112	.778	166	33	34	0	350	31.8
63-64—St. Louis	12	494	226	93	.412	79	66	.835	174	33	44	0	252	21.0
64-65—St. Louis	4	95	41	15	.366	20	16	.800	24	8	10	0	46	11.5
Totals	88	3545	1834	766	.418	915	708	.774	1304	241	277	1	2240	25.5

NBA ALL-STAR GAME RECORD

Season—Team	Min.	FGA	FGM	Pct.	FTA	FTM	Pct.	Reb.	Ast.	PF	Disq.	Pts.
1955—Milwaukee	27	14	3	.214	4	2	.500	9	2	0	0	8
1956—St. Louis	31	17	7	.412	7	6	.857	24	7	4	0	20
1957—St. Louis	31	18	8	.444	6	5	.833	11	2	2	0	21
1958—St. Louis	38	21	10	.476	10	8	.800	26	1	1	0	28
1959—St. Louis	34	21	8	.381	9	9	1.000	16	5	1	0	25
1960—St. Louis	28	15	4	.267	6	3	.500	14	2	2	0	11
1961—St. Louis	32	22	13	.591	7	3	.429	9	0	2	0	29
1962—St. Louis	37	20	10	.500	5	5	1.000	27	2	5	0	25
1963—St. Louis	32	16	7	.438	12	11	.917	13	0	1	0	25
1964—St. Louis	36	15	6	.400	9	7	.778	17	2	3	0	19
1965—St. Louis	34	14	5	.357	5	3	.600	12	0	4	0	13
Totals	360	193	81	.420	80	62	.775	178	23	25	0	224

NBA COACHING RECORD

	Regular Season			
Sea. Club	W.	L.	Pct.	Pos.
1961-62—St. Louis	4	2	.667	...†

†Western Division.

Elected to Naismith Memorial Basketball Hall of Fame, 1970. . . . Named to NBA 25th and 35th Anniversary All-Time Teams, 1970 and 1980. . . . NBA Most Valuable Player, 1956 and 1959. . . . Named to All-NBA First Team, 1955, 1956, 1957, 1958, 1959, 1960, 1961, 1962, 1963, 1964. . . . All-NBA Second Team, 1965. . . . NBA Rookie of the Year, 1955. . . . Holds NBA championship series game records for most free-throw attempts, 24, and most free throws made, 19, vs. Boston, April 9, 1958. . . . Holds NBA championship series record for most field goals made in one half,

13, vs. Boston, April 9, 1957. . . . Shares NBA championship series record for most field goals made in one quarter, 8, vs. Boston, April 12, 1958. . . . Shares NBA championship series record for most free-throw attempts in one quarter, 11, vs. Boston, April 9, 1958. . . . NBA All-Star Game MVP, 1956, 1958, 1962. . . . NBA All-Star Game co-MVP, 1959. . . . Holds NBA All-Star Game records for most rebounds in one game, 27, in 1962, and most rebounds in one quarter, 10, in 1962. . . . Shares NBA All-Star Game record for most rebounds in one half, 16, in 1962. . . . Member of NBA championship team, 1958. . . . Led NBA in scoring, 1956 and 1959. . . . Led NBA in rebounding, 1956.

JAMES C. POLLARD
(Jim)

Born July 9, 1922 at Oakland, Calif. Height 6:05. Weight 185.
High School—Oakland, Calif., Tech.
College—Stanford University, Stanford, Calif.
Signed by Minneapolis NBL, 1947.

—COLLEGIATE RECORD—

Year	G.	Min.	FGA	FGM	Pct.	FTA	FTM	Pct.	Reb.	Pts.	Avg.
40-41†						Statistics Unavailable					
41-42	23	....	...	103	....	48	35	.729	....	241	10.5
Varsity Totals	23	....	...	103	....	48	35	.729	....	241	10.5

Note: In military service during 1942-43, 1943-44 and 1944-45 seasons. Played with Alameda, Calif., Coast Guard team.

AMERICAN BASKETBALL LEAGUE RECORD
(Amateur Athletic Union League)

Year—Team	G	FG	FT	Pts.	Avg.
45-46—San Diego Dons	15	84	55	223	14.9
46-47—Oakland Bittners	20	..	..	279	14.0

(Led league in scoring both seasons.)

NBL AND NBA REGULAR SEASON RECORD

Sea.—Team	G.	Min.	FGA	FGM	Pct.	FTA	FTM	Pct.	Reb.	Ast.	PF	Disq.	Pts.	Avg.
47-48—Minn-N L	59	....	....	310	....	207	140	.676	....	....	147	....	760	12.9
48-49—Minneapolis	53	....	792	314	.396	227	156	.687	....	142	144	....	784	14.8
49-50—Minneapolis	66	....	1140	394	.346	242	185	.764	....	252	143	....	973	14.7
50-51—Minneapolis	54	....	728	256	.352	156	117	.750	484	184	157	4	629	11.6
51-52—Minneapolis	65	2545	1155	411	.356	260	183	.704	593	234	199	4	1005	15.5
52-53—Minneapolis	66	2403	933	333	.357	251	193	.769	452	231	194	3	859	13.0
53-54—Minneapolis	71	2483	882	326	.370	230	179	.778	500	214	161	0	831	11.7
54-55—Minneapolis	63	1960	749	265	.354	186	151	.812	458	160	147	3	681	10.8
Totals	497	....	....	2609	....	1759	1304	.741	....	....	1292	....	6522	13.1

NBA PLAYOFF RECORD

Sea.—Team	G.	Min.	FGA	FGM	Pct.	FTA	FTM	Pct.	Reb.	Ast.	PF	Disq.	Pts.	Avg.
48-49—Minneapolis	10	....	147	43	.293	62	44	.710	....	39	31	....	130	13.0
49-50—Minneapolis	12	....	175	50	.286	62	44	.710	....	56	36	....	144	12.0
50-51—Minneapolis	7	....	108	35	.324	30	25	.833	62	27	27	1	95	13.6
51-52—Minneapolis	11	469	173	70	.405	50	37	.740	71	33	34	1	177	16.1
52-53—Minneapolis	12	455	167	62	.371	62	48	.774	86	49	37	2	172	14.3
53-54—Minneapolis	13	543	155	56	.361	60	48	.800	110	41	27	0	160	12.3
54-55—Minneapolis	7	257	104	33	.317	46	33	.717	78	14	13	0	99	14.1
Totals	72	....	1029	349	.339	372	279	.750	....	259	205	....	977	13.6

NBA ALL-STAR GAME RECORD

Season—Team	Min.	FGA	FGM	Pct.	FTA	FTM	Pct.	Reb.	Ast.	PF	Disq.	Pts.
1951—Minneapolis	..	11	2	.182	0	0	.000	4	5	1	0	4
1952—Minneapolis	29	17	2	.118	0	0	.000	11	5	3	0	4
1954—Minneapolis	41	22	10	.455	5	3	.600	3	3	3	0	23
1955—Minneapolis	27	19	7	.368	3	3	1.000	4	0	1	0	17
Totals (4 games)	..	69	21	.304	8	6	.750	22	13	8	0	48

NBA COACHING RECORD

	Regular Season				Playoffs	
Sea. Club	W.	L.	Pct.	Pos.	W.	L.
1959-60—Minneapolis	14	25	.359	3	5	4
1961-62—Chicago	18	62	.225	5	..	..
Totals (2 years)	32	87	.269		5	4

ABA COACHING RECORD

	Regular Season				Playoffs	
Sea. Club	W.	L.	Pct.	Pos.	W.	L.
1967-68—Minnesota	50	28	.641	2	4	6
1968-69—Miami	43	35	.551	2	5	7
1969-70—Miami	5	15	.250	...	..	..
Totals (3 years)	98	78	.557		9	13

COLLEGIATE COACHING RECORD

Sea.	Club	Regular Season W.	L.	Pct.	Pos.
1955-56	—La Salle	15	10	.600	
1956-57	—La Salle	17	9	.653	
1957-58	—La Salle	16	9	.640	

Elected to Naismith Memorial Basketball Hall of Fame, 1977. . . . Named to All-NBA First Team, 1949 and 1950. . . . All-NBA Second Team, 1952 and 1954. . . . Member of NBA championship teams, 1949, 1950, 1952, 1953, 1954. . . . Member of NBL championship team, 1948. . . . Member of NCAA Division I championship team, 1942.

WILLIS REED JR.

Born June 25, 1942 at Hico, La. Height 6:10. Weight 240.
High School—Lillie, La., West Side.
College—Grambling College, Grambling, La.
Drafted by New York on second round, 1964 (10th pick).

—COLLEGIATE RECORD—

Year	G.	Min.	FGA	FGM	Pct.	FTA	FTM	Pct.	Reb.	Pts.	Avg.
60-61	35	....	239	146	.611	122	86	.705	312	378	10.8
61-62	26	....	323	189	.585	102	80	.784	380	458	17.6
62-63	33	....	489	282	.565	177	135	.763	563	699	21.2
63-64	28	....	486	301	.619	199	143	.719	596	745	26.6
Totals	122	....	1537	918	.597	600	444	.740	1851	2280	18.7

NBA REGULAR SEASON RECORD

Sea.—Team	G.	Min.	FGA	FGM	Pct.	FTA	FTM	Pct.	Reb.	Ast.	PF	Disq.	Pts.	Avg.
64-65—New York	80	3042	1457	629	.432	407	302	742	1175	133	339	14	1560	19.5
65-66—New York	76	2537	1009	438	.434	399	302	.757	883	91	323	13	1178	15.5
66-67—New York	78	2824	1298	635	.489	487	358	.735	1136	126	293	9	1628	20.9
67-68—New York	81	2879	1346	659	.490	509	367	.721	1073	159	343	12	1685	20.8
68-69—New York	82	3108	1351	704	.521	435	325	.747	1191	190	314	7	1733	21.1
69-70—New York	81	3089	1385	702	.507	464	351	.756	1126	161	287	2	1755	21.7
70-71—New York	73	2855	1330	614	.462	381	299	.785	1003	148	228	1	1527	20.9
71-72—New York	11	363	137	60	.438	39	27	.692	96	22	30	0	147	13.4
72-73—New York	69	1876	705	334	.474	124	92	.742	590	126	205	0	760	11.0

									—Rebounds—									
Sea.—Team	G.	Min.	FGA	FGM	Pct.	FTA	FTM	Pct.	Off.	Def.	Tot.	Ast.	PF	Dq.	Stl.	Blk.	Pts.	Avg.
73-74—N. Y.	19	500	184	84	.457	53	42	.792	47	94	141	30	49	0	12	21	210	11.1
Totals	650	23073	10202	4859	.476	3298	2465	.747			8414	1186	2411	58			12183	18.7

NBA PLAYOFF RECORD

Sea.—Team	G.	Min.	FGA	FGM	Pct.	FTA	FTM	Pct.	Reb.	Ast.	PF	Disq.	Pts.	Avg.
66-67—New York	4	148	80	43	.538	25	24	.960	55	7	19	1	110	27.5
67-68—New York	6	210	98	53	.541	30	22	.733	62	11	24	1	128	21.3
68-69—New York	10	429	198	101	.510	70	55	.786	141	19	40	1	257	25.7
69-70—New York	18	732	378	178	.471	95	70	.737	248	51	60	0	426	23.7
70-71—New York	12	504	196	81	.413	39	26	.667	144	27	41	0	188	15.7
72-73—New York	17	486	208	97	.466	21	18	.857	129	30	65	1	212	12.5

									—Rebounds—									
Sea.—Team	G.	Min.	FGA	FGM	Pct.	FTA	FTM	Pct.	Off.	Def.	Tot.	Ast.	PF	Dq.	Stl.	Blk.	Pts.	Avg.
73-74—N.Y.	11	132	45	17	.378	5	3	.600	4	18	22	4	26	0	2	0	37	3.4
Totals	78	2641	1203	570	.474	285	218	.765			801	149	275	4			1358	17.4

NBA ALL-STAR GAME RECORD

Season—Team	Min.	FGA	FGM	Pct.	FTA	FTM	Pct.	Reb.	Ast.	PF	Disq.	Pts.
1965—New York	25	11	3	.273	2	1	.500	5	1	2	0	7
1966—New York	23	11	7	.636	2	2	1.000	8	1	3	0	16
1967—New York	17	6	2	.333	0	0	.000	9	1	0	0	4
1968—New York	25	14	7	.500	3	2	.667	8	1	4	0	16
1969—New York	14	8	5	.625	0	0	.000	4	2	2	0	10
1970—New York	30	18	9	.500	3	3	1.000	11	0	6	1	21
1971—New York	27	16	5	.313	6	4	.667	13	1	3	0	14
Totals	161	84	38	.452	16	12	.750	58	7	20	1	88

NBA COACHING RECORD

Sea. Club	Regular Season W.	L.	Pct.	Pos.	Playoffs W.	L.
1977-78—New York	43	39	.524	2†	2	4
1978-79—New York	6	8	.429	..†	..	..
1987-88—New Jersey	7	21	.250	..†	..	..
1988-89—New Jersey	26	56	.317	5†	..	..
Totals (4 seasons)	82	124	.398		2	4

†Atlantic Division.

Assistant, Atlanta Hawks, 1985-87, and Sacramento Kings, 1987-88.

COLLEGIATE COACHING RECORD

Sea.	Club	Regular Season W.	L.	Pct.	Pos.
1981-82	—Creighton	7	20	.259	‡8
1982-83	—Creighton	8	19	.296	‡10
1983-84	—Creighton	17	14	.548	‡4
1984-85	—Creighton	20	11	.645	‡4
Totals (4 seasons)		52	64	.448	

‡Missouri Valley Conference.

Elected to Naismith Memorial Basketball Hall of Fame, 1981.... NBA Most Valuable Player, 1970.... Named to All-NBA First Team, 1970.... All NBA Second Team, 1967, 1968, 1969, 1971.... NBA All-Defensive First Team, 1970. ... NBA Rookie of the Year, 1965.... NBA All-Rookie Team, 1965.... NBA Playoff MVP, 1970 and 1973.... NBA All-Star Game MVP, 1970.... Member of NBA championship teams, 1970 and 1973.... Member of NAIA championship team, 1961.... Elected to NAIA Basketball Hall of Fame, 1970.

OSCAR PALMER ROBERTSON
(Big O)

Born November 24, 1938 at Charlotte, Tenn. Height 6:05. Weight 220.

High School—Indianapolis, Ind., Crispus Attucks.

College—University of Cincinnati, Cincinnati, O.

Drafted by Cincinnati on first round (territorial choice), 1960.

Traded by Cincinnati to Milwaukee for Flynn Robinson and Charlie Paulk, April 21, 1970.

—COLLEGIATE RECORD—

Year	G.	Min.	FGA	FGM	Pct.	FTA	FTM	Pct.	Reb.	Pts.	Avg.
56-57†	13	....	...	151	....	178	127	.713	....	429	33.0
57-58	28	1085	617	352	.571	355	280	.789	425	984	35.1
58-59	30	1172	650	331	.509	398	316	.794	489	978	32.6
59-60	30	1155	701	369	.526	361	273	.756	424	1011	33.7
Varsity Totals	88	3412	1968	1052	.535	1114	869	.780	1338	2973	33.8

NBA REGULAR SEASON RECORD

Sea.—Team	G.	Min.	FGA	FGM	Pct.	FTA	FTM	Pct.	Reb.	Ast.	PF	Disq.	Pts.	Avg.
60-61—Cincinnati	71	3012	1600	756	.473	794	653	.822	716	690	219	3	2165	30.5
61-62—Cincinnati	79	3503	1810	866	.478	872	700	.803	985	899	258	1	2432	30.8
62-63—Cincinnati	80	3521	1593	825	.518	758	614	.810	835	758	293	1	2264	28.3
63-64—Cincinnati	79	3559	1740	840	.483	938	800	.853	783	868	280	3	2480	31.4
64-65—Cincinnati	75	3421	1681	807	.480	793	665	.839	674	861	205	2	2279	30.4
65-66—Cincinnati	76	3493	1723	818	.475	881	742	.842	586	847	227	1	2378	31.3
66-67—Cincinnati	79	3468	1699	838	.493	843	736	.873	486	845	226	2	2412	30.5
67-68—Cincinnati	65	2765	1321	660	.500	660	576	.873	391	633	199	2	1896	29.2
68-69—Cincinnati	79	3461	1351	656	.486	767	643	.838	502	772	231	2	1955	24.7
69-70—Cincinnati	69	2865	1267	647	.511	561	454	.809	422	558	175	1	1748	25.3
70-71—Milwaukee	81	3194	1193	592	.496	453	385	.850	462	668	203	0	1569	19.4
71-72—Milwaukee	64	2390	887	419	.472	330	276	.836	323	491	116	0	1114	17.4
72-73—Milwaukee	73	2737	983	446	.454	281	238	.847	360	551	167	0	1130	15.5

Sea.—Team	G.	Min.	FGA	FGM	Pct.	FTA	FTM	Pct.	—Rebounds— Off.	Def.	Tot.	Ast.	PF	Dq.	Stl.	Blk.	Pts.	Avg.
73-74—Milw.	70	2477	772	338	.438	254	212	.835	71	208	279	446	132	0	77	4	888	12.7
Totals	1040	43866	19620	9508	.485	9185	7694	.838			7804	9887	2931	18			26710	25.7

NBA PLAYOFF RECORD

Sea.—Team	G.	Min.	FGA	FGM	Pct.	FTA	FTM	Pct.	Reb.	Ast.	PF	Disq.	Pts.	Avg.
61-62—Cincinnati	4	185	81	42	.519	39	31	.795	44	44	18	1	115	28.8
62-63—Cincinnati	12	570	264	124	.470	154	133	.864	156	108	41	0	381	31.8
63-64—Cincinnati	10	471	202	92	.455	127	109	.858	89	84	30	0	293	29.3
64-65—Cincinnati	4	195	89	38	.427	39	36	.923	19	48	14	0	112	28.0
65-66—Cincinnati	5	224	120	49	.408	68	61	.897	38	39	20	1	159	31.8
66-67—Cincinnati	4	183	64	33	.516	37	33	.892	16	45	9	0	99	24.8
70-71—Milwaukee	14	520	210	102	.486	69	52	.754	70	124	39	0	256	18.3
71-72—Milwaukee	11	380	140	57	.407	36	30	.833	64	83	29	0	144	13.1
72-73—Milwaukee	6	256	96	48	.500	34	31	.912	28	45	21	1	127	21.2

Sea.—Team	G.	Min.	FGA	FGM	Pct.	FTA	FTM	Pct.	—Rebounds— Off.	Def.	Tot.	Ast.	PF	Dq.	Stl.	Blk.	Pts.	Avg.
73-74—Milw.	16	689	200	90	.450	52	44	.846	15	39	54	149	46	0	15	4	224	14.0
Totals	86	3673	1466	675	.460	655	560	.855			578	769	267	3			1910	22.2

NBA ALL-STAR GAME RECORD

Season—Team	Min.	FGA	FGM	Pct.	FTA	FTM	Pct.	Reb.	Ast.	PF	Disq.	Pts.
1961—Cincinnati	34	13	8	.615	9	7	.778	9	14	5	0	23
1962—Cincinnati	37	20	9	.450	14	8	.571	7	13	3	0	26
1963—Cincinnati	37	15	9	.600	4	3	.750	3	6	5	0	21
1964—Cincinnati	42	23	10	.435	10	6	.600	14	8	4	0	26
1965—Cincinnati	40	18	8	.444	13	12	.923	6	8	5	0	28
1966—Cincinnati	25	12	6	.500	6	5	.833	10	8	0	0	17

OSCAR ROBERTSON

Season—Team	Min.	FGA	FGM	Pct.	FTA	FTM	Pct.	Reb.	Ast.	PF	Disq.	Pts.
1967—Cincinnati	34	20	9	.450	10	8	.800	2	5	4	0	26
1968—Cincinnati	22	9	7	.778	7	4	.571	1	5	2	0	18
1969—Cincinnati	32	16	8	.500	8	8	1.000	6	5	3	0	24
1970—Cincinnati	29	11	9	.818	4	3	.750	6	4	3	0	21
1971—Milwaukee	24	6	2	.333	3	1	.333	2	2	3	0	5
1972—Milwaukee	24	9	3	.333	10	5	.500	3	3	4	0	11
Totals	380	172	88	.512	98	70	.714	69	81	41	0	246

Elected to Naismith Memorial Basketball Hall of Fame, 1979. . . . Named to NBA 35th Anniversary All-Time Team, 1980. . . . NBA Most Valuable Player, 1964. . . . Named to All-NBA First Team, 1961, 1962, 1963, 1964, 1965, 1966, 1967, 1968, 1969. . . . All-NBA Second Team, 1970 and 1971. . . . NBA Rookie of the Year, 1961. . . . Holds NBA record for most free throws attempted, 22, and most free throws made, 19, in one half, vs. Baltimore, December 27, 1964. . . . Shares NBA record for most free throws attempted in one quarter, 16, vs. Baltimore, December 27, 1964. . . . NBA all-time leader in free throws made, assists and rebounds by guard. . . . NBA All-Star Game MVP, 1961, 1964, 1969. . . . Shares NBA All-Star Game records for most career free throws attempted; most free throws made in one game, 12, in 1965. . . . Member of NBA championship team, 1971. . . . Led NBA in assists, 1961, 1962, 1964, 1965, 1966, 1969. . . . Led NBA in free-throw percentage, 1964 and 1968. . . . THE SPORTING NEWS College Player of the Year, 1958, 1959, 1960. . . . Named to THE SPORTING NEWS All-America First Team, 1958, 1959, 1960. . . . Led NCAA in scoring, 1958, 1959, 1960. . . . Member of U.S. Olympic team, 1960.

GUY WILLIAM RODGERS JR.

Born September 1, 1935 at Philadelphia, Pa. Height 6:00. Weight 185.

High School—Philadelphia, Pa., Northeast.

College—Temple University, Philadelphia, Pa.

Drafted by Philadelphia on first round (territorial choice), 1958.

Philadelphia franchise transferred to San Francisco, 1962.

Traded by San Francisco to Chicago for a draft choice, cash and two players to be designated, September 7, 1966. Jim King and Jeff Mullins sent to San Francisco to complete deal.

Traded by Chicago to Cincinnati for Flynn Robinson, cash and two draft choices, October 20, 1967.

Selected from Cincinnati by Milwaukee in expansion draft, May 6, 1968.

—COLLEGIATE RECORD—

Year	G.	Min.	FGA	FGM	Pct.	FTA	FTM	Pct.	Reb.	Pts.	Avg.
54-55†	15	....	...	...	....	...	...	....	....	278	18.5
55-56	31	....	552	243	.440	155	87	.561	186	573	18.5
56-57	29	....	565	216	.382	224	159	.710	202	591	20.4
57-58	30	....	564	249	.441	171	105	.614	199	603	20.1
Varsity Totals	90	....	1681	708	.421	550	351	.638	587	1767	19.6

NBA REGULAR SEASON RECORD

Sea.—Team	G.	Min.	FGA	FGM	Pct.	FTA	FTM	Pct.	Reb.	Ast.	PF	Disq.	Pts.	Avg.
58-59—Philadelphia	45	1565	535	211	.394	112	61	.545	281	261	132	1	483	10.7
59-60—Philadelphia	68	2483	870	338	.388	181	111	.613	391	482	196	3	787	11.6
60-61—Philadelphia	78	2905	1029	397	.386	300	206	.687	509	677	262	3	1000	12.3
61-62—Philadelphia	80	2650	749	267	.356	182	121	.599	348	643	312	12	655	8.2
62-63—San Francisco	79	3249	1150	445	.387	286	208	.725	394	825	296	7	1098	14.1
63-64—San Francisco	79	2695	923	337	.365	280	198	.707	328	556	245	4	872	11.0
64-65—San Francisco	79	2699	1225	465	.380	325	223	.686	323	565	256	4	1153	14.6
65-66—San Francisco	79	2902	1571	586	.373	407	296	.727	421	846	241	6	1468	18.6
66-67—Chicago	81	3063	1377	538	.391	475	383	.806	346	908	243	1	1459	18.0
67-68—Chi.-Cinn.	79	1546	426	148	.347	133	107	.805	150	380	167	1	403	5.1
68-69—Milwaukee	81	2157	862	325	.377	232	184	.793	226	561	207	2	834	10.3
69-70—Milwaukee	64	749	191	68	.356	90	67	.744	74	213	73	1	203	3.2
Totals	892	28663	10908	4125	.378	3003	2165	.721	3791	6917	2630	45	10415	11.7

NBA PLAYOFF RECORD

Sea.—Team	G.	Min.	FGA	FGM	Pct.	FTA	FTM	Pct.	Reb.	Ast.	PF	Disq.	Pts.	Avg.
59-60—Philadelphia	9	370	136	49	.360	36	20	.555	77	54	39	3	118	13.1
60-61—Philadelphia	3	121	57	21	.368	20	11	.550	21	15	16	2	53	17.7
61-62—Philadelphia	13	482	145	52	.359	55	35	.636	7	88	57	3	139	11.6
63-64—San Francisco	12	419	173	57	.329	47	33	.702	58	90	46	1	147	12.3
66-67—Chicago	3	97	40	15	.375	5	4	.800	6	18	11	0	34	11.3
69-70—Milwaukee	7	68	14	4	.286	12	9	.750	4	21	7	0	17	2.4
Totals	47	1557	565	198	.350	175	112	.640	173	286	176	9	508	10.8

NBA ALL-STAR GAME RECORD

Season—Team	Min.	FGA	FGM	Pct.	FTA	FTM	Pct.	Reb.	Ast.	PF	Disq.	Pts.
1963—San Francisco	17	6	3	.500	2	1	.500	2	4	2	0	7
1964—San Francisco	22	6	3	.500	0	0	.000	2	2	4	0	6
1966—San Francisco	34	11	4	.364	0	0	.000	7	11	4	0	8
1967—Chicago	28	4	0	.000	1	1	1.000	2	8	3	0	1
Totals	101	27	10	.370	3	2	.667	13	25	13	0	22

Led NBA in assists, 1963 and 1967. . . . Named to THE SPORTING NEWS All-America First Team, 1958.

WILLIAM FELTON RUSSELL
(Bill)

Born February 12, 1934 at Monroe, La. Height 6:10. Weight 220.
High School—Oakland, Calif., McClymonds.
College—University of San Francisco, San Francisco, Calif.
Drafted by Boston on first round, 1956. (3rd pick—Boston traded Ed Macauley and Cliff Hagan to St. Louis for its first-round choice, April 29, 1956.)

—COLLEGIATE RECORD—

Year	G.	Min.	FGA	FGM	Pct.	FTA	FTM	Pct.	Reb.	Pts.	Avg.
52-53†	23	....	...	...	....	...	...	....	...	461	20.0
53-54	21	....	309	150	.485	212	117	.552	403	417	19.9
54-55	29	....	423	229	.541	278	164	.590	594	622	21.4
55-56	29	....	480	246	.513	212	105	.495	609	597	20.6
Varsity Totals	79	....	1212	625	.516	702	386	.550	1606	1636	20.7

NBA REGULAR SEASON RECORD

Sea.—Team	G.	Min.	FGA	FGM	Pct.	FTA	FTM	Pct.	Reb.	Ast.	PF	Disq.	Pts.	Avg.
56-57—Boston	48	1695	649	277	.427	309	152	.492	943	88	143	2	706	14.7
57-58—Boston	69	2640	1032	456	.442	443	230	.519	1564	202	181	2	1142	16.6
58-59—Boston	70	2979	997	456	.457	428	256	.598	1612	222	161	3	1168	16.7
59-60—Boston	74	3146	1189	555	.467	392	240	.612	1778	277	210	0	1350	18.2
60-61—Boston	78	3458	1250	532	.426	469	258	.550	1868	268	155	0	1322	16.9
61-62—Boston	76	3433	1258	575	.457	481	286	.594	1790	341	207	3	1436	18.9
62-63—Boston	78	3500	1182	511	.432	517	287	.555	1843	348	189	1	1309	16.8
63-64—Boston	78	3482	1077	466	.433	429	236	.550	1930	370	190	0	1168	15.0
64-65—Boston	78	3466	980	429	.438	426	244	.573	1878	410	204	1	1102	14.1
65-66—Boston	78	3386	943	391	.415	405	223	.551	1779	371	221	4	1005	12.9
66-67—Boston	81	3297	870	395	.454	467	285	.610	1700	472	258	4	1075	13.4
67-68—Boston	78	2953	858	365	.425	460	247	.537	1451	357	242	2	977	12.5
68-69—Boston	77	3291	645	279	.433	388	204	.526	1484	374	231	2	762	9.9
Totals	963	40726	12930	5687	.440	5614	3148	.561	21620	4100	2592	24	14522	15.1

NBA PLAYOFF RECORD

Sea.—Team	G.	Min.	FGA	FGM	Pct.	FTA	FTM	Pct.	Reb.	Ast.	PF	Disq.	Pts.	Avg.
56-57—Boston	10	409	148	54	.365	61	31	.508	244	32	41	1	139	13.9
57-58—Boston	9	355	133	48	.361	66	40	.606	221	24	24	0	136	15.1
58-59—Boston	11	496	159	65	.409	67	41	.612	305	40	28	1	171	15.5
59-60—Boston	13	572	206	94	.456	75	53	.707	336	38	38	1	241	18.5
60-61—Boston	10	462	171	73	.427	86	45	.523	299	48	24	0	191	19.1
61-62—Boston	14	672	253	116	.458	113	82	.726	370	70	49	0	314	22.4
62-63—Boston	13	617	212	96	.453	109	72	.661	326	66	36	0	264	20.3
63-64—Boston	10	451	132	47	.356	67	37	.552	272	44	33	0	131	13.1
64-65—Boston	12	561	150	79	.527	76	40	.526	302	76	43	2	198	16.5
65-66—Boston	17	814	261	124	.475	123	76	.618	428	85	60	0	324	19.1
66-67—Boston	9	390	86	31	.360	52	33	.635	198	50	32	1	95	10.6
67-68—Boston	19	869	242	99	.409	130	76	.585	434	99	73	1	274	14.4
68-69—Boston	18	829	182	77	.423	81	41	.506	369	98	65	1	195	10.8
Totals	165	7497	2335	1003	.430	1106	667	.603	4104	770	546	8	2673	16.2

NBA ALL-STAR GAME RECORD

Season—Team	Min.	FGA	FGM	Pct.	FTA	FTM	Pct.	Reb.	Ast.	PF	Disq.	Pts.
1958—Boston	26	12	5	.417	3	1	.333	11	2	5	0	11
1959—Boston	27	10	3	.300	1	1	1.000	9	1	4	0	7
1960—Boston	27	7	3	.429	2	0	.000	8	3	1	0	6
1961—Boston	28	15	9	.600	8	6	.750	11	1	2	0	24
1962—Boston	27	12	5	.417	3	2	.667	12	2	2	0	12
1963—Boston	37	14	8	.571	4	3	.750	24	5	3	0	19
1964—Boston	42	13	6	.462	2	1	.500	21	2	4	0	13
1965—Boston	33	12	7	.583	9	3	.333	13	5	6	1	17
1966—Boston	23	6	1	.167	0	0	.000	10	2	2	0	2
1967—Boston	22	2	1	.500	0	0	.000	5	5	2	0	2
1968—Boston	23	4	2	.500	0	0	.000	9	8	5	0	4
1969—Boston	28	4	1	.250	2	1	.500	6	3	1	0	3
Totals	343	111	51	.459	34	18	.529	139	39	37	1	120

NBA COACHING RECORD

	Regular Season				Playoffs	
Sea. Club	W.	L.	Pct.	Pos.	W.	L.
1966-67—Boston	60	21	.741	2†	4	5
1967-68—Boston*	54	28	.659	2†	12	7
1968-69—Boston*	48	34	.585	4†	12	6
1973-74—Seattle	36	46	.439	3‡	..	..
1974-75—Seattle	43	39	.524	2‡	4	5
1975-76—Seattle	43	39	.524	2‡	2	4
1976-77—Seattle	40	42	.488	4‡	..	..
1987-88—Sacramento	17	41	.293	..‡	..	..
Totals (8 seasons)	341	290	.540		34	27

*Won NBA championship. †Eastern Division. ‡Pacific Division.

BILL RUSSELL

Selected as "Greatest Player in the History of the NBA" by Professional Basketball Writers' Association of America, 1980. . . . Elected to Naismith Memorial Basketball Hall of Fame, 1974. . . . Named to NBA 25th and 35th Anniversary All-Time Teams, 1970 and 1980. . . . NBA Most Valuable Player, 1958, 1961, 1962, 1963, 1965. . . . Named to All-NBA First Team, 1959, 1963, 1965. . . . All-NBA Second Team, 1958, 1960, 1961, 1962, 1964, 1966, 1967, 1968. . . . NBA All-Defensive First Team, 1969. . . . Holds NBA record for most rebounds in one half, 32, vs. Philadelphia, November 16, 1957. . . . NBA all-time playoff leader in rebounds. . . . Holds NBA championship series game record for most rebounds, 40, vs. St. Louis, March 29, 1960, and vs. Los Angeles, April 18, 1962. . . . Holds NBA championship series game record for most free throws attempted in one half, 15, vs. St. Louis, April 11, 1961. . . . Holds NBA championship series game record for most rebounds in one quarter, 19, vs. Los Angeles, April 18, 1962. . . . NBA All-Star Game MVP, 1963. . . . Member of NBA championship teams, 1957, 1959, 1960, 1961, 1962, 1963, 1964, 1965, 1966, 1968 (also coach), 1969 (also coach). . . . Led NBA in rebounding, 1957, 1958, 1964, 1965. . . . NCAA Tournament Most Outstanding Player, 1955. . . . Member of NCAA championship teams, 1955 and 1956. . . . Member of U.S. Olympic team, 1956. . . . One of only seven players to average over 20 points and 20 rebounds per game during NCAA career.

ADOLPH SCHAYES
(Dolph)

Born May 19, 1928 at New York, N. Y. Height 6:08. Weight 220.
High School—Bronx, N. Y., DeWitt Clinton.
College—New York University, New York, N. Y.
Drafted by Tri-Cities NBL, 1948.

NBL draft rights obtained by Syracuse from Tri-Cities, 1948; Syracuse franchise transferred to Philadelphia, 1963.

—COLLEGIATE RECORD—

Year	G.	Min.	FGA	FGM	Pct.	FTA	FTM	Pct.	Reb.	Pts.	Avg.
44-45	11	....	...	46	....	...	23	....	....	115	10.5
45-46	22	....	...	54	....	...	41	....	....	149	6.8
46-47	21	....	...	66	....	...	63	....	....	195	9.3
47-48	26	....	...	124	....	...	108	....	....	356	13.7
Totals	80	....	...	290	....	...	235	....	....	815	10.2

NBL AND NBA REGULAR SEASON RECORD

Sea.—Team	G.	Min.	FGA	FGM	Pct.	FTA	FTM	Pct.	Reb.	Ast.	PF	Disq.	Pts.	Avg.
48-49—Syr. NBL	63	....	....	272	...	369	267	.724	....	....	232	..	811	12.8
49-50—Syracuse	64	....	903	348	.385	486	376	.774	....	259	225	..	1072	16.8
50-51—Syracuse	66	....	930	332	.357	608	457	.752	1080	251	271	9	1121	17.0
51-52—Syracuse	63	2004	740	263	.355	424	342	.807	773	182	213	5	868	13.8
52-53—Syracuse	71	2668	1002	375	.367	619	512	.827	920	227	271	9	1262	17.8
53-54—Syracuse	72	2655	973	370	.380	590	488	.827	870	214	232	4	1228	17.1
54-55—Syracuse	72	2526	1103	422	.383	587	489	.833	887	213	247	6	1333	18.5
55-56—Syracuse	72	2517	1202	465	.387	632	542	.858	891	200	251	9	1472	20.4
56-57—Syracuse	72	2851	1308	496	.379	691	625	.904	1008	229	219	5	1617	22.5
57-58—Syracuse	72	2918	1458	581	.398	696	629	.904	1022	224	244	6	1791	24.9
58-59—Syracuse	72	2645	1304	504	.387	609	526	.864	962	178	280	9	1534	21.3
59-60—Syracuse	75	2741	1440	578	.401	597	533	.892	959	256	263	10	1689	22.5
60-61—Syracuse	79	3007	1595	594	.372	783	680	.868	960	296	296	9	1868	23.6
61-62—Syracuse	56	1480	751	268	.357	319	286	.896	439	120	167	4	822	14.7
62-63—Syracuse	66	1438	575	223	.388	206	181	.879	375	175	177	2	627	9.5
63-64—Phila.	24	350	143	44	.308	57	46	.807	110	48	76	3	134	5.6
Totals	1059	....	15427	6135	.380	8273	6979	.844	11256	3072	3664	90	19249	18.2

NBA PLAYOFF RECORD

Sea.—Team	G.	Min.	FGA	FGM	Pct.	FTA	FTM	Pct.	Reb.	Ast.	PF	Disq.	Pts.	Avg.
48-49—Syr. NBL	6	....	....	27	...	42	32	.762	....	....	26	..	86	14.3
49-50—Syracuse	11	...	148	57	.385	101	74	.733	....	28	43	..	188	17.1
50-51—Syracuse	7	....	105	47	.448	64	49	.766	102	20	28	2	143	20.4
51-52—Syracuse	7	248	91	41	.451	78	60	.769	90	15	34	2	142	20.3
52-53—Syracuse	2	58	16	4	.250	13	10	.769	17	1	7	0	18	9.0
53-54—Syracuse	13	374	140	64	.457	108	80	.741	136	24	40	1	208	16.0
54-55—Syracuse	11	363	167	60	.359	106	89	.840	141	40	48	3	209	19.0
55-56—Syracuse	8	310	142	52	.366	83	73	.880	111	27	27	0	177	22.1
56-57—Syracuse	5	215	95	29	.305	55	49	.891	90	14	18	0	107	21.4
57-58—Syracuse	3	131	64	25	.391	36	30	.833	45	6	10	0	80	26.7
58-59—Syracuse	9	351	195	78	.400	107	98	.916	117	41	36	0	254	28.2
59-60—Syracuse	3	126	66	30	.454	30	28	.933	48	8	10	0	88	29.3
60-61—Syracuse	8	308	152	51	.335	70	63	.900	91	21	32	2	165	20.6
61-62—Syracuse	5	95	66	24	.364	13	9	.692	35	5	21	0	57	11.5
62-63—Syracuse	5	108	44	20	.455	12	11	.917	28	7	17	0	51	10.2
Totals	103	2687	1491	609	.390	918	755	.822	1051	257	397	10	1973	19.2

NBA ALL-STAR GAME RECORD

Season—Team	Min.	FGA	FGM	Pct.	FTA	FTM	Pct.	Reb.	Ast.	PF	Disq.	Pts.
1951—Syracuse	..	10	7	.700	2	1	.500	14	3	1	0	15
1952—Syracuse	Selected—Injured, Did Not Play											
1953—Syracuse	26	7	2	.286	4	4	1.000	13	3	3	0	8

Season—Team	Min.	FGA	FGM	Pct.	FTA	FTM	Pct.	Reb.	Ast.	PF	Disq.	Pts.
1954—Syracuse	24	3	1	.333	6	4	.667	12	1	1	0	6
1955—Syracuse	29	12	6	.500	3	3	1.000	13	1	4	0	15
1956—Syracuse	25	8	4	.500	10	6	.600	4	2	2	0	14
1957—Syracuse	25	6	4	.667	1	1	1.000	10	1	1	0	9
1958—Syracuse	39	15	6	.400	6	6	1.000	9	2	4	0	18
1959—Syracuse	22	14	3	.214	8	7	.875	13	1	6	1	13
1960—Syracuse	27	19	8	.421	3	3	1.000	10	0	3	0	19
1961—Syracuse	27	15	7	.467	7	7	1.000	6	3	4	0	21
1962—Syracuse	4	0	0	.000	0	0	.000	1	0	3	0	0
Totals	248	109	48	.440	50	42	.840	105	17	32	1	138

NBA COACHING RECORD

	Regular Season				Playoffs	
Sea. Club	W.	L.	Pct.	Pos.	W.	L.
1963-64—Philadelphia	34	46	.425	3†	2	3
1964-65—Philadelphia	40	40	.500	3†	6	5
1965-66—Philadelphia	55	25	.688	1†	1	4
1970-71—Buffalo	22	60	.268	4‡	..	..
1971-72—Buffalo	0	1	.000	..‡	..	..
Totals (5 seasons)	151	172	.467		9	12

†Eastern Division. ‡Atlantic Division.

Elected to Naismith Memorial Basketball Hall of Fame, 1972. . . . Named to NBA 25th Anniversary All-Time Team, 1970. . . . All-NBA First Team, 1952, 1953, 1954, 1955, 1957, 1958. . . . All-NBA Second Team, 1950, 1951, 1956, 1959, 1960, 1961. . . . Member of NBA championship team, 1955. . . . Led NBA in rebounding, 1951. . . . Led NBA in free-throw percentage, 1958, 1960, 1962. . . . NBA Coach of the Year, 1966. . . . Former NBA Supervisor of Referees. . . . Father of Milwaukee Bucks center Dan Schayes.

WILLIAM WALTON SHARMAN
(Bill)

Born May 25, 1926 at Abilene, Tex. Height 6:01. Weight 190.

High Schools—Lomita, Calif., Narbonne (Soph.) and Porterville, Calif. (Jr. and Sr.)

College—University of Southern California, Los Angeles, Calif.

Drafted by Washington on second round, 1950.

Selected by Fort Wayne in dispersal draft of Washington franchise, January 8, 1951. (Did not report to Fort Wayne).

Traded by Fort Wayne with Bob Brannum to Boston for NBA rights to Charlie Share, 1951.

Signed as player-coach by Los Angeles of American Basketball League, 1961.

—COLLEGIATE PLAYING RECORD—

Year	G.	Min.	FGA	FGM	Pct.	FTA	FTM	Pct.	Reb.	Pts.	Avg.
46-47	10	....	....	....	....	....	....	....	....	41	4.1
47-48	24	....	....	100	....	44	38	.864	....	238	9.9
48-49	24	....	....	142	....	125	98	.784	....	382	15.9
49-50	24	....	421	171	.406	129	104	.806	....	446	18.6
Totals	82	....	....	....	....	....	...	....	....	1107	13.5

NOTE: In military service during 1944-45 and 1945-46 seasons.

NBA REGULAR SEASON RECORD

Sea.—Team	G.	Min.	FGA	FGM	Pct.	FTA	FTM	Pct.	Reb.	Ast.	PF	Disq.	Pts.	Avg.
50-51—Washington	31	....	361	141	.391	108	96	.889	96	39	86	3	378	12.2
51-52—Boston	63	1389	628	244	.389	213	183	.859	221	151	181	3	671	10.7
52-53—Boston	71	2333	925	403	.436	401	341	.850	288	191	240	7	1147	16.2
53-54—Boston	72	2467	915	412	.450	392	331	.844	255	229	211	4	1155	16.0
54-55—Boston	68	2453	1062	453	.427	387	347	.897	302	280	212	2	1253	18.4
55-56—Boston	72	2698	1229	538	.438	413	358	.867	259	339	197	1	1434	19.9
56-57—Boston	67	2403	1241	516	.416	421	381	.905	286	236	188	1	1413	21.1
57-58—Boston	63	2214	1297	550	.424	338	302	.893	295	167	156	3	1402	22.3
58-59—Boston	72	2382	1377	562	.408	367	342	.932	292	179	173	1	1466	20.4
59-60—Boston	71	1916	1225	559	.456	291	252	.866	262	144	154	2	1370	19.3
60-61—Boston	61	1538	908	383	.422	228	210	.921	223	146	127	0	976	16.0
Totals	711	21793	11168	4761	.426	3559	3143	.883	2779	2101	1925	27	12665	17.8

—DID YOU KNOW—

That high-profile colleges North Carolina, Nevada-Las Vegas, Georgetown, DePaul, Oklahoma, Kentucky, Indiana, North Carolina State and Notre Dame did not have any players selected in the 1990 draft?

NBA PLAYOFF RECORD

Sea.—Team	G.	Min.	FGA	FGM	Pct.	FTA	FTM	Pct.	Reb.	Ast.	PF	Disq.	Pts.	Avg.
51-52—Boston	1	27	12	7	.583	1	1	1.000	3	7	4	0	15	15.0
52-53—Boston	6	201	60	20	.333	32	30	.938	15	15	26	1	70	11.7
53-54—Boston	6	206	81	35	.432	50	43	.860	25	10	29	2	113	18.3
54-55—Boston	7	290	110	55	.500	38	35	.921	38	38	24	1	145	20.7
55-56—Boston	3	119	46	18	.391	17	16	.941	7	12	7	0	52	17.3
56-57—Boston	10	377	197	75	.381	64	61	.953	35	29	23	1	211	21.1
57-58—Boston	11	406	221	90	.407	56	52	.929	54	25	28	0	232	21.1
58-59—Boston	11	322	193	82	.425	59	57	.966	36	28	35	0	221	20.1
59-60—Boston	13	364	209	88	.421	53	43	.811	45	20	22	1	219	16.8
60-61—Boston	10	261	133	68	.511	36	32	.889	27	17	22	0	168	16.8
Totals	78	2573	1262	538	.426	406	370	.911	285	201	220	6	1446	18.5

NBA ALL-STAR GAME RECORD

Season—Team	Min.	FGA	FGM	Pct.	FTA	FTM	Pct.	Reb.	Ast.	PF	Disq.	Pts.
1953—Boston	26	8	5	.625	1	1	1.000	4	0	2	0	11
1954—Boston	30	9	6	.667	4	2	.500	2	3	3	0	14
1955—Boston	18	10	5	.500	5	5	.500	4	2	4	0	15
1956—Boston	24	8	2	.250	4	3	.750	7	2	6	1	7
1957—Boston	23	17	5	.294	2	2	1.000	3	2	2	0	10
1958—Boston	25	19	6	.316	3	3	1.000	4	3	2	0	15
1959—Boston	24	12	3	.250	6	5	.833	2	0	1	0	11
1960—Boston	26	21	8	.381	1	1	1.000	6	2	1	0	17
Totals	196	104	40	.385	26	22	.846	32	14	21	1	100

COLLEGIATE COACHING RECORD

	Regular Season			
Sea. Club	W.	L.	Pct.	Pos.
1962-63—Cal St.-Los Ang.	10	12	.454	4§
1963-64—Cal St.-Los Ang.	17	8	.680	2§

§California Collegiate Athletic Association.

NBA COACHING RECORD

	Regular Season				Playoffs	
Sea. Club	W.	L.	Pct.	Pos.	W.	L.
1966-67—San Francisco	44	37	.543	1†	9	6
1967-68—San Francisco	43	39	.524	3†	4	6
1971-72—Los Angeles*	69	13	.841	1‡	12	3
1972-73—Los Angeles	60	22	.732	1‡	9	8
1973-74—Los Angeles	47	35	.573	1‡	1	4
1974-75—Los Angeles	30	52	.366	5‡	..	..
1975-76—Los Angeles	40	42	.488	4‡	..	..
Totals (7 seasons)	333	240	.581		35	27

*Won NBA Championship. †Western Division. ‡Pacific Division.

ABL AND ABA COACHING RECORD

	Regular Season				Playoffs	
Sea. Club	W.	L.	Pct.	Pos.	W.	L.
1961-62—LA-Clev. ABL	43	26	.615	..	5	2
1968-69—Los Ang. ABA	33	45	.423	5†	..	..
1969-70—Los Ang. ABA	43	41	.512	4†	10	7
1970-71—Utah ABA*	57	27	.679	2†	12	6
Totals (4 seasons)	176	139	.559		27	15

Note: Los Angeles Jets had 24-15 record when they folded after first half of season. Sharman then guided the Cleveland Pipers to ABL championship.

*Won ABA Championship. †Western Division.

ABL REGULAR SEASON RECORD

			—2-Point—			—3-Point—									
Sea.—Team	G.	Min.	FGM	FGA	Pct.	FGM	FGA	Pct.	FTM	FTA	Pct.	Reb.	Ast.	Pts.	Avg.
61-62—Los Angeles	19	346	80	35	.438	8	1	.125	37	34	.919	43	37	107	5.6

RECORD AS BASEBALL PLAYER

Year Club	League	Pos.	G.	AB.	R.	H.	2B.	3B.	HR.	RBI.	B.A.	PO.	A.	E.	F.A.
1950—Elmira	East.	OF	10	38	5	11	2	0	1	11	.289	17	0	1	.944
1950—Pueblo	West.	OF	111	427	65	123	22	8	11	70	.288	214	16	10	.958
1951—Fort Worth	Texas	OF	157	570	84	163	18	5	8	53	.286	254	11	2	.993
1952—St. Paul	A. A.	OF	137	411	63	121	16	4	16	77	.294	215	15	3	.987
1953—Mobile	S. Assoc.	OF	90	228	21	48	8	1	5	17	.211	136	6	2	.986
1954—		(Out of Organized Ball)													
1955—St. Paul	A. A.	OF-3B	133	424	59	124	15	0	11	58	.292	183	100	11	.963

Elected to Naismith Memorial Basketball Hall of Fame, 1974. . . . Named to NBA 25th Anniversary All-Time Team, 1970. . . . All-NBA First Team, 1956, 1957, 1958, 1959. . . . All-NBA Second Team, 1953, 1955, 1960. . . . NBA All-Star Game MVP, 1955. . . . Holds NBA All-Star Game record for most field goals attempted in one quarter, 12, in 1960. . . . Member of NBA championship teams, 1957, 1959, 1960, 1961. . . . Led NBA in free-throw percentage, 1953, 1954, 1955, 1956, 1957, 1959, 1961. . . . NBA Coach of the Year, 1972. . . . Coach of NBA championship team, 1972. . . . ABA Co-Coach of the Year, 1970. . . . Coach of ABA championship team, 1971. . . . Coach of ABL championship team, 1962. . . . Named to THE SPORTING NEWS All-America First Team, 1950. . . . THE SPORTING NEWS All-America Third Team, 1949.

PAUL THERON SILAS

Born July 12, 1943 at Prescott, Ariz. Height 6:07. Weight 230.
High School—Oakland, Calif., McClymonds.
College—Creighton University, Omaha, Neb.
Drafted by St. Louis on second round, 1964 (12th pick).

Traded by Atlanta to Phoenix for Gary Gregor, May 8, 1969.

Traded by Phoenix to Boston, September 19, 1972, to complete deal in which Phoenix acquired draft rights to Charlie Scott, March 14, 1972.

Traded by Boston to Denver in three-team deal, in which Curtis Rowe was traded by Detroit to Boston, and Ralph Simpson was traded by Denver to Detroit, October 20, 1976.

Traded by Denver with Willie Wise and Marvin Webster to Seattle for Tom Burleson, Bob Wilkerson and a 1977 2nd round draft choice, May 24, 1977.

Signed by San Diego as Veteran Free Agent, May 21, 1980; Seattle received a 1985 2nd round draft choice as compensation.

Played in Eastern Basketball League with Wilkes Barre, 1965-66.

—COLLEGIATE RECORD—

Year	G.	Min.	FGA	FGM	Pct.	FTA	FTM	Pct.	Reb.	Pts.	Avg.
60-61†	21	....	...	225	....	119	96	.807	568	546	26.0
61-62	25	....	524	213	.406	215	125	.581	563	551	22.0
62-63	27	....	531	220	.414	228	133	.583	557	573	21.2
63-64	29	....	529	210	.397	194	117	.603	631	537	18.5
Varsity Totals	81	....	1584	643	.406	637	375	.589	1751	1661	20.5

NBA REGULAR SEASON RECORD

Sea.—Team	G.	Min.	FGA	FGM	Pct.	FTA	FTM	Pct.	Reb.	Ast.	PF	Disq.	Pts.	Avg.
64-65—St. Louis	79	1243	375	140	.373	164	83	.506	576	48	161	1	363	4.6
65-66—St. Louis	46	586	173	70	.405	61	35	.574	236	22	72	0	175	3.8
66-67—St. Louis	77	1570	482	207	.429	213	113	.531	669	74	208	4	527	6.9
67-68—St. Louis	82	2652	871	399	.458	424	299	.705	958	162	243	4	1097	13.4
68-69—Atlanta	79	1853	575	241	.419	333	204	.613	745	140	166	0	686	8.7
69-70—Phoenix	78	2836	804	373	.464	412	250	.607	916	214	266	5	996	12.8
70-71—Phoenix	81	2944	789	338	.428	416	285	.685	1015	247	227	3	961	11.9
71-72—Phoenix	80	3082	1031	485	.470	560	433	.773	955	343	201	2	1403	17.5
72-73—Boston	80	2618	851	400	.470	380	266	.700	1039	251	197	1	1066	13.3

Sea.—Team	G.	Min.	FGA	FGM	Pct.	FTA	FTM	Pct.	—Rebounds— Off.	Def.	Tot.	Ast.	PF	Dq.	Stl.	Blk.	Pts.	Avg.
73-74—Boston	82	2599	772	340	.440	337	264	.783	334	581	915	186	246	3	63	20	944	11.5
74-75—Boston	82	2661	749	312	.417	344	244	.709	348	677	1025	224	229	3	60	22	868	10.6
75-76—Boston	81	2662	740	315	.426	333	236	.709	365	660	1025	203	227	3	56	33	866	10.7
76-77—Denver	81	1959	572	206	.360	255	170	.667	236	370	606	132	183	0	58	23	582	7.2
77-78—Seattle	82	2172	464	184	.397	186	109	.586	289	377	666	145	182	0	65	16	477	5.8
78-79—Seattle	82	1957	402	170	.423	194	116	.598	259	316	575	115	177	3	31	19	456	5.6
79-80—Seattle	82	1595	299	113	.378	136	89	.654	204	232	436	66	120	0	25	5	315	3.8
Totals	1254	34989	9949	4293	.432	4748	3196	.673			12357	2572	3105	32	358	138	11782	9.4

NBA PLAYOFF RECORD

Sea.—Team	G.	Min.	FGA	FGM	Pct.	FTA	FTM	Pct.	Reb.	Ast.	PF	Disq.	Pts.	Avg.
64-65—St. Louis	4	42	10	4	.400	4	3	.750	18	1	6	0	11	2.8
65-66—St. Louis	7	80	18	5	.278	11	8	.727	34	2	11	0	18	2.6
66-67—St. Louis	8	122	36	9	.250	18	11	.611	52	6	17	0	29	3.6
67-68—St. Louis	6	178	51	22	.431	38	27	.711	57	21	17	0	71	11.8
68-69—Atlanta	11	258	58	21	.362	37	19	.514	92	21	32	0	61	5.5
69-70—Phoenix	7	286	109	46	.422	32	21	.656	111	30	29	1	113	16.1
72-73—Boston	13	512	120	47	.392	50	31	.620	196	39	39	0	125	9.6

Sea.—Team	G.	Min.	FGA	FGM	Pct.	FTA	FTM	Pct.	—Rebounds— Off.	Def.	Tot.	Ast.	PF	Dq.	Stl.	Blk.	Pts.	Avg.
73-74—Boston	18	574	126	50	.397	53	44	.830	53	138	191	47	51	2	13	9	144	8.0
74-75—Boston	11	405	92	42	.457	25	16	.640	46	84	130	40	45	1	12	2	100	9.1
75-76—Boston	18	741	154	69	.448	69	56	.812	78	168	246	42	67	1	24	6	194	10.8
76-77—Denver	6	141	33	14	.424	24	13	.542	16	24	40	16	23	1	2	4	41	6.8
77-78—Seattle	22	605	94	33	.351	60	41	.683	73	114	187	36	59	0	12	6	107	4.9
78-79—Seattle	17	418	54	21	.389	46	31	.674	40	58	98	19	44	1	9	5	73	4.3
79-80—Seattle	15	257	43	13	.302	13	11	.846	33	42	75	15	29	0	9	2	37	2.5
Totals	163	4619	998	396	.397	480	332	.692			1527	335	469	7	81	34	1124	6.9

NBA ALL-STAR GAME RECORD

Season—Team	Min.	FGA	FGM	Pct.	FTA	FTM	Pct.	—Rebounds— Off.	Def.	Tot.	Ast.	PF	Dq.	Stl.	Blk.	Pts.
1972—Phoenix	15	6	0	.000	3	2	.667			9	1	1	0			2
1975—Boston	15	4	2	.500	2	2	1.000	0	2	2	2	2	0	4	0	6
Totals	30	10	2	.200	5	4	.800			11	3	3	0			8

EBL REGULAR SEASON RECORD

Sea.—Team	G.	Min.	—2-Point— FGM	FGA	Pct.	—3-Point— FGM	FGA	Pct.	FTM	FTA	Pct.	Reb.	Ast.	Pts.	Avg.
65-66—Wilkes Barre EBL	5	....	25	....	....	0	0	.000	13	21	.619	85	9	63	12.6

NBA COACHING RECORD

Sea.	Club	Regular Season W.	L.	Pct.	Pos.
1980-81	San Diego	36	46	.439	5†
1981-82	San Diego	17	65	.207	6†
1982-83	San Diego	25	57	.305	6†
	Totals (3 seasons)	78	168	.317	

†Pacific Division.

Named to NBA All-Defensive First Team, 1975 and 1976. . . . NBA All-Defensive Second Team, 1971, 1972, 1973. . . . Member of NBA championship teams, 1974, 1976, 1979. . . . Holds NCAA record for most rebounds in 3-year career. . . . Led NCAA in rebounding, 1963. . . . One of only seven players to average over 20 points and 20 rebounds per game during NCAA career.

NATHANIEL THURMOND
(Nate)

Born July 25, 1941 at Akron, O. Height 6:11. Weight 235.
High School—Akron, O., Central.
College—Bowling Green State University, Bowling Green, O.
Drafted by San Francisco on first round, 1963.

Franchise named changed to Golden State, 1971.
Traded by Golden State to Chicago for Clifford Ray, cash and a 1975 1st round draft choice, September 3, 1974.
Traded by Chicago with Rowland Garrett to Cleveland for Steve Patterson and Eric Fernsten, November 27, 1975.

—COLLEGIATE RECORD—

Year	G.	Min.	FGA	FGM	Pct.	FTA	FTM	Pct.	Reb.	Pts.	Avg.
59-60†	17	....	....	....	....	....	....	....	208	225	13.2
60-61	24	....	427	170	.398	129	87	.674	449	427	17.8
61-62	25	....	358	163	.455	113	67	.593	394	393	15.7
62-63	27	....	466	206	.442	197	124	.629	452	536	19.9
Varsity Totals	76	....	1251	539	.431	439	278	.633	1295	1356	17.8

NBA REGULAR SEASON RECORD

Sea.—Team	G.	Min.	FGA	FGM	Pct.	FTA	FTM	Pct.	Reb.	Ast.	PF	Disq.	Pts.	Avg.
63-64—San Fran.	76	1966	554	219	.395	173	95	.549	790	86	184	2	533	7.0
64-65—San Fran.	77	3173	1240	519	.419	357	235	.658	1395	157	232	3	1273	16.5
65-66—San Fran.	73	2891	1119	454	.406	428	280	.654	1312	111	223	7	1188	16.3
66-67—San Fran.	65	2755	1068	467	.437	445	280	.629	1382	166	183	3	1214	18.7
67-68—San Fran.	51	2222	929	382	.411	438	282	.644	1121	215	137	1	1046	20.5
68-59—San Fran.	71	3208	1394	571	.410	621	382	.615	1402	253	171	0	1524	21.5
69-70—San Fran.	43	1919	824	341	.414	346	261	.754	762	150	110	1	943	21.9
70-71—San Fran.	82	3351	1401	623	.445	541	395	.730	1128	257	192	1	1641	20.0
71-72—Golden St.	78	3362	1454	628	.432	561	417	.743	1252	230	214	1	1673	21.4
72-73—Golden St.	79	3419	1159	517	.446	439	315	.718	1349	280	240	2	1349	17.1

									—Rebounds—									
Sea.—Team	G.	Min.	FGA	FGM	Pct.	FTA	FTM	Pct.	Off.	Def.	Tot.	Ast.	PF	Dq.	Stl.	Blk.	Pts.	Avg.
73-74—Gld. St.	62	2463	694	308	.444	287	191	.666	249	629	878	165	179	4	41	179	807	13.0
74-75—Chicago	80	2756	686	250	.364	224	132	.589	259	645	904	328	271	6	46	195	632	7.9
75-76—Chi.-Clev.	78	1393	337	142	.421	123	62	.504	115	300	415	94	160	1	22	98	346	4.4
76-77—Cleveland	49	997	246	100	.407	106	68	.642	121	253	374	83	128	2	16	81	268	5.5
Totals	964	35875	13105	5521	.421	5089	3395	.667			14464	2575	2624	34	125	553	14437	15.0

NBA PLAYOFF RECORD

Sea.—Team	G.	Min.	FGA	FGM	Pct.	FTA	FTM	Pct.	Reb.	Ast.	PF	Disq.	Pts.	Avg.
63-64—San Fran.	12	410	98	42	.429	53	36	.679	148	12	46	0	120	10.0
66-67—San Fran.	15	690	215	93	.433	91	52	.571	346	47	52	1	238	15.9
68-69—San Fran.	6	263	102	40	.392	34	20	.588	117	28	18	0	100	16.7
71-71—San Fran.	5	192	97	36	.371	20	16	.800	51	15	20	0	88	17.6
71-72—Golden St.	5	230	122	53	.434	28	21	.750	89	26	12	0	127	25.4
72-73—Golden St.	11	460	161	64	.398	40	32	.800	145	40	30	1	160	14.5

									—Rebounds—									
Sea.—Team	G.	Min.	FGA	FGM	Pct.	FTA	FTM	Pct.	Off.	Def.	Tot.	Ast.	PF	Dq.	Stl.	Blk.	Pts.	Avg.
74-75—Chicago	13	254	38	14	.368	37	18	.486	24	63	87	31	36	0	5	21	46	3.5
75-76—Chi.-Cle.	13	375	79	37	.468	32	13	.406	38	79	117	28	52	2	6	29	87	6.7
76-77—Cleveland	1	1	0	0	.000	0	0	.000	0	1	1	0	0	0	0	1	0	0.0
Totals	81	2875	912	379	.416	335	208	.621			1101	227	266	4	11	51	966	11.9

NBA ALL-STAR GAME RECORD

Season—Team	Min.	FGA	FGM	Pct.	FTA	FTM	Pct.	Reb.	Ast.	PF	Disq.	Pts.
1965—San Francisco	10	2	0	.000	0	0	.000	3	0	1	0	0
1966—San Francisco	33	16	3	.188	3	1	.000	16	1	1	0	7
1967—San Francisco	42	16	7	.438	4	2	.500	18	0	1	0	16
1968—San Francisco					Selected—Injured, Did Not Play							
1970—San Francisco					Selected—Injured, Did Not Play							
1973—Golden State	14	5	2	.400	0	0	.000	4	1	2	0	4

Season—Team	Min.	FGA	FGM	Pct.	FTA	FTM	Pct.	—Rebounds— Off.	Def.	Tot.	Ast.	PF	Dq.	Stl.	Blk.	Pts.
1974—Golden St.	5	4	2	.500	1	0	.000	1	2	3	0	0	0	0	0	4
Totals	104	43	14	.326	8	3	.375			44	2	5	0			31

Elected to Naismith Memorial Basketball Hall of Fame, 1984. . . . Named to NBA All-Defensive First Team, 1969 and 1971. . . . NBA All-Defensive Second Team, 1972, 1973, 1974. . . . NBA All-Rookie Team, 1964. . . . Holds NBA record for most rebounds in one quarter, 18, vs. Baltimore, February 28, 1965. . . . Named to THE SPORTING NEWS All-America First Team, 1963. . . . Holds NCAA Tournament record for most rebounds in one game, 31, vs. Mississippi State, 1963.

JOHN KENNEDY TWYMAN
(Jack)

Born May 11, 1934 at Pittsburgh, Pa. Height 6:06. Weight 210.
High School—Pittsburgh, Pa., Central Catholic.
College—University of Cincinnati, Cincinnati, O.
Drafted by Rochester on second round, 1955 (10th pick).

Rochester franchise transferred to Cincinnati, 1957.

—COLLEGIATE RECORD—

Year	G.	Min.	FGA	FGM	Pct.	FTA	FTM	Pct.	Reb.	Pts.	Avg.
51-52	16	....	83	27	.325	27	13	.481	55	67	4.2
52-53	24	716	323	136	.421	143	89	.622	362	361	15.0
53-54	21	777	443	174	.393	145	110	.759	347	458	21.8
54-55	29	1097	628	285	.454	192	142	.740	478	712	24.6
Totals	90	....	1477	622	.421	507	354	.698	1242	1598	17.8

NBA REGULAR SEASON RECORD

Sea.—Team	G.	Min.	FGA	FGM	Pct.	FTA	FTM	Pct.	Reb.	Ast.	PF	Disq.	Pts.	Avg.
55-56—Rochester	72	2186	987	417	.422	298	204	.685	466	171	239	4	1038	14.4
56-57—Rochester	72	2338	1023	449	.439	363	276	.760	354	123	251	4	1174	16.3
57-58—Cincinnati	72	2178	1028	465	.452	396	307	.775	464	110	224	3	1237	17.2
58-59—Cincinnati	72	2713	1691	710	.420	558	437	.783	653	209	277	6	1857	25.8
59-60—Cincinnati	75	3023	2063	870	.422	762	598	.785	664	260	275	10	2338	31.2
60-61—Cincinnati	79	2920	1632	796	.488	554	405	.731	669	225	279	5	1997	25.3
61-62—Cincinnati	80	2991	1542	739	.479	435	353	.815	638	323	315	5	1831	22.9
62-63—Cincinnati	80	2523	1335	641	.480	375	304	.811	598	214	286	7	1586	19.8
63-64—Cincinnati	68	2004	993	447	.450	228	189	.829	364	137	267	7	1083	19.9
64-65—Cincinnati	80	2236	1081	479	.443	239	198	.828	383	137	239	4	1156	14.5
65-66—Cincinnati	73	943	498	224	.450	117	95	.812	168	60	122	1	543	7.4
Totals	823	26055	13873	6237	.450	4325	3366	.778	5421	1969	2774	56	15840	19.2

NBA PLAYOFF RECORD

Sea.—Team	G.	Min.	FGA	FGM	Pct.	FTA	FTM	Pct.	Reb.	Ast.	PF	Disq.	Pts.	Avg.
57-58—Cincinnati	2	74	45	15	.333	12	7	.583	22	1	6	0	37	18.5
61-62—Cincinnati	4	149	78	34	.436	8	8	1.000	29	12	18	0	76	19.0
62-63—Cincinnati	12	410	205	92	.449	77	65	.844	98	30	47	1	249	20.8
63-64—Cincinnati	10	354	176	83	.472	49	29	.796	87	16	41	1	205	20.5
64-65—Cincinnati	4	97	48	19	.396	11	11	1.000	17	3	16	0	49	12.3
65-66—Cincinnati	2	11	4	2	.500	2	1	.500	2	0	3	0	5	2.5
Totals	34	1095	556	245	.441	159	131	.824	255	62	131	2	621	18.3

NBA ALL-STAR GAME RECORD

Season—Team	Min.	FGA	FGM	Pct.	FTA	FTM	Pct.	Reb.	Ast.	PF	Disq.	Pts.
1957—Rochester	17	8	1	.125	3	1	.333	0	1	1	0	3
1958—Cincinnati	25	13	8	.615	2	2	1.000	3	0	3	0	18
1959—Cincinnati	23	12	8	.667	4	2	.500	8	3	4	0	18
1960—Cincinnati	28	17	11	.647	8	5	.625	5	1	4	0	27
1962—Cincinnati	8	6	4	.667	3	3	1.000	1	2	0	0	11
1963—Cincinnati	16	12	6	.500	0	0	.000	4	1	2	0	12
Totals	117	68	38	.559	20	13	.650	21	8	14	0	89

Elected to Naismith Memorial Basketball Hall of Fame, 1982. . . . Named to All-NBA Second Team, 1960 and 1962. . . . Led NBA in field-goal percentage, 1958.

CHESTER WALKER
(Chet)

Born February 22, 1940 at Benton Harbor, Mich. Height 6:07. Weight 220.
High School—Benton Harbor, Mich.
College—Bradley University, Peoria, Ill.
Drafted by Syracuse on second round, 1962 (14th pick).

Franchise transferred from Syracuse to Philadelphia, 1963.

Traded with Shaler Halimon by Philadelphia to Chicago for Jim Washington and a player to be named later, September 2, 1969.

—COLLEGIATE RECORD—

Year	G.	Min.	FGA	FGM	Pct.	FTA	FTM	Pct.	Reb.	Pts.	Avg.
58-59†	15	....	264	146	.553	93	56	.602	246	348	23.2
59-60	29	....	436	244	.560	234	144	.615	388	632	21.8
60-61	26	....	423	238	.563	250	180	.720	327	656	25.2
61-62	26	....	500	268	.536	236	151	.640	321	687	26.4
Varsity Totals	81	....	1359	750	.552	720	475	.660	1036	1975	24.4

NBA REGULAR SEASON RECORD

Sea.—Team	G.	Min.	FGA	FGM	Pct.	FTA	FTM	Pct.	Reb.	Ast.	PF	Disq.	Pts.	Avg.
62-63—Syracuse	78	1992	751	352	.469	362	253	.699	561	83	220	3	957	12.3
63-64—Philadelphia	76	2775	1118	492	.440	464	330	.711	784	124	232	3	1314	17.3
64-65—Philadelphia	79	2187	936	377	.403	388	288	.742	528	132	200	2	1042	13.2
65-66—Philadelphia	80	2603	982	443	.451	468	335	.716	636	201	238	3	1221	15.3
66-67—Philadelphia	81	2691	1150	561	.488	581	445	.766	660	188	232	4	1567	19.3
67-68—Philadelphia	82	2623	1172	539	.460	533	387	.726	607	157	252	3	1465	17.9
68-69—Philadelphia	82	2753	1145	554	.484	459	369	.804	640	144	244	0	1477	18.0
69-70—Chicago	78	2726	1249	596	.477	568	483	.850	604	192	203	1	1675	21.5
70-71—Chicago	81	2927	1398	650	.465	559	480	.859	588	179	187	2	1780	22.0
71-72—Chicago	78	2588	1225	619	.505	568	481	.847	473	178	171	0	1719	22.0
72-73—Chicago	79	2455	1248	597	.478	452	376	.832	395	179	166	1	1570	19.9

									—Rebounds—									
Sea.—Team	G.	Min.	FGA	FGM	Pct.	FTA	FTM	Pct.	Off.	Def.	Tot.	Ast.	PF	Dq.	Stl.	Blk.	Pts.	Avg.
73-74—Chicago	82	2661	1178	572	.486	502	439	.875	131	275	406	200	201	1	68	4	1583	19.3
74-75—Chicago	76	2452	1076	524	.487	480	413	.860	114	318	432	169	181	0	49	6	1461	19.2
Totals	1032	33433	14628	6876	.470	6384	5079	.796			7314	2126	2727	23	117	10	18831	18.2

NBA PLAYOFF RECORD

Sea.—Team	G.	Min.	FGA	FGM	Pct.	FTA	FTM	Pct.	Reb.	Ast.	PF	Disq.	Pts.	Avg.
62-63—Syracuse	5	130	53	27	.509	30	22	.733	47	9	8	0	76	15.2
63-64—Philadelphia	5	190	77	30	.390	46	34	.739	52	13	15	0	94	18.8
64-65—Philadelphia	11	469	173	83	.480	75	57	.760	79	18	38	0	223	20.3
65-66—Philadelphia	5	181	64	24	.375	31	25	.806	37	15	18	0	73	14.6
66-67—Philadelphia	15	551	246	115	.467	119	96	.807	114	32	44	0	326	21.7
67-68—Philadelphia	13	485	210	86	.410	112	76	.679	96	24	44	1	248	19.1
68-69—Philadelphia	4	109	43	23	.535	12	8	.667	23	8	5	0	54	13.5
69-70—Chicago	5	178	83	35	.422	33	27	.818	42	11	14	0	97	19.4
70-71—Chicago	7	234	100	44	.440	24	17	.708	50	22	20	0	105	15.0
71-72—Chicago	4	97	38	16	.421	16	13	.813	14	4	7	0	45	11.3
72-73—Chicago	7	229	121	42	.347	37	33	.892	62	14	15	0	117	16.7

									—Rebounds—									
Sea.—Team	G.	Min.	FGA	FGM	Pct.	FTA	FTM	Pct.	Off.	Def.	Tot.	Ast.	PF	Dq.	Stl.	Blk.	Pts.	Avg.
73-74—Chicago	11	403	159	81	.509	79	68	.861	26	35	61	18	26	0	10	1	230	20.9
74-75—Chicago	13	432	164	81	.494	75	66	.880	10	50	60	24	32	2	13	1	228	17.5
Totals	105	3688	1531	687	.449	689	542	.787			737	212	286	3	23	2	1916	18.2

NBA ALL-STAR GAME RECORD

Season—Team	Min.	FGA	FGM	Pct.	FTA	FTM	Pct.	Reb.	Ast.	PF	Disq.	Pts.
1964—Philadelphia	12	5	2	.400	0	0	.000	0	0	1	0	4
1966—Philadelphia	25	10	3	.300	3	2	.667	6	4	2	0	8
1967—Philadelphia	22	9	6	.667	4	3	.750	4	1	2	0	15
1970—Chicago	17	3	1	.333	2	2	1.000	2	1	2	0	4
1971—Chicago	19	9	3	.333	5	4	.800	3	1	1	0	10
1973—Chicago	16	5	1	.200	2	2	1.000	1	0	2	0	4

								—Rebounds—								
Season—Team	Min.	FGA	FGM	Pct.	FTA	FTM	Pct.	Off.	Def.	Tot.	Ast.	PF	Dq.	Stl.	Blk.	Pts.
1974—Chicago	14	5	4	.800	4	4	1.000	0	2	2	1	1	0	0	0	12
Totals	125	46	20	.435	20	17	.850			18	8	11	0			57

Named to NBA All-Rookie Team, 1963. . . . Led NBA in free-throw percentage, 1971. . . . Member of NBA championship team, 1967. . . . Named to THE SPORTING NEWS All-America First Team, 1962. . . . THE SPORTING NEWS All-America Second Team, 1961.

WILLIAM THEODORE WALTON
(Bill)

Born November 5, 1952 at La Mesa, Calif. Height 6:11. Weight 235.

High School—La Mesa, Calif., Helix.

College—University of California at Los Angeles, Los Angeles, Calif.

Drafted by Portland on first round, 1974 (1st pick).

Missed entire 1978-79, 1980-81, 1981-82 and 1987-88 seasons due to injury.

Signed by San Diego as a Veteran Free Agent, May 13, 1979; Portland received Kevin Kunnert, Kermit Washington, a 1980 1st round draft choice and cash as compensation, September 18, 1979.

Traded by Los Angeles Clippers to Boston for Cedric Maxwell, a 1986 1st round draft choice and cash, September 6, 1985.

—COLLEGIATE RECORD—

Year	G.	Min.	FGA	FGM	Pct.	FTA	FTM	Pct.	Reb.	Pts.	Avg.
70-71†	20	....	266	155	.686	82	52	.634	321	362	18.1
71-72	30	....	372	238	.640	223	157	.704	466	633	21.1
72-73	30	....	426	277	.650	102	59	.569	506	612	20.4
73-74	27	....	349	232	.665	100	58	.580	398	522	19.3
Varsity Totals	87	....	1147	747	.651	425	273	.642	1370	1767	20.3

NBA REGULAR SEASON RECORD

									—Rebounds—									
Sea.—Team	G.	Min.	FGA	FGM	Pct.	FTA	FTM	Pct.	Off.	Def.	Tot.	Ast.	PF	Dq.	Stl.	Blk.	Pts.	Avg.
74-75—Portland	35	1153	345	177	.513	137	94	.686	92	349	441	167	115	4	29	94	448	12.8
75-76—Portland	51	1687	732	345	.471	228	133	.583	132	549	681	220	144	3	49	82	823	16.1
76-77—Portland	65	2264	930	491	.528	327	228	.697	211	723	934	245	174	5	66	211	1210	18.6
77-78—Portland	58	1929	882	460	.522	246	177	.720	118	648	766	291	145	3	60	146	1097	18.9
79-80—San Diego	14	337	161	81	.503	54	32	.593	28	98	126	34	37	0	8	38	194	13.9
82-83—San Diego	33	1099	379	200	.528	117	65	.556	75	248	323	120	113	0	34	119	465	14.1
83-84—San Diego	55	1476	518	288	.556	154	92	.597	132	345	477	183	153	1	45	88	668	12.1
84-85—L.A. Clippers	67	1647	516	269	.521	203	138	.680	168	432	600	156	184	0	50	140	676	10.1
85-86—Boston	80	1546	411	231	.562	202	144	.713	136	408	544	165	210	1	38	106	606	7.6
86-87—Boston	10	112	26	10	.385	15	8	.533	11	20	31	9	23	0	1	10	28	2.8
Totals	468	13250	4900	2552	.521	1683	1111	.660	1103	3820	4923	1590	1298	17	380	1034	6215	13.3

Three-Point Field Goals: 1983-84, 0-for-2. 1984-85, 0-for-2. Totals, 0-for-4.

NBA PLAYOFF RECORD

									—Rebounds—									
Sea.—Team	G.	Min.	FGA	FGM	Pct.	FTA	FTM	Pct.	Off.	Def.	Tot.	Ast.	PF	Dq.	Stl.	Blk.	Pts.	Avg.
76-77—Portland	19	755	302	153	.507	57	39	.684	56	232	288	104	80	3	20	64	345	18.2
77-78—Portland	2	49	18	11	.611	7	5	.714	5	17	22	4	1	0	3	3	27	13.5
85-86—Boston	16	291	93	54	.581	23	19	.826	25	78	103	27	45	1	6	12	127	7.9
86-87—Boston	12	102	25	12	.480	14	5	.357	9	22	31	10	23	0	3	4	29	2.4
Totals	49	1197	438	230	.525	101	68	.673	95	349	444	145	149	4	32	83	528	10.8

Three-Point Field Goals: 1985-86, 0-for-1.

NBA ALL-STAR GAME RECORD

								—Rebounds—								
Season—Team	Min.	FGA	FGM	Pct.	FTA	FTM	Pct.	Off.	Def.	Tot.	Ast.	PF	Dq.	Stl.	Blk.	Pts.
1977—Portland	Selected—Injured, Did Not Play															
1978—Portland	31	14	6	.429	3	3	1.000	2	8	10	2	3	0	3	2	15

Named NBA Most Valuable Player, 1978. . . . All-NBA First Team, 1978. . . . All-NBA Second Team, 1977. . . . NBA All-Defensive First Team, 1977 and 1978. . . . NBA Playoff MVP, 1977. . . . Member of NBA championship teams, 1977 and 1986. . . . Recipient of NBA Sixth Man Award, 1986. . . . Shares NBA championship series game record for most blocked shots, 8, vs. Philadelphia, June 5, 1977. . . . Led NBA in blocked shots, 1977. . . . Led NBA in rebounding, 1977. . . . THE SPORTING NEWS College Player of the Year, 1972, 1973, 1974. . . . Named to THE SPORTING NEWS All-America First Team, 1972, 1973, 1974. . . . NCAA Division I Tournament Most Outstanding Player, 1972 and 1973. . . . Member of NCAA Division I championship teams, 1972 and 1973. . . . Holds NCAA tournament record for highest field-goal percentage in one year (minimum of 40 made), 76.3 percent (45-of-59), 1973. . . . Holds NCAA tournament record for highest field-goal percentage in career (minimum of 60 made), 68.6 percent (109-of-159), 1972 through 1974. . . . Brother of former National Football League tackle Bruce Walton.

JERRY ALAN WEST

Born May 28, 1938 at Cheylan, W. Va. Height 6:02. Weight 185.
High School—East Bank, W. Va.
College—West Virginia University, Morgantown, W. Va.
Drafted by Minneapolis on first round, 1960 (2nd pick).

Minneapolis franchise transferred to Los Angeles, 1960.

—COLLEGIATE RECORD—

Year	G.	Min.	FGA	FGM	Pct.	FTA	FTM	Pct.	Reb.	Pts.	Avg.
56-57†	17	....	...	114	....	...	104	....	....	332	19.5
57-58	28	799	359	178	.496	194	142	.732	311	498	17.8
58-59	34	1210	656	340	.518	320	223	.697	419	903	26.6
59-60	31	1129	645	325	.504	337	258	.766	510	908	29.3
Varsity Totals	93	3138	1660	843	.508	851	623	.732	1240	2309	24.8

NBA REGULAR SEASON RECORD

Sea.—Team	G.	Min.	FGA	FGM	Pct.	FTA	FTM	Pct.	Reb.	Ast.	PF	Disq.	Pts.	Avg.
60-61—Los Angeles	79	2797	1264	529	.419	497	331	.666	611	333	213	1	1389	17.6
61-62—Los Angeles	75	3087	1795	799	.445	926	712	.769	591	402	173	4	2310	30.8

JERRY WEST

Sea.—Team	G.	Min.	FGA	FGM	Pct.	FTA	FTM	Pct.	Reb.	Ast.	PF	Disq.	Pts.	Avg.
62-63—Los Angeles	55	2163	1213	559	.461	477	371	.778	384	307	150	1	1489	27.1
63-64—Los Angeles	72	2906	1529	740	.484	702	584	.832	443	403	200	2	2064	28.7
64-65—Los Angeles	74	3066	1655	822	.497	789	648	.821	447	364	221	2	2292	31.0
65-66—Los Angeles	79	3218	1731	818	.473	977	840	.860	562	480	243	1	2476	31.3
66-67—Los Angeles	66	2670	1389	645	.464	686	602	.878	392	447	160	1	1892	28.7
67-68—Los Angeles	51	1919	926	476	.514	482	391	.811	294	310	152	1	1343	26.3
68-69—Los Angeles	61	2394	1156	545	.471	597	490	.821	262	423	156	1	1580	25.9
69-70—Los Angeles	74	3106	1673	831	.497	785	647	.824	338	554	160	3	2309	31.2
70-71—Los Angeles	69	2845	1351	667	.494	631	525	.832	320	655	180	0	1859	26.9
71-72—Los Angeles	77	2973	1540	735	.477	633	515	.814	327	747	209	0	1985	25.8
72-73—Los Angeles	69	2460	1291	618	.479	421	339	.805	289	607	138	0	1575	22.8

									—Rebounds—								
Sea.—Team	G.	Min.	FGA	FGM	Pct.	FTA	FTM	Pct.	Off.	Def.	Tot.	Ast.	PF	Dq.	Stl.	Blk.	Pts.	Avg.
73-74—L. A.	31	967	519	232	.447	198	165	.833	30	86	116	206	80	0	81	23	629	20.3
Totals	932	36571	19032	9016	.474	8801	7160	.814			5376	6238	2435	17			25192	27.0

NBA PLAYOFF RECORD

Sea.—Team	G.	Min.	FGA	FGM	Pct.	FTA	FTM	Pct.	Reb.	Ast.	PF	Disq.	Pts.	Avg.
60-61—Los Angeles	12	461	202	99	.490	106	77	.726	104	63	39	0	275	22.9
61-62—Los Angeles	13	557	310	144	.465	150	121	.807	88	57	38	0	409	31.5
62-63—Los Angeles	13	538	286	144	.503	100	74	.740	106	61	34	0	362	27.8
63-64—Los Angeles	5	206	115	57	.496	53	42	.792	36	17	20	0	156	31.2
64-65—Los Angeles	11	470	351	155	.442	155	137	.884	63	58	37	0	447	40.6
65-66—Los Angeles	14	619	357	185	.518	125	109	.872	88	79	40	0	479	34.2
66-67—Los Angeles	1	1	0	0	.000	0	0	.000	1	0	0	0	0	0.0
67-68—Los Angeles	15	622	313	165	.527	169	132	.781	81	82	47	0	462	30.8
68-69—Los Angeles	18	757	423	196	.463	204	164	.804	71	135	52	1	556	30.9
69-70—Los Angeles	18	830	418	196	.469	212	170	.802	66	151	55	1	562	31.2
71-72—Los Angeles	15	608	340	128	.376	106	88	.830	73	134	39	0	344	22.9
72-73—Los Angeles	17	638	336	151	.449	127	99	.780	76	132	49	1	401	23.6

									—Rebounds—								
Sea.—Team	G.	Min.	FGA	FGM	Pct.	FTA	FTM	Pct.	Off.	Def.	Tot.	Ast.	PF	Dq.	Stl.	Blk.	Pts.	Avg.
73-74—L. A.	1	14	9	2	.222	0	0	.000	0	2	2	1	1	0	0	0	4	4.0
Totals	153	6321	3460	1622	.469	1507	1213	.805			855	970	451	3			4457	29.1

NBA ALL-STAR GAME RECORD

Season—Team	Min.	FGA	FGM	Pct.	FTA	FTM	Pct.	Reb.	Ast.	PF	Disq.	Pts.
1961—Los Angeles	25	8	2	.250	6	5	.833	2	4	3	0	9
1962—Los Angeles	31	14	7	.500	6	4	.667	3	1	2	0	18
1963—Los Angeles	32	15	5	.333	4	3	.750	7	5	1	0	13
1964—Los Angeles	42	20	8	.400	1	1	1.000	4	5	3	0	17
1965—Los Angeles	40	16	8	.500	6	4	.667	5	6	2	0	20
1966—Los Angeles	11	5	1	.200	2	2	1.000	1	0	2	0	4
1967—Los Angeles	30	11	6	.545	4	4	1.000	3	6	3	0	16
1968—Los Angeles	32	17	7	.412	4	3	.750	6	6	4	0	17
1969—Los Angeles					Selected—Injured, Did Not Play							
1970—Los Angeles	31	12	7	.583	12	8	.667	5	5	3	0	22
1971—Los Angeles	20	4	2	.500	3	1	.333	1	9	1	0	5
1972—Los Angeles	27	9	6	.667	2	1	.500	6	5	2	0	13
1973—Los Angeles	20	6	3	.500	0	0	.000	4	3	2	0	6
1974—Los Angeles					Selected—Injured, Did Not Play							
Totals	341	137	62	.453	50	36	.720	47	55	28	0	160

NBA COACHING RECORD

	Regular Season				Playoffs	
Sea. Club	W.	L.	Pct.	Pos.	W.	L.
1976-77—Los Angeles	53	29	.646	1†	4	7
1977-78—Los Angeles	45	37	.549	4†	1	2
1978-79—Los Angeles	47	35	.573	3†	3	5
Totals (3 seasons)	145	101	.589		8	14

†Pacific Division.

Elected to Naismith Memorial Basketball Hall of Fame, 1979. . . . Named to NBA 35th Anniversary All-Time Team, 1980. . . . All-NBA First Team, 1962, 1963, 1964, 1965, 1966, 1967, 1970, 1971, 1972, 1973. . . . All-NBA Second Team, 1968 and 1969. . . . NBA All-Defensive First Team, 1970, 1971, 1972, 1973. . . . NBA All-Defensive Second Team, 1969. . . . NBA Playoff MVP, 1969. . . . Holds NBA record for most free throws made in one season, 1966. . . . NBA all-time playoff leader in free throws made and scoring average. . . . Holds NBA playoff game record for most free throws made in one half, 14, vs. Baltimore, April 5, 1965. . . . NBA All-Star Game MVP, 1972. . . . Member of NBA championship team, 1972. . . . Led NBA in assists, 1972. . . . Led NBA in scoring, 1970. . . . Named to THE SPORTING NEWS All-America First Team, 1959 and 1960. . . . NCAA Tournament Most Outstanding Player, 1959. . . . Member of U.S. Olympic team, 1960.

PAUL DOUGLAS WESTPHAL

Born November 30, 1950 at Torrance, Calif. Height 6:04. Weight 195.

High School—Redondo Beach, Calif., Aviation.

College—University of Southern California, Los Angeles, Calif.

Drafted by Boston on first round, 1972 (10th pick).

Traded by Boston with 1975 and 1976 2nd round draft choices to Phoenix for Charlie Scott, May 23, 1975.

Traded by Phoenix to Seattle for Dennis Johnson, June 4, 1980.
Signed by New York as a Veteran Free Agent, March 12, 1982.
Waived by New York, June 20, 1983; signed by Phoenix as a free agent, September 27, 1983.
Waived by Phoenix, October 12, 1984.

—COLLEGIATE RECORD—

Year	G.	Min.	FGA	FGM	Pct.	FTA	FTM	Pct.	Reb.	Pts.	Avg.
68-69†	19	....	262	134	.511	119	87	.731	106	355	18.7
69-70	26	....	277	147	.531	110	84	.764	68	378	14.5
70-71	26	....	328	157	.479	150	109	.727	84	423	16.3
71-72	14	....	219	106	.484	95	72	.758	74	284	20.3
Varsity Totals	66	....	824	410	.498	355	265	.746	226	1085	16.4

NBA REGULAR SEASON RECORD

									—Rebounds—									
Sea.—Team	G.	Min.	FGA	FGM	Pct.	FTA	FTM	Pct.	Off.	Def.	Tot.	Ast.	PF	Dq.	Stl.	Blk.	Pts.	Avg.
72-73—Boston	60	482	212	89	.420	86	67	.779			67	69	88	0			245	4.1
73-74—Boston	82	1165	475	238	.501	153	112	.732	49	94	143	171	173	1	39	34	588	7.2
74-75—Boston	82	1581	670	342	.510	156	119	.763	44	119	163	235	192	0	78	33	803	9.8
75-76—Phoenix	82	2960	1329	657	.494	440	365	.830	74	185	259	440	218	3	210	38	1679	20.5
76-77—Phoenix	81	2600	1317	682	.518	439	362	.825	57	133	190	459	171	1	134	21	1726	21.3
77-78—Phoenix	80	2481	1568	809	.516	487	396	.813	41	123	164	437	162	0	138	31	2014	25.2
78-79—Phoenix	81	2641	1496	801	.535	405	339	.837	35	124	159	529	159	1	111	26	1941	24.0
79-80—Phoenix	82	2665	1317	692	.525	443	382	.862	46	141	187	416	162	0	119	35	1792	21.9
80-81—Seattle	36	1078	500	221	.442	184	153	.832	11	57	68	148	70	0	46	14	601	16.7
81-82—New York	18	451	194	86	.443	47	36	.766	9	13	22	100	61	1	19	8	210	11.7
82-83—New York	80	1978	693	318	.459	184	148	.804	19	96	115	439	180	1	87	16	798	10.0
83-84—Phoenix	59	865	313	144	.460	142	117	.824	8	35	43	148	69	0	41	6	412	7.0
Totals	823	20947	10084	5079	.504	3166	2596	.820			1580	3591	1705	8	1022	262	12809	15.6

Three-Point Field Goals: 1979-80, 26-for-93 (.280). 1980-81, 6-for-25 (.240). 1981-82, 2-for-8 (.250). 1982-83, 14-for-48 (.292). 1983-84, 7-for-26 (.269). Totals, 55-for-200 (.275).

NBA PLAYOFF RECORD

									—Rebounds—									
Sea.—Team	G.	Min.	FGA	FGM	Pct.	FTA	FTM	Pct.	Off.	Def.	Tot.	Ast.	PF	Dq.	Stl.	Blk.	Pts.	Avg.
72-73—Boston	11	109	39	19	.487	7	5	.714			7	9	24	1			43	3.9
73-74—Boston	18	241	100	46	.460	15	11	.733	6	15	21	31	37	0	8	2	103	5.7
74-75—Boston	11	183	81	38	.469	18	12	.667	5	8	13	32	21	0	6	2	88	8.0
75-76—Phoenix	19	685	323	165	.511	93	71	.763	14	33	47	96	61	1	34	9	401	21.1
77-78—Phoenix	2	66	47	22	.468	9	8	.889	3	3	6	19	4	0	1	0	52	26.0
78-79—Phoenix	15	534	287	142	.495	66	52	.788	7	26	33	64	38	0	15	5	336	22.4
79-80—Phoenix	8	253	142	69	.486	32	28	.875	2	8	10	31	20	0	11	3	167	20.9
82-83—New York	6	156	50	22	.440	13	10	.769	0	8	8	34	13	0	2	2	57	9.5
83-84—Phoenix	17	222	80	30	.375	32	28	.875	3	5	8	37	23	0	12	0	90	5.3
Totals	107	2449	1149	553	.481	285	225	.789			153	353	241	2	89	23	1337	12.5

Three-Point Field Goals: 1979-80, 1-for-12 (.083). 1982-83, 3-for-8 (.375). 1983-84, 2-for-9 (.222). Totals, 6-for-29 (.207).

NBA ALL-STAR GAME RECORD

								—Rebounds—							
Season—Team	Min.	FGA	FGM	Pct.	FTA	FTM	Pct.	Off.	Def.	Tot.	Ast.	PF	Dq.	Stl.	Blk.	Pts.
1977—Phoenix	31	16	10	.625	0	0	.000	0	1	1	6	2	0	3	2	20
1978—Phoenix	24	14	9	.643	5	2	.400	0	0	0	5	4	0	1	1	20
1979—Phoenix	21	12	8	.667	2	1	.500	0	1	1	5	0	0	0	0	17
1980—Phoenix	27	14	8	.571	6	5	.833	1	0	1	5	5	0	2	1	21
1981—Seattle	25	12	8	.667	3	3	1.000	2	2	4	3	3	0	0	1	19
Totals	128	68	43	.632	16	11	.688	3	4	7	24	14	0	6	5	97

Three-Point Field Goals: 1980, 0-for-2.

Named to All-NBA First Team, 1977, 1979, 1980. . . . All-NBA Second Team, 1978. . . . Member of NBA championship team, 1974. . . . NBA Comeback Player of the Year, 1983. . . . Named to THE SPORTING NEWS All-America Second Team, 1972.

JOSEPH HENRY WHITE
(Jo Jo)

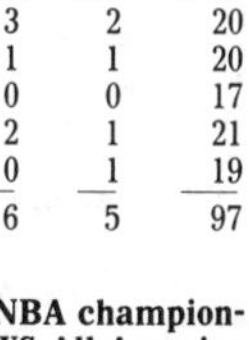

Born November 16, 1946 at St. Louis, Mo. Height 6:03. Weight 190.
High Schools—St. Louis, Mo., Vashon (Soph.) and McKinley (Jr.-Sr.)
College—University of Kansas, Lawrence, Kan.
Drafted by Boston on first round, 1969 (9th pick).

Traded by Boston to Golden State for a 1979 1st round draft choice, January 30, 1979.
Sold by Golden State to Kansas City, September 10, 1980.
Played in Continental Basketball Association with Topeka Sizzlers, 1987-88.

—COLLEGIATE RECORD—

Year	G.	Min.	FGA	FGM	Pct.	FTA	FTM	Pct.	Reb.	Pts.	Avg.
64-65†	2	....	34	11	.324	15	11	.733	25	33	16.5
65-66†	6	....	88	35	.398	27	18	.667	32	88	14.7
65-66	9	....	112	44	.393	26	14	.538	68	102	11.3
66-67	27	....	416	170	.409	72	59	.819	150	399	14.8
67-68	30	....	462	188	.407	115	83	.722	107	459	15.3
68-69	18	....	286	134	.469	79	58	.734	84	326	18.1
Varsity Totals	84	....	1276	536	.420	292	214	.733	409	1286	15.3

CBA REGULAR SEASON RECORD

			—2-Point—			—3-Point—									
Sea.—Team	G.	Min.	FGM	FGA	Pct.	FGM	FGA	Pct.	FTM	FTA	Pct.	Reb.	Ast.	Pts.	Avg.
87-88—Topeka	5	122	12	27	.444	0	3	.000	4	6	.667	6	21	28	5.6

NBA REGULAR SEASON RECORD

Sea.—Team	G.	Min.	FGA	FGM	Pct.	FTA	FTM	Pct.	Reb.	Ast.	PF	Disq.	Pts.	Avg.
69-70—Boston	60	1328	684	309	.452	135	111	.822	169	145	132	1	729	12.2
70-71—Boston	75	2787	1494	693	.464	269	215	.799	376	361	255	5	1601	21.3
71-72—Boston	79	3261	1788	770	.431	343	285	.831	446	416	227	1	1825	23.1
72-73—Boston	82	3250	1665	717	.431	228	178	.781	414	498	185	2	1612	19.7

									—Rebounds—									
Sea.—Team	G.	Min.	FGA	FGM	Pct.	FTA	FTM	Pct.	Off.	Def.	Tot.	Ast.	PF	Dq.	Stl.	Blk.	Pts.	Avg.
73-74—Boston	82	3238	1445	649	.449	227	190	.837	100	251	351	448	185	1	105	25	1488	18.1
74-75—Boston	82	3220	1440	658	.457	223	186	.834	84	227	311	458	207	1	128	17	1502	18.3
75-76—Boston	82	3257	1492	670	.449	253	212	.838	61	252	313	445	183	2	107	20	1552	18.9
76-77—Boston	82	3333	1488	638	.429	383	333	.869	87	296	383	492	193	5	118	22	1609	19.6
77-78—Boston	46	1641	690	289	.419	120	103	.858	53	127	180	209	109	2	49	7	681	14.8
78-79—Bos.-G.S.	76	2338	910	404	.444	158	139	.880	42	158	200	347	173	1	80	7	947	12.5
79-80—Golden State	78	2052	706	336	.476	114	97	.851	42	139	181	239	186	0	88	13	770	9.9
80-81—Kansas City	13	236	82	36	.439	18	11	.611	3	18	21	37	21	0	11	1	83	6.4
Totals	837	29941	13884	6169	.444	2471	2060	.834			3345	4095	2056	21	686	112	14399	17.2

Three-Point Field Goals: 1979-80, 1-for-6 (.167)

NBA PLAYOFF RECORD

Sea.—Team	G.	Min.	FGA	FGM	Pct.	FTA	FTM	Pct.	Reb.	Ast.	PF	Disq.	Pts.	Avg.
71-72—Boston	11	432	220	109	.495	48	40	.833	59	58	31	0	258	23.5
72-73—Boston	13	583	300	135	.450	54	49	.907	54	83	44	2	319	24.5

									—Rebounds—									
Sea.—Team	G.	Min.	FGA	FGM	Pct.	FTA	FTM	Pct.	Off.	Def.	Tot.	Ast.	PF	Dq.	Stl.	Blk.	Pts.	Avg.
73-74—Boston	18	765	310	132	.426	46	34	.739	17	58	75	98	56	1	15	2	298	16.6
74-75—Boston	11	462	227	100	.441	33	27	.818	18	32	50	63	32	0	11	4	227	20.6
75-76—Boston	18	791	371	165	.445	95	78	.821	12	59	71	98	51	0	23	1	408	22.7
76-77—Boston	9	395	201	91	.453	33	28	.848	10	29	39	52	27	0	14	0	210	23.3
Totals	80	3428	1629	732	.449	309	256	.828			348	452	241	3	63	7	1720	21.5

NBA ALL-STAR GAME RECORD

Season—Team	Min.	FGA	FGM	Pct.	FTA	FTM	Pct.	Reb.	Ast.	PF	Disq.	Pts.
1971—Boston	22	10	5	.500	0	0	.000	9	2	2	0	10
1972—Boston	18	15	6	.400	2	0	.000	4	3	1	0	12
1973—Boston	18	7	3	.429	0	0	.000	5	5	0	0	6

								—Rebounds—								
Season—Team	Min.	FGA	FGM	Pct.	FTA	FTM	Pct.	Off.	Def.	Tot.	Ast.	PF	Dq.	Stl.	Blk.	Pts.
1974—Boston	22	12	6	.500	3	1	.333	2	4	6	4	1	0	2	1	13
1975—Boston	13	2	1	.500	6	5	.833	0	1	1	4	1	0	0	0	7
1976—Boston	16	7	3	.429	0	0	.000	0	1	1	1	1	0	2	0	6
1977—Boston	15	7	5	.714	0	0	.000	0	1	1	2	0	0	0	0	10
Totals	124	60	29	.483	11	6	.545			27	21	6	0	4	1	64

Named to All-NBA Second Team, 1975 and 1977. . . . NBA All-Rookie Team, 1970. . . . NBA Playoff MVP, 1976. . . . Member of NBA championship teams, 1974 and 1976. . . . Named to THE SPORTING NEWS All-America First Team, 1968 and 1969. . . . Member of U. S. Olympic team, 1968.

GEORGE HARRY YARDLEY

Born November 23, 1928 at Hollywood, Calif. Height 6:05. Weight 195.

High School—Balboa, Calif.

College—Stanford University, Stanford, Calif.

Drafted by Ft. Wayne on first round, 1950.

Played with the San Francisco Stewart Chevrolets in the National Industrial Basketball League, an Amateur Athletic Union League, during 1950-51 season. (Finished third in the league in scoring with a 13.1-point averge on 104 field goals and 53 field goals for 261 points in 20 games.)

In military service during 1951-52 and 1952-53 seasons. Played with Los Alamitos, Calif., Naval Air Station.

Signed by Ft. Wayne NBA, 1953.

Ft. Wayne franchise transferred to Detroit, 1957.

Traded by Detroit to Syracuse for Ed Conlin, February 13, 1959.

Played in American Basketball League with Los Angeles, 1961-62.

—COLLEGIATE RECORD—

Year	G.	Min.	FGA	FGM	Pct.	FTA	FTM	Pct.	Reb.	Pts.	Avg.
46-47†					Statistics Unavailable						
47-48	18	....	...	22	....	20	8	.400	....	52	2.9
48-49	28	....	377	126	.334	131	93	.710	....	345	12.3
49-50	25	....	452	164	.363	130	95	.731	....	423	16.9
Varsity Totals	71	....	...	312	....	281	196	.698	....	820	11.5

NBA REGULAR SEASON RECORD

Sea.—Team	G.	Min.	FGA	FGM	Pct.	FTA	FTM	Pct.	Reb.	Ast.	PF	Disq.	Pts.	Avg.
53-54—Ft. Wayne	63	1489	492	209	.425	205	146	.712	407	99	166	3	564	9.0
54-55—Ft. Wayne	60	2150	869	363	.418	416	310	.745	594	126	205	7	1036	17.3
55-56—Ft. Wayne	71	2353	1067	434	.407	492	365	.742	686	159	212	2	1233	17.4
56-57—Ft. Wayne	72	2691	1273	522	.410	639	503	.787	755	147	231	2	1547	21.5
57-58—Detroit	72	2843	1624	673	.414	808	655	.811	768	97	226	3	2001	27.8
58-59—Det.-Syr.	61	1839	1042	446	.428	407	317	.779	431	65	159	2	1209	19.8
59-60—Syracuse	73	2390	1214	549	.452	462	377	.816	570	123	227	3	1475	20.2
Totals	472	15755	7581	3196	.422	3429	2673	.780	4211	816	1426	22	9065	19.2

NBA PLAYOFF RECORD

Sea.—Team	G.	Min.	FGA	FGM	Pct.	FTA	FTM	Pct.	Reb.	Ast.	PF	Disq.	Pts.	Avg.
53-54—Ft. Wayne	4	107	33	16	.485	12	10	.833	24	3	10	0	42	10.5
54-55—Ft. Wayne	11	420	143	57	.399	79	60	.759	99	36	37	2	174	15.8
55-56—Ft. Wayne	10	406	183	77	.421	98	76	.776	139	26	25	0	230	23.0
56-57—Ft. Wayne	2	85	53	24	.453	11	9	.818	19	8	7	0	57	28.5
57-58—Detroit	7	254	127	52	.409	67	60	.896	72	17	26	0	164	23.4
58-59—Syracuse	9	333	189	83	.439	70	60	.857	87	21	29	0	226	25.1
59-60—Syracuse	3	88	39	15	.385	12	10	.833	17	1	9	0	40	13.3
Totals	46	1693	767	324	.422	349	285	.817	457	112	143	2	933	20.3

NBA ALL-STAR GAME RECORD

Season—Team	Min.	FGA	FGM	Pct.	FTA	FTM	Pct.	Reb.	Ast.	PF	Disq.	Pts.
1955—Fort Wayne	22	11	4	.364	4	3	.750	4	2	2	0	11
1956—Fort Wayne	19	7	3	.429	3	2	.667	6	1	1	0	8
1957—Fort Wayne	25	10	4	.400	1	1	1.000	9	0	2	0	9
1958—Detroit	32	15	8	.533	5	3	.600	9	1	1	0	19
1959—Detroit	17	8	2	.250	2	2	1.000	4	0	3	0	6
1960—Syracuse	16	9	5	.556	2	1	.500	3	0	4	0	11
Totals	131	60	26	.433	17	12	.706	35	4	13	0	64

ABL REGULAR SEASON RECORD

			—2-Point—			—3-Point—								
Sea.—Team	G.	Min.	FGM	FGA	Pct.	FGM	FGA	Pct.	FTM	FTA	Pct.	Reb.	Ast.	Pts.	Avg.
1961-62—L.A.	25	948	378	159	.421	37	14	.378	148	122	.824	172	65	482	19.2

Named to All-NBA First Team, 1958. . . . All-NBA Second Team, 1957. . . . Led league in scoring in 1958 when he became first NBA player ever to score over 2,000 points in a season.

MAX ZASLOFSKY

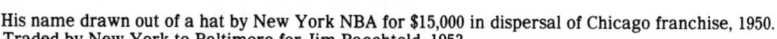

Born December 7, 1925 at Brooklyn, N. Y. Height 6:02. Weight 170.

Died October 15, 1985.

High School—Brooklyn, N. Y., Thomas Jefferson.

College—St. John's University, Brooklyn, N. Y.

Signed as free agent by Chicago BAA, 1946.

His name drawn out of a hat by New York NBA for $15,000 in dispersal of Chicago franchise, 1950.
Traded by New York to Baltimore for Jim Baechtold, 1953.
Traded by Baltimore to Milwaukee, November, 1953.
Traded by Milwaukee to Fort Wayne, December, 1953.
Coached in ABA with New Jersey Americans and New York Nets, 1967-68 and 1968-69.

—COLLEGIATE PLAYING RECORD—

Year	G.	Min.	FGA	FGM	Pct.	FTA	FTM	Pct.	Reb.	Pts.	Avg.
45-46	18	....	...	59	....	38	22	.579	...	140	7.8

NOTE: Played only one year of college basketball. In Military Service during 1944-45 season.

NBA REGULAR SEASON RECORD

Sea.—Team	G.	Min.	FGA	FGM	Pct.	FTA	FTM	Pct.	Reb.	Ast.	PF	Disq.	Pts.	Avg.
46-47—Chicago	61	....	1020	336	.329	278	205	.737	...	40	121	...	877	14.4
47-48—Chicago	48	....	1156	373	.323	333	261	.784	...	29	125	...	1007	21.0
48-49—Chicago	58	....	1216	425	.350	413	347	.840	...	149	156	...	1197	20.6
49-50—Chicago	68	....	1132	397	.351	381	321	.843	...	155	185	...	1115	16.4
50-51—New York	66	....	853	302	.354	298	231	.775	228	136	150	...	835	12.7
51-52—New York	66	....	958	322	.336	380	287	.755	194	156	183	...	931	14.1
52-53—New York	29	....	320	123	.384	142	98	.690	75	55	81	...	344	11.9

Sea.—Team	G.	Min.	FGA	FGM	Pct.	FTA	FTM	Pct.	Reb.	Ast.	PF	Disq.	Pts.	Avg.
53-54—Balt.-Mil.-F.W.	65	....	756	278	.368	357	255	.714	160	154	142	...	811	12.5
54-55—Fort Wayne	70	....	821	269	.328	352	247	.702	191	203	130	...	785	11.2
55-56—Fort Wayne	9	....	81	29	.358	35	30	.857	16	16	18	...	88	9.8
Totals	540	...	8313	2854	.343	2969	2282	.769	...	1093	1291	...	7990	14.8

NBA PLAYOFF RECORD

Sea.—Team	G.	Min.	FGA	FGM	Pct.	FTA	FTM	Pct.	Reb.	Ast.	PF	Disq.	Pts.	Avg.
46-47—Chicago	11	....	199	60	.302	44	29	.659	...	4	26	..	149	13.5
47-48—Chicago	5	....	88	30	.341	47	37	.787	...	0	17	..	97	19.4
48-49—Chicago	2	....	49	15	.306	18	14	.778	...	6	3	..	44	22.0
49-50—Chicago	2	....	32	15	.469	18	15	.833	...	6	7	..	45	22.5
50-51—New York	14	....	217	88	.406	100	74	.740	58	38	43	..	250	17.9
51-52—New York	14	....	185	69	.373	110	89	.809	44	23	51	..	227	16.2
53-54—Fort Wayne	4	....	36	11	.306	15	13	.867	3	6	7	..	35	8.8
54-55—Fort Wayne	11	....	44	18	.409	20	16	.750	16	18	20	..	52	4.7
Totals	63	....	850	306	.360	372	287	.772	...	101	174	..	899	14.3

NBA ALL-STAR GAME RECORD

Season—Team	Min.	FGA	FGM	Pct.	FTA	FTM	Pct.	Reb.	Ast.	PF	Disq.	Pts.
1952—New York	....	7	3	.429	5	5	1.000	4	2	0	0	11

ABA COACHING RECORD

	Regular Season			
Sea. Club	W.	L.	Pct.	Pos.
1967-68—New Jersey	36	42	.462	4T†
1968-69—New York	17	61	.218	5†
Totals (2 seasons)	53	103	.339	

†Eastern Division.

Named to All-NBA First Team, 1947, 1948, 1949, 1950. . . . Led NBA in scoring, 1948. . . . Led NBA in free-throw percentage, 1950.

COACHES

ALVIN A. ATTLES
(Al)

Born November 7, 1936 at Newark, N. J. Height 6:00. Weight 185.
High School—Newark, N. J., Weequahic.
College—North Carolina A&T State University, Greensboro, N. C.
Drafted by Philadelphia on fifth round, 1960 (39th pick).

Philadelphia franchise transferred to San Francisco, 1962.

COLLEGIATE PLAYING RECORD

Year	G.	Min.	FGA	FGM	Pct.	FTA	FTM	Pct.	Reb.	Pts.	Avg.
56-57	Statistics Unavailable										
57-58	Statistics Unavailable										
58-59	29	....	225	105	.467	91	56	.615	....	266	9.2
59-60	24	....	301	190	.631	71	47	.662	80	427	17.8

NBA REGULAR SEASON RECORD

Sea.—Team	G.	Min.	FGA	FGM	Pct.	FTA	FTM	Pct.	Reb.	Ast.	PF	Disq.	Pts.	Avg.
60-61—Philadelphia	77	1544	543	222	.409	162	97	.599	214	174	235	5	541	7.0
61-62—Philadelphia	75	2468	724	343	.474	267	158	.592	355	333	279	8	844	11.3
62-63—San Fran.	71	1876	630	301	.478	206	133	.646	205	184	253	7	735	10.4
63-64—San Fran.	70	1883	640	289	.452	275	185	.673	236	197	249	4	763	10.9
64-65—San Fran.	73	1733	662	254	.384	274	171	.624	239	205	242	7	679	9.3
65-66—San Fran.	79	2053	724	364	.503	252	154	.611	322	225	265	7	882	11.2
66-67—San Fran.	70	1764	467	212	.454	151	88	.583	321	269	265	13	512	7.3
67-68—San Fran.	67	1992	540	252	.467	216	150	.694	276	390	284	9	654	9.8
68-69—San Fran.	51	1516	359	162	.451	149	95	.638	181	306	183	3	419	8.2
69-70—San Fran.	45	676	202	78	.386	113	75	.664	74	142	103	0	231	5.1
70-71—San Fran.	34	321	54	22	.407	41	24	.585	40	58	59	2	68	2.0
Totals	712	17826	5545	2499	.451	2106	1330	.632	2463	2483	2417	65	6328	8.9

NBA PLAYOFF RECORD

Sea.—Team	G.	Min.	FGA	FGM	Pct.	FTA	FTM	Pct.	Reb.	Ast.	PF	Disq.	Pts.	Avg.
60-61—Philadelphia	3	110	26	12	.462	14	5	.357	12	9	14	0	29	9.7
61-62—Philadelphia	12	338	76	28	.368	31	17	.548	55	27	54	4	73	6.1
63-64—San Fran.	12	386	144	58	.403	56	30	.536	37	30	54	5	146	12.2
66-67—San Fran.	15	237	46	20	.435	16	6	.375	62	38	45	1	46	3.1
67-68—San Fran.	10	277	62	25	.403	30	23	.767	53	70	49	2	73	7.3
68-69—San Fran.	6	109	21	7	.333	4	1	.250	18	21	17	0	15	2.5
70-71—San Fran.	4	47	7	4	.571	7	4	.571	8	11	13	0	12	3.0
Totals	62	1504	382	154	.403	158	86	.544	245	206	246	12	394	6.4

NBA COACHING RECORD

	Regular Season				Playoffs	
Sea. Club	W.	L.	Pct.	Pos.	W.	L.
1969-70—San Francisco	8	22	.267	6†	..	..
1970-71—San Francisco	41	41	.500	2‡	1	4
1971-72—Golden State	51	31	.622	2‡	1	4
1972-73—Golden State	47	35	.573	2‡	5	6
1973-74—Golden State	44	38	.537	2‡	..	..
1974-75—Golden State*	48	34	.585	1‡	12	5
1975-76—Golden State	59	23	.720	1‡	7	6
1976-77—Golden State	46	36	.561	3‡	5	5
1977-78—Golden State	43	39	.524	5‡	..	..
1978-79—Golden State	38	44	.463	6‡	..	..
1979-80—Golden State	18	43	.295	6‡	..	..
1980-81—Golden State	39	43	.476	4‡	..	..
1981-82—Golden State	45	37	.549	4‡	..	..
1982-83—Golden State	30	52	.366	5‡	..	..
Totals (14 seasons)	557	518	.518		31	30

†Western Division. ‡Pacific Division.
*Won NBA championship.

Coach of NBA championship team, 1975.

ARNOLD JACOB AUERBACH
(Red)

Born September 20, 1917 at Brooklyn, N. Y. Height 5:10. Weight 170.
High School—Brooklyn, N. Y., Eastern District.
Colleges—Seth Low Junior College, New York, N. Y., and George Washington University, Washington, D. C.

—COLLEGIATE PLAYING RECORD—

Seth Low JC

Year	G.	Min.	FGA	FGM	Pct.	FTA	FTM	Pct.	Reb.	Pts.	Avg.
Statistics Unavailable											

George Washington

Year	G.	Min.	FGA	FGM	Pct.	FTA	FTM	Pct.	Reb.	Pts.	Avg.
37-38	17	....	...	22	....	12	8	.667	....	52	3.1
38-39	20	....	...	54	....	19	12	.632	....	120	6.0
39-40	19	....	...	69	....	39	24	.727	....	162	8.5
Totals	56	....	...	145	....	64	44	.688	....	334	6.0

COLLEGIATE COACHING RECORD

Assistant, Duke University, 1949-50.

NBA COACHING RECORD

	Regular Season				Playoffs	
Sea. Club	W.	L.	Pct.	Pos.	W.	L.
1946-47—Washington	49	11	.817	1†	2	4
1947-48—Washington	28	20	.583	4†	..	..
1948-49—Washington	38	22	.633	1†	6	5
1949-50—Tri-Cities	28	29	.491	3‡	1	2
1950-51—Boston	39	30	.565	2†	0	2
1951-52—Boston	39	27	.591	2†	1	2
1952-53—Boston	46	25	.568	3†	3	3
1953-54—Boston	42	30	.583	2T†	2	4
1954-55—Boston	36	36	.500	3†	3	4
1955-56—Boston	39	33	.542	2†	1	2
1956-57—Boston	44	28	.611	*1†	7	3
1957-58—Boston	49	23	.681	1†	6	5
1958-59—Boston	52	20	.722	*1†	8	3
1959-60—Boston	59	16	.787	*1†	8	5
1960-61—Boston	57	22	.722	*1†	8	2
1961-62—Boston	60	20	.750	*1†	8	6
1962-63—Boston	58	22	.725	*1†	8	5
1963-64—Boston	59	21	.738	*1†	8	2
1964-65—Boston	62	18	.775	*1†	8	4
1965-66—Boston	54	26	.675	*2†	11	6
Totals (20 seasons)	938	479	.662		99	69

*Won NBA Championship. †Eastern Division. ‡Western Division.

Selected as the "Greatest Coach in the History of the NBA" by the Professional Basketball Writers' Association of America, 1980. . . . Elected to the Naismith Memorial Basketball Hall of Fame, 1968. . . . Named NBA Coach of the Year, 1965. . . . NBA Executive of the Year, 1980. . . . Winningest coach in history of NBA. . . . Coach of NBA championship teams, 1957, 1959, 1960, 1961, 1962, 1963, 1964, 1965, 1966.

LAWRENCE R. COSTELLO

Born July 2, 1931 at Minoa, N. Y. Height 6:01. Weight 188.
High School—Minoa, N. Y.
College—Niagara University, Niagara Falls, N. Y.
Drafted by Philadelphia on second round, 1954.

Sold by Philadelphia to Syracuse, October 10, 1957.
Syracuse franchise moved to Philadelphia, 1963.
Drafted by Milwaukee from Philadelphia in expansion draft, May 6, 1968.
Played in Eastern Basketball League with Wilkes-Barre Barons, 1965-66.

—COLLEGIATE PLAYING RECORD—

Year	G.	Min.	FGA	FGM	Pct.	FTA	FTM	Pct.	Reb.	Pts.	Avg.
50-51†	Statistics Unavailable										
51-52	28	....	...	131	....	87	58	.667	....	320	11.4
52-53	28	....	...	185	....	191	140	.733	....	510	18.2
53-54	29	....	...	160	....	152	125	.822	....	445	15.3
Totals	85	....	...	476	....	430	323	.751	....	1275	15.0

NBA REGULAR SEASON RECORD

Sea.—Team	G.	Min.	FGA	FGM	Pct.	FTA	FTM	Pct.	Reb.	Ast.	PF	Disq.	Pts.	Avg.
54-55—Philadelphia	19	463	139	46	.331	32	26	.813	49	78	37	0	118	6.2
55-56—Philadelphia	Did Not Play—Military Service													
56-57—Philadelphia	72	2111	497	186	.374	222	175	.788	323	236	182	2	547	7.6
57-58—Syracuse	72	2746	888	378	.426	378	320	.847	378	317	246	3	1076	14.9
58-59—Syracuse	70	2750	948	414	.437	349	280	.802	365	379	263	7	1108	15.8
59-60—Syracuse	71	2469	822	372	.453	289	249	.862	388	449	234	4	993	14.0
60-61—Syracuse	75	2167	844	407	.482	338	270	.799	292	413	286	9	1084	14.5
61-62—Syracuse	63	1854	726	310	.427	295	247	.837	245	359	220	5	867	13.7
62-63—Syracuse	78	2066	660	285	.432	327	288	.881	237	334	263	4	858	11.0
63-64—Philadelphia	45	1137	408	191	.476	170	147	.865	105	167	150	3	529	11.8
64-65—Philadelphia	64	1967	695	309	.445	277	243	.877	169	275	242	10	861	13.5
66-67—Philadelphia	49	976	293	130	.444	133	120	.902	103	140	141	2	380	7.8
67-68—Philadelphia	28	492	148	67	.453	81	67	.827	51	68	62	0	201	7.2
Totals	706	21198	7068	3095	.438	2891	2432	.841	2705	3215	2326	49	8622	12.2

NBA PLAYOFF RECORD

Sea.—Team	G.	Min.	FGA	FGM	Pct.	FTA	FTM	Pct.	Reb.	Ast.	PF	Disq.	Pts.	Avg.
56-57—Philadelphia	2	16	8	3	.375	1	0	.000	5	2	3	0	6	3.0
57-58—Syracuse	3	134	34	10	.294	14	14	1.000	25	12	6	0	34	11.3
58-59—Syracuse	9	361	121	54	.446	61	51	.836	53	54	40	2	159	17.7
59-60—Syracuse	3	122	47	20	.425	12	10	.833	14	20	15	1	50	16.7
60-61—Syracuse	8	269	103	42	.408	55	47	.854	35	52	39	3	131	16.4
61-62—Syracuse	5	167	51	22	.431	33	29	.879	16	28	21	0	73	14.6
62-63—Syracuse	5	134	37	16	.432	23	19	.826	4	23	27	2	51	10.2

Sea.—Team	G.	Min.	FGA	FGM	Pct.	FTA	FTM	Pct.	Reb.	Ast.	PF	Disq.	Pts.	Avg.
63-64—Philadelphia	5	36	14	3	.214	10	10	1.000	3	4	14	1	16	3.2
64-65—Philadelphia	10	207	53	22	.415	16	11	.688	12	20	43	2	55	5.5
66-67—Philadelphia	2	25	8	6	.750	5	5	1.000	4	3	2	0	17	8.5
Totals	52	1471	476	198	.416	230	196	.852	171	218	210	11	592	11.4

NBA ALL-STAR GAME RECORD

Season—Team	Min.	FGA	FGM	Pct.	FTA	FTM	Pct.	Reb.	Ast.	PF	Disq.	Pts.
1958—Syracuse	17	6	0	.000	1	1	1.000	1	4	2	0	1
1959—Syracuse	18	8	3	.375	1	1	1.000	3	3	1	0	7
1960—Syracuse	20	9	5	.556	0	0	.000	4	2	1	0	10
1961—Syracuse	5	2	1	.500	0	0	.000	0	0	2	0	2
1962—Syracuse	Selected—Injured, Did Not Play											
1965—Philadelphia	11	7	2	.286	0	0	.000	1	2	2	0	4
Totals	71	32	11	.344	2	2	1.000	9	11	8	0	24

EBL REGULAR SEASON RECORD

			—2-Point—			—3-Point—									
Sea.—Team	G.	Min.	FGM	FGA	Pct.	FGM	FGA	Pct.	FTM	FTA	Pct.	Reb.	Ast.	Pts.	Avg.
65-66—Wilkes-Barre	12	....	54	...	....	2	...	....	53	59	.898	22	83	167	13.9

NBA COACHING RECORD

	Regular Season				Playoffs	
Sea. Club	W.	L.	Pct.	Pos.	W.	L.
1968-69—Milwaukee	27	55	.329	7†	..	..
1969-70—Milwaukee	56	26	.683	2†	5	5
1970-71—Milwaukee	66	16	.805	*1†	12	2
1971-72—Milwaukee	63	19	.768	1‡	6	5
1972-73—Milwaukee	60	22	.732	1‡	2	4
1973-74—Milwaukee	59	23	.720	1‡	11	5
1974-75—Milwaukee	38	44	.463	4‡	..	..
1975-76—Milwaukee	38	44	.463	1‡	1	2
1976-77—Milwaukee	3	15	.167	6‡	..	..
1978-79—Chicago	20	36	.357	3‡	..	..
Totals (10 seasons)	430	300	.589		37	23

*Won NBA championship. †Eastern Division. ‡Midwest Division.

COLLEGIATE COACHING RECORD

	Regular Season			
Sea. Club	W.	L.	Pct.	Pos.
1980-81—Utica	13	12	.520	..
1981-82—Utica	4	22	.154	..
1982-83—Utica	11	15	.423	..
1983-84—Utica	11	15	.423	..
1984-85—Utica	15	12	.556	..
1985-86—Utica	13	14	.481	..
1986-87—Utica	10	16	.385	..
Totals (7 seasons)	77	106	.421	

NOTE: Costello coached the Milwaukee Does of the Women's Professional Basketball League during 1979-80 season. He also coached at Minoa, N. Y., High School during 1965-66 season.

Named to All-NBA Second Team, 1961.... Led NBA in free-throw percentage, 1963 and 1965.... Member of NBA championship team, 1967.... Coach of NBA championship team, 1971.

WILLIAM JOHN CUNNINGHAM
(Billy)

Born June 3, 1943 at Brooklyn, N. Y. Height 6:07. Weight 210.

High School—Brooklyn, N. Y., Erasmus.

College—University of North Carolina, Chapel Hill, N. C.

Drafted by Philadelphia on first round, 1965.

Signed by Carolina ABA as a free agent, August, 1969.
Returned to Philadelphia, 1974.

—COLLEGIATE PLAYING RECORD—

Year	G.	Min.	FGA	FGM	Pct.	FTA	FTM	Pct.	Reb.	Pts.	Avg.
61-62†	10	....	162	81	.500	78	45	.577	127	207	20.7
62-63	21	....	380	186	.489	170	105	.618	339	477	22.7
63-64	24	....	526	233	.443	249	157	.631	379	623	26.0
64-65	24	....	481	237	.493	213	135	.634	344	609	25.4
Varsity Totals	69	....	1387	656	.473	632	397	.628	1062	1709	24.8

NBA REGULAR SEASON RECORD

									—Rebounds—									
Sea.—Team	G.	Min.	FGA	FGM	Pct.	FTA	FTM	Pct.	Off.	Def.	Tot.	Ast.	PF	Dq.	Stl.	Blk.	Pts.	Avg.
65-66—Philadelphia	80	2134	1011	431	.426	443	281	.634			599	207	301	12			1143	14.3
66-67—Philadelphia	81	2168	1211	556	.459	558	383	.686			589	205	260	2			1495	18.5
67-68—Philadelphia	74	2076	1178	516	.438	509	368	.723			562	187	260	3			1400	18.9
68-69—Philadelphia	82	3345	1736	739	.426	754	556	.737			1050	287	329	10			2034	24.8

Sea.—Team	G.	Min.	FGA	FGM	Pct.	FTA	FTM	Pct.	—Rebounds— Off.	Def.	Tot.	Ast.	PF	Dq.	Stl.	Blk.	Pts.	Avg.
69-70—Philadelphia	81	3194	1710	802	.469	700	510	.729			1101	352	331	15			2114	26.1
70-71—Philadelphia	81	3090	1519	702	.462	620	455	.734			946	395	328	5			1859	23.0
71-72—Philadelphia	75	2900	1428	658	.461	601	428	.712			918	443	295	12			1744	23.3
74-75—Philadelphia	80	2859	1423	609	.428	444	345	.777	130	596	726	442	270	4	91	35	1563	19.5
75-76—Philadelphia	20	640	251	103	.410	88	68	.773	29	118	147	107	57	1	24	10	274	13.7
Totals	654	22406	11467	5116	446	4717	3394	.720			6638	2625	2431	64	115	45	13626	20.8

NBA PLAYOFF RECORD

Sea.—Team	G.	Min.	FGA	FGM	Pct.	FTA	FTM	Pct.	—Rebounds— Off.	Def.	Tot.	Ast.	PF	Dq.	Stl.	Blk.	Pts.	Avg.
65-66—Philadelphia	4	69	31	5	.161	13	11	.846			18	10	11	0			21	5.3
66-67—Philadelphia	15	339	221	83	.376	90	59	.656			93	33	53	1			225	15.0
67-68—Philadelphia	3	86	43	24	.558	17	14	.824			22	10	16	1			62	20.7
68-69—Philadelphia	5	217	117	49	.419	38	24	.632			63	12	24	1			122	24.4
69-70—Philadelphia	5	205	123	61	.496	36	24	.667			52	20	19	0			146	29.2
70-71—Philadelphia	7	301	142	67	.472	67	47	.701			108	40	28	0			181	25.9
Totals	39	1217	677	289	.427	261	179	.686			356	125	151	3			757	19.4

NBA ALL-STAR GAME RECORD

Season—Team	Min.	FGA	FGM	Pct.	FTA	FTM	Pct.	—Rebounds— Off.	Def.	Tot.	Ast.	PF	Dq.	Stl.	Blk.	Pts.
1969—Philadelphia	22	10	5	.500	0	0	.000			5	1	3	0			10
1970—Philadelphia	28	13	7	.538	5	5	1.000			4	2	3	0			19
1971—Philadelphia	19	8	2	.250	2	1	.500			4	3	1	0			5
1972—Philadelphia	24	13	4	.308	8	6	.750	—	—	10	3	4	0	—	—	14
Totals	93	44	18	.409	15	12	.800			23	9	11	0			48

ABA REGULAR SEASON RECORD

Sea.—Team	G.	Min.	—2-Point— FGM	FGA	Pct.	—3-Point— FGM	FGA	Pct.	FTM	FTA	Pct.	Reb.	Ast.	Pts.	Avg.
72-73—Carolina	84	3248	757	1534	.493	14	49	.286	472	598	.789	1012	530	2028	24.1
73-74—Carolina	32	1190	252	529	.476	1	8	.125	149	187	.797	331	150	656	20.5
Totals	116	4438	1009	2063	.489	15	57	.263	621	785	.791	1343	680	2684	23.1

ABA PLAYOFF RECORD

Sea.—Team	G.	Min.	—2-Point— FGM	FGA	Pct.	—3-Point— FGM	FGA	Pct.	FTM	FTA	Pct.	Reb.	Ast.	Pts.	Avg.
72-73—Carolina	12	472	111	219	.507	1	4	.250	57	83	.687	142	61	282	23.5
73-74—Carolina	3	61	9	29	.310	0	2	.000	4	5	.800	16	6	22	7.3
Totals	15	533	120	248	.484	1	6	.167	61	88	.693	158	67	304	20.3

ABA ALL-STAR GAME RECORD

Sea.—Team	Min.	—2-Point— FGM	FGA	Pct.	—3-Point— FGM	FGA	Pct.	FTM	FTA	Pct.	Reb.	Ast.	Pts.	Avg.
1973—Carolina	20	9	11	.818	0	1	.000	0	0	.000	6	4	18	18.0

NBA COACHING RECORD

Sea. Club	Regular Season W.	L.	Pct.	Pos.	Playoffs W.	L.
1977-78—Philadelphia	53	23	.697	1†	6	4
1978-79—Philadelphia	47	35	.573	2†	5	4
1979-80—Philadelphia	59	23	.720	2†	12	6
1980-81—Philadelphia	62	20	.756	1T†	9	7
1981-82—Philadelphia	58	24	.707	2†	12	9
1982-83—Philadelphia*	65	17	.793	1†	12	1
1983-84—Philadelphia	52	30	.634	2†	2	3
1984-85—Philadelphia	58	24	.707	2†	8	5
Totals (8 seasons)	454	196	.698		66	39

*Won NBA championship. †Atlantic Division.

Elected to Naismith Memorial Basketball Hall of Fame, 1985. . . . Named to All-NBA First Team, 1969, 1970, 1971. . . . All-NBA Second Team, 1972. . . . NBA All-Rookie Team, 1966. . . . Member of NBA championship team, 1967. . . . Coach of NBA championship team, 1983. . . . ABA Most Valuable Player, 1973. . . . ABA All-Star First Team, 1973. . . . Led ABA in steals, 1973. . . . Named to THE SPORTING NEWS All-America Second Team, 1965.

ALEXANDER MURRAY HANNUM
(Alex)

Born July 19, 1923 at Los Angeles, Calif. Height 6:07. Weight 225.
High School—Los Angeles, Calif., Hamilton.
College—University of Southern California, Los Angeles, Calif.
Signed by Oshkosh NBL, 1948.

Sold by Oshkosh NBA to Syracuse NBA, 1949.
Traded with Fred Scolari by Syracuse to Baltimore for Red Rocha, 1951.
Sold by Baltimore to Rochester during 1951-52 season.
Sold by Rochester to Milwaukee, 1954.

Milwaukee franchise moved to St. Louis, 1955.
Released by St. Louis, signed by Ft. Wayne, 1956.
Released by Ft. Wayne, December 12, 1956; signed by St. Louis, December 17, 1956.
Played for Los Angeles Shamrocks, an Amateur Athletic Union team, during 1945-46 season (averaged 9.8 points per game).

—COLLEGIATE PLAYING RECORD—

Year	G.	Min.	FGA	FGM	Pct.	FTA	FTM	Pct.	Reb.	Pts.	Avg.
41-42†	Statistics Unavailable										
42-43	15	....	....	23	....	20	9	.450	....	55	3.7
43-44-45-46	In Military Service.										
46-47	24	....	....	....	....	....	....	....	....	251	10.5
47-48	23	....	...	108	....	...	...	....	....	263	11.4
Varsity Totals	62	....	....	....	...	...	....	....	....	569	9.2

NBA REGULAR SEASON RECORD

Sea.—Team	G.	Min.	FGA	FGM	Pct.	FTA	FTM	Pct.	Reb.	Ast.	PF	Disq.	Pts.	Avg.
48-49—Oshkosh NBL	62	....	....	126	...	191	113	.592	...	...	188	...	365	5.9
49-50—Syracuse	64	....	488	177	.363	186	128	.688	...	129	264	...	482	7.5
50-51—Syracuse	63	....	494	182	.368	197	107	.543	301	119	271	...	471	7.5
51-52—Balt.-Roch.	66	....	462	170	.368	138	98	.710	336	133	271	...	438	6.6
52-53—Rochester	68	....	360	129	.358	133	88	.662	279	81	258	...	346	5.1
53-54—Rochester	72	....	503	175	.348	164	102	.622	350	105	279	...	452	6.3
54-55—Milwaukee	53	....	358	126	.352	107	61	.570	245	105	206	...	313	5.9
55-56—St. Louis	71	....	453	146	.322	154	93	.604	344	157	271	...	385	5.4
56-57—Ft. W.-St. Louis	59	....	223	77	.345	56	37	.661	158	28	135	...	191	3.2
Totals	578	....	....	1308	....	1326	827	.624	...	...	2143	...	3443	6.0

NBA PLAYOFF RECORD

Sea.—Team	G.	Min.	FGA	FGM	Pct.	FTA	FTM	Pct.	Reb.	Ast.	PF	Disq.	Pts.	Avg.
49-50—Syracuse	11	....	86	38	.442	34	17	.500	....	10	50	....	93	8.5
50-51—Syracuse	7	....	39	17	.436	10	8	.800	47	17	37	3	42	6.0
51-52—Rochester	6	146	42	16	.381	13	8	.615	26	8	30	3	40	6.7
52-53—Rochester	3	52	10	4	.400	8	3	.375	4	2	16	1	11	3.7
53-54—Rochester	6	107	29	12	.414	24	15	.625	22	5	28	3	39	6.5
55-56—St. Louis	8	159	66	21	.318	35	19	.543	29	10	36	3	61	7.6
56-57—St. Louis	2	6	2	0	.000	0	0	.000	0	0	2	0	0	0.0
Totals	43	....	274	108	.394	124	70	.565	....	52	199	....	286	6.7

NBA COACHING RECORD

Sea. Club	Regular Season W.	L.	Pct.	Pos.	Playoffs W.	L.
1956-57—St. Louis	15	16	.484	1T†	6	4
1957-58—St. Louis	41	31	.569	*1†	8	3
1960-61—Syracuse	38	41	.481	3‡	4	4
1961-62—Syracuse	41	39	.513	3‡	2	3
1962-63—Syracuse	48	32	.600	2‡	2	3
1963-64—San Francisco	48	32	.600	1†	5	7
1964-65—San Francisco	17	63	.213	5†	..	..
1965-66—San Francisco	35	45	.438	4†	..	..
1966-67—Philadelphia	68	13	.840	*1‡	11	4
1967-68—Philadelphia	62	20	.756	1‡	7	6
1969-70—San Diego	18	38	.321	7†	..	..
1970-71—San Diego	40	42	.488	3§	..	..
Totals (12 Seasons)	471	412	.533		45	34

*Won NBA Championship.

ABA COACHING RECORD

Sea. Club	Regular Season W.	L.	Pct.	Pos.	Playoffs W.	L.
1968-69—Oakland*	60	18	.769	1†	12	4
1971-72—Denver	34	50	.405	4†	3	4
1972-73—Denver	47	37	.560	3†	1	4
1973-74—Denver	37	47	.440	4T†	0	0
Totals (4 seasons)	178	152	.539		16	12

*Won ABA Championship.
†Western Division. ‡Eastern Division. §Pacific Division.

NBA Coach of the Year, 1964. . . . Coach of NBA championship teams, 1958 and 1967. . . . ABA Coach of the Year, 1969. . . . Coach of ABA championship team, 1969.

THOMAS W. HEINSOHN
(Tom)

Born August 26, 1934 at Jersey City, N. J. Height 6:07. Weight 218.
High School—Union City, N. J., St. Michael's.
College—Holy Cross College, Worcester, Mass.
Drafted by Boston on first round (territorial choice), 1956.

—COLLEGIATE RECORD—

Year	G.	Min.	FGA	FGM	Pct.	FTA	FTM	Pct.	Reb.	Pts.	Avg.
52-53†	15	....	...	97	....	...	70	....	....	264	17.6

Year	G.	Min.	FGA	FGM	Pct.	FTA	FTM	Pct.	Reb.	Pts.	Avg.
53-54	28	....	364	175	.481	142	94	.662	300	444	15.9
54-55	26	....	499	232	.465	215	141	.656	385	605	23.3
55-56	27	....	630	254	.403	304	232	.763	569	740	27.4
Varsity Totals	81	....	1493	661	.443	661	467	.707	1254	1789	22.1

NBA REGULAR SEASON RECORD

Sea.—Team	G.	Min.	FGA	FGM	Pct.	FTA	FTM	Pct.	Reb.	Ast.	PF	Disq.	Pts.	Avg.
56-57—Boston	72	2150	1123	446	.397	343	271	.790	705	117	304	12	1163	16.2
57-58—Boston	69	2206	1226	468	.382	394	294	.746	705	125	274	6	1230	17.8
58-59—Boston	66	2089	1192	465	.390	391	312	.798	638	164	271	11	1242	18.8
59-60—Boston	75	2420	1590	673	.423	386	283	.734	794	171	275	8	1629	21.7
60-61—Boston	74	2256	1566	627	.400	424	325	.767	732	141	260	7	1579	21.3
61-62—Boston	79	2383	1613	692	.429	437	358	.819	747	165	280	2	1742	22.1
62-63—Boston	76	2004	1300	550	.423	407	340	.835	569	95	270	4	1440	18.9
63-64—Boston	76	2040	1223	487	.398	342	283	.827	460	183	268	3	1257	16.5
64-65—Boston	67	1706	954	365	.383	229	182	.795	399	157	252	5	912	13.6
Totals	654	19254	11787	4773	.405	3353	2648	.790	5749	1318	2454	58	12194	18.6

NBA PLAYOFF RECORD

Sea.—Team	G.	Min.	FGA	FGM	Pct.	FTA	FTM	Pct.	Reb.	Ast.	PF	Disq.	Pts.	Avg.
56-57—Boston	10	370	231	90	.390	69	49	.710	117	20	40	1	229	22.9
57-58—Boston	11	349	194	68	.351	72	56	.778	119	18	52	3	192	17.5
58-59—Boston	11	348	220	91	.414	56	37	.661	98	32	41	0	219	19.9
59-60—Boston	13	423	267	112	.419	80	60	.750	126	27	53	2	284	21.8
60-61—Boston	10	291	201	82	.408	43	33	.767	99	20	36	1	197	19.7
61-62—Boston	14	445	291	116	.399	76	58	.763	115	34	58	4	290	20.7
62-63—Boston	13	413	270	123	.456	98	75	.765	116	15	55	2	321	24.7
63-64—Boston	10	308	180	70	.412	42	34	.810	80	26	36	0	174	17.4
64-65—Boston	12	276	181	66	.365	32	20	.625	84	23	46	1	152	12.7
Totals	104	3223	2035	818	.402	568	422	.743	954	215	417	14	2058	19.8

NBA ALL-STAR GAME RECORD

Season—Team	Min.	FGA	FGM	Pct.	FTA	FTM	Pct.	Reb.	Ast.	PF	Disq.	Pts.
1957—Boston	23	17	5	.294	2	2	1.000	7	0	3	0	12
1961—Boston	19	16	2	.125	0	0	.000	6	1	4	0	4
1962—Boston	13	11	4	.364	2	2	1.000	2	1	4	0	10
1963—Boston	21	11	6	.545	4	3	.750	2	1	4	0	15
1964—Boston	21	12	5	.417	0	0	.000	3	0	5	0	10
1965—Boston				Selected—Injured, Did Not Play								
Totals	97	67	22	.328	8	7	.875	20	3	20	0	51

NBA COACHING RECORD

	Regular Season				Playoffs	
Sea. Club	W.	L.	Pct.	Pos.	W.	L.
1969-70—Boston	34	48	.415	6†	..	..
1970-71—Boston	44	38	.537	3‡	..	..
1971-72—Boston	56	26	.683	1‡	5	6
1972-73—Boston	68	14	.829	1‡	7	6
1973-74—Boston	56	26	.683	*1‡	12	6
1974-75—Boston	60	22	.732	1‡	6	5
1975-76—Boston	54	28	.659	*1‡	12	6
1976-77—Boston	44	38	.537	2‡	5	4
1977-78—Boston	11	23	.324	3‡	..	..
Totals (9 seasons)	427	263	.619		47	33

*Won NBA Championship. †Eastern Division. ‡Atlantic Division.

Elected to Naismith Memorial Basketball Hall of Fame, 1985. . . . Named to All-NBA Second Team, 1961, 1962, 1963, 1964. . . . NBA Rookie of the Year, 1957. . . . Member of NBA championship teams, 1957, 1959, 1960, 1961, 1962, 1963, 1964, 1965. . . . NBA Coach of the Year, 1973. . . . Coach of NBA championship teams, 1974 and 1976.

WILLIAM HOLZMAN
(Red)

Born August 10, 1920 at Brooklyn, N. Y. Height 5:10. Weight 175.

High School—Brooklyn, N. Y., Franklin Lane.

Colleges—University of Baltimore, Baltimore, Md., and City College of New York, New York, N. Y.

Signed by Rochester NBL, 1945.

Acquired by Milwaukee NBA from Rochester NBA, 1953.
Played in American Basketball League with New York 1945-46.

—COLLEGIATE PLAYING RECORD—

Baltimore

Year	G.	Min.	FGA	FGM	Pct.	FTA	FTM	Pct.	Reb.	Pts.	Avg.
38-39						Statistics Unavailable					

CCNY

Year	G.	Min.	FGA	FGM	Pct.	FTA	FTM	Pct.	Reb.	Pts.	Avg.
39-40	Did Not Play—Transfer Student										
40-41	21	....	...	96	....	...	37	....	....	229	10.9
41-42	18	....	...	87	....	...	51	....	....	225	12.5
Varsity Totals	39	....	...	183	....	...	88	....	...	454	11.6

NOTE: In Military Service during 1942-43, 1943-44 and 1944-45 seasons. Played at Norfolk, Va., Naval Training Station and scored 305 points in 1942-43 and 258 points in 1943-44.

NBL AND NBA REGULAR SEASON RECORD

Sea.—Team	G.	Min.	FGA	FGM	Pct.	FTA	FTM	Pct.	Reb.	Ast.	PF	Disq.	Pts.	Avg.
45-46—Roch. NBL	34	....	....	144	....	115	77	.669	....	....	54	....	365	10.7
46-47—Roch. NBL	44	....	....	227	....	139	74	.532	....	....	68	....	528	12.0
47-48—Roch. NBL	60	....	....	246	....	182	117	.643	....	....	58	....	609	10.2
48-49—Rochester	60	....	691	225	.326	157	96	.611	....	149	93	....	546	9.1
49-50—Rochester	68	....	625	206	.330	210	144	.686	....	200	67	....	556	8.2
50-51—Rochester	68	....	561	183	.326	179	130	.726	152	147	94	0	496	7.3
51-52—Rochester	65	1065	372	104	.280	85	61	.718	106	115	95	1	269	4.1
52-53—Rochester	46	392	149	38	.255	38	27	.711	40	35	56	2	103	2.2
53-54—Milwaukee	51	649	224	74	.330	73	48	.658	46	75	73	1	196	3.8
Totals	496	....	....	1447	....	1178	774	.666	....	....	658	....	3668	7.4

NBL AND NBA PLAYOFF RECORD

Sea.—Team	G.	Min.	FGA	FGM	Pct.	FTA	FTM	Pct.	Reb.	Ast.	PF	Disq.	Pts.	Avg.
45-46—Roch. NBL	7	....	....	30	....	31	21	.677	....	....	10	....	81	11.6
46-47—Roch. NBL	11	....	....	42	....	29	22	.759	....	....	22	....	106	9.6
47-48—Roch. NBL	10	....	....	35	....	15	10	.667	....	....	6	....	80	8.0
48-49—Rochester	4	....	40	18	.450	6	5	.833	....	13	3	....	41	10.3
49-50—Rochester	2	....	9	3	.333	2	1	.500	....	0	3	....	7	3.5
50-51—Rochester	14	....	76	31	.408	34	23	.676	19	20	14	....	85	6.1
51-52—Rochester	6	65	15	3	.200	6	1	.167	6	2	3	0	7	1.2
52-53—Rochester	2	14	5	1	.200	4	1	.250	1	1	4	0	3	1.5
Totals	56	....	....	163	....	127	84	.661	....	....	65	....	410	7.3

NBA COACHING RECORD

	Regular Season				Playoffs	
Sea. Club	W.	L.	Pct.	Pos.	W.	L.
1953-54—Milwaukee	10	16	.385	4†	..	..
1954-55—Milwaukee	26	46	.361	4†	..	..
1955-56—St. Louis	33	39	.458	2T†	4	4
1956-57—St. Louis	14	19	.424	1†	..	..
1967-68—New York	28	17	.622	3‡	2	4
1968-69—New York	54	28	.659	3‡	6	4
1969-70—New York*	60	22	.732	1‡	12	7
1970-71—New York	52	30	.634	1§	7	5
1971-72—New York	48	34	.667	2§	9	7
1972-73—New York*	57	25	.695	2§	12	5
1973-74—New York	49	33	.598	2§	5	7
1974-75—New York	40	42	.488	3§	1	2
1975-76—New York	38	44	.463	4§	..	..
1976-77—New York	40	42	.488	3§	..	..
1978-79—New York	25	43	.368	4§	..	..
1979-80—New York	39	43	.476	3T§	..	..
1980-81—New York	50	32	.610	3§	0	2
1981-82—New York	33	49	.402	5§	..	..
Totals (18 seasons)	696	604	.535		58	47

*Won NBA championship.
†Western Division. ‡Eastern Division. §Atlantic Division.

Elected to Naismith Memorial Basketball Hall of Fame, 1985. . . . NBA Coach of the Year, 1970. . . . Coach of NBA championship teams, 1970 and 1973. . . . Member of NBL championship team, 1946. . . . Member of NBA championship team, 1951. . . . Named to NBL All-Star First Team, 1946 and 1948. . . . NBL All-Star Second Team, 1947.

JOHN KUNDLA

Born July 3, 1916 at Star Junction, Pa. Height 6:02. Weight 180.
High School—Minneapolis, Minn., Central.
College—University of Minnesota, Minneapolis, Minn.

—COLLEGIATE PLAYING RECORD—

Year	G.	Min.	FGA	FGM	Pct.	FTA	FTM	Pct.	Reb.	Pts.	Avg.
35-36†	Statistics unavailable										
36-37	15	....	...	53	....	53	34	.641	....	140	9.3
37-38	20	....	...	62	....	77	41	.532	....	165	8.3
38-39	17	....	...	71	....	63	40	.635	....	182	10.7
Varsity Totals	52	....	...	186	....	193	115	.596	....	487	9.4

NBA COACHING RECORD

	Regular Season				Playoffs	
Sea. Club	W.	L.	Pct.	Pos.	W.	L.
1948-49—Minneapolis	44	16	.733	*2†	8	2
1949-50—Minneapolis	51	17	.750	*1T†	10	2
1950-51—Minneapolis	44	24	.647	1†	3	4
1951-52—Minneapolis	40	26	.606	*2†	9	4
1952-53—Minneapolis	48	22	.686	*1†	9	3
1953-54—Minneapolis	46	26	.639	*1†	9	4
1954-55—Minneapolis	40	32	.556	2†	3	4
1955-56—Minneapolis	33	39	.458	2T†	1	2
1956-57—Minneapolis	34	38	.472	1T†	2	3
1957-58—Minneapolis	10	23	.303	4†	..	..
1958-59—Minneapolis	33	39	.458	2†	6	7
Totals (11 seasons)	423	302	.583		60	35

*Won NBA Championship. †Western Division.

COLLEGIATE COACHING RECORD

	Regular Season			
Sea. Club	W.	L.	Pct.	Pos.
1946-47—St. Thomas	11	11	.500	....
1959-60—Minnesota	12	12	.500	3T
1960-61—Minnesota	10	13	.435	4T
1961-62—Minnesota	10	14	.417	7
1962-63—Minnesota	12	12	.500	4T
1963-64—Minnesota	17	7	.708	3
1964-65—Minnesota	19	5	.792	2
1965-66—Minnesota	14	10	.583	5T
1966-67—Minnesota	9	15	.375	9
1967-68—Minnesota	7	17	.292	9T
Totals (10 seasons)	121	116	.511	

NBL COACHING RECORD

	Regular Season				Playoffs	
Sea. Club	W.	L.	Pct.	Pos.	W.	L.
1947-48—Minneapolis	43	17	.717	1†	8	2

†Western Division.

Coach of NBA championship teams, 1950, 1952, 1953, 1954.

JOSEPH BOHOMIEL LAPCHICK
(Joe)

Born April 12, 1900 at Yonkers, N. Y. Height 6:05½. Weight 185.

Died August 10, 1970.

Did not play high school or college basketball.

Played with independent teams, including the Original Celtics, in 1917-18 through 1919-20; 1923-24 through 1925-26 and 1931-32 through 1935-36 seasons.

PRO RECORD

Year Team	League	G	FG	FT	Pts.	Avg.
1920-21—Holyoke	IL	11	14	40	68	6.2
1921-22—Schenectady-Troy	NYSL	32	12	95	119	3.7
1921-22—Brooklyn	MBL	10	6	20	32	3.2
1922-23—Brooklyn	MBL	33	34	109	177	5.4
1922-23—Troy	NYSL	24	13	59	85	3.5
1926-27—New York	NBL	..	..	..	..	7.3
1926-27—Brooklyn	ABL	32	35	131	201	6.3
1927-28—New York	ABL	47	103	110	316	6.7
1928-29—Cleveland	ABL	39	51	86	188	4.8
1929-30—Cleveland	ABL	52	47	92	186	3.6
1930-31—Cleveland-Toledo	ABL	30	22	49	93	3.1
ABL Pro Totals		200	258	468	984	4.9

COLLEGIATE COACHING RECORD

	Regular Season			
Sea. Club	W.	L.	Pct.	Pos.
1936-37—St. John's	12	7	.632	....
1937-38—St. John's	15	4	.789	....
1938-39—St. John's	18	4	.818	....
1939-40—St. John's	15	5	.750	....
1940-41—St. John's	11	6	.647	....
1941-42—St. John's	16	5	.762	....
1942-43—St. John's	21	3	.875	....
1943-44—St. John's	18	5	.783	....
1944-45—St. John's	21	3	.875	....
1945-46—St. John's	17	6	.739	....
1946-47—St. John's	16	7	.696	....
1956-57—St. John's	14	9	.609	....
1957-58—St. John's	18	8	.692	....
1958-59—St. John's	20	6	.769	....
1959-60—St. John's	17	8	.680	....
1960-61—St. John's	20	5	.800	....
1961-62—St. John's	21	5	.808	....
1962-63—St. John's	9	15	.375	....
1963-64—St. John's	14	11	.560	....
1964-65—St. John's	21	8	.724	....
Totals (20 seasons)	334	130	.720	

NBA COACHING RECORD

	Regular Season				Playoffs	
Sea. Club	W.	L.	Pct.	Pos.	W.	L.
1947-48—New York	26	22	.542	2†	1	2
1948-49—New York	32	28	.533	2†	3	3
1949-50—New York	40	28	.588	2†	3	2
1950-51—New York	36	30	.545	3†	8	6
1951-52—New York	37	29	.561	3†	8	6
1952-53—New York	47	23	.671	1†	6	5
1953-54—New York	44	28	.611	1†	0	4
1954-55—New York	38	34	.528	2†	1	2
1955-56—New York	26	25	.510		....	....
Totals (9 seasons)	326	247	.569		30	30

†Eastern Division

Elected to Naismith Memorial Basketball Hall of Fame, 1966.

—DID YOU KNOW—

That when the Sacramento Kings selected four players in the first round of the 1990 NBA draft, they became the first team in history to have four No. 1 draft picks in the same year?

JOHN MATTHEW MacLEOD

Born October 3, 1937 at New Albany, Ind. Height 6:00. Weight 170.
High School—Clarksville, Ind., New Providence.
College—Bellarmine College, Louisville, Ky.

—COLLEGIATE PLAYING RECORD—

Year	G.	Min.	FGA	FGM	Pct.	FTA	FTM	Pct.	Reb.	Pts.	Avg.
55-56					Statistics Unavailable						
56-57	10	....	...	0	....	...	1	....	....	1	0.1
57-58	8	....	...	2	....	10	3	.300	....	7	0.8
58-59	5	....	...	2	....	....	4	....	....	8	1.6

COLLEGIATE COACHING RECORD

	Regular Season			
Sea. Club	W.	L.	Pct.	Pos.
1967-68—Oklahoma	13	13	.500	3T§
1968-69—Oklahoma	7	19	.269	8§
1969-70—Oklahoma	9	19	.321	3§
1970-71—Oklahoma	19	8	.704	2§
1971-72—Oklahoma	14	12	.538	3§
1972-73—Oklahoma	18	8	.692	4§
Totals (6 seasons)	80	79	.503	

Assistant coach at Oklahoma, 1966-67. §Big Eight Conference.

NBA COACHING RECORD

	Regular Season				Playoffs	
Sea. Club	W.	L.	Pct.	Pos.	W.	L.
1973-74—Phoenix	30	52	.366	4†	..	..
1974-75—Phoenix	32	50	.390	4†	..	..
1975-76—Phoenix	42	40	.512	3†	10	9
1976-77—Phoenix	34	48	.415	5†	..	..
1977-78—Phoenix	49	33	.598	2†	0	2
1978-79—Phoenix	50	32	.610	2†	9	6
1979-80—Phoenix	55	27	.671	3†	3	5
1980-81—Phoenix	57	25	.695	1†	3	4
1981-82—Phoenix	46	36	.561	3†	2	5
1982-83—Phoenix	53	29	.646	2†	1	2
1983-84—Phoenix	41	41	.500	4†	9	8
1984-85—Phoenix	36	46	.439	3†	0	3
1985-86—Phoenix	32	50	.390	3T†	..	..
1986-87—Phoenix	22	34	.393	...†	..	..
1987-88—Dallas	53	29	.646	2‡	10	7
1988-89—Dallas	38	44	.463	4‡	..	..
1989-90—Dallas	5	6	.455	..‡	..	..
Totals (17 seasons)	675	622	.520		47	51

†Pacific Division. ‡Midwest Division.

JOHN T. RAMSAY (Jack)

Born February 21, 1925 at Philadelphia, Pa. Height 6:01. Weight 180.
High School—Upper Darby, Pa.
Colleges—St. Joseph's University, Philadelphia, Pa., and Villanova University, Villanova, Pa.

Played with San Diego Dons, an Amateur Athletic Union team, during 1945-46 season. Played in Eastern Basketball League with Harrisburg and Sunbury, 1949 through 1955.

—COLLEGIATE PLAYING RECORD—

St. Joseph's

Year	G.	Min.	FGA	FGM	Pct.	FTA	FTM	Pct.	Reb.	Pts.	Avg.
42-43					Statistics Unavailable						
46-47	21	....	214	72	.336	32	20	.625	....	164	7.8
47-48	14	....	....	60	....	...	38	....	....	158	11.3
48-49	23	....	...	75	....	...	52	....	....	202	8.8

NOTE: In military service (Navy) during 1943-44, 1944-45 and 1945-46 seasons.

COLLEGIATE COACHING RECORD

	Regular Season			
Sea. Club	W.	L.	Pct.	Pos.
1955-56—St. Joseph's	23	6	.793	..
1956-57—St. Joseph's	17	7	.708	..
1957-58—St. Joseph's	18	9	.667	..
1958-59—St. Joseph's	22	5	.815	..
1959-60—St. Joseph's	20	7	.741	1
1960-61—St. Joseph's	25	5	.833	1
1961-62—St. Joseph's	18	10	.643	1
1962-63—St. Joseph's	23	5	.821	2
1963-64—St. Joseph's	18	10	.643	2
1964-65—St. Joseph's	26	3	.897	1
1965-66—St. Joseph's	24	5	.828	1
Totals (11 seasons)	234	72	.765	

NBA COACHING RECORD

Sea.	Club	Regular Season W.	L.	Pct.	Pos.	Playoffs W.	L.
1968-69	Philadelphia	55	27	.671	2†	1	4
1969-70	Philadelphia	42	40	.512	4†	1	4
1970-71	Philadelphia	47	35	.573	2‡	3	4
1971-72	Philadelphia	30	52	.366	3‡	..	..
1972-73	Buffalo	21	61	.256	3‡	..	..
1973-74	Buffalo	42	40	.512	3‡	2	4
1974-75	Buffalo	49	33	.598	2‡	3	4
1975-76	Buffalo	46	36	.561	2T‡	4	5
1976-77	Portland*	49	33	.598	2§	14	5
1977-78	Portland	58	24	.707	1§	2	4
1978-79	Portland	45	37	.549	4§	1	2
1979-80	Portland	38	44	.463	4§	1	2
1980-81	Portland	45	37	.549	3§	1	2
1981-82	Portland	42	40	.512	5§	..	..
1982-83	Portland	46	36	.561	4§	3	4
1983-84	Portland	48	34	.585	2§	2	3
1984-85	Portland	42	40	.512	2§	4	5
1985-86	Portland	40	42	.488	2§	1	3
1986-87	Indiana	41	41	.500	4x	1	3
1987-88	Indiana	38	44	.463	6x	..	..
1988-89	Indiana	0	7	.000	..x	..	..
Totals (21 seasons)		864	783	.525		44	58

*Won NBA championship. †Eastern Division. ‡Atlantic Division. §Pacific Division. xCentral Division.

Coach of NBA championship team, 1977.

PATRICK JAMES RILEY
(Pat)

Born March 20, 1945 at Rome, N. Y. Height 6:04. Weight 205.
High School—Schenectady, N. Y., Linton.
College—University of Kentucky, Lexington, Ky.
Drafted by San Diego on first round, 1967 (7th pick).

Selected from San Diego by Portland in expansion draft, May 11, 1970.
Sold by Portland to Los Angeles, October 9, 1970.
Traded by Los Angeles to Phoenix for draft rights to John Roche and a 1976 2nd round draft choice, November 3, 1975.

—COLLEGIATE RECORD—

Year	G.	Min.	FGA	FGM	Pct.	FTA	FTM	Pct.	Reb.	Pts.	Avg.
63-64†	16	....	259	120	.463	146	93	.637	235	333	20.8
64-65	25	825	370	160	.432	89	55	.618	212	375	15.0
65-66	29	1078	514	265	.516	153	107	.699	259	637	22.0
66-67	26	953	373	165	.442	156	122	.782	201	452	17.4
Varsity Totals	80	2856	1257	590	.469	398	284	.714	672	1464	18.3

NBA REGULAR SEASON RECORD

Sea.—Team	G.	Min.	FGA	FGM	Pct.	FTA	FTM	Pct.	Reb.	Ast.	PF	Disq.	Pts.	Avg.
67-68—San Diego	80	1263	660	250	.379	202	128	.634	177	138	205	1	628	7.9
68-69—San Diego	56	1027	498	202	.406	134	90	.672	112	136	146	1	494	8.8
69-70—San Diego	36	474	180	75	.417	55	40	.727	57	85	68	0	190	5.3
70-71—Los Angeles	54	506	254	105	.413	87	56	.644	54	72	84	0	266	4.9
71-72—Los Angeles	67	926	441	197	.447	74	55	.743	127	75	110	0	449	6.7
72-73—Los Angeles	55	801	390	167	.428	82	65	.793	65	81	126	0	399	7.3

Sea.—Team	G.	Min.	FGA	FGM	Pct.	FTA	FTM	Pct.	—Rebounds— Off.	Def.	Tot.	Ast.	PF	Dq.	Stl.	Blk.	Pts.	Avg.
73-74—Los Angeles	72	1361	667	287	.430	144	110	.764	38	90	128	148	173	1	54	3	684	9.5
74-75—Los Angeles	46	1016	523	219	.419	93	69	.742	25	60	85	121	128	0	36	4	507	11.0
75-76—LA-Phoe.	62	813	301	117	.389	77	55	.714	16	34	50	57	112	0	22	6	289	4.7
Totals	528	8187	3914	1619	.414	948	668	.705			855	913	1152	3	112	13	3906	7.4

NBA PLAYOFF RECORD

Sea.—Team	G.	Min.	FGA	FGM	Pct.	FTA	FTM	Pct.	Reb.	Ast.	PF	Disq.	Pts.	Avg.
68-69—San Diego	5	76	37	16	.432	6	5	.833	11	2	13	0	37	7.4
70-71—Los Angeles	7	135	69	29	.420	11	8	.727	15	14	12	0	66	9.4
71-72—Los Angeles	15	244	99	33	.333	16	12	.750	29	14	37	0	78	5.2
72-73—Los Angeles	7	53	27	9	.333	0	0	.000	5	7	10	0	18	2.6

Sea.—Team	G.	Min.	FGA	FGM	Pct.	FTA	FTM	Pct.	—Rebounds— Off.	Def.	Tot.	Ast.	PF	Dq.	Stl.	Blk.	Pts.	Avg.
73-74—Los Angeles	5	106	50	18	.360	4	3	.750	3	3	6	10	11	0	4	0	39	7.8
75-76—Phoenix	5	27	15	6	.400	1	1	1.000	0	0	0	5	3	0	0	0	13	2.6
Totals	44	641	297	111	.374	38	29	.763			66	52	86	0	4	0	251	5.7

NBA COACHING RECORD

Sea.	Club	Regular Season W.	L.	Pct.	Pos.	Playoffs W.	L.
1981-82	Los Angeles*	50	21	.704	1†	12	2
1982-83	Los Angeles	58	24	.707	1†	8	7
1983-84	Los Angeles	54	28	.659	1†	14	7
1984-85	L.A. Lakers*	62	20	.756	1†	15	4
1985-86	L.A. Lakers	62	20	.756	1†	8	6
1986-87	L.A. Lakers*	65	17	.793	1†	15	3
1987-88	L.A. Lakers*	62	20	.756	1†	15	9
1988-89	L.A. Lakers	57	25	.695	1†	11	4
1989-90	L.A. Lakers	63	19	.768	1†	4	5
Totals (9 seasons)		533	194	.733		102	47

*Won NBA championship. †Pacific Division.

Member of NBA championship team, 1972. . . . Coach of NBA championship teams, 1982, 1985, 1987, 1988. . . . Named NBA Coach of the Year, 1990. . . . Son of former major league catcher and minor league manager Leon Riley. . . . Brother of former National Football League defensive back Lee Riley. . . . Drafted by Dallas Cowboys in 11th round of 1967 NFL draft.